CLYMER®

# HARLEY-DAVIDSON

## FLH/FLT/FXR EVOLUTION • 1984-1994

*The world's finest publisher of mechanical how-to manuals*

**PRIMEDIA**
Business Directories & Books

*P.O. Box 12901, Overland Park, Kansas 66282-2901*

FIRST EDITION
First Printing August, 1992
Second Printing August, 1993

SECOND EDITION
First Printing June, 1995
Second Printing May, 1997
Third Printing September, 1998
Fourth Printing October, 2000
Fifth Printing January, 2002
Sixth Printing September, 2003

Printed in U.S.A.

CLYMER and colophon are registered trademarks of PRIMEDIA Business Magazines & Media Inc.

ISBN: 0-89287-633-6

Library of Congress: 94-77640

*AUTHOR: Clymer staff.*

*TECHNICAL PHOTOGRAPHY: Ron Wright.*

*TECHNICAL ILLUSTRATIONS: Steve Amos.*

*TECHNICAL ASSISTANCE: American Motorcycle Institute (www.amiwrench.com) and the AMI Harley-Davidson specialty program. Special thanks to following at AMI: President Lamar Williams; Program Director James Watts; Instructor David A. Walker and graduate Bill Eaton for his tuning experience. We also want to acknowledge the assistance of Robison Harley-Davidson Sales and his technicians for the use of their shops at 508 International Speedway Blvd., Daytona Beach, FL 32114.*

*TOOLS AND EQUIPMENT: K & L Supply at www.klsupply.com.*

*PRODUCTION: Shirley Renicker.*

*COVER: Mark Clifford Photography at www.markclifford.com.*

# CLYMER PUBLICATIONS

## PRIMEDIA Business Magazines & Media

**President & Chief Executive Officer** Charles McCurdy
**Senior Vice President, Sales Operation** John French
**Vice President, PRIMEDIA Business Directories & Books** Bob Moraczewski

### EDITORIAL

***Managing Editor***
James Grooms

***Associate Editor***
Jason Beaver

***Technical Writers***
Ron Wright
Ed Scott
George Parise
Mark Rolling
Michael Morlan
Jay Bogart

***Editorial Production Manager***
Dylan Goodwin

***Senior Production Editors***
Greg Araujo
Shirley Renicker

***Production Editors***
Holly Messinger
Shara Pierceall
Darin Watson

***Associate Production Editor***
Susan Hartington

***Technical Illustrators***
Steve Amos
Errol McCarthy
Mitzi McCarthy
Bob Meyer
Mike Rose

### MARKETING/SALES AND ADMINISTRATION

***Publisher***
Shawn Etheridge

***Marketing Manager***
Elda Starke

***Advertising & Promotions Coordinators***
Melissa Abbott
Wendy Stringfellow

***Art Directors***
Chris Paxton
Tony Barmann

***Sales Managers***
Ted Metzger, Manuals
Dutch Sadler, Marine
Matt Tusken, Motorcycles

***Sales Coordinator***
Marcia Jungles

***Operations Manager***
Patricia Kowalczewski

***Customer Service Manager***
Terri Cannon

***Customer Service Supervisor***
Ed McCarty

***Customer Service Representatives***
Susan Kohlmeyer
April LeBlond
Courtney Hollars
Jennifer Lassiter
Ernesto Suarez
Shawna Davis

***Warehouse & Inventory Manager***
Leah Hicks


***The following books and guides are published by PRIMEDIA Business Directories & Books.***

The Electronics Source Book

**More information available at *primediabooks.com***

# CONTENTS

# QUICK REFERENCE DATA

## TIRE PRESSURE (FLT AND FXR)*

| | Front psi | Front kg/cm² | Rear psi | Rear kg/cm² |
|---|---|---|---|---|
| Rider only | | | | |
| 1984-1985 | | | | |
| FLT/C | ** | ** | ** | ** |
| FLHT/C (K101A) | 28 | 1.9 | 36 | 2.5 |
| FXRS (K291T) | 30 | 2.1 | 36 | 2.5 |
| FXRT (K291T) | 30 | 2.1 | 36 | 2.5 |
| 1986-on | | | | |
| FLT | 36 | 2.5 | 36 | 2.5 |
| FXR | 30 | 2.1 | 36 | 2.5 |
| Rider with one passenger | | | | |
| 1984-1985 | | | | |
| FLT/C and FLHT/C | 28 | 1.9 | 36 | 2.5 |
| FXRS | 30 | 2.1 | 40 | 2.8 |
| FXRT | 30 | 2.1 | 30 | 2.1 |
| FLT with sidecar | 28 | 1.9 | 40 | 2.8 |
| 1986-on | | | | |
| FLT | 36 | 2.5 | 40 | 2.8 |
| FXR | 30 | 2.1 | 40 | 2.8 |

* Tire pressures listed in this table are for original equipment tires. See your dealer or tire manufacturer when equipping your model with non-stock tires.
** Not specified.

## TIRE PRESSURE (FXWG, FXEF AND FXSB)*

| | Front psi | Front kg/cm² | Rear psi | Rear kg/cm² |
|---|---|---|---|---|
| Rider only | | | | |
| FXEF and FXSB | | | | |
| K181 | 30 | 2.1 | 32 | 2.2 |
| K291T | 36 | 2.5 | 36 | 2.5 |
| FXWG | 30 | 2.1 | 32 | 2.2 |
| Rider with one passenger | | | | |
| FXEF and FXSB | | | | |
| K181 | 30 | 2.1 | 32 | 2.2 |
| K291T | 36 | 2.5 | 40 | 2.8 |
| FXWG | | | | |
| "F" rib | 30 | 2.1 | 32 | 2.2 |
| K101A | — | — | 28 | 1.9 |

* Tire pressures listed in this table are for original equipment tires. See your dealer or tire manufacturer when equipping your model with non-stock tires.

## ENGINE OIL

| Type | HD rating | Viscosity | Ambient operating temperature |
|---|---|---|---|
| HD Multigrade | HD 240 | SAE 10W/40 | Below 40° F |
| HD Multigrade | HD 240 | SAE 20W/50 | +40° F to 100° F |
| HD Regular | HD 240 | SAE 50 | +60° F to 100° F Heavy* |
| HD Extra | HD 240 | SAE 60 | +80° F to 100° F Heavy* |

* Not recommended for use when ambient temperature is below 50° F.

## RECOMMENDED LUBRICANTS AND FLUIDS*

| | |
|---|---|
| Brake fluid | DOT 5 |
| Fork oil | HD Type E or equivalent |
| Battery top up | Distilled water |
| Transmission | HD transmission or equivalent |
| Clutch | HD lubricant or equivalent |
| Drive chain | |
| Enclosed drive chain | SAE 50 or SAE 60 wt. |
| Open drive chain (without O-rings) | Any commerical chain lubricant |
| Open drive chain (with O-rings) | Commercial chain lubricant recommended for O-ring chains |

## ENGINE, CLUTCH AND TRANSMISSION OIL CAPACITIES

| | |
|---|---|
| Oil tank | |
| FLT | 4.0 qt. (3.8 L, 3.3 imp. qt.) |
| FXR | 3.0 qt. (2.8 L, 2.5 imp. qt.) |
| FXEF, FXSB and FXWG | 4.0 qt. |
| Transmission | |
| 1986-1990 | 16 oz. (473 ml, 0.42 imp. qt.) |
| 1991-on | 20-24 oz. (591-710 ml, 0.41 imp. qt.) |
| Primary chain case | |
| Early 1984 | — |
| Late 1984-1990 | 1.5 qt. (1.4 L, 1.2 imp. qt.) |
| 1991-on | 38-44 oz. (1.1-1.3 L, 1.0-1.1 imp. qt.) |

* See text for correct check and refill procedure.

## FUEL TANK CAPACITY

| | Total | | | Reserve | | |
|---|---|---|---|---|---|---|
| | U.S. gal. | Liters | Imp. gal. | U.S. gal. | Liters | Imp.gal. |
| FLT | | | | | | |
| 1984-1988 | 5.0 | 18.9 | 4.2 | 0.7 | 2.6 | 0.6 |
| 1989-on | 5.0 | 18.9 | 4.2 | 0.9 | 3.4 | 0.7 |
| FXR | 4.2 | 15.9 | 3.5 | 0.4 | 1.5 | 0.3 |
| FXEF and FXSB | 4.2 | 15.9 | 3.5 | 1.0 | 3.8 | 0.8 |
| FXWG | 5.2 | 19.7 | 4.3 | 1.2 | 4.5 | 1.0 |

## FRONT FORK OIL CAPACITY

| | Wet | | Dry | |
|---|---|---|---|---|
| | U.S. oz. | cc | U.S. oz. | cc |
| FLT | 7 3/4 | 229.2 | 8 1/2 | 251.3 |
| FXR | | | | |
| 1984-1987 FXR and FXRS | 6 1/4 | 184.8 | 7.0 | 206.9 |
| 1984-1987 FXRD and FXRT | 7.0 | 206.9 | 7 3/4 | 229.2 |
| 1987 FXRSE | 10.5 | 310.5 | 11.5 | 339.2 |
| 1987-on FXLR | 9.2 | 272 | 10.2 | 300.9 |
| 1988-on FXR, FXRS | 9.2 | 272 | 10.2 | 300.9 |
| 1988-on FXRT, FXRS-SP | 10.5 | 310.5 | 11.5 | 339.2 |
| FXLR | 9.2 | 272 | 10.2 | 300.9 |
| FXEF | 5.0 | 147.8 | 6.5 | 192.2 |
| FXSB | 7.5 | 221.8 | 6.75 | 199.6 |
| FXWG | 10.2 | 300.9 | 11.2 | 330.4 |

## ENGINE TUNE-UP SPECIFICATIONS

| | |
|---|---|
| Engine compression | 90 psi |
| Spark plugs | |
| Type | HD 5R6A or equivalent |
| Gap | 0.038-0.043 in. |
| Ignition timing | |
| Type | Electronic |
| Timing specifications | |
| Early 1984 | |
| Range | 5°-50° BTDC |
| Start | 5° BTDC |
| Fast idle | 35° BTDC |
| @ 1,800-2,800 rpm | 50° BTDC |
| Late 1984-on | |
| Range | 0° –35° BTDC |
| Start | 5° BTDC |
| Fast idle | 35° BTDC |

## CARBURETOR IDLE SPEED SPECIFICATIONS

| | |
|---|---|
| FLT and FXR | |
| 1984-1989 carburetor | |
| 1984-1987 | |
| Slow idle | 900-950 rpm |
| Fast idle | 1,500 rpm |
| 1988-1989 | |
| Slow idle | 1,000 rpm |
| Fast idle | 1,500 rpm |
| 1990-on | |
| Idle | 1,000 rpm |
| FXEF, FXSB and FXWG | |
| Slow idle | 1,000-1,050 rpm |
| Fast idle | 1,500-1,550 rpm |

## CARBURETOR SPECIFICATIONS

| | Main jet | Pilot jet |
|---|---|---|
| FLT | | |
| Early 1984 | 165 | 50 |
| Late 1984-1986 | 175 | 50 |
| 1987 | 170 | 50 |
| 1988-1989 | | |
| 49-state | 165 | 52 |
| California | 140 | 42 |
| 1990-1991 | | |
| 49-state | 185 | 45 |
| California | 165 | 42 |
| 1992-1993 | | |
| 49-state | 175 | 40 |
| California | 160 | 40 |
| 1994 | | |
| 49-state | 175 | 42 |
| California | 165 | 42 |
| HDI* | 175 | 40 |

(continued)

**CARBURETOR SPECIFICATIONS (continued)**

| | Main jet | Pilot jet |
|---|---|---|
| FXR | | |
| 1984-1985 | 160 | 50 |
| 1986 | 170 | 50 |
| 1987 | 165 | 50 |
| 1988-1989 | | |
| 49-state | 165 | 52 |
| California | 140 | 42 |
| 1990-1991 | | |
| 49-state | 185 | 45 |
| California | 165 | 42 |
| 1992-1993 | | |
| 49-state | 165 | 40 |
| California | 160 | 40 |
| 1994 | | |
| 49-state | 165 | 42 |
| California | 165 | 42 |
| HDI* | 165 | 40 |
| FXWG | | |
| 1985 | 165 | 50 |
| 1986 | 170 | 50 |
| FXEF and FXSB | | |
| 1985 | 165 | 50 |

*HDI: International models.

**BATTERY CAPACITY**

| | |
|---|---|
| 1984-1990 | 12 volt, 19 amp hr. |
| 1991-on | |
| FLT | 12 volt, 20 amp hr. |
| FXR | 12 volt, 19 amp hr. |

**ELECTRICAL SPECIFICATIONS**

| | |
|---|---|
| Battery capacity | |
| FLT | 20 AH @ 10 hour rate |
| | 22 AH @ 20 hour rate |
| FXR | 19 AH @ 10 hour rate |
| | 21 AH @ 20 hour rate |
| FXWG, FXEF and FXSB | 19 AH |
| Ignition coil | |
| Primary resistance | 2.5-3.1 ohms |
| Secondary resistance | |
| 1986-1992 | 11,250-13,750 ohms |
| 1993-on | 10,000-12,500 ohms |
| Alternator | |
| Stator coil resistance | |
| 1984-1988 | 0.2-0.4 ohms |
| 1989-on | 0.1-0.2 ohms |
| AC output | |
| FLT and FXR | |
| 1984-1988 | 19-23 amps @ 2,000 rpm |
| 1989-1990 | 29-32 amps @ 2,000 rpm |
| 1991-on | 26-32 amps @ 3,000 rpm |
| FXWG, FXEF and FXSB | 19-26 amps @ 2,000 rpm |

(continued)

## ELECTRICAL SPECIFICATIONS (continued)

| | |
|---|---|
| Starter current draw | |
| 1984-1988 | 45 amps max. @ 10.0 volts |
| 1990-on | 90 amps max. @ 11.5 volts |
| Starter current draw test (test) | |
| 1984-1988 | 40-50 amps max. |
| 1989-1992 | 150 amps max. |
| 1993-on | |
| Range | 160-180 |
| Maximum | 200 |

## CIRCUIT BREAKER RATINGS

| Circuit | Rating (amps) |
|---|---|
| Main (battery) | 30 |
| Ignition | 15 |
| Lights | 15 |
| Accessory | |
| FLHS | 10* |
| Accessory | 15 |
| Radio | 15* |
| Constant | 15* |
| Cruise | 15* |

* FLT and FXR models only.

## CIRCUIT BREAKER RATINGS (1994 FLT)

| Circuit | Rating (amps) | Color code | Terminal |
|---|---|---|---|
| Main | 50 | None | Threaded |
| Lights | 15 | Light blue | Blade type |
| Accessory | 15 | Light blue | Blade type |
| Ignition | 15 | Light blue | Blade type |
| Constant | 15 | Light blue | Blade type |

## BLADE TYPE FUSES (1993-ON FLT)

| Circuit | Rating (amps) | Color code |
|---|---|---|
| CB power | 3 | Violet |
| CB memory | 1 | Charcoal |
| Fender tip | | |
| 1994 FLHT/U | 1 | Charcoal |
| Pod power | 5 | Tan |
| Radio | | |
| 1994 Ultras | 10 | Red |
| Radio memory | | |
| 1994 | 1 | Charcoal |

## DRY CLUTCH SPECIFICATIONS

| Item | Specification |
|---|---|
| Type | Dry, multiple disc |
| Spring adjustment | 1 1/32-1 7/8 in. (26.2-47.6 mm) from spring collar edge |
| Spring free length | 1 47/64-1 45/64 in. (44.04-43.26 mm) |
| Friction disc | |
| Minimum lining thickness | 1/32 in. (0.8 mm) |
| Warpage limit | 0.010 in. (0.25 mm) |
| Steel disc warpage limit | 0.010 in. (0.25 mm) |
| Clutch screw adjustment | See text |
| Clutch hand lever free play | 1/16 in. (1.59 mm) |

## WET CLUTCH SPECIFICATIONS (1985-1989)

| | |
|---|---|
| Type | Wet, multiple disc |
| Clutch hand lever free play | 1/8-3/16 in. (3.17-4.76 mm) |
| Steel disc | |
| Minimum thickness | 0.044 in. (1.12 mm) |
| Warpage limit | 0.011 in. (0.30 mm) |
| Friction plate | |
| Minimum lining thickness | 0.078 in. (1.98 mm) |

## WET CLUTCH SPECIFICATIONS (1990-ON)

| | |
|---|---|
| Type | Wet, multiple disc |
| Clutch hand lever free play | |
| 1990 | 1/8-3/16 in. (3.17-4.76 mm) |
| 1991-on | 1/16-1/8 in. (1.6-3.2 mm) |
| Steel disc | |
| Warpage limit | 0.006 in. (0.15 mm) |
| Friction plate assembly | |
| Minimum lining thickness (assembly) | 0.661 in. (16.8 mm)* |

* See text for procedures on measuring friction plates.

## BRAKE SPECIFICATIONS

| | in. | mm |
|---|---|---|
| Brake pad minimum thickness | | |
| Front and rear | 0.062 | 1.57 |
| Brake disc (front and rear) | | |
| FLT and FXR | See text | |
| FXWG, FXEF and FXSB | | |
| Minimum thickness | 0.205 | 5.21 |
| Outside diameter | 11.50 | 292.1 |

## FRONT WHEEL TIGHTENING TORQUES

| | ft.-lb. | N•m |
|---|---|---|
| Front axle | | |
| FLT | 50-55 | 69-76 |
| FXR | | |
| 1984-1992 | 50 | 69 |
| 1993-on | 50-55 | 66-76 |
| FXWG, FXEF and FXSB | 50-55 | 69-76 |
| Front axle slider cap nuts | | |
| FLT | 9-13 | 12.4-17.9 |
| FXR | | |
| FXLR and 1987 FXRSE | 7-9 | 9.6-12.4 |
| All other models | 9-13 | 12.4-17.9 |
| FXWG, FXEF and FXSB | 9-13 | 12.4-17.9 |
| Front brake caliper | 25-30 | 34.5-41.4 |

## REAR WHEEL TIGHTENING TORQUES

| | ft.-lb. | N•m |
|---|---|---|
| Rear axle | 60-65 | 82.8-89.7 |
| Rear sprocket | | |
| FLT and FXR | | |
| 1984-1991 | | |
| Grade 5 bolts | 45-50 | 62.1-69 |
| Grade 8 bolts | 65-70 | 89.7-96.6 |
| 1992 | 45-55 | 55.2-75 |
| 1993-on | 55-65 | 75-88 |
| FXWG, FXEF and FXSB | | |
| Laced wheel | | |
| FXWG | 40-45 | 55.2-62.1 |
| FXEF and FXSB | 35 | 48.3 |
| Alloy wheel | | |
| Grade 5 bolts | 45-50 | 62.1-69 |
| Grade 8 bolts | 65-70 | 89.7-96.6 |

## MOTORCYCLE INFORMATION

MODEL:______________________________ YEAR:______________

VIN NUMBER:__________________________________________

ENGINE SERIAL NUMBER:_________________________________

CARBURETOR SERIAL NUMBER OR I.D. MARK:_________________

## CHAPTER ONE

# GENERAL INFORMATION

This Clymer shop manual covers all Harley-Davidson FLH, FLT and FXR models from 1984-1994 and all 1985 FXSB and FXEF models and 1985-1986 FXWG models.

Troubleshooting, tune-up, maintenance and repair are not difficult, if you know what tools and equipment to use and what to do. Step-by-step instructions guide you through jobs ranging from simple maintenance to complete engine and suspension overhaul.

This manual can be used by anyone from a first time do-it-yourselfer to a professional mechanic. Detailed drawings and clear photographs give you all the information you need to do the work right.

Some of the procedures in this manual require the use of special tools. The resourceful mechanic can, in many cases, think of acceptable substitutes for special tools–there is always another way. This can be as simple as using a few pieces of threaded rod, washers and nuts to remove or install a bearing or fabricating a tool from scrap material. However, using a substitute for a special tool is not recommended as it can be dangerous and may damage the part. If you find that a tool can be designed and safely made, but will require some type of machine work, you may want to search out a local community college or high school that has a machine shop curriculum. Shop teachers sometimes welcome outside work that can be used as practical shop applications for advanced students.

**Table 1** lists model coverage.

General specifications are listed in **Tables 2 and 3** while gross vehicle weight ratings are listed in **Table 4**. Fuel tank capacity is listed in **Table 5**.

U.S. to metric conversion is given in **Table 6**.

Critical torque specifications are found in table form at the end of each chapter (as required). The general torque specifications listed in **Table 7** can be used when a torque specification is not listed for a specific component or assembly.

Inch tap drill sizes can be found in **Table 8**.

A wind chill chart is found in **Table 9** that can be used to better prepare yourself when riding your Harley in cold weather.

## MANUAL ORGANIZATION

This chapter provides general information useful to Harley vehicle owners and mechanics. In addition, information in this chapter discusses the tools and techniques for preventive maintenance, troubleshooting and repair.

Chapter Two provides methods and suggestions for quick and accurate diagnosis and repair of problems. Troubleshooting procedures discuss typical symptoms and logical methods to pinpoint the trouble.

Chapter Three explains all periodic lubrication and routine maintenance necessary to keep your Harley operating well. Chapter Three also includes recommended tune-up procedures, eliminating the need to consult other chapters constantly on the various assemblies.

Subsequent chapters describe specific systems, providing disassembly, repair, assembly and adjustment procedures in simple step-by-step form. If a repair is impractical for a home mechanic, it is so indicated. It is usually faster and less expensive to take such repairs to a dealer or competent repair shop. Specifications concerning a specific system are included at the end of the appropriate chapter.

## NOTES, CAUTIONS AND WARNINGS

The terms NOTE, CAUTION and WARNING have specific meanings in this manual. A NOTE provides additional information to make a step or procedure easier or clearer. Disregarding a NOTE could cause inconvenience, but would not cause damage or personal injury.

A CAUTION emphasizes areas where equipment damage could occur. Disregarding a CAUTION could cause permanent mechanical damage; however, personal injury is unlikely.

A WARNING emphasizes areas where personal injury or even death could result from negligence. Mechanical damage may also occur. WARNINGS *are to be taken seriously*. In some cases, serious injury and death have resulted from disregarding similar warnings.

## SAFETY FIRST

Professional mechanics can work for years and never sustain a serious injury. If you observe a few rules of common sense and safety, you can enjoy many safe hours servicing your own machine. If you ignore these rules you can hurt yourself or damage the equipment.

1. Never use gasoline as a cleaning solvent.

*WARNING*

*Gasoline should only be stored in an approved safety gasoline storage container, properly labeled. Spilled gasoline should be wiped up immediately.*

2. Never smoke or use a torch in the vicinity of flammable liquids, such as cleaning solvent, in open containers.
3. If welding or brazing is required on the machine, remove the fuel tanks to a safe distance, at least 50 feet (127 cm) away.
4. Use the proper sized wrenches to avoid damage to fasteners and injury to yourself.
5. When loosening a tight or stuck nut, be guided by what would happen if the wrench should slip. Be careful; protect yourself accordingly.
6. When replacing a fastener, make sure to use one with the same measurements and strength as the old one. Incorrect or mismatched fasteners can result in damage to your Harley and possible personal injury. Beware of fastener kits that are filled with cheap and poorly made nuts, bolts, washers and cotter pins. Refer to *Fasteners* in this chapter for additional information.
7. Keep all hand and power tools in good condition. Wipe greasy and oily tools after using them. They are difficult to hold and can cause injury. Replace or repair worn or damaged tools.
8. Keep your work area clean and uncluttered.
9. Wear safety goggles during all operations involving drilling, grinding, the use of a cold chisel or *any* time you feel unsure about the safety of your eyes. Safety goggles (**Figure 1**) should also be worn when solvent and compressed air are used to clean parts.

*WARNING*

*The improper use of compressed air is very dangerous. Using compressed air to dust off your clothes, bike or workbench can cause flying particles to be*

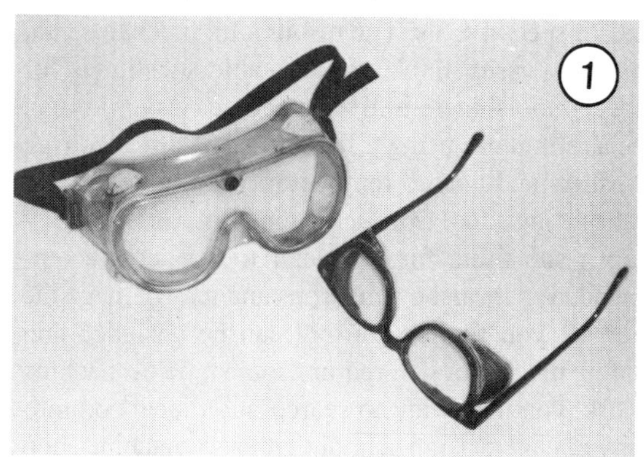

*blown into your eyes or skin. **Never** direct or blow compressed air into your skin or through any body opening (including cuts) as this can cause severe injury or death. Compressed air should be used carefully; never allow children to use or play with compressed air.*

10. Keep an approved fire extinguisher nearby (**Figure 2**). Be sure it is rated for gasoline (Class B) and electrical (Class C) fires.

11. When drying bearings or other rotating parts with compressed air, never allow the air jet to rotate the bearing or part. The air jet is capable of rotating them at speeds far in excess of those for which they were designed. The bearing or rotating part is very likely to disintegrate and cause serious injury and damage. To prevent bearing damage when using compressed air, hold the inner bearing race (**Figure 3**) by hand.

12. Never work on the upper part of the bike while someone is working underneath it.

13. Never carry sharp tools in your pockets.

14. There is always a right way and wrong way to use tools. Learn to use them the right way.

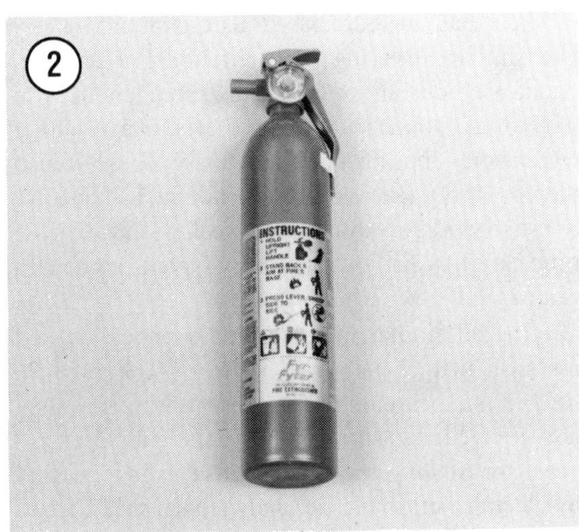


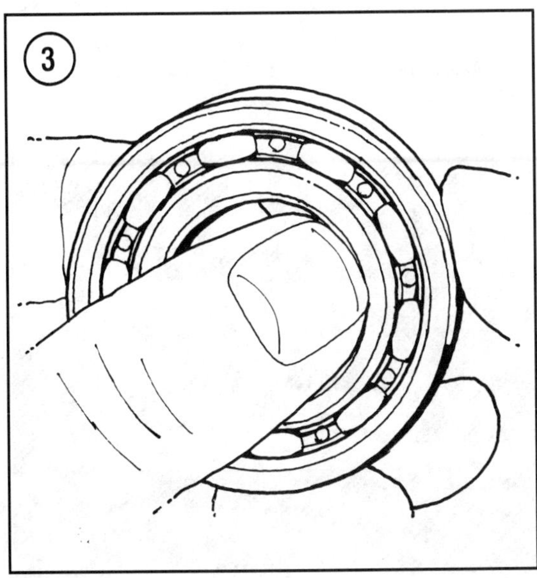


## SERVICE HINTS

Most of the service procedures covered are straightforward and can be performed by anyone reasonably handy with tools. It is suggested, however, that you consider your own capabilities carefully before attempting any operation involving major disassembly.

1. "Front," as used in this manual, refers to the front of the motorcycle; the front of any component is the end closest to the front of the motorcycle. The "left-" and "right-hand" side refer to the position of the parts as viewed by a rider sitting on the seat and facing forward. For example, the throttle control is on the right-hand side. These rules are simple, but confusion can cause a major inconvenience during service.

2. Whenever servicing the engine or transmission, or when removing a suspension component, the bike should be secured in a safe manner. If the bike is to be parked on its jiffy stand, check the stand to make sure it is secure and not damaged. Block the front and rear wheels if they remain on the ground. A small hydraulic jack and a block of wood can be used to raise the chassis, or you can use a commercial type of stand. If the transmission is not going to be worked on and the drive chain or drive belt is connected to the rear wheel, shift the transmission into first gear.

3. Repairs go much faster and easier if the bike is clean before you begin work. There are special cleaners for washing the engine and related parts. Spray or brush on the cleaning solution, following the manufacturer's directions. Rinse parts with a garden hose. Clean all oily or greasy parts with cleaning solvent as you remove them.

*WARNING*

*Never use gasoline as a cleaning agent. It presents an extreme fire hazard. Be sure to work in a well-ventilated area when using cleaning solvent. Keep a fire extinguisher, rated for gasoline fires, handy in any case.*

4. Much of the labor charged for by mechanics is to remove and disassemble other parts to reach the defective unit. It is usually possible to perform the preliminary operations yourself and then take the defective unit to the dealer for repair.

5. Once you have decided to tackle the job yourself, read the entire section *completely* while looking at the actual parts before starting the job. Make sure you have identified the proper procedure. Study the illustrations and text until you have a good idea of what is involved in completing the job satisfactorily. If special tools or replacement parts are required, make arrangements to get them before you start. It is frustrating and time-consuming to get partly into a job and then be unable to complete it.

*NOTE*

*Some of the procedures or service specifications listed in this manual may not be applicable if your Harley has been modified or if it has been equipped with non-stock equipment. When modifying or installing non-stock equipment, file all printed instruction or technical information regarding the new equipment in a folder or notebook for future reference. If your Harley was purchased second hand, the previous owner may have installed non-stock parts. If necessary, consult with your dealer or the accessory manufacturer on components that may change tuning or repair procedures.*

6. Simple wiring checks can be easily made at home, but knowledge of electronics is almost a necessity for performing tests with complicated test gear.

*CAUTION*

*Improper testing can sometimes damage an electrical component.*

7. Disconnect the negative battery cable (**Figure 4**) when working on or near the electrical, clutch or starter systems and before disconnecting any wires. On all models covered in this manual, the negative terminal will be marked with a minus (–) sign and the positive terminal with a plus (+) sign.

*WARNING*

*Never disconnect the positive battery cable unless the negative cable has been disconnected. Disconnecting the positive cable while the negative cable is still connected may cause a spark. This could ignite the hydrogen gas given off by the battery, causing an explosion.*

8. During disassembly, keep a few general cautions in mind. Force is rarely needed to get things apart. If parts are a tight fit, such as a bearing in a case, there is usually a tool designed to separate them. Never use a screwdriver to pry parts with machined surfaces such as crankcase halves. You will mar the surfaces and end up with leaks.

9. Make diagrams (or take a Polaroid picture) wherever similar-appearing parts are found. For instance, crankcase bolts are often not the same length. You may think you can remember where everything came from—but mistakes are costly. There is also the possibility that you may be sidetracked and not return to work for days or even weeks—in which the time carefully laid out parts may have become disturbed.

10. Tag all similar internal parts for location and mark all mating parts for position (A, **Figure 5**). Record number and thickness of any shims as they are removed; measure with a vernier caliper or micrometer. Small parts such as bolts can be identified by placing them in plastic sandwich bags (B, **Figure 5**). Seal and label them with masking tape.

11. Place parts from a specific area of the engine (e.g. cylinder head, cylinder, clutch, primary drive, etc.) into plastic boxes (C, **Figure 5**) to keep them separated.

12. When disassembling transmission shaft assemblies, use an egg flat (type that restaurants get their eggs in) (D, **Figure 5**) and set the parts from the shaft in one of the depressions in the same order in which it was removed.

13. Wiring should be tagged with masking tape and marked as each wire is removed. Again, do not rely on memory alone, especially if the wiring was changed by a previous owner.

14. Finished surfaces should be protected from physical damage or corrosion. Keep gasoline off painted surfaces.

15. Use penetrating oil on frozen or tight bolts, then strike the bolt head a few times with a hammer and punch (use a screwdriver on screws). Avoid the use of heat where possible, as it can warp, melt or affect the temper of parts. Heat also ruins finishes, especially paint and plastics.

16. No parts removed or installed (other than bushings and bearings) in the procedures given in this manual should require unusual force during disassembly or assembly. If a part is difficult to remove or install, find out why before proceeding.

17. Cover all openings after removing parts or components to prevent dirt, small tools, etc. from falling in.

18. Recommendations are occasionally made to refer service or maintenance to a Harley-Davidson dealer or independent Harley-Davidson repair shop. In these cases, the work will be done more quickly and economically than if you performed the job yourself.

19. In procedural steps, the term "replace" means to discard a defective part and replace it with a new or

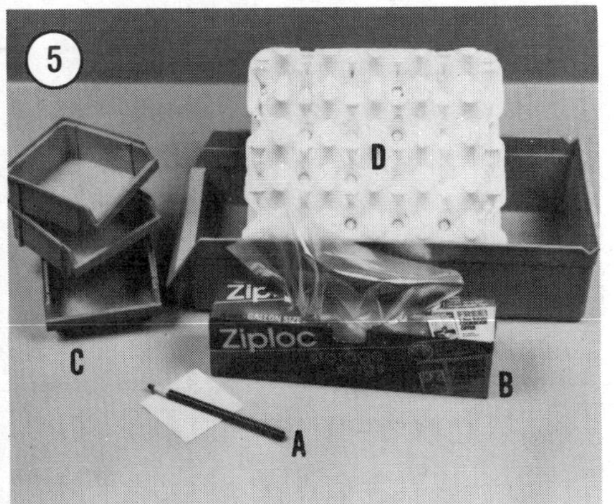


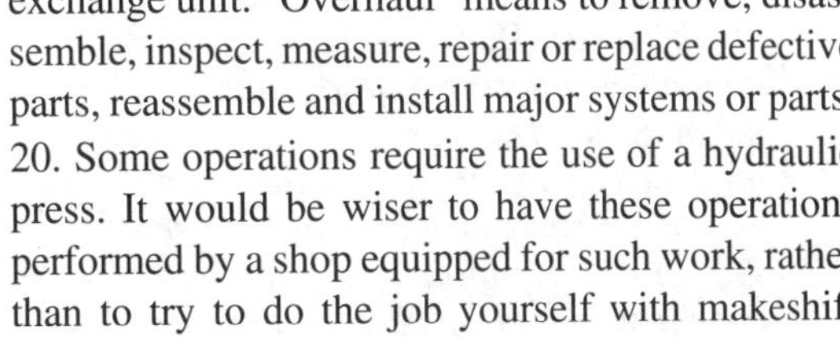

exchange unit. "Overhaul" means to remove, disassemble, inspect, measure, repair or replace defective parts, reassemble and install major systems or parts.

20. Some operations require the use of a hydraulic press. It would be wiser to have these operations performed by a shop equipped for such work, rather than to try to do the job yourself with makeshift equipment that may damage your machine.

21. When assembling parts, be sure all shims and washers are replaced exactly as they came out.

22. Whenever a rotating part butts against a stationary part, look for a shim or washer.

23. Use new gaskets if there is any doubt about the condition of the old ones.

24. If it becomes necessary to purchase gasket material to make a gasket, measure the thickness of the old gasket (at an uncompressed point) and purchase gasket material with the same approximate thickness.

25. Heavy grease can be used to hold small parts in place if they tend to fall out during assembly. However, keep grease and oil away from electrical and brake components.

26. Never use wire to clean out jets and air passages. They are easily damaged. Use compressed air to blow out the carburetor only if the diaphragm has been removed first.

27. A baby bottle makes a good measuring device. Get one that is graduated in fluid ounces and cubic centimeters. After it has been used for this purpose, do *not* let a child drink out of it as there will always be an oil residue in it.

28. Take your time and do the job right. Do not forget that a newly rebuilt engine must be broken in just like a new one.

## SERIAL NUMBERS

Harley-Davidson makes frequent changes during a model year, some minor, some relatively major. All Harley models in this manual can be identified by their individual 17 digit Vehicle Identification Number (VIN): for example, 1HD1BJL11LM110001. This number is stamped into the steering head (**Figure 6**) and recorded on a label placed on the right front frame downtube. The engine is identified with an abbreviated VIN number stamped onto the left-hand crankcase at the base of the rear cylinder block (**Figure 7**): for example, BJLM110001.

*NOTE*
*When Harley-Davidson makes a running change during a production year, the bikes, depending on where they are produced during production, are identified as an early or late model for that year. For example, if a production change was made during the 1985 production run, the bikes, depending on where they were manufactured during the actual run, would be referred to as an Early 1985 or Late 1985 model. If you run across this type of designation in this manual that pertains to your model, give your Harley-Davidson dealer a call and have them identify your model with its 17 digit VIN number.*

## PARTS REPLACEMENT

When you order parts from the dealer or other parts distributor, always order by the full 17 digit VIN number. Compare new parts to old before purchasing them. If they are not alike, have the parts manager explain the difference to you.

## TORQUE SPECIFICATIONS

Torque specifications throughout this manual are given in foot-pounds (ft.-lb.) as well as the metric equivalent in newton-meters (N•m).

**Table 7** lists general torque specifications for nuts and bolts that are not listed in the respective chapters. To use the table, first determine the size of the bolt or nut. Use a vernier caliper and measure the inside dimensions of the threads of the nut (**Figure 8**) and across the threads for a bolt (**Figure 9**).

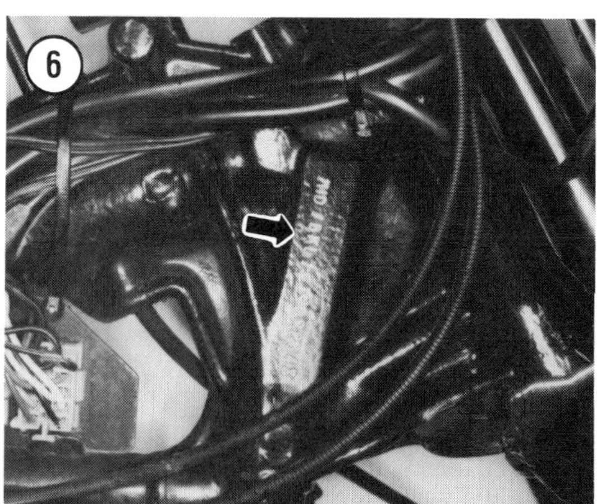
6

## FASTENERS

The materials and designs of the various fasteners used on your Harley are not arrived at by chance or

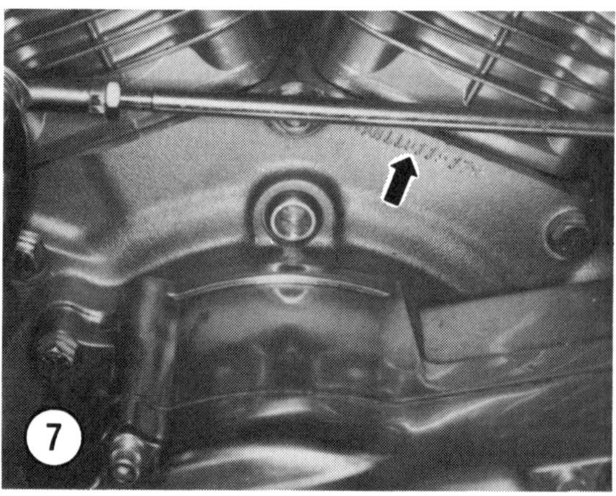
7

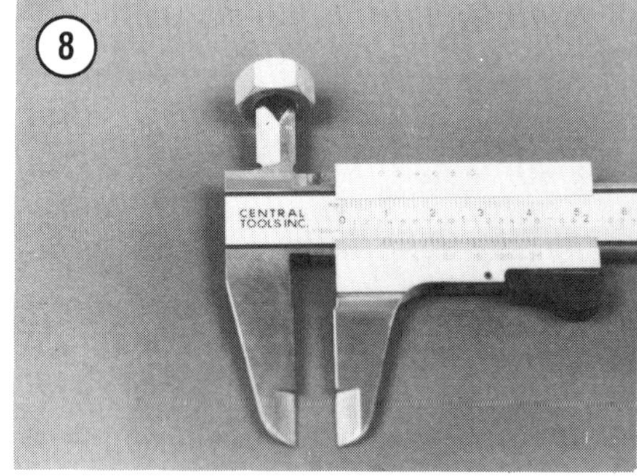

8

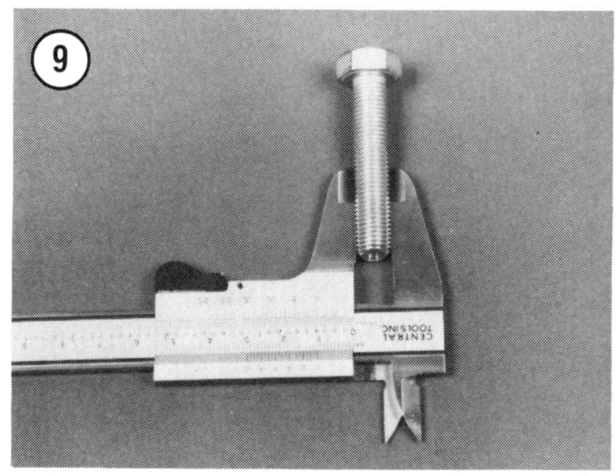
9

accident. Fastener design determines the type of tool required to work the fastener. Fastener material is carefully selected to decrease the possibility of physical failure.

Nuts, bolts and screws are manufactured in a wide range of thread patterns. To join a nut and bolt, the diameter of the bolt and the diameter of the hole in the nut must be the same. It is just as important that the threads on both be properly matched.

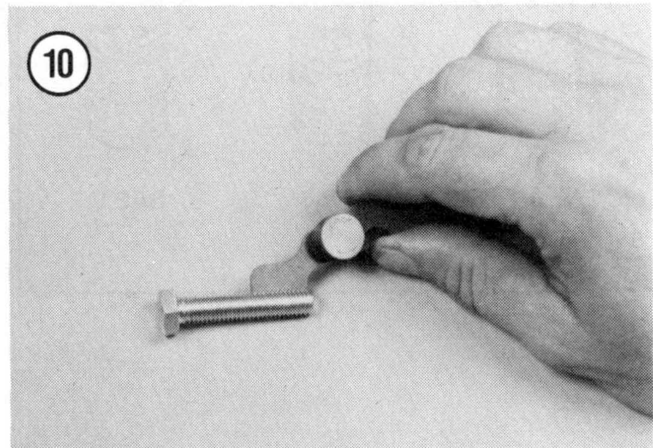


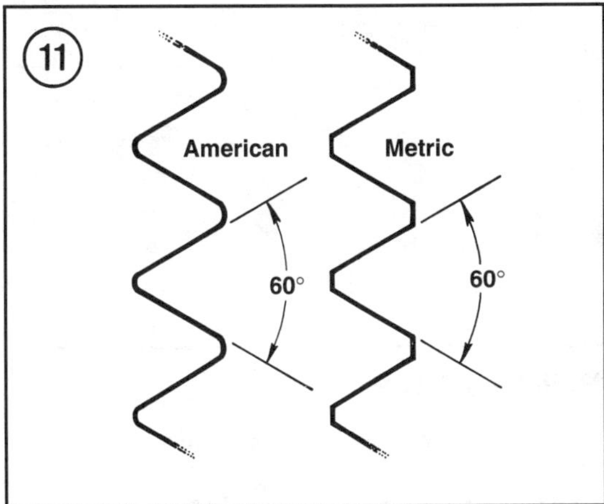


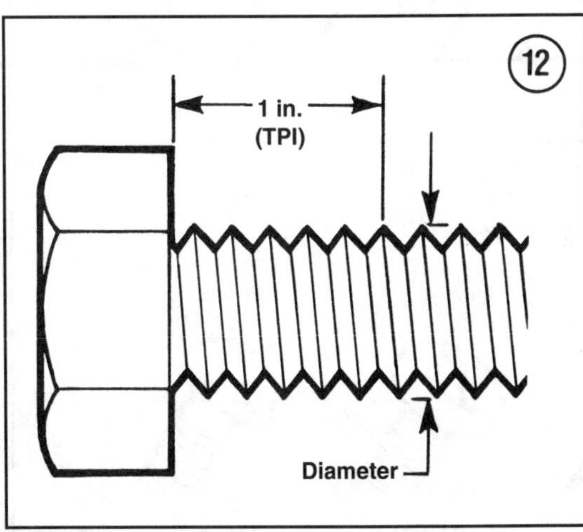


The best way to tell if the threads on 2 fasteners are matched is to turn the nut on the bolt (or the bolt into the threaded hole in a piece of equipment) with fingers only. Be sure both pieces are clean. If much force is required, check the thread condition on each fastener. If the thread condition is good but the fasteners jam, the threads are not compatible. A thread pitch gauge (**Figure 10**) can also be used to determine pitch. Harley-Davidson motorcycles are manufactured with American standard fasteners. The threads are cut differently than metric fasteners (**Figure 11**).

Most threads are cut so that the fastener must be turned clockwise to tighten it. These are called right-hand threads. Some fasteners have left-hand threads; they must be turned counterclockwise to be tightened. Left-hand threads are used in locations where normal rotation of the equipment would tend to loosen a right-hand threaded fastener.

## American Threads

American threads come in a coarse or fine thread. Because both coarse and fine threads are used for general use, it is important to match the threads correctly so you do not strip the threads and damage one or both fasteners.

American fasteners are normally described by diameter, threads per inch (TPI) and length; **Figure 12** shows the first 2 specifications. For example, 3/8-16 × 2 indicates a bolt 3/8 in. in diameter with 16 threads per inch, 2 inches long. The measurement across 2 flats on the head of the bolt or screw (**Figure 13**) indicates the proper wrench size to be used. **Figure 9** shows how to determine bolt diameter.

Markings found on American bolt heads indicate tensile strength. For example, a bolt with no head marking is usually made of mild steel, while a bolt with 2 or more markings indicates a higher grade material. **Figure 14** indicates the various head markings with SAE grade identification. When torquing SAE bolts not listed in a torque specification table, refer to the head marking (**Figure 13**) and then to **Table 7** for the torque specification.

### Determining Bolt Length

When purchasing a bolt from a dealer or parts store, it is important to know how to specify bolt length. The correct way to measure bolt length is to measure the length starting from underneath the bolt head to the end of the bolt (**Figure 15**). Always measure bolt length in this manner to avoid purchasing bolts that are too long.

### Machine Screws

Machine screw refers to a numbering system used to identify screws smaller than 1/4 of an inch. Ma-

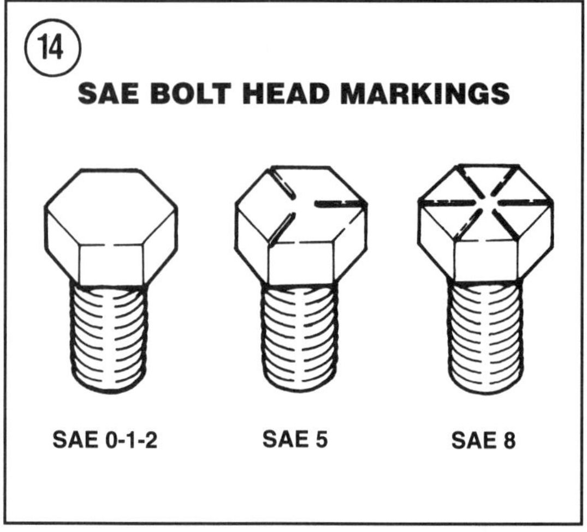


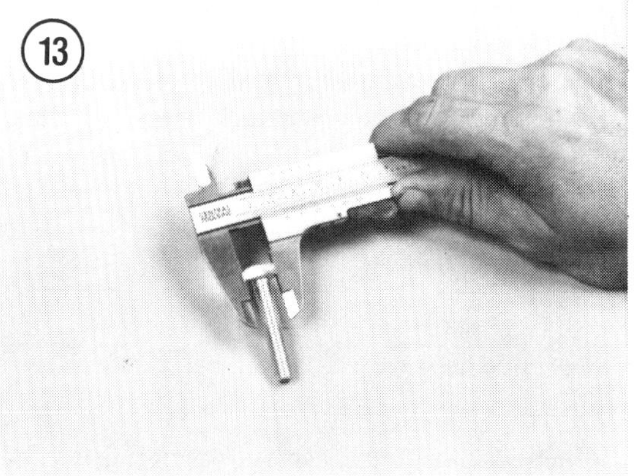


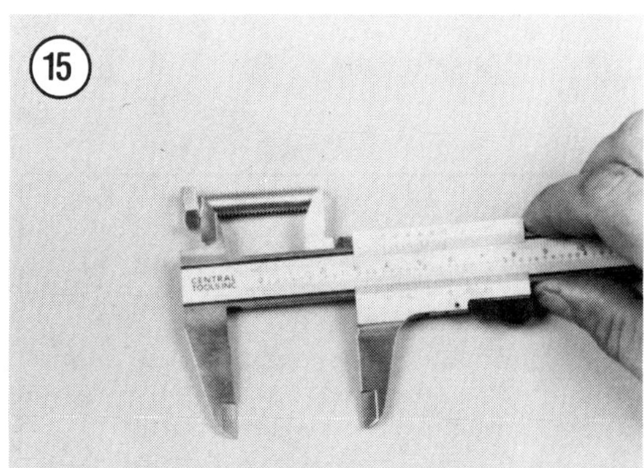


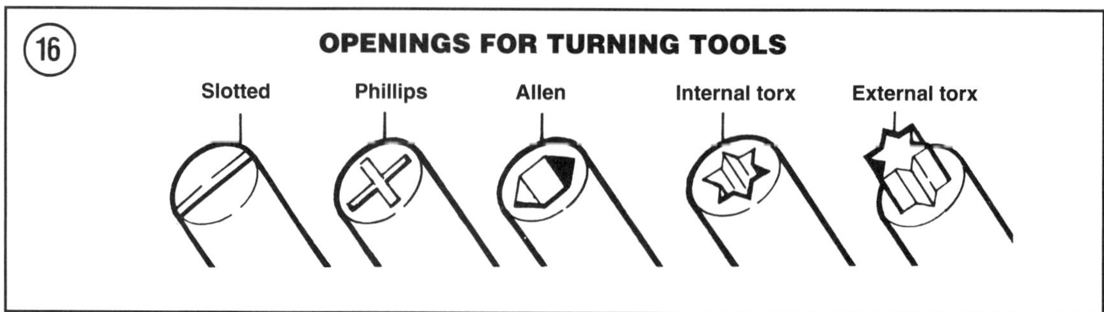


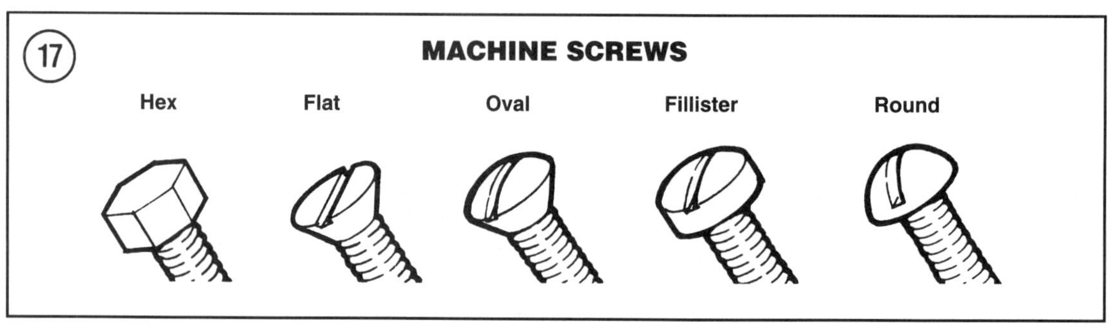

chine screws are identified by gauge size (diameter) and threads per inch. For example, 12-28 indicates a 12 gauge screw with 28 threads per inch.

There are many different types of machine screws. **Figure 16** shows a number of screw heads requiring different types of turning tools. Heads are also designed to protrude above the metal (round) or to be slightly recessed in the metal (flat). See **Figure 17**.

### Bolts

Commonly called bolts, the technical name for these fasteners is cap screw. Refer to *American Threads* in this section for additional information.

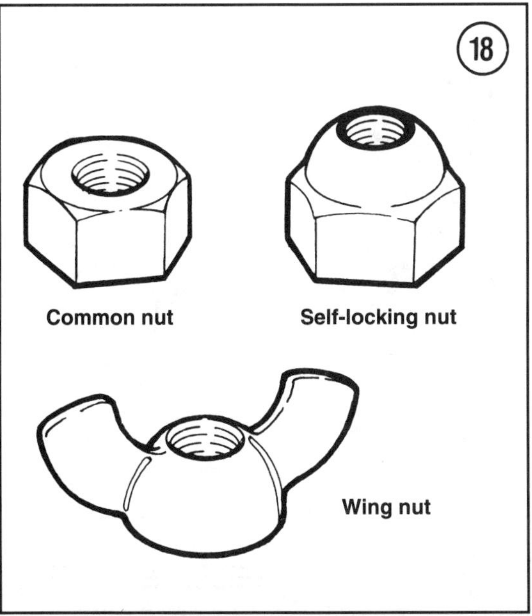


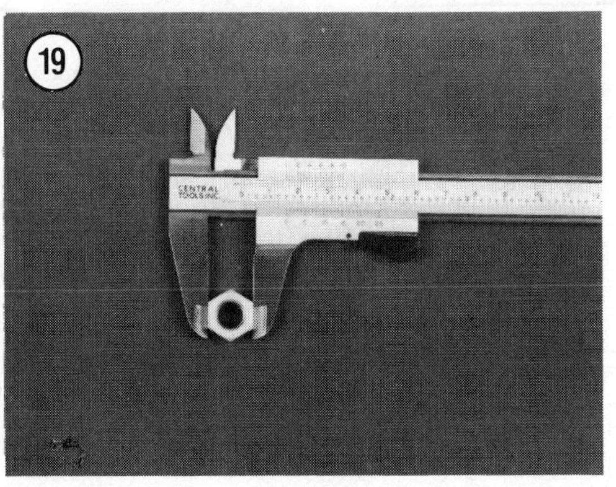


### Nuts

Nuts are manufactured in a variety of types and sizes. Most are hexagonal (6-sided) and fit on bolts, screws and studs with the same diameter and pitch.

**Figure 18** shows several types of nuts. The common nut is generally used with a lockwasher. Self-locking nuts have a nylon insert which prevents the nut from loosening; no lockwasher is required. Wing nuts are designed for fast removal by hand. Wing nuts are used for convenience in non-critical locations.

To indicate the size of a nut, manufacturers specify the diameter of the opening and the thread pitch. This is similar to bolt specifications, but without the length dimension. The measurement across 2 flats on the nut (**Figure 19**) indicates the proper wrench size to be used.

### Self-locking Fasteners

Several types of bolts, screws and nuts incorporate a system that develops an interference between the bolt, screw, nut or tapped hole threads. Interference is achieved in various ways: by distorting threads, coating threads with dry adhesive or nylon, distorting the top of an all-metal nut, using a nylon insert in the center or at the top of a nut, etc.

Self-locking fasteners offer greater holding strength and better vibration resistance. Some self-locking fasteners can be reused if in good condition. Others, like the nylon insert nut, form an initial locking condition when the nut is first installed; the nylon forms closely to the bolt thread pattern, thus reducing any tendency for the nut to loosen. When the nut is removed, the locking efficiency is greatly reduced. For greatest safety, it is recommended that you install new self-locking fasteners whenever they are removed.

### Washers

There are 2 basic types of washers: flat washers and lockwashers. Flat washers are simple discs with a hole to fit a screw or bolt. Lockwashers are designed to prevent a fastener from working loose due to vibration, expansion and contraction. Lockwashers should be installed between the bolt head or nut and a flat washer (**Figure 20**). **Figure 21** shows several types of washers. Washers are also used in the following functions:

a. As spacers.
b. To prevent galling or damage of the equipment by the fastener.
c. To help distribute fastener load during torquing.
d. As fluid seals (copper or laminated washers).

Note that flat washers are often used between a lockwasher and a fastener to provide a smooth bearing surface. This allows the fastener to be turned easily with a tool.

*NOTE*
*As much care should be given to the selection and purchase of washers as that given to bolts, nuts and other fasteners. Beware of washers that are made of thin and weak materials. These will deform and crush the first time they are used in a high torque application.*

## Cotter Pins

Cotter pins (**Figure 22**) are used to secure fasteners in a special location. The threaded stud, bolt or axle must have a hole in it. Its nut or nut lock piece has castellations around its upper edge into which the cotter pin fits to keep it from loosening. When *properly* installed, a cotter pin is a positive locking device.

The first step in properly installing a cotter pin is to purchase one that will fit snugly when inserted through the nut and the mating thread part. This should not be a problem when purchasing cotter pins through a Harley-Davidson dealer; you can order them by their respective part numbers. However, when you stop off at your local hardware or automotive store, keep this in mind. The cotter pin should not be so tight that you have to drive it in and out, but you do not want it so loose that it can move or float after it is installed.

Before installing a cotter pin, tighten the nut to the recommended torque specification. If the castellations in the nut do not line up with the hole in the bolt or axle, tighten the nut until alignment is achieved. Do not loosen the nut to make alignment. Insert a *new* cotter pin through the nut and hole, then tap the head lightly to seat it. Bend one arm over the flat on the nut and the other against the top of the

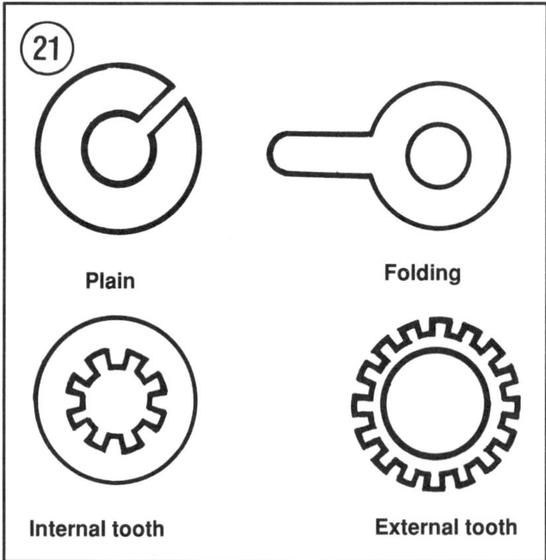


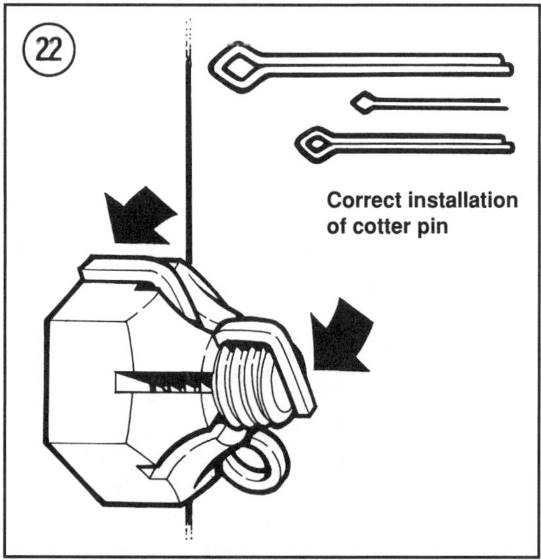

axle or bolt (**Figure 22**). Cut the arms to a suitable length to prevent them from snagging on clothing, or worse, your hands, arms or legs; the exposed arms will cut flesh easily. When the cotter pin is bent and its arms cut to length, it should be tight. If you can wiggle the cotter pin, it is improperly installed.

Cotter pins should not be reused as their ends may break and allow the cotter pin to fall out and perhaps the fastener to unscrew itself.

### Circlips

Circlips can be of internal or external design. They are used to retain items on shafts (external type) or within tubes (internal type). In some applications, circlips of varying thicknesses are used to control the end play of parts assemblies. These are often called selective circlips. Circlips should be replaced during installation, as removal weakens and deforms them.

Two basic styles of circlips are available: machined and stamped circlips. Machined circlips (**Figure 23**) can be installed in either direction (shaft or housing) because both faces are machined, thus creating two sharp edges. Stamped circlips (**Figure 24**) are manufactured with one sharp edge and one rounded edge. When installing stamped circlips in a thrust situation, the sharp edge must face away from the part producing the thrust. When installing circlips, observe the following:

a. Circlips should be removed and installed with circlip pliers. See *Circlip Pliers* in this chapter.
b. Compress or expand circlips only enough to install them.
c. After the circlip is installed, make sure it is completely seated in its groove.

Transmission circlips become worn with use and increase side play. For this reason, always use new circlips whenever a transmission is to be reassembled.

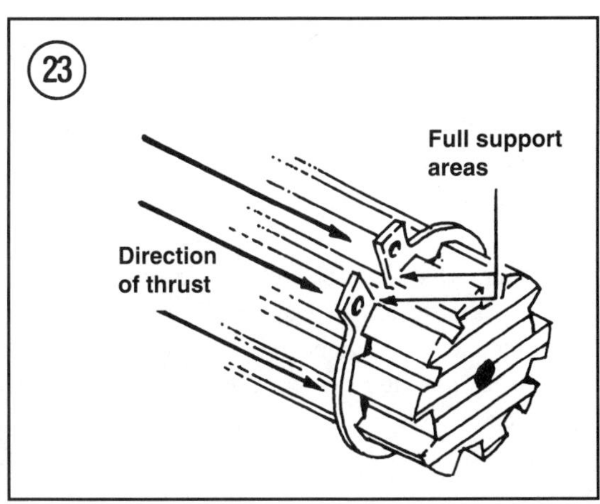


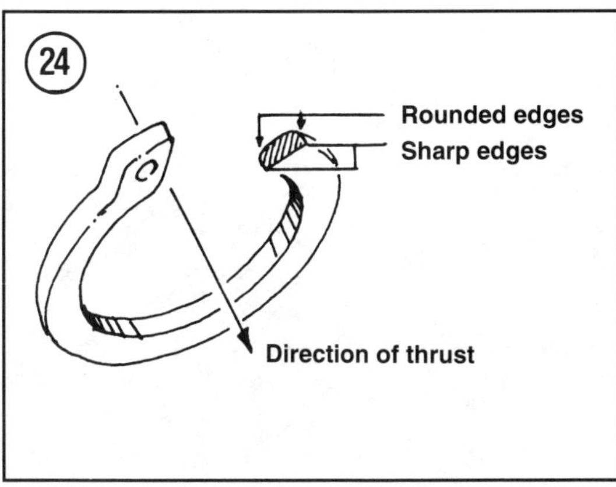


## LUBRICANTS

Periodic lubrication assures long life for any type of equipment. The *type* of lubricant used is just as important as the lubrication service itself, although in an emergency the wrong type of lubricant is better than none. The following paragraphs describe the types of lubricants most often used on motorcycle equipment. Be sure to follow the manufacturer's recommendations for lubricant types.

If any unique lubricant is recommended by Harley-Davidson, it is specified in the service procedure.

Generally, all liquid lubricants are called "oil." They may be mineral-based (including petroleum bases), natural-based (vegetable and animal bases), synthetic-based or emulsions (mixtures). "Grease" is an oil to which a thickening base has been added so that the end product is semi-solid. Grease is often classified by the type of thickener added; lithium soap is commonly used.

### Engine Oil

Four-cycle oil for motorcycle and automotive engines is graded by the American Petroleum Institute (API) and the Society of Automotive Engineers (SAE) in several categories. Oil containers display these ratings on the top or label (**Figure 25**).

API oil grade is indicated by letters; oils for gasoline engines are identified by an "S."

Viscosity is an indication of the oil's thickness. The SAE uses numbers to indicate viscosity; thin oils have low numbers while thick oils have high numbers. A "W" after the number indicates that the viscosity testing was done at low temperature to simulate cold-weather operation. Engine oils fall into the 5W-30 and 20W-50 range.

Multi-grade oils (for example 10W-40) are less viscous (thinner) at low temperatures and more viscous (thicker) at high temperatures. This allows the oil to perform efficiently across a wide range of engine operating conditions. The lower the number, the better the engine will start in cold climates. Higher numbers are usually recommended for engines running in hot weather conditions.

### Grease

Greases are graded by the National Lubricating Grease Institute (NLGI). Greases are graded by number according to the consistency of the grease; these range from No. 000 to No. 6, with No. 6 being the most solid. A typical multipurpose grease is NLGI No. 2. For specific applications, equipment manufacturers may require grease with an additive such as molybdenum disulfide (MOS2).

Also recommended for axle and swing arm pivot shafts is an anti-seize lubricant (**Figure 26**). This is necessary to prevent the pivot points from corroding and locking up.

## RTV GASKET SEALANT

Room temperature vulcanizing (RTV) sealant is used on some pre-formed gaskets and to seal some components. RTV is a silicone gel supplied in tubes and can be purchased in a number of different colors.

Moisture in the air causes RTV to cure. Always place the cap on the tube as soon as possible when using RTV. RTV has a shelf life of one year and will not cure properly when the shelf life has expired. Check the expiration date on RTV tubes before using and keep partially used tubes tightly sealed.

### Applying RTV Sealant

Clean all gasket residue from mating surfaces. Surfaces should be clean and free of oil and dirt. Remove all RTV gasket material from blind attaching holes, as it can cause a "hydraulic" effect and affect bolt torque.

Apply RTV sealant in a continuous bead. Circle all mounting holes unless otherwise specified. Torque mating parts within 10 minutes after application.

## THREADLOCK

A chemical locking compound should be used on all bolts and nuts, even if they are secured with lockwashers. A locking compound will lock fasteners against vibration loosening and seal against leaks. Loctite 242 (blue) and 271 (red) are recommended for many threadlock requirements described in this manual (**Figure 27**).

Loctite 242 (blue) is a medium strength threadlock and component disassembly can be performed with normal hand tools. Loctite 271 (red) is a high strength threadlock and heat or special tools, such as a press or puller, may be required for component disassembly.

### Applying Threadlock

Surfaces should be clean and free of oil, grease, dirt and other residue; clean threads with an aerosol electrical contact cleaner before applying the Loctite. When applying Loctite, use a small amount. If too much is used, it can work its way down the threads and stick parts together not meant to be stuck.

## GASKET REMOVER

Stubborn gaskets can present a problem during engine service as they can take a long time to remove. Consequently, there is the added problem of secondary damage occurring to the gasket mating surfaces from the incorrect use of gasket scraping tools. To quickly and safely remove stubborn gaskets, use a spray gasket remover. Spray gasket remover can be purchased through automotive parts houses. Follow the manufacturer's directions for use.

## EXPENDABLE SUPPLIES

Certain expendable supplies are required during maintenance and repair work. These include grease, oil, gasket cement, wiping rags and cleaning solvent. Ask your dealer for the silicone lubricants, contact cleaner and other products which make maintenance simpler and easier. Cleaning solvent or kerosene is available at some service stations or hardware stores.

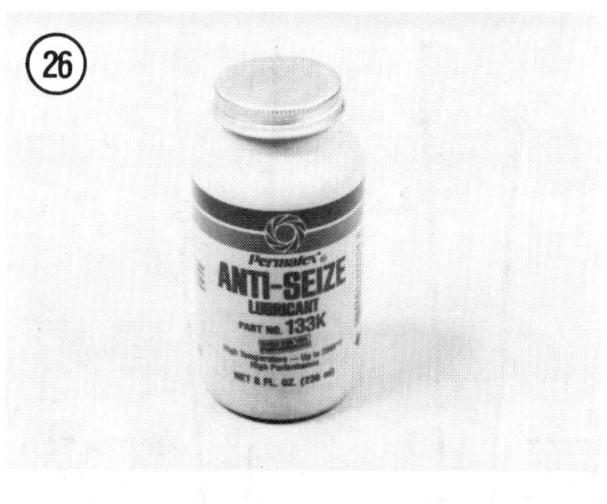

## BASIC HAND TOOLS

Many of the procedures in this manual can be carried out with simple hand tools and test equipment familiar to the average home mechanic. Keep your tools clean and in a tool box. Keep them organized with the sockets and related drives together, the open-end combination wrenches together, etc. After using a tool, wipe off dirt and grease with a clean cloth and return the tool to its correct place.

Top quality tools are essential; they are also more economical in the long run. If you are now starting to build your tool collection, stay away from the "advertised specials" featured at some parts houses, discount stores and chain drug stores. These are usually a poor grade tool that can be sold cheaply and that is exactly what they are—*cheap*. They are usually made of inferior material, and are thick, heavy and clumsy. Their rough finish makes them difficult to clean and they usually don't last very long. If it is ever your misfortune to use such tools, you will probably find out that the wrenches do not fit the heads of bolts and nuts correctly and damage the fastener.

Quality tools are made of alloy steel and are heat treated for greater strength. They are lighter and better balanced than cheap ones. Their surface is smooth, making them a pleasure to work with and easy to clean. The initial cost of good quality tools may be more but they are cheaper in the long run. Don't try to buy everything in all sizes in the beginning; do it a little at a time until you have the necessary tools.

The following tools are required to perform virtually any repair job. Each tool is described and the recommended size given for starting a tool collection. Additional tools and some duplicates may be added as you become familiar with your Harley. Harley-Davidson motorcycles are built with American standard fasteners. If you are starting your collection now, buy American sizes.

### Screwdrivers

The screwdriver is a very basic tool, but if used improperly it will do more damage than good. The slot on a screw has a definite dimension and shape. Through improper use or selection, a screwdriver can damage the screw head, making removal of the screw difficult. A screwdriver must be selected to conform to the shape of the screw head used. Two basic types of screwdrivers are required: standard (flat- or slot-blade) screwdrivers (**Figure 28**) and Phillips screwdrivers (**Figure 29**).

Note the following when selecting and using screwdrivers:

a. The screwdriver must always fit the screw head. If the screwdriver blade is too small for the screw slot, damage may occur to the screw slot and screwdriver. If the blade is too large, it cannot engage the slot properly and will result in damage to the screw head.

b. Standard screwdrivers are identified by the length of their blade. A 6-inch (15.2 cm) screwdriver has a blade six inches (15.2 cm) long. The width of the screwdriver blade will vary, so make sure that the blade engages the screw slot the complete width of the screw.

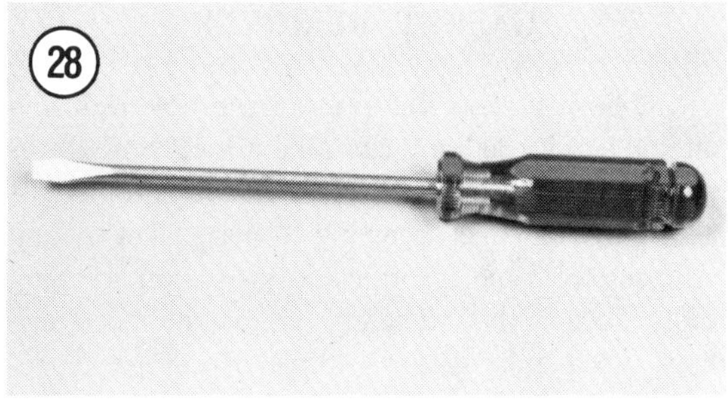


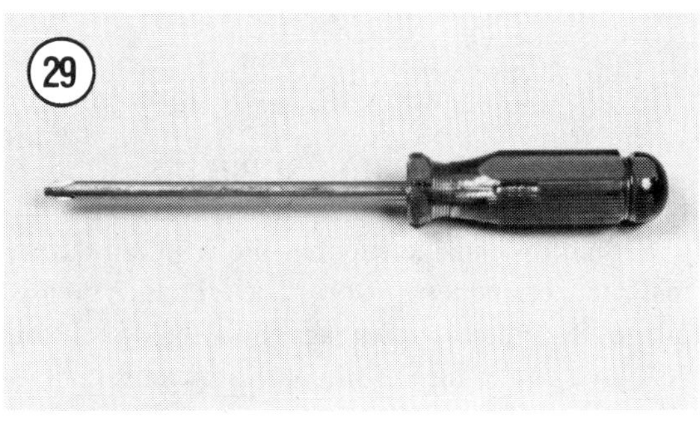


30

CORRECT TAPER AND SIZE

TAPER TOO STEEP

FRONT

SIDE

CORRECT WAY TO GRIND BLADE

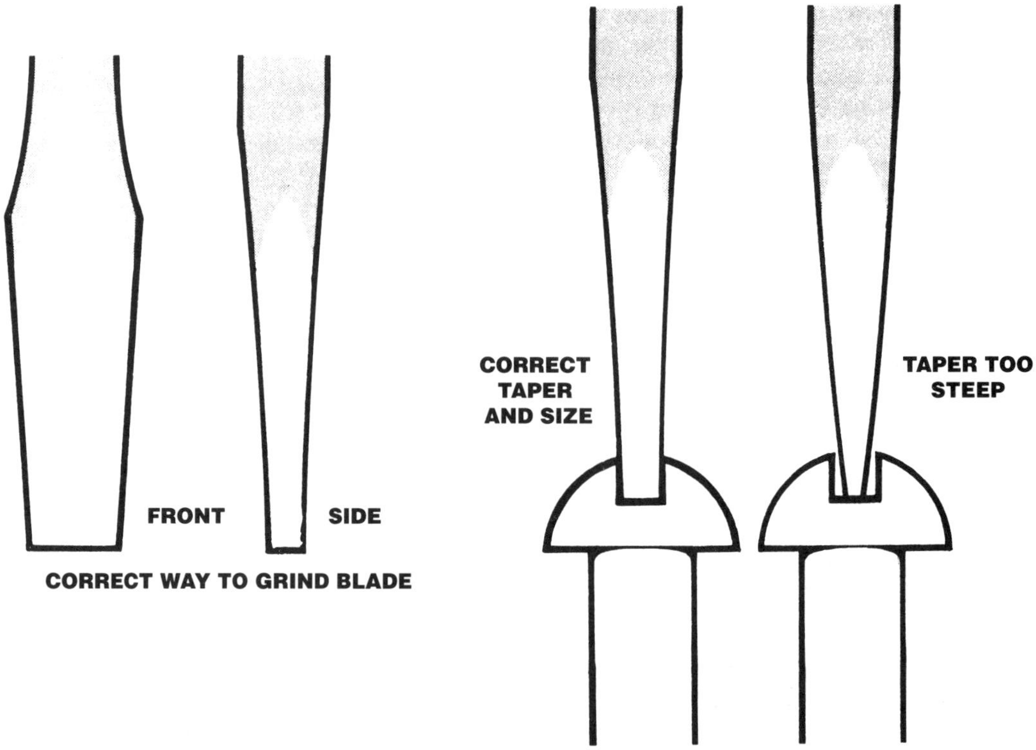

c. Phillips screwdrivers are sized according to their point size. They are numbered one, two, three and four. The degree of taper determines the point size; the No. 1 Phillips screwdriver will be the most pointed. The points become more blunt as their number increases.

*NOTE*
*You should also be aware of another screwdriver similar to the Phillips, and that is the Reed and Prince tip. Like the Phillips, the Reed and Prince screwdriver tip forms an "X" but with one major exception, the Reed and Prince tip has a much more pointed tip. The Reed and Prince screwdriver should never be used on Phillips screws and vice versa. Intermixing these screwdrivers will cause damage to the screw and screwdriver. If you have both types in your tool box and they are similar in appearance, you may want to identify them by painting the screwdriver shank underneath the handle.*

d. When selecting screwdrivers, note that you can apply more power with less effort with a longer screwdriver than with a short one. Of course, there will be situations where only a short handled screwdriver can be used. Keep this in mind though, when having to remove tight screws.

e. Because the working end of a screwdriver receives quite a bit of abuse, you should purchase screwdrivers with hardened-tips. The extra money will be well spent.

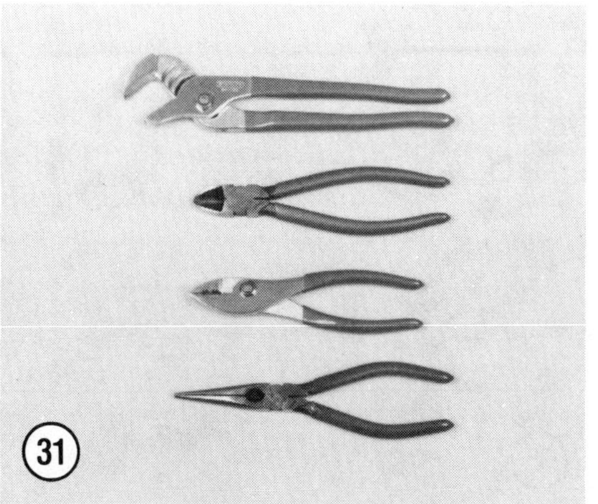
31

Screwdrivers are available in sets which often include an assortment of common and Phillips blades. If you buy them individually, buy at least the following:

a. Common screwdriver—5/16 × 6 in. blade.
b. Common screwdriver—3/8 × 12 in. blade.
c. Phillips screwdriver—size 2 tip, 6 in. blade.
d. Phillips screwdriver—size 3 tip, 6 and 8 in. blade.

Use screwdrivers only for driving screws. Never use a screwdriver for prying or chiseling metal. Do not try to remove a Phillips, Torx or Allen head screw with a standard screwdriver (unless the screw has a combination head that will accept either type); you can damage the head so that the proper tool will be unable to remove it.

Keep screwdrivers in the proper condition and they will last longer and perform better. Always keep the tip of a standard screwdriver in good condition. **Figure 30** shows how to grind the tip to the proper shape if it becomes damaged. Note the symmetrical sides of the tip.

## Pliers

Pliers come in a wide range of types and sizes. Pliers are useful for cutting, bending and crimping. They should never be used to cut hardened objects or to turn bolts or nuts. **Figure 31** shows several pliers useful in repairing your Harley.

Each type of pliers has a specialized function. Slip-joint pliers are general purpose pliers and are used mainly for holding things and for bending. Needlenose pliers are used to hold or bend small objects. Water pump pliers can be adjusted to hold various sizes of objects; the jaws remain parallel to grip around objects such as pipe or tubing. There are many more types of pliers.

*CAUTION*
*Pliers should not be used for loosening or tightening nuts or bolts. The pliers sharp teeth will grind off the nut or bolt corners and damage it.*

*CAUTION*
*If slip-joint or water pump pliers are going to be used to hold an object with a finished surface, wrap the object with tape or cardboard for protection.*

### Vise-grip Pliers

Vise-grip pliers (**Figure 32**) are used to hold objects very tightly while another task is performed on the object. While Vise-grip pliers work well, caution should be followed with their use. Because Vise-grip pliers exert more force than regular pliers, their sharp jaws can permanently scar the object. In addition, when Vise-grip pliers are locked into position, they can crush or deform thin-walled material.

Vise-grip pliers are available in many types for more specific tasks.

### Circlip Pliers

Circlip pliers (**Figure 33**) are special in that they are only used to remove or install circlips. When purchasing circlip pliers, there are two kinds to choose from. External pliers (spreading) are used to remove circlips that fit on the outside of a shaft. Internal pliers (squeezing) are used to remove circlips which fit inside a housing.

*WARNING*
*Because circlips can sometimes slip and "fly off" during removal and installation, always wear safety glasses when servicing them.*

### Box-end, Open-end and Combination Wrenches

Box-end and open-end wrenches (**Figure 34**) are available in sets or separately in a variety of sizes. The size number stamped near the end refers to the distance between 2 parallel flats on the hex head bolt or nut.

Box-end wrenches are usually superior to open-end wrenches. Open-end wrenches grip the nut on only 2 flats. Unless a wrench fits well, it may slip and round off the points on the nut. The box-end wrench grips on all 6 flats. Both 6-point and 12-point openings on box-end wrenches are available. The

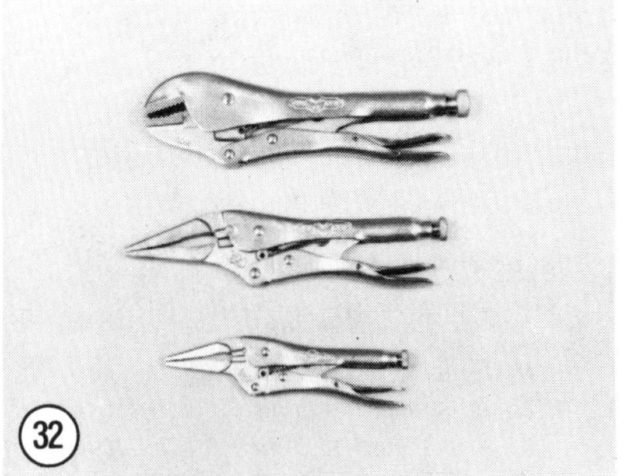
32

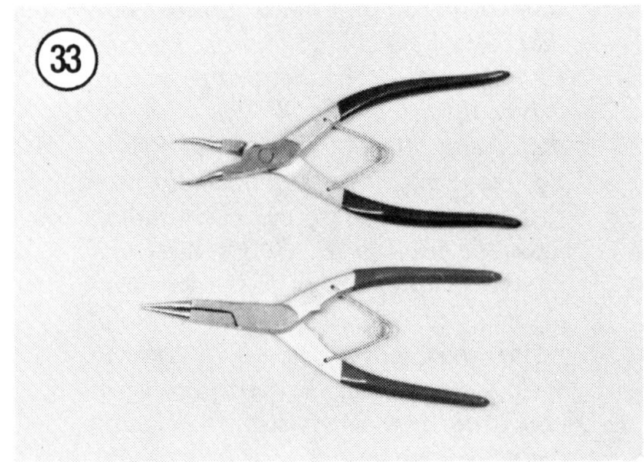
33

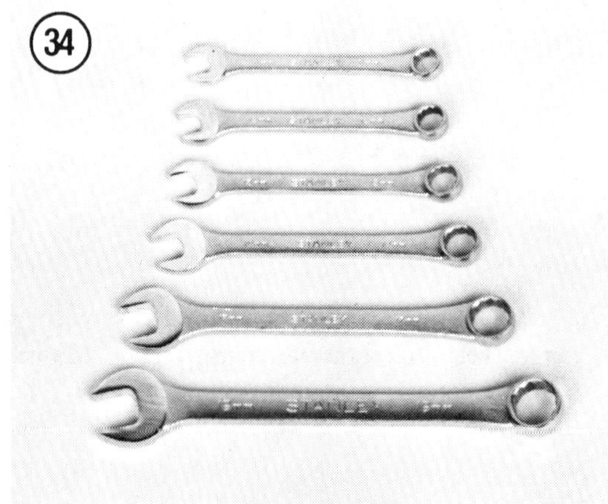
34

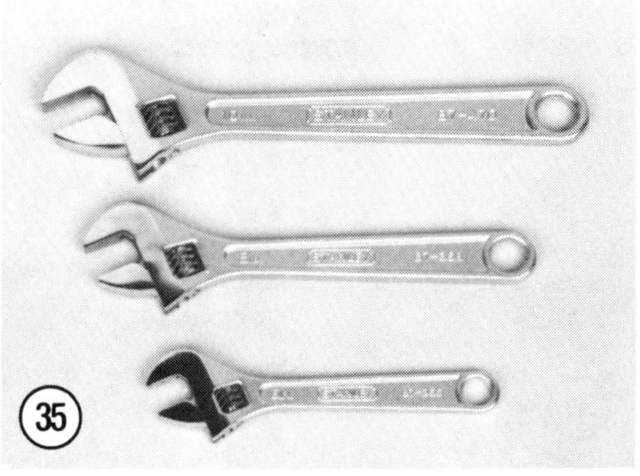
35

6-point gives superior holding power; the 12-point allows a shorter swing.

Combination wrenches which are open on one side and boxed on the other are also available. Both ends are the same size.

No matter what style of wrench you choose, proper use is important to prevent personal injury. When using a wrench, get into the habit of pulling the wrench toward you. This technique will reduce the risk of injuring your hand if the wrench should slip. If you have to push the wrench away from you to loosen or tighten a fastener, open and push with the palm of your hand; your fingers and knuckles will be out of the way if the wrench slips. Before using a wrench, always think ahead as to what could happen if the wrench should slip or if the fastener strips or breaks.

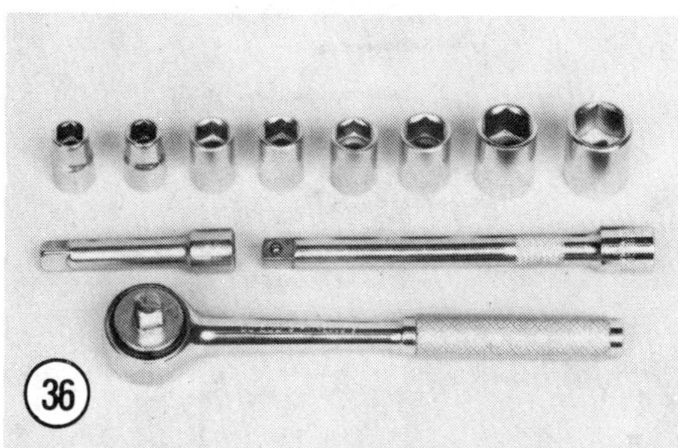


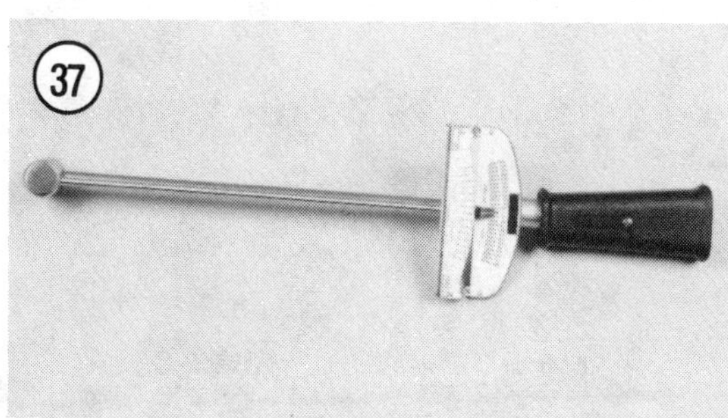


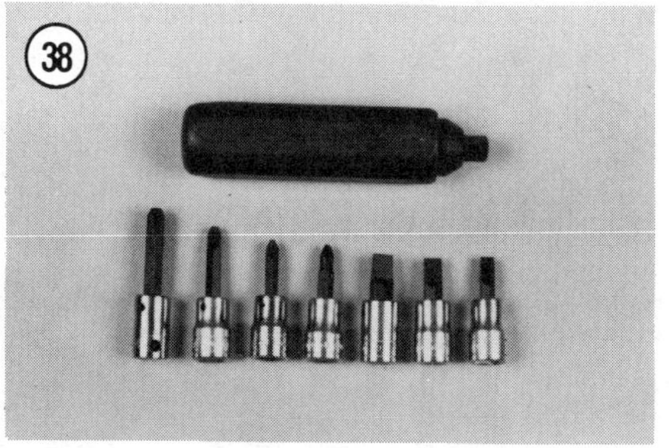


## Adjustable Wrenches

An adjustable wrench can be adjusted to fit nearly any nut or bolt head which has clear access around its entire perimeter. Adjustable wrenches are best used as a backup wrench to keep a large nut or bolt from turning while the other end is being loosened or tightened with a proper wrench. See **Figure 35**.

Adjustable wrenches have only two gripping surfaces which makes them more subject to slipping off the fastener and damaging the part and possibly your hand. See *Box-end, Open-end and Combination Wrenches* in this chapter.

These wrenches are directional; the solid jaw must be the one transmitting the force. If you use the adjustable jaw to transmit the force, it will loosen and possibly slip off.

Adjustable wrenches come in all sizes but something in the 6 to 8 inch range is recommended as an all-purpose wrench.

## Socket Wrenches

This type is undoubtedly the fastest, safest and most convenient to use. Sockets which attach to a ratchet handle (**Figure 36**) are available with 6-point or 12-point openings and 1/4, 3/8, 1/2 and 3/4 in. drives. The drive size indicates the size of the square hole which mates with the ratchet handle.

## Torque Wrench

A torque wrench (**Figure 37**) is used with a socket to measure how tightly a nut or bolt is installed. They come in a wide price range and with either 3/8 or 1/2 in. square drives. The drive size indicates the size of the square drive which mates with the socket.

## Impact Driver

This tool makes removal of tight fasteners easy and eliminates damage to bolts and screw slots. Impact drivers and interchangeable bits (**Figure 38**) are available at most large hardware and motorcycle dealers. Don't purchase a cheap one as they don't work as well and require more force than a moderately priced one. Sockets can also be used with a hand impact driver. However, make sure the socket is designed for use with an impact driver or air tool. Do not use regular hand-type sockets, as they may shatter during use.

## Hammers

The correct hammer (**Figure 39**) is necessary for repairs. Use only a hammer with a face (or head) of rubber or plastic or the soft-faced type that is filled with buckshot. These are sometimes necessary in engine teardowns. *Never* use a metal-faced hammer on engine or suspension parts, as severe damage will result in most cases. Ball-peen or machinist's hammers will be required when striking another tool, such as a punch or impact driver. When striking a hammer against a punch, cold chisel or similar tool, the face of the hammer should be at least 1/2 in. larger than the head of the tool. When it is necessary to strike hard against a steel part without damaging it, a brass hammer should be used. A brass hammer can be used because brass will give when striking a harder object. Brass hammers are used when truing crankshafts.

When using hammers, note the following:

a. *Always* wear safety glasses when using a hammer.
b. Inspect hammers for damaged or broken parts. Repair or replace the hammer as required. Do *not* use a hammer with a taped handle.
c. Always wipe oil or grease off of the hammer *before* using it.
d. The head of the hammer should always strike the object squarely. Do not use the side of the hammer or the handle to strike an object.
e. Always use the correct hammer for the job.

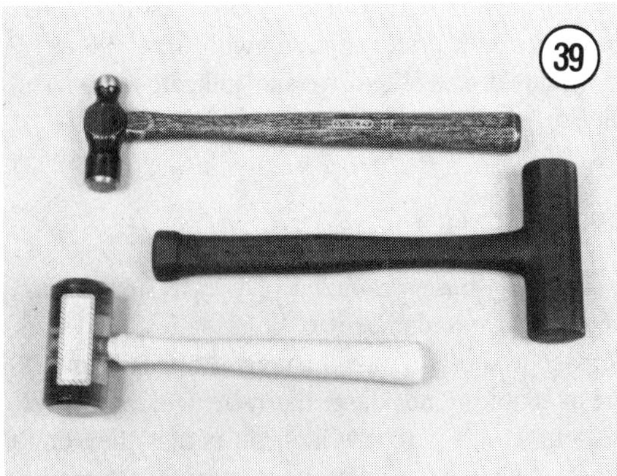

39

## Allen Wrenches

Allen wrenches (**Figure 40**) are available in sets or separately in a variety of sizes. These sets come in SAE and metric size, so be sure to buy a SAE set. Allen bolts are sometimes called socket bolts.

Harley-Davidson uses Allen bolts throughout the bike. Sometimes the bolts are difficult to reach and it is suggested that a variety of Allen wrenches be

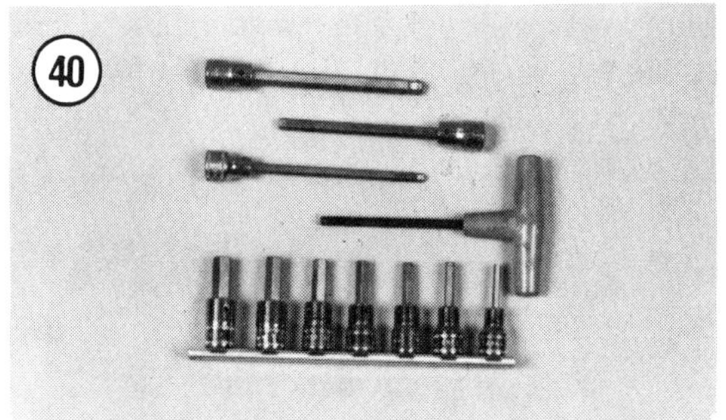

40

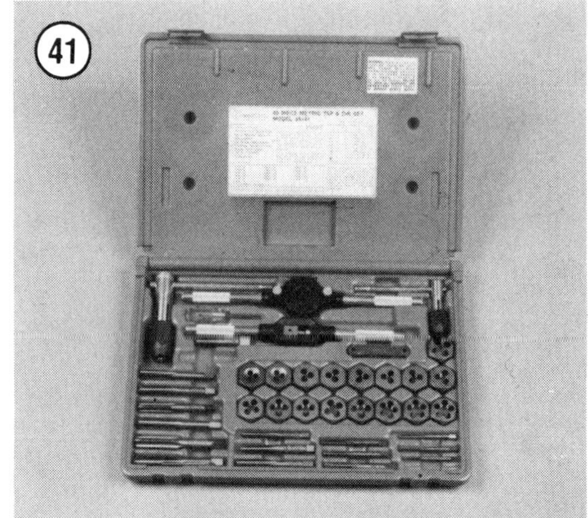

41

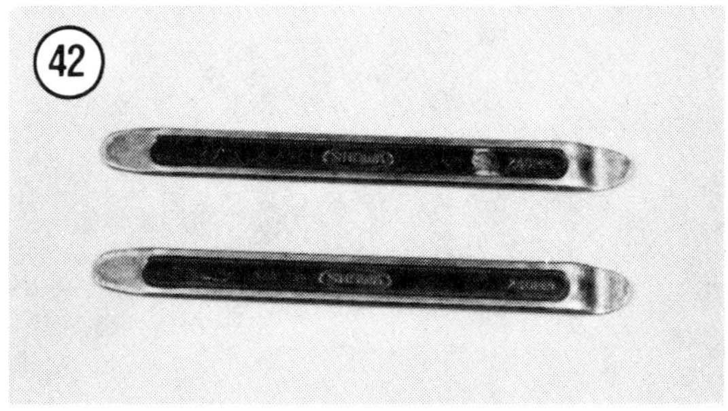

42

purchased (e.g. socket driven, T-handle and extension type) as shown in **Figure 40**.

### Tap and Die Set

A complete tap and die set (**Figure 41**) is a relatively expensive tool. But when you need a tap or die to clean up a damaged thread, there is really no substitute. Be sure to purchase one for American Standard (SAE) threads when working on your Harley.

### Tire Levers

When changing tires, use a good set of tire levers (**Figure 42**). Never use a screwdriver in place of a tire lever; refer to Chapter Ten for tire changing procedures using these tools. Before using the tire levers, check the working ends of the tool and remove any burrs. Don't use a tire lever for prying anything but tires. **Figure 42** shows a regular pair of 10 in. (25.4 cm) long tire levers. However, for better leverage when changing tires on your Harley, you may want to invest in a set of 16 in. (40.6 cm) long tire irons. These can be ordered through your dealer.

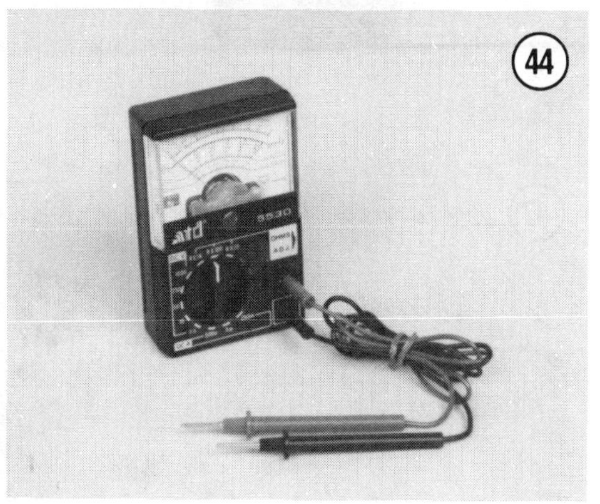


### Bike Stand

Because your Harley is not equipped with a centerstand, you will need some type of bike stand to raise its wheels off of the ground. And when raising your Harley, you do not want to improvise a bike stand with available materials to just get you by. Consider the physical damage that would occur if your bike falls onto a cement floor.

There are a number of accessory bike stands that can be used to raise and support your Harley safely during service. Most are designed for shop use only. The bike stand shown in **Figure 43** was made out of heavy duty pipe. Aftermarket stands are available that are both useful and innovative. Along with using it in your shop or garage, some stands can be folded into a compact size and packed with your travel gear and taken along for emergency use on the road. When selecting a bike stand, make sure that it can be used on Harley-Davidson motorcycles. Always check the stability of the bike stand before walking away from the bike or when working on it.

### Drivers and Pullers

These tools are used to remove and install oil seals, bushings, bearings and gears. These will be called out during service procedures in later chapters as required.

## TEST EQUIPMENT

### Multimeter or Volt-ohm Meter

This instrument (**Figure 44**) is invaluable for electrical system troubleshooting and service. A few of its functions may be duplicated by homemade test equipment, but for the serious mechanic it is a must. Its uses are described in the applicable section of the book.

## Compression Gauge

An engine with low compression cannot be properly tuned and will not develop full power. A compression gauge measures engine compression. The one shown in **Figure 45** has a flexible stem with an extension that can allow you to hold it while cranking the engine over. Press-in rubber tipped types (**Figure 46**) are also available. Open the throttle all the way when checking engine compression. See Chapter Three.

## Cylinder Leak Down Tester

By positioning a cylinder on its compression stroke so that both valves are closed and then pressurizing the cylinder, you can isolate engine problem areas (eg. leaking valve, damaged head gasket, broke, worn or stuck piston rings) by listening for escaping air through the carburetor, exhaust pipe, cylinder head mating surface, etc. To perform this procedure, a leak down tester and air compressor are required. This procedure is described in Chapter Three as it pertains to the Harley-Davidson Evolution engines. Cylinder leak down testers can be purchased through Harley-Davidson dealers, accessory tool manufacturers and automotive tool suppliers.

## Battery Hydrometer

A hydrometer (**Figure 47**) is the best way to check a battery's state of charge. A hydrometer measures the weight or density of the sulfuric acid in the battery's electrolyte in specific gravity.

## Portable Tachometer

A portable tachometer is necessary for tuning (**Figure 48**). Ignition timing and carburetor adjustments must be performed at specified engine speeds. The best instrument for this purpose is one with a low range of 0-1,000 or 0-2,000 rpm and a high range of 0-4,000. Extended range (0-6,000 or 0-8,000 rpm) instruments lack accuracy at lower speeds. The instrument should be capable of detecting 25 rpm on the low range.

## Timing Light

Suitable timing lights range from inexpensive neon bulb types to powerful xenon strobe lights (**Figure 49**). A light with an inductive pickup is recommended to prevent any possible damage to ignition wiring.

45

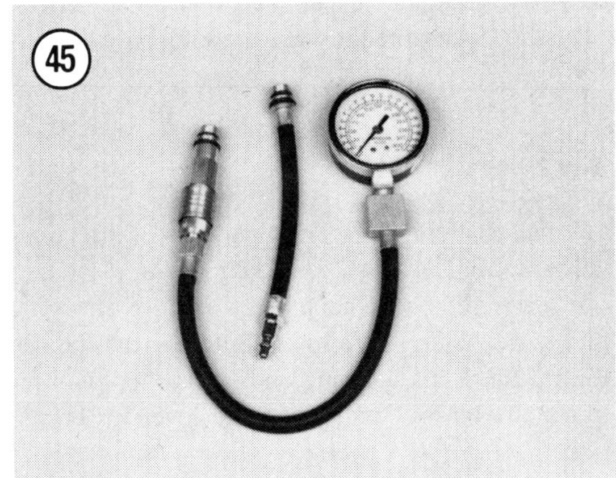

46

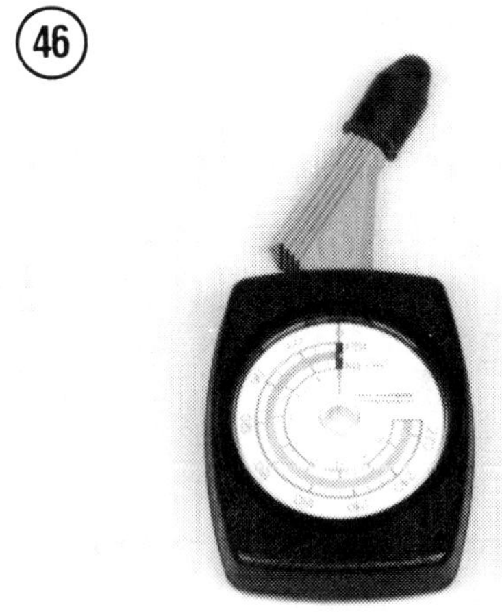

47

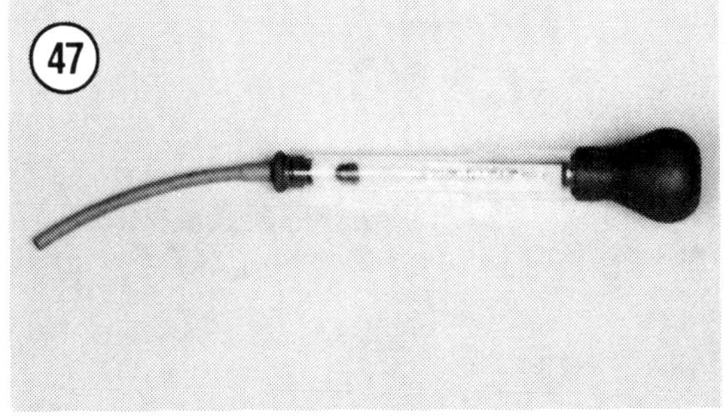

## PRECISION MEASURING TOOLS

Measurement is an important part of servicing your Harley. When performing many of the service procedures in this manual, you will be required to make a number of measurements. These include basic checks such as engine compression and spark plug gap. As you become more involved with engine disassembly and service, measurements will be required to determine the condition of the piston and cylinder bore, crankshaft runout and so on. When making these measurements, the degree of accuracy will dictate which tool is required. Precision measuring tools are expensive. If this is your first experience at engine service, it may be more worthwhile to have the checks made at a dealer. However, as your skills and enthusiasm increase for doing your own service work, you may want to begin purchasing some of these specialized tools. The following is a description of the measuring tools required during engine overhaul.

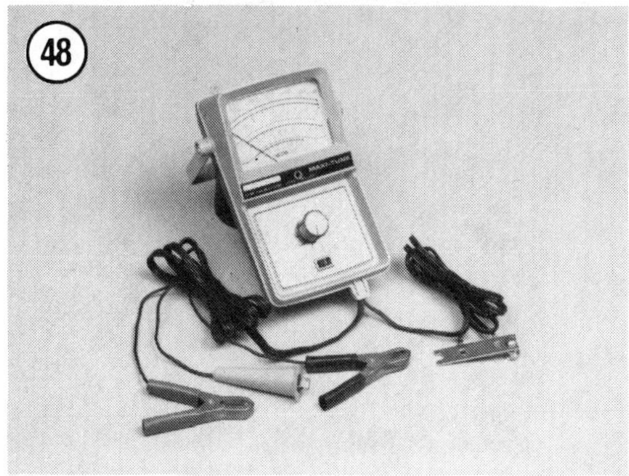


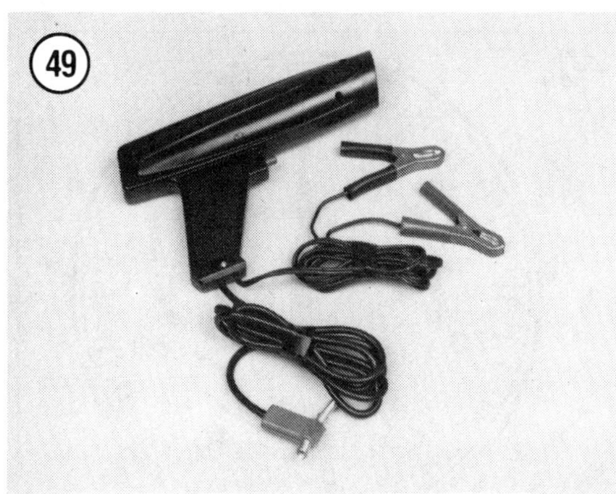


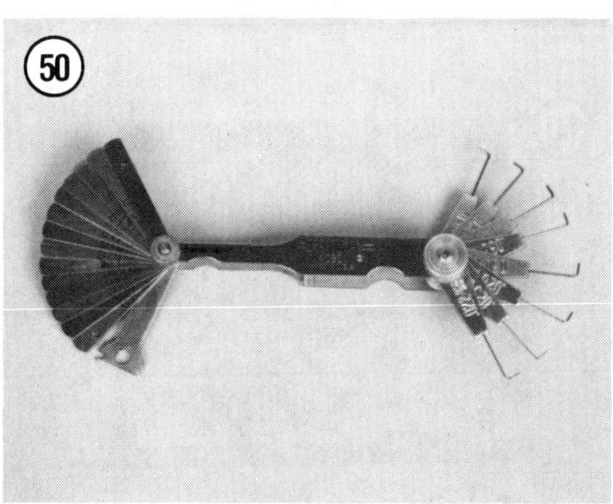


### Feeler Gauge

The feeler gauge (**Figure 50**) is made of either a piece of a flat or round hardened steel of a specified thickness. Wire gauges are used to measure spark plug gap. Flat gauges are used for all other measurements.

### Vernier Caliper

This tool (**Figure 51**) is invaluable when it is necessary to measure inside, outside and depth measurements with close precision. It can be used to measure the thickness of shims and thrust washers. It is perhaps the most often used measuring tool in the motorcycle service shop. Vernier calipers are available in a wide assortment of styles and price ranges.

### Outside Micrometers

The outside micrometer (**Figure 52**) is used for very exact measurements of close-tolerance components. It can be used to measure the outside diameter of a piston as well as for shims and thrust washers. Outside micrometers will be required to transfer measurements from bore, snap and small hole gauges. Micrometers can be purchased individually or in a set.

### Dial Indicator

Dial indicators (**Figure 53**) are precision tools used to check crankshaft and drive shaft runout limits. For motorcycle repair, select a dial indicator with a continuous dial (**Figure 54**).

### Cylinder Bore Gauge

The cylinder bore gauge is a very specialized precision tool. The gauge set shown in **Figure 55** is comprised of a dial indicator, handle and a number of length adapters to adapt the gauge to different bore sizes. The bore gauge can be used to make cylinder bore measurements such as bore size, taper and out-of-round. An outside micrometer must be used together with the bore gauge to determine bore dimensions.

### Telescoping Gauges

Telescoping gauges (**Figure 56**) can be used to measure hole diameters from approximately 5/16 in. to 6 in. Like the small hole gauge, the telescoping gauge does not have a scale gauge for direct readings. Thus an outside micrometer is required to determine bore dimensions.

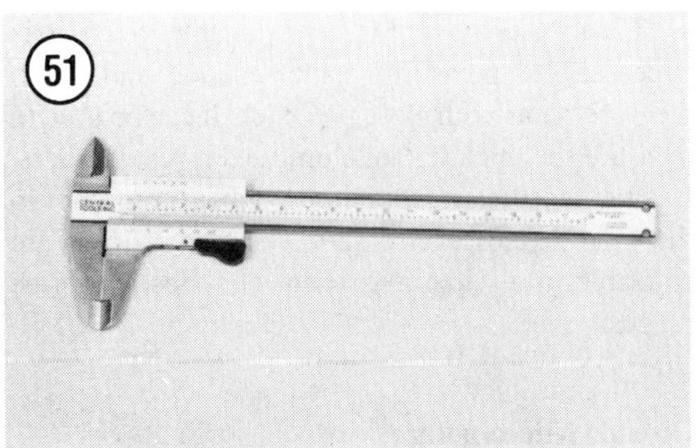


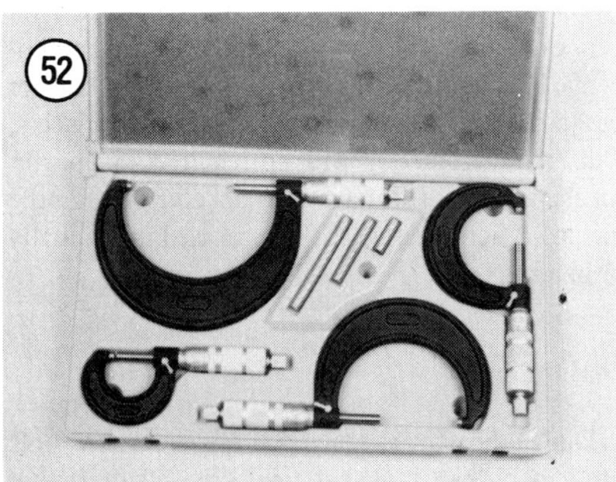


### Small Hole Gauges

A set of small hole gauges (**Figure 57**) allows you to measure a hole, groove or slot ranging in size up to 1/2 in. An outside micrometer must be used to-

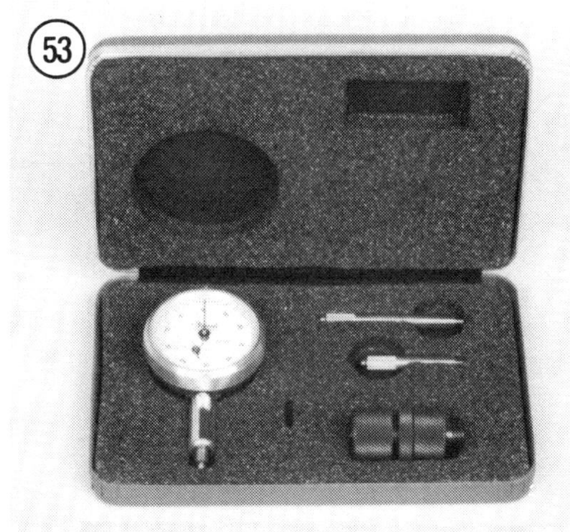

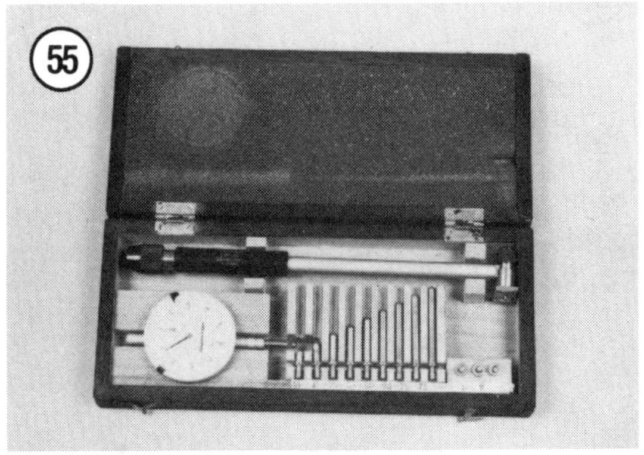

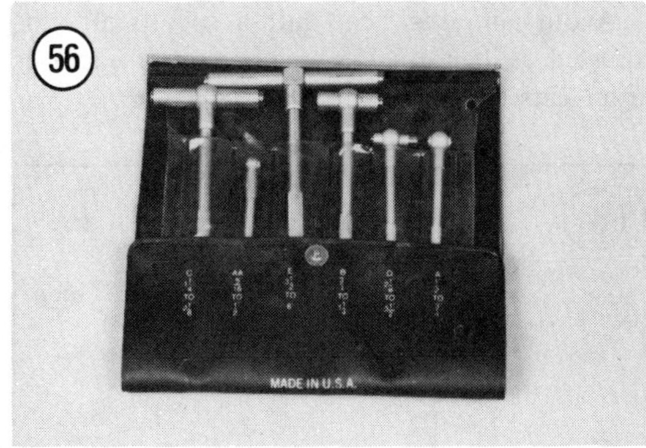


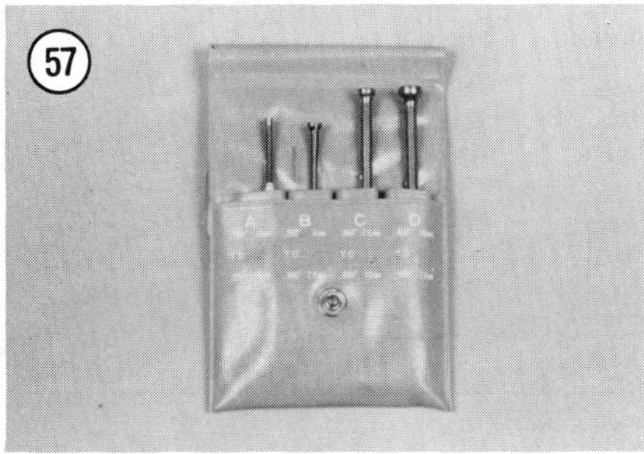


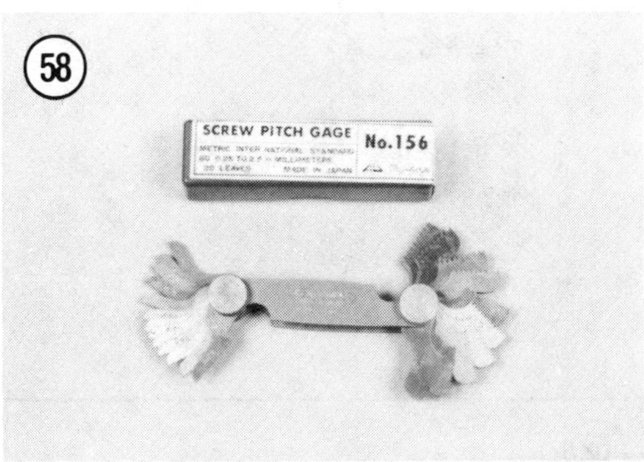


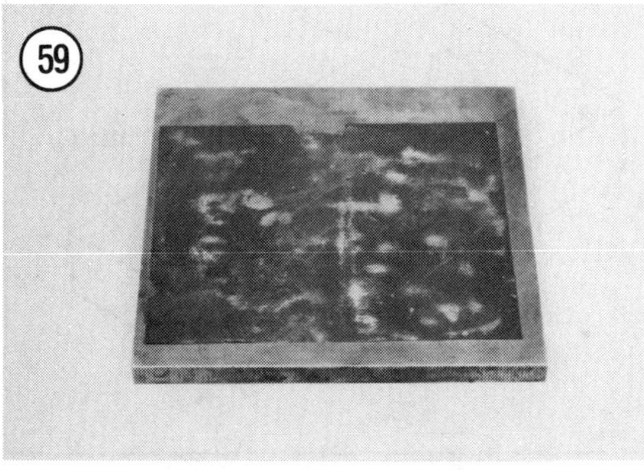


gether with the small hole gauge to determine bore dimensions.

## Screw Pitch Gauge

A screw pitch gauge (**Figure 58**) determines the thread pitch of bolts, screws, studs, etc. The gauge is made up of a number of thin plates. Each plate has a thread shape cut on one edge to match one thread pitch. When using a screw pitch gauge to determine a thread pitch size, try to fit different blade sizes onto the bolt thread until both threads match.

## Surface Plate

A surface plate can be used to check the flatness of parts or to provide a perfectly flat surface for minor resurfacing of cylinder head or other critical gasket surfaces. While industrial quality surface plates are quite expensive, the home mechanic can improvise. A thick metal plate can be put to use as a surface plate. The metal surface plate shown in **Figure 59** has a piece of sandpaper glued to its surface that is used for cleaning and smoothing cylinder head and crankcase mating surfaces.

*NOTE*
*Check with a local machine shop on the availability and cost of having a metal plate resurfaced for use as a surface plate.*

# CLEANING SOLVENT

With the environmental concern that is prevalent today concerning the disposal of hazardous solvents, the home mechanic should select a water soluble, biodegradable solvent. These solvents can be purchased through dealers, automotive parts houses and large hardware stores.

Selecting a solvent is only one of the problems facing the home mechanic when it comes to cleaning parts. You need some type of tank to clean parts as well as to store the solvent. There are a number of manufacturers offering different types and sizes of parts cleaning tanks. While a tank may seem a luxury to the home mechanic, you will find that it will quickly pay for itself through its efficiency and convenience. When selecting a parts washer, look for one that can recycle and store the solvent, as well as separate the sludge and contamination from the clean solvent. Most important, check the warranty, if any, as it pertains to the tank's pump. Like most tools, when purchasing a parts washer, you get what you pay for.

*WARNING*

*Having a stack of clean shop rags on hand is important when performing engine work. However, to prevent the possibility of fire damage from spontaneous combustion from a pile of solvent-soaked rags, store them in a sealed metal container until they can be washed or discarded.*

*NOTE*

*To avoid absorbing solvent and other chemicals into your skin while cleaning parts, wear a pair of petroleum-resistant rubber gloves. These can be purchased through industrial supply houses or well-equipped hardware stores.*

## OTHER SPECIAL TOOLS

A few other special tools may be required for major service. These are described in the appropriate chapters and are available from Harley-Davidson dealers or other manufacturers as indicated.

## MECHANIC'S TIPS

### Removing Frozen Nuts and Screws

When a fastener rusts and cannot be removed, several methods may be used to loosen it. First, apply penetrating oil such as Liquid Wrench or WD-40 (available at hardware or auto supply stores). Apply it liberally and let it penetrate for 10-15 minutes. Rap the fastener several times with a small hammer; do not hit it hard enough to cause damage. Reapply the penetrating oil if necessary.

For frozen screws, apply penetrating oil as described, then insert a screwdriver in the slot and rap the top of the screwdriver with a hammer. This loosens the rust so the screw can be removed in the normal way. If the screw head is too chewed up to use this method, grip the head with Vise-grip pliers and twist the screw out.

Avoid applying heat unless specifically instructed, as it may melt, warp or remove the temper from parts.

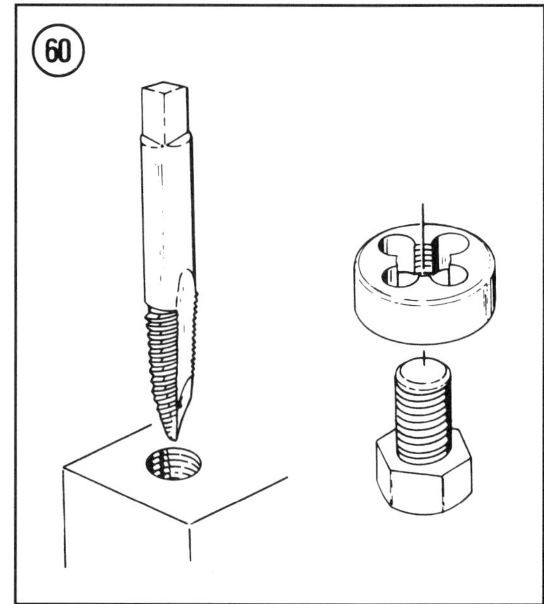


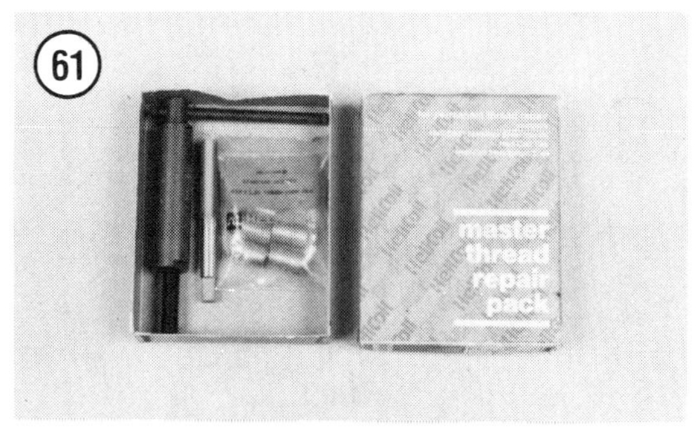


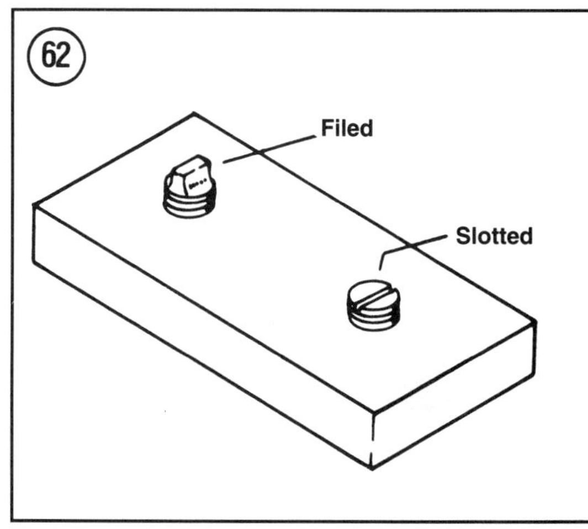

### Remedying Stripped Threads

Occasionally, threads are stripped through carelessness or impact damage. Often the threads can be cleaned up by running a tap (for internal threads on nuts) or die (for external threads on bolts) through the threads. See **Figure 60**. To clean or repair spark plug threads, a spark plug tap can be used.

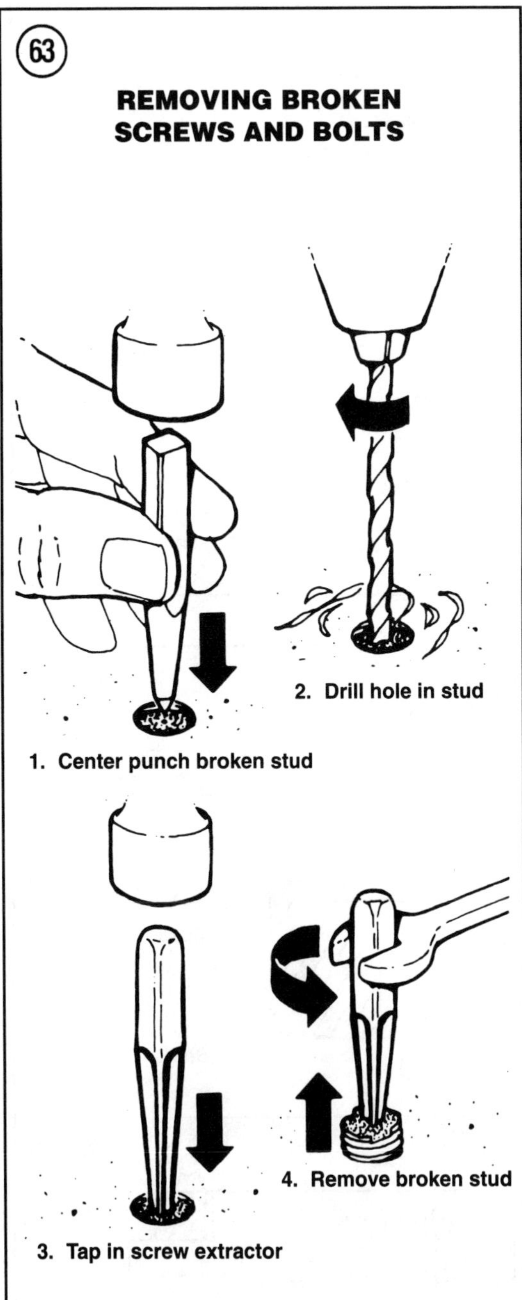


If an internal thread is damaged, it may be necessary to install a Helicoil (**Figure 61**) or some other type of thread insert. These kits have all of the necessary parts to repair a damaged internal thread.

If it is necessary to drill and tap a hole, refer to **Table 8** for SAE tap drill sizes.

### Removing Broken Screws or Bolts

When the head breaks off a screw or bolt, several methods are available for removing the remaining portion.

If a large portion of the remainder projects out, try gripping it with Vise-grip pliers. If the projecting portion is too small, file it to fit a wrench or cut a slot in it to fit a screwdriver. See **Figure 62**.

If the head breaks off flush, use a screw extractor. To do this, centerpunch the exact center of the remaining portion of the screw or bolt. Drill a small hole in the screw and tap the extractor into the hole. Back the screw out with a wrench on the extractor. See **Figure 63**.

### Removing Broken or Damaged Studs

If a stud is broken or the threads severely damaged, perform the following. A tube of Loctite 271 (red), 2 nuts, 2 wrenches and a new stud will be required during this procedure (**Figure 64**).

*NOTE*

*The following steps describe general procedures for replacing a typical stud. However, if you are replacing cylinder studs, refer to **Cylinder Stud Replacement** in Chapter Four. Do **not** use the following steps to replace cylinder studs. The improper installation of cylinder studs can cause cylinder head leakage.*

1. Thread two nuts onto the damaged stud. Then tighten the 2 nuts against each other so that they are locked.

*NOTE*

*If the threads on the damaged stud do not allow installation of the 2 nuts, you will have to remove the stud with a pair of Vise-grip pliers.*

2. Turn the bottom nut counterclockwise and unscrew the stud.
3. Threaded holes with a bottom surface should be blown out with compressed air as dirt buildup in the bottom of the hole may prevent the stud from being torqued properly. If necessary, use a bottoming tap to true up the threads and to remove any deposits.
4. Install 2 nuts on the top half of the new stud as in Step 1. Make sure they are locked securely.
5. Coat the bottom half of a new stud with Loctite 271 (red).
6. Turn the top nut clockwise and thread the new stud securely.
7. Remove the nuts and repeat for each stud as required.
8. Follow Loctite's directions on cure time before assembling the component.

## BALL BEARING REPLACEMENT

Ball bearings (**Figure 65**) are used throughout your Harley's engine and chassis to reduce power loss, heat and noise resulting from friction. Because ball bearings are precision made parts, they must be maintained by proper lubrication and maintenance. When a bearing is found to be damaged, it should be replaced immediately. However, when installing a new bearing, care should be taken to prevent damage to the new bearing. While bearing replacement is described in the individual chapters where applicable, the following can be used as a guideline.

*NOTE*
*Unless otherwise specified, install bearings with the manufacturer's mark*

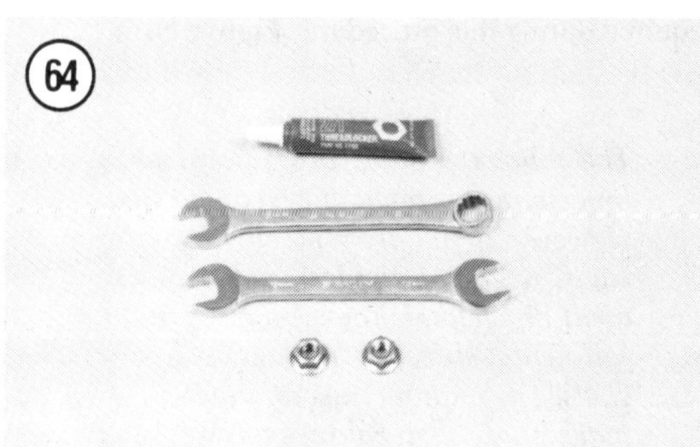

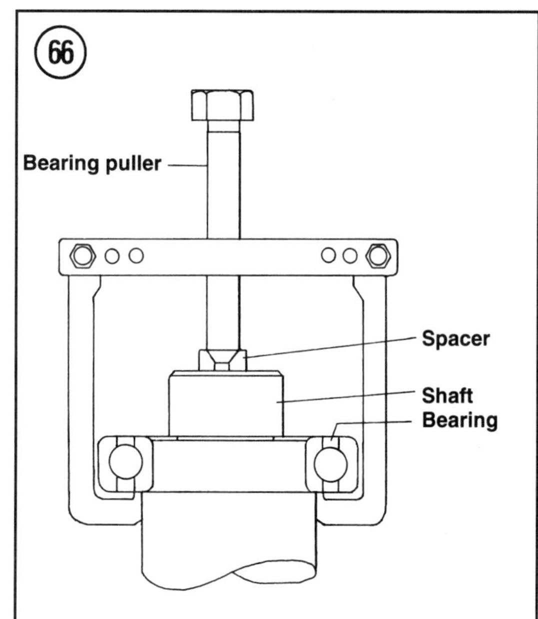


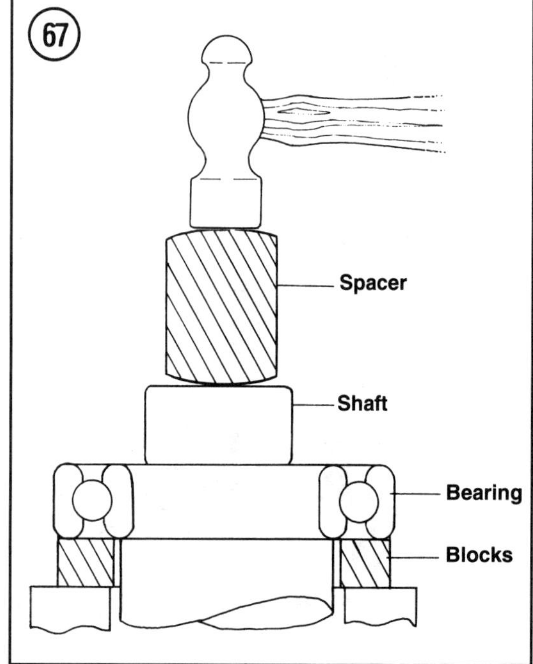

*or number on the bearing facing outward.*

## Bearing Removal

While bearings are normally removed only when damaged, there may be times when it is necessary to remove a bearing that is in good condition. Depending on the situation, you may be able to remove the bearing without damaging it. However, bearing removal in some situations, no matter how careful you are, will cause bearing damage. Care should always be given to bearings during their removal to prevent secondary damage to the shaft or housing. Note the following when removing bearings.

1. When using a puller to remove a bearing on a shaft, care must be taken so that shaft damage does not occur. Always place a piece of metal between the end of the shaft and the puller screw. In addition, place the puller arms next to the inner bearing race. See **Figure 66**.
2. When using a hammer to remove a bearing on a shaft, do not strike the hammer directly against the shaft. Instead, use a brass or aluminum spacer between the hammer and shaft (**Figure 67**). In addition, make sure to support *both* bearing races with wood blocks as shown in **Figure 67**.
3. The most ideal method of bearing removal is with a hydraulic press. However, certain procedures must be followed or damage may occur to the bearing, shaft or case half. Note the following when using a press:
    a. Always support the inner and outer bearing races with a suitable size wood or aluminum spacer ring (**Figure 68**). If only the outer race is supported, the balls and/or the inner race will be damaged.
    b. Always make sure the press ram (**Figure 68**) aligns with the center of the shaft. If the ram is not centered, it may damage the bearing and/or shaft.
    c. The moment the shaft is free of the bearing, it will drop to the floor. Secure or hold the shaft to prevent it from falling.

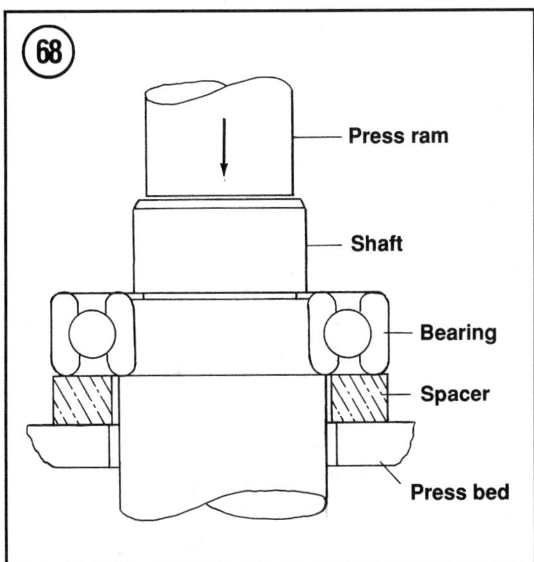


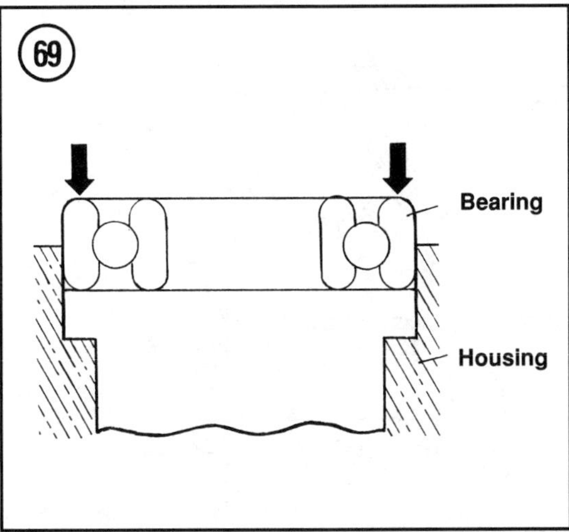


## Bearing Installation

1. When installing a bearing in a housing, pressure must be applied to the *outer* bearing race (**Figure 69**). When installing a bearing on a shaft, pressure must be applied to the *inner* bearing race (**Figure 70**).
2. When installing a bearing as described in Step 1, some type of driver will be required. Never strike the bearing directly with a hammer or the bearing will be damaged. When installing a bearing, a piece of pipe or a socket with an outer diameter that matches the bearing race will be required. **Figure 71** shows the correct way to use a socket and hammer when installing a bearing over a shaft.
3. Step 1 describes how to install a bearing in a case half and over a shaft. However, when installing a bearing over a shaft and into a housing at the same

time, a snug fit will be required for both outer and inner bearing races. In this situation, a spacer must be installed underneath the driver tool so that pressure is applied evenly across *both* races. See **Figure 72**. If the outer race is not supported as shown in **Figure 72**, the balls will push against the outer bearing track and damage it.

### Shrink Fit

1. *Installing a bearing over a shaft*: When a tight fit is required, the bearing inside diameter will be smaller than the shaft. In this case, driving the bearing on the shaft using normal methods may cause bearing damage. Instead, the bearing should be heated before installation. Note the following:

a. Secure the shaft so that it can be ready for bearing installation.

b. Clean the bearing surface on the shaft of all residue. Remove burrs with a file or sandpaper.

c. Fill a suitable pot or beaker with clean mineral oil. Place a thermometer (rated higher than 248° F[120° C]) in the oil. Support the thermometer so that it does not rest on the bottom or side of the pot.

d. Remove the bearing from its wrapper and secure it with a piece of heavy wire bent to hold it in the pot. Hang the bearing in the pot so that it does not touch the bottom or sides of the pot.

e. Turn the heat on and monitor the thermometer. When the oil temperature rises to approximately 248° F (120° C), remove the bearing from the pot and quickly install it. If necessary, place a socket on the inner bearing race and tap the bearing into place. As the bearing chills, it will tighten on the shaft so you must work quickly when installing it. Make sure the bearing is installed all the way.

2. *Installing a bearing in a housing*: Bearings are generally installed in a housing with a slight interference fit. Driving the bearing into the housing using normal methods may damage the housing or cause bearing damage. Instead, the housing should be heated before the bearing is installed. Note the following:

*CAUTION*

*Before heating the crankcases in this procedure to remove the bearings, wash the cases thoroughly with detergent and water. Rinse and rewash the cases as required to remove all traces of oil and other chemical deposits.*

a. The housing must be heated to a temperature of about 212° F (100° C) in an oven or on a hot plate. An easy way to check to see that it

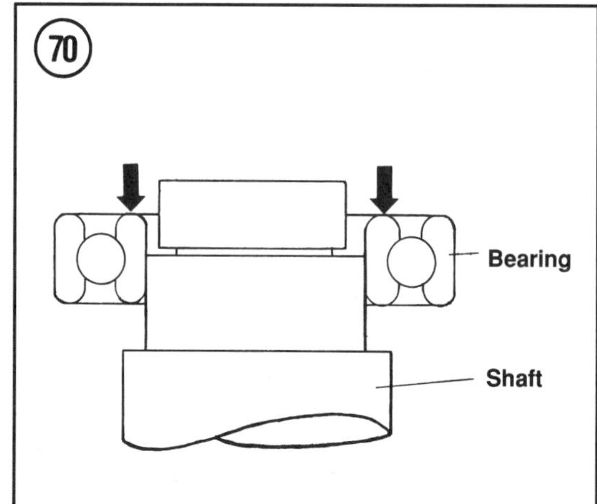


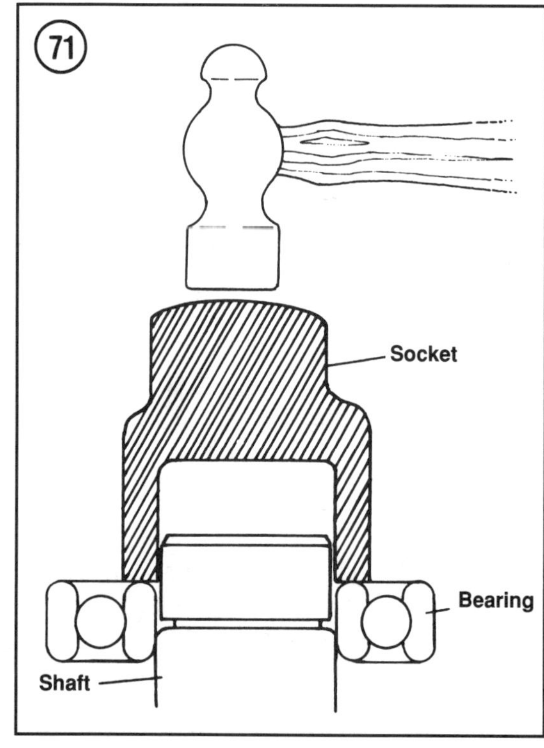

is at the proper temperature is to drop tiny drops of water on the case as it heats; if they sizzle and evaporate immediately, the temperature is correct. Heat only one housing at a time.

*CAUTION*
*Do not heat the housing with a torch (propane or acetylene)—never bring a flame into contact with the bearing or housing. The direct heat will destroy the case hardening of the bearing and will likely warp the housing.*

b. Remove the housing from the oven or hot plate and hold onto the housing with a kitchen pot holder, heavy gloves or heavy shop cloths—*it is hot.*

*NOTE*
*A suitable size socket and extension works well for removing and installing bearings.*

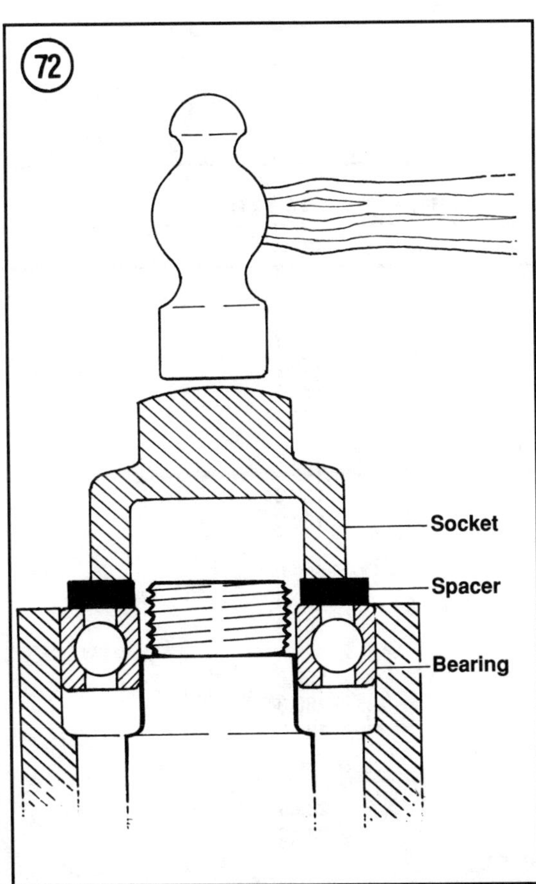


c. Hold the housing with the bearing side down and tap the bearing out. Repeat for all bearings in the housing.

d. While heating the housing halves, place the new bearings in a freezer if possible. Chilling them will slightly reduce their overall diameter while the hot housing assembly is slightly larger due to heat expansion. This will make installation much easier.

*NOTE*
*Always install bearings with the manufacturer's mark or number facing outward.*

e. While the housing is still hot, install the new bearing(s) into the housing. Install the bearings by hand, if possible. If necessary, lightly tap the bearing(s) into the housing with a socket placed on the outer bearing race. *Do not* install new bearings by driving on the inner bearing race. Install the bearing(s) until it seats completely.

## OIL SEALS

Oil seals (**Figure 73**) are used to contain oil, water, grease or combustion gasses in a housing or shaft. Improper removal of a seal can damage the housing

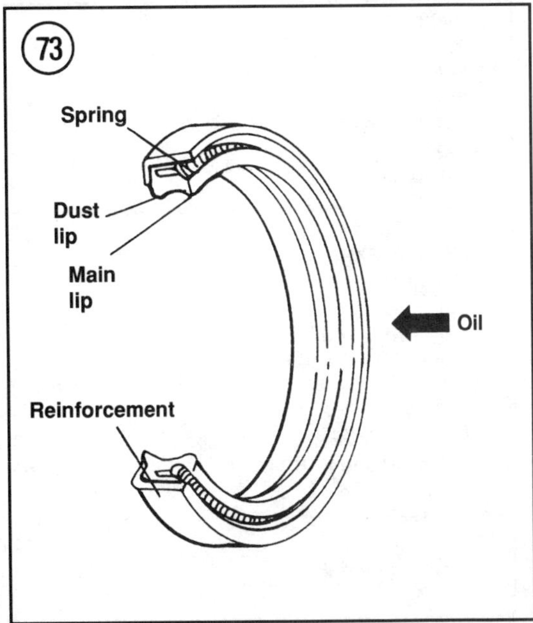

or shaft. Improper installation of the seal can damage the seal. Note the following:

a. Prying is generally the easiest and most effective method of removing a seal from a housing. However, always place a rag underneath the pry tool to prevent damage to the housing.
b. Grease should be packed in the seal lips before the seal is installed.
c. Oil seals should always be installed so that the manufacturer's numbers or marks face out.
d. Oil seals should be installed with a socket placed on the outside of the seal as shown in **Figure 74**. Make sure the seal is driven squarely into the housing. Never install a seal by hitting against the top of the seal with a hammer.

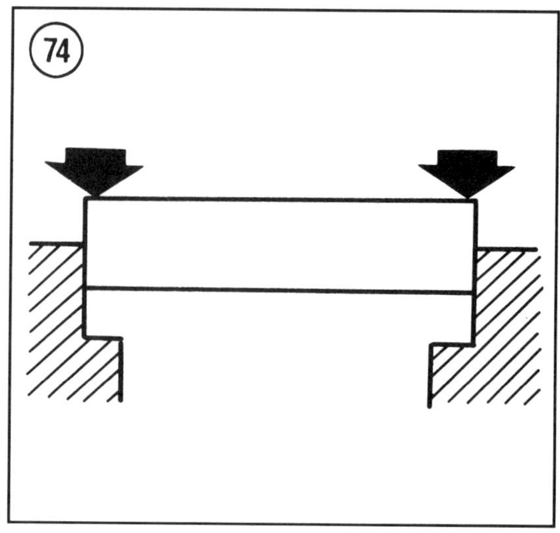


**Table 1 MODEL IDENTIFICATION**

| |
|---|
| 1984-1994 |
| FLH (all models) |
| FXR (all models) |
| FLT (all models) |
| 1985 |
| FXEF |
| FXSB |
| 1985-1986 |
| FXWG |

**Table 2 GENERAL SPECIFICATIONS (FLH, FLT AND FXR)**

| Item | in. | cm |
|---|---|---|
| Wheel base | | |
| 1984-1985 | | |
| FLHT/C | 62.9 | 159.7 |
| FLT/C | 62.9 | 159.7 |
| FXRT | 64.7 | 164.3 |
| FXRS | 63.13 | 160.3 |
| 1986-1990 | | |
| FLTC | 62.94 | 159.8 |
| FLHT/C and FLHS | 62.94 | 159.8 |
| FXR and FXRS | 63.13 | 160.3 |
| 1991-1992 | | |
| FLT | 62.94 | 159.8 |
| FXR, FXRS and FXLR | 63.13 | 160.3 |
| FXRT, FXRSP and FXRS/CON | 64.7 | 164.3 |
| 1993-on | | |
| FLT | 62.94 | 159.8 |
| FXR and FXLR | 63.13 | 160.3 |
| FXRS-SP and FXRS/CON | 64.7 | 164.3 |
| Length | | |
| 1984-1985 | | |
| FXRS | 91.65 | 232.8 |
| All other models | 94.2 | 239.3 |

(continued)

**Table 2 GENERAL SPECIFICATIONS (FLH, FLT AND FXR) (continued)**

| Item | in. | cm |
|---|---|---|
| Length (continued) | | |
| 1986-1990 | | |
| FLT | 94.25 | 239.4 |
| FXR and FXRS | 91.65 | 232.8 |
| FXLR | 91.6 | 232.6 |
| FXRD | 98.0 | 248.9 |
| FXRT | 94.2 | 239.3 |
| FXRT/SE/SP/CON | 93.2 | 236.7 |
| 1991-1992 | | |
| FLT | 94.25 | 239.4 |
| FXR and FXRS | 91.65 | 232.8 |
| FXRT | 94.2 | 239.3 |
| FXLR | 91.6 | 232.6 |
| FXRSP and FXRS/CON | 93.2 | 236.7 |
| 1993-on | | |
| FLT | 94.25 | 239.4 |
| FXR and FXLR | 91.63 | 232.7 |
| FXRS-SP and FXRS/CON | 93.2 | 236.7 |
| Width | | |
| 1984-1985 | | |
| FLT | 37.0 | 93.9 |
| FXRT | 34.5 | 87.6 |
| FXRS | 31.0 | 78.7 |
| 1986-1992 | | |
| FLTC | 37.0 | 93.9 |
| FLHT/C and FLHS | 39.0 | 99.1 |
| FXR and FXRS | 31.0 | 78.7 |
| FXRT and FXRD | 34.5 | 87.6 |
| FXRS/SE/SP/CON | 31.0 | 78.7 |
| 1993-on | | |
| FLTC Ultra | 37.0 | 93.9 |
| FLHTC and FLHTC Ultra | 39.0 | 99.1 |
| FXR | 31.0 | 78.7 |
| Overall height | | |
| 1984-1985 | | |
| FLHT/C | 60.5 | 153.6 |
| FLT/C | 59.0 | 149.8 |
| FXRT | 59.5 | 151.1 |
| FXRS | 48.0 | 121.9 |
| 1986-1992 | | |
| FLTC | 58.75 | 149.2 |
| FLHT/C and FLHS | 61.0 | 154.9 |
| FXR, FXRS and FXLR | 48.0 | 121.9 |
| FXRT and FXRD | 59.5 | 151.1 |
| FXRS/SE/SP/CON | 50.0 | 127.0 |
| 1993-on | | |
| FLTC Ultra | 58.75 | 149.2 |
| FLHTC and FLHTC Ultra, FLHS | 61.0 | 154.9 |
| FXR and FXLR | 48.0 | 121.9 |
| FXRS-SP and FXRS/CON | 50.0 | 127.0 |
| Seat height | | |
| 1984-1985 | | |
| FXRS | 28.10 | 71.4 |
| All other models | 28.0 | 71.1 |

(continued)

**Table 2 GENERAL SPECIFICATIONS (FLH, FLT AND FXR) (continued)**

| Item | in. | cm |
|---|---|---|
| Seat height (continued) | | |
| 1986-1992 | | |
| FLTC | 29.6 | 75.2 |
| FLHT/C and FLHS | 28.0 | 71.1 |
| FXR, FXRS and FXLR | 26.5 | 67.3 |
| FXRT | 27.75 | 70.5 |
| FXRD | 28.25 | 71.7 |
| FXRS/SE/SP/CON | 27.5 | 69.8 |
| 1993-on | | |
| FLTC Ultra | 29.62 | 75.2 |
| FLHTC and FLHTC Ultra | 28.0 | 71.1 |
| FLHS | 27.0 | 68.6 |
| Ground clearance | | |
| 1984-1985 | | |
| FLHT/C and FLT/C | 5.1 | 12.9 |
| FXRT | 6.0 | 15.2 |
| FXRS | 5.25 | 13.3 |
| 1986-1992 | | |
| FLT | 5.12 | 13.0 |
| FXR, FXRS and FXLR | 5.25 | 13.3 |
| FXRT, FXRD, FSRS/SE/SP/CON | 6.0 | 15.2 |
| 1993-on | | |
| FLT | 5.12 | 13.0 |
| FXR and FXLR | 5.25 | 13.3 |
| FXRS-SP and FXRS/CON | 6.0 | 15.2 |
| | **lb.** | **kg** |
| Dry weight | | |
| 1984-1985 | | |
| FLT/C | 741 | 336.1 |
| FLHT/C | 712 | 322.9 |
| FXRT | 640 | 290.3 |
| FXRS | 575 | 260.8 |
| 1986-1992 | | |
| FLTC | 741 | 336.1 |
| FLHT/C and FLHS | 722 | 327.5 |
| FXR, FXRS and FXLR | 575 | 260.8 |
| FXRT | 640 | 290.3 |
| FXRD | 672 | 304.8 |
| 1993-on | | |
| FLHTC Ultra and FLTC Ultra | 765 | 347.3 |
| FLHTC | 741 | 336.1 |
| FLHS | 692 | 314.2 |
| FXR | 575 | 260.8 |

**Table 3 GENERAL SPECIFICATIONS (FX)**

| Item | in. | cm |
|---|---|---|
| Wheel basee | | |
| FXEF | 63.0 | 160.0 |
| FXSB | 63.50 | 161.3 |
| FXWG | 65.0 | 165.1 |
| Length | | |
| FXEF | 91.50 | 232.4 |
| FXSB | 92.0 | 233.7 |
| FXWG | 93.0 | 236.2 |

(continued)

**Table 3 GENERAL SPECIFICATIONS (FX) (continued)**

| Item | in. | cm |
|---|---|---|
| Width | | |
| FXEF | 33.75 | 85.7 |
| FXSB | 29.0 | 73.6 |
| FXWG | 47.0 | 119.4 |
| Overall height | | |
| FXEF | 45.75 | 116.2 |
| FXSB | 41.75 | 106.0 |
| FXWG | 47.0 | 119.4 |
| | **lb.** | **kg** |
| Dry weight | | |
| All FX | 527 | 239.0 |

**Table 4 GROSS VEHICLE WEIGHT RATINGS**

| | lb. | kg |
|---|---|---|
| Gross vehicle weight rating (GVWR)* | | |
| 1984-1985 | | |
| FLT | 1,180 | 535.2 |
| FXR | 1,085 | 492.2 |
| 1986-1992 | | |
| FLT | 1,180 | 535.2 |
| FXR | 1,085 | 492.2 |
| FXEF, FXSB and FXWG | 1,085 | 492.2 |
| 1993-on | | |
| FLT | 1,197 | 543.4 |
| FXR | 1,085 | 492.4 |
| Gross axle weight ratings (GAWR) | | |
| Front axle | | |
| 1986-1992 | | |
| FLT | 410 | 185.9 |
| FXR | 390 | 176.9 |
| FXEF, FXSB and FXWG | 390 | 176.9 |
| 1993-on | | |
| FLT | 427 | 193.9 |
| FXR | 390 | 176.9 |
| Rear axle | | |
| FLT | 770 | 349.3 |
| FXR | 695 | 315.2 |
| FXEF, FXSB and FXWG | 695 | 315.2 |

*GVWR is the maximum allowable vehicle weight. This weight includes combined vehicle, rider(s) and accessory weight.

**Table 5 FUEL TANK CAPACITY**

| | Total | | | Reserve | | |
|---|---|---|---|---|---|---|
| | U.S. gal. | Liters | Imp. gal. | U.S. gal. | Liters | Imp. gal. |
| FLT | | | | | | |
| 1984-1988 | 5.0 | 18.9 | 4.2 | 0.7 | 2.6 | 0.6 |
| 1989-on | 5.0 | 18.9 | 4.2 | 0.9 | 3.4 | 0.7 |
| FXR | 4.2 | 15.9 | 3.5 | 0.4 | 1.5 | 0.3 |
| FXEF and FXSB | 4.2 | 15.9 | 3.5 | 1.0 | 3.8 | 0.8 |
| FXWG | 5.2 | 19.7 | 4.3 | 1.2 | 4.5 | 1.0 |

**Table 6 DECIMAL AND METRIC EQUIVALENTS**

| Fractions | Decimal in. | Metric mm | Fractions | Decimal in. | Metric mm |
|---|---|---|---|---|---|
| 1/64 | 0.015625 | 0.39688 | 33/64 | 0.515625 | 13.09687 |
| 1/32 | 0.03125 | 0.79375 | 17/32 | 0.53125 | 13.49375 |
| 3/64 | 0.046875 | 1.19062 | 35/64 | 0.546875 | 13.89062 |
| 1/16 | 0.0625 | 1.58750 | 9/16 | 0.5625 | 14.28750 |
| 5/64 | 0.078125 | 1.98437 | 37/64 | 0.578125 | 14.68437 |
| 3/32 | 0.09375 | 2.38125 | 19/32 | 0.59375 | 15.08125 |
| 7/64 | 0.109375 | 2.77812 | 39/64 | 0.609375 | 15.47812 |
| 1/8 | 0.125 | 3.1750 | 5/8 | 0.625 | 15.87500 |
| 9/64 | 0.140625 | 3.57187 | 41/64 | 0.640625 | 16.27187 |
| 5/32 | 0.15625 | 3.96875 | 21/32 | 0.65625 | 16.66875 |
| 11/64 | 0.171875 | 4.36562 | 43/64 | 0.671875 | 17.06562 |
| 3/16 | 0.1875 | 4.76250 | 11/16 | 0.6875 | 17.46250 |
| 13/64 | 0.203125 | 5.15937 | 45/64 | 0.703125 | 17.85937 |
| 7/32 | 0.21875 | 5.55625 | 23/32 | 0.71875 | 18.25625 |
| 15/64 | 0.234375 | 5.95312 | 47/64 | 0.734375 | 18.65312 |
| 1/4 | 0.250 | 6.35000 | 3/4 | 0.750 | 19.05000 |
| 17/64 | 0.265625 | 6.74687 | 49/64 | 0.765625 | 19.44687 |
| 9/32 | 0.28125 | 7.14375 | 25/32 | 0.78125 | 19.84375 |
| 19/64 | 0.296875 | 7.54062 | 51/64 | 0.796875 | 20.24062 |
| 5/16 | 0.3125 | 7.93750 | 13/16 | 0.8125 | 20.63750 |
| 21/64 | 0.328125 | 8.33437 | 53/64 | 0.828125 | 21.03437 |
| 11/32 | 0.34375 | 8.73125 | 27/32 | 0.84375 | 21.43125 |
| 23/64 | 0.359375 | 9.12812 | 55/64 | 0.859375 | 22.82812 |
| 3/8 | 0.375 | 9.52500 | 7/8 | 0.875 | 22.22500 |
| 25/64 | 0.390625 | 9.92187 | 57/64 | 0.890625 | 22.62187 |
| 13/32 | 0.40625 | 10.31875 | 29/32 | 0.90625 | 23.01875 |
| 27/64 | 0.421875 | 10.71562 | 59/64 | 0.921875 | 23.41562 |
| 7/16 | 0.4375 | 11.11250 | 15/16 | 0.9375 | 23.81250 |
| 29/64 | 0.453125 | 11.50937 | 61/64 | 0.953125 | 24.20937 |
| 15/32 | 0.46875 | 11.90625 | 31/32 | 0.96875 | 24.60625 |
| 31/64 | 0.484375 | 12.30312 | 63/64 | 0.984375 | 25.00312 |
| 1/2 | 0.500 | 12.70000 | 1 | 1.00 | 25.40000 |

**Table 7 GENERAL TORQUE SPECIFICATIONS (FT.-LB.)***

| | Body Size or Outside Diameter | | | | | | | | | |
|---|---|---|---|---|---|---|---|---|---|---|
| **Type**** | **1/4** | **5/16** | **3/8** | **7/16** | **1/2** | **9/16** | **5/8** | **3/4** | **7/8** | **1** |
| SAE 2 | 6 | 12 | 20 | 32 | 47 | 69 | 96 | 155 | 206 | 310 |
| SAE 5 | 10 | 19 | 33 | 54 | 78 | 114 | 154 | 257 | 382 | 587 |
| SAE 7 | 13 | 25 | 44 | 71 | 110 | 154 | 215 | 360 | 570 | 840 |
| SAE 8 | 14 | 29 | 47 | 78 | 119 | 169 | 230 | 380 | 600 | 700 |

*Convert ft.-lb. specificatin to N•m by multiplying by 1.3558.
**Fastener strength of SAE bolts can be determined by the bolt head "grade markings." Unmarked bolt heads and cap screws are usually to be mild steel. More "grade markings" indicate higher fastener quality.

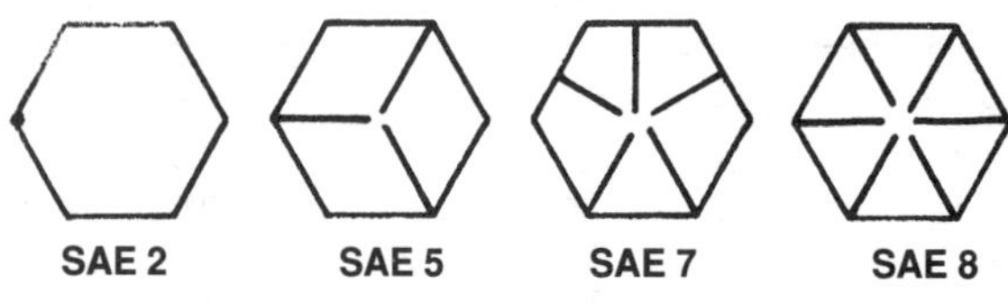

**Table 8 AMERICAN TAP DRILL SIZES**

| Tap thread | Drill size | Tap thread | Drill size |
|---|---|---|---|
| #0-80 | 3/64 | 1/4-28 | No. 3 |
| #1-64 | No. 53 | 5/16-18 | F |
| #1-72 | No. 53 | 5/16-24 | I |
| #2-56 | No. 51 | 3/8-16 | 5/16 |
| #2-64 | No. 50 | 3/8-24 | Q |
| #3-48 | 5/64 | 7/16-14 | U |
| #3-56 | No. 46 | 7/16-20 | W |
| #4-40 | No. 43 | 1/2-13 | 27/64 |
| #4-48 | No. 42 | 1/2-20 | 29/64 |
| #5-40 | No. 39 | 9/16-12 | 31/64 |
| #5-44 | No. 37 | 9/16-18 | 33/64 |
| #6-32 | No. 36 | 5/8-11 | 17/32 |
| #6-40 | No. 33 | 5/18-18 | 37/64 |
| #8-32 | No. 29 | 3/4-10 | 21/32 |
| #8-36 | No. 29 | 3/4-16 | 11/16 |
| #10-24 | No. 25 | 7/8-9 | 49-64 |
| #10.32 | No. 21 | 7/8-14 | 13/16 |
| #12-24 | No. 17 | 1-8 | 7/8 |
| #12-28 | No. 15 | 1-14 | 15/16 |
| 1/4-20 | No. 8 | | |

**Table 9 WINDCHILL FACTOR**

| Estimated Wind Speed in MPH | Actual Thermometer Reading (° F)* | | | | | | | | | | | |
|---|---|---|---|---|---|---|---|---|---|---|---|---|
| | 50 | 40 | 30 | 20 | 10 | 0 | –10 | –20 | –30 | –40 | –50 | –60 |
| | Equivalent Temperature (° F)* | | | | | | | | | | | |
| Calm | 50 | 40 | 30 | 20 | 10 | 0 | –10 | –20 | –30 | –40 | –50 | –60 |
| 5 | 48 | 37 | 27 | 16 | 6 | –5 | –15 | –26 | –36 | –47 | –57 | –68 |
| 10 | 40 | 28 | 16 | 4 | –9 | –21 | –33 | –46 | –58 | –70 | –83 | –95 |
| 15 | 36 | 22 | 9 | –5 | –18 | –36 | –45 | –58 | –72 | –85 | –99 | –112 |
| 20 | 32 | 18 | 4 | –10 | –25 | –39 | –53 | –67 | –82 | –96 | –110 | –124 |
| 25 | 30 | 16 | 0 | –15 | –29 | –44 | –59 | –74 | –88 | –104 | –118 | –133 |
| 30 | 28 | 13 | –2 | –18 | –33 | –48 | –63 | –79 | –94 | –109 | –125 | –140 |
| 35 | 27 | 11 | –4 | –20 | –35 | –49 | –67 | –82 | –98 | –113 | –129 | –145 |
| 40 | 26 | 10 | –6 | –21 | –37 | –53 | –69 | –85 | –100 | –116 | –132 | –148 |
| ** | **Little Danger** (for properly clothed person) | | | | **Increasing Danger** | | | **Great Danger** | | | | |
| | | | | | • Danger from freezing of exposed flesh • | | | | | | | |

* To convert Fahrenheit (°F) to Celsius (°C), use the following formula: °C = 5/9 × (°F - 32).
** Wind speeds greater than 40 mph have little additional effect.

# CHAPTER TWO

# TROUBLESHOOTING

Every motorcycle engine requires an uninterrupted supply of fuel and air, proper ignition and adequate compression. If any of these are lacking, the engine will not run.

Diagnosing mechanical problems is relatively simple if you use orderly procedures and keep a few basic principles in mind.

The troubleshooting procedures in this chapter analyze typical symptoms and show logical methods of isolating causes. These are not the only methods. There may be several ways to solve a problem, but only a systematic approach can guarantee success.

Never assume anything. Do not overlook the obvious. If you are riding along and the bike suddenly quits, check the easiest, most accessible problem spots first. Is there gasoline in the tank? Has a spark plug wire fallen off?

If nothing obvious turns up in a quick check, look a little further. Learning to recognize and describe symptoms will make repairs easier for you or a mechanic at the shop. Describe problems accurately and fully. Saying "it won't run" isn't the same thing as saying "it quit at high speed and won't start," or "it sat in my garage for 3 months and then wouldn't start."

Gather as many symptoms as possible to aid in diagnosis. Note whether the engine lost power gradually or all at once. Remember that the more complicated a machine is, the easier it is to troubleshoot because symptoms point to specific problems.

After the symptoms are defined, areas which could cause problems are tested and analyzed. Guessing at the cause of a problem may provide the solution, but it can easily lead to frustration, wasted time and a series of expensive, unnecessary parts replacements.

You do not need fancy equipment or complicated test gear to determine whether repairs can be attempted at home. A few simple checks could save a large repair bill and lost time while the bike sits in a dealer's service department. On the other hand, be realistic and do not attempt repairs beyond your abilities. Service departments tend to charge heavily for putting together a disassembled engine that may have been abused. Some won't even take on such a job—so use common sense, don't get in over your head.

**Table 1** and **Table 2** (electrical specifications) are at the end of the chapter.

## OPERATING REQUIREMENTS

An engine needs 3 basics to run properly: correct fuel/air mixture, compression and a spark at the correct time (**Figure 1**). If one or more is missing, the engine will not run. If all three engine basics are present, but one or more is not working properly, the engine may start, but it will not run properly.

The electrical system is the weakest link of the 3 basics. More problems result from electrical breakdowns than from any other source. Keep that in mind before you begin tampering with carburetor adjustments and the like.

If the machine has been sitting for any length of time and refuses to start, check and clean the spark plugs and then look to the gasoline delivery system. This includes the fuel tank, fuel shutoff valve and fuel line to the carburetor. Gasoline deposits may have formed and gummed up the carburetor jets and air passages. Gasoline tends to lose its potency after standing for long periods. Condensation may contaminate the fuel with water. Drain the old fuel (fuel tank, fuel lines and carburetor) and try starting with a fresh tankful.

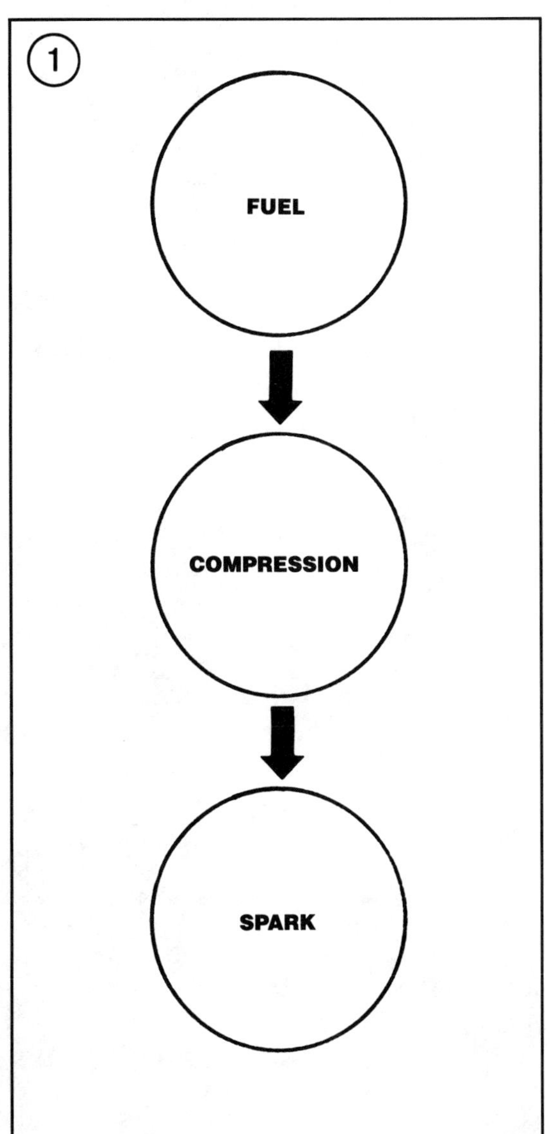


## TROUBLESHOOTING INSTRUMENTS

Chapter One lists the instruments needed and gives instruction on their use.



## TESTING ELECTRICAL COMPONENTS

Most dealers and parts houses will not accept returns on electrical parts purchased from them. When testing electrical components, make sure that you perform the test procedures as described in this chapter and that your test equipment is working properly. If a test result shows that the component is defective but the reading is close to the service limit, have the component tested by a Harley-Davidson dealer to verify the test result before purchasing a new electrical component.

## EMERGENCY TROUBLESHOOTING

When the bike is difficult to start, or won't start at all, it doesn't help to wear down the battery using the starter or your leg and foot on kickstart models. Check for obvious problems even before getting out your tools. Go down the following list step by step. If the bike still will not start, refer to the appropriate troubleshooting procedures which follow in this chapter. As described under *Operating Requirements*, the engine requires 3 basics before it will start and run properly. The following procedure will illustrate steps for checking each of the 3 basic engine principles.

1. Visually inspect the bike for gas or oil leakage, loose wires or other abnormal conditions. If you did not find anything that could cause a starting problem, proceed with the following.
2. Make sure the engine STOP switch is not in the OFF position (**Figure 2**).

*WARNING*
*Do **not** use an open flame to check the fuel tank. A serious explosion is certain to result.*

3. Is there fuel in the tank? Open the filler cap and rock the bike. Listen for fuel sloshing around.

*NOTE*
*If the engine has not been run for some time, gasoline deposits may have gummed up carburetor jets and air pas-*

*sages. In addition, gasoline tends to lose its potency after standing for long periods or you may find water in the tank. Drain the old gas and try starting with a fresh tankful.*

4. Is the fuel supply valve (**Figure 3**) in the ON position? If the fuel level in the tank is low, turn the valve to RESERVE to be sure you get the last remaining gas.

5. Is the choke (**Figure 4**) in the correct position? The choke knob should be pulled out when starting a cold engine and pushed in when restarting a warm or hot engine. If the choke does not seem to be operating correctly, adjust it as described in Chapter Three.

*NOTE*

*The condition of your engine's spark plugs is a deciding factor in its performance and an important reference point during troubleshooting and general maintenance. To avoid mixups when removing the spark plugs in Step 6, make sure to identify each plug so that you know which cylinder it came from.*

6. After attempting to start the engine, immediately remove the spark plugs (**Figure 5**) and check their firing tips. Refer to Chapter Three for information on reading spark plugs. Fuel should be present on both plugs firing tips; this indicates that fuel is being pumped from the fuel tank to the engine. If there is no sign of fuel on the plugs, suspect a fuel delivery problem; refer to *Fuel System* in this chapter. If it appears that there is water on the plugs, water has probably entered the engine from contaminated fuel or there is water in the crankcase.

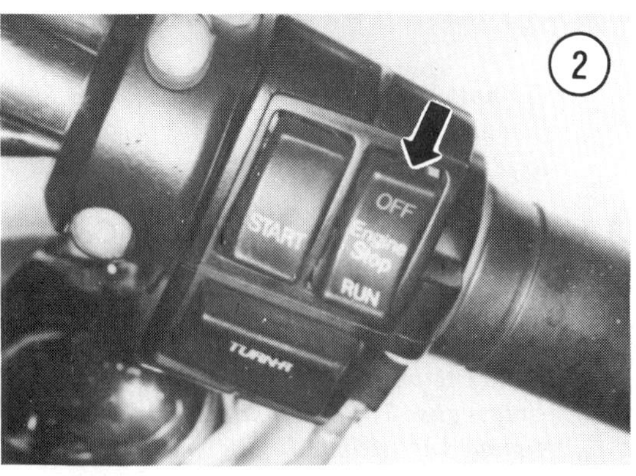

2

7. Perform a spark test as described under *Engine Fails to Start (Spark Test)* in this chapter. If there is a strong spark, perform Step 8.

8. Check cylinder compression as follows:

a. Turn the fuel valve OFF.

b. Remove and ground the spark plugs against the cylinder head. The spark plugs must be grounded when performing the following steps or the ignition system will be permanently damaged.

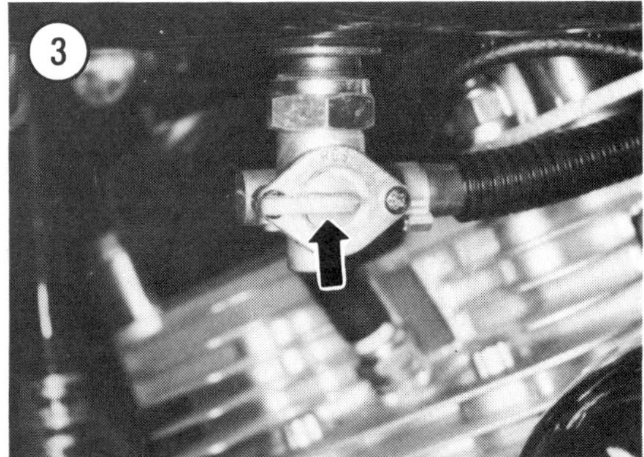
3

4

5

*WARNING*
*When grounding the spark plugs, make sure the plugs are placed away from the spark plug holes in the cylinder head. Because you will be placing your fingers over the cylinder head spark plug holes, you could be shocked if you accidentally touch a plug while cranking the engine.*

c. Put your finger over one of the spark plug holes.
d. Crank the engine with the starter button. Rising pressure in the cylinder should force your finger off of the spark plug hole. This indicates that the cylinder probably has sufficient cylinder compression to start the engine.
e. Repeat for the opposite cylinder.
f. Lack of cylinder compression indicates a problem with that cylinder. This could be worn or damaged piston rings or valves(s). Refer to *Engine* in this chapter.

*NOTE*
*Engine compression can be checked more accurately with a compression gauge as described in Chapter Three.*

6

7

g. Reinstall the spark plugs.

### Engine Fails to Start (Spark Test)

Perform the following spark test to determine if the ignition system is operating properly.
1. Remove the spark plugs.
2. Connect the spark plug wire and connector to the spark plug and touch the spark plug base to a good ground like the engine cylinder head. Position the spark plug so you can see the electrodes. See **Figure 6**. Repeat for the other spark plug.
3. Crank the engine over with the starter. A fat blue spark should be evident across the spark plug electrodes.

*WARNING*
*Do not hold the spark plug, wire or connector or a serious electrical shock may result. If necessary, use a pair of insulated pliers to hold the spark plug or wire. The high voltage generated by the ignition system could produce serious or fatal shocks.*

4. If the spark is good, check for one or more of the following possible malfunctions:
   a. Obstructed fuel line or fuel filter.
   b. Leaking head gasket(s).
   c. Low compression.
5. If the spark is not good, check for one or more of the following:
   a. Loose electrical connections.
   b. Dirty electrical connections.
   c. Loose or broken ignition coil ground wire.
   d. Broken or shorted high tension lead to the spark plug.
   e. Discharged battery.
   f. Disconnected or damaged battery connection.
   g. Damaged ignition system component.

### Engine is Difficult to Start

Check for one or more of the following possible malfunctions:
   a. Fouled spark plug(s).
   b. Improperly adjusted choke.
   c. Intake manifold air leak (**Figure 7**).
   d. Contaminated fuel system.
   e. Improperly adjusted carburetor.
   f. Weak ignition unit.

g. Weak ignition coil(s).
h. Poor compression.
i. Engine oil too heavy.

### Engine Will Not Crank

Check for one or more of the following possible malfunctions:

a. Discharged battery.
b. Damaged starter motor.
c. Seized piston(s).
d. Seized crankshaft bearings.
e. Broken connecting rod.

## ENGINE PERFORMANCE

In the following check list, it is assumed that the engine runs, but is not operating at peak performance. This will serve as a starting point from which to isolate a performance malfunction.

### Engine Turns Over But Will Not Start

a. Empty fuel tank.
b. Inoperative fuel shutoff valve.
c. Obstructed fuel line or fuel shutoff valve.
d. Loose or damaged battery connections.
e. Incorrect ignition timing.
f. Faulty ignition components.
g. Fouled spark plugs.
h. Loose or damaged ignition coil cables or wires.
i. Stuck valve(s).
j. Incorrect push rod length.
k. On 1994 FLT models, the automatic fuel supply valve vacuum hose is damaged, disconnected or pinched closed.
l. Engine flooded.
m. Incorrect engine oil viscosity for winter operation (too heavy).

### Engine is Difficult to Start

a. Carburetor incorrectly adjusted.
b. Fouled or improperly gapped spark plug(s).
c. Leaking head gasket(s).
d. Obstructed fuel line or fuel shutoff valve.
e. Obstructed fuel filter.
f. Battery nearly discharged.
g. Loose battery connection.
h. Incorrect ignition timing.
i. Faulty ignition components.
j. Choke stuck open.
k. Sticking valves.
l. Faulty vacuum operated electric switch (VOES).
m. Plugged fuel tank vent hose.
n. Plugged vapor valve (if so equipped).

### Engine Runs but Misses

a. Fouled or improperly gapped spark plugs.
b. Improper carburetor main jet selection.
c. Incorrect ignition timing.
d. Faulty ignition components.
e. Obstructed fuel line or fuel shutoff valve.
f. Obstructed fuel filter.
g. Clogged carburetor jets.
h. Battery nearly discharged.
i. Loose battery connection.
j. Short circuit due to damaged wiring or insulation.
k. Water in fuel.
l. Weak or damaged valve springs.
m. Damaged valve(s).
n. Dirty electrical connections.
o. Faulty vacuum operated electric switch (VOES).

### Engine Overheating

a. Incorrect carburetor adjustment or jet selection.
b. Ignition timing retarded. This could be due to improper adjustment or defective ignition component(s).
c. Faulty vacuum operated electric switch (VOES).
d. Improper spark plug heat range.
e. Damaged or blocked cooling fins.
f. Low oil level.
g. Oil not circulating properly.
h. Valves leaking.
i. Heavy engine carbon deposit.

### Smoky Exhaust and Engine Runs Roughly

a. Clogged air filter element.

b. Carburetor adjustment incorrect—mixture too rich.
c. Choke not operating correctly.
d. Water or other contaminants in fuel.
e. Clogged fuel line.
f. Spark plugs fouled.
g. Damaged ignition coil.
h. Damaged ignition module or sensor.
i. Loose or defective ignition circuit wire.
j. Short circuit from damaged wire insulation.
k. Loose battery cable connection.
l. Incorrect cam timing.
m. Intake manifold or air cleaner air leak.

### Engine Loses Power

a. Carburetor incorrectly adjusted.
b. Engine overheating.
c. Ignition timing incorrect due to damaged ignition component(s).
d. Incorrectly gapped spark plugs.
e. Obstructed muffler.
f. Dragging brake(s).

### Engine Lacks Acceleration

a. Carburetor mixture too lean.
b. Clogged fuel line.
c. Ignition timing incorrect due to damaged ignition component(s).
d. Dragging brake(s).

### Front or Rear Cylinder Spark Plug Fouls Consistently

a. Worn valve guide(s).
b. Damaged valve guide(s).
c. Worn or damaged valve guide oil seal(s).
d. Worn piston rings.
e. Damaged piston rings.
f. Incorrect spark plug heat range.
g. Incorrect fuel mixture.
h. Incorrect enrichener (choke) operation.

## STARTING SYSTEM

The starting system consists of the battery, starter motor, starter relay, solenoid, start switch, starter mechanism and related wiring.

When the ignition switch is turned on and the start button pushed in, current is transmitted from the battery to the starter relay. When the relay is activated, it in turn activates the starter solenoid which mechanically engages the starter with the engine.

Starting system problems are relatively easy to find. In most cases, the trouble is a loose or corroded electrical connection.



### Troubleshooting Preparation

Before troubleshooting the starting system, make sure that:

a. The battery is fully charged.
b. Battery cables are proper size and length. Replace cables that are damaged, severely corroded or undersize.
c. All electrical connections are clean and tight.
d. The wiring harness is in good condition, with no worn or frayed insulation or loose harness sockets.
e. The fuel tank is filled with an adequate supply of fresh gasoline.
f. The spark plugs are in good condition and properly gapped.
g. The ignition system is correctly timed and adjusted.

Troubleshooting is intended only to isolate a malfunction to a certain component. If further bench testing is required, remove the suspect component and test it further.

### Troubleshooting (1984-1988)

Perform the steps listed under *Troubleshooting Preparation*. When making the following voltage checks, test results must be within 1/2 volt of battery voltage.

*CAUTION*

*Never operate the starter motor for more than 30 seconds at a time. Allow the starter to cool for approximately 15 seconds before reusing it. Failing to allow the starter motor to cool after continuous starting attempts can damage the starter.*

*1984 and late 1985-1988 models*

When making the following voltage tests, you will be isolating individual components to check voltage flow into a component (input side) and then checking voltage through the component (output side).

1. Turn on the ignition switch and depress the start button. If the solenoid and relay do not click, perform Step 2. If only the solenoid clicks, perform Step 3. If only the relay clicks, perform Step 4.

2. If the solenoid and relay did not click when performing Step 1, perform the following checks. When making the following checks, first connect the black voltmeter lead to a good ground, then connect the red voltmeter lead to the point in the circuit described in each of the following tests. When both voltmeter leads are connected, turn the ignition switch ON and depress the start button while observing the voltmeter scale. Turn the ignition switch OFF and disconnect the voltmeter after making the test. Refer to **Figure 8** for starter relay terminal contact numbers.

a. Connect the black voltmeter lead across the No. 85 (FX and FXR) or the No. 86 (FLT) starter relay terminal (ground). Then connect the red voltmeter lead across the No. 86 (FX and FXR) or the No. 85 (FLT) starter relay terminal. If the voltage reading is low, check for loose or damaged wiring at the starter relay and start switch. If battery voltage is indicated, the starter relay is defective. Confirm by bench testing the starter relay as described in this chapter.
b. Connect the black voltmeter lead to ground, then connect the red voltmeter lead separately across the start switch input and output terminals; battery voltage should be shown during each test. Low input voltage indicates a damaged stop switch. Low output voltage indicates a damaged start switch.
c. Connect the black voltmeter lead to ground, then check input and output voltage at the stop switch; battery voltage should be shown during each test. Low input voltage indicates damaged or faulty wiring to the ignition switch. Low output voltage indicates a faulty stop switch.
d. Connect the black voltmeter lead to ground and the red voltmeter lead to the ignition circuit breaker input side (copper stud). Repeat to check voltage on circuit breaker output side. Battery voltage should be shown when making each test. Low input voltage indicates a problem in the wiring from the ignition switch and circuit breaker. Low output voltage indicates a damaged ignition circuit breaker.
e. Connect the black voltmeter lead to ground and the red voltmeter lead to the main circuit breaker input side (copper stud). Repeat voltage check on output side. Battery voltage should be shown during each test. Low input voltage indicates a problem in the wiring from the main circuit breaker to the battery. Low output voltage indicates a damaged main circuit breaker.
f. Connect the black voltmeter lead to ground and the red lead to the ignition terminal on the ignition switch. A low reading indicates a damaged ignition switch.
g. Connect the black voltmeter lead to the battery terminal on the ignition switch. Low voltage indicates a problem in the wiring from the main circuit to the switch.

3. If only the solenoid clicked when performing Step 1, perform the following checks. When making the following tests, first connect the black voltmeter lead to a good ground, then connect the red voltmeter lead to the point in the circuit described in each of the following tests. When both voltmeter leads are connected, turn the ignition switch ON and depress the start button while observing the voltmeter scale. Turn the ignition switch OFF and disconnect the voltmeter after making the test.

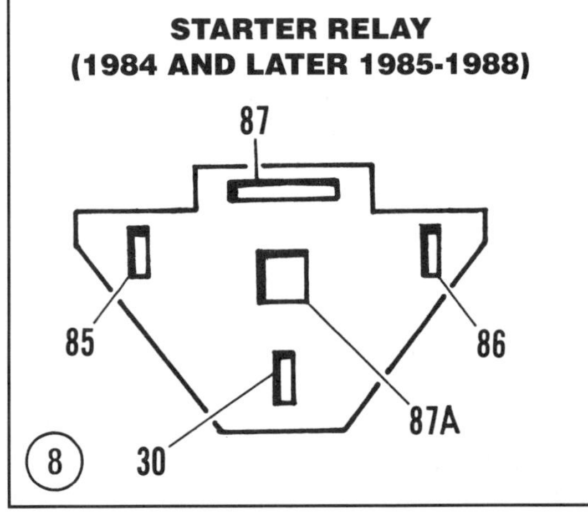

a. Connect the black voltmeter lead to ground and the red lead to the starter wire at the starter; battery voltage should be indicated. A low reading indicates a problem in the wiring from the solenoid to the starter.

b. Connect the black voltmeter lead to ground and the red lead to the *long* solenoid terminal; battery voltage should be indicated. A low reading indicates a problem in the wiring from the battery to the solenoid.

c. Connect the black voltmeter lead to ground and the red lead to the *short* solenoid terminal; battery voltage should be indicated. A low reading indicates solenoid damage or a problem in the starter drive system.

4. If only the starter relay clicked when performing Step 1, perform the following checks. When making the following tests, first connect the black voltmeter lead to a good ground, then connect the red voltmeter lead to the point in the circuit described in each of the following tests. When both voltmeter leads are connected, turn the ignition switch ON and depress the start button while observing the voltmeter scale. Turn the ignition switch OFF and disconnect the voltmeter after making the test.

a. Connect the black voltmeter lead to ground and the red lead to the starter relay No. 30 terminal (**Figure 8**); meter should read battery voltage. A low reading indicates a problem in the main circuit breaker wiring.

b. Connect the black voltmeter lead to ground and the red lead to the starter relay No. 87 terminal (**Figure 8**); meter should show battery voltage. A low reading indicates a damaged starter relay. Confirm by bench testing the starter relay as described in this chapter.

c. Connect the black voltmeter to ground and the red lead to the center solenoid terminal; meter should show battery voltage. A low reading indicates a problem in the wiring between the solenoid and starter relay.

9 **STARTER RELAY INTERNAL WIRING (EARLY 1985)**

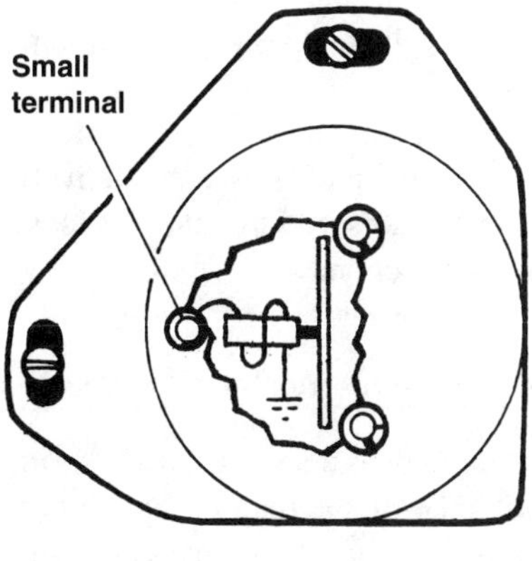

Small terminal

### *Early 1985 models*

When making the following voltage tests, you will be isolating individual components to check voltage flow into a component (input side) and then checking voltage through the component (output side).

1. Turn on the ignition switch and depress the start button. If the solenoid and relay do not click, perform Step 2. If only the solenoid clicks, perform Step 3. If only the relay clicks, perform Step 4.

2. If the solenoid and relay did not click when performing Step 1, perform the following checks. When making the following checks, first connect the black voltmeter lead to a good ground, then connect the red voltmeter lead to the point in the circuit described in each of the following tests. When both voltmeter leads are connected, turn the ignition switch ON and depress the start button while observing the voltmeter scale. Turn the ignition switch OFF and disconnect the voltmeter after making the test. Refer to **Figure 9** for starter relay test points.

a. Connect the black voltmeter lead across the starter relay base (ground) and the red lead across the small starter relay terminal. A low reading indicates a problem in the wiring at the relay base (ground), small terminal on relay or at the start switch. If battery voltage is indicated, the starter relay is defective. Confirm by bench testing the starter relay as described in this chapter.

b. Connect the black voltmeter lead to ground and the red voltmeter lead separately across the start switch input and output sides; battery voltage should be shown during each test. Low input voltage indicates a damaged stop switch. Low output voltage indicates a damaged start switch.

c. Connect the black voltmeter lead to ground, then check input and output voltage at the stop switch; battery voltage should be shown during each test. Low input voltage indicates damaged or faulty wiring to the ignition switch. Low output voltage indicates a faulty stop switch.

d. Connect the black voltmeter lead to ground and the red voltmeter lead to the ignition circuit breaker input side (copper stud). Repeat to check voltage on circuit breaker output side. Battery voltage should be shown when making each test. Low input voltage indicates a problem in the wiring from the ignition switch and circuit breaker. Low output voltage indicates a damaged ignition circuit breaker.

e. Connect the black voltmeter lead to ground and the red voltmeter lead to the main circuit breaker input side (copper stud). Repeat to check voltage on output side. Battery voltage should be shown when making each test. Low input voltage indicates a problem in the wiring from the main circuit breaker to the battery. Low output voltage indicates a damaged main circuit breaker.

f. Connect the black voltmeter lead to ground and the red lead to the ignition terminal on the ignition switch. A low reading indicates a damaged ignition switch.

g. Connect the black voltmeter lead to the battery terminal on the ignition switch. Low voltage indicates a problem in the wiring from the main circuit to the switch.

3. If only the solenoid clicked when performing Step 1, perform the following checks. When making the following checks, first connect the black voltmeter lead to a good ground, then connect the red voltmeter lead to the point in the circuit described in each of the following tests. When both voltmeter leads are connected, turn the ignition switch ON and depress the start button while observing the voltmeter scale. Turn the ignition switch OFF and disconnect the voltmeter after making the test.

a. Connect the black voltmeter lead to ground and the red lead to the starter wire at the starter; battery voltage should be indicated. A low reading indicates a problem in the wiring from the solenoid to the starter.

b. Connect the black voltmeter lead to ground and the red lead to the short/large solenoid terminal; battery voltage should be indicated. A low reading indicates solenoid damage. Confirm by bench testing the solenoid as described in this chapter. If the solenoid tests okay, check the starter drive system for damage.

4. If only the starter relay clicked when performing Step 1, perform the following checks. During testing, first connect the black voltmeter lead to a good ground, then connect the red voltmeter lead to the point in the circuit described in each of the following tests. When both voltmeter leads are connected, turn the ignition switch ON and depress the start button while observing the voltmeter scale. Turn the ignition switch OFF and disconnect the voltmeter after making the test.

a. Connect the black voltmeter lead to ground and the red lead to the starter relay battery terminal; meter should read battery voltage. A low reading indicates a problem in the wiring between the starter relay and battery.

b. Connect the black voltmeter lead to ground and the red lead to the starter relay-to-solenoid terminal at the starter relay. No battery voltage indicates a damaged starter relay.

c. Connect the black voltmeter lead to ground and the red lead to the long/large solenoid terminal. Low battery voltage indicates a problem in the wiring from the solenoid to the starter relay.

d. Connect the black voltmeter lead to ground and the red lead to the small solenoid terminal. A low voltage reading indicates a problem between the jumper wire at the solenoid.

### *1989 and later models*

The basic starter-related troubles are:

a. Engine cranks very slowly or not at all.
b. Starter spins but does not crank engine.
c. Starter will not disengage when start button is released.
d. Loud grinding noises when starter runs.

Starter system problems are relatively easy to find. In most cases, the trouble is a loose or dirty electrical connection.

### *Engine cranks very slowly or not at all*

1. If the starter does not work, check the intensity of the headlight with the ignition switch turned on. If the headlight is dim or does not come on at all, the

battery and connecting wires are most likely at fault. Check the battery with a hydrometer as described in Chapter Nine. Check wiring for breaks, shorts and dirty connections. If the battery is okay, check the starter connections at the battery, solenoid and start switch. Check continuity between the battery and ignition switch with an ohmmeter.

2. If the headlight is bright but dims or goes out when the start button is pressed, check for a corroded or loose connection at the battery. Wiggle the battery terminals and recheck. If the starter turns over, you've found the problem. Clean and/or replace corroded or damaged cables as required.

3. If the headlight remains bright or dims only slightly when cranking, the trouble may be in the starter, solenoid or wiring. Check the start switch, engine run switch, starter relay and the solenoid. Check each switch by bypassing it with a jumper wire. If the starter spins, check the solenoid and wiring to the ignition switch.

4. If the headlight dims severely when the start button is pressed, the battery is nearly dead or the starter is shorted to ground.

#### *Starter spins but does not crank engine*

1. Remove the starter. See Chapter Nine.

2. Check the starter pinion gear. If the teeth are chipped or worn, inspect the clutch flywheel ring gear for the same problems.

3. If the pinion gear and overrunning clutch are in good condition, disassemble the starter and check the armature shaft for corrosion. See Chapter Nine.

4. If there is no corrosion, suspect a damaged overrunning clutch assembly:

   a. The overrunning clutch rollers and/or compression spring is damaged.
   b. The overrunning clutch, idler gear and solenoid gear teeth are damaged.
   c. Pinion gear shaft does not slide smoothly during engagement.
   d. The overrunning clutch assembly fails to operate after the engine has started.

#### *Starter will not disengage when start button is released*

1. A sticking solenoid can cause this problem, which may be due to a worn solenoid return spring or other internal damage. If the solenoid is damaged, it must be replaced as a unit.

2. On high-mileage models, the pinion gear can jam on a worn clutch ring gear. Unable to return, the starter will continue to run. This condition usually requires ring gear replacement.

3. Check the start switch and starter relay for internal damage.

#### *Loud grinding noises when starter runs*

This can be caused by improper meshing of the starter pinion and clutch ring gear or by a broken overrunning clutch mechanism. Remove and inspect the starter as described in Chapter Nine.

### Component Testing

This section describes testing of individual starting system components. Refer to Chapter Nine for starter service.

### Starter Relay Testing

Starter relay testing will require an ohmmeter, jumper wires and a fully charged 12-volt battery.

1. Disconnect and remove the starter relay from the starting circuit on the bike. See Chapter Nine.

2. Connect an ohmmeter and 12-volt battery between the relay terminals as shown in **Figure 10** (early 1985), **Figure 11** (1984 and all late 1985-1990 models) or **Figure 12** (1991-on). This setup will energize the relay.

CAUTION

*On 1991-on models, the No. 85 terminal must be connected to the negative battery terminal as shown in **Figure 12**. Otherwise, the diode connected across the relay winding will be damaged.*

3. Check for continuity through the relay contacts (**Figures 10-12**) with the ohmmeter while the relay coil is energized. The ohmmeter should show continuity. If there is no continuity, replace the relay.

### Starter Current Draw Test

This test will determine whether current is flowing in the starter circuit, and whether the current flow is excessive because of a short in the circuit or from a mechanical problem in the starter drive mechanism. An induction ammeter will be required for this test. Current draw specifications are listed in **Table 1**.

*NOTE*
*The battery should be fully charged when performing the following test.*

1. Shift the transmission into NEUTRAL.

2. Disconnect the 2 spark plug caps at the spark plugs. Then ground the plug caps with 2 extra spark plugs. Do not remove the spark plugs in the cylinder heads.

3. Connect an induction ammeter to the starting circuit as shown in **Figure 13** (1984-1988) or **Figure 14** (1989-on).

4. Turn the ignition switch ON and press the start button for approximately 10 seconds. Note the ammeter reading.

*NOTE*
*Initially, the current draw will be very high when the start button is first pressed, then it will drop to a normal level. This second level or reading is the one you should refer to during this test.*

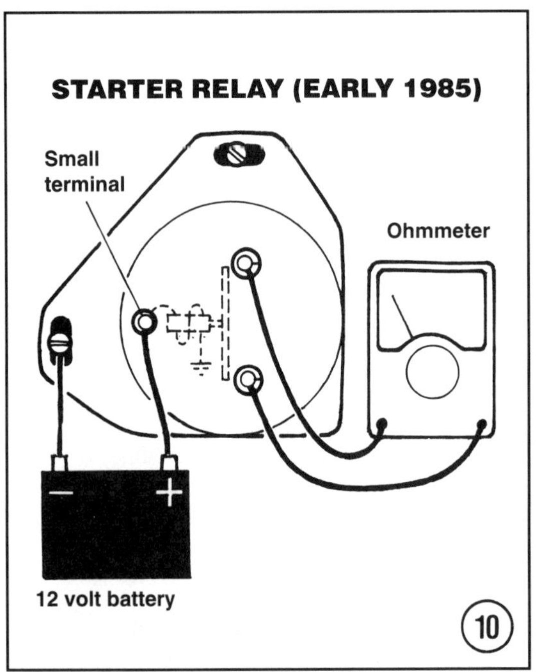


5. If the current draw exceeds the specified current draw (bench test) listed in **Table 1**, suspect a faulty starter or starter drive mechanism. Remove and service these components as described in Chapter Nine.

6. Disconnect the ammeter and the 2 jumper cables.

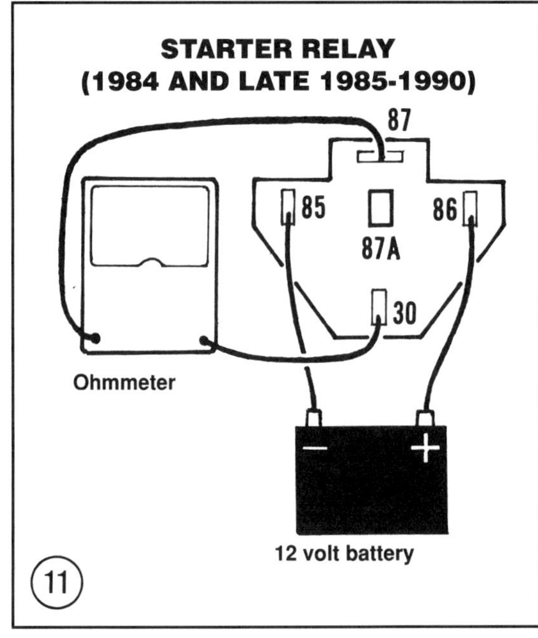


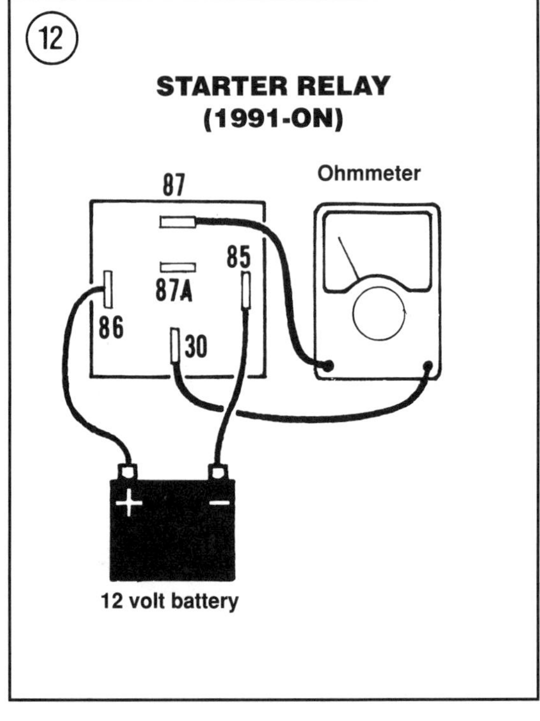

## Solenoid Testing (1984-1988)

The solenoid can be tested while mounted on the motorcycle. **Figures 15-19** identify solenoid terminals for 1984-1988 models. Refer to the drawing for your model and compare it to the actual wiring arrangement on your bike. An ohmmeter will be required to perform the following tests.

1. Disconnect the negative battery cable.

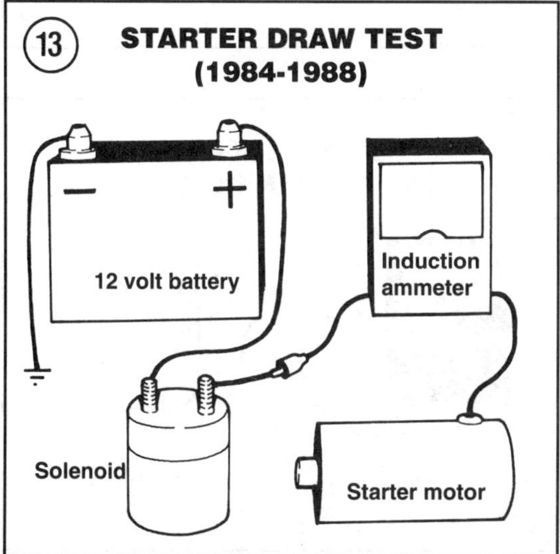


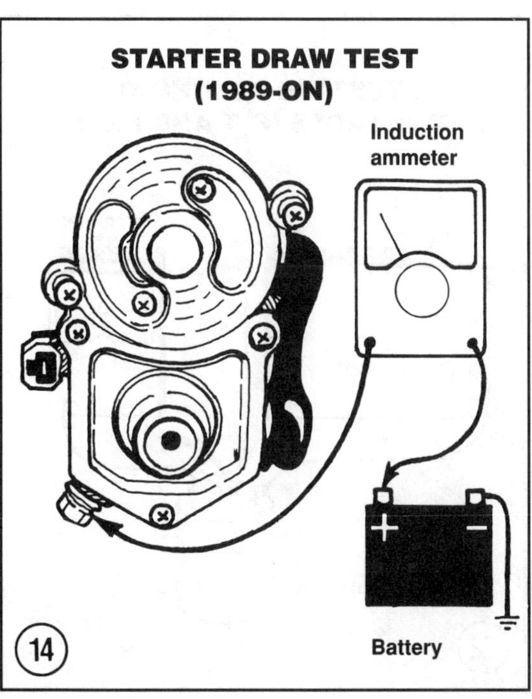


2. Locate the solenoid on your bike. Label and disconnect all of the cables at the solenoid. See **Figures 15-19**.

*NOTE*
*Set the ohmmeter on the R × 1 scale when performing the following tests. Then cross the test leads and adjust the meter needle until it reads zero.*

3. *Pull-in coil test*: Connect an ohmmeter between the small and the short/large terminal on the solenoid (**Figure 20**). There should be continuity (no measurable resistance).

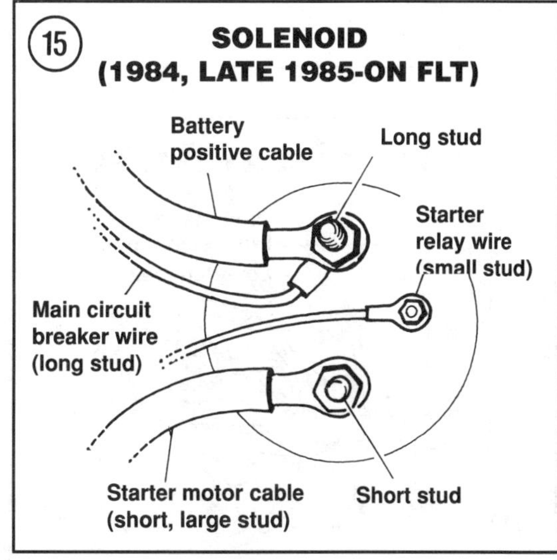


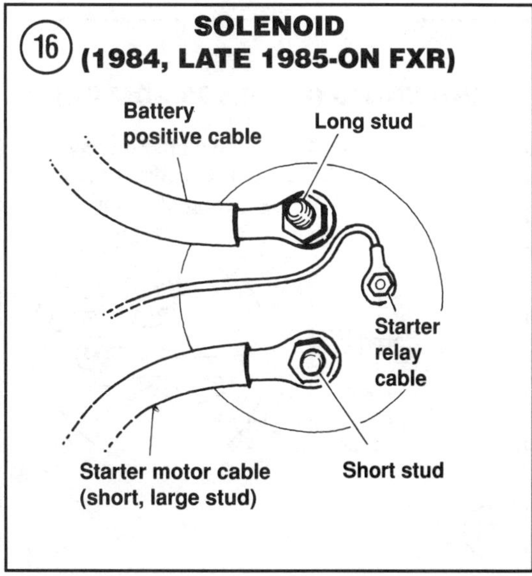

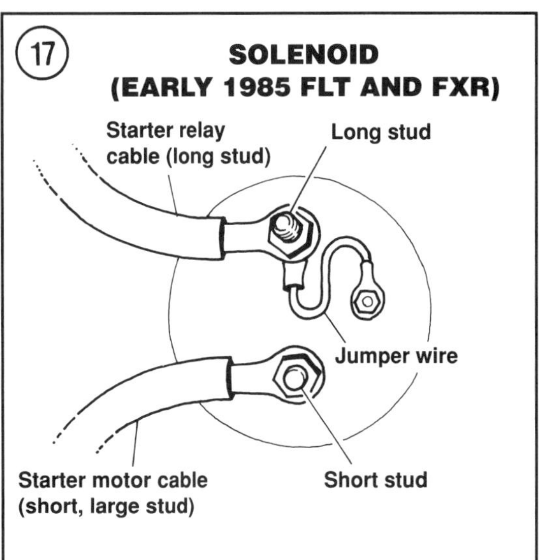
17
SOLENOID
(EARLY 1985 FLT AND FXR)
Starter relay
cable (long stud)
Long stud
Jumper wire
Starter motor cable
(short, large stud)
Short stud

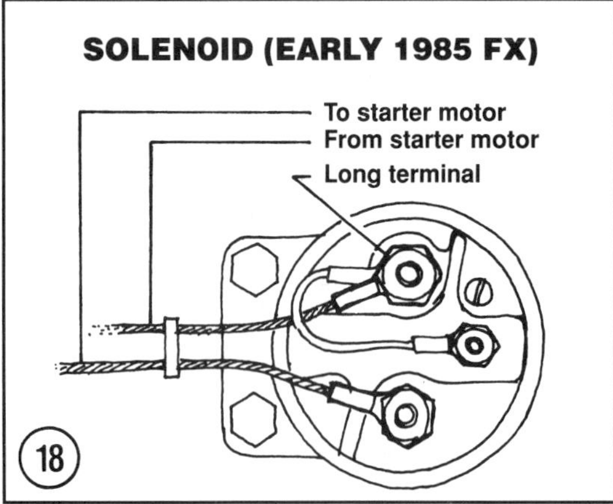
SOLENOID (EARLY 1985 FX)
To starter motor
From starter motor
Long terminal
18

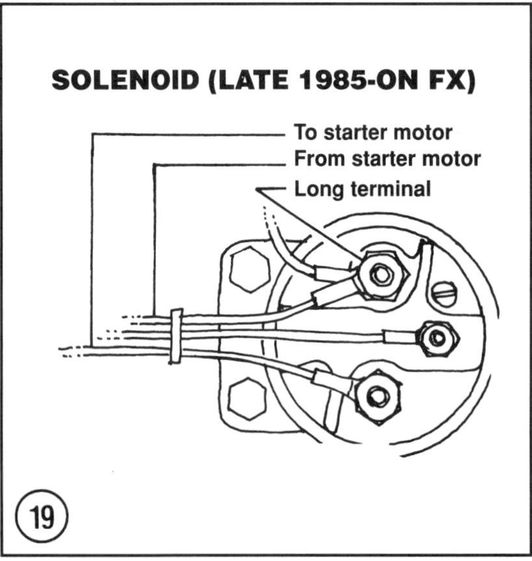
SOLENOID (LATE 1985-ON FX)
To starter motor
From starter motor
Long terminal
19

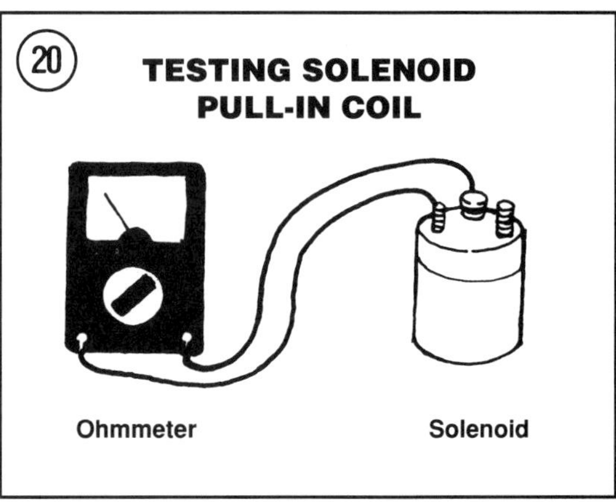
20
TESTING SOLENOID
PULL-IN COIL
Ohmmeter
Solenoid

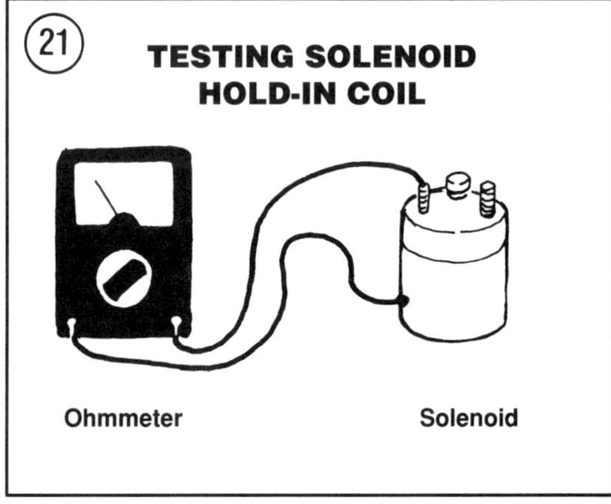
21
TESTING SOLENOID
HOLD-IN COIL
Ohmmeter
Solenoid

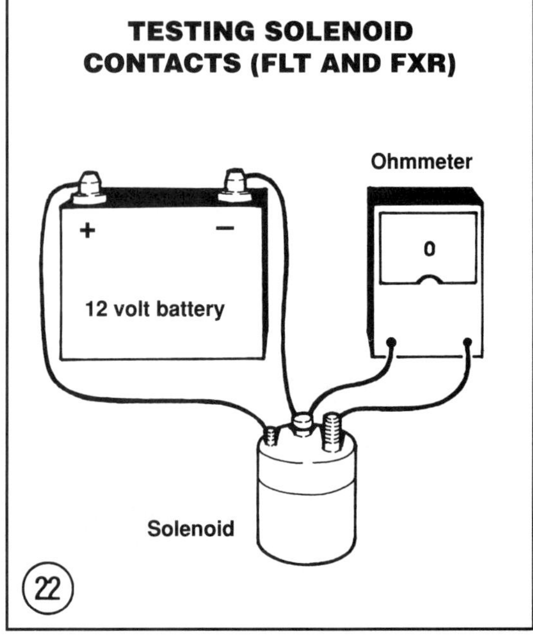
TESTING SOLENOID
CONTACTS (FLT AND FXR)
Ohmmeter
+
–
0
12 volt battery
Solenoid
22

4. *Hold-in coil test*: Connect one ohmmeter lead to the small diameter solenoid terminal and touch the opposite lead onto the solenoid body (**Figure 21**). There should be continuity (no measurable resistance).

5. *FLT and FXR*: Connect a battery to the solenoid as shown in **Figure 22**. The solenoid should click when both battery cables are connected. With the battery still connected, connect an ohmmeter between the 2 large coil terminals. There should be continuity (no measurable resistance).

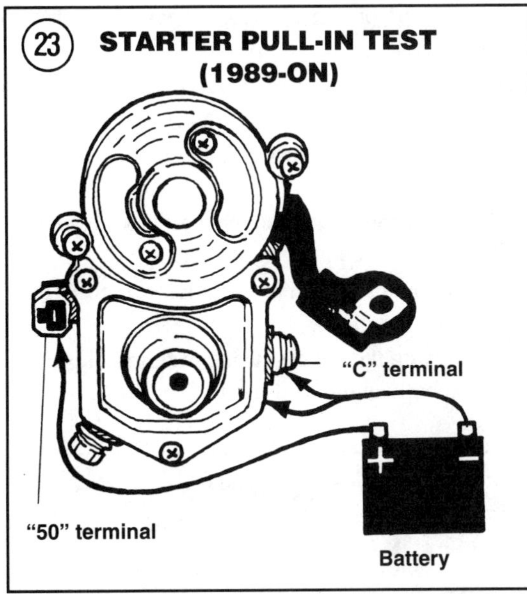


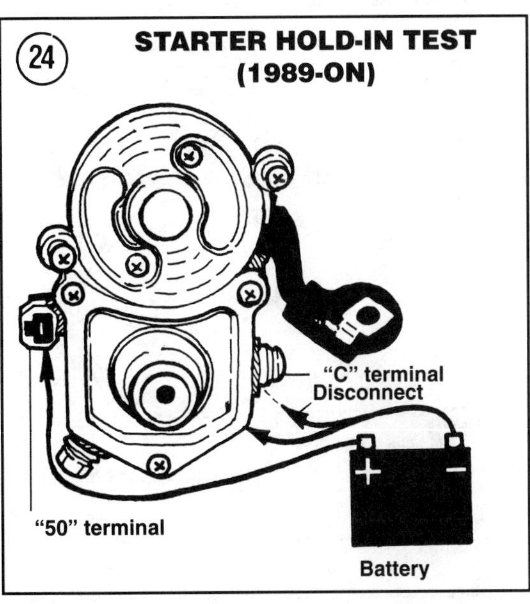


6. Replace the solenoid if it failed any one test in Steps 3-5.

7. Reverse Steps 1 and 2 after testing or replacing the solenoid.

2

### Solenoid Testing (1989-on)

A fully charged 12-volt battery and 4 jumper wires will be required to make the following tests.

1. Remove the starter motor as described in Chapter Nine. The solenoid must be installed on the starter during the following tests. Do not remove it.

2. Disconnect the "C" wire terminal at the starter motor (**Figure 23**) before performing the following tests.

*CAUTION*
*When battery voltage is applied to the solenoid and starter in the following tests, do not leave the jumper cables connected to the solenoid for more than 3-5 seconds. Failure to observe this caution can cause solenoid damage.*

3. Connect a battery to the starter motor as shown in **Figure 23**. The starter shaft should *pull* into the housing. Then disconnect the jumper wire at the "C" starter terminal (**Figure 24**). The starter shaft should *remain* in the housing. Quickly reconnect the jumper wire at the "C" starter terminal and disconnect the jumper wire at the "50" starter terminal (**Figure 25**);

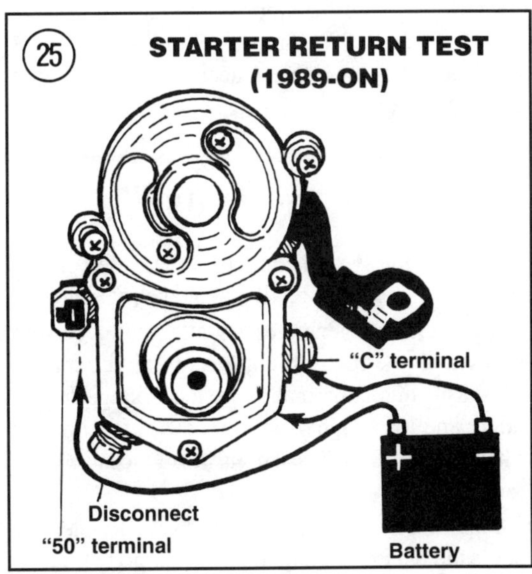

the starter shaft should *return* to its original position. Disconnect the jumper wires from the starter and solenoid.

4. Replace the solenoid if the starter shaft failed to operate properly as described in Step 3.

### Free Running Current Draw Test (1989-on)

A fully charged 12-volt battery, induction ammeter, 14 gauge jumper cable and 3 heavy jumper cables (6 gauge minimum) will be required to make the following tests.

1. Remove the starter motor as described in Chapter Nine. The solenoid must be installed on the starter during the following test. Do not remove it.

2. Mount the starter motor in a vise with soft jaws.

3. Connect a heavy jumper cable between the starter mounting flange and the negative battery terminal (**Figure 26**).

4. Connect a heavy jumper cable between the positive battery terminal and the induction ammeter (**Figure 26**).

5. Connect another cable between the induction ammeter and the "M" terminal on the starter solenoid (**Figure 26**).

6. Connect a 14 gauge jumper cable between the positive battery terminal and the solenoid "50" terminal.

7. Read the current indicated on the ammeter. Ammeter should read 90 amps maximum. If current reading exceeds 90 amps, disassemble starter as described in Chapter Nine. Check for severely worn or damaged parts.

## CHARGING SYSTEM

The charging system consists of the battery, alternator and a solid state rectifier/voltage regulator.

The alternator generates an alternating current (AC) which the rectifier converts to direct current (DC). The regulator maintains the voltage to the battery and load (lights, ignition, etc.) at a constant voltage regardless of variations in engine speed and load.

A malfunction in the charging system generally causes the battery to remain undercharged.

### Service Precautions

Before servicing the charging system, observe the following precautions to prevent damage to any charging system component.

1. Never reverse battery connections. Instantaneous damage may occur.

2. Do not short across any connection.

3. Never attempt to polarize an alternator.

4. Never start the engine with the alternator disconnected from the voltage regulator/rectifier, unless instructed to do so in testing.

5. Never start or run the engine with the battery disconnected.

6. Never attempt to use a high-output battery charger to assist in engine starting.

7. Before charging battery, remove it from the motorcycle.

8. Never disconnect the voltage regulator connector with the engine running.

9. Do not mount the voltage regulator/rectifier unit at another location.

10. Make sure the battery negative terminal is connected to both engine and frame.

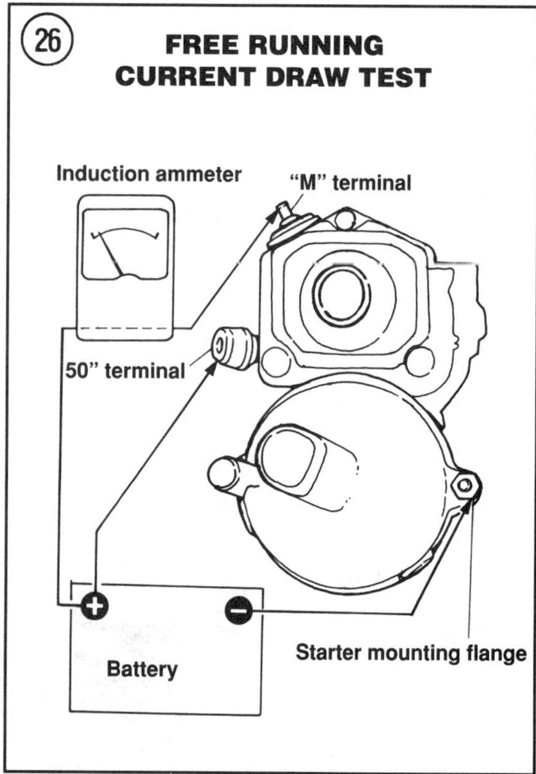

### Testing

Whenever the charging system is suspected of trouble, make sure the battery is fully charged before going any further. Clean and test the battery as described in Chapter Nine. If the battery is in good condition, test the charging system as follows.

If your battery runs down when the motorcycle is not being ridden or it runs down when riding the motorcycle, perform the *Current Draw Test*. If the battery runs down when the motorcycle is not being used, perform the *Voltage Regulator/Rectifier Test* in this chapter.

### Current Draw Test (FLT and FXR) (Battery Runs Down When Bike is Not Being Ridden)

*NOTE*
*Because the clock and radio memory (if so equipped) are energized at all times, the battery may run down if the bike is not run during a one to two week time period. To prevent battery drain, disconnect the negative battery cable or trickle charge the battery.*

1. To perform this test, the battery must be fully charged. Use a hydrometer to check the specific gravity as described in Chapter Nine, and bring the battery up to full charge, if required.

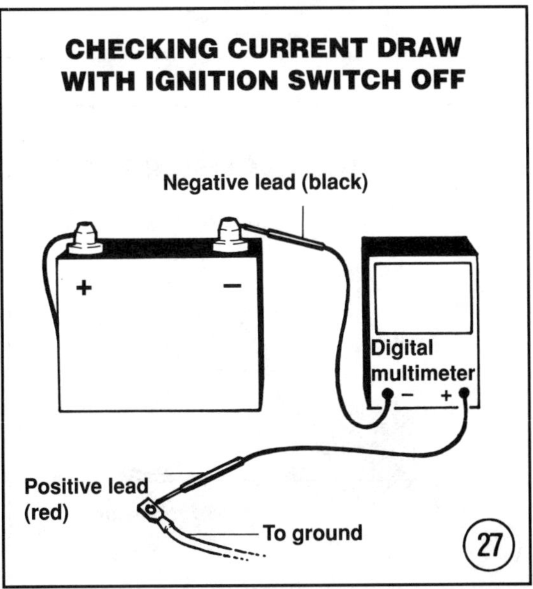


2. Switch the ignition switch OFF.
3. Disconnect the negative battery cable at the battery.

*NOTE*
*The Harley-Davidson Digital multimeter (part No. HD-35500) or equivalent must be used when performing the following test.*

4. Connect the positive (red) multimeter lead to the negative battery terminal and the negative (black) multimeter lead to the battery ground cable. Refer to **Figure 27** for these test connections.
5. With the ignition switch and all lights and accessories turned OFF, read the meter for your bike's current draw and compare it to the specification for your model in **Table 2**. Readings exceeding the specification indicate excessive current draw.
6. If excessive current draw is noted, perform the following. If your model does not have a clock, radio or CB, the regulator is probably faulty.
   a. Refer to the wiring diagram for your model and check the charging system wires and connectors for shorts or other damage.
   b. Check the radio, clock, CB and regulator wiring. Unplug each of these electrical connectors separately and check for a change in the meter reading. If the meter reading changes when one of these connectors has been disconnected from the electrical system, you have isolated the damaged component. Check the electrical connections carefully before testing the individual component.
7. After completing the test, disconnect the multimeter and reconnect the negative battery cable.

### Current Draw Test (Battery Runs Down When Bike is Being Ridden)

This test will check your electrical systems current draw. An induction load tester (**Figure 28**) will be required for this test. If you do not have the proper test equipment, have the test performed by a Harley-Davidson dealer or an independent service shop familiar with Harley service.
1. To perform this test, the battery must be fully charged. Use a hydrometer to check the specific gravity as described in Chapter Nine, and bring the battery up to full charge, if required.

*NOTE*
*Follow the manufacturer's instructions closely when using their test equipment. You should not leave the load switch ON for more than 20 seconds at a time, or tester damage may occur from overheating.*

2. Connect an induction load tester into your bike's electrical circuit as shown in **Figure 29**.
3. Turn the ignition switch on. Then turn on all electrical accessories and switch the headlight beam to HIGH.
4. Read the amp reading (current draw) on the induction load tester and compare it to the alternator output for your model listed in **Table 1**. Amp reading registering on load tester should be 3.5 amps less than the alternator output specified for your model listed in **Table 1**. For example, if current draw exceeds 18.5 amps on 1984-1988 models or 28.5 amps on 1989 and later models, your bike's existing current draw exceeds the charging system output. Under this condition, the battery will continually run down. Excessive current draw can be caused by an excessive number of electrical accessories (added to your bike) or by a short circuit.
5. The combined current draw of your bike's stock accessories and any add-on equipment may be causing the excessive current draw. To check, disconnect all of the accessory equipment and repeat the test; if the current draw is now within specifications (Step 3), you have found the problem. However, if you have not added any electrical equipment, the excessive current draw may be due to a short circuit.

*NOTE*
*To reduce current draw when adding electrical accessories to your Harley, contact Kriss Mfg. & Machine Inc. and request information on their Star-Less Power Reducer. This is a sealed electrical device that can be installed to your Harley's electrical system to reduce current draw by 32% or 18%. For more information, write to Kriss Mfg. & Machine Inc., P.O. Box 35331, Tucson, Arizona, 85740.*

### Voltage Regulator/Rectifier Test

1. Turn the ignition switch and all electrical accessories OFF when performing this test.

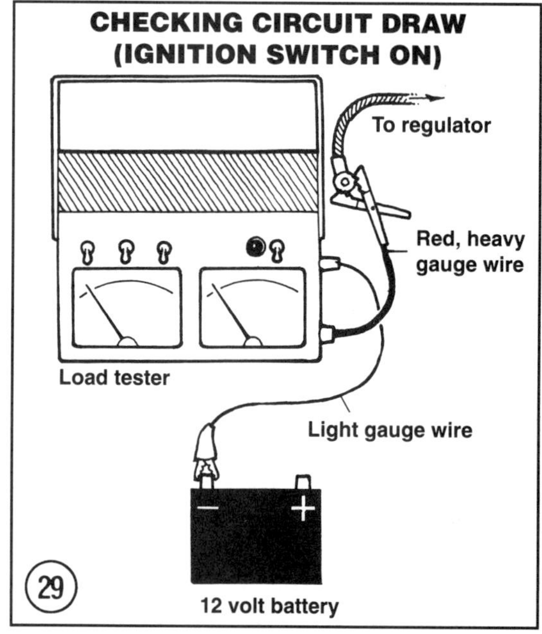


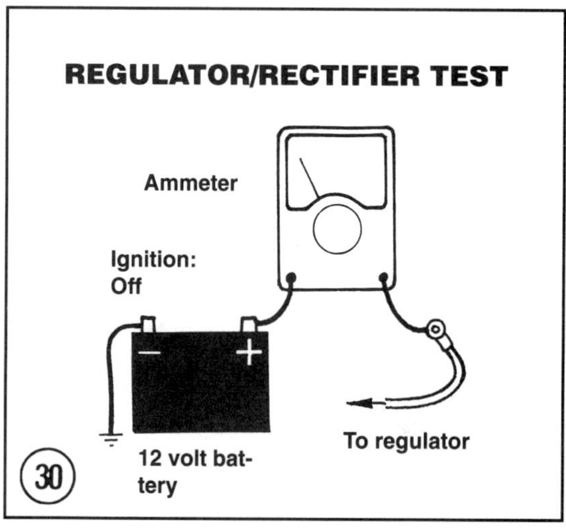

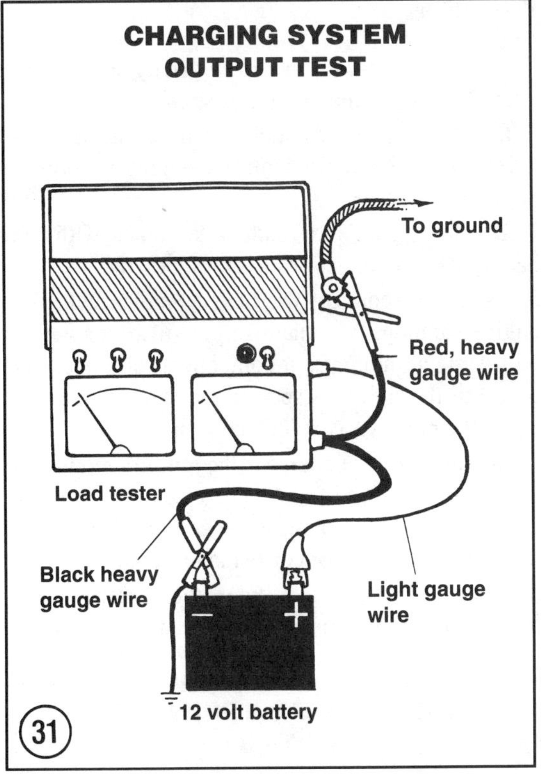

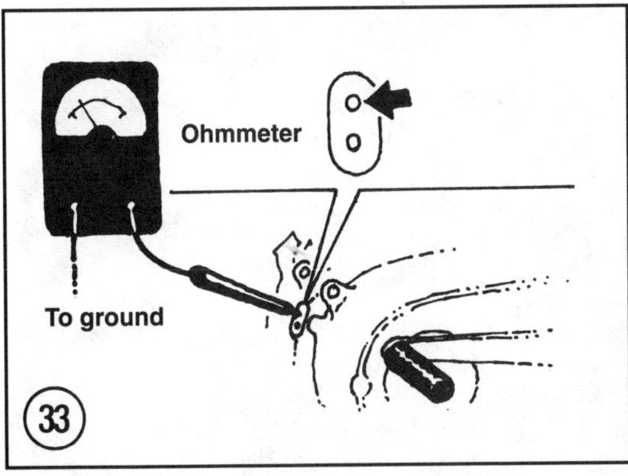


2. Connect an ammeter between the battery positive terminal and the regulator. See **Figure 30**. The reading should not exceed 3 milliamps.

3. If the amp reading is excessive, the regulator/rectifier is damaged and must be replaced.

4. Remove all test equipment and reconnect all electrical leads.

### Charging System Output Test

An induction load tester will be required for this test procedure.

1. To perform this test, the battery must be fully charged. Use a hydrometer to check the specific gravity as described in Chapter Nine, and bring the battery up to full charge, if required.

*NOTE*
*Follow the manufacturer's instructions closely when using their test equipment. Do not leave the load switch ON for more than 20 seconds at a time, or tester damage may occur from overheating.*

2. Connect an induction load tester to your bike as shown in **Figure 31**.

3. Start the engine and slowly bring its speed up to 2,000 rpm while reading the load tester scale. With the engine idling at 2,000 rpm, operate the load tester switch until the voltage scale reads 13.0 volts. Then read the current output scale. For the charging system output to be correct, it must read as follows:
   a. *1984-1988*: 19-23 amps.
   b. *1989-on*: 29-32 amps.

4. With the engine still running at 2,000 rpm, turn the load switch off and read the load tester voltage scale. Battery voltage must not exceed 15 volts. If volt reading exceeds 15 volts, voltage regulator is damaged.

5. Turn the engine off and then disconnect the load tester from the bike.

6. If output voltage is incorrect, test the stator as described under *Stator Check* in this chapter.

### Stator Check

1. With ignition turned off, disconnect the regulator/rectifier connector from the stator at the crankcase. See **Figure 32**.

2. Connect an ohmmeter between either stator pin and ground (**Figure 33**). Set the ohmmeter to the

2

R × 1 scale. The ohmmeter should read infinity (no continuity). If the reading is incorrect, the stator is grounded and must be replaced.

3. Connect an ohmmeter between both stator pins. Set the ohmmeter to the R × 1 scale. The ohmmeter should read 0.2-0.4 (1984-1988) or 0.10-0.12 (1989-on) ohms. If there was no needle movement, or if the resistance is higher than specified, the stator must be replaced.

4. Check the stator AC output as follows:
   a. Disconnect the regulator/rectifier connector (**Figure 32**).
   b. Connect an AC voltmeter across the stator sockets as shown in **Figure 34**.
   c. Start the engine and slowly increase idle speed. When the stator and rotor are functioning normally, the AC meter scale will read 19-26 volts (1984-1988) or 16-20 volts (1989-on) per each 1,000 rpm. Note the bike's tachometer reading when reading the voltmeter scale.
   d. An incorrect reading in sub-step c indicates a defective stator or rotor.
   e. A correct reading in sub-step c indicates a defective regulator/rectifier.

5. Reconnect the regulator/rectifier connector (**Figure 32**).

## IGNITION SYSTEM

All Harley-Davidson models in this manual are equipped with a solid state transistorized ignition system that uses no breaker points. This system provides a longer life for the components and delivers a more efficient spark throughout the entire speed range of the engine than breaker point systems.

Most problems involving failure to start, poor driveability or rough running are caused by trouble in the ignition system.

Note the following symptoms:

a. Engine misses.
b. Stumbles on acceleration (misfiring).
c. Loss of power at high speed (misfiring).
d. Hard starting or failure to start.
e. Rough idle.

Most of the symptoms can also be caused by a carburetor that is dirty, worn or improperly adjusted.

### Precautions

Several precautions should be strictly observed to avoid damage to the ignition system.

1. Do not reverse the battery connections. This reverses polarity and can damage the ignition components.
2. Do not "spark" the battery terminals with the battery cable connections to check polarity.
3. Do not disconnect the battery cables with the engine running. A voltage surge will occur which will damage the ignition components and possibly burn out the lights. A spark may occur which can cause the battery to explode and spray acid.
4. Do not crank the engine if the ignition module is not grounded to the frame. The black wire leading out of the ignition module is the ground wire. Check the end of the wire for corrosion or damage.
5. Do not crank the engine unless the spark plugs are grounded to the engine. When the spark plugs are

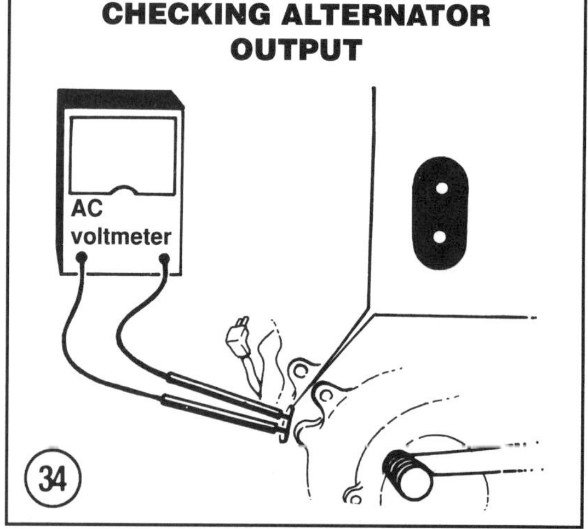

installed in the cylinder heads, both plug caps must be installed on the spark plugs (**Figure 35**). When cranking the engine with the plugs removed, both plugs must be installed in their caps and placed against the engine, grounding them (**Figure 36**).
6. Whenever working on any part of the ignition system, first turn the ignition switch OFF or disconnect the battery negative (–) lead. This is done to prevent damage to the ignition system components from an accidental short circuit.
7. Keep all connections between the various units clean and tight. Be sure that the wiring connections are pushed together firmly to help keep out moisture.
8. Make sure all ground wires are properly attached and free of oil and corrosion.

### Troubleshooting Preparation

If you suspect a problem with the ignition system, perform the following procedures in order.
1. Check the wiring harness and all plug-in connections to make sure that all terminals are free of corrosion, all connectors are tight and the wiring insulation is in good condition.
2. Check all electrical components that are grounded to the engine for a good ground. See wiring diagrams at the end of this book for ground connections for your model. These will include the ignition module, battery-to-frame and engine-to-frame ground wires and straps.
3. Make sure that all ground wires are properly connected and that the connections are clean and tight. Clean connectors with electrical contact cleaner.
4. Check remainder of the wiring for disconnected wires and short or open circuits.
5. Check the ignition circuit breaker to make sure it is not defective.
6. Make sure the fuel tank has an adequate supply of fuel and that the fuel is reaching the carburetors.
7. The battery must be fully charged. Use a hydrometer to check the specific gravity as described in Chapter Nine, and bring the battery up to full charge, if required.
8. Check spark plug cable routing. Make sure the cables are properly connected to their respective spark plugs. If cable routing is correct, perform the *Engine Fails to Start (Spark Test)* in this chapter. If there is no spark or only a weak one, recheck with a new spark plug(s). If the condition remains the same with new spark plugs and if all external wiring connections are good, the problem is most likely in the ignition system; perform the following tests. If a spark is obtained, the problem is not in the ignition or coil. Check the fuel system.

### Ignition Test (No Spark at Spark Plug)

Refer to **Figure 37** (1984-1990), **Figure 38** (1991-1993 and 1994 FXR) or **Figure 39** (1994 FLT) when performing these procedures.
1. Check the battery charge as described in Chapter Nine. If okay, proceed to Step 2.
2. Check that the black ignition module ground lead is fastened securely. Check also that the battery ground lead is fastened and in good condition.

*NOTE*
*When performing the following test procedures, it will be necessary to fabricate a test jumper from 2 lengths of 16 ga. wire, 3 alligator clips and a 0.33 MFD capacitor; see* ***Figure 40****. The test jumper should be long enough to reach from the ignition coil to a good engine ground.*

*NOTE*
*A voltmeter is required to perform the following tests.*

3. Perform the following:

a. Connect the red voltmeter lead to the white (1984-1993 and 1994 FXR) or white/black (1994 FLT) wire and the black voltmeter lead to ground (**Figure 41**).
b. Turn the ignition switch ON. The voltmeter should read 11-13 volts. Turn the ignition switch OFF. Interpret results as follows.
c. Voltage correct: Proceed to Step 4.
d. Voltage incorrect: Check the main and ignition circuit breakers. Also check for loose or damaged ignition system wiring.

4. Perform the following:
   a. Disconnect the blue (1984-1990) or pink (1991-on) wire from the ignition coil terminal (**Figure 42**).
   b. Turn the ignition switch ON.
   c. Connect the black voltmeter lead to ground. Then connect the red voltmeter lead alternately to the white (1984-1993 and 1994 FXR) or white/black (1994 FLT) wire) and then to the blue or pink ignition coil terminals (**Figure 42**). The voltmeter should be 12 volts at each wire. Turn the ignition switch OFF. Interpret results as follows.
   d. Voltage correct: Proceed to Step 5.
   e. Voltage incorrect: Check the ignition coil resistance as described in this chapter. If the resistance is okay, proceed to Step 5.
5. Perform the following:
   a. Disconnect the blue (1984-1990) or pink (1991-on) wire from the ignition coil terminal (**Figure 43**).

**37**

**IGNITION SYSTEM (1984-1990)**

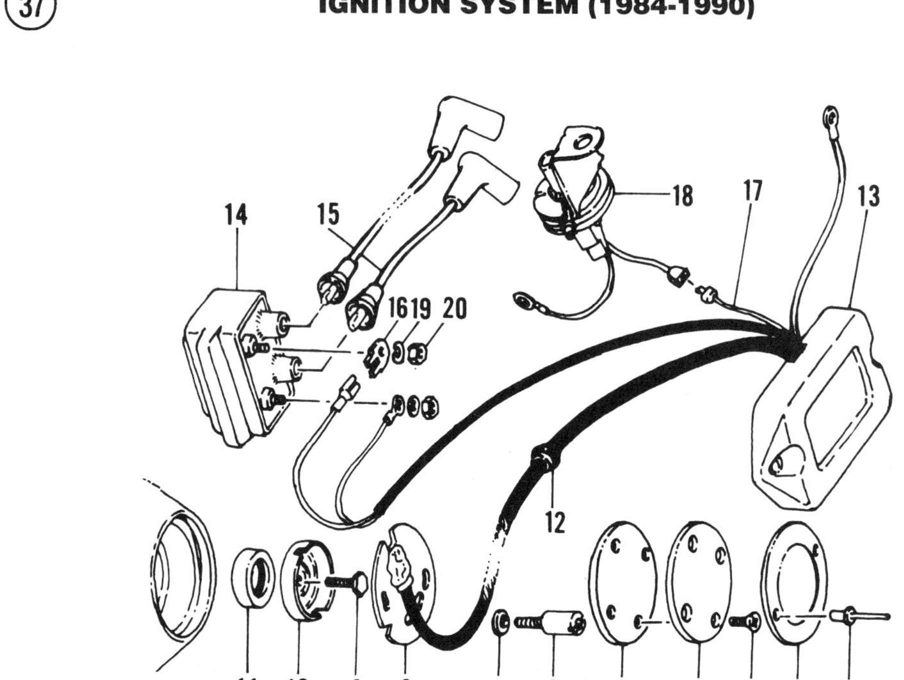


1. Outer cover rivet (2)
2. Outer cover
3. Inner cover screw (2)
4. Inner cover
5. Gasket
6. Sensor plate screw (2)
7. Washer (2)
8. Sensor plate
9. Rotor screw and star washer
10. Rotor
11. Camshaft oil seal
12. Connector
13. Ignition coil module
14. Ignition coil
15. Spark plug cable (2)
16. Ignition coil terminal
17. V.O.E.S. wire
18. Vacuum operated electric switch
19. Washer
20. Nut

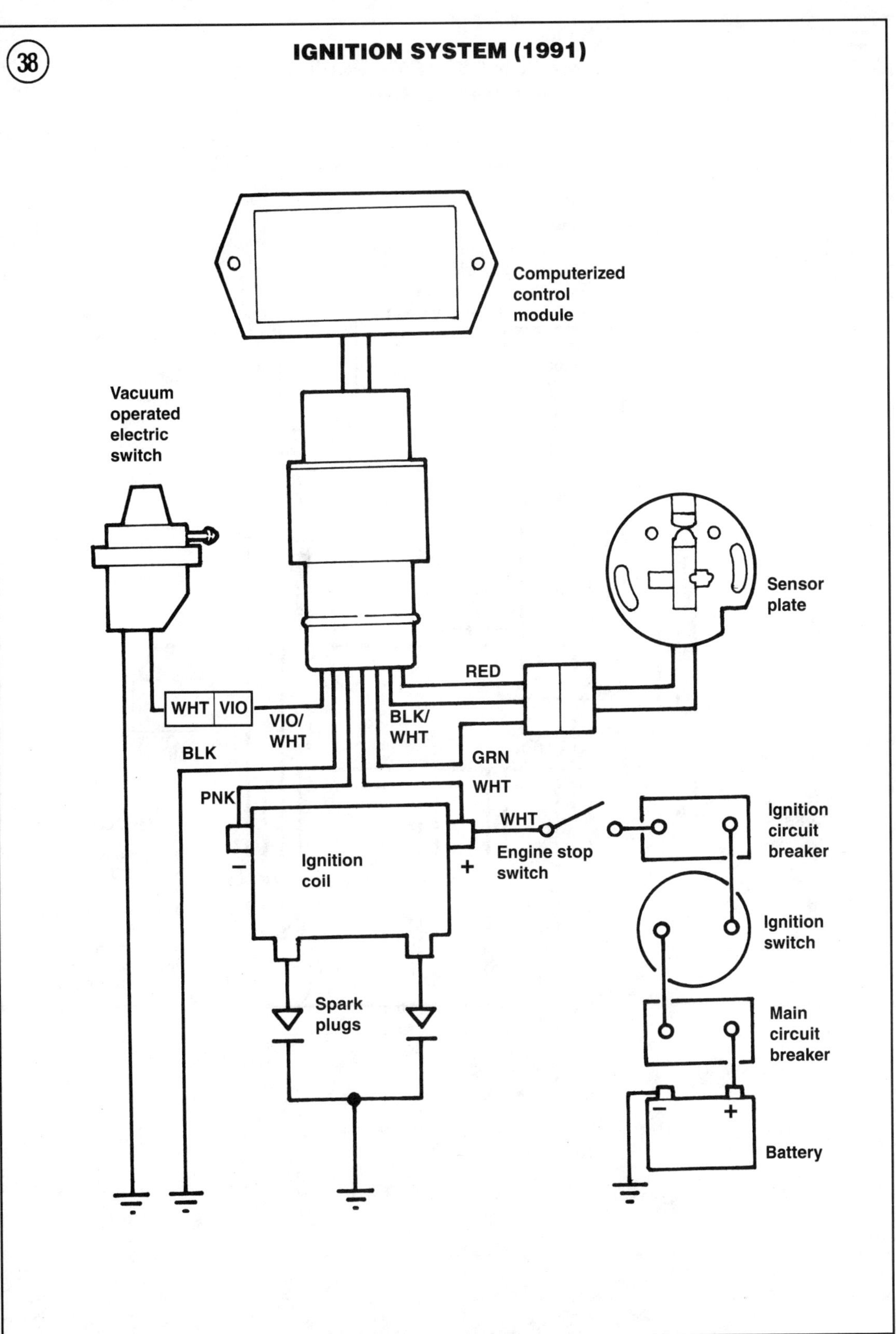
38
IGNITION SYSTEM (1991)
Computerized
control
module
Vacuum
operated
electric
switch
Sensor
plate
RED
WHT
VIO
VIO/
WHT
BLK/
WHT
BLK
GRN
WHT
PNK
WHT
Ignition
circuit
breaker
−
Ignition
coil
+
Engine stop
switch
Ignition
switch
Spark
plugs
Main
circuit
breaker
−
+
Battery

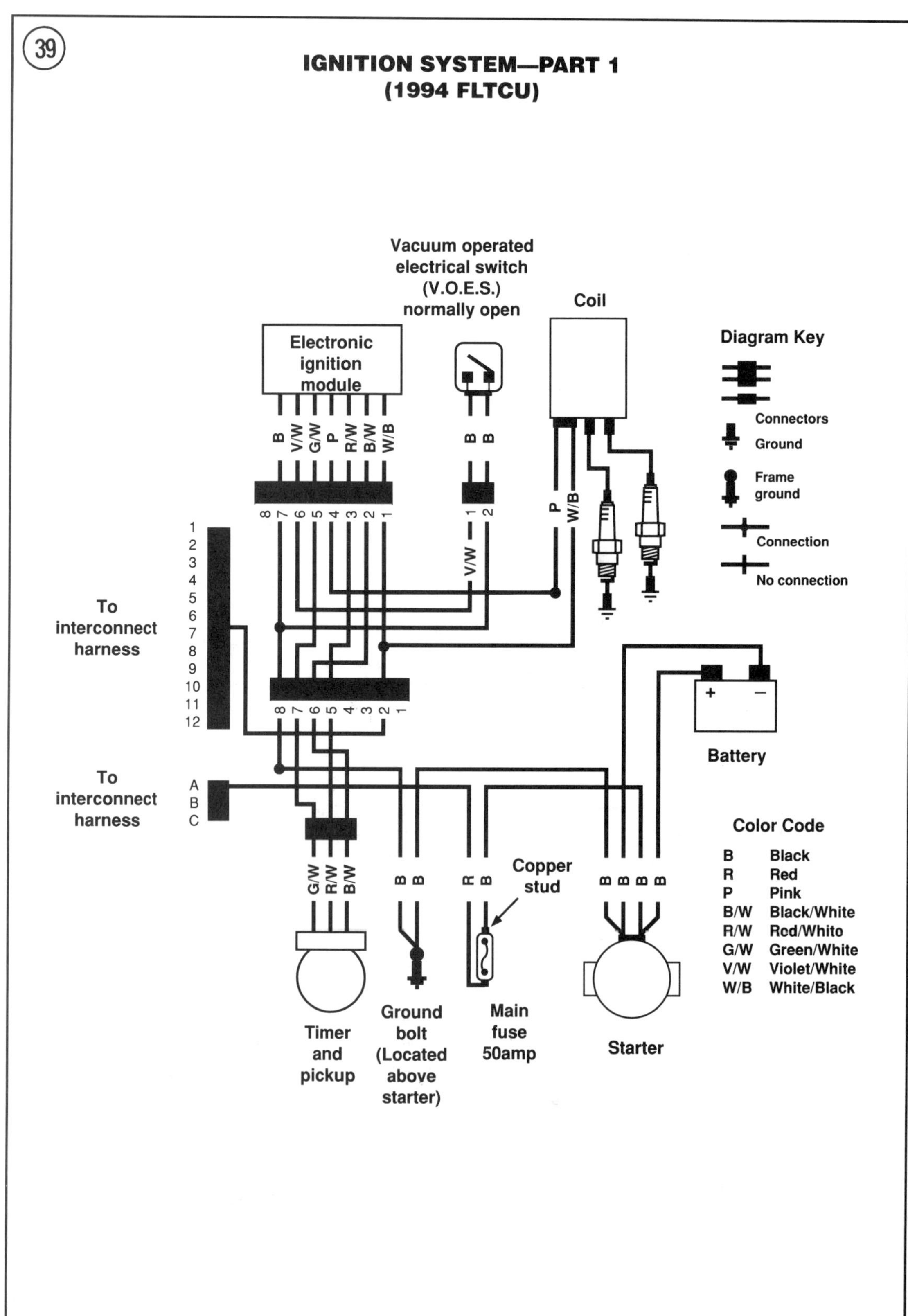
39
IGNITION SYSTEM—PART 1
(1994 FLTCU)
Vacuum operated
electrical switch
(V.O.E.S.)
normally open
Coil
Electronic
ignition
module
Diagram Key
Connectors
Ground
Frame
ground
Connection
No connection
B V/W G/W P R/W B/W W/B
B B
P W/B
V/W
To
interconnect
harness
1 2 3 4 5 6 7 8 9 10 11 12
Battery
To
interconnect
harness
A B C
G/W R/W B/W
B B
R B
Copper
stud
B B B B
Color Code
B Black
R Red
P Pink
B/W Black/White
R/W Red/White
G/W Green/White
V/W Violet/White
W/B White/Black
Timer
and
pickup
Ground
bolt
(Located
above
starter)
Main
fuse
50amp
Starter

(39) (continued)

## IGNITION SYSTEM—PART 2A (1994 FLTCU)

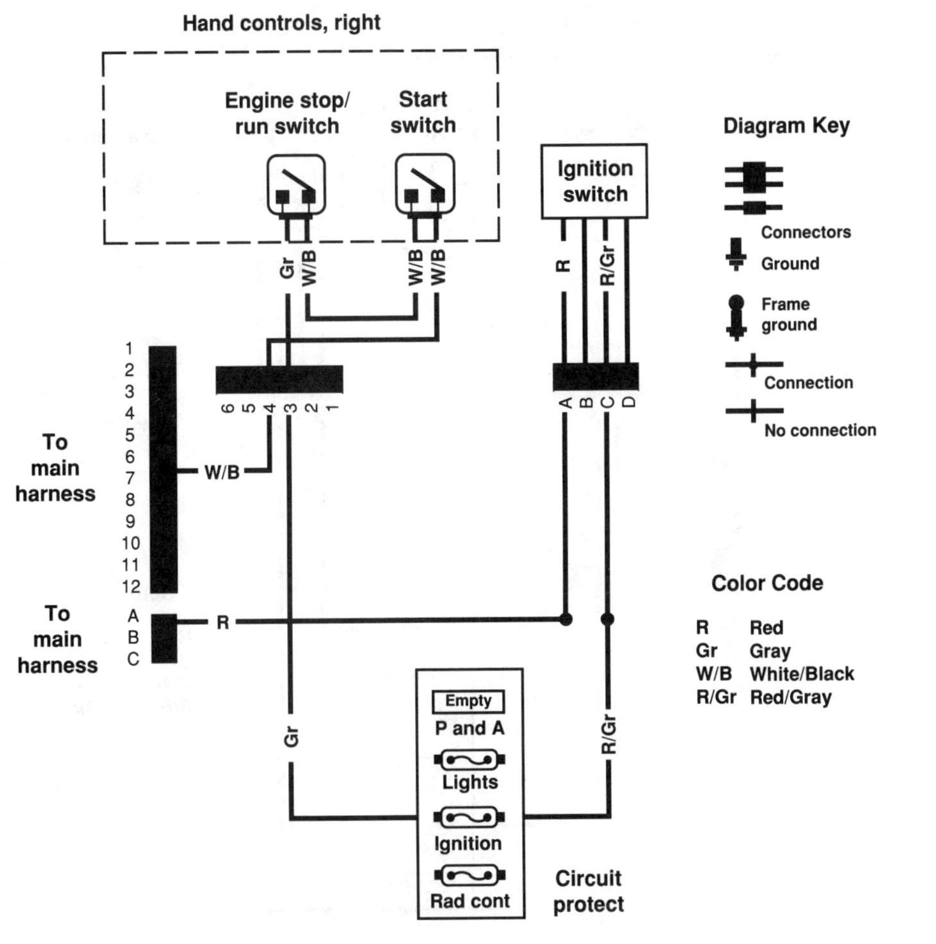

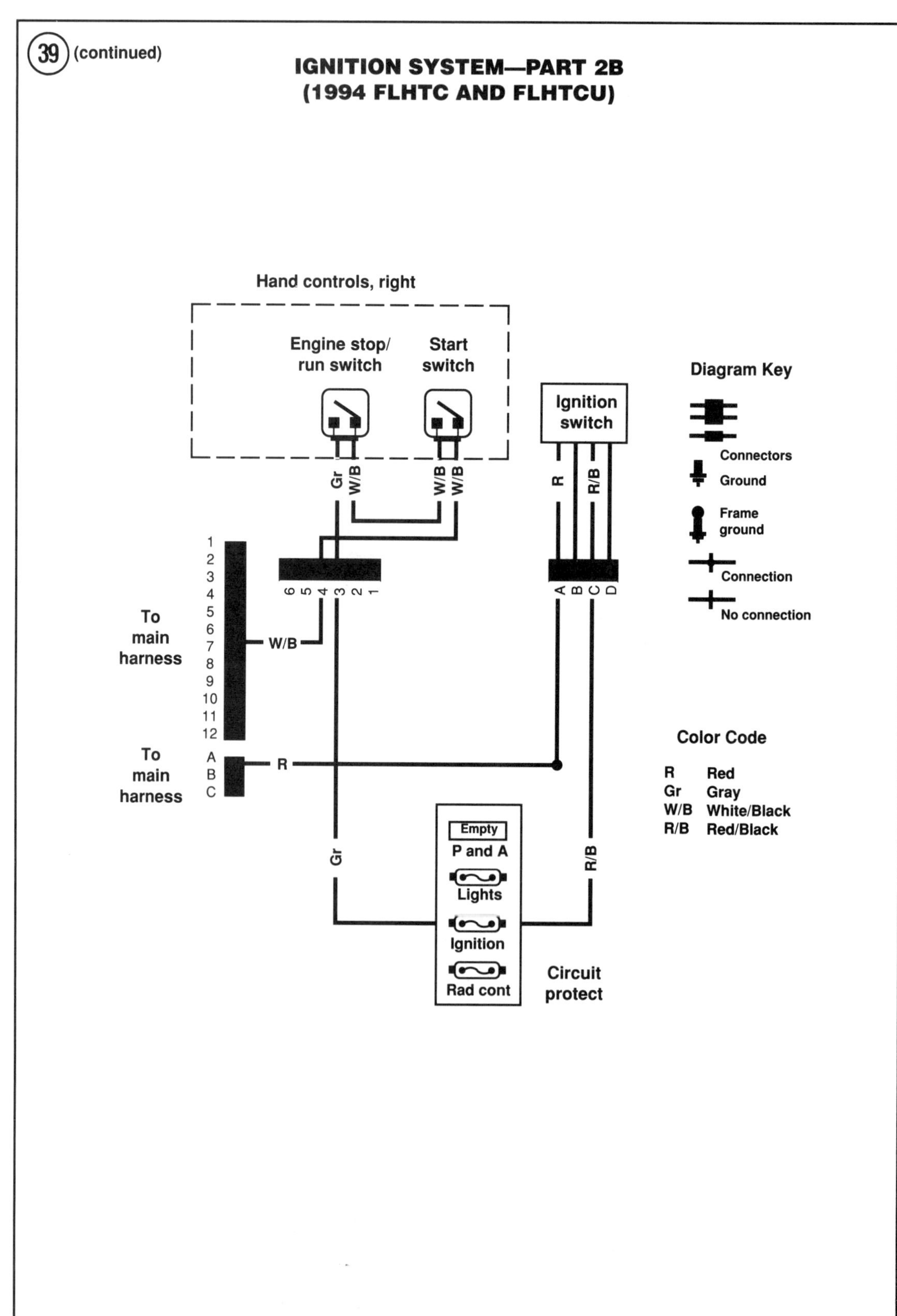

39 (continued)
IGNITION SYSTEM—PART 2B
(1994 FLHTC AND FLHTCU)
Hand controls, right
Engine stop/
run switch
Start
switch
Ignition
switch
Gr
W/B
W/B
W/B
R
R/B
1
2
3
4
5
6
7
8
9
10
11
12
To
main
harness
W/B
6 5 4 3 2 1
A B C D
To
main
harness
A
B
C
R
Gr
R/B
Empty
P and A
Lights
Ignition
Rad cont
Circuit
protect
Diagram Key
Connectors
Ground
Frame
ground
Connection
No connection
Color Code
R Red
Gr Gray
W/B White/Black
R/B Red/Black

b. Remove one of the spark plugs. Then connect the spark plug wire and connector to the spark plug and touch the spark plug base to a good ground like the engine cylinder head. Position the spark plug so you can see the electrodes.

c. Turn the ignition switch ON.

d. Connect the 2 jumper wires to a good engine ground (**Figure 43**). Then momentarily touch the jumper wire with the capacitor to the ignition coil blue or pink terminal while observing the spark plug firing tip. The spark plug should spark. Turn the ignition switch OFF and remove the jumper wire assembly. Interpret results as follows.

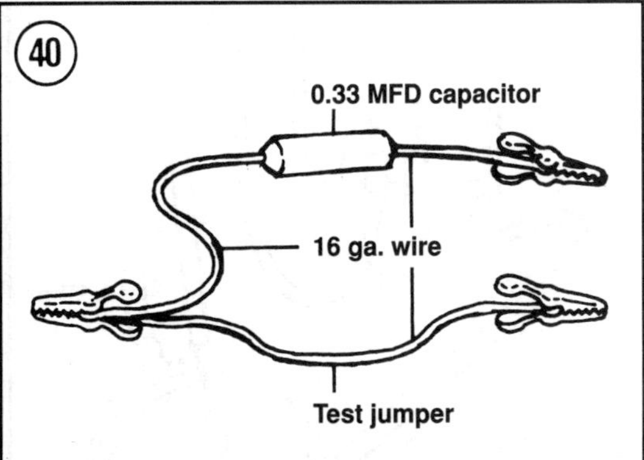


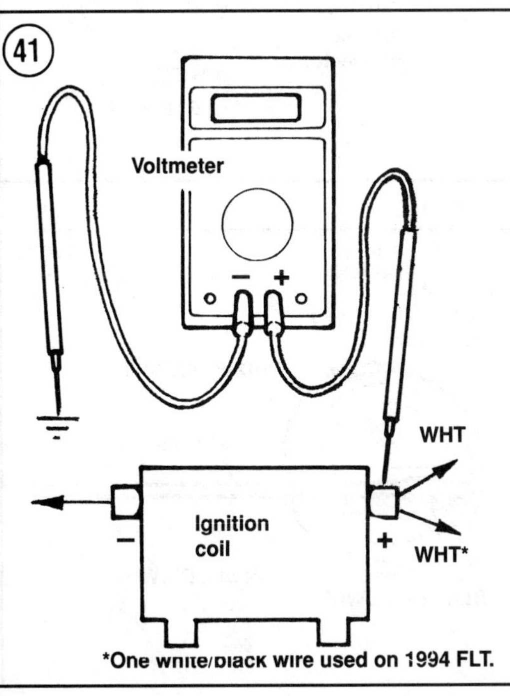


e. Spark: Proceed to Step 6.

f. No spark: Replace the ignition coil.

g. Do not reinstall the spark plug at this time.

6. Perform the following:

a. Reconnect the ignition coil blue (1984-1990) or pink (1991-on) wire to its terminal on the ignition coil.

b. Turn the ignition switch ON.

c. Disconnect the sensor plate electrical connector.

d. Connect the red voltmeter lead to the ignition module red (1984-1993 and 1994 FXR) or red/white (1994 FLT) wire socket and the black voltmeter lead to the ignition module black (1984-1990) or black/white (1991-on) pin (**Figure 44**). The voltmeter should read 4.5-5.5 volts. Disconnect the voltmeter and turn the ignition switch OFF. Interpret results as follows.

e. Voltage correct: Proceed to Step 7.

f. Voltage incorrect: Check the ignition module ground wire and the module for loose connections or damage. If okay, proceed to Step 7.

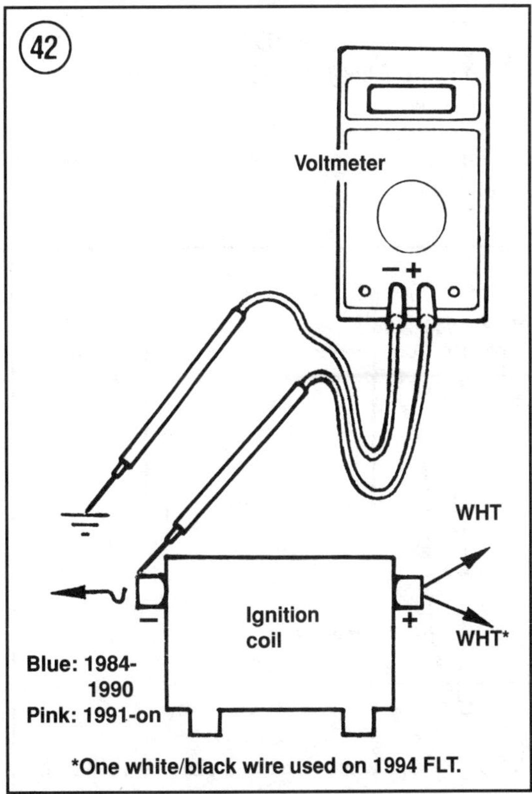

7. Turn the ignition switch ON. Then momentarily ground a screwdriver across the ignition module green or green/white and the black or black/white connector pins (**Figure 45**). There should be a strong spark at the spark plug firing tip as the screwdriver is *removed* from the connector pins. Interpret results as follows.

a. Spark: Check the sensor resistance as described in this chapter.

b. No spark: Check the ignition module resistance as described in this chapter.

8. Install and reconnect all parts removed for this procedure. If there is still no spark, either retest or have a Harley-Davidson dealer check the ignition system.

## Ignition Test (Intermittent Ignition Problems)

Intermittent problems are usually caused by temperature or vibration variances. Perform the following.

### *Temperature test*

*NOTE*
*Steps 1-4 must be performed on a cold engine.*

1. Remove the outer timing cover as described in Chapter Nine.

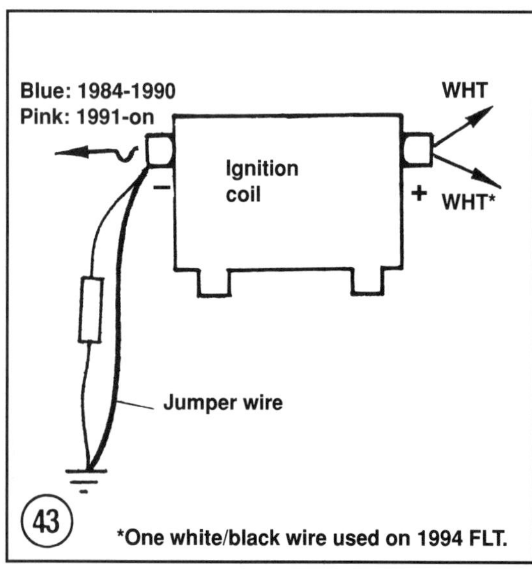


2. Remove the inner timing cover and gasket (**Figure 46**).

3. Start the engine.

4. Spray the sensor (**Figure 47**) with a cooling spray (available at electronic supply stores). If the engine dies, replace the sensor as described in Chapter Nine.

5. Allow the engine to warm to normal operating temperature. Then apply heat to the sensor with a

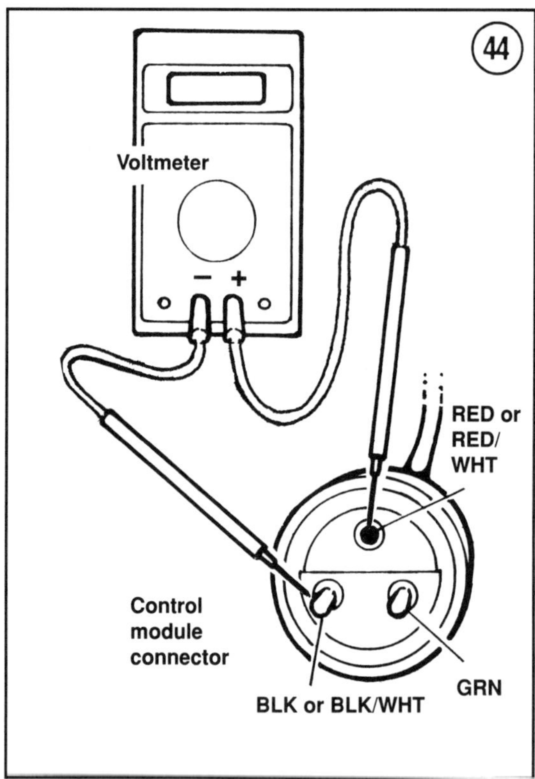


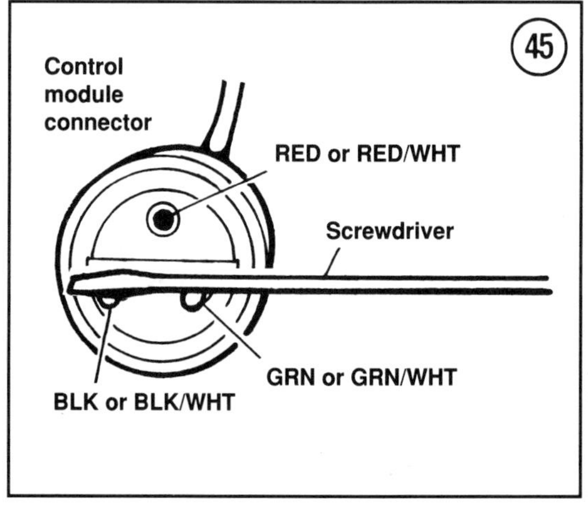

46

47

blow dryer. If the engine dies, replace the sensor as described in Chapter Nine.

6. Remove the left-hand side cover. With the engine running, apply heat to the ignition module with a blow dryer or heat gun. If the engine dies, replace the module as described in Chapter Nine.

7. Install the inner timing cover, gasket and outer timing cover as described in Chapter Nine.



### *Vibration test*

Read this procedure completely through before starting. Refer to **Figure 48** (1984-1993 and 1994 FXR) or **Figure 39** (part 1 and part 2 [1994 FLT]).

1. Check the battery connections. Retighten or repair as required.

2. On 1984-1993 and 1994 FXR, check the module ground wire connection. If necessary, remove the ground wire at the frame and scrape all paint away from its mounting point. Reinstall the ground wire with a star washer.

3. Start the engine and retest. If there is still an intermittent problem, proceed to Step 4.

4A. On 1984-1993 and 1994 FXR, disconnect the white *ignition stop switch* wire terminal at the igni-

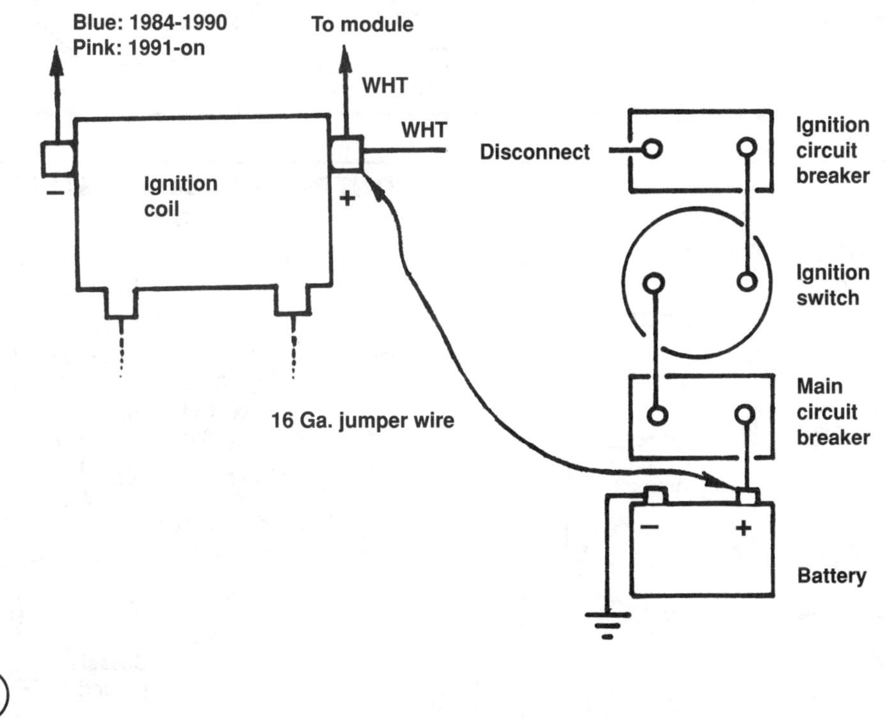

48

Blue: 1984-1990
Pink: 1991-on
To module
WHT
WHT
Ignition coil
−
+
Disconnect
Ignition circuit breaker
Ignition switch
Main circuit breaker
16 Ga. jumper wire
Battery
−
+

tion coil. Do not disconnect the ignition coil-to-ignition module white wire.

4B. On 1994 FLT, do not disconnect the ignition coil white/black wire.

5A. On 1984-1993 and 1994 FXR, connect a 16 ga. jumper wire from the positive battery terminal to the white ignition coil terminal.

5B. On 1994 FLT, connect a 16 ga. jumper wire from the positive battery terminal to the white/black ignition coil terminal.

*WARNING*
*Steps 4 and 5 have by-passed the ignition stop switch. When performing Step 6, the engine can only be stopped by removing the jumper wire. Test by removing the jumper wire before riding the bike. Test ride the bike on a paved surface in a secluded area away from all traffic. If you do not feel that you can perform this test safely, or if you do not have access to a safe riding area, refer testing to a Harley-Davidson dealer.*

6. Test ride the bike. If the intermittent problem has stopped, there is a problem with the ignition kill switch. If the problem continues, the vibration may be caused by loose connections in the starter circuit safety switches.

7. Remove the jumper wire and reconnect the white or white/black wire at the ignition coil terminal.

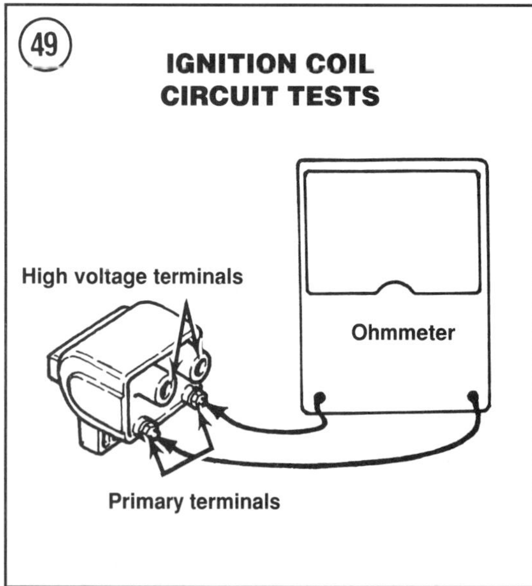


### Ignition Coil Testing

If the coil condition is doubtful, there are several checks which can be made. Disconnect the coil secondary and primary wires before testing.

*NOTE*
*When switching between ohmmeter scales in the following tests, always*

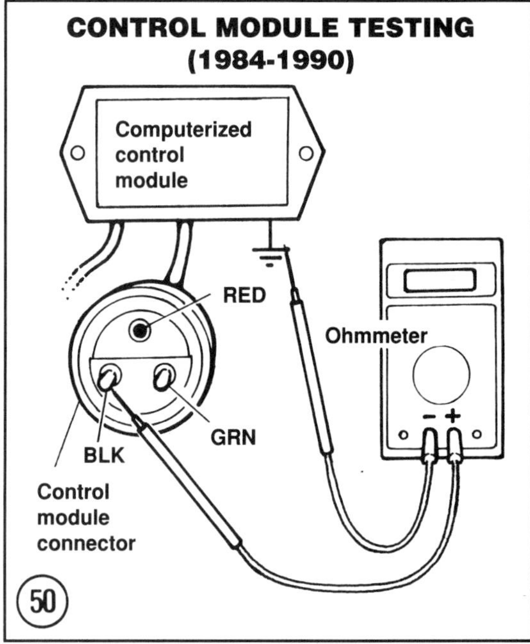


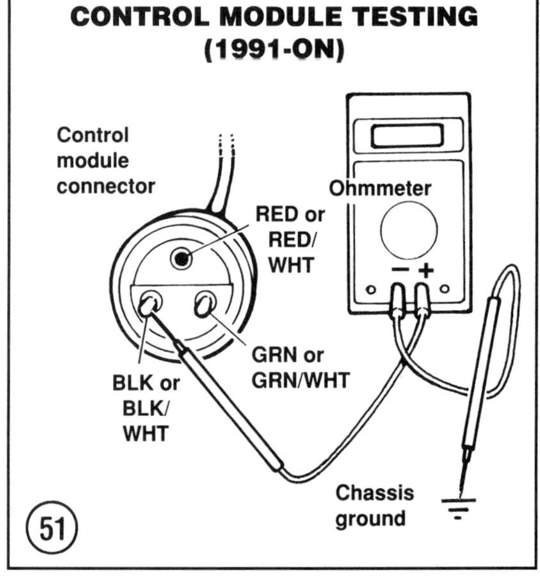

*cross the test leads and zero the needle to assure a correct reading.*

1. Set an ohmmeter on R × 1. Measure the coil primary resistance between both coil primary terminals (**Figure 49**). Compare reading to specification listed in **Table 1**.
2. Set the ohmmeter on R × 100. Measure the coil secondary resistance between both high voltage terminals (**Figure 49**). Compare reading with **Table 1**.
3. Replace the coil if it does not test within specifications in Step 1 or Step 2.

## Ignition Module and Sensor Resistance Testing

The following tests should be performed with the Harley-Davidson KMT multimeter (part No. HD-35500). If any other meter is used, the results may be different than the specified values listed in these tests. If you do not have the Harley-Davidson multimeter, it is suggested that you do not purchase replacement parts based upon your meter's test results as electrical components normally cannot be returned.

*NOTE*
*In the following tests, the red ohmmeter lead is always considered to be the positive lead and the black ohmmeter lead is the negative lead. Refer to the instructions provided with the KMT multimeter for proper operation.*

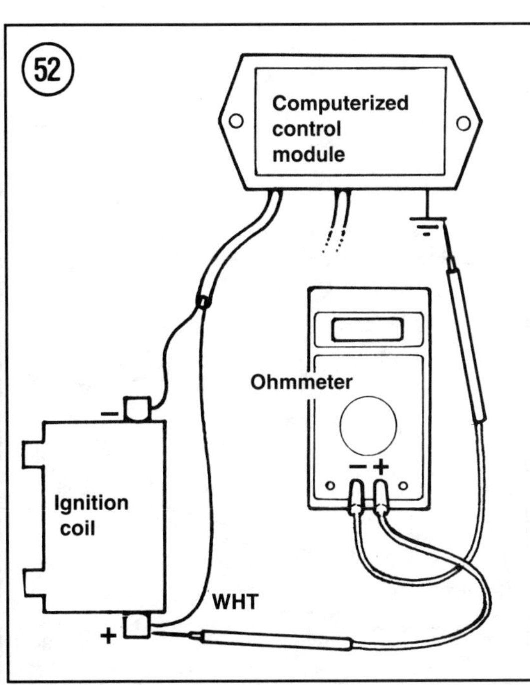


### *Ignition module ground test—all models*

Refer to **Figure 50** (1984-1990) or **Figure 51** (1991-on) when performing this procedure.
1. Disconnect the module to sensor connector.
2. Connect the red ohmmeter lead to the black (1984-1990) or black/white (1991-on) module pin and the black ohmmeter lead to ground.
3. The correct resistance reading is 0-1 ohms. If the reading exceeds 1 ohm, replace the module.
4. Reconnect the connector.

### *Power supply diode test—1984-1990*

Refer to **Figure 52** when performing this procedure.
1. Disconnect the white ignition coil-to-module connector.
2. Set the ohmmeter on the R × 100 scale.
3. Connect the red ohmmeter lead to the white ignition coil connector and the black lead to the module ground wire. The correct resistance is 800-1300 ohms.
4. Switch the test leads in Step 3. The ohmmeter should indicate infinite resistance.
5. Replace the module if either reading is not within specifications.
6. Remove the ohmmeter and reconnect the ignition coil-to-module connector.

### *Coil driver transistor check—1984-1990*

Refer to **Figure 53** when performing this procedure.
1. Disconnect the blue ignition coil-to-module connector.
2. Set the ohmmeter on the R × 100 scale.
3. Connect the red ohmmeter lead to the blue ignition coil connector and the black lead to the module ground wire. The ohmmeter should indicate infinite resistance.
4. Switch the test leads in Step 3. The correct resistance is 400-800 ohms.
5. Replace the module if either reading is not within specifications.

6. Disconnect the ohmmeter and reconnect the ignition coil-to-module connector.

### *Ignition sensor ground test—1984-1990*

Refer to **Figure 54** when performing this procedure.

1. Disconnect the module to sensor connector.
2. Set the ohmmeter on the R × 1 scale.
3. Connect the red ohmmeter lead to the sensor connector red pin and the ohmmeter black lead onto the sensor plate.
4. The ohmmeter should read infinite resistance.
5. Repeat Step 3 by checking at the sensor connector black and green pins. In each case, the ohmmeter should read infinite resistance.
6. If the ohmmeter showed continuity in either test, replace the sensor plate.
7. Disconnect the ohmmeter and reconnect the module to sensor connector.

### *Ignition sensor output test—1984-1990*

Refer to **Figure 55** for this procedure.

1. Disconnect the ignition module to sensor plate electrical connector.
2. Set the ohmmeter on the R × 100 scale.
3. Connect the red ohmmeter lead to the sensor connector green pin and the ohmmeter black lead to the sensor connector black pin. The meter should show infinite resistance.
4. Switch the test leads in Step 3. The correct resistance is 300-750 ohms.
5. If any of the meter readings differ from the stated values, replace the sensor plate.
6. Disconnect the ohmmeter and reconnect the ignition module-to-sensor plate connector.

### *Ignition module harness resistance test—1991-on*

Refer to **Figure 56** (1991-1993 and 1994 FXR) or **Figure 39** (1994 FLT).

1. Turn the ignition stop switch (at handlebar) to the OFF position.
2. Disconnect the 7-prong ignition module electrical connector.
3. Disconnect the sensor plate 3-prong electrical connector.

*NOTE*
*When making the following resistance tests, cross the ohmmeter test leads and zero the needle.*

4. Set the ohmmeter to the R × 1 scale.
5. On 1991-1993 and 1994 FXR models, connect the red ohmmeter lead to the No. 4 ignition module

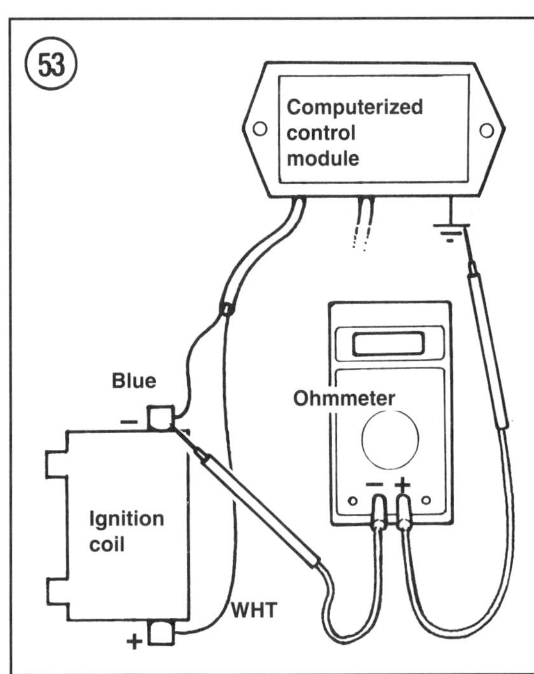


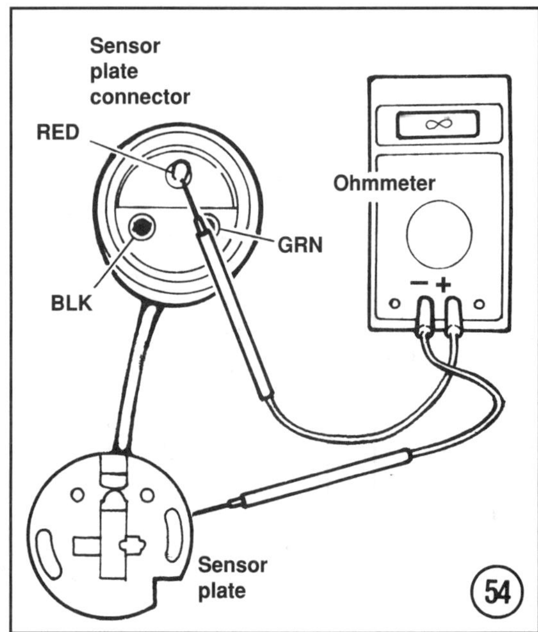

connector socket (on the wiring harness side, not on the module side). On 1994 FLT models, connect the red ohmmeter lead to pin No. 7 (black wire) on the ignition module connector (on the wiring harness side, not on the module side). Connect the black ohmmeter lead to a good engine ground. Wiggle the wiring harness and read the resistance indicated on the ohmmeter. It should be 0-1 ohms. Note the following:

a. If the resistance reading is correct, perform Step 6.
b. If a high resistance reading is obtained, check for dirty or loose-fitting terminals or a bare or damaged wire; clean and repair as required.

6. Connect the red ohmmeter lead to the No. 1 ignition module connector socket (on the wiring harness side, not on the module side). Connect the black ohmmeter lead to a good engine ground. Wiggle the wiring harness and read the ohmmeter scale. It should be infinity (high resistance). Note the following:

a. If the reading is infinity, perform Step 7.
b. If the meter shows a resistance reading, the wire is shorting out to ground. Repair the wire and retest.
c. On 1991-1993 and 1994 FXR models, repeat this test for the following ignition module sockets: No. 2, 3, 5, 6 and 7.
d. On 1994 FLT models, repeat this test for the following ignition module connectors: No. 2, 3, 4, 5 and 6.

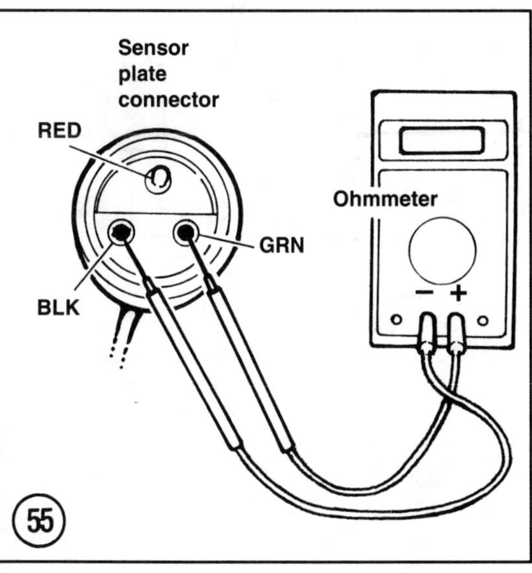


7. Check each of the ignition module socket wires (except No. 4 on 1991-1993 and 1994 FXR or No. 7 on 1994 FLT) for continuity with an ohmmeter set on the R × 1 scale. The reading for each wire should be 0-1 ohm. An infinite reading indicates that there is an open in the wire; check for a dirty, loose-fitting or a damaged connector or wire.

8. Reconnect the ignition module and sensor plate electrical connectors.

## FUEL SYSTEM

The fuel system consists of the fuel tank, fuel valve, fuel lines and carburetor (**Figure 57**). The throttle and choke cables and the throttle grip should also be included in the operation of the fuel system.

During engine operation, fuel will flow from the fuel tank, through the fuel valve and into the carburetor where it is mixed with air before entering the engine. If fuel is entering the carburetor incorrectly (too much or too little), the engine will not run properly.

Many owners automatically assume that the carburetor is at fault when the engine does not run properly. While fuel system problems are not uncommon, carburetor adjustment is seldom the answer. In many cases, adjusting the carburetor only compounds the problem by making the engine run worse.

Fuel system troubleshooting should start at the fuel tank and work through the system, reserving the carburetor as the final point. Most fuel system problems result from an empty fuel tank, sour fuel, a dirty air filter or clogged carburetor jets.

### Identifying Carburetor Conditions

The following list can be used as a guide when distinguishing between rich and lean carburetor conditions.

When the engine is running rich, one or more of the following conditions may be present:

a. The spark plug(s) will foul.
b. The engine will miss and run rough when it is running under a load.
c. As the throttle is increased, the exhaust smoke becomes more excessive.
d. With the throttle open, the exhaust will sound choked or dull. Bringing the motorcycle to a dead stop and trying to clear the exhaust with

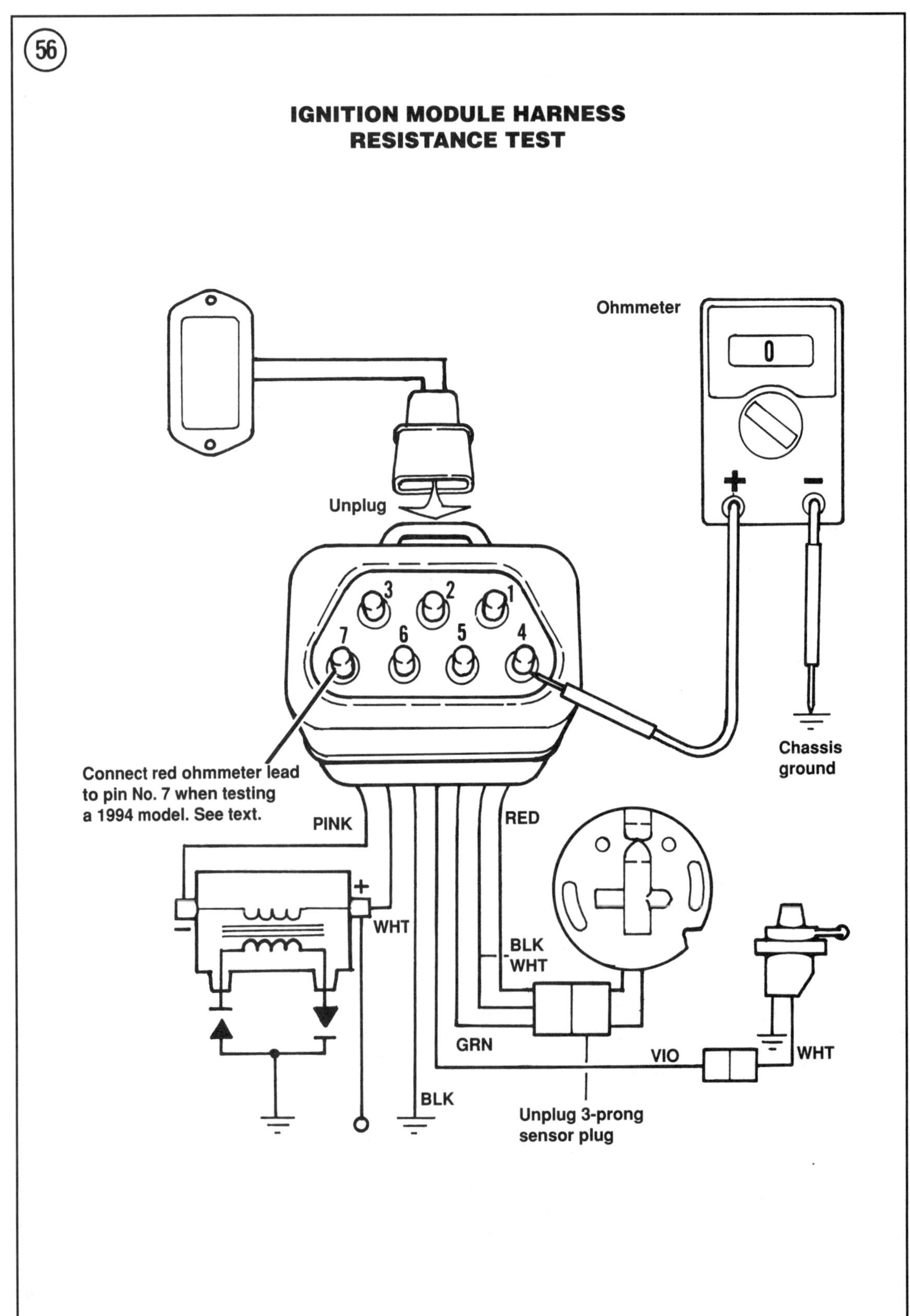
56
IGNITION MODULE HARNESS
RESISTANCE TEST
Ohmmeter
0
+
-
Unplug
3
2
1
7
6
5
4
Chassis
ground
Connect red ohmmeter lead
to pin No. 7 when testing
a 1994 model. See text.
PINK
RED
+
-
WHT
BLK
WHT
GRN
VIO
WHT
BLK
Unplug 3-prong
sensor plug

the throttle held wide open does not clear up the sound.

When the engine is running lean, one or more of the following conditions may be present:

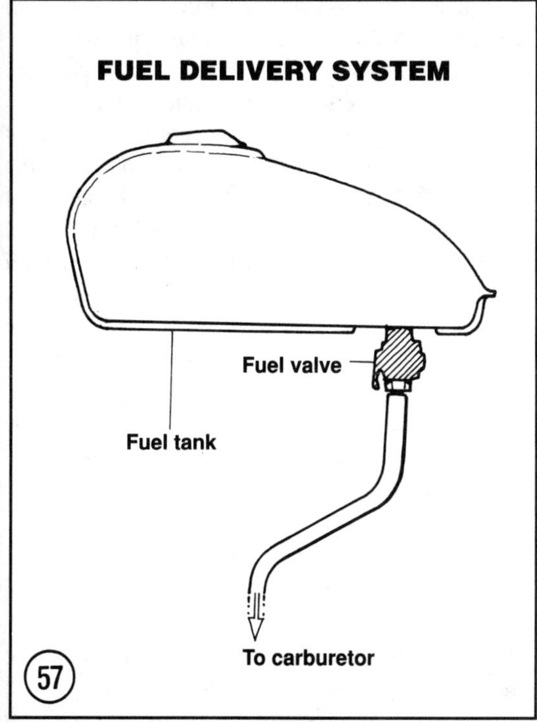


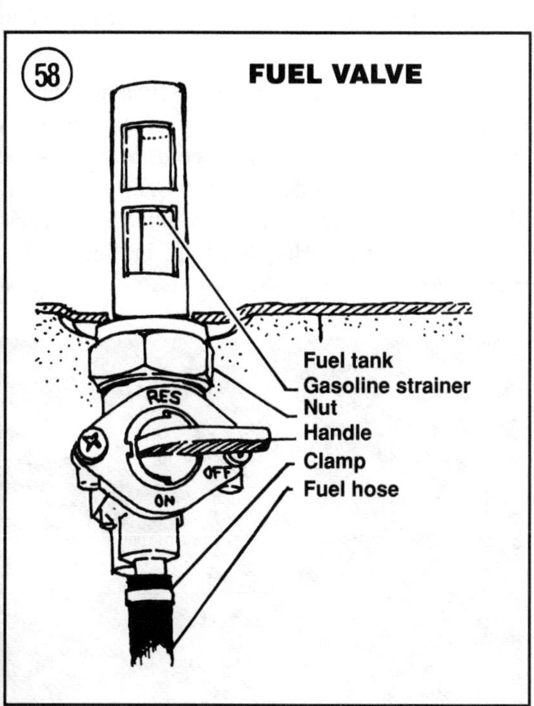


a. The spark plug firing end will become very white or blistered in appearance.
b. The engine overheats.
c. Acceleration is slower.
d. Flat spots are felt during operation that feel much like the engine is trying to run out of gas.
e. Engine power is reduced.
f. At full throttle, engine rpm will not be steady.



## Troubleshooting

Fuel system problems should be isolated to the fuel tank, fuel valve and filter, fuel hoses, external fuel filter (if used) or carburetor. The following procedures assume that the ignition system is working properly and is correctly adjusted.

### *Fuel delivery system*

Check fuel flow. Remove the fuel tank caps and look into the tank. If fuel is present, disconnect the battery ground cable as a safety precaution. Then check that the fuel valve is turned OFF. Disconnect the fuel hose at the carburetor and put the hose into a container to catch any discharged fuel.

*NOTE*
*Make sure there is a sufficient supply of fuel in each tank to allow the fuel valve to work in its normal operating position.*

*WARNING*
*Make sure there are no open flames in the area when performing the following.*

The fuel valve controls fuel flow from the fuel tank to the carburetor. The fuel valve on all models is a 3-position valve (**Figure 58**). Because a gravity-feed type fuel delivery system is used, fuel should always be present at the fuel valve. Turn the fuel valve so that the end of the handle faces down (valve in normal operating position). Fuel should flow into the container. Turn the fuel valve so that the end of the handle faces up (valve in RESERVE). Fuel should flow into the container. If there is no fuel present at the hose:

a. The fuel valve may be shut off or blocked by rust or foreign matter. If fuel flows in the RESERVE but not in the ON position, the fuel level in the tank may be too low. If the fuel level is high enough to flow in the ON position, the ON side of the valve is clogged. This would also hold true if the RESERVE side failed to work properly.

b. The fuel hose may be plugged or kinked. Remove the fuel hose and then clear the hose by passing a stiff piece of wire or a rod (less than 1/4 in. [6.35 mm] in diameter) through the hose.

*WARNING*
*When reconnecting the fuel hose, make sure the hose is inserted through the nylon hose insulator (**Figure 59**). Do not operate the engine without the insulator properly installed.*

c. The fuel tank is not properly vented. Check by opening the fuel tank cap. If fuel flows with the cap open, check for a plugged vent.

If fuel flow is present, fuel is reaching the carburetor. Examine the fuel in the container for rust or dirt that could clog or restrict the fuel valve filter and the carburetor jets. If there is evidence of contamination, it will be necessary to clean and flush the fuel tanks, fuel valve assembly, hoses and carburetor. Refer to Chapter Eight for fuel system service.

If you are getting a good fuel flow from the fuel tank to the carburetor and the fuel is not contaminated with dirt or rust, refer to the troubleshooting chart in **Figure 60** or **Figure 61** for additional information.

***Fuel level system***

The fuel supply system is shown in **Figure 62** (1984-1989) and **Figure 63** (1990-on). Proper carburetor operation is dependent on a constant and correct carburetor fuel level. As fuel is drawn from the float bowl during engine operation, the float level in the bowl drops. As the float drops, the float needle moves away from its seat and allows fuel to flow through the seat into the float bowl. Fuel entering the float bowl will cause the float to rise and push against the float needle. When the fuel level reaches a predetermined level, the needle is pushed against the float seat to prevent the float bowl from overfilling.

If the float needle doesn't close, the engine will run rich or flood with fuel. Symptoms of this problem are rough running, excessive black smoke and poor acceleration. This condition will sometimes clear up when the engine is run at wide open throttle, as the fuel is being used up before the float bowl can overfill. As the engine speed is reduced, however, the rich running condition repeats itself.

**Figure 60** (1984-1989) and **Figure 61** (1990-on) list several problems that can cause fuel overflow. In most instances, it can be as simple a small piece of dirt trapped between the needle and seat or an incorrect float level. If you see fuel flowing out of the overflow tube connected at the bottom of the float bowl, the float valve is being held open. First check the position of the fuel valve. Turn the fuel lever OFF if it was left in the ON or RESERVE position. Then tap on the carburetor (not too hard) and turn the fuel valve back on. If the fuel flow stopped running out of the overflow tube, you may have dislodged whatever it was holding the needle off of its seat. If fuel continues to flow from the overflow tube, it will be necessary to remove and service the carburetor. See Chapter Eight.

***Starter or choke system***

A cold engine requires a very rich mixture. The choke used on 1984-1989 models consists of a choke valve and a fast idle cam. On 1990 and later models, a cable actuated enrichener valve is used for cold-starting.

Carburetor chokes can also present a problem by causing difficult cold starting. If your engine has become difficult to start when cold, first check the choke adjustment as described in Chapter Three. If the choke adjustment is correct, refer to the possible causes listed under "Hard Starting" in **Figure 60** or **Figure 61**.

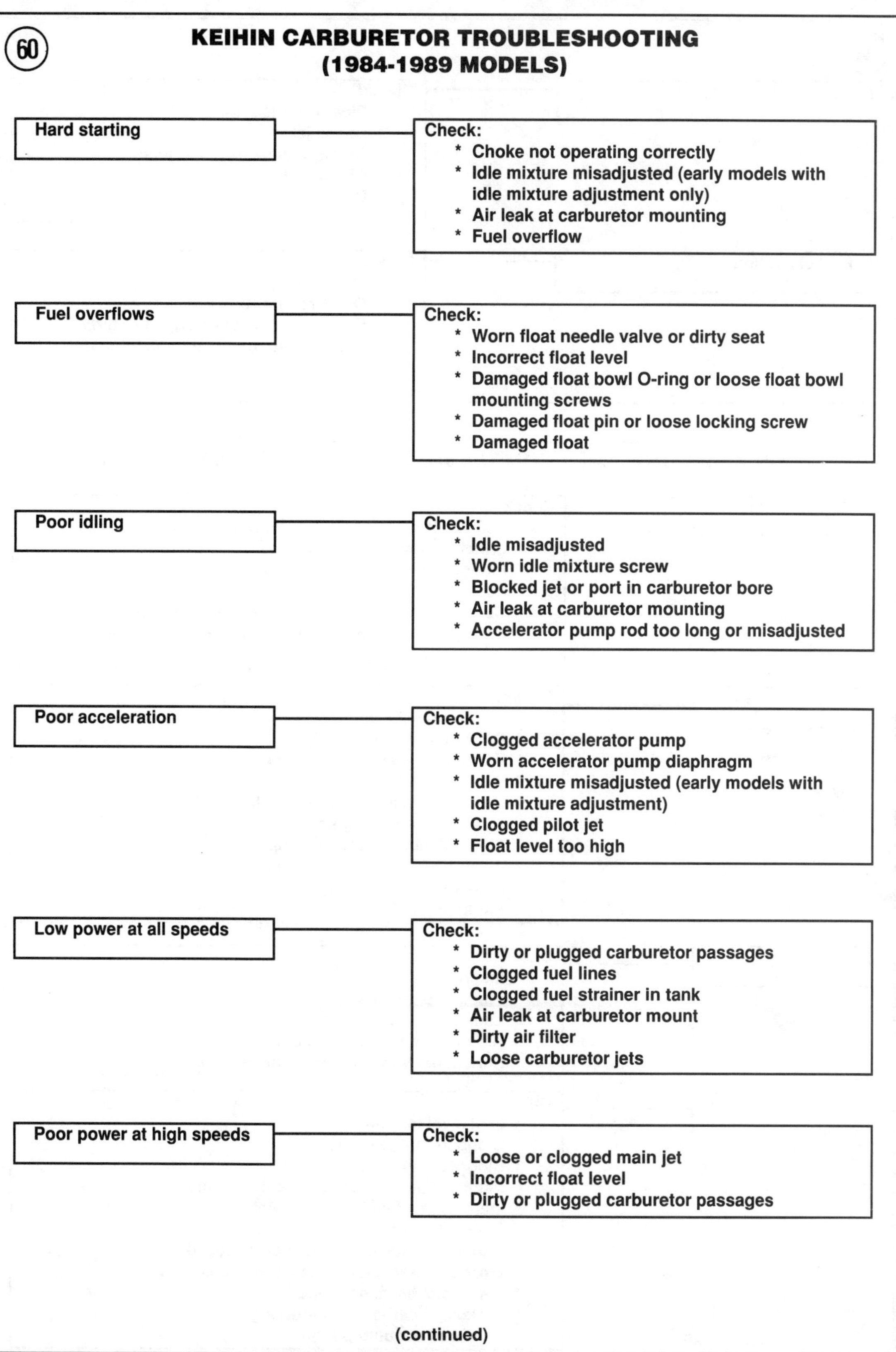

**60** KEIHIN CARBURETOR TROUBLESHOOTING (1984-1989 MODELS)

|  |  |
|---|---|
| Hard starting | Check:<br>* Choke not operating correctly<br>* Idle mixture misadjusted (early models with idle mixture adjustment only)<br>* Air leak at carburetor mounting<br>* Fuel overflow |
| Fuel overflows | Check:<br>* Worn float needle valve or dirty seat<br>* Incorrect float level<br>* Damaged float bowl O-ring or loose float bowl mounting screws<br>* Damaged float pin or loose locking screw<br>* Damaged float |
| Poor idling | Check:<br>* Idle misadjusted<br>* Worn idle mixture screw<br>* Blocked jet or port in carburetor bore<br>* Air leak at carburetor mounting<br>* Accelerator pump rod too long or misadjusted |
| Poor acceleration | Check:<br>* Clogged accelerator pump<br>* Worn accelerator pump diaphragm<br>* Idle mixture misadjusted (early models with idle mixture adjustment)<br>* Clogged pilot jet<br>* Float level too high |
| Low power at all speeds | Check:<br>* Dirty or plugged carburetor passages<br>* Clogged fuel lines<br>* Clogged fuel strainer in tank<br>* Air leak at carburetor mount<br>* Dirty air filter<br>* Loose carburetor jets |
| Poor power at high speeds | Check:<br>* Loose or clogged main jet<br>* Incorrect float level<br>* Dirty or plugged carburetor passages |

(continued)

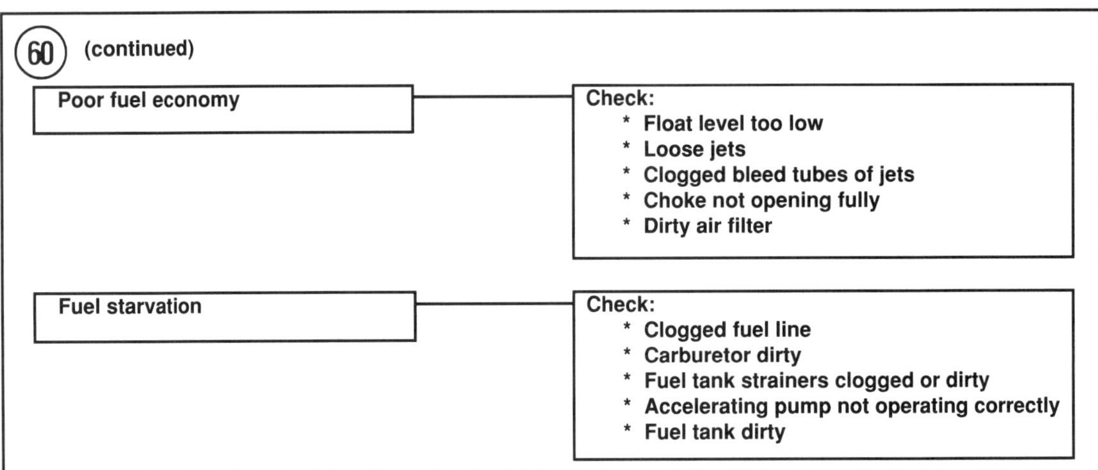

**60** (continued)

**Poor fuel economy**

Check:
* Float level too low
* Loose jets
* Clogged bleed tubes of jets
* Choke not opening fully
* Dirty air filter

**Fuel starvation**

Check:
* Clogged fuel line
* Carburetor dirty
* Fuel tank strainers clogged or dirty
* Accelerating pump not operating correctly
* Fuel tank dirty

## CV CARBURETOR TROUBLESHOOTING (1990-ON MODELS)

**Hard starting**

Check:
* Fuel overflow from float assembly
* Enrichener system inoperative
* Plugged pilot jet and/or passage
* Fuel overflow
* Contaminated or restricted fuel supply system
* Damaged or inoperative vacuum operated fuel valve on 1994 FLT

**Fuel overflows**

Check:
* Incorrect fuel level
* Damaged float assembly
* Worn float needle valve or dirty seat
* Incorrect float alignment
* Damaged float bowl O-ring or loose float bowl mounting screws
* Plugged vent in fuel tank cap
* Incorrect fuel tank cap installed (non-vent type)
* Plugged fuel tank vent or vent system

**Poor idling**

Check:
* Incorrect idle speed
* Plugged pilot jet system
* Loose pilot jet
* Air leak at carburetor mounting
* Enrichener valve nut loose or damaged

**Poor acceleration**

Check:
* Fuel level too low
* Clogged fuel passages
* Clogged jets
* Plugged fuel tank vent or vent system
* Incorrect fuel tank cap installed (non-vent type)
* Enrichener valve nut loose or damaged
* Worn or damaged needle jet or needle
* Throttle cable misadjusted
* Air leak at carburetor mounting
* Damaged vacuum piston

**61** (continued)

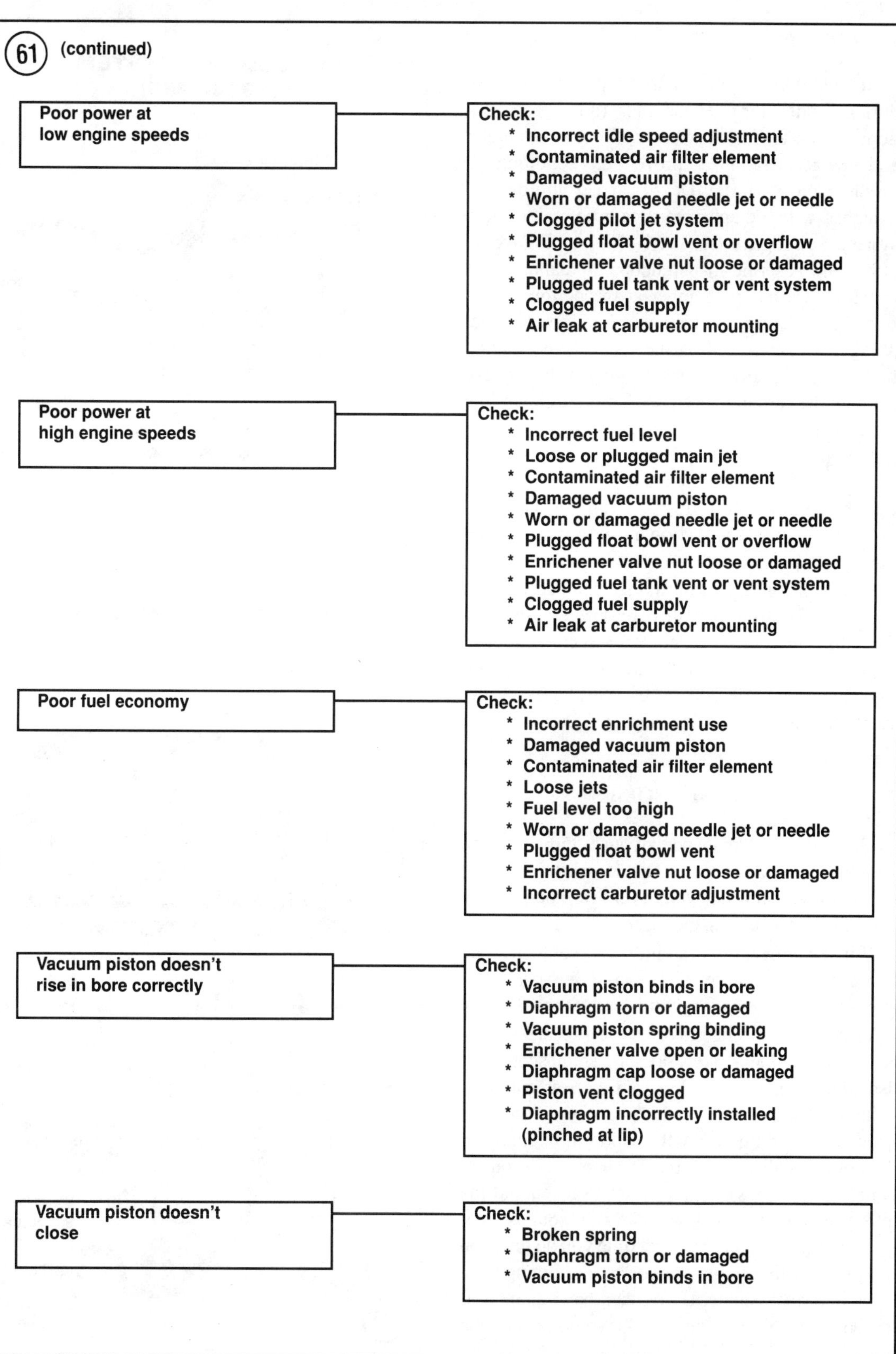
61 (continued)
Poor power at low engine speeds
Check:
* Incorrect idle speed adjustment
* Contaminated air filter element
* Damaged vacuum piston
* Worn or damaged needle jet or needle
* Clogged pilot jet system
* Plugged float bowl vent or overflow
* Enrichener valve nut loose or damaged
* Plugged fuel tank vent or vent system
* Clogged fuel supply
* Air leak at carburetor mounting
Poor power at high engine speeds
Check:
* Incorrect fuel level
* Loose or plugged main jet
* Contaminated air filter element
* Damaged vacuum piston
* Worn or damaged needle jet or needle
* Plugged float bowl vent or overflow
* Enrichener valve nut loose or damaged
* Plugged fuel tank vent or vent system
* Clogged fuel supply
* Air leak at carburetor mounting
Poor fuel economy
Check:
* Incorrect enrichment use
* Damaged vacuum piston
* Contaminated air filter element
* Loose jets
* Fuel level too high
* Worn or damaged needle jet or needle
* Plugged float bowl vent
* Enrichener valve nut loose or damaged
* Incorrect carburetor adjustment
Vacuum piston doesn't rise in bore correctly
Check:
* Vacuum piston binds in bore
* Diaphragm torn or damaged
* Vacuum piston spring binding
* Enrichener valve open or leaking
* Diaphragm cap loose or damaged
* Piston vent clogged
* Diaphragm incorrectly installed (pinched at lip)
Vacuum piston doesn't close
Check:
* Broken spring
* Diaphragm torn or damaged
* Vacuum piston binds in bore

*Accelerator pump system*

Because the carburetor cannot supply enough fuel during sudden throttle openings (quick acceleration), a lean air/fuel mixture will cause hesitation and poor acceleration. To prevent this condition, all of the factory Harley-Davidson carburetors are equipped with a diaphragm type accelerator pump system. See **Figure 64** (1984-1989) or **Figure 65** (1990-on). A spring-loaded neoprene diaphragm is installed in a pump chamber at the bottom of the float bowl. During sudden acceleration, the diaphragm is compressed by the pump lever, forcing fuel out of the pump chamber through a check valve and into the carburetor venturi. This additional fuel richens the existing air/fuel mixture to prevent engine hesitation. The diaphragm spring returns the diaphragm to its uncompressed position, allowing the chamber to refill with fuel. The check valve prevents fuel from back flowing into the chamber during pump operation.

If your bike hesitates during sudden acceleration or if it suffers from overall poor acceleration, perform the checks listed under "Poor Acceleration" in **Figure 60** or **Figure 61**. If the accelerator pump system is faulty, it will necessary to service the carburetor as described in Chapter Eight.

## ENGINE NOISES

Often the first evidence of an internal engine problem is a strange noise. That knocking, clicking or tapping sound which you never heard before may be warning you of impending trouble.

While engine noises can indicate problems, they are difficult to interpret correctly; inexperienced mechanics can be seriously misled by them.

Professional mechanics often use a special stethoscope (which looks like a doctor's stethoscope) for isolating engine noises. You can do nearly as well with a "sounding stick" which can be an ordinary piece of doweling, a length of broom handle or a section of small hose. By placing one end in contact with the area to which you want to listen and the other end near your ear, you can hear sounds emanating from that area. The first time you do this, you may be horrified at the strange sounds coming from even a normal engine. If you can, have an experienced friend or mechanic help you sort out the noises.

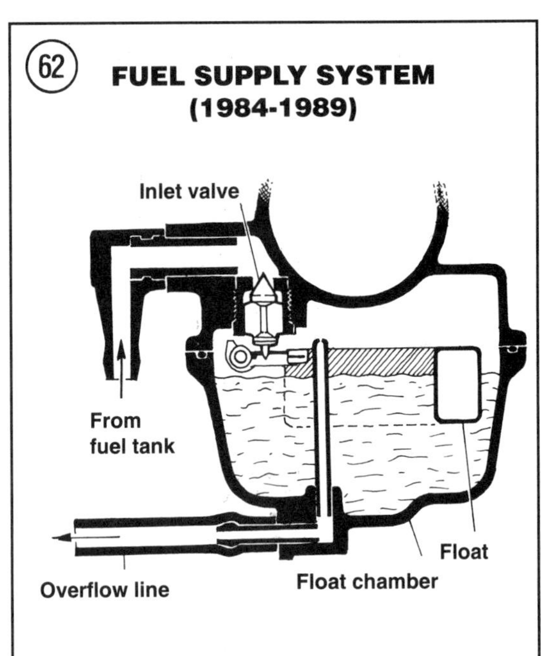


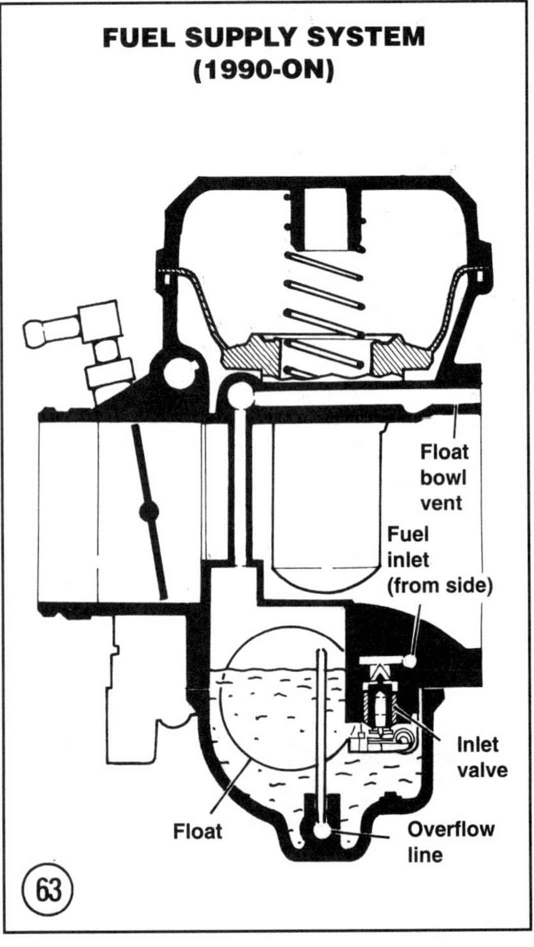

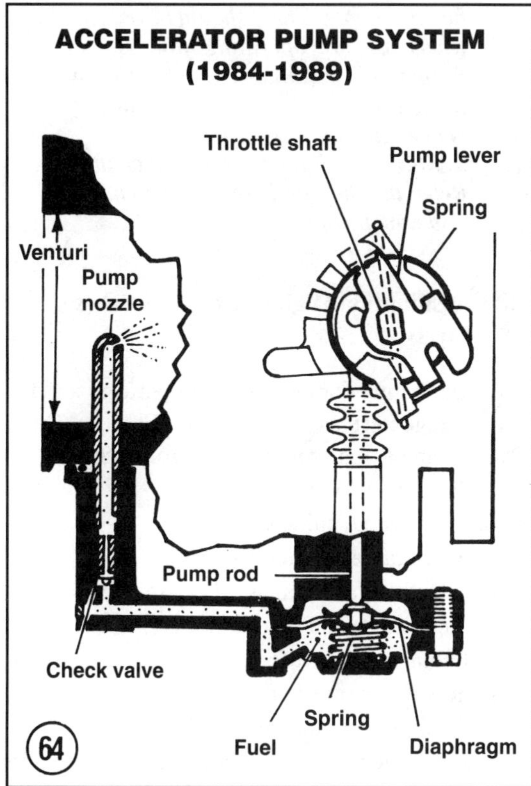


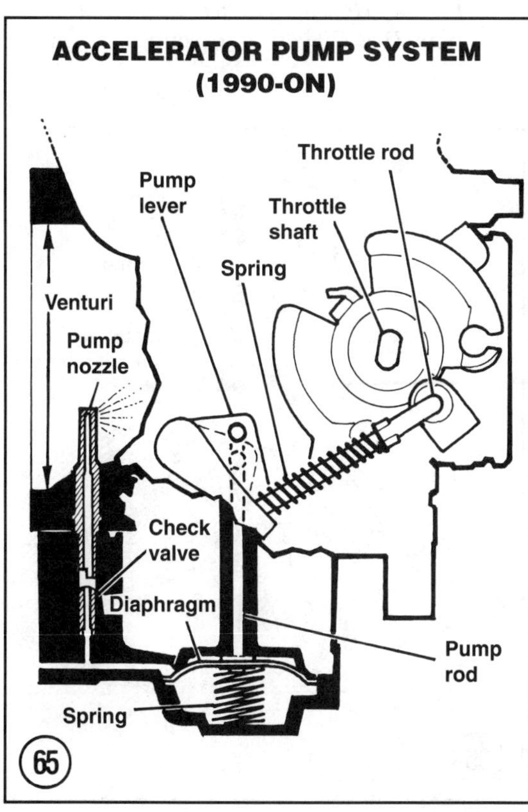


Consider the following when troubleshooting engine noises:

1. *Knocking or pinging during acceleration*—Caused by using a lower octane fuel than recommended. May also be caused by poor fuel. Pinging can also be caused by a spark plug of the wrong heat range. Refer to *Correct Spark Plug Heat Range* in Chapter Three.
2. *Slapping or rattling noises at low speed or during acceleration*—May be caused by piston slap, i.e., excessive piston-cylinder wall clearance.
3. *Knocking or rapping while decelerating*—Usually caused by excessive rod bearing clearance.
4. *Persistent knocking and vibration*—Usually caused by worn main bearing(s).
5. *Rapid on-off squeal*—Compression leak around cylinder head gasket(s) or spark plugs.
6. *Valve train noise*—Check for the following:
   a. Bent push rod(s).
   b. Defective tappets.
   c. Valve sticking in guide.
   d. Worn cam gears and/or cam.
   e. Low oil pressure—probably caused by obstructed oil screen. Also check oil feed pump operation.
   f. Damaged rocker arm or shaft. Rocker arm may be binding on shaft.

## ENGINE LUBRICATION

An improperly operating engine lubrication system will quickly lead to engine damage. The engine oil tank should be checked weekly and the tank refilled, as described in Chapter Three. Oil pump service is covered in Chapter Four.

### Oil Light

The oil light will come on when the ignition switch is turned to ON before starting the engine. After the engine is started, the oil light should go off when the engine speed is above idle.

If the oil light does not come on the when the ignition switch is turned to ON and the engine is not running, check for a burned out oil light bulb. If the bulb is okay, check the oil pressure switch as described in Chapter Nine.

If the oil light remains on when the engine speed is above idle, turn the engine off and check the oil level in the oil tank. If the oil level is satisfactory, check the following:

a. Check for a plugged tappet screen (**Figure 66**). Remove and service the screen as described in Chapter Three.
b. Oil may not be returning to the oil tank from the return line. Check for a clogged or damaged return line or a damaged oil pump. Refer to the oil routing diagram for your model as listed under *Oil Tank Inspection* in Chapter Three.
c. If you are operating your Harley in conditions where the ambient temperature is below freezing, ice and sludge may be blocking the oil feed pipe. This condition will prevent the oil from circulating properly.

*NOTE*
*Because water is formed during combustion, it can collect in the engine if the engine is run at moderate speeds for short periods of time, especially during winter months. If you ride your bike for short trips and then turn the engine off and allow it to cool before it has reached maximum operating temperature, water that is formed each time the engine is started will accumulate in the engine's lubrication system. This buildup of water, as it mixes with the oil, will form sludge deposits. Sludge is a thick, creamy substance that will clog oil feed and return systems (oil filter, tappet screen, lines, etc.). Sludge will accelerate engine wear and result in engine failure. In addition, when the ambient temperature falls below freezing, water in the tank and oil lines will freeze, thus preventing proper oil circulation and lubrication. To prevent sludge buildup in your engine, note the following:*
*1. When operating your Harley in cold/freezing weather, note how long you actually run the engine—the engine is colder in winter months and will take longer to warm up. Run the engine for longer periods so that it can reach maximum operating temperature. This will allow water that has formed in the engine to vaporize and to be blown out through the engine breather.*
*2. Change the engine oil more frequently. The oil change intervals specified in Chapter Three should be reduced when you are operating your Harley during cold weather. This step can interrupt sludge accumulation and prevent engine damage.*
*3. Flush the oil tank at each oil change. Refer to Chapter Three for oil change and tank flush procedures.*

### Oil Consumption High or Engine Smokes Excessively

Check engine compression and perform a cylinder leakage test as described in Chapter Three. Causes can be one or more of the following:

a. Worn valve guides.
b. Worn valve guide seals.
c. Worn or damaged piston rings.
d. Breather valve damaged or timed incorrectly.
e. Restricted oil tank return line.
f. Oil tank overfilled.
g. Restricted oil filter.
h. Leaking cylinder head surfaces.
i. Insufficient primary chain case vacuum on dry clutch models only (early 1984). Perform the *Primary Housing Vacuum Check (Early 1984 With Dry Clutch)* as described in Chapter Five.

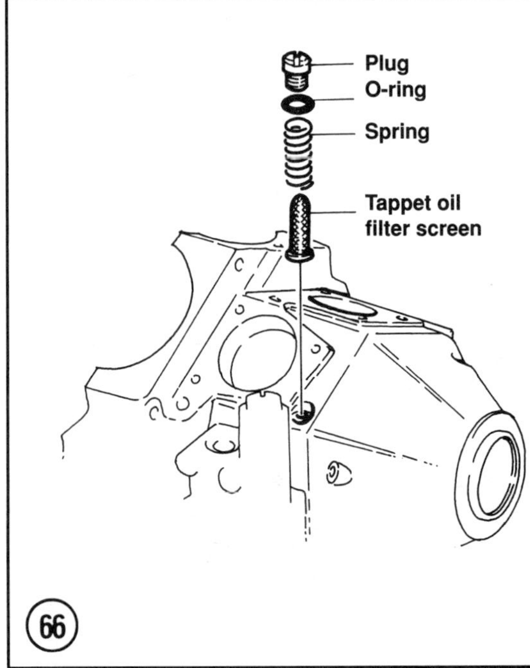

### Oil Fails to Return to Oil Tank

a. Oil lines or fittings restricted or damaged.
b. Oil pump damaged or operating incorrectly.
c. Empty oil tank.
d. Restricted oil filter.

### Excessive Engine Oil Leaks

a. Clogged air cleaner breather hose.
b. Restricted or damaged oil return line to oil tank.
c. Loose engine parts.
d. Damaged gasket sealing surfaces.
e. Restricted air cleaner breather hose.
f. Oil tank overfilled.

## CLUTCH

The three basic clutch troubles are:
a. Clutch noise.
b. Clutch slipping.
c. Improper clutch disengagement or dragging.

All clutch troubles, except adjustments, require partial clutch disassembly to identify and cure the problem. The troubleshooting chart in **Figure 67** lists clutch troubles and checks to make. Refer to Chapter Five for clutch service procedures.

## TRANSMISSION

The basic transmission troubles are:
a. Excessive gear noise.
b. Difficult shifting.
c. Gears pop out of mesh.
d. Incorrect shift lever operation.

Transmission symptoms are sometimes hard to distinguish from clutch symptoms. The troubleshooting chart in **Figure 68** lists transmission troubles and checks to make. Refer to Chapter Six or Chapter Seven for transmission service procedures. Be sure that the clutch is not causing the trouble before working on the transmission.

## ELECTRICAL PROBLEMS

If bulbs burn out frequently, the cause may be excessive vibration, loose connections that permit sudden current surges, or the installation of the wrong type of bulb.

Most light and ignition problems are caused by loose or corroded ground connections. Check these prior to replacing a bulb or electrical component.

2

## EXCESSIVE VIBRATION

This can be difficult to find without disassembling the engine. Usually this is caused by loose engine mounting hardware. High speed vibration may be due to a bent axle shaft or loose or faulty suspension components. Vibration can also be caused by the following conditions:
a. Broken frame.
b. Severely worn primary chain.
c. Tight primary chain links.
d. Loose transmission mounting bolts.
e. Loose transmission sub-mounting plate bolts.
f. Improperly balanced wheel(s).
g. Defective or damaged wheel(s).
h. Defective or damaged tire(s).
i. Internal engine wear or damage.

## FRONT SUSPENSION AND STEERING

Poor handling may be caused by improper tire pressure, a damaged or bent frame or front steering components, worn wheel bearings or dragging brakes. Possible causes for suspension and steering malfunctions are listed below.

### Irregular or Wobbly Steering

a. Loose wheel axle nut(s).
b. Loose or worn steering head bearings.
c. Excessive wheel hub bearing play.
d. Damaged cast wheel.
e. Spoke wheel out of alignment.
f. Unbalanced wheel assembly.
g. Worn hub bearings.
h. Incorrect wheel alignment.
i. Bent or damaged steering stem or frame (at steering neck).
j. Tire incorrectly seated on rim.
k. Excessive front end loading from non-standard equipment.

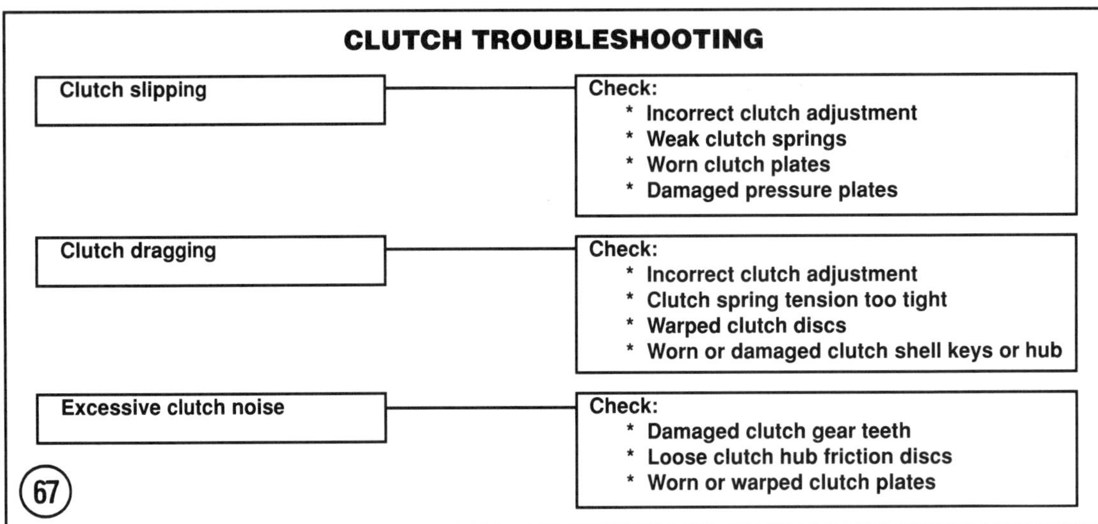


## TRANSMISSION TROUBLESHOOTING

|  |  |
|---|---|
| Excessive gear noise | Check:<br>* Worn bearings<br>* Worn or damaged gears<br>* Excessive gear backlash |
| Difficult shifting | Check:<br>* Damaged gears<br>* Damaged shift forks<br>* Damaged shift drum<br>* Damaged shift lever assembly<br>* Incorrect mainshaft and countershaft engagement<br>* Incorrect clutch disengagement |
| Gears pop out of mesh | Check:<br>* Worn gear or transmission shaft splines<br>* Shift forks worn or bent<br>* Worn dog holes in gears<br>* Insufficient shift lever spring tension<br>* Damaged shift lever linkage |
| Incorrect shift lever operation | Check:<br>* Bent shift lever<br>* Bent or damaged shift lever shaft<br>* Damaged shift lever linkage or gears |
| Incorrect shifting after engine reassembly | Check:<br>* Missing transmission shaft shims<br>* Incorrectly installed parts<br>* Shift forks bent during reassembly<br>* Incorrectly assembled transmission<br>* Incorrect clutch adjustment<br>* Incorrectly assembled shift linkage assembly |

68

### Stiff Steering

a. Low front tire air pressure.
b. Bent or damaged steering stem or frame (at steering neck).
c. Loose or worn steering head bearings.

### Stiff or Heavy Fork Operation

a. Incorrect fork springs.
b. Incorrect fork oil viscosity.
c. Excessive fork oil capacity.
d. Bent fork tubes.

### Poor Fork Operation

a. Worn or damaged fork tubes.
b. Fork oil capacity low.
c. Bent or damaged fork tubes.
d. Contaminated fork oil.
e. Incorrect fork springs.
f. Heavy front end loading from non-standard equipment.

### Poor Rear Shock Absorber Operation

a. Weak or worn springs.
b. Damper unit leaking.
c. Shock shaft worn or bent.
d. Incorrect rear shock springs.
e. Rear shocks adjusted incorrectly.
f. Heavy rear end loading from non-standard equipment.
g. Incorrect loading.

## BRAKE PROBLEMS

All models are equipped with front and rear disc brakes. Good brakes are vital to the safe operation of any vehicle. Perform the maintenance specified in Chapter Three to minimize brake system problems. Brake system service is covered in Chapter Thirteen. When refilling the front and rear master cylinders, use only DOT 5 brake fluid.

### Insufficient Braking Power

Worn brake pads or disc, air in the hydraulic system, glazed or contaminated pads, low brake fluid level or a leaking brake line or hose can cause this problem. Visually check for leaks. Check for worn brake pads. Check also for a leaking or damaged primary cup seal in the master cylinder. Bleed and adjust the brakes. Rebuild a leaking master cylinder or brake caliper. Brake drag will result in excessive heat and brake fade. See *Brake Drag* in this section.

### Spongy Brake Feel

This problem is generally caused by air in the hydraulic system. Bleed and adjust the brakes.

### Brake Drag

Check brake adjustment, looking for insufficient brake pedal and/or hand lever free play. Also check for worn, loose or missing parts in the brake calipers. Check the brake disc for excessive runout.

### Brakes Squeal or Chatter

Check brake pad thickness and disc condition. Make sure that the pads are not loose; check that the anti-rattle springs are properly installed and in good condition. Clean off any dirt on the pads. Loose components can also cause this. Check for:

a. Warped brake disc.
b. Loose brake disc.
c. Loose caliper mounting bolts.
d. Loose front axle nut.
e. Worn wheel bearings.
f. Damaged hub.

**Tables 1 and 2 are on the following page.**

**Table 1 ELECTRICAL SPECIFICATIONS**

| | |
|---|---|
| Battery capacity | |
| FLT | 20 AH @ 10 hour rate |
| | 22 AH @ 20 hour rate |
| FXR | 19 AH @ 10 hour rate |
| | 21 AH @ 20 hour rate |
| FXWG, FXEF and FXSB | 19 AH |
| Ignition coil | |
| Primary resistance | 2.5-3.1 ohms |
| Secondary resistance | |
| 1986-1992 | 11,250-13,750 ohms |
| 1993-on | 10,000-12,500 ohms |
| Alternator | |
| Stator coil resistance | |
| 1984-1988 | 0.2-0.4 ohms |
| 1989-on | 0.1-0.2 ohms |
| AC output | |
| FLT and FXR | |
| 1984-1988 | 19-23 amps @ 2,000 rpm |
| 1989-1990 | 29-32 amps @ 2,000 rpm |
| 1991-on | 26-32 amps @ 3,000 rpm |
| FXWG, FXEF and FXSB | 19-26 amps @ 2,000 rpm |
| Starter current draw | |
| 1984-1988 | 45 amps max. @ 10.0 volts |
| 1990-on | 90 amps max. @ 11.5 volts |
| Starter current draw test (test) | |
| 1984-1988 | 40-50 amps max. |
| 1989-1992 | 150 amps max. |
| 1993-on | |
| Range | 160-180 |
| Maximum | 200 |

**Table 2 CURRENT DRAW (FLT AND FXR)**

| Model | Meter reading (milliamperes) |
|---|---|
| 1986-1987 | |
| FLT/C and FLHT/C | Less than 40 |
| FXRT | Less than 40 |
| 1988-on | |
| FLTC and FLHTC[1] | Less than 10 |
| 1989-on | |
| FLTC Ultra and FLHTC Ultra[2] | Less than 15 |
| 1984-on (without clock and radio) | Less than 3 |

[1] Radio memory only.
[2] Radio and CB memory.

# CHAPTER THREE

# PERIODIC LUBRICATION, MAINTENANCE AND TUNE-UP

The service life and operation of your Harley-Davidson will depend on the maintenance it receives. This is easy to understand, once you realize that a motorcycle, even in normal use, is subjected to tremendous heat, stress and vibration. When neglected, any bike becomes unreliable and actually dangerous to ride.

All motorcycles require attention before and after riding them. The time spent on basic maintenance and lubrication will provide you with the utmost in safety and performance as well as maintaining and actually increasing your Harley's monetary value. Minor problems found during these inspections are simple and inexpensive to correct. If they are not found and corrected at this time they could lead to major and more expensive problems later on. Letting things go is a bad and costly habit to get into. Harley-Davidson motorcycles are some of the most well designed and manufactured motorcycles sold today. Maintain the image by maintaining your bike.

Regular cleaning of the bike is also very important. It makes routine maintenance a lot easier by not having to work your way through a build-up of road dirt to get to a component for adjustment or replacement. Routine cleaning also allows you to find damaged components or leaks which can be repaired or replaced before they break or cause secondary damage.

If this is your first bike, start out by doing simple tune-up, lubrication and maintenance. Tackle more involved jobs as you become more acquainted with the bike.

Certain maintenance tasks and checks should be performed weekly. Others should be performed at certain time or mileage intervals. Still others should be done whenever certain symptoms appear. Some maintenance procedures are included under *Tune-up* at the end of this chapter. Detailed instructions will be found there. Other steps are described in the following chapters. Chapter references are included with these steps.

The service procedures and intervals shown in **Table 1** are recommended by Harley-Davidson. **Tables 1-9** are located at the end of the chapter.

## ROUTINE SAFETY CHECKS

The following safety checks should be performed prior to the first ride of the day.

### General Inspection

1. Inspect the engine for signs of oil or fuel leakage.
2. Check the tires for embedded stones. Pry them out with a suitable tool.
3. Make sure all lights work.

*NOTE*

*At least check the brake light. It can burn out anytime. Motorists can't stop as quickly as you and need all the warning you can give.*

4. Inspect the fuel lines and fittings for wetness.

5. Check the fuel level in the fuel tank and top off, if required.
6. Check the operation of the front and rear brakes. Add DOT 5 brake fluid to the front and rear master cylinders as required.
7. Check the operation of the clutch. If necessary, adjust the clutch free-play as described in this chapter.
8. Check the throttle operation. The hand throttle should move smoothly with no sign of roughness, sticking or tightness. The throttle should snap back when released. Adjust throttle free play, if necessary, as described in this chapter.
9. Check the rear brake pedal. It should move smoothly. If necessary, adjust free play as described in this chapter.
10. Inspect the front and rear suspension. Make sure they have a good solid feel with no looseness.
11. Check the exhaust system for damage.

*CAUTION*
*When checking the tightness of the exposed fasteners on your Harley, do* ***not*** *include the cylinder head bolts in this process. Harley-Davidson lists a specific bolt tightening sequence to prevent cylinder head and cylinder distortion, head leakage and stud failure. When tightening the cylinder head bolts, follow the procedure described in Chapter Four.*

### Engine Oil Tank Level

Refer to *Periodic Lubrication* in this chapter.

### Tire Pressure

Tire pressure must be checked with the tires cold. Correct tire pressure, listed in **Table 2** and **Table 3**, varies with the load you are carrying. Refer to *Tire Pressure* in this chapter.

### Battery

Remove the battery and check the battery electrolyte level. The level must be maintained within the MIN and MAX battery markings (**Figure 1**).

For complete details, see *Battery* in Chapter Nine.

### Lights and Horn

With the engine running, check the following.
1. Pull the front brake lever and check that the brake light comes on.
2. Push the rear brake pedal down and check that the brake light comes on soon after you have begun depressing the pedal.
3. Check to see that the headlight and taillight are on.
4. Move the dimmer switch up and down between the high and low positions, and check to see that both headlight elements are working.
5. Push the turn signal switch to the left position and right position and check that all 4 turn signal lights are working.
6. Check that all fender, saddlebags and Tour-pak lights work properly, if so equipped.
7. Push the horn button and make sure that the horn blows loudly.
8. If the horn or any light failed to work properly, refer to Chapter Nine.

## MAINTENANCE INTERVALS

The services and intervals shown in **Table 1** are recommended by the factory. Strict adherence to these recommendations will go a long way toward insuring long service from your Harley. If the bike

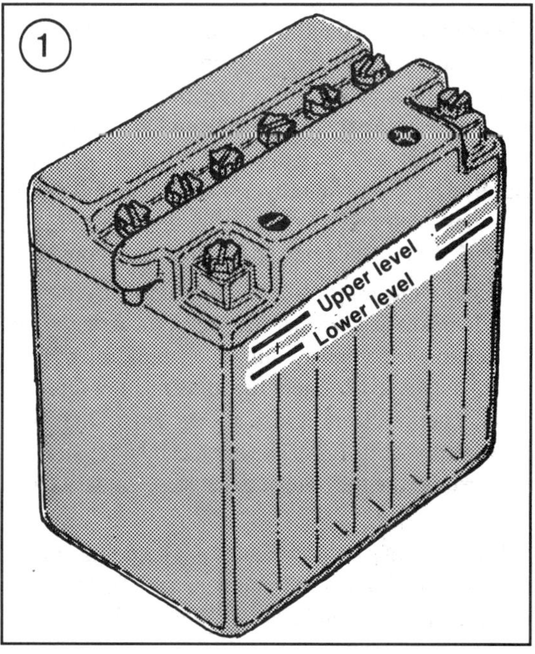

is run in an area of high humidity, the lubrication service must be done more frequently to prevent possible rust damage.

For convenient maintenance of your motorcycle, most of the services shown in **Table 1** are described in this chapter. Those procedures which require more than minor disassembly or adjustment are covered elsewhere in the appropriate chapter. The *Table of Contents* and *Index* can help you to locate a particular service procedure.

## CLEANING YOUR HARLEY

Regular cleaning of your Harley is important. It makes routine maintenance a lot easier by not having to work your way through built-up dirt to get to a component for adjustment or replacement. It also makes the bike look like new even though it may have many thousands of miles on it.

If you ride in rural areas or where there is a lot of rain or road salt residue in the winter, clean the bike more often in order to maintain the painted, plated and polished surfaces in good condition. Keep a good coat of wax on the bike during the winter to prevent premature weathering of all finishes.

Washing the bike should be done in a gentle way to avoid damage to the painted and plated finishes and to components that are not designed to withstand high-pressure water. Try to avoid using the coin-operated car wash systems as the cleaning agents may be harmful to the plastic parts on the bike. Also the rinse cycle is usually fairly high pressure and will force water into areas that should be kept dry.

Use a mild detergent (mild liquid dish washing detergent) or a commercial car washing detergent available at most auto parts outlets. Be warned, these detergents will remove some of the wax that you have applied to the finish. Follow the manufacturer's instructions for the correct detergent-to-water mixture.

If the lower end of the engine and frame are covered with oil, grease or road dirt, spray this dirt with a commercial cleaner like Gunk Cycle Cleaner, or equivalent. Keep this cleaner off of the plastic components as it may damage the finish. Follow the manufacturer's instructions and rinse with *plenty of cold water*. Do not allow any of this cleaner residue to settle in any pockets as it will stain or destroy the finish of most painted parts.

Use a commercial tar-stain remover to remove any severe road dirt and tar stains. Be sure to rinse all areas thoroughly with plenty of clean water to make sure all of the tar-stain remover is rinsed off of all surfaces.

Prior to washing the plastic and painted surfaces of the bike make sure the surfaces are cool. Do not wash a hot bike as you will probably end up with streaks since the soap suds will start to dry prior to being rinsed off.

*CAUTION*

*Do not allow water (especially under pressure) to enter the air intake, brake assemblies, electrical switches and connectors, instrument cluster, wheel bearing areas, swing arm bearings or any other moisture-sensitive areas of the bike.*

After all of the heavily soiled areas are cleaned off, use the previously described detergent, warm water and a soft natural sponge and carefully wash down the entire bike, including the wheels and tires. Always wet the bike down *before* washing with a detergent soaked sponge or rag. This will remove dirt from sensitive areas and prevent scratching. Don't use too much detergent as it will be difficult to rinse off all of the soap suds thoroughly. After all areas have been washed, rinse off the soap suds with *low-pressure cold water*. Make sure all of the detergent residue is thoroughly rinsed off.

*NOTE*

*Before washing the fuel tank, check for small pebbles, metal shavings or dirt stuck to or partially hidden in your sponge and rags. These objects may scratch and mar the tank's finish. As you wash your bike, rinse the sponge or rag frequently to remove accumulated dirt.*

If you have access to compressed air, *gently* blow excess water from areas where the water may have collected. Do not force the water into any of the sensitive areas mentioned in the previous *CAUTION*. Gently dry off the bike with a chamois, a clean soft Turkish towel or an old plain T-shirt (no transfers or hand-painted designs, these may scratch the tank).

If your Harley is equipped with a windshield, be careful when cleaning it; windshields can be easily

3

scratched or damaged. Do not use a cleaner with an abrasive or a combination cleaner and wax. Never use gasoline or cleaning solvent. These products will either scratch or totally destroy the surface finish of the windshield.

Clean the windshield with a soft cloth or natural sponge and plenty of water. Dry thoroughly with a soft cloth or chamois—do not press hard.

*WARNING*

*The brake components may have gotten wet. If they are damp or wet they will not be operating at their optimum effectiveness. Be prepared to take a longer distance to stop the bike right after washing the bike. Ride slowly and lightly apply the brakes to dry off the pads.*

Start the engine and let it reach normal operating temperature. Take the bike out for a *slow and careful* ride around to blow off any residual water. Bring the bike back to the wash area and dry off any residual water streaks from the painted and plated surfaces.

Once the bike is thoroughly dry, get out the polish, wax and Armour All and give the bike a good polish and wax job to protect the painted, plated and polished surfaces.

## TIRES AND WHEELS

### Tire Pressure

Tire pressure should be checked and adjusted to maintain the tire profile, good traction and handling and to get the maximum life out of the tire. A simple, accurate gauge (**Figure 2**) can be purchased for a few dollars and should be carried in your motorcycle tool kit. The appropriate tire pressures are shown in **Table 2** and **Table 3**.

*NOTE*

*After checking and adjusting the air pressure, make sure to reinstall the air valve cap (**Figure 3**). The cap prevents small pebbles and dirt from collecting in the valve stem; these could allow air leakage or result in incorrect tire pressure readings.*

### Tire Inspection

The tires take a lot of punishment so inspect them periodically for excessive wear, deep cuts, imbedded objects such as stones, nails, etc. If you find a nail or other object in a tire, mark its location with a light crayon prior to removing it. This will help to locate the hole for repair. Refer to Chapter Ten for tire changing and repair information.

Check local traffic regulations concerning minimum tread depth. Measure with a tread depth gauge (**Figure 4**) or small ruler. As a guideline, replace tires when the tread depth is 5/16 in. (7.94 mm) or less.

### Wire Spoke Tension

On wire spoked wheels, the spokes should be checked frequently for loosening or breakage. Loose spokes can cause spoke, rim and hub breakage. Spokes can be checked by one of the two following methods:

a. Tone: Tap each spoke with a screwdriver or spoke wrench (**Figure 5**) and listen for a variation in tone between the different spokes. The higher pitch of sound it makes, the tighter the spoke. The lower the sound frequency, the looser the spoke. A "ping" is good; a "clunk" says the spoke is loose.

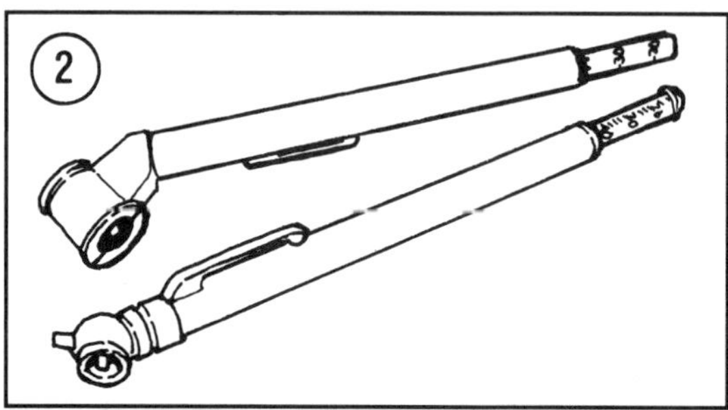

2

3

b. Feel: Grab two spokes near their cross point, then squeeze and check tension. Tight spokes will not give or flex as much as loose spokes.
c. If one or more spokes are loose, tighten them as described in Chapter Ten.

### Rim Inspection

Frequently inspect the wheel rims. If a rim has been damaged, it might have been knocked out of alignment. Improper wheel alignment can cause severe vibration and result in an unsafe riding condition. If the rim portion of an alloy wheel is damaged, the wheel must be replaced as it cannot be repaired. Refer to Chapter Ten for rim service.

## PERIODIC LUBRICATION

### Oil

Oil is graded according to its viscosity, which is an indication of how thick it is. The Society of Automotive Engineers (SAE) system distinguishes oil viscosity by numbers. Thick oils have higher viscosity numbers than thin oils. For example, an SAE 5 oil is a thin oil while an SAE 90 oil is relatively thick.

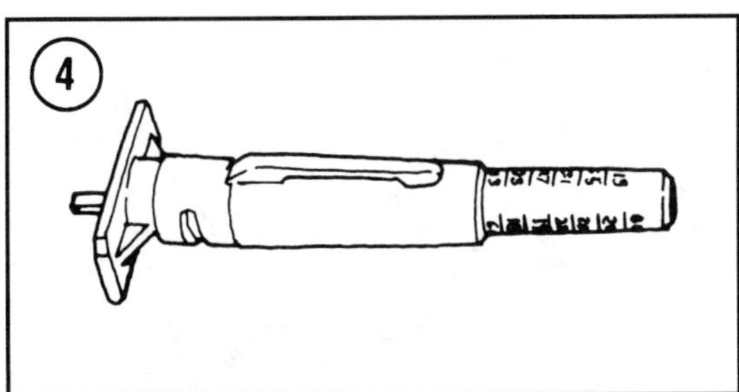

4

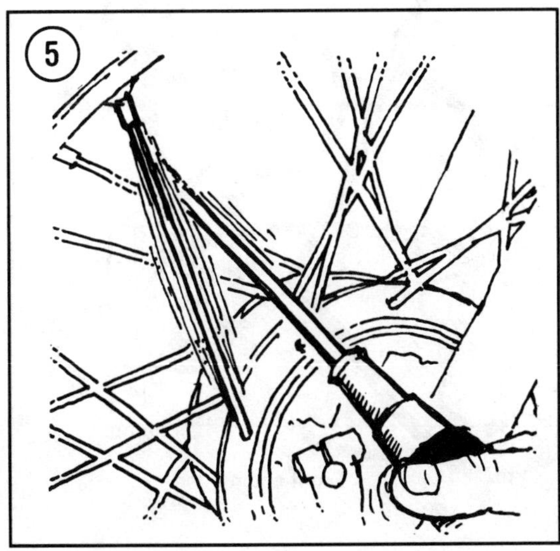

5

### Grease

A good quality grease (preferably waterproof) should be used (**Figure 6**). Water does not wash grease off parts as easily as it washes oil off. In addition, grease maintains its lubricating qualities better than oil on long and strenuous rides.

### Oil Tank Inspection

Before checking the oil level, inspect the oil tank for cracks or other damage. If oil seepage is noted on or near the tank, find and repair the problem. Check all of the oil tank mounting bolts for loose or missing fasteners; replace or tighten fasteners as required. Check the hose connections on the tank. Each hose should be secured with a hose clamp. Check each hose for swelling, cracks or damage and replace immediately; otherwise, oil leakage may occur and cause engine damage. Refer to the following diagram for your model:

a. **Figure 7**: Early 1984 FLT and FXR.
b. **Figure 8**: Late 1984-1990 FLT and FXR.
c. **Figure 9**: 1985-1986 FXWG, FXEF and FXSB.
d. **Figure 10**: 1991 FLT and FXR.
e. **Figure 11**: 1992-on FXR.
f. **Figure 12**: 1992 FLT.
g. **Figure 13**: 1993-on FLT.

6

## Oil Tank Level Check (All Models Except 1993-on FLT)

A remote oil tank is mounted on the right-hand side of the bike. The oil level in the tank should be checked prior to each ride as oil consumption is relative to engine speed and engine tune. In addition, the engine will consume less oil and run cooler when the oil level in the tank is kept relatively high.

Engine oil level is checked with the dipstick mounted in the tank filler cap.

1. Start and run the engine for approximately 10 minutes or until the engine has reached normal operating temperature. Then turn the engine off and allow the oil to settle in the tank.

2A. On FXR models, park the bike on its jiffy stand. If the bike is held straight up when checking the oil level, an incorrect reading will be obtained.

2B. On FLT, FXWG, FXES and FXEF models, have an assistant support the bike so that it stands straight up. If the bike is supported on its jiffy stand when checking the oil level, an incorrect reading will be obtained.

3A. On FXR models, the oil level can be checked by observing the oil tank sight gauge. The oil level is correct when it is above the top of the sight gauge. If you can see the oil level in the sight gauge, the oil level in the tank is low.

*NOTE*
*On FXR models, it will be necessary to raise or remove the seat to access the dipstick in the top of the oil tank.*

3B. On all models, wipe off the oil tank filler cap and the area around the cap with a clean rag, then remove the filler cap and dipstick. Wipe the dipstick off with a clean rag and reinsert the filler cap all the way into the oil tank. Withdraw the filler cap once again and check oil level on dipstick. Oil level

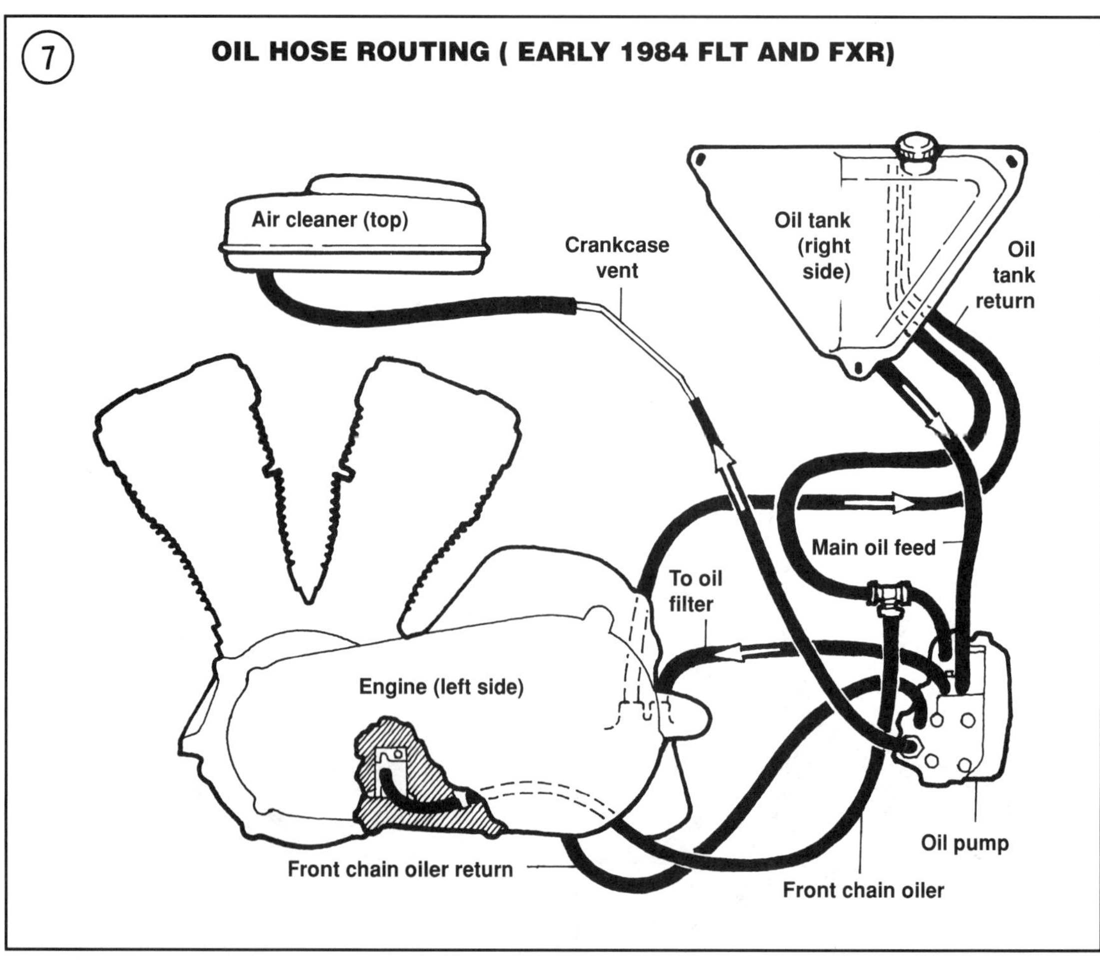

8

**OIL HOSE ROUTING (LATE 1984-1990 FLT AND FXR)**

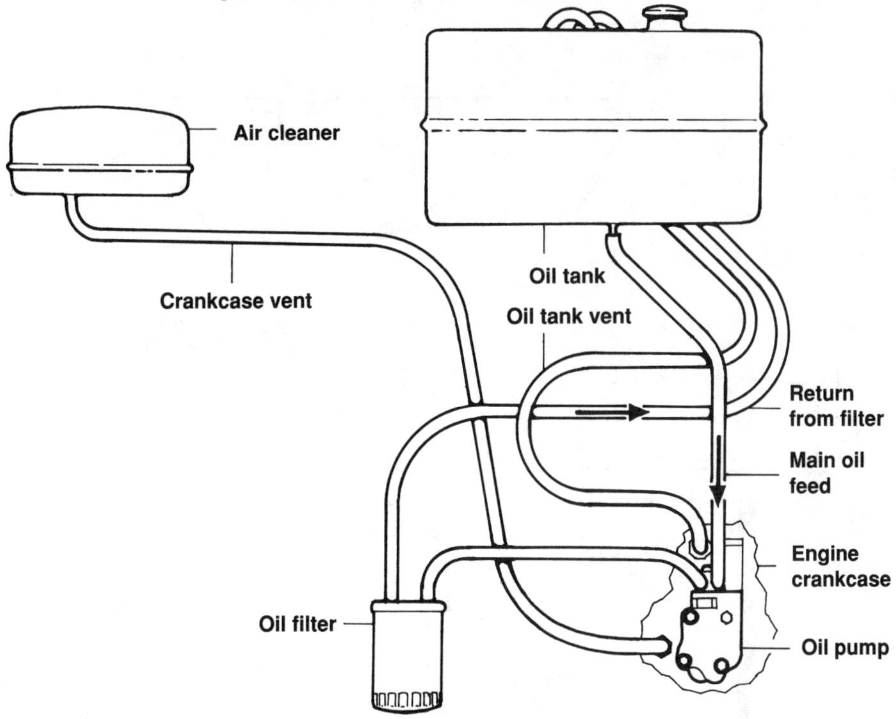

9

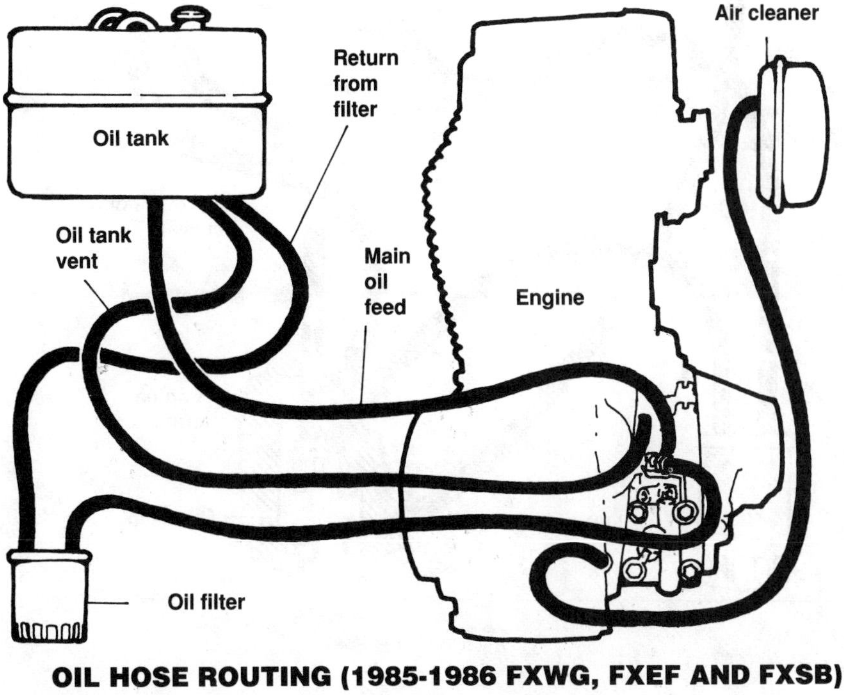

**OIL HOSE ROUTING (1985-1986 FXWG, FXEF AND FXSB)**

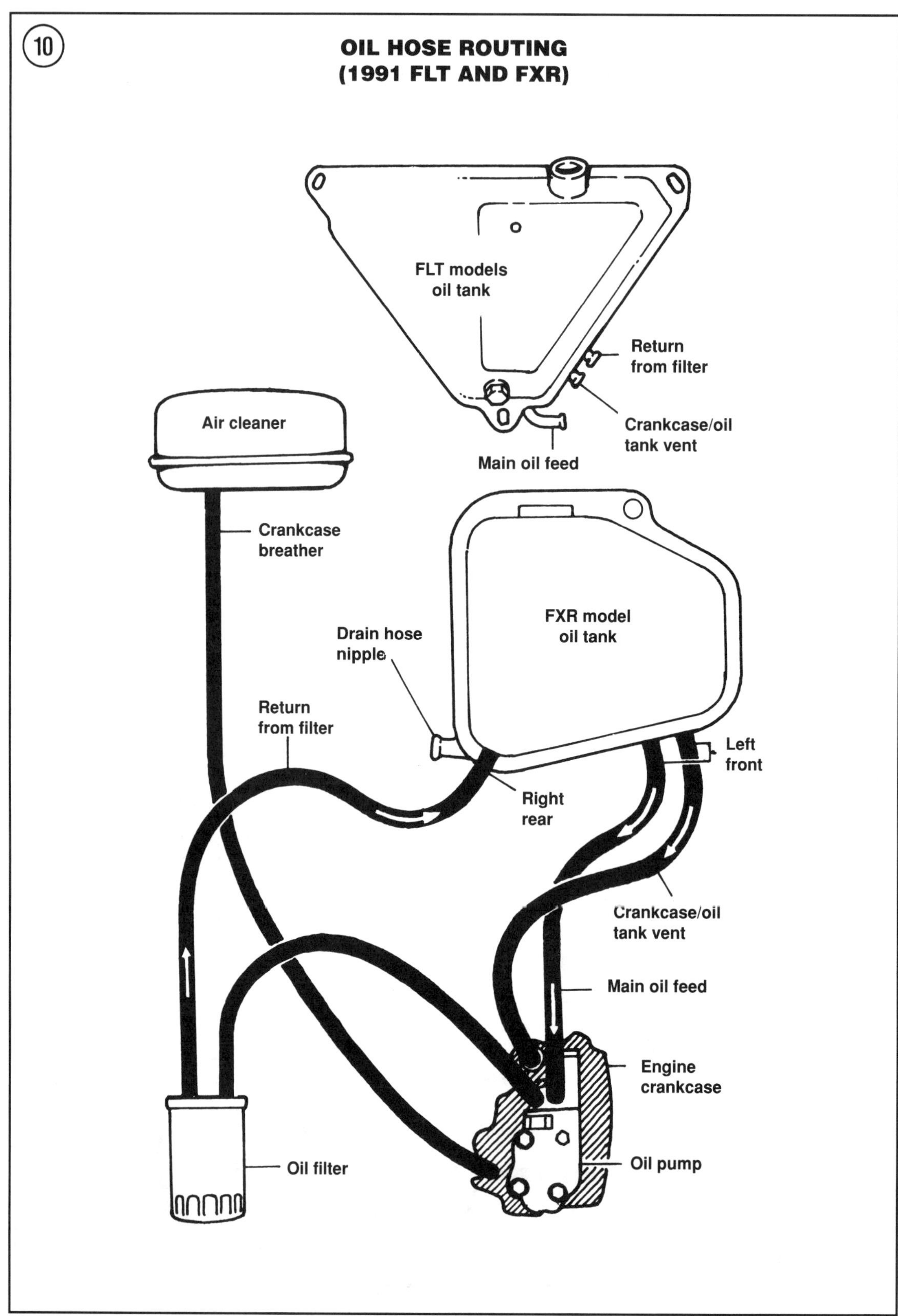
10
OIL HOSE ROUTING
(1991 FLT AND FXR)
FLT models
oil tank
Return
from filter
Crankcase/oil
tank vent
Main oil feed
Air cleaner
Crankcase
breather
FXR model
oil tank
Drain hose
nipple
Return
from filter
Left
front
Right
rear
Crankcase/oil
tank vent
Main oil feed
Engine
crankcase
Oil pump
Oil filter

(11)

**OIL HOSE ROUTING (1992 FXR-ON)**

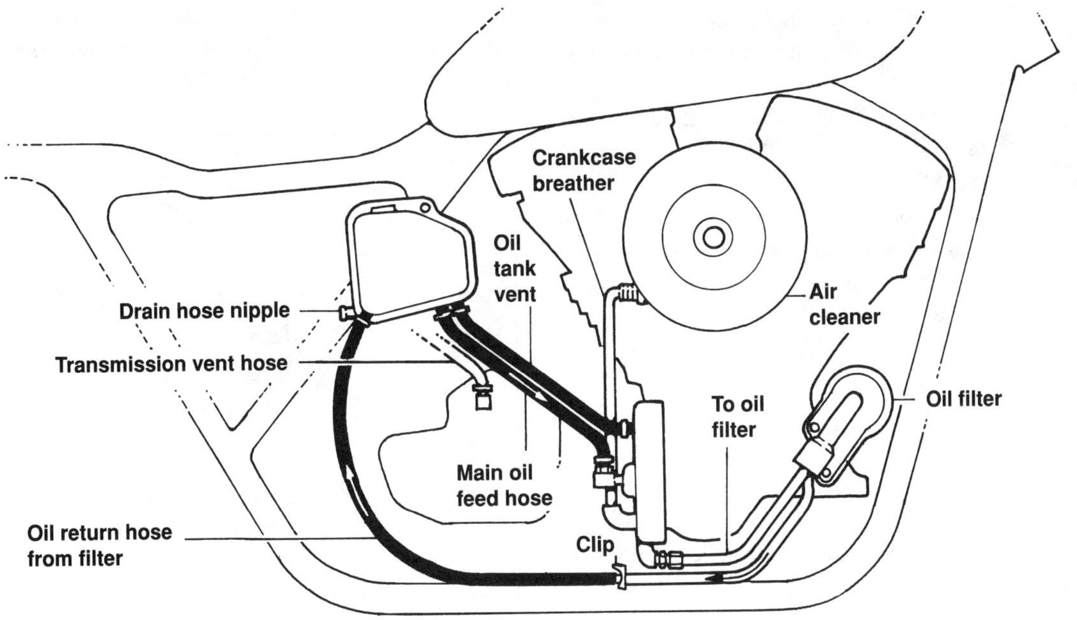

Crankcase breather
Oil tank vent
Air cleaner
Drain hose nipple
Transmission vent hose
To oil filter
Oil filter
Main oil feed hose
Oil return hose from filter
Clip

(12)

**OIL HOSE ROUTING (1992 FLT)**

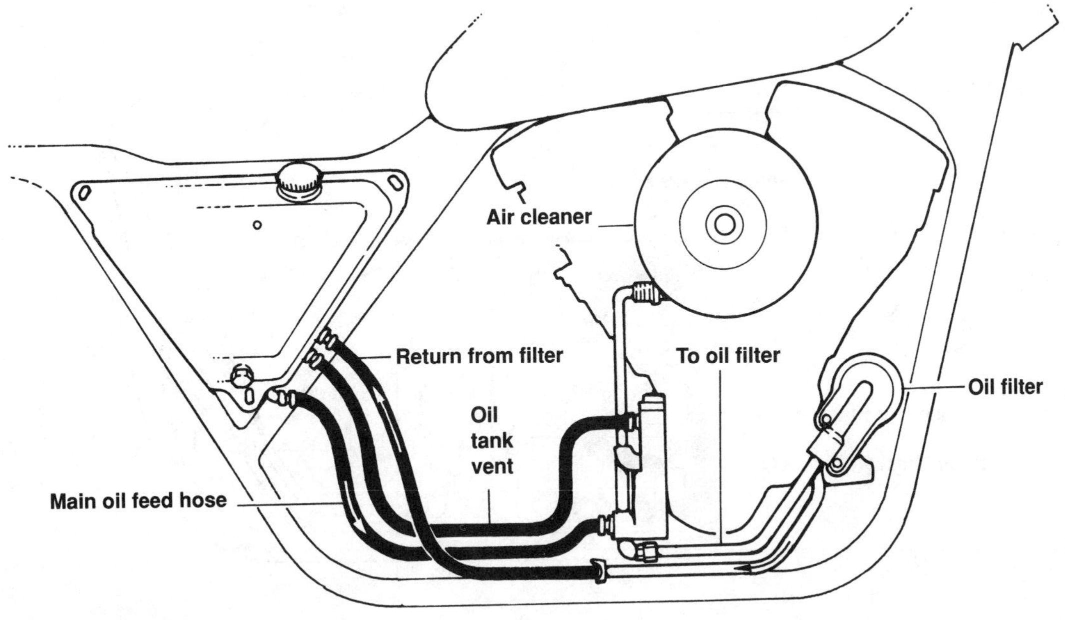

Air cleaner
Return from filter
To oil filter
Oil filter
Oil tank vent
Main oil feed hose

should be above "REFILL" dipstick mark. See **Figure 14**.

4. If the oil level in the tank is low, perform the following:
   a. The oil tank is full when the hot oil level in the tank is level with the upper mark on the dipstick (**Figure 14**).
   b. Do not overfill beyond the specified point as the oil will overflow and an air space is required in the tank.
   c. Add the recommended weight engine oil indicated in **Table 4** to correct the oil level.
   d. Reinstall the filler cap.
   e. Close the seat on FXR models.

5. As a safety precaution, check the oil tank drain plug or hose for tightness.

## Engine Oil Level Check (1993-on FLT)

The engine oil level should be checked prior to each ride.

Engine oil level is checked with the dipstick mounted in the transmission (**Figure 15**).

1. Start and run the engine for approximately 10 minutes or until the engine has reached normal operating temperature. Then turn the engine off and allow the oil to settle in the oil pan.

14

Upper mark (full)
Lower mark (add oil)

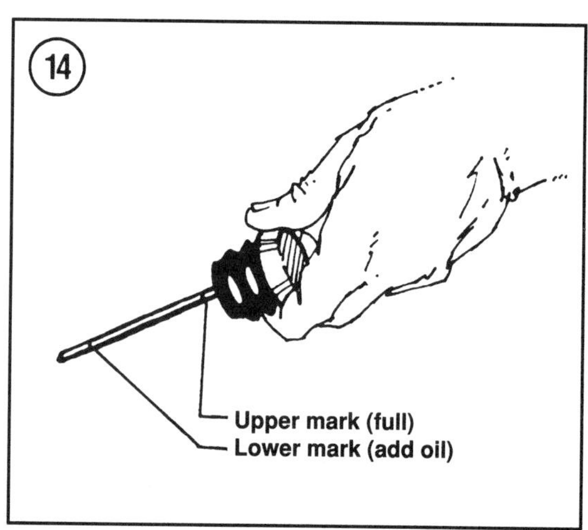

13

**OIL HOSE ROUTING (1993-ON FLT)**

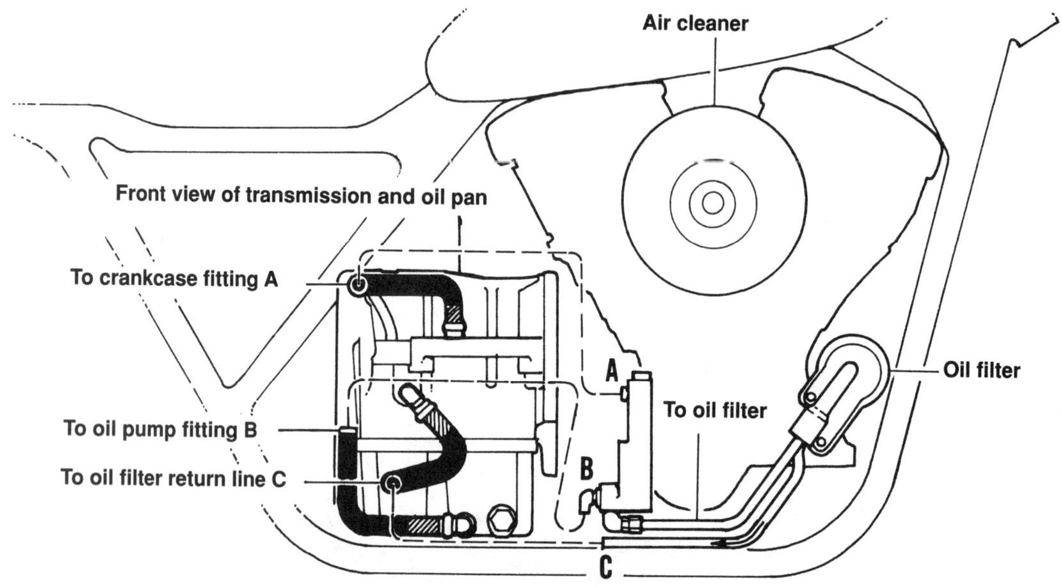

Air cleaner
Front view of transmission and oil pan
To crankcase fitting A
To oil pump fitting B
To oil filter return line C
A
B
C
To oil filter
Oil filter

2. Park the bike on its jiffy stand. If the bike is held straight up when checking the oil level, an incorrect reading will be obtained.
3. Wipe off the filler cap and the area around the cap with a clean rag, then remove the filler cap and dipstick. Wipe off the dipstick with a clean rag and reinsert the filler cap all the way into the fill spout. Withdraw the filler cap once again and check the oil level on dipstick. Oil level should be above "ADD QUART" dipstick mark. See **Figure 15**. Reinstall the filler cap.
4. If the oil level is low, perform the following:
   a. Add the recommended weight engine oil indicated in **Table 4** to correct the oil level.
   b. Reinstall the filler cap.
   c. Do not overfill beyond the specified point as an air space is required in the oil pan.

### Engine Oil and Filter Change

The factory-recommended oil and filter change interval is specified in **Table 1**. This assumes that the motorcycle is operated in moderate climates. In extreme climates, oil should be changed more often. The time interval is more important than the mileage interval because combustion acids, formed by gasoline and water vapor, will contaminate the oil even if the motorcycle is not run for several months. If a motorcycle is operated under dusty conditions, the oil will get dirty more quickly and should be changed more frequently than recommended.

Oil for motorcycle and automotive engines is graded by the American Petroleum Institute (API) and the Society of Automotive Engineers (SAE) in several categories. Oil containers display these ratings on the top of the oil can or on the bottle label (**Figure 16**).

Use only a detergent oil with an API rating of SE or SF. Try to use the same brand of oil at each change. Refer to **Table 4** for correct oil viscosity to use under anticipated ambient temperatures (not engine oil temperature).

To change the engine oil and filter you will need the following:

a. Drain pan.
b. Funnel.
c. Can opener or pour spout (can-type only).
d. Wrench (for drain plug models).
e. Correct quantity of oil (**Table 5**).
f. Oil filter element.

There are a number of ways to discard the used oil safely. The easiest way is to pour it from the drain

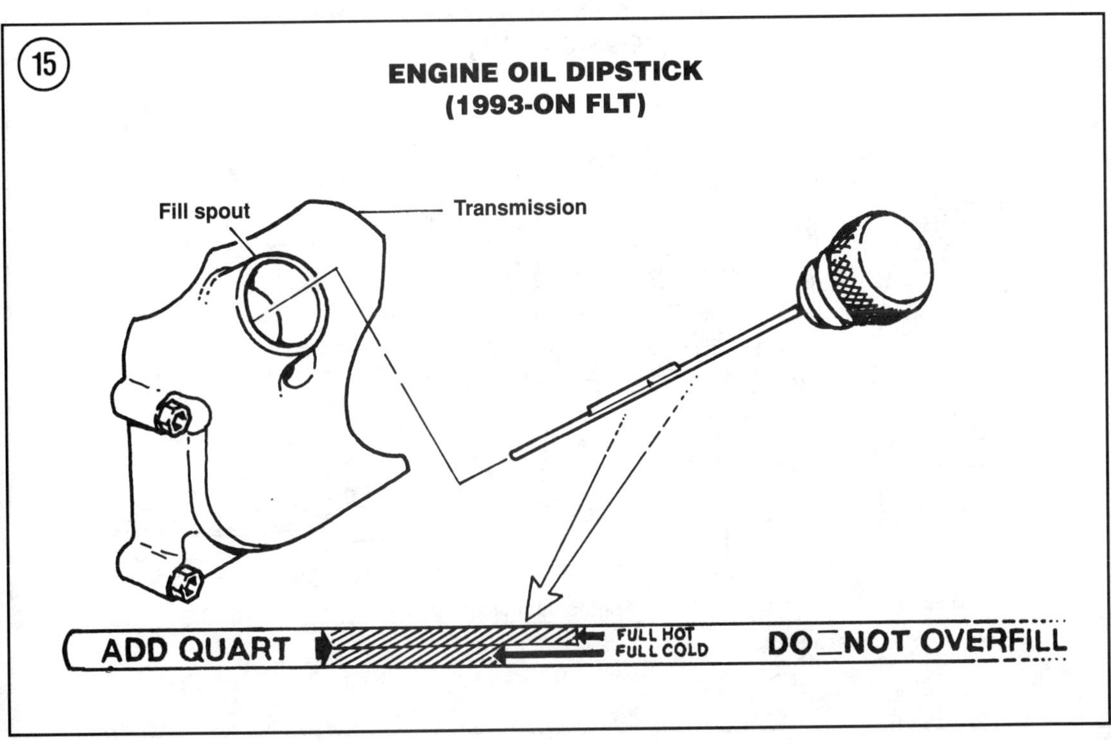

pan into a gallon plastic bleach, juice or milk container for disposal.

NOTE

*Never dispose of motor oil in the trash or pour it on the ground, or down a storm drain. Many service stations accept used motor oil. Many waste haulers provide curbside used motor oil collection. Do not combine other fluids with motor oil to be recycled. To find a recycling location contact the American Petroleum Institute (API) at* ***www.recycleoil.org****.*

1. Start and run the engine for approximately 10 minutes or until the engine has reached normal operating temperature. Then turn the engine off and allow the oil to settle in the tank. Support the bike so that the oil can drain completely.

NOTE

*There are 2 important reasons for draining the engine oil while it is hot. First, hot oil will drain more quickly. Second, contaminants in the oil will drain with it, instead of settling in the bottom of the oil tank, ready to mix with the new oil.*

NOTE

*Before removing the oil tank cap, thoroughly clean off all dirt and oil around it.*

2A. On 1993-on FLT models: Place a drain pan underneath the oil pan and remove the engine drain plug and gasket at the front of the oil pan (**Figure 17**). Allow the oil to drain completely.

2B. On all other models, place a drain pan beside the bike, then remove the oil tank drain plug and gasket (**Figure 18**) or remove the drain hose clamp at the drain hose connected to the bottom of the oil tank (**Figure 19**). Use a funnel and drain the oil into the pan.

3. *Models with dry clutch:* Remove the primary case drain plug located underneath the clutch cover and

17

**ENGINE AND TRANSMISSION DRAIN PLUGS (1993-ON FLT)**

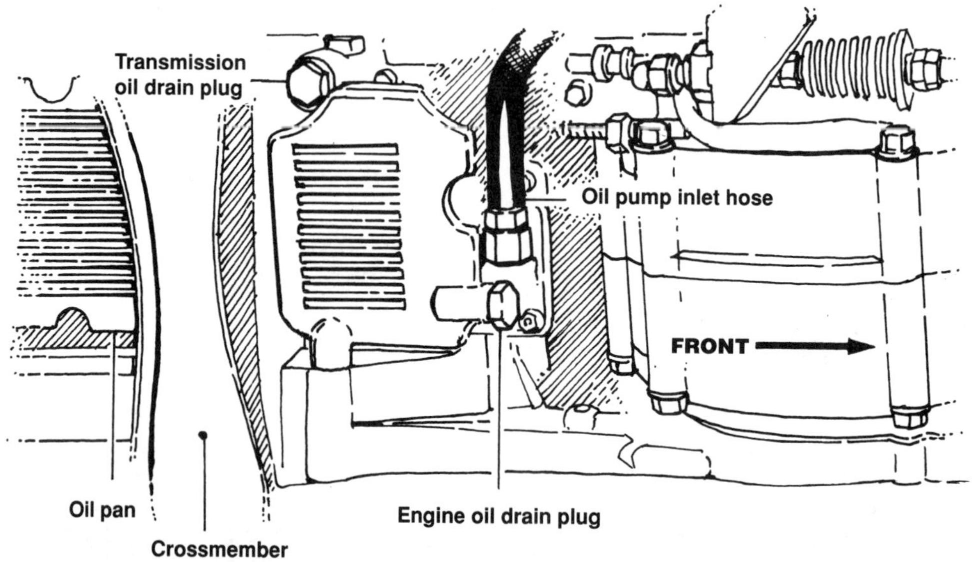

Transmission oil drain plug
Oil pump inlet hose
FRONT
Oil pan
Crossmember
Engine oil drain plug

drain the primary case. Reinstall the drain plug and washer.

4. Service the oil filter as follows:
   a. Remove the filter with a filter wrench.
   b. Pour any trapped oil out of the oil filter and discard it.
   c. Wipe the crankcase gasket surface with a clean, lint-free cloth.
   d. Coat the neoprene gasket on the new filter with clean oil (**Figure 20**).

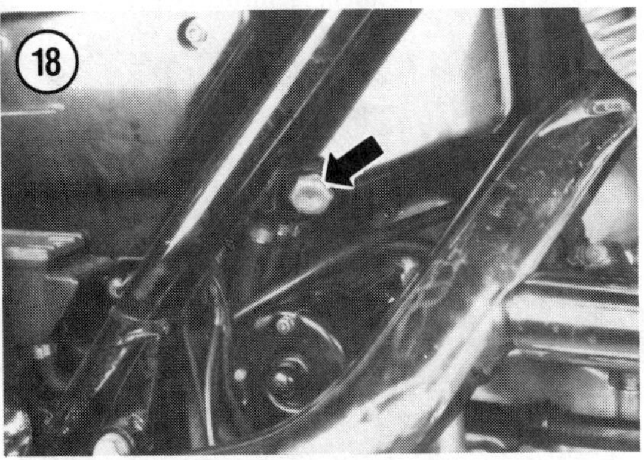


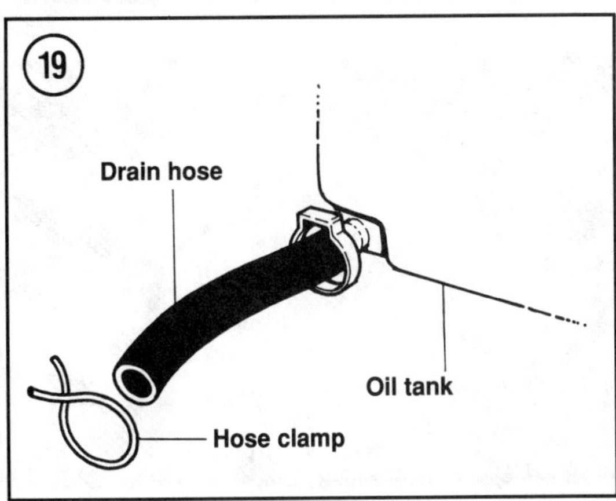


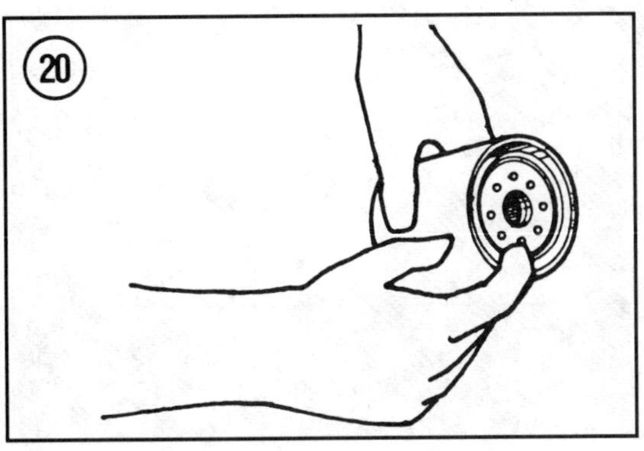


   e. Screw the filter onto the crankcase *by hand* until the filter gasket just touches the base, i.e., until you feel the slightest resistance when turning the filter. Then tighten the filter *by hand* 1/4-1/2 turn more.

*CAUTION*
*Do not overtighten and do not use a filter wrench or the filter may leak.*



5. On models with oil tank, flush the oil tank at the first 500 miles (new bike or after rebuilding engine) and at every second oil change thereafter.

6A. On 1993-on FLT models, reinstall the oil pan drain plug and gasket. Tighten securely.

6B. On all other models, reinstall the oil tank drain plug and gasket or reinstall the drain hose clamp onto the drain hose.

7. Fill the oil pan (1993-on FLT) or oil tank (all other models) with the correct viscosity (**Table 4**) and quantity (**Table 5**) of oil.

8. Insert the filler cap into the oil tank or oil pan.

9. Clean the tappet oil screen as described under *Tappet Oil Screen Cleaning* in this chapter.

10. Start the engine and check for oil leaks around the oil filter, drain plug or drain hose.

11. When engine is at normal operating temperature, turn it off and recheck the oil level as described in this chapter. Add oil, if required.

### Oil Tank Flushing (Except 1993-on FLT)

At the first 500 miles (new bike or after rebuilding the engine), and at every second oil change during warm riding weather, flush the oil tank before refilling it with new oil. During colder weather, the oil tank should be flushed at each oil change.

1. Drain the oil tank as previously described.

2. ID all oil hoses at the oil tank so you don't mix them up during reassembly. See **Figures 7-12**. Then remove the oil tank fasteners and remove the oil tank from the bike.

*CAUTION*
*Total flushing of the oil tank while it is mounted on the bike is difficult. Sludge broken loose from the tank and not removed during flushing will pass through the main oil feed line and into the oil pump; there it will clog oil passages and cause engine seizure.*

3. Reinstall the oil tank drain plug (if used) and plug all tank hose openings.
4. Fill the oil tank 3/4 full with kerosene.
5. Vigorously swish the tank from side to side to break loose sludge and sediment accumulation in the tank.
6. Remove the dipstick from the top of the tank and drain the tank. Using a small flashlight, check the tank for sludge and sediment deposits that did not drain out. Repeat this step until *all* of these deposits are removed. If necessary, break hard deposits loose with a wooden dowel or similar tool inserted into the tank.
7. When the tank is clean, pour some clean engine oil into the tank and shake the tank once again to cover the tank walls with the oil. Then drain and discard the oil.
8. Clean the filler cap/dipstick assembly before installing it back into the tank.
9. Remove the plugs from the oil tank hoses and reinstall the oil tank. Tighten all tank mounting bolts or nuts securely. Wipe the oil hoses off before reconnecting them onto the tank. Reconnect the oil hoses, following your ID marks and the hose routing diagrams in **Figures 7-12** for your model.

### Transmission Oil Check

Inspect the transmission oil level at the interval listed in **Table 1**. If the bike has just been run, allow it to cool down (approximately 10 minutes), then check the oil level. When checking the transmission oil level, do not allow any dirt or foreign matter to enter the case opening.
1. Park the bike on a level surface and support it so that it is standing straight up. Do not support it with its jiffy stand or an incorrect reading will be obtained.
2. Wipe the area around the transmission filler cap. See **Figure 21** (4-speed), **Figure 22** (early model 5-speed) or **Figure 23** (late model 5-speed).
3A. *4-speed with oil level plug*: Remove the oil level plug from transmission cover. The oil should be level with the level plug opening. Reinstall the oil level plug.
3B. *4-speed without oil level plug*: The oil should be level with the filler cap opening.
3C. *5-speed*: Wipe the dipstick off and reinsert it back into the transmission housing; do not screw the cap in place, rest it on the housing and then withdraw it. The oil level should be between the 2 dipstick marks. See **Figure 24**.
4. If the oil level is low, add the recommended type of oil listed in **Table 6**. Do not overfill.
5. Inspect the filler cap O-ring. Replace if worn or damaged.
6. Install the oil filler cap and its O-ring.
7. Wipe off any spilled oil from the transmission case.

### Transmission Oil Change

Change the transmission oil at the intervals specified in **Table 1**.

To change the transmission oil, you will need the following:

a. Drain pan.

b. Funnel.

c. Box-end wrench for drain plug.

d. Transmission oil; see **Table 6** for quantity.

1. Ride the bike until the transmission oil reaches normal operating temperature. Usually 10-15 minutes of stop and go riding is sufficient. Shut the engine off.

*NOTE*
*There are 2 important reasons for draining the transmission oil while it is hot. First, hot oil will drain more quickly. Second, contaminants in the oil will drain with it, instead of settling in the bottom of the transmission case, ready to mix with the new oil.*

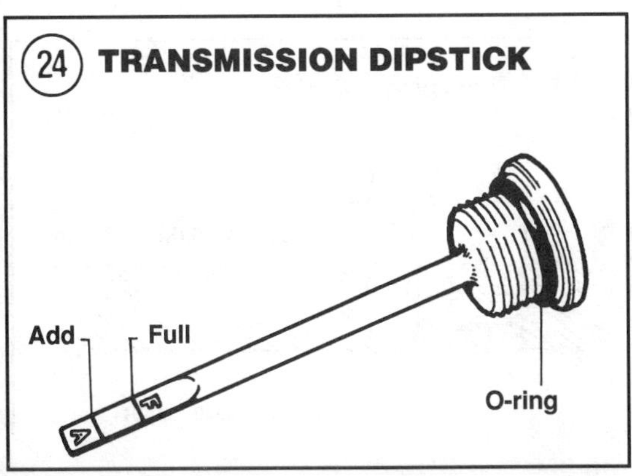

24 TRANSMISSION DIPSTICK

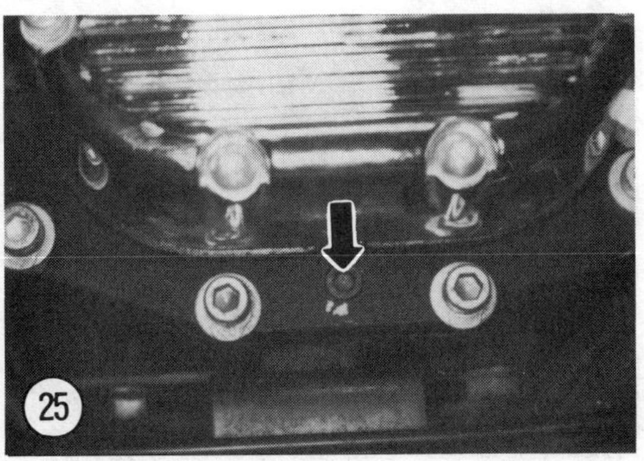
25

2. Park the bike on a level surface and support it so that it is standing straight up. Do not support it with its jiffy stand.
3. Wipe the area around the filler cap clean and unscrew the filler cap and O-ring. See **Figure 21**, **Figure 22** or **Figure 23**.
4. Place a drain pan underneath the transmission drain plug.
5A. *4-speed*: Remove the drain plug and gasket from the bottom of the transmission case. Allow the oil to drain for 10 minutes.
5B. *5-speed*: Remove the drain plug from the transmission side cover (**Figure 25** [early models]) or the drain plug and gasket (late models) from underneath the center of the transmission housing. Allow the oil to drain for 10 minutes.

*WARNING*
*If some of the oil spills onto the ground, wipe it up immediately so that it cannot contact the rear tire.*

6. Check the drain plug gasket for damage and replace if necessary.
7. The drain plug is magnetic. Check the plug (**Figure 26**) for metal debris that may indicate transmission wear, then wipe the plug off. Replace the plug if the head and/or threads are damaged.
8A. Install the drain plug and its gasket into the bottom of the transmission housing and tighten securely.

*CAUTION*
*On models where the drain plug screws into the side cover (**Figure 25**), the plug uses tapered threads. Overtightening the plug can lock it into the cover so tight that the Allen wrench will round*

26

3

*out the socket head when you try to remove it. Save your muscles for tightening axle nuts and tighten the plug as described in Step 8B.*

8B. If the transmission plug screws into the transmission side cover (**Figure 25**), install and tighten it until a distance of 0.16-0.18 in. (4.06-4.57 mm) is maintained from the top of the plug head to the side cover surface; see **Figure 27**.

9. Refill the transmission through the side cover hole (**Figure 21**, **Figure 22** or **Figure 23**) with the recommended quantity (**Table 5**) and type (**Table 6**) transmission oil.

10. Install the filler cap and O-ring and tighten securely.

11. Remove the oil drain pan from underneath the transmission and dispose of the oil as outlined under *Engine Oil and Filter Change* in this chapter.

12. Ride the bike until the transmission oil reaches normal operating temperature. Then shut the engine off.

13. Check the transmission oil level as described in this chapter and readjust the level if necessary.

### Front Fork Oil Change

The fork oil should be changed at the intervals specified in **Table 1**.

1. Place a drain pan beside one fork tube and remove the drain screw and washer. See **Figure 28**, typical. Apply the front brake lever and push down on the forks and release. Repeat this procedure until all of the fork oil is drained.

2. Inspect the sealing washer on the drain screw; replace if necessary.

3. Reinstall the drain screw and washer. Tighten securely.

4. Repeat Steps 1-3 for the opposite fork tube.

CAUTION

*Do not allow the fork oil to come in contact with any of the brake components.*

5. Raise and secure the front end so that the front tire clears the ground. Both fork tubes should be fully extended.

CAUTION

*Make sure the vehicle is supported securely.*

6. On FLT models, remove the instrument panel and handlebar.

7. On 1986-on FLHT models, remove the front light bar and outer fairing.

8A. On all FLT and FXR models with air forks, bleed the air from the front forks, then remove the banjo bolt from the fork tube.

NOTE

*The fork caps on non-air forks are under pressure from the fork springs. Remove the caps slowly and carefully in Step 8B.*

8B. On all other models, remove the fork cap from one fork tube. See **Figure 29**, typical.

9. Insert a small funnel into the opening in the fork tube.

NOTE

*If the fork has been disassembled, refill with "dry" quantity; otherwise, refill with "wet" quantity. See **Table 7**.*

NOTE

*To measure the correct amount of fluid, use a baby bottle. These bottles have*

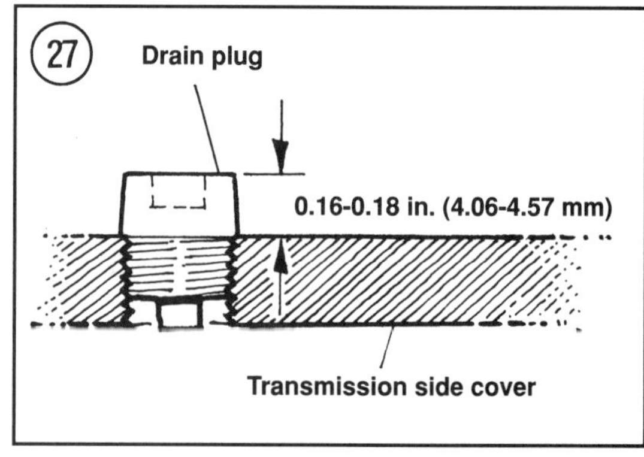

*measurements in fluid ounces (oz.) and cubic centimeters (cc) imprinted on the side. Mark the bottle with "Shop Use Only" after using it.*

10. Fill the fork tube with the correct viscosity and quantity of fork oil. Refer to **Table 6** and **Table 7**. Remove the small funnel.
11. Check the condition of the fork cap O-ring (if so equipped), and replace it if necessary.
12. Reinstall the fork cap and O-ring or the banjo bolt.
13. Repeat for the opposite fork tube.
14. Install all parts previously removed.
15. Road test the bike and check for leaks.

### Control Cables

The control cables should be lubricated at the intervals specified in **Table 1**. They should also be inspected for fraying, and the cable sheath should be checked for chafing. Replace damaged cables.

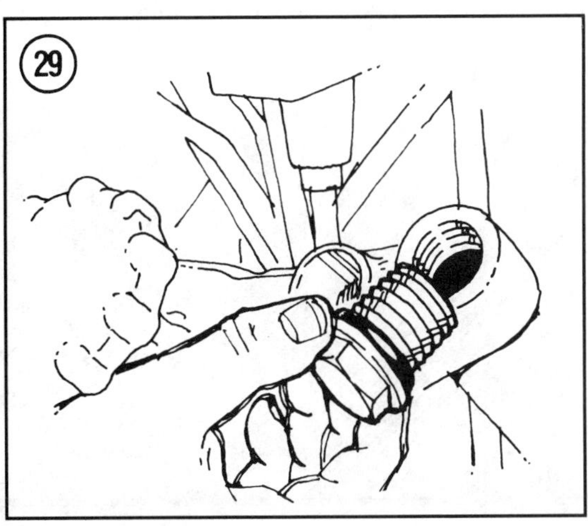


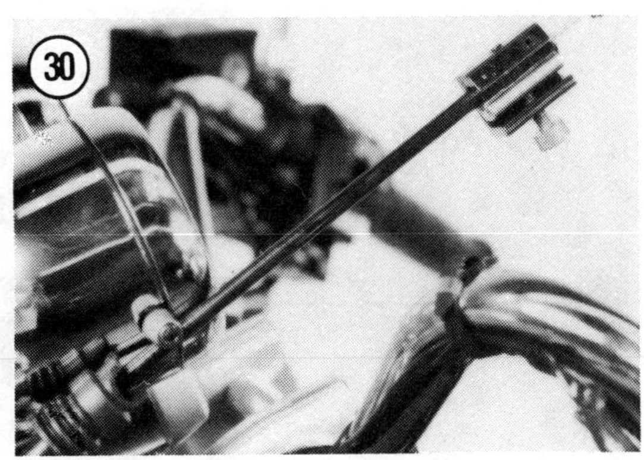


They can be lubricated with any of the popular cable lubricants and a cable lubricator.

NOTE
*The main cause of cable breakage or cable stiffness is improper lubrication. Maintaining the cables as described in this section will assure long cable service life.*



NOTE
*The enrichener (choke) cable on 1990 and later models must have sufficient cable resistance to work properly. Do not lubricate the enrichener cable or its conduit.*

1. Disconnect the clutch cable from the left-hand side handlebar. Disconnect the throttle cable(s) from the throttle grip.
2. Attach a lubricator to the cable following the manufacturer's instructions (**Figure 30**).

NOTE
*Place a shop cloth at the end of the cable(s) to catch all excess lubricant that will flow out.*

3. Insert the nozzle of the lubricant can into the lubricator, press the button on the can and hold it down until the lubricant begins to flow out of the other end of the cable. If lubricant squirts out around the lubricator, it is not clamped to the cable properly. Loosen and reposition the cable lubricator.

NOTE
*If the lubricant does not flow out of the other end of the cable, check the cable for fraying, bending or other damage. Replace the cable if damaged.*

4. Remove the lubricator, reconnect and adjust the cable(s) as described in this chapter.

### Speedometer Cable Lubrication

Lubricate the cable every year or whenever needle operation is erratic.

1. Disconnect the speedometer cable from underneath the speedometer.
2. Pull the cable from the sheath.
3. If the grease is contaminated, thoroughly clean off all old grease.

4. Thoroughly coat the cable with a good grade of multi-purpose grease and reinstall into the sheath.

5. Make sure the cable is correctly seated into the drive unit. If not, it will be necessary to disconnect the cable at its lower connection and reattach.

## Primary Chain Lubrication (Dry Clutch Models)

The primary chain is lubricated through a metering tube (**Figure 31**) connected to an oil line attached to the oil pump. Oil flow is controlled by a fixed metering orifice; adjustment of the oil flow is not possible. Excess oil that collects in the primary cover is drawn back into the engine through the gearcase breather. Whenever the primary chain is adjusted, check to see that oil drops out of the metering tube as follows.

1. Remove the clutch inspection cover (**Figure 32**).

2. Start the engine and check that oil comes out of the metering tube (**Figure 31**).

3. Turn the engine off.

4. If oil did not flow out of the metering tube in Step 2, check and clean the oil hose and oil tube.

## Primary Chain Lubrication (Wet Clutch)

Oil in the primary housing lubricates the clutch, primary chain and both chain sprockets.

### *Inspection*

1. Park the bike on a level surface and support it so that it is standing straight up. Do not support it with its jiffy stand.

2. Remove the clutch inspection cover (A, **Figure 33**) and O-ring.

3. The oil level should be level with the bottom of the clutch opening or at the bottom of the clutch diaphragm spring (**Figure 34**).

4. If necessary, add Harley-Davidson Primary Chaincase Lubricant or equivalent through the opening (**Figure 34**) to correct the level.

5. Install the clutch inspection cover together with its O-ring.

### *Oil change*

1. Ride the bike until the primary chaincase oil reaches normal operating temperature. Usually 10-15 minutes of stop and go riding is sufficient. Shut the engine off.

NOTE

*There are 2 important reasons for draining the oil while it is hot. First, hot oil will drain more quickly. Second, contaminants in the oil will drain with it, instead of settling in the bottom of the primary housing, ready to mix with the new oil.*

2. Park the bike on a level surface and support it so that it is standing straight up. Do not support it with its jiffy stand.

3. Place a drain pan under the chaincase and remove the drain plug. The drain plug is at the right-hand side of the primary chaincase. See B, **Figure 33**.

4. Allow the oil to drain for at least 10 minutes.

5. Reinstall the drain plug, making sure you do not overtighten it.

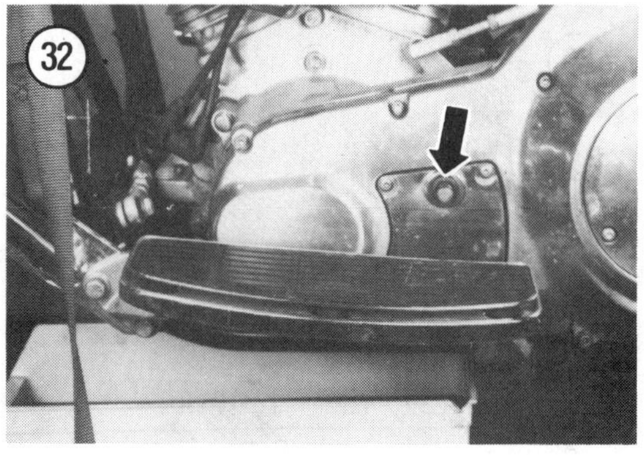

6. Remove the clutch inspection cover (A, **Figure 33**) and refill the primary housing as described in this chapter.

## Drive Chain Lubrication (Open Chain)

1. Support the bike with the rear wheel off of the ground.
2. Shift the transmission to NEUTRAL.

*NOTE*

*If your Harley is equipped with an O-ring drive chain, lubricate it with a chain lubricant specified for use on O-ring chains. Using another type of lubricant may cause the O-rings to swell and deteriorate.*

3. Oil the bottom chain run with a commercial chain lubricant. Concentrate on getting the lubricant down between the side plates, pins, bushings and rollers of each chain link. Rotate the wheel and oil the entire chain.
4. Wipe any excess lubricant off of the swing arm, wheel and tire with a rag.

## Drive Chain Lubrication (Enclosed Chain)

The rear drive chain is enclosed in a housing/cover assembly (**Figure 35**). The drive chain is lubricated by the oil held in the housing assembly. Oil capacity used in the rear cover is not specified. Instead, oil capacity is determined by the oil level in the rear cover. Check and adjust oil capacity as follows:

1. Park the bike so that it is upright, not resting on its jiffy stand.
2. Check the housing's oil level by removing the oil level bolt and O-ring from the lower cover (**Figure 36**). If the oil level is correct, oil will be level with the hole; reinstall the bolt and O-ring. If the oil level is low, proceed to Step 3.
3. Fill the drive chain housing with oil as follows:

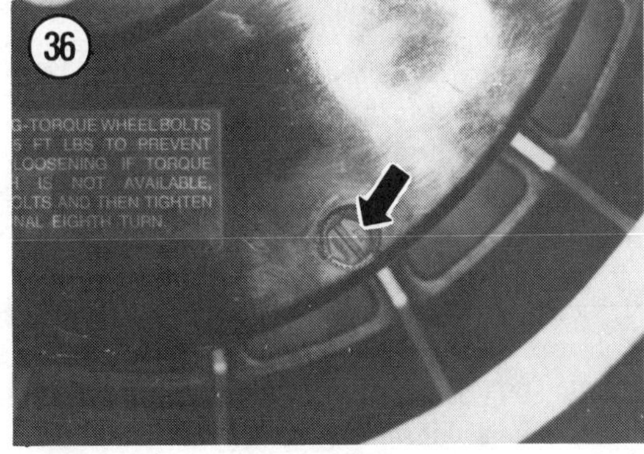

a. Wipe the top cover off with a shop rag, then carefully pry the oil filler plug out with a small screwdriver (**Figure 37**). Do not gouge the upper cover when removing the plug.

b. Slowly fill the housing with SAE 50 or SAE 60 weight engine oil until it begins to drain out of the oil level hole, then install the oil level bolt and O-ring.

*CAUTION*
*Do not install transmission oil into the chain housing. Some oils will damage the chain boots and seals.*

c. Wipe the lower cover off with a shop rag after installing the plug.

d. Snap the oil filler plug into the top cover. Make sure the plug seats in the cover hole completely.

4. Check the chain housing for oil leaks.

5. Check the tire carefully for oil that may have contacted it when you were checking or filling the rear cover. Oil must be wiped off the tire before riding the bike.

### Steering Head Lubrication (All Models Except 1991-on FLT and 1992-on FXR)

The steering bearings must be removed from the steering head, cleaned and lubricated at the intervals specified in **Table 1**. Complete lubrication will require removal of the steering head assembly. Refer to Chapter Eleven.

### Steering Head Lubrication (1991-on FLT and 1992-on FXR)

On 1991-on FLT and 1992 FXR models, a grease fitting (**Figure 38**) is installed on the left-hand side of the steering head that allows periodic lubrication of the steering bearings without having to remove them. All 1993-on FXR models have a grease fitting hole installed in the right-hand side of the steering head. The hole is tapped and sealed with a plug.

1. On FLHTC and FLHS models, remove the headlight assembly.

2. On 1993-on FXR models, remove the grease fitting plug and install a grease fitting.

3. Wipe the grease fitting and the grease gun nozzle with a clean rag.

4. Snap the grease gun nozzle onto the fitting. Slowly pump the gun until grease starts to ooze out between the upper and lower steering head bearings.

5. Remove the grease gun and wipe up all excess grease.

6. On FLHTC and FLHS models, install the headlight assembly.

7. On 1993-on FXR models, remove the grease fitting and reinstall the plug.

### Rear Swing Arm Pivot Shaft Lubrication (FXWG, FXEF and FXSB)

A grease fitting is installed in the middle of the swing arm on the bottom side that allows periodic

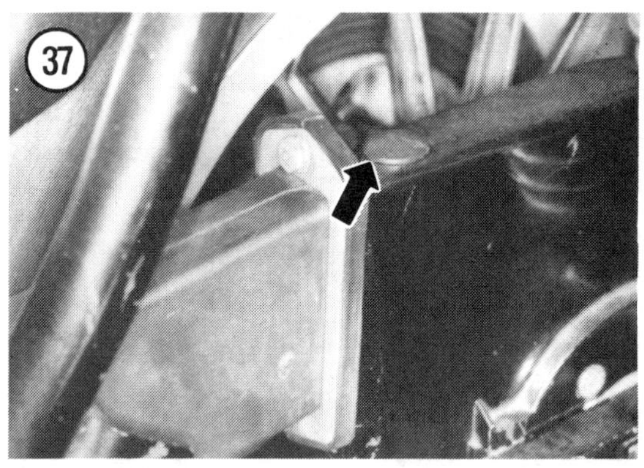

37

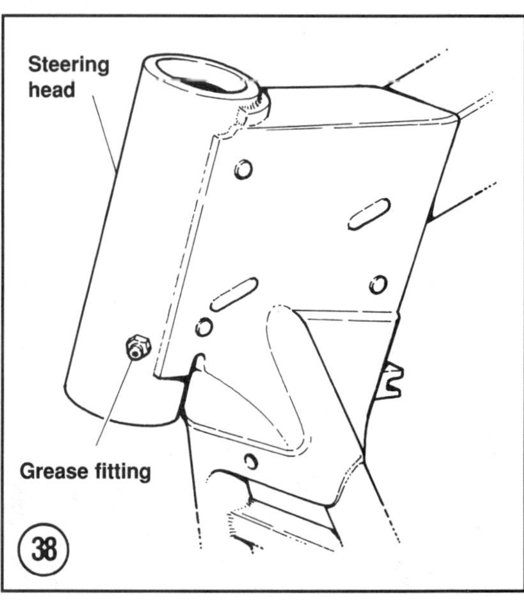


38

lubrication of the swing arm pivot shaft and bearings without having to remove the swing arm.

1. Park the bike on its jiffy stand.

2. Wipe the grease fitting and the grease gun nozzle with a clean rag.

3. Snap the grease gun nozzle onto the fitting. Slowly pump the gun until grease fills the area between the bearings.

*NOTE*
*If the grease fitting will not take the grease, it may be plugged. Remove the fitting and clean or replace it.*

4. Remove the grease gun and wipe up all excess grease.

### Rear Brake Pedal and Shift Linkage Lubrication

On some models, a grease fitting is installed on the brake pedal and/or shift linkage mounting bracket that allows periodic lubrication of the respective pivot shaft.

1. Wipe the grease fitting and the grease gun nozzle with a clean rag.

2. Snap the grease gun nozzle onto the fitting. Slowly pump the gun until grease starts to ooze out of the pivot shaft area.

*NOTE*
*If the grease fitting will not take the grease, it is probably plugged. Remove the fitting and clean or replace it.*

3. Remove the grease gun and wipe up all excess grease.

### Miscellaneous Lubrication Points

Lubricate the clutch lever, front brake lever, rear brake lever, jiffy stand pivot and footrest pivot points. Use SAE 10W/30 motor oil.

## PERIODIC MAINTENANCE

The following items should be checked at the maintenance intervals listed in **Table 1**.

### Front Rubber Mount Inspection (FLT and FXR)

Check the front rubber engine mount for cracks or damage. Check the area between the large metal washer and the frame for damage. If the rubber mount is damaged, replace it.

*NOTE*
*The vehicle's alignment should be checked by a Harley-Davidson dealer after replacing the front rubber mount.*

### Engine Stabilizer Links (FLT and FXR)

Check the engine stabilizer links for looseness or damage. Check end play by moving the links along their mounting axis. Replace the links if their end play is 0.025 in. (0.63 mm) or more.

### Primary Chain Adjustment

*NOTE*
*As the primary chain stretches and wears in use, the chain will become tighter at one point. The chain must be checked and adjusted at this point.*

1. Disconnect the negative battery cable.

2. Remove the gearshift lever, if necessary.

3. Remove the primary chain inspection cover and gasket (**Figure 39**).

*NOTE*
*The following steps show chain adjustment with the primary cover removed. The adjustment can be made through the inspection cover removed in Step 3.*

4. Check chain free play at the upper chain run midway between the sprockets (**Figure 40**). Chain free play should be 5/8 to 7/8 in. (15.87-22.22 mm) on a cold engine and 3/8 to 5/8 in. (9.52-15.87 mm) on a hot engine. If necessary, adjust chain as follows.
5. Loosen the chain adjuster shoe nut or bolt (**Figure 34**) approximately 2 turns.
6. Move the shoe assembly up or down to correct free play.
7. Tighten the bolt or nut (**Figure 40**) and recheck free play.
8. Install the inspection cover (**Figure 39**) with a new gasket.
9. Install the shift lever, if necessary.

## Open Drive Chain Inspection/Adjustment

*NOTE*
*As the drive chain stretches and wears in use, the chain will become tighter at one point. The chain must be checked and adjusted at this point.*

1. Turn the rear wheel and check the chain for its tightest point. Mark this spot and turn the wheel so that the mark is located on the lower chain run, midway between both sprockets.
2. Push the chain up midway between the sprockets on the lower chain run and check free play (**Figure 41**). The correct free play is 1/2-5/8 in. (12.7-15.87 mm) with a rider mounted on the seat.
3. If chain adjustment is incorrect, adjust it as follows:
   a. Loosen the rear axle nut (**Figure 42**).
   b. Turn each axle adjuster (**Figure 43**) in or out to adjust chain free play. Turn axle adjusters in equal amounts to maintain rear wheel alignment.
   c. When the chain free play is correct, check chain alignment with the tool shown in **Figure 44**; you can make this tool out of 1/8 in. (3.17 mm) aluminum or brass rod. Measure from the center of the swing arm pivot shaft to the center of the rear axle. Slide the rubber grommet along the tool until it aligns with the center of the axle. Now check alignment on the opposite side, comparing the rubber grommet position with the center of the axle. The alignment on both sides of the axle must be the same. If necessary, adjust the axle with the axle adjusters, while at the same time maintaining correct chain free play.
   d. Tighten the axle nut to 60-65 ft.-lb. (82.8-89.7 N•m).

4. If you cannot adjust the drive chain within the limits of the chain adjusters, it is excessively worn and stretched and must be replaced. If the chain can be adjusted, but you feel it may be worn, pull the chain away from the rear sprocket as shown in

40

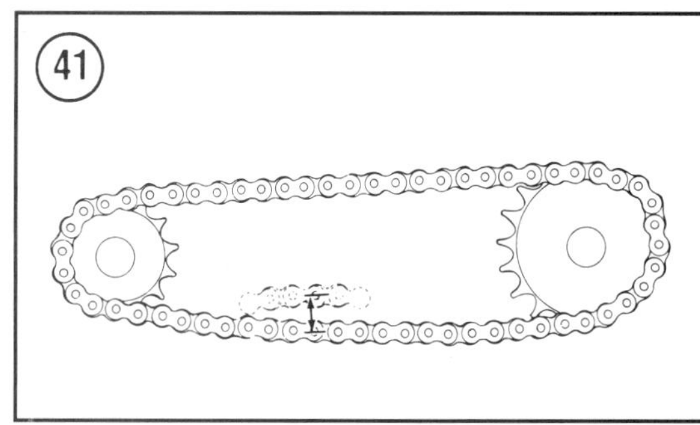
41

42

**Figure 45**. If more than 1/2 of a sprocket tooth is exposed, the chain is worn. Always replace both sprockets when replacing the drive chain; never install a new chain over worn sprockets.

*WARNING*
*Excessive free play or a worn chain can result in chain breakage; this could cause a serious accident.*

5. After adjusting the drive chain, adjust the rear brake pedal free play as described in this chapter.

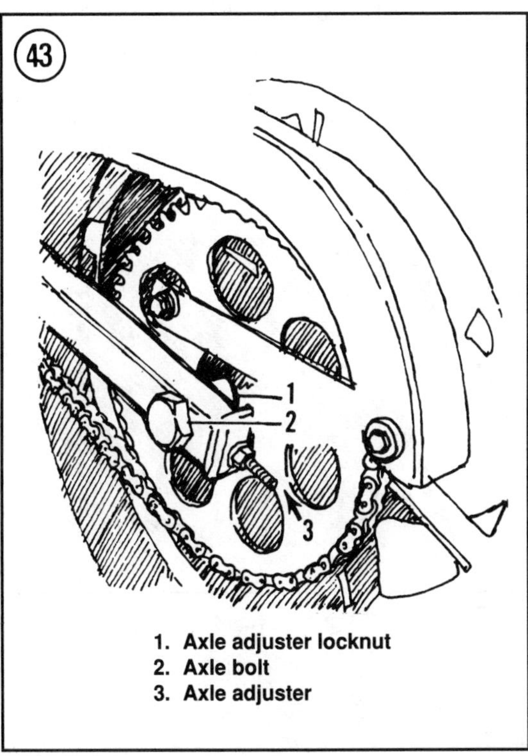


1. Axle adjuster locknut
2. Axle bolt
3. Axle adjuster

### Enclosed Drive Chain Inspection/Adjustment

*NOTE*
*As the drive chain stretches and wears in use, the chain will become tighter at one point. The chain must be checked and adjusted at this point.*

1. Remove the bolts holding the upper chain cover (**Figure 46**) in place and slide the cover forward to expose as much of the upper chain run as possible. Use Bunji cords to hold the cover in place.
2. Turn the rear wheel and check the chain for its tightest point. Mark this spot and turn the wheel so that the mark is located on the upper chain run, midway between both sprockets.
3. Push the chain up midway between the sprockets on the upper chain run and check free play. The correct free play is 1/2 in. (12.7 mm) with a rider mounted on the seat.
4. If chain adjustment is incorrect, adjust it as follows:
   a. Loosen the rear axle nut (**Figure 47**).

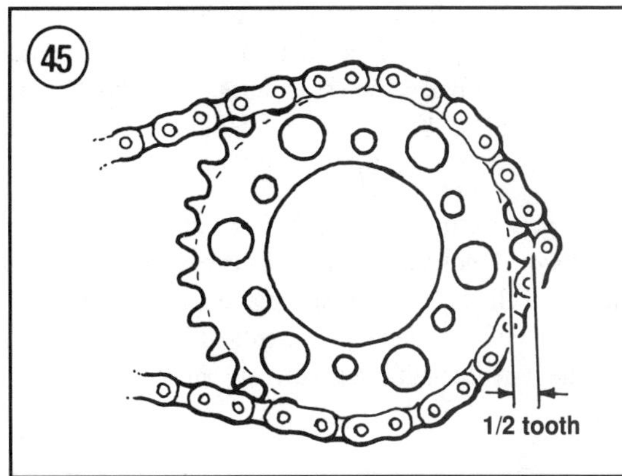


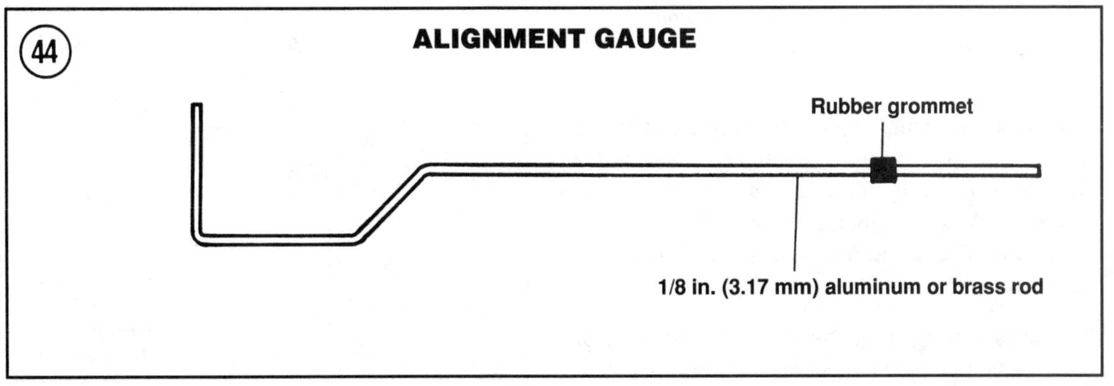

b. Loosen the anchor bolt locknut and loosen the anchor bolt (**Figure 47**), if so equipped.

c. Turn each axle adjuster in or out to adjust chain free play. Turn axle adjusters in equal amounts to maintain rear wheel alignment.

d. When the chain free play is correct, check chain alignment with the tool shown in **Figure 44**; you can make this tool out of 1/8 in. (3.17 mm) aluminum or brass rod. Measure from the center of the swing arm pivot shaft to the center of the rear axle. Slide the rubber grommet along the tool until it aligns with the center of the axle. Now check alignment on the opposite side, comparing the rubber grommet position with the center of the axle. The alignment on both sides of the axle must be the same. If necessary, adjust the axle with the axle adjusters, while at the same time maintaining correct chain free play.

e. Tighten the axle nut to 60-65 ft.-lb. (82.8-89.7 N•m). Tighten the chain adjuster locknuts securely.

f. Tighten the anchor bolt (**Figure 47**) until the rubber plug in the center of the bolt just starts to compress, then stop and tighten the locknut to 20 ft.-lb. (27.6 N•m). Hold the bolt with a wrench when tightening the locknut.

5. If you cannot adjust the drive chain within the limits of the chain adjusters, it is excessively worn and stretched and must be replaced. Always replace both sprockets when replacing the drive chain; never install a new chain over worn sprockets.

*WARNING*
*Excessive free play or a worn chain can result in chain breakage; this could cause a serious accident.*

6. Release the chain cover and apply a coating of RTV silicone sealant to the chain cover and to the chain housing mating surface. Secure the cover with its screws. Wipe up all of the chain oil that may have leaked out. Check the rear wheel for oil that may have run onto it.

7. After adjusting the drive chain, adjust the rear brake pedal free play as described in this chapter.

## Drive Chain Cleaning and Inspection

Because the enclosed drive chain runs in a bath of oil and is not subjected to dirt and other road conditions, it does not require periodic cleaning.

1. Remove the drive chain as follows:

a. Loosen the rear axle nut and the chain adjusters and push the rear wheel forward.

b. Locate the master link, then remove the outer link clip (**Figure 48**).

c. Remove the master link with a chain breaking tool and separate the drive chain.

d. Using the master link, connect one end of an old chain to the original chain. Then pull the original chain out from around the front sprocket. Disconnect and remove the original chain.

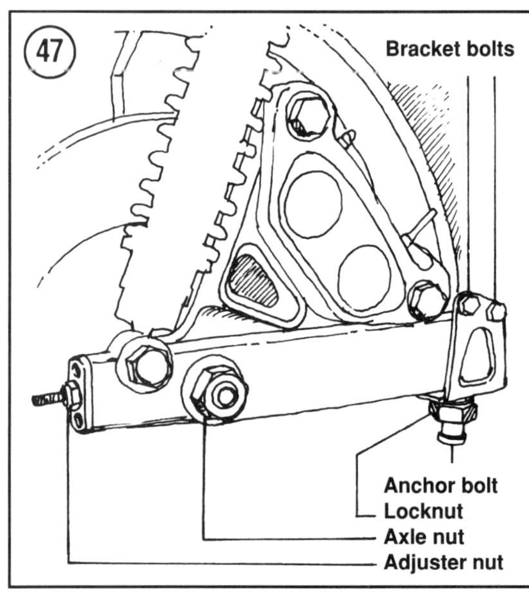

*CAUTION*
*Kerosene should be used to clean O-ring drive chains (**Figure 49**). Do not use gasoline or other solvents as these will cause the O-rings to swell and deteriorate, damaging the chain.*

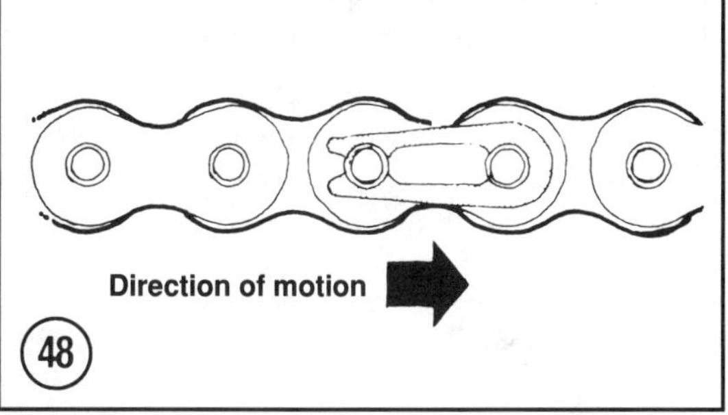


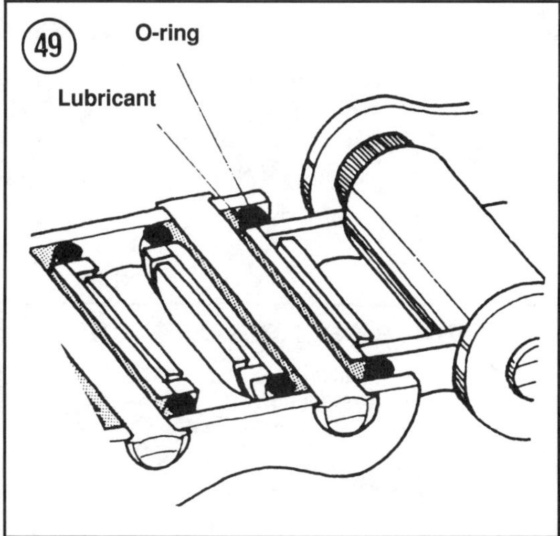


2A. *O-ring chains*: These chains should not be soaked in any type of solvent. Instead, wipe the outer chain surfaces with a rag soaked with kerosene.

2B. *Non O-ring chains*: Soak the chain in a pan of kerosene or solvent for approximately 15-30 minutes. Move it around and flex it to remove dirt trapped between the pins and rollers. Scrub the rollers and side plates with a stiff brush and rinse away loosened grit. Rinse it a couple of times to make sure all dirt is washed out.

3. Hang up the chain and allow it to dry thoroughly.

*NOTE*
*Place an empty can underneath the chain to catch the kerosene or solvent as it drips and runs off the chain.*

4. After cleaning the chain, examine it for the following conditions (**Figure 50**). If the chain is damaged or severely worn, replace it.

a. Excessive wear.
b. Loose pins.
c. Damaged rollers.
d. Damaged plates.
e. Dry plates.
f. On O-ring chains, check for worn, damaged or missing O-rings (**Figure 49**).

*CAUTION*
*Always check both sprockets when the drive chain is removed. If wear is visible on the teeth, replace the sprocket. Never install a new chain over worn sprockets or a worn chain over new sprockets.*

3

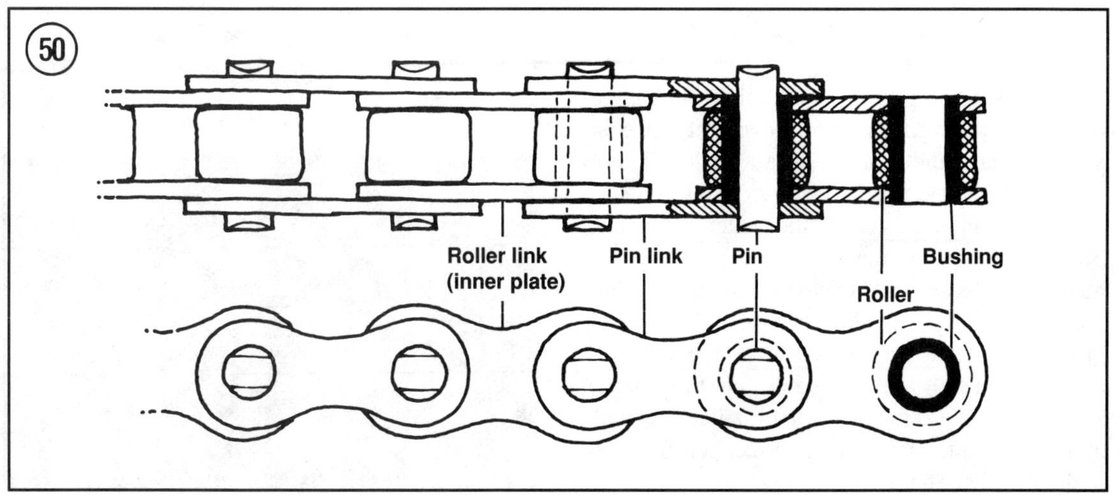

5. Reverse Step 1 to install the drive chain. Reconnect the drive chain with a new master link and side plate. Then install the master link spring clip with its closed end facing in the direction of chain travel (**Figure 48**). Make sure the clip seats in the link grooves completely.

### Final Drive Belt Adjustment

The final drive belt (**Figure 51**) stretches very little after the first 500 miles (800 km) of operation, but it should be inspected for tension and alignment according to the maintenance schedule (**Table 1**). If the belt appears severely worn or wearing incorrectly, inspect it as described in Chapter Twelve.

1. With a force of 10 lbs. (4.5 kg) applied to the middle of the lower belt strand, the top belt strand should deflect 5/16-3/8 in.(7.9-9.5 mm) (FLT and FXR) or 3/8-1/2 in. (9.5-12.7 mm) (FXWG and FXSB) with the rear wheel on the ground and one rider mounted on the bike. See **Figure 52**. If the belt tension is incorrect, adjust as follows:

NOTE
*A belt tension gauge can be used to apply pressure against the belt when checking it in Step 1.*

2. Remove the cotter pin (if used) and loosen the rear axle nut.
3. *1985 models*: Loosen the brake anchor locknut and the anchor nut (**Figure 47**).
4. Turn each axle adjuster (**Figure 43**) in or out as required, in equal amounts to maintain rear wheel alignment. Recheck belt free play as described in Step 1.
5. When belt free play is correct, check belt alignment with the alignment tool shown in **Figure 44**; you can make the tool out of 1/8 in. (3.17 mm) aluminum or brass rod. Measure from the center of the swing arm pivot shaft to the center of the axle. Slide the rubber grommet along the tool until it aligns with the center of the axle. Now check alignment on the opposite side, comparing the rubber grommet position with the center of the axle. The alignment on both sides of the axle must be the same. If necessary, adjust the belt with the adjusters, while at the same time maintaining correct belt free play as described in Step 1.

6A. *Pre-1989 models*: Tighten the axle nut to 60-65 ft.-lb. (82.8-89.7 N•m).

6B. *1989-on models*: Tighten the axle nut to 60 ft.-lb.(82.8 N•m) If necessary, tighten the nut to align the hole in the axle with the slot in the nut, but do not exceed 65 ft.-lb. (89.7 N•m); do not loosen the nut to align the hole and slot. Install a new cotter pin through the nut and axle and bend its arms over to lock it.

7. *1985 models*: Tighten the anchor bolt (**Figure 47**) until the rubber plug in the center of the bolt just starts to compress, then stop and tighten the locknut

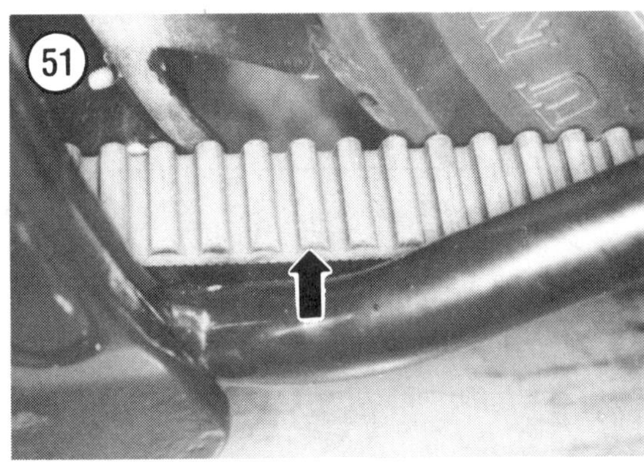


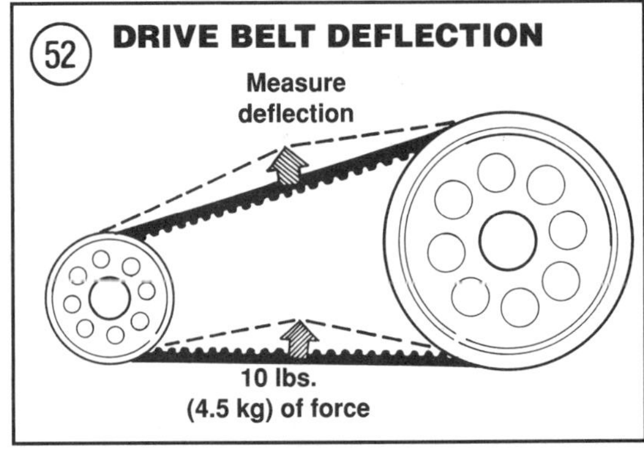


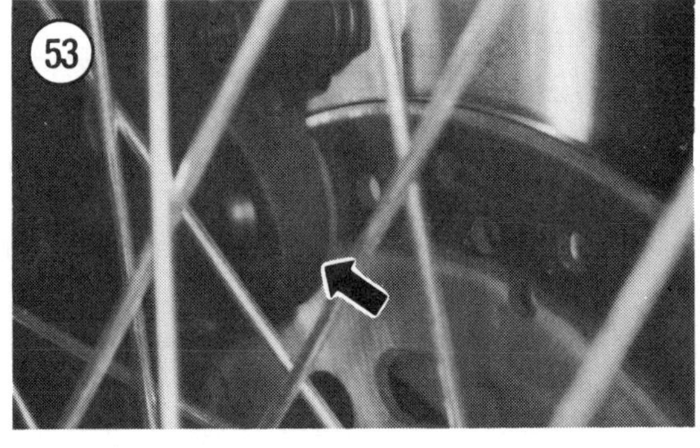

to 20 ft.-lb. (27.6 N•m). Hold the bolt with a wrench when tightening the locknut.

## Disc Brake Inspection

The hydraulic brake fluid in the disc brake master cylinder should be checked every month. The disc brake pads should be checked at the intervals specified in **Table 1**. Using a flashlight, check the brake pad friction material on each pad; see **Figure 53**, typical. If the thickness of the friction material is 1/16 in. (1.58 mm) or less, replace the brake pads as described in Chapter Thirteen.

## Disc Brake Fluid Level

1A. *Front brake:* The fluid level in the reservoir should be level with the gasket surface. To check, level the master cylinder assembly by turning the handlebar assembly.

1B. *Rear brake:* The fluid level in the reservoir should be 1/8 in. (3.17 mm) below the gasket surface. To check, level the bike.

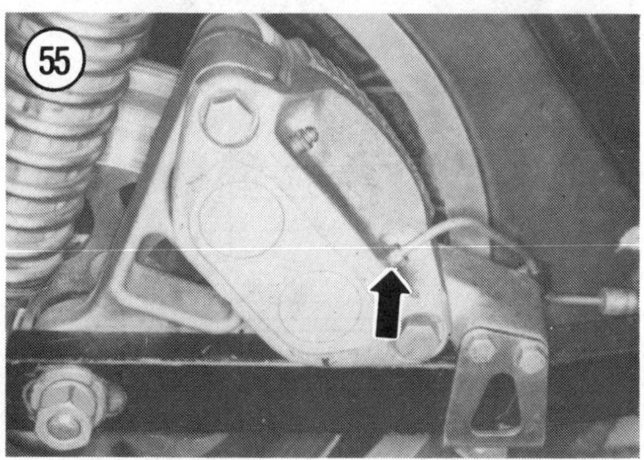


2. Wipe the master cylinder cover with a clean shop cloth.

3. Remove the cover screws and cover (**Figure 54**, typical) and lift the diaphragm or gasket out of the housing. If necessary, correct the level by adding fresh DOT 5 brake fluid.

*WARNING*
*Use brake fluid clearly marked DOT 5 only and specified for disc brakes. Others may vaporize and cause brake failure.*

4. Reinstall all parts.

*NOTE*
*If the brake fluid was so low as to allow air in the hydraulic system, the brakes will have to be bled. Refer to Chapter Thirteen.*

## Disc Brake Lines and Seals

Check brake lines between the master cylinder and the brake caliper; see **Figure 55**, typical. If there is any leakage, tighten the connections and bleed the brakes as described in Chapter Thirteen. If this does not stop the leak or if a line is damaged, cracked or chafed, replace the line and seals and bleed the brake.

## Disc Brake Fluid Change

Every time the reservoir cap is removed, a small amount of dirt and moisture enters the brake fluid. The same thing happens if a leak occurs or when any part of the hydraulic system is loosened or disconnected. Dirt can clog the system and cause unnecessary wear. Water in the fluid vaporizes at high temperatures, impairing the hydraulic action and reducing brake performance.

To change brake fluid, follow the brake bleeding procedure in Chapter Thirteen. Continue adding new fluid to the master cylinder and bleeding at the calipers until the fluid leaving the calipers is clean and free of contaminants and air bubbles.

*WARNING*
*Use brake fluid clearly marked DOT 5 only. Others may vaporize and cause brake failure.*

### Front Disc Brake Adjustment

The front disc brake does not require periodic adjustment.

### Rear Brake Adjustment (All Models)

Because the brakes are your Harley's primary safety system, brake adjustment is not a procedure to be taken lightly. When adjusting the rear brake, accuracy must be followed.

*WARNING*
*After adjusting the rear brake, make sure the brake is operating properly before riding the motorcycle. Make your test ride a short one.*

#### *FLT*

On 1984-1991 models, brake pedal adjustment is a two part procedure: brake pedal height and pushrod free play. On 1992 and later models, brake pedal adjustment consists of brake pedal height only—pushrod free play is built-in on all 1992 and later model master cylinders.

A minimum clearance of 2 1/4 in. (57.1 mm) must be maintained between the brake pedal and footboard (**Figure 56**). This clearance should be checked when the brake pedal height, footboard position or master cylinder pushrod free play is changed.

*WARNING*
*Insufficient brake pedal clearance may cause the pedal to contact the footboard before the brake is fully applied. This condition may prevent you from stopping safely when applying the rear brake and could cause you to lose control.*

1A. To adjust footboard position, loosen footboard adjustment bolts and reposition footboard, using bolts in guide slots, to obtain the correct pedal to footboard clearance (**Figure 56**). Tighten bolts and recheck adjustment. Then mount bike and check that the footboard and brake pedal positions are correct.

1B. To change brake pedal height, remove the clevis screw and pull the clevis off of the brake pedal shaft. Rotate the clevis on the brake rod (clockwise or counterclockwise) to change its position on the brake rod. Reinstall the clevis onto the brake pedal shaft and remeasure pedal clearance. Install clevis screw and tighten securely when pedal clearance is correct.

2A. *1984-1991*: When brake pedal clearance is correct, check and adjust pushrod free play as follows:

**56 REAR BRAKE PEDAL CLEARANCE (FLT)**

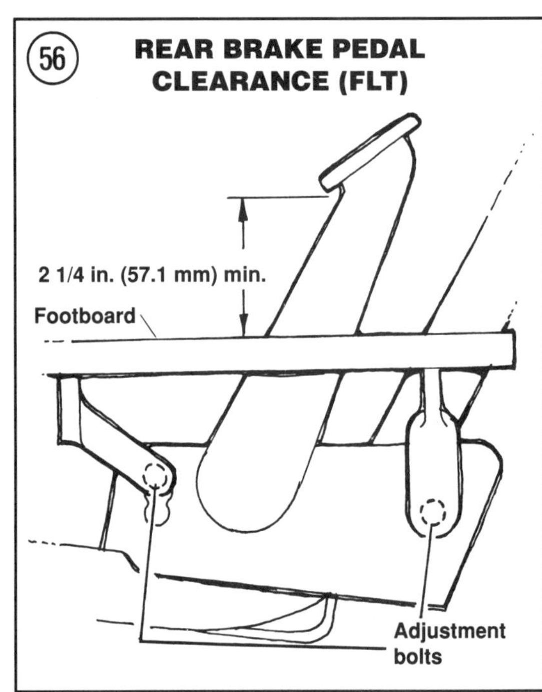


**57 REAR BRAKE FREE PLAY ADJUSTMENT (FLT)**

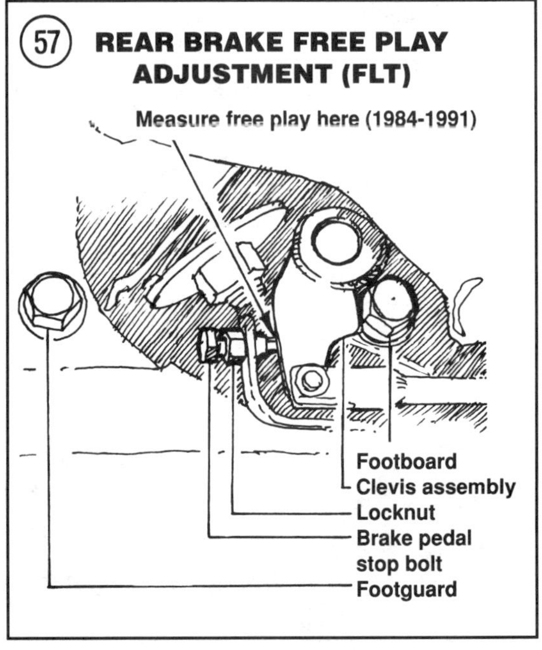

a. With the brake pedal at rest, measure clearance between the end of the stop bolt and the clevis assembly as shown in **Figure 51**. Correct pushrod free play is 3/32-1/8 in. (2.38-3.17 mm).

b. To adjust free play, loosen the stop bolt locknut and turn the stop bolt as required. Tighten locknut and recheck clearance.

*WARNING*
*Insufficient pushrod free play may cause brake drag and incorrect brake operation.*

2B. *1992-on*: To make minor adjustments in brake pedal height, perform the following:

a. Loosen the pushrod locknut (**Figure 58**).



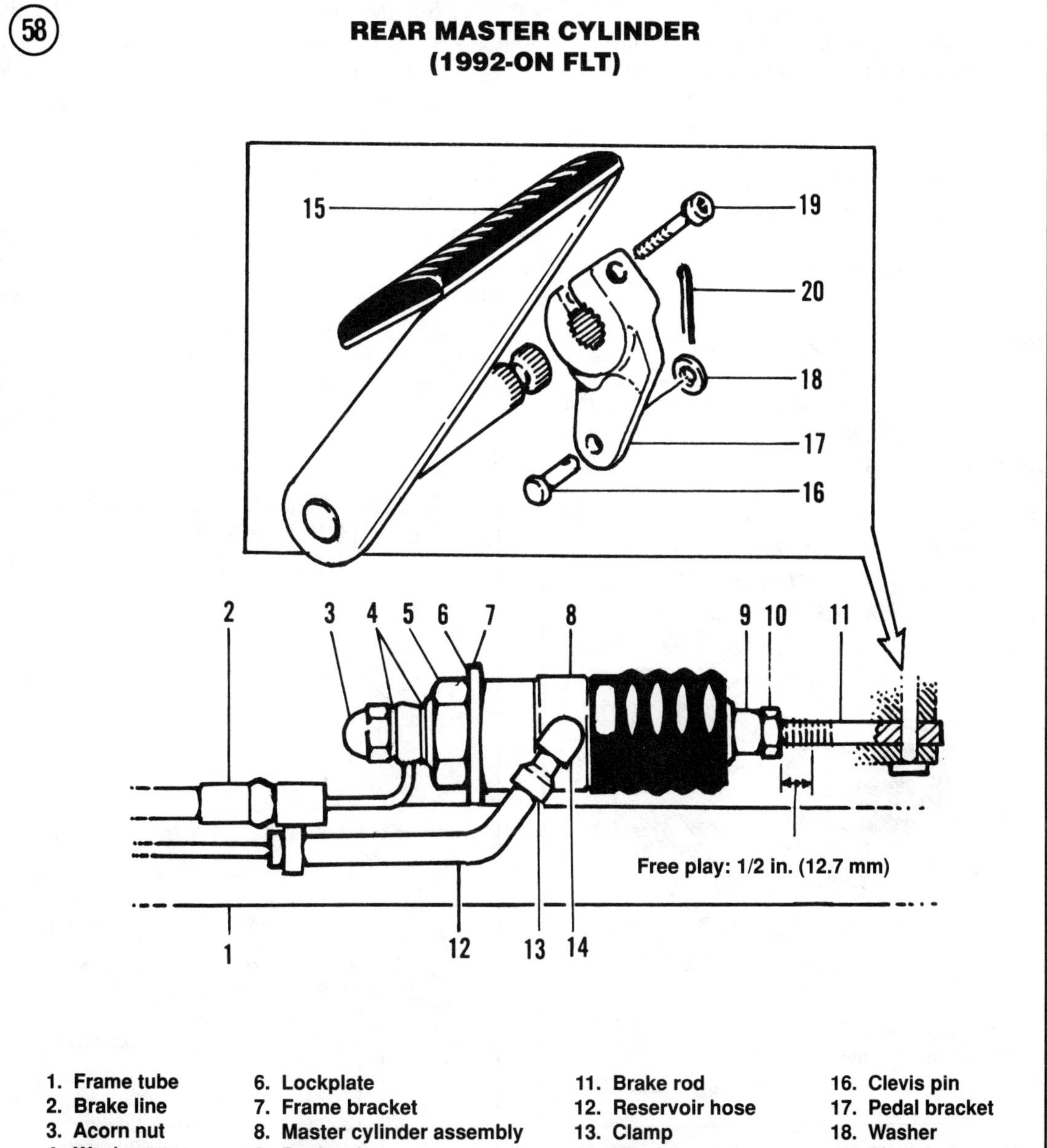

b. Turn the pushrod as required to change pedal height. Tighten the locknut.
c. Measure the length of the exposed threads on the brake rod as shown in **Figure 58**. There should be no more than 1/2 in. (12.7 mm) of threads showing. If necessary, loosen the pushrod locknut and readjust the pushrod until less than 1/2 in. (12.7 mm) of threads are exposed. Tighten the locknut and remeasure.

*WARNING*
*More than 1/2 in. (12.7 mm) of threads exposed on the brake rod indicate insufficient thread engagement between the brake rod and pushrod. This may allow the brake rod and pushrod to disengage, causing loss of rear brake. This may cause you to loose control.*

3. Recheck brake pedal height.

### *1984-Early 1987 FXR except FXRD*

Brake pedal adjustment is a two part procedure: brake pedal height and pushrod free play.

1. Park the bike on level ground.

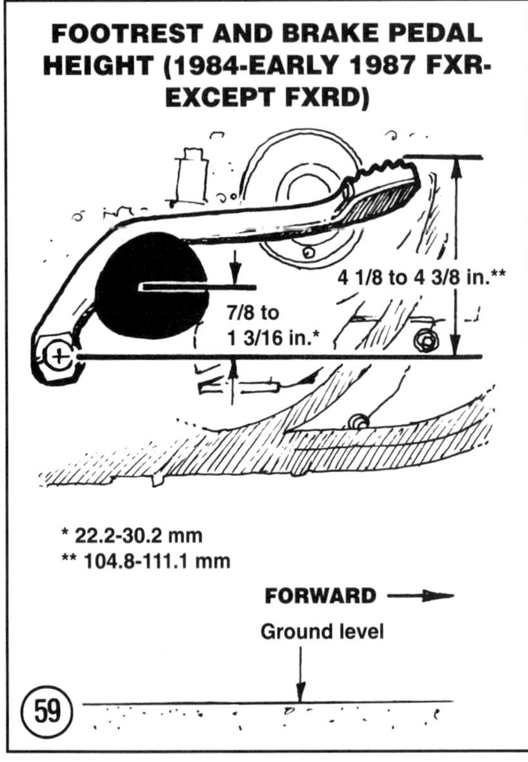


2. Check that the brake pedal is in the at-rest position.
3. Determine brake pedal height as follows:
   a. Place a ruler on the ground next to the brake pedal pivot shaft. Measure the distance from the ground up to the center of the brake pedal pivot shaft; record distance.
   b. Measure the distance from the ground up to the top of the brake pedal; record distance.
   c. Subtract sub-step a from sub-step b. The difference should be 4 1/8 to 4 3/8 in. (104.8-111.1 mm). If the difference is incorrect, perform Step 4. If the difference is correct, perform Step 6.
4. Measure the distance from the center of the footpeg rubber to the brake pedal pivot shaft center line (**Figure 59**); the correct distance is 7/8 to 1 3/16 in. (22.2-30.2 mm). If necessary, loosen the footpeg mounting bolts and adjust footpeg position to obtain the correct distance measurement. Tighten bolts and recheck. Make sure that the brake pedal arm does not contact the footpeg mounting bracket. Perform Step 5.

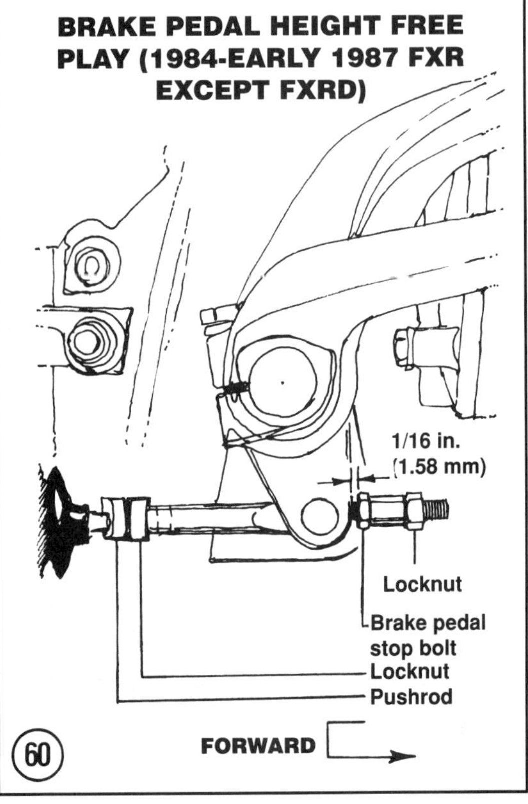

5. Measure the distance from the top of the brake pedal to the brake pedal pivot shaft center line (**Figure 59**); the correct distance is 4 1/8 to 4 3/8 in. (104.8-111.1 mm). If the distance is incorrect, perform the following.

a. Loosen the rear brake pedal stop bolt locknut and turn the stop bolt in either direction until the correct brake pedal height is achieved.
b. Hold onto the stop bolt and tighten the locknut securely.
c. Recheck the height distance and readjust if necessary.

WARNING
*An improperly adjusted brake pedal could cause the pedal to contact the exhaust pipe before the brake is fully applied. This condition may prevent you from stopping safely when applying the rear brake and could cause you to lose control.*

6. Measure pushrod free play between the brake pedal arm and the brake pedal stop bolt as shown in **Figure 60**. The correct free play is 1/16 in. (1.58 mm). If the free play is incorrect, perform the following.

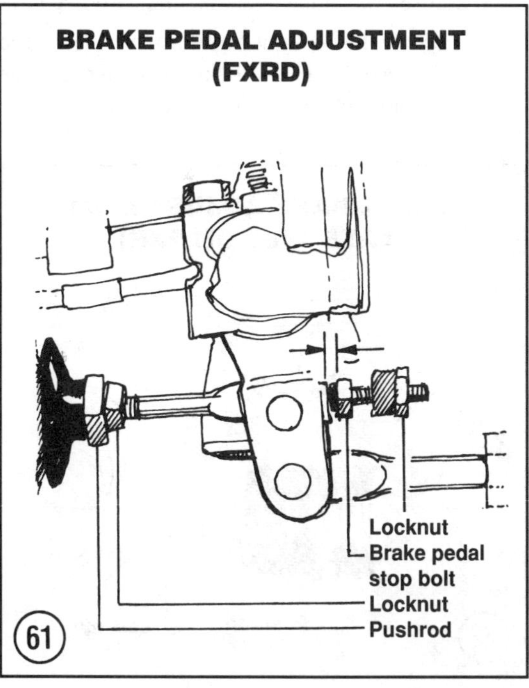


a. Loosen the pushrod locknut and turn the pushrod in either direction until the free play is correct.
b. Hold onto the pushrod and tighten the locknut securely.
c. Recheck the free play and readjust if necessary.

WARNING
*Insufficient pushrod free play may cause brake drag and incorrect brake operation.*

### *FXRD*

Brake pedal adjustment is a two part procedure: brake pedal height and pushrod free play.

1. Park the bike on level ground.
2. Check that the brake pedal is in the at-rest position.
3. There is no set brake pedal height measurement. Instead, brake pedal height should be set to rider preference. Perform the following:

WARNING
*Insufficient brake pedal clearance may cause the pedal to contact the footboard before the brake is fully applied. This condition may prevent you from stopping safely when applying the rear brake and could cause you to lose control.*

a. Sit on the bike and operate the rear brake pedal with your foot. Determine at what position the brake pedal feels the most comfortable.
b. If adjustment is necessary, loosen the brake pedal stop bolt locknut (**Figure 61**) and turn the stop bolt in either direction until the correct brake pedal height is achieved.
c. Hold onto the stop bolt and tighten the locknut securely.
d. Recheck the height distance and readjust if necessary.

4. Measure free play between the brake pedal arm and the brake pedal stop bolt as shown in **Figure 61**. The correct free play is 1/16 in. (1.58 mm). If the free play is incorrect, perform the following.

a. Loosen the pushrod locknut and turn the pushrod in either direction until the free play is correct.

b. Hold onto the pushrod and tighten the locknut securely.
c. Recheck the free play and readjust if necessary.

*WARNING*
*If you cannot obtain 1/16 in. (1.58 mm) pushrod free play, the brake pedal may be positioned incorrectly. Check brake pedal position and readjust if necessary. Insufficient pushrod free play can cause brake drag.*

### *Late 1987-on FXR*

Rear brake adjustment on these models consists of setting the brake pedal height in proper relationship with the footpeg.

1. Park the bike on level ground.
2. Check that the brake pedal is in the at-rest position.
3. Determine brake pedal height as follows:
   a. Place a ruler on the ground next to the brake pedal pivot shaft. Measure the distance from the ground up to the center of the brake pedal pivot shaft; record distance.
   b. Measure the distance from the ground up to the top of the brake pedal; record distance.
   c. Subtract sub-step a from sub-step b. The difference should be 4 1/8 to 4 3/8 in. (104.8-111.1 mm). If the difference is incorrect, perform Step 4. If the difference is correct, perform Step 5.

*WARNING*
*When adjusting the master cylinder pushrod in Step 4, sufficient thread engagement between the brake rod and pushrod must be maintained. Otherwise, these parts could disconnect and cause complete loss of the rear brake.*

4. Loosen the pushrod locknut and turn the pushrod (**Figure 62**) in either direction until the brake pedal height is correct. Hold onto the pushrod and tighten the locknut securely. Recheck the brake pedal height and readjust if necessary.
5. Measure the distance from the center of the footpeg rubber to the brake pedal pivot shaft center line (**Figure 59**); the correct distance is 7/8 to 1 3/16 in. (22.2-30.2 mm). If necessary, loosen the footpeg mounting bolts and adjust footpeg position to obtain the correct distance measurement. Tighten bolts and recheck. Make sure that the brake pedal arm does not contact the footpeg mounting bracket.
6. There is no rear brake free play adjustment on these models. Free play is built into the master cylinder. To check free play, push the brake pedal down by hand. A small amount of free play should be felt. If there is no free play, check the brake pedal assembly for damage. If the pedal assembly is okay, the rear master cylinder may require service; refer to Chapter Thirteen.

### *FXWG*

1. Place the motorcycle on its jiffy stand.
2. Check that the brake pedal is in the at-rest position.
3. See **Figure 63**. Measure the distance between the brake pedal and the footrest. It should be 0.26-0.50 in. (6.6-12.7 mm). To adjust, loosen the locknut and adjust the stop bolt as required. Tighten the locknut and recheck.
4. Work the brake pedal by hand. When the brake pedal is adjusted correctly, the pushrod will move approximately 1/16 in. (1.58 mm) before it contacts the master cylinder piston. If necessary, adjust as follows:
   a. Loosen the brake pedal locknut (**Figure 63**).
   b. Loosen the locknut and turn the clevis rod (**Figure 63**) counterclockwise to increase free play or clockwise to decrease it.

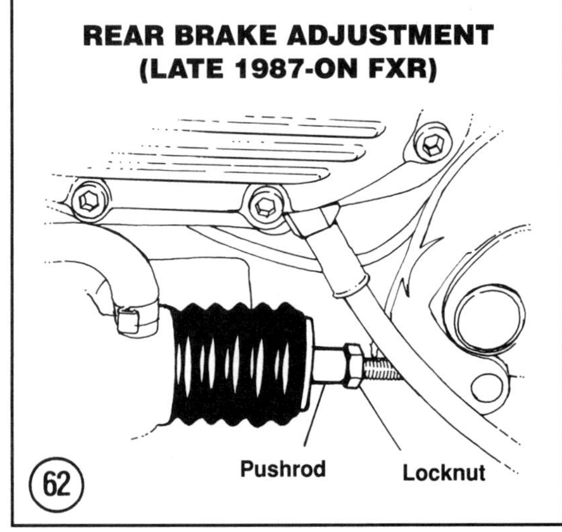

c. Tighten the locknut and recheck the adjustment.

*WARNING*
*Do not ride the motorcycle until you are sure the rear brake adjustment is correct and that the pedal does not interfere with the rear exhaust system or footboard (if so equipped). This condition may prevent you from stopping safely when applying the rear brake and could cause you to lose control.*

### *FXEF and FXSB*

1. Check that the brake pedal is in the at-rest position.
2. Work the brake pedal by hand. When the brake pedal is adjusted correctly, the pushrod will have 1/16 in. (1.58 mm) free play before it contacts the master cylinder piston.
3. If the free play is incorrect, perform the following:
   a. Loosen the pushrod locknut and turn the pushrod in either direction until the free play is correct.
   b. Hold onto the pushrod and tighten the locknut securely.
   c. Recheck the free play and readjust if necessary.

*WARNING*
*If you cannot obtain 1/16 in. (1.58 mm) pushrod free play, the brake pedal may be positioned incorrectly. Check brake pedal position and readjust if necessary. Insufficient pushrod free play can cause brake drag.*

### Clutch Adjustment (Early 1984 Dry Clutch Models)

Check and adjust the clutch at the interval indicated in **Table 1**. If the clutch slips when engaged or if the bike creeps forward when in gear, the clutch release mechanism is out of adjustment.

Refer to **Figure 64** when performing this procedure.

1. Loosen the locknut at the engine.
2. Turn the adjust sleeve as required to produce approximately 1/16 in. (1.58 mm) clutch lever free

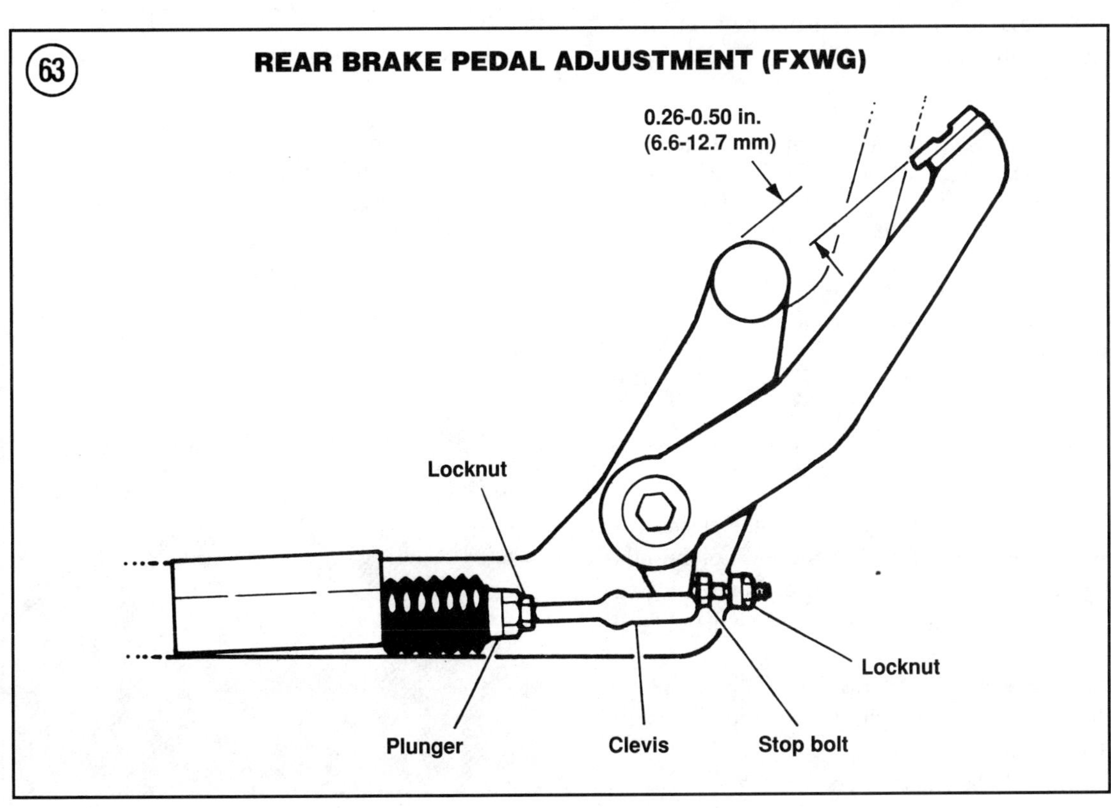

play before the clutch starts to release. See **Figure 65**.

3. Tighten the locknut.

4. If the sleeve adjustment has been taken up, perform the following adjustment.

5. Loosen the locknut and turn the adjust sleeve clockwise to loosen the clutch cable. Then disconnect the clutch cable from the release arm.

6. Remove the clutch inspection cover (**Figure 66**).

7. Loosen the pushrod locknut (1, **Figure 67**).

8. Turn the clutch adjusting screw (2, **Figure 67**) clockwise until all free play is removed from the release arm, then back it out 1/4 turn. Tighten the locknut and install the clutch inspection cover.

9. Reconnect the clutch cable at the release arm.

10. Perform Steps 1-3 to adjust the clutch cable.

11. If the clutch still slips after making this adjustment, perform the *Clutch Disc Adjustment* in this chapter.

**Clutch Disc Adjustment (Early 1984 Dry Clutch Models)**

1. Shift the transmission into NEUTRAL.

2. Remove the clutch inspection cover (**Figure 66**).

3. Turn the clutch spring adjusting nuts (**Figure 67**) clockwise 1/2 turn.

*WARNING*

*When starting the bike in Step 4, keep hands, feet and all clothing away from the clutch opening. Check that the transmission is in NEUTRAL.*

4. Start the engine and allow it to idle. Then test the clutch by shifting transmission into gear. If clutch slips or drags, repeat Step 3.

*CAUTION*

*Do not increase clutch spring tension any more than necessary.*

5. Measure the distance between the spring collar and the outer disc (**Figure 67**) at each of the adjusting nut positions. The distance should be greater than 7/8 in. (22.2 mm). A new clutch will be adjusted so that this distance is 1 1/32 in. (26.2 mm). If the distance is equal to or less than 7/8 in. (22.2 mm), the clutch may not disengage. Refer to Chapter Five and service the clutch.

6. Reinstall the clutch inspection cover.

**Clutch Adjustment (Wet Clutch with 4-speed Transmission)**

1. Park the vehicle so that it is straight up.

2. Disconnect the clutch cable at the release lever (at engine).

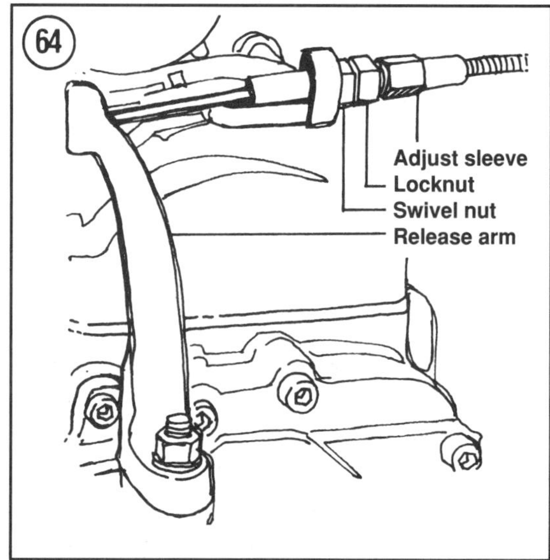


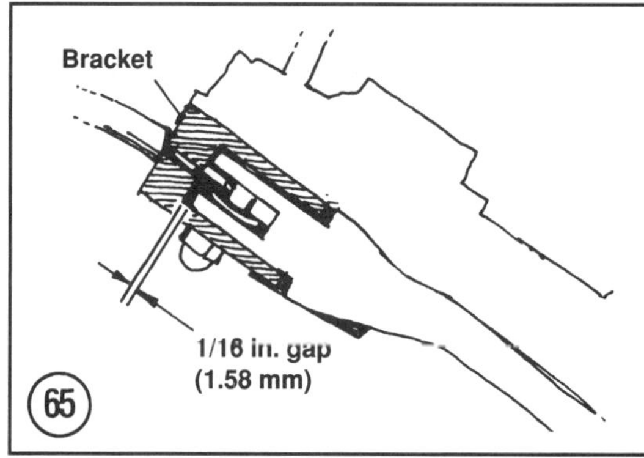

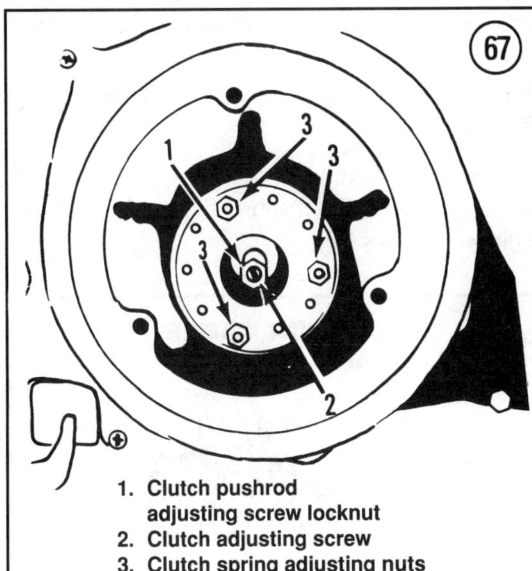


1. Clutch pushrod adjusting screw locknut
2. Clutch adjusting screw
3. Clutch spring adjusting nuts

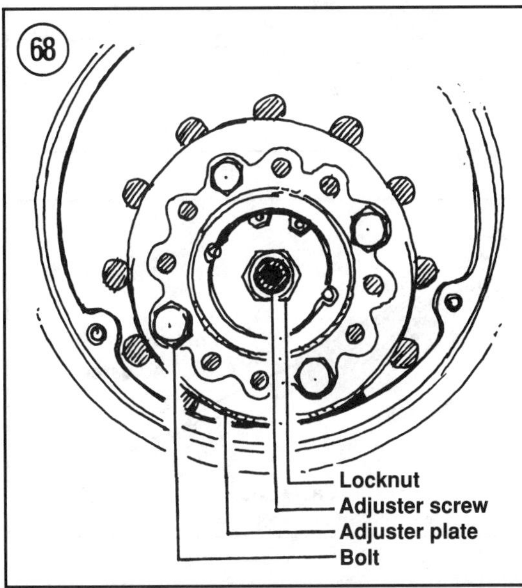

3. Remove the clutch inspection cover (**Figure 66**).
4. Refer to **Figure 68**. Loosen the clutch adjuster screw locknut (**Figure 69**).

*NOTE*
*When performing Step 5, lightly push on the release lever to remove any pushrod free play.*

5. Turn the adjuster screw (**Figure 68**) to position the release lever 13/16 in. (20.6 mm) from the transmission cover as shown in **Figure 70**.
6. Hold the adjuster screw in position with an Allen wrench and tighten the locknut (**Figure 68**).
7. Reconnect the clutch cable at the release lever.
8. Loosen the clutch cable adjusting screw locknut (**Figure 71**). Turn the adjusting screw (**Figure 71**) in either direction to obtain 1/16 in. (1.58 mm) free play at the clutch hand lever (**Figure 65**). Tighten the locknut.
9. Check the primary chaincase oil level as described in this chapter before reinstalling the clutch inspection cover.
10. Install the clutch inspection cover.

### Clutch Adjustment (Late 1984-1989 Wet Clutch with 5-speed Transmission)

1A. *Late 1984-1986*: Loosen the locknut and turn the adjust sleeve clockwise to loosen the clutch cable (**Figure 64**).

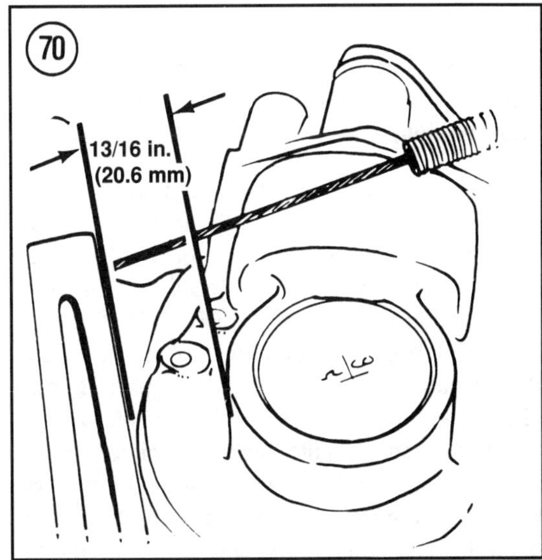


3

1B. *1987-1989*: Locate the clutch cable adjuster and slide the rubber boot away from the adjuster (**Figure 72**). Loosen the cable locknut and turn the adjuster to provide as much cable slack as possible.
2. Support the bike so that it sits straight up.
3. Remove the clutch inspection cover (**Figure 66**).
4. Refer to **Figure 68** and perform the following:
   a. Loosen the clutch pushrod adjusting screw locknut.
   b. Turn the clutch adjusting screw clockwise to remove all pushrod free play.
   c. Turn the clutch adjusting screw 3/4 turn counterclockwise. Then hold the screw securely and tighten the locknut.
5. Check the primary chaincase oil level as described in this chapter before reinstalling the clutch inspection cover.
6. Reinstall the clutch inspection cover.
7. Pull the clutch handlebar lever 3 to 4 times to seat the clutch release mechanism.

*NOTE*
*When turning the clutch cable adjuster in Step 8, pull the clutch cable away from the clutch hand lever bracket.*

8. Turn the clutch cable adjuster (**Figure 64** or **Figure 72**) until there is 1/8-3/16 in. (3.17-4.76 mm) free play between the clutch hand lever bracket and the outer clutch cable end as shown in **Figure 73**.
9. Tighten the clutch cable locknut. On 1987-1989 models, slide rubber boot over cable adjuster.
10. If clutch slips or drags, perform the *Clutch Diaphragm Spring Adjustment* in this chapter.

### Clutch Diaphragm Spring Adjustment (Late 1984-1989 Wet Clutch with 5-speed Transmission)

1. Park the vehicle so that it is straight up.
2A. *Late 1984-1986*: Loosen the locknut and turn the adjust sleeve clockwise to loosen the clutch cable (**Figure 64**). Then disconnect the cable from the release arm.
2B. *1987-1989*: Locate the clutch cable adjuster and slide the rubber boot away from the adjuster (**Figure 72**). Loosen the cable locknut and turn the adjuster to provide as much cable slack as possible.
3. Remove the clutch inspection cover (**Figure 66**).
4. Refer to **Figure 68**. Loosen the clutch adjuster screw locknut (**Figure 69**) and turn the adjuster screw counterclockwise to provide clutch pushrod free play.
5. Lay a straightedge across the diaphragm spring (**Figure 74**).
6. The spring should be flat within 0.010 in. (0.25 mm). See **Figure 75**. If spring flatness is incorrect, adjust as follows.

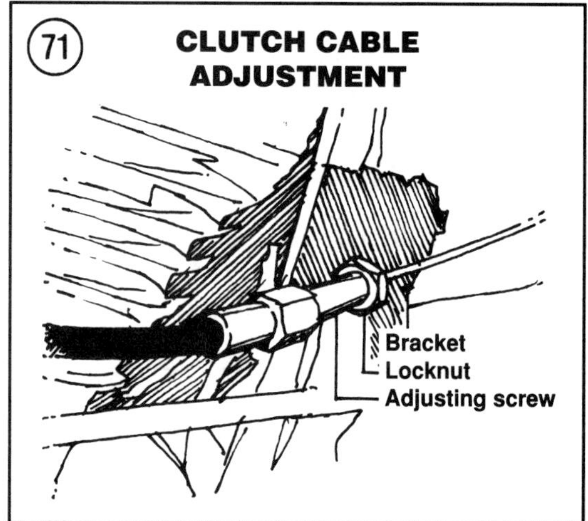


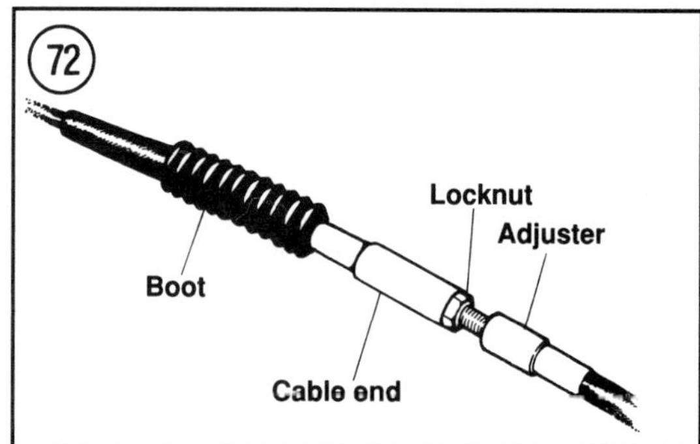


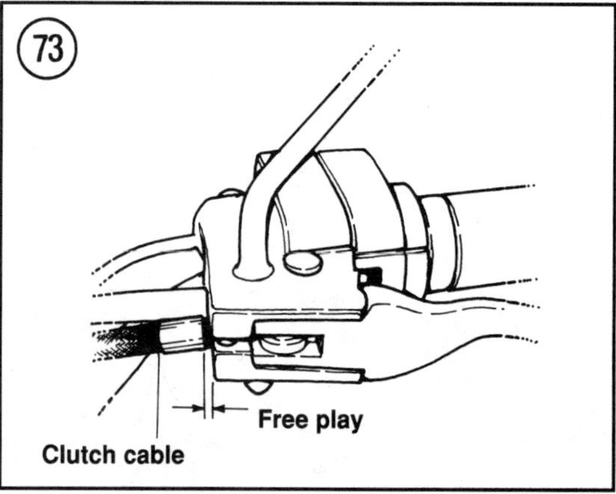

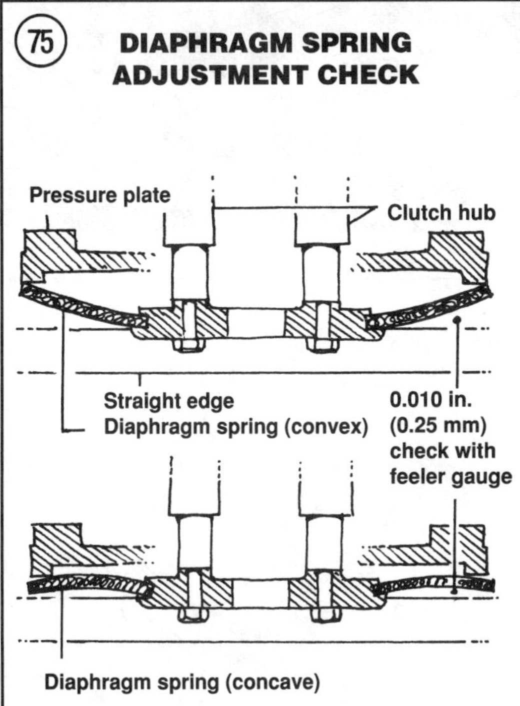

*NOTE*

*Spring compression adjustment is performed by removing the adjuster plate (**Figure 76**) and reinstalling it using one of the 3 different hole positions for least, middle and greatest compression. See **Figure 77**.*

7. Loosen the 4 adjuster plate bolts (**Figure 76**) in a crisscross pattern 1/2 to 1 turn. Continue until all spring tension is removed. Then remove the bolts and spring adjuster and position the spring adjuster plate at the mounting holes that will give the correct clutch adjustment. Referring to **Figure 77**, note the following:

   a. If the spring is bowed outward more than 0.010 in. (0.25 mm), position the adjuster plate at the next hole that offers greater compression.

   b. If the spring is dished inward more than 0.010 in. (0.25 mm), position the adjuster plate at the next hole that offers less compression.

   c. The factory spring position is flat to 0.010 in. (0.25 mm) concave. No adjustment required at this position. See **Figure 75**.

8. Install the 4 adjuster plate bolts. Tighten them in a crisscross pattern to 6.5-8 ft.-lb. (9-11 N•m). Recheck the adjustment. If adjustment is correct, remove the 4 adjuster plate bolts and apply Loctite 222 (purple) to the bolt threads. Reinstall the bolts and tighten to 6.5-8 ft.-lb. (9-11 N•m).

9. Adjust clutch as previously described.

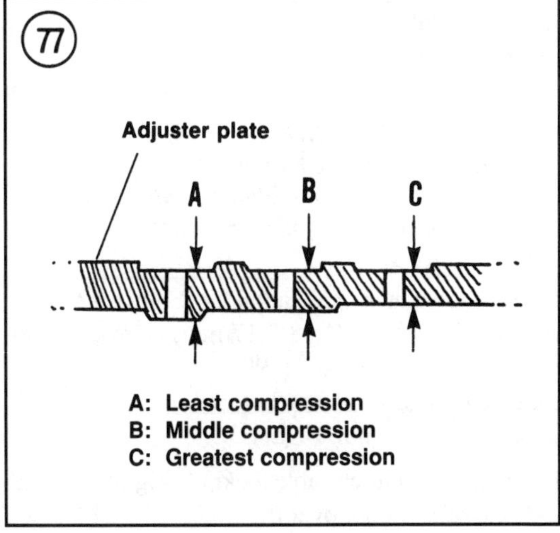

### Clutch Adjustment (1990-on)

*CAUTION*
*Because the clutch adjuster screw clearance increases with engine temperature, clutch adjustment must be made when the clutch is cold (room temperature). If the clutch is adjusted when the engine is hot, insufficient pushrod clearance may result and cause clutch slippage.*

1. Locate the clutch cable adjuster. Then slide the rubber boot away from the adjuster (**Figure 72**).
2. Loosen the cable locknut and turn the adjuster to provide as much cable slack as possible.
3. Support the bike so that it sits straight up.
4. Remove the clutch inspection cover (**Figure 66**) from the left-hand side.
5. Refer to **Figure 78** and perform the following:
   a. Loosen the clutch pushrod adjusting screw locknut.
   b. Turn the clutch adjuster screw clockwise to remove all pushrod free play.
   c. Turn the clutch adjuster screw 1/2-3/4 turn counterclockwise. Then hold the screw and tighten the locknut.
6. Reinstall the clutch inspection cover.
7. Check the primary chaincase oil level as described in this chapter before reinstalling the clutch inspection cover.
8. Install the clutch inspection cover.
9. Pull the clutch handlebar lever 3 times to seat the clutch release mechanism.

*NOTE*
*When turning the clutch cable adjuster in Step 10, pull the clutch cable away from the clutch hand lever bracket.*

10. Turn the clutch cable adjuster (**Figure 72**) until there is 1/16-1/8 in. (1.58-3.17 mm) (1990) or 1/8-3/16 in. (3.17-4.76 mm) (1991) free play between the clutch hand lever bracket and the outer clutch cable end as shown in **Figure 73**.
11. Tighten the clutch cable locknut (**Figure 72**) and slide the rubber boot over the cable adjuster.

### Throttle Cable(s)

Check the throttle cables from grip to carburetors. Make sure they are not kinked or chafed. Replace it if necessary.

Make sure that the throttle grip rotates smoothly from fully closed to fully open. Check at center, full left and full right position of steering.

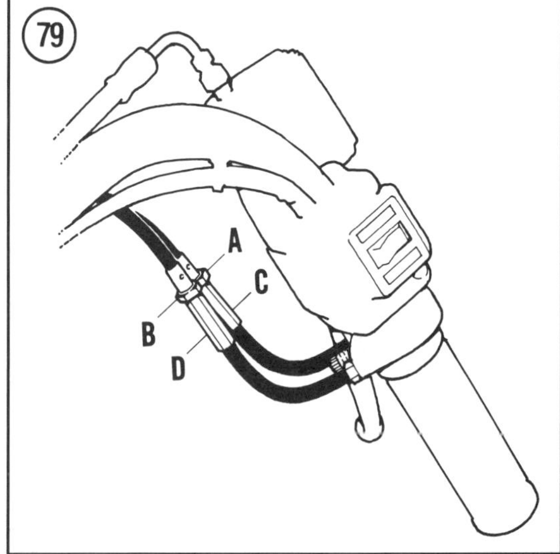

### Throttle Cable Adjustment (Cruise Control Models)

Refer to Chapter Fourteen.

### Throttle Cable Adjustment (Non-Cruise Control Models)

Refer to **Figure 79** for this procedure.

1. Loosen both cable adjuster locknuts (A and B, **Figure 79**), then turn the cable adjusters (C and D) clockwise as far as possible.
2. With the motorcycle's front wheel pointing straight ahead, open the throttle fully with the throttle grip and hold it in this position. Then turn the throttle cable adjuster (C, **Figure 79**) counterclockwise until the throttle cam stop just touches the stop boss cast into the carburetor body. If you are not sure if the throttle valve is fully open, turn the pulley by hand to see if there is more movement. Tighten the throttle cable adjuster locknut (A, **Figure 79**). Release the throttle grip.
3. With the motorcycle's front wheel turned all the way to the right, lengthen the throttle cable adjuster (D, **Figure 79**) until the lower end of the cable just contacts the spring in the outer cable fitting. Tighten the locknut (B, **Figure 79**).
4. Start the engine and rev it several times. Release the throttle and make sure the rpm returns to idle. If the rpm does not return to idle, loosen the cable adjuster locknut (B, **Figure 79**) and turn the cable adjuster (D, **Figure 79**) clockwise as required. Tighten the cable adjuster (B, **Figure 79**).
5. Support the bike so that the front wheel is off the ground. Start the engine and allow it to idle, then turn the handlebar from side to side. Engine rpm must not rise above idle throughout the handlebar movement.

If the rpm rises above idle, readjust the throttle cables. If this does not fix the problem, check the throttle cables for proper routing or possible damage.

*WARNING*
*Do not ride the motorcycle until the throttle cable adjustment is correct. A sticking or improperly adjusted throttle cable can cause you to lose control.*

### Choke Cable Adjustment (1984-1989)

1. Operate the choke lever (**Figure 80**) and check for smooth operation of the cable and choke mechanism.
2. Slide the lever (**Figure 80**) all the way to the closed position. Then pull the choke arm (**Figure 81**) at the carburetor to make sure it is at the end of its travel. If you can move the choke lever an additional amount, it must be adjusted as follows.
3. Loosen the clutch cable clamping screw (**Figure 81**) and move the cable sheath *up* until the choke lever is fully closed. Hold the choke lever in this position and tighten the cable clamping screw (**Figure 81**).
4. Slide the choke lever all the way to the fully open position.
5. If proper adjustment cannot be achieved using this procedure, the cable has stretched and must be replaced.

### Enrichener/Choke Cable Adjustment (1990-on)

The enrichener knob (**Figure 82**) should move from full open to full close without any sign of binding. The knob should also stay in its fully closed or fully open position without creeping. If the knob does not stay in position, adjust tension on the cable by turning the knurled plastic nut behind the enrichener knob (**Figure 83**) as follows:

*NOTE*
*The enrichener cable must have sufficient cable resistance to work properly. Do not lubricate the enrichener cable or its conduit.*

1. Loosen the hex nut behind the mounting bracket. Then move the cable to free it from the mounting bracket slot.
2. Hold the cable across its flats with a wrench and turn the knurled plastic nut counterclockwise to reduce cable resistance. The knob should slide inward freely.
3. Turn the knurled plastic nut clockwise to increase cable resistance. Continue adjustment until the knob remains stationary when pulled all the way out. Knob movement should be smooth and without any sign of roughness.
4. Reinstall the cable into the slot in the mounting bracket. Tighten the hex nut to secure the cable to the mounting bracket.

### Fuel Shutoff Valve/Filter

Refer to Chapter Eight for complete details on removal, cleaning and installation of the fuel shutoff valve.

### Fuel Line Inspection

Inspect the fuel lines from the fuel tank to the carburetor. If any are cracked or starting to deteriorate they must be replaced. Make sure the small hose clamps are in place and holding securely. Check the hose fittings for looseness.

*WARNING*
*A damaged or deteriorated fuel line presents a very dangerous fire hazard to both the rider and the bike if fuel should spill onto a hot engine or exhaust pipe.*

### Exhaust System

Check all fittings for exhaust leakage. Do not forget the crossover pipe connections. Tighten all bolts and nuts; replace any gaskets as necessary. Removal and installation procedures are described in Chapter Eight.

### Air Cleaner Removal/Installation

A clogged air cleaner can decrease the efficiency and life of the engine. Never run the bike without the air cleaner installed; even minute particles of dust can cause severe internal engine wear.

The service intervals specified in **Table 1** should be followed with general use. However, the air cleaner should be serviced more often if the bike is ridden in dusty areas.

The air filter on all models is installed on the right-hand side of the bike. See **Figure 84** (1984-1985 FLT), **Figure 85** (1984-1985 FXR and 1985 FX), **Figure 86** (1986-1989), **Figure 87** (1990) or **Figure 88** (1991-on).

1. Remove the air filter cover screw(s) and washer(s). Then remove the cover and filter.
2. Clean the filter as described in this chapter.
3. If necessary, remove the air filter housing.
4. Installation is the reverse of these steps. If the backing plate assembly was removed, install a new carburetor gasket. Reconnect the hose to the air filter housing.

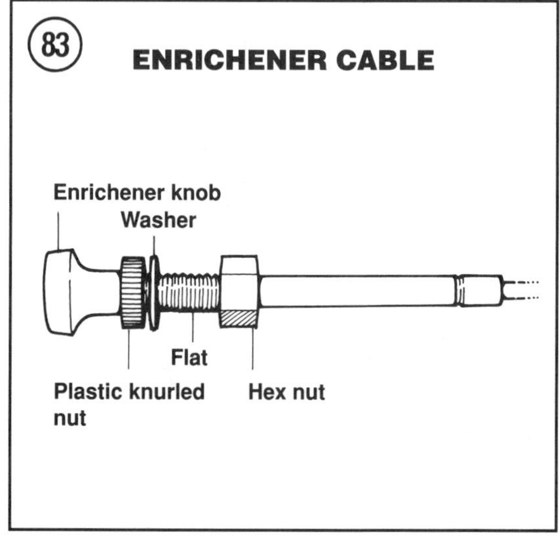

## Air Filter Cleaning (1984-1990)

These models are equipped with a foam air filter. To work properly, the filter must be properly cleaned and oiled.

Refer to **Figures 84-87** for your model when performing this procedure.

1. Remove the air filter as described in this chapter.

2. Remove the wire mesh from inside the filter.

3. Inspect the air filter element for damage. If the filter element is torn or damaged, it must be replaced. A more thorough inspection will take place after the filter is cleaned.

*WARNING*
*Never clean the air filter in gasoline or low flash point cleaning solvent. If this type of cleaner is used, the residual solvent or vapors could cause a fire or explosion after the filter is reinstalled*



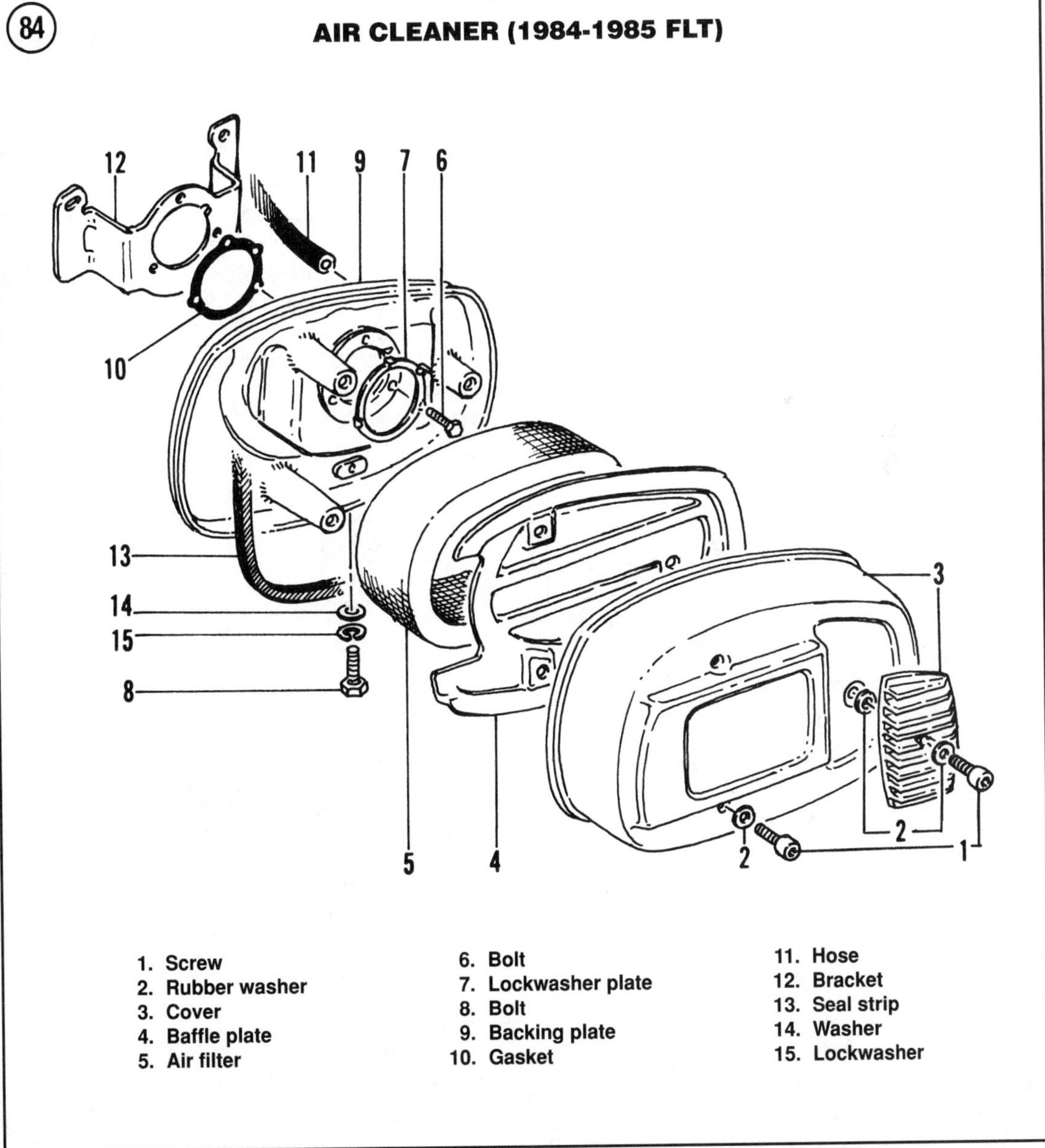

*and the engine started. Do not clean the filter in any type of solvent.*

CAUTION

*Do not wring or twist the filter when cleaning it. This harsh action could damage a filter pore or tear the filter loose at a seam. This would allow unfiltered air to enter the engine and cause severe and rapid wear.*

4. Submerge the filter into a solution of soap and water and gently work the cleaner into the filter pores. Soak and gently squeeze the filter to clean it.
5. Rinse the filter under warm water while soaking and gently squeezing it.
6. Repeat Step 3 and Step 4 two or three times or until there are no signs of dirt being rinsed from the filter.
7. Inspect the filter; if it is torn or damaged in any area, it must be replaced. Do *not* run the bike with a damaged filter as it may allow dirt to enter the engine.
8. Set the filter aside and allow it to dry thoroughly.

CAUTION

*A damp filter will not trap fine dust. Make sure the filter is completely dry before oiling it.*

9. Properly oiling an air filter element is a messy job. You may want to wear a pair of disposable rubber gloves when performing this procedure. Oil the filter as follows:

a. Purchase a box of gallon size recloseable storage bags. The bags can be used when cleaning the filter as well as for storing engine and carburetor parts during disassembly.
b. Place the cleaned filter into a storage bag.
c. Pour engine oil onto the filter to soak it.
d. Gently squeeze and release the filter element to soak oil into the filter's pores. Repeat until all of the filter's pores are discolored with oil.
e. Remove the filter from the bag and check the pores for uneven oiling. This is indicated by light or dark areas. If necessary, soak the filter and squeeze it again.

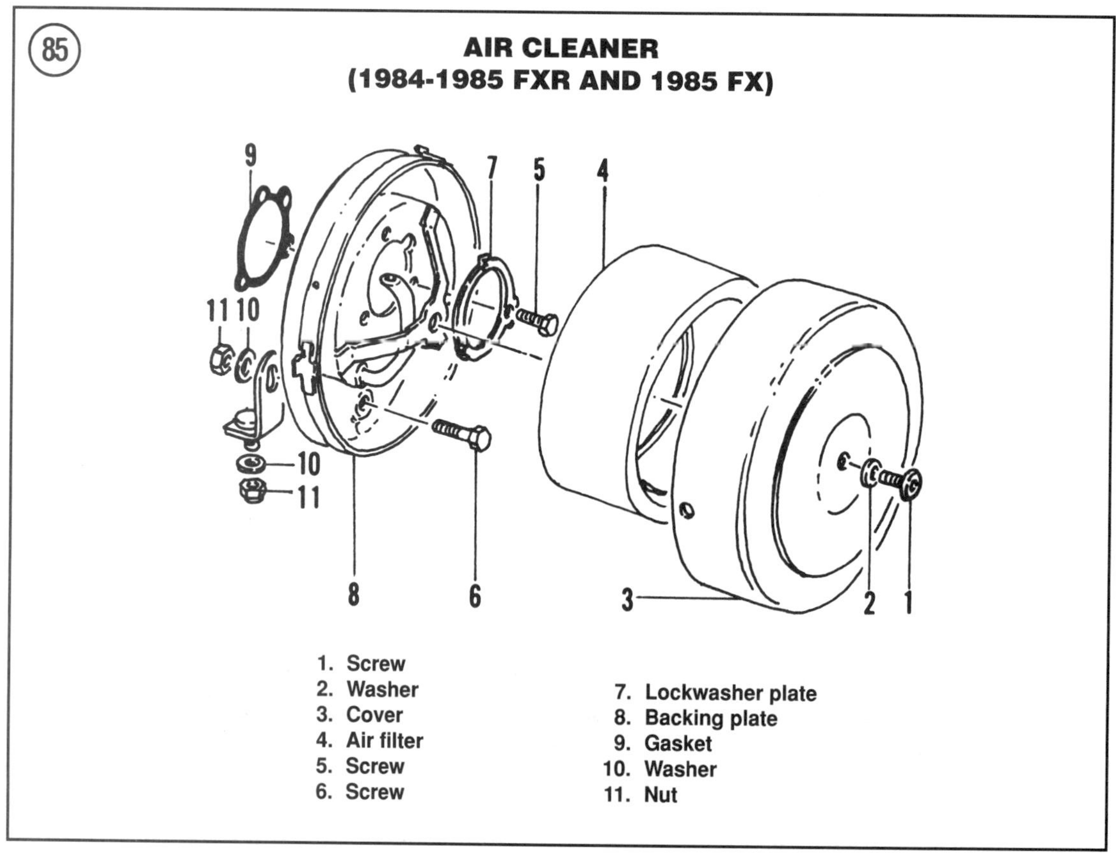

f. When the filter oiling is even, squeeze the filter element a final time.

10. Remove the filter from the bag.

11. Reinstall wire mesh frame into the filter.

12. Clean out the inside of the air box with a shop rag and cleaning solvent. Remove any foreign matter that may have passed through a torn filter.

*NOTE*

*When cleaning the inside of air box, do not to allow any dirt or other debris to run into the carburetor.*

13. Install the air filter as described in this chapter.

14. Pour the leftover oil from the bag back into the oil bottle for reuse. Label the oil bottle "Air Filter Use Only."

15. Dispose of the plastic bag.

**Air Filter Cleaning (1991-on)**

These models are equipped with a gauze air filter element.

Refer to **Figure 88** when performing this procedure.

1. Remove the air filter as described in this chapter.

2. Inspect the element for damage. If the element is torn or damaged, it must be replaced.

*WARNING*

*Never clean the air filter in gasoline or low flash point cleaning solvent. If this type of cleaner is used, the residual solvent or vapors could cause a fire or explosion after the filter is reinstalled*



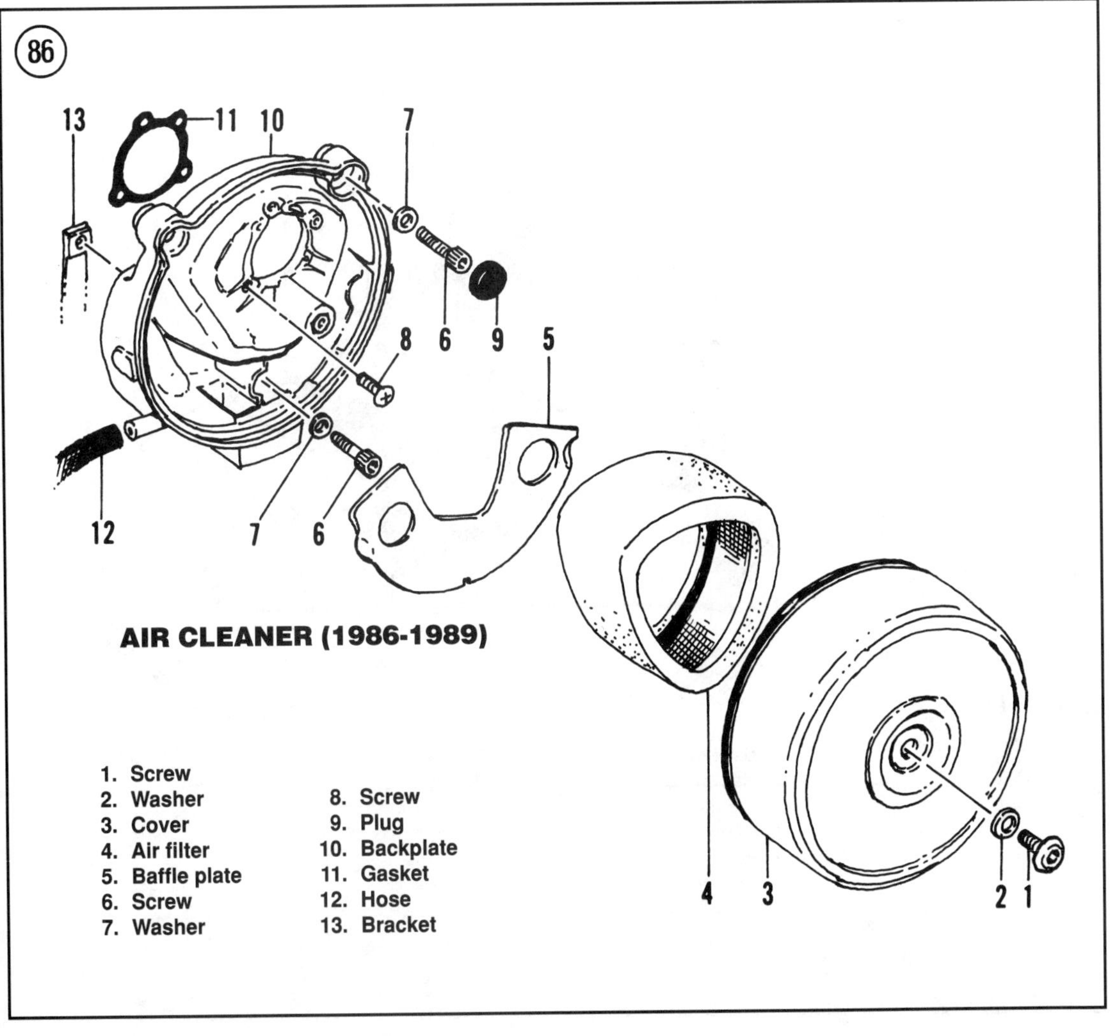


AIR CLEANER (1986-1989)

1. Screw
2. Washer
3. Cover
4. Air filter
5. Baffle plate
6. Screw
7. Washer
8. Screw
9. Plug
10. Backplate
11. Gasket
12. Hose
13. Bracket

*and the engine started. Do not clean the element in any type of solvent.*

3. Fill a pan with hot soapy water and place the filter in it for approximately 30 minutes. Swish the filter around to help removed trapped dirt and oil.
4. Remove the filter and hold it up to a strong light. Check the filter pores for dirt and oil. Repeat Step 3 until you can no longer see dirt and oil in the filter pores. If the filter cannot be cleaned by soaking, it must be replaced.

*CAUTION*
*Do **not** use high air pressure to dry the filter, as this will damage it.*

*CAUTION*
*In the next step, do not direct compressed air toward the outer surface of the filter. The normal air flow through the air filter, when the engine is running, is from the outer surface through the filter and out through the inner surface. Thus, during normal operation, dirt is collected on the outer filter surface. If air pressure is directed to the outer surface it will force the dirt and dust into the pores of the filter, restricting air flow.*

5. *Gently* apply compressed air toward the inner surface of the element to remove all loosened dirt and dust from the filter. This is reversing the normal air flow through the filter.
6. Inspect the filter; if it is torn or damaged in any area, it must be replaced. Do *not* run the bike with a damaged filter as it may allow dirt to enter the engine.

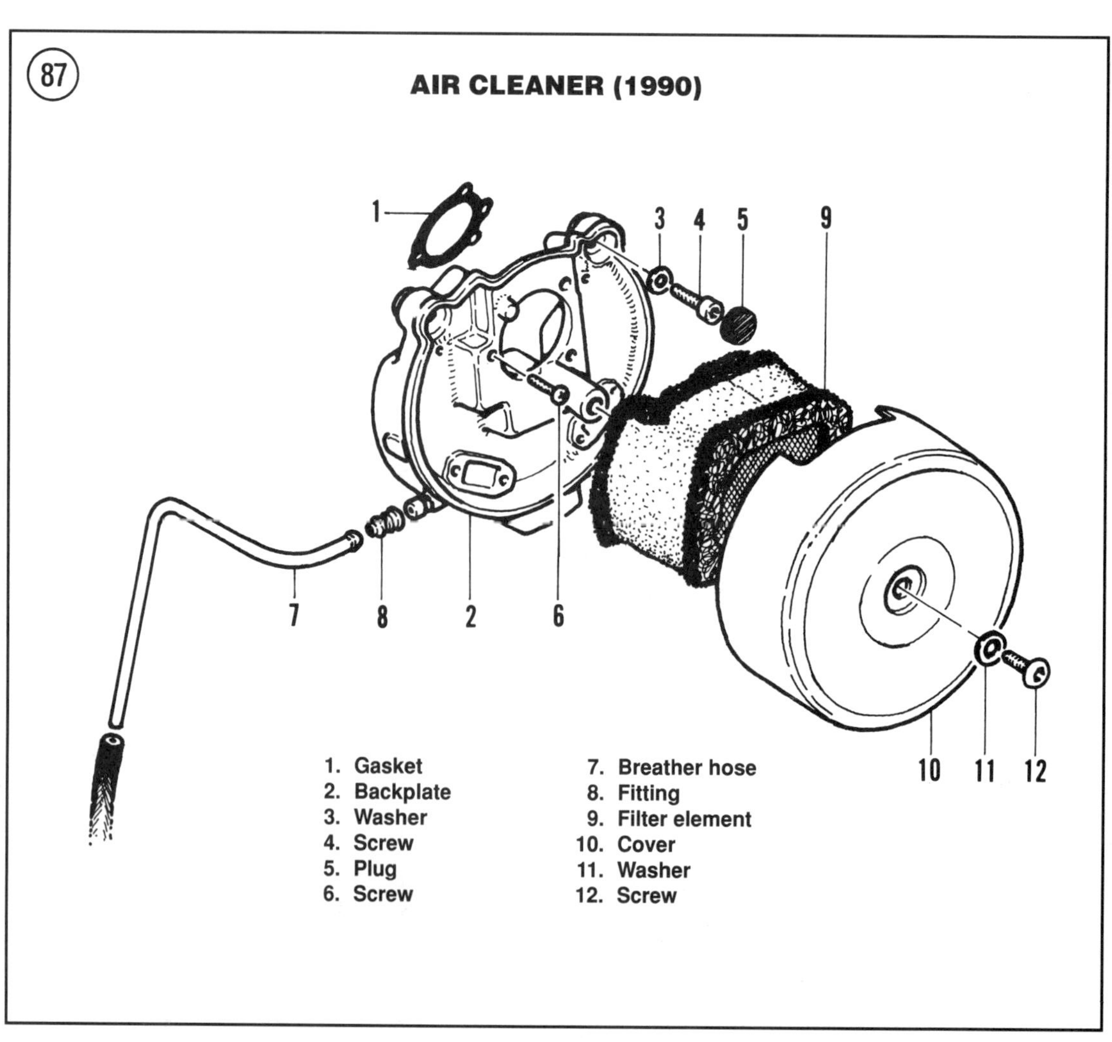

7. Clean out the inside of the air box with a shop rag and cleaning solvent. Remove any foreign matter that may have passed through a torn filter.

NOTE
*When cleaning the inside of the air box, do not allow any dirt or other debris to run into the carburetor.*

8. Allow the filter to dry completely, then reinstall it as described in this chapter.

CAUTION
*Running the engine with a damp air filter will allow air to pass through it. Make sure the filter is dry before installing it.*

## Oil Tappet Screen Cleaning

After every oil change or at the intervals specified in **Table 1**, remove the oil tappet screen located under the plug on the cam case near the rear cylinder tappet block. See **Figure 89**. Clean the screen in solvent. Replace the screen if damaged. Reverse to install.

## Wheel Bearings

The wheel bearings should be cleaned and repacked at the intervals specified in **Table 1**.

Refer to Chapter Ten for complete service procedures.

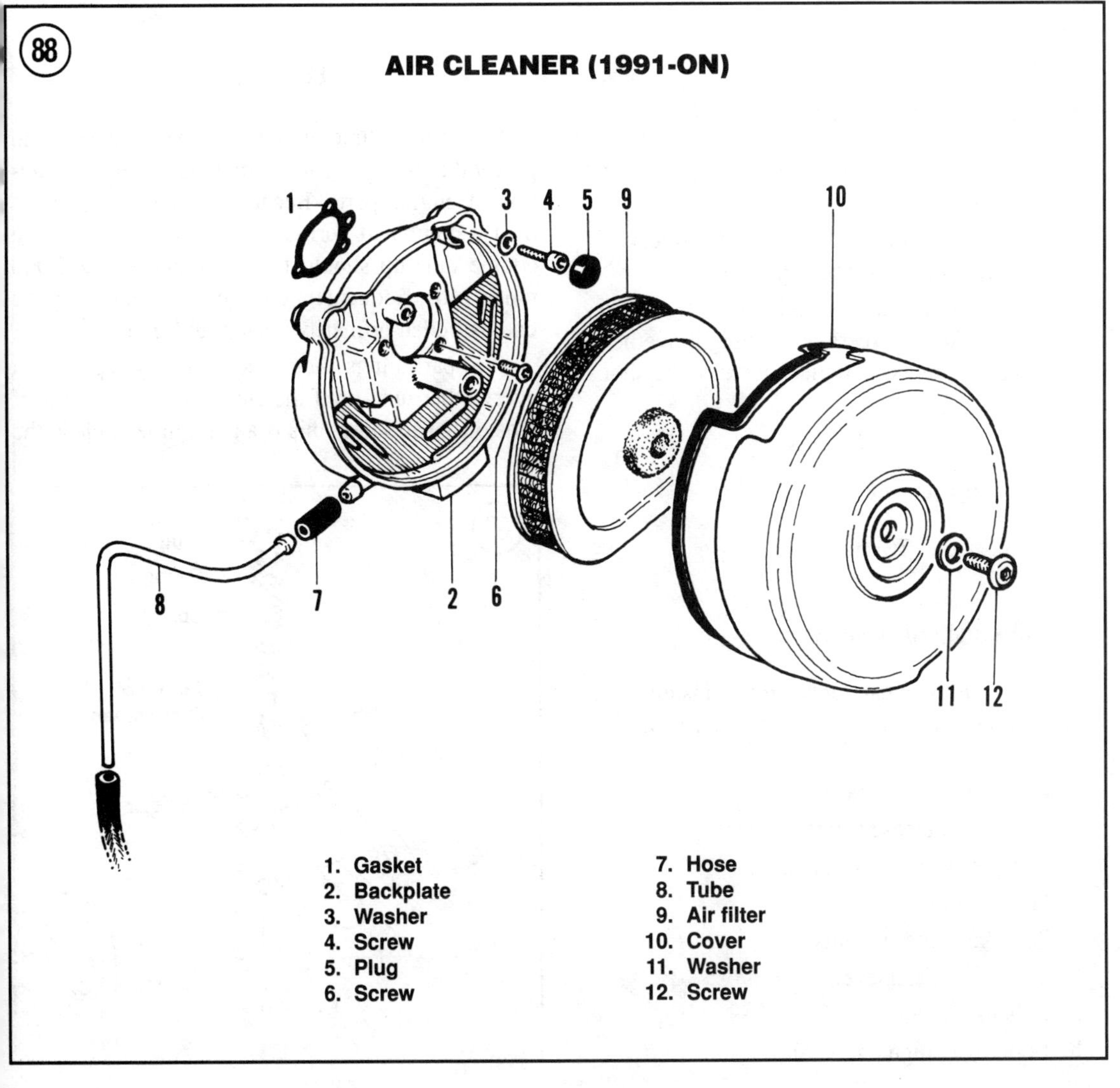

### Steering Play

The steering head should be checked for looseness at the intervals specified in **Table 1**. Adjustment procedures are given in Chapter Eleven.

### Front Suspension Check

Periodically check the front fork mounting bolts for tightness. Refer to Chapter Eleven for torque specifications.

### Rear Suspension Check

Periodically check the rear shock absorber and rear suspension swing arm pivot shaft bolts for tightness. Refer to Chapter Twelve for torque specifications and procedures.

### Rear Shock Absorber Check

Check the rear shock absorbers at the interval listed in **Table 1**.

1. Check the rear shock absorbers for fluid leaks. If a shock is leaking, it must be replaced.
2. Grasp the shock absorber and twist it from side-to-side, checking for excessive bushing movement. If the bushings are worn, replace them or the shock absorber.

### Air Shock Adjustment

Rcfcr to Chaptcr Twclvc.

### Nuts, Bolts and Other Fasteners

Constant vibration can loosen many fasteners on a motorcycle. Check the tightness of all fasteners, especially those on:

a. Engine mounting hardware.
b. Engine crankcase covers.
c. Handlebar and front forks.
d. Gearshift lever.
e. Sprocket bolts and nuts.
f. Brake pedal and lever.
g. Exhaust system.
h. Lighting equipment.

### Electrical Equipment and Switches

Check all of the electrical equipment and switches for proper operation.

### Cruise Control Operational Check

The cruise control system should be checked for proper operation.

### Rear Brake Caliper Pins and Boots

Check the brake caliper boots for tearing or other damage. The caliper pins should be removed and lubricated at the specified interval (**Table 1**). See Chapter Thirteen for service procedures.

## TUNE-UP

A complete tune-up restores performance and power that is lost due to normal wear and deterioration of engine parts. Because engine wear occurs over a combined period of time and mileage, the engine tune-up should be performed every 5,000 miles. More frequent tune-ups may be required if the bike is ridden primarily in stop-and-go traffic.

The spark plugs should be routinely replaced at every other tune-up if the electrodes show signs of erosion. In addition, this is a good time to clean the

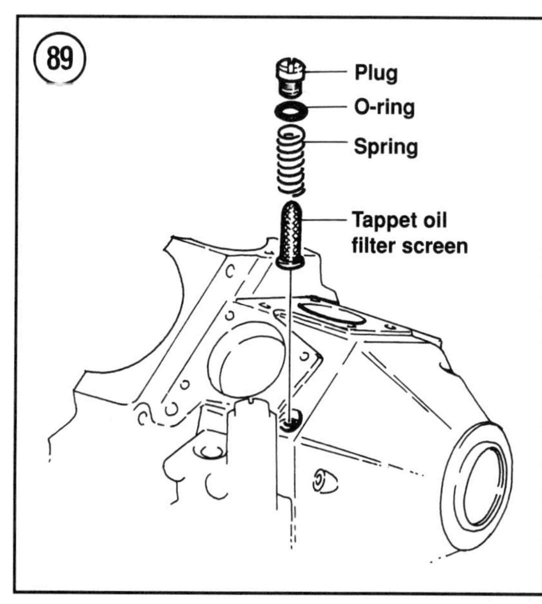

air filter element. Have the new parts on hand before you begin.

**Table 8** summarizes tune-up specifications.

Because different systems in an engine interact, the procedures should be done in the following order:

a. Clean or replace the air filter element.

b. Check engine compression.

c. Check or replace the spark plugs.

d. Check the ignition timing.

e. Adjust carburetor idle speed.

To perform a tune-up on your Harley, you will need the following tools:

a. Spark plug wrench.

b. Socket wrench and assorted sockets.

c. Compression gauge.

d. Spark plug wire feeler gauge and gapper tool.

e. Ignition timing light.

## Air Cleaner

The air cleaner element should be cleaned or replaced prior to doing other tune-up procedures. Complete procedures are described in this chapter.

3

## Compression Test

At every tune-up check cylinder compression. Record the results and compare them at the next check. A running record will show trends in deterioration so that corrective action can be taken before complete failure.

The results, when properly interpreted, can indicate general cylinder, piston ring and valve condition.

1. Warm the engine to normal operating temperature, then turn it off.
2. Remove the spark plugs (**Figure 90**) and reinstall them in their caps. Place the spark plugs against the cylinder to ground them.
3. Connect the compression tester to one cylinder following manufacturer's instructions (**Figure 91**).
4. Set the choke and throttle valves so that they are completely open.
5. Have an assistant crank the engine over until there is no further rise in pressure.
6. Record the reading and remove the tester.
7. Repeat Steps 3-6 for the other cylinder.

When interpreting the results, actual readings are not as important as the difference between the readings. Standard compression pressure is shown in **Table 8.** Pressure should not vary from cylinder to cylinder by more than 10 percent. Greater differences indicate worn or broken rings, leaky or sticky valves, blown head gasket or a combination of all.

If compression readings do not differ between cylinders by more than 10 percent, the rings and valves are in good condition. If a low reading (10 percent or more) is obtained on one of the cylinders, it indicates valve or ring trouble. To determine which, pour about a teaspoon of engine oil through the spark plug hole onto the top of the piston. Turn the engine over once to distribute some of the oil, then take another compression test and record the reading. If the compression increases significantly, the valves are good but the rings are defective on that cylinder. If compression does not increase, the valves require servicing. A valve could be hanging open but not burned or a piece of carbon could be on a valve seat.

*NOTE*
*If the compression is low, the engine cannot be tuned to maximum performance. The worn parts must be replaced and the engine rebuilt.*

8. Reinstall the spark plugs and reconnect their caps.

## Cylinder Leakage Test

A cylinder leakage test can determine engine problems from leaking valves, blown head gaskets or broken, worn or stuck piston rings. A cylinder leakage test is performed by applying compressed air to the cylinder and then measuring the percent of leakage. A cylinder leakage tester and an air compressor are required to perform this test.

Follow the manufacturer's directions along with the following information when performing a cylinder leakage test.

1. Start and run the engine until it reaches normal operating temperature.
2. Remove the air cleaner assembly. Then set the throttle and choke valves in their wide open position.
3. Remove the ignition timing inspection plug from the crankcase (**Figure 92**).
4. Set the piston for the cylinder being tested to TDC on its compression stroke. Reinstall the timing plug.
5. Remove the spark plugs (**Figure 90**).

*NOTE*
*The engine may want to turn over when air pressure is applied to the cylinder. To prevent this from happening, shift the transmission into fifth gear and lock the rear brake pedal so that the rear brake is applied.*

6. Make a cylinder leakage test following the manufacturer's instructions. Listen for leaking air while noting the following:
   a. Air leaking through the exhaust pipe indicates a leaking exhaust valve.
   b. Air leaking through the carburetor indicates a leaking intake valve.

   *NOTE*
   *Air leaking through the valves can also be caused by pushrods that are too long.*

   c. Air leaking through the ignition timing inspection hole indicates worn or broken piston rings, a leaking cylinder head gasket or a worn piston.
7. Repeat for the other cylinder.

## Correct Spark Plug Heat Range

Spark plugs are available in various heat ranges that are hotter or colder than the spark plugs originally installed at the factory.

Select plugs in a heat range designed for the loads and temperature conditions under which the engine will operate. Using incorrect heat ranges can cause piston seizure, scored cylinder walls or damaged piston crowns.

In general, use a hotter plug for low speeds, low loads and low temperatures. Use a colder plug for high speeds, high engine loads and high temperatures.

*NOTE*
*In areas where seasonal temperature variations are great, a "two-plug system" —a cold plug for hard summer riding and a hot plug for slower winter operation may prevent spark plug and engine problems.*

The reach (length) of a plug is also important. A longer than normal plug could interfere with the valves and pistons causing permanent and severe damage. Refer to **Figure 93**. **Table 8** lists the standard heat range spark plug recommended by Harley-Davidson.

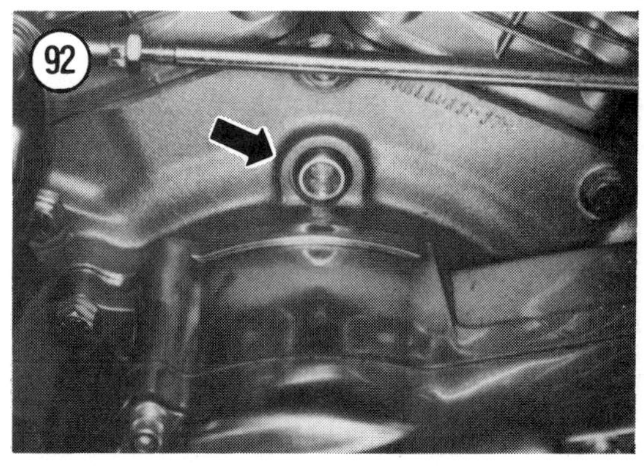

### Spark Plug Cleaning/Replacement

*CAUTION*
*Do not turn the engine over with the starter or try to run the engine with any of the spark plug leads disconnected. If this is done, components within the ignition system could be damaged.*

1. Grasp the spark plug leads as near to the plug as possible and pull them off the plugs.
2. Blow away any dirt that has accumulated in the spark plug wells (**Figure 90**).

*CAUTION*
*If any dirt falls into the cylinder when the plugs are removed, it could cause serious engine damage.*

*NOTE*
*Keep the spark plugs in the order in which they were removed (front and rear). If one of the spark plugs shows signs of abnormal engine operation, it is a good idea to know its cylinder position.*

3. Remove the spark plugs with a spark plug wrench.

*NOTE*
*If plugs are difficult to remove, apply penetrating oil such as WD-40 or Liquid Wrench around base of plugs and let it soak in about 10-20 minutes.*

4. Inspect spark plug carefully. Look for plugs with broken center porcelain, excessively eroded electrodes and excessive carbon or oil fouling (**Figure 94**). Replace worn or fouled spark plugs.

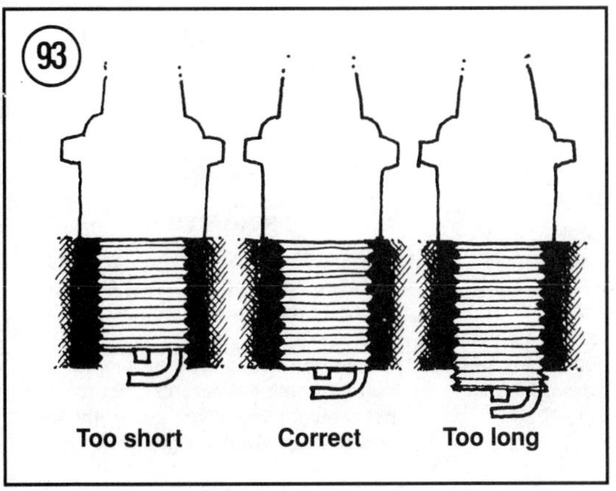


*NOTE*
*For optimum performance, replace both spark plugs at the same time.*

*NOTE*
*Spark plug cleaning with the use of a sand-blast type device is not recommended. While this type of cleaning is thorough, the plug must be perfectly free of all abrasive cleaning material when done. If not, it is possible for the cleaning material to fall into the engine during operation and cause damage.*

### Spark Plug Gapping and Installation

New plugs should be carefully gapped to ensure a reliable, consistent spark. You must use a special spark plug gapping tool.

1. Remove the new plug from its box. Screw on the small piece that may be loose in the box (**Figure 95**).
2. Insert a wire gauge between the center and the side electrode of each plug (**Figure 96**). The correct gap is listed in **Table 8**. If the gap is correct, you will feel a slight drag as you pull the wire through. If there is no drag, or the gauge won't pass through, bend the side electrode *with the gapping tool* (**Figure 97**) to set the proper gap (**Table 8**).
3. Put a small drop of anti-seize compound on the threads of each spark plug.
4. Screw each spark plug in by hand until it seats. Very little effort is required. If force is necessary, you have the plug cross-threaded or the spark plug threads in the cylinder head are damaged or contaminated with carbon or other debris; unscrew it and try again.
5. Tighten the spark plugs to 14 ft.-lb. (19.3 N•m). If you don't have a torque wrench, turn the plug an additional 1/4 to 1/2 turn after the gasket has made contact with the head. If you are reinstalling old spark plugs and are reusing the old gaskets, tighten the plug an additional 1/4 turn after the gasket makes contact with the cylinder head.

*NOTE*
*Do not overtighten. This will only squash the gasket and destroy its sealing ability. Overtightening may also cause thread damage in the cylinder head.*

3

## SPARK PLUG CONDITION

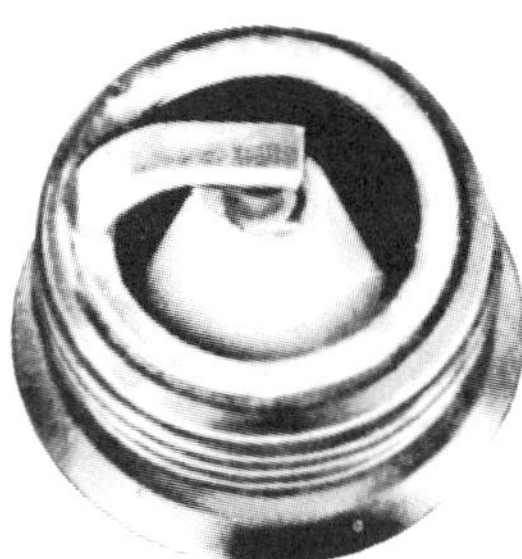

**NORMAL**

- Identified by light tan or gray deposits on the firing tip.
- Can be cleaned.

**GAP BRIDGED**

- Identified by deposit buildup closing gap between electrodes.
- Caused by oil or carbon fouling. If deposits are not excessive, the plug can be cleaned.

**OIL FOULED**

- Identified by wet black deposits on the insulator shell bore and electrodes.
- Caused by excessive oil entering combustion chamber through worn rings and pistons, excessive clearance between valve guides and stems, or worn or loose bearings. Can be cleaned. If engine is not repaired, use a hotter plug.

**CARBON FOULED**

- Identified by black, dry fluffy carbon deposits on insulator tips, exposed shell surfaces and electrodes.
- Caused by too cold a plug, weak ignition, dirty air cleaner, too rich a fuel mixture, or excessive idling. Can be cleaned.

**LEAD FOULED**

- Identified by dark gray, black, yellow, or tan deposits or a fused glazed coating on the insulator tip.
- Caused by highly leaded gasoline. Can be cleaned.

**WORN**

- Identified by severely eroded or worn electrodes.
- Caused by normal wear. Should be replaced.

**FUSED SPOT DEPOSIT**

- Identified by melted or spotty deposits resembling bubbles or blisters.
- Caused by sudden acceleration. Can be cleaned.

**OVERHEATING**

- Identified by a white or light gray insulator with small black or gray brown spots and with bluish-burnt appearance of electrodes.
- Caused by engine overheating, wrong type of fuel, loose spark plugs, too hot a plug, or incorrect ignition timing. Replace the plug.

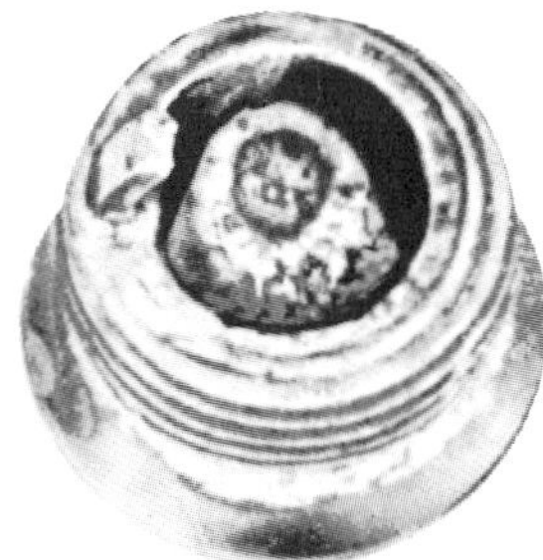

**PREIGNITION**

- Identified by melted electrodes and possibly blistered insulator. Metallic deposits on insulator indicate engine damage.
- Caused by wrong type of fuel, incorrect ignition timing or advance, too hot a plug, burned valves, or engine overheating. Replace the plug.

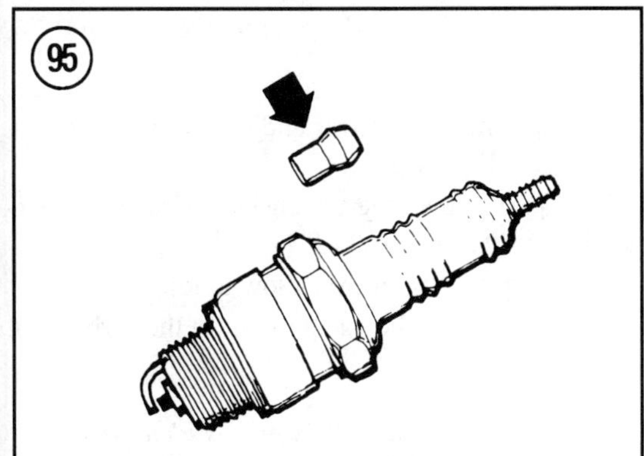


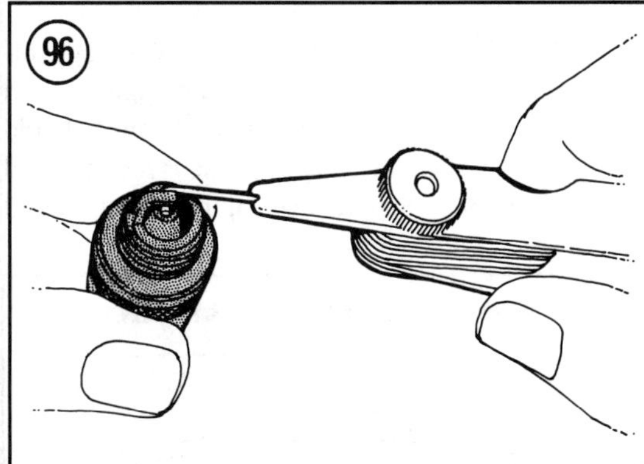


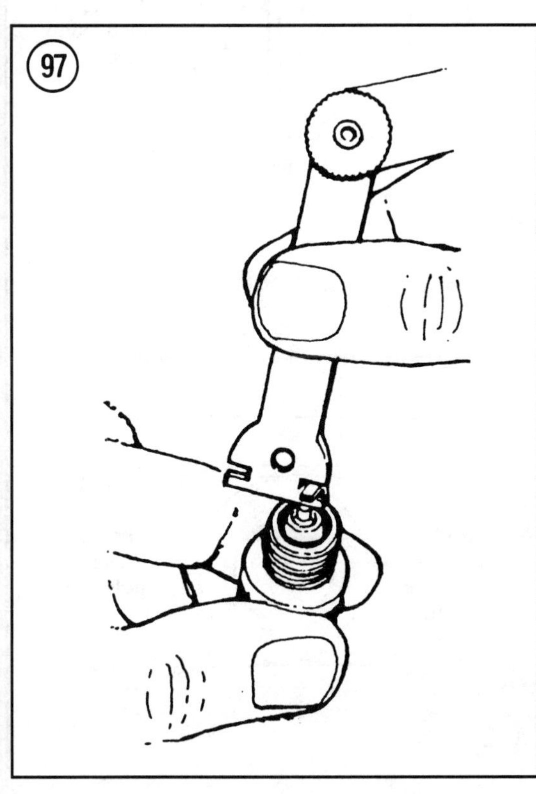


6. Install each spark plug wire. Make sure it goes to the correct spark plug.

### Reading Spark Plugs

Much information about engine and spark plug performance can be determined by careful examination of the spark plugs. This information is more valid after performing the following steps.

1. Ride bike a short distance at full throttle in third or fourth gear.
2. Turn off kill switch before closing throttle and simultaneously pull in clutch. Coast and brake to a stop. Do not downshift transmission while stopping.
3. Remove one spark plug at a time, as described in this chapter, and examine it. Compare it to the following and to **Figure 94**:
   a. If the plug has a light tan or grey colored deposit and no abnormal gap wear or electrode erosion is evident, the plug and the engine are running properly.
   b. If the plug is covered with soft, dry soot deposits, the engine is running rich.
   c. If the plug is brightly colored from overheating, the engine is running lean.
   d. If the plug exhibits a black insulator tip, a damp and oily film over the firing end and a carbon layer over the entire nose, it is oil fouled.

*NOTE*

*If the spark plug was fouled, refer to Chapter Two for information on troubleshooting engine and fuel systems.*

4. If the existing spark plug is okay, reinstall it. If not, replace with a new one.
5. Repeat for the other spark plug. Replace both plugs as a set for maximum performance.

## IGNITION SERVICE

### Ignition Timing Inspection and Adjustment

1. Remove the plug from the timing hole on the left side of the engine (**Figure 92**). A clear plastic viewing plug is available from Harley-Davidson dealers to minimize oil spray. Make sure the plug doesn't contact the flywheel.

3

2. Connect a portable tachometer following the manufacturer's instructions. The bike's tach is not accurate enough in the low rpm range for this adjustment.
3. Connect an inductive clamp-on timing light to the front cylinder spark plug wire following the manufacturer's instructions.

NOTE
*Make sure the vacuum hose is connected to the carburetor and the vacuum operated electric switch (VOES) when checking ignition timing.*

4. Start the engine and allow to idle at 1,300-1,500 rpm. If necessary, adjust idle as described in this chapter.
5. Aim the timing light at the timing inspection hole. At 1,300-1,500 rpm, the front cylinder's advance mark should appear in the center of the inspection window. **Figure 98** shows the single drilled dot that shows full advance for the front cylinder. If the mark does not align, stop the engine and adjust the ignition timing, starting with Step 7.
6. If the ignition timing is correct, reinstall the timing hole plug (**Figure 92**) and proceed to Step 17.
7. Drill out the outer cover pop rivets (1, **Figure 99**) with a 3/8 in. (9.5 mm) drill bit. See **Figure 100**.
8. Using a punch, lightly tap the rivets out of the outer cover (**Figure 101**).
9. Remove the outer cover (**Figure 102**).
10. If necessary, lightly tap the rivets out of the inner cover (**Figure 103**).
11. Remove the inner cover screws and remove the inner cover (**Figure 104**).
12. Remove the gasket (**Figure 105**).
13. Remove any remaining rivet bits from the ignition housing.
14. Loosen the timing plate sensor plate screws (**Figure 106**) just enough to allow the plate to rotate. Start the engine and turn the plate as required so that the advanced mark is aligned as described in Step 5. Make sure idle speed specified in Step 5 is maintained when checking timing. Tighten the screws and recheck ignition timing.
15. Install the gasket and inner cover.

NOTE
*When installing pop rivets to secure the outer cover, make sure to use the headless type shown in **Figure 107**. The end of a normal pop rivet will break off on installation and damage the timing mechanism.*

16. Install the outer cover and secure with the new rivets. See **Figure 108**.
17. As part of the tune-up, check the vacuum operated electric switch (VOES) as follows:
   a. Start the engine and allow to idle.
   b. Disconnect the vacuum line at the carburetor.

NOTE
*The carburetor VOES port is identified in **Figure 109** (1984-1989) and **Figure 110** (1990-on).*

   c. Plug the carburetor VOES port with your finger. With the port blocked, the engine speed should decrease and the ignition timing should retard. When the vacuum hose is reconnected to the VOES port, the engine speed should

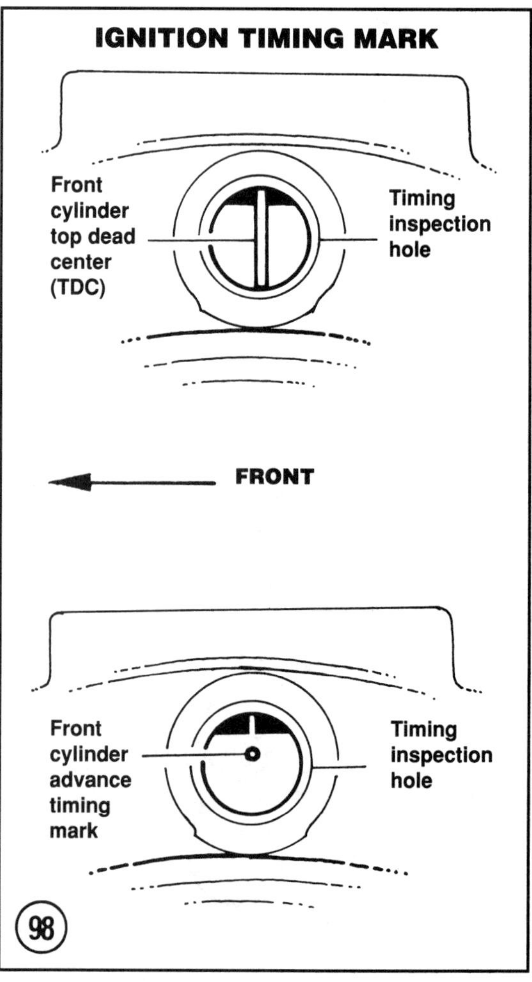

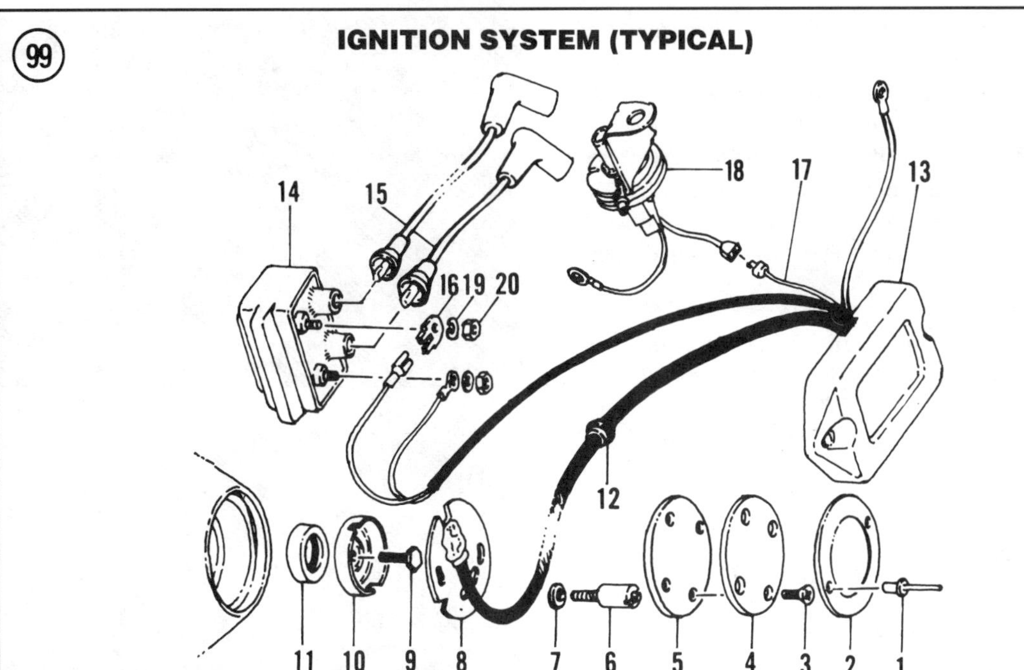


1. Outer cover rivet (2)
2. Outer cover
3. Inner cover screw
4. Inner cover
5. Gasket
6. Sensor plate screw (2)
7. Washer (2)
8. Sensor plate
9. Rotor screw and star washer
10. Rotor
11. Camshaft oil seal
12. Connector
13. Ignition module
14. Ignition coil
15. Spark plug cable (2)
16. Ignition coil terminal
17. VOES wire
18. Vacuum operated electric switch
19. Washer
20. Nut

increase and the ignition timing should advance.

d. If the engine failed to operate as described in sub-step c, check the VOES wire connection (**Figure 99**) at the ignition module. Also check the VOES ground wire for looseness or damage. If the wire connections are okay, have the VOES tested by a Harley-Davidson dealer.

*CAUTION*

*The vacuum operated electric switch (VOES) must be tested at each tune-up and replaced if malfunctioning. A damaged VOES switch will allow too high a spark advance and will cause severe engine knock and damage.*

## CARBURETOR ADJUSTMENTS

### Slow and Fast Idle Adjustment (1984-1989)

*NOTE*

*The motorcycle must be parked in an upright position when performing this procedure.*

1. Attach a tachometer to the engine following the manufacturer's instructions.
2. Start the engine and warm it to normal operating temperature. When the engine can run without the choke (**Figure 111**), proceed to Step 3.
3. With the engine idling, compare the tachometer reading to the slow idle speed specification listed in **Table 9**. If the tachometer reading is incorrect, set the slow idle speed with the throttle stop screw (**Figure 112**).
4. The idle mixture is set and sealed at the factory. It is not adjustable.
5. Rev the engine a couple of times and release the throttle. Engine rpm should return to the slow idle speed set in Step 3. If necessary, readjust the slow idle speed by turning the throttle stop screw (**Figure 112**).
6. Pull the choke knob (**Figure 111**) out to its first detent and compare the tachometer reading to the fast idle speed specification listed in **Table 9**. If the tachometer reading is incorrect, set the fast idle speed with the fast idle screw. Then push the choke knob all the way in and check that the idle drops to the slow idle speed (**Table 9**). If the choke does not

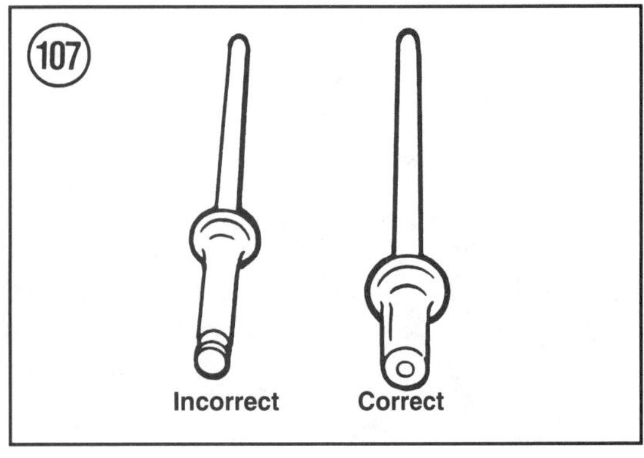

operate correctly, adjust it as described in this chapter.

7. Disconnect and remove the tachometer.

### Idle Speed Adjustment (1990-on)

*NOTE*
*The motorcycle must be parked in an upright position when performing this procedure.*

1. Attach a tachometer to the engine following the manufacturer's instructions.

2. Start the engine and warm it to normal operating temperature. When the engine can run without the choke, proceed to Step 3. Check that the enrichener valve is closed (enrichener knob all the way in).

3. With the engine idling, compare the tachometer reading to the idle speed specification listed in **Table 9**. If the tachometer reading is incorrect, set the idle speed with the throttle stop screw (**Figure 113**).

108

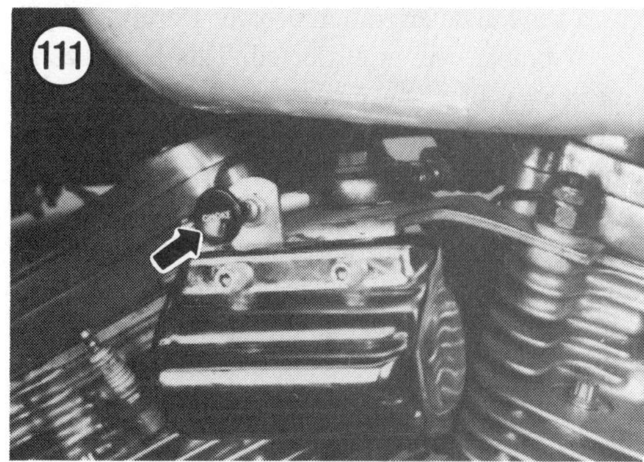
111

109

112

110

113

4. The idle mixture is set and sealed at the factory. It is not adjustable.

5. Rev the engine a couple of times and release the throttle. The idle speed should return to the speed set in Step 3. If necessary, readjust the idle speed by turning the throttle stop screw (**Figure 113**).

6. Disconnect and remove the tachometer.

## STORAGE

Several months of inactivity can cause problems and a general deterioration of your Harley's condition if proper care is neglected. This is especially true in areas of weather extremes. Storing your bike is not difficult or time consuming, but it can become expensive if it is not done properly or avoided altogether. Proper storage is one of the most important aspects in protecting the substantial investment of time and money you've made in your Harley, as well as to prepare for the next riding season. Whether you put your Harley away for a few months or put it away for a number of winter months, you must prepare it carefully.

### Preparation for Storage

Careful preparation of your Harley will minimize deterioration and make it easier to return it to service later. Use the following procedure.

1. Wash your bike thoroughly, then start and run the engine until all traces of moisture are gone. Wax all painted and polished surfaces.

*NOTE*

*There are 2 ways to prevent the fuel system from plugging up. The first method is to drain the fuel tank and then run the engine until all of the fuel in the carburetor and fuel line is used up. The second method is to add a fuel stabilizer to the fuel tank, then following the manufacturer's directions, you basically start and run the engine long enough so that the stabilizer has a good chance to reach the carburetor float bowl, thereby stabilizing the entire fuel system. Unstabilized fuel will form a gum and varnish deposits that will plug the fuel valve and carburetor passages.*

*WARNING*

*Because of the flammable nature that exists around gasoline, you should not store a motorcycle in a home garage where it is in the presence of open flames—pilot lights, electric motors, sparks, etc.*

2A. If you are adding a commercial fuel stabilizer to the fuel system, fill the fuel tank and then add the stabilizer to the tank, following the manufacturer's directions, Make sure to run the engine long enough so that the stabilizer has a chance of reaching the carburetor float bowl.

2B. Drain the fuel tank and carburetor of all fuel. Store the fuel in a can approved for gasoline storage. Then spray the inside of the fuel tank with a commercial type rust preventative, following the manufacturer's instructions for use and application.

3. Perform the lubrication procedures described in this chapter.

*NOTE*

*Steps 4A and 4B describe two methods for protecting the engine from rust and corrosion during engine storage. Many riders avoid these steps by starting and running their bike's engine every few weeks. They feel that short term running keeps everything lubricated while at the same time preventing the carburetor from blocking up. Wrong! Because water is a by-product of combustion, short start-ups like this are probably more harmful to the engine than doing nothing at all.*

4A. To fog the engine:

*WARNING*

*The exhaust gases are poisonous. Do not run the engine in a closed area. Make sure there is plenty of ventilation.*

a. Purchase a commercial engine fogging oil. Fog the engine following the manufacturer's instructions while noting the following.
b. Start the engine and allow it to warm to a normal operating temperature. If you are using a gasoline stabilizer, use it now. Turn the engine off.
c. Remove the air filter element.

*NOTE*
*A cloud of smoke will develop in sub-step d. This is normal.*

d. Start the engine once again and allow it to idle. Then spray the fogging oil into the carburetor. Do this until the engine stalls or emits smoke.
e. Turn the ignition switch off.
f. Reinstall the air filter element and its cover.

4B. To hand lubricate the engine top end:

a. Start the engine and allow it to warm to normal operating temperature. If you are using a gasoline stabilizer, use it now. Turn the engine off.
b. Remove both spark plugs.
c. Pour 1 to 2 tablespoons of engine oil into *each* spark plug hole.
d. Crank or turn the engine over five or six revolutions to distribute the oil.
e. Reinstall the spark plugs and reconnect the plug caps.

*CAUTION*
*During the storage period, do not run the engine.*

5A. *1984-on FXR and 1984-1992 FLT*: While the engine oil is hot, drain the oil tank and then flush it as described in this chapter. Then go to the oil pump and locate the oil feed line fitting marked with an "F." Follow this oil line from the oil pump to the bottom of the oil tank. Disconnect the oil line at the oil tank and plug the oil line and the bottom of the tank. Doing so will prevent oil from seeping past the oil pump check ball and filling the lower crankcase area with oil. Now replace the oil filter and refill the oil tank with new engine oil as described in this chapter.

5B. *1993-on FLT*: While the engine oil is hot, drain the engine oil as described in this chapter. Replace the oil filter and reinstall new engine oil as described in this chapter.

*NOTE*
*Draining the old used oil is important because it contains moisture, acids and other contaminants that can damage the engine during storage.*

6. Change the transmission oil as described in this chapter.
7. Remove the battery and coat the cable terminals with petroleum jelly; see Chapter Nine for battery service. Check the electrolyte level and refill with distilled water. Store the battery in an area above freezing temperatures and trickle charge it once a month. Keep the electrolyte level above the battery plates.

*WARNING*
*Make sure the battery is stored where young children cannot find it.*

8. Plug the exhaust pipes to prevent moisture from entering (or mice from building a nest in the pipe). Then place a note on the handlebar to remind you to remove the plugs before restarting the engine next season.
9. Spray all vinyl and rubber parts with a rubber preservative.
10. Spray the unpainted surfaces with a rust preservative.
11. Repack the wheel bearings as described in Chapter Ten.
12. Clean the brake drums and brake linings. See Chapter Thirteen.
13. Adjust the primary chain as described in this chapter.
14. Adjust the drive chain as described in this chapter.
15. Inflate the tires to the tire pressure reading specified in **Table 2**. If the bike is going to be stored longer than 1 month, support the bike so that all weight is off both tires. Support the bike securely and in a safe manner.
16. Cover the bike with a heavy cover that will provide adequate protection from dust and damage. Do not cover with a plastic tarp as moisture can collect and cause rusting.

### Once A Month

1. Recharge the battery with a 1 amp charger until it is fully charged; see Chapter Nine.
2. Check the electrolyte level and keep it above the battery plates.

### Removal from Storage

Preparing your Harley for use after storage should be relatively easy if proper storage procedures were followed.

1. Remove the plugs from the end of the exhaust pipes.
2. Gap and install 2 new spark plugs.
3. Service the air filter as described in this chapter.
4. Drain the oil that was installed prior to storing the bike. If the oil line and oil tank was plugged off, remove the plugs and reconnect the oil line. Secure the oil line with its clamp. Refill the oil tank or engine with new engine oil as described in this chapter.
5. Service the oil filter as described in this chapter.
6. Reinstall the battery, making sure the vent hose is properly attached and routed. Check the electrolyte level and refill with distilled water.
7. Check the primary and drive chain adjustments as described in this chapter. Readjust if necessary.
8. Perform the lubrication procedures described in this chapter.
9. Inflate the tires to their correct pressure for the load you will be carrying.
10. Check all of the control cables for proper adjustment.
11. Check the brake fluid level on models with rear disc brake. Refill with DOT 5 brake fluid.
12. Make sure that both brakes are working correctly.
13. Make a thorough check of the bike for loose or missing nuts, bolts or screws.
14. Without starting the engine, shift the transmission into 3rd or 4th gear, disengage the clutch and push the bike back and forth a few times. This is to make sure the clutch is disengaging properly. If not, service the clutch as described in Chapter Five.
15. If the fuel tank was drained, refill it with fresh gasoline.

*WARNING*
*The exhaust gases are poisonous. Do not run the engine in a closed area. Make sure there is plenty of ventilation.*

16. Start the engine and check for fuel or exhaust leaks. Make sure the lights and all switches work properly.

**Table 1 PERIODIC MAINTENANCE[1]**

| Interval | Service |
|---|---|
| **Initial 500 miles (800 km); thereafter every 2,500 miles (4,000 km)** | Check brake pad wear<br>Check brake disc wear<br>Inspect fuel valve, fuel lines and all fittings for leaks<br>Check engine idle speed<br>Check battery fluid level; refill with distilled water<br>Check electrical equipment and switches for proper operation<br>Check throttle operation<br>Operate and check choke cable operation<br>Check tire pressure and tread wear |
| **Initial 500 miles (800 km); thereafter every 5,000 miles (8,000 km)** | Change engine oil and replace oil filter<br>Clean, inspect and reoil air filter (1985-1990)<br>Inspect and clean air filter (1991)<br>Inspect tappet oil screen<br>Check rear drive chain or belt tension; adjust if necessary<br>Inspect primary chain<br>Check primary chain tension; adjust if necessary<br>Change primary chaincase oil<br>Check clutch adjustment; adjust if necessary<br>Change transmission housing oil<br>Check brake fluid level; refill with DOT 5 brake fluid<br>Check rear brake pedal adjustment; adjust if necessary<br>Perform general lubrication to equipment specified in this chapter<br>Check ignition timing<br>Check vacuum operated electric switch (V.O.E.S)<br>Check rear swing arm pivot shaft tightness<br>Check engine mount bolt tightness<br>Check rubber engine mount on FLT and FXR<br>Check engine stabilizer links on FLT and FXR<br>Inspect rear shock absorbers<br>Check air suspension components<br>Check all electrical equipment and switches<br>Check cruise control operation and equipment<br>Check all exposed fasteners for tightness[2]<br>Lubricate rear swing arm bearing<br>Lubricate rear swing arm pivot shaft and bearings on FX models |
| **Initial 500 miles (800 km) and first 5,000 miles (8,000 km) thereafter every 10,000 miles (16,000 km)** | Check steering bearing adjustment |
| **Every 2,500 miles (4,000 km)** | Check engine oil level<br>Check primary chaincase oil level<br>Check transmission housing oil level |
| **Every 5,000 miles (8,000 km)** | Inspect rear brake caliper mounting pins and boots; lubricate pins and boots during reassembly<br>Inspect and lubricate rear brake and shifter linkage assembly<br>Lubricate throttle control sleeve<br>Lubricate speedometer cable |
| **Initial 5,000 miles (8,000 km); thereafter every 10,000 miles (16,000 km)** | Inspect spark plug gap and condition |

(continued)

3

**Table 1 PERIODIC MAINTENANCE[1] (continued)**

| | |
|---|---|
| **Every 10,000 miles (16,000 km)** | Replace spark plugs<br>Change front fork oil<br>Lubricate steering bearings<br>Inspect and lubricate wheel bearings |

1. This maintenance schedule should be considered a guide to general maintenance and lubrication intervals. Harder than normal use and exposure to mud, water, high humidity, etc., will naturally dictate more frequent attention to most maintenance items.
2. Except cylinder head bolts. Cylinder head bolts should be tightened by following the procedure listed in Chapter Four. Improper tightening of the cylinder head bolts may cause head leakage.

**Table 2 TIRE PRESSURE (FLT AND FXR)***

| | Front | | Rear | |
|---|---|---|---|---|
| | psi | $kg/cm^2$ | psi | $kg/cm^2$ |
| Rider only | | | | |
| 1984-1985 | | | | |
| FLT/C | ** | ** | ** | ** |
| FLHT/C (K101A) | 28 | 1.9 | 36 | 2.5 |
| FXRS (K291T) | 30 | 2.1 | 36 | 2.5 |
| FXRT (K291T) | 30 | 2.1 | 36 | 2.5 |
| 1986-on | | | | |
| FLT | 36 | 2.5 | 36 | 2.5 |
| FXR | 30 | 2.1 | 36 | 2.5 |
| Rider with one passenger | | | | |
| 1984-1985 | | | | |
| FLT/C and FLHT/C | 28 | 1.9 | 36 | 2.5 |
| FXRS | 30 | 2.1 | 40 | 2.8 |
| FXRT | 30 | 2.1 | 30 | 2.1 |
| FLT with sidecar | 28 | 1.9 | 40 | 2.8 |
| 1986-on | | | | |
| FLT | 36 | 2.5 | 40 | 2.8 |
| FXR | 30 | 2.1 | 40 | 2.8 |

* Tire pressures listed in this table are for original equipment tires. See your dealer or tire manufacturer when equipping your model with non-stock tires.
** Not specified.

**Table 3 TIRE PRESSURE (FXWG, FXEF AND FXSB)***

| | Front | | Rear | |
|---|---|---|---|---|
| | psi | $kg/cm^2$ | psi | $kg/cm^2$ |
| Rider only | | | | |
| FXEF and FXSB | | | | |
| K181 | 30 | 2.1 | 32 | 2.2 |
| K291T | 36 | 2.5 | 36 | 2.5 |
| FXWG | 30 | 2.1 | 32 | 2.2 |
| Rider with one passenger | | | | |
| FXEF and FXSB | | | | |
| K181 | 30 | 2.1 | 32 | 2.2 |
| K291T | 36 | 2.5 | 40 | 2.8 |
| FXWG | | | | |
| "F" rib | 30 | 2.1 | 32 | 2.2 |
| K101A | — | — | 28 | 1.9 |

* Tire pressures listed in this table are for original equipment tires. See your dealer or tire manufacturer when equipping your model with non-stock tires.

**Table 4 ENGINE OIL**

| Type | HD rating | Viscosity | Ambient operating temperature |
|---|---|---|---|
| HD Multigrade | HD 240 | SAE 10W/40 | Below 40° F |
| HD Multigrade | HD 240 | SAE 20W/50 | +40° F to 100° F |
| HD Regular | HD 240 | SAE 50 | +60° F to 100° F Heavy* |
| HD Extra | HD 240 | SAE 60 | +80° F to 100° F Heavy* |

* Not recommended for use when ambient temperature is below 50° F.

**Table 5 ENGINE, CLUTCH AND TRANSMISSION OIL CAPACITIES**

| | |
|---|---|
| Oil tank | |
| FLT | 4.0 qt. (3.8 L, 3.3 imp. qt.) |
| FXR | 3.0 qt. (2.8 L, 2.5 imp. qt.) |
| FXEF, FXSB and FXWG | 4.0 qt. |
| Transmission | |
| 1986-1990 | 16 oz. (473 ml, 0.42 imp. qt.) |
| 1991-on | 20-24 oz. (591-710 ml, 0.41 imp. qt.) |
| Primary chain case | |
| Early 1984 | — |
| Late 1984-1990 | 1.5 qt. (1.4 L, 1.2 imp. qt.) |
| 1991-on | 38-44 oz. (1.1-1.3 L, 1.0-1.1 imp. qt.) |

* See text for correct check and refill procedure.

**Table 6 RECOMMENDED LUBRICANTS AND FLUIDS***

| | |
|---|---|
| Brake fluid | DOT 5 Silicone based |
| Fork oil | HD Type E or equivalent |
| Battery top up | Distilled water |
| Transmission | HD transmission or equivalent |
| Clutch | HD lubricant or equivalent |
| Drive chain | |
| Enclosed drive chain | SAE 50 or SAE 60 |
| Open drive chain (without O-rings) | Any commerical chain lubricant |
| Open drive chain (with O-rings) | Commercial chain lubricant recommended for O-ring chains |

**Table 7 FRONT FORK OIL CAPACITY**

| | Wet | | Dry | |
|---|---|---|---|---|
| | U.S. oz. | cc | U.S. oz. | cc |
| FLT | 7.75 | 229.2 | 8.5 | 251.3 |
| FXR | | | | |
| 1984-1987 FXR and FXRS | 6.25 | 184.8 | 7.0 | 206.9 |
| 1984-1987 FXRD and FXRT | 7.0 | 206.9 | 7.75 | 229.2 |
| 1987 FXRSE | 10.5 | 310.5 | 11.5 | 339.2 |
| 1987-on FXLR | 9.2 | 272 | 10.2 | 300.9 |
| 1988-on FXR, FXRS | 9.2 | 272 | 10.2 | 300.9 |
| 1988-on FXRT, FXRS-SP FXRS-CON | 10.5 | 310.5 | 11.5 | 339.2 |
| FXLR | 9.2 | 272 | 10.2 | 300.9 |
| FXEF | 5.0 | 147.8 | 6.5 | 192.2 |
| FXSB | 7.5 | 221.8 | 6.75 | 199.6 |
| FXWG | 10.2 | 300.9 | 11.2 | 330.4 |

**Table 8 ENGINE TUNE-UP SPECIFICATIONS**

| | |
|---|---|
| Engine compression | 90 psi |
| Spark plugs | |
| Type | HD 5R6A or equivalent |
| Gap | 0.038-0.043 in. |
| Ignition timing | |
| Type | Electronic |
| Timing specifications | |
| Early 1984 | |
| Range | 5°-50° BTDC |
| Start | 5° BTDC |
| Fast idle | 35° BTDC |
| @ 1,800-2,800 rpm | 50° BTDC |
| Late 1984-on | |
| Range | 0°–35° BTDC |
| Start | 5° BTDC |
| Fast idle | 35° BTDC |

**Table 9 CARBURETOR IDLE SPEED SPECIFICATIONS**

| | |
|---|---|
| FLT and FXR | |
| 1984-1989 carburetor | |
| 1984-1987 | |
| Slow idle | 900-950 rpm |
| Fast idle | 1,500 rpm |
| 1988-1989 | |
| Slow idle | 1,000 rpm |
| Fast idle | 1,500 rpm |
| 1990-on | |
| Idle | 1,000 rpm |
| FXEF, FXSB and FXWG | |
| Slow idle | 1,000–1,050 rpm |
| Fast idle | 1,500–1,550 rpm |

## CHAPTER FOUR

# ENGINE



All models are equipped with the V2 Evolution Engine, an air-cooled 4-cycle, overhead-valve V-twin engine. The engine has three major assemblies: engine, crankcase and gearcase. Viewed from the engine's right side, engine rotation is clockwise.

Both cylinders fire once in 720° of crankshaft rotation. The rear cylinder fires 315° after the front cylinder. The front cylinder fires again in another 405°. Note that one cylinder is always on its exhaust stroke when the other fires on its compression stroke.

This chapter provides complete service and overhaul procedures, including information for disassembly, removal, inspection, service and reassembly of the engine.

Work on the engine requires considerable mechanical ability. You should carefully consider your own capabilities before attempting any operation involving major disassembly of the engine.

Much of the labor charge for dealer repairs involves the removal and disassembly of other parts to reach the defective component. Even if you decide not to tackle the entire engine overhaul after studying the text and illustrations in this chapter, it can be cheaper to perform the preliminary operations yourself and then take the engine to your dealer. Since dealers have lengthy waiting lists for service (especially during the spring and summer season), this practice can reduce the time your unit is in the shop. If you have done much of the preliminary work, your repairs can be scheduled and performed much quicker.

General engine specifications are listed in **Table 1. Tables 1-4** are found at the end of the chapter.

## SERVICE PRECAUTIONS

Whenever you work on your Harley, there are several precautions that should be followed to help with disassembly, inspection and reassembly.

1. Before beginning the job, re-read Chapter One of this manual. You will do a better job with this information fresh in your mind.

2. In the text there is frequent mention of the left-hand and right-hand side of the engine. This refers to the engine as it is mounted in the frame, not as it sits on your workbench.

3. Always replace a worn or damaged fastener with one of the same size, type and torque requirements. Make sure to identify each bolt before replacing it. Bolt threads should be lubricated with engine oil, unless otherwise specified, before torque is applied. If a tightening torque is not listed in **Table 3** (end of this chapter), refer to the torque and fastener information in Chapter One.

*NOTE*
*All of the washers and fasteners used in the Evolution engine are hardened. Make sure to use exact replacement fasteners as described in Step 3.*

4. Use special tools where noted. In some cases, it may be possible to perform the procedure with makeshift tools, but this procedure is not recommended. The use of makeshift tools can damage the components and may cause serious personal injury. Where special tools are required, these may be purchased through any Harley-Davidson dealer. Other tools can be purchased through your dealer, or from a motorcycle or automotive accessory store.

5. Before removing the first bolt and to prevent frustration during installation, get a number of boxes, plastic bags and containers to store the parts as they are removed (**Figure 1**). Also have on hand a roll of masking tape and a permanent, waterproof marking pen to label each part or assembly as required. If your Harley was purchased secondhand and it appears that some of the wiring may have been changed or replaced, label each electrical connection before disconnecting it.

6. Use a vise with protective jaws to hold parts. If protective jaws are not available, insert wooden blocks on either side of the part(s) before clamping them in the vise.

7. Remove and install pressed-on parts with an appropriate mandrel, support and hydraulic press. **Do not** try to pry, hammer or otherwise force them on or off.

8. Refer to the **Table 3** at the end of the chapter for torque specifications. Proper torque is essential to assure long life and satisfactory service from components.

9. Discard all O-rings and oil seals during disassembly. Apply a small amount of grease to the inner lips of each oil seal to prevent damage when the engine is first started.

10. Keep a record of all shims and where they came from. As soon as the shims are removed, inspect them for damage and write down their thickness and location.

11. Work in an area where there is sufficient lighting and room for component storage.

## SPECIAL TOOLS

Where special tools are required or recommended for engine overhaul, the tool part numbers are provided. Harley-Davidson tool numbers have a "HD" prefix. These tools can be purchased through Harley-Davidson dealers. Tools unique to Harley-Davidson service can also be purchased through accessory manufacturers.

## SERVICING ENGINE IN FRAME

Many components can be serviced while the engine is mounted in the frame:

a. Rocker arm cover.
b. Cylinder head.
c. Cylinder and piston.
d. Camshaft.
e. Gearshift mechanism.
f. Clutch.
g. Transmission.
h. Carburetor.
i. Starter motor and gears.

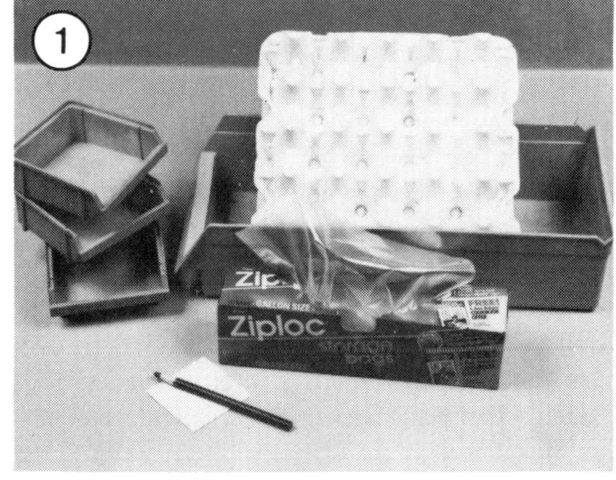


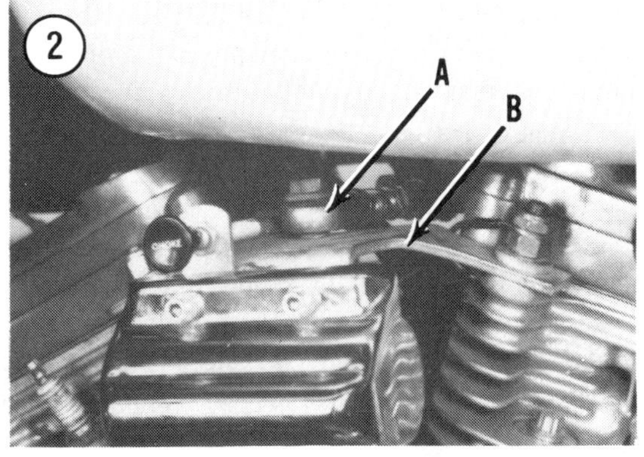

j. Alternator and electrical systems.

## ENGINE

*WARNING*

*Because of the explosive and flammable conditions that exist around gasoline, always observe the following precautions.*

*1. Disconnect the negative battery cable.*

*2. Gasoline dripping onto a hot engine component may cause a fire. Always allow the engine to cool completely before working on any fuel system component.*

*3. Spilled gasoline should be wiped up immediately with dry rags. Then store the rags in a suitable metal container until they can be cleaned or disposed of. Do not store gas or solvent-soaked rags in an open container.*

*4. Do not service any fuel system component while in the vicinity of open flames, sparks or while anyone is smoking.*

*5. Always have a fire extinguisher close at hand when working on the engine.*

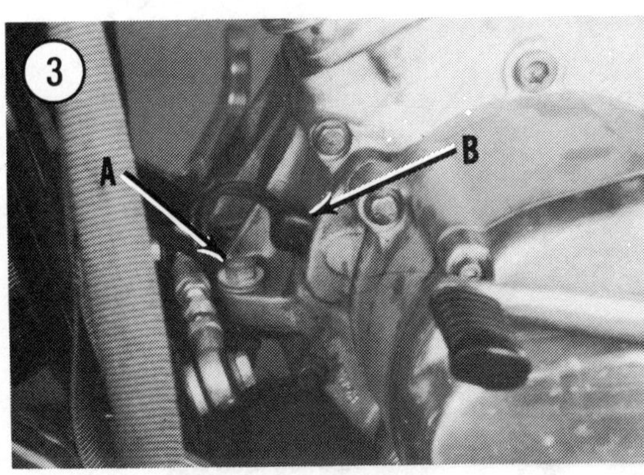


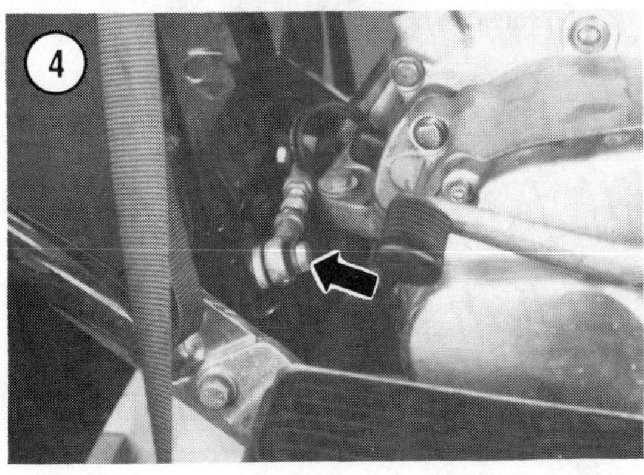


### Engine Removal/Installation (FLT and FXR Models)

1. Thoroughly clean the engine exterior of dirt, oil and foreign material, using one of the cleaners designed for this purpose.
2. If the engine is going to be disassembled, check engine compression and perform a leak down test as described in Chapter Three. Record the measurements so that you can refer to them later.

*NOTE*

*Because the Harley-Davidson models in this manual are not equipped with centerstands, the bike must be secured with a jack or bike stand placed underneath the frame. Block the front and rear wheels to prevent the bike from rolling when removing the engine.*

3. Disconnect the negative battery cable.
4. Remove the fuel tank as described in Chapter Eight.
5. Remove the air cleaner assembly. See Chapter Three.
6. Remove the carburetor as described in Chapter Eight.
7. Remove the exhaust system as described in Chapter Eight.
8. Remove the upper cylinder stabilizer bar from the cylinder head bracket and frame. See A, **Figure 2**. It is not necessary to loosen the stabilizer bar jam nuts.
9. On FXR models, remove the ignition switch.
10. On FLT models, remove the right-hand side lower footboard attaching bolts.
11. Remove the front engine mount center bolt (A, **Figure 3**).
12. Remove the front stabilizer outer end bolt (**Figure 4**).
13. Remove the front engine mount bolts. Then remove the front engine mount with stabilizer attached.
14. Remove the rocker arm covers as described in this chapter.

15. Remove the cylinder heads and cylinder as described in this chapter.
16. On FLT models, remove the left footboard and rear bracket.
17. On FXR models, remove the footrest brackets.
18. On wet clutch models, drain the primary chaincase oil as described in Chapter Three.
19. On FXR models, remove the shift lever.
20. Remove the primary housing as described in Chapter Five.
21. Disconnect the charging system wire connector at the engine crankcase (B, **Figure 3**).
22. Remove the clutch cable bracket at the engine.
23. Disconnect the oil sending unit wire.
24. Drain the oil tank as described in Chapter Three.
25. Label and disconnect the engine-to-oil tank oil lines. Refer to the illustration for your model:
    a. **Figure 5**: Early 1984 FLT and FXR.
    b. **Figure 6**: Late 1984-1990 FLT and FXR.
    c. **Figure 7**: 1991 FLT and FXR.
    d. **Figure 8**: 1992-on FXR.
    e. **Figure 9**: 1992 FLT.
    f. **Figure 10**: 1993-on FLT.
26. Remove the rear engine mount bolts.
27. Check the engine to make sure all wiring, hoses and other components have been disconnected or removed.

*NOTE*
*If the fairing is installed on FXRT models, the front rocker box and the 2 lower fairing support bracket bolts must be removed before removing the engine from the frame. After removing the 2 fairing bolts, raise the fairing approximately one inch and then support its right hand side so that it cannot interfere with engine removal. If you are not*

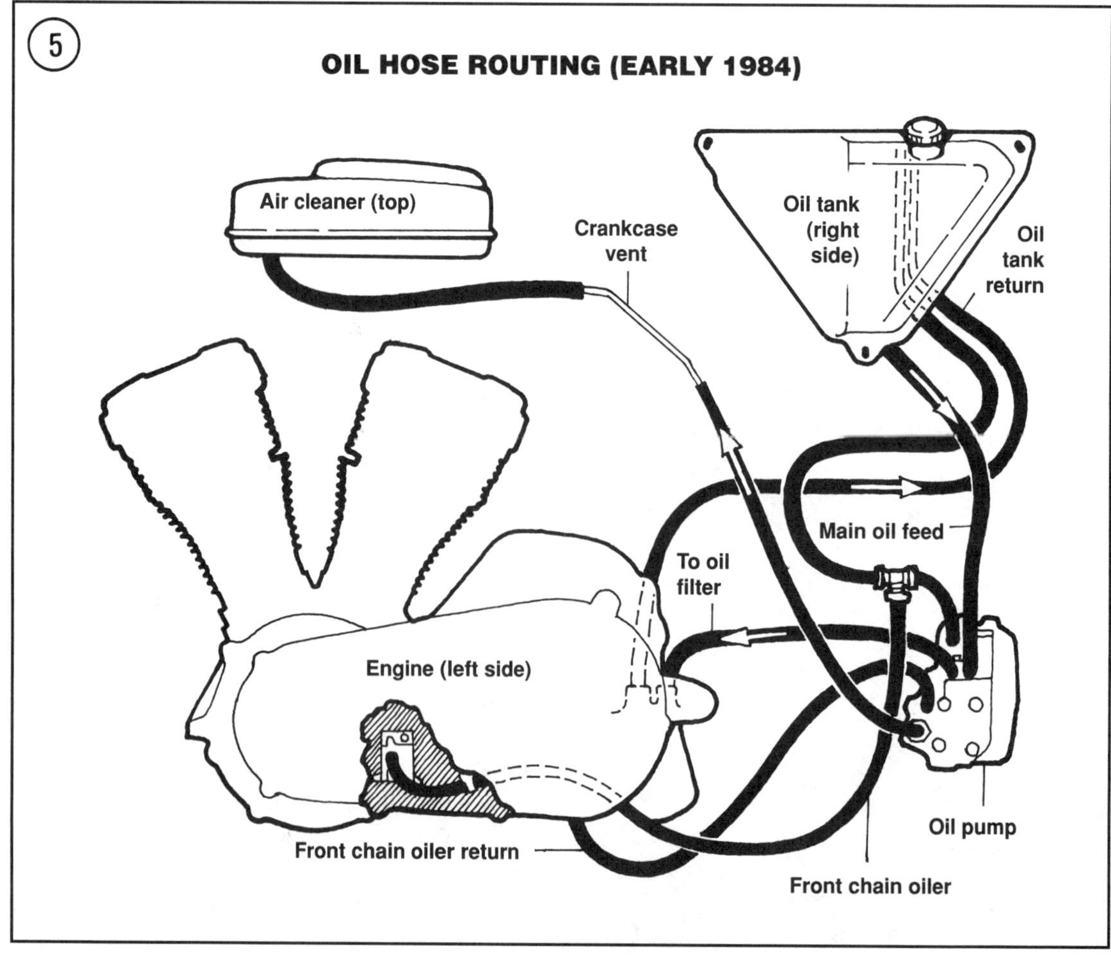

*going to remove the front rocker box, remove the fairing instead.*

*NOTE*
*A minimum of 2 people or a hoist will be required to remove the engine in Step 28.*

28. Remove the engine from the right-hand side of the frame.
29. Place the engine in an engine stand or take it to a workbench for further disassembly.
30. Install by reversing these removal steps. Note the following.
31. After installing the engine in the frame, install the rear engine mounting fasteners and tighten finger-tight.
32. Install the front engine mount and stabilizer. Tighten bolts, washers and nuts finger-tight.
33. Install the primary housing mounting bolts and tighten finger-tight.
34. Tighten the engine mounting bolts in the following order:
    a. Tighten the primary housing-to-engine mounting bolts as described in Chapter Five. Install new safety wire or bend the lockwasher tabs over the bolt heads as required.
    b. Tighten the rear mounting bolts to the torque specification listed in **Table 3**.
35. Adjust the primary chain as described in Chapter Three.
36. Use new hose clamps when reconnecting the oil line hoses.
37. Install a new oil filter and refill the engine oil tank as described in Chapter Three.
38. *Wet clutch models*: Refill the primary chaincase as described in Chapter Three.
39. Adjust the choke or enrichener and the throttle cables as described in Chapter Three.
40. If the rear master cylinder brake hose was disconnected, bleed the rear brake as described in Chapter Thirteen.
41. Tighten the front engine mount and stabilizer bolt. Have a Harley-Davidson dealer check vehicle alignment.
42. If the footboard was loosened or removed, check rear brake pedal adjustment as described in Chapter Three.

4

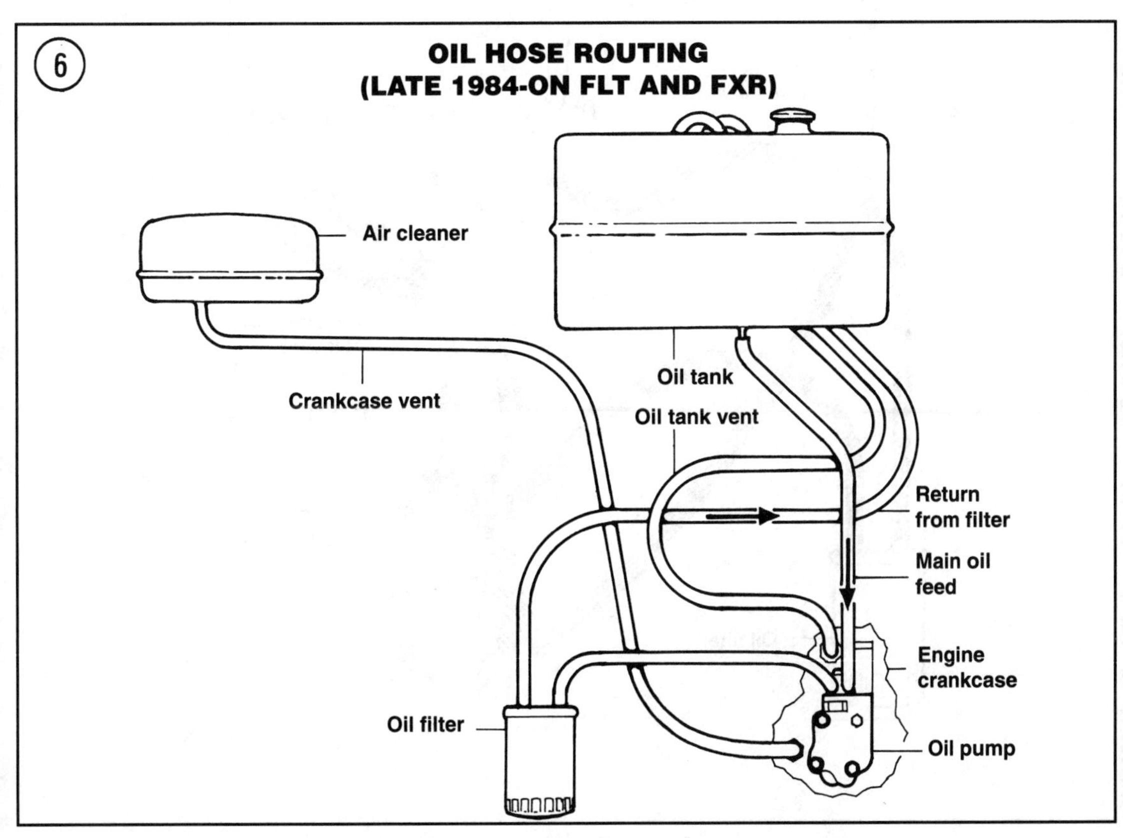

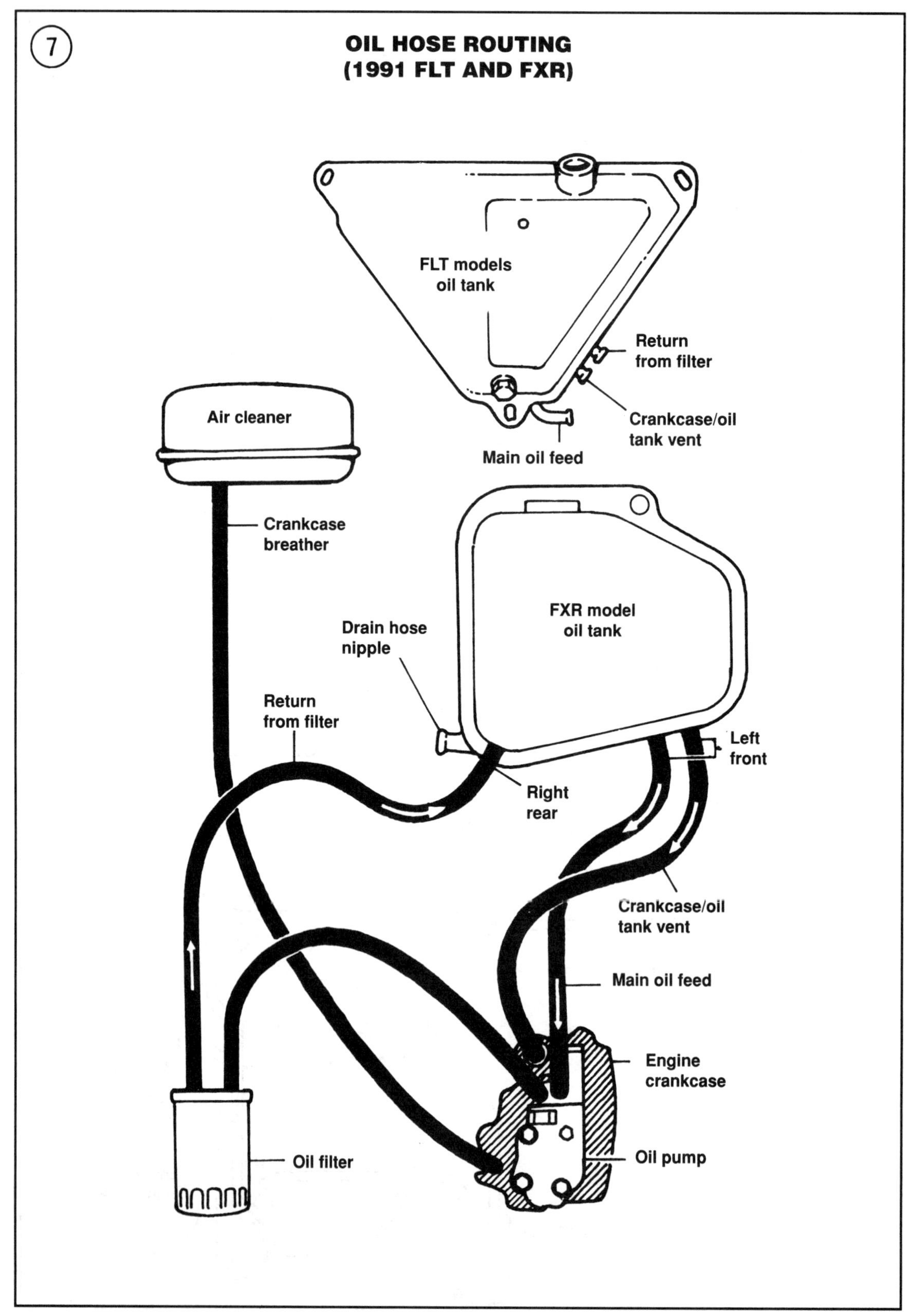
7
OIL HOSE ROUTING
(1991 FLT AND FXR)
FLT models
oil tank
Return
from filter
Crankcase/oil
tank vent
Main oil feed
Air cleaner
Crankcase
breather
FXR model
oil tank
Drain hose
nipple
Return
from filter
Left
front
Right
rear
Crankcase/oil
tank vent
Main oil feed
Engine
crankcase
Oil pump
Oil filter

8
OIL HOSE ROUTING
(1992-ON FXR)
Crankcase breather
Oil tank vent
Air cleaner
Drain hose nipple
Transmission vent hose
Oil filter
To oil filter
Main oil feed hose
Oil return hose from filter
Clip

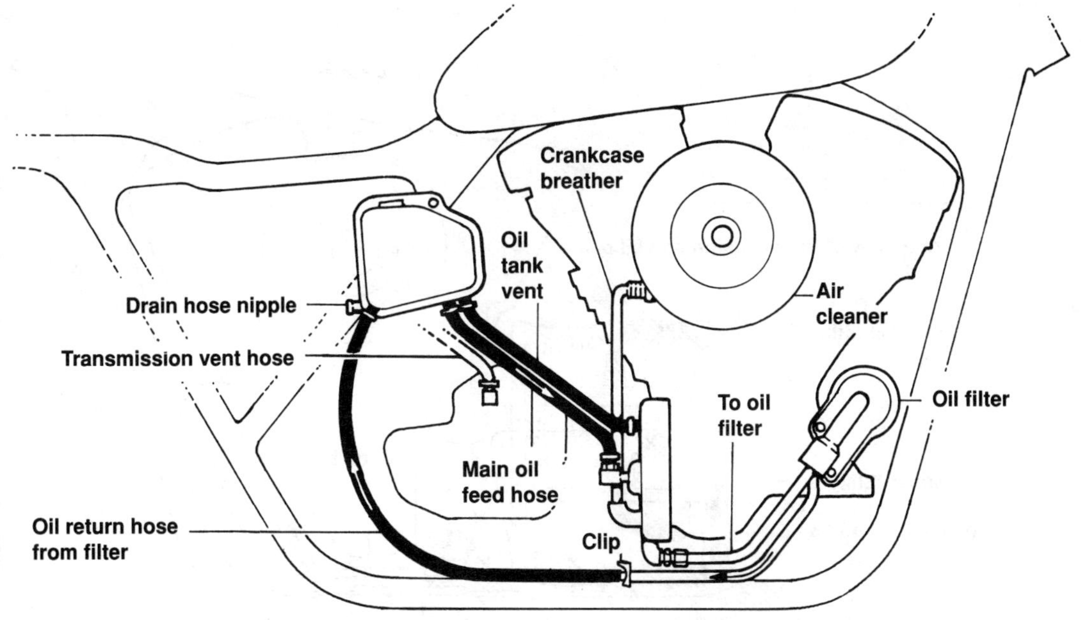

9
OIL HOSE ROUTING
(1992 FLT)
Air cleaner
Return from filter
To oil filter
Oil filter
Oil tank vent
Main oil feed hose

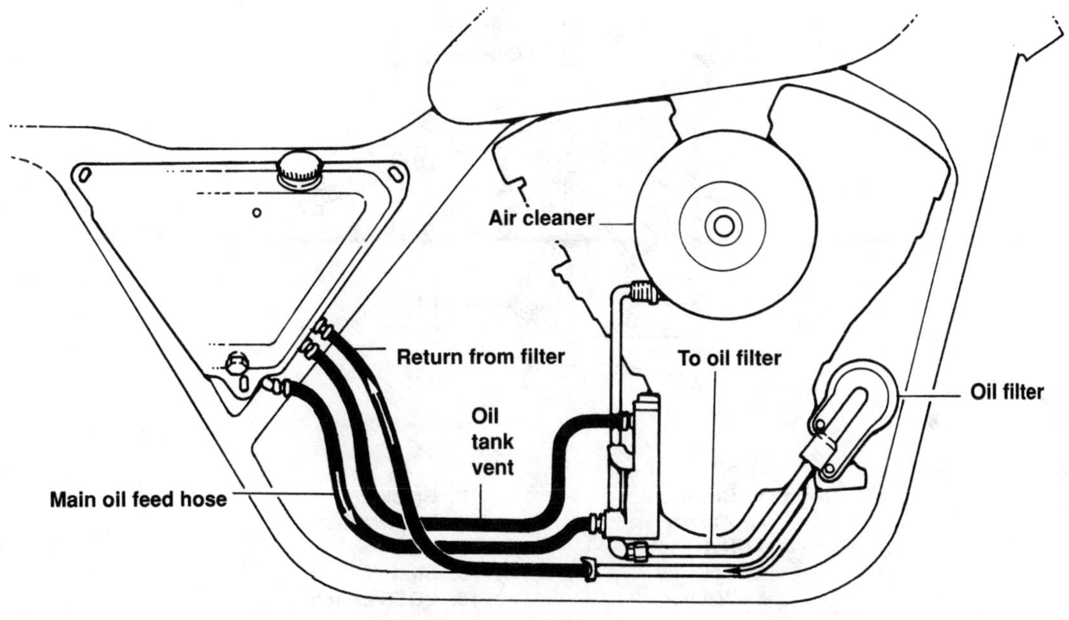

10

**OIL HOSE ROUTING (1993-ON FLT)**

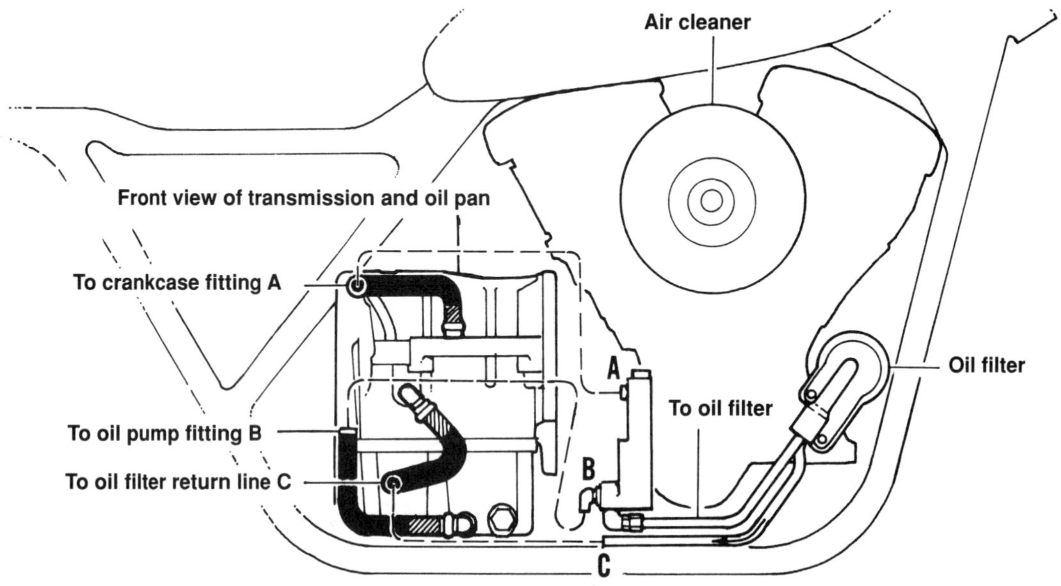
Air cleaner
Front view of transmission and oil pan
To crankcase fitting A
To oil pump fitting B
To oil filter return line C
A
B
C
To oil filter
Oil filter

11

**UPPER CYLINDER HEAD BRACKET (FX)**

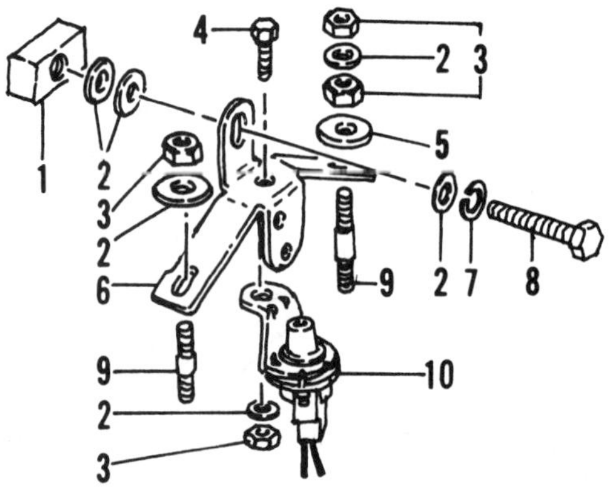
1
2
3
4
5
6
7
8
9
10

1. Block
2. Washer
3. Nut
4. Bolt
5. Washer
6. Bracket
7. Lockwasher
8. Bolt
9. Stud
10. VOES switch

43. Reconnect the negative battery cable.
44. Start the engine and check for leaks.

## Engine Removal/Installation (FX Models)

1. Thoroughly clean the engine exterior of dirt, oil and foreign material, using one of the cleaners designed for this purpose.
2. If the engine is going to be disassembled, check engine compression and perform a leak down test as described in Chapter Three. Record the measurements so that you can refer to them later.

NOTE

*Because Harley-Davidson models in this manual are not equipped with centerstands, the bike must be secured with a jack or bike stand placed underneath the frame. Block the front and rear wheels to prevent the bike from rolling when removing the engine.*

12

13

14

3. Disconnect the negative battery cable.
4. Remove the fuel tank as described in Chapter Eight.
5. Remove the air cleaner assembly. See Chapter Three.
6. Remove the carburetor as described in Chapter Eight.
7. Remove the exhaust system as described in Chapter Eight.

NOTE

*The upper cylinder head bracket (**Figure 11**) is installed with special washers between the bracket and frame. Mark these washers and install them in the same position during reassembly. Likewise, ID all electrical wire brackets and ground wires at the bracket mounting bolts and nuts.*

8. Remove the upper cylinder head bracket assembly. See **Figure 11**, typical.
9. Remove the rocker arm covers as described in this chapter.
10. Remove the cylinder heads and cylinders as described in this chapter.
11. On models without forward foot controls, remove the following components:
   a. Right-hand footrest assembly.
   b. Brake pedal.
   c. Master cylinder assembly. See Chapter Thirteen.
12. On wet clutch models, drain the primary chaincase oil as described in Chapter Three.
13. Remove the primary drive system (**Figure 12**) as described in Chapter Five.
14. Remove the flywheel and stator plate as described in Chapter Nine.
15. Remove the inner primary housing-to-engine mounting bolts as described in Chapter Five. See **Figure 13**, typical.
16. Remove the clutch cable bracket at the engine.
17. Disconnect the wire at the oil pressure switch (**Figure 14**).
18. Drain the oil tank as described in Chapter Three.

19. Label and disconnect the engine-to-oil tank oil lines. See **Figure 15**.

20. Remove the front and rear engine mounting bolts.

21. Check the engine to make sure all wiring, hoses and other components have been disconnected or removed.

*NOTE*
*A minimum of 2 people or an engine hoist must be used when removing the engine.*

22. Remove the engine from the right-hand side.

23. Place the engine in an engine stand or take it to a workbench for further disassembly.

24. Install by reversing these removal steps. Note the following:

25. After installing the engine in the frame, install the engine mounting bolts and nuts and tighten finger-tight.

26. Install the primary housing mounting bolts and tighten finger-tight.

27. Tighten the engine mounting bolts in the following order:

a. Tighten the rear mounting bolts to the torque specification listed in **Table 3**.
b. Check that the front frame pad and the engine mounting boss are properly aligned (**Figure 16**).
c. Tighten the front mounting bolts to the torque specification listed in **Table 3**.
d. Tighten the primary housing-to-engine mounting bolts as described in Chapter Five. Install new safety wire or bend the lockwasher tabs over the bolt heads as required.
e. Install the upper cylinder head bracket and its spacers (**Figure 11**). Check bracket alignment with the engine. Shim the bracket as required, then tighten the mounting nuts to the torque specification listed in **Table 3**.

28. Adjust the primary chain as described in Chapter Three.

29. Use new hose clamps when reconnecting the oil line hoses.

30. Install a new oil filter and refill the engine oil tank as described in Chapter Three.

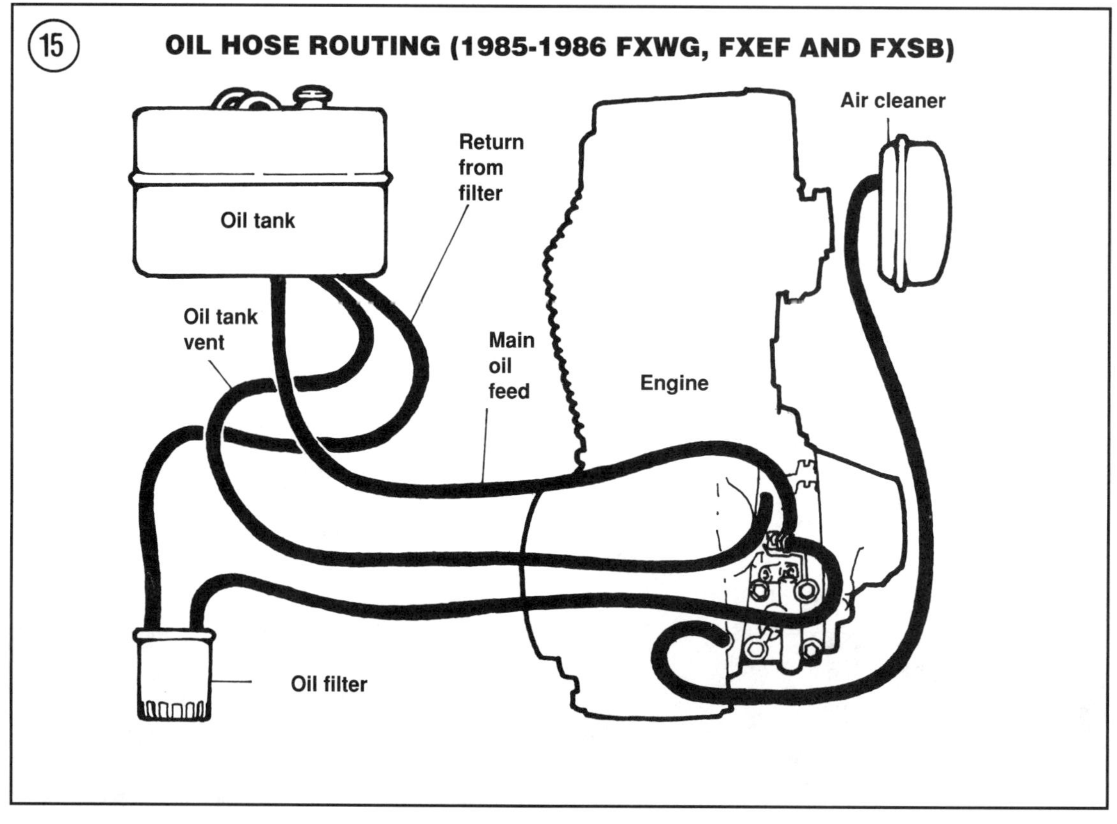

31. *Wet clutch models*: Refill the primary chaincase as described in Chapter Three.
32. Adjust the choke and throttle cables as described in Chapter Three.
33. If the rear master cylinder brake hose was disconnected, bleed the rear brake as described in Chapter Thirteen.
34. If the footboard was loosened or removed, check rear brake pedal adjustment as described in Chapter Three.
35. Start the engine and check for leaks.

## ROCKER ARM COVER/ CYLINDER HEAD

Refer to **Figure 17** and **Figure 18** when performing procedures in this section.

### Removal

This procedure describes rocker arm and cylinder head removal. The cylinder head can be removed with the engine in the frame.
1. Perform Steps 1-8 under *Engine Removal.*
2. Remove the spark plugs.
3. Remove the ignition coil bracket assembly (**Figure 19**).
4. Remove the 4 upper rocker arm cover bolts, washers and the copper or fiber washers.
5. Remove the upper rocker arm cover (**Figure 20**).
6. Remove the middle rocker arm cover (**Figure 21**). Discard the gaskets.
7. Using a screwdriver (**Figure 22**), pry the spring cap retainer downward and remove it. Repeat for each pushrod.
8. Rotate the engine until both valves are closed (on the cylinder head being removed).

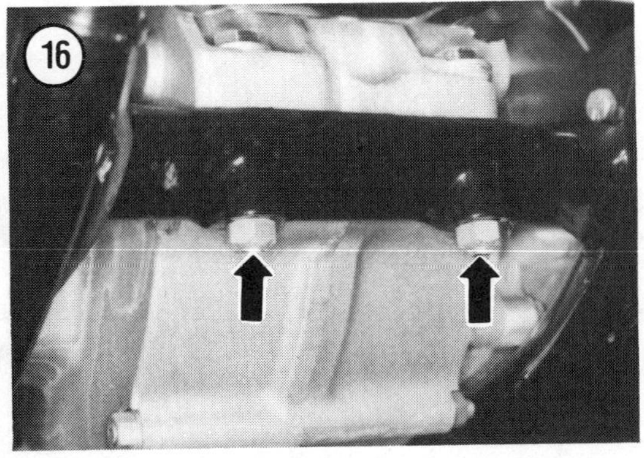


*NOTE*
*Valve position can be determined by observing the rocker arm position (**Figure 23**).*

*NOTE*
*While performing the following steps, mark the individual parts during removal so that they can be reinstalled into their original positions.*

9. Remove the rocker arm cover bolts (A, **Figure 24**) and lift the cover off of the cylinder head (B, **Figure 24**).

*NOTE*
*Mark each pushrod as to its top and bottom position and its position in the cylinder head. The pushrods must be installed in their original positions during reassembly.*

10. Refer to **Figure 25**. Remove each pushrod (**Figure 26**).
11. Remove the pushrod cover assemblies (**Figure 27**).
12. Remove the upper (**Figure 28**) and lower (**Figure 29**) pushrod cover gaskets.
13. Remove the carburetor and intake manifold as described in Chapter Eight.
14. Loosen the cylinder head bolts 1/8 turn at a time in the crisscross pattern shown in **Figure 30**.
15A. *1984-1987*: Remove the cylinder head bolts and washers. See **Figure 31**, typical.
15B. *1988-on*: Remove the cylinder head bolts.
16. Tap the cylinder head with a rubber mallet to free it. Then remove the cylinder head (**Figure 32**).
17. Repeat Steps 1-16 and remove the opposite cylinder head.
18. Disassemble and inspect the rocker arm/cylinder head assembly as described in this chapter.

### Installation

Refer to **Figure 17** and **Figure 18** for this procedure.
1. Clean the cylinder head (**Figure 33**) and cylinder (**Figure 34**) mating surfaces of all gasket residue.
2. Install 2 new O-rings over the dowel pins in the cylinder. See **Figure 35**.

4

(17)

**ROCKER ARM ASSEMBLY**

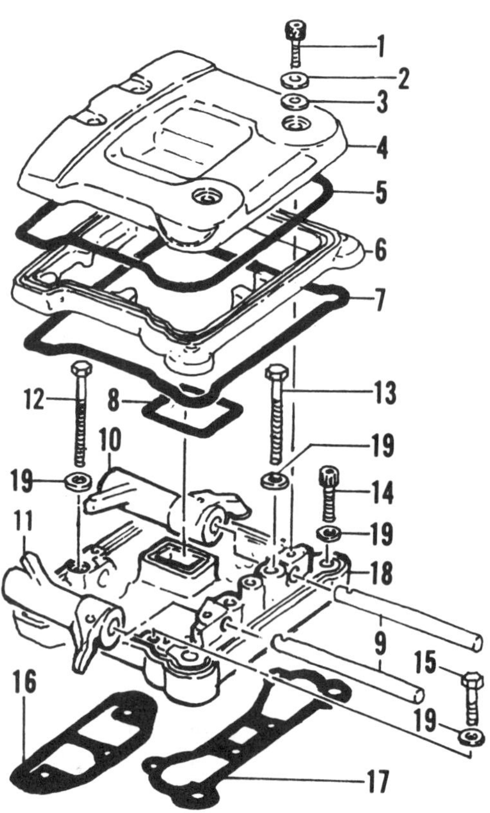


1. Bolt
2. Washers (not used on models)
3. Seals
4. Upper cover
5. Gasket
6. Middle cover
7. Gasket
8. Gasket
9. Rocker arm shafts
10. Rocker arm
11. Rocker arm
12. Bolt
13. Bolt
14. Bolt
15. Bolt
16. Gasket
17. Gasket
18. Lower cover
19. Washers

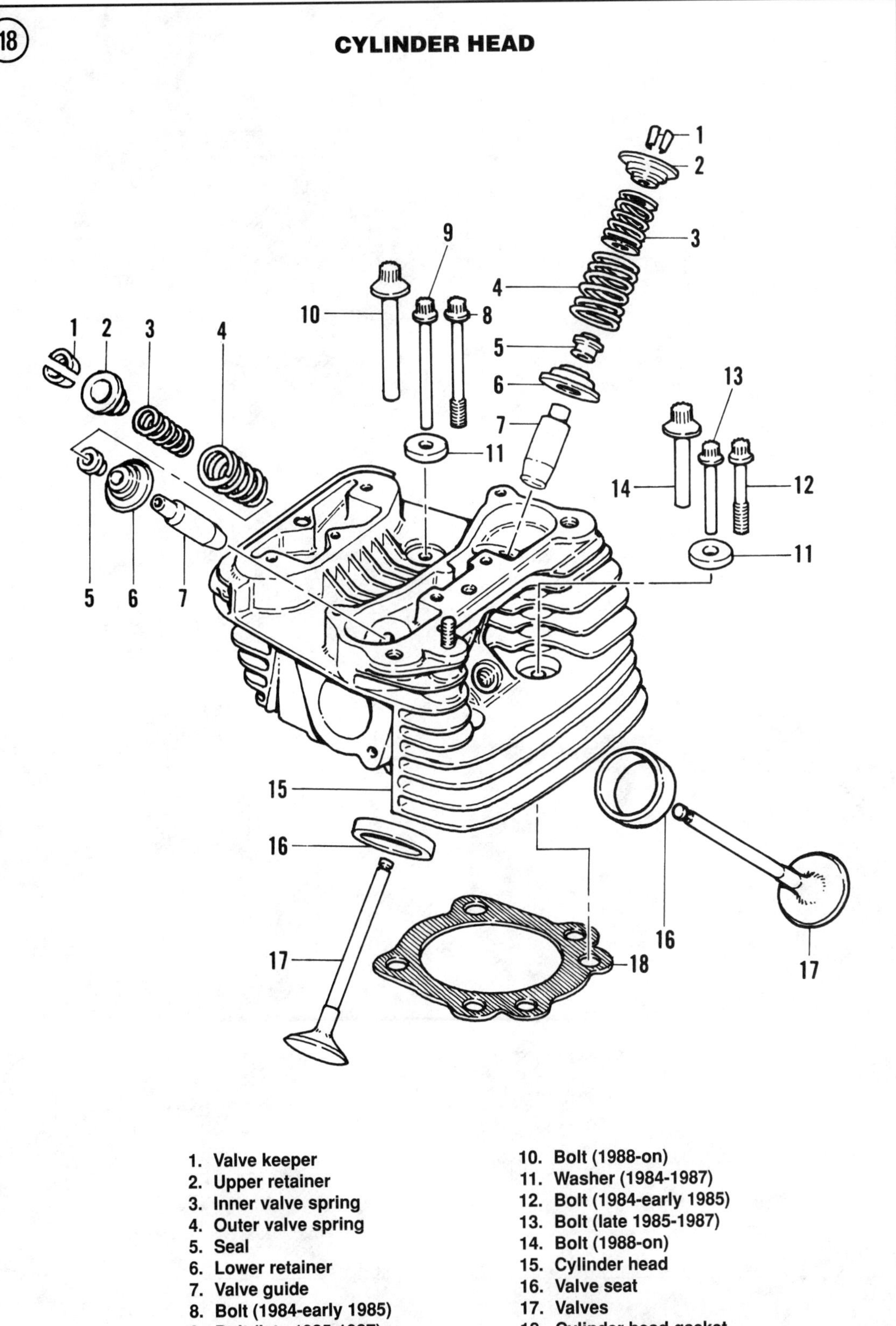


1. Valve keeper
2. Upper retainer
3. Inner valve spring
4. Outer valve spring
5. Seal
6. Lower retainer
7. Valve guide
8. Bolt (1984-early 1985)
9. Bolt (late 1985-1987)
10. Bolt (1988-on)
11. Washer (1984-1987)
12. Bolt (1984-early 1985)
13. Bolt (late 1985-1987)
14. Bolt (1988-on)
15. Cylinder head
16. Valve seat
17. Valves
18. Cylinder head gasket

*CAUTION*

*The cylinder dowel pin O-rings installed in Step 2 must be installed before installing the cylinder head gasket in Step 3 to ensure correct alignment of the cylinder head gasket. If this procedure is not followed, the cylinder head gasket may leak.*

3. Install a new cylinder head gasket, making sure the oil return holes in the gasket line up with the oil holes in the cylinder head. See **Figure 36**.

*NOTE*

*Make sure the bolt holes in the cylinder head are clean and unobstructed.*

4. Install the cylinder head, allowing the dowel pins to align the cylinder head as you install it onto the cylinder. See **Figure 32**.

*NOTE*

*To ensure proper torque readings, clean all cylinder head bolts and washers (1984-1987) in solvent and then dry thoroughly. Replace damaged fasteners as required.*

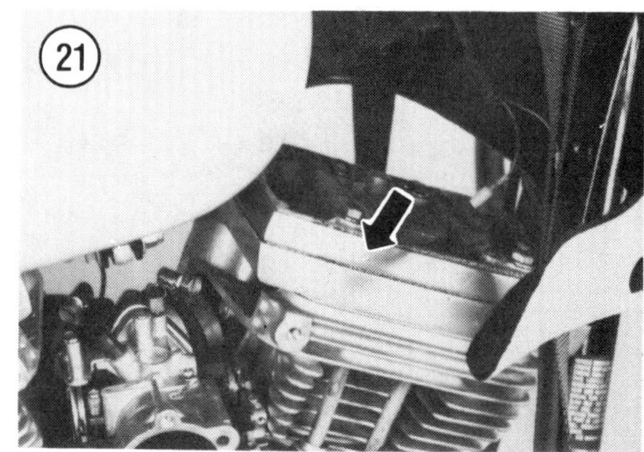

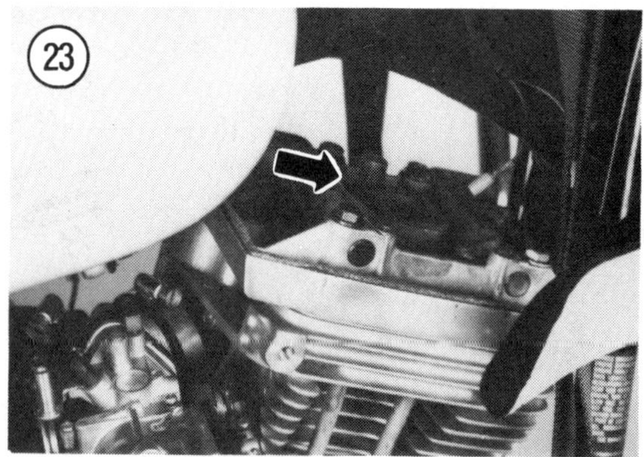


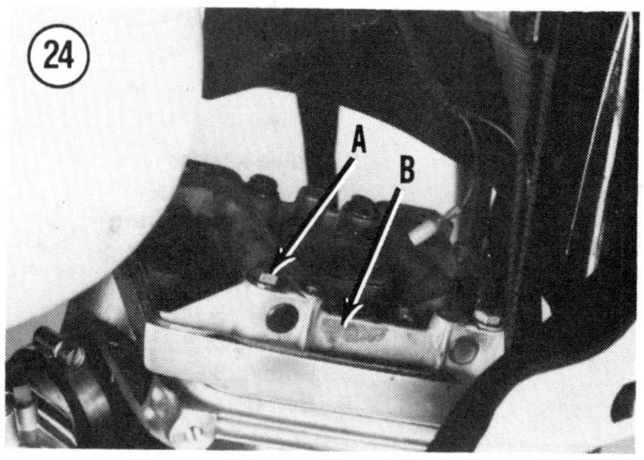

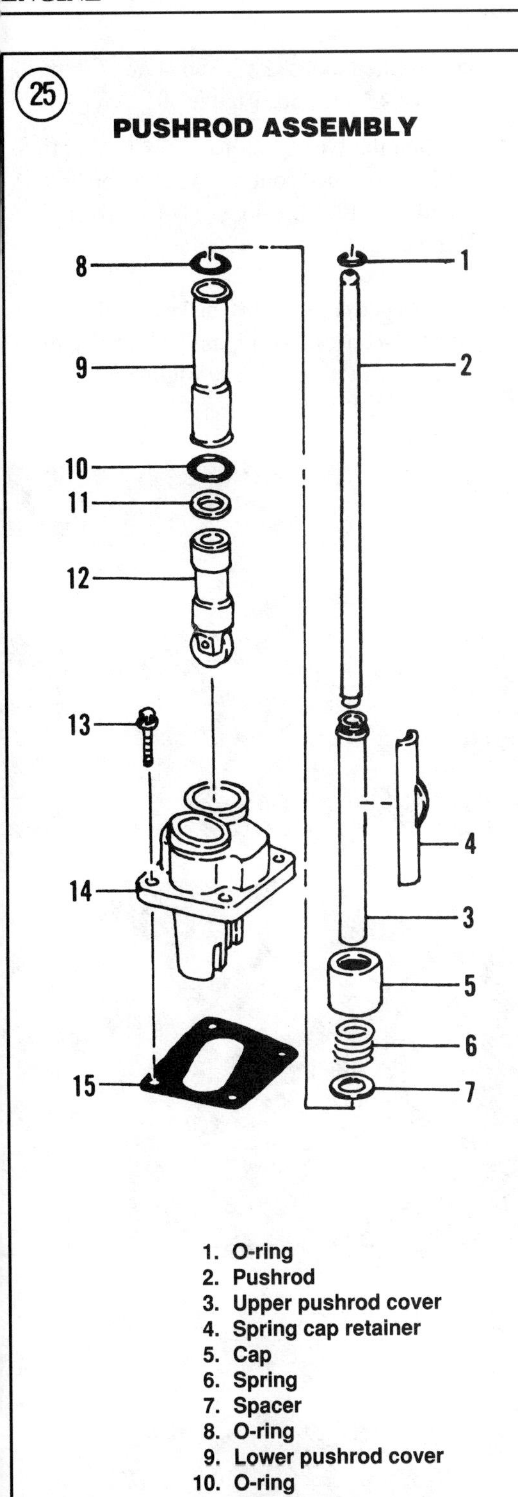
25
PUSHROD ASSEMBLY
1
2
3
4
5
6
7
8
9
10
11
12
13
14
15
1. O-ring
2. Pushrod
3. Upper pushrod cover
4. Spring cap retainer
5. Cap
6. Spring
7. Spacer
8. O-ring
9. Lower pushrod cover
10. O-ring
11. Spacer
12. Tappet
13. Bolt
14. Tappet guide
15. Gasket

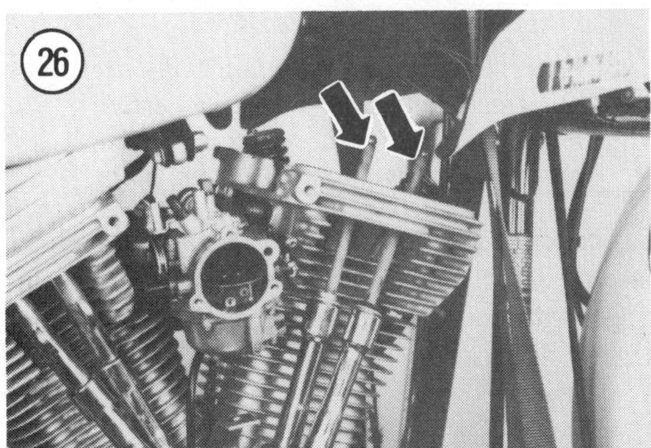
26

27

28

29

*NOTE*
*The cylinder head mounting bolts are not interchangeable between certain model years. When replacing bolts, make sure to purchase the correct bolts.*

5. Coat cylinder head bolt threads and the bottom face of each bolt head with oil and install them finger-tight only. Make sure to install washers on 1984-1987 models.

*NOTE*
*The cylinder head bolts and washers (**Figure 37**, typical) are made of Grade 8 material. Do not substitute these items with a part made of a lower grade material. If replacement is required, purchase new parts from a Harley-Davidson dealer. Late style cylinder head washers cannot be used on early style cylinder head bolts. When replacing cylinder head fasteners, have a Harley-Davidson dealer confirm the style and type of fastener required for your model.*

*CAUTION*
*Failure to follow the torque pattern and sequence in Step 6 may cause cylinder head distortion and gasket leakage.*

6. Tighten the cylinder head bolts in the following order:
   a. Using a torque wrench, tighten the No. 1 bolt to 7-9 ft.-lb. (9.6-12.4 N•m). Then continue and tighten bolts 2, 3 and 4 to 7-9 ft.-lb. (9.6-12.4 N•m). See **Figure 30**.
   b. Tighten the No. 1 bolt to 12-14 ft.-lb. (16.5-19.3 N•m). Then continue and tighten bolts 2, 3 and 4 to 12-14 ft.-lb. (16.5-19.3 N•m). See **Figure 30**.
   c. Using a pen (**Figure 38**), make a vertical mark on the No. 1 bolt head and a matching mark on the cylinder head. See **Figure 39**. Repeat for each bolt.

30

**Front cylinder head**

1 3
2 4

**Rear cylinder head**

2 4
1 3

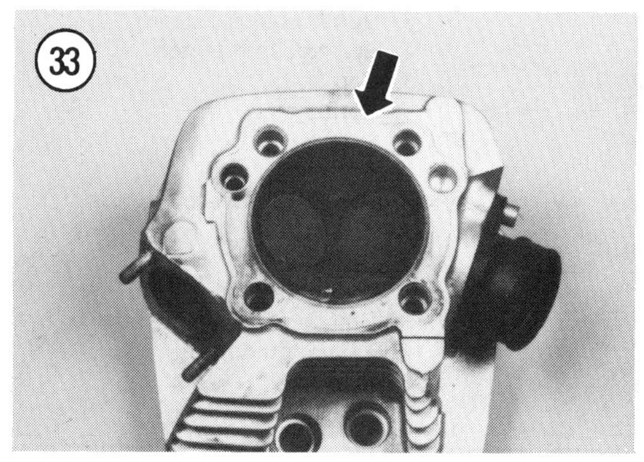

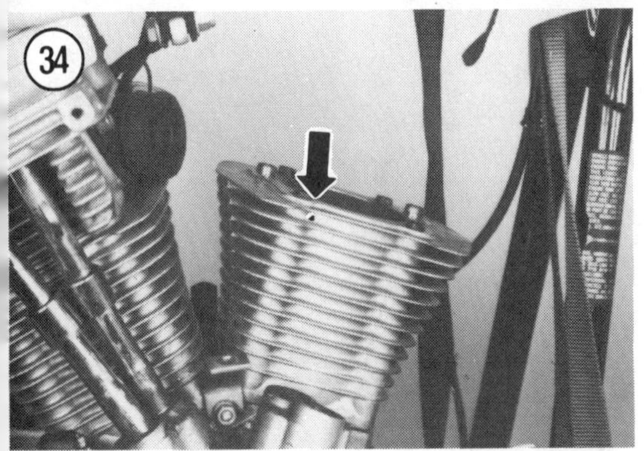


d. Following the torque sequence in **Figure 30**, turn each bolt head 1/4 turn clockwise, using the match marks as a guide. See **Figure 40**.
e. When all match marks are aligned as shown in **Figure 40**, the torque sequence is complete.
f. Repeat for the opposite cylinder head.

*NOTE*
*The rocker boxes and gaskets are not interchangeable between certain model years. When installing gaskets or replacing rocker boxes, make sure to pur-*



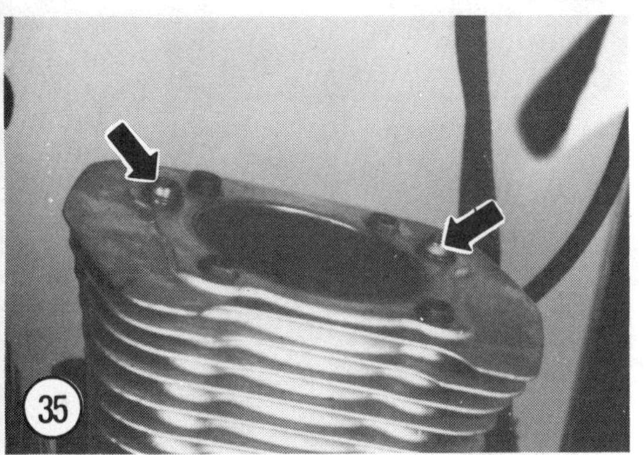

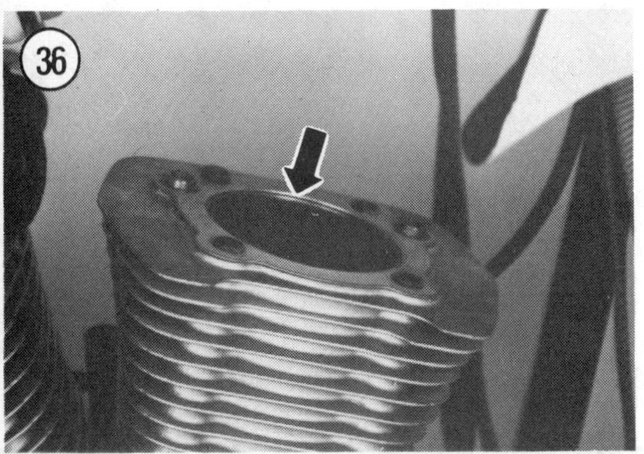


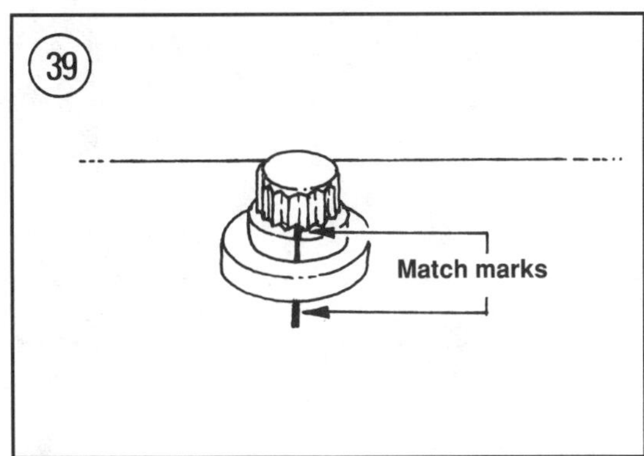


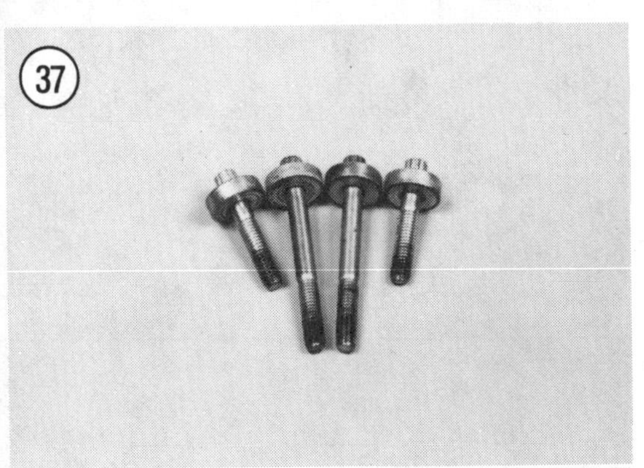


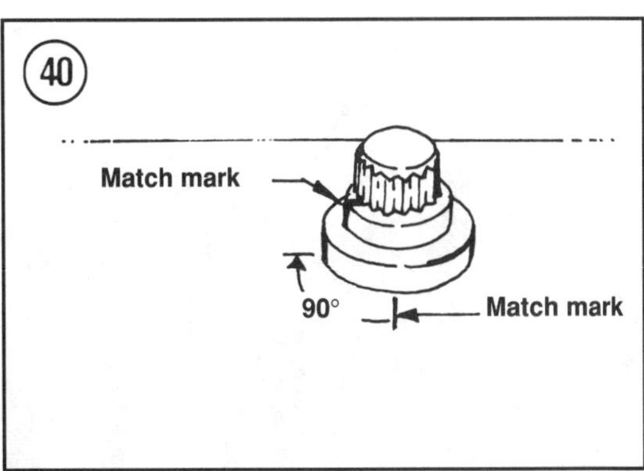

*chase parts for your Harley's model year.*

7. Install 2 new lower rocker arm cover gaskets with the bead on the gaskets facing up. See **Figure 41**.

*NOTE*
*If a valve train component has been replaced or if the valves and seats have been reconditioned, the length of each pushrod must be checked and adjusted by a Harley-Davidson dealer as special tools are required.*

8. Install new upper (**Figure 28**) and lower (**Figure 29**) pushrod O-rings.
9. Install the lower pushrod covers (**Figure 27**).

*NOTE*
*The pushrods are color coded for proper installation: rear exhaust—purple, rear intake—blue, front intake—yellow, front exhaust—green.*

10. Install the pushrods (**Figure 26**) in their original positions, using the marks made prior to removal.

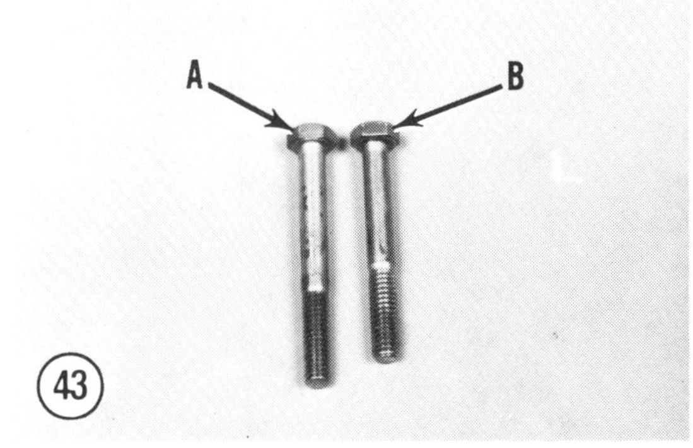

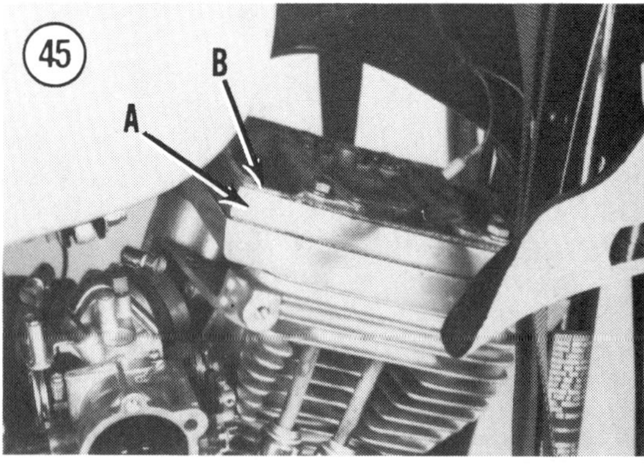


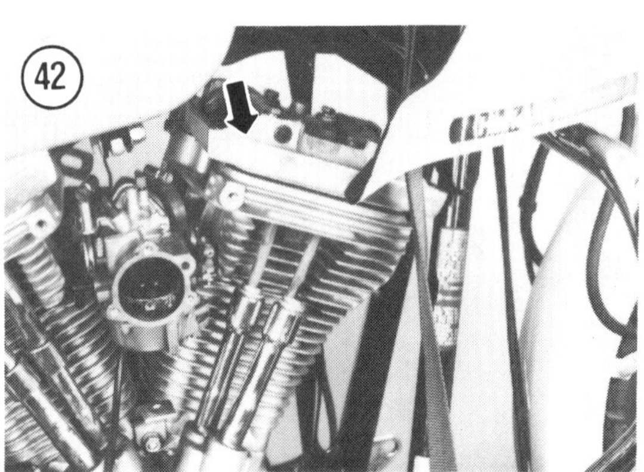


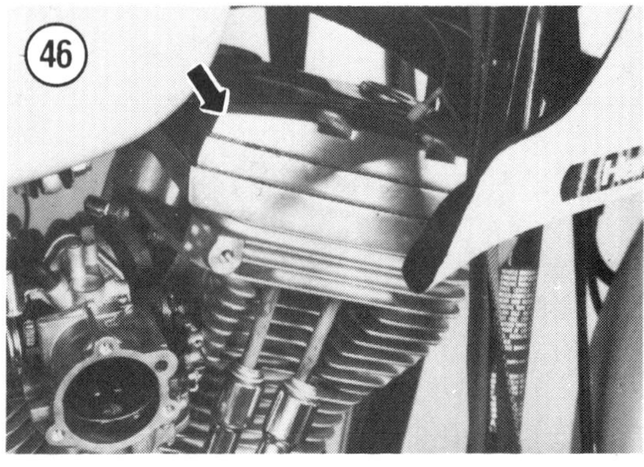

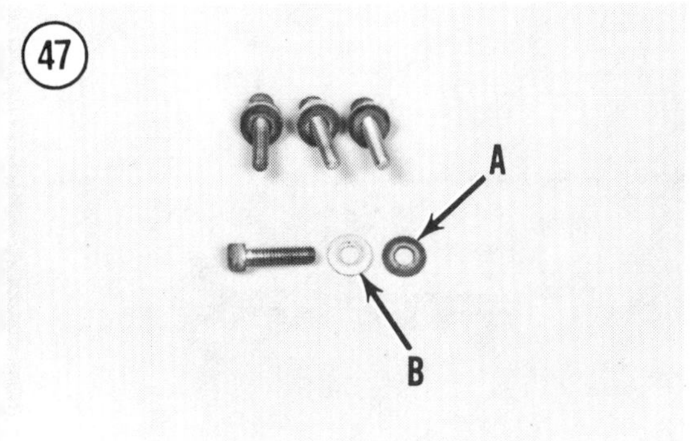

*NOTE*

*Before installing the rocker arm cover in Step 11, make sure that the cam is positioned with its face circle facing up.*

11. Position the rocker arm cover (**Figure 42**) onto the cylinder head.

12. The rocker arm cover bolt sizes are different. Install the longer bolts (A, **Figure 43**) on the right-hand side.

*NOTE*

*If the right-hand bolts do not drop into position correctly, the rocker arm shafts are not aligned properly. Refer to* ***Rocker Arm*** *in this chapter.*

13. Tighten the rocker cover bolts in a crisscross pattern to the torque specification listed in **Table 3**. Tighten the bolts in small increments to help bleed the lifters.

14. Check that the pushrods spin freely.

*CAUTION*

*If the pushrods do not spin freely, do not start the engine as the valves could be damaged. If the valves are tight, have the pushrods gauged by a Harley-Davidson dealer.*

15. Install 2 new rocker arm cork gaskets at the positions shown in **Figure 44**.

16. Position the middle rocker arm cover (A, **Figure 45**) onto the engine. Then install a new cork gasket (B, **Figure 45**).

17. Install the rocker arm cover (**Figure 46**). Then install the 4 cover screws with the steel and new copper or fiber washers.

*NOTE*

*The copper or fiber washers (A,* ***Figure 47****) must be installed under the steel washers (B,* ***Figure 47****).*

18. Check that the middle rocker arm cover is spaced evenly on all sides, then tighten the cover screws to 10-13 ft.-lb. (13.8-17.9 N•m) in a crisscross pattern.

19. Push the upper pushrod cover up (**Figure 48**) and seat it in the rocker arm cover (**Figure 49**). Then position the spring cap retainer as shown in **Figure 50**. Place a screwdriver under the retainer. Then lift the screwdriver up slightly and slide the retainer into position.

20. Reverse Steps 1-8 under *Engine Installation*.

### Rocker Arm Removal/Inspection/Installation

Label all parts before disassembly so they will be installed in their original positions. Refer to **Figure 17** for this procedure.

1. See **Figure 51**. Remove the rocker arm shafts (A) and remove the rocker arms (B).

2. Clean all parts in solvent. Blow compressed air through all oil passages to make sure they are clear.

3. Examine the rocker arm pads and ball sockets (**Figure 52**) for pitting and excessive wear; replace the rocker arms if necessary.

4. Measure the rocker arm shaft with a micrometer (**Figure 53**) where it rides in the lower rocker arm cover. Then measure the rocker arm shaft bore (**Figure 54**) in the lower rocker arm cover. Subtract the shaft O.D. from the bore I.D. to obtain rocker arm shaft clearance. Replace worn parts if the clearance exceeds the specifications in **Table 2**.

5. Measure the rocker arm bushing inside diameter (**Figure 55**) with a small hole gauge. Bushing re-

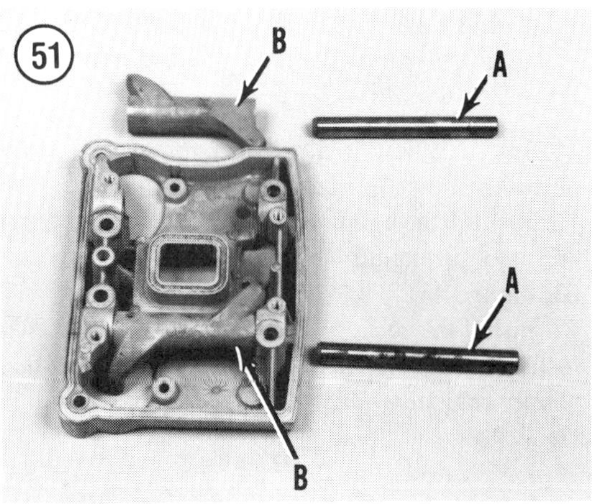

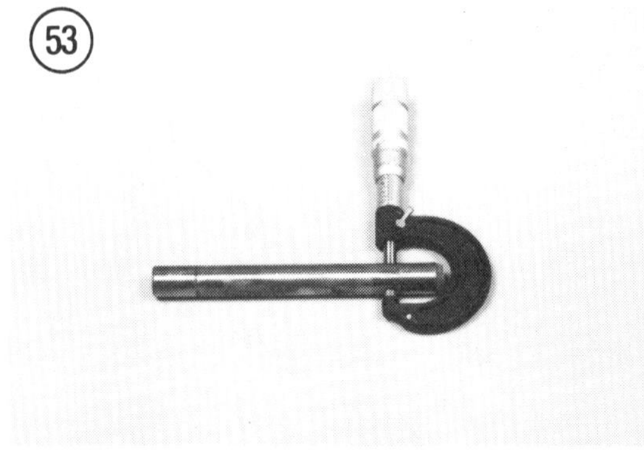


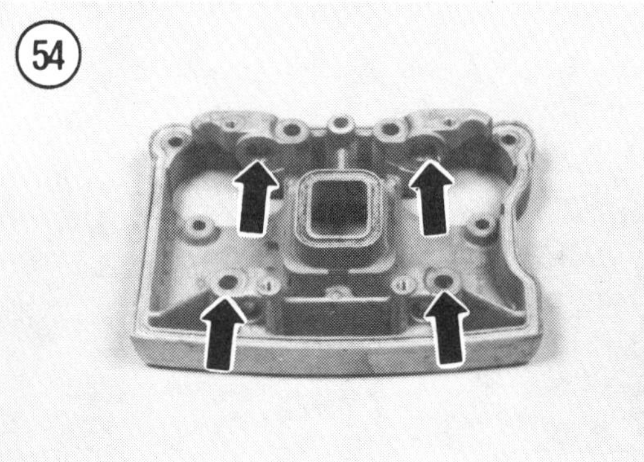


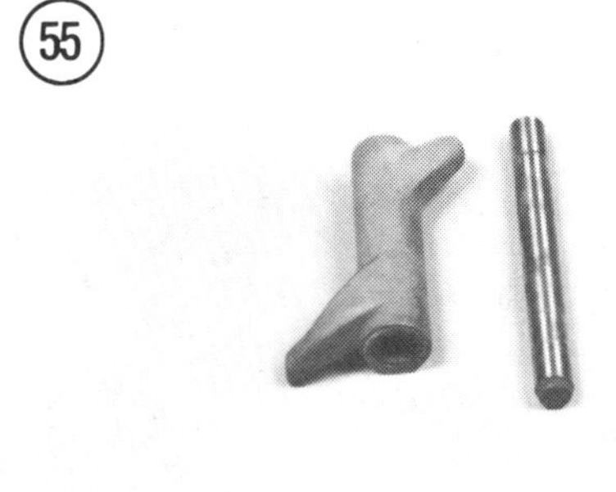

placement should be referred to a Harley-Davidson dealer as the new bushings must be reamed to size after installation.

6. After completing Steps 3-5 and replacing worn parts (if required), perform the following:

a. Install the rocker arms and rocker arm shafts into the lower cover (**Figure 56**).

b. Check the rocker arm end clearance with a feeler gauge (**Figure 57**).

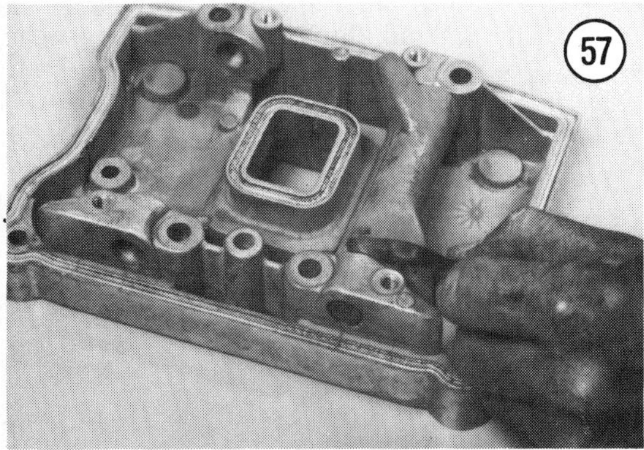


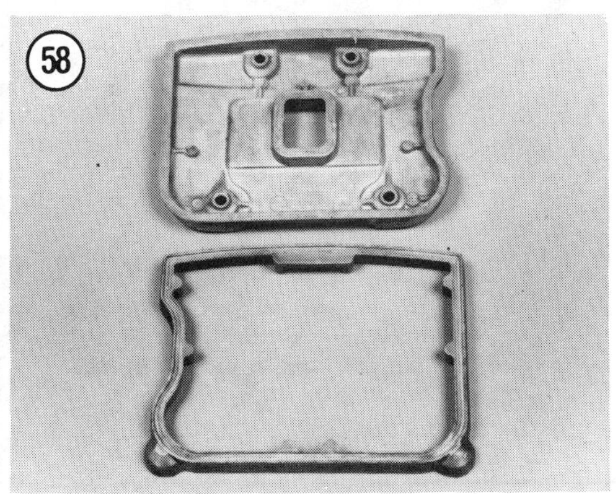

c. Replace the rocker arm or lower cover or both parts if the end clearance exceeds specifications (**Table 2**).

7. Inspect the upper and middle cover gasket surfaces (**Figure 58**) for damage or warpage. Replace parts as necessary.

8. Assemble the rocker arm assembly as follows:

*NOTE*
*Following the ID marks made during disassembly, install parts in their original positions.*

a. Place the rocker arms into the rocker arm cover (B, **Figure 51**).

b. Install the rocker arm shafts partway so that the machined notch in each shaft faces to the right-hand side (**Figure 59**) of the cover. Then turn each shaft so that the machined notch aligns with the bolt hole slot in the cover. This allows the cover bolts to be installed correctly during cover installation. In addition, the cover bolts engage the shaft machined notch and lock the shafts in position during engine operation.

### Cylinder Head Inspection

Refer to **Figure 18** for this procedure.

1. Without removing valves, remove all carbon deposits from the combustion chambers (**Figure 60**) with a wire brush.

*CAUTION*
*If the combustion chambers are cleaned while the valves are removed, make sure to keep the scraper or wire brush away from the valve seats to prevent damaging the seat surfaces. A damaged or*

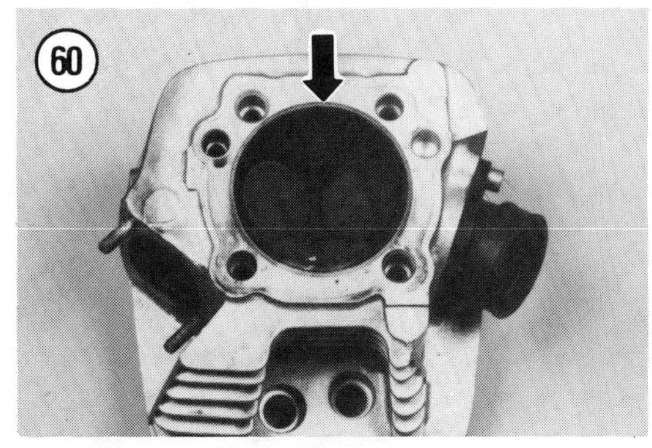


4

*even slightly scratched valve seat will cause poor valve seating.*

2. Examine the spark plug threads in the cylinder head (**Figure 61**) for damage. If damage is minor or if the threads are dirty or clogged with carbon, use a spark plug thread tap to clean the threads following the manufacturer's instructions. If thread damage is severe, refer further service to a Harley-Davidson dealer or machine shop.

3. After all carbon is removed from combustion chambers, valve ports and the spark plug thread holes are repaired, clean the entire head in solvent. Use compressed air, if available, to dry the head thoroughly and to remove small debris from passages.

4. Clean away all carbon on the piston crowns. Do not remove the carbon ridge at the top of the cylinder bore.

5. See **Figure 62**. Check for cracks in the combustion chamber (A) and exhaust ports (B). A cracked head must be replaced.

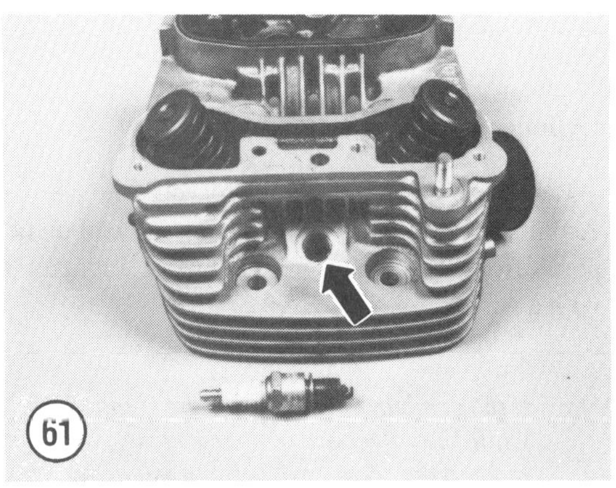


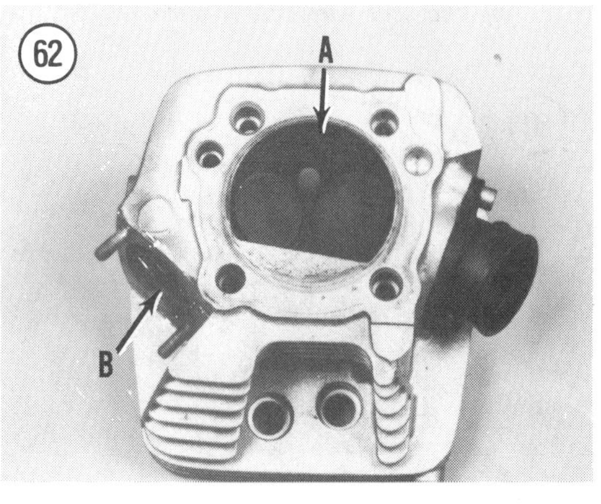


6. After the head has been thoroughly cleaned, place a straightedge across the gasket surface at several points (**Figure 63**). Measure warp by inserting a feeler gauge between the straightedge and cylinder head at each location. Maximum allowable warpage is listed in **Table 2**. If warpage exceeds this limit, refer service to your dealer.

7. Check the rocker arm cover mating surface using the procedure in Step 6. There should be no warpage.

8. Check the valves and valve guides as described under *Valves and Valve Components* in this chapter.

9. Check the pushrods (**Figure 64**) for bending, wear or damage. Check the pushrod ends for wear. Replace if necessary.

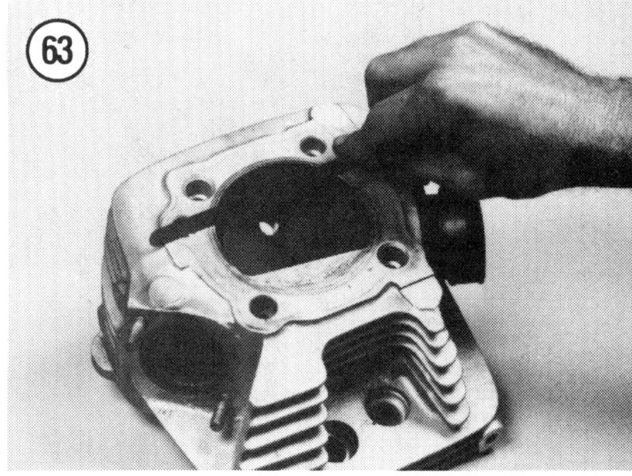

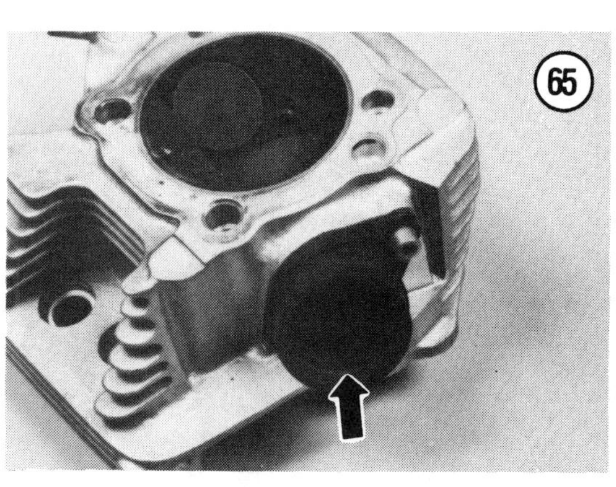

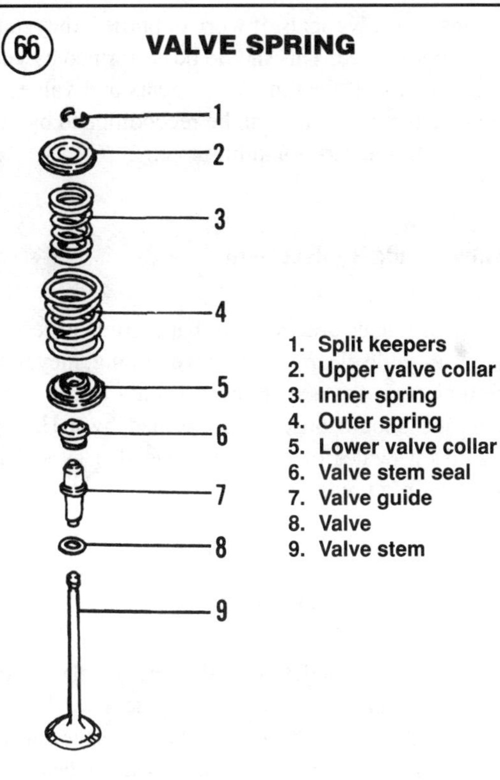


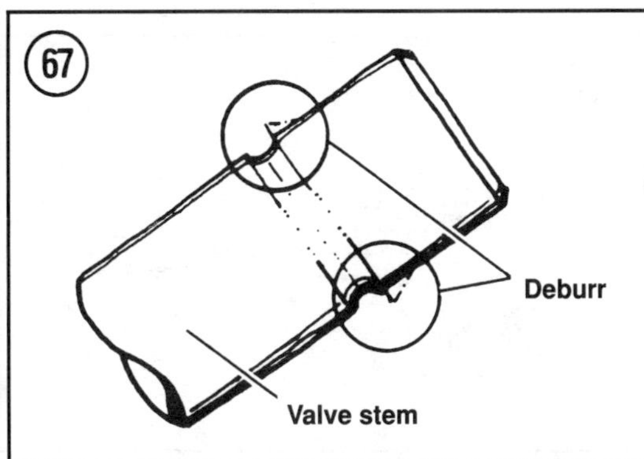


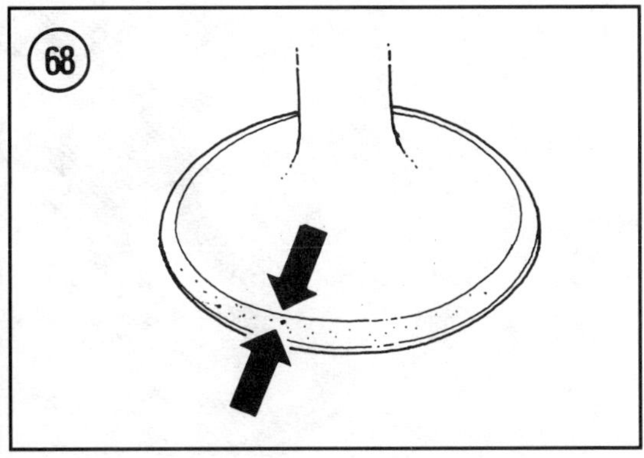


10. *1984-1989*: Check the intake manifolds (**Figure 65**) for cracks or tear damage that could allow unfiltered air to enter the engine. Also check the manifold bolts for tightness. If you removed the manifold, install it with a new gasket.

## VALVES AND VALVE COMPONENTS

General practice among those who do their own service is to remove the cylinder heads and take them to a dealer or machine shop for inspection and service. Since the cost is low relative to the required effort and equipment, this is the best approach, even for experienced mechanics.

Refer to **Figure 66** for this procedure.

*CAUTION*
*All component parts of each valve assembly must be kept together. Do not mix with like components from other valves or excessive wear may result.*

1. Remove the cylinder head(s) as described in this chapter.
2. Install a valve spring compressor squarely over the valve retainer with other end of tool placed against valve head.
3. Tighten valve spring compressor until split valve keeper separates. Lift out split keeper with needlenose pliers.
4. Gradually loosen valve spring compressor and remove from head. Lift off valve retainer.

*CAUTION*
*Remove any burrs from the valve stem grooves before removing the valve (**Figure 67**); otherwise the valve guides will be damaged.*

5. Remove inner and outer springs, retainer and valve.
6. Repeat Steps 2-5 and remove remaining valves.
7. Remove and discard all of the valve guide oil seals.

### Inspection

1. Clean valves with a wire brush and solvent.
2. Inspect the contact surface of each valve for burning (**Figure 68**). Minor roughness and pitting can be removed by lapping the valve as described in this chapter. Excessive unevenness to the contact

4

surface is an indication that the valve is not serviceable. The contact surface of the valve may be ground on a valve grinding machine, but it is best to replace a burned or damaged valve with a new one.

3. Inspect the valve stems for wear and roughness.

4. Measure valve stem O.D. with a micrometer (**Figure 69**). Record O.D. for each valve.

5. Remove all carbon and varnish from the valve guides with a stiff spiral wire brush.

> *NOTE*
> *Step 6 requires special measuring equipment. If you do not have the required measuring devices, proceed to Step 8.*

6. Measure each valve guide at top, center and bottom with a small hole gauge. Record I.D. for each valve guide.

7. Subtract the measurement made in Step 4 from the measurement made in Step 6. The difference is the valve guide-to-valve stem clearance. See specifications in **Table 2** for specified clearance. Replace any guide and valve that is not within tolerance.

8. Insert each valve in its guide. Hold the valve just slightly off its seat and rock it sideways. If it rocks more than slightly, the guide is probably worn and should be replaced. As a final check, take the head to a dealer and have the valve guides measured.

9. Measure the valve spring free length with a vernier caliper (**Figure 70**). All should be of length specified in **Table 2** with no bends or other distortion. Replace defective springs.

10. Check the valve spring retainer and split keepers. Replace worn or damaged parts as required.

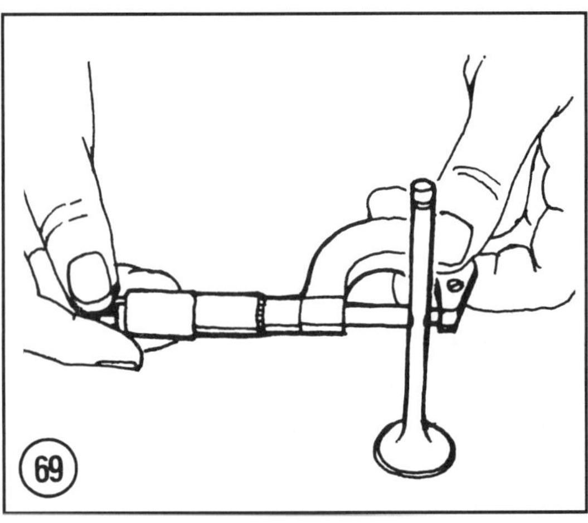


11. Inspect valve seats. If worn or burned, they must be reconditioned. This should be performed by your dealer or local machine shop. Seats and valves in near-perfect condition can be reconditioned by lapping with fine carborundum paste.

### Valve Guide Replacement

When guides are worn so that there is excessive stem-to-guide clearance or valve tipping, they must be replaced. Replace all, even if only one is worn. This job should only be performed by a Harley-Davidson dealer or qualified specialist as special tools are required.

### Valve Seat Reconditioning

This job is best left to your dealer or local machine shop. They have the special equipment and knowledge for this exacting job. You can still save considerable money by removing the cylinder head and taking just the head to the shop.

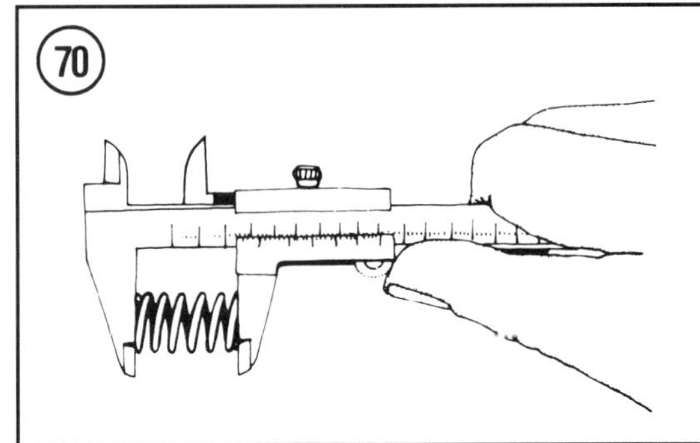


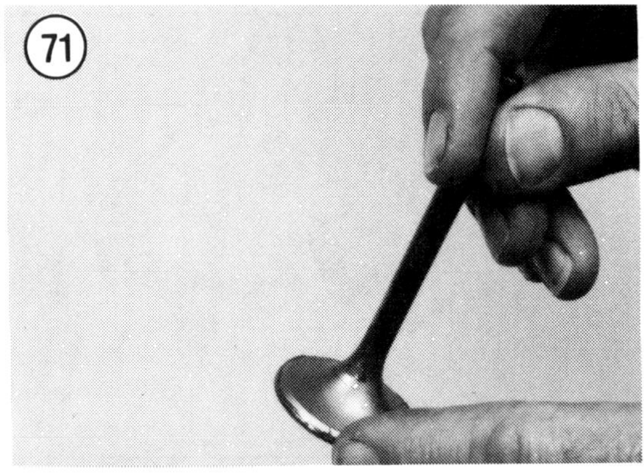

### Valve Lapping

Valve lapping is a simple operation which can restore the valve seal without machining if the amount of wear or distortion is not too great.

1. Smear a light coating of fine grade valve lapping compound on seating surface of valve (**Figure 71**).
2. Insert the valve into the head.
3. Wet the suction cup of the lapping stick (**Figure 72**) and stick it onto the head of the valve. Lap the valve to the seat by spinning tool between hands while lifting and moving valve around seat 1/4 turn at a time.
4. Wipe off valve and seat frequently to check progress of lapping. Lap only enough to achieve a precise seating ring around valve head (**Figure 73**).
5. Closely examine valve seat in cylinder head. It should be smooth and even with a smooth, polished seating "ring."
6. Thoroughly clean the valves and cylinder head in solvent to remove all grinding compound. Any compound left on the valves or the cylinder head will end up in the engine and cause premature and rapid engine wear.
7. After the lapping has been completed and the valve assemblies have been reinstalled into the head the valve seal should be tested. Check the seal of each valve by pouring solvent into each of the intake and exhaust ports. There should be no leakage past the seat. If leakage occurs, combustion chamber (**Figure 60**) will appear wet. If fluid leaks past any of the seats, disassemble that valve assembly and repeat the lapping procedure until there is no leakage.

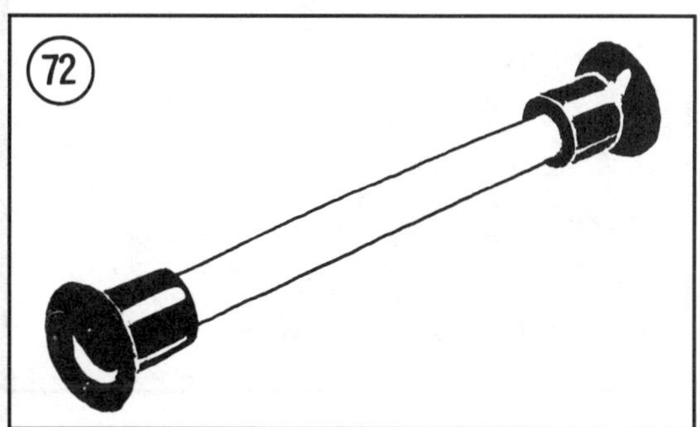

72

73

### Installation

1. Lap valves as described in this chapter.
2. Coat a valve stem with oil and insert the valve into its valve guide in cylinder head.
3. Install the bottom retainer.
4. Install new valve guide seals as follows:
   a. Place a protective cover over the end of the valve stem (covering the valve keeper groove on valve stem).
   b. Apply a small amount of RC 620 Loctite (green) to the outside portion on the valve guide near the top.

*CAUTION*
*Installing the valve guide seals without the protective cover described in substep c will cause seal damage.*

   c. Wipe the protective cover with oil and place a new valve guide seal on the cover. Then use a socket and carefully drive the seal over the cover and onto the valve stem. Drive the seal squarely onto the valve stem until it bottoms out against the valve guide. Do not continue to drive it after it bottoms out or you will damage it.

*NOTE*
*Harley-Davidson sells a valve seal installation tool (part No. HD-34643) and driver handle (part No. HD-34740) that can be used to install the valve guide seals accurately.*

5. Install valve springs. Then install the upper valve spring retainer.
6. Push down on upper valve spring collar with the valve spring compressor and install valve keepers. After releasing tension from compressor, examine valve keepers (**Figure 74**) and make sure they are seated correctly.
7. Repeat to install the remaining valve guide seals and valves.

4

*CAUTION*
*Do not remove the valve after installing it as it will damage the valve seal. If you must remove the valve, install a new seal.*

## CYLINDER

### Removal

Refer to **Figure 75** when performing the following.

1. Remove the cylinder head as described in this chapter.
2. Remove all dirt and foreign material from the cylinder base.
3. Remove the 2 dowel pins and O-rings (**Figure 76**) from the top of the cylinder.
4. Turn the engine over until the piston is at bottom dead center (BDC).
5. Loosen the cylinder by tapping around the perimeter with a rubber or plastic mallet.
6. Pull the cylinder straight up (**Figure 77**) and off the piston and cylinder studs.
7. Stuff clean shop rags into the crankcase opening to prevent objects from falling undetected into the crankcase.
8. Install a 6 inch rubber hose over each stud. This will protect both the piston and studs from damage.

*CAUTION*
*While the cylinder is removed, use care when working around the cylinder studs to avoid bending or damaging them. The slightest bend could cause a stud failure later during engine operation.*

9. Repeat Steps 1-8 for the other cylinder.

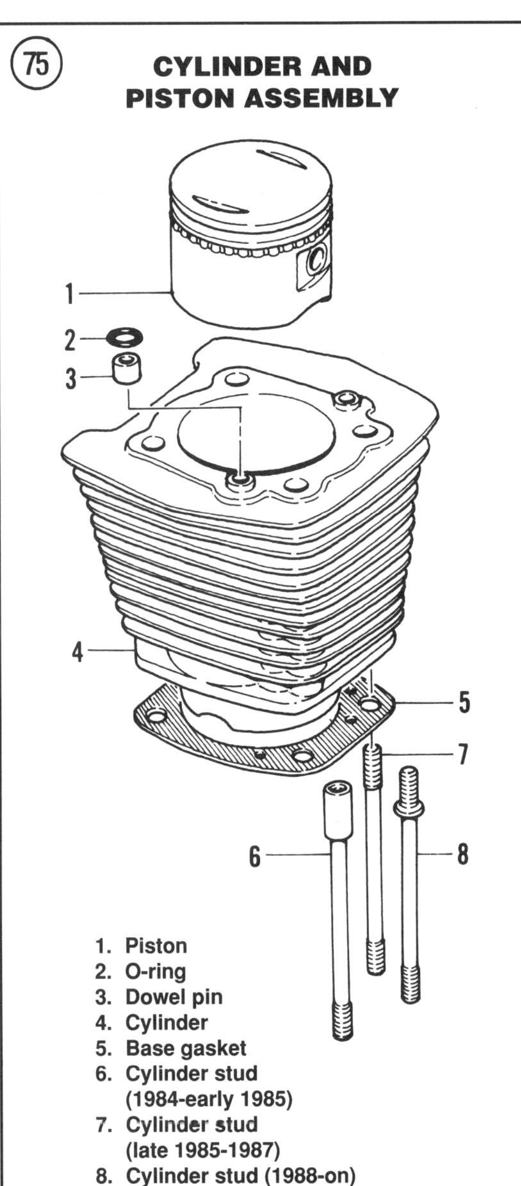


1. Piston
2. O-ring
3. Dowel pin
4. Cylinder
5. Base gasket
6. Cylinder stud (1984-early 1985)
7. Cylinder stud (late 1985-1987)
8. Cylinder stud (1988-on)

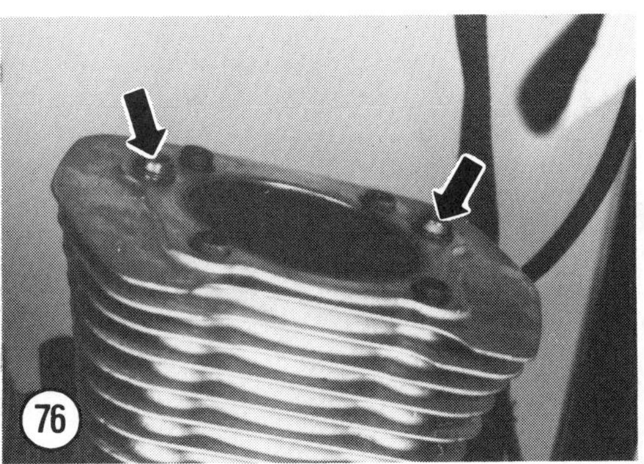

## Inspection

The pistons on all models cannot be accurately measured with standard measuring instruments and techniques. This is because the piston has a complex shape due to its design and manufacturing. Furthermore, the piston bore is offset. Piston-to-cylinder clearance is checked by measuring the cylinder bore only. If a cylinder is worn, the cylinder must be bored to specific factory specifications—not to match a particular piston size as with conventional methods. All service related to cylinder and piston matching should be referred to a Harley-Davidson dealer.

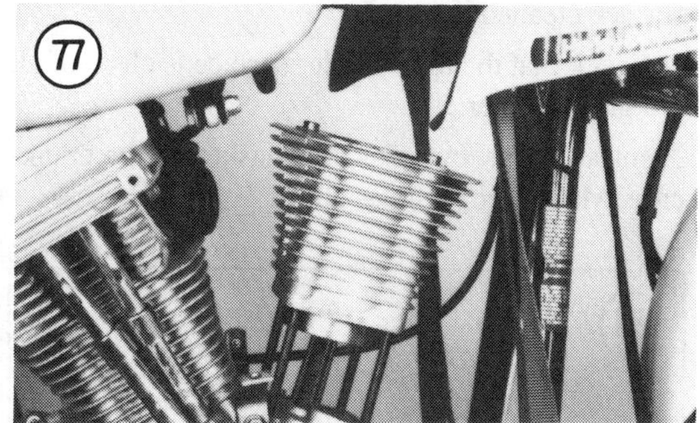


The following procedure requires the use of highly specialized and expensive measuring instruments. If such instruments are not readily available, have the measurements performed by a dealer or qualified machine shop.

*NOTE*
*Harley-Davidson recommends clamping the cylinder between torque plates (part No. HD-33446) (**Figure 78**) when making cylinder measurements and performing boring and honing operations. This arrangement simulates the distortion imparted on a cylinder when it is torqued down by the cylinder head and cylinder bolts. Measurements made without the engine torque plate can vary by 0.001 in. (0.02 mm). If you do not have access to the torque plates, refer service to a Harley-Davidson dealer.*

1. Thoroughly clean the cylinder with solvent and dry with compressed air. Lightly oil the cylinder bore to prevent rust after performing Step 2.
2. Check the cylinder's top (**Figure 79**) and bottom (**Figure 80**) gasket surfaces with a straightedge and



78

Bolt
Torque plate
Cylinder
Top
Middle
Bottom
Torque plate
Nut

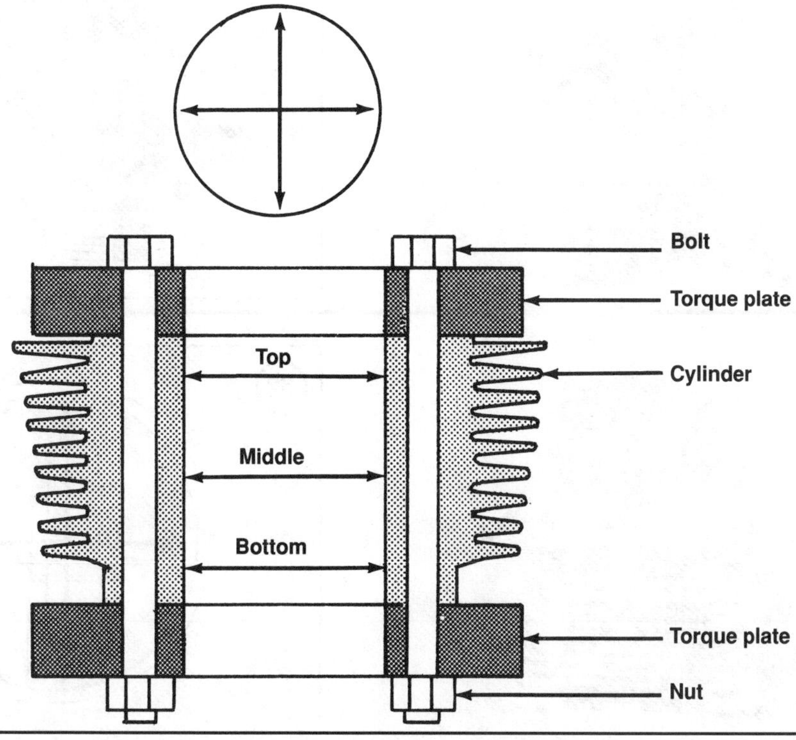

feeler gauge. Replace the cylinder if the following specifications are exceeded:

a. Top cylinder surface: 0.006 in. (0.15 mm)

b. Bottom cylinder surface: 0.008 in. (0.20 mm)

3. Install a new cylinder head and base gasket onto the cylinder and clamp the cylinder between the torque plates (**Figure 78**). Install the torque plate bolts, making sure they engage the gaskets properly. Tighten the torque plate bolts following the procedure and torque specification given for the cylinder heads as described in this chapter.

4. Measure the cylinder bores with a bore gauge (**Figure 81**) or inside micrometer at the points shown in **Figure 82**. Initial measurement should be made at a distance of 0.500 in. (12.7 mm) below the top of the cylinder. The 0.500 in. (12.7 mm) depth distance represents the start of the ring path area; do not take readings that are out of the ring path area.

5. Measure in 2 axes—in line with the piston pin and at 90° to the pin. If the taper or out-of-round is greater than specifications (**Table 2**), the cylinders must be rebored to the next oversize and new pistons and rings installed. Rebore both cylinders even though only one may be worn.

6. Check the cylinder walls for scuffing, scratches or other damage; if evident, the cylinders should be rebored and the pistons replaced.

7. Have your dealer confirm all cylinder measurements before you order replacement parts or have the cylinders honed or bored.

## Installation

Refer to **Figure 75** when performing this procedure.

1. If the base gasket is stuck to the bottom of the cylinder, it should be removed and the cylinder surface cleaned thoroughly.

2. Check that the top cylinder surface is clean of all old gasket material.

3. Install a new cylinder base gasket on the crankcase. Make sure all holes align.

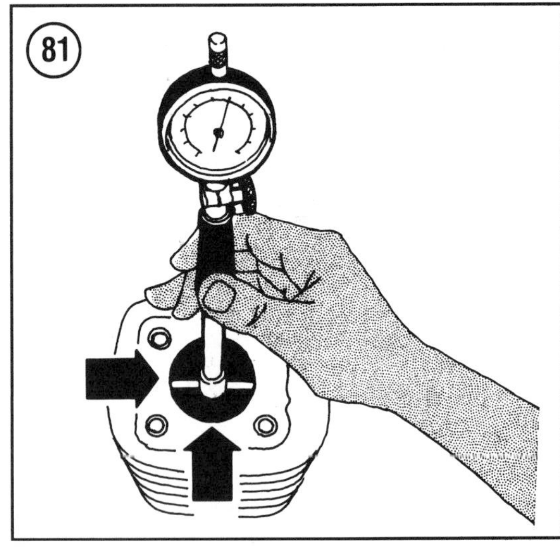


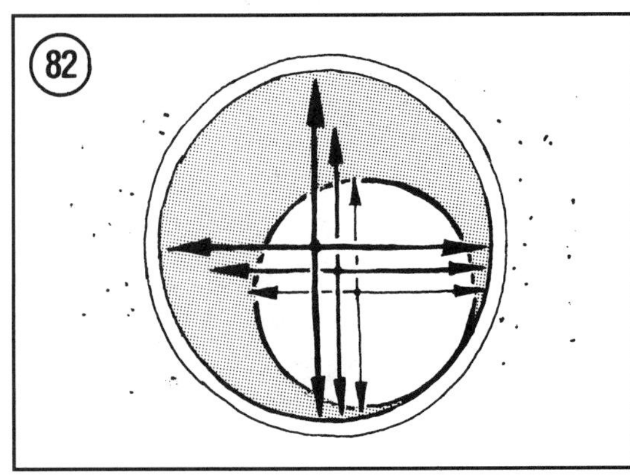

4. Turn the engine over until the piston is at top dead center (TDC).

5. Lubricate the cylinder bores and pistons liberally with engine oil.

6. Compress the rings with a ring compressor (**Figure 83**) or with aircraft type hose clamps of appropriate diameter. Tighten the compressor just enough to compress the rings.

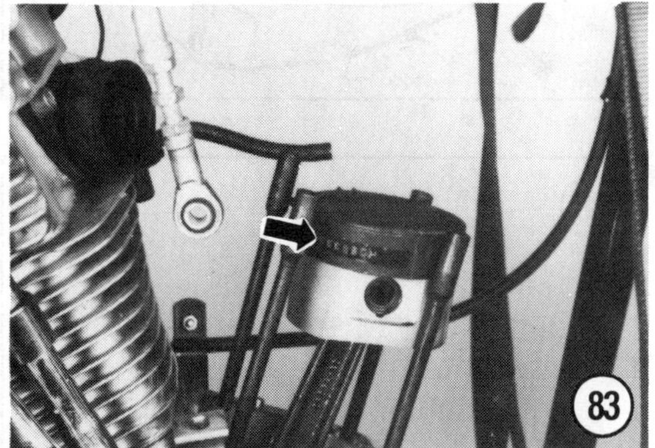

83

84

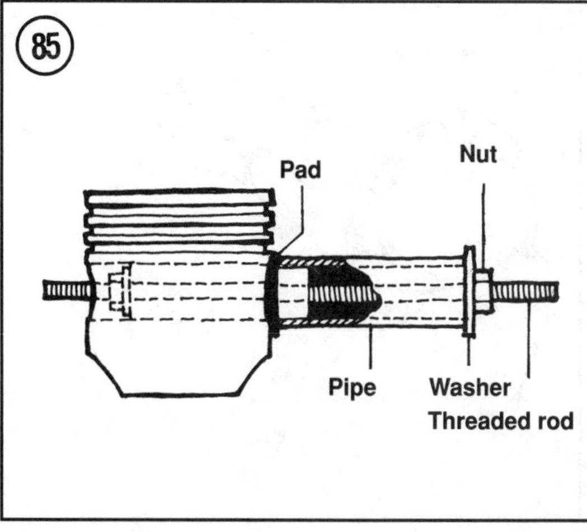


85

*CAUTION*

*Don't tighten the clamp any more than necessary to compress the rings. If the rings can't slip through easily, the clamp may gouge the rings and piston.*

7. Carefully align the cylinder over the piston and slide it down (**Figure 77**). Once the rings are positioned in the cylinder, remove the ring compressor or hose clamp installed in Step 6.
8. Rotate the cylinder as necessary and slide it over the crankcase studs.
9. Install the cylinder dowel pins, O-rings and cylinder head as described in this chapter.



## PISTONS AND PISTON RINGS

### Piston Removal/Installation

1. Remove the cylinder head and cylinder as described in this chapter.
2. Stuff the crankcase with clean shop rags to prevent objects from falling into the crankcase.
3. Lightly mark the pistons with an F (front) or R (rear) so they will be installed into the correct cylinder. Also mark the piston crown with an arrow pointing to the front of the bike. Because the piston pins are offset in the pistons, the pistons must not be installed backwards.
4. Remove the piston rings as described under *Piston Ring Replacement* in this chapter.

*WARNING*

*Because the piston pin retaining rings are highly compressed in the piston pin ring groove, safety glasses must be worn during their removal and installation.*

5. Using an awl, pry the piston pin retaining rings (**Figure 84**) out of the piston. Place your thumb over the hole to help prevent the rings from flying out during removal.
6. Support the piston and push out the piston pin. If the piston is difficult to remove, use a homemade tool as shown in **Figure 85**.
7. Inspect the piston as described in this chapter.
8. Coat the connecting rod bushing, piston pin and piston with assembly oil.
9. Place the piston over the connecting rod, following the ID marks made prior to removal. New pistons should be installed so that the nub on the piston

pin boss (**Figure 86**) faces toward the left-hand side (clutch side) of the bike. If the piston has an arrow cast into the piston crown, install it so that the arrow faces toward the front of the bike.

*NOTE*
*The piston markings described in Step 9 are for O.E.M. Harley-Davidson pistons. If you are using aftermarket pistons, follow the manufacturer's directions for piston alignment and installation.*

10. Insert the piston pin and tap it with a plastic mallet until it starts into the connecting rod bushing. Hold the rod so that the lower end does not take any shock. If the pin does not slide easily, use the homemade tool (**Figure 85**) but eliminate the piece of pipe. Tap the pin in until it is centered in the piston.

*WARNING*
*Safety glasses should be worn when installing the piston pin retaining rings in Step 11.*

11. Install *new* piston pin retaining rings. If the retaining rings are difficult to install, use the piston pin retaining ring installer (HD-34623). Turn each retaining ring so that its gap faces away from the slot in the bottom of the piston. Make sure each retaining ring seats fully in its piston groove.

12. Install rings as described under *Piston Ring Replacement* in this chapter.

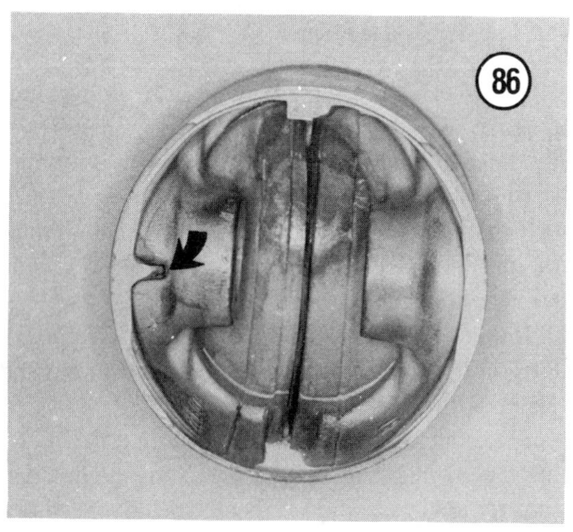

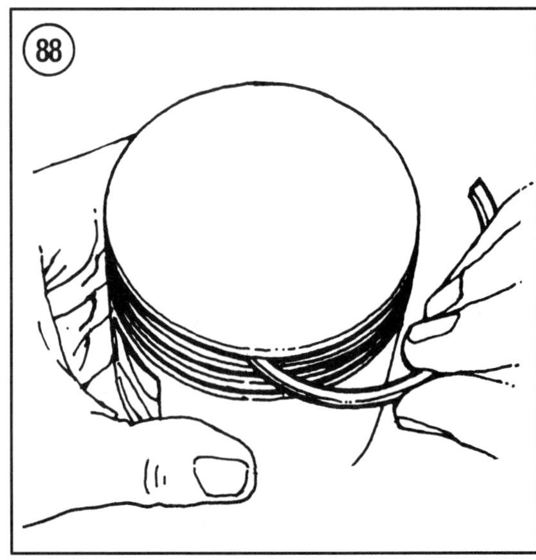


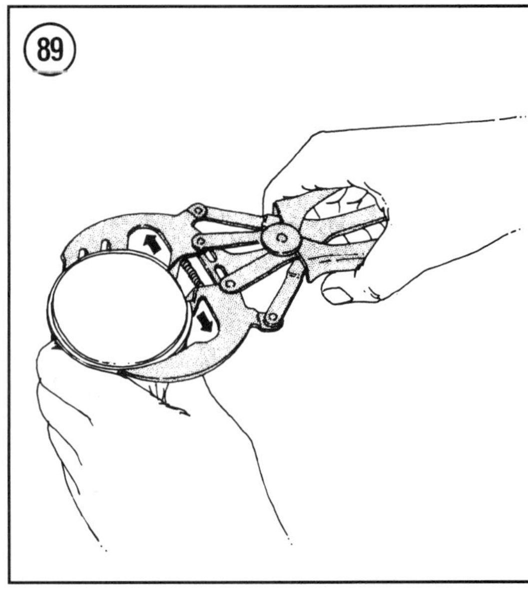

## Piston Inspection

1. Carefully clean the carbon from the piston crown with a soft scraper (**Figure 87**). Do not remove or damage the carbon ridge around the circumference of the piston above the top ring.

*CAUTION*
*Do not wire brush piston skirts.*

2. Using a broken piston ring, remove all carbon deposits from the piston ring grooves (**Figure 88**). Make sure you do not remove metal from the piston ring grooves when cleaning them.
3. Examine each ring groove for burrs, dented edges and wide wear. Pay particular attention to the top compression ring groove, as it usually wears more than the others.
4. Check cylinder clearance as described in this chapter. Replace worn or damaged parts as required.



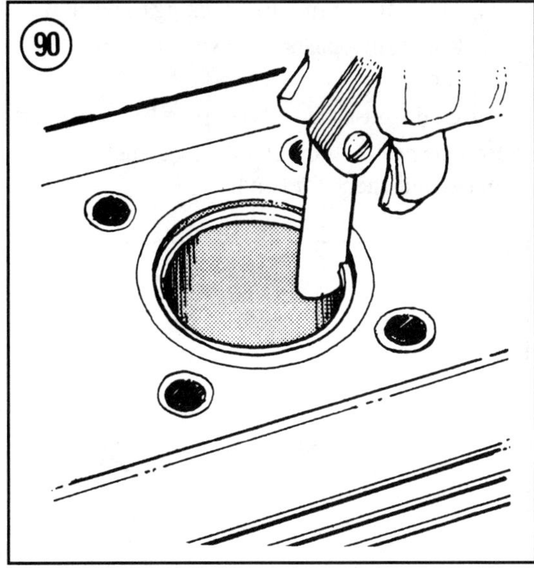


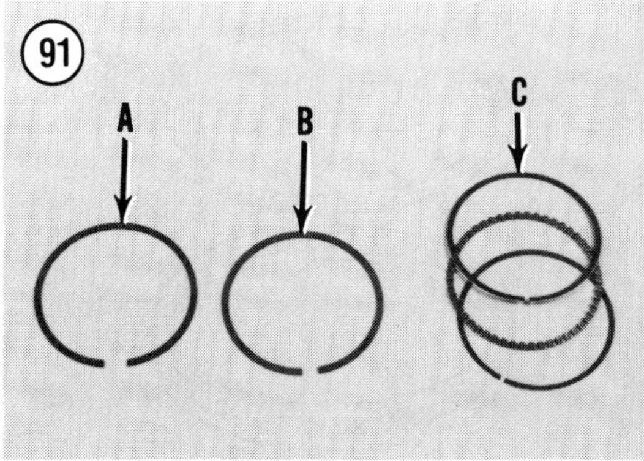


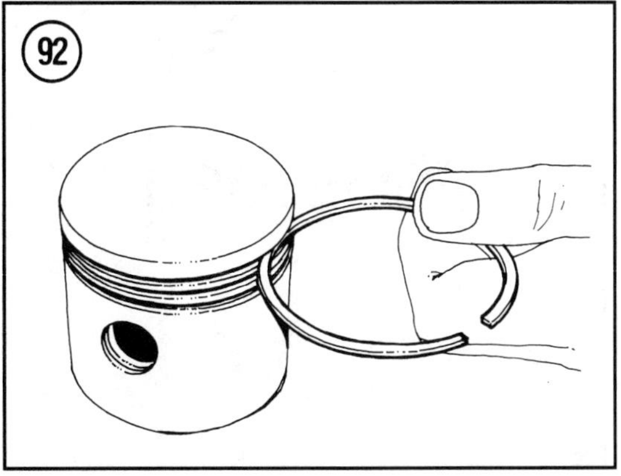


## Piston Ring Replacement

*NOTE*
*ID the piston rings as they are removed in Step 1 so that they can be reinstalled in their original positions.*

1. Remove the old rings with a ring expander tool (**Figure 89**).
2. Inspect ring grooves carefully for burrs, nicks, or broken or cracked lands. Replace piston if necessary.
3. Check end gap of each ring. To check ring, insert the ring into the top of the cylinder bore and square it with the cylinder wall by tapping it with the piston. Insert a feeler gauge as shown in **Figure 90**. Compare gap with specifications in **Table 2**. Replace ring if gap is too large.

*NOTE*
*The piston ring end gap specifications listed in **Table 2** do not apply to oversize piston rings.*

*NOTE*
*The oil control ring expander spacer does not have a wear specification. If the oil control ring rails show wear, all 3 oil control rings (C, **Figure 91**) should be replaced as a set.*

4. Roll each ring around its piston groove (as shown in **Figure 92**) to check for binding.
5. Install oil ring in oil ring groove with a ring expander tool (**Figure 89**).
6. If you are installing the original rings, install them according to the ID marks made while removing

them. If you are installing new compression rings, note the following:

a. The top compression ring (A, **Figure 91**) does not have a dot. The second compression ring (B, **Figure 91**) has a dot that must face upward when installing the ring.
b. Install the second compression ring, then install the top compression ring.

*NOTE*
*When installing oversize compression rings, check the number to make sure the correct rings are being installed. The ring numbers should be the same as the piston oversize number.*

7. Check side clearance of each ring as shown in **Figure 93**. Compare with specifications in **Table 2**.
8. Distribute ring gaps around piston as shown in **Figure 94**.

## PUSHRODS

### Removal/Installation

Remove and install pushrods as described under *Cylinder Head Removal/Installation.*

### Inspection

Refer to **Figure 95** for this procedure.

1. Disassemble the pushrod cover as follows:
   a. Remove the lower pushrod cover (**Figure 96**).
   b. Remove the O-ring (**Figure 97**).
   c. Remove the spacer (**Figure 98**).
   d. Remove the spring (**Figure 99**).
   e. Remove the cap (**Figure 100**).
2. Check the pushrod cover assembly (**Figure 101**) as follows:
   a. Check the spring for sagging or cracking.
   b. Check the spacer for deformation or damage.
   c. Check the O-ring for cracking or wear.
   d. Check the pushrod covers for cracking or damage.
3. Check the pushrod ends (**Figure 102**) for wear.
4. Roll the pushrods on a flat surface, such as a piece of glass, and check for bending.

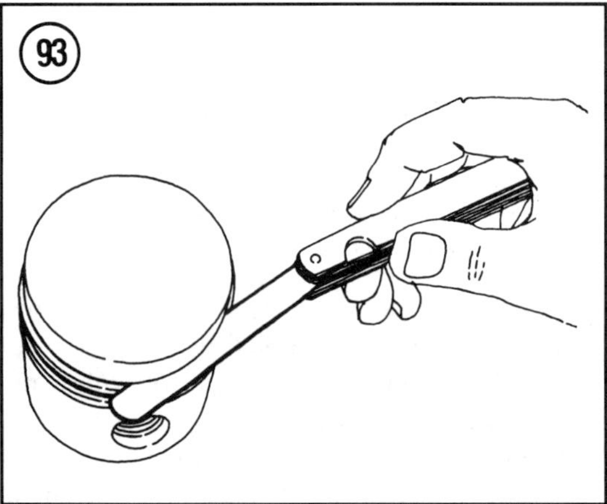


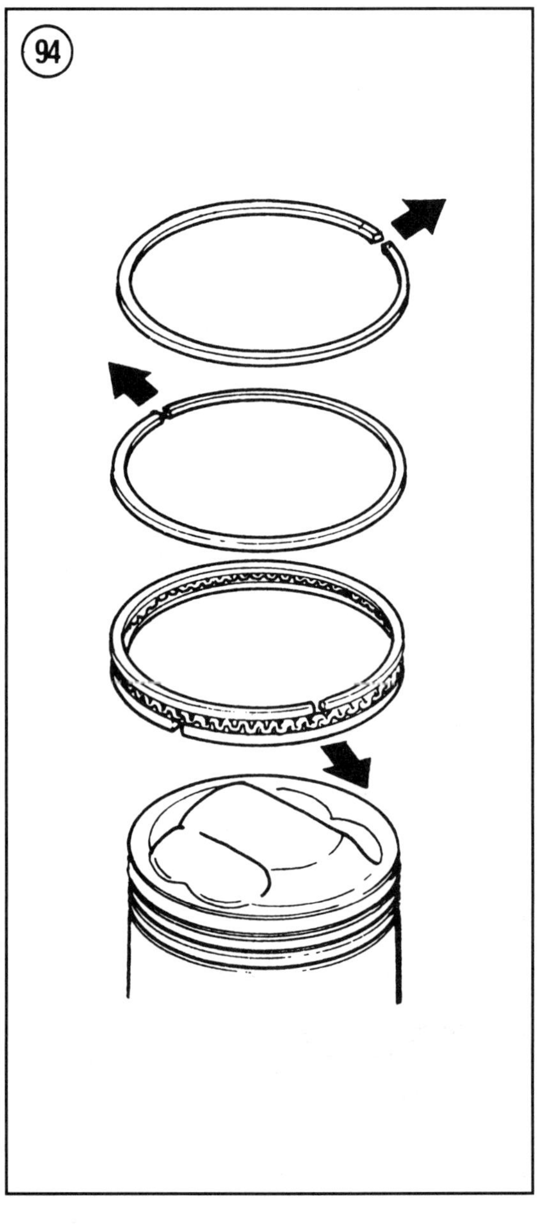

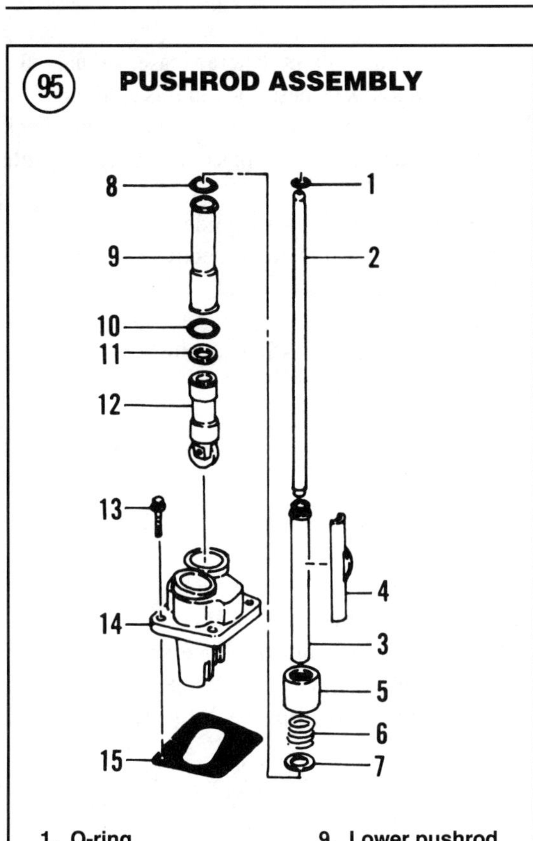
95
PUSHROD ASSEMBLY
1
2
3
4
5
6
7
8
9
10
11
12
13
14
15
1. O-ring
2. Pushrod
3. Upper pushrod cover
4. Spring cap retainer
5. Cap
6. Spring
7. Spacer
8. O-ring
9. Lower pushrod cover
10. O-ring
11. Spacer
12. Tappet
13. Screw
14. Tappet guide
15. Gasket

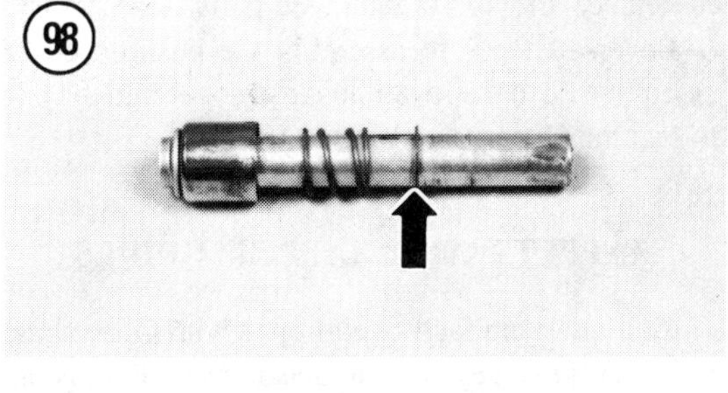
98



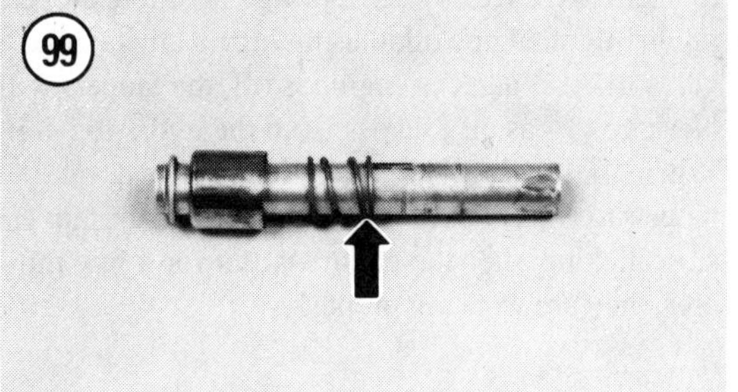
99

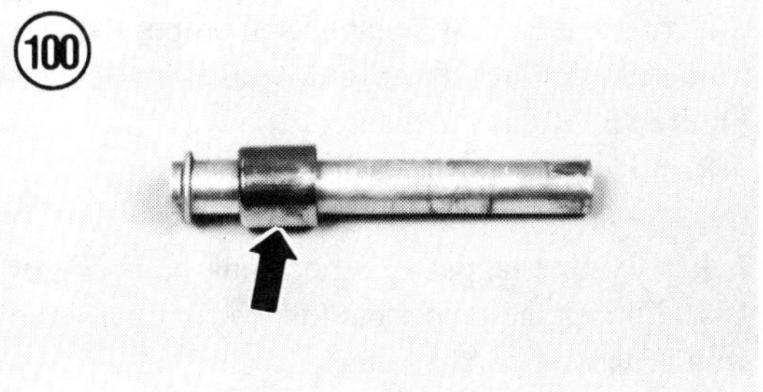
100

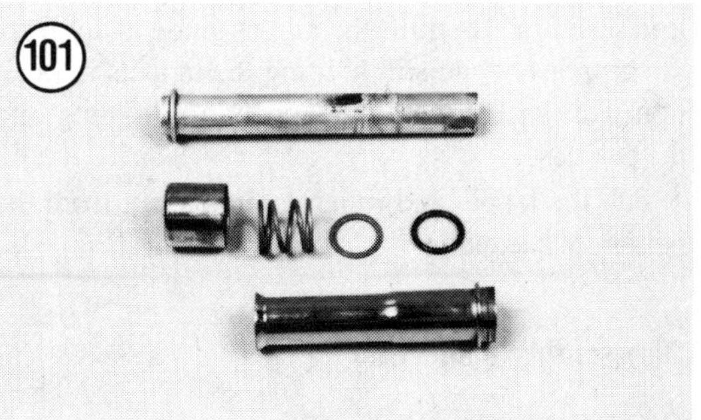
101

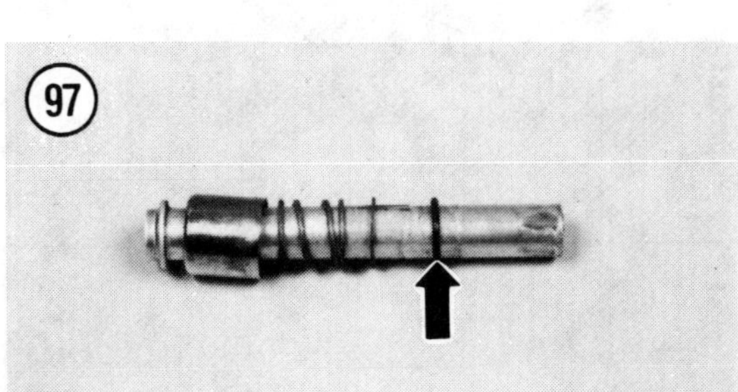
96

102

5. Replace all worn or damaged parts as necessary.
6. Reverse Step 1 to assembly the pushrod cover assembly. Push the lower pushrod cover into the cap to seat the O-ring. See **Figure 103**.

## TAPPETS AND TAPPET GUIDES

All models are factory equipped with tappets and rollers (**Figure 95**). The tappets consist of a piston, cylinder and check valve. During operation, tappets pump full of engine oil, thus taking up all play in the valve train. When the engine is off, the tappets will "leak down" as oil escapes from the hydraulic unit. When the engine is started, it is normal for the tappets to click until they refill with oil. If the tappets stop clicking after the engine is run for a few minutes, they are working properly.

### Removal

During removal, store tappets in proper sequence for installation in their original positions. Refer to **Figure 95** for this procedure.

1. Remove the pushrods as described under *Cylinder Head Removal* in this chapter.
2. Remove the tappet guide housing bolts (**Figure 104**). Loosen the tappet guide by striking it lightly with a plastic-tipped hammer.
3. Use your fingers and push the tappet and roller assembly against the side of the tappet guide to hold it in position. Then lift the tappet guide away from the gearcase while still holding the tappets in position. This will prevent the tappets from falling into the gearcase.
4. Pull the tappet and roller assembly out from the bottom of the guide.

### Disassembly/Inspection

1. Clean all of the parts, except the tappet and roller assembly, in solvent.
2. Blow out all tappet guide and hydraulic oil passages with compressed air.
3. Clean the tappet guide oil channel openings with a piece of wire.
4. Check the tappet rollers for pitting, scoring, galling or excessive wear. If the rollers are worn excessively, check the cam lobes for the same wear conditions. The cam lobes can be observed through the tappet guide hole in the crankcase. Replace the cam, if necessary, as described in this chapter.
5. Clean the roller with contact cleaner. Then check the roller end clearance. Replace if excessive (**Table 2**).
6. Measure tappet O.D. and guide I.D. to determine tappet guide fit. Compare to specifications in **Table 2** and replace parts as required.
7. If dirt has entered the tappet, replace it.
8. After inspection, soak the tappets in clean engine oil before reinstallation.

### Installation

1. Slide the tappets through the bottom of the tappet guide.
2. Install a new tappet guide gasket. Do not install any type of sealer on the gasket.
3. Hold the tappets with your fingers or use wire and install the tappet guide onto the gearcase. Do not allow the tappets to drop into the gearcase.

*NOTE*
*The tappets can be installed into their guide facing in either direction.*

4. Install the Tappet Guide Alignment Tool (part No. HD-33443) into the tappet screw hole closest to the tappet oil feed hole. Then install the 3 tappet block

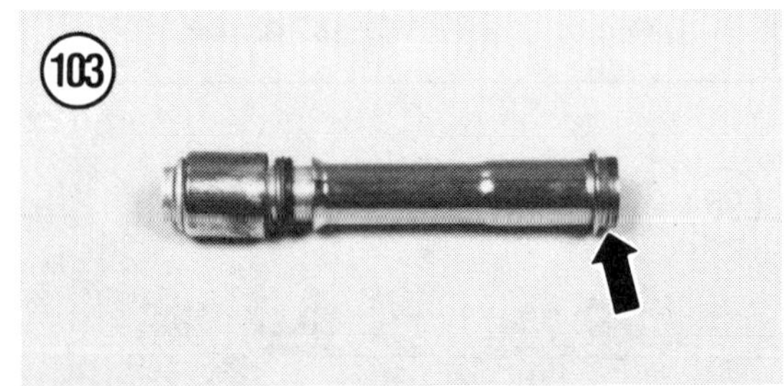
103

104

mounting screws and tighten them securely. Remove the alignment tool and then install and tighten the remaining tappet block mounting screw.

5. Tighten the tappet guide retaining screws securely.
6. Have a dealer check pushrod length.
7. Install the pushrods as described in this chapter.

### Tappet Oil Screen

The tappet oil screen should be cleaned at specified service intervals. See Chapter Three for complete information.

*CAUTION*
*Failure to clean the tappet oil screen as described in Chapter Three will cause premature tappet wear.*

## OIL PUMP

The oil pump is installed at the rear of the gearcase. The pump consists of 2 sections: a feed pump which supplies oil under pressure to the engine components, and a scavenger pump which returns oil to the oil tank from the engine.

### Removal/Disassembly

Refer to **Figure 105** for this procedure.

*NOTE*
*Label all gears and Woodruff keys during removal so that they can be installed in their original positions.*

1. Drain the engine oil tank as described in Chapter Three.

*NOTE*
*When disconnecting the oil lines in Step 2, make sure to tag each line so that it may be returned to its original position.*

2A. On 1984-1991 models, disconnect the oil lines from the oil pump. Plug the ends of the lines to prevent oil leakage and contamination. On 1991 models, discard the one-piece band clamps as new clamps must be used during installation. Refer to the illustration for your model:

a. **Figure 106**: Early 1984 FLT and FXR.
b. **Figure 107**: Late 1984-1990 FLT and FXR.
c. **Figure 108**: 1991 FLT and FXR.
d. **Figure 109**: 1985-1986 FX.

2B. On 1992-on FXR (**Figure 110**), 1992 FLT (**Figure 111**) and 1993-on FLT (**Figure 112**) models, perform the following:

a. Disconnect the oil tank vent line at the oil pump.
b. Disconnect the main oil feed hose at the oil pump.
c. Disconnect the oil filter-to-oil pump cover manifold oil hose as described under *Oil Filter Mount (1992-on)* in this chapter.

3. Remove the bolts securing the oil pump cover and remove the cover. See **Figure 113**.
4. Remove the snap ring, gear, Woodruff key and idler gear.

*CAUTION*
*When performing the following steps, make sure the drive gear shaft is not pushed into the gearcase; otherwise, the Woodruff key on the end of the shaft could fall into the gearcase.*

5. Remove the oil pump body mounting bolts. Then slide the oil pump body off the drive gear shaft.
6. Remove the drive gear, Woodruff key and the idler gear.
7. Remove the check valve spring cover screw, check valve spring and the check valve ball.
8. Remove the bypass valve plug, bypass valve spring and the bypass valve.
9. Inspect the oil pump as described under *Inspection* in this chapter.
10. Assembly is the reverse of these steps. Note the following.

*CAUTION*
*Never use "homemade" gaskets to check and reassemble the oil pump. Factory gaskets are made to a specified thickness with holes placed accurately to pass oil through the oil pump. Gaskets of the incorrect thickness can cause loss of oil pressure and severe engine damage.*

11. Coat all parts with fresh engine oil prior to installation, then place them on a clean lint-free cloth until their reassembly.
12. Install new circlips during assembly.

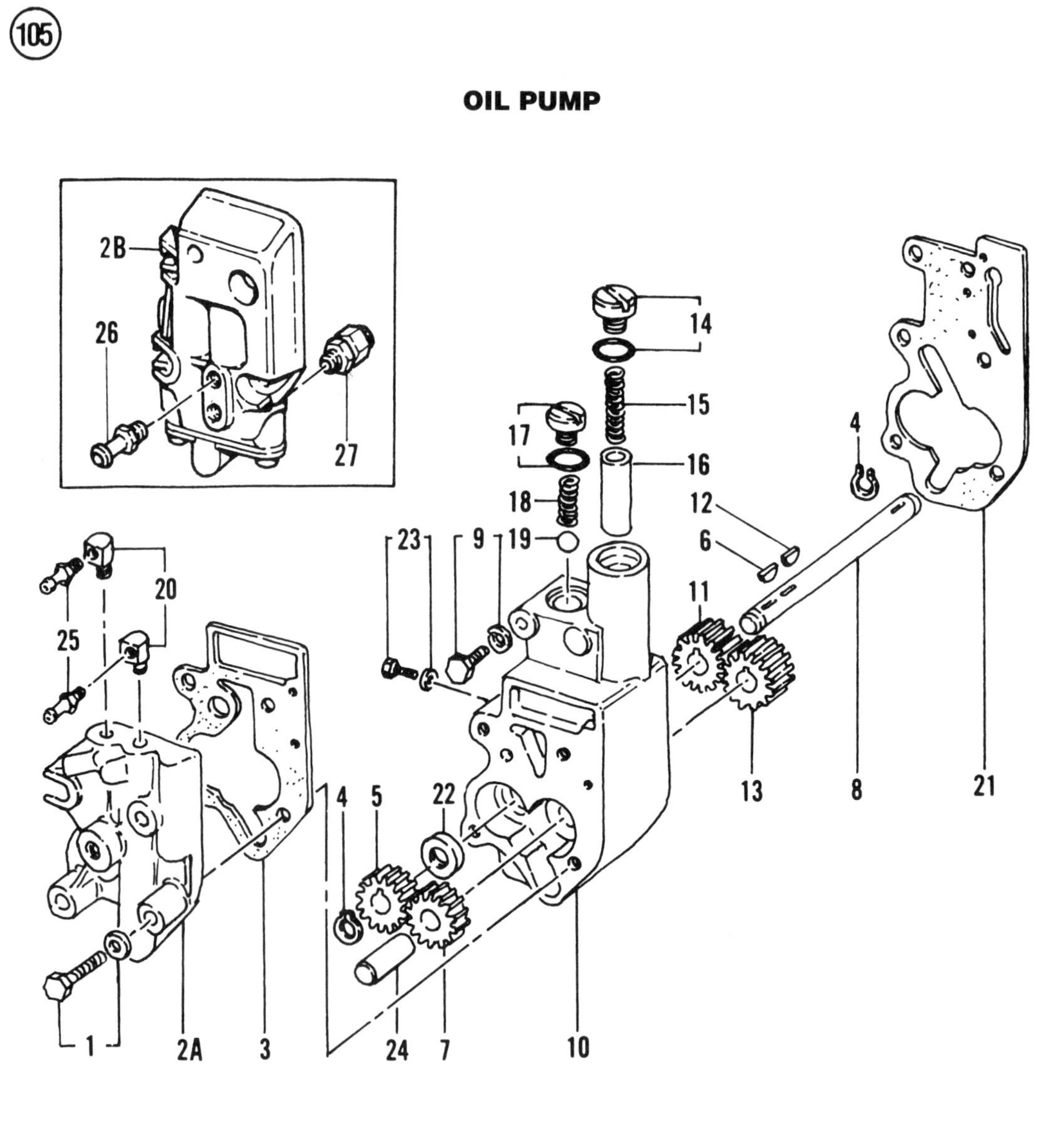


1. Cover bolts and lockwashers
2A. Oil pump cover (1984-1991)
2B. Oil pump cover (1992-on)
3. Cover gasket
4. Snap ring
5. Drive gear
6. Woodruff key
7. Idler gear
8. Oil pump gear drive shaft
9. Oil pump body mounting bolts/lockwashers
10. Oil pump body
11. Drive gear
12. Gear key
13. Idler gear
14. Valve plug and O-ring
15. Bypass valve spring
16. Bypass valve
17. Check valve spring cover
18. Check valve spring
19. Check valve ball
20. Oil line elbow
21. Gasket
22. Seal
23. Plug and gasket
24. Idler shaft
25. Oil line nipple
26. Hose nipple
27. Compression nut fitting

13. Tighten the valve plug (14, **Figure 105**) to 80-110 in.-lb. (9.2-12.6 N•m).
14. Tighten the oil pump body mounting bolts (9, **Figure 105**) to 60-85 in.-lb. (6.9-9.7 N•m).

*CAUTION*
*Do not overtighten the bolts in Step 15 as this will eliminate the pump gear side clearance and could cause the pump to seize, resulting in engine seizure.*

15. Tighten the oil pump body and oil pump cover bolts to 90-120 in.-lb. (10.3-13.8 N•m).
16. Refill the engine oil tank as described in Chapter Three.
17A. On 1984-1991 models, reconnect the oil lines to the oil pump. On 1991 models, install new one-piece band clamps. Tighten hose clamp with Harley-Davidson hose clamp tool (part No. HD-97087-65A) or equivalent. On all other models, replace damaged hose clamps as required and tighten securely. Refer to the illustration for your model:

a. **Figure 106**: Early 1984 FLT and FXR.
b. **Figure 107**: Late 1984-1990 FLT and FXR.
c. **Figure 108**: 1991 FLT and FXR.
d. **Figure 109**: 1985-1986 FX.

17B. On 1992-on FXR (**Figure 110**), 1992 FLT (**Figure 111**) and 1993-on FLT (**Figure 112**) models, perform the following:

a. Reconnect the oil tank vent line at the oil pump.
b. Reconnect the main oil feed hose at the oil pump.
c. Reconnect the oil filter-to-oil pump cover manifold oil hose as described under *Oil Filter Mount (1992-On)* in this chapter.

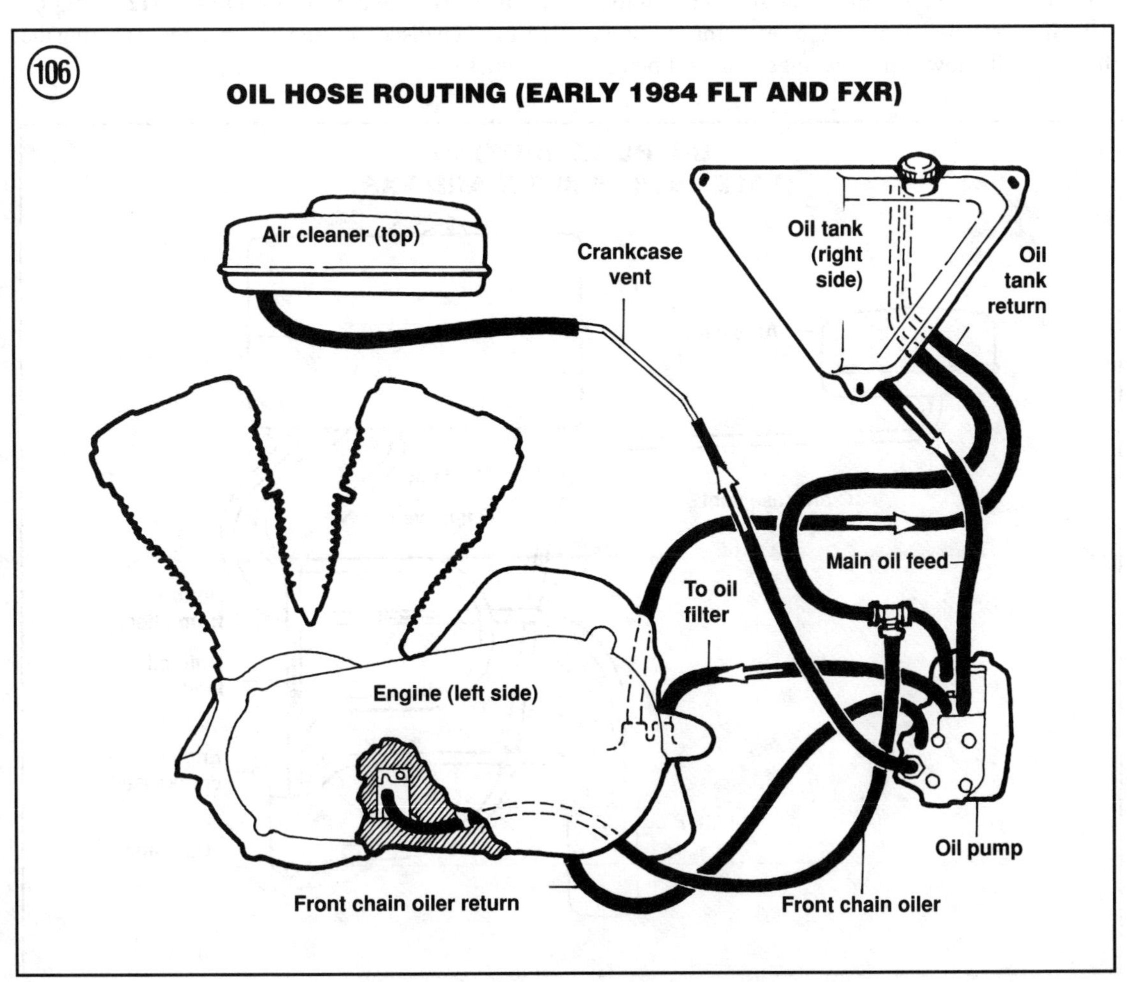

### Inspection

1. Clean all parts thoroughly in solvent.
2. Inspect the check valve ball and spring (**Figure 114**) for wear or damage. Replace the check valve spring cover screw O-ring if damaged. Replace parts as necessary.
3. Check the bypass valve spring plunger and spring (**Figure 115**) for wear and damage.
4. Check the drive shaft (A, **Figure 116**) for cracks, scoring or wear. Also check the drive shaft keyways (B, **Figure 116**) for cracking. Replace the drive shaft if necessary.
5. Check the oil pump gears (**Figure 117**) and the drive gear (**Figure 118**) for cracks, scoring or excessive wear.
6. Replace the oil seal (A, **Figure 119**) if it appears worn or damaged. The seal lip must face toward the feed gears.
7. Check the oil pump idler gear shaft (B, **Figure 119**). If it is loose, replace the oil pump body as slippage will allow metal shavings in the oil pump. A new shaft can be pressed in, but in most cases, the oil pin has wallowed the shaft bore in the housing.
8. Check the oil pump body machined surface (**Figure 120**) for nicks or gouging.
9. Assemble the feed and scavenger gears. See **Figure 121** and **Figure 122**. Lay a straightedge across the gears and measure the height of the gears in relation to the gasket surface. The gear faces should extend above the pump body 0.003-0.004 in. (0.076-0.102 mm). Perform this check for both the feed and scavenger gears. If this clearance is incorrect, the oil pump must be replaced.

## OIL FILTER MOUNT (1992-ON)

Refer to **Figure 123** when performing procedures in this section. Refer to **Figure 110** (1992-on FXR), **Figure 111** (1992 FLT) or **Figure 112** (1993-on FLT) when disconnecting and then reconnecting the oil lines.

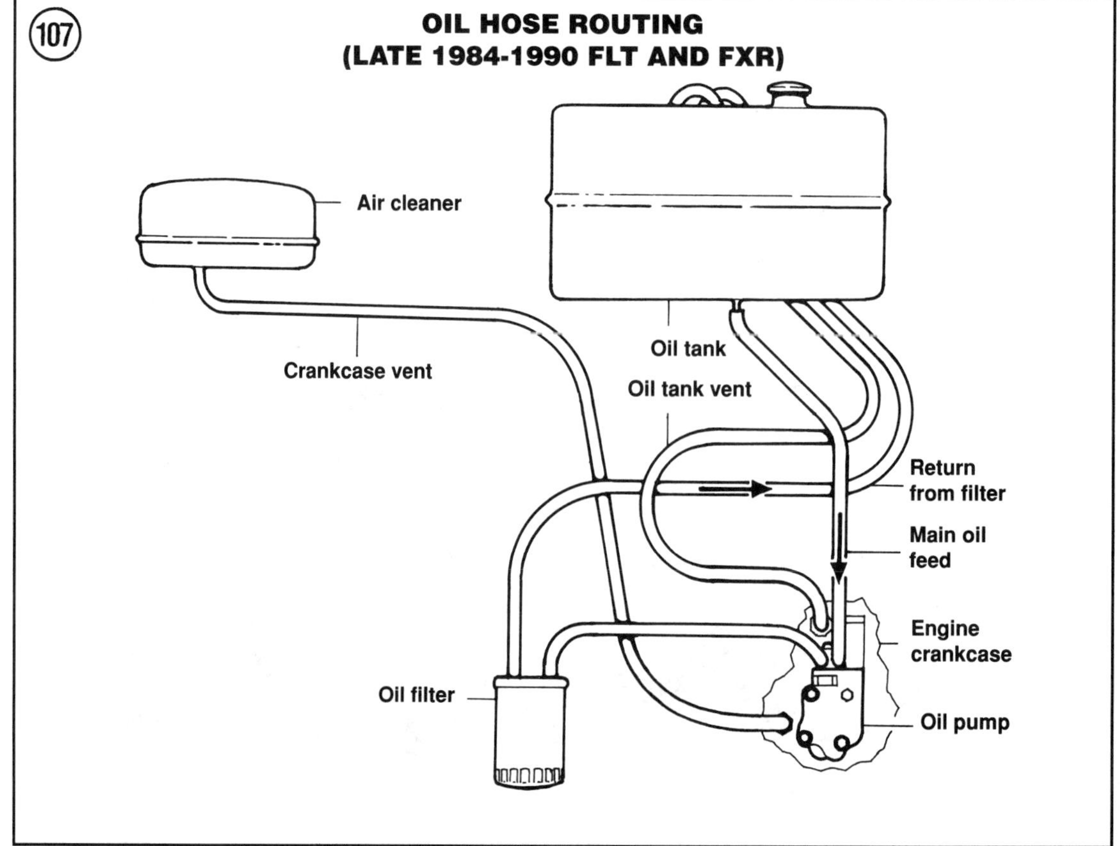

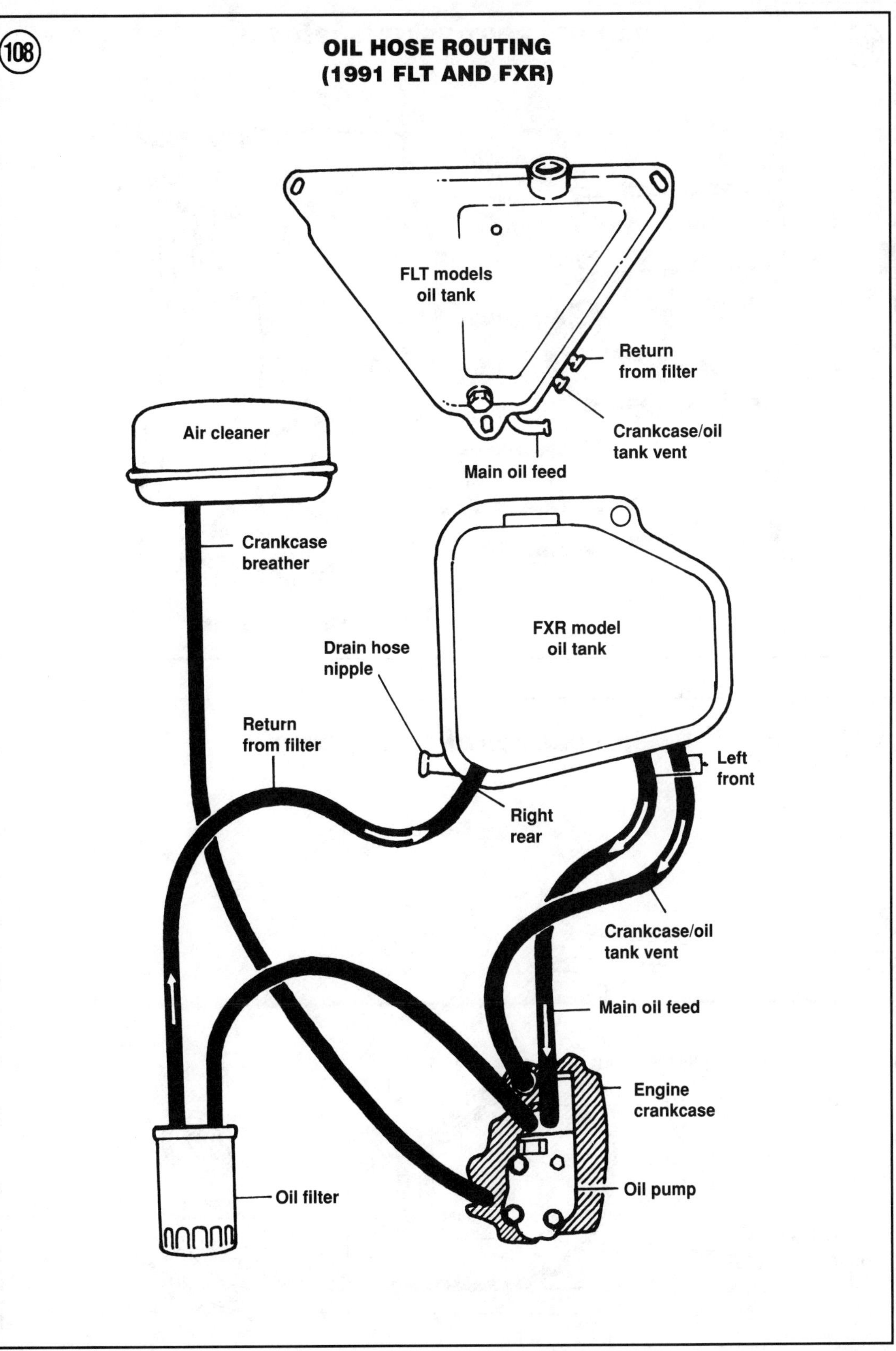
108
OIL HOSE ROUTING
(1991 FLT AND FXR)
FLT models
oil tank
Return
from filter
Crankcase/oil
tank vent
Main oil feed
Air cleaner
Crankcase
breather
FXR model
oil tank
Drain hose
nipple
Return
from filter
Left
front
Right
rear
Crankcase/oil
tank vent
Main oil feed
Engine
crankcase
Oil pump
Oil filter

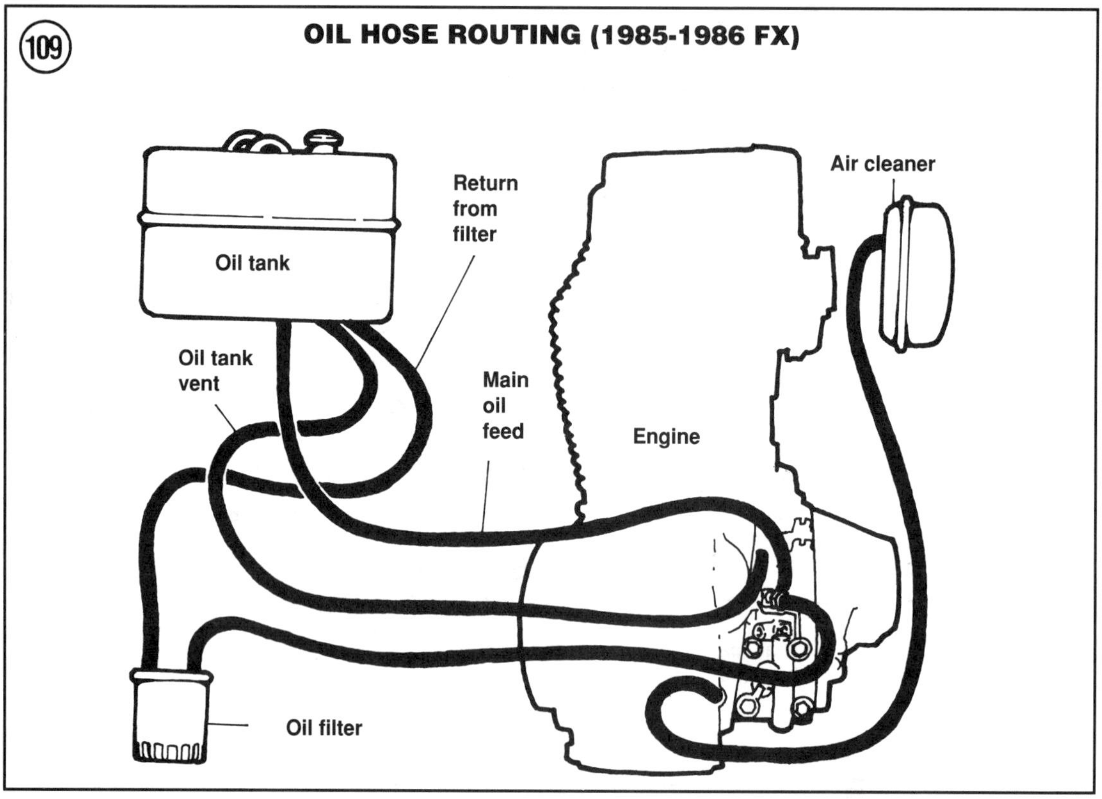
109
OIL HOSE ROUTING (1985-1986 FX)
Return from filter
Air cleaner
Oil tank
Oil tank vent
Main oil feed
Engine
Oil filter

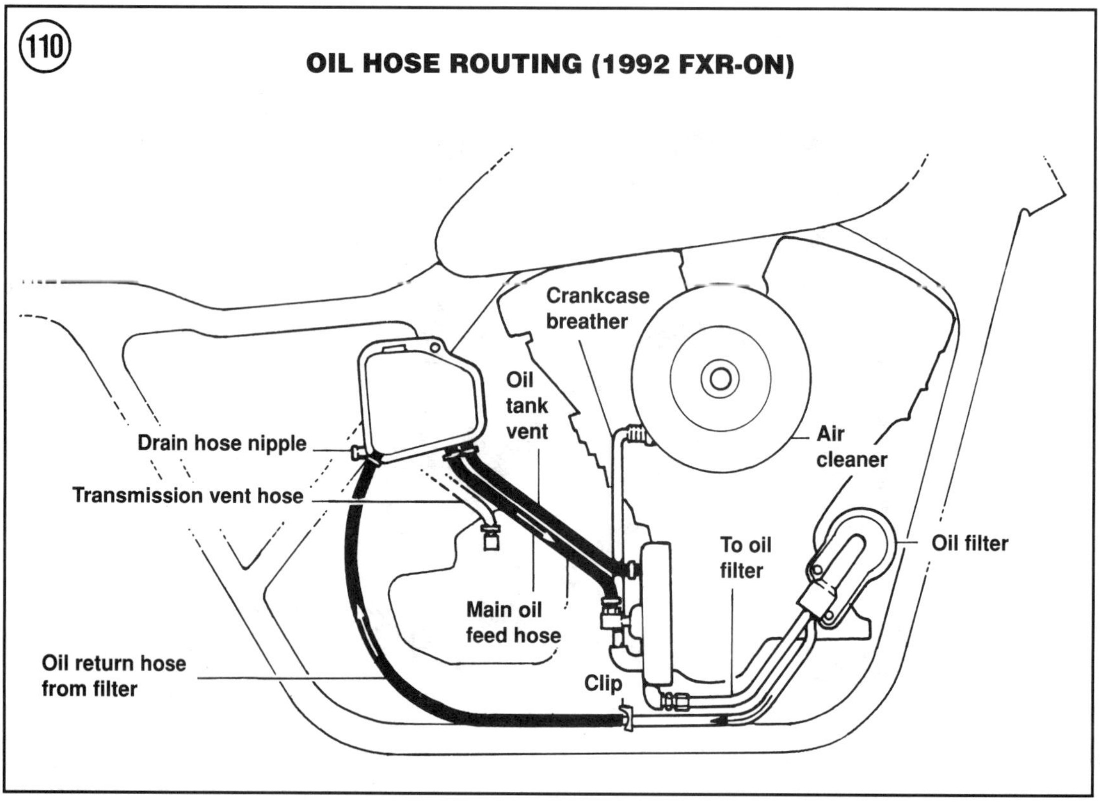
110
OIL HOSE ROUTING (1992 FXR-ON)
Crankcase breather
Oil tank vent
Drain hose nipple
Air cleaner
Transmission vent hose
To oil filter
Oil filter
Main oil feed hose
Oil return hose from filter
Clip

(111)

**OIL HOSE ROUTING (1992 FLT)**

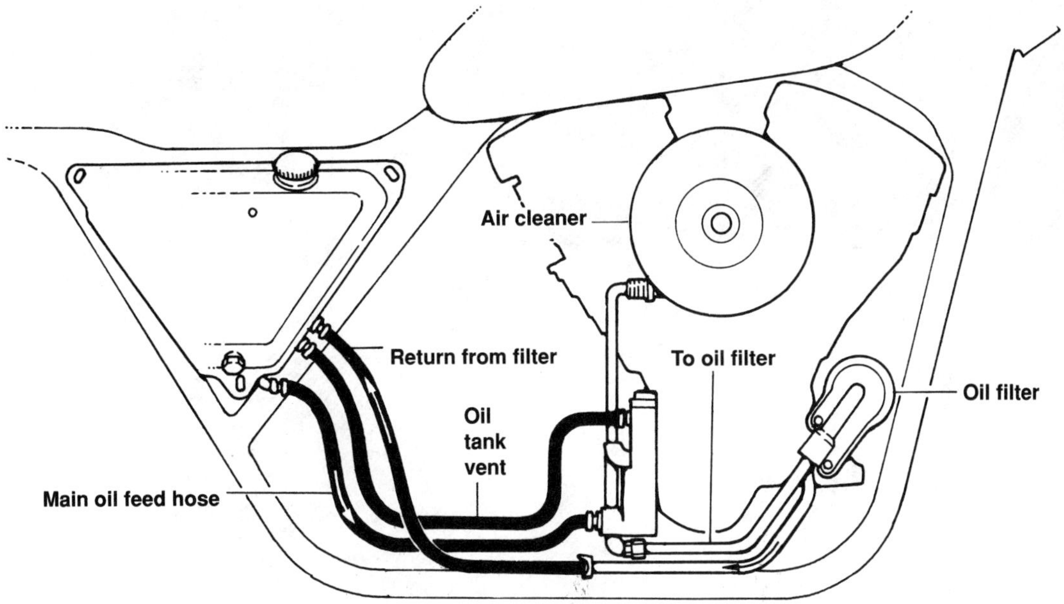

Air cleaner
Return from filter
To oil filter
Oil filter
Oil tank vent
Main oil feed hose

(112)

**OIL HOSE ROUTING (1993-ON FLT)**

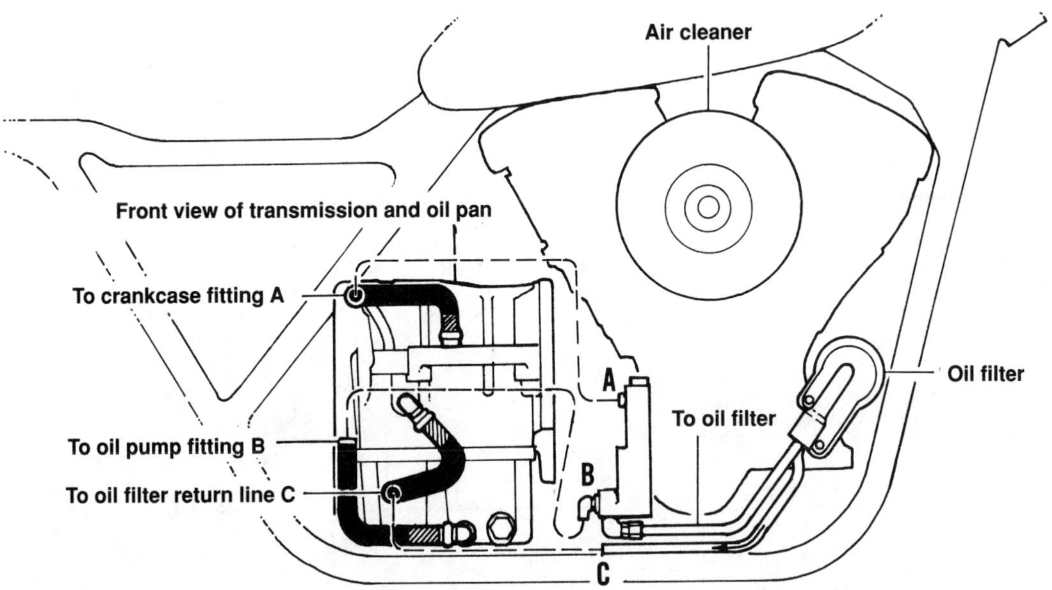

Air cleaner
Front view of transmission and oil pan
To crankcase fitting A
A
Oil filter
To oil filter
To oil pump fitting B
B
To oil filter return line C
C

113

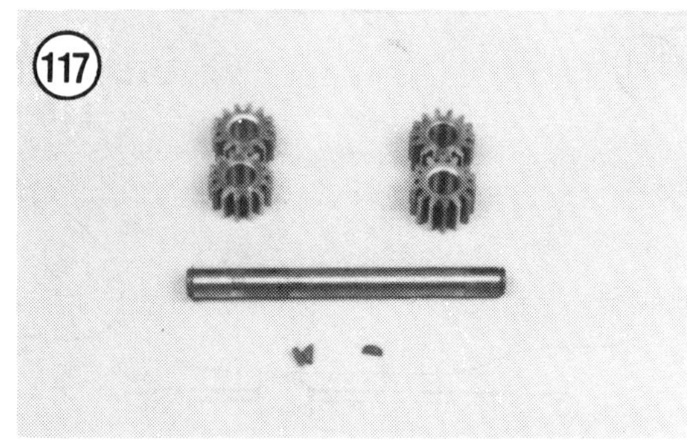
117

114

118

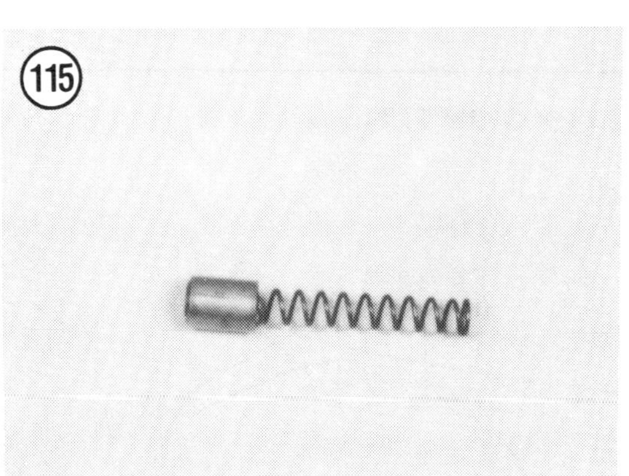
115

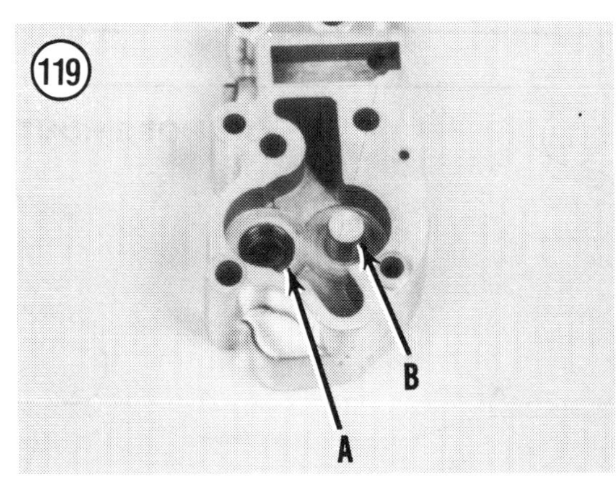
119
B
A

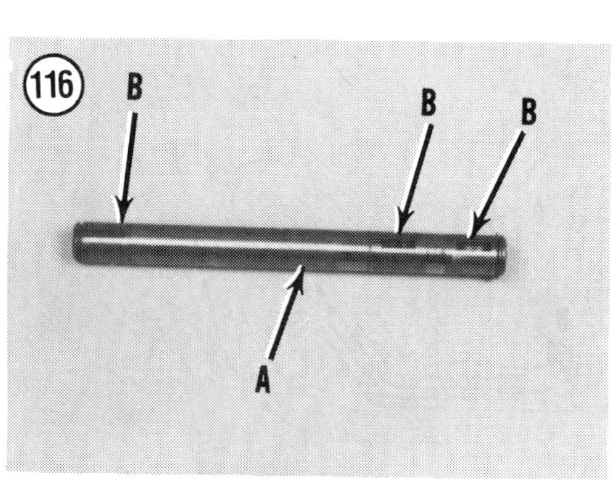
116
B
B
B
A

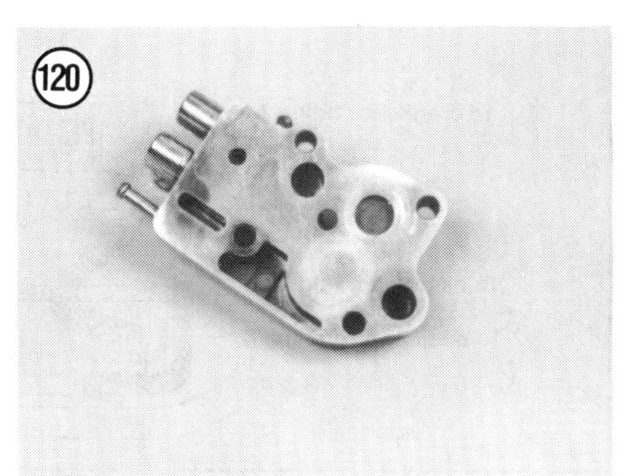
120

### Removal

1. Park the bike on a level surface.
2. Drain the oil tank or engine oil (oil pan) and remove the oil filter as described in Chapter Three.
3. Loosen the oil filter line compression nut at the oil pump cover manifold until it sets on the oil line.
4. Remove the oil pump cover manifold mounting bolts and washers and remove the manifold and O-rings from the oil pump cover.
5. Remove the oil line clamp nut, washer and spacer.
6. Loosen the oil line compression fittings at the oil filter mount. Then remove the oil lines from the oil filter mount.
7. Remove the oil filter mount screws and washers and remove the oil filter mount.
8. Remove the upper compression nut seals from the oil lines. If necessary, remove the upper compression nuts.
9. Loosen, then remove the compression nut fitting from the oil pump cover manifold.

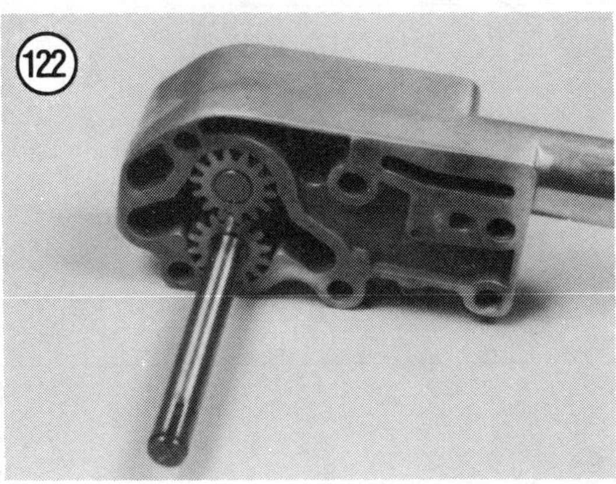


10. Remove the lower seal and compression nut from the oil line.
11. If necessary, remove the oil filter adapter from the oil filter mount.
12. If necessary, remove the hose nipple from the oil pump cover.

### Inspection

1. Inspect the oil lines for cracks or other damage.
2. If you replace the oil lines, make sure to remove the rubber sleeves from the oil lines and install them on the new lines in the same position.
3. Clean the compression nuts and compression nut fitting in solvent and dry thoroughly.
4. Replace worn or damaged parts as required.

4

### Installation

1. Make sure all parts are clean and dry prior to installing them.
2. If removed, install the hose nipple (2, **Figure 123**) as follows:
   a. On FXR models, install the hose nipple in the upper pump cover hole (1, **Figure 123**).
   b. On FLT models, install the hose nipple in the lower pump cover hole (1, **Figure 123**).
3. If removed, install the compression nut fitting (7, **Figure 123**) as follows:
   a. Apply Loctite 242 (blue) to the compression nut fitting threads prior to installation.
   b. Install the compression nut fitting and tighten to the torque specification in **Table 3**.
4. If removed, install the oil filter adapter into the oil filter mount.
5. Install the oil filter mount and its mounting screws and washers. Tighten the oil filter mount screws to the torque specification in **Table 3**.
6. Slide the oil line compression nut (9, **Figure 123**) and seal (8, **Figure 123**) onto the oil line.
7. Install the 2 compression fitting oil seals (18, **Figure 123**) into the oil filter mount.
8. Install the upper oil line compression nut fittings (17, **Figure 123**) into the oil filter mount. Tighten the fittings finger-tight only.
9. Insert the oil lines (14 and 15, **Figure 123**) into their respective compression nut fittings until they bottom out.

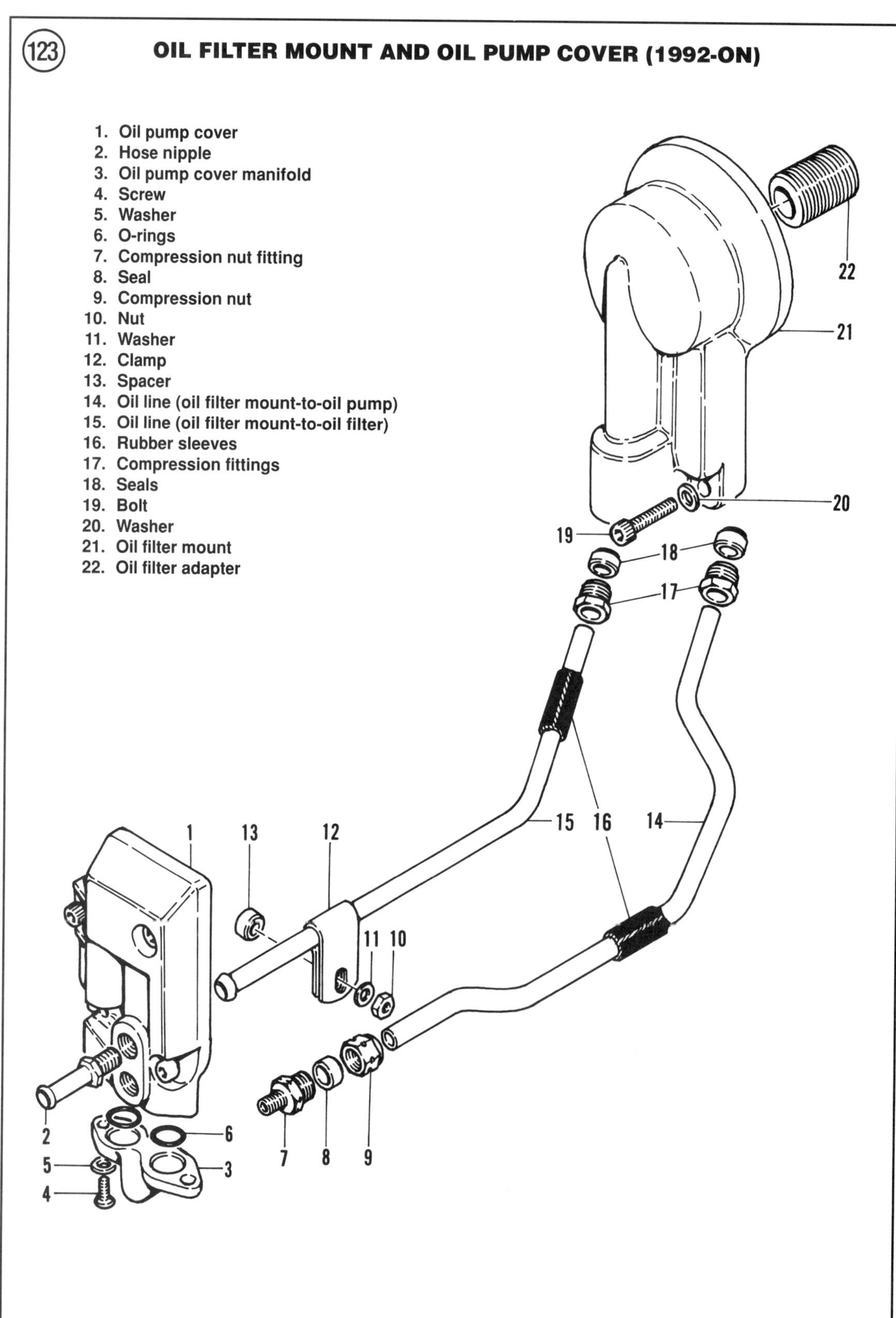
123
OIL FILTER MOUNT AND OIL PUMP COVER (1992-ON)
1. Oil pump cover
2. Hose nipple
3. Oil pump cover manifold
4. Screw
5. Washer
6. O-rings
7. Compression nut fitting
8. Seal
9. Compression nut
10. Nut
11. Washer
12. Clamp
13. Spacer
14. Oil line (oil filter mount-to-oil pump)
15. Oil line (oil filter mount-to-oil filter)
16. Rubber sleeves
17. Compression fittings
18. Seals
19. Bolt
20. Washer
21. Oil filter mount
22. Oil filter adapter
22
21
20
19
18
17
15
16
14
1
13
12
11
10
2
6
5
3
4
7
8
9

10. Assemble the oil line clamp, spacer, washer and nut as shown in **Figure 123**; do not tighten the nut at this time.

11. Slide the oil pump manifold compression nut onto the oil line (15, **Figure 123**).

12. Install 2 new O-rings onto the oil pump cover manifold and place the manifold onto the bottom of the oil pump cover. Install the manifold screws and washers and tighten to the torque specification in **Table 3**.

13. Thread the compression nut (9, **Figure 123**) onto the compression nut fitting; tighten nut until it bottoms out on fitting.

14. Tighten the upper oil line compression fittings (17, **Figure 113**) until the hex portion on fittings seat against the oil filter mount.

15. Tighten the oil line securing nut (10, **Figure 123**) securely.

16. Install the oil filter and fill the oil tank or oil pan as described in Chapter Three.

17. Start the engine and check for leaks.

## GEARCASE COVER AND TIMING GEARS

Refer to **Figure 124** (1984-1992) or **Figure 125** (1993-on) when performing procedures in this section.

### Removal

1. Remove the pushrods, valve tappets and guides as described in this chapter.

2. Remove the tappet oil screen cap and O-ring. Then remove the spring and screen. See **Figure 126**.

3. Remove the electronic ignition sensor plate and rotor as described in Chapter Nine.

4. Place an oil drain pan underneath the gearcase cover.

*NOTE*
*The gearcase cover screws are different lengths. To ease reassembly, draw an outline of the gearcase cover on cardboard, and then punch a hole along the outline to represent the position of each screw. Then, as you remove the screws from the gearcase, install them into the appropriate hole in the cardboard.*

5A. On 1984-1992 models, remove the gearcase cover as follows:

a. Remove the gearcase cover screws.
b. The gearcase cover is located by snug dowel pins and must be worked off carefully. Tap the cover lightly with a soft-faced hammer at the point where the cover projects beyond the crankcase and remove it (**Figure 127**).
c. Remove the gasket.

5B. On 1993-on models, remove the gearcase cover as follows:

a. Fabricate the puller shown in **Figure 128**.
b. Mount the puller onto the gearcase cover and secure it with 2 screws (**Figure 129**).
c. Operate the puller pressure screw and remove the gearcase cover and gasket.
d. Remove the puller from the gearcase cover.

6. Remove the cam gear (**Figure 130**).

7. Remove the cam gear spacer washer (1984-1987) and the cam gear thrust washer (**Figure 131**).

8. Remove the breather valve washer (**Figure 132**) and the breather gear (**Figure 133**).

9A. On 1984-1992 models, remove the pinion gear shaft nut and gear as follows:

*NOTE*
*The pinion gear shaft nut has left-hand threads. Turn the nut clockwise to remove it.*

a. Remove the pinion gear shaft nut (**Figure 134**) using the Pinion Shaft Nut Socket (part No. HD-94555-55A).
b. Remove the pinion gear (**Figure 135**) using the pinion gear puller (part No. HD-96830-51A).

9B. On 1993-on models, remove the pinion gear shaft nut and gear as follows:

*NOTE*
*The pinion gear shaft nut has right-hand threads. Turn the nut counterclockwise to remove it.*

a. Remove the pinion gear shaft nut (14, **Figure 125**) with a socket.
b. Remove the pinion gear (13, **Figure 125**).

10A. On 1984-1992 models, remove the following parts in order:

(124)

**GEARCASE ASSEMBLY**
**(1984-1992)**

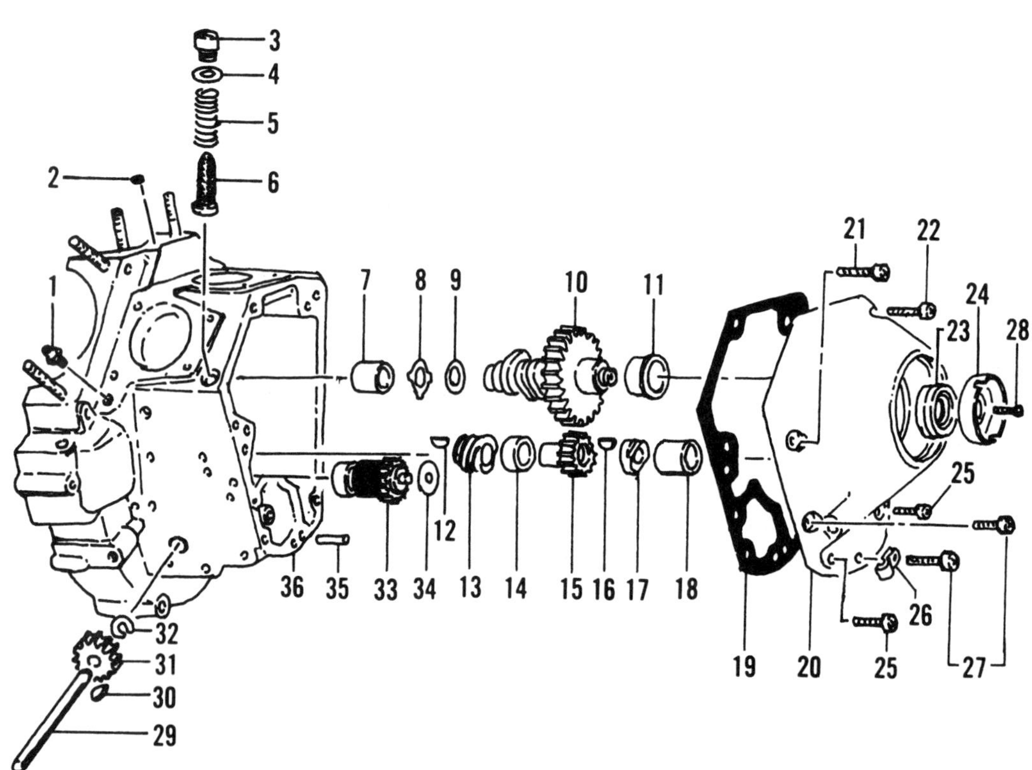


1. Oil pressure switch
2. Plug
3. Oil screen cap
4. O-ring
5. Spring
6. Oil screen
7. Camshaft needle bearing
8. Cam gear thrust washer
9. Cam gear spacer washer (1984-1987)
10. Cam gear
11. Camshaft bushing
12. Woodruff key
13. Oil pump pinion shaft gear
14. Pinion gear spacer
15. Pinion gear
16. Woodruff key
17. Pinion shaft nut
18. Pinion shaft bushing
19. Gasket
20. Gearcase cover
21. Screw (1 3/4 in.)
22. Screw (1 1/4 in.)
23. Camshaft oil seal
24. Rotor
25. Screw (1 in.)
26. Clip
27. Screw (1 1/4 in.)
28. Rotor bolt
29. Oil pump shaft
30. Woodruff key
31. Oil pump drive gear
32. Oil pump drive gear lock ring
33. Breather gear
34. Breather gear spacer
35. Dowel pin
36. Gearcase

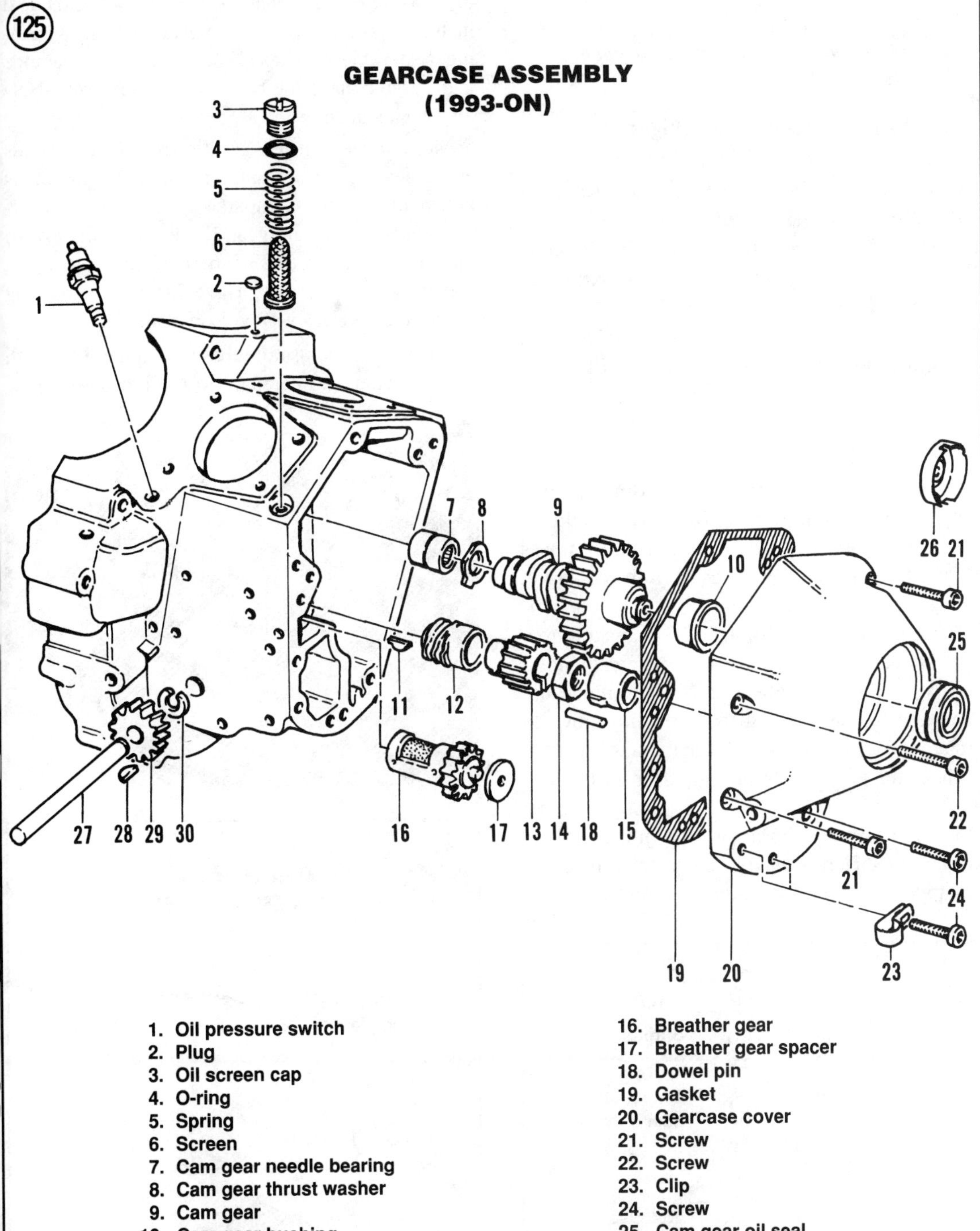


1. Oil pressure switch
2. Plug
3. Oil screen cap
4. O-ring
5. Spring
6. Screen
7. Cam gear needle bearing
8. Cam gear thrust washer
9. Cam gear
10. Cam gear bushing
11. Woodruff key
12. Oil pump pinion shaft gear
13. Pinion gear
14. Pinion shaft nut
15. Pinion shaft bushing
16. Breather gear
17. Breather gear spacer
18. Dowel pin
19. Gasket
20. Gearcase cover
21. Screw
22. Screw
23. Clip
24. Screw
25. Cam gear oil seal
26. Rotor
27. Oil pump shaft
28. Woodruff key
29. Oil pump drive gear
30. Oil pump drive gear lock ring

*NOTE*
*1990-1992 models use a single Woodruff key for the pinion and oil pump gears.*

a. *1984-1989:* Woodruff key (**Figure 136**).
b. Pinion gear spacer (**Figure 137**).
c. Oil pump pinion shaft gear (**Figure 138**).
d. Woodruff key (**Figure 139**).

10B. On 1993-on models, remove the oil pump pinion shaft gear (12, **Figure 125**) and Woodruff key (11, **Figure 125**).

11. If required, remove the oil pump drive gear and oil pump as described in this chapter.

## Inspection

1. Thoroughly clean gearcase compartment, cover and components with solvent. Blow out all oil passages with compressed air. Make sure that all traces of gasket compound are removed from the gasket mating surfaces.

2. Check the oil screen (**Figure 126**) to make sure it is not blocked or damaged. Test the screen by holding it upside down and filling it with engine oil. Watch the screen to see that the oil flows evenly through the screen. If not, replace the screen.

3. Check the pinion gear and cam gear bushings in the gearcase cover for grooving, pitting or other wear. If the bushings appear visibly worn, have them replaced by a Harley-Davidson dealer. If the bushings appear okay, perform Step 4.

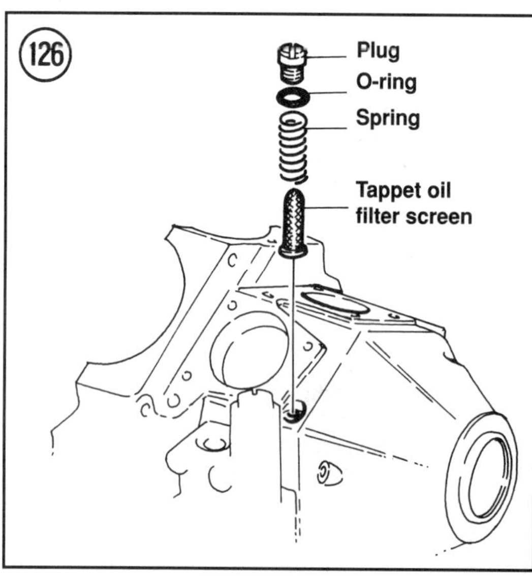


4. Measure the cam gear (A, **Figure 140**) O.D. and its bushing I.D. to check cam gear shaft fit in bushing. See **Table 2** for specifications. If the clearance is excessive, have the bushings replaced by a Harley-Davidson dealer.

5. Measure the cam gear (A, **Figure 140**) small ends at the bearing surface and near the cam gear lobes with a micrometer. Compare the 2 different measuring points on the cam gear. If the camshaft is worn more than 0.003 in. (0.08 mm), replace the camshaft and its needle bearing. Have the needle bearing replaced by a Harley-Davidson dealer.

6. Measure the camshaft lobes (B, **Figure 140**) with a micrometer and compare to the lobes on a new

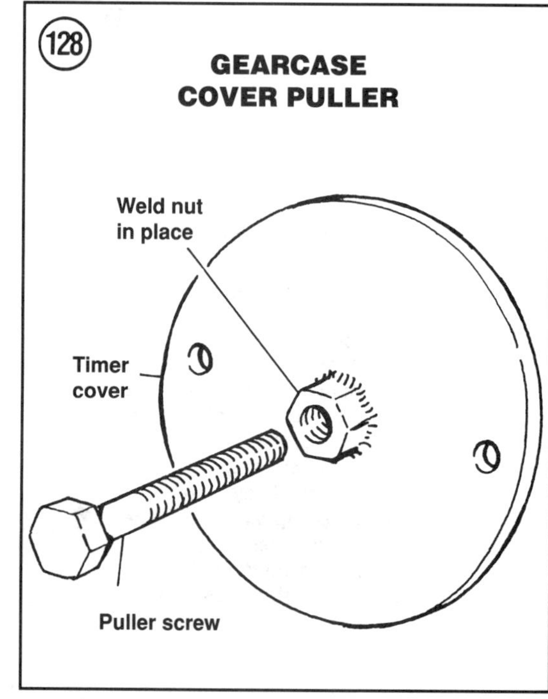

Evolution cam. If the camshaft lobes are worn more than 0.006 in. (0.15 mm), replace the camshaft.

*NOTE*
*Camshafts used in early V-twin models cannot be used in Evolution engines and vice versa. Do not use a non-Evolution cam when comparing lobe wear in Step 6.*

7. Check the cam gear oil seal (**Figure 141**) in the gearcase cover. If worn, carefully pry it out of the

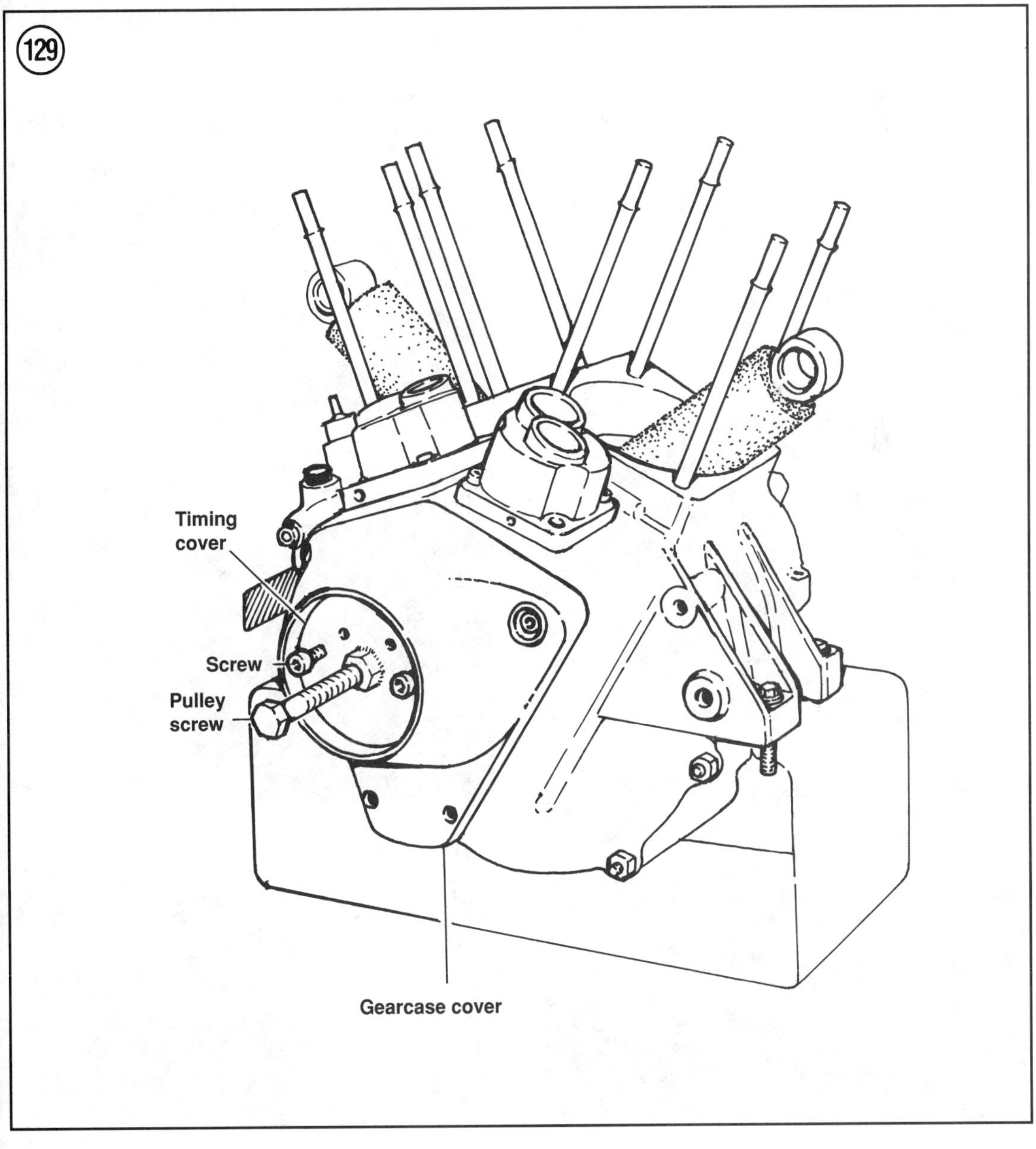

129

Timing cover

Screw

Pulley screw

Gearcase cover

case. Install a new seal by driving it into the gearcase cover using a suitable size drift or socket placed on the outside portion of the seal.

8. Inspect the breather gear (**Figure 142**) teeth for damage. Also check the screen for debris or damage and clean with solvent if necessary. Replace the breather gear if necessary.

9. Check all gears for signs of wear or damage; replace if necessary. If the cam gears appear okay, check the gear mesh as follows:

a. Assemble the cam gear (10, **Figure 124**) and pinion gears (13 and 15, **Figure 124**) in the gearcase. Do not install the cam gear spacer (9, **Figure 124**).

*NOTE*
*The cam gear spacer is not used on 1988 and later models.*

b. Install the gearcase cover (**Figure 127**) and secure it with a minimum of 3 screws. Tighten the screws securely.

c. Check the gear mesh through the tappet guide hole (**Figure 143**) by hand. Gear mesh is correct when there is no play between the gears and the cam gear can be moved back and forth with slight drag.

d. If gear mesh is incorrect, replace the cam and pinion gears.

*NOTE*
*Cam and pinion gears are color-coded by their pitch diameters. Replacement gears must be matched or abnormal gear noise will result. When replacing these gears, have gears matched by a Harley-Davidson dealer.*

131

132

133

134

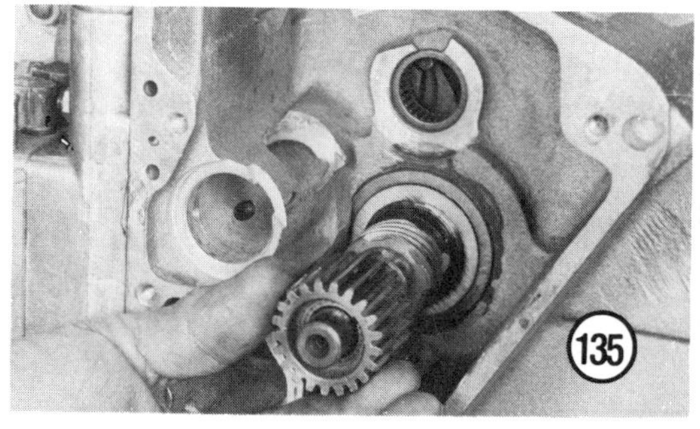
135

## Assembly

Refer to **Figure 124** when performing this procedure.

1. Assembly is the reverse of disassembly, plus the following.

2. Before final assembly of gearcase components, check the breather gear end play as follows:

a. Install the breather gear (**Figure 144**) and a new cover gasket on the gearcase.

b. Install the spacer (**Figure 145**) on the breather gear.

c. Lay a straightedge across the gearcase at the breather gear spacer. Then using a feeler gauge, measure the clearance between the straightedge and the spacer. See **Figure 146**.

d. Subtract 0.006 in. (0.15 mm) from the clearance determined in sub-step c. This is the amount the gearcase gasket will compress.

e. An end play clearance of 0.001-0.016 in. (0.02-0.41 mm) is correct. If the clearance

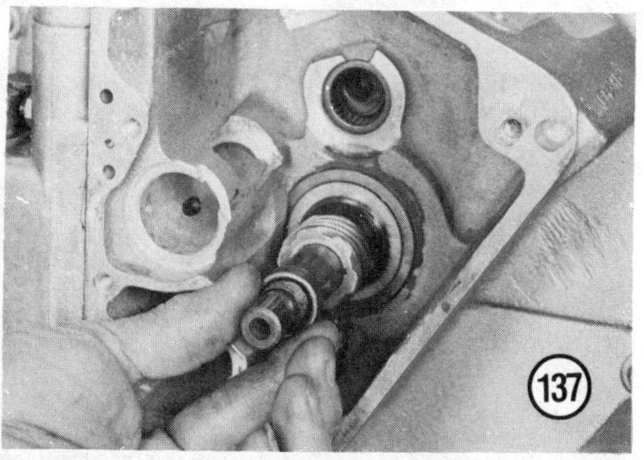


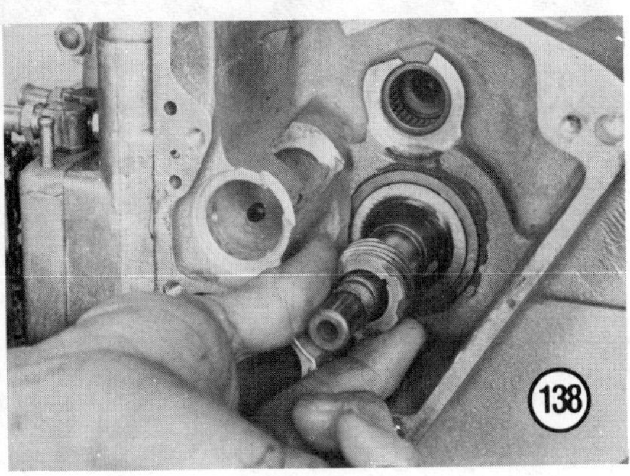

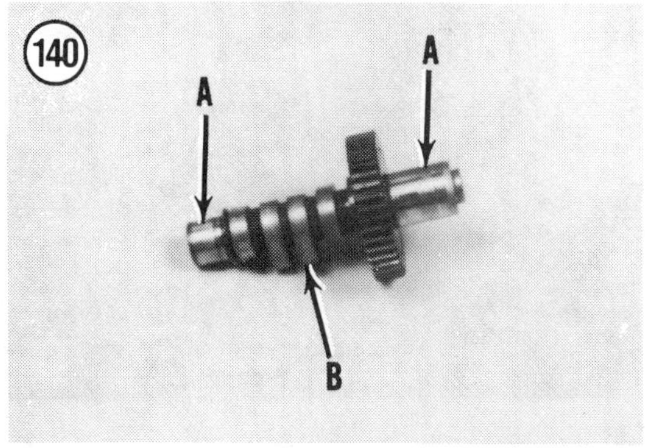


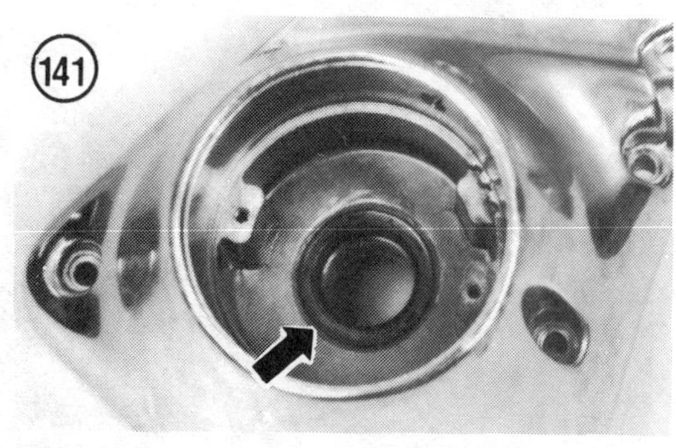

exceeds this amount, install a thicker spacer (**Figure 147**). Spacers are available in various thicknesses from Harley-Davidson dealers.

3. Before final assembly of gearcase components, check the cam gear end play as follows:

a. Install the cam gear thrust washer, cam gear spacer washer (1984-1987) (**Figure 148**) and the cam gear (**Figure 149**).

b. Install the gearcase cover (**Figure 127**) and a new gasket. Install a minimum of 3 gearcase cover screws. Tighten the screws securely.

c. Measure the cam gear end play between the gear shaft and the thrust washer with a feeler gauge inserted through the gearcase tappet hole (**Figure 150**).

d. *1984-1987*: An end play clearance of 0.001-0.016 in. (0.02-0.41 mm) is correct. If the clearance exceeds this amount, install a suitable size spacer (**Figure 151**) to bring the clearance within specifications. Spacers in different thicknesses are available from Harley-Davidson dealers.

142

143

144

145

146

147

e. *1988-on*: An end play clearance of 0.001-0.050 in. (0.02-1.27 mm) is correct. If the clearance exceeds this amount, check for worn or damaged parts.

4. Slide the cam gear thrust washer and cam gear spacer washer (1984-1987) onto the end of the cam gear.

5. Install the oil pump pinion shaft gear Woodruff key (**Figure 139**) on 1984-1989 models. 1990 and later models use a single Woodruff key for the pinion and oil pump gears.

148

149

150

*NOTE*

*On 1984 and early 1985 models, install the oil pump pinion shaft gear (**Figure 138**) so that the chamfer on the gear faces toward the inside of the engine. On late 1985 and later models, the oil pump pinion shaft gears are chamfered on both sides and the gear can be installed either way.*

6. Slide the oil pump pinion shaft gear (**Figure 138**) onto the shaft, making sure to align the keyway in the gear with the Woodruff key.

7. On 1984-1992 models, install the pinion gear spacer (**Figure 137**) onto the end of the pinion gear.

8. Install the oil pump drive gear Woodruff key. Then install the oil pump drive gear and secure it with a new lock ring.

9. Install the breather gear spacer onto the end of the breather gear (**Figure 145**).

10. Install the cam, breather and pinion gears so that the timing marks on the gears align as shown in **Figure 149**.

11A. On 1984-1992 models, perform the following:

*NOTE*

*The pinion shaft uses left-hand thread. Turn the nut counterclockwise to tighten it.*

a. Put 2 drops of Loctite 262 (red) on the pinion shaft nut before installing and tightening it.

b. Install the pinion shaft nut and tighten it to 35-45 ft.-lb. (47-61 N•m). Use the pinion shaft nut socket (HD-94555-55A) to tighten the pinion shaft nut.

c. After tightening the pinion shaft nut, check that the pinion shaft spacer has noticeable end play. If not, remove the pinion shaft nut and

151

4

the pinion shaft gear and reinstall. Make sure the timing marks in Step 10 are correct.

11B. On 1993-on models, perform the following:

*NOTE*
*The pinion shaft nut uses right-hand threads. Turn the nut clockwise to tighten it.*

a. Put 2 drops of Loctite 262 (red) on the pinion shaft nut before installing and tightening it.
b. Install the pinion shaft nut and tighten to 35-45 ft.-lb. (47-61 N•m).

12. Turn the gear train to make sure all gears rotate freely. Any binding should be corrected before completing engine reassembly.

13. Coat a new gearcase gasket with a non-hardening gasket sealer and install it.

14. Install the gearcase and screws. Tighten the screws to 80-110 in.-lb. (9.2-12.6 N•m).

15. Pour approximately 1/4 pint (0.12 L) of engine oil through the tappet guide hold to provide initial gear train lubrication.

16. Install the ignition components as described in Chapter Nine.

## CRANKCASE AND CRANKSHAFT

Crankcases must be disassembled to service the crankshaft, connecting rod bearings, pinion shaft bearings and sprocket shaft bearings. This section describes basic checks and procedures that can be performed in the home shop. Bearing and crankshaft service should be referred to a Harley-Davidson dealer equipped to handle such repairs.

### Crankshaft End Play Check

It is recommended that crankshaft end play be measured before completely disassembling the crankcase. Crankshaft end play is a measure of sprocket shaft bearing wear.

1. Remove the engine from the frame as described in this chapter.
2. Mount the crankcase in a suitable fixture (**Figure 152**).
3. Install the bearing installation tool (part No. HD-97225-55) onto the sprocket shaft to preload the bearing races. See **Figure 152**.
4. Attach a dial indicator so that the probe touches against the end of the crankshaft (**Figure 152**).
5. Turn and pull on the sprocket shaft while noting the end play registering on the dial indicator. If end play exceeds limit in **Table 2**, the inner bearing

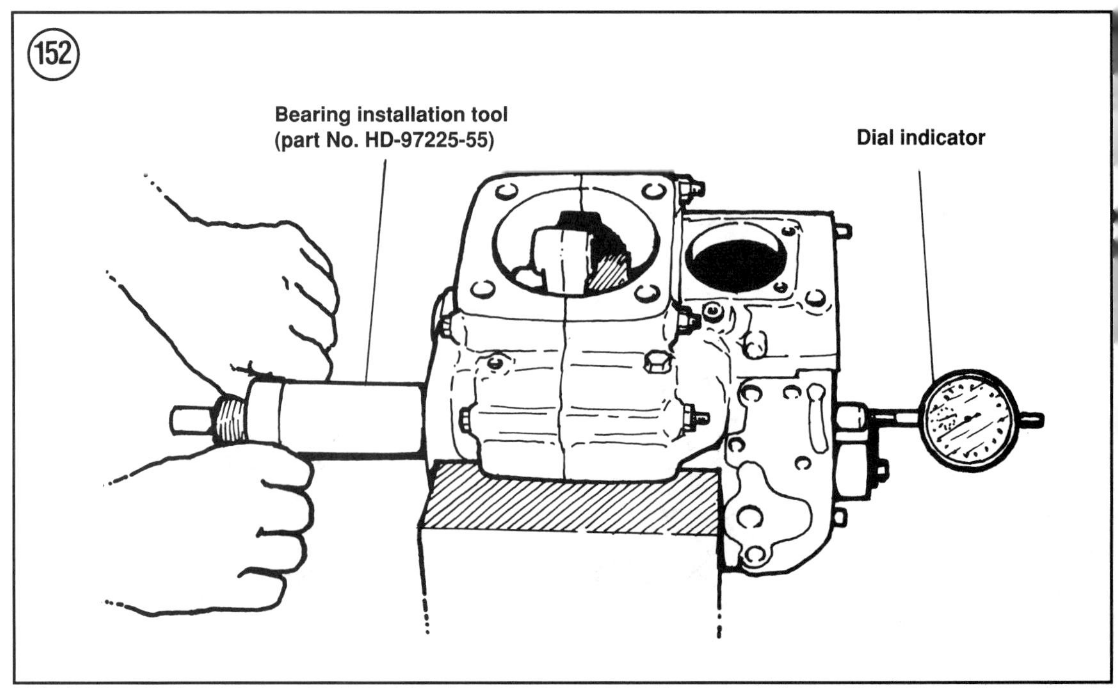

spacer (4, **Figure 153**) must be replaced by selecting a different spacer from the chart in **Table 4**.

## Disassembly

Refer to **Figure 153** for this procedure.

1. Remove the engine from the frame as described in this chapter.

*CAUTION*
*After removing the cylinders, slip rubber hoses over the cylinder studs to prevent their damage during the following service procedures. In addition, do not lift the crankcase assembly by grabbing the cylinder studs. Bent or damaged cylinder studs may cause oil leakage.*

2. Disassemble and remove the gearcase assembly as described in this chapter.
3. Check the crankshaft end play as described in this chapter.

*NOTE*
*When removing the crankcase bolts and studs in Step 4, note that the top center stud (4, **Figure 154**) and the right bottom studs (5, **Figure 154**) are matched and fitted to the crankcase holes for correct crankcase alignment. During their removal, mark them so they can be reinstalled in their original positions.*

4. See **Figure 154**. Remove the crankcase bolts and studs.
5. Lay the crankcase assembly on wood blocks so that right-hand side faces up.
6. Tap the crankcase with a plastic mallet and remove the right-hand crankcase half.
7. Remove the pinion shaft spiral lock ring (**Figure 155**).
8. Grasp the 2 bearing washers and remove the washers, bearings and retainers as an assembly (**Figure 156**). Store the complete assembly in a plastic bag.

4

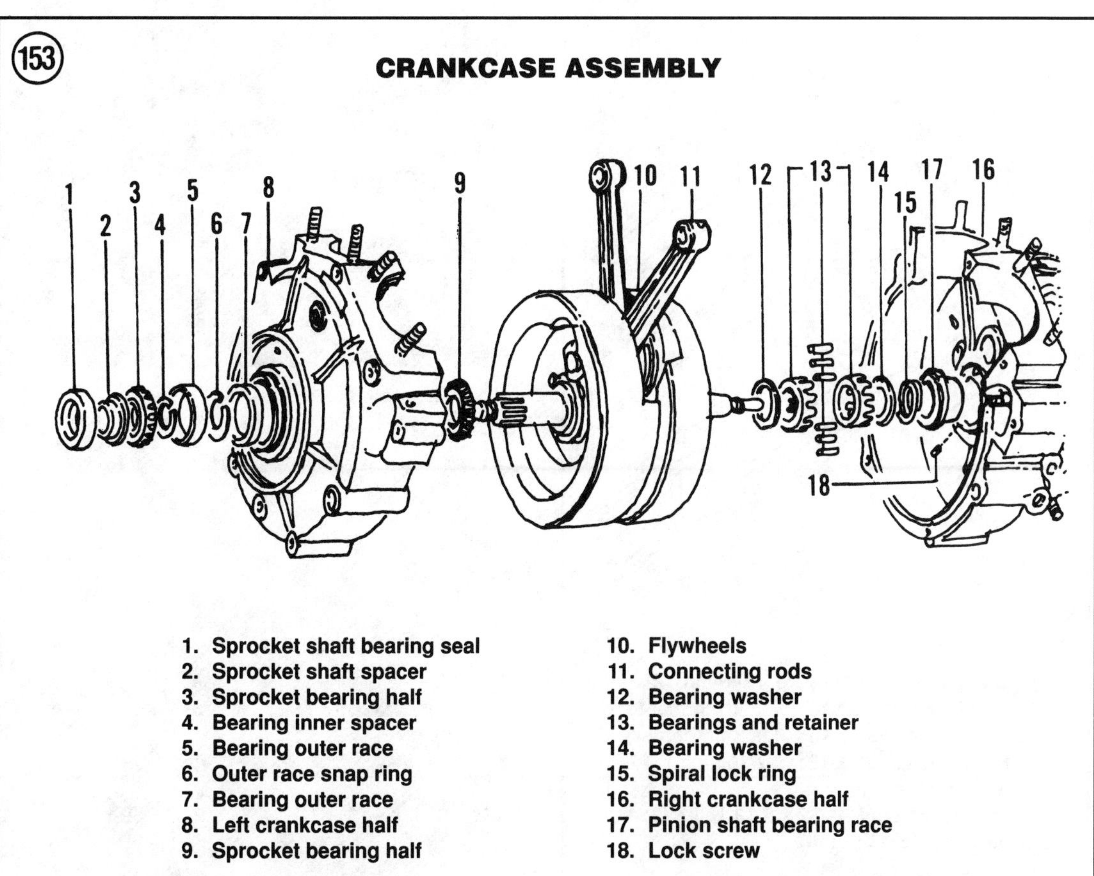


1. Sprocket shaft bearing seal
2. Sprocket shaft spacer
3. Sprocket bearing half
4. Bearing inner spacer
5. Bearing outer race
6. Outer race snap ring
7. Bearing outer race
8. Left crankcase half
9. Sprocket bearing half
10. Flywheels
11. Connecting rods
12. Bearing washer
13. Bearings and retainer
14. Bearing washer
15. Spiral lock ring
16. Right crankcase half
17. Pinion shaft bearing race
18. Lock screw

*NOTE*
*Further disassembly of the crankcase/flywheel assembly is not recommended. A hydraulic press is required to separate the crankshaft from the left-hand crankcase half. Furthermore, additional equipment is required to install and line ream new bearings properly.*

9. Check connecting rod side play with a feeler gauge as shown in **Figure 157**. If the side play is not within the specifications in **Table 2**, refer service to a Harley-Davidson dealer.

10. Refer crankcases to a Harley-Davidson dealer for inspection and repair.

11. Installation is the reverse of these steps, noting the following.

12. If the crankshaft was removed, have it pressed into the left-hand crankcase by a Harley-Davidson dealer.

(154) **CRANKCASE STUDS**

1. **Crankcase stud bolt, 3/8 × 3-1/4 in. (2)**
2. **Crankcase stud, 5/16 × 5 in. (right center)**
3. **Crankcase stud, 5/16 × 6 in. (left center)**
4. **Crankcase stud, 5/16 × 5-7/16 in. (2) (top and top right)**
5. **Crankcase stud, 11/32 × 5-13/16 in. (2) (left and right bottom)**

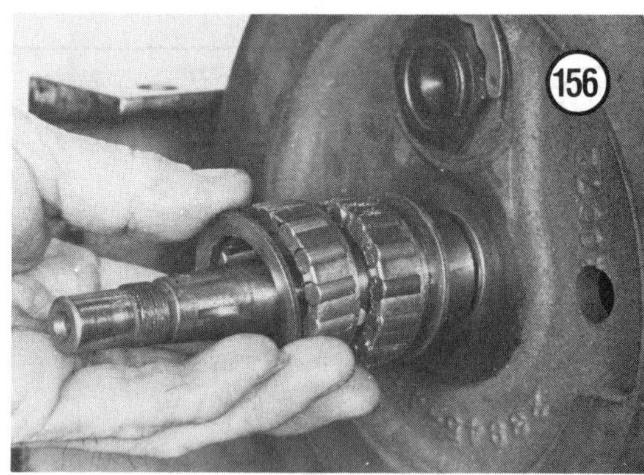

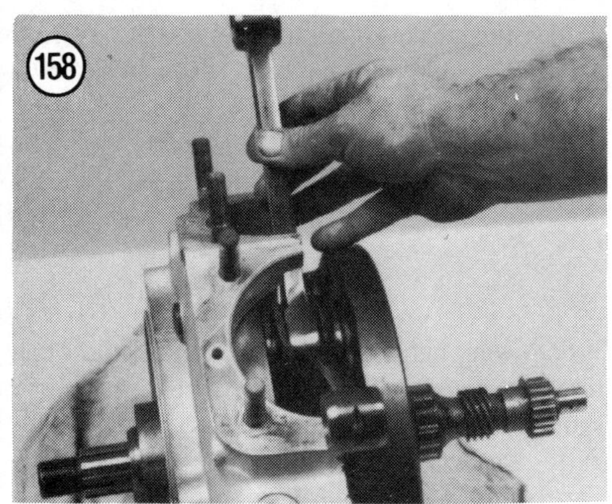

158

**CRANKCASE TORQUE SEQUENCE**

2
4
7
6
8
5
3
1

159

160

13. Make sure rods are aligned as shown in **Figure 158** before assembling the right-hand crankcase.
14. Referring to **Figure 153**, install the bearing washer, bearings and retainer and the bearing washer. See **Figure 156**.
15. Install a new spiral lock ring (**Figure 155**) in the pinion shaft groove.
16. Coat the crankcase mating surfaces with Harley-Davidson Crankcase Sealant (part No. HD-99650-81) or 3M #800.
17. Align the crankcase halves and install the right-hand crankcase.
18. Referring to **Figure 154**, tap the No. 4 and No. 5 bolts into the crankcase. These bolts are used for alignment and must be installed first.
19. Install the remaining studs and bolts (**Figure 154**).
20. Install the stud nuts and tighten as follows:
    a. Install the stud nuts and tighten finger-tight.

*NOTE*
*The following torque procedure must be followed to ensure crankcase longevity.*

    b. Tighten the crankcase nuts to 10 ft.-lb. (14 N•m) in the order shown in **Figure 159**.
    c. Install the cylinders and cylinder heads as described in this chapter, the perform sub-step d.
    d. Tighten the crankcase nuts to 15-17 ft.-lb. (20-35 N•m) in the order shown in **Figure 159**.

21. Install the sprocket shaft spacer (2, **Figure 153**). Then install a new sprocket shaft bearing seal (**Figure 160**). On dry clutch models, the seal lip must face toward the flywheels. On wet clutch models, the seal lip must face away from the flywheels. Press the seal into place with the Sprocket Shaft Seal Installation Tool (part No. HD-39361) (**Figure 161**) or equivalent.
22. Recheck flywheel end play as described in this chapter.

### Cylinder Stud Replacement

Bent or damaged cylinder studs must be replaced to prevent cylinder head and cylinder leakage. The following tools will be required to replace the cylinder studs:

a. Air or electric impact wrench.
b. 0.313 in. diameter steel ball.

*NOTE*
*For steel ball, use Harley-Davidson steel ball (part No. 8860).*

1. If the engine is assembled, stuff some clean shop rags into the crankcase opening to prevent abrasive particles from falling into the engine.
2. Remove the damaged stud with a stud remover.
3. Clean the crankcase threads and the new stud with solvent or contact cleaner. Blow dry.

*NOTE*
*The cylinder studs have a shoulder on the upper end; see **Figure 162**.*

4. Measuring from the top of the stud, paint a mark that is 5.75 in. (146.05 mm) down the stud; see **Figure 163**.
5. Drop the 0.313 in. diameter steel ball into a cylinder head bolt and thread the bolt onto the top of the new stud.
6. Hand-thread the new stud into the crankcase, then install it with an air gun until the paint mark on the stud aligns with the crankcase base gasket surface.

*CAUTION*
*Do not use a breaker bar or ratchet to install the studs. These tools will bend the stud, damaging it.*

7. Remove the cylinder head bolt and steel ball from the cylinder stud.

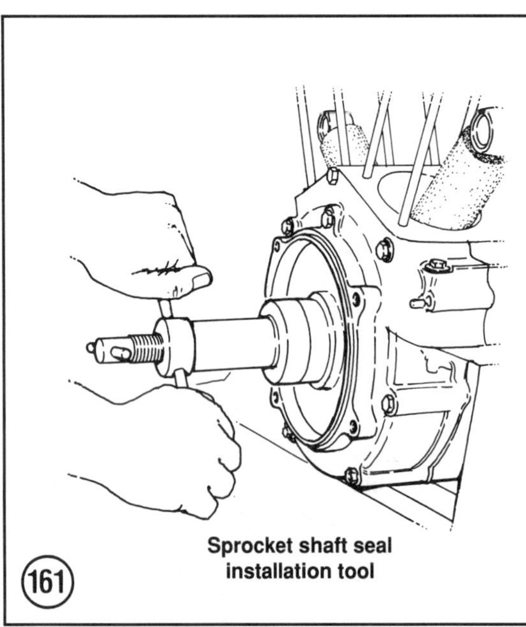


8. Measure the stud's installed height with a vernier caliper. The stud's installed height should be 5.670-5.770 in. (144.02-146.56 mm).
9. Place a protective hose over the stud.
10. Repeat Steps 2-9 for each stud.

## ENGINE BREAK-IN

Following cylinder servicing (new pistons, new rings, etc.) and major lower end work, the engine should be broken in just as though it were new. The performance and service life of the engine depends greatly on a careful and sensible break-in.

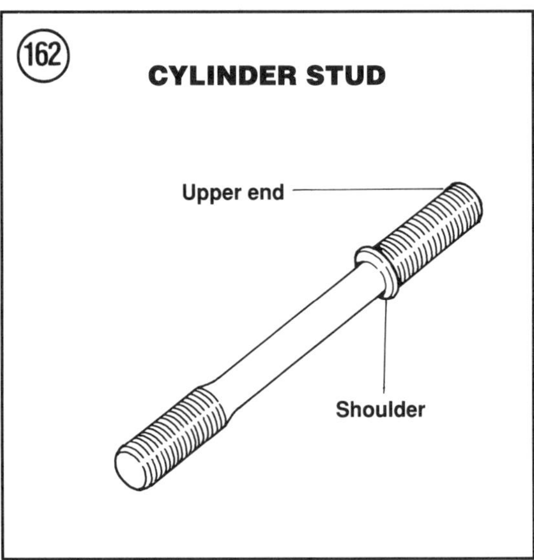


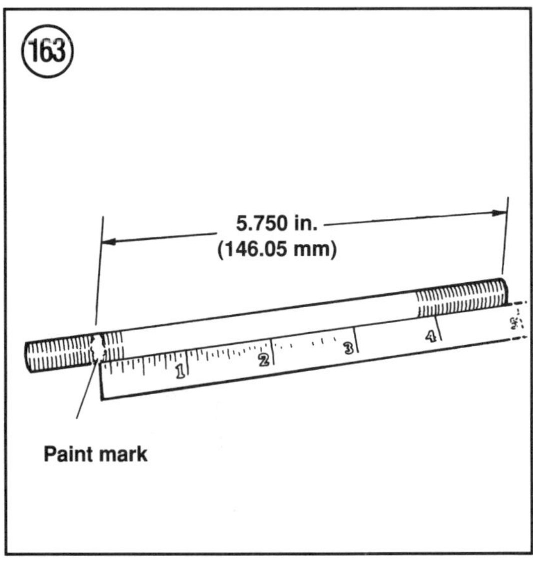

For the first 500 miles (800 km), no more than one-third throttle should be used and the speed should be varied as much as possible within the one-third throttle limit. Prolonged, steady running at one speed, no matter how moderate, is to be avoided as is hard acceleration.

Following the 500-mile (800 km) service, increasingly more throttle can be used but full throttle should not be used until the motorcycle has covered at least 1,000 miles (1,600 km) and then it should be limited to short bursts until 1,500 miles (2,400 km) have been logged.

During engine break-in, oil consumption will be higher than normal. It is important to frequently check and correct the oil level in the tank, making sure to maintain a 1 in. (25.4 mm) air gap in the top of the tank.

### 500 Mile (800 km) Service

It is essential that the oil tank be drained, flushed and refilled and the oil filter serviced after the first 500 break-in miles (800 km). In addition, it is a good idea to repeat this service at the completion of break-in (about 1,500 miles [2,400 km]) to ensure that all of the particles produced during break-in are removed from the lubrication system. The small added expense may be considered a smart investment that will pay off in increased engine life.

4

**Table 1 GENERAL ENGINE SPECIFICATIONS**

| | |
|---|---|
| Engine type | Air cooled, 4-stroke, OHV, V-twin |
| Number of cylinders | 2 |
| Bore and stroke | 3.498 × 4.250 in. (88.85 × 107.95 mm) |
| Displacement | 81.6 cu. in. (1,340 cc) |
| Compression ratio | 8.5:1 |
| Lubrication system | Forced feed oiling system |

**Table 2 ENGINE SERVICE SPECIFICATIONS**

| | Specification | | Wear limit | |
|---|---|---|---|---|
| | in. | mm | in.[1] | mm[1] |
| Cylinder head | | | | |
| Warpage | 0-0.006 | 0-0.15 | 0.006 | 0.15 |
| Valve seat in head | 0.0045-0.0020 | 0.114-0.051 | 0.0020[2] | 0.051[2] |
| Valve guide ID | 0.0033-0.0020 | 0.084-0.051 | 0.0020[2] | 0.051[2] |
| Valves | | | | |
| Fit in guide | | | | |
| Intake | 0.0008-0.0026 | 0.020-0.066 | 0.0035 | 0.089 |
| Exhaust | 0.0015-0.0033 | 0.038-0.084 | 0.0040 | 0.102 |
| Seat width | | | | |
| 1984 | 0.040-0.062 | 1.02-1.57 | 0.062 | 1.57 |
| 1985-on | 0.040-0.062 | 1.02-1.57 | 0.090 | 2.29 |
| Stem length from cylinder head boss | 1.990-2.024 | 50.55-51.41 | 2.034 | 51.66 |
| Valve springs | | | | |
| Outer springs | | | | |
| Free length | 2.105-2.177 | 53.47-55.3 | 2.177 | 55.30 |
| Compression | | | | |
| Closed—1.751-1.848 in. (44.47-46.94 mm) | 72-92 lbs. | 33-42 kg | — | — |
| Open—1.282-1.378 in. (32.56-35.00 mm) | 183-207 lbs. | 83-94 kg | — | — |
| Inner springs | | | | |
| Free length | 1.926-1.996 | 48.92-50.70 | 1.996 | 50.70 |
| Compression | | | | |

(continued)

**Table 2 ENGINE SERVICE SPECIFICATIONS (continued)**

| | Specification in. | Specification mm | Wear limit in.[1] | Wear limit mm[1] |
|---|---|---|---|---|
| Compression (continued) | | | | |
| Closed—1.577-1.683 in. | | | | |
| (40.06-42.75 mm) | 38-49 lbs. | 17.24-22.23 | — | — |
| Open—1.107-1.213 in. | | | | |
| (28.12-30.81 mm) | 98-112 lbs. | 44.45-50.80 | — | — |
| Stem-to-face eccentricity | — | — | 0.002 | 0.05 |
| Rocker arm | | | | |
| End clearance | 0.003-0.013 | 0.08-0.33 | 0.025 | 0.63 |
| Shaft clearance | 0.0005-0.002 | 0.013-0.050 | 0.0035 | 0.089 |
| Bushing fit in rocker arm | 0.004-0.002 | 0.10-0.05 | — | — |
| Rocker arm shaft | | | | |
| Shaft fit in rocker cover | 0.0007-0.0022 | 0.018-0.056 | 0.0035 | 0.089 |
| Piston | | | | |
| Clearance in cylinder | | | | |
| 1984-early 1985 | 0.0008-0.0023 | 0.020-0.058 | 0.0053 | 0.135 |
| Late 1985-on[3] | 0.00075-0.00175 | 0.019-0.044 | 0.0053 | 0.135 |
| Piston pin | | | | |
| Pin fit in piston | 0.0002-0.0006 | 0.005-0.015 | 0.001 | 0.02 |
| Piston rings | | | | |
| Compression ring end gap | 0.007-0.020 | 0.18-0.51 | 0.030 | 0.76 |
| Oil control ring rail gap | 0.009-0.052 | 0.23-1.32 | 0.065 | 1.65 |
| Compression ring | | | | |
| side clearance | | | | |
| Top | 0.002-0.0045 | 0.05-0.11 | 0.006 | 0.15 |
| 2nd | 0.0016-0.0041 | 0.041-0.104 | 0.006 | 0.15 |
| Oil control ring | | | | |
| side clearance | 0.0016-0.0076 | 0.041-0.193 | 0.008 | 0.20 |
| Cylinder bore sizes | | | | |
| Taper | | | 0.002 | 0.05 |
| Out-of-round | | | 0.003 | 0.08 |
| Bore | | | | |
| Standard | 3.4980[4] | 88.849[4] | 3.501 | 88.925 |
| 0.005 in. (0.13 mm) oversize | 3.5030[4] | 88.976[4] | 3.506 | 89.052 |
| 0.010 in. (0.25 mm) oversize | 3.5080[4] | 89.103[4] | 3.511 | 89.179 |
| 0.020 in. (0.51 mm) oversize | 3.5180[4] | 89.357[4] | 3.521 | 89.433 |
| 0.030 in. (0.76 mm) oversize | 3.5280[4] | 89.611[4] | 3.531 | 89.687 |
| Tappets | | | | |
| Guide fit in crankcase | 0.000-0.004 | 0.00-0.10 | — | — |
| Fit in guide | 0.0008-0.002 | 0.020-0.051 | 0.003 | 0.08 |
| Roller end clearance | — | — | 0.015 | 0.38 |
| Connecting rods | | | | |
| Piston pin fit | 0.0003-0.0007 | 0.008-0.018 | 0.001 | 0.03 |
| Side play @ crankshaft | 0.005-0.025 | 0.13-0.63 | 0.030 | 0.76 |
| Fit on crankpin | 0.0004-0.0017 | 0.010-0.043 | 0.002 | 0.05 |
| Gearcase | | | | |
| Breather gear end play | See text | — | — | — |
| Cam gear shaft fit | | | | |
| in bushing | 0.00075-0.00175 | 0.0190-0.0444 | 0.003 | 0.08 |
| Cam gear shaft fit | | | | |
| in bearing | 0.0005-0.0025 | 0.013-0.063 | 0.005 | 0.13 |
| Cam gear end play | See text | — | — | — |
| Oil pump drive shaft fit | | | | |
| in crankcase bushing | 0.0004-0.0025 | 0.010-0.063 | 0.0035 | 0.089 |
| Flywheels | | | | |
| Runout (@ rim) | 0.000-0.010 | 0.00-0.25 | 0.015 | 0.38 |
| Runout (@ shaft) | 0.000-0.002 | 0.00-0.05 | 0.003 | 0.08 |
| End play | 0.001-0.005 | 0.02-0.13 | 0.006 | 0.15 |

(continued)

**Table 2 ENGINE SERVICE SPECIFICATIONS (continued)**

| | Specification in. | Specification mm | Wear limit in.[1] | Wear limit mm[1] |
|---|---|---|---|---|
| Sprocket shaft bearing | | | | |
| Cup fit in crankcase | 0.0032-0.0012 | 0.081-0.030 | — | — |
| Cone fit on shaft | 0.0015-0.0005 | 0.038-0.013 | — | — |
| Pinion shaft bearing | | | | |
| Roller bearing fit | 0.0002-0.0009 | 0.005-0.023 | — | — |
| Cover bushing fit | 0.001-0.0025 | 0.025-0.063 | 0.0035 | 0.089 |

[1] Part should be considered worn if measurement exceeds wear limit specification, unless otherwise noted; see below.
[2] Part should be considered worn if measurement is less than the wear limit specification.
[3] Specifies clearance of KSG pistons.
[4] ± 0.0002 in. (0.005 mm)



**Table 3 ENGINE TIGHTENING TORQUES**

| | ft.-lb. | in.-lb. | N•m |
|---|---|---|---|
| Cylinder head bolts | See text | — | — |
| Spark plug | 18-22 | — | 24.8-30.4 |
| Rocker cover bolts | | | |
| 1/4 in. | 10-13 | — | 13.8-17.9 |
| 5/16 in. | 15-18 | — | 20.7-24.8 |
| Sprocket shaft nut | | | |
| 1984-early 1985 | 290-320 | — | 400.2-441.6 |
| Late 1985-on | — | — | — |
| Crankpin nut | 180-210 | — | 248.4-289.8 |
| Pinion shaft nut | | | |
| 1984-1990 | 140-170 | — | 193.2-234.6 |
| 1991 | — | — | — |
| Pinion gear nut | 35-45 | — | 48.3-62.1 |
| Crankcase stud nut | 15-19 | — | 20.7-26.2 |
| Crankcase bolt | 15-19 | — | 20.7-26.2 |
| Oil pump cover bolts | — | 90-120 | 10.3-13.8 |
| Tappet guide bolts | — | 90-120 | 10.3-13.8 |
| Gearcase cover screws | — | 90-120 | 10.3-13.8 |
| Tappet screen plug | — | 90-120 | 10.3-13.8 |
| Timer screws | — | 15-30 | 1.7-3.4 |
| Rear engine mounting bolts | 33-38 | — | 45.5-52.4 |
| Front engine mounting bolts | 33-38 | — | 45.5-52.4 |
| Top center engine mounting nuts (FX) | 35-40 | — | 48.3-55.2 |
| Upper engine mounting bracket screw | 28-35 | — | 38-43 |
| Compression nut fitting | | | |
| 1992-on | 8-12 | — | 11-16 |
| Oil filter mount screws | | | |
| 1992-on | 13-17 | — | 18-23 |
| Oil pump cover manifold screws | | | |
| 1992-on | — | 70-80 | 7.9-9.0 |

**Table 4 INNER BEARING SPACER SIZE**

| Part No. | Spacer size (in.)* |
|---|---|
| 9120 | 0.0925-0.0915 |
| 9121 | 0.0945-0.0935 |
| 9122 | 0.0965-0.0955 |
| 9123 | 0.0985-0.0975 |
| 9124 | 0.1005-0.0995 |
| 9125 | 0.1025-0.1015 |
| 9126 | 0.1045-0.1035 |
| 9127 | 0.1065-0.1055 |
| 9128 | 0.1085-0.1075 |
| 9129 | 0.1101-0.1095 |
| 9130 | 0.1125-0.1115 |
| 9131 | 0.1145-0.1135 |
| 9132 | 0.1165-0.1155 |
| 9133 | 0.1185-0.1175 |
| 9134 | 0.1205-0.1195 |

* Multiply specification by 25.4 to find millimeter (mm) equivalent.

## CHAPTER FIVE

# CLUTCH, PRIMARY DRIVE AND STARTER DRIVE

The primary drive, clutch, transmission and final drive systems make up the power train assembly on your Harley-Davidson. This chapter describes service to the primary drive, clutch and starter drive assemblies. Transmission and final drive service are described in separate chapters.

The primary drive system uses sprockets and a primary drive chain to transmit power from the engine to the transmission. This system is designed to allow the engine sprocket to turn faster than the clutch sprocket (engine sprocket is smaller than clutch sprocket). This ratio difference increases engine torque and reduces the amount of power flowing into the transmission and final drive systems.

An external chain primary drive assembly is used on all Harley-Davidson V-twin engines. This system is used because the Harley engine is a non-unit engine; that is, the engine and transmission do not share a common case. The primary drive assembly is mounted inside the primary chain case, a sealed housing mounted on the left-hand side of the bike. The chain case contains the engine compensating sprocket, clutch and clutch sprocket, primary chain, chain adjuster, solenoid and starter drive mechanism. The engine and clutch turn in the same direction.

Abnormal gear noises are usually the first sign of trouble with the primary sprockets and chain. If you notice an increase in the primary chain case noise level, first check the oil level (wet clutch), then check the primary chain tension for looseness and for a damaged chain tensioner assembly. If necessary, remove the primary chain case cover and inspect the primary drive assembly. The primary chain and sprockets can be replaced without major engine disassembly.

The clutch is mounted in the primary housing between the engine sprocket and transmission. The clutch allows the rider to control power from the engine into the transmission by disengaging the clutch from the transmission when shifting from one gear to another. A dry clutch is used on early 1984 FLT and FXR models. All late 1984 and later models use a wet clutch. If the clutch should slip or drag, first perform the clutch adjustments described in Chapter Three. If adjustment does not solve the problem, service the clutch assembly as described in this chapter.

The starter drive mechanism is mounted in the chain case housing on 1984-1988 models. Starting with 1989 models, the starter drive mechanism was changed; a starter jackshaft assembly is mounted in the chain case housing. Refer to Chapter Eight for starter motor service.

Specifications are found in **Tables 1-5**. All tables are found at the end of the chapter.

## DRY CLUTCH (EARLY 1984 FLT AND FXR)

Refer to **Figure 1** when performing procedures in this section.

### Removal

1. Disconnect the negative battery cable.

2A. *FLT*: Remove the left footboard and the rear bracket.

2B. *FXR*: Remove the shifter lever (**Figure 2**) and the footrest bracket.

3. Remove the primary chain case cover screws. Then tap the cover (**Figure 3**) with a plastic-faced mallet to break the gasket seal. Pull the cover off of the engine and transmission housings.

4. The engine must be locked to prevent the crankshaft from turning when loosening the compensating sprocket nut (**Figure 4**). Lock the engine by shifting the transmission into gear. Then hold the compensating sprocket cover with a chain wrench. Wrap the compensating sprocket cover with shim stock to prevent damage from the chain wrench. If these tools are not available, an air gun and socket will be necessary.

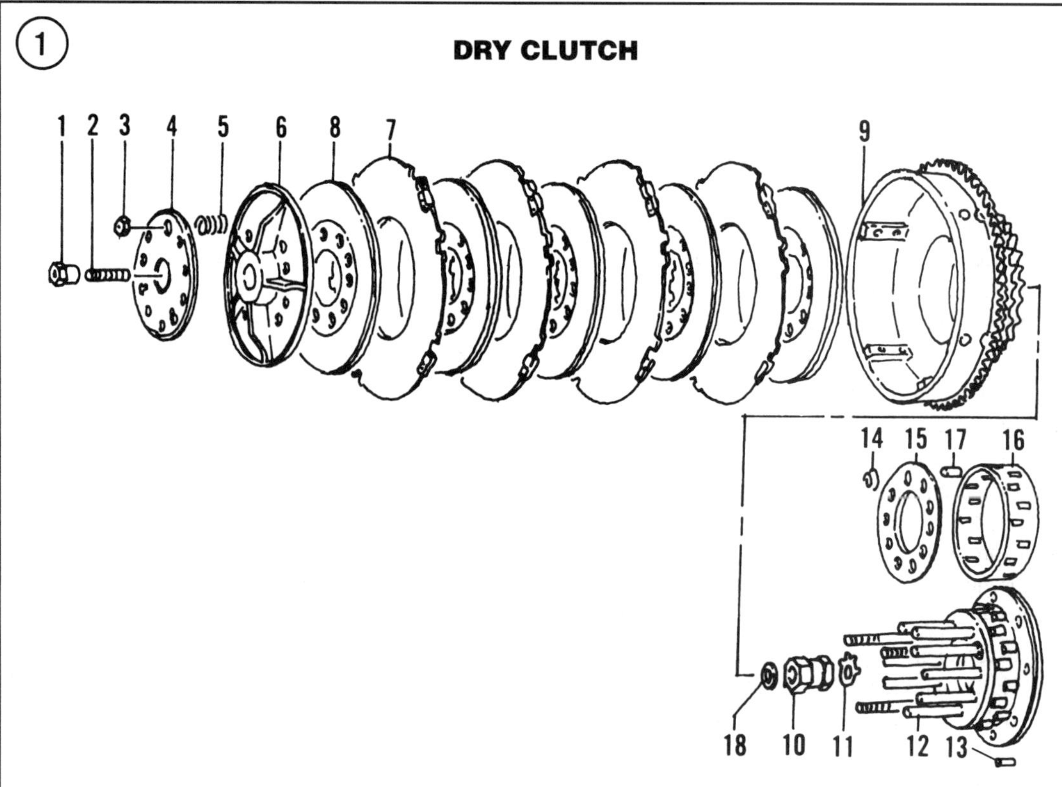

5. After locking the engine, use a large socket and breaker bar or air gun to loosen the compensating sprocket nut (**Figure 4**).

6. Refer to **Figure 5**. Remove the following parts in order:

   a. Nut (**Figure 4**).
   b. Cover (5, **Figure 5**).
   c. Sliding cam (**Figure 6**).

7. Remove the pushrod adjuster screw locknut (**Figure 7**).

8. Place a flat washer (1/8 in. thick, 1 3/4 in. O.D. and 3/8 in. I.D.) over the pushrod adjusting screw (**Figure 8**). Then reinstall the adjuster screw locknut removed in Step 8.

9. Refer to **Figure 8**. Tighten the push rod adjusting screw locknut until the clutch spring adjusting nuts are loose. Then remove the clutch spring nuts.

*NOTE*

*Do not disassemble the parts in Step 10 unless replacement is required. Disassembly is described under **Clutch, Inspection** in this chapter.*

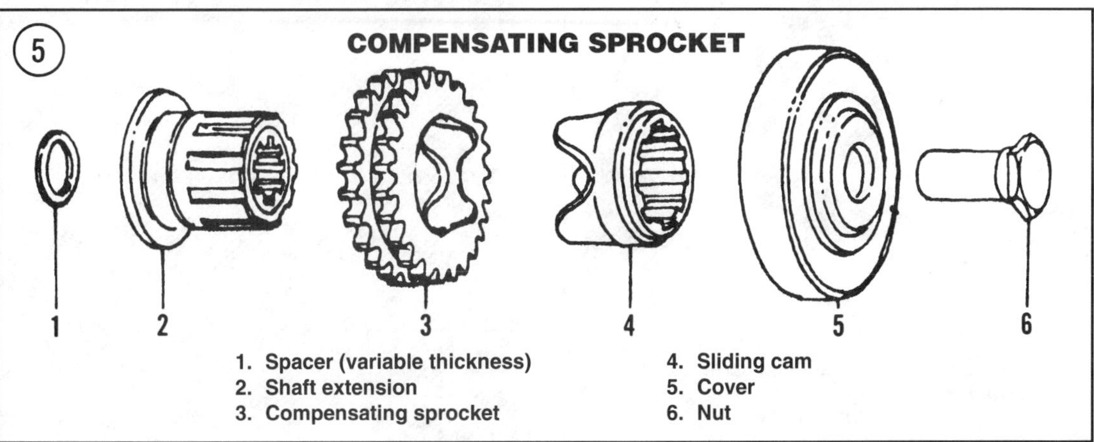

10. Remove the pressure plate, clutch springs and the releasing disc as an assembly. See **Figure 1**.

11. Remove the friction (**Figure 9**) and steel (**Figure 10**) clutch plates in order.

12. Referring to **Figure 11**, remove the primary chain adjuster bolt and remove the chain adjuster assembly. See **Figure 12**.

13. Remove the oil hose from the primary chain adjuster fitting.

14. Remove the clutch shell, compensating sprocket and primary chain as one unit (**Figure 13**).

*NOTE*
*The clutch nut uses left-hand threads. Turn the nut clockwise to loosen it.*

15. Pry back the clutch hub lockwasher tab, then loosen the clutch nut (A, **Figure 14**) by turning it *clockwise*. Remove the nut and its lockwasher.

16. Attach the clutch hub puller (part No. HD-95960-41) to the clutch hub (**Figure 15**). Then turn the puller's center bolt clockwise and remove the clutch hub (B, **Figure 14**).

17. Remove the clutch hub Woodruff key (**Figure 16**) from groove in mainshaft.

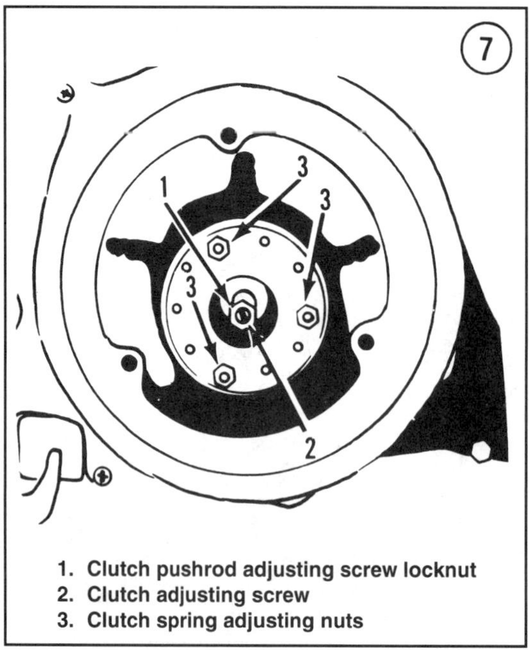

1. Clutch pushrod adjusting screw locknut
2. Clutch adjusting screw
3. Clutch spring adjusting nuts

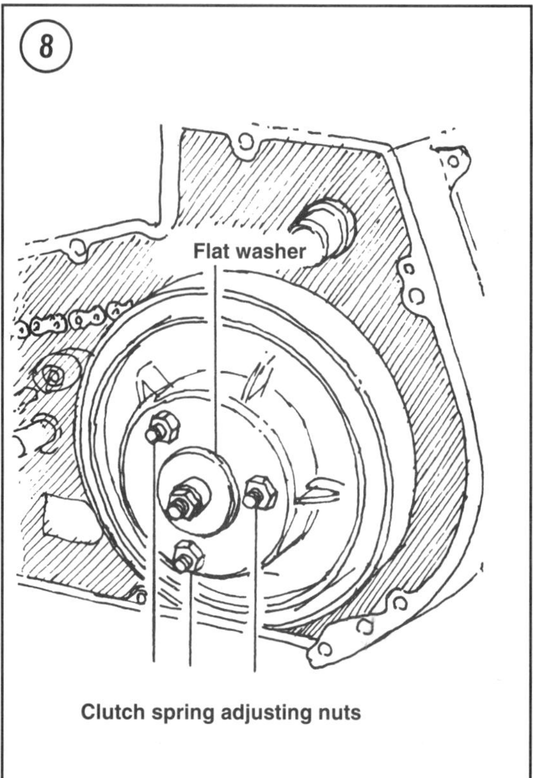

Clutch spring adjusting nuts

## Inspection

1. Clean all clutch parts in a non-oil based solvent and thoroughly dry with compressed air.
2. To disassemble the pressure plate assembly:
   a. Install 3 bolts through the original pressure plate-to-clutch hub bolt holes. The bolts should be long enough to allow removal of the parts while under compression.
   b. Secure each nut with a flat washer and nut. Tighten all nuts in a crisscross pattern until the clutch springs compress slightly.
   c. Remove the adjuster locknut and remove the adjuster screw.
   d. Loosen the 3 nuts in a crisscross pattern. Loosen the nuts 1/2 to 1 turn at a time to release spring tension evenly.
   e. After loosening the nuts, remove the washers and 3 bolts. Then separate the pressure plate and remove the clutch springs.
3. Measure the free length of each clutch spring as shown in **Figure 17**. Replace any springs that are too short (**Table 1**).
4. Inspect steel clutch plates (A, **Figure 18**) for warping or wear grooves. Replace if necessary.

5. Inspect friction plates (B, **Figure 18**) for a shiny appearance or signs of oil soaking. Also check the plates for worn or grooved lining surfaces. Measure each plate (**Figure 19**) and compare thickness to the specifications in **Table 1**. Replace plates if thickness meets or exceeds minimum thickness.

6. Check for loose clutch plate rivets; replace if necessary.

7. Check the clutch shell inner bearing race (A, **Figure 20**) for grooves, wear or damage. Also check the clutch shell plate tabs (B, **Figure 20**) for looseness or damage. If found, replace the clutch shell.

8. Check the clutch shell gear teeth (**Figure 21**) for wear or damage. Replace the clutch shell if necessary.

9. Spin the clutch hub roller bearing assembly (A, **Figure 22**) by hand. If bearing assembly appears rough, disassemble it by removing the 3 bearing plate springs (B, **Figure 22**). Then slide the bearing plate off the hub pins and remove the bearing retainer. Check all parts for wear or damage; replace parts as required.

10. Pry the pushrod seal out of the hub nut. Install a new seal by tapping it into place.

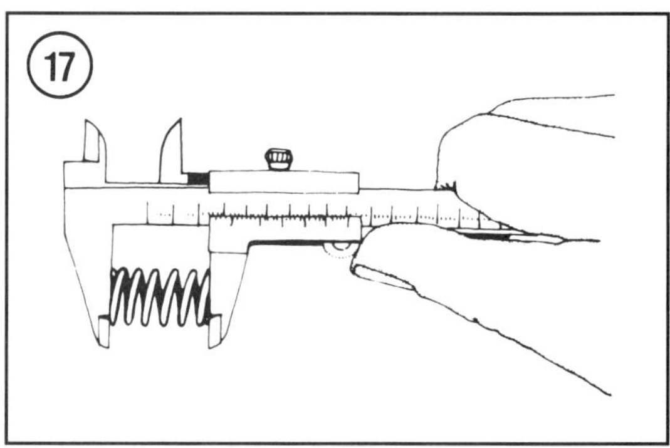


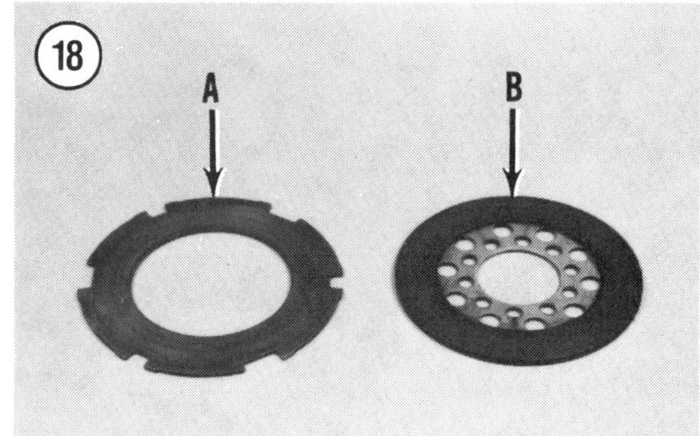


### Installation

1. Install the Woodruff key (**Figure 16**) into the mainshaft keyway.

2. Install the pushrod, if removed.

3. Slide the clutch hub assembly (B, **Figure 14**) onto the mainshaft.

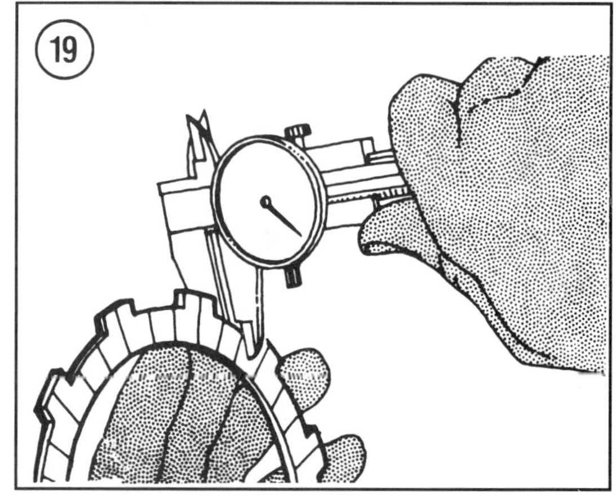


*NOTE*
*The clutch nut uses left-hand threads. Turn the nut counterclockwise to tighten it.*

4. Thread the clutch nut onto the mainshaft by turning the nut *counterclockwise*. Using a torque wrench, tighten the nut to the torque specification listed in **Table 4**. Use the same tools and procedures to prevent the mainshaft from turning as used during disassembly. Bend the lockwasher tab over the nut to lock it.

*NOTE*
*Grease the clutch shell bearing before installing the clutch shell in Step 5.*

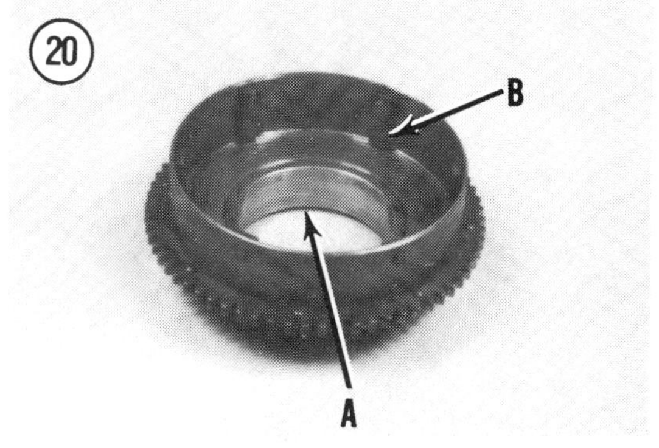

5. Install the clutch shell, primary chain and the compensating sprocket as an assembly. See **Figure 13**.

6. Refer to **Figure 5**. Install the following parts in order:

  a. Washer (if removed).
  b. Shaft extension (if removed).
  c. Sliding cam (**Figure 6**).
  d. Cover (**Figure 5**).

7. Install the compensating sprocket nut (**Figure 4**) and tighten it to 80-100 ft.-lb. (110.4-138 N•m).

*NOTE*
*To prevent the friction material on the friction plates from absorbing moisture, Harley-Davidson recommends spraying these plates with a silicone spray lubricant before reassembling the clutch. Do not use a silicone spray that contains penetrating oil or any type of petroleum products as clutch slippage will occur. Ask your dealer to recommend a lubricant that can work in the dry clutch.*

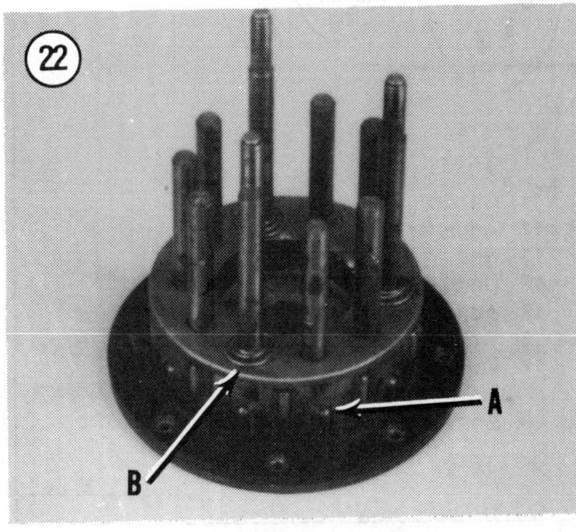


8. Install the friction and steel clutch plates in the order shown in **Figure 1**. Install the steel clutch plates (**Figure 10**) with the side stamped *OUT* facing outward.

9. If the pressure plate unit was disassembled, assemble as follows:

  a. Place the clutch hub on the workbench so that the bolts face up (**Figure 22**).
  b. Install the retaining disc on the hub.
  c. Install the clutch springs on the hub pins and studs.
  d. Place the pressure plate over the clutch spring. Because of stud hole arrangement, plate collar in pressure plate will fit only one way.
  e. Screw the pushrod adjuster locknut onto the adjuster screw until the screw is flush with the top of the nut. Install a 1 3/4 in. washer under the nut and thread the adjusting screw into the releasing disc.
  f. Tighten the nut to compress the clutch springs.
  g. Install the 3 clutch spring adjusting nuts.
  h. Remove the adjust screw locknut and remove the 1 3/4 in. washer. Then reinstall the locknut.
  i. Tighten the 3 adjusting nuts in a crisscross pattern until the distance from the releasing disc to the pressure plate is exactly 1 1/32 in. (26.19 mm). Tighten the adjusting locknut to maintain this distance.

10. Install the primary chain adjuster (**Figure 11**).

11. Adjust the primary drive chain as described in Chapter Three.

12. Check primary chain alignment as described in this chapter.

13. Install the primary chain cover dowel pin, if removed.

14. Install the primary chain cover using a new gasket.

15. Install all parts previously removed.

16. Perform the *Primary Housing Vacuum Check (Early 1984 Models With Dry Clutch)* as described in this chapter.

## WET CLUTCH (LATE 1984-1989)

This section describes service to the wet clutch installed on late 1984-1989 models. If you have a

**WET CLUTCH
(LATE 1984-1989)**

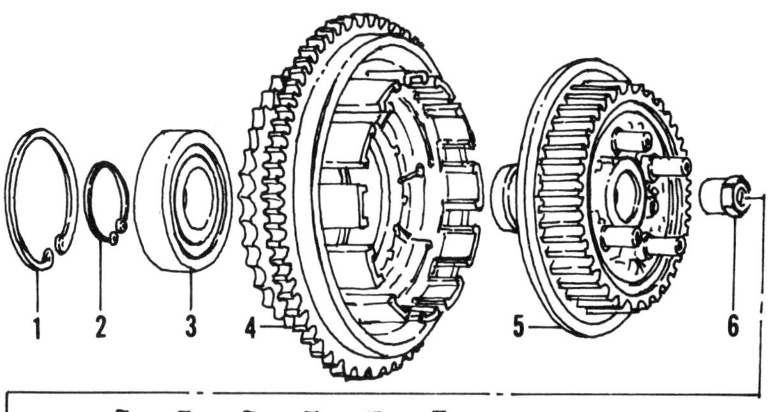


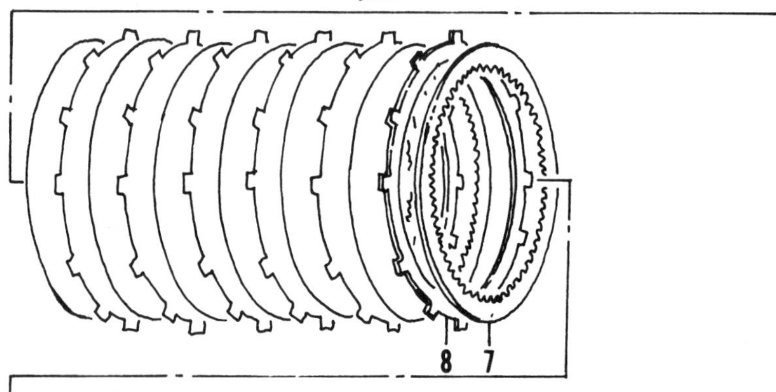


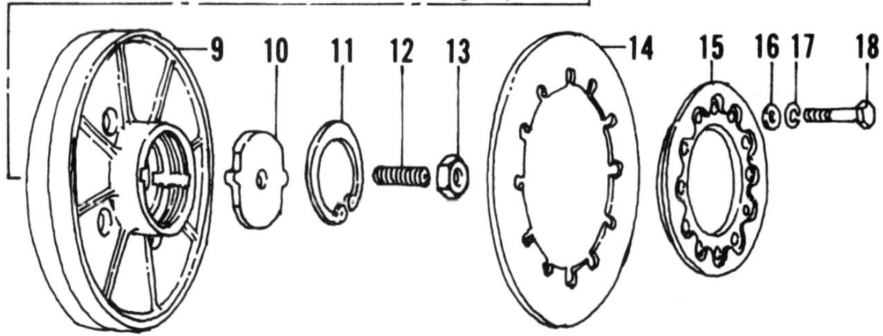


1. Circlip
2. Circlip
3. Pilot bearing
4. Clutch shell
5. Inner clutch hub
6. Nut
7. Steel clutch plate
8. Friction clutch plate
9. Pressure plate
10. Release plate
11. Circlip
12. Adjuster screw
13. Nut
14. Diaphragm spring
15. Adjuster plate
16. Washer
17. Lockwasher (late 1984-early 1985 only)
18. Bolt

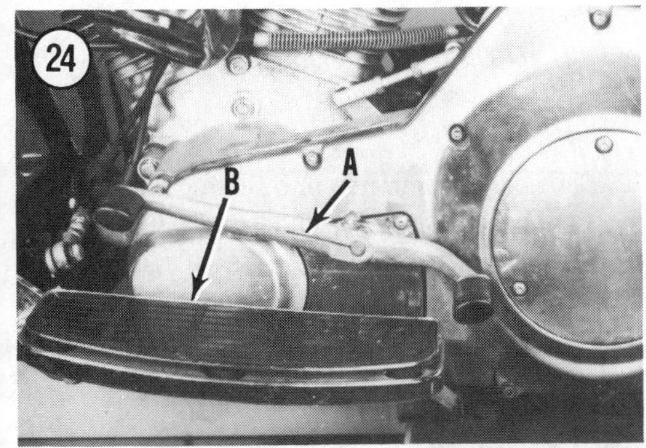

1990 or later model, refer to *Wet Clutch (1990-On)* in this chapter. Refer to **Figure 23** when performing procedures in this section.

**Removal/Installation**

1. Disconnect the negative battery cable.
2. Clean the primary chain case cover thoroughly of all dirt, oil and road debris before removing it.
3. Refer to **Figure 24**. Remove the gearshift pedal (A) and the left-hand running board (B).
4. Place a drain pan under the primary cover and remove the drain plug (**Figure 25**). Allow the oil to drain.
5. Remove the primary chain case cover screws and cover (**Figure 26**). Remove the dowel pin.
6. Loosen and remove the 4 adjuster plate bolts (A, **Figure 27**) in a crisscross pattern.
7. Remove the adjuster plate (B, **Figure 27**) and the diaphragm spring (C, **Figure 27**).
8. Remove the circlip and the release plate from the pressure plate (**Figure 28**).
9. Remove the pressure plate (**Figure 29**).

5

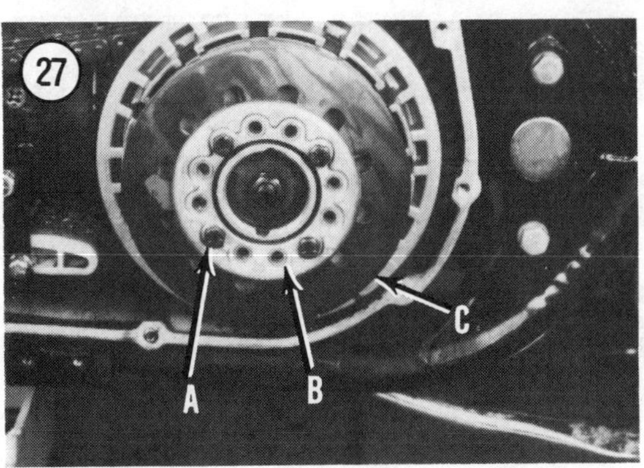

10. Remove the steel (**Figure 30**) and friction (**Figure 31**) plates.
11. Remove the pushrod (**Figure 32**).

*NOTE*
*The clutch nut uses left-hand threads. Turn the nut clockwise to loosen it.*

*NOTE*
*Step 12 describes removal of the clutch nut. For additional information on loosening the clutch nut, refer to Step 7A and Step 7B under **Clutch Removal (Clutch is not Disassembled)** for 1990 and later models in this chapter.*

12. Shift the transmission into first gear and apply the rear brake. Turn the clutch nut (**Figure 33**) *clockwise* and remove it.

30

31

32

33

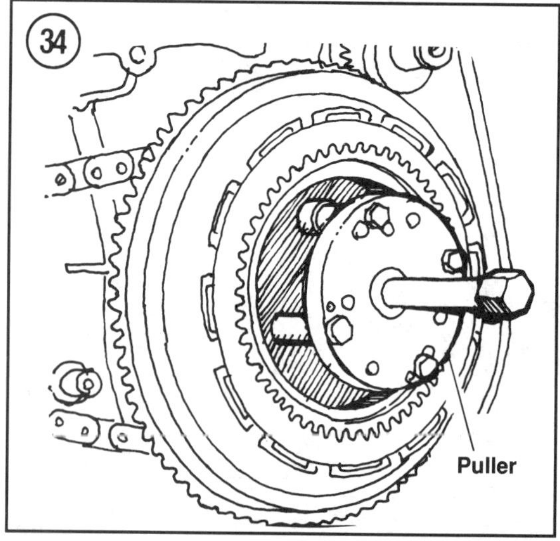

34

35

13. Attach the puller (part No. HD-95960-52B) to the clutch hub. See **Figure 34**.

14. Remove the primary chain adjuster bolt or nut. See **Figure 35**.

15. The engine must be locked to prevent the crankshaft from turning when loosening the compensating sprocket nut (**Figure 36**). Lock the engine by shifting the transmission into gear. Then hold the compensating sprocket cover with a chain wrench. Wrap the compensating sprocket cover with shim stock to prevent damage from the chain wrench. If these tools are not available, an air gun and socket will be necessary.

16. After locking the engine, use a large socket and breaker bar or air gun to loosen the compensating sprocket nut (**Figure 37**).

17. Refer to **Figure 36**. Remove the following parts in order:

a. Nut (**Figure 37**).

b. Cover (**Figure 36**).

c. Sliding cam (**Figure 38**).

d. Turn the clutch hub puller pressure screw to pull the clutch hub and remove the clutch shell (with clutch hub attached), primary chain (with adjuster) and compensating sprocket at the same time. See **Figure 39**.



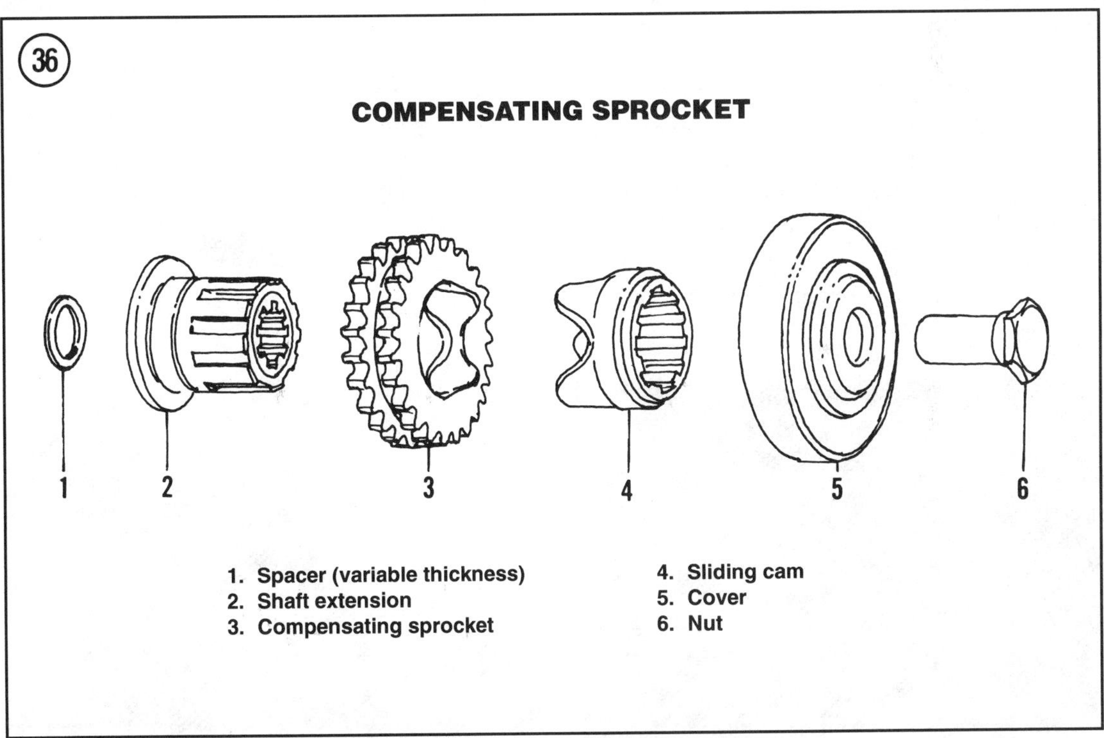

e. Remove the shaft extension and washer, if necessary.

18. Disassembly of the clutch shell and hub assembly is not required unless parts are damaged and require replacement.

19. Remove the Woodruff key.

## Inspection

1. Clean all clutch parts in a non-oil based solvent and thoroughly dry with compressed air.

2. Inspect the friction plates (**Figure 40**) for worn or grooved lining surfaces. Measure each plate (**Figure 41**) and compare to the specifications in **Table 2**. Replace the friction plates as a set if one plate is found too thin.

3. Check each steel plate (**Figure 42**) for thickness with a vernier caliper (**Figure 43**). Also check each steel plate for flatness with a feeler gauge and straightedge in several places (**Figure 44**). Replace any plate that is too thin or warped beyond specifications (**Table 2**).

4. Check the diaphragm spring (**Figure 45**) for wear or damage. Replace if necessary.

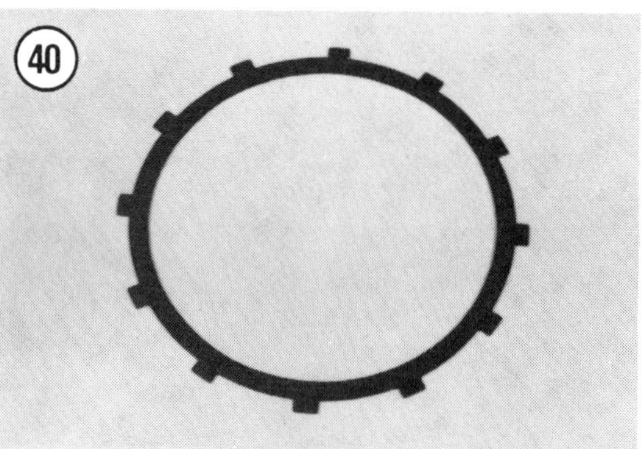


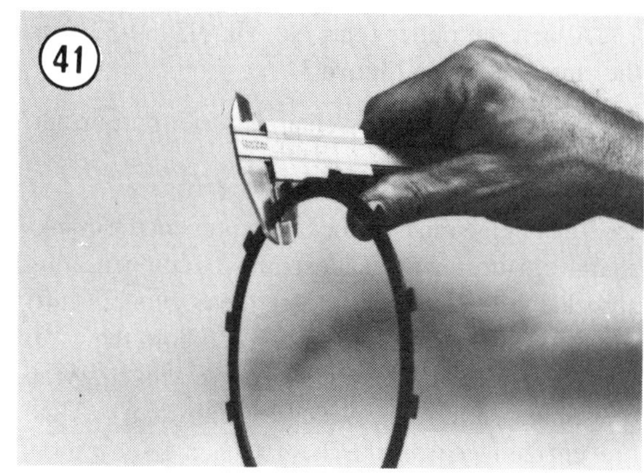

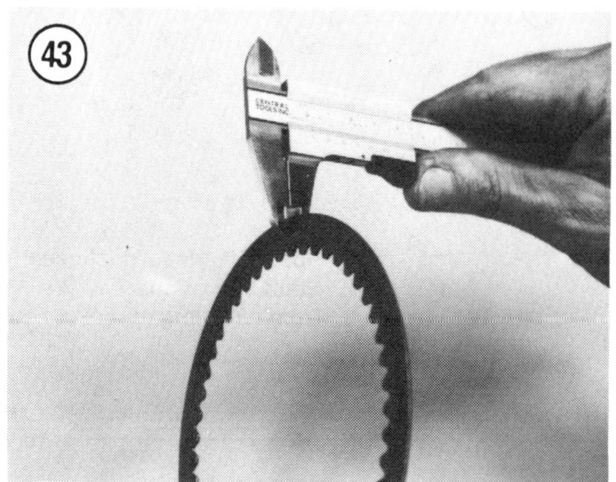


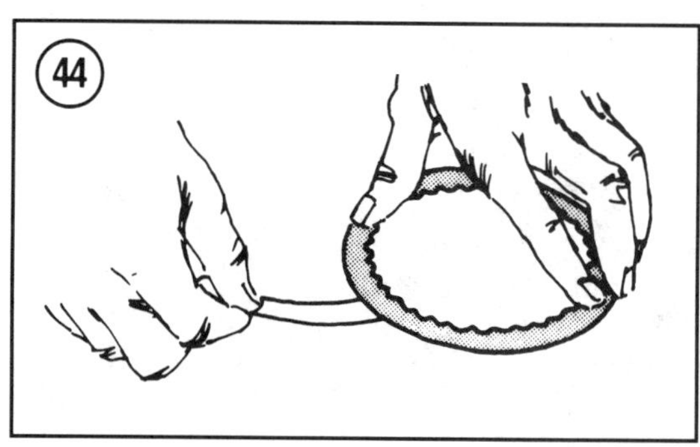

45

46

47

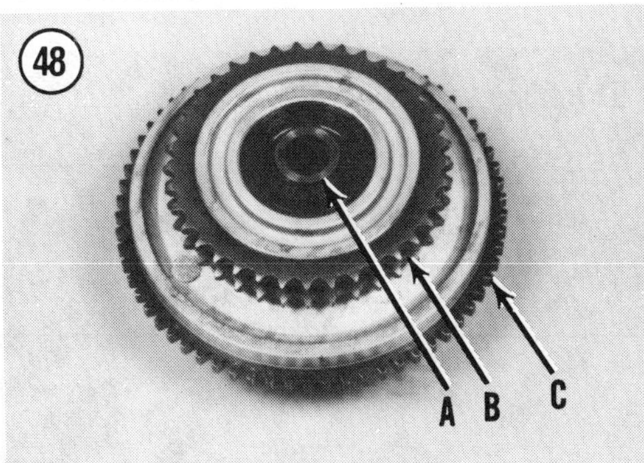

48

5. Check the pressure plate surfaces (**Figure 46** and **Figure 47**) for wear or cracking. Replace if necessary.

*NOTE*

*The clutch shell assembly consists of the inner clutch hub, clutch shell and pilot bearing. Because of the possibility of damaging the pilot bearing when removing it, do not disassemble these parts unless it is necessary to replace worn or damaged parts or to access the parts for closer inspection. A press is required for disassembly and reassembly.*

6. Check the pilot bearing (A, **Figure 48**) for wear by holding the clutch hub and turning the clutch shell by hand. If the bearing appears worn, replace it as described in this chapter.
7. Check the clutch shell teeth (B and C, **Figure 48**) for wear or damage. Also check the inner clutch hub splines (**Figure 49**) for wear or damage. If worn or damaged parts are detected, disassemble the clutch shell assembly as described in this chapter.

**Clutch Shell Disassembly/Reassembly**

The clutch hub and shell should not be separated unless replacement of the hub, shell or bearing is required. Disassembly of the hub and shell may damage the pilot bearing; bearing replacement will be required during reassembly. A press is required for this procedure.

Read this procedure completely through before starting disassembly. Refer to **Figure 23**.

1. Remove the circlip from the clutch shell groove.
2. Remove the circlip from the clutch hub groove.
3. Support the clutch hub and shell in a press and press the clutch hub out of the bearing. Remove the clutch shell from the press.
4. Support the clutch shell in the press and press the bearing out of the shell. Discard the bearing if severely worn, damaged or if damaged during removal.
5. Discard worn or damaged parts. Clean reusable and new parts (except bearing) in solvent and dry thoroughly.
6. Place the clutch shell into the press. Then align the bearing with the clutch shell and press bearing into shell until bearing bottoms out against lower

shoulder. When pressing the bearing into the clutch shell, press only on the outer bearing race. Installing the bearing by pressing on its inner race will damage the bearing. Refer to *Ball Bearing Replacement* in Chapter One for additional information.

7. Install the bearing circlip into the clutch shell groove. Make sure the circlips seats in the groove completely.

8. Press the clutch hub into the clutch shell as follows:

   a. Place the clutch shell in a press. Support the inner bearing race with a sleeve as shown in **Figure 50**.

*CAUTION*

*Failure to support the inner bearing race as described in sub-step a will cause bearing and clutch shell damage. Refer to **Figure 50** to make sure the inner bearing race is supported properly.*

   b. Align the clutch hub with the bearing and press the clutch hub into the bearing (**Figure 50**) until the clutch hub shoulder seats against the bearing.

   c. Using circlip pliers, install the clutch hub circlip. Make sure the circlip seats in the clutch hub groove completely.

9. After completing assembly, hold the clutch hub and rotate the clutch shell by hand. The shell should turn smoothly with no sign of roughness or binding. If the clutch shell binds or turns roughly, the bearing may have been damaged during reassembly.

## Installation

Refer to **Figure 23** when installing the clutch assembly.

1. Install the Woodruff key (**Figure 51**) into the mainshaft.

*NOTE*

*Check to make sure that the Woodruff key is parallel with the mainshaft taper.*

2. Install the clutch shell and hub, primary chain and compensating sprocket and cam as an assembly. *Make sure* the Woodruff key is not knocked out of alignment during installation.

*NOTE*

*The clutch nut uses left-hand threads. Turn the nut counterclockwise to tighten.*

*CAUTION*

*Overtightening the clutch nut can damage the clutch hub and pilot bearing.*

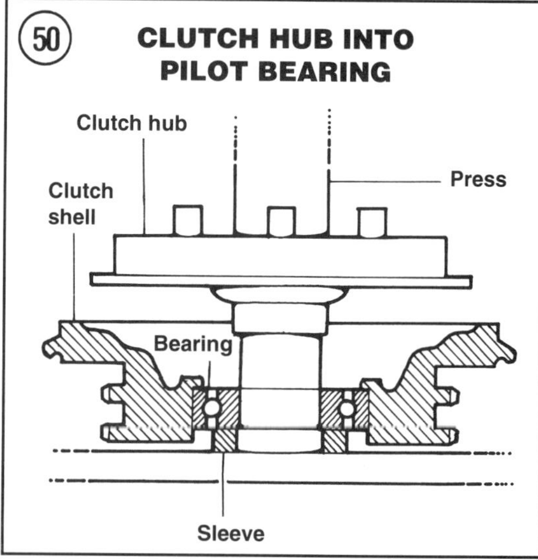

3. Apply a few drops of Loctite 262 (red) to the clutch nut threads and thread the nut onto the mainshaft by turning the nut *counterclockwise*. Using a torque wrench, tighten the nut to the torque specification listed in **Table 4**. Use the same tools and procedures to prevent the mainshaft from turning as used during disassembly.
4. Refer to **Figure 36**. Install the following parts in order:
   a. Washer (if removed).
   b. Shaft extension (if removed).
   c. Sliding cam.
   d. Cover.

CAUTION
*The compensating sprocket nut is tightened to a high torque specification. Make sure you hold the sprocket securely when tightening the nut in Step 5.*

5. Apply a few drops of Loctite 262 (red) to the compensating sprocket nut and then install the nut and tighten to the torque specification listed in **Table 4**. Use the same tools and procedures to prevent the crankshaft from turning as used during disassembly.
6. Soak all friction plates in clean engine oil before reassembly.
7. Install the clutch plates in the order shown in **Figure 23**.
8. Thread the pushrod into the release plate, if removed.

NOTE
*If the release plate was removed from the pressure plate (**Figure 46**), reinstall it into the pressure plate and then secure it with the beveled circlip; install the circlip so that its beveled edge faces outward. Make sure the circlip seats in the pressure plate groove completely.*

9. Install the pressure plate (**Figure 28**).
10. Install the spring diaphragm (C, **Figure 27**) with its convex side facing outward.
11. Install the adjuster plate (B, **Figure 27**).
12. Install the washer(s) onto each of the clutch hub bolts.

NOTE
*Late 1984-Early 1985 models use a flat washer and a lockwasher on each of the clutch hub bolts. Late 1985 and later models do not use the lockwasher.*

13. Apply a few drops of Loctite 222 (purple) to threads on each of the clutch hub bolts. Then install the bolts through the adjuster and pressure plates and thread into the clutch hub. Tighten the bolts in a crisscross pattern to 6.5-8 ft.-lb. (9-11 N•m).
14. Adjust the clutch as described in Chapter Three.

NOTE
*If new clutch components were installed, readjust the clutch at the first 500 mile (800 km) interval.*

15. Assemble and secure the primary chain adjust shoe assembly as described in this chapter.
16. Adjust the primary chain as described in Chapter Three.
17. Check primary chain alignment as described in this chapter.
18. Install the primary chain case cover dowel pin, if removed.
19. Install the primary chain case cover (**Figure 26**) together with a *new* gasket. Install the cover screws and washers and tighten each screw securely.
20. Refill the primary chain housing with the correct type and quantity oil as described in Chapter Three.
21. Check the clutch inspection cover O-ring and the primary chain inspection cover gasket for wear or damage; replace as required.
22. Install the clutch inspection cover with its O-ring. Install the primary chain inspection cover and its gasket. Tighten all of the cover screws securely.
23. Install all external parts previously removed.
24. Ride the bike a short distance and check the cover for oil leaks.

5

## WET CLUTCH (1990-ON)

This section describes service to the wet clutch installed on 1990 and later models. If you are servicing a late 1984-1989 model, refer to *Wet Clutch (Late 1984-1989)* in this chapter. Refer to **Figure 52** when performing procedures in this section.

### Preliminary Steps

Complete disassembly of the clutch will require the use of the Harley-Davidson Spring Compression Tool (part No. HD-38515) or equivalent. If you do not have access to the compression tool, you can remove the clutch intact from the bike and then take it to a Harley-Davidson dealer or independent repair shop for disassembly and service. Do not attempt to disassemble the clutch without the special tool. Observe the *WARNING* in the following procedures.

## Clutch Removal (Clutch is Not Disassembled)

This procedure describes removal of the clutch unit only. If you wish to disassemble the clutch while it is installed on the bike, refer to *Clutch Disassembly on Bike* in this chapter.

1. Disconnect the negative battery cable.
2. Shift the transmission into 5th gear.

3A. *FLT*: Remove the left footboard and the rear bracket.

3B. *FXR*: Remove the shifter lever and the footrest bracket.

4. Clean the primary chain case cover thoroughly of all dirt, oil and road debris before removing it.

5. Place a drain pan under the primary cover and remove the drain plug (**Figure 25**). Allow the oil to drain completely.

6. Remove the primary case cover screws and cover (**Figure 53**). If the case appears to be stuck, make sure all of the cover screws have been removed. Then lightly tap the cover to break the gasket seal. Remove the 2 dowel pins.

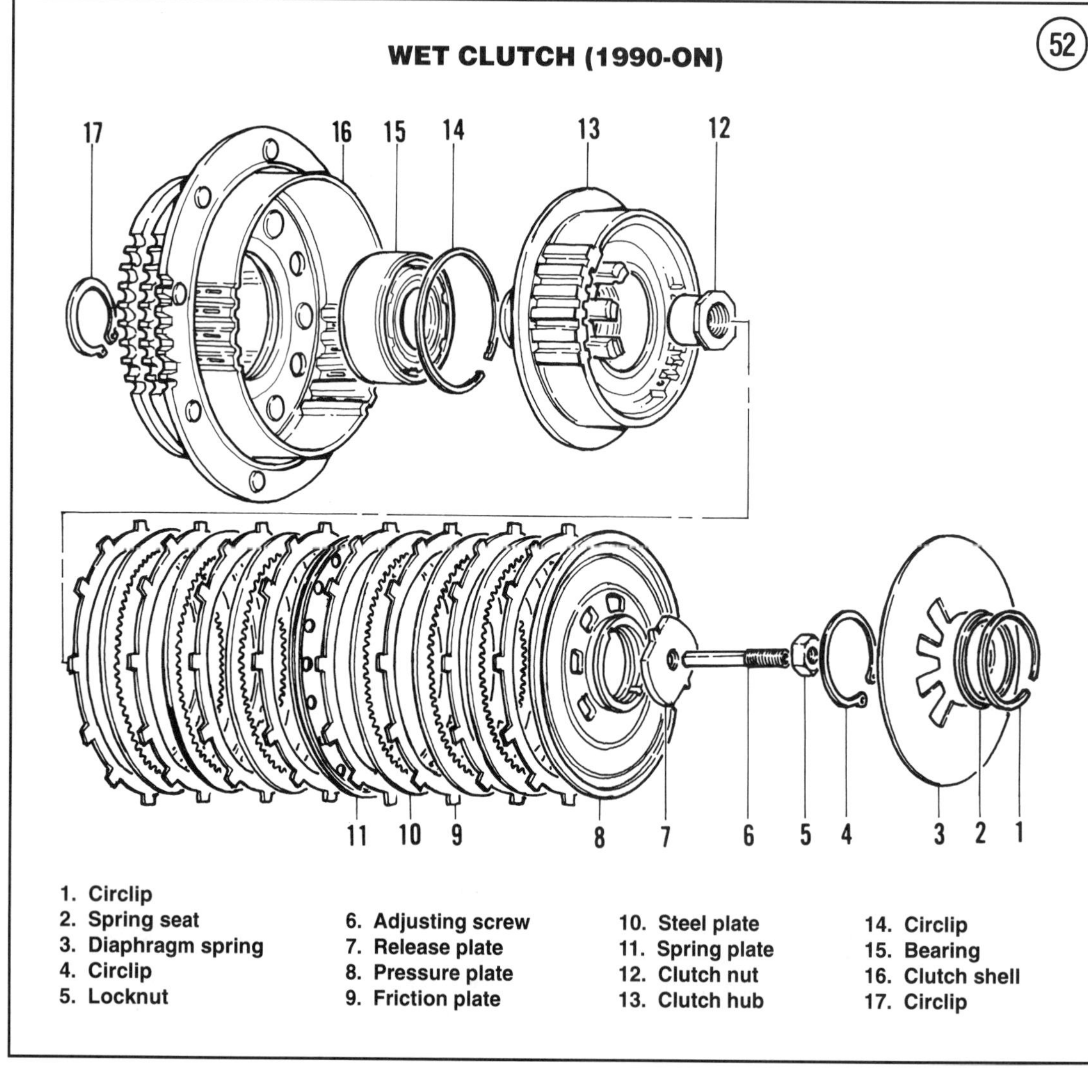

53

54

55

56

7. Remove the circlip holding the adjust screw plate in position, then remove the adjust screw plate (**Figure 54**), adjust screw and nut.

*NOTE*
*The 2 notches cast in the pressure plate can be used to help pry the circlip out when removing it.*

*NOTE*
*An air gun is the simplest way to remove the clutch and compensating sprocket nuts. However, if you do not have an air gun, Step 8 describes 2 methods that can be used to remove the clutch nut (**Figure 55**).*

*CAUTION*
*The clutch hub nut is secured with Loctite 262 (red) and tightened to a high torque reading. It will be tight. To loosen the clutch hub nut safely, make sure to read the procedure completely through first, and then perform the steps in order.*

8A. *Method 1*: This method is recommended by Harley-Davidson. Remove the clutch hub nut (**Figure 55**) as follows:

a. The transmission should be in 5th gear when loosening the clutch hub nut. See Step 1.
b. Have an assistant apply the rear brake hard.
c. Remove the clutch hub nut with a 1 3/16 in. socket. The clutch hub nut uses left-hand threads, so turn the nut *clockwise* to remove it.

8B. *Method 2*: This method of removing the clutch and compensating sprocket nuts uses a homemade clutch bar that fits between the compensating sprocket and clutch shell gear teeth. **Figure 56** shows the bar in use. The clutch bar can be made of steel or aluminum; the ends of the bar must be bent as shown in **Figure 57** to engage the teeth on both gears properly. Remove the clutch hub nut (**Figure 55**) as follows:

a. Fit the clutch bar so that the ends of the bar engage the compensating sprocket and clutch shell gear teeth (**Figure 56**).
b. Remove the clutch hub nut with a 1 3/16 in. socket. The clutch hub nut uses left-hand threads, so turn the nut *clockwise* to remove it.

9. Remove the nut and washer from the center bolt and remove the adjusting shoe (**Figure 58**).

*NOTE*
*If you made the clutch bar in Step 8B, you can use it to hold the compensating sprocket and clutch shell while loosening the compensating sprocket nut.*

10. Remove the compensating sprocket nut (**Figure 59**) as follows:

*CAUTION*
*The compensating nut is secured with Loctite 262 (red) and torqued to 150-165 ft.-lb. (207-228 N•m). The nut is tight. To loosen the compensating nut safely, read the following procedure completely through first, and then perform the steps in order.*

a. The transmission should be in 5th gear when loosening the compensating sprocket nut. See Step 1.
b. Hold the compensating sprocket cover with a chain wrench. Wrap the compensating sprocket cover with shim stock to prevent damage from the chain wrench. If these tools are not available, an air gun and socket will be required.
c. Loosen and remove the compensating sprocket nut (**Figure 59**), spacer, cover and sliding cam. See **Figure 36**.

11. Remove the clutch assembly, compensating sprocket, primary chain and adjuster bracket at the same time.

### Clutch Disassembly on Bike

This procedure describes disassembly of the clutch while it is mounted on the bike. Compensating sprocket and primary chain removal is not required. Read this procedure completely through before starting disassembly.

1. Disconnect the negative battery cable.

2A. *FLT*: Remove the left footboard and the rear bracket.

2B. *FXR*: Remove the shifter lever (**Figure 2**) and the footrest bracket.

3. Clean the primary chain case cover thoroughly of all dirt, oil and road debris before removing it.

4. Place a drain pan under the primary cover and remove the drain plug (**Figure 25**). Allow the oil to drain.

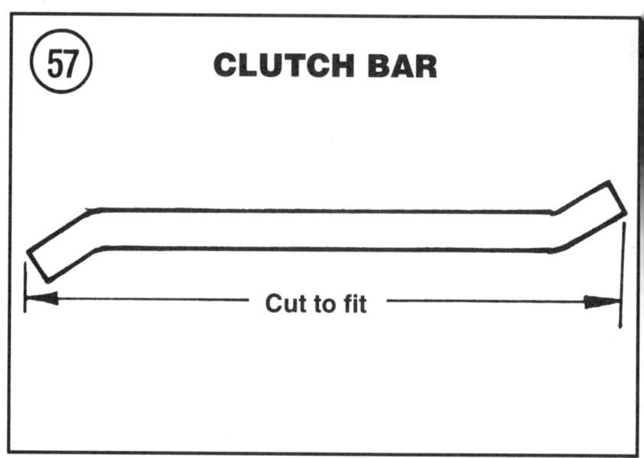


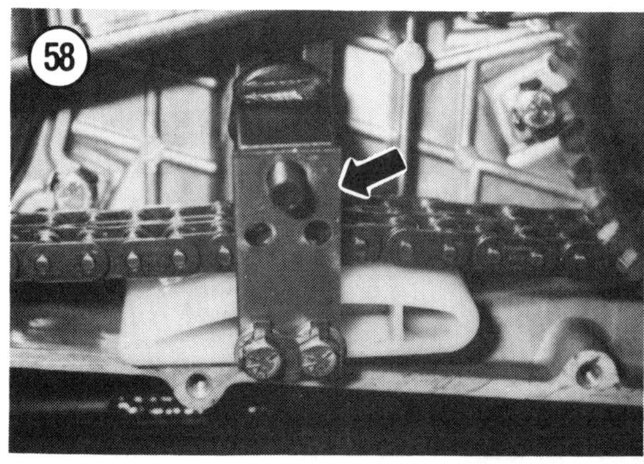

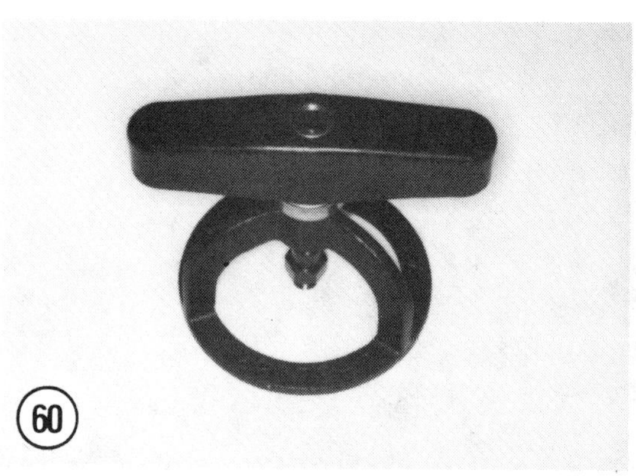

5. Remove the primary case cover screws and cover (**Figure 37**). If the case appears to be stuck, make sure all of the cover screws have been removed. Then lightly tap the cover to break the gasket seal. Remove the 2 dowel pins.

6. Loosen the clutch adjust screw locknut with a socket (**Figure 54**). Then remove the adjust screw and locknut.

*WARNING*

*The Harley-Davidson Spring Compression Tool (part No. HD-38515 [**Figure 60**]) or equivalent must be used when disassembling the clutch in the following steps. The clutch diaphragm spring is under considerable pressure and will fly off, possibly causing severe personal injury, if the tool is not used.*

7. Align the compression tool with the clutch assembly and thread the forcing screw on the tool into the release plate until the hex head on the forcing screw bottoms out against the release plate (**Figure 61**). Then turn the compression tool handle *clockwise* to compress the diaphragm tool while at the same time moving the clutch spring seat inward and away from the large circlip. When the clutch spring seat has been moved away from the circlip, remove the circlip with circlip pliers or carefully pry it out with a small screwdriver (**Figure 62**).

8. After removing the circlip in Step 6, remove the spring compression tool from the clutch with the diaphragm spring and pressure plate still attached (**Figure 63**).

*NOTE*

*Do not loosen the spring compression tool to remove the diaphragm spring or pressure plate unless these parts require close inspection or replacement. Loosening and removing the compression tool will require repositioning of the diaphragm spring during reassembly. This step will not be required as long as the compression tool is not removed from these parts.*

9. Remove the friction and steel clutch plates (and the spring plate) from the clutch assembly in order (**Figure 64**). Note the spring plate installed between the 4th and 5th friction plate (**Figure 65**).

5

*NOTE*
*Further removal steps are not required unless it is necessary to remove the clutch hub and shell assembly. Remove these parts as described under **Clutch Removal (Clutch Is Not Disassembled)** in this chapter. See **Figure 66**.*

## Inspection

Refer to **Figure 52** when performing the following.

1. Clean all parts (except friction plates and bearing) in a non-oil based solvent and thoroughly dry with compressed air. Place all cleaned parts on lint-free paper towels.
2. Check each steel plate (A, **Figure 67**) for visual damage such as cracks or wear grooves. Then place each plate on a surface plate and check for warpage with a feeler gauge. Replace the steel plates as a set if any one plate is warped more than 0.006 in. (0.15 mm).

*NOTE*
*A piece of glass can be used as a surface plate when measuring warpage in Step 2.*

3. Inspect the friction plates (B, **Figure 67**) for worn or grooved lining surfaces; replace the friction plates as a set if any 1 plate is damaged. If the friction plates do not show visual wear or damage, wipe each plate thoroughly with a lint-free cloth to remove as much oil from the plates as possible. Then stack each of the 8 friction plates on top of each other and measure the thickness of the plate assembly with a vernier caliper or micrometer. Replace the friction plates as an assembly if the combined minimum thickness of the 8 plates is less than 0.661 in. (16.79 mm).

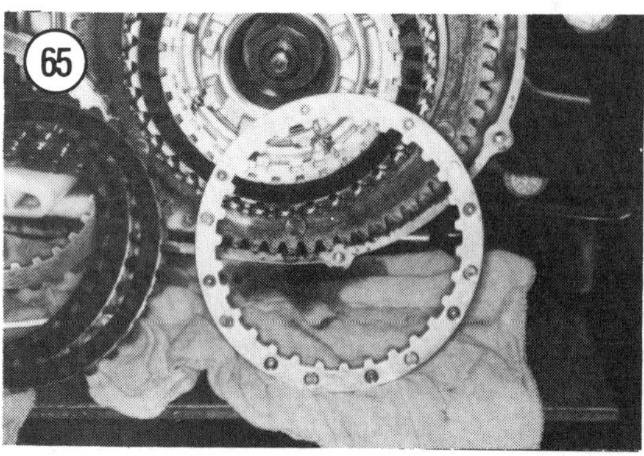
65

4. Check the spring plate (C, **Figure 67**) for cracks or damage. Check each of the rivets (**Figure 68**) for looseness or damage. Replace the spring plate if necessary.
5. Check the diaphragm spring for cracks or damage. Check also for bent or damaged tabs. Replace the diaphragm spring if necessary.
6. A double-row ball bearing is pressed into the clutch shell and the clutch hub is pressed into the

66

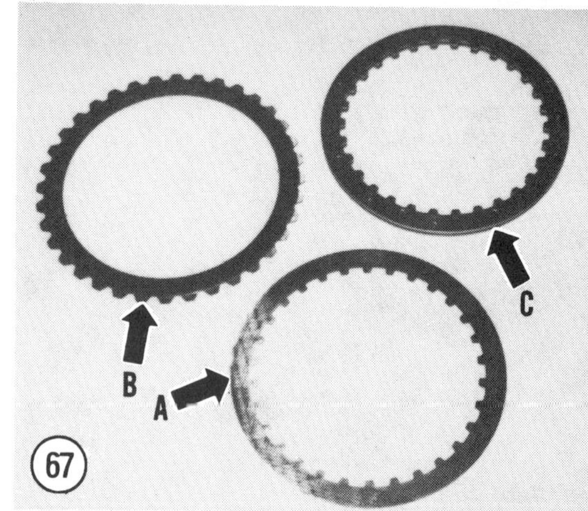

67

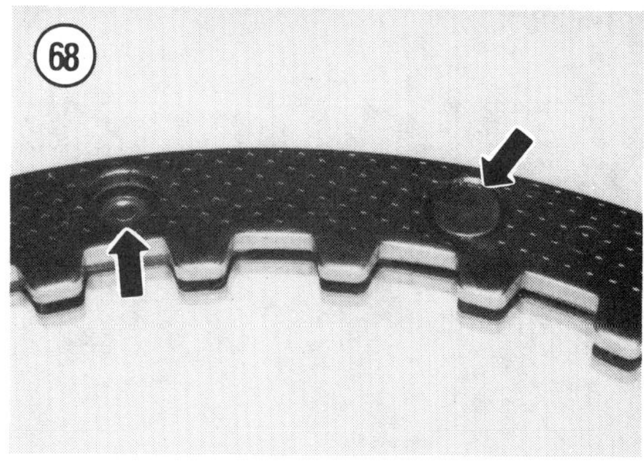
68

bearing. Hold the clutch hub and rotate the clutch shell by hand. The shell should turn smoothly with no sign of roughness or tightness. If the clutch shell binds or turns roughly, the bearing is damaged and must be replaced. Refer to Step 10.

7. The steel clutch plate inner teeth mesh with the clutch hub splines (**Figure 69**). Check the splines for cracks or galling. They must be smooth for chatter-free clutch operation. If the clutch hub splines are damaged, the clutch hub must be replaced; refer to Step 10.

8. The friction plates (B, **Figure 67**) have tabs that slide in the clutch shell grooves. Inspect the shell grooves for cracks or wear grooves. The grooves must be smooth for chatter-free clutch operation. If the clutch shell grooves are damaged or worn severely, the clutch shell must be replaced; refer to Step 10.



9. Check the primary chain sprocket and the starter ring gear on the clutch shell for cracks, deep scoring, excessive wear or heat discoloration. If either the sprocket or ring gear are severely worn or damaged, replace the clutch shell; refer to Step 10. If the sprocket is worn, also check the primary chain and the compensating sprocket as described in this chapter.

10. If the clutch hub, shell or bearing require replacement, refer to *Clutch Hub and Shell Disassembly/Reassembly* in this chapter.

## Clutch Hub and Shell Disassembly/Reassembly

The clutch hub and shell should not be separated unless replacement of the hub, shell or bearing is required. Disassembly of the hub and shell will damage the double-row ball bearing; bearing replacement will be required during reassembly. A press is required for this procedure.

Read this procedure completely through before starting disassembly. Refer to **Figure 52** when performing this procedure.

1. Remove the clutch plates from the clutch hub and shell assembly, if they have not been previously removed. Refer to *Clutch Disassembly on Bike*.

2. Remove the circlip from the clutch hub groove with circlip pliers (**Figure 70**).

3. Support the clutch hub and shell in a press (**Figure 71**) and press the clutch hub out of the bearing. See **Figure 72**. Remove the clutch shell from the press.

*WARNING*
*The clutch hub is a sub-assembly held together with a circlip (**Figure 73**). The parts making up the clutch hub are not serviceable; if the clutch hub is damaged, replace it as a single unit. When handling and servicing the clutch hub, do **not** remove this circlip. The clutch hub is under considerable pressure and removal of the circlip would allow the clutch hub to fly apart under extreme force. This could result in severe personal injury.*

73

4. Locate the circlip (**Figure 74**) securing the bearing in the clutch shell. Carefully remove the circlip from the clutch shell groove.

*NOTE*
*When removing the bearing in Step 5, note that the bearing must be removed through the front side of the shell. The clutch shell is manufactured with a shoulder on the rear (primary chain) side.*

74

5. Support the clutch shell in the press and press the bearing out of the shell. Discard the bearing.
6. Discard worn or damaged parts. Clean reusable and new parts (except bearing) in solvent and dry thoroughly.
7. Place the clutch shell into the press. Then align the bearing with the clutch shell and press bearing into shell until bearing bottoms out against lower shoulder (**Figure 75**). When pressing the bearing into the clutch shell, press only on the outer bearing race. Installing the bearing by pressing on its inner race will damage the bearing. Refer to *Ball Bearing Replacement* in Chapter One for additional information.

75

8. Install the bearing circlip into the clutch shell groove (**Figure 74**). Make sure the circlip seats in the groove completely. See **Figure 76**.
9. Press the clutch hub into the clutch shell as follows:
   a. Place the clutch shell in a press. Support the inner bearing race with a sleeve as shown in **Figure 77**.

*CAUTION*
*Failure to support the inner bearing race as described in sub-step a will cause bearing and clutch shell damage.*

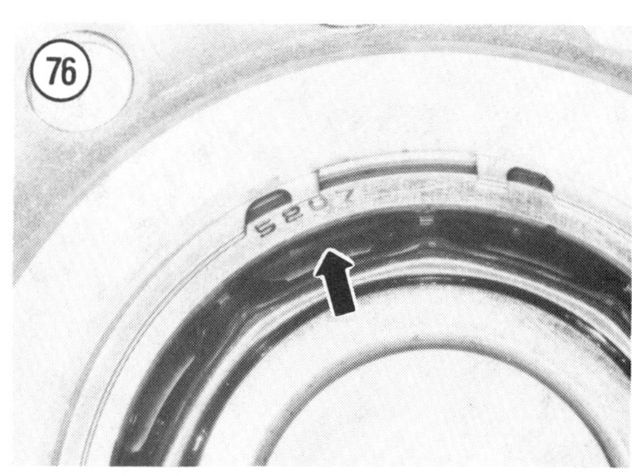
76

*Refer to **Figure 77** to make sure the inner bearing race is supported properly.*

b. Align the clutch hub with the bearing and press the clutch hub into the bearing until the clutch hub shoulder seats against the bearing.

c. Using circlip pliers, install the clutch hub circlip (**Figure 70**). Make sure the circlip seats in the clutch hub groove completely.

10. After completing assembly, hold the clutch hub and rotate the clutch shell by hand. The shell should turn smoothly with no sign of roughness or binding. If the clutch shell binds or turns roughly, the bearing may have been damaged during reassembly.

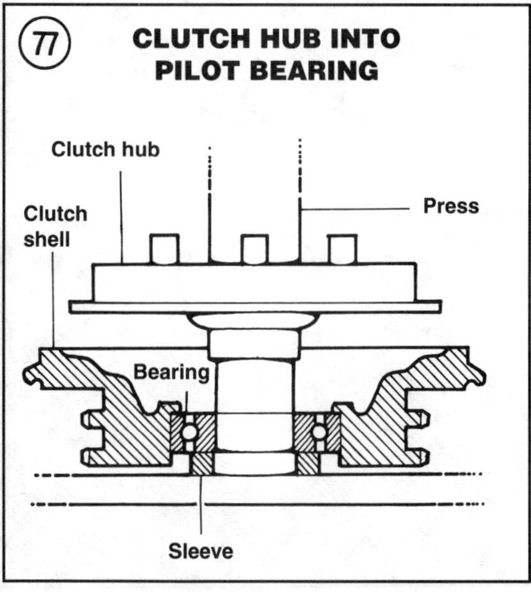

## Clutch Assembly

This section describes clutch assembly. After assembly, the clutch will be installed back onto the bike. If you did not disassemble the clutch assembly, refer to *Clutch Installation*.

Refer to **Figure 52** when performing this procedure.

1. Soak all of the clutch plates in clean primary chain case oil for approximately 5 minutes before installing them.

*NOTE*
*Before installing the clutch plates, count the number of each plate. You should have 8 friction plates, 6 steel plates and 1 spring plate.*

2. Align the tabs on a friction plate with the clutch shell grooves and install the plate. Then align the inner teeth on a steel plate with the clutch hub grooves and install the plate. Repeat until all of the clutch plates have been installed. The spring plate (**Figure 65**) should be installed between the 4th and 5th friction plate. The last plate installed should be a friction plate.

*NOTE*
*During clutch removal, you had the option of whether or not to remove the spring compression tool from the diaphragm spring and pressure plate after removing the pressure plate assembly. If the spring compression tool was not removed from the diaphragm spring and pressure plate (**Figure 78**), proceed to Step 4. If the spring compression tool was removed and the diaphragm spring was separated from the pressure plate, proceed to Step 3.*

3. Assemble the pressure plate and diaphragm spring as follows:

a. If the release plate was removed from the pressure plate, install it onto the pressure plate by aligning its tabs with the slots in the pressure plate. Secure the release plate by installing the circlip into the pressure plate groove. Make sure the circlip seats in the groove completely. Do not thread the adjust screw and locknut into the release plate at this time.

b. Align the teeth on the pressure plate with the clutch hub, then insert the pressure plate into the clutch hub.

c. The diaphragm spring is not flat, but instead it has a convex side (side that curves outward). Install the diaphragm spring onto the pressure plate so that the convex side faces *away* from the pressure plate—the convex side must face out. After installing the diaphragm spring, you will note that there is room for the diaphragm spring to move around within the pressure plate; this area within the pressure plate is called the spring pocket. For the diaphragm spring to be properly installed, it must be centered within the pressure plate spring pocket. Center the diaphragm spring by hand and hold it in position.

d. The clutch spring seat has a lip on one side. Install the spring seat onto the face of the diaphragm spring so that the lip faces out.

*WARNING*
*The following steps describe installation of the diaphragm spring circlip. Because of the force required to compress the diaphragm spring in order to install the circlip, the Harley-Davidson Spring Compression Tool (part No. HD-38515 [**Figure 60**]) or equivalent must be used. Severe personal injury could occur if the special tool is not used.*

e. Align the compression tool with the clutch hub and thread the center screw on the tool into the release plate until the hex head on the forcing screw bottoms out against the release plate (**Figure 79**). Then check that the diaphragm spring is still centered within the clutch hub spring pocket as described in sub-step c. If necessary, reposition the diaphragm spring. When the diaphragm spring position is correct, proceed to sub-step f.

f. Turn the compression tool handle *clockwise* to compress the diaphragm spring and move the clutch spring seat inward to access the clutch hub circlip groove. Then install the diaphragm spring circlip into the clutch hub groove, making sure the ends of the circlip do not overhang the bosses or posts on the end of the clutch hub.

g. After making sure the circlip is seated completely in the clutch hub groove and positioned as described in sub-step f, slowly turn the compression tool handle *counterclockwise* while checking that the clutch spring seat lip seats inside the circlip. After all tension has been removed from the compression tool, remove it from the release plate.

h. Thread the adjust screw and locknut into the release plate (**Figure 80**).

79

80

81

4. If the compression tool was not removed from the diaphragm spring, install the diaphragm spring as follows:

a. Align the teeth on the pressure plate (**Figure 81**) with the clutch hub, then insert the pressure plate into the clutch hub.

b. Turn the compression tool handle *clockwise* to compress the diaphragm spring and move the clutch spring seat inward to access the clutch hub circlip groove. Then install the diaphragm spring circlip into the clutch hub groove, making sure the ends of the circlip do not overhang the bosses or posts on the end of the clutch hub.

c. After making sure the circlip is seated completely in the clutch hub groove and positioned as described in sub-step b, slowly turn the compression tool handle *counterclockwise* while checking that the clutch spring seat lip seats inside the circlip. After all tension has been removed from the compression tool, remove it from the release plate.

d. Thread the adjust screw and locknut into the release plate (**Figure 80**).



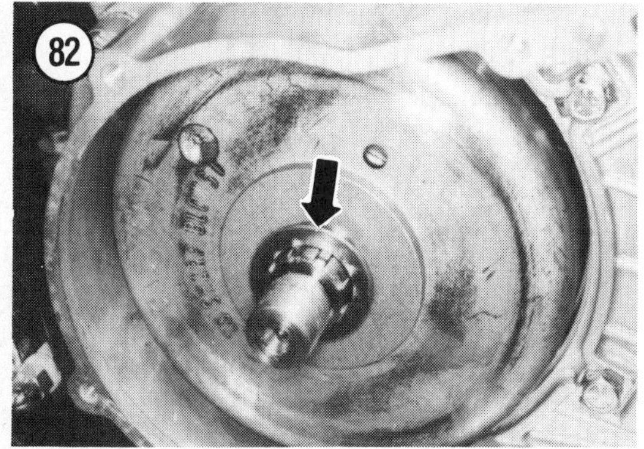

82

83

84

### Clutch Installation

1. Clean the primary chain case housing and the chain case cover gasket surfaces of all gasket residue. Wipe all oil residue out of the bottom of the chain case cover and housing.

2. Assemble the clutch assembly as described in the previous section.

3. Clean the crankshaft threads, compensating sprocket nut, clutch hub nut and mainshaft threads of all Loctite residue.

4. Install the sprocket shaft spacer (**Figure 82**) and the compensating sprocket shaft extension (**Figure 83**), if previously removed.

5. The compensating sprocket, primary chain, chain adjuster and clutch are installed as an assembly. Assemble the compensating sprocket and clutch shell sprocket with the primary chain. Likewise, engage the chain tensioner with the chain.

6. Lift the primary drive assembly as a unit and slide the compensating sprocket and clutch shell into the chain case. Make sure the chain tension assembly is still attached to the chain. See **Figure 84**.

NOTE

*The clutch hub nut uses left-hand threads. Turn the nut counterclockwise to tighten it.*

7. Apply 2 drops of Loctite 262 (red) to the clutch hub nut threads and thread the nut onto the mainshaft by turning the nut *counterclockwise*. Using a torque wrench, tighten the nut to the torque specifications listed in **Table 4**. Use the same tools and procedures to prevent the mainshaft from turning as used during disassembly.

*CAUTION*
*The compensating sprocket is tightened to a high torque specification. Make sure you hold the sprocket securely when tightening the nut in Step 8.*

8. Apply 2 drops of Loctite 262 (red) to the compensating sprocket nut threads and thread the nut onto the crankshaft threads. Using the same tools and procedures to prevent the compensating sprocket from turning, tighten the nut to the torque specification listed in **Table 4**.
9. Adjust the clutch as described in Chapter Three.

*NOTE*
*If new clutch components were installed, readjust the clutch at the first 500 mile (800 km) interval.*

10. Assemble and secure the primary chain adjust shoe assembly as described in this chapter.
11. Adjust the primary chain as described in Chapter Three.
12. Check the primary chain alignment as described under *Primary Chain Alignment* in this chapter.
13. Install the 2 primary chain case cover dowel pins, if they have not been previously installed.
14. Install the primary chain case cover together with a *new* gasket. Install the cover screws and washers and tighten each screw securely.
15. Refill the primary chain housing with the correct type and quantity of oil as described in Chapter Three.
16. Check the clutch inspection cover O-ring and the primary chain inspection gasket for wear or damage; replace as required.
17. Install the clutch inspection cover with its O-ring. Install the primary chain inspection cover with its gasket. Install the cover Allen screws and washers and tighten securely.

*NOTE*
*The clutch inspection cover Allen head screws are longer than the primary chain inspection cover screws.*

18. Ride the bike a short distance and check the cover for oil leaks.

## PRIMARY CHAIN

### Removal/Installation

Remove the primary chain as described under the clutch removal procedure for your model in this chapter.

### Inspection

Refer to the procedures in Chapter Three to lubricate and adjust the chain. If the chain cannot be adjusted within the specifications in Chapter Three, it must be replaced.

Always replace the primary drive chain (A, **Figure 85**) if it is worn or damaged. Attempting to repair a worn chain can cause expensive engine damage. If the primary drive chain is worn, also check the compensating sprocket (B, **Figure 85**) and the clutch shell driven sprocket (C, **Figure 85**) for wear or damage. Replace parts as necessary.

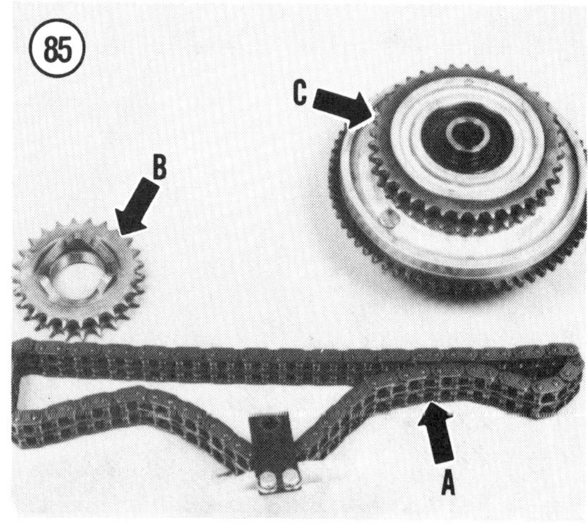

### Adjustment Shoe Replacement

If the primary chain cannot be adjusted properly and the adjustment shoe (**Figure 86**) appears worn, replace it as follows.

1. Remove the primary chain case cover as described under clutch removal for your model in this chapter.
2. Remove the top shoe bracket bolt and remove the bracket.
3. Pry back the locking tabs and remove the adjusting shoe mounting bolts. Remove the old adjusting shoe and install a new one. Lock the new adjusting shoe in place by bending the lockwasher tabs over the mounting bolts.
4. Adjust the primary chain as described in Chapter Three.
5. Install the primary chain case cover as described under the clutch inspection procedure for your model in this chapter.

### Alignment

The compensating sprocket is aligned with the clutch sprocket by a spacer placed between the alternator rotor and the shaft extension (**Figure 87**). The same spacer should be reinstalled any time the compensating sprocket is removed. However, if the primary chain is wearing on one side or if new clutch components were installed that could affect alignment, perform the following.

#### *Wet clutch*

1. Disconnect the negative battery cable.
2. Remove the primary chain, compensating sprocket and clutch shell as described in this chapter.
3. Determine spacer thickness as follows:
   a. Install the clutch hub.
   b. Measure the distance from the alternator rotor hub to the primary drive housing gasket surface (A, **Figure 88**).
   c. Measure the distance from the clutch disc friction surface to the primary drive housing gasket surface (B, **Figure 88**).
   d. Subtract measurement B from A to obtain spacer thickness C.
   e. Select the proper spacer thickness from **Table 5**.
4. Reinstall all parts as described in this chapter.

#### *Dry clutch*

1. Remove the primary cover as described under the clutch removal procedure for your model.

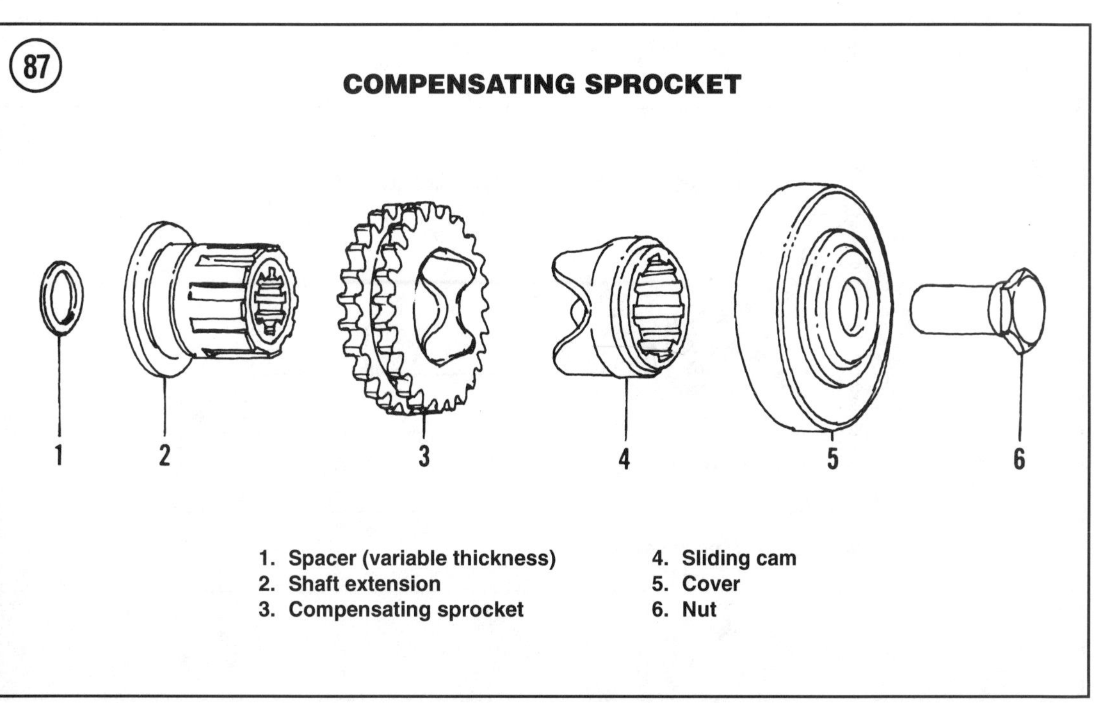

2. Check and adjust the primary chain tension as described in Chapter Three.
3. Push the primary chain toward the engine as far as it will go at the sprockets as shown in **Figure 89**. This pushes the chain clearance to the inside of the sprockets.
4. Place a straightedge across the primary cover gasket surface near the engine compensating sprocket and measure the distance from the chain link side plates to the straightedge. Record this measurement.
5. Repeat Step 4 by measuring the distance at the clutch sprocket.
6. The difference between Step 4 and Step 5 should be within 0.030 in. (0.76 mm). If the clearance exceeds 0.030 in. (0.76 mm), replace the spacer (**Figure 87**) with a suitable size spacer. Spacers are available through Harley-Davidson dealers.

## COMPENSATING SPROCKET

### Removal/Installation

Remove and install the compensating sprocket as described under *Clutch Removal/Installation*.

### Inspection

Refer to **Figure 87** for this procedure.
1. Clean all parts in solvent, then blow dry.
2. Visually check the cam surfaces (A, **Figure 90**) for cracks, deep scoring or excessive wear.
3. Check the compensating sprocket gear teeth (B, **Figure 90**) for cracks or excessive wear.

*NOTE*
*If the compensating sprocket gear teeth are worn, also check the primary chain and clutch shell gear teeth for wear. See **Figure 85**.*

4. Check the shaft extension splines (**Figure 91**) for wear or galling.
5. Inspect the cover (**Figure 92**) for damage.
6. Visually inspect the nut (**Figure 93**) for galling or wear and the threads for damage.
7. Replace any worn or damaged part.
8. If any component was replaced, check the primary chain alignment as described in this chapter.

## PRIMARY CHAIN CASE

The primary chain case houses the compensating sprocket assembly, primary chain, chain adjuster and clutch.

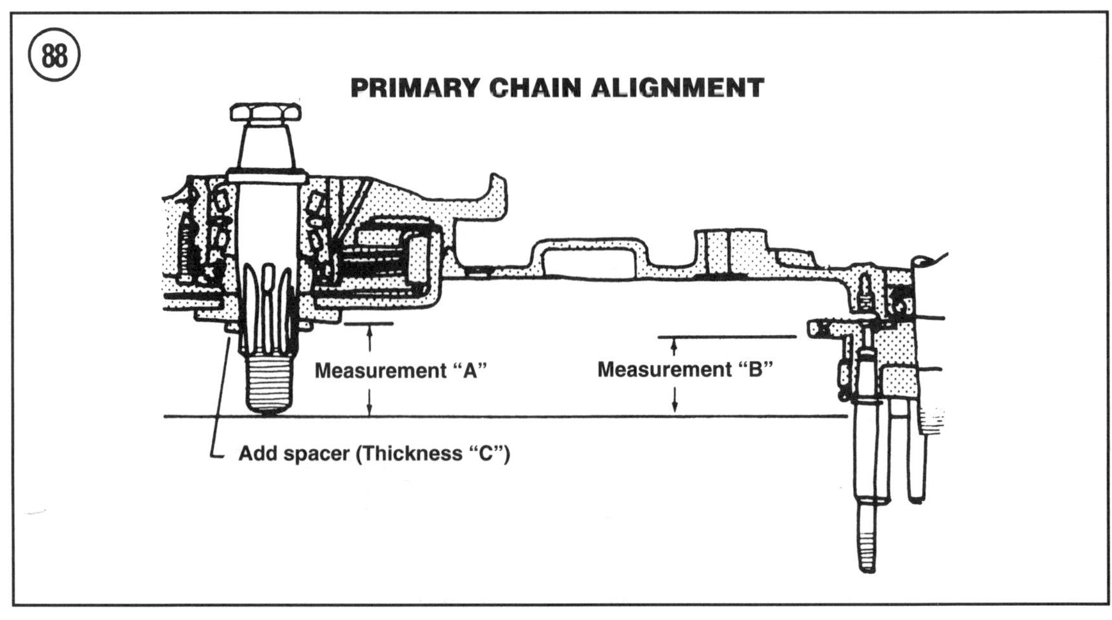

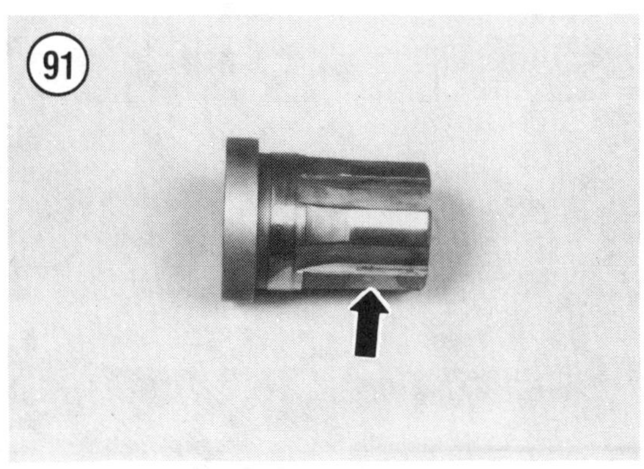


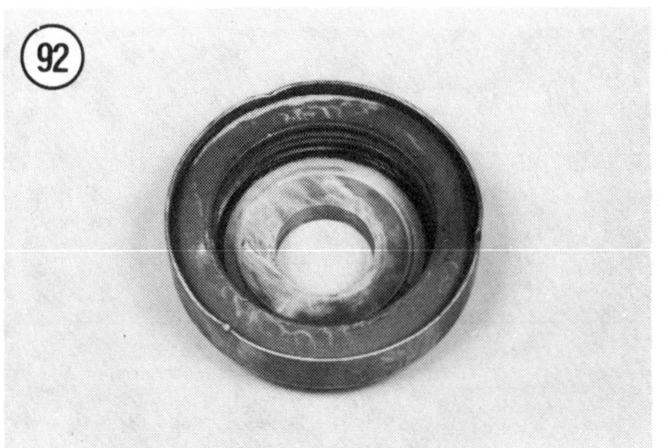


## Removal (1984-1988 FLT and FXR)

1. Remove the clutch, primary chain and compensating sprocket as described under the clutch removal procedure for your model in this chapter.
2. Remove the solenoid and plunger as described in Chapter Nine.
3. Remove the starter drive housing as described in this chapter.
4. *1984*: Using the Rear Chain Boot Remover (Harley-Davidson part No. HD-97101-81), remove the screws securing the chain boot to the primary chain case.

5

NOTE
*On early 1984 models, label the vent hoses before disconnecting them in the following steps.*

5. *Early 1984 models*: Disconnect the chain oil hose at the oil pump. Then find the T-fitting next to the oil pump that has the 2 attached vent hoses. Disconnect the crankcase and oil pump vent hoses from the T-fitting.
6. Perform the following:
   a. Cut any safety wire (**Figure 94**) used to lock the engine case bolts.
   b. Remove the primary-to-transmission case bolts. See **Figure 95** or **Figure 96**.

NOTE
*On models with 2 bolts (**Figure 96**) at the rear of the housing, remove the 2 bolts from behind the case.*

   c. Remove the primary housing-to-engine case bolts. See **Figure 97** or **Figure 98**.
   d. On early 1984 models, pull the primary case out slightly and disconnect the remaining vent

hose from the rear of the primary case. Then on all models, rotate the primary case clockwise on the mainshaft and remove it. On 1985-1988 models, pull the primary case away from the engine and remove it. See **Figure 99**.

7. Inspect the primary chain case assembly as described in this chapter.

## Installation (1984-1988 FLT and FXR)

1. Replace the alternator O-ring (**Figure 100**) if worn or damaged.

2. On models in which the mainshaft bearing is not held in place with circlips, wipe the outer bearing surface with Loctite Retaining Compound No. 601 and install the bearing into the primary chain case. On later models, install the bearing and secure it with the 2 circlips.

3. Install a new inner chain case gasket on early models.

4. Carefully align the chain case with the mainshaft and slide the chain case onto the mainshaft.

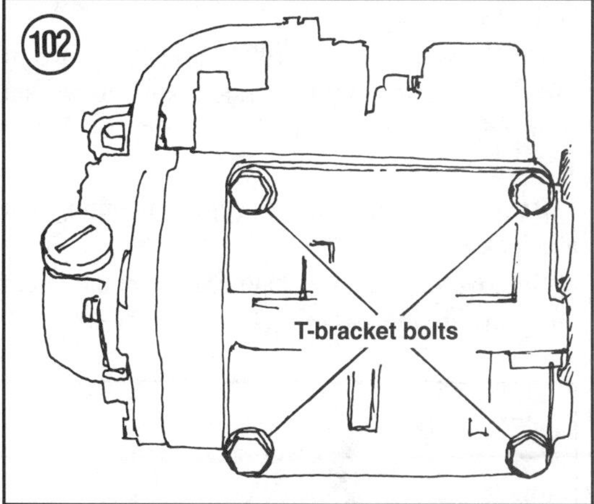

*NOTE*

*Use the ID marks made on the vent hoses prior to their disassembly when performing Step 3.*

5. *Early 1984 models*: Connect the oil return hose at its fitting on the bottom/rear of the primary housing. Then route the chain oiler and vent hoses between the engine and transmission housings. Reconnect the chain oil hose to its fitting on the oil pump. Connect the vent hoses from the oil tank and oil pump to the fitting on the primary vent hose.

*CAUTION*

*The following procedures should be followed in order to ensure that the transmission is properly aligned with the engine. Improper alignment could cause chain and transmission failure.*

6. Install the inner primary case to transmission bolts and lock tabs. Tighten 3/8 in. bolts to 21-27 ft.-lb.(29-37 N•m). Tighten 5/16 in. bolts to 13-16 ft.-lb. (18-22 N•m). After tightening bolts, check that the mainshaft (**Figure 101**) turns freely. When mainshaft is turning properly, bend the lock tabs over the bolt heads to lock the bolts.

7. Install the chain case to engine mounting bolts finger-tight.

8A. *1984-1986*: Loosen the 4 engine T-bracket-to-transmission bolts (**Figure 102**).

8B. *1987-1988*: Loosen the 2 engine-to-transmission 3/8 in. bolts.

9. Tighten the chain case-to-engine bolts to 16-18 ft.-lb. (22-25 N•m). On 1984 models, safety wire the 2 inner bolts. See **Figure 103** and **Figure 104**.

*NOTE*

*Always install safety wire so that it tightens the bolt.* ***Figure 105*** *shows how*

5

*safety wire two bolts by the double twist method. Always use stainless steel wire approved for safety wiring.*

10A. *1984-1986*: Tighten the 4 engine T-bracket-to-transmission bolts to 13-16 ft.-lb. (18-22 N•m).
10B. *1987-1988*: Tighten the 2 engine-to-transmission 3/8 in. bolts to 35-38 ft.-lb. (48.3-52.4 N•m).
11. Install the starter and starter drive housing as described in this chapter.
12. Install the solenoid as described in this chapter.
13. Coat the rear chain boots and the chain case and transmission case mating surfaces with 3M 750 Silicone Sealant. Install the housing bolts and tighten in a crisscross pattern to 3-4 ft.-lb. (4.1-5.5 N•m).
14. Install the clutch, primary chain and compensating sprocket as described in this chapter.
15. On dry clutch models, perform the *Primary Housing Vacuum Check (Early 1984 with Dry Clutch)* in this chapter.

### Primary Housing Vacuum Check (Early 1984 with Dry Clutch)

The primary housing must be checked for air tightness after reassembly.

1. Remove one of the clutch inspection cover screws and thread the Vacuum Gauge (part No. HD 96950-68) into the screw hole.
2. Start the engine and allow it to idle. The vacuum gauge should read 9 inches of water vacuum (minimum).
3. Locate the 3/8 in. (9.5 mm) vent hose connected between the chain case and the tee connector. Pinch this hose closed and bring the engine idle speed up to 1,500 rpm. The vacuum gauge should now read 25 inches of water vacuum.
4. If the vacuum gauge shows a lower reading, there is an air leak into the primary housing.
5. Pinch all of the oil lines running to the primary housing. Pinch the hoses as close to the housing as possible.

*CAUTION*

*Do not apply more than 10 psi (0.7 kg/cm$^2$) of compressed air into the primary housing.*

6. Pressurize the housing with 10 psi (0.7 kg/cm$^2$) of compressed air. Now listen for air leaks at the following locations:
   a. All O-ring and gasket surfaces.
   b. All hose and oil seal fittings.
   c. Starter drive and solenoid mounting areas.
   d. Timing inspection hole.
   e. Transmission filler hole.
   f. Along the primary chain case housing and cover (possible cracks or casting defects).
7. Leaking areas must be repaired before putting the bike back into service.

### Removal (1989-on FLT and FXR)

Refer to **Figure 106** when performing this procedure.

1. Remove the clutch, primary chain and compensating sprocket as described under the clutch removal procedure for your model in this chapter.
2. Remove the starter jackshaft as described in this chapter.
3. Remove the starter motor as described in Chapter Nine.
4. Bend the lock tab away from each of the mounting bolts.
5. Remove the chain case-to-transmission mounting bolts and lock tabs.
6. On all models except 1993-on FLT, remove the lower chain case-to-transmission bolt and washers from behind the transmission housing (4, **Figure 107**).
7. Remove the chain case-to-engine mounting bolts and lock tabs.
8. Remove the primary chain case from the engine and transmission assemblies.

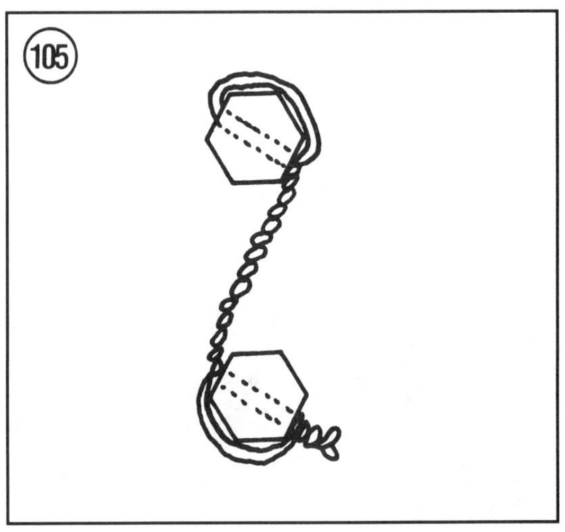

9. Inspect the primary chain case assembly as described in this chapter.

### Installation (1989-1992 FLT and FXR)

1. Replace the alternator O-ring (**Figure 100**) if worn or damaged.

*CAUTION*

*Wipe the inner chain case oil seal lip with chain case oil before installing the chain case in Step 2. When installing the chain case, work the oil seal carefully along the mainshaft so that you don't damage it. Wrap the mainshaft splines with tape to protect the inner chain case oil seal when installing it over the mainshaft.*

2. Carefully align the chain case with the mainshaft and slide the chain case onto the mainshaft.

*CAUTION*

*The following procedures should be followed in order to ensure that the transmission is properly aligned with the engine. Improper alignment could cause chain and transmission failure.*



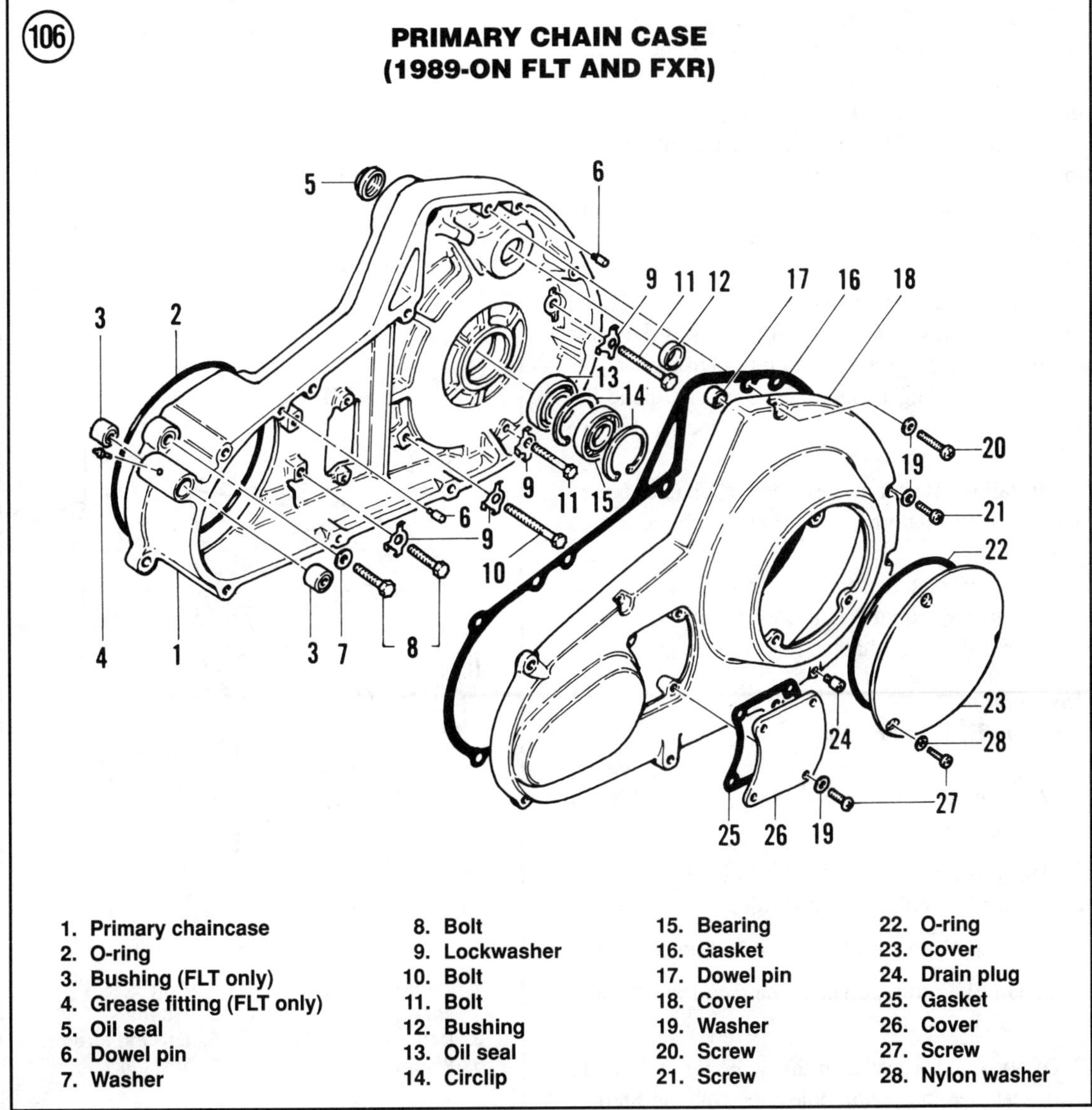


(106) **PRIMARY CHAIN CASE (1989-ON FLT AND FXR)**

1. Primary chaincase
2. O-ring
3. Bushing (FLT only)
4. Grease fitting (FLT only)
5. Oil seal
6. Dowel pin
7. Washer
8. Bolt
9. Lockwasher
10. Bolt
11. Bolt
12. Bushing
13. Oil seal
14. Circlip
15. Bearing
16. Gasket
17. Dowel pin
18. Cover
19. Washer
20. Screw
21. Screw
22. O-ring
23. Cover
24. Drain plug
25. Gasket
26. Cover
27. Screw
28. Nylon washer

*NOTE*
*Replace damaged lockwashers as required.*

3. Install the primary case-to-transmission mounting bolts finger-tight.
4. Install the bolt, lockwasher, ground cable and lockwasher onto the back of the transmission housing as shown in **Figure 107**. Tighten finger-tight.
5. Tighten bolts installed in Steps 3 and 4 to 13-16 ft.-lb. (18-22 N•m). Then check that the mainshaft turns freely.

*NOTE*
*Recheck that the alternator O-ring is still in position.*

6. Install the chain case-to-engine mounting bolts and lockwashers. Tighten bolts finger-tight.
7. Loosen the 2 engine-to-transmission 3/8 in. mounting bolts (**Figure 107**).
8. Tighten the chain case-to-engine mounting bolts to 16-18 ft.-lb. (22-25 N•m).
9. Tighten the 2 engine-to-transmission 3/8 in. mounting bolts (loosened in Step 7) to 33-37 ft.-lb. (45.5-51.1 N•m).
10. Check that the mainshaft turns freely. If the mainshaft binds or turns roughly, loosen the bolts tightened in Steps 8 and 9 and retighten them.
11. Where folding lockwashers are used, bend the lockwasher tab over the bolt head to lock it (**Figure 108**).
12. Install the starter as described in Chapter Nine.
13. Install the starter jackshaft as described in this chapter.
14. Install the clutch, engine compensating sprocket, chain adjuster, primary chain and primary case cover as described in this chapter.

***Installation (1993-on FLT and FXR)***

1. Replace the alternator O-ring (**Figure 100**) if worn or damaged.
2. Apply silicone sealer to the following primary chain case bolt holes (inboard side):

a. 2 rear chain case-to-engine bolt holes.
b. On FLT models, 3 chain case-to-transmission bolt holes.

3. Apply silicone sealer to the 4 (FXR) or 5 (FLT) bolts installed in the bolt holes described in Step 2.

*NOTE*
*The use of silicone sealer as described in Steps 2 and 3 helps to prevent primary chain case oil leaks.*

*CAUTION*
*The following procedures should be followed in order to ensure that the transmission and engine are properly aligned. This is especially important if the engine and/or transmission were previously removed from the frame. Improper alignment will cause primary chain wear and possible transmission damage.*

4. If the engine and/or transmission was previously removed and installed, perform the following:

a. Make sure the bike is supported securely. Then block the engine and transmission so that they don't sag at their mating surfaces.

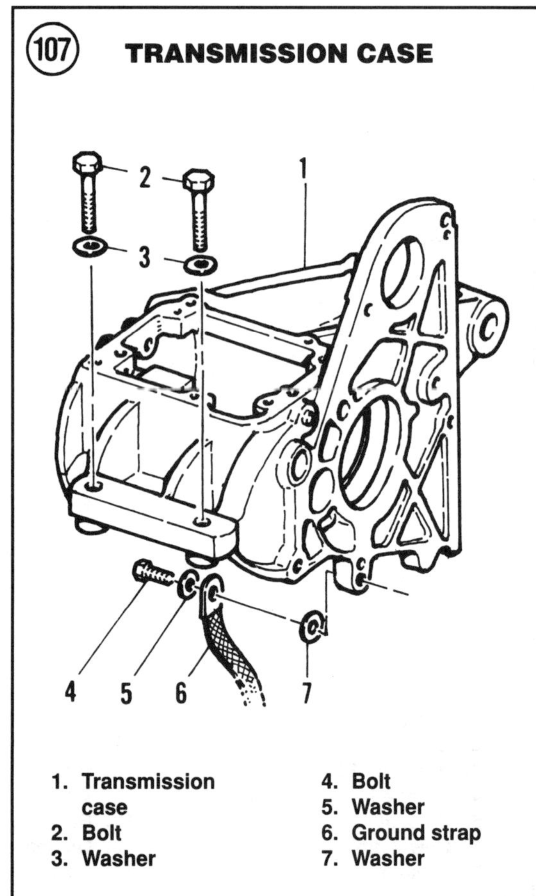


1. Transmission case
2. Bolt
3. Washer
4. Bolt
5. Washer
6. Ground strap
7. Washer

b. Loosen, but do not remove, the engine-to-transmission mounting bolts if they were previously tightened.

NOTE
*All models continue with Step 5.*

CAUTION
*Wrap the mainshaft splines with tape to protect the inner chain case oil seal when installing it over the mainshaft.*

5. Apply oil to the primary chain case oil seal lip.
6. Align the chain case with the mainshaft and slide the chain case into position against the engine and transmission.

NOTE
*Before proceeding with Step 7, check that the alternator O-ring (**Figure 100**) did not get knocked off of the crankcase.*

NOTE
*Initially, install all bolts finger-tight. Do not tighten until specified in procedure.*

7. Install the 2 front outer mounting bolts (8A, **Figure 106**) and washers.
8. Install the 2 front inner mounting bolts (8B) and their lockwashers.
9. Tighten the bolts installed in Steps 7 and 8 to 18-21 ft.-lb. (24-28 N•m).
10. Install the chain case-to-transmission mounting bolts; see 10 and 11, **Figure 106**. On FXR models, install the bottom, inboard bolt and ground cable as shown in **Figure 107**. Tighten these bolts to 18-21 ft.-lb.. (24-28 N•m).
11. Check that the mainshaft turns freely. Also check for crankcase-to-frame distortion. If there is no binding or other abnormal conditions, continue with Step

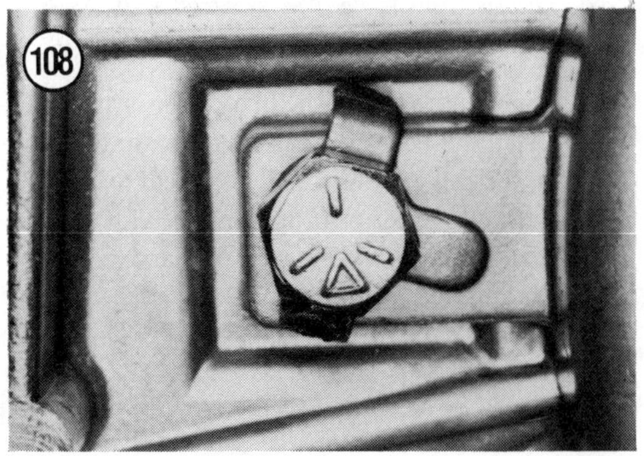


12. If binding is noted, loosen all of the bolts previously tightened and repeat Steps 7-10.
12. If upper engine-to-transmission mounting bolts (**Figure 107**) are loose, tighten as follows:
   a. Tighten the right-hand transmission mounting bolt to 33-38 ft.-lb. (45-52 N•m).
   b. Tighten the left-hand transmission mounting bolt to 33-38 ft.-lb. (45-52 N•m).
13. Where folding lcckwashers are used, bend the lockwasher tab over the bolt head to lock it (**Figure 108**).
14. Install the starter motor as described in Chapter Nine.
15. Install the starter jackshaft as described in this chapter.
16. Install the clutch, engine compensating sprocket, chain adjuster, primary chain and primary chain case cover as described in this chapter.

5

### Removal (1985-1986 FX)

1. Remove the clutch, primary chain and compensating sprocket as described under the clutch removal procedure for your model in this chapter.
2. Remove the solenoid and plunger as described in Chapter Nine.
3. Remove the starter drive housing as described in this chapter.
4. Loosen the lower engine-to-frame mounting bolts and nuts.
5. Loosen the transmission-to-frame mounting bolts and nuts.
6. Perform the following:
   a. Cut any safety wire (**Figure 94**) used to lock the engine case bolts.
   b. Remove the primary-to-transmission case bolts. See **Figure 95** or **Figure 96**.
   c. Remove the primary housing-to-engine case bolts. See **Figure 97** or **Figure 98**.
   d. Pull the primary case away from the engine and remove it. See **Figure 99**.
7. Inspect the primary chain case assembly as described in this chapter.

### Installation (1985-1986 FX)

1. Replace the alternator O-ring (**Figure 100**) if worn or damaged.

*NOTE*
*Wipe the inner chain case oil seal lip with chain case oil before installing the chain case in Step 2. When installing the chain case, work the oil seal carefully along the mainshaft so that you don't damage it.*

2. Carefully align the chain case with the mainshaft and slide the chain case onto the mainshaft.

*CAUTION*
*The following procedures should be followed in order to ensure that the transmission is properly aligned with the engine. Improper alignment could cause chain and transmission failure.*

3. Loosen the engine and transmission frame mounting fasteners if they were not loosened during removal.
4. Install the primary case-to-transmission mounting bolts finger-tight.

*NOTE*
*The 2 primary case-to-engine mounting bolts with the drilled head should be installed into the rear engine mounting holes.* ***Figure 94*** *shows these 2 bolts.*

5. Install the primary case-to-engine mounting bolts finger-tight. See **Figure 97** or **Figure 98**.
6. Tighten the primary case-to-engine mounting bolts to 18-22 ft.-lb. (24.8-30.4 N•m). See **Figure 97** or **Figure 98**.
7. Align the primary case with the transmission housing.

*NOTE*
*Before tightening the primary case-to-transmission bolts, check the bolts for binding by screwing them in and out by hand. Likewise, check the mainshaft (**Figure 101**) for binding by turning it by hand. If the bolts or mainshaft show any sign of binding, you must reposition the primary case where it mounts on the transmission. If necessary, loosen the primary case-to-engine mounting bolts and start over. When there is no apparent binding when the engine mounting bolts are tight, proceed to Step 8.*

8. Tighten the primary case-to-transmission mounting bolts to 18-22 ft.-lb. (24.8-30.4 N•m). Bend the lockwasher tab over the bolt head to lock it.
9. Tighten the lower engine-to-frame mounting bolts and nuts to 33-38 ft.-lb. (45.5-52.4 N•m).
10. Tighten the transmission-to-frame mounting bolts to 33-38 ft.-lb. (45.5-52.4 N•m).

*NOTE*
*Recheck that the mainshaft (**Figure 101**) turns freely with no sign of binding.*

11. Safety wire the 2 rear primary case-to-engine bolts as shown in **Figure 103** and **Figure 104**.

*CAUTION*
*Always install safety wire so that it tightens the bolt.* ***Figure 105*** *shows the correct way to safety wire two bolts by the double twist method. Always use stainless steel wire approved for safety wiring.*

12. Install the starter and starter drive housing as described in this chapter.
13. Install the solenoid and plunger as described in Chapter Nine.
14. Install the clutch, engine compensating sprocket, chain adjuster, primary chain and primary case cover as described in this chapter.

**Inspection (Early Models with Dry Clutch)**

1. Clean the primary case in solvent and dry thoroughly.
2. Check the gasket surface on both sides of the housing for cracks or other damage.
3. Check the primary case bearing. Turn the inner bearing race by hand and check for excessive play, roughness or noise; both conditions indicate a worn or damaged bearing. To replace the bearing:

*NOTE*
*The bearing is held in position with a chemical locking compound.*

a. Remove the bearing with a puller or press.
b. Clean the bearing mounting area in the case thoroughly to remove all chemical residue.
c. Wipe the outer bearing surface with Loctite Retaining Compound No. 601 and press the bearing into the housing.

*NOTE*
*Follow the manufacturer's cure time before reassembling the primary housing.*

## Inspection (Late Models with Wet Clutch)

1. Clean the primary case in solvent and dry thoroughly.

NOTE
*On early models, remove the circlip before removing the oil seal.*

2. Check the inner primary case oil seal for wear or damage. If the seal is damaged, carefully pry it out of the primary case with a screwdriver. Place a rag underneath the screwdriver to avoid damaging the case.
3. Check the primary case bearing (15, **Figure 106**). Turn the inner bearing race by hand and check for excessive play, roughness or noise. To replace the bearing:
   a. Remove the inner and outer bearing circlips (14, **Figure 106**), if used.

NOTE
*If your model does not use an inner circlip, note the position of the bearing in the primary case for reassembly.*

   b. Support the primary case and press the bearing out.
   c. Install the outer circlip (clutch side), if used. Make sure the circlip is fully seated in the groove.

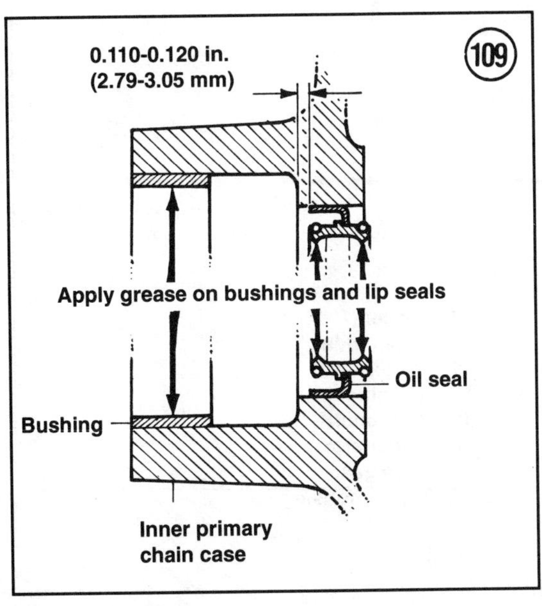


CAUTION
*If the outer circlip is used on your model, support the circlip when pressing the bearing into the primary case in the next step. The force required to press the bearing into the primary case may force the circlip out of its groove, damaging the primary case.*

   d. Support the primary case and outer circlip (if used) in a press. Then press the bearing into the primary case. If the outer circlip is used, press the bearing until it seats against the circlip. If the outer circlip is not used, press the bearing to the same depth recorded prior to removal.
   e. Install the inner circlip, if used. Make sure the circlip is fully seated in the groove.
   f. Recheck circlip installation.

4. Install a new inner primary case oil seal with a bearing driver or socket; install oil seal so that it seats against the bearing (early models) or circlip (late models). On early models, install the outer circlip.

NOTE
*Before removing needle bearing or bushings in Step 5, note their positions in the primary housing. If they are countersunk or installed flush with the housing, they must be reinstalled accordingly. If countersunk in housing, record depth measurement.*

5. If the primary cover bushing is worn, remove it with a suitable driver. Then press a new bushing into the cover until it is flush or within 0.030 in. (0.76 mm) below its mounting boss.

6A. *1989*: Inspect the primary housing, jackshaft bushing, oil seal and scraper and the primary cover bushing for wear or damage. Replace as follows:
   a. Remove the bushing with a suitable driver or press. Then press new bushing into housing so that it is flush or within 0.010 in. (0.25 mm) below its mounting boss.
   b. To replace the oil seal, first drive the oil seal and scraper out of housing and discard both parts. Install a new seal to the dimensions shown in **Figure 109**. The oil scraper is no longer used.

6B. *1990-on*: Check the primary housing jackshaft bushing and oil seal for damage. If worn or damaged, remove the oil seal and bushing and discard them both. Install new parts to the dimensions shown in **Figure 109**.

7. *FLT*: Check the 2 front bushings installed in the primary housing; see **Figure 106**, typical. If these bushings are worn or damaged, remove them with a suitable driver. Install the 2 new bushings so that the outer edge of each bushing is flush with or within 0.030 in. (0.76 mm) from the outside edge of the primary housing. Check the grease fitting (**Figure 106**) for damage or contamination.

## ELECTRIC STARTER DRIVE (1984-1988 FLT AND FXR)

Refer to **Figure 110** when performing procedures in this section.

### Removal

1. Disconnect the negative battery cable.
2. Remove the primary cover as described in this chapter.

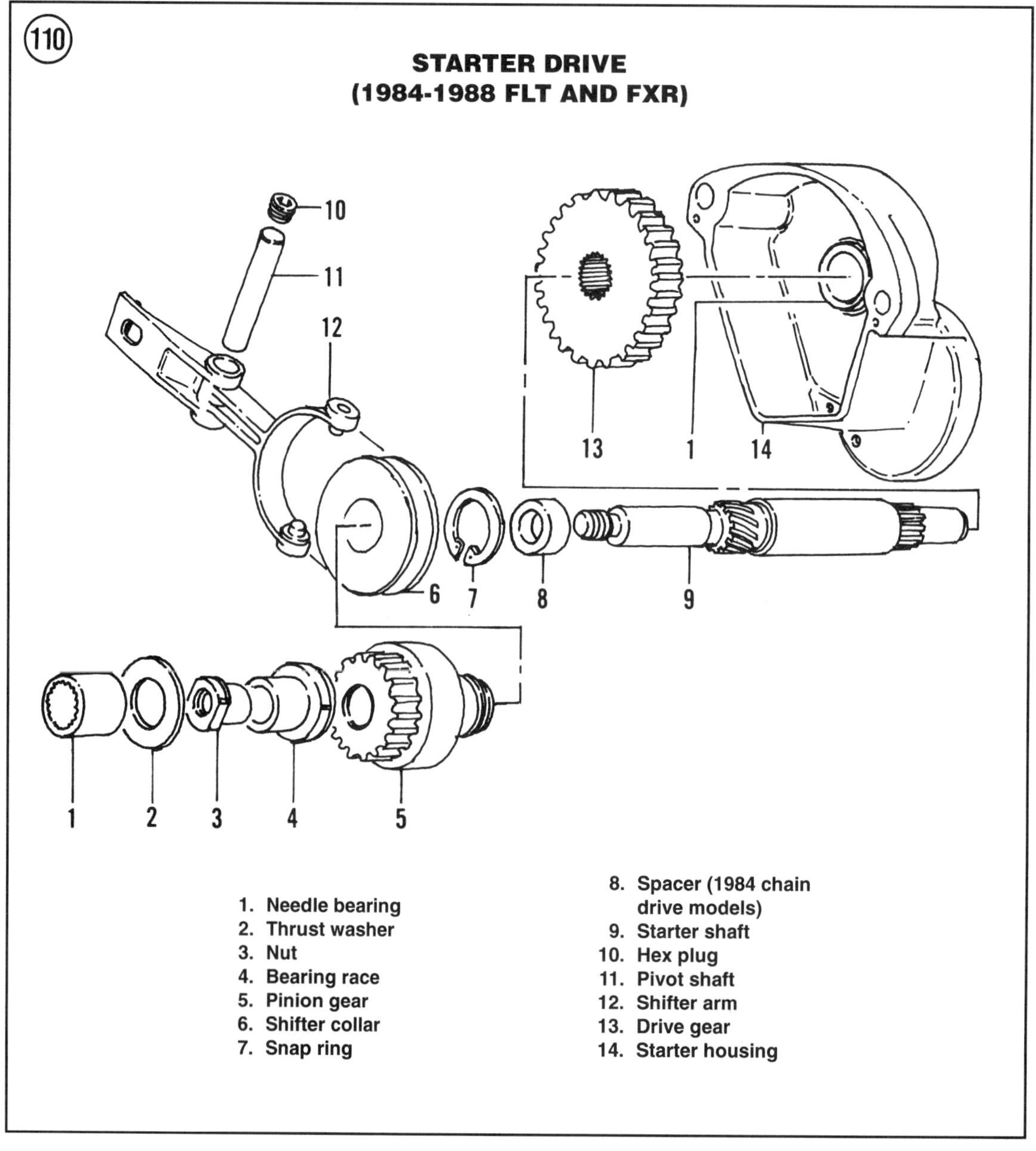


1. Needle bearing
2. Thrust washer
3. Nut
4. Bearing race
5. Pinion gear
6. Shifter collar
7. Snap ring
8. Spacer (1984 chain drive models)
9. Starter shaft
10. Hex plug
11. Pivot shaft
12. Shifter arm
13. Drive gear
14. Starter housing

*NOTE*
*If the clutch has been removed, it is not necessary to remove the starter or starter housing. Proceed to Step 4. If the clutch is not going to be removed, proceed to Step 3.*

3. Remove the starter (Chapter Nine).
4. Remove the solenoid (Chapter Nine).
5. Remove the thrust washer and remove the starter shaft.
6. Remove the hex plug, shaft and shifter arm.

**Inspection**

1. Check the pinion gear for worn, chipped or broken teeth. Replace the gear if necessary.
2. Check pinion gear operation by attempting to turn the gear in both directions. It should only turn in one direction.
3. Check the needle bearings in the cover and starter housing for wear or damage. Rotate the bearings with your fingers and check for noise, roughness or looseness. Replace the bearings, using suitable bearing tools.
4. Lubricate the needle bearings with a high temperature grease.
5. To disassemble the pinion gear shaft assembly, perform the following:
   a. Secure the pinion shaft in a vise with soft jaws.

*NOTE*
*The pinion shaft nut uses left-hand threads.*

   b. Remove the pinion shaft nut by turning it clockwise.
   c. Remove the bearing race.
   d. Remove the pinion gear and collar as one assembly. Then, if necessary, separate them by removing the circlip.
   e. Remove the spacer on chain drive models.
   f. Inspect the components as described in this section.
6. Assemble the pinion gear and shaft assembly by reversing Step 5, and noting the following:
   a. Lubricate all parts with a high-temperature grease.
   b. Install the bearing race so that its lip faces against the pinion gear.
   c. Tighten the pinion shaft nut securely.

**Installation**

1. Assemble the pinion gear and shaft assembly as described under *Inspection.*
2. Install the starter shaft assembly.
3. Install the thrust washer.
4. Lightly grease the pivot shaft with a high-temperature grease.
5. Install the shifter arm pivot shaft and hex plug.
6. Install the solenoid (Chapter Nine).
7. Install the starter. See Chapter Nine.
8. Install the primary chain cover as described in this chapter.

5

## ELECTRIC STARTER DRIVE (1985 CHAIN DRIVE FX MODELS)

Refer to **Figure 111** when performing procedures in this section.

**Removal**

1. Disconnect the negative battery cable.
2. Remove the starter as described in Chapter Nine.
3. Remove the primary cover as described in this chapter.
4. Remove the drive gear housing bolts and remove the drive gear housing.
5. Remove the oil deflector and gasket.
6. Working from the left-hand side, disengage the shifter lever fingers from the shifter collar. Then remove the pinion gear and shaft assembly.
7. To remove the shifter lever, perform the following:
   a. Remove the battery and battery carrier as described in Chapter Nine.
   b. Remove the oil tank mounting brackets.
   c. Remove the solenoid as described in Chapter Nine.
   d. Remove the shifter lever screw and remove the shifter lever.

**Inspection**

1. Check the drive gear for worn, chipped or broken teeth. Replace the gear if necessary.

*NOTE*
*If the drive gear is worn, check the starter gear for wear or damage.*

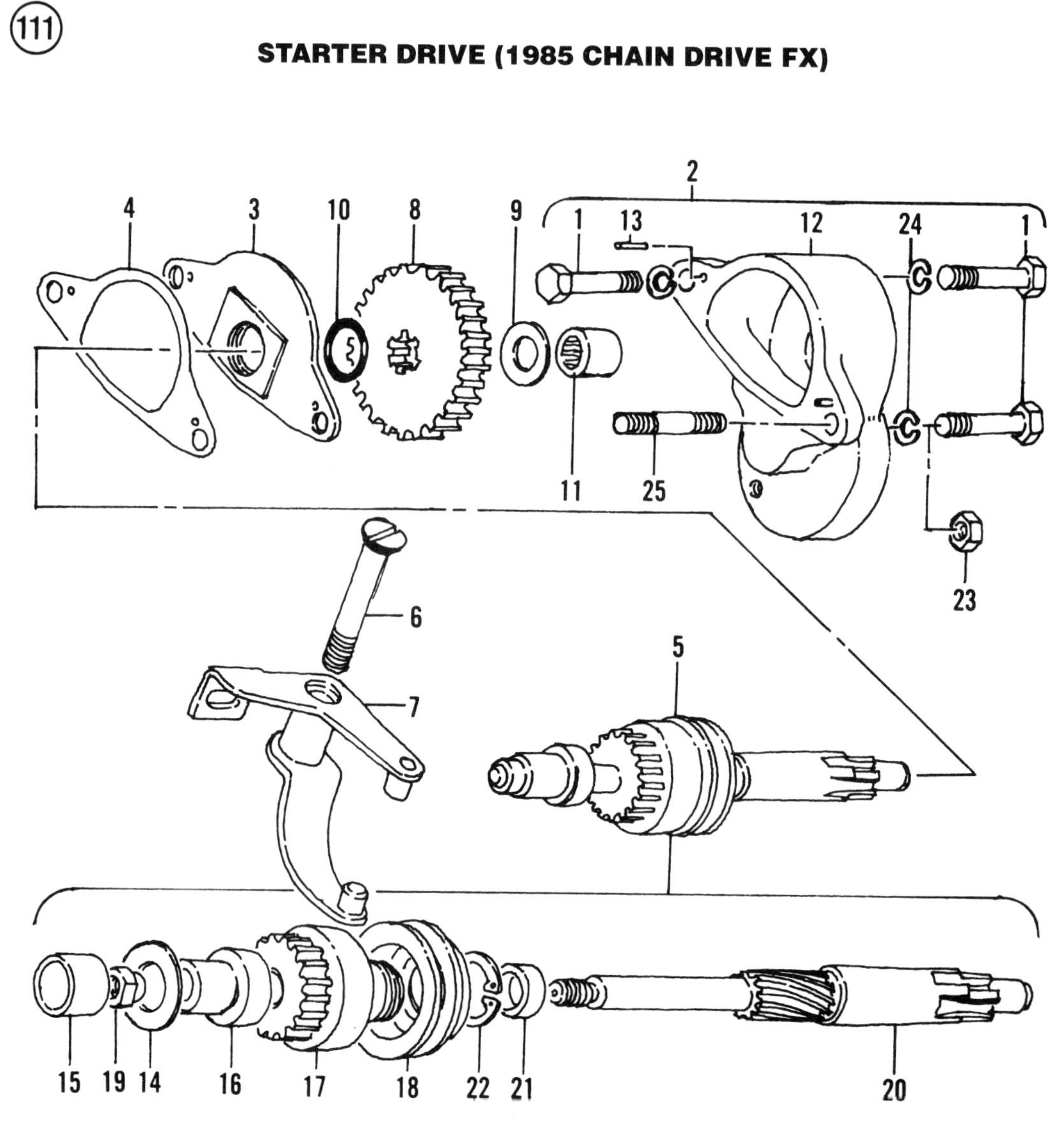


(111)

**STARTER DRIVE (1985 CHAIN DRIVE FX)**

1. Bolt
2. Drive gear housing assembly
3. Oil deflector
4. Gasket
5. Pinion gear and shaft assembly
6. Shifter lever screw
7. Shifter lever
8. Drive gear
9. Thrust washer
10. O-ring
11. Bearing (in drive gear housing)
12. Drive gear housing
13. Locating pin
14. Thrust washer
15. Bearing (in primary cover)
16. Pinion shaft collar
17. Pinion gear
18. Shifter collar
19. Pinion shaft nut (left hand thread)
20. Pinion shaft
21. Spacer
22. Circlip
23. Nut
24. Lockwasher
25. Stud

2. Check the drive gear thrust washer for damage or cupping. Replace the washer if necessary.

3. Check the drive gear housing needle bearing for wear or damage. Rotate the bearing with your fingers and check for noise, roughness or looseness. If the bearing's condition is doubtful, replace it. Replace the bearing with press.

4. Lubricate the needle bearing with a high temperature grease.

5. Install the drive gear and thrust washer in the drive housing.

6. Inspect the pinion gear needle bearing installed in the primary cover as described in Step 3. See **Figure 112**. Also check the pinion shaft collar bearing surface. If the bearing or collar is worn, replace them both. Replace the bearing as described in Step 3.

7. Check the pinion gear for worn, chipped or broken teeth. Replace the gear if necessary.

NOTE

*If the pinion gear is worn, check the clutch ring gear as described in this chapter under **Clutch Inspection**.*

8. Check the shifter collar groove and the shifter lever fingers for wear. Replace both parts if either is worn.

9. To disassemble the pinion gear shaft assembly, perform the following:

   a. Secure the pinion shaft in a vise with soft jaws.

   NOTE

   *The pinion shaft nut uses left-hand threads.*

   b. Remove the pinion shaft nut by turning it clockwise.
   c. Remove the washer and pinion shaft collar.
   d. Remove the slide pinion gear and shifter collar as one unit.
   e. Remove the spacer.
   f. If necessary, remove the circlip and separate the pinion gear and shifter collar.
   g. Inspect components as described in this section.

10. Assemble the pinion gear and shaft assembly by reversing Step 9. Note the following:

   a. Inspect all parts for wear and damage as described in this procedure. Replace parts as necessary.
   b. Install the circlip.
   c. Lubricate all parts with a high-temperature grease.

5

### Installation

1. Assemble the pinion gear and shaft assembly as described under *Inspection*.
2. Install the pinion shaft assembly. Engage the shifter lever fingers with the shifter collar drum.
3. Install the shifter lever assembly into the inner primary case. Lubricate the shifter lever screw with a high temperature grease and install it through the shifter lever. Tighten the screw securely.
4. Install the drive gear housing (with gear). See **Figure 113**.
5. Install a new O-ring in the oil deflector.
6. Install the oil deflector into the drive gear housing.
7. Install a new gasket on the oil deflector.
8. Install the primary cover as described in this chapter.
9. Install the solenoid and starter as described in Chapter Nine.
10. Reinstall the battery and the oil tank mounting brackets.

114

**STARTER DRIVE (1985-1986 BELT DRIVE FX)**

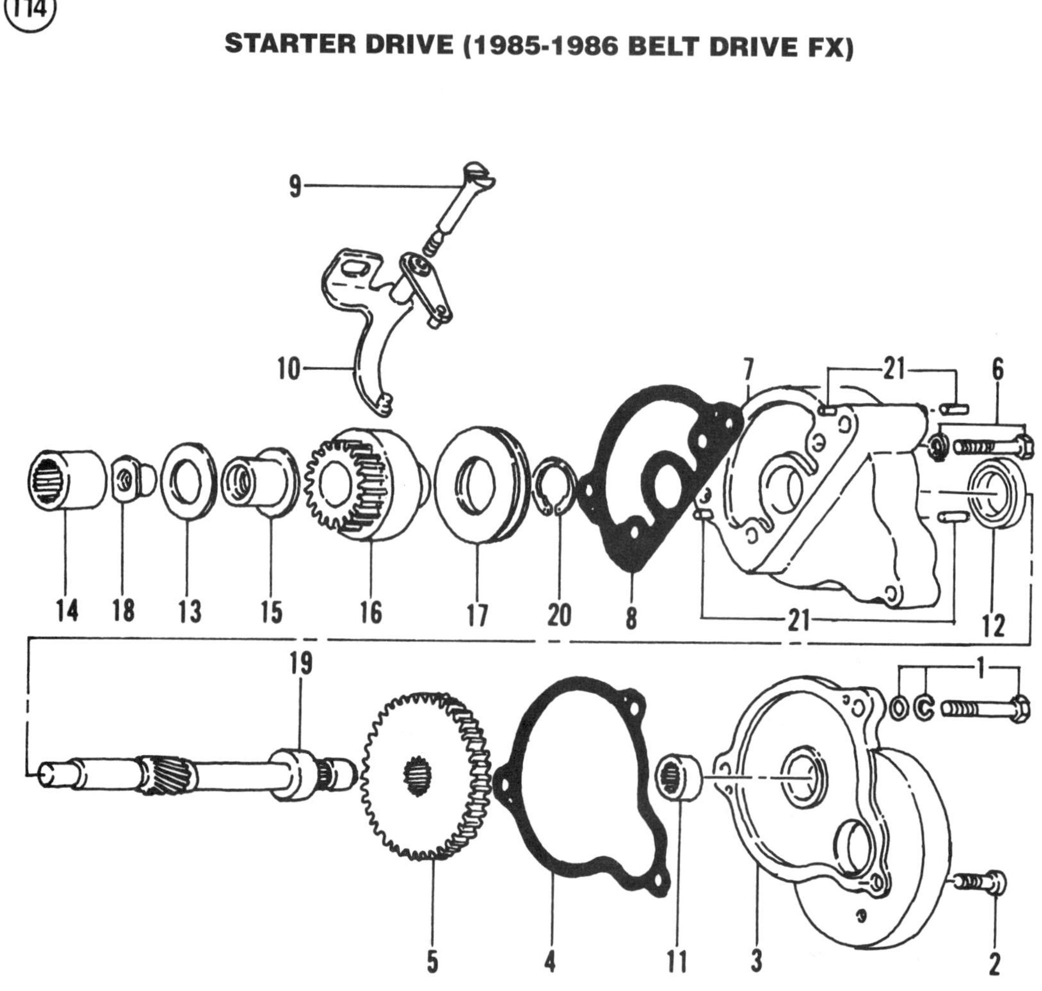


1. Bolt, lockwasher and washer
2. Allen head bolt
3. Outer drive gear housing half
4. Gasket
5. Drive gear
6. Bolt and lockwasher
7. Inner drive gear housing half
8. Gasket
9. Shifter lever screw
10. Shifter lever
11. Bearing (in outer drive gear housing)
12. Seal (inner drive gear housing)
13. Thrust washer
14. Bearing (in outer primary cover)
15. Pinion shaft collar
16. Pinion gear
17. Shifter collar
18. Pinion shaft nut (left hand thread)
19. Pinion shaft (1985)
20. Circlip
21. Locating pins

## ELECTRIC STARTER DRIVE (1985-1986 BELT DRIVE FX MODELS)

Refer to **Figure 114** when performing procedures in this section.

### Removal

1. Disconnect the negative battery cable.
2. Remove the starter as described in Chapter Nine.
3. Remove the primary cover as described in this chapter.
4. Remove the outer drive gear housing bolts and Allen screw.
5. Remove the outer drive housing, gasket and drive gear.
6. Remove the inner drive housing bolts and remove the housing and gasket.
7. Working from the left-hand side, disengage the shifter lever fingers from the shifter collar. Then remove the pinion gear and shaft assembly.
8. Remove the solenoid (Chapter Nine) and the shifter lever screw to remove the shifter lever.

### Inspection

1. Check the drive gear for worn, chipped or broken teeth. Replace the gear if necessary.

*NOTE*
*If the drive gear is worn, check the starter gear.*

2. Inspect the inner drive gear housing seal for wear or damage. If necessary, remove the seal by prying it out of the housing with a screwdriver. Install the new seal with a large socket placed on the outside seal surface. Install the seal with the lip side facing toward the drive gear.
3. Grasp the locating pins on both sides of the inner drive gear housing. The pins should be tight. If not, check the pin locations to make sure the housing is not cracked.
4. Check the inner drive gear housing needle bearing for wear or damage. Rotate the bearing with your fingers and check for noise, roughness or looseness. If the bearing's condition is doubtful, replace it. Replace the bearing with a press.
5. Lubricate the needle bearings with a high-temperature grease.
6. Inspect the pinion gear needle bearing installed in the outer drive gear housing as described in Step 4. Also check the pinion shaft collar bearing surface. If bearing or collar is worn, replace them both. Replace the bearing as described in Step 4.
7. Check the pinion gear for worn, chipped or broken teeth. Replace the gear if necessary.

*NOTE*
*If the pinion gear is worn, check the clutch ring gear as described in this chapter under **Clutch Inspection**.*

8. Check the shifter collar groove and the shifter lever fingers for wear. Replace both parts if any one part is worn.
9. To disassemble the pinion gear shaft assembly, perform the following:
   a. Secure the pinion shaft in a vise with soft jaws.

   *NOTE*
   *The pinion shaft nut uses left-hand threads.*

   b. Turn the pinion shaft nut clockwise to remove it.
   c. Remove the washer and pinion shaft collar.
   d. Remove the slide pinion gear and shifter collar as one unit.
   e. If necessary, remove the circlip and separate the pinion gear and shifter collar.
   f. Inspect components as described in this section.
10. Assemble the pinion gear and shaft assembly by reversing Step 9. Note the following:
    a. Inspect all parts for wear and damage as described in this procedure. Replace parts as necessary.
    b. Install a new circlip.
    c. Lubricate all parts with a high-temperature grease.

### Installation

1. Assemble the pinion gear and shaft assembly as described under *Inspection*.
2. Install the shifter lever assembly into the inner primary case. Lubricate the shifter lever screw with a high-temperature grease and install it through the shifter lever. Tighten the screw securely.
3. Install the pinion shaft assembly. Engage the shifter lever fingers with the shifter collar.

4. Glue a new gasket onto the inner drive gear housing.

5. Install the inner drive gear housing over the pinion shaft assembly and install onto the primary case. Install the mounting bolts and tighten securely.

6. Lubricate the drive gear with a high-temperature grease and slide it onto the pinion shaft.

7. Glue a new gasket onto the outer drive gear housing. Then install the housing and tighten the mounting bolts and Allen screw securely.

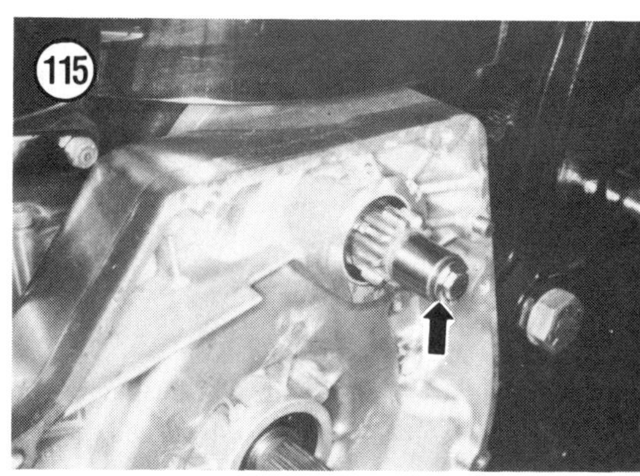


116

**STARTER JACKSHAFT (1989)**

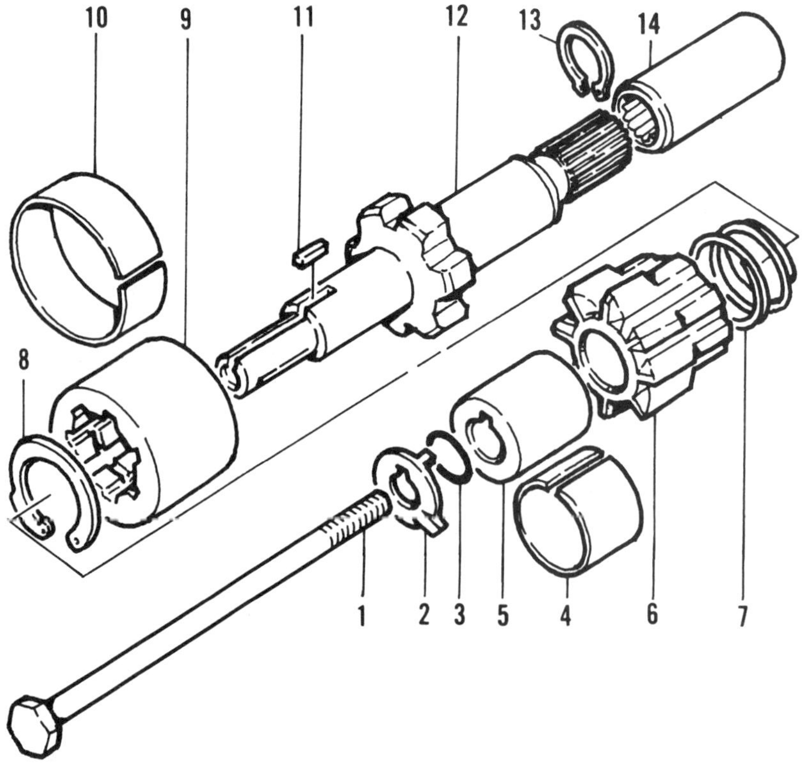

10 9 11 12 13 14 8 1 2 3 5 4 6 7

1. Jackshaft bolt
2. Lockplate
3. O-ring
4. Bushing
5. Sleeve
6. Pinion gear
7. Spring
8. Circlip
9. Coupling
10. Bushing
11. Key
12. Jackshaft
13. Circlip
14. Coupling

8. Install the starter motor as described in Chapter Nine.
9. Wipe the thrust washer with grease and slide it onto the pinion shaft collar.
10. Install the primary cover as described in this chapter.
11. Install the solenoid as described in Chapter Nine.

## STARTER JACKSHAFT (1989-ON)

The starter jackshaft is mounted in the primary chain case (**Figure 115**). The 1989 jackshaft assembly is not interchangeable with 1990 and later models.

### Removal/Disassembly (1989)

Refer to **Figure 116** for this procedure.

1. Disconnect the negative battery cable.
2. Remove the clutch as described in this chapter.
3. Remove the starter-to-jackshaft coupling if it did not come off with the starter
4. Pry the lockplate tab away from the jackshaft bolt. Then hold the pinion gear and loosen the jackshaft bolt. Withdraw the jackshaft bolt, lockplate and O-ring from the jackshaft.
5. Slide the jackshaft assembly out of the primary housing.
6. Disassemble the jackshaft as follows:
   a. Slide the sleeve off of the jackshaft and remove the key from the jackshaft if it did not come off with the sleeve.
   b. Remove the pinion gear.
   c. Slide the coupling off the jackshaft, then remove the spring from inside the coupling. If necessary, remove the circlip from inside the coupling.
   d. If necessary, remove the circlip from the jackshaft.
7. Clean and inspect the starter jackshaft assembly as described in this chapter.

### Assembly/Installation (1989)

Refer to **Figure 116** when performing this procedure.

1. Prior to assembly, perform the *Inspection* procedure to make sure all worn or defective parts have been replaced. All parts should be thoroughly cleaned before installation or assembly.

*NOTE*
*Install new circlips during assembly.*

2. Install the circlip onto the jackshaft, if previously removed.
3. Install the circlip into the coupling and slide the coupling onto the jackshaft. Place the spring inside the coupling.

*NOTE*
*Make sure that the side of the coupling with the circlip faces toward the starter after installing it. If the coupling is reversed, the pinion gear cannot engage the clutch ring gear.*

4. Slide the pinion gear onto the jackshaft, with the small OD end facing inward.
5. Install the key in the jackshaft keyway.
6. Align the keyway in the sleeve with the key and slide the sleeve onto the jackshaft.
7. Slide the lockplate and O-ring onto the jackshaft bolt, then insert the bolt into the jackshaft.
8. Align the inner tab on the lockplate with the keyway in the jackshaft, then tighten the bolt finger-tight.

*CAUTION*
*The inner lockplate tab must be installed in the jackshaft keyway. The lockplate serves 2 purposes; it prevents the key from sliding out of the sleeve and locks the jackshaft bolt to prevent it from backing out of the jackshaft. Install a new lockplate, if one of the tabs is cracked or broken.*

9. Slide the jackshaft-to-starter coupling onto the end of the jackshaft.
10. Slide the jackshaft into the primary chain case, with the pinion gear facing outward. Make sure the coupling engages the starter shaft as the jackshaft assembly is installed.
11. Hold the pinion gear and tighten the jackshaft bolt to 7-9 ft.-lb. (9.6-12.4 N•m). Bend the lockplate tab against the jackshaft bolt head to lock it. If the lockplate tab does not align with one of the bolt head

5

flats, tighten the bolt until the 2 parts align with each other; do not loosen the bolt to align the tab.

12. Install the clutch as described in this chapter.

13. Reconnect the negative battery cable.

### Removal/Disassembly (1990-on)

Refer to **Figure 117** for this procedure.

1. Disconnect the negative battery cable.
2. Remove the clutch as described in this chapter.
3. Pry the lockplate tab (2) away from the bolt (1).
4. Hold the pinion gear and loosen the bolt. Then remove the bolt, lockplate, thrust washer and O-ring (1990-1992).
5. Remove the pinion gear (5).
6. Remove the spring (6) and coupling(8).
9. Remove the coupling circlip (7) if necessary.

10A. On 1990-1993 models, remove the coupling and circlip (10 and 11).

10B. On 1994 models, to remove the coupling and circlip (10 and 11):

a. Remove the starter motor as described in Chapter Nine.
b. Remove the coupling and circlip.

CAUTION

*If the starter motor is not removed prior to removing the coupling and circlip on 1994 models, the primary chain case oil seal will be damaged.*

11. Clean and inspect the jackshaft assembly as described in this chapter.

### Assembly/Installation (1990-on)

Refer to **Figure 117** when performing this procedure.

1. Prior to assembly, perform the *Inspection* procedure to make sure all worn or defective parts have

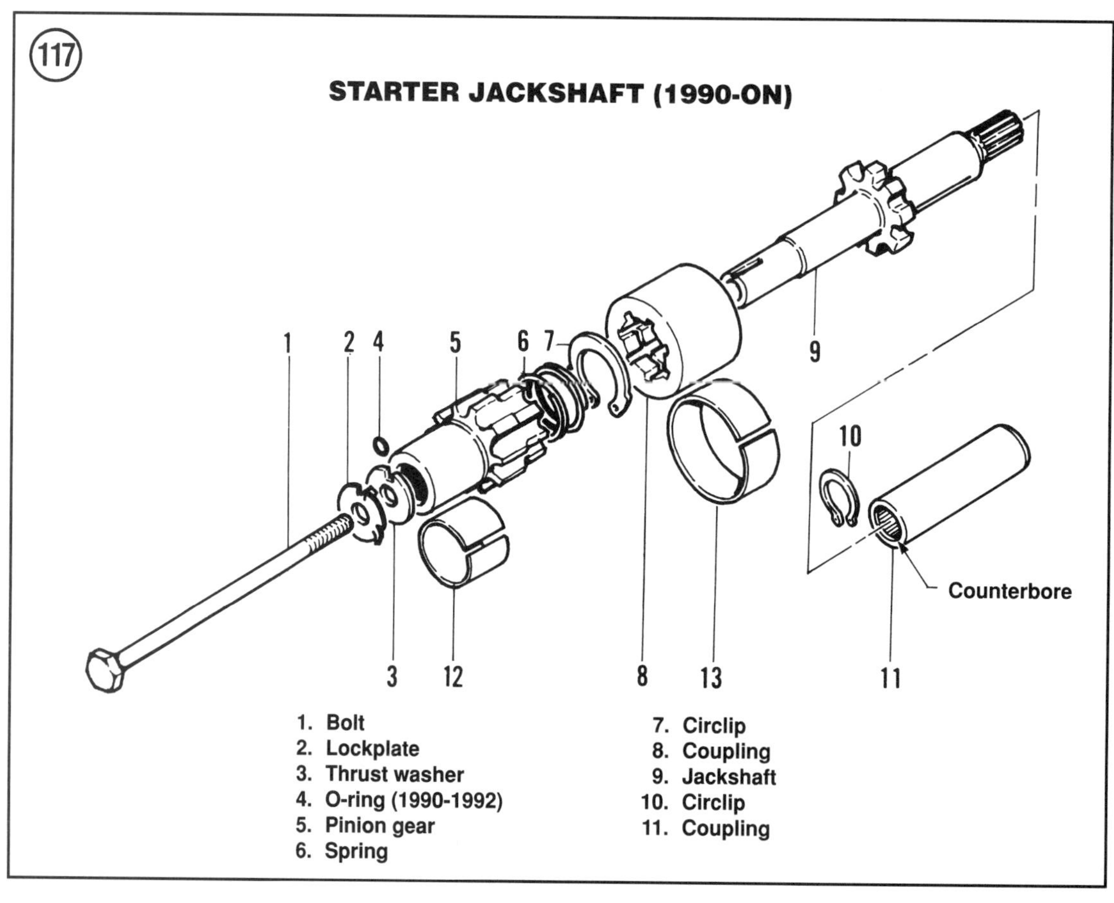

been replaced. All parts should be thoroughly cleaned before installation or assembly.

*NOTE*
*Install new circlips during assembly.*

2. Install the circlip (7, **Figure 117**) inside the coupling (8).
3. Install the coupling (11) onto the starter output shaft with the coupling's counterbore facing toward the jackshaft.

*CAUTION*
*On 1994 models, the coupling (11) must be installed before installing the jackshaft. Otherwise, the primary chain case oil seal will be damaged.*

4. Install spring (6) inside coupling. Slide coupling onto jackshaft.
5. Install pinion gear (5) on jackshaft (9).
6. Install lockplate (2), thrust washer (3) and O-ring (4 [1990-1992]) onto the bolt.
7. Insert the bolt into the jackshaft.
8. Install the circlip (10), if previously removed, onto the jackshaft groove.
9. Insert the jackshaft assembly into the iner primary assembly.
10. Align the lockplate tab and thrust washer slot with the jackshaft keyway. Screw the bolt (1) into the starter shaft.

*CAUTION*
*The lockplate tab must be installed in the jackshaft keyway to hold the lockplate and thrust washer in place.*

11. Hold the pinion gear and tighten the bolt (1) to 7-9 ft.-lb. (9-12 N•m).
12. Bend the lockplate tab against the bolt head.
13. Install the clutch as described in this chapter.
14. Reconnect negative battery cable.

## Inspection (All Models)

1. Clean all jackshaft components thoroughly in solvent. Dry with compressed air, if available.
2. Visually check the jackshaft surfaces for cracks, deep scoring, excessive wear or discoloration. Check the keyway slot and circlip grooves for damage.
3. Check the jackshaft and pinion gear teeth for cracks, severe wear or damage.
4. Check the O-ring for hardening or damage.
5. Check the spring for stretching or damage.
6. Check the jackshaft bolt and jackshaft threads for stripping, cross-threading or deposit buildup. If necessary, use a tap to true up jackshaft threads and remove any deposits. Replace the jackshaft bolt if threads or bolt head are damaged.
7. Check the large coupling for surface damage. Check the spline and the circlip groove inside the coupling for damage.
8. On 1989 models, inspect the small sleeve for surface damage. Check the keyway inside the sleeve for damage. Check the key for damage.
9. Inspect the lockplate closely for cracked, broken or weak alignment and lock tabs.
10. Replace worn or damaged parts as required.

5

**Table 1 DRY CLUTCH SPECIFICATIONS**

| Item | Specification |
|---|---|
| Type | Dry, multiple disc |
| Spring adjustment | 1 1/32-1 7/8 in. (26.2-47.6 mm) from spring collar edge |
| Spring free length | 1 47/64-1 45/64 in. (44.04-43.26 mm) |
| Friction plates | |
| Minimum lining thickness | 1/32 in. (0.8 mm) |
| Warpage limit | 0.010 in. (0.25 mm) |
| Steel disc warpage limit | 0.010 in. (0.25 mm) |
| Clutch screw adjustment | See text |
| Clutch hand lever free play | 1/16 in. (1.59 mm) |

**Table 2 WET CLUTCH SPECIFICATIONS (1985-1989)**

| | |
|---|---|
| Type | Wet, multiple disc |
| Clutch hand lever free play | 1/8-3/16 in. (3.17-4.76 mm) |
| Steel disc | |
| Minimum thickness | 0.044 in. (1.12 mm) |
| Warpage limit | 0.011 in. (0.30 mm) |
| Friction plate | |
| Minimum lining thickness | 0.078 in. (1.98 mm) |

**Table 3 WET CLUTCH SPECIFICATIONS (1990-ON)**

| | |
|---|---|
| Type | Wet, multiple disc |
| Clutch hand lever free play | |
| 1990 | 1/8-3/16 in. (3.17-4.76 mm) |
| 1991-on | 1/16-1/8 in. (1.6-3.2 mm) |
| Steel disc | |
| Warpage limit | 0.006 in. (0.15 mm) |
| Friction plate assembly | |
| Minimum lining thickness (assembly) | 0.661 in. (16.8 mm)* |

* See text for procedures on measuring friction plates.

**Table 4 CLUTCH TIGHTENING TORQUES**

| | ft.-lb. | N•m |
|---|---|---|
| Compensating sprocket nut | | |
| 1984-1990 | 90-100 | 124.2-138 |
| 1991 | 150-165 | 207-227.7 |
| Clutch hub nut | | |
| 1984-1990 | 50-60 | 69-82.8 |
| 1991 | 70-80 | 96.6-110.4 |
| Primary cover screws | 9-10 | 12.4-13.8 |
| Primary chaincase to engine | | |
| FLT and FXR | 16-18 | 22-24.8 |
| FXWG, FXEF and FXSB | 18-22 | 24.8-30.3 |
| Jackshaft bolt | | |
| 1989-on | 7-9 | 9.6-12.4 |

**Table 5 PRIMARY CHAIN ALIGNMENT**

| Dimension C | Spacer thickness |
|---|---|
| 0.2500-0.2812 in. (6.35-7.14 mm) | 0.060 in. (1.52 mm) |
| 0.2812-0.3125 in. (7.14-7.94 mm) | 0.090 in. (2.29 mm) |
| 0.3125-0.3427 in. (7.94-8.70 mm) | 0.120 in. (3.05 mm) |
| 0.3437-0.3750 in. (8.73-9.52 mm) | 0.150 in. (3.81 mm) |
| 0.3750-0.4063 in. (9.52-10.32 mm) | 0.180 in. (4.57 mm) |
| 0.4062-0.4375 in. (10.32-11.11 mm) | 0.210 in. (5.33 mm) |

# CHAPTER SIX

# 4-SPEED TRANSMISSION



The 4-speed Harley-Davidson transmission and shifter assembly is mounted in a separate housing and can be completely disassembled and serviced without having to disassemble the engine. Removal of the transmission housing, however, will first require removal of the primary drive assembly; see Chapter Five. The 4-speed transmission was used on FXWG, FXEF and FXSB models.

The transmission service procedures in this chapter are arranged by sub-assembly—shifter assembly and transmission. Before servicing the transmission or shifter assembly, make sure the problem is not due to a faulty clutch adjustment or a problem with the primary drive system.

An external shift linkage assembly connects the gearshift lever to the transmission. The shift linkage assembly requires adjustment to compensate for normal wear to the linkage/shifter mechanism components or when the transmission housing has been removed from the bike.

A ratchet-type kickstarter assembly is mounted in the transmission right-hand side cover. The kickstarter mechanism can be removed with the transmission mounted on the bike.

This chapter includes all service procedures for the 4-speed transmission and kickstarter. **Table 1** and **Table 2** are at the end of the chapter.

## TRANSMISSION

### Removal/Installation

1. Drain the transmission oil as described in Chapter Three.
2. Remove the battery and battery carrier as described in Chapter Three.
3. Remove the passenger grab strap and seat.
4. Remove the master cylinder reservoir mount bracket at the transmission end cover.
5. Remove the starter as described in Chapter Nine.
6. Remove the primary housing as described in Chapter Five.
7. Remove the left side oil tank mounting nuts.
8. Disconnect the shifter rod end from the shift lever (FXEF and FXSB) or from the shifter linkage (FXWG).
9. Disconnect the clutch cable from the release lever.
10. Disconnect the wiring at the solenoid.
11. Disconnect the speedometer drive cable and housing at the transmission (if so equipped).
12. Disconnect the neutral indicator switch wire at the transmission.

13A. *Chain drive*: Disconnect the drive chain master link and remove the drive chain.

13B. *Belt drive*: Loosen the rear axle and the belt adjusters and remove the drive belt.

*NOTE*
*The transmission can be removed with its mounting plate attached.*

14. Remove the transmission mounting plate-to-frame bolts.

15. Remove the starter relay and wiring.

16. Remove the brake line bracket.

17. Remove the transmission-to-frame mounting bolt from underneath the right side.

18. *FXEF and FXSB:* Remove the master cylinder alignment plate, if necessary.

19. *FXWG:* Remove the rear brake line clip from the transmission end cover.

20. Remove the transmission and mounting plate from the left side.

21. Installation is the reverse of these steps. Note the following.

22. Install the transmission assembly in the frame and install the mounting hardware. Tighten the mounting plate bolt to 30-33 ft.-lb. (41.4-45.5 N•m).

23. Tighten the transmission-to-mounting plate bolts to 21-27 ft.-lb. (28.9-37.3 N•m).

24. Tighten the transmission-to-frame right-hand mounting bolt to 21-27 ft.-lb. (28.9-37.3 N•m).

25. When installing the footrest and brake pedal assembly, make sure the brake pushrod seats in the rear brake master cylinder. See Chapter Thirteen.

26. Refill the transmission with the correct type and quantity of oil as described in Chapter Three.

27. Adjust the primary chain as described in Chapter Three.

28. Check primary chain alignment as described in Chapter Five.

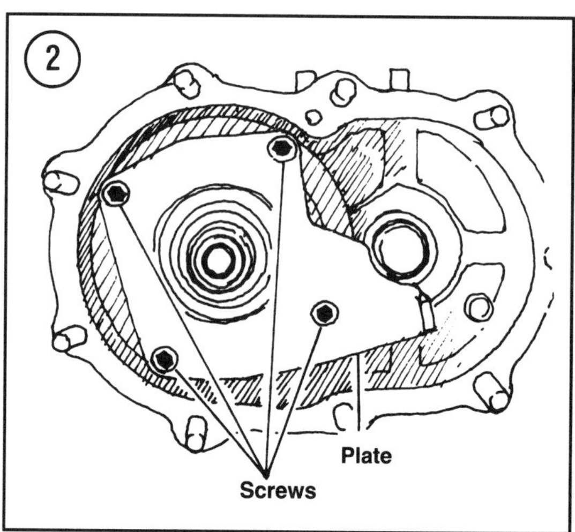


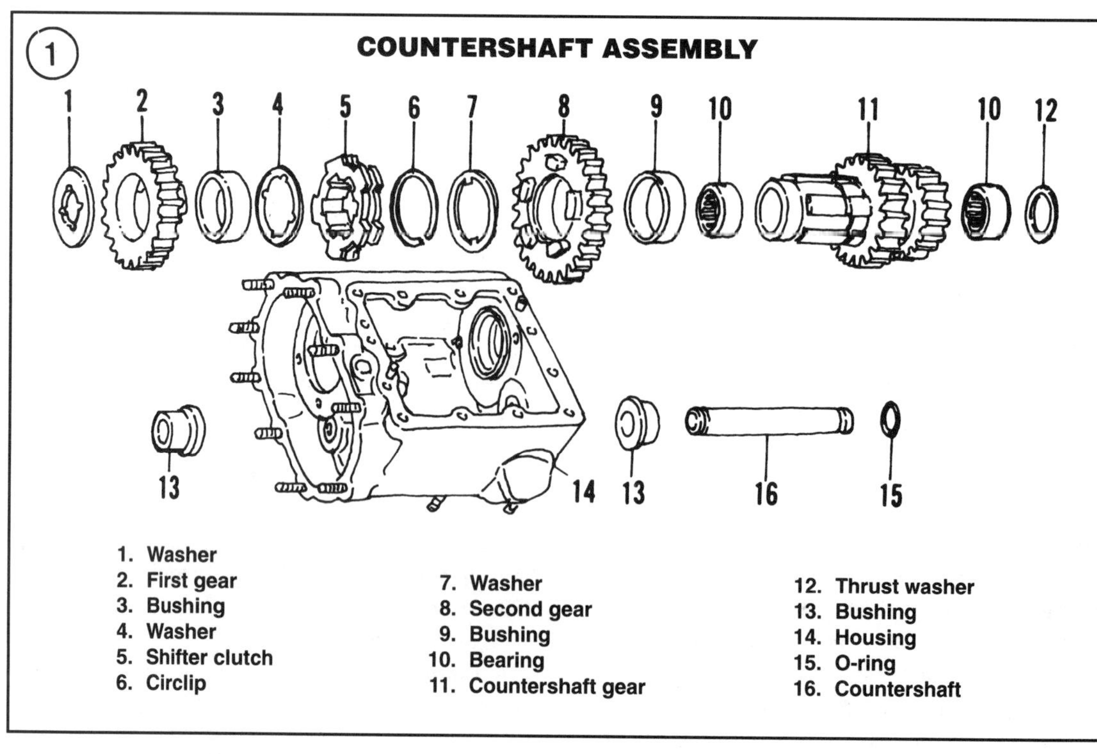

3

4

5

6

29. When reconnecting the drive chain with its master link, make sure the closed end of the master link clip faces toward normal chain travel.
30. Adjust the rear drive chain or drive belt as described in Chapter Three.
31. Adjust the clutch as described in Chapter Three.

### Countershaft Disassembly

Refer to **Figure 1** for this procedure.

1. Remove the following assemblies as described in this chapter.
   a. Transmission.
   b. Shifter cover.
   c. Side cover.
   d. Shift forks.
2. Referring to **Figure 2**, remove the retaining plate screws and remove the retaining plate.
3. While holding the gear cluster (**Figure 3**) with one hand, withdraw the countershaft through the side cover (**Figure 4**).
4. Lift the gear cluster out of the housing (**Figure 5**).
5. Remove the thrust washer from the transmission case (B, **Figure 6**).
6. Remove the following parts in order:
   a. First gear (**Figure 7**).
   b. Bushing (if necessary).
   c. Washer (**Figure 8**).
   d. Shifter clutch (**Figure 9**).
7. Using a pointed tool, carefully pry the retaining ring from the gear cluster (**Figure 10**). Then remove the following parts in order:
   a. Washer (**Figure 11**).
   b. Second gear (**Figure 12**).
   c. Bushing (**Figure 13**).
8. Remove the thrust washer (12, **Figure 1**).

7

6

9. The countershaft bearings are single unit needle bearings. Replace the bearings as described under *Inspection*.

### Inspection

1. Examine gears for worn or chipped teeth, pitting, scoring or other damage. See **Figure 14** and **Figure 15**.
2. Examine shifter clutch (**Figure 16**) for rounded edges or severe wear.

11

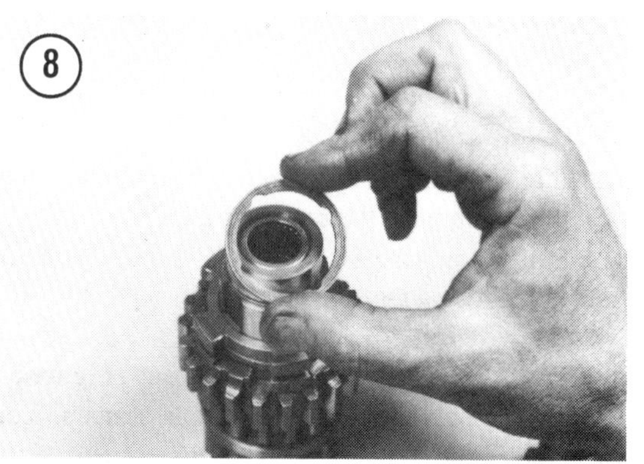
8

12

9

13

10

14

3. Check gear dogs for wear or rounded edges (**Figure 17**).

4. Examine gear and shaft splines (**Figure 18**) for wear or rounded edges.

5. Slip gears on shafts and check for free movement without appreciable play.

6. Replace worn or damaged thrust washers.

7. Check the countershaft gear needle bearings (**Figure 19**) for wear or roughness. If worn or damaged, they must be replaced as follows:

CAUTION

*The Harley-Davidson countershaft gear bearing installer (part No. HD-34733)* ***must*** *be used to install the countershaft gear bearings. The tool is shown in* ***Figure 20****. The Harley-Davidson tool is designed so that all loading applied to the bearing during installation is placed on the outer edge of the bearing race. This prevents the type of damage that normally occurs to needle bearings when they are installed with a socket. Driving the bearings in with a socket will damage them.*

a. Support the countershaft and remove the old bearings with a bearing remover or drive them out with a long drift.

6

NOTE

*Align both needle bearings with countershaft gear so that ID mark stamped on end of bearing faces out.*

b. Install the new bearings with the Harley-Davidson tool (part No. HD-34733) and a press as shown in **Figure 20**.

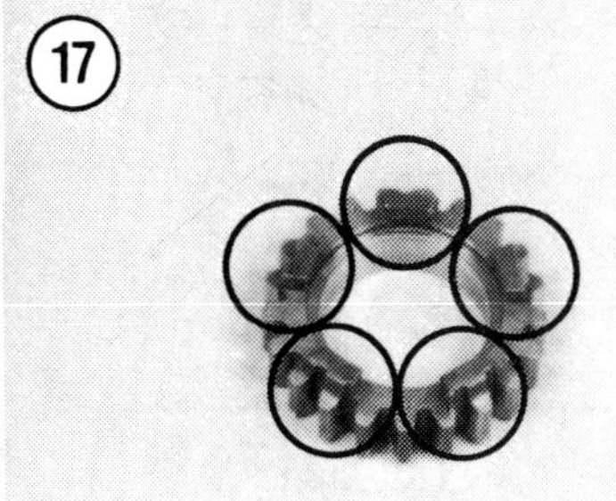

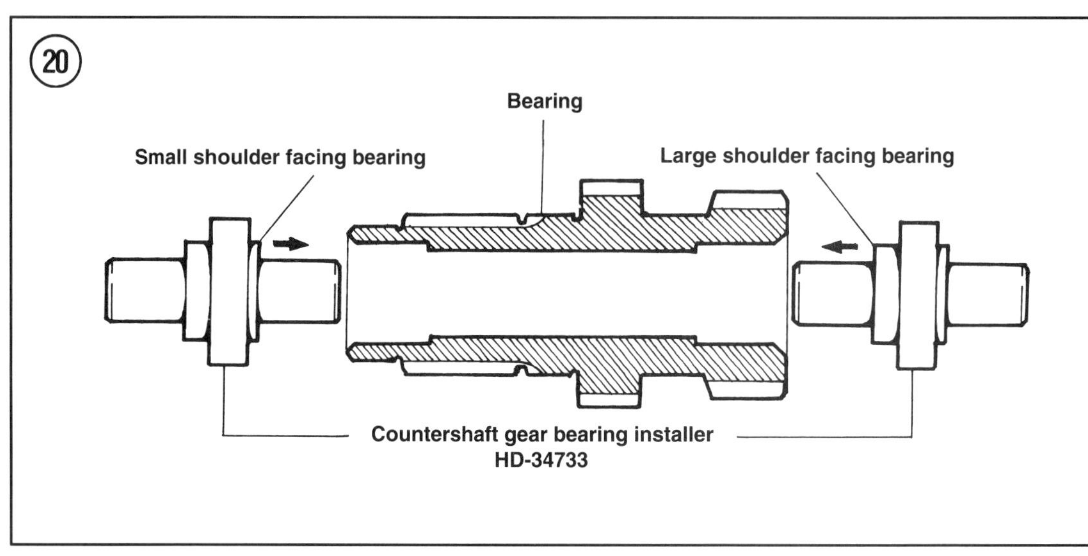

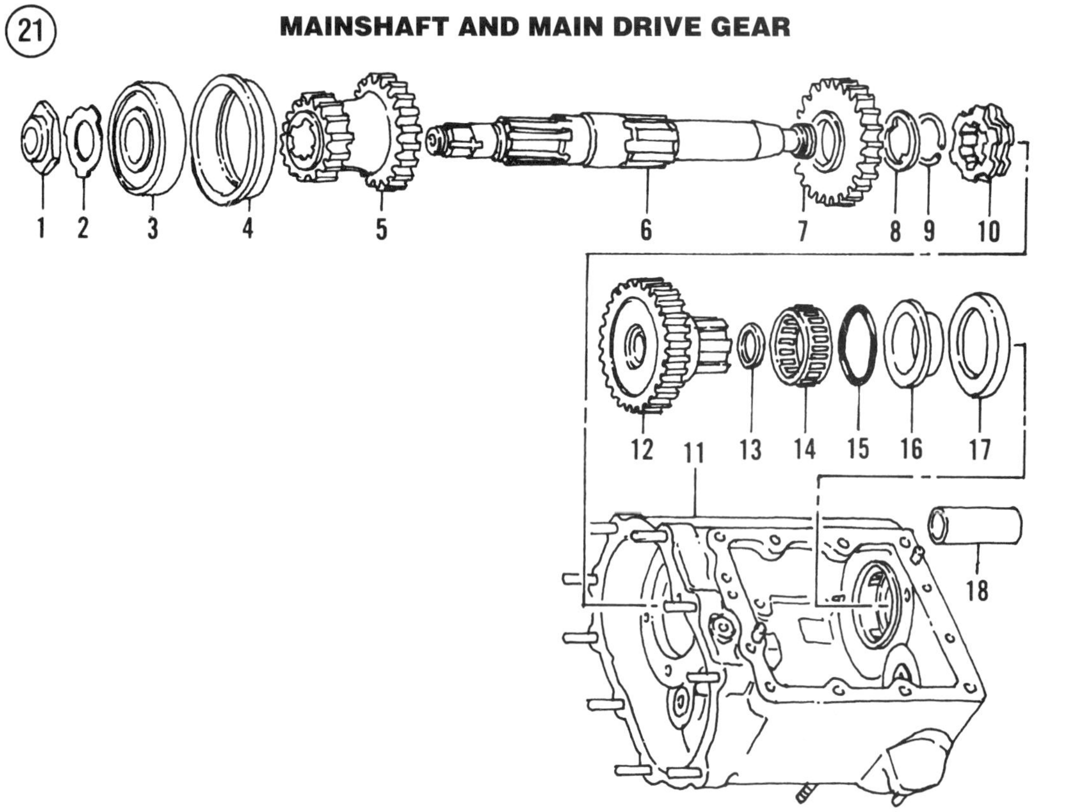

21

**MAINSHAFT AND MAIN DRIVE GEAR**

1. Nut
2. Lockwasher
3. Bearing
4. Bearing housing
5. 1st/2nd gear combination
6. Mainshaft
7. 3rd gear
8. Washer
9. Circlip
10. Shifter clutch
11. Housing
12. Main drive gear
13. Oil seal
14. Bearing
15. O-ring
16. Spacer
17. Oil seal
18. Bushing

8. Inspect the transmission housing bushings and oil seals as described in this chapter.

### Countershaft Assembly/Installation

1. Coat all parts with engine oil prior to assembly.
2. Slide on the bushing and install second gear (**Figure 12**).
3. Install the washer (**Figure 11**).
4. Install a new circlip (**Figure 10**). Make sure the circlip seats completely in the gear cluster groove.
5. Install the shifter clutch (**Figure 9**), washer (**Figure 8**), bushing and first gear (**Figure 7**).
6. Install the thrust washer (A, **Figure 6**) into its recess.
7. Coat the countershaft end thrust washer (B, **Figure 6**) with grease and install it in the transmission case.
8. Install a new O-ring on the countershaft (15, **Figure 1**).
9. Install the gear cluster in the transmission case (**Figure 5**). Hold it in position with one hand.
10. Insert the countershaft through the gear cluster from the sprocket side of the transmission case. The O-ring should be on the sprocket side (**Figure 1**).
11. Measure the gear end play between the washer and the countershaft gear with a feeler gauge. Correct end play is listed in **Table 1**. If the end play is incorrect, replace the washer (1, **Figure 1**) with a suitable size washer. Washers are available in the following sizes: 0.074, 0.078, 0.082, 0.085, 0.090, 0.095 and 0.100 in. (1.88, 1.98, 2.08, 2.16, 2.29, 2.41 and 2.54 mm).

*NOTE*

*If the mainshaft does not require removal, perform Step 12. If mainshaft removal is required, remove it now as described in this chapter.*

12. Install the retaining plate (**Figure 2**). Tighten the screws to 7-9 ft.-lb. (9.7-12.4 N•m).

### Mainshaft Removal/Disassembly

Refer to **Figure 21** for this procedure.

1. Remove the transmission case as described in this chapter.
2. *Late 1984-1985*: Remove the bearing race from the end of the mainshaft with the Bearing Race Puller & Installation Tool (part No. HD-34902). See **Figure 22**.
3. Remove countershaft as described in this chapter.

*NOTE*

*The mainshaft retaining plate (**Figure 2**) was removed during countershaft removal.*

4. Using a brass or rawhide mallet, drive the mainshaft (**Figure 23**) out of the transmission case

6

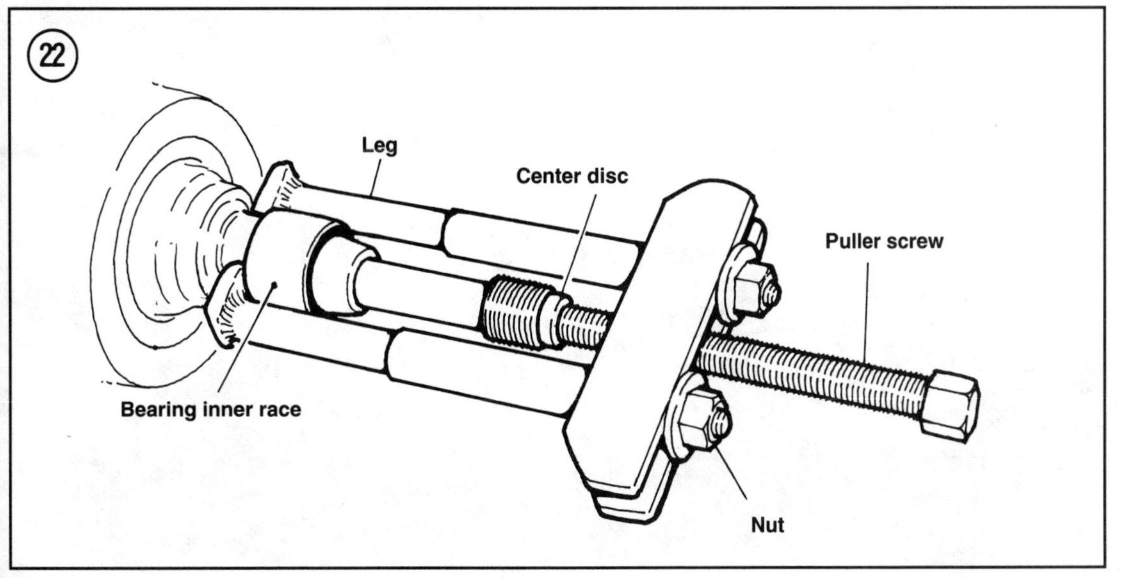

through the side cover end until second gear almost contacts the case.

5. Pry the circlip (**Figure 24**) between the washer and shifter clutch out of its groove and slide it on the mainshaft splines. See **Figure 25**.

6. Slide the mainshaft out of the case while at the same time sliding third gear (**Figure 26**), washer (**Figure 27**), circlip (**Figure 28**) and the shifter clutch (**Figure 29**) off the shaft. Then remove the parts through the case opening.

7. If necessary, remove the main drive gear from the transmission case as described in this chapter.

8. If removal of the bearing (A, **Figure 30**) and the first/second gear combination (B, **Figure 30**) is required, perform the following:

   a. Clamp the mainshaft in a vise with soft jaws (i.e., Harley-Davidson copper jaws [part No. HD-96798-43]).

   b. Bend the lockwasher tab away from the mainshaft nut, then remove the nut and lockwasher.

   c. Support first/second gear combination in a press. Then press off the bearing, bearing housing and first/second gear.

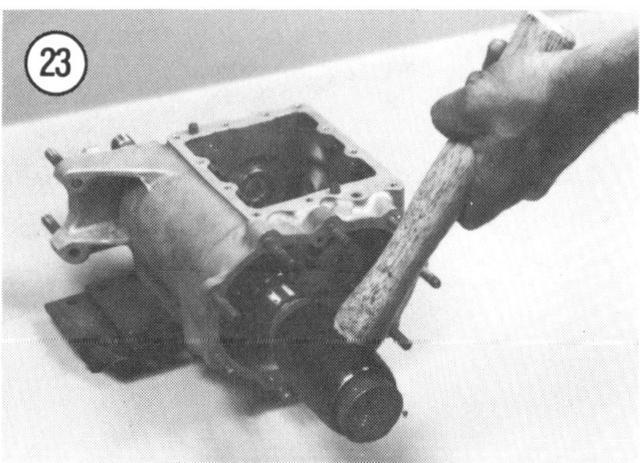

23

24

## Mainshaft Inspection

1. Examine gears for worn or chipped teeth, pitting, scoring or other damage. See **Figure 31**.

2. Examine dog clutches (**Figure 32**) for rounded edges or severe wear.

3. Slip gears on shafts and check for free movement without appreciable play.

4. Replace worn or damaged thrust washers.

25

26

27

5. Inspect the main drive gear bushing for cracks or severe wear. If bushing is worn or damaged, have it replaced by a Harley-Davidson dealer.

*CAUTION*
*Improper bushing installation can cause bushing and mainshaft failure from improper lubrication. In addition, honing may be required to obtain correct main drive gear-to-mainshaft clearance after installing a new bushing. Refer bushing replacement to a Harley-Davidson dealer.*

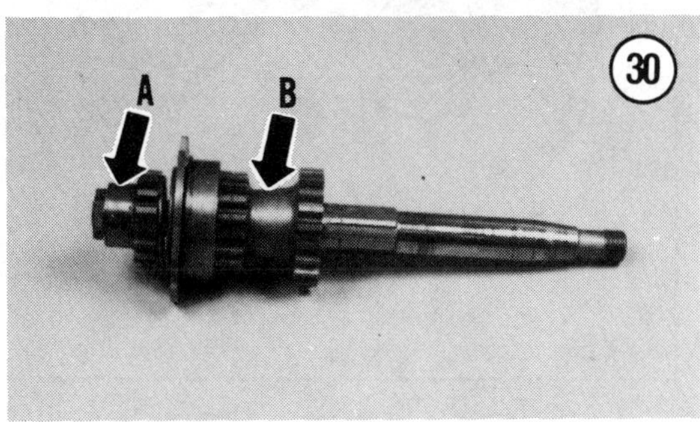

## Mainshaft Assembly/Installation

1. Coat all parts with transmission oil prior to assembly.
2. Install the main drive gear in the transmission case as described in this chapter.
3. Install the first/second combination and bearing onto the mainshaft, if previously removed, as follows:
   a. Align the lettered side on the bearing with the flange end on the bearing housing and press the bearing into the bearing housing.
   b. Slide the first/second combination gear and the bearing housing onto the mainshaft. The lettered side of the bearing must face out when installed on the mainshaft. See **Figure 21**.

*NOTE*
*The support block described in sub-step c should have the following dimensions: 1 in. (25.4 mm) I.D. × 1 3/8 in. (34.9 mm) O.D. × 2 1/4 in. (57.1 mm) long.*

   c. Install the support block over the end of the mainshaft so that it rests against the inner bearing race and place the assembly into a press. Press the bearing onto the mainshaft.
   d. Support the mainshaft in a vise with soft jaws. Install the lockwasher and nut onto the end of the mainshaft. Tighten the nut to 50-60 ft.-lb. (69-82.8 N•m), then bend the lockwasher tab over a flat on the nut to lock it.

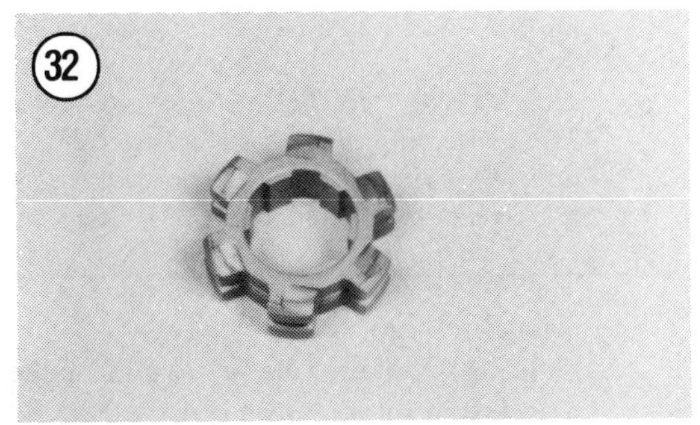


6

*NOTE*
*If only the mainshaft nut was loosened, tighten the mainshaft nut as described in Step 3, sub-step d.*

4. Install the mainshaft into the transmission and slide it so that second gear barely contacts the case.
5. Slide the following parts on the mainshaft:
   a. Bushing.
   b. Third gear (**Figure 26**).
   c. Washer (**Figure 27**).
   d. New circlip (**Figure 28**).

*NOTE*
*Make sure the circlip seats in the mainshaft groove completely.*

   e. Shifter clutch (**Figure 29**).

*NOTE*
*Install the shifter clutch so that the word HIGH on one side faces toward the main drive gear.*

6. Lightly tap the mainshaft into the transmission case until the bearing housing flange seats against the case.
7. Install the countershaft as described in this chapter.
8. Install the retaining plate (**Figure 33**). Tighten the screws to 7-9 ft.-lb. (9.7-12.4 N•m).
9. *Late 1984-1985*: Install the bearing race as follows:

*NOTE*
*The Harley-Davidson Bearing Race Puller & Installation Tool (part No. HD-34902) will be required to install the bearing race onto the mainshaft.*

   a. Slide the bearing race (**Figure 34**) onto the mainshaft so that the chamfered edge on the race faces inward (toward transmission housing).

*NOTE*
*The sleeve pilot installed in sub-step b uses left-hand threads. Turn the sleeve pilot counterclockwise to install it.*

   b. Thread the sleeve pilot onto the end of the mainshaft (**Figure 34**).
   c. Slide the sleeve over the sleeve pilot and rest it against the bearing race (**Figure 35**). Then secure the sleeve with the washer and nut (**Figure 35**).
   d. Place a wrench on the end of the sleeve pilot threads (flat portion) and tighten the nut to push the bearing race onto the mainshaft. Install the bearing race so that its inside edge is 0.200 in. (5.08 mm) from the main drive gear. Before measuring the bearing race to main drive gear clearance, pull the main drive gear towards the end of the mainshaft.
   e. When the bearing race is properly installed, remove the installation tool.

## Main Drive Gear Removal/Installation

Refer to **Figure 21** for this procedure.

1. Remove the countershaft and mainshaft as described in this chapter.
2. If the countershaft sprocket was not removed during transmission case removal, remove it as follows:

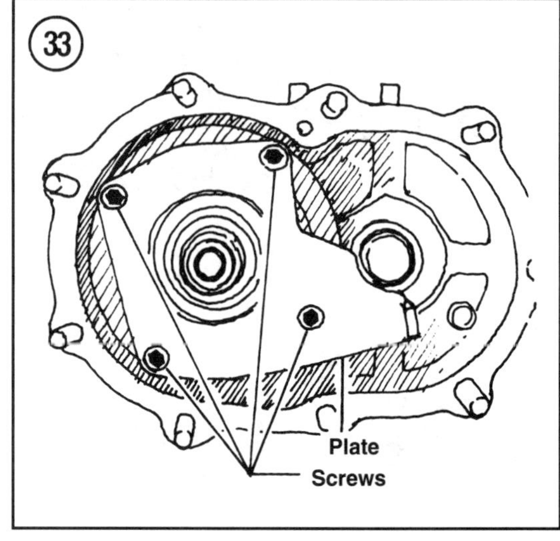


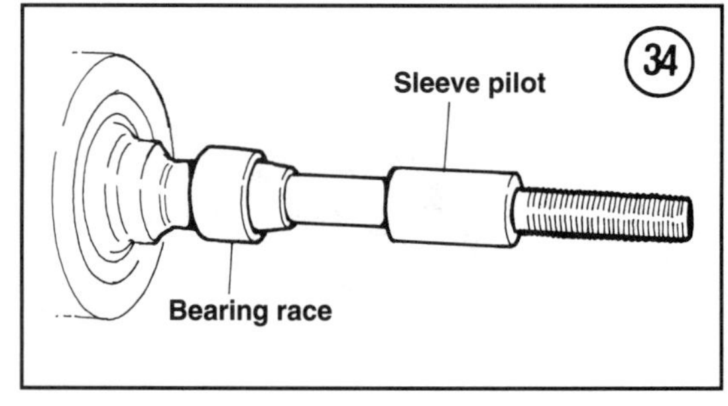

a. Hold the sprocket with a chain wrench or a universal holding tool.
b. Remove the set screw that locks against the sprocket nut.

*NOTE*
*The sprocket nut uses left-hand threads. Turn the nut counterclockwise to remove it.*

c. Loosen the sprocket nut.
d. Remove the lockwasher, if used.
e. Remove the sprocket.

3. Measure the main drive gear end play with a dial indicator. Correct end play is listed in **Table 1**. If the end play is incorrect, replace the main drive gear.

4. Push the main drive gear (**Figure 36**) into the case, then remove it through the shifter cover opening.

5. Remove the main drive gear oil seal (**Figure 37**) by carefully prying it out of the transmission housing.

6. Remove the main drive gear spacer and bearing case.

7. Examine gears for worn or chipped teeth, pitting, scoring or other damage.

8. Examine gear and shaft splines for wear or rounded edges.

9. Remove the drive gear oil seal by prying it out with a sharp tool or a small screwdriver.

6

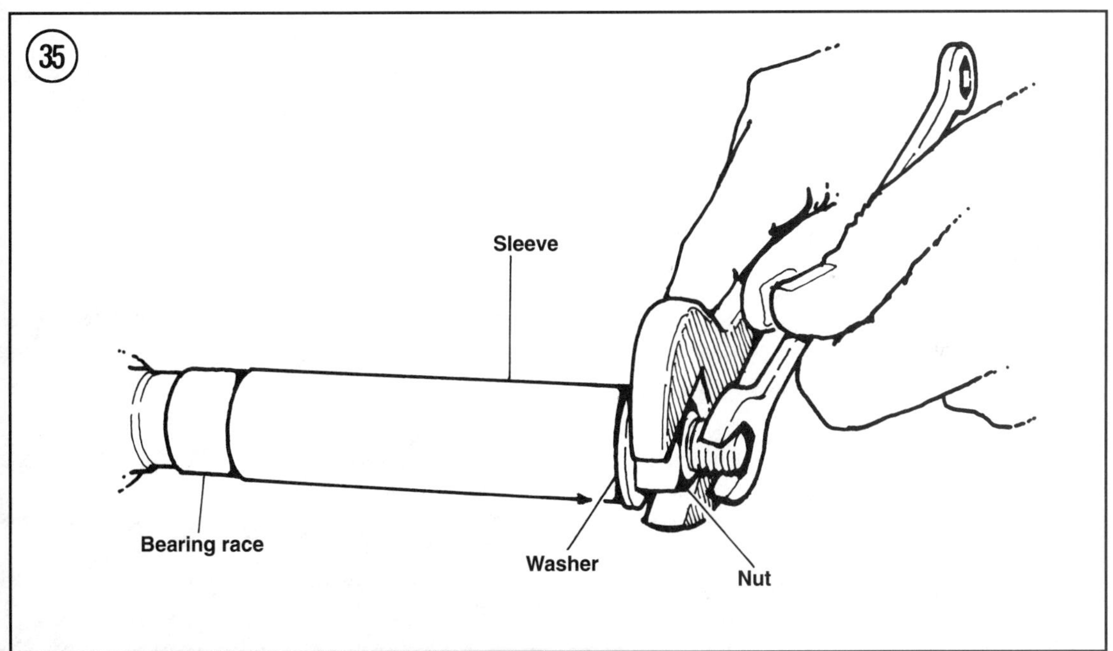

10. Check the needle bearing (14, **Figure 21**) for wear or roughness. If worn or damaged, replace as follows:
   a. Remove the spacer (16, **Figure 21**) if it was not previously removed.
   b. Press the bearing out of the transmission housing.
   c. Lubricate the new bearing's outer race with a light weight oil.
   d. Align the bearing with the bore in the housing so that the ID mark on the bearing faces toward the bearing installer.

*CAUTION*
*The bearing installer tool described in sub-step e ensures correct bearing installation. Installing the bearing without the Harley-Davidson Main Drive Gear Bearing Installer (part No. HD-33428) can cause bearing damage.*

   e. Install the bearing with a press and the Harley-Davidson tool (part No. HD-33428). The small diameter center guide on the bearing installer should fit into the bearing cavity when installing the bearing. Press the bearing in until the tool bottoms against the steel sleeve insert. When the tool bottoms out, the bearing is installed to its specified depth.

11. Install a new main drive gear oil seal and spacer as shown in **Figure 21**.
12. Carefully tap the main drive gear into the transmission housing (**Figure 38**) until the flange on the bearing housing seats against the transmission housing.
13. Lightly oil a new drive gear seal. Then install the seal into the end of the drive gear using a piece of pipe with a 1 in. (25.4 mm) I.D. and a 1 3/16 in. (30.2 mm) O.D.

### Main Drive Gear Oil Seal Replacement (With Transmission Installed)

The main drive gear oil seal (**Figure 39**) can be replaced with the transmission installed in the frame.

1. Remove the countershaft sprocket.
2. Remove the primary chain case as described in Chapter Five.
3. Pry the oil seal from the transmission as shown in **Figure 40**.
4. Carefully install the new oil seal over the shaft (**Figure 41**) and align it with the seal bore in the transmission housing.
5. Install the new seal by driving it squarely into the transmission housing.
6. Install all parts previously removed.

### Transmission Housing

Remove the transmission mounting plate bolts (**Figure 42**) and remove the plate. Reverse to install. Tighten the nuts securely.

38

39

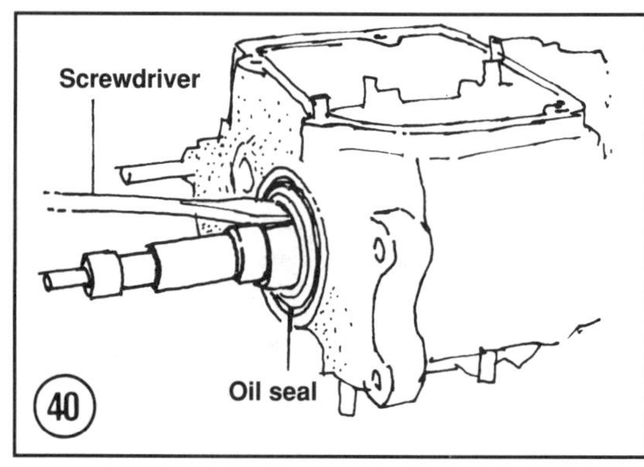

40

## SHIFTER COVER

### Removal

The shifter cover can be removed with the transmission installed on the motorcycle. If transmission repairs are also required, remove the transmission and shifter cover as one unit. This procedure describes removal of the shifter cover only.

Refer to **Figure 43** for this procedure.

1. Remove the battery and batter carrier.
2. Drain the oil tank as described in Chapter Three. Then remove the oil tank.
3. Remove the bolts and washers attaching the shift cover to the transmission; the bolt from the hole shown with an arrow in **Figure 43** can be loosened, but not removed. To remove the bolt, the shifter shaft cover must be removed first.
4. Lift the shifter cover off of the transmission housing. Discard the shifter cover gasket.
5. Installation is the reverse of these steps. Note the following.
6. Install a new shift cover gasket during installation.

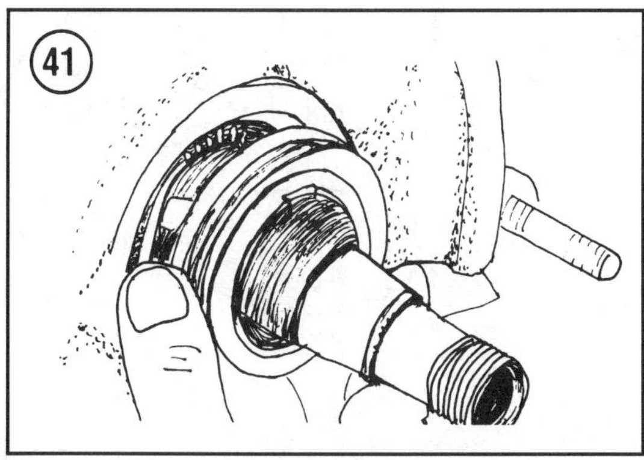

7. Lightly coat the shift cover mounting bolts with Loctite Lock N' Seal. Tighten the mounting bolt to 13-16 ft.-lb. (17.9-22.1 N•m).
8. Adjust the shift linkage as described in this chapter.

### Disassembly

Refer to **Figure 43** for this procedure.

1. Remove the neutral indicator switch and washer.
2. Remove the shifter shaft cover bolts and washers.
3. Remove the shift lever bolt and washer.
4. Remove the shifter linkage assembly from the transmission cover.
5. Remove remaining shifter cover bolt.
6. If necessary, remove the top plug from the shift cover as follows:
   a. Drill a 1/4 in. (6.35 mm) hole through the top plug. Drill only far enough to penetrate completely through the top plug.
   b. Pry the top plug off of the shift cover with a punch inserted through the drilled hole.
   c. Discard the top plug; a new plug must be installed during reassembly.
7. Remove the shift cam retaining ring and washer through the top plug hole opening and remove the shifter cam and pawl assembly.
8. Disassemble the shifter cover (**Figure 44**) as follows:
   a. Remove the cam follower and spring from the cam follower body.
   b. Pry back the lockwasher tabs and remove the cam follower body bolts.
   c. Lift the cam follower body out of the shift cover.
   d. Remove the screws, pawl stops and remove the long springs.

### Inspection

1. Thoroughly clean all parts (except neutral switch) in solvent, then blow dry.

*NOTE*

*When parts have been disassembled and cleaned, visually inspect them for any signs of wear, cracks, breakage or other damage. If there is any doubt as to the condition of any part, replace it with a new one.*

(43)

**SHIFTER COVER**

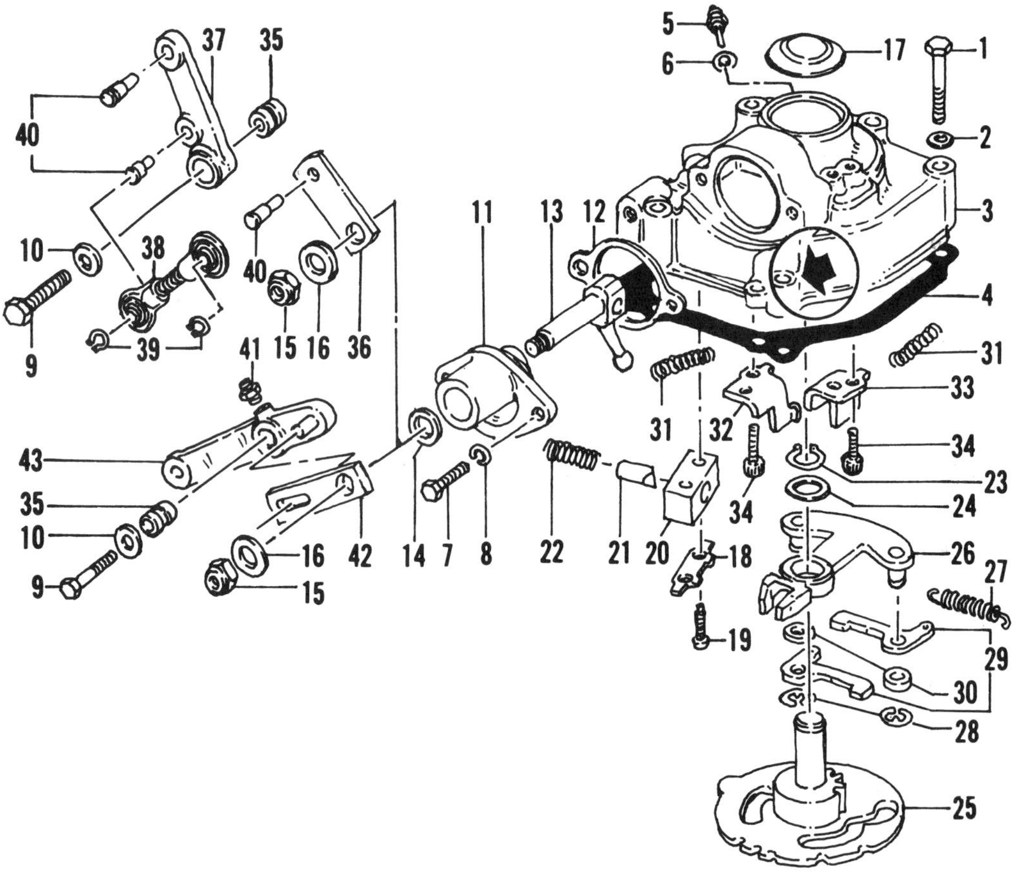

1. Bolt
2. Washer
3. Shift cover
4. Gasket
5. Neutral indicator switch
6. Washer
7. Bolt
8. Lockwasher
9. Bolt
10. Washer
11. Shifter shaft cover
12. Gasket
13. Shifter shaft
14. Oil seal
15. Nut
16. Washer
17. Plug
18. Lockplate
19. Bolt
20. Plunger body
21. Plunger
22. Spring
23. Retaining ring
24. Thrust washer
25. Shifter cam
26. Pawl carrier
27. Shifter pawl spring
28. Retaining ring
29. Pawl
30. Spacer
31. Pawl carrier spring
32. Shift pawl stop, rear
33. Shift pawl stop, front
34. Socket head screw
35. Bushing
36. Shift lever arm (FXEF and FXSB)
37. Shift lever (FXEF and FXSB)
38. Shift linkage arm (FXEF and FXSB)
39. Retaining ring (2) (FXEF and FXSB)
40. Pivot pin (3) (FXEF and FXSB)
41. Grease fitting
42. Shift lever arm (FXWG)
43. Shift lever (1985 FXWG)

2. Replace any circlips and retaining rings that were removed during disassembly as removal sometimes deforms and weakens them.

3. Check the shift cam slots for worn or grooved cam slots. Excessive wear will result in difficult shifting.

4. Check pawl stops for breakage or surface cracks.

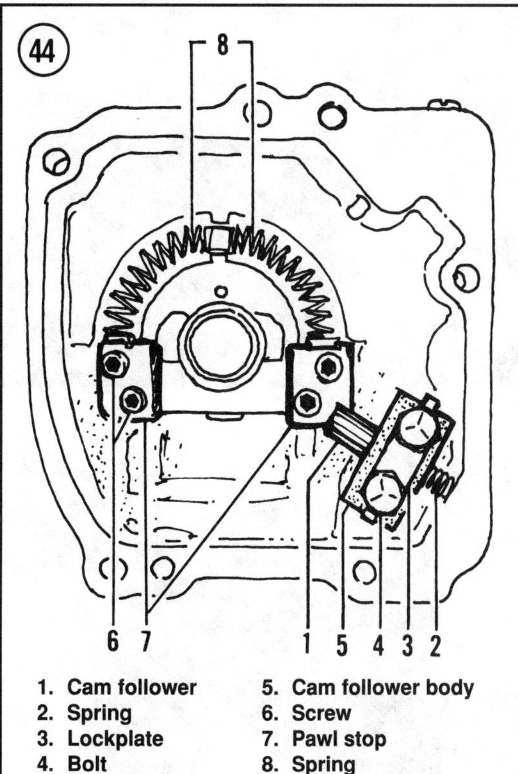


1. Cam follower
2. Spring
3. Lockplate
4. Bolt
5. Cam follower body
6. Screw
7. Pawl stop
8. Spring

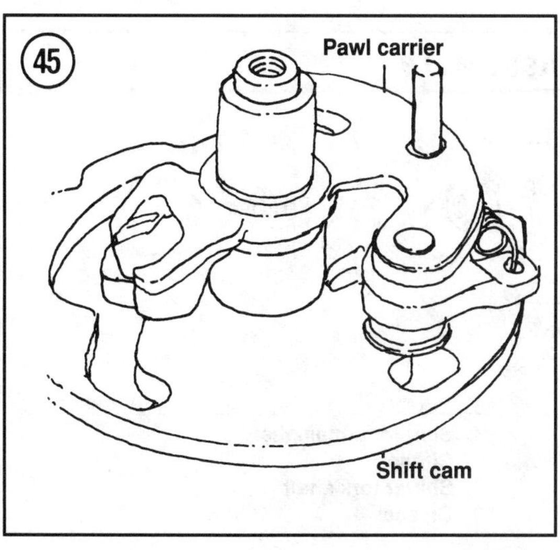


**Assembly**

1. Lubricate the pawl stop springs with multi-purpose grease.
2. Install the pawl stops and secure with the Allen bolts.
3. Install the pawl stop springs.
4. Install the cam follower body, lockwasher and bolts. Tighten the bolts and bend the lockwasher tabs over the bolts to lock them.
5. Install the spring and cam follower into the cam follower body.
6. Coat the neutral switch threads with Loctite Pipe Sealant With Teflon. Install the neutral switch and washer and tighten to 5-10 ft.-lb. (6.9-13.8 N•m).
7. Refer to **Figure 45**. Slide the pawl assembly on the shift cam. Engage the pawls with the shift cam gear teeth.
8. Install the shift cam and pawl assembly into the shift cover. Position the tab on the pawl assembly between the pawl stop springs.
9. Install the shift cam washer and a new circlip.
10. Coat a new top plug with Seal-All. Then place the top plug in the cover and seat it with a ball peen hammer.
11. Assemble the shift linkage using a new circlip. Tighten all linkage bolts securely.

## SHIFT FORKS

**Removal/Disassembly**

Refer to **Figure 46** for this procedure.

1. Remove the shifter cover as described in this chapter.
2. Remove the shifter finger rollers (**Figure 47**) from each shifter finger.
3. Remove the circlip (**Figure 48**) from the end of the shifter fork shaft.
4. Tap the shifter fork shaft with a drift and remove it from the housing (**Figure 49**).
5. Remove the shift forks (**Figure 50**).

*NOTE*
*Do not disassemble the forks unless replacement of a part is necessary.*

*NOTE*
*When disassembling the shift fork assemblies, label each sub-assembly as they are not interchangeable (**Figure 51**).*

6

6. Loosen and remove the shift finger nuts (**Figure 52**) and remove them. Then disassemble the shift forks in the order shown in **Figure 46**.

7. Repeat Step 4 for the opposite shift finger assembly.

### Inspection

1. Clean all parts in solvent.

2. Inspect each shift fork (**Figure 52**) for signs of wear or damage. Make sure the forks slide smoothly on the shifter fork shaft. Replace any worn forks.

3. Check for any arc-shaped wear or burn marks on the shift forks (**Figure 53**). If this is apparent, the shift fork has come in contact with the gear, indicating that the fingers are worn beyond use and the fork must be replaced.

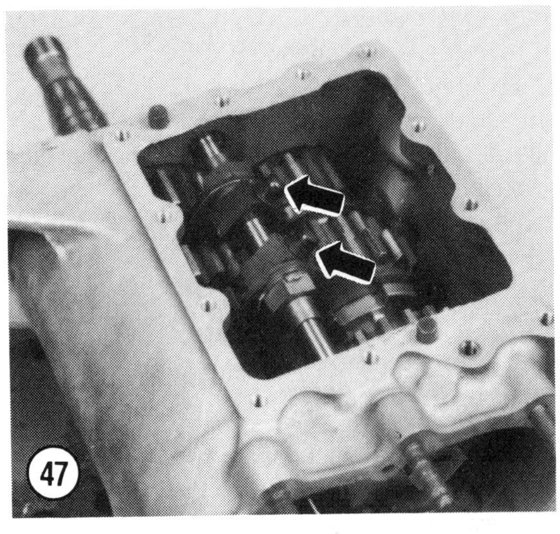


4. Roll the shift fork shaft (**Figure 54**) on a flat surface and check for bending. If the shaft is bent, it must be replaced.

5. Install each shift finger on the shift shaft (**Figure 55**). The shift fingers should slide smoothly without any sign of binding.

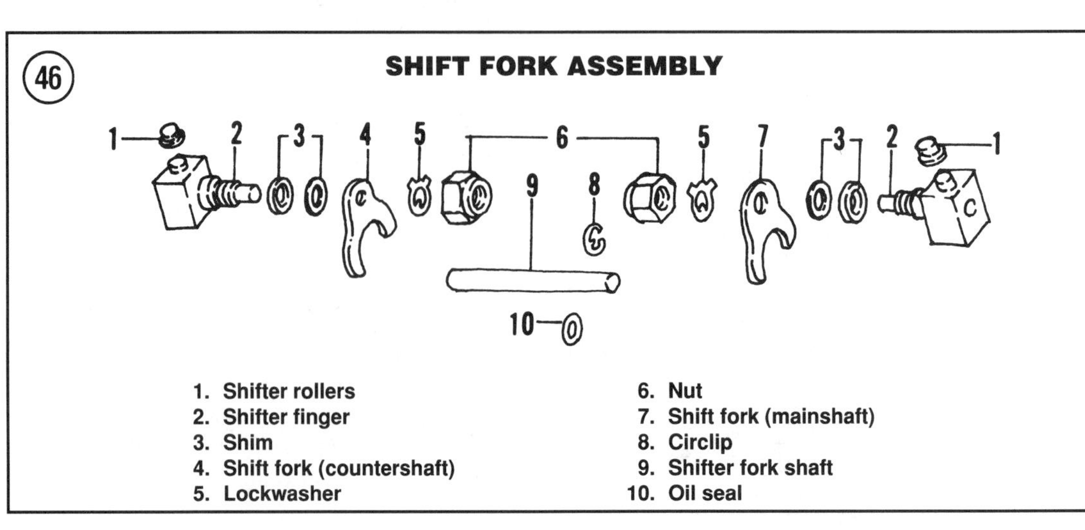

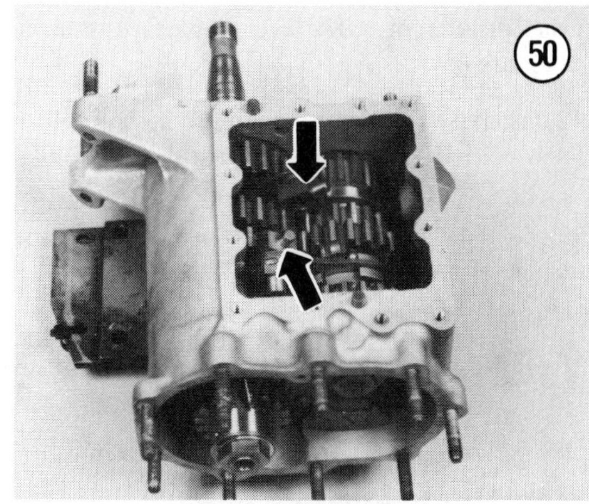

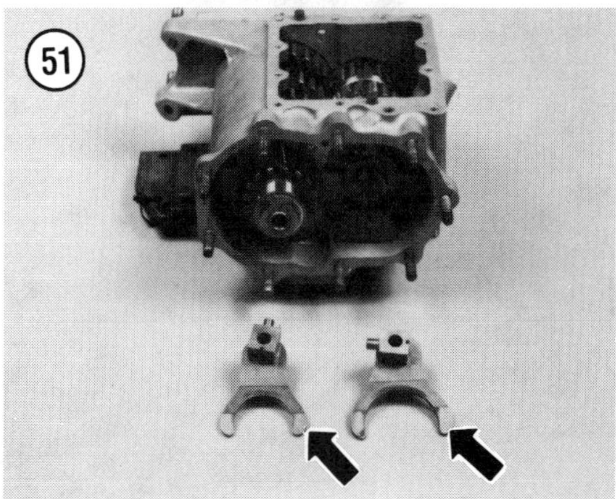

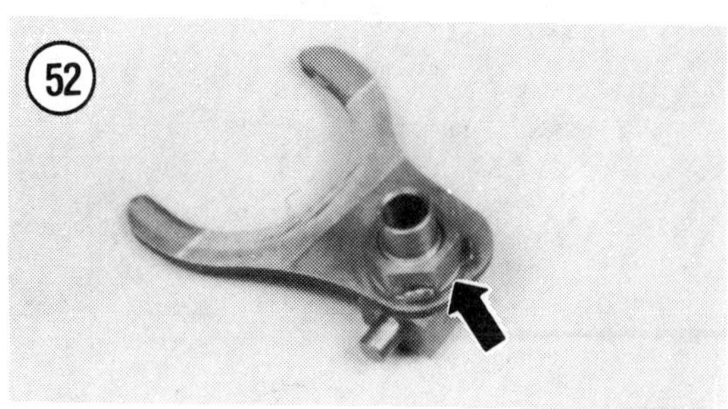

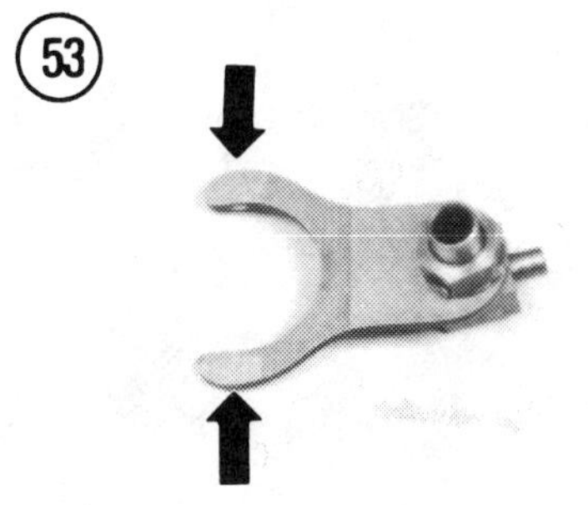

### Assembly

*NOTE*

*If any part was replaced, the shifter clutch clearance must be checked and adjusted. Because this procedure requires special tools, refer clearance check to a Harley-Davidson dealer.*

1. Coat all bearing and sliding surfaces with assembly oil.
2. Install the spacer(s), shift fork, lockwasher and nut on the shift finger. Tighten the nut to 10-12 ft.-lb. (13.8-16.5 N•m). Bend the lockwasher tab against the nut to lock it.

*CAUTION*

*Do not exceed the torque specifications in Step 2 as this could cause the shift finger to bind on the shift shaft.*

3. Position the shift fork assemblies (**Figure 56** and **Figure 57**) in the transmission case. See **Figure 50**. Engage the shift forks with their respective gears.
4. Slide the shift shaft through the transmission case (**Figure 58**) and through the shift fork assemblies (**Figure 49**). Secure the shaft with a new circlip (**Figure 59**). See **Figure 48**.
5. Install the shift rollers (**Figure 47**) onto the shift fingers.

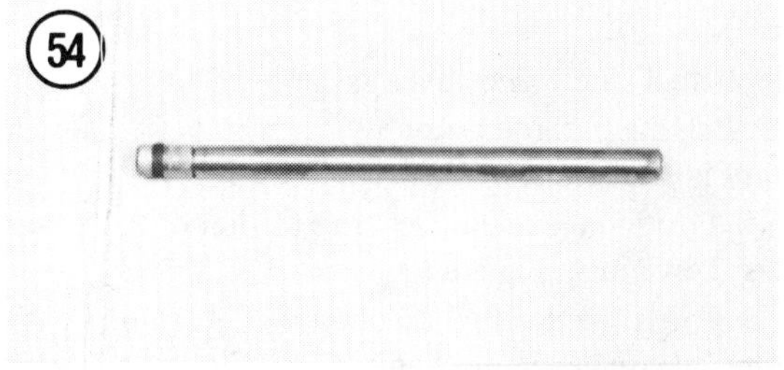

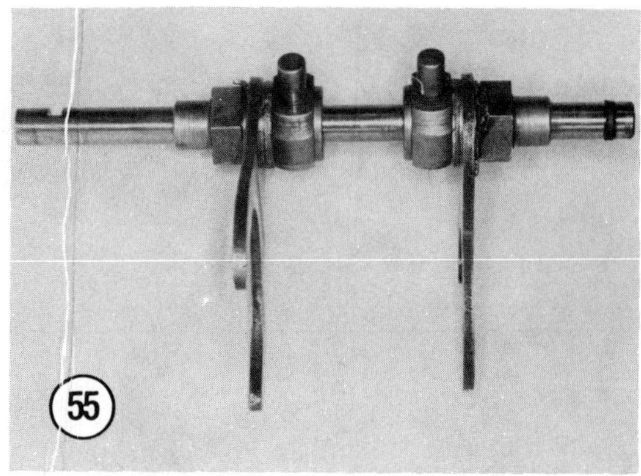

6

6. If any part was replaced, have the shift fork adjustment checked by a Harley-Davidson dealer.

## KICKSTARTER AND STARTER CLUTCH

### Removal/Disassembly

Refer to **Figure 60** for this procedure.

1. Disconnect the negative battery cable.
2A. *FXSB*: Perform the following:
   a. Remove the exhaust pipes. See Chapter Eight.
   b. Remove the brake pedal assembly.
   c. Remove the master cylinder and reservoir. See Chapter Thirteen.
2B. *FXWG*: Perform the following:
   a. Remove the exhaust pipes. See Chapter Eight.
   b. Remove the rear brake line support clip.
   c. Remove the starter motor bracket.
   d. Remove the master cylinder reservoir. See Chapter Thirteen.
3. Drain the transmission oil as described in Chapter Three.
4. Remove the kickstarter pedal.
5. Remove the side cover mounting bolts and remove the side cover (**Figure 61**).
6. If necessary, disassemble the side cover as described in this chapter.
7. Installation is the reverse of these steps. Note the following.
8. Install a new side cover gasket.
9. Pull the pushrod assembly partway out as shown in **Figure 62**.
10. Position the release lever to the left of the cover as shown in A, **Figure 63**.
11. Align the pushrod oil slinger (**Figure 64**) with the release lever mechanism (B, **Figure 63**) and

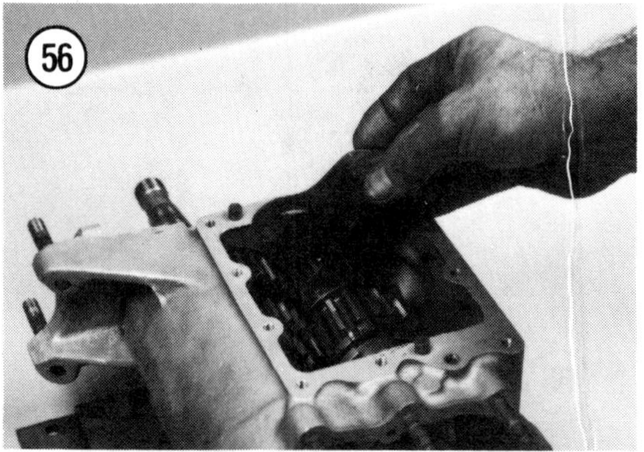


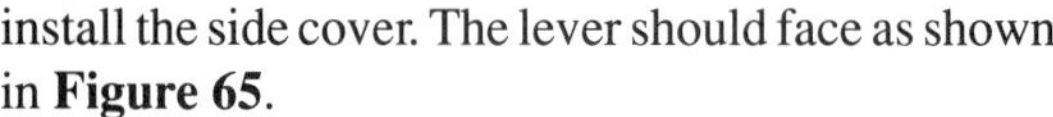
install the side cover. The lever should face as shown in **Figure 65**.

12. Install the side cover mounting bolts and tighten them to 13-16 ft.-lb. (17.9-22.1 N•m).

13. Refill the transmission with the correct type and quantity of oil as described in Chapter Three.

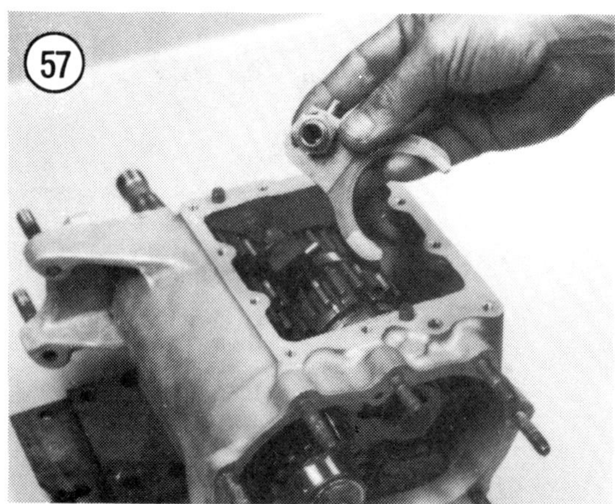

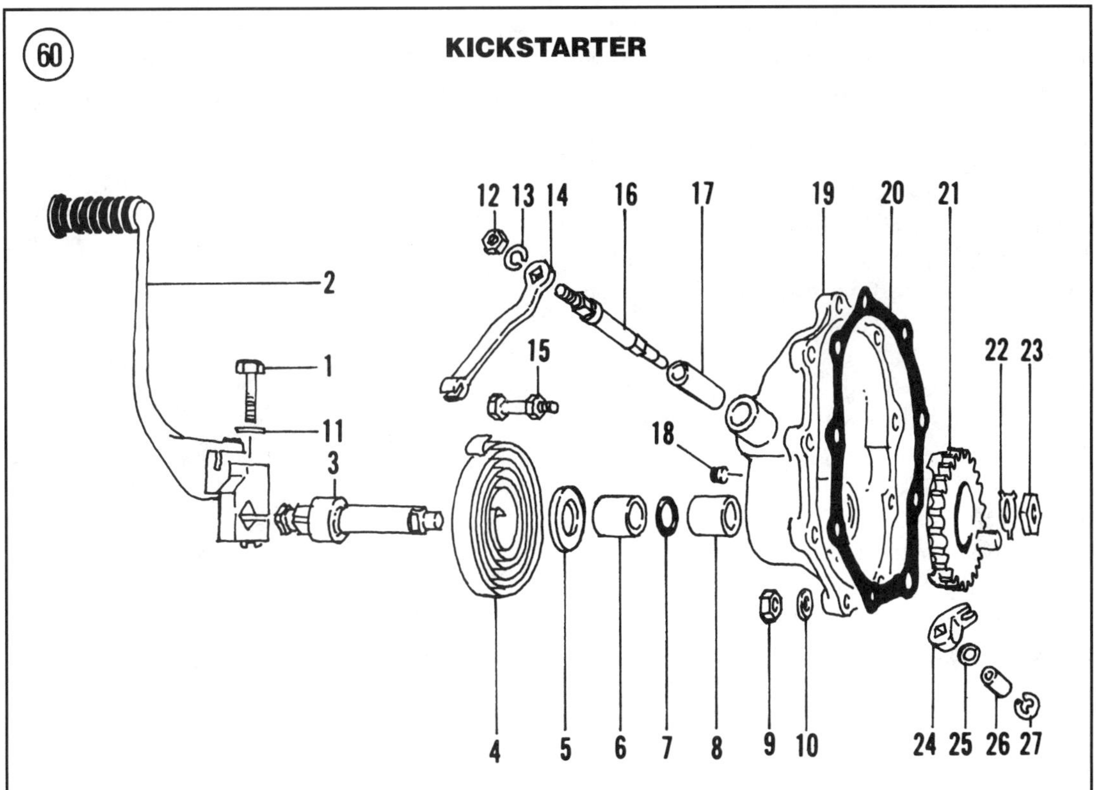

(60)

## KICKSTARTER

1. Bolt
2. Kickstarter
3. Crankshaft
4. Spring
5. Thrust washer
6. Bushing
7. O-ring
8. Bushing
9. Nut
10. Washer
11. Washer
12. Nut
13. Lockwasher
14. Release lever
15. Stud
16. Shaft
17. Bushing
18. Screw
19. Side cover
20. Gasket
21. Starter crank gear
22. Lockwasher
23. Nut
24. Release finger
25. Washer
26. Bushing
27. Circlip

(61)

(62)

14. Reinstall all parts previously removed. If a brake line was disconnected, bleed the rear brake as described in Chapter Thirteen.

### Disassembly

Refer to **Figure 60** for this procedure.

1. Clamp the end of the kickstarter shaft in a vise with soft jaws. Then, from inside the cover, pry back the kickstarter shaft lockwasher and remove the nut (A, **Figure 66**).
2. Using a universal type claw puller (**Figure 67**), remove the kickstarter gear. See B, **Figure 66**.
3. Support the side cover in a vise or on wood blocks. Do not block the kickstarter shaft or spring. Drive the kickstarter shaft out of the cover using a plastic hammer. Remove the thrust washer (5, **Figure 60**).
4. Remove the release lever nut and washer.
5. Pull the release lever off of the shaft with a universal type claw puller.
6. Remove the clip. Then remove the shaft from the cover.
7. Remove the release finger and washer.

### Inspection

1. Clean all components thoroughly with solvent. Remove any gasket residue from the cover-to-transmission machined surfaces. Check the threads in the transmission case to be sure they are clean. If dirty or damaged, use a tap to true up the threads and remove any deposits.

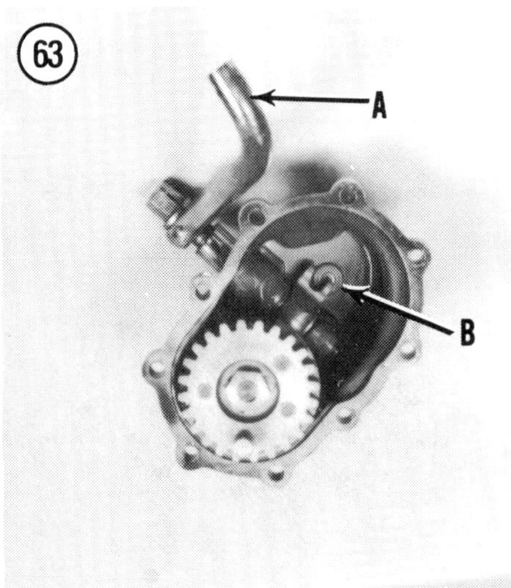


2. Visually check the shaft surfaces for cracks, deep scoring, excessive wear or heat discoloration.
3. Check the kickstarter gear for worn or damaged gear teeth.
4. If oil leaks out of the side cover along the kickstarter shaft, the oil seal must be replaced by removing the front bushing with a blind hole bearing remover and slide hammer. Have the new bushings

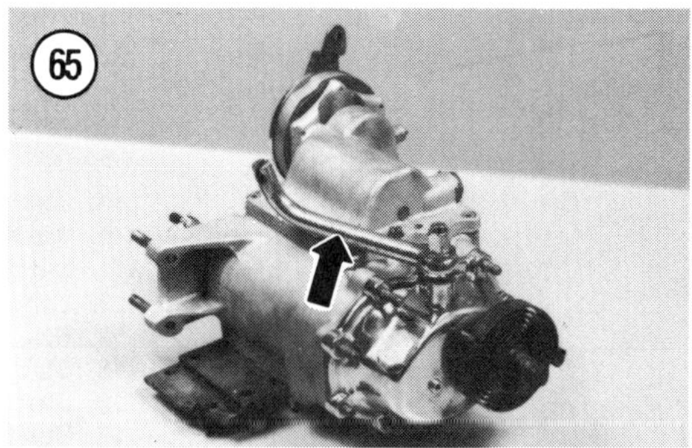


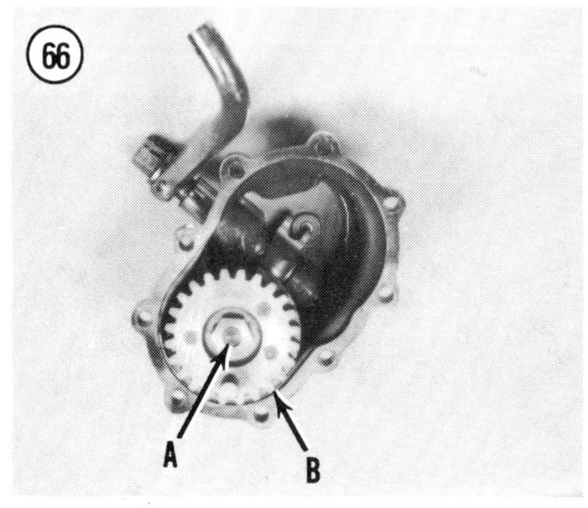

installed by a Harley-Davidson dealer or machine shop as a press is required.

5. Check the kickstarter spring. If it is damaged or broken, replace it by performing the following:

   a. Remove the kickstarter shaft as described in this chapter.

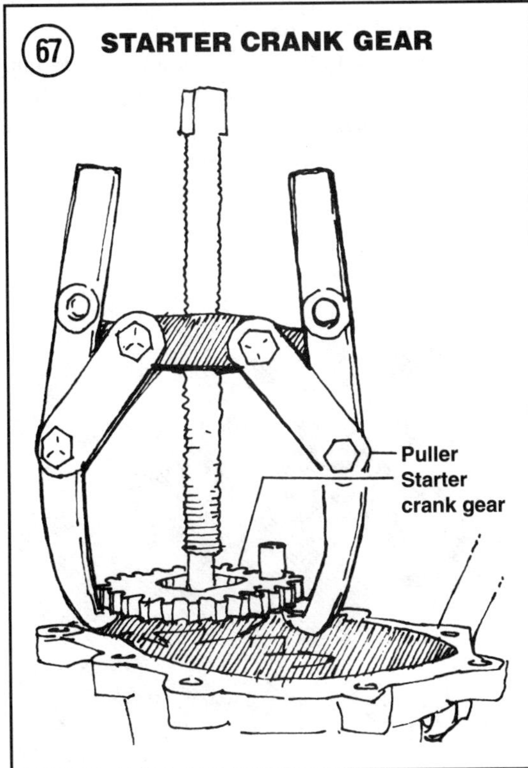


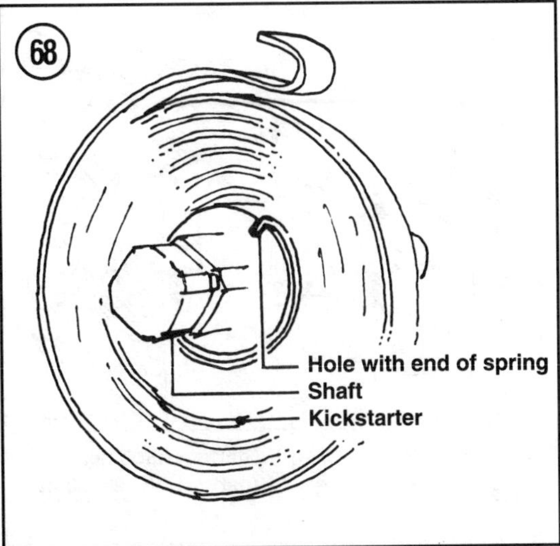


   b. Lift the outer spring hook off of the shaft spring stop.
   c. Tap the spring off the kickstarter shaft with a punch and hammer.
   d. Install the new spring, so that the outer spring hook faces to the left-hand side when looking at the kickstarter crank end. See **Figure 68**.

### Assembly

Refer to **Figure 60** for this procedure.

1. Assemble the release finger as follows:
   a. Install the washer and release finger into the side cover.
   b. Insert the release lever shaft into the side cover and through the release finger and washer. Secure the shaft with a new circlip.
   c. Install the release lever. Then install the lock-washer and the nut. Tighten the nut until the release lever bottoms on the shaft.

2. Install the washer on the kickstarter shaft so that the chamfered side of the washer faces the spring.

3. See **Figure 69**. Install the kickstarter gear as follows:
   a. Turn the kickstarter shaft so that the flat side is straight up (12 o'clock).

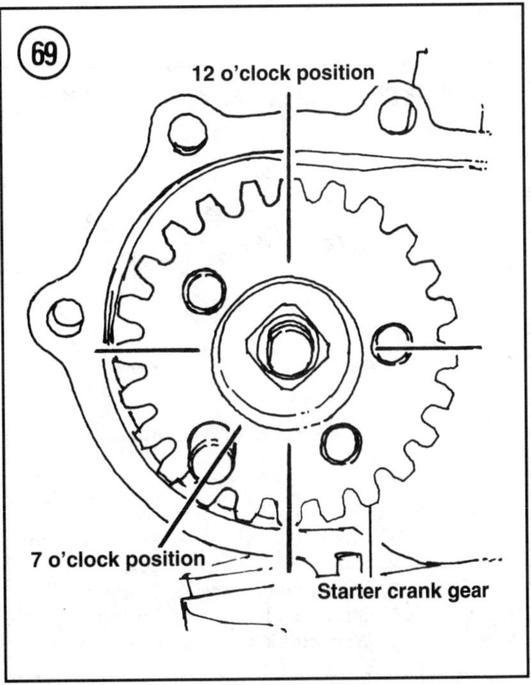


6

b. Slide the kickstarter gear onto the shaft. When installed correctly, the kickstarter gear dowel pin is in the 7 o'clock position.

4. Hold the kickstarter shaft in a vise with soft jaws as during disassembly.

5. Engage the end of the kickstarter spring with the stud on the side cover.

6. Press the kickstarter gear onto the kickstarter shaft.

7. Install the kickstarter gear lockwasher and nut. Tighten the nut to 30-40 ft.-lb. (41.4-55.2 N•m). Bend the lockwasher tab over the nut to lock it.

## Starter Clutch Removal/Inspection/Installation

Refer to **Figure 70** for this procedure.

1. Remove the kickstarter side cover as described in this chapter.

2. Remove the pushrod (**Figure 62**).

3. Lock the transmission into 2 gears at once.

4. Bend the lockwasher tab away from the starter clutch nut (**Figure 71**).

5. Remove the starter clutch with the Harley-Davidson starter clutch puller (part No. HD-95650-42). See **Figure 72**.

6. Remove the Woodruff key, starter clutch gear and spring.

**STARTER CLUTCH ASSEMBLY**

1. Pushrod
2. Nut
3. Lockwasher
4. Starter clutch
5. Woodruff key
6. Starter clutch gear
7. Bushing
8. Spring
9. Housing

(70)

7. Check the starter gear and starter clutch teeth. Teeth should be sharp and show no signs of cracking, scoring or excessive wear. Replace starter clutch and starter gear if teeth are rounded or if the kickstarter has been slipping.

8. Visually check the starter clutch for cracks, deep scoring and excessive wear.

9. Slide the starter gear on the mainshaft and check play by hand; the gear should just be loose enough to slide under spring pressure. If gear is loose, replace the bushing in the gear with a press. Do not attempt to drive a new bushing into the gear with a socket and hammer.

10. Installation is the reverse of these steps. Note the following:

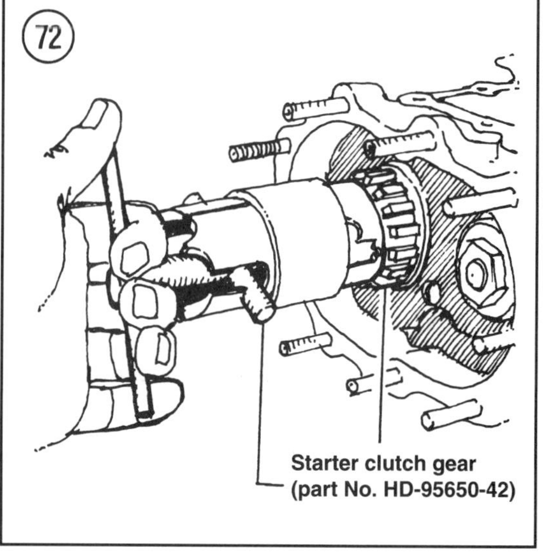

a. Lubricate the mainshaft with engine oil.
b. Install the spring and starter gear onto the mainshaft.
c. Push the starter gear toward the transmission and release it. The spring should be able to push the gear forward. If the gear is tight, the gear bushing should be reamed. Refer this service to a Harley-Davidson dealer.
d. Press the starter clutch onto the mainshaft.
e. Tighten the starter clutch nut to 34-42 ft.-lb. (46.9-57.9 N•m). Bend the lockwasher tab over the nut to lock it.

## SIDE COVER (ELECTRIC START)

### Removal/Disassembly

Refer to **Figure 73** for this procedure.

1. Disconnect the negative battery cable.
2. Drain the transmission oil as described in Chapter Three.

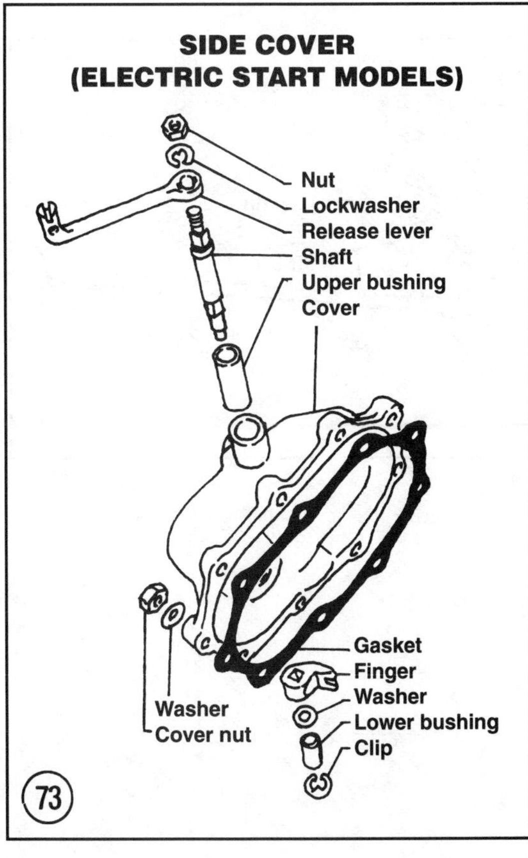


3. Remove the exhaust system as described in Chapter Eight.
4. Remove the rear master cylinder reservoir. See Chapter Thirteen.
5. Remove the starter bracket.
6. Remove the side cover mounting bolts and remove the side cover and gasket.
7. If necessary, disassemble the side cover as described in this chapter.
8. Installation is the reverse of these steps. Note the following.
9. Install a new side cover gasket.
10. Pull the pushrod assembly partway out as shown in **Figure 62**.
11. Position the release lever to the left of the cover as shown in A, **Figure 63**.
12. Align the pushrod oil slinger (**Figure 64**) with the release lever mechanism (B, **Figure 63**) and install the side cover. The lever should face as shown in **Figure 65**.
13. Install the side cover mounting bolts and tighten them to 13-16 ft.-lb. (17.9-22.1 N•m).
14. Refill the transmission with the correct type and quantity of oil as described in Chapter Three.

### Disassembly/Inspection/Reassembly

Refer to **Figure 73** for this procedure.

1. Remove the release lever nut and washer.
2. Pull the release lever off of the shaft with a universal type claw puller.
3. Remove the clip. Then remove the shaft from the cover.
4. Remove the release finger and washer.
5. Clean all components thoroughly with solvent. Remove any gasket residue from the cover-to-transmission machined surfaces. Check the threads in the transmission case to be sure they are clean. If dirty or damaged, use a tap to true up the threads and remove any deposits.
6. Visually check the shaft surfaces for cracks, deep scoring, excessive wear or heat discoloration.
7. Slide the shaft release lever shaft into the side cover. Check the shaft-to-bushing wear by moving the shaft back and forth. If there is excessive shaft wear, replace the upper and lower bushings with a blind hole bearing remover and slide hammer. Use a press to install the new bushing.
8. Assemble the release finger as follows:

a. Install the washer and release finger into the side cover.
b. Insert the release lever shaft into the side cover and through the release finger and washer. Secure the shaft with a new circlip.
c. Install the release lever. Then install the lock-washer and the nut. Tighten the nut until the release lever bottoms on the shaft.

## SHIFTER ADJUSTMENT

Shifter adjustment is required to compensate for component wear or whenever the transmission has been removed.

### Shift Linkage Adjustment (FXWG)

Refer to **Figure 74**.

1. Remove the retaining clip securing the shifter rod to the shift lever.
2. Slide the shift linkage rod off of the clevis pin.
3. Loosen the locknut and turn the shift linkage rod as required so that the shift linkage can travel its full limit without interference.
4. Tighten the locknut.
5. Reconnect the shift linkage rod and secure it with a new retaining clip.

### Shift Linkage Adjustment (FXEF and FXSB)

Refer to **Figure 75**.

1. Remove the retaining clip securing the shifter rod to the clevis pin. Then pull the shifter rod off of the clevis pin.
2. Loosen the shifter rod locknut and turn the shifter rod end as required so that the shift pedal travels through all gear positions without interference. Tighten the locknut.

3. Reconnect the shifter rod and secure it with a new retaining clip.

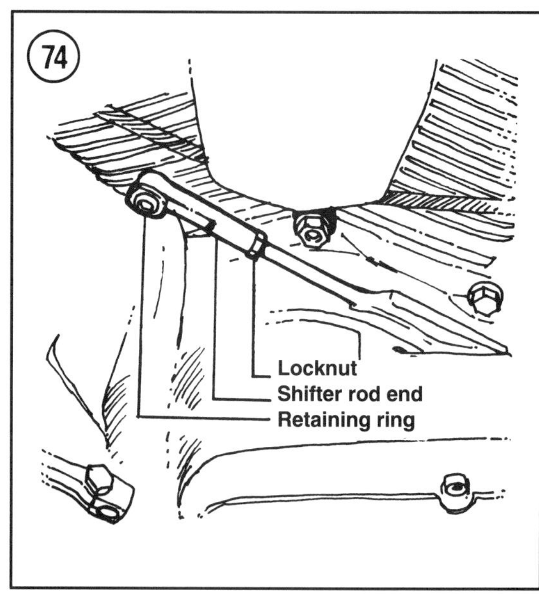


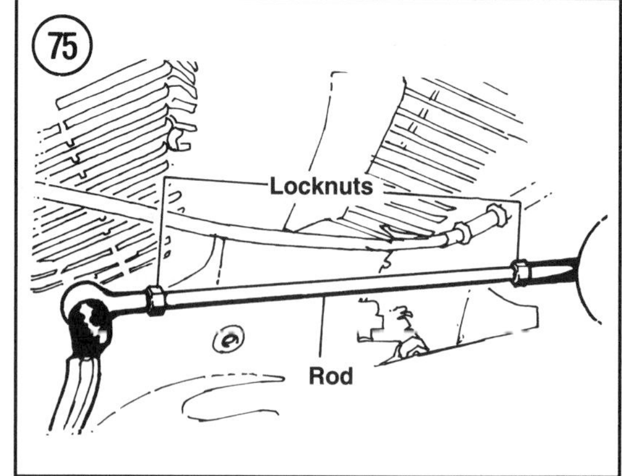

**Table 1 4-SPEED TRANSMISSION SPECIFICATIONS**

| | Specification | | Wear limit | |
|---|---|---|---|---|
| | in. | mm | in. | mm |
| Mainshaft main drive gear | | | | |
| End play | 0.010-0.035 | 0.25-0.89 | 0.035 | 0.89 |
| Bushing fit on mainshaft | 0.0018-0.0032 | 0.046-0.081 | 0.004 | 0.10 |
| Mainshaft | | | | |
| Third gear end play | 0.005-0.021 | 0.13-0.53 | 0.021 | 0.53 |
| Shift fork clutch gear spacing | 0.100-0.110 | 2.54-2.79 | 0.110 | 2.79 |
| Countershaft | | | | |
| Gear end play | 0.004-0.012 | 0.10-0.30 | 0.015 | 0.38 |
| Second gear end play | 0.003-0.017 | 0.08-0.43 | 0.020 | 0.51 |
| Shift fork clutch gear spacing | 0.080-0.090 | 2.03-2.29 | 0.090 | 2.29 |
| Gear backlash | 0.003-0.006 | 0.08-0.15 | 0.010 | 0.25 |



**Table 2 TRANSMISSION TIGHTENING TORQUES**

| Item | ft.-lb. | N•m |
|---|---|---|
| Drain screw | 12-15 | 16.5-20.7 |
| Primary cover screws | 18-22 | 24.8-30.4 |
| Transmission sprocket | 80-90 | 110.4-124.2 |
| Mainshaft ball bearing nut | 50-60 | 69-82.8 |
| Retaining plate screws | 7-9 | 9.7-12.4 |
| Shift clutch nut* | 34-42 | 46.9-57.9 |
| Starter crankcase nut | 18-22 | 24.8-30.4 |
| Transmission end cover stud nut | 13-16 | 17.9-22.1 |
| Shift fork nut | 10-12 | 13.8-16.5 |
| Neutral switch | 5-10 | 6.9-13.8 |
| Top cover bolts | 13-16 | 17.9-22.1 |
| Frame to transmission bolt | 21-27 | 28.9-37.3 |
| Sprocket nut locking screw | 50-60 in.-lb. | 5.7-6.9 |

* Kickstarter models only.

# CHAPTER SEVEN

# 5-SPEED TRANSMISSION

The 5-speed Harley-Davidson transmission and shifter assembly is mounted in a separate housing and can be completely disassembled and serviced without having to disassemble the engine or remove the transmission housing. The 5-speed transmission is used on all 1984 and later FLT and FXR models.

The transmission service procedures in this chapter are arranged by sub-assembly—shifter assembly and transmission. Before servicing the transmission or shifter assembly, make sure the problem is not due to a faulty clutch adjustment or a problem with the primary drive system.

An external shift linkage assembly connects the gearshift lever to the transmission. The shift linkage assembly requires adjustment to compensate for normal wear to the linkage/shifter mechanism components or when the transmission housing has been removed from the bike.

This chapter provides service procedures for the 5-speed transmission. **Tables 1-3** are found at the end of the chapter.

## PRODUCTION GEARS (1994 MODELS)

During the 1994 production year, two types of transmission gear sets were produced by Harley-Davidson—domestic ratios (U.S., Canada and Japan) and HDI ratios (Harley-Davidson International). Domestic ratio gears can be identified by a 0.03 in. (0.76 mm) radius groove machined in the center of each gear tooth. Motorcycles with HDI ratios are equipped with high contact ratio (HCR) gears installed on the mainshaft and countershaft 2nd through 5th gears. HDI ratio gears do not have grooved gear teeth.

*CAUTION*
*Domestic and HDI ratio gears should not be intermixed. Running both types of gears in a single transmission assembly will damage mating gears.*

## SHIFT CAM ASSEMBLY

The shifter cam is mounted to the top of the transmission case, directly underneath the transmission top cover (**Figure 1**).

*NOTE*
*Late 1991 and later models are equipped with a new style shifter cam (8,* ***Figure 1****) that does not require the use of the inner thrust washer (11,* ***Figure 1****). Early and late style shifter cams can be identified by the neutral indicator actuator (A,* ***Figure 2****) mounted on the shifter cam. A cast neutral indicator actuator is used on early style shifter cams. Later style shifter cams use a pressed-in pin. In addition, on models with the late style shifter cam, 2 locating dowel pins are used to locate the left-hand support block (10,* ***Figure 1****) to the transmission case.*

### Removal

1. Disconnect the negative battery cable.
2. Remove the battery.

3. Drain and remove the engine oil tank (Chapter Three).
4. *1984-1986*: Disconnect the clutch cable at the engine (**Figure 3**).
5. Disconnect the neutral switch wire at the switch (**Figure 4**).
6. Remove the transmission top cover mounting bolts and remove the cover and gasket. See **Figure 5**.
7. Remove the shift cam mounting bolts (**Figure 6**) and lift the shift cam assembly out of the transmission. See **Figure 7**.
8. Slide the left side support block (**Figure 8**) off the shift cam. On late 1991-on models, remove the 2 dowel pins.

*NOTE*
*On 1984-early 1991 models, label all of the thrust washers removed in the following steps so you don't mix them up during reassembly.*

9. Refer to **Figure 9**. Remove the shift cam circlip (A) and outer thrust washer (B).

1

**SHIFT CAM ASSEMBLY**

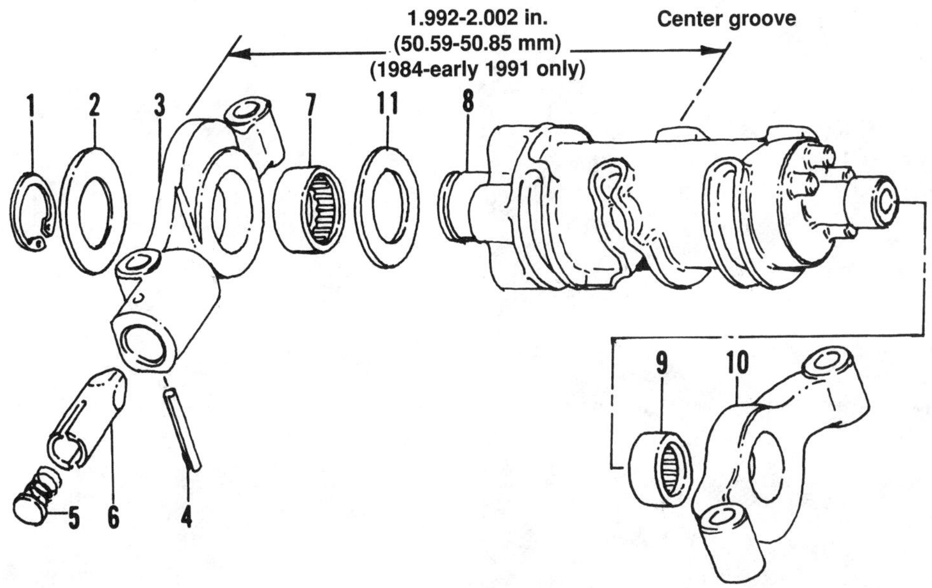

1.992-2.002 in.
(50.59-50.85 mm)
(1984-early 1991 only)
Center groove

1. Circlip
2. Outer thrust washer
3. Right support block
4. Roll pin
5. Spring
6. Cam follower
7. Bearing
8. Shifter cam
9. Bearing
10. Left support block
11. Inner thrust washer (1984-early 1991)

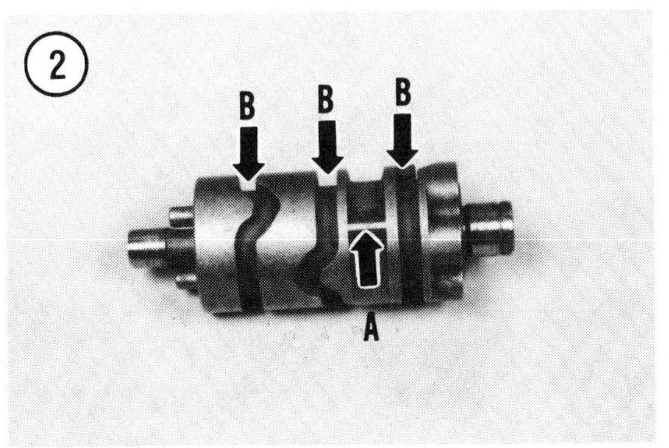

10. Remove the right-hand support block (**Figure 10**).

11. On 1984-early 1991 models, remove the inner thrust washer (**Figure 11**) from the shift cam.

## Inspection

1. Clean all parts (except support block bearings) in solvent.

2. Check the grooves in the shift cam (B, **Figure 2**) for wear or roughness. If any of the groove profiles have excessive wear or damage, replace the shift cam.

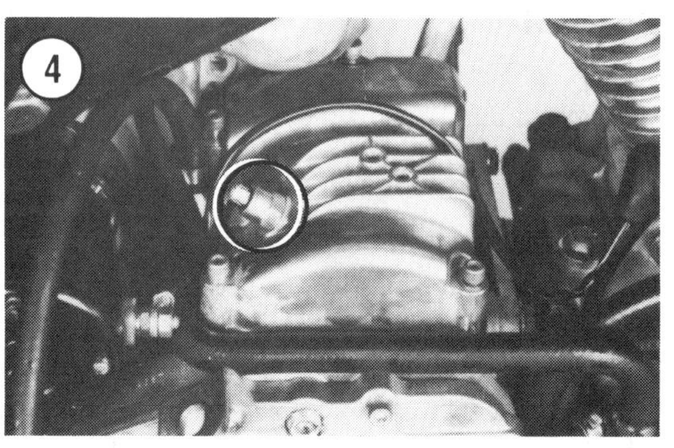

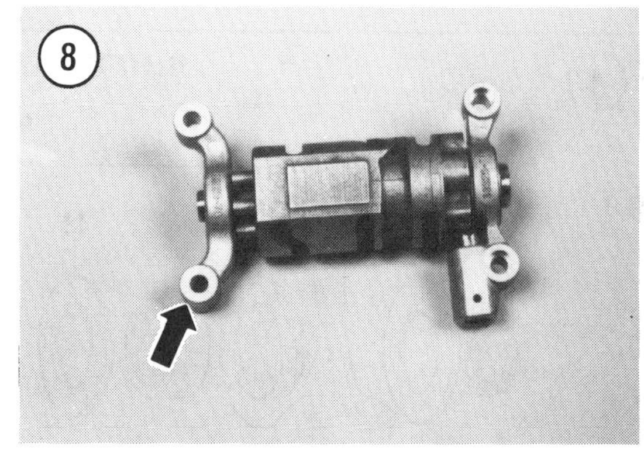

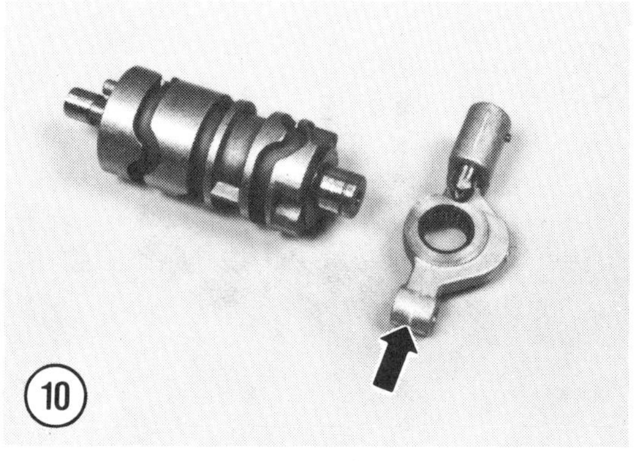

3. Check the support block bearings. See **Figure 12** and **Figure 13**. Make sure the bearings operate smoothly with no signs of wear or damage.
4. Check the support blocks for wear or damage. Replace if necessary.

### Installation

Refer to **Figure 1** when performing this procedure.
1. Coat all bearing and sliding surfaces with assembly oil.

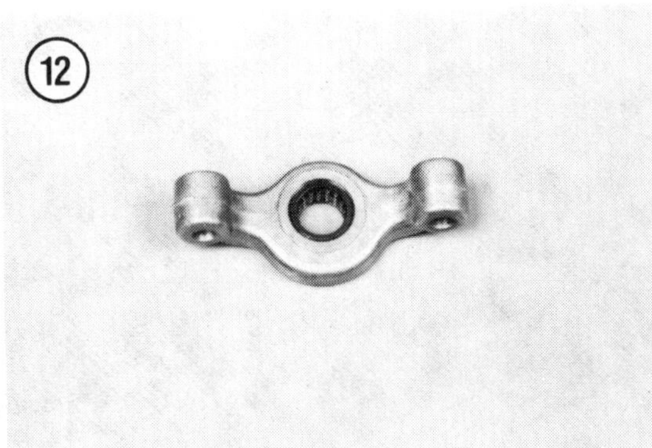


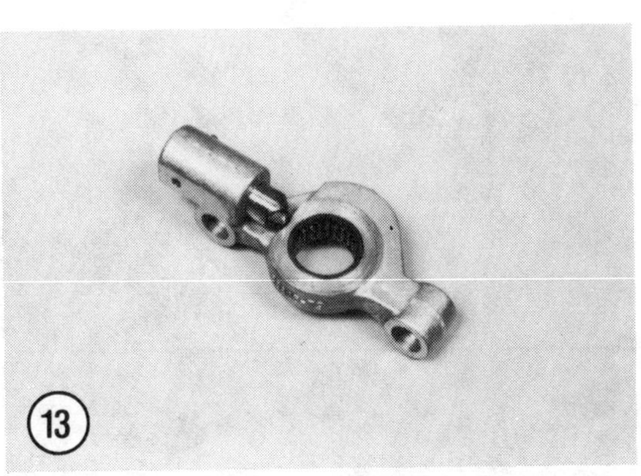


2. On 1984-early 1991 models, install the inner thrust washer (**Figure 11**). On all models, install right support block (**Figure 10**) on the shifter cam.
3. On 1984-early 1991 models, check shift drum position as follows:
   a. Install the shifter drum/right support block onto the transmission case. Engage the right support block with its dowel pins.
   b. Turn the shifter drum to its neutral position. The neutral indicator ramp mounted on the shifter drum, as shown in **Figure 14**, can be used as a reference point.
   c. Push the shifter drum so that it fits snug against the right support block thrust washer.
   d. Measure from the outer bearing support machined surface to the nearest edge of the center shifter cam groove as shown in **Figure 14**. The correct distance is 1.992-2.002 in. (50.59-50.85 mm).
   e. If the distance is incorrect, replace the inner thrust washer (11, **Figure 1**) with a different thickness thrust washer. Different thickness thrust washers are available from Harley-Davidson dealers.
   f. Remove the shifter drum/right support block from the transmission case.
4. Install the outer thrust washer (B, **Figure 9**) and a new circlip (A, **Figure 9**).

*NOTE*
*After installing the circlip, make sure the outer thrust washer (2, **Figure 1**) can be rotated by hand.*

5. Measure shifter cam end play as follows:

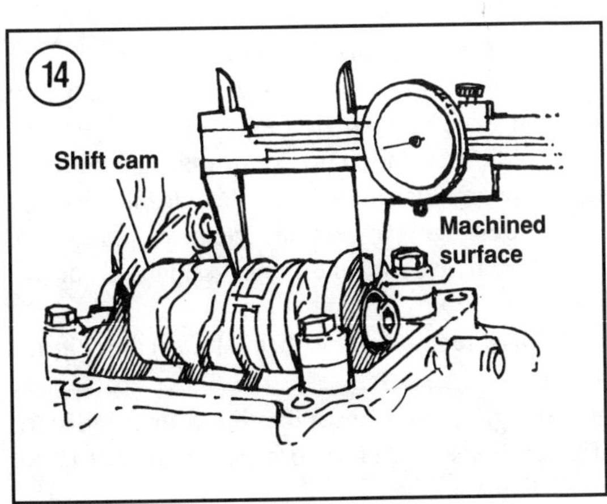


7

a. Install the shifter drum/right support block onto the transmission case. Engage the right support block with its dowel pins.
b. Measure end play between the outer thrust washer and shifter cam (**Figure 15**). Correct end play measurement is 0.001-0.004 in. (0.025-0.010 mm).
c. If necessary, correct end play by replacing the outer thrust washer (2, **Figure 1**) with a suitable thickness thrust washer.

*CAUTION*
*On 1984-early 1991 models, do not correct shifter cam end play by changing the inner thrust washer (11, **Figure 1**) clearance. This washer is used to set shift cam position only. Late 1991-on models do not use the inner thrust washer.*

*NOTE*
*Inner and outer thrust washers are available from Harley-Davidson dealers in the following thicknesses: 0.017 in. (0.43 mm), 0.020 in. (0.51 mm), 0.022 in. (0.56 mm), 0.025 in. (0.63 mm), 0.028 in. (0.71 mm), 0.031 in. (0.79 mm), 0.035 in. (0.89 mm) and 0.039 in. (0.99 mm).*

d. Remove the shifter drum/right support block from the transmission case.

6. Install the left support block (**Figure 8**) onto the shifter cam.

*NOTE*
*The numbers on the left support block should face down (toward transmission) when shifter cam assembly is installed.*

7. Align the shift fork pins (**Figure 16**) with the shifter cam slots and install the shifter cam into position. See **Figure 7**. On 1984-early 1991 models, engage the transmission case dowel pins with the right support block mounting holes. On late 1991-on models, engage the left and right support block mounting holes with the transmission case dowel pins.
8. Engage the shift lever with the shifter cam (**Figure 17**).
9. Install the shifter cam mounting bolts (**Figure 6**). Tighten bolts in a crisscross pattern to 7-9 ft.-lb. (9-12 N•m).

*NOTE*
*On 1984-early 1991 models, check that the left support block is not cocked or binding on its bearing.*

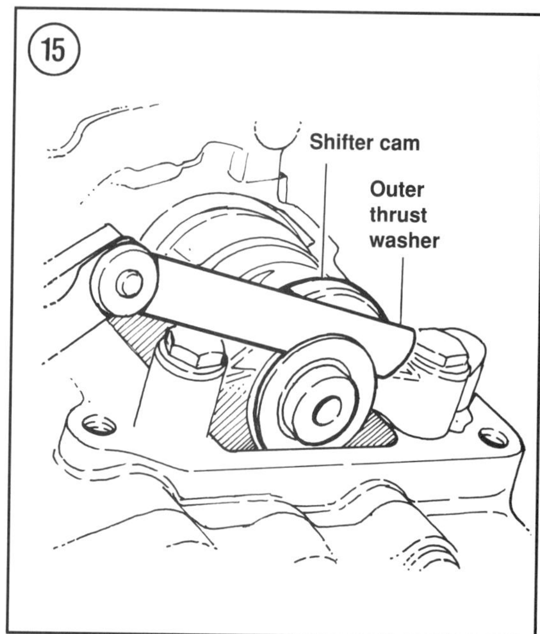

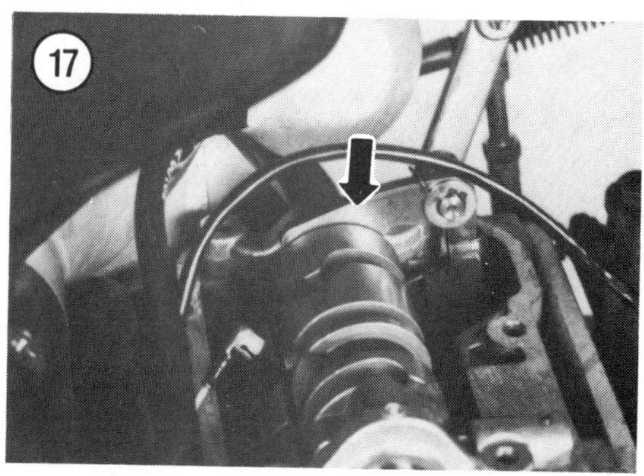

*CAUTION*
*On all models, overtightening the shifter cam mounting bolts can distort the cam follower and cause shifting problems.*

10. Perform the *Gear Engagement Check/Adjustment* procedure in this chapter.
11. Install the top cover (**Figure 5**) using a new gasket.
12. Reconnect the neutral switch wire (**Figure 4**) at the switch.

13. Install all parts previously removed.

## SHIFT FORKS

### Removal

Refer to **Figure 18** when performing this procedure.

1. Remove the shift cam as described in this chapter.
2. Remove the right-hand side shift shaft case plug (**Figure 19**).

*NOTE*
*Mark all shift forks during removal as they are different and must be reinstalled in their original position.*

3. Slide the shift shaft (**Figure 20**) out of the transmission case and remove the shift forks (**Figure 21**) from the transmission.

### Inspection

1. Inspect each shift fork (**Figure 22**) for signs of wear or damage. Replace worn or damaged shift forks as required.



18

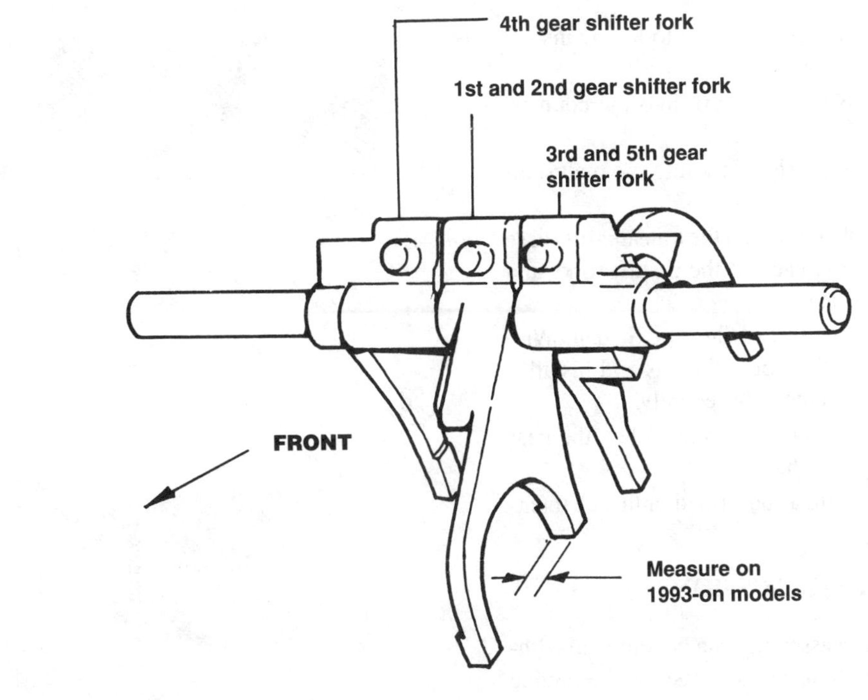

4th gear shifter fork
1st and 2nd gear shifter fork
3rd and 5th gear shifter fork
FRONT
Measure on 1993-on models

2A. On 1984-1992 models, check the shift forks for wear and bending. Place the shift forks on a flat surface at the points where they contact the sliding gear grooves (A, **Figure 23**) and measure flatness with a feeler gauge. Replace any shift fork that is worn or bent more than 0.020 in. (0.51 mm).

2B. On 1993-on models, measure the width of each shift fork finger where it contacts the sliding gear groove (**Figure 18**). The finger width service limit is 0.165 in. (4.19 mm). Replace shift fork(s) if finger width is equal to or less than the service limit.

3. Check for any arc-shaped wear or burn marks on the shift forks (B, **Figure 23**). If this is apparent, the shift fork has come in contact with the gear, indicating that the fingers are worn beyond use and the forks must be replaced.

4. Roll the shift fork shaft on a flat surface and check for bending. If the shaft is bent, it must be replaced.

5. Install each shift fork on the shift shaft. The shift fingers should slide smoothly without any sign of binding.

### Assembly

1. Coat all bearing and sliding surfaces with assembly oil.

2. Refer to **Figure 18** and **Figure 24**. Install the shift forks as follows:

   a. Insert the No. 1 shift fork into the mainshaft first gear.

   b. Install the No. 2 shift fork into the countershaft third gear.

   c. Install the No. 3 shift fork into the mainshaft second gear.

3. Insert the shift shaft through the transmission case (**Figure 20**), through each of the 3 shift forks and into the transmission case.

4. Apply a light coat of Loctite Pipe Sealant With Teflon on the shift shaft plug threads and install it (**Figure 19**). Tighten the plug securely.

5. Check that forks move smoothly when the gear position is changed by hand.

6. Install the shift cam as described in this chapter.

## TRANSMISSION

The transmission assembly can be removed without removing the transmission case or the engine assembly from the frame.

20

21

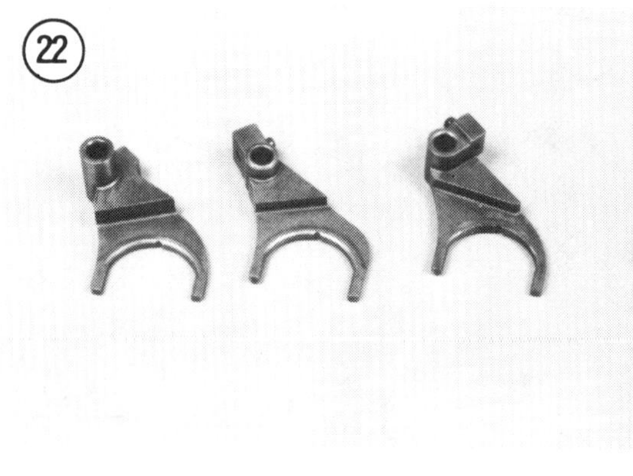

22

23

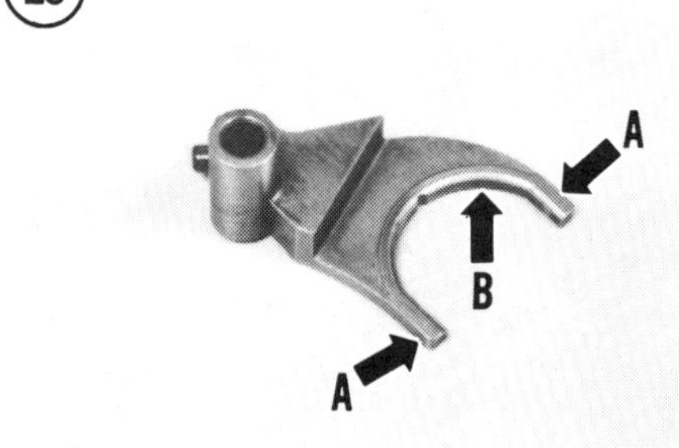

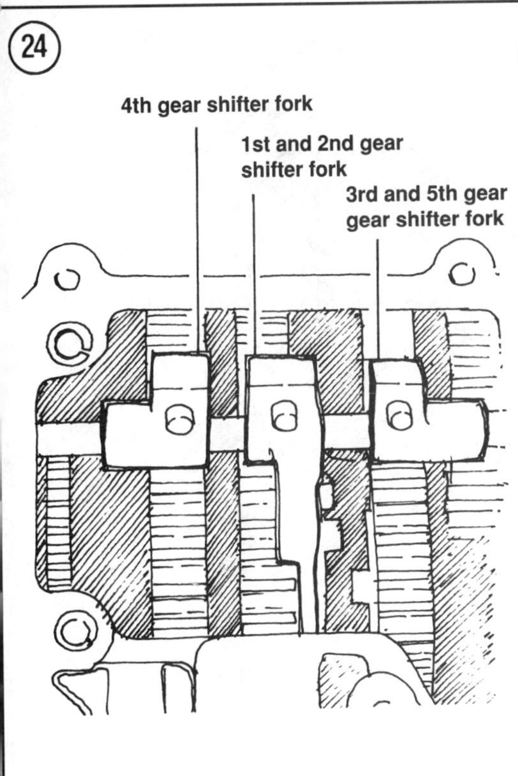

### Removal

1. Remove the exhaust pipes. See Chapter Eight.
2. Drain the transmission oil as described in Chapter Three.
3. Remove the clutch as described in Chapter Five.
4. Remove the shift forks as described in this chapter. See **Figure 24**.
5. Remove the clutch arm (**Figure 25**).
6A. *1986*: Remove the transmission side cover (**Figure 26**).
6B. *1987-on*: Remove the transmission side cover as described in this chapter.
7. Remove the roller (**Figure 27**) and pushrod (**Figure 28**).
8. Turn the transmission by hand and mesh the transmission into 2 gears at the same time so that the shafts cannot rotate.
9. Loosen the countershaft and mainshaft locknuts and spacers. See **Figure 29**.

*NOTE*
*On all models, the transmission can be removed without removing the main drive gear. However, if main drive gear removal is required, the Bearing Race Puller and Installation Tool (part No. HD-34902) will be required. See **Figure 30** and **Figure 31**.*

*NOTE*
*The main drive gear bearing will have to be replaced if the main drive gear is removed. Removal of the main drive gear damages its bearing.*

10. To remove the main drive gear:
    a. Remove the primary chain case as described in Chapter Five.

7

b. Install the bearing race puller onto the bearing inner race as shown in **Figure 32**.

c. Remove the bearing inner race from the transmission mainshaft. See **Figure 33**.

d. On 1984-early 1991 models, remove the sprocket nut locking screw (**Figure 34**). On late 1991-on models, remove the 2 locking screws and lockplate (**Figure 35**).

e. Have an assistant apply the rear brake.

NOTE
*The countershaft nut uses left-hand threads. Turn the nut clockwise to remove it.*

f. Using a deep socket, loosen and remove the countershaft nut (A, **Figure 36**).

NOTE
*Harley-Davidson dealers sell a deep socket (part No. HD-94660-37) that can be used to remove the countershaft nut.*

g. Loosen the rear axle adjuster to obtain as much drive belt slack as possible.

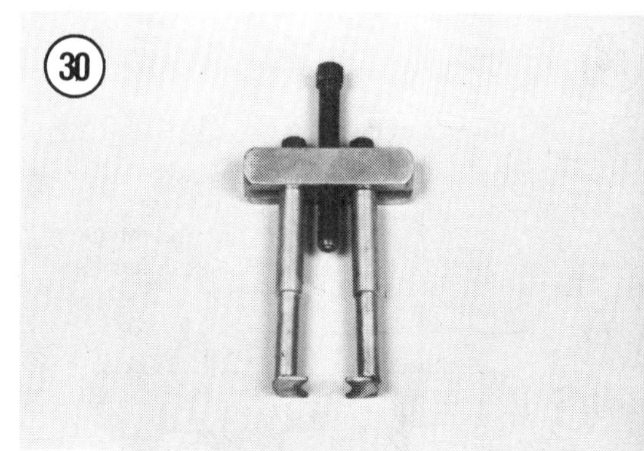


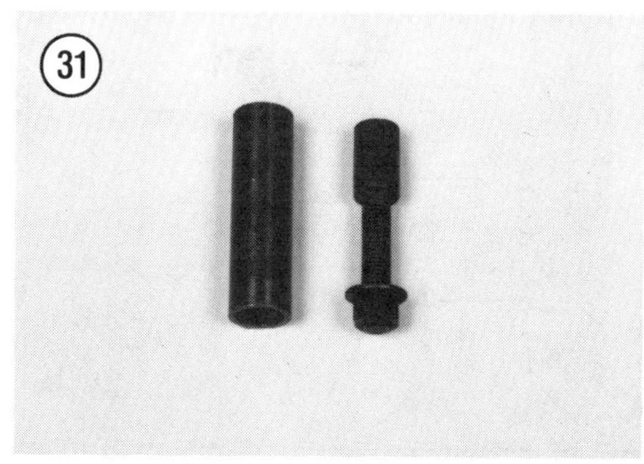

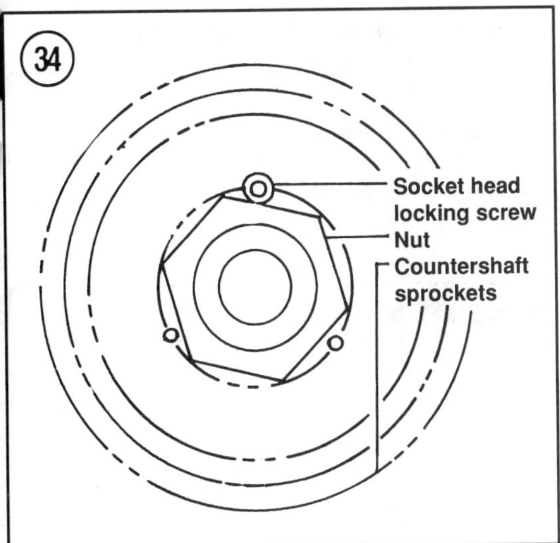


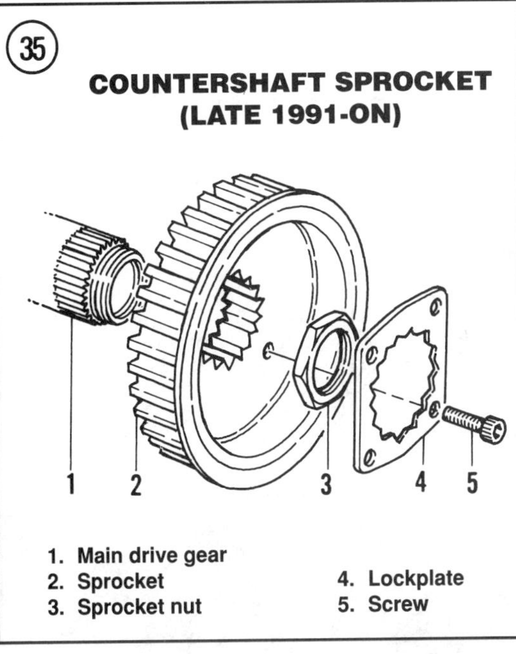

h. Remove the countershaft sprocket (B, **Figure 36**).

CAUTION

*Wrap the mainshaft clutch hub splines on 1990 and later models with tape to prevent the splines from damaging the inner primary housing oil seal.*

11. Remove the transmission access cover mounting fasteners (**Figure 37**). Then remove the access cover

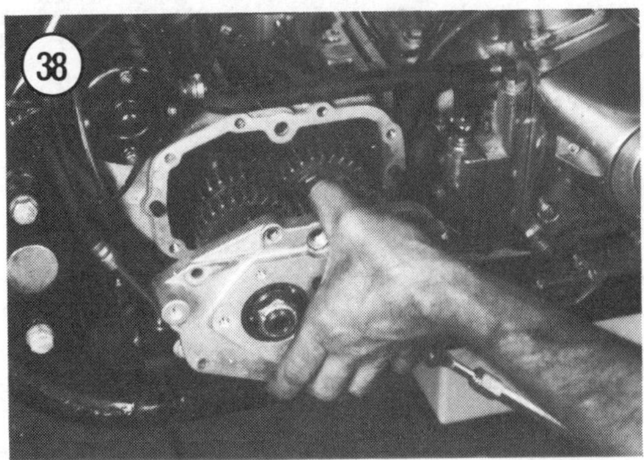

7

(**Figure 38**) together with the countershaft and mainshaft as an assembly. See **Figure 39**.

### Transmission Shafts Removal/Installation

Refer to **Figure 40** for this procedure.

1. Remove the countershaft and mainshaft nuts (**Figure 41**) loosened during transmission removal. Then remove the washers and transmission shafts from the access cover. See **Figure 42**.

2. Remove the pushrod and clutch release bearing assembly from the mainshaft.

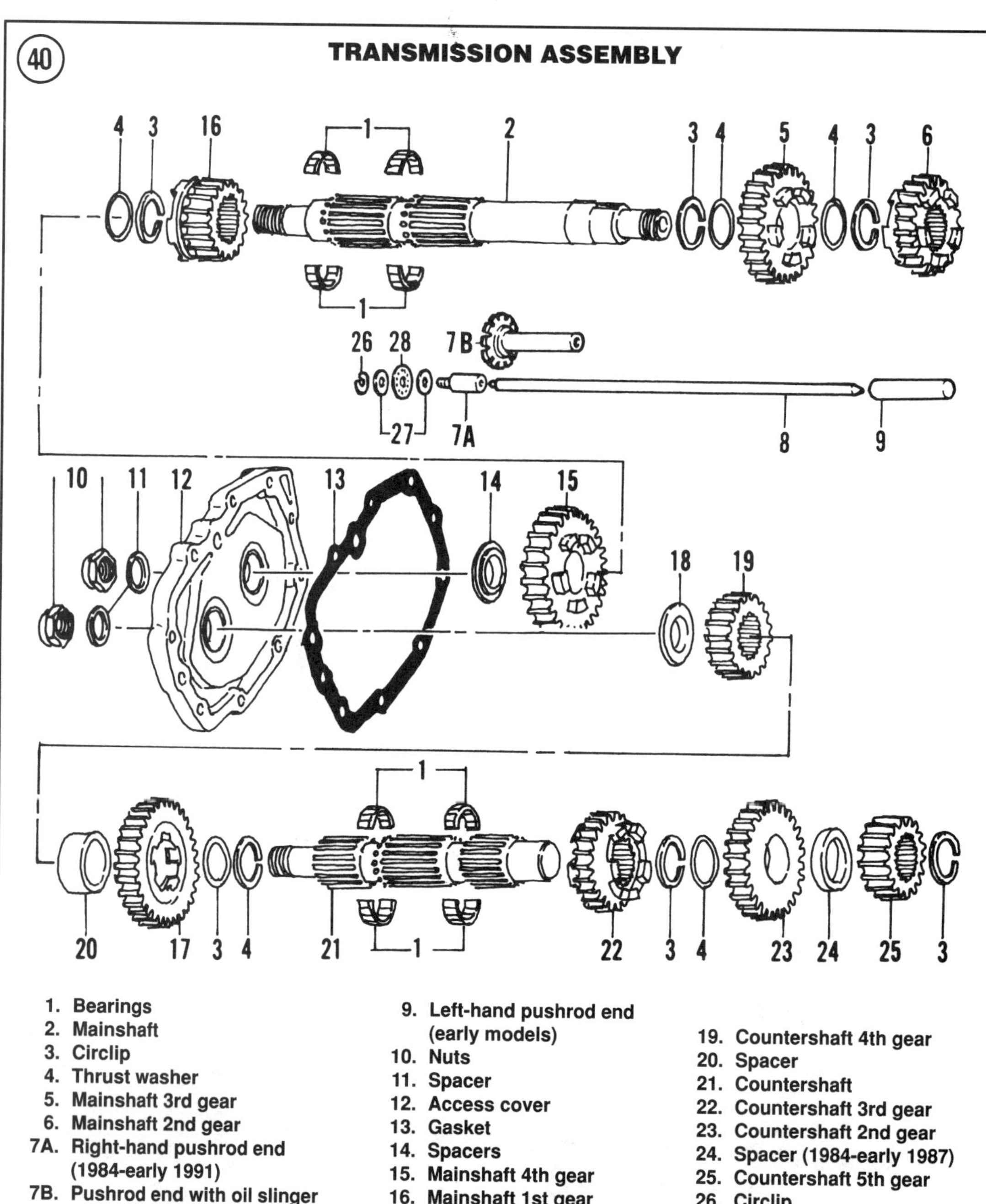

41

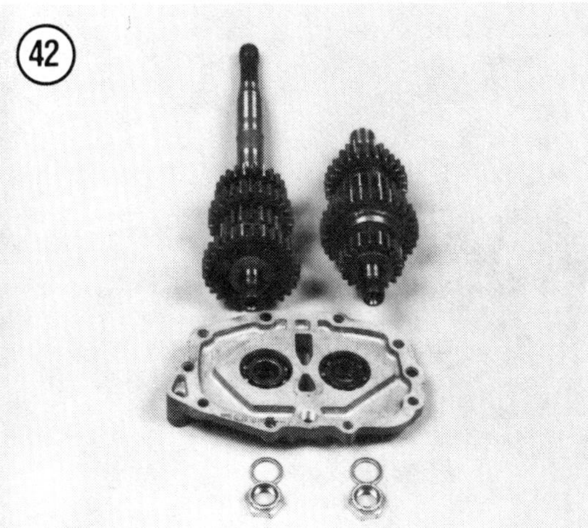
42

3. Assemble by reversing these steps. Tighten the countershaft and mainshaft nuts after installing the transmission assembly into the transmission housing.

## Countershaft Disassembly/Reassembly

Refer to **Figure 40** for this procedure.

1. Disassemble the countershaft as follows:
   a. Spacer (**Figure 43**).
   b. Countershaft 4th gear (**Figure 44**).
   c. Spacer (**Figure 45**).
   d. Countershaft 1st gear (**Figure 46**).
   e. Bearings (**Figure 47**).
   f. Thrust washer (**Figure 48**).
   g. Circlip (**Figure 49**).
   h. Countershaft 3rd gear (**Figure 50**).
   i. Circlip (**Figure 51**).
   j. Countershaft 5th gear (**Figure 52**).

NOTE
*The spacer (**Figure 53**) is used on 1986-early 1987 models only.*

   k. Spacer (**Figure 53**).

7

43

44

45

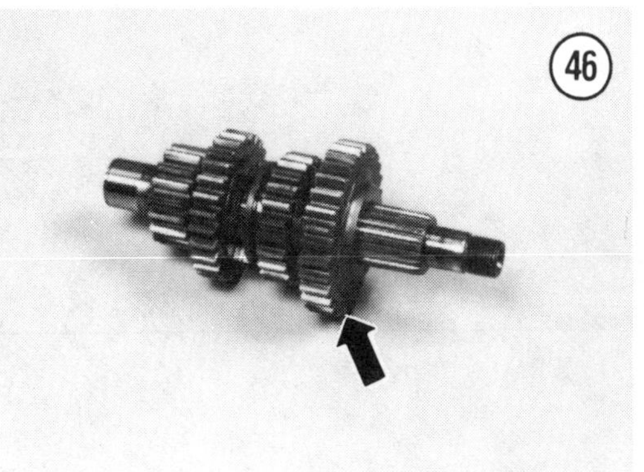
46

l. Countershaft 2nd gear (**Figure 54**).

m. Bearings (**Figure 55**).

n. Thrust washer (**Figure 56**).

o. Circlip (**Figure 57**).

2. Inspect the countershaft assembly as described under *Inspection* in this chapter.

3. Assemble the countershaft by reversing Step 1, noting the following:

   a. Make sure all circlips seat completely in their grooves.

   b. Make sure the bearing halves are installed correctly (**Figure 58**).

47

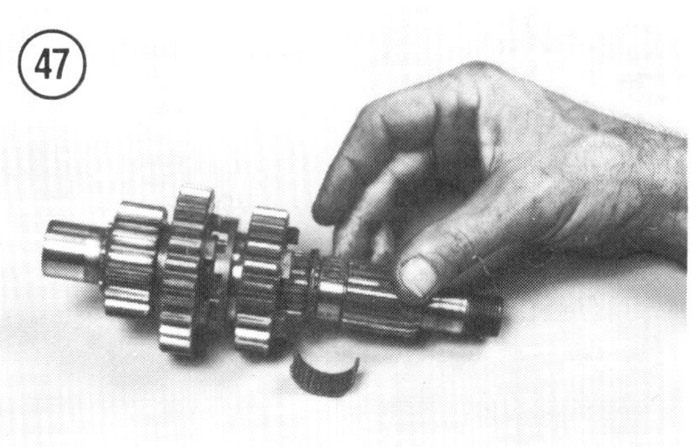

50

48

51

49

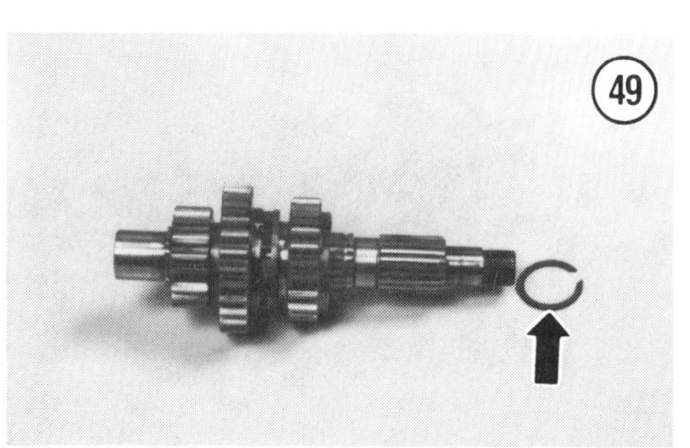

52

53

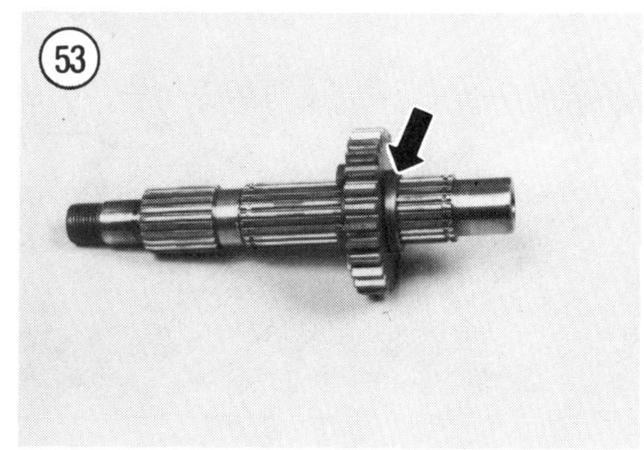

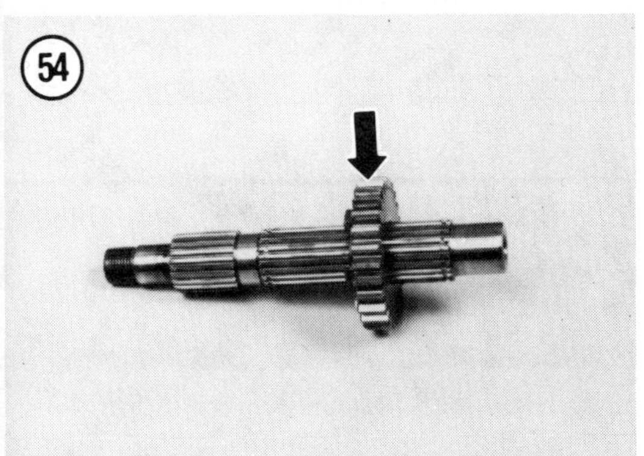


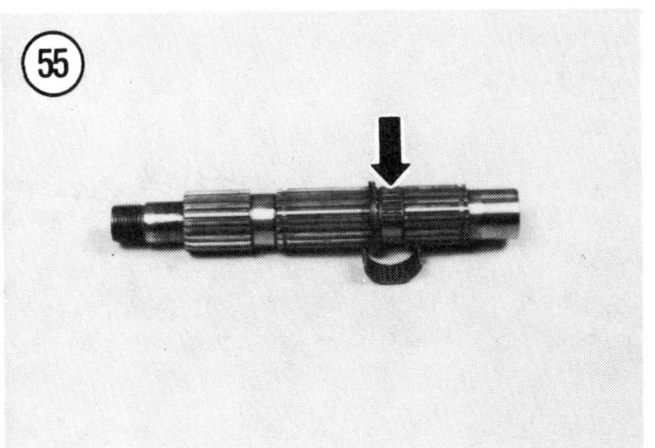


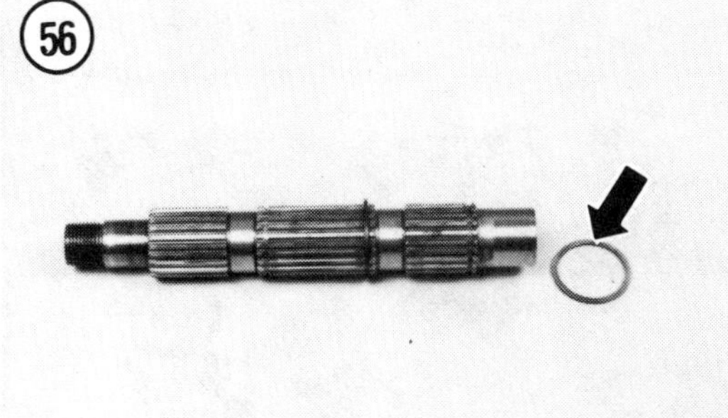


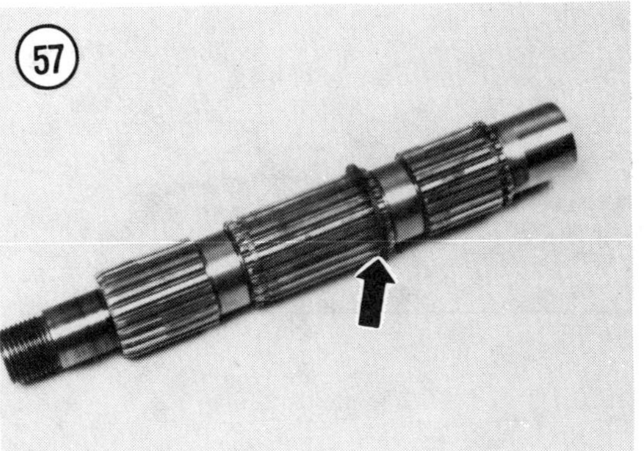


c. Make sure all gears are correctly installed. See **Figure 59**.

*NOTE*
*If you have a 1986-early 1987 model and you replaced countershaft 5th gear, do not install the spacer (**Figure 53**). Confirm this with your dealer when purchasing the new 5th gear.*

**Mainshaft Disassembly/Reassembly**

Refer to **Figure 40** for this procedure.

1. Disassemble the mainshaft as follows:
   a. Mainshaft spacer (**Figure 60**).

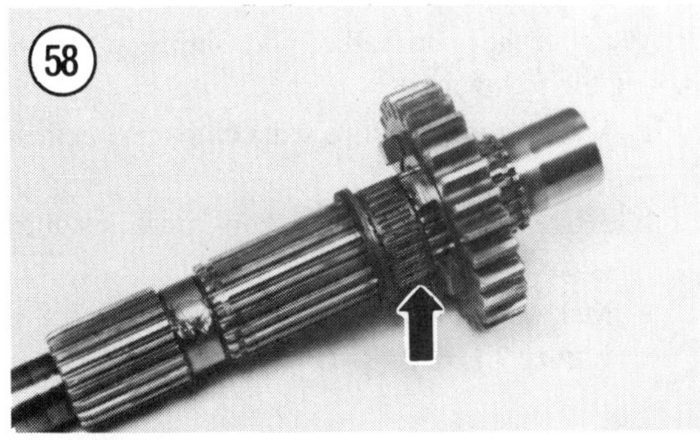


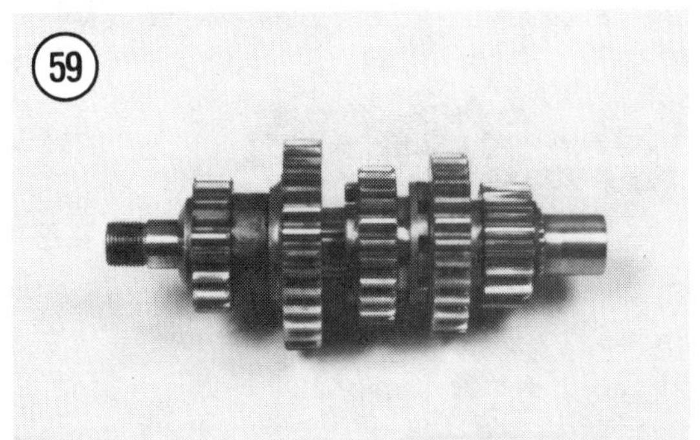

b. Mainshaft 4th gear (**Figure 61**).
c. Bearings (**Figure 62**).
d. Thrust washer (**Figure 63**).
e. Mainshaft 2nd gear (**Figure 64**).
f. Circlip (**Figure 65**).
g. Mainshaft 1st gear (**Figure 66**).
h. Circlip (**Figure 67**).
i. Thrust washer (**Figure 68**).
j. Mainshaft 3rd gear (**Figure 69**).
k. Bearings (**Figure 70**).
l. Thrust washer (**Figure 71**).
m. Circlip (**Figure 72**).

2. Inspect the mainshaft assembly as described under *Inspection* in this chapter.

3. Assemble the mainshaft by reversing Step 1 while noting the following:
   a. Make sure all circlips seat completely in their grooves.
   b. Make sure the bearing halves are installed correctly (**Figure 58**).
   c. Make sure all gears are correctly installed. See **Figure 73**.

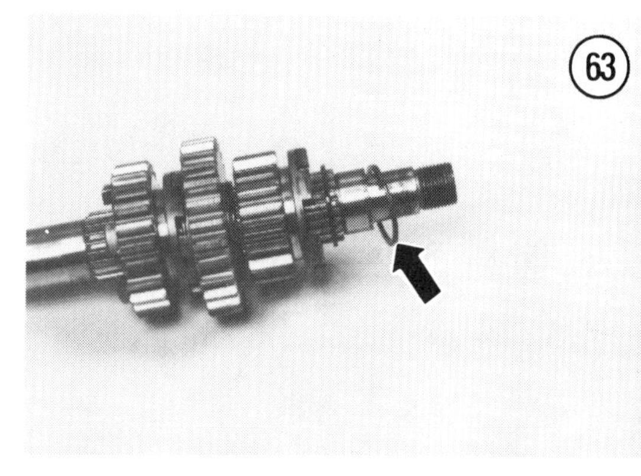
63

64

61

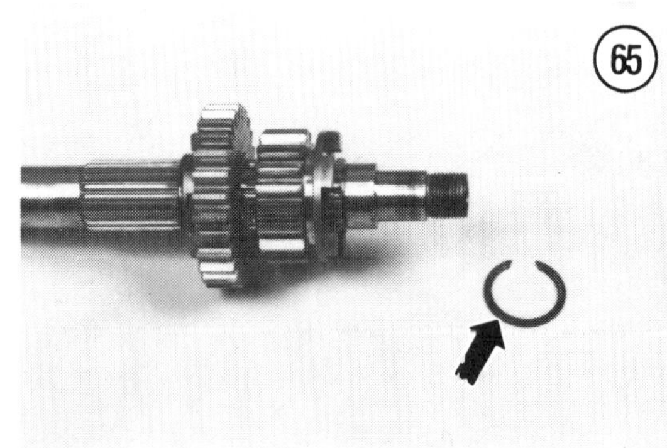
65

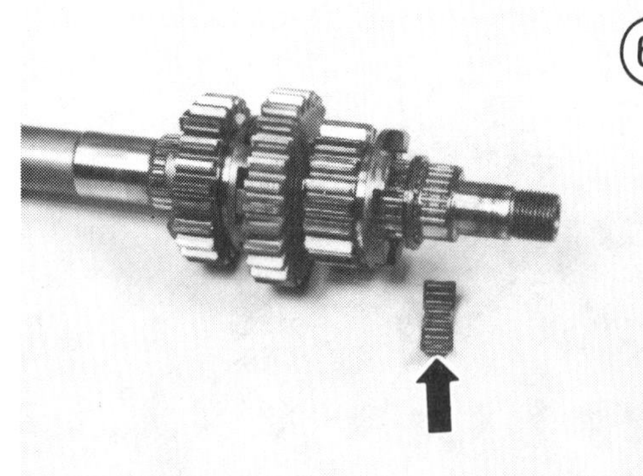
62

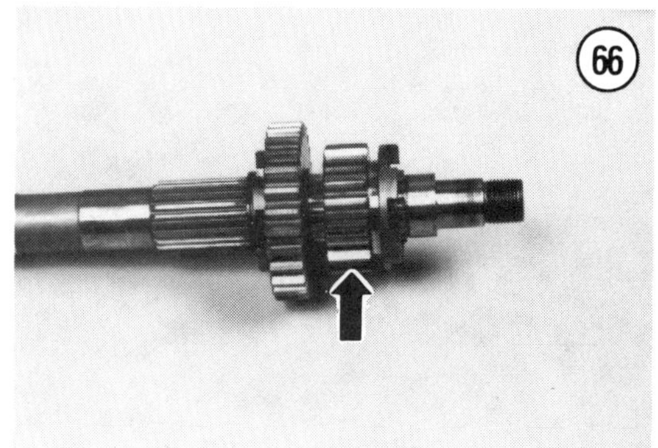
66

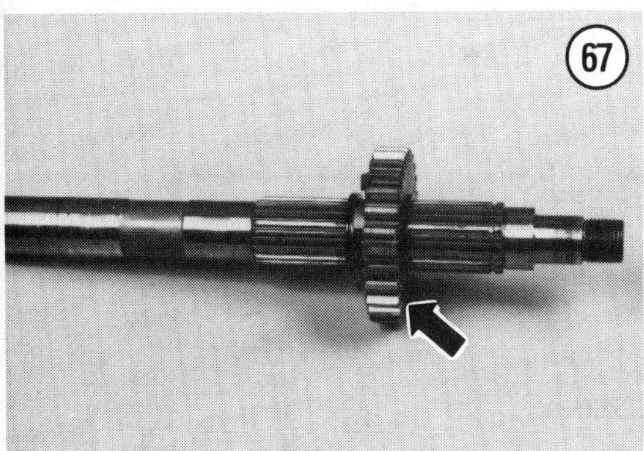


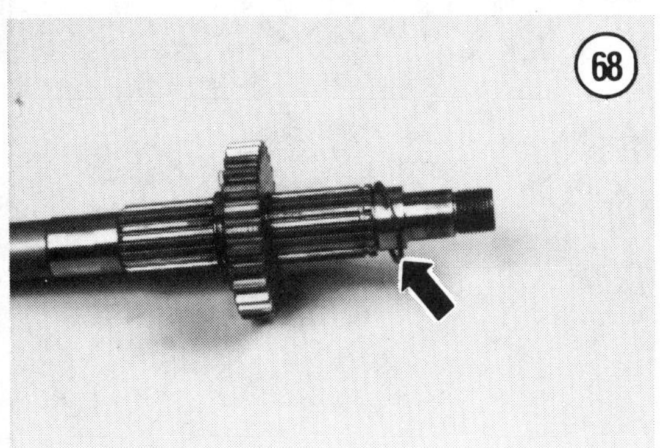


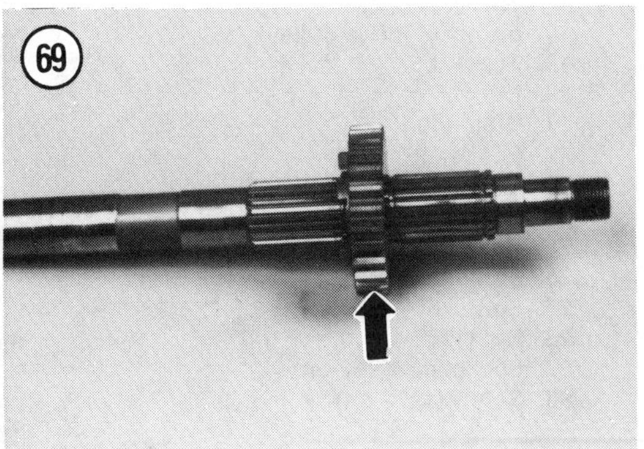


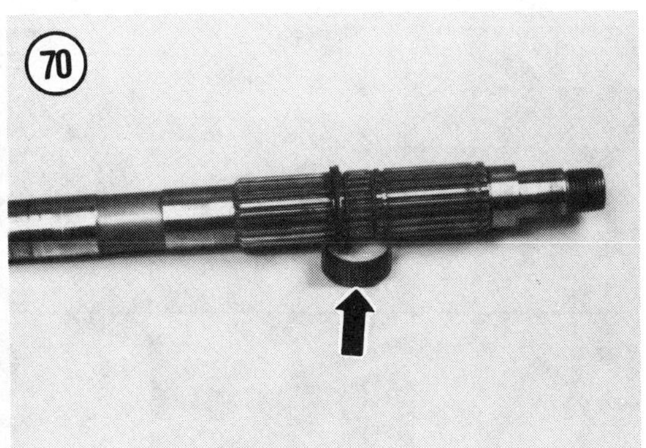


## Main Drive Gear Removal/Inspection/Installation

Refer to **Figure 74** for this procedure.

1. Place the transmission case in a press.

2. Using the Main Drive Gear Remover and Installer (part No. HD-35316), remove the main drive gear (**Figure 75**). Remove the gear through the access cover opening (**Figure 76**).

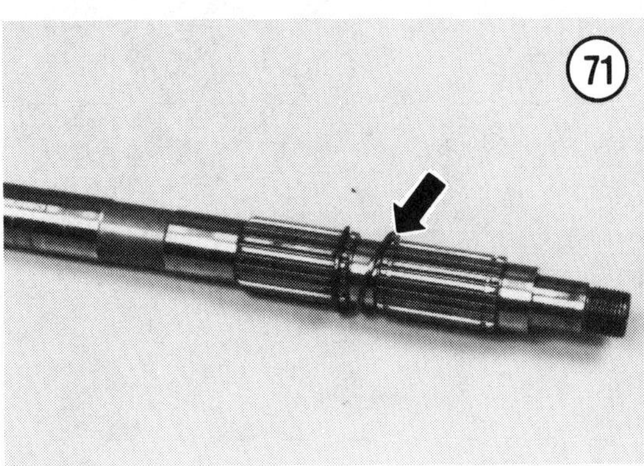


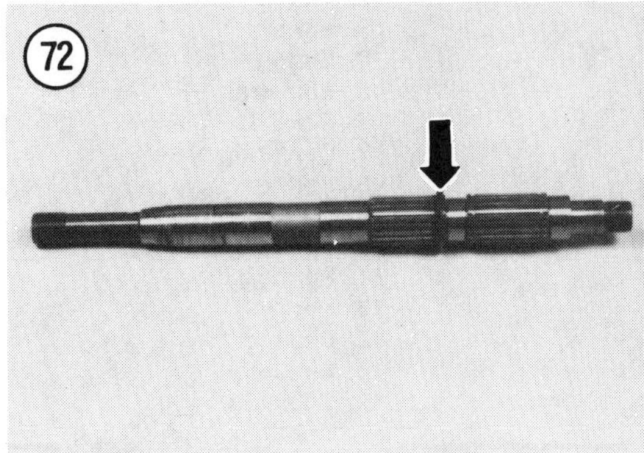


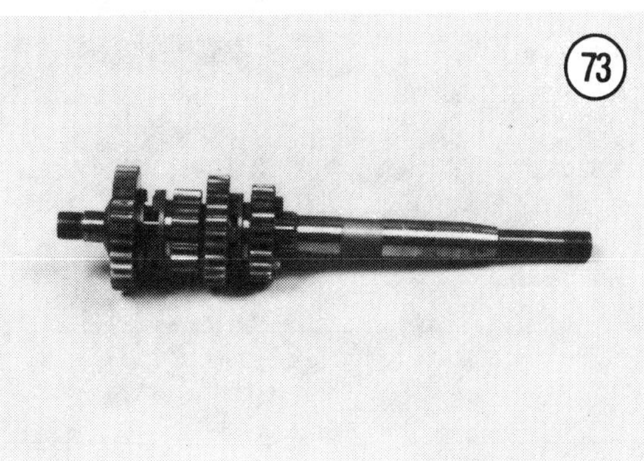

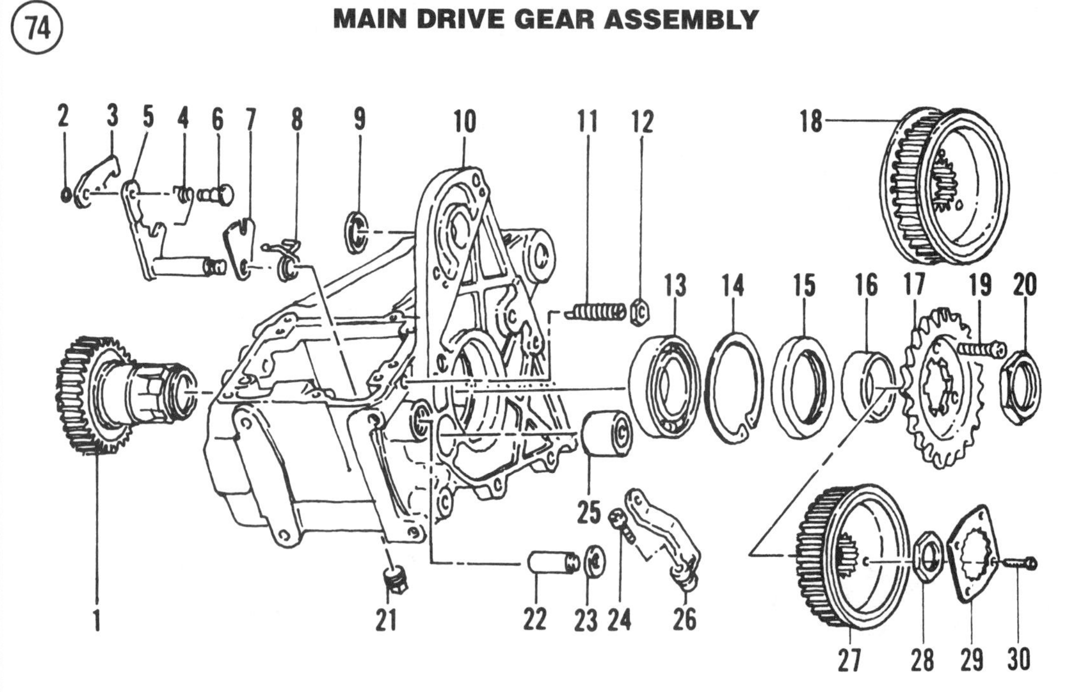

**74** MAIN DRIVE GEAR ASSEMBLY

1. Main drive gear
2. Circlip
3. Pawl
4. Spring
5. Shift arm
6. Pin
7. Centering plate
8. Spring
9. Oil seal
10. Transmission case
11. Spring
12. Nut
13. Bearing
14. Circlip
15. Oil seal
16. Spacer
17. Sprocket
18. Sprocket (drive pulley)
19. Screw
20. Nut
21. Drain plug
22. Spacer
23. Oil seal
24. Screw
25. Bearing
26. Shifter lever
27. Sprocket (1992-on)
28. Nut (1992-on)
29. Lockplate (1992-on)
30. Screw (1992-on)

75

76

*NOTE*
*If the main drive gear remover/installer is not used to remove the main drive gear, check the housing bearing for damage.*

3. Check the main drive gear (**Figure 77**) and shaft splines (**Figure 78**) for wear or damage. Replace if necessary.

4. Check the needle bearings (**Figure 79**) on the inside of the main drive gear. If these bearings are questionable, check the transmission mainshaft bearing race surface for pitting or wear grooves. If such wear is found, have a Harley-Davidson dealer replace the main drive gear needle bearings and seal.

5. Place the main drive gear into the transmission and align with the bearing.

6. Install the main drive gear using the main drive gear installation tool (part No. HD-34723).



### Transmission Inspection

1. Examine gears for worn or chipped teeth, pitting, scoring or other damage. See **Figure 80**.

2. Examine dog clutches (**Figure 81**) for chips and rounded edges or wear.

3. Check the shafts for worn or damaged splines or damaged circlip grooves. See **Figure 82**.

4. Slip gears on shafts and check for free movement without appreciable play.

5. Replace worn or damaged thrust washers.

6. Check the needle bearings (**Figure 83**) for wear or roughness.

7. Check the access cover bearings (**Figure 84**) for wear or roughness. If replacement is required, perform the following:

a. Remove the circlips from the access cover grooves.
b. Remove the bearings with a press.
c. Clean the access cover in solvent and dry thoroughly.
d. Align the new bearings with the access cover so that the ID number on each bearing faces toward the outside of the access cover.
e. When pressing in the new bearings, support the opposite side of the access cover at the bearing bores with a flat plate; otherwise you may damage the access cover when pressing the bearings in.
f. Install the bearing circlips into the access cover grooves. Make sure each circlip seats in its groove completely.

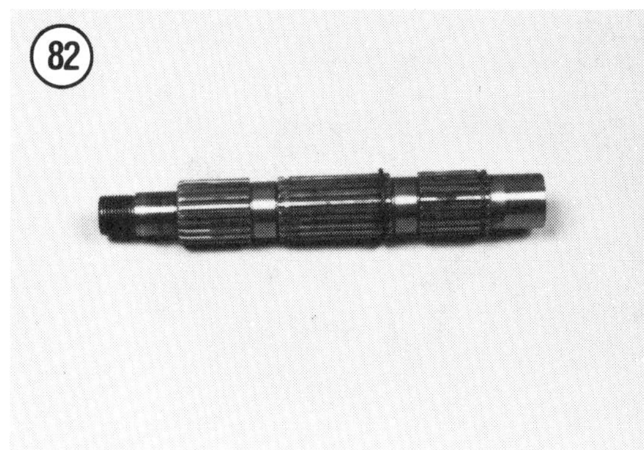

### Transmission Installation

1. If the main drive gear was removed, install it as described in this chapter.

*CAUTION*
*Wrap the mainshaft clutch hub splines on 1990 and later models with tape to prevent the splines from damaging the inner primary housing oil seal.*

2. Install the transmission assembly (**Figure 85**) into the transmission case, using a new access cover gasket. Install and tighten the access cover bolts and screws as follows:
   a. 5/16 in. bolts: 13-16 ft.-lb. (17.9-22.1 N•m).
   b. 1/4 in. screws: 7-9 ft.-lb. (9.7-12.4 N•m).
3. Lock the transmission into two different gears.
4. Tighten the countershaft and mainshaft locknuts to 27-33 ft.-lb. (37.3-45.5 N•m). See **Figure 86**.
5. Install the spacer and countershaft sprocket on the main drive gear (**Figure 87**). Apply a drop of Loctite 262 (red) to the countershaft sprocket nut threads and install the nut hand-tight.

*NOTE*
*The sprocket nut uses left-hand threads. Turn the sprocket nut counterclockwise to tighten it.*

6. Using the same socket as during removal, tighten the sprocket nut to the torque specification in **Table 3**.
7A. On 1984-early 1991 models, locate a lockscrew hole in the sprocket that most closely matches that

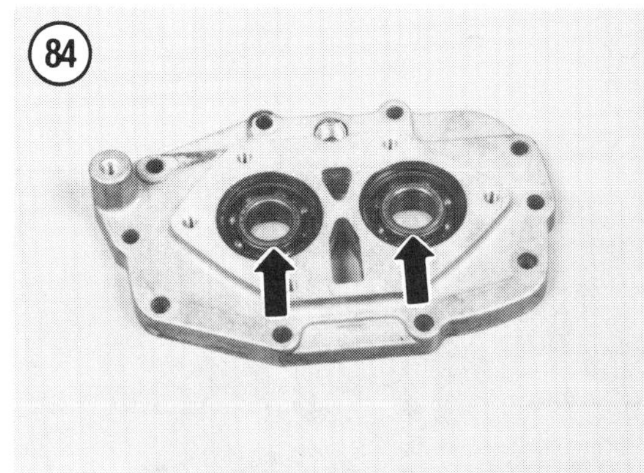

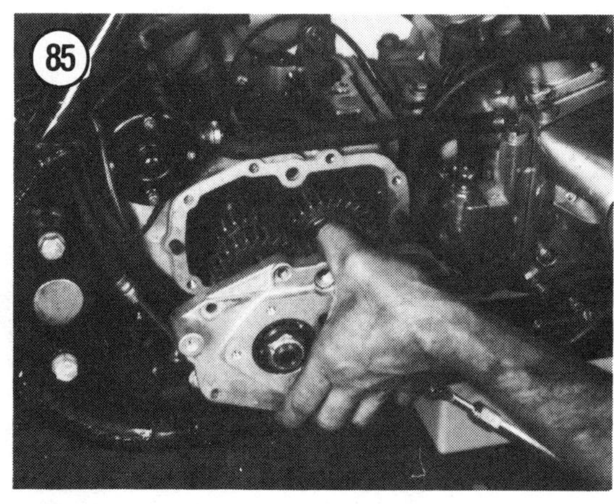

alignment in **Figure 88**. If none of the tapped holes align, turn the sprocket counterclockwise to obtain correct alignment. Coat the lockscrew threads with Loctite 242 (blue) and screw it into the sprocket and main drive gear tapped threads. Tighten the lockscrew to 50-60 in.-lb. (5.7-6.9 N•m) on 1984-1992 models or to 7-9 ft.-lb. (9-12 N•m) on 1993-on models.

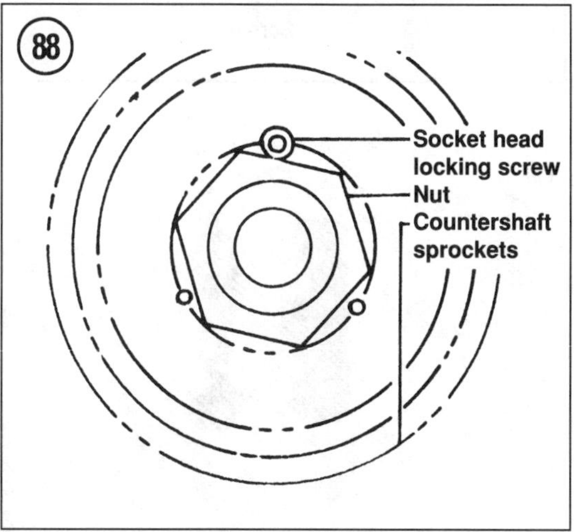


*WARNING*
*Do not exceed 120 ft.-lb. (163 N•m) or loosen the sprocket nut when aligning the lockscrew threads.*

7B. On late 1991-on models, install the lockplate (**Figure 89**) and align 2 of the lockplate holes with the 2 tapped holes in the sprocket (**Figure 90**). If you cannot get the holes to align, turn the sprocket counterclockwise to obtain correct alignment. Coat the lockscrew threads with Loctite 242 (blue). Then install the screws and tighten to 7-9 ft.-lb. (9-12 N•m).

*WARNING*
*Do not exceed 120 ft.-lb. (163 N•m) or loosen the sprocket nut when aligning the lockscrew threads.*

8. Install the main drive gear bearing race as follows, using the puller and installation tool part No. HD-34902 (**Figure 91**).

a. Measure the length of the bearing inner race. Early 1985 models have a race 0.8975-0.8125 in. (22.796-20.637 mm) long. Late 1985 and later models have a race that is 0.9950-1.000 in. (25.273-25.4 mm) long. Length of race will determine its final installation position.

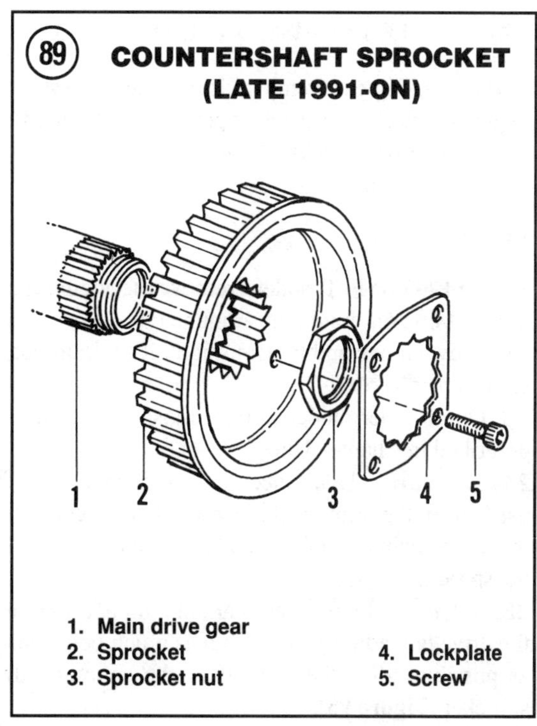


7

b. Slide the bearing inner race on the mainshaft (**Figure 92**). The bearing's chamfered edge should face toward the transmission.
c. Thread the tool's sleeve pilot onto the mainshaft (the mainshaft uses left-hand threads).
d. Slide the sleeve over the sleeve pilot and rest it against the bearing race (**Figure 93**).
e. Place a suitable size washer over the adapter screw and install the nut.

*NOTE*
*The installation specification described in sub-step f must be maintained to align the bearing inner race properly with the bearing outer race in the primary chain case.*

f. Place a wrench on the end of the sleeve pilot screw flats. Then tighten the large nut until the bearing inner race inside edge is 0.200 in. (5.08 mm) (early 1985 models with the 0.8975-0.8125 in. [22.796-20.637 mm] long race) or 0.100 in. (2.54 mm) (late 1985 and later models with the 0.9950-1.000 in. [25.273-25.4 mm] long race) from the drive gear. See **Figure 94**.

9. Install the shift forks as described in this chapter.
10. Install all parts previously removed.

## TRANSMISSION CASE

Transmission case removal is only necessary if it requires replacement or when performing extensive frame repair or replacing a frame.

### Removal

1A. On 1993-on FLT models, remove the engine and transmission oil drain plugs mounted in the oil pan and allow engine and transmission oil to drain out; see Chapter Three.
1B. On all other models, drain transmission oil as described in Chapter Three.
2A. *Chain drive*: Disconnect the rear chain boots (if used) from the primary chaincase. Then disconnect the drive chain master link and pull the chain off of the sprocket.
2B. *Belt drive*: Loosen the rear axle nut and loosen the drive belt adjusters to obtain as much belt slack as possible. Slide the belt off of the countershaft sprocket (**Figure 95**).
3. If necessary, remove the main drive gear and transmission shafts as described in this chapter.
4. Remove the starter as described in Chapter Nine.
5. Disconnect the foot shifter rod from the shifter arm.
6. Remove the shifter lever from the shifter arm.
7. If necessary, remove the shift arm as described later in this chapter.
8. Label and then disconnect the oil hoses at the transmission case and oil filter mount (early models).
9A. On 1993-on FLT models, disconnect the following hoses (**Figure 96**):

a. Transmission case-to-crankcase hose.

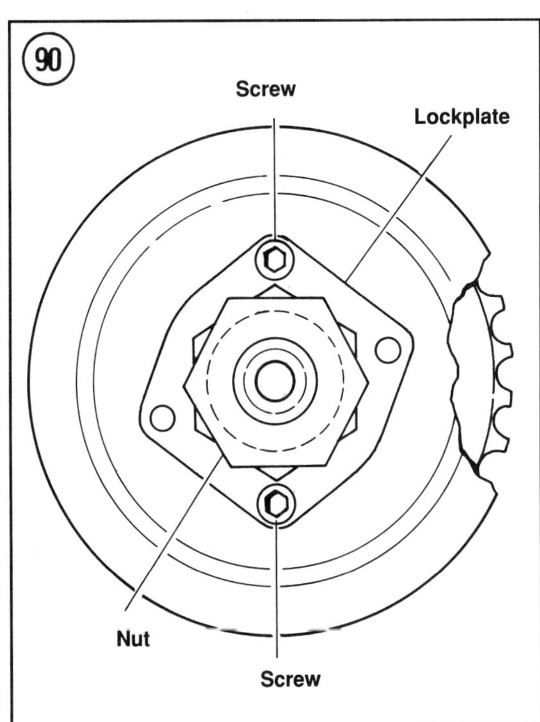


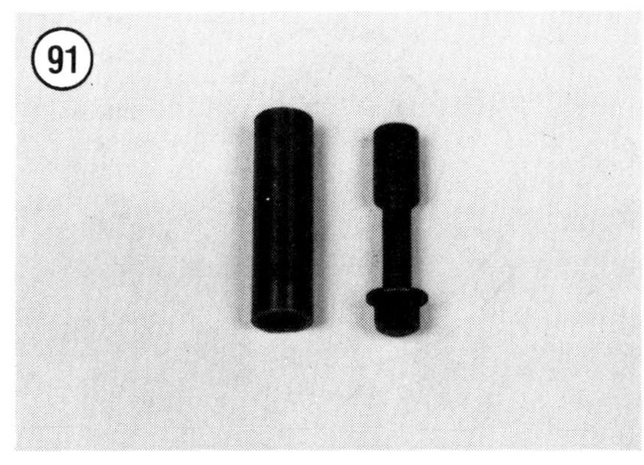

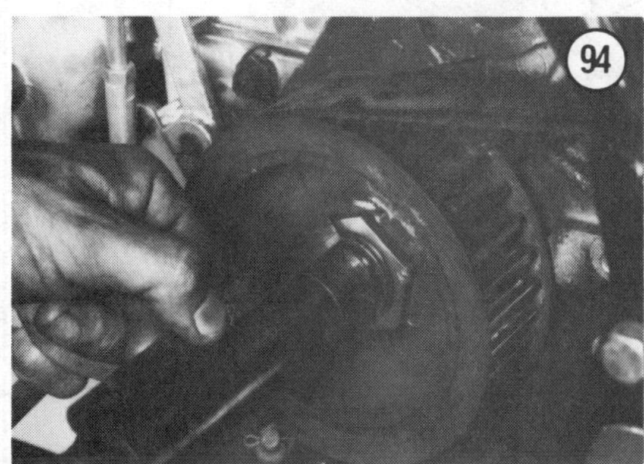

b. Oil pan-to-oil pump hose.
c. Transmission case-to-oil filter hose.

9B. On all other models, disconnect the transmission vent hose.

10A. *1984*: Unscrew and remove the oil filter at the bottom of the transmission case.

10B. *1985-on except 1993-on FLT*: Label the engine oil hoses at the oil filter mount. Then remove the oil filter mount.

11. Support the engine with wood blocks and a suitable jack.

*CAUTION*
*On 1993-on FLT models, do not damage the oil pan when positioning the jack.*

12. Remove the swing arm pivot shaft covers (**Figure 97**).

*NOTE*
*Harley-Davidson has used 3 different types of pivot shafts since 1984. Refer to* ***Figure 94*** *and the following procedure for your model year.*

13A. *1984-early 1986*: The pivot shaft on these models is threaded on both ends; each end is secured with a washer and nut. Remove the pivot shaft as follows:

a. Remove the cover plug from the end of the pivot shaft mounting brackets on FXR models.
b. Remove the right-hand pivot shaft nut and spacer.
c. Remove the pivot shaft mounting brackets on FXR models or remove the left- and right-hand passenger footpeg mounting brackets on FLT models.
d. Align the end of an aluminum or brass rod and tap the pivot shaft out of the swing arm.

13B. *Late 1986-1988*: A dual pivot shaft assembly is used on these models. The left- and right-hand pivot shafts thread onto a center stud (**Figure 98**). Remove the pivot shafts as follows:

a. Remove the cover plug from the end of the pivot shaft mounting brackets on FXR models. If you have a 1987-1988 FXR, remove the spring clips installed inside the mounting bracket access hole (**Figure 98**).
b. Hold the left-hand pivot bolt with a wrench and loosen the right-hand pivot bolt.

7

96

## OIL PAN ASSEMBLY (1993-ON FLT)

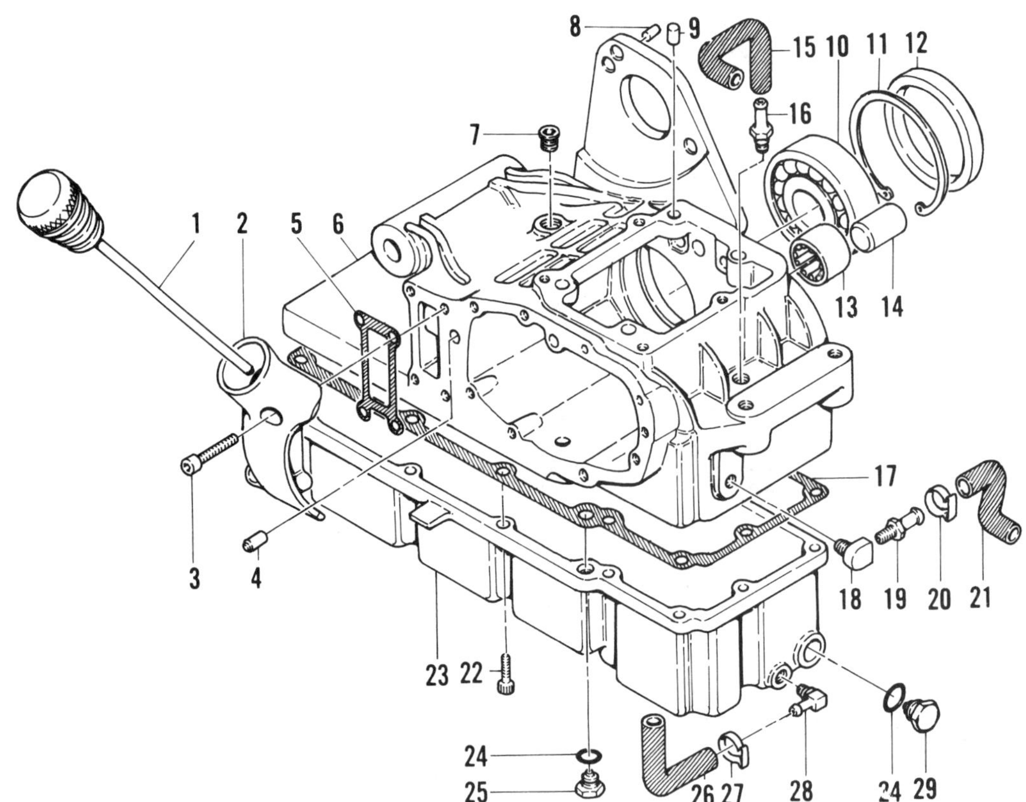


1. Oil filler cap
2. Oil filter spout
3. Bolt
4. Dowel pin
5. Gasket
6. Transmission housing
7. Plug
8. Dowel pin
9. Pillow block pin
10. Bearing
11. Circlip
12. Oil seal
13. Needle bearing
14. Spacer
15. Transmission housing-to-crankcase hose
16. Hose fitting
17. Gasket
18. Hose fitting adapter
19. Hose fitting
20. Hose clamp
21. Transmission housing-to-oil filter hose
22. Bolt
23. Oil pan
24. O-ring
25. Transmission oil plug
26. Oil pan-to-oil pump hose
27. Hose clamp
28. Hose fitting
29. Engine oil drain plug

97

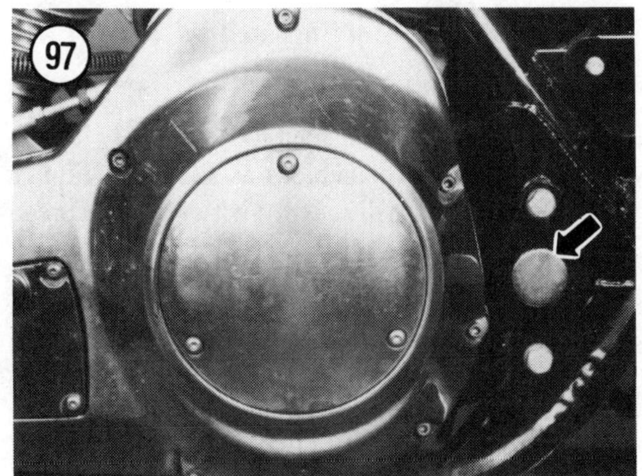

c. Remove the pivot shaft mounting brackets on FXR models or remove the left- and right-hand passenger footpeg mounting brackets on FLT models.

d. Select a piece of aluminum or brass rod with an O.D. larger than the center stud O.D. Selecting the proper size rod to use will prevent you from damaging the threads on the center stud. Insert the rod through the swing arm from the right-hand side, center it against the center stud and carefully tap the center stud and left-hand pivot shaft out of the swing arm.

**REAR SWING ARM** (98)

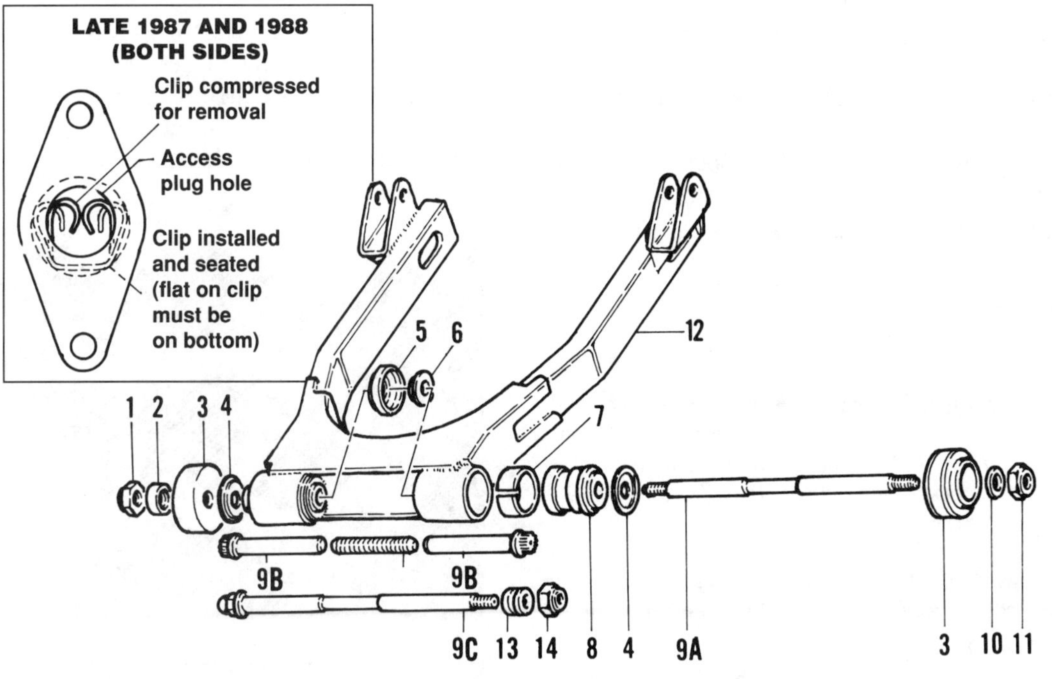

LATE 1987 AND 1988
(BOTH SIDES)
Clip compressed for removal
Access plug hole
Clip installed and seated (flat on clip must be on bottom)
1
2
3
4
5
6
7
12
9B
9B
9C
13
14
8
4
9A
3
10
11


1. Nut
2. Washer (early models)
3. Rubber mount
4. Nylon washer
5. Plastic ring
6. Washer
7. Tolerance ring
8. Clevebloc
9A. Pivot shaft (1984-early 1986)
9B. Pivot bolt (late 1986-1988)
9C. Pivot shaft (1989-on)
10. Washer (1984-early 1986)
11. Nut (1984-early 1986)
12. Swing arm
13. Cup washer (1989-on)
14. Nut (1989-on)

13C. *1989-on*: The swing arm pivots on a pivot shaft installed from the right-hand side (**Figure 98**). Remove the pivot shaft as follows:

a. Remove the cover plug from the end of the pivot shaft mounting brackets on FXR models.
b. Hold the right-hand pivot shaft nut with a wrench and loosen the left-hand nut. Then remove the nut and the cup washer.
c. Remove the pivot shaft mounting brackets on FXR models or remove the left- and right-hand passenger footpeg mounting brackets on FLT models.
d. Align the end of an aluminum or brass rod and tap the pivot shaft out of the swing arm.
e. Remove the pivot shaft.

14. Remove the bolts and washers securing the engine to the transmission.
15. Remove the transmission-to-primary chain case mounting bolts and locking tabs.
16. On some 1993-on FLT models, it may be necessary to remove the oil fill spout (**Figure 96**). To do so, remove the oil fill spout mounting bolts and remove the oil fill spout and gasket.
17. Remove the transmission housing (**Figure 95**).

## Installation

*NOTE*
*If the main drive gear was not removed from the transmission case, slip the drive belt around the transmission sprocket as the case is installed into the frame.*

1. Install the transmission housing into the frame. Install the bolts and nuts and tighten finger-tight at this time.
2. Install the swing arm at the back of the transmission. If the swing arm will not fit into the transmission, it will be necessary to spread the clevebloc bushings apart. Perform the following:

a. Install the Clevebloc Spreading Tool (part No. HD-33805) between the cleveblocs as shown in **Figure 100**.

*NOTE*
*The clevebloc spreading tool is shown in **Figure 100**. If you don't have the Harley-Davidson tool, you can substitute with a piece of threaded rod, 2 large washers and 2 nuts.*

b. Assemble the threaded rod, nuts and washers between the cleveblocs as shown in **Figure 100**, then turn the nuts with a wrench to spread the cleveblocs apart approximately 4 9/16 in. (115.9 mm).
c. Remove the tool and check the swing arm fit at the back of the transmission. When the swing arm fits into the transmission correctly, proceed to Step 3 for your model.

3A. *1984-early 1986*: Install the pivot shaft assembly as follows:

a. Lay the pivot shaft assembly out in the order shown in **Figure 98**. Reclean and dry parts as required before assembly.
b. Identify the left side of the pivot shaft and slide the left-hand rubber mount (with shoulder facing outward) onto the pivot shaft. Then install the washer and nut onto the pivot shaft; tighten nut until it bottoms out on shaft threads.

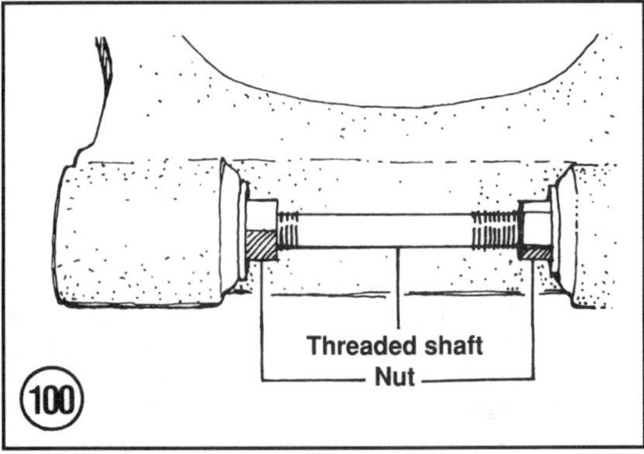

c. Slide the nylon washer onto the pivot shaft and seat it against the rubber mount so that the smaller diameter on the washer faces inward.
d. Wipe the pivot shaft with Loctite Anti-Seize or equivalent.
e. Install the pivot shaft through the swing arm from the left-hand side.
f. Install the right-hand nylon washer (smaller washer diameter facing inward), rubber mount (shoulder facing outward), washer and nut. Tighten nut finger-tight at this time.

*NOTE*
*If you have a late 1986-1988 model and you replaced the swing arm pivot shaft assembly with a 1989 or later pivot shaft assembly, perform Step 3C.*

3B. *Late 1986-1988*: Install the pivot shaft assembly as follows:

a. Lay the pivot shaft assembly out in the order shown in **Figure 98**. Reclean and dry parts as required before assembly.
b. Install the left-hand pivot shaft onto the center stud.
c. Coat the pivot shaft and center stud with Loctite Anti-Seize.
d. Slide the left-hand rubber mount (with shoulder facing outward) onto the pivot shaft.
e. Slide the nylon washer onto the pivot shaft and seat it against the rubber mount so that the smaller diameter on the washer faces inward.
f. Install the pivot shaft through the swing arm from the left-hand side.
g. Coat the right-hand pivot shaft with Loctite Anti-Seize, then install the right-hand nylon washer (smaller washer diameter facing inward) and the right-hand rubber mount (shoulder facing outward) onto the pivot shaft.
h. Insert the right-hand pivot shaft through the swing arm and thread it into the center stud finger-tight.

3C. *1989-on*: Install the pivot shaft assembly as follows:

a. Lay the pivot shaft assembly out in the order shown in **Figure 98**. Reclean and dry parts as required before assembly.
b. Wipe the pivot shaft with Loctite Anti-Seize.
c. Slide the right-hand rubber mount (with shoulder facing outward) onto the pivot shaft.
d. Slide the right-hand nylon washer (with smaller washer diameter facing inward) onto the pivot shaft.
e. Insert the pivot shaft through the swing arm from the right-hand side.
f. Install the left-hand nylon washer (smaller diameter facing inward), rubber mount (shoulder facing outward) and cup washer onto the pivot shaft. Then install the pivot shaft nut and tighten finger-tight.

4. Install passenger footpeg mounting bracket on FLT models. When installing mounting brackets, make sure roll pin in each bracket engages hole in rubber mount.
5. Install the pivot shaft mounting brackets on FXR models. When installing brackets, make sure roll pin in each bracket engages hole in rubber mount.
6. On 1984-early 1986 models, make sure the flat on the pivot shaft engages the flat on the right-hand rubber mount.
7. If passenger footpegs were removed, position footpegs so that they fold at a 45° angle, then tighten their mounting nuts to 20-25 ft.-lb. (27.6-34.5 N•m).

8A. *1984-early 1986*: Hold the left-hand pivot shaft nut with a wrench and tighten the right-hand nut to 45 ft.-lb. (62.1 N•m).

8B. *late 1986-1988*: Hold the left pivot bolt with a wrench and tighten the right-hand pivot bolt to 85 ft.-lb. (117.3 N•m). After tightening pivot bolts, install the clip into each mounting bracket so that the flat on the clip faces toward the bottom of the bracket; see **Figure 98**.

*NOTE*
*If a 1989 or later pivot shaft assembly was installed on a late 1986-1988 model (to replace the 3-piece pivot shaft assembly), do not install the clips into the mounting brackets as described in Step 8B.*

8C. *1989-on*: Hold the right-hand pivot nut with a wrench and tighten the left-hand nut to 45 ft.-lb. (62.1 N•m).

9. Install the shift arm assembly into the transmission housing, if removed, as described in this chapter.
10. Install the main drive gear into the transmission housing as described in this chapter.
11. On FLT models, if removed, install the oil fill spout (**Figure 96**) as follows:

a. Remove gasket residue from mating surfaces.
b. Install the oil spout gasket with the cutout side at the bottom; see **Figure 96**.
c. Install the oil spout and its mounting bolts. Tighten mounting bolts to 7-9 ft.-lb. (9-12 N•m).

*CAUTION*
*If the oil spout gasket is installed incorrectly, the oil spout will leak.*

12. Install the shifter cam and forks as described in this chapter.
13. Install the transmission top and right-hand side covers.
14. Install the primary housing assembly as described in Chapter Five.
15. Install the starter motor as described in Chapter Nine.
16A. *1984-1990*: Install the transmission-to-primary housing mounting bolts and lockwashers. Tighten 3/8 in. bolts to 21-27 ft.-lb. (28.9-37.2 N•m). Tighten 5/16 in. bolts to 13-16 ft.-lb. (17.9-22.1 N•m). On 1984 models, secure the 2 lock tabs and bolts with safety wire.
16B. *1991-on*: Install the transmission-to-primary housing mounting bolts and lockwashers. Tighten bolts to 18-21 ft.-lb. (24-28 N•m).
17A. On 1993-on FLT models, reconnect the following hoses (**Figure 96**):
a. Transmission case-to-crankcase hose.
b. Oil pan-to-oil pump hose.
c. Transmission case-to-oil filter hose.
17B. On all other models, reconnect the transmission vent hose.
18A. *Chain drive*: Coat the rear chain boots (if used) and their mating surfaces on the primary housing and transmission with RTV silicone sealant. Secure the boots to the housing and tighten screws in a crisscross pattern.
18B. *Belt drive*: Adjust the drive belt as described in Chapter Three.
19. Tighten the transmission-to-engine mounting bolts to 33-37 ft.-lb. (45-50 N•m).
20. Connect the foot shifter rod to the shifter arm.
21. *1984*: Connect the oil hoses to the oil filter inlet and outlet ports.
22. *1985-on*: Install the oil filter mount and its mounting bolt.
23. Wipe the oil filter seal with clean engine oil and screw the filter onto the filter mount.
24. Adjust the following:
a. Perform the transmission adjustments as described in this chapter.
b. Adjust the rear drive chain as described in Chapter Three.
c. Readjust the rear drive belt as described in Chapter Three.
25. Install the remaining parts previously removed to access the transmission housing.
26. Refill the transmission and primary housings with the correct type and quantity of oil as described in Chapter Three. On 1993-on FLT models, refill the engine oil as described in Chapter Three.

*NOTE*
*Recheck the pivot shaft nut torque every 5,000 miles (8,000 km).*

### Shift Arm Disassembly/Inspection/Assembly

Refer to **Figure 74** for this procedure.
1. Loosen the shift lever screw at the bottom of the transmission case and slide the shift lever off of the shift arm.
2. Loosen the shift lever adjusting screw and turn it counterclockwise until it clears the centering plate. Then pull the shift arm assembly out of the transmission case.
3. Remove the circlip and remove the pawl and spring.
4. Slide the spring and centering plate off of the shift arm.
5. The pawl pin is a press fit. If removal is necessary, drive it out with a suitable size punch.
6. Check the shift pawl and centering plate for wear. Replace the pawl if its ends are damaged. Replace the centering plate if its adjustment slot is elongated.
7. Check the springs for wear or damage. Assemble the pawl and spring on the shift arm pin. If the spring will not hold the pawl on the cam, replace it.
8. Place the centering plate on the shift lever.
9. Assemble the springs, pin and pawl. Secure with a new circlip.
10. Install the shift arm assembly into the transmission housing.
11. Align the adjusting screw with the centering plate slot.
12. Slide the shift lever on the shift arm. Install the screw, making sure it engages the slot in the shift lever, and tighten to 18-22 ft.-lb. (24.8-30.4 N•m).

## TRANSMISSION OIL PAN (1993-ON FLT)

Refer to **Figure 96** when servicing the oil pan.

### Removal

To remove the oil pan with the transmission case mounted in the frame, perform the following.

1. Support the bike securely.
2. Drain the engine and transmission as described in Chapter Three.
3. Disconnect the oil pan-to-oil pump hose at the front of the oil pan.

NOTE
*A long 3/16 in. ball hex socket driver can be used to remove the oil pan mounting bolts in Step 4.*

4. Loosen, then remove the oil pan mounting bolts.
5. Remove the engine oil dipstick.

CAUTION
*The engine oil dipstick must be removed prior to removing the oil pan. Otherwise, dipstick will contact oil pan and be damaged during pan's removal.*

6. Remove the oil pan from the transmission case.

NOTE
*If the oil pan contacts the frame cross member and cannot be removed, the front engine mount must be disconnected. To do this, perform Step 7.*

7. To disconnect the front engine mount (**Figure 101**) and remove the oil pan, perform the following:
   a. Remove the left/hand regulator bracket bolt.
   b. Loosen the right-hand regulator bracket bolt.
   c. Pivot the left end of the regulator bracket forward.
   d. Remove the front engine nut, bolt and washers.



101

**FRONT ENGINE MOUNT (1993-ON FLT)**

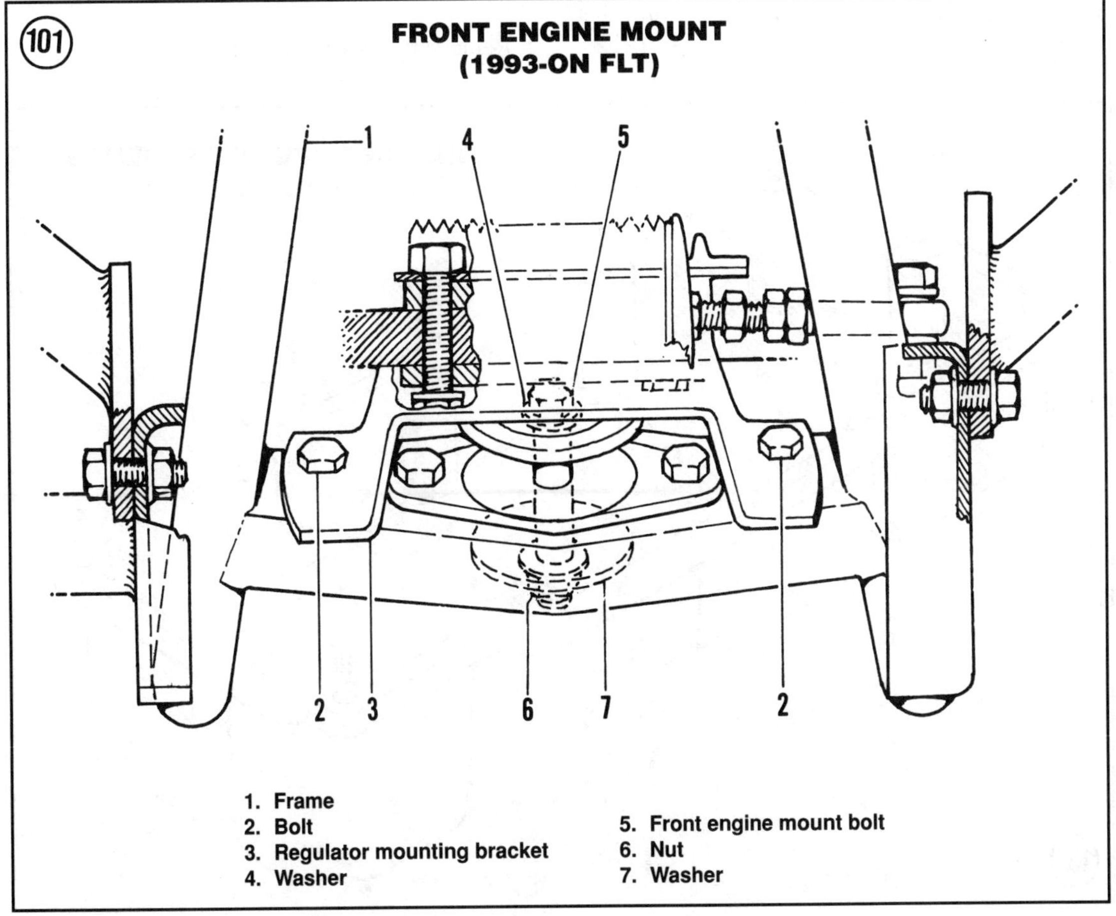


1. Frame
2. Bolt
3. Regulator mounting bracket
4. Washer
5. Front engine mount bolt
6. Nut
7. Washer

e. Carefully raise the front of the engine to support it.
f. Slide the oil pan forward and remove it.

8. Remove all gasket residue from the oil pan and transmission case gasket surfaces.
9. Clean the oil pan in solvent and dry thoroughly.

### Installation

1. Apply a thin coat of Hylomar gasket sealer to the oil pan gasket surface.
2. Place a new gasket onto the oil pan. Allow the sealer to dry slightly (tacky feel) before installing the oil pan.
3. Install the oil pan and gasket. Install the oil pan mounting bolts; tighten bolts 2 turns after making initial thread engagement. Check that gasket is centered correctly on oil pan.
4. Tighten all oil pan bolts finger-tight. Then tighten bolts in the numerical order shown in **Figure 102** to 7-9 ft.-lb. (9-12 N•m).
5. If front engine bolt was removed, perform the following:
   a. Remove wood blocks supporting engine.
   b. Install the front engine mount bolt, washers and nut. Torque bolt to 35-45 ft.-lb. (47-61 N•m).
   c. Pivot regulator mounting bracket back until bolt holes align. Install left-hand bolt. Tighten both regulator mounting bracket mounting bolts to 15-19 ft.-lb. (20-26 N•m).
6. Reconnect the oil pan-to-oil pump hose at the front of the oil pan.
7. Refill the engine oil and transmission oil as described in Chapter Three. Check the oil pan for leaks.

*WARNING*
*Do not ride the motorcycle if the oil pan is leaking.*

## TRANSMISSION SIDE COVER (1987-ON)

### Removal

1. Remove the exhaust system.

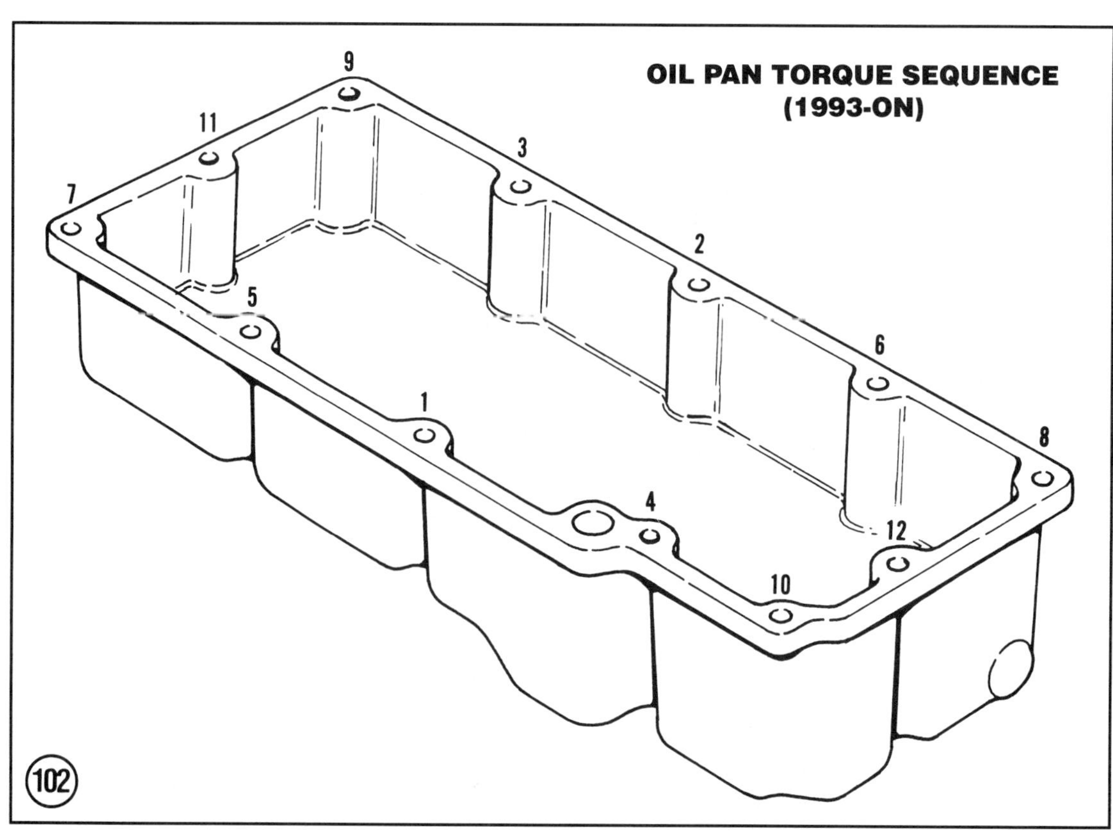

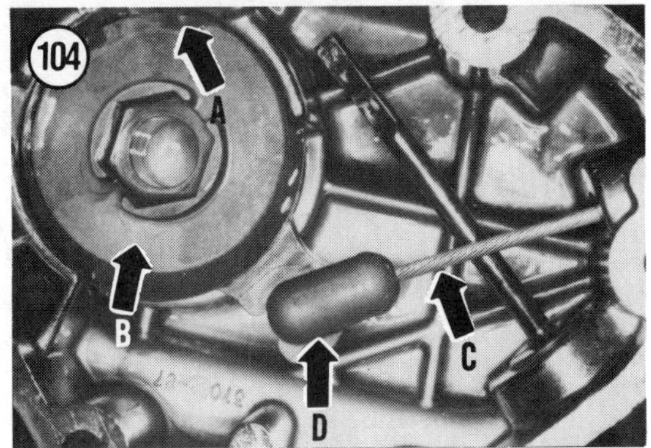

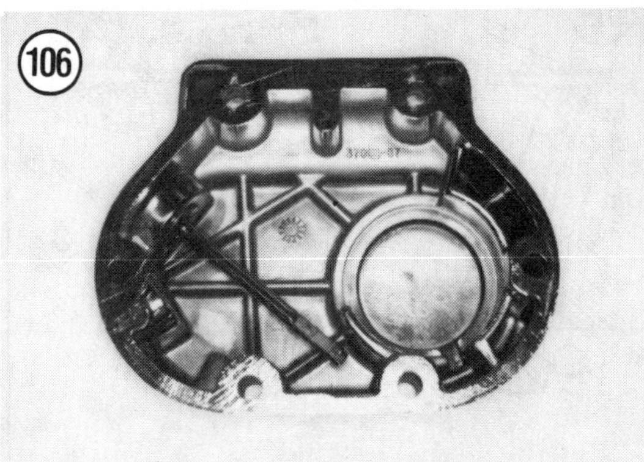


2. Drain the transmission oil as described under *Transmission Oil Change* in Chapter Three.
3. Remove the transmission fill plug/dipstick assembly.
4. Loosen the clutch cable adjuster locknut and turn the adjuster to provide as much slack in the cable as possible.
5. Remove the side cover bolts and remove the side cover (**Figure 103**).
6. Refer to **Figure 104**. Perform the following:
   a. Remove the circlip (A, **Figure 104**).
   b. Remove the inner ramp and coupling (B) from the side cover.
   c. Disconnect the clutch cable (C) from the ball and ramp coupling (D).
   d. If necessary, remove the cable fitting from the side cover.

### Inspection

1. Wash the side cover and all components thoroughly in solvent and dry thoroughly.
2. Check the release mechanism balls and the ramp ball socket surfaces for cracks, deep scoring or excessive wear (**Figure 105**).
3. Check the hub ramp for looseness.
4. Check the side cover (**Figure 106**) for cracks or damage. Check the clutch cable threads and the coupling circlip groove for damage. Check the ramp bore in the side cover for severe wear, lips or grooves that could catch the ramps and bind them sideways, causing improper clutch adjustment.
5. Replace worn or damaged parts.

### Assembly/Installation

1. If removed, screw the clutch cable guide into the side cover. Do not tighten it at this point.
2. Refer to **Figure 104**. Perform the following:
   a. Align the tang on the outer ramp with the slot in the side cover and install the outer ramp (**Figure 107**). B, **Figure 104** shows the outer ramp installed.
   b. Place a steel ball in each of the outer ramp slots. There are a total of 3 balls used in this assembly. **Figure 108** shows the outer ramp with the 3 balls installed.
   c. Attach the clutch cable (C, **Figure 104**) coupling onto the end of the inner ramp (D, **Figure 104**).
   d. Install the inner ramp into the side cover.

e. Secure the inner and outer ramp assembly with the large circlip (A, **Figure 104**).

*NOTE*
*The circlip opening must be installed so that it faces to the right of the outer ramp tang slot.*

f. Attach the clutch cable to the side cover.

3. Install the side cover using a new gasket. Install the side cover bolts and tighten to 10-12 ft.-lb. (13.8-16.6 N•m).
4. Refill the transmission oil as described in Chapter Three.
5. Install the exhaust system.
6. Adjust the clutch as described in Chapter Three.

## TRANSMISSION ADJUSTMENTS

Shift linkage adjustment should only be required if the linkage rod is damaged or if the gears do not engage properly.

### Shift Linkage Adjustment (FLT)

1. Disconnect one end of the shifter rod. See **Figure 109**.
2. Loosen the locknuts on the end of the shifter rod disconnected in Step 1. Then turn the shifter rod until the gears engage properly.
3. Reconnect the shifter rod and tighten the locknuts to 20-24 ft.-lb. (27.6-33.1 N•m).

*CAUTION*
*The foot shifter pedal must not contact the footboard when shifting the transmission. Contact would cause incomplete gear engagement or transmission damage. Harley-Davidson recommends a minimum clearance of 3/8 in. (9.5 mm) between the shifter pedal and the floorboard.*

### Shift Linkage Adjustment (FXR)

*NOTE*
*One end of the ball joint rod (**Figure 110**) has left-hand threads. When the ball joint rod is turned, it will either shorten or lengthen the shifter pedal position.*

1. Hold the ball joint flat with a wrench and loosen the locknuts (**Figure 110**).
2. Turn the ball joint until the gears engage properly.
3. Tighten both locknuts to 20-24 ft.-lb. (27.6-33.1 N•m).

107

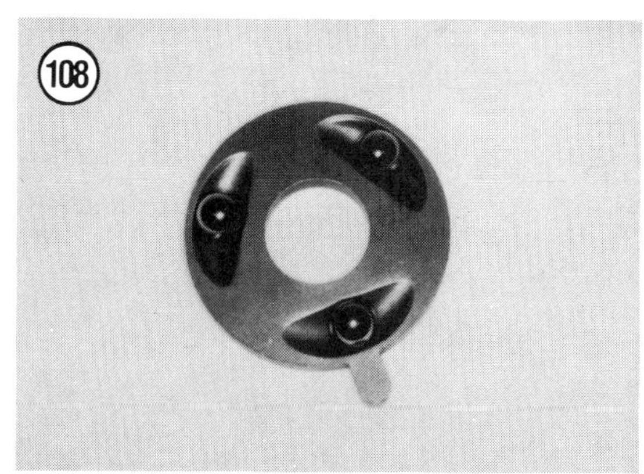
108

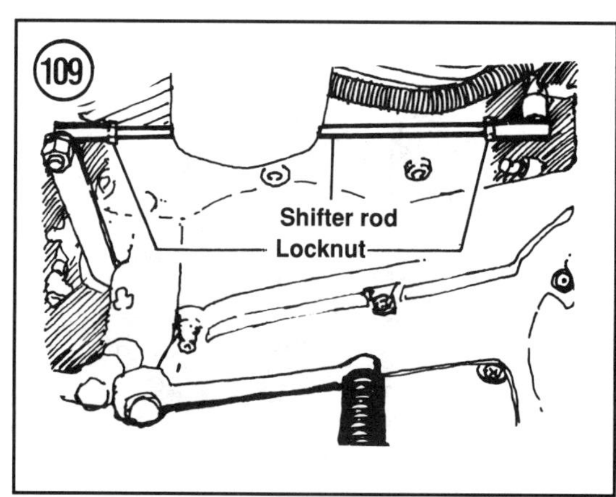

109

110

111

112

113

## Gear Engagement Check/Adjustment

When the transmission gears do not engage properly, perform the following checks (sub-steps a-d) before proceeding to Step 1.

a. Check clutch adjustment and operation. See Chapter Three.
b. Check the shift linkage adjustment as described in this chapter. If the shift linkage appears to be correct, check the shift linkage rod for damage or interference.
c. Check the shift forks for wear or damage as described in this chapter.
d. If these checks do not solve the shifting problem, perform the following procedures.

1. Disconnect the negative battery cable.
2. *1984-1986*: Disconnect the clutch cable at the engine (**Figure 111**).
3. Disconnect the neutral switch wire at the switch (**Figure 112**).
4. Remove the transmission top cover mounting bolts and remove the top cover and gasket. See **Figure 113**.
5. Shift the transmission into third gear.

*NOTE*

*Third gear can be easily found by pushing the motorcycle forward and shifting the transmission until third gear is reached. Then set the jiffy stand and continue the procedure.*

6. Move the shifter lever (**Figure 114**) to check for free play and spring pressure in both directions.
7. The gear engagement is correct if the spring pressure is the same in both directions and there is approximately 0.010 in. (0.25 mm) clearance between the shifter pawl arms and the shift cam pins

114

7

as shown in **Figure 115**. If necessary, adjust the gear engagement as described in Step 8.

8. Refer to **Figure 116**. Loosen the adjusting screw locknut and turn the bolt in 1/4 turn increments or less (clockwise or counterclockwise) until the shifter lever travel spring pressure is equal on both sides and the 0.010 in. (0.25 mm) clearance is maintained. Tighten the locknut and recheck the adjustment.

9. Reinstall all previously removed parts as described in this chapter.

10. *1986*: Adjust the clutch after reconnecting the clutch cable (**Figure 111**). Refer to Chapter Three.

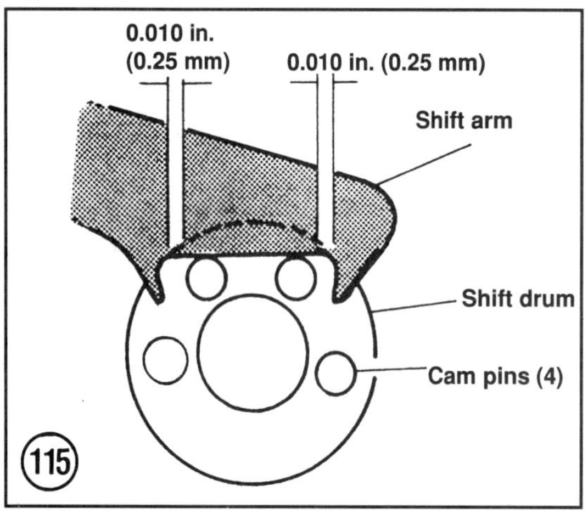


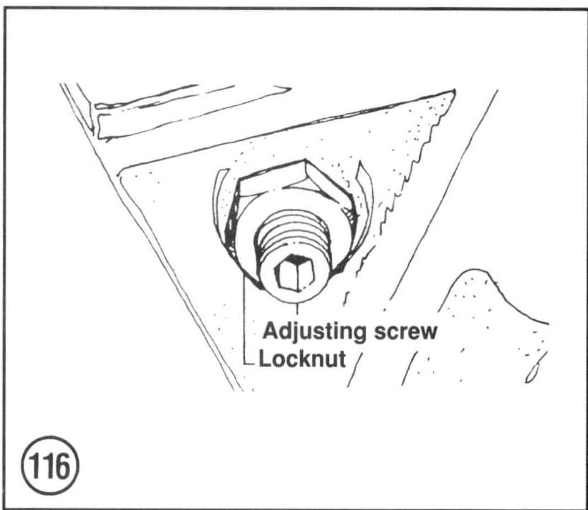

**Table 1 5-SPEED TRANSMISSION SPECIFICATIONS**

| | Specifications in. | mm |
|---|---|---|
| Mainshaft | | |
| Runout | 0.000-0.003 | 0.00-0.08 |
| End play | 0.000 | 0.00 |
| 1st gear clearance | 0.0000-0.0080 | 0.00-0.20 |
| 2nd gear clearance | 0.0000-0.0080 | 0.00-0.20 |
| 3rd gear | | |
| Clearance | 0.0003-0.0019 | 0.008-0.048 |
| End play | 0.0050-0.0420 | 0.127-1.067 |
| 4th gear | | |
| Clearance | 0.0003-0.0019 | 0.008-0.048 |
| End play | 0.0050-0.0310 | 0.127-0.787 |
| Mainshaft drive gear (5th) | | |
| End play | 0.000 | 0.00 |
| Fit on mainshaft | 0.00001-0.0009 | 0.0002-0.0229 |
| Fit in bearing | | |
| Loose | 0.0001 | 0.002 |
| Tight | 0.0009 | 0.023 |
| Bearing fit in housing | | |
| 1984-1992 | | |
| Loose | 0.000140 | 0.002 |
| Tight | 0.0004 | 0.010 |
| 1993-on | | |
| Loose | 0.0003 | 0.008 |
| Tight | 0.0017 | 0.043 |
| Countershaft | | |
| Runout | 0.000-0.003 | 0.00-0.08 |
| End play | 0.000 | 0.00 |
| 1st gear | | |
| Clearance | 0.0003-0.0019 | 0.008-0.048 |
| End play | 0.0050-0.3900 | 0.127-0.990 |
| 2nd gear | | |
| Clearance | 0.0003-0.0019 | 0.008-0.048 |
| End play | 0.0050-0.0440 | 0.127-1.118 |
| 3rd gear clearance | 0.0000-0.0080 | 0.000-0.200 |
| 4th gear | | |
| Clearance | 0.0000-0.0080 | 0.000-0.200 |
| End play | 0.0050-0.0390 | 0.127-0.991 |
| 5th gear | | |
| Clearance | 0.0000-0.0080 | 0.000-0.200 |
| End play | 0.0050-0.0440 | 0.127-0.102 |
| Shifter cam assembly | | |
| Shifter cam end play | 0.0001-0.004 | 0.002-0.102 |
| Right edge of middle cam groove to right support block | See text | – |
| Shift forks | | |
| Shift fork taper | 0.000-0.020 | 0.00-0.51 |
| Shift fork to cam groove end play | 0.0017-0.0019 | 0.043-0.048 |
| Shift fork to gear groove end play | 0.0010-0.0011 | 0.025-0.0279 |
| Side door bearing | | |
| Fit on mainshaft | | |
| Loose | 0.0001 | 0.002 |
| Tight | 0.0007 | 0.018 |
| Fit on countershaft | | |
| Loose | 0.00001 | 0.0002 |
| Tight | 0.0008 | 0.020 |
| Fit on side door (tight) | 0.0014-0.0001 | 0.035-0.002 |

**Table 2 SHIFT DOG CLEARANCE**

| Gears | Min. in. | Min. mm | Max. in. | Max. mm |
|---|---|---|---|---|
| 2nd-5th | 0.035 | 0.89 | 0.139 | 3.53 |
| 2nd-3rd | 0.035 | 0.89 | 0.164 | 4.16 |
| 1st-4th | 0.035 | 0.89 | 0.152 | 3.86 |
| 1st-3rd | 0.035 | 0.89 | 0.157 | 3.99 |

**Table 3 TRANSMISSION TIGHTENING TORQUES**

| | ft.-lb. | N•m |
|---|---|---|
| All 1/4 in. fasteners | 7-9 | 9.7-12.4 |
| Front bracket mounting bolts | 33-38 | 45.5-52.4 |
| Rear mounting bracket bolts | 13-16 | 17.9-22.1 |
| Support block bolts | 7-9 | 9.7-12.4 |
| Side door mounting screws | | |
| 5/16 in. | 13-16 | 17.9-22.1 |
| 1/4 in. | 7-9 | 9.7-12.4 |
| Neutral indicator switch | 3-5 | 4.1-6.9 |
| Top cover mounting bolts | 7-9 | 9.7-12.4 |
| Side cover mounting bolts | 7-9 | 9.7-12.4 |
| Mainshaft/countershaft side door nuts | 27-33 | 37.3-45.5 |
| Shifter arm screw | 18-22 | 24.8-30.4 |
| Shifter arm adjusting screw locknut | 20-24 | 27.6-33.1 |
| Countershaft sprocket nut | 110-120 | 149-163 |
| Clutch cable bracket screws | 6-8 | 8.3-11 |
| Clutch release arm nut | 8-10 | 11.0-13.8 |
| Pivot shaft nut | 45 | 61 |
| Front transmission housing mounting bolts | | |
| 1993-on | 33-38 | 45-52 |
| Filler cap and dipstick | 25-75 in.-lb. | 2.8-8.5 |

# CHAPTER EIGHT

# FUEL, EXHAUST AND EMISSION CONTROL SYSTEMS



This chapter includes service procedures for all parts of the fuel, exhaust and emission control systems.

Carburetor specifications are listed in **Table 1** (end of chapter).

## AIR CLEANER

The air cleaner must be cleaned or replaced at the intervals specified in Chapter Three (or more frequently in dusty areas).

Refer to Chapter Three for air cleaner service.

## CARBURETOR (1984-1989)

### Service

Major carburetor service (removal and cleaning) should be performed when poor engine performance and/or hesitation is observed. Carburetor rejetting should be attempted only if you're experienced in this type of "tuning" work; a bad guess could result in costly engine damage or, at best, poor performance.

If, after servicing the carburetors and making adjustments as described in this chapter, the motorcycle does not perform correctly (and assuming that other factors affecting performance are correct, such as ignition timing and condition, valve adjustment, etc.), the motorcycle should be checked by a dealer or a qualified performance tuning specialist.

### Removal/Installation

1. Remove the air cleaner as described in Chapter Three.
2. Turn the fuel valve off.
3. Disconnect the throttle (**Figure 1**) and choke (**Figure 2**) cables at the carburetor.

4. Disconnect the fuel hose at the fuel valve (**Figure 3**).
5. Label and disconnect all hoses at the carburetor.
6. Remove the carburetor mounting screws and remove the carburetor (**Figure 4**) and insulator block.
7. Examine the intake manifolds on the cylinder head for cracks or damage that would allow unfiltered air to enter the engine. Damaged parts should be replaced.
8. Install by reversing these removal steps. Tighten the carburetor mounting screws securely.

*CAUTION*
*Make sure all carburetor mounting points are well secured and air-tight. Any leaks around the engine intake manifold or air filter housing can easily cause serious engine damage from dirt or a too-lean fuel mixture.*

9. Connect the fuel line and turn the fuel shutoff valve to the ON position. Check for fuel leaks and correct before starting the engine.
10. Adjust the throttle and choke cables as described in Chapter Three.

## Disassembly

Refer to **Figure 5** for this procedure.

*CAUTION*
*Fuel will spill when the float bowl is removed in Step 1. Work over a workbench so the fuel can be wiped up.*

1. Remove the float bowl (**Figure 6**).
2. Remove the accelerating pump housing at the bottom of the float bowl (**Figure 7**). Then remove the spring (**Figure 8**) and diaphragm (**Figure 9**).
3. Remove the O-ring (**Figure 10**) from the accelerating pump housing.
4. Remove the following parts from the float bowl:
   a. Overflow hose (**Figure 11**).
   b. Rubber boot (**Figure 12**).
   c. O-ring (**Figure 13**).
5. Remove the float pin screw (**Figure 14**) and withdraw the float pin and float (**Figure 15**).
6. Detach the fuel valve (**Figure 16**) from the float and remove the clip (**Figure 17**).
7. Remove the accelerator pump rod from the float bowl.
8. Unscrew and remove the main jet (**Figure 18**).
9. Remove the pilot jet plug (**Figure 19**). Then unscrew and remove the pilot jet (**Figure 20**).

10. If necessary, remove the cable guide (**Figure 21**) at the top of the carburetor housing.

11. The throttle (**Figure 22**) and choke (**Figure 23**) valve assemblies are matched to the individual carburetor during manufacturing. Do not remove them from the carburetor. If these parts are damaged, the carburetor must be replaced.

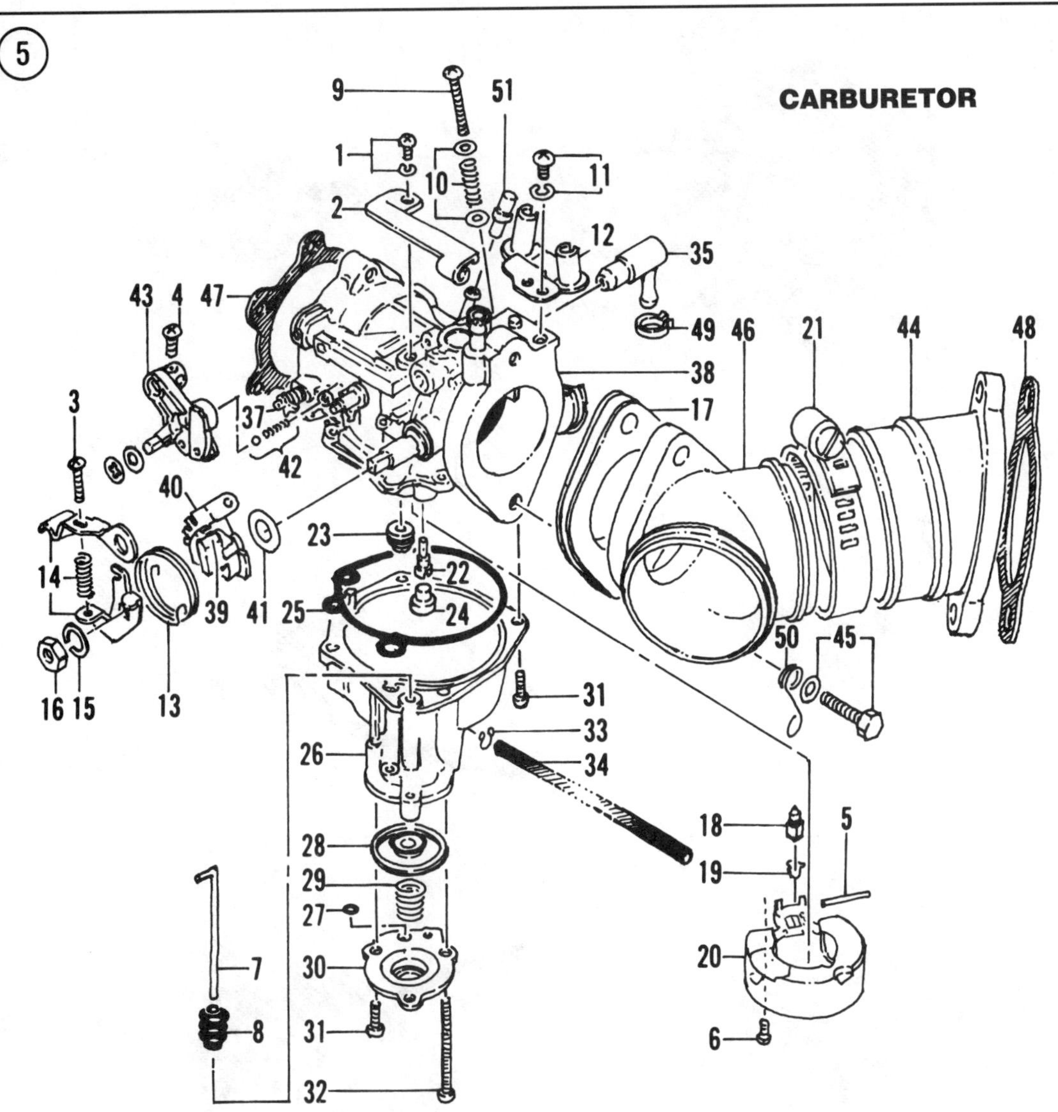


1. Screw and washer
2. Choke cable bracket
3. Fast idle adjusting screw
4. Choke cable screw
5. Float pin
6. Float retaining screw
7. Accelerating pump rod
8. Rubber boot
9. Throttle stop screw
10. Springs and washers
11. Screw and washer
12. Throttle cable bracket
13. Spring
14. Fast idle cam assembly
15. Lockwasher
16. Nut
17. Insulator block
18. Inlet valve
19. Clip
20. Float assembly
21. Clamp
22. Pilot jet
23. Main jet
24. Plug
25. Rubber gasket
26. Float bowl
27. O-ring (accelerating pump)
28. Accelerating pump diaphragm
29. Accelerating pump spring
30. Accelerating pump housing
31. Screw and washer
32. Screw and washer
33. Overflow line clip
34. Overflow line
35. Fuel inlet fitting
36. Choke plate (not shown)
37. Choke lever shaft
38. Housing
39. Accelerating pump rod hole
40. Rocker arm
41. Washer
42. Choke detent ball and spring
43. Fast idle cam
44. Compliance fitting
45. Mounting bolt and lockwasher
46. Intake manifold
47. Gasket
48. Gasket
49. Clamp
50. Cable guide
51. Cap (evap. purge port)

8

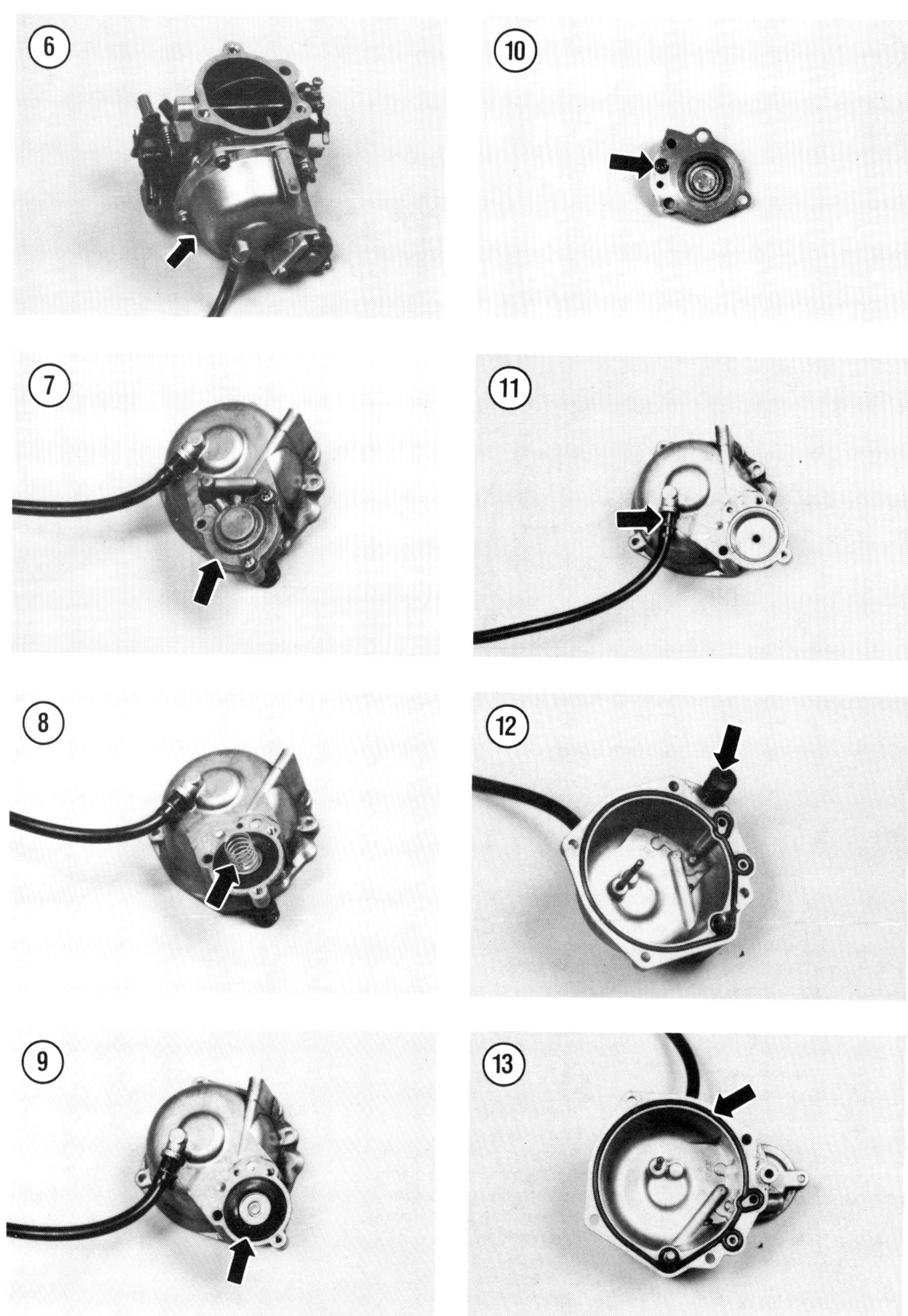
6
10
7
11
8
12
9
13

14

18

15

19

16

20

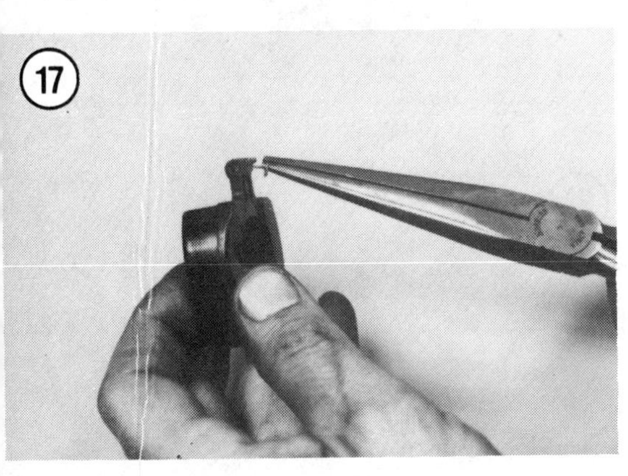
17

21

### Inspection

*CAUTION*
*Before cleaning plastic or rubber components, make sure that the cleaning agent is compatible with these materials. Some types of solvents can cause permanent damage. Carburetor cleaner use is described in Step 1.*

1. Clean all metal parts that were removed from the carburetor body in a good grade of carburetor cleaner. This solution is available at most automotive supply stores, in a small, resealable tank with a dip basket. If it is tightly sealed when not in use, the solution will last for several cleanings. Follow the manufacturer's instructions for correct soaking time.

*CAUTION*
*Do not soak the carburetor body in a tank of carburetor cleaner. The cleaner can damage the non-removable rubber seals used at the throttle plate shaft assembly.*

2. Remove all parts from the cleaner and blow dry with compressed air. Blow out the jets with compressed air. *Do not* use a piece of wire to clean them as minor gouges in a jet can alter the flow rate and upset the air/fuel mixture.
3. Make sure all fuel and air openings are clear. Blow out with compressed air if necessary.
4. Check the float assembly for leaks. Place the float in a container of water and try to sink it. There should be no bubbles. Replace the float assembly if it leaks.
5. Check the float needle and seat contact areas. Both contact surfaces should appear smooth without any gouging or other apparent damage. Replace both needle and seat as a set if any one part is worn or damaged.
6. A damaged accelerating pump diaphragm will cause poor acceleration. Hold the diaphragm up to a strong light and check the diaphragm for pin holes, cracks or other damage (**Figure 24**). Replace if necessary.
7. Replace the pump rod if bent or worn.
8. O-rings tend to become hardened after prolonged use and heat and lose their ability to seal properly. Inspect all O-rings and replace if necessary.
9. Inspect the pilot jet for wear or damage that may have occurred during removal. Check the slot in the top of the jet for cracks or breakage. Do not install a damaged pilot jet.

### Assembly

Refer to **Figure 5** when performing this procedure.

1. Prior to assembly, perform the *Inspection* procedure to make sure all worn or damaged parts have been repaired or replaced. All parts should be thoroughly cleaned before assembly.

*NOTE*
*Before installing new jets, double check the jet size and compare to the old jet.*

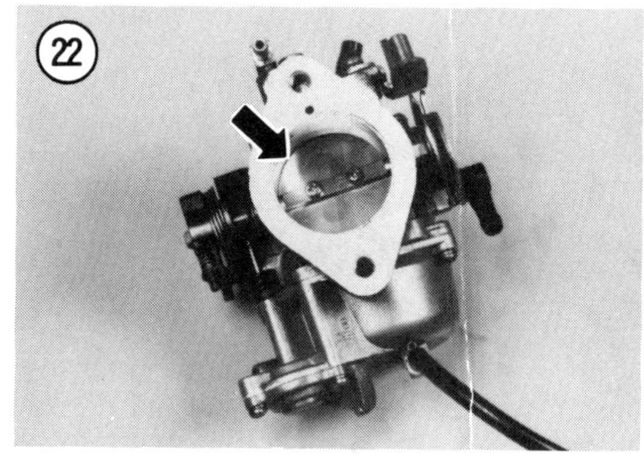


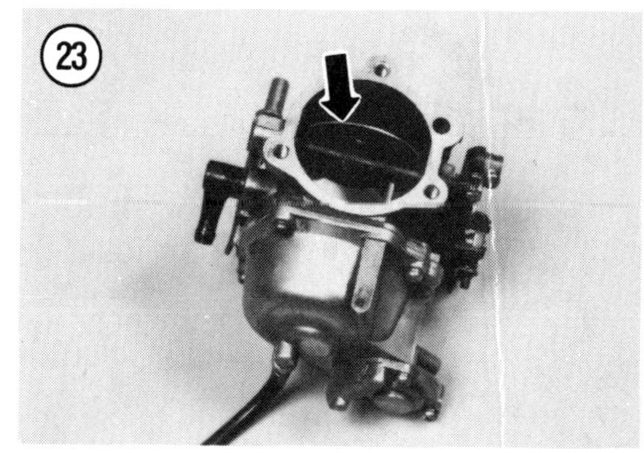


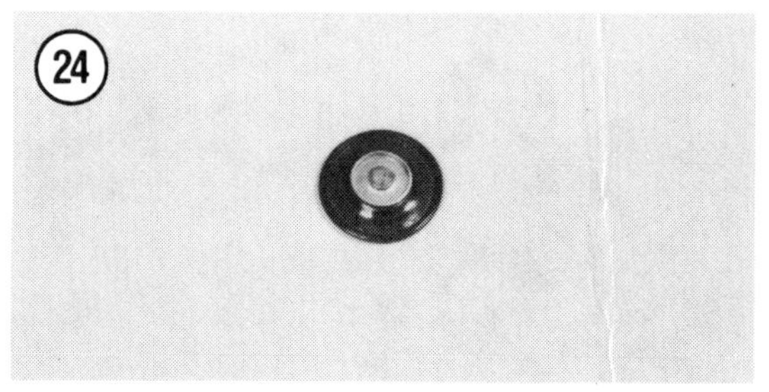

*If you are not rejetting the carburetor, make sure to install the same size jet(s).*

2. Drop the pilot jet (**Figure 20**) into the passage and tighten it with the same screwdriver used during removal.
3. Install the pilot jet plug (**Figure 19**).
4. Install the main jet (**Figure 18**).

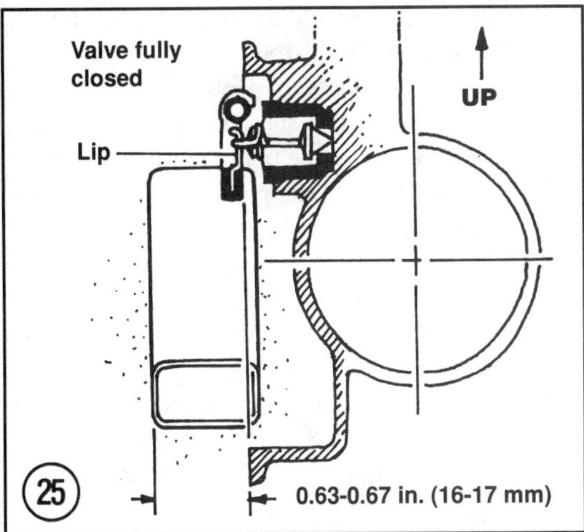


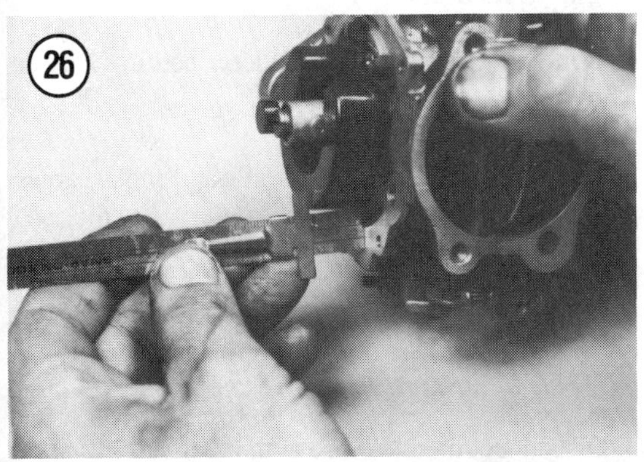


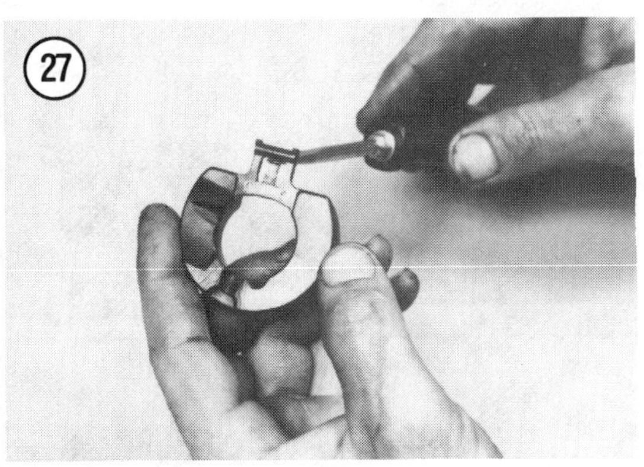


5. Attach the fuel valve (**Figure 17**) onto the float arm and install the float onto the carburetor so that the valve drops into its seat. Align the float pivot arm with the 2 carburetor mounting posts and slip the pin through the float pivot arm and mounting posts. See **Figure 15**.
6. Check the float level as described in this chapter.
7. Assemble and install the float bowl as follows:
   a. Install the O-ring into the cover passageway hole (**Figure 10**).
   b. Insert the accelerator pump diaphragm into the accelerator pump housing in the bottom of the float bowl. Make sure the diaphragm seats around the bowl groove. See **Figure 9**.
   c. Install the spring into the accelerator pump cover (**Figure 8**).
   d. Align the cover assembly with the diaphragm and bowl and install the cover assembly. Install the screws and lockwashers and tighten securely.
   e. Insert the accelerator pump nozzle into the float bowl, if removed.
   f. Install the boot onto the float bowl (**Figure 12**).
   g. Install a new float bowl O-ring. Then align the float bowl with the carburetor and install the float bowl. Install the float bowl screws and lockwasher and tighten them in a crisscross pattern to prevent warpage.
   h. Insert the pump rod through the boot on the float bowl and engage the rod with the diaphragm. Then connect the pump rod with the lever assembly.
   i. If the drain hose was removed from the float bowl, install it now.



### Float Level Measurement

1. Remove the carburetor as described in this chapter.
2. Remove the float bowl as described in this chapter.
3. Turn the carburetor to position the float bowl as shown in **Figure 25**. Measure the float height from the face of the bowl mounting flange surface to the bottom float surface (**Figure 26**). Float height should be 0.63-0.67 in. (16-17 mm). Bend the float tang with a screwdriver to adjust. See **Figure 27**.
4. Reinstall the float bowl and install the carburetor as described in this chapter.

## CARBURETOR (1990-ON)

### Service

Major carburetor service (removal and cleaning) should be performed when poor engine performance and/or hesitation is observed. Carburetor rejetting should be attempted only if you're experienced in this type of "tuning" work; a bad guess could result in costly engine damage or, at best, poor performance.

If after servicing the carburetors and making adjustments as described in this chapter, the motorcycle does not perform correctly (and assuming that other factors affecting performance are correct, such as ignition timing and condition, valve adjustment, etc.), the motorcycle should be checked by a dealer or a qualified performance tuning specialist.

### Vacuum Piston Inspection

If you suspect that the vacuum piston is not operating properly (failing to rise or close properly), perform the following procedures before removing the carburetor from the bike:

1. Check vacuum piston rise as follows:
   a. Remove the air cleaner assembly so that you can see the vacuum piston.

NOTE

*__Figure 28__ shows the vacuum piston with the carburetor removed for clarity. The carburetor must be installed on the bike when performing the following.*

WARNING

*When you are checking vacuum piston operation with the engine running as described in sub-step b, __protect__ your eyes from a possible back-fire by __wearing safety glasses__ and standing a safe distance away from the carburetor. Have an assistant operate the throttle; do not operate the throttle and watch the vacuum piston at the same time. You will be too close to the carburetor.*

   b. With the engine running and properly warmed up, have an assistant open and close the throttle several times while you watch vacuum piston operation. The vacuum piston should rise and lower when the throttle is opened and closed. Turn the engine off.
   c. With the engine off, lift the vacuum piston all the way up the carburetor bore with your finger and release it. Note how the piston traveled upward in the bore. The piston should move smoothly with no sign of roughness or binding.
2. Check piston closing as follows:
   a. With the engine off, lift the vacuum piston all the way up the carburetor bore with your finger and release it. Note how the piston drops in the bore. It should drop smoothly and come to a stop at the bottom of the bore.
   b. Without touching the piston after releasing it in sub-step a, observe the bottom of the piston in relation to the piston bore in the carburetor. The lower edge of the piston should align or rest with the horizontal groove at the bottom end of the piston bore track.
3. If the vacuum piston failed to operate properly as described in these steps, refer to Chapter Two for carburetor troubleshooting.

### Removal/Installation

1. Remove the air cleaner as described in Chapter Three.
2. Turn the fuel valve off.
3. Label and disconnect the throttle and choke cables at the carburetor.

NOTE

*On FLTC and FLHTC Ultra models, disconnect the cruise control servo cable at the carburetor.*

4. Disconnect the fuel hose at the fuel valve.

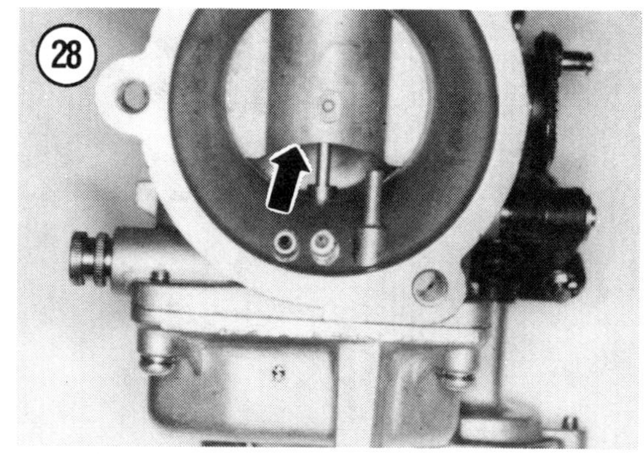

5. Label and disconnect all hoses at the carburetor.
6. Pull the carburetor off of its seal ring and manifold.

*NOTE*
*The front and rear intake manifold flanges (**Figure 29**) have different part numbers. ID the flanges during removal so that you don't mix them up during reassembly.*

7. Remove the manifold Allen bolts and nuts and remove the manifold, the 2 flanges and 2 intake manifold seals (**Figure 29**).
8. Check the intake manifold seals (**Figure 29**) for wear, deterioration or other damage. Replace the seals if necessary.
9. Inspect the carburetor seal ring (**Figure 29**) and replace it if it is worn or damaged.
10. Install by reversing these removal steps, plus the following.
11. Install the intake manifold as follows:
   a. Install the front and rear flanges onto the intake manifold so that the slot in each flange can align with the cylinder head stud (**Figure 29**).

*CAUTION*
*Do not tighten the manifold nuts and bolts until the manifold, flanges and carburetor are aligned with each other. Attempting to align the assembly after tightening the bolts will damage the manifold seals.*

   b. Install an intake manifold seal into the front and rear manifold-to-cylinder head openings.
   c. Install the intake manifold onto the cylinder heads, then install the washer and nut on each stud. Tighten finger-tight.
   d. Install the intake manifold Allen bolts and washers (if used). Tighten finger-tight.
   e. Install the carburetor seal ring onto the intake manifold, then insert the carburetor into the seal ring.
   f. Align the manifold, flanges and carburetors as an assembly. When the assembly is properly aligned, remove the carburetor.
   g. Tighten the mounting screws and nuts securely.
   h. Install the carburetor into the seal ring in the manifold so that it is in a vertical position.

*NOTE*
*The float bowl overflow hose should be routed between the rear cylinder pushrods and then down between the engine oil pump cover and crankcase.*

*CAUTION*
*Make sure all carburetor mounting points are well secured and air-tight. Any leaks around the engine manifold or air filter housing can easily cause serious engine damage from dirt or a too-lean fuel mixture.*

12. Adjust the throttle and choke cables as described in Chapter Three.

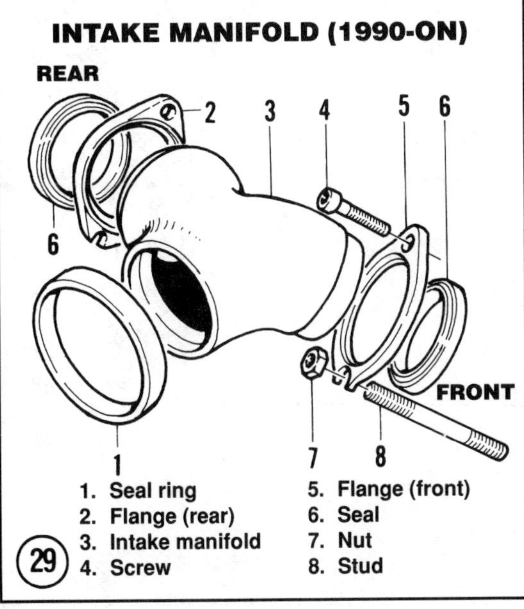


### Disassembly

When servicing the carburetor, you will be working with a number of small parts that can easily become lost. As the carburetor is disassembled, store the parts in a metal pan or tray.

Refer to **Figure 30** for this procedure.

*NOTE*
*The throttle cable bracket shown in **Figure 30** is used on FXR, FX and early FLT models. The throttle cable bracket used on late-model FLT models has an*

8

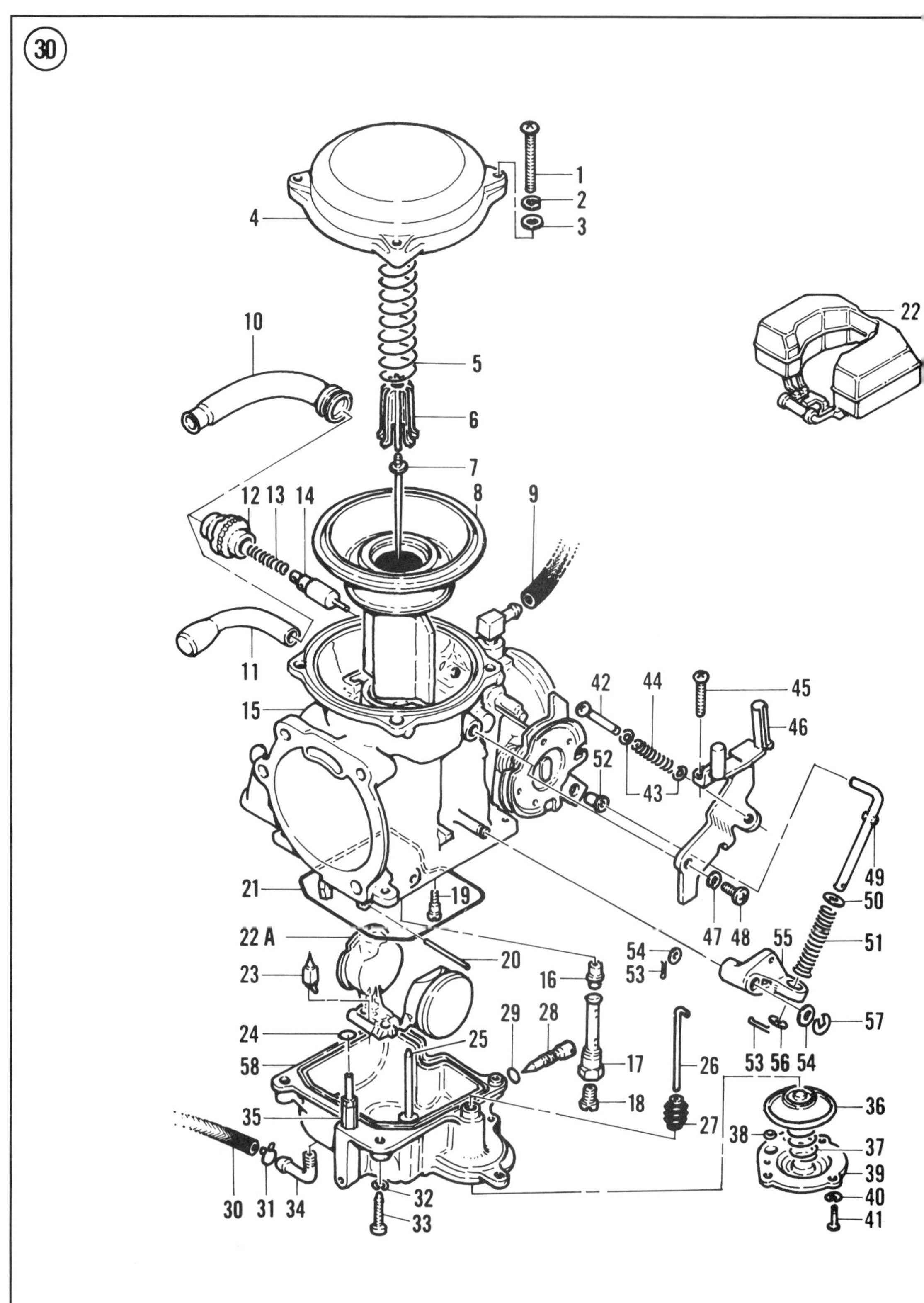
30
1
2
3
4
5
6
7
8
9
10
11
12
13
14
15
16
17
18
19
20
21
22
22 A
23
24
25
26
27
28
29
30
31
32
33
34
35
36
37
38
39
40
41
42
43
44
45
46
47
48
49
50
51
52
53
54
55
56
57
58

**CARBURETOR (1990-ON)**

1. Screw
2. Lockwasher
3. Flat washer
4. Cover
5. Spring
6. Spring seat
7. Jet needle
8. Vacuum piston
9. Vacuum hose
10. Cable guide
11. Starter cap
12. Cable sealing cap
13. Spring
14. Enrichener valve
15. Body
16. Needle jet
17. Needle jet holder
18. Main jet
19. Pilot jet
20. Float pin
21. O-ring

22A. Float (1990-1991)
22B. Float (1992-on)

23. Fuel valve and clip
24. O-ring
25. Overflow pipe
26. Rod
27. Boot
28. Drain screw
29. O-ring
30. Hose
31. Clamp
32. Lockwasher
33. Screw
34. Fitting
35. Accelerator pump nozzle
36. Diaphragm
37. Spring
38. O-ring
39. Cover
40. Lockwasher
41. Screw
42. Idle adjust screw
43. Washer
44. Spring
45. Screw
46. Throttle cable bracket
47. Washer
48. Screw
49. Rod
50. Washer
51. Spring
52. Collar
53. Cotter pin
54. Washer
55. Lever
56. Washer
57. E-clip
58. Float bowl

*additional tab that is used to mount the cruise control servo cable.*

1. Disconnect the overflow hose from the float bowl (**Figure 31**).

2. Unscrew and remove the enrichener cable (**Figure 32**).

3. Remove the screws and washers securing the throttle cable bracket to the carburetor. Remove the bracket (**Figure 33**).

31

32

33

8

4. Remove the remaining cover screws and washers and remove the cover (**Figure 34**) and spring (**Figure 35**).

5. Remove the vacuum piston (**Figure 36**) from the carburetor housing. Do not damage the jet needle sticking out of the bottom of the vacuum piston.

*NOTE*

*An accelerator pump diaphragm is installed in a separate chamber on the bottom side of the float bowl. The accelerator pump reduces engine hesitation by injecting a fine spray of fuel into the carburetor intake passage during sudden acceleration. Because the pump is synchronized with the throttle plate, note the position of the throttle and pump rods when removing the float bowl in the following steps.*

6. Remove the accelerator pump diaphragm as follows:

a. Remove the screws and lockwashers holding the pump cover (**Figure 37**) to the float bowl and remove the cover.

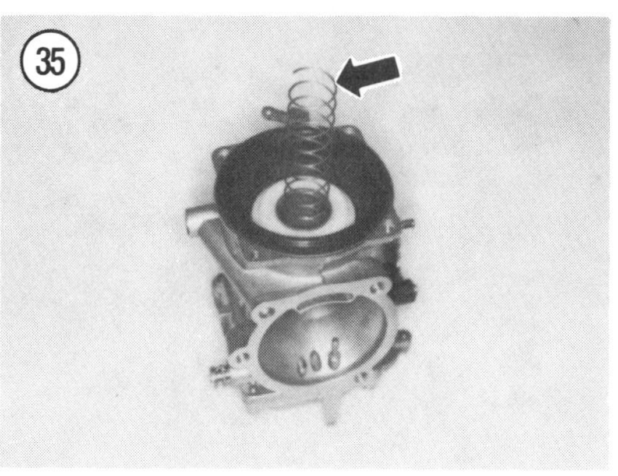


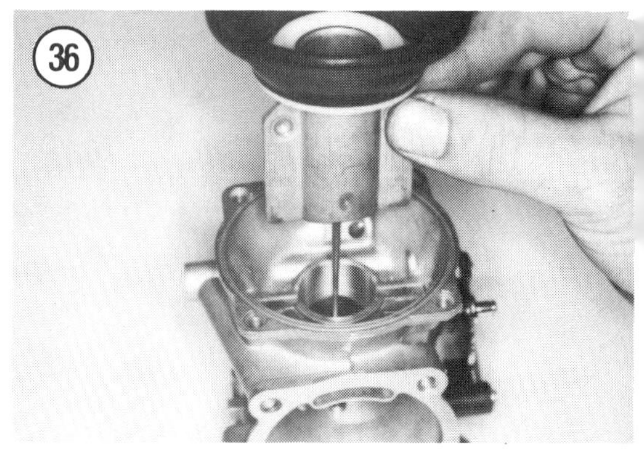


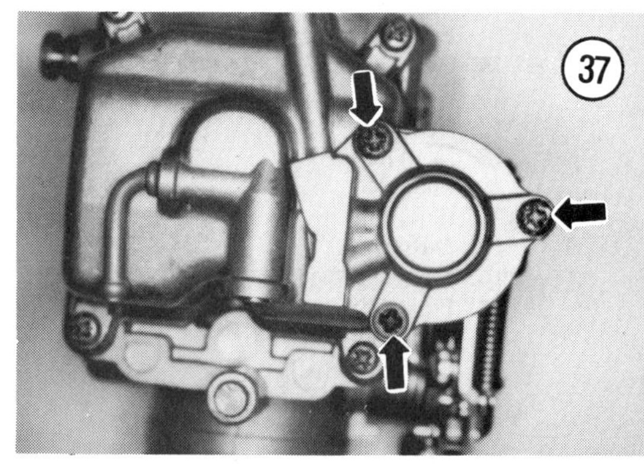

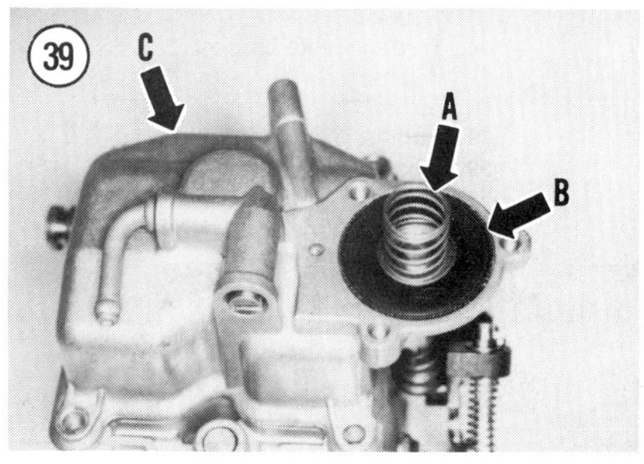

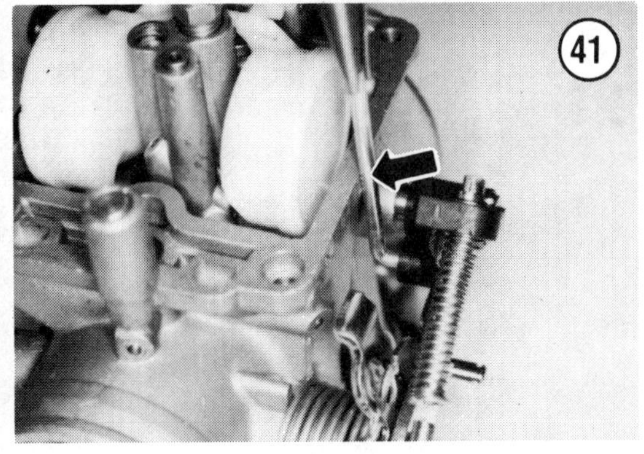


   b. Remove the small pump cover O-ring (**Figure 38**).

   c. Remove the spring (A, **Figure 39**) and diaphragm (B, **Figure 39**).

7. Remove the float bowl as follows:

   a. Remove the screws and washers securing the float bowl (C, **Figure 39**) to the carburetor. Remove the float bowl from the carburetor while allowing the pump rod (**Figure 40**) to withdraw from the boot on the bowl.

   b. Disconnect the pump rod from the lever assembly on the carburetor (**Figure 41**).

   c. Carefully pull the boot (**Figure 42**) off of the float bowl.

8A. On 1984-1991 models, remove the float pin (**Figure 43**) and lift off the float and needle valve assembly (**Figure 44**).

8B. On 1992 models, remove the float pin (**Figure 45**) and lift off the float and needle valve assembly (**Figure 46**).

9. The main jet is screwed into the top of the needle jet holder. Either remove the main jet (**Figure 47**) and then the needle jet (**Figure 48**) or remove the needle jet with the main jet attached.

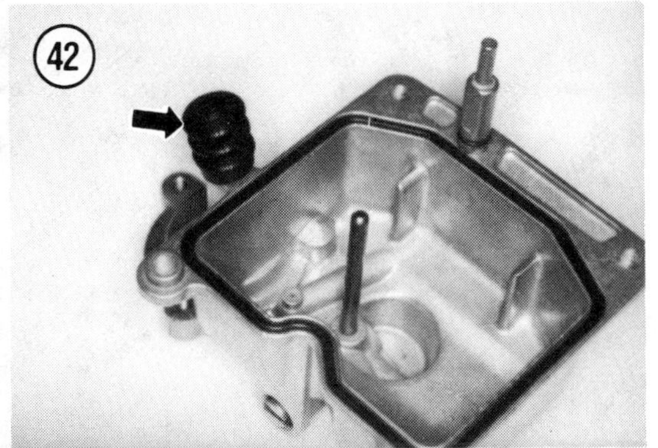

8

10. Remove the needle jet from the needle jet bore in the carburetor (**Figure 49**).
11. Using a flat-tipped screwdriver that fits the pilot jet slot, loosen and remove the pilot jet (**Figure 50**).

*CAUTION*
*If the screwdriver used to remove the pilot jet is too small, you may break the slots at the top of the jet and damage it. If necessary, grind a screwdriver tip to fit.*

*NOTE*
*Replacement parts are not available for the throttle plate (**Figure 51**) assembly. Do not remove it.*

## Inspection

*CAUTION*
*Before cleaning plastic or rubber components, make sure that the cleaning agent is compatible with these materials. Some types of solvents can cause permanent damage. Carburetor cleaner use is described in Step 1.*

1. Clean all metal parts that were removed from the carburetor body in a good grade of carburetor cleaner. This solution is available at most automotive supply stores, in a small, resealable tank with a dip basket. If it is tightly sealed when not in use, the solution will last for several cleanings. Follow the manufacturer's instructions for correct soaking time.

*CAUTION*
*Do not soak the carburetor body in a tank of carburetor cleaner. The cleaner can damage the non-removable rubber seals used at the throttle plate shaft assembly.*

46

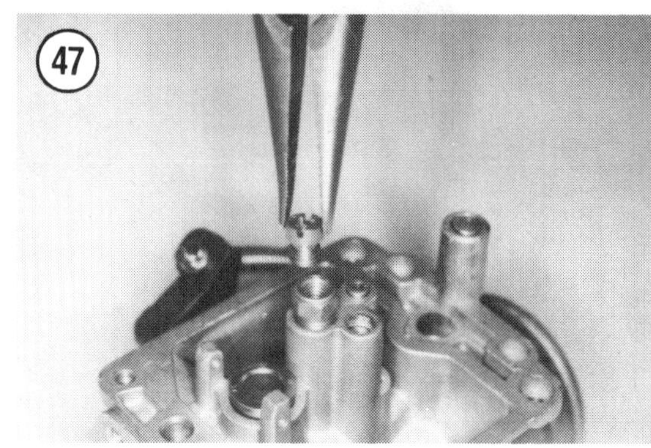
47

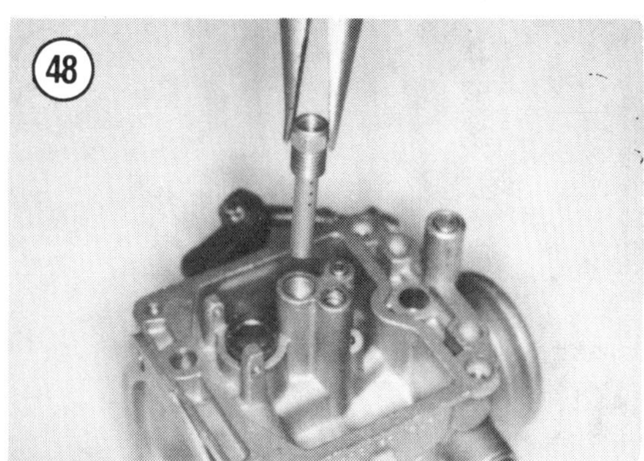
48

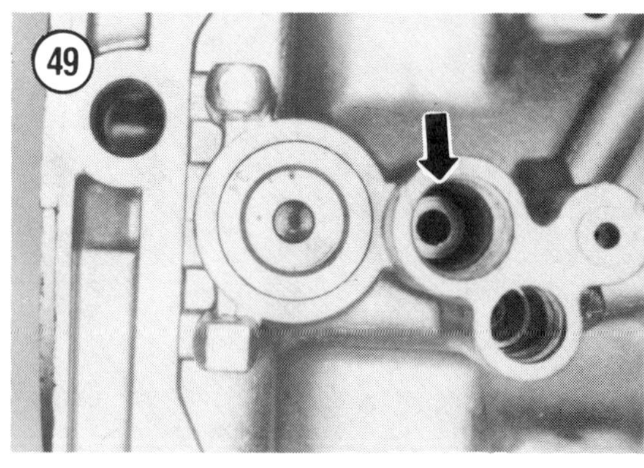
49

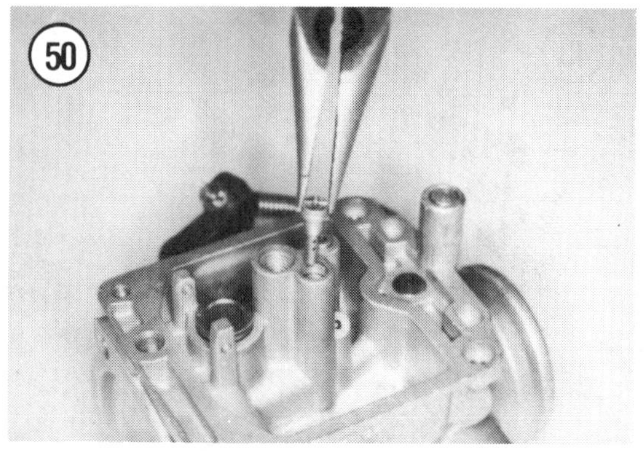
50

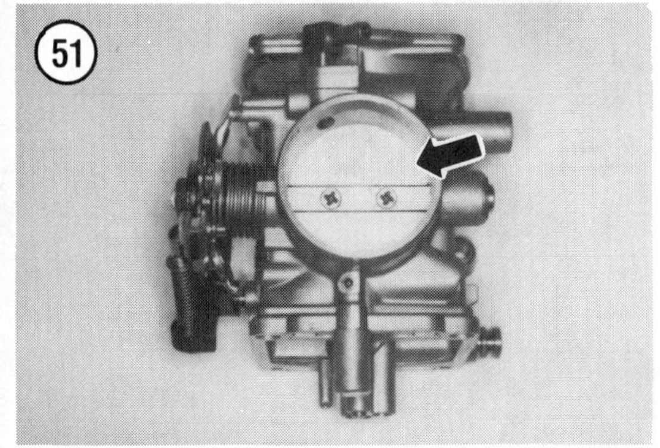
51

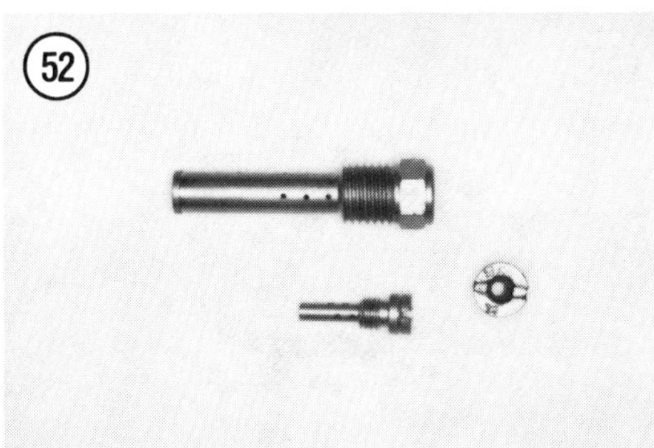
52

2. Remove all parts from the cleaner and blow dry with compressed air. Blow out the jets (**Figure 52**) with compressed air. *Do not* use a piece of wire to clean them as minor gouges in a jet can alter the flow rate and upset the air/fuel mixture.

3. Make sure the needle jet holder (**Figure 52**) bleed tube orifices are clear.

4. Make sure all fuel and air openings are clear. Blow out with compressed air if necessary.

5. Check the float assembly; see A, **Figure 53** (1984-1991) or **Figure 54** (1992-on). Place the float in a container full of water and push it down. There should be no bubbles. Replace the float if it leaks.

6. Check the float needle (B, **Figure 53**) and seat (**Figure 55**) contact areas. Both contact surfaces should appear smooth without any gouging or other apparent damage. Replace the needle if damaged. The seat is a permanent part of the carburetor housing; if damaged the housing must be replaced.

7. A damaged accelerating pump diaphragm (**Figure 56**) will cause poor acceleration. Hold the diaphragm up to a strong light and check the diaphragm for pin holes, cracks or other damage (**Figure 24**). Replace if necessary.

8

53

55

54

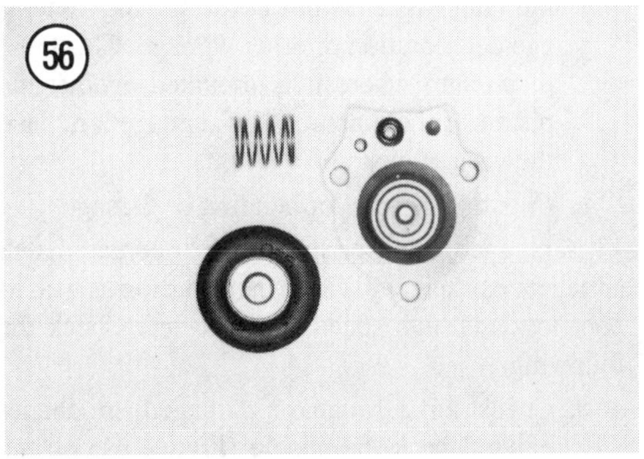
56

8. Remove the accelerator pump nozzle and its O-ring (**Figure 57**) from the float bowl. Clean the nozzle with compressed air.

9. Replace the pump rod if bent or worn.

10. O-rings tend to become hardened after prolonged use and heat and lose their ability to seal properly. Inspect all O-rings and replace if necessary. When replacing an O-ring, make sure the new O-ring fits in its groove properly. See **Figure 58**, typical.

11. Inspect the pilot jet (**Figure 52**) for wear or damage that may have occurred during removal. Check the slot in the top of the jet for cracks or breakage. Do not install a damaged pilot jet.

*NOTE*

*Step 12 describes bench checks that should be performed on the vacuum piston. Operational checks with the vacuum installed in the carburetor and with the engine running are described in this chapter.*

12. Bench check the vacuum piston as follows:
   a. Check the spring (**Figure 59**) for fatigue, stretching, distortion or other damage.
   b. Check the vacuum passage through the bottom of the piston (**Figure 60**) for contamination. Clean passage if blocked.
   c. The sides of the piston ride in grooves machined in the carburetor bore. Check these sides for roughness, nicks, cracks or distortion. If the piston sides are damaged, check the mating grooves in the carburetor for damage. Minor roughness can be removed with emery cloth or by buffing. If the sides are severely damaged, replace the vacuum piston.
   d. Hold the vacuum piston up to a light and check the diaphragm for pin holes, tearing, cracks, age deterioration or other damage. Check the diaphragm where it is mounted against the piston. If the diaphragm is damaged, replace the vacuum piston.
   e. Check jet needle for bending or damage.

13. A plugged, improperly seating or contaminated enrichener system will cause hard starting as well as poor low and high speed performance. Check the following:
   a. Check for a rough or damaged enrichener valve. Check the needle (**Figure 61**) on the

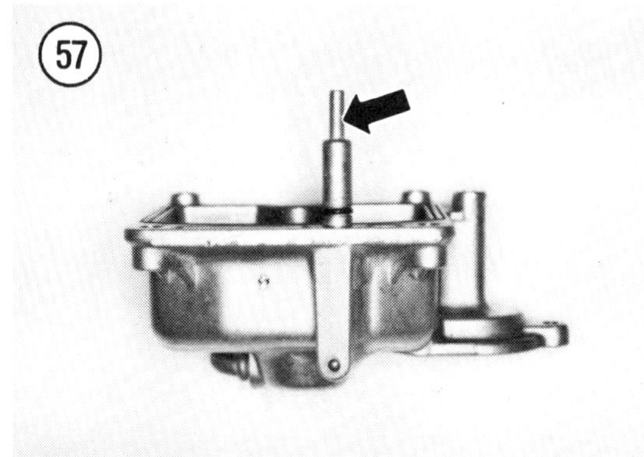


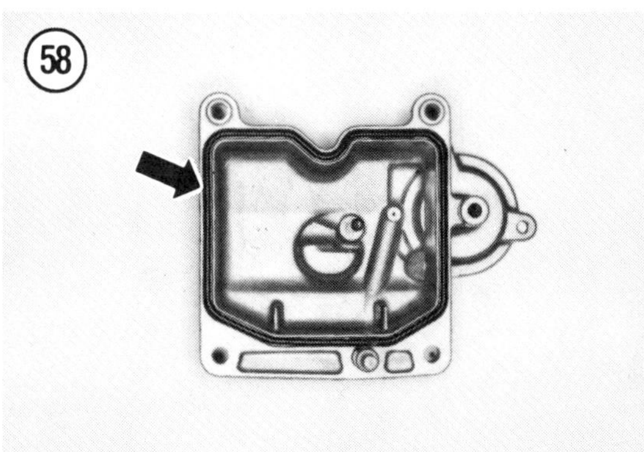


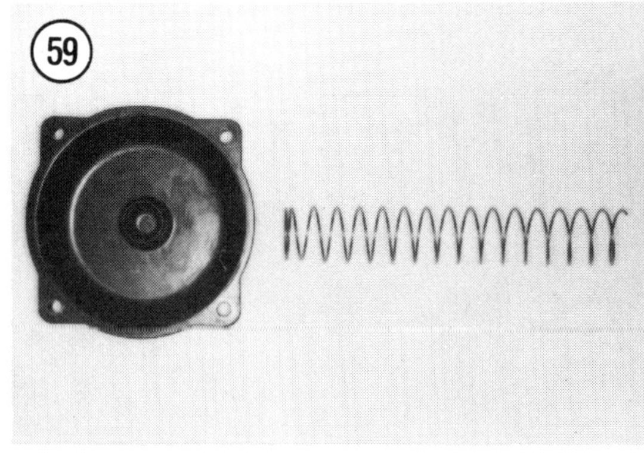


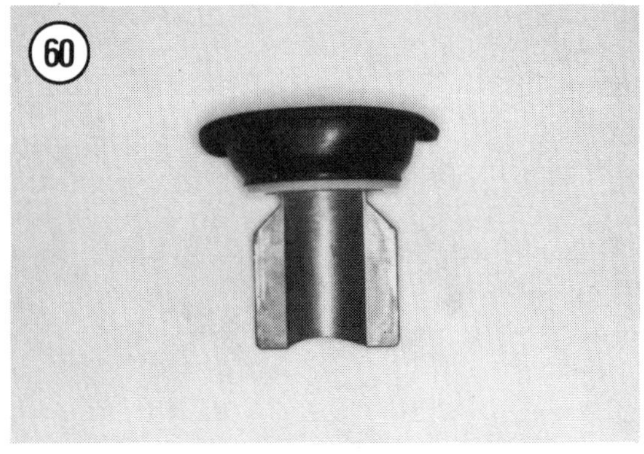

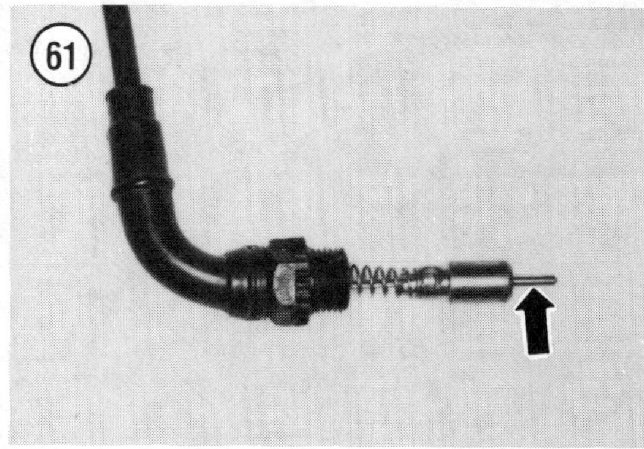

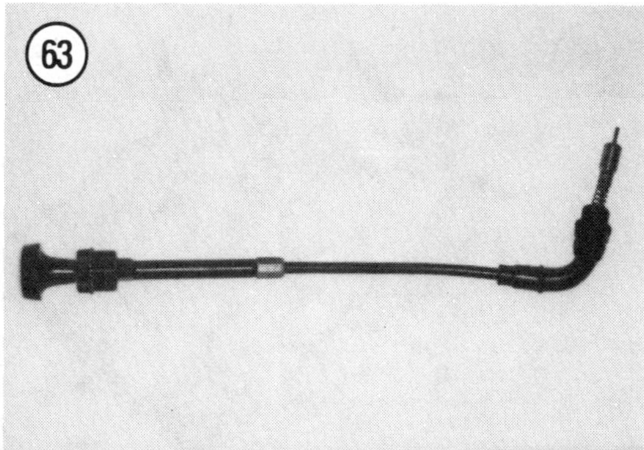

end of the enrichener valve for bending or contamination.

b. Check the enrichener valve spring for fatigue, stretching or distortion.

c. The enrichener valve chamber (A, **Figure 62**) in the carburetor must be clean. Clean the chamber carefully, making sure the enrichener valve air inlet and the air/fuel passages are clear.

d. Check the enrichener valve cable (**Figure 63**) for kinks or other damage.

14. Check the throttle rod (**Figure 64**) and all external carburetor components for missing or damaged parts.

15. Check that the throttle valve shaft E-clip (B, **Figure 62**) is properly secured in the groove on the end of the shaft.

### Assembly

Refer to **Figure 30** when performing this procedure.

1. Prior to assembly, perform the *Inspection* procedure to make sure all worn or damaged parts have been repaired or replaced. All parts should be thoroughly cleaned before assembly.



*NOTE*

*Before installing new jets, double check the jet size and compare to the old jet. If you are not rejetting the carburetor, make sure to install the same size jet(s).*

2. Drop the pilot jet (**Figure 50**) into the passage and tighten with the same screwdriver used during removal.

3. The needle jet has 2 different sides and can be installed incorrectly. Install the needle jet into its passage (**Figure 49**) so that the end with the larger opening faces up toward the vacuum piston chamber (top of carburetor).

4. Install the needle jet holder (**Figure 48**) into the main jet passage and tighten securely.

5. Install the main jet (**Figure 47**) onto the end of the needle jet holder and tighten securely.

6A. On 1984-1991 models, install the float as follows:

a. Install the fuel valve onto the float (**Figure 65**) and position the float onto the carburetor so that the valve drops into its seat.

b. Align the float pivot arm with the 2 carburetor mounting posts and slip the pin through the float pivot arm and mounting posts (**Figure 66**).

6B. On 1992-on models, install the float as follows:

a. Install the fuel valve onto the float (**Figure 67**) and position the float onto the carburetor so that the valve drops into its seat.

b. Align the float pivot arm with the 2 carburetor mounting posts and slip the pin through the float pivot arm and mounting posts (**Figure 68**).

7. Check float level as described in this chapter.

8. Assemble and install the float bowl as follows:

a. Insert the accelerator pump nozzle into the float bowl. Install the O-ring onto the nozzle. See **Figure 57**.

b. Install the rubber boot (A, **Figure 69**) and O-ring (B, **Figure 69**) onto the float bowl.

c. Connect the pump rod onto the lever assembly on the carburetor (**Figure 70**).

d. Insert the pump rod through the boot on the float bowl and engage the rod with the diaphragm while installing the float bowl (**Figure 71**). Then check that the pump rod is still attached to the lever assembly as shown in

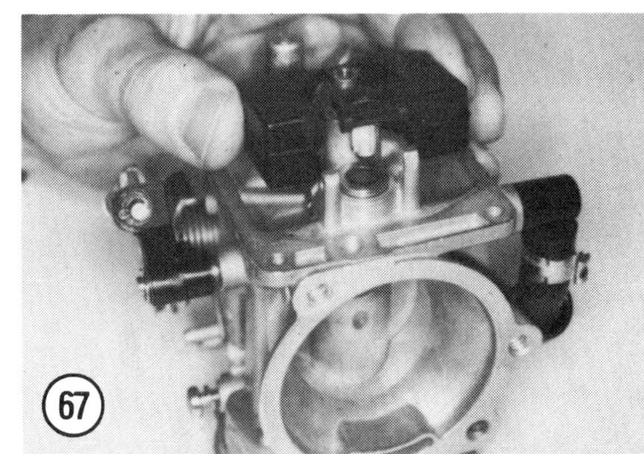
67

68

65

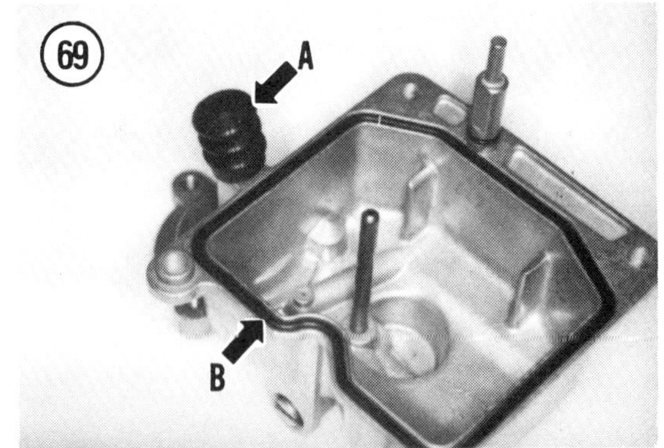

69

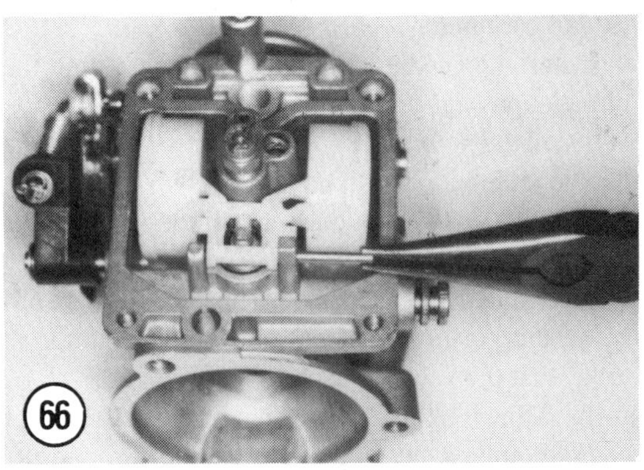
66

70

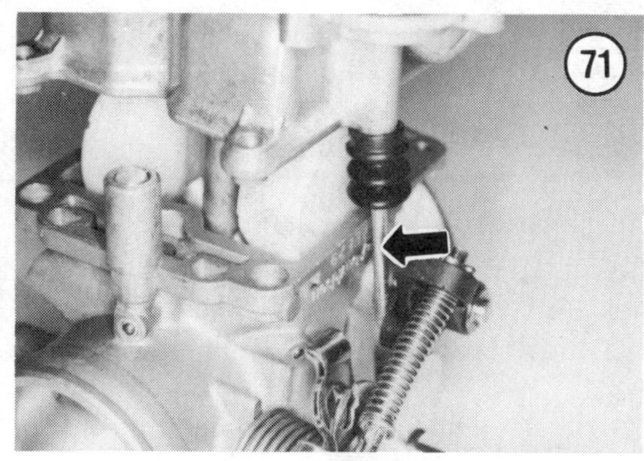

71

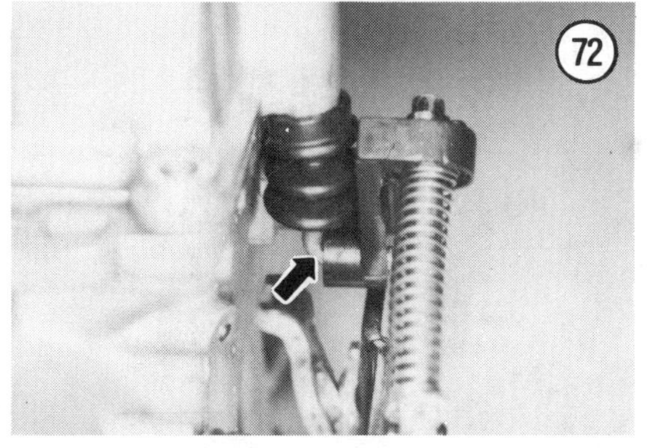

72

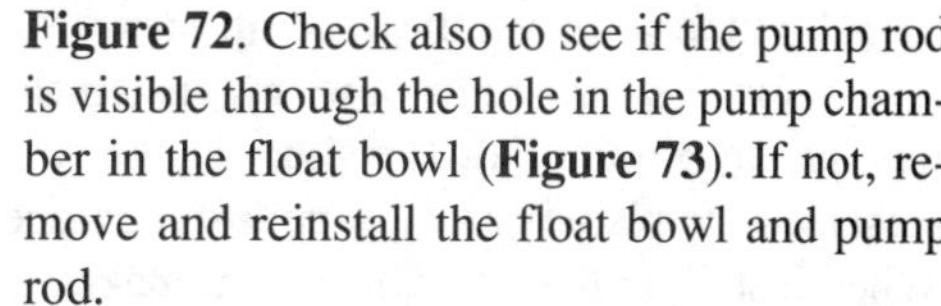

**Figure 72**. Check also to see if the pump rod is visible through the hole in the pump chamber in the float bowl (**Figure 73**). If not, remove and reinstall the float bowl and pump rod.

e. Install the float bowl screws and washers and tighten securely in a crisscross pattern.

9. Install the accelerator pump diaphragm assembly as follows:

a. Insert the accelerator pump diaphragm into the bottom of the float bowl. Make sure the diaphragm seats around the bowl groove (**Figure 74**).
b. Install the spring into the center of accelerator pump diaphragm (**Figure 75**).
c. Install the O-ring into the cover passageway hole (**Figure 76**).
d. Align the cover assembly with the diaphragm and bowl and install the cover assembly. Install the screws and lockwashers and tighten securely. See **Figure 77**.

10. Drop the jet needle through the center hole in the vacuum piston. Install the spring seat over the top of the needle to secure it.

8

73

75

74

76

11. Align the slides on the vacuum piston with the grooves in the carburetor bore and install the vacuum piston (**Figure 78**). The slides on the piston are offset, so the piston can only be installed one way. When installing the vacuum piston, make sure the jet needle drops through the needle jet.

12. Seat the outer edge of the vacuum piston into the groove at the top of the carburetor piston chamber.

13. Insert the spring (**Figure 79**) into the vacuum piston so that the end of the spring fits over the spring seat.

14. Align the free end of the spring with the carburetor top and install the top onto the carburetor, compressing the spring.

15. Hold the carburetor top in place and lift the vacuum piston with your finger. The piston should move smoothly. If the piston movement is rough or sluggish, the spring may be improperly installed. Remove the top and reinstall the spring.

16. Install the 3 carburetor top screws, lockwashers and flat washers finger-tight (**Figure 80**).

17. Install the throttle cable bracket (A, **Figure 81**) onto the carburetor so that the end of the idle speed screw engages the top of the throttle cam stop (B,

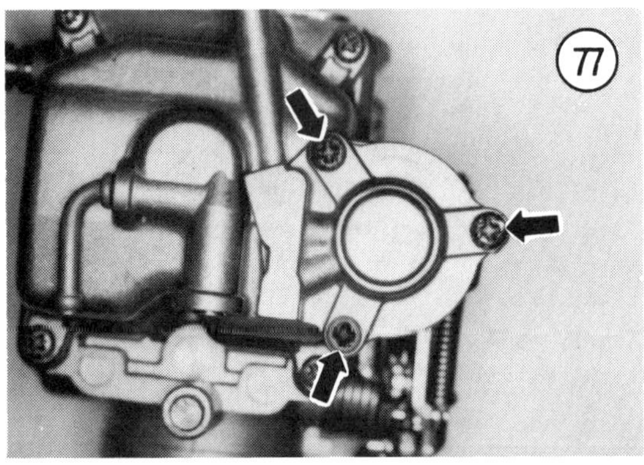
77

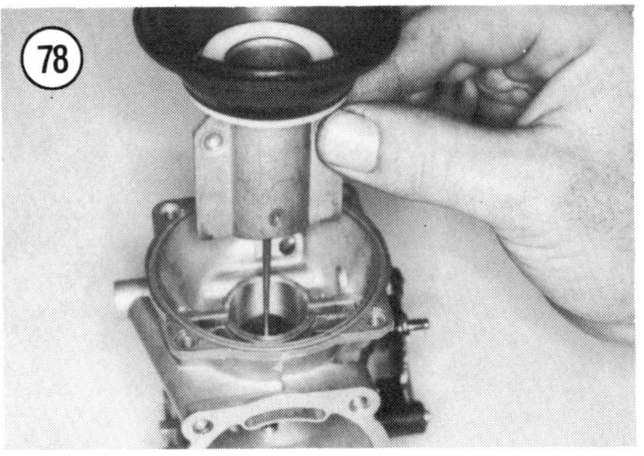
78

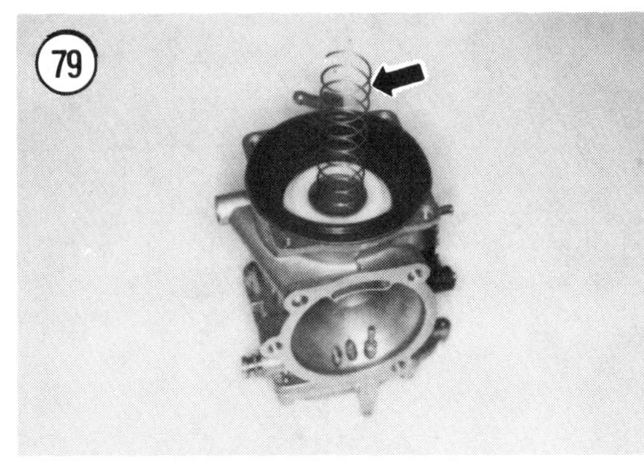
79

80

81

82

**Figure 81**). Hold the bracket in place and install the bracket's side mounting screw and washer; tighten screw securely. Then install the upper bracket mounting screw (**Figure 82**), lockwasher and flat washer finger-tight.

18. Tighten the 4 carburetor cap screws securely in a crisscross pattern.

19. Align the enrichener valve needle with the needle passage in the carburetor (**Figure 83**) and install the enrichener valve. Tighten the valve nut securely.

20. Install the float bowl overflow hose and secure it with its clamp.

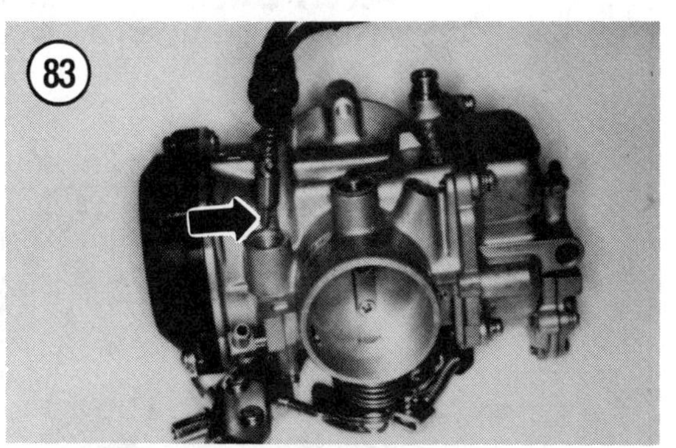

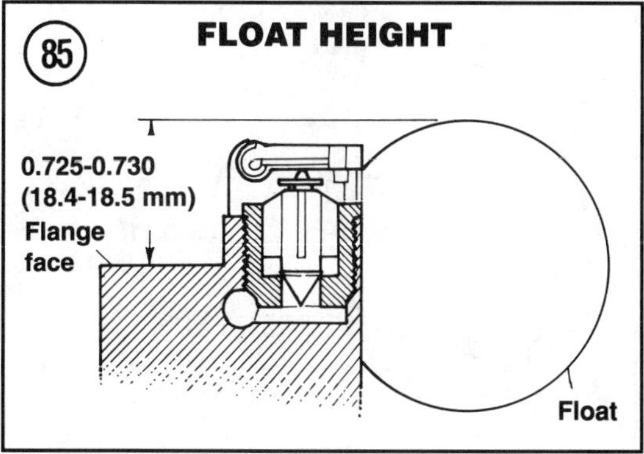


### Float Level Adjustment (1984-Early 1991)

An incorrect float level can cause flooding as well as poor fuel economy and acceleration.

The carburetor must be removed and partially disassembled for this adjustment.

*NOTE*

*1990-early 1991 model carburetors are equipped with a 3-sided fuel valve. Starting with late 1991 models (production date June, 1991), carburetors are equipped with a 4-sided fuel valve. If you have a 1991 model and it is equipped with a 3-sided fuel valve, service the float level as described in the following steps. If your 1991 model is equipped with a 4-sided fuel valve, refer to **Float Level Adjustment (Late 1991-on)** in this chapter.*

1. Remove the carburetor as described in this chapter.
2. Remove the float bowl as described in this chapter.
3. One-piece floats are used in the carburetor. Before checking the float level, check that the 2 float halves (**Figure 84**) are aligned at an equal height with each other. If the float halves are not in alignment, remove the float and check it for damage.
4. Turn the carburetor to position the float bowl as shown in **Figure 85**. Measure the float height from the face of the bowl mounting flange surface to the bottom float surface (**Figure 85**). Do not apply pressure to the float when measuring. The correct float height is 0.725-0.730 in. (18.4-18.5 mm).
5. If the float height is incorrect, remove the float pin and float.
6. Bend the float tang with a screwdriver to adjust.
7. Reinstall the float and the float pin and recheck the float level. Repeat until the float level is correct.
8. Reinstall the float bowl and carburetor as described in this chapter.

### Float Adjustment (Late 1991-on)

An incorrect float level can cause flooding as well as poor fuel economy and acceleration.

The carburetor must be removed and partially disassembled for this adjustment.

1. Remove the carburetor as described in this chapter.

2. Remove the float bowl as described in this chapter.
3. One-piece floats are used in the carburetor. Before checking the float level, check that the 2 float halves (**Figure 86**) are aligned at an equal height with each other. If the float halves are not in alignment, remove the float and check for damage.
4. Place the carburetor intake spigot on a flat surface as shown in **Figure 87**. This is the base position.
5. Tilt the carburetor counterclockwise 15-20° as shown in **Figure 88**. At this position, the float will come to rest as the float pin compresses without compressing the pin return spring.

*NOTE*
*If the carburetor is tilted less than 15° or more than 20°, the following carburetor measurements will be incorrect.*

6. Measure from the carburetor flange surface to the top of the float with a caliper or float gauge as shown in **Figure 88**. When measuring float level, make sure you do not compress the float. The correct float level measurement is as follows:
   a. 1991: 0.690-0.730 in. (17.5-18.5 mm).
   b. 1992-on: 0.413-0.453 in. (10.5-11.5 mm).
7. If the float level is incorrect, remove the float pin and float. With a screwdriver, bend the tab on the float hinge that contacts the fuel valve.
8. Reinstall the float and the float pin and recheck the float level. Repeat until the float level is correct.
9. Reinstall the float bowl and carburetor as described in this chapter.

## CARBURETOR REJETTING

Do not try to solve a poor running engine problem by rejetting the carburetor if all of the following conditions hold true.

1. The engine has held a good tune in the past with the standard jetting.
2. The engine has not been modified (this includes the addition of accessory exhaust systems).
3. The motorcycle is being operated in the same geographical region under the same general climatic conditions as in the past.
4. The motorcycle was and is being ridden at average highway speeds.

If those conditions all hold true, the chances are that the problem is due to a malfunction in the carburetor or in another component that needs to be adjusted or repaired. Changing carburetion jet size

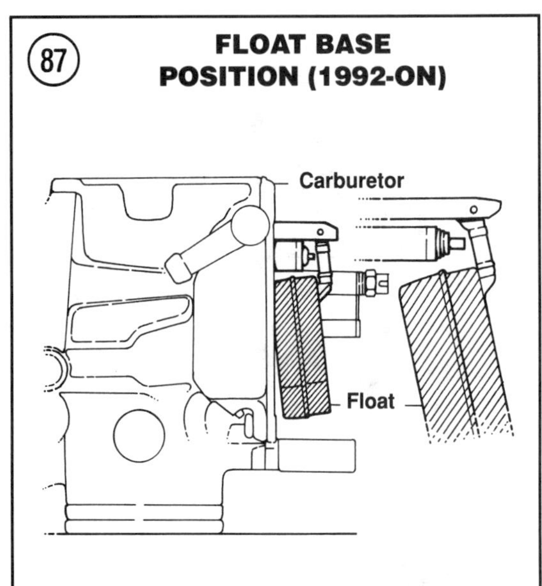


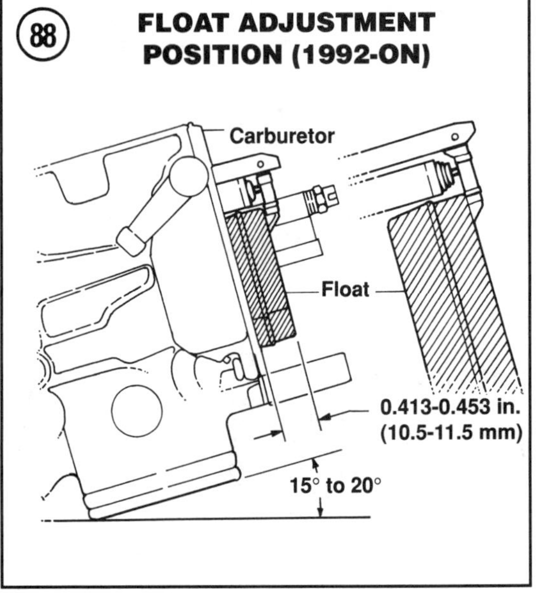

probably won't solve the problem. Rejetting the carburetor may be necessary if any of the following conditions hold true.

1. A non-standard type of air filter element is being used.

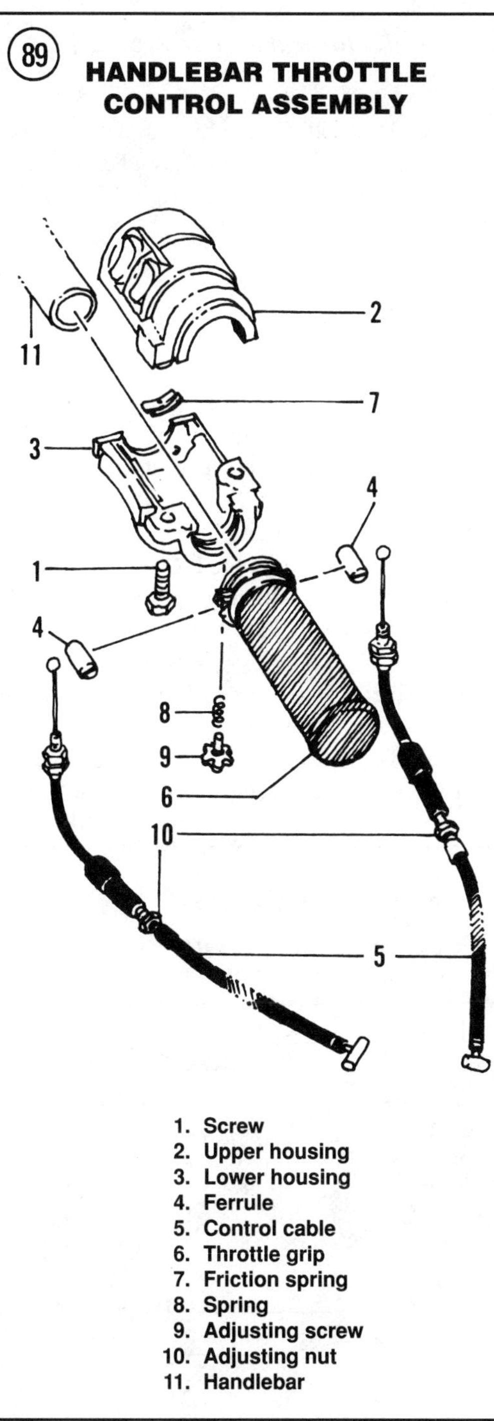


**89 HANDLEBAR THROTTLE CONTROL ASSEMBLY**

1. Screw
2. Upper housing
3. Lower housing
4. Ferrule
5. Control cable
6. Throttle grip
7. Friction spring
8. Spring
9. Adjusting screw
10. Adjusting nut
11. Handlebar

2. A non-standard exhaust system is installed on the motorcycle.
3. Any of the following engine components have been modified: pistons, cam, valves, compression ration, etc.

NOTE
*When installing accessory engine equipment, manufacturers often enclose guidelines on rejetting the carburetor.*

4. The motorcycle is in use at considerably higher or lower altitudes or in a considerably hotter or colder climate than in the past.
5. The motorcycle is being operated at considerably higher speeds than before and changing to colder spark plugs does not solve the problem.
6. Someone has previously changed the carburetor jetting.
7. The motorcycle has never held a satisfactory engine tune.

## THROTTLE AND IDLE CABLE REPLACEMENT (NON-CRUISE CONTROL MODELS)

All models use a dual throttle cable arrangement. The throttle cable is installed into the right-hand anchor slot at the top of the throttle housing. The idle cable is installed into the left-hand anchor slot at the top of the throttle housing. See **Figure 89**, typical.

NOTE
*You can identify the throttle and idle cables by checking the size of the threads used on each cable's threaded adjuster. The throttle cable uses a 5/16-18 threaded adjuster. The threaded adjuster on the idle cable uses 1/4-20 threads.*

1. Remove the fuel tank as described in this chapter.
2. Remove the air filter. See Chapter Three.

NOTE
*Make a diagram of each cable's routing path **before** removing the cables from the bike. Also ID the cable guides or plastic ties on the diagram where used.*

3. Loosen the friction adjusting screw.
4. Loosen the cable adjust nuts and turn the cable adjuster to obtain as much cable slack as possible.
5. Remove the screws securing the upper and lower right-hand switch/throttle housing together and

separate the housing from the handlebar (**Figure 89**).

6. Loosen the cable locknuts at the lower switch housing.

7. Unhook the cables from the throttle grip and remove the ferrule from the end of each cable.

8. Unscrew each cable and remove it from the lower housing assembly.

9. At the carburetor, hold the lever up with one hand and disengage the cable end. Slip the cable out through the carburetor bracket. See **Figure 90**, typical. Repeat for the other cable.

10. Cut any plastic ties used to route the cables.

NOTE
*The piece of string attached in the next step will be used to pull the new cables back through the frame so they will be routed in exactly the same position as the old ones.*

11. Tie a piece of heavy string or cord (approximately 7 ft. [213.3 cm] long) to the *carburetor* end of one throttle cable. Wrap this end with masking or duct tape. Do not use an excessive amount of tape as it must be pulled through the frame loop during removal. Tie the other end of the string to the frame.

12. At the throttle grip end of the cables, carefully pull the cables (and attached string) out through the frame. Make sure the attached string follows the same path as the cable through the frame.

13. Remove the tape and untie the string from the old cables. Do not remove the string.

14. Clean the throttle in solvent and dry thoroughly. Check the throttle slots for cracks or other damage. Replace the throttle if necessary.

15. The friction adjust screw is secured to the lower switch housing with a circlip. If necessary, remove the friction spring, circlip, spring and friction adjust screw. Check these parts for wear or damage. Replace damaged parts and reverse to install. Make sure the circlip seats in the friction screw completely.

16. Clean the right-hand handlebar with solvent or electrical contact cleaner.

17. Wipe the right-hand handlebar and the inside of the throttle grip with graphite.

18. Lubricate the throttle cables as described in Chapter Three.

19. Tie the string to the new throttle cables and wrap it with tape.

20. Carefully pull the string back through the frame, routing the new cables through the same path as the old cables.

21. Remove the tape and untie the string from the cables and the frame.

NOTE
*The throttle cable uses a 5/16-18 threaded cable adjuster.*

22. Screw the throttle cable into the lower switch housing and fit the ferrule onto the end of the cable. Then insert the ferrule into the right-hand anchor slot at the top of the throttle.

NOTE
*The idle cables uses a 1/4-20 threaded cable adjuster.*

23. Screw the idle cable into the lower switch housing and fit the ferrule onto the end of the cable. Then insert the ferrule into the left-hand anchor slot at the top of the throttle.

24. Assemble the upper and lower switch housings and slide the throttle grip onto the handlebar. Install the housing screws and tighten securely. Operate the throttle and make sure both cables move in and out properly.

25. Locate the 2 cable support sleeves on the carburetor; one cable sleeve is longer than the other. Install the idle cable onto the *longer* support sleeve; attach the end of the cable onto the cable spool.

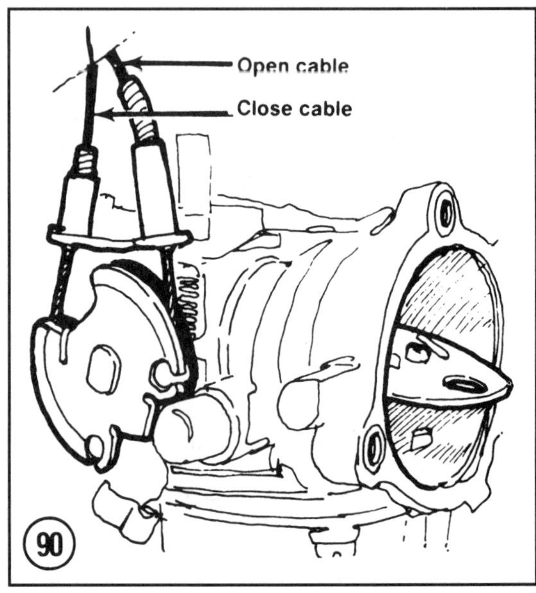


90

Install the throttle cable onto the *shorter* support sleeve; attach the end of the cable onto the cable spool.

26. Reinstall all cable guides and clamps.

27. Operate the throttle grip and make sure the carburetor throttle linkage is operating correctly and with no binding. If operation is incorrect or there is binding, carefully check that the cables are attached correctly and there are no tight bends in the cables.

28. Adjust the throttle and idle cables as described in Chapter Three.

29. Install the fuel tank and seat.

30. Start the engine and turn the handlebar from side to side. Do not operate the throttle. If the engine speed increases as the handlebar assembly is turned, the throttle cables are routed incorrectly. Remove the seat and fuel tank and recheck the cable routing.

91

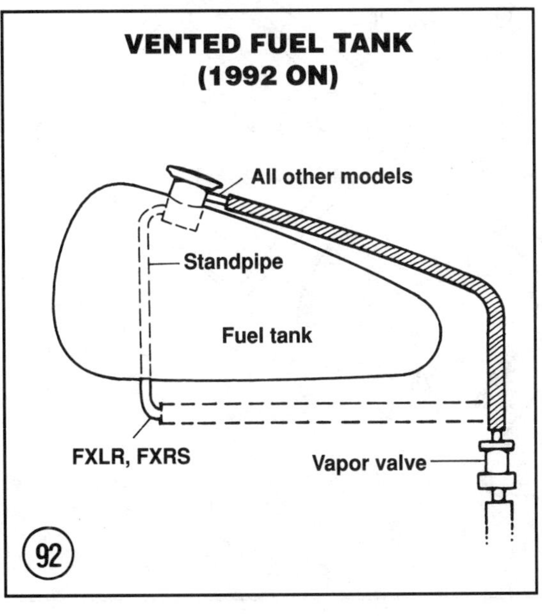

92

*WARNING*
*Do **not** ride the bike until you are sure the throttle cables are routed properly.*

31. Test ride the bike slowly at first and make sure the throttle is operating correctly.

## THROTTLE AND IDLE CABLE REPLACEMENT (CRUISE CONTROL MODELS)

Refer to Chapter Fourteen.

## CHOKE/ENRICHENER CABLE REPLACEMENT

A choke cable is used on 1984-1989 models. An enrichener cable is used on 1990 and later models.

1. Remove the air cleaner assembly, if necessary, to access the cable at the carburetor.

2. Disconnect the cable at both ends and remove the cable.

3. Installation is the reverse of these steps. On 1990 and later models, align the enrichener valve needle with the needle passage in the carburetor (**Figure 91**) and install the enrichener valve. Tighten the valve nut securely.

4. Adjust the choke or enrichener cable as described in Chapter Three.



## FUEL TANK

When removing the fuel tank in the following procedure, keep track of all fasteners and rubber bushings so that you don't lose or mix them up during installation.

### Fuel Tank Venting (1984-1991)

On 1984-1991 models, the fuel tank(s) are vented through the fuel cap.

### Fuel Tank Venting (1992-on)

All 1992-on fuel tanks are vented through a vapor valve. On 1992-on FXLR and 1992 FXRS models, the vent tube is connected to a standpipe mounted in the bottom of the fuel tank. On all other models, a vent nozzle is installed in the tank's filler neck. See **Figure 92**.

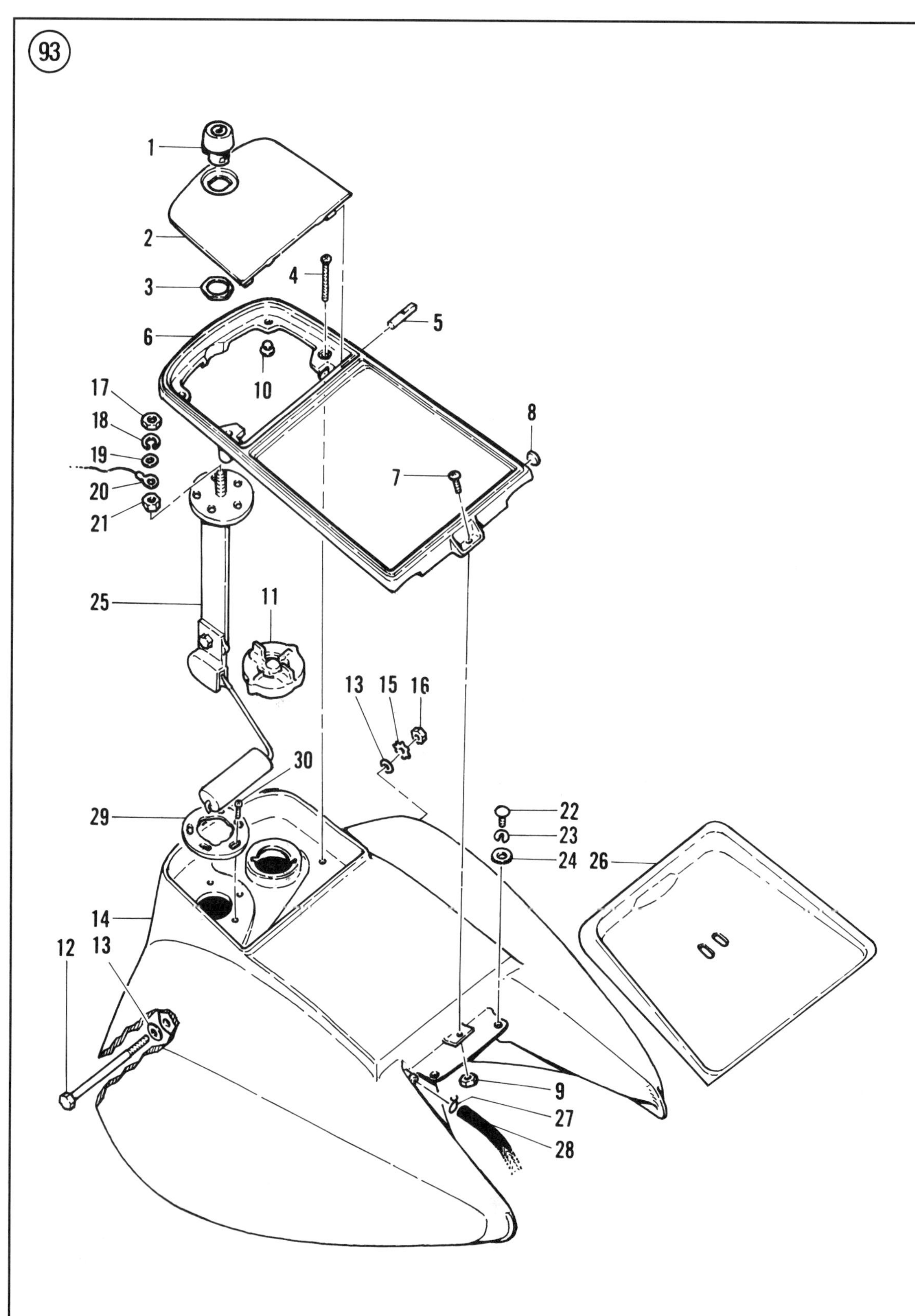
93
1
2
3
4
5
6
7
8
9
10
11
12
13
14
15
16
17
18
19
20
21
22
23
24
25
26
27
28
29
30

**FUEL TANK (1984-1988 FLT)**

1. Lock
2. Cover
3. Nut
4. Screw
5. Pin
6. Panel
7. Screw
8. Spacer
9. Nut
10. Bumper
11. Cap
12. Bolt
13. Washer
14. Fuel tank
15. Washer
16. Nut
17. Nut
18. Lockwasher
19. Washer
20. Fuel gauge wire
21. Nut
22. Screw
23. Lockwasher
24. Washer
25. Fuel gauge
26. Panel
27. Clip
28. Hose
29. Gasket
30. Screw

The vapor valve prevents fuel from flowing through the vent opening when the motorcycle is dropped or positioned at a low angle.

When replacing the vapor valve, note the following:

a. The vapor valve must be installed in a vertical position.
b. The vapor valve has 2 different end fittings. The long fitting must be installed at the top.

*CAUTION*

*If the vapor valve is installed incorrectly, excessive pressure may build in the fuel tank.*

### Removal/Installation (1984-on FLT)

*WARNING*

*Gasoline is very volatile and presents an extreme fire hazard. Be sure to work in a well-ventilated area away from any open flames (including pilot lights on household appliances). Do not allow anyone to smoke in the area. Have a fire extinguisher rated for gasoline fires handy.*

Refer to **Figure 93** (1984-1988, typical) or **Figure 94** (1989-on, typical) when performing this procedure.

1. Disconnect the negative battery cable.
2. Disconnect the fuel line at the fuel shutoff valve. Connect a longer hose to the shutoff valve fitting and place the open end of the hose in a safety approved fuel storage tank. Turn the shutoff valve to RESERVE and drain the fuel into the tank. Don't lose the fuel line insulator.
3. Disconnect the hoses from the fuel tank.
4. Remove the seat.
5. *1989-on*: Open the fuel tank cap cover and remove the screws securing the console to the fuel tank. Then carefully lift the console off of the fuel tank and place it on the frame behind the fuel tank.

*NOTE*

*On 1989 and later models, do not remove the nut holding the yellow wire to the center of the fuel gauge sender. If this nut is removed, the fuel gauge sender will fall into the fuel tank.*

8

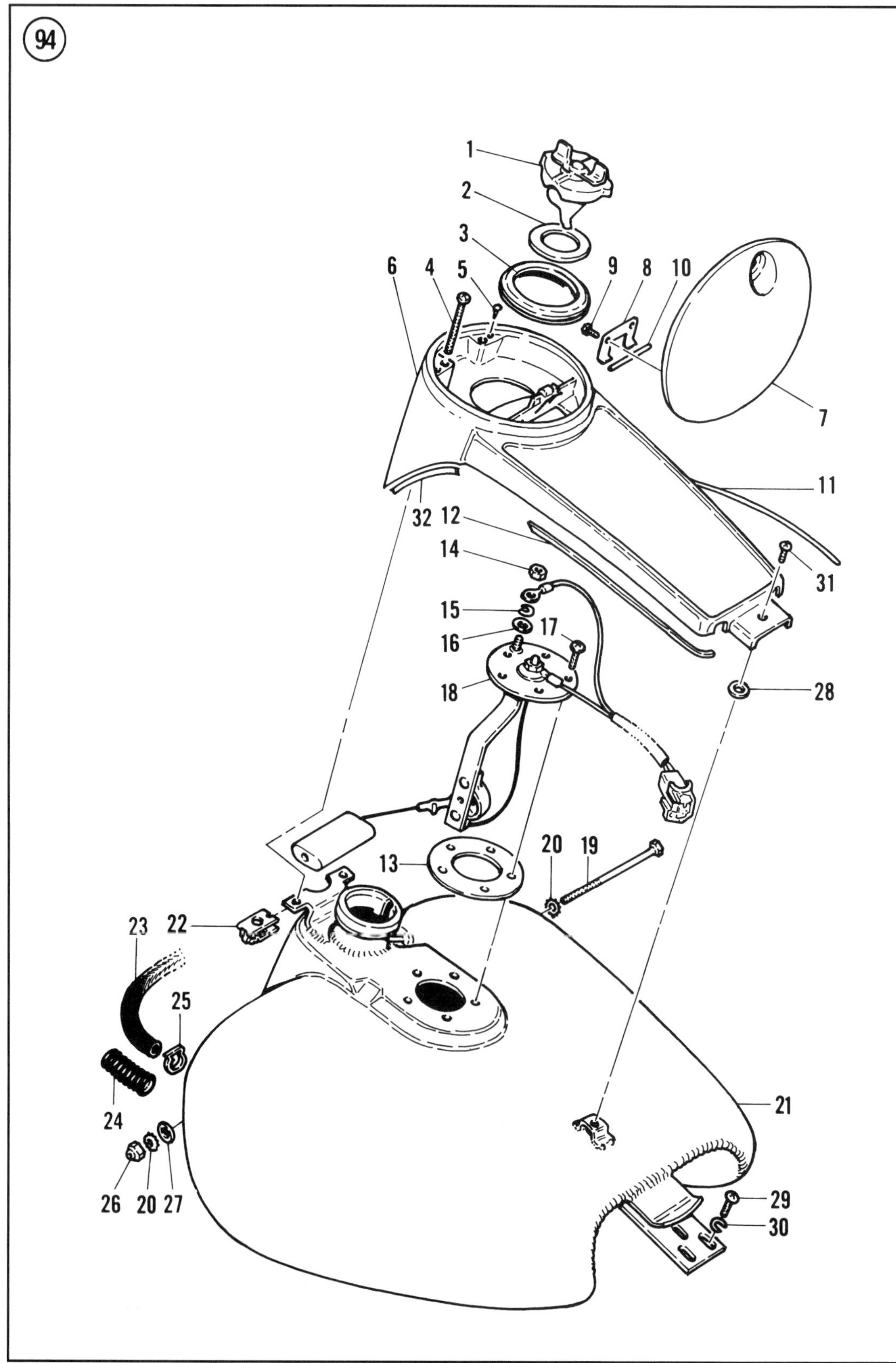

94
1
2
3
6
4
5
9
8
10
7
11
32
12
14
31
15
17
16
28
18
20
19
13
23
22
25
24
21
26
20
27
29
30

**FUEL TANK (1989-ON FLT)**

1. Cap
2. Gasket
3. Boot
4. Screw
5. Bumper
6. Console
7. Cover
8. Bracket
9. Screw
10. Pin
11. Trim
12. Trim
13. Gasket
14. Nut
15. Lockwasher
16. Washer
17. Screw
18. Fuel gauge
19. Bolt
20. Washer
21. Fuel tank
22. Nut
23. Hose
24. Insulator
25. Hose clamp
26. Nut
27. Washer
28. Washer
29. Screw
30. Lockwasher
32. Screw
32. Trim

6. Disconnect the fuel gauge sender electrical connector wires.
7. Remove the front and rear fuel tank fasteners.
8. Carefully lift and remove the fuel tank from the frame.
9. Drain any remaining fuel in the tank into the fuel storage tank.
10. Installation is the reverse of these steps. Note the following.

*NOTE*
*If you are installing an OEM replacement fuel tank on 1991 FLT and FXR California models, refer to* ***Fuel Tank Vent Modification (1991 FLT and FXR California Models)*** *in this chapter prior to installing the new tank.*

11. Position the fuel tank on the frame tubes and install the washers, bolts and nuts in their original mounting positions.
12. Remove the drain tube from the fuel tank and reconnect the fuel line. Secure the fuel line with a new hose clamp. Make sure the insulator is placed over the fuel line before reconnecting it.
13. Refill the tank and check for leaks.

8

### Removal/Installation (All FXR Models except 1988-on FXRS)

*WARNING*
*Gasoline is very volatile and presents an extreme fire hazard. Be sure to work in a well-ventilated area away from any open flames (including pilot lights on household appliances). Do not allow anyone to smoke in the area. Have a fire extinguisher rated for gasoline fires handy.*

Refer to **Figure 95** and **Figure 96** when performing this procedure.

1. Disconnect the negative battery cable.
2. Disconnect the fuel line at the fuel shutoff valve. Connect a longer hose to the shutoff valve fitting and place the open end of the hose in a safety approved fuel storage tank. Turn the shutoff valve to RESERVE and drain the fuel into the tank. Don't lose the fuel line insulator.
3. Disconnect the hoses from the fuel tank.
4. Remove the fuel tank center panel screws and gas cap. Remove the rear center panel fasteners, if used.

5. Lift the center panel slightly and disconnect the fuel gauge wire at the sending unit and the power supply wire from the main wire harness.

6. On models with a speedometer mounted on the console, disconnect the speedometer power supply wire and the speedometer light ground wire. Then disconnect the speedometer cable.

7. Remove the front fuel tank mounting fasteners.

8. Disconnect the fuel gauge ground wire attached to a clip under the console. Then remove the mounting bolt and washer and remove the center panel.

9. Open and secure the seat or remove the seat.

10. Remove the rear fuel tank mounting fasteners.

CAUTION
*When removing the fuel tank in Step 11, do not pull on or damage the main wiring harness.*

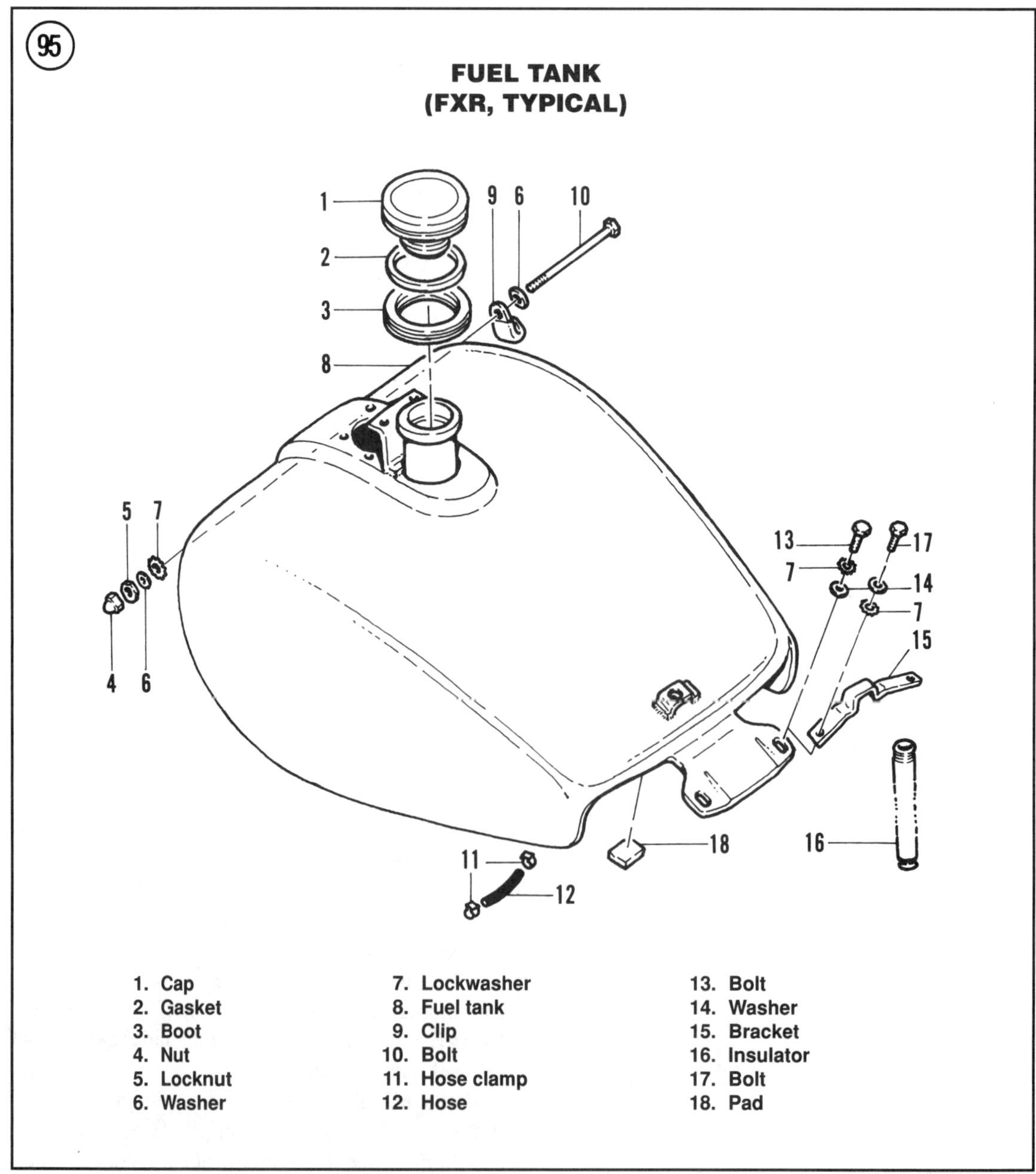

**FUEL TANK INSTRUMENTS (FXR, TYPICAL)**

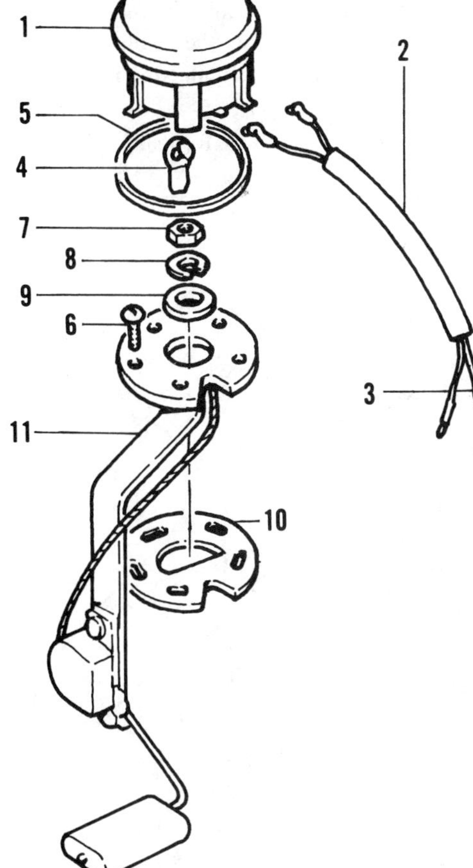


1. Fuel gauge indicator
2. Wire harness
3. Terminal ring
4. Bulb
5. Gasket
6. Screw
7. Nut
8. Lockwasher
9. Washer
10. Gasket
11. Fuel gauge

96

11. Carefully remove the fuel tank from the frame.
12. Drain any remaining fuel in the tank into the fuel storage tank.
13. Installation is the reverse of these steps. Note the following.

*NOTE*
*If you are installing an OEM replacement fuel tank on 1991 FLT and FXR California models, refer to* ***Fuel Tank Vent Modification (1991 FLT and FXR California Models)*** *in this chapter prior to installing the new tank.*

14. Position the fuel tank on the frame tube and install the washers, bolts and nuts in their original mounting positions.
15. Remove the drain tube from the fuel tank and reconnect the fuel line. Secure the fuel line with a new hose clamp. Make sure the insulator is placed over the fuel line before reconnecting it.
16. Refill the tank and check for leaks.

8

**Removal/Installation (1988-on FXRS)**

*WARNING*
*Gasoline is very volatile and presents an extreme fire hazard. Be sure to work in a well-ventilated area away from any open flames (including pilot lights on household appliances). Do not allow anyone to smoke in the area. Have a fire extinguisher rated for gasoline fires handy.*

Refer to **Figure 95** and **Figure 96** when performing this procedure.

1. Disconnect the negative battery cable.
2. Disconnect the fuel line at the fuel shutoff valve. Connect a longer hose to the shutoff valve fitting and place the open end of the hose in a safety approved fuel storage tank. Turn the shutoff valve to RESERVE and drain the fuel into the tank. Don't lose the fuel line insulator.
3. Disconnect the hoses from the fuel tank.
4. Remove the screws securing the instrument panel to the fuel tank. Then lift the panel and disconnect the speedometer cable and electrical leads.
5. Remove the front fuel tank mounting fasteners.
6. Open and secure the seat.
7. Remove the rear fuel tank mounting fasteners.

*CAUTION*
*When removing the fuel tank in Step 8, do not pull on or damage the main wiring harness.*

8. Carefully remove the fuel tank from the frame.
9. Drain any remaining fuel in the tank into the fuel storage tank.
10. Installation is the reverse of these steps. Note the following.

*NOTE*
*If you are installing an OEM replacement fuel tank on 1991 FLT and FXR California models, refer to **Fuel Tank Vent Modification (1991 FLT and FXR California Models)** in this chapter prior to installing the new tank.*

11. Position the fuel tank on the frame tube and install the washers, bolts and nuts in their original mounting positions.

12. Remove the drain tube from the fuel tank and reconnect the fuel line. Secure the fuel line with a new hose clamp. Make sure the insulator is placed over the fuel line before reconnecting it.

13. Refill the tank and check for leaks.

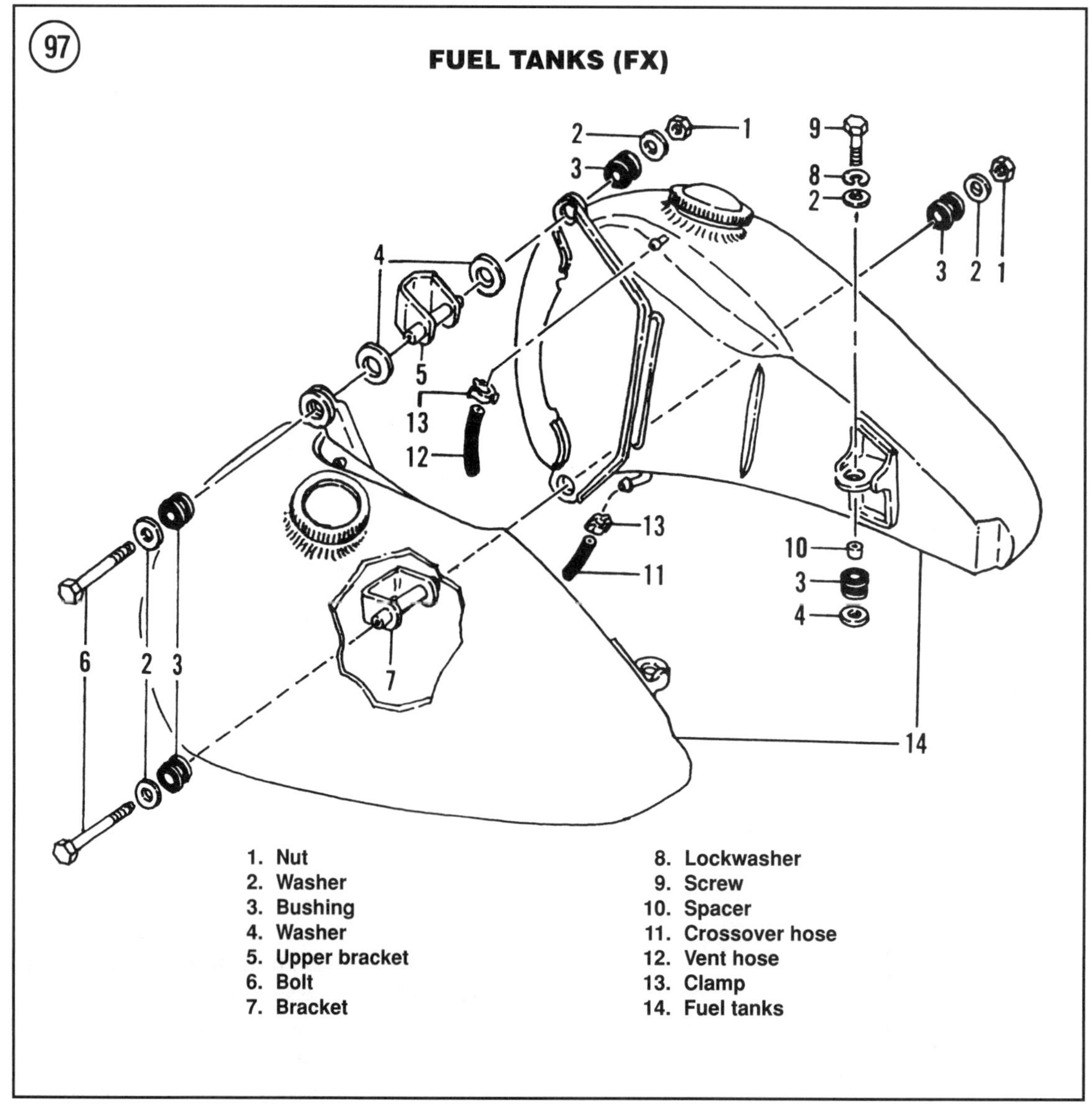

### Removal/Installation (1985-1986 FX)

*WARNING*
*Gasoline is very volatile and presents an extreme fire hazard. Be sure to work in a well-ventilated area away from any open flames (including pilot lights on household appliances). Do not allow anyone to smoke in the area. Have a fire extinguisher rated for gasoline fires handy.*

Two steel fuel tanks are bolted to the upper frame tube and to each other; see **Figure 97**, typical. Rubber bushings are used at almost all tank mounting points. A 3-way fuel shutoff valve is mounted on the left-hand fuel tank; the tanks are connected by a crossover line. The gas caps on both tanks are non-vented. Fuel tank venting is provided by a hose connected to the inside of each tank.

1. Disconnect the negative battery cable.
2. Remove the odometer knob and screw from the instrument panel.
3. Remove the choke knob and nuts, if so equipped.

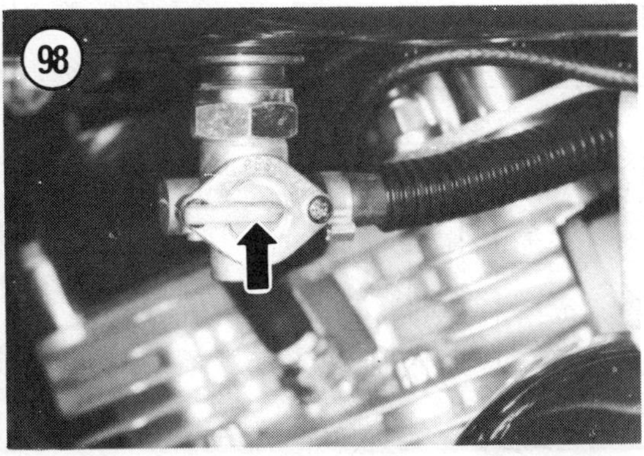
98

99

4. Remove the trim panel at the bottom of the tanks.
5. Remove the instrument panel mounting fasteners and lift the instrument panel off of the fuel tanks.
6. Disconnect the fuel line at the fuel shutoff valve (**Figure 98**). Connect a longer hose to the shutoff valve fitting and place the open end of the hose in a gasoline fuel tank. Turn the shutoff valve to RESERVE and drain the fuel into the tank. Don't lose the fuel line insulator.

*NOTE*
*Before disconnecting the crossover fuel line in Step 7, be prepared to plug both tank fittings after the hose is disconnected. The crossover tube can be plugged with a bolt or golf tee. The other fuel tank can be plugged by installing a separate piece of hose, plugged in one end, on the crossover tank fitting.*

7. Disconnect the crossover fuel line (**Figure 99**). Plug the crossover fuel line and plug the other tank's fuel fitting.
8. Remove the front upper and lower mounting bolts, washers and nuts.
9. Remove the rear bolts, washers and spacers securing the tanks to the frame.
10. Disconnect the upper vent line from the fuel tanks.
11. Check the fuel tanks for any remaining fasteners and remove the tanks from the frame.

*NOTE*
*After removing the tanks, store them in a safe place—away from open flame or objects that could fall and damage them.*

12. Drain any remaining fuel left in the tanks into the storage tank.
13. Installation is the reverse of these steps. Note the following.
14. Position the fuel tanks on the frame tubes and install the washers, bolts and nuts in their original mounting positions. The large ID washers fit over the left- and right-hand ends on the upper bracket spacer tube and over the tapped anchor insert at the rear tank brackets.
15. Tighten the front and rear bolts securely.
16. Route the crossover tube over the lower front tank bracket and reconnect it at the other tank. Secure the line with new clamps.

17. Remove the drain tube from the fuel tank and reconnect the fuel line. Secure the fuel line with a new hose clamp. Make sure the insulator is placed over the fuel line before reconnecting it.
18. Refill the tanks and check for leaks.

### Inspection

1. Inspect all of the fuel and vent lines for cracks, age deterioration or damage. Replace damaged lines with the same type and size material. The fuel line must be flexible and strong enough to withstand engine heat and vibration.
2. Check the fuel line insulator for damage.
3. Check for damaged or missing rubber dampers.
4. Remove the fuel tank cap(s) and inspect the inside of the tank for rust or contamination. If there is a rust buildup inside the tank, clean and flush the tank as described in this chapter.
5. Inspect the fuel tank for leaks. If fuel was noted on the outside of the tank, and it was not spilled during refilling, the tank is leaking. If the leakage point is small, repair the leak as described in this chapter. If the leak is large, or if it cannot be repaired with a tank sealant, replace the fuel tank.

### Fuel Tank Vent Modification (1991 FLT and FXR California Models)

When installing an OEM replacement fuel tank on 1991 FLT and FXR California models, a 0.03-0.06 in. (0.76-1.5 mm) hole must be drilled through the vapor tube cap. Confirm this with your Harley-Davidson dealer upon purchasing the new tank. To drill the cap:

a. First center punch the cap and drill through the cap with a 1/16 in. drill bit (**Figure 100**).
b. Remove the fuel cap and use compressed air to remove all chips from the fuel tank.
c. Reinstall the fuel cap.

### Fuel Tank Flushing

While the fuel tanks require little in the way of service, moisture can build in the tanks. From this moisture, rust will form on the interior of the tank. If allowed to go unchecked, it will build and then mix with the gas in the tank, causing fuel supply and carburetion problems as it works its way through the fuel line and into the carburetor. If rust has formed in the tank(s), perform the following.

1. Remove and drain the fuel tank(s)as described in this chapter.
2. Remove the fuel shutoff valve as described in this chapter. While the valve is off the tank, clean it as described in this chapter.
3. Plug all of the tank openings.

**FUEL TANK VENT MODIFICATION (1991 FLT AND FXR CALIFORNIA MODELS)**

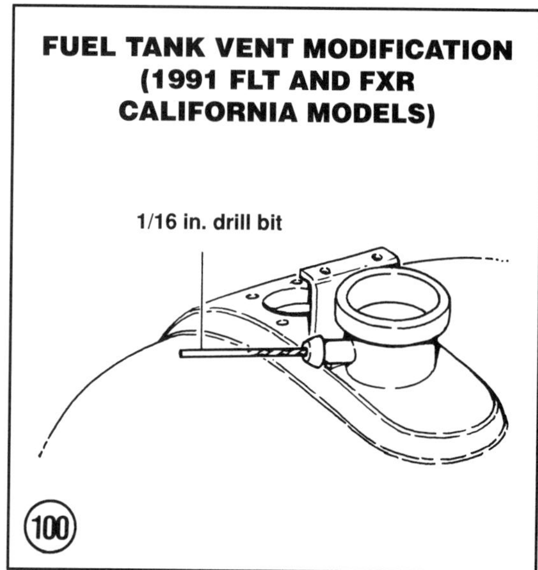


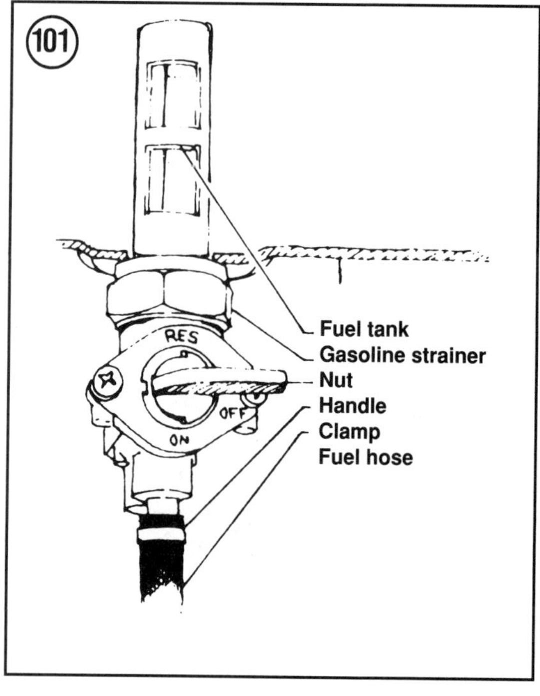

*NOTE*

*The following steps describe the use of soap and water to clean the tank. If you plan to use a commercial fuel tank cleaning agent, follow the manufacturer's instructions.*

4. To help break up the rust buildup, add a number of non-ferrous balls or pellets into the tank. Count the number of balls put into the tank so that you can be sure all of the balls are removed after cleaning.

*WARNING*

*Do not use metal balls to loosen fuel tank deposits. Metal balls can produce a spark that could ignite fumes trapped in the tank, causing a serious explosion and possible personal injury.*

5. Prepare a soap and water solution and pour it into the tank. Install the fuel cap and shake the tank to move the balls around and break up the rust deposits.
6. After cleaning the inside of the tank, pour the tank's contents into a container so that you can count the balls added previously.
7. If necessary, repeat Steps 5 and 6 until all of the rust has been removed. If the rust buildup is difficult to remove, you may have to use a commercial cleaning agent.

*NOTE*

*If you are going to put the tank into storage, pour an equal amount of fuel and oil into each tank. This will prevent rust buildup during storage. Drain and flush the tanks before starting the engine.*

8. After all of the rust has been removed and the tank has been thoroughly flushed, allow it to air dry before installing it.

### Repairing Minor Tank Leaks (Pin Hole Size)

Small pin hole size leaks can be repaired with a commercial fuel tank sealant. Follow the manufacturer's instructions. If the leak cannot be repaired with the sealant, refer further service to your dealer.

*WARNING*

*Welding a metal tank is serious business, as any trace of fuel left in the tank can cause it to explode. If the tank must be welded, refer service to your dealer. Do not attempt this repair at home. A tank explosion can cause severe personal injury.*

## FUEL SHUTOFF VALVE (ALL 1984-1994 EXCEPT 1994 FLT)

A 3-way fuel shutoff valve is mounted onto the left-hand fuel tank. A replaceable fuel strainer is mounted at the top of the shutoff valve.

### Removal/Installation and Filter Cleaning

The fuel filter removes particles which might otherwise enter into the carburetor and possibly cause the float needle to remain in the open position.

Refer to **Figure 101** for this procedure.

*WARNING*

*Gasoline is very volatile and presents an extreme fire hazard. Be sure to work in a well-ventilated area away from any open flames (including pilot lights on household appliances). Do not allow anyone to smoke in the area and have a fire extinguisher rated for gasoline fires handy.*

1. Disconnect the battery negative lead.
2. Turn the fuel valve to OFF.
3. To drain the fuel tank:
   a. Disconnect the fuel line at the fuel shutoff valve.
   b. Connect a drain hose to the fuel valve that can reach from the valve to a gasoline storage tank.
   c. Turn fuel valve handle to RESERVE and drain the fuel into the storage tank.
   d. Disconnect the drain hose at the fuel valve.
4. Loosen the fuel valve nut and remove the valve and gasket from the fuel tank. Catch any gas that may leak from the fuel tank after the valve is removed.
5. Check the fuel strainer for contamination or damage. If the strainer cannot be thoroughly cleaned, replace it. Install a new gasket when installing a new strainer.

*NOTE*
*If the strainer is contaminated, the fuel tank may require cleaning and flushing. Refer to* ***Fuel Tank Flushing*** *in this chapter.*

6. Inspect the condition of the gasket; replace if necessary.

7. Clean the fuel tank threads of all sealant.

8. Coat the shutoff valve threads with Loctite Pipe Sealant With Teflon and insert the valve into the tank. Tighten valve nut as follows:

a. 1993-on FXR and 1993 FLT: Tighten valve nut to 18 ft.-lb. (24 N•m).

*WARNING*
*On 1993-on FXR and 1993 FLT models, do not turn the fuel valve nut more than 2 turns or the nut will bottom-out on the fuel tank threads. This may cause the fuel valve to leak gasoline, creating a fire hazard.*

b. On all other models, tighten fuel valve nut securely.

9. Remove the drain tube from the fuel tank and reconnect the fuel line. Secure the fuel line with a new hose clamp. Make sure the insulator is placed over the fuel line before reconnecting the fuel line.

10. Refill the fuel tank(s).

11. Check the area around the fuel valve and hoses carefully to make sure no fuel is leaking.

## VACUUM OPERATED FUEL VALVE (1994 FLT)

These models are equipped with a vacuum operated fuel valve (**Figure 102**).

### Removal/Installation and Filter Cleaning

*WARNING*
*Gasoline is very volatile and presents an extreme fire hazard. Be sure to work in a well-ventilated area away from any open flames (including pilot lights on*

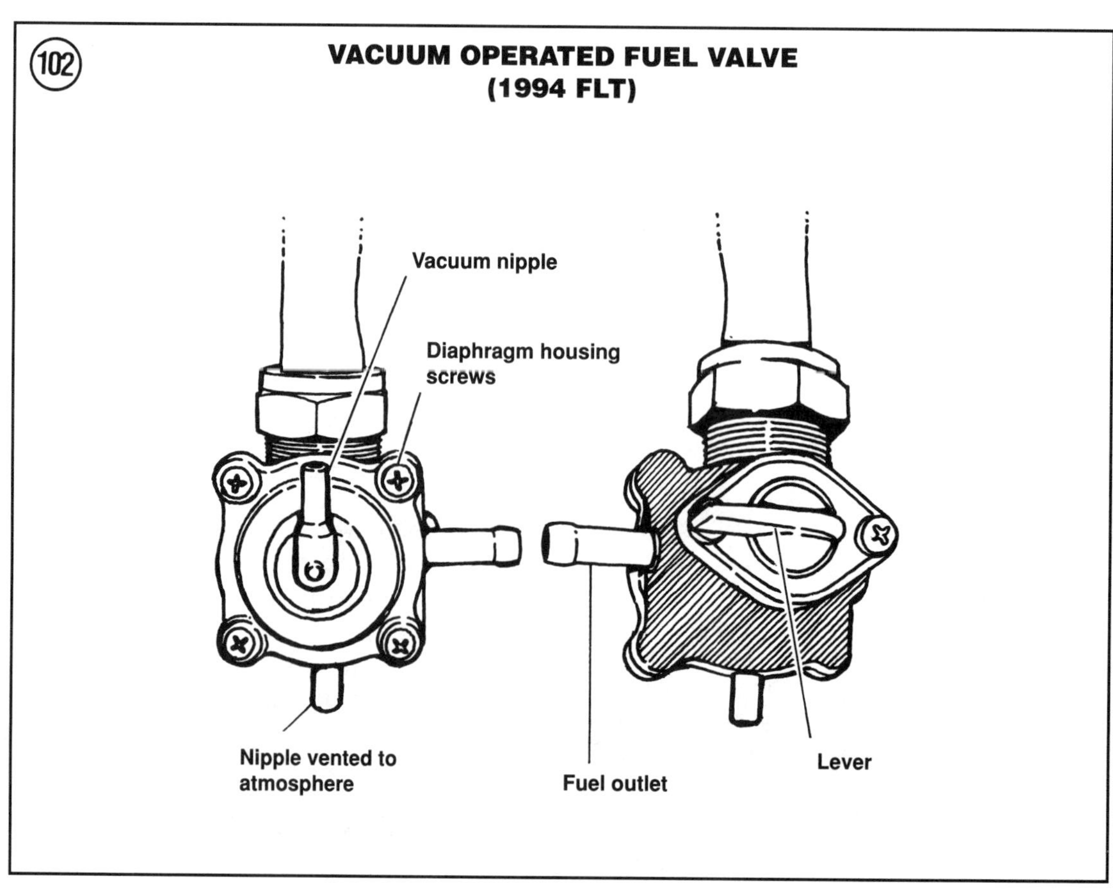

*household appliances). Do not allow anyone to smoke in the area and have a fire extinguisher rated for gasoline fires handy.*

1. Disconnect the battery negative lead.
2. Turn the fuel valve handle OFF—horizontal valve handle position.
3. Disconnect the fuel line at the fuel shutoff valve.
4. Disconnect the vacuum line at the fuel shutoff valve.
5. To drain the fuel tank:
   a. Connect a drain hose to the fuel valve that can reach from the valve to a gasoline storage tank.
   b. Turn fuel valve handle to RESERVE—up valve handle position.
   c. Connect a hand-operated vacuum pump to the fuel shutoff valve vacuum hose nipple.
   d. Apply a vacuum of 1-10 in. (HG) or just enough vacuum to obtain a good fuel flow through the shutoff valve.

*CAUTION*

*Applying more than 10 in. (HG) to the shutoff valve will damage the valve diaphragm.*

   e. With the vacuum applied, allow the tank to drain. Then disconnect the drain hose and vacuum hose at the fuel valve.
6. Loosen the fuel valve nut and remove the valve and gasket from the fuel tank. Catch any gas that may leak from the fuel tank after the valve is removed.
7. Check the fuel strainer for contamination or damage. If the strainer cannot be thoroughly cleaned, replace it. Install a new gasket when installing a new strainer.

103

*NOTE*

*If the strainer is contaminated, the fuel tank may require cleaning and flushing. Refer to* ***Fuel Tank Flushing*** *in this chapter.*

8. Inspect the fuel valve gasket; replace if necessary.
9. Clean the fuel tank threads of all sealant.
10. Coat the shutoff valve threads with Loctite Pipe Sealant With Teflon and insert the valve into the tank. Tighten valve nut to 18 ft.-lb. (24 N•m).

*WARNING*

*Do not turn the fuel valve nut more than 2 turns after initial thread engagement or the nut will bottom-out on the fuel tank threads. This may cause the fuel valve to leak gasoline, creating a fire hazard.*

11. Reconnect the vacuum and fuel lines at the fuel shutoff valve. Secure the both lines with new hose clamps. Make sure the insulator is placed over the fuel line before reconnecting the fuel line.
12. Refill the fuel tank.
13. Check the area around the fuel valve and hoses carefully to make sure no fuel is leaking.

## EXHAUST SYSTEM

### Removal/Installation

A number of exhaust systems have been used on the Harley-Davidson models covered in this manual. This procedure presents a general guideline for exhaust system removal and installation. See **Figure 103**, typical.

The O.E.M. exhaust system consists of exhaust pipes, mufflers, chrome covers, hose clamps, pipe gaskets, studs, washers and nuts.

Each exhaust pipe clamps to its respective cylinder head exhaust port with a flange plate and 2 nuts. Knitted steel gaskets (**Figure 104**) are placed between the cylinder exhaust pipe and cylinder head to prevent exhaust leakage. The 5/16 in. (7.9 mm) O.D. exhaust pipe studs are threaded with a fine thread (5/16-24) on one end and a coarse thread (5/16-18) on the opposite end. The coarse thread end threads into the cylinder head. The fine thread end is used to secure the 2 exhaust pipe flange mounting nuts.

1. Secure the bike on a suitable stand.
2. The exhaust pipe covers are held to the pipes with hose clamps. These clamps rust easily, so before

removing them, spray each clamp with WD-40 or a similar lubricant to help prevent thread strippage when loosening them. Hold a rag behind the clamp when spraying it to prevent the lubricant from contacting the engine or other components. Turn the hose clamp screws until the clamp is disconnected from around the pipe, then remove the covers.

3. Remove the bolts and washers securing the muffler to the support tube.
4. Loosen the muffler clamp bolts at the exhaust pipe and remove the muffler by twisting it off the exhaust pipe.

*NOTE*
*Rust that forms between the muffler and exhaust pipe mating surfaces can make muffler removal difficult.*

5. Loosen the hose clamp connecting the front and rear exhaust pipes.
6. Remove the nuts and washers securing the exhaust pipe flange at the cylinder head (**Figure 105**).
7. Slide the rear cylinder exhaust flange off of the cylinder head studs and remove the rear exhaust pipe. Repeat to remove the front cylinder exhaust pipe. Stuff the exhaust port openings with a clean rag until reassembly. Note the gasket and exhaust washer, if used, where the 2 exhaust pipes join. Discard the gasket.

*CAUTION*
*If the exhaust flanges (**Figure 106**) do not slide off of the cylinder head studs easily in Step 7, the flange plate is distorted, a condition usually caused by overtightened flange nuts. **Figure 107** shows a distorted or bowed flange. If a flange is severely distorted, the distance between the flange holes is reduced, causing the flange to wedge against the stud. The edge of the flange will dig into the stud threads as you try to slide it off, damaging the threads in the process. If a flange is tight, remove one of the cylinder head studs using the 2 nut technique (see Chapter One) before the stud threads are damaged, or if necessary, with a pair of Vise-grips. The stud can be reinstalled before installing the exhaust pipe. The flange can either be removed from the exhaust pipe and flattened, or replaced as described later in this chapter.*

105

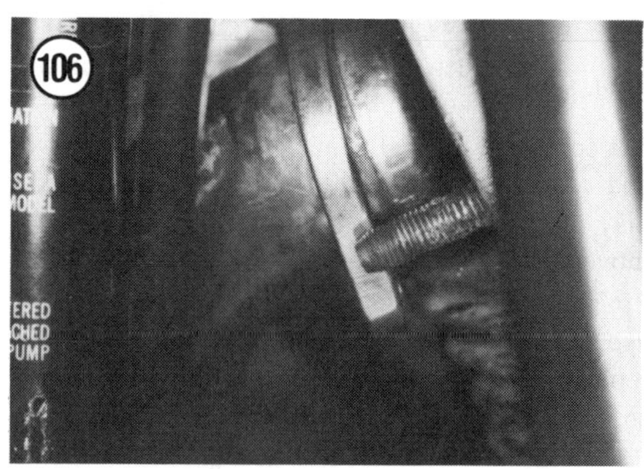
106

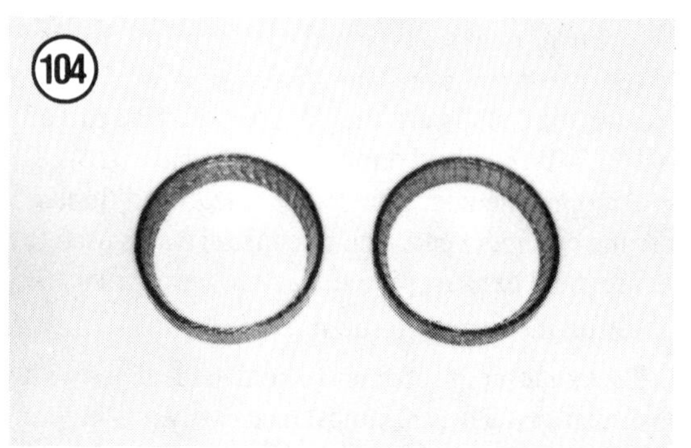
104

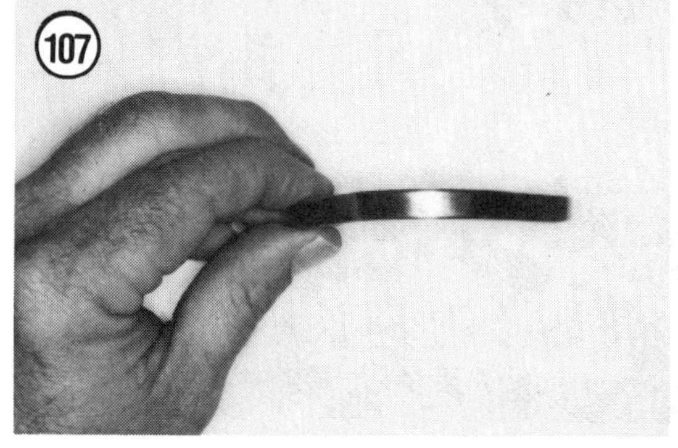
107

8. Remove and discard the exhaust port gaskets (**Figure 108**).
9. Inspect the exhaust system as described in this chapter.
10. Install by reversing these removal steps. Note the following.
11. Before installing the new exhaust port gasket, scrape the gasket and the pipe fitting surfaces in the port (**Figure 109**) with a knife blade or similar tool to remove all carbon residue—removing the carbon will assure a good gasket fit. Wipe the port with a rag, then align the new gasket with the port and push it into place. The new gasket should fit snugly in the port (**Figure 108**). Repeat for the other exhaust port and gasket.
12. If an exhaust flange was removed from its pipe, check that the retaining ring holding the flange to the exhaust pipe fits on the pipe tightly.

NOTE

*If you had to remove or discard an exhaust stud, install the stud now. Refer to **Stud Replacement** in Chapter One.*

13. Install the front cylinder exhaust pipe by inserting the end of the pipe into the exhaust port and sliding the flange over the studs. Install the washer and nut onto each stud. Tighten the nuts finger-tight only.
14. Repeat Step 13 to install the rear cylinder exhaust pipe, while inserting the crossover tube into the mating tube on the front exhaust pipe. If a gasket and exhaust washer were used where the 2 exhaust pipes mate, install a new gasket and the exhaust washer.
15. Install the mufflers onto the exhaust pipes, twisting them back and forth if necessary. Install the muffler bolts, lockwashers and flat washers and tighten the bolts finger-tight.

NOTE

*Harley-Davidson does not list a torque specification for the exhaust pipe flange nuts. The nuts used are 5/16-24, grade 2 steel. Cross-referencing this information with the General Torque Specifications torque table in Chapter One, the nuts should not be tightened more than 12 ft.-lb. (16.5 N•m).*

16. Starting at the exhaust pipe flange, tighten the exhaust pipe nuts to 12 ft.-lb. (16.5 N•m) with a torque wrench. Then work your way rearward and tighten the exhaust pipe and then the muffler mounting bolts securely. Do not overtighten the flange nuts or you may distort the flange.

NOTE

*By tightening the exhaust pipe fasteners as described in Step 16 (front to rear), you can minimize exhaust leaks at the cylinder heads.*

17. Wipe the exhaust pipes and mufflers off with a clean rag to remove all traces of oil and grease, then polish the exhaust pipes.
18. Install the exhaust pipe covers and tighten securely with their hose clamps. Then clean and polish the covers.

NOTE

*If you are installing new pipes, check with the pipe manufacturer and your dealer for information regarding tuning changes that may be required with the new pipes. You want the carburetor jetting and ignition timing to be as spot-on as possible before starting the engine to prevent exhaust pipe bluing. If the pipes are new (have not been installed on a running engine), you may want to coat the inside of the exhaust pipes with a*

108

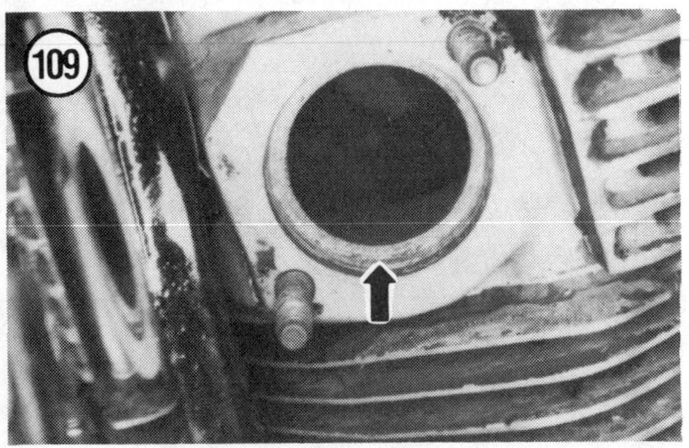
109

8

*special sealer, such as DYNO-KOTE Pipe Bluing Preventative, before installing them. See your dealer for additional information.*

19. Start the engine and check for leaks. Some smoke will be evident after starting, especially if WD-40 was used on the hose clamps (prior to removal) or if oil and grease residue was not wiped off of the exhaust pipes and mufflers.

## Inspection

1. Check the exhaust pipe for cracks or spots that have rusted through. A damaged or leaking pipe should be replaced.
2. Remove all rust from all pipe and muffler mating surfaces.
3. Check the hose clamps for damage or severe rusting. Clean or repair clamps as required.
4. If the exhaust flange is distorted, repair or replace it before reinstalling it. Perform the following:
   a. Each exhaust flange is secured to its exhaust pipe with a retaining ring. Pry the ring out of its groove and remove the flange. Discard the ring. See **Figure 110**.
   b. Examine the flange for distortion or other damage; the flange must be flat to fit properly onto the exhaust studs. If the flange is not severely distorted, you may be able to hammer or press it flat. If not, install a new flange. Make sure you do not damage the edges or holes in the flange when straightening it.
   c. If you straightened a flange, check its fit on the exhaust studs before installing it onto the pipe.

*NOTE*
*Chrome replacement flanges are available from accessory manufacturers.*

   d. Clean the end of the pipe to remove all rust and other debris. If you are reinstalling a used flange, clean the inside of the flange thoroughly.
   e. Slide the flange on the exhaust pipe so that the shoulder on the flange faces toward the retaining ring groove. Install a new retaining ring and check its fit; it must be secure in the groove.
   f. Repeat for the other exhaust pipe and flange, if required.

5. Replace worn or damaged exhaust pipe cover hose clamps as required (**Figure 111**).
6. Store the exhaust pipes in a safe place until they are reinstalled.

## Exhaust System Care

The exhaust system greatly enhances the appearance of any motorcycle. And more importantly, the exhaust system is a vital key to the motorcycle's operation and performance. As the owner, you should periodically inspect, clean and polish the exhaust system. Special chemical cleaners and preservatives compounded for exhaust systems are available at most motorcycle shops.

Severe dents which cause gas flow restrictions require the replacement of the damaged part.

Problems occurring within the exhaust pipes are normally caused by rust from the collection of water in the pipe. Periodically, or whenever the exhaust pipes are removed, turn the pipes to remove any trapped water.

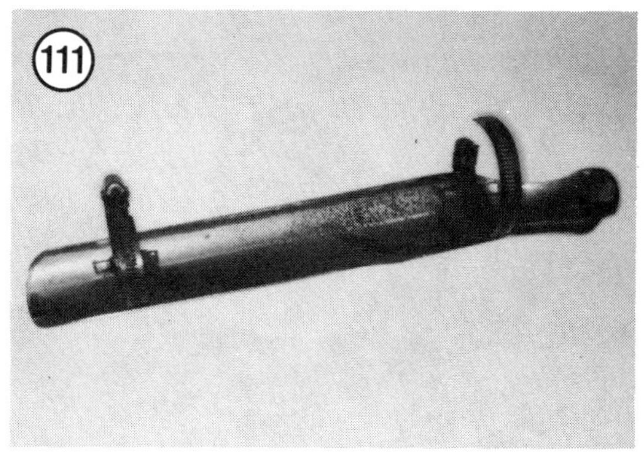

## EMISSION CONTROL (1985-1991 CALIFORNIA MODELS)

All 1985 and later models sold in California are equipped with an evaporative emission control system. This system prevents gasoline vapors from escaping into the atmosphere.

When the engine is not running, fuel vapor from the fuel tank is routed through the vapor valve and stored in a carbon canister. When the engine is running, these vapors are drawn through a purge hose and into the carburetor where they are burned in the combustion chambers. The vapor valve also prevents gasoline vapors from escaping from the carbon canister if the bike should fall onto its side.

During the 1988 model year, a set of reed valves and a vacuum operated valve (VOV) were added to the system. The reed valves are installed in the carburetor backplate to prevent vapors from the carbon canister from escaping into the atmosphere when the engine is not running. The VOV vents fuel vapors from the carburetor float bowl to the atmosphere when the engine is not running; when the engine is turned off, the VOV closes off the carburetor vent tube, preventing vapors from escaping into the atmosphere. A damaged VOV can cause the engine to run lean at high speeds. If you have a 1988 or later model and the engine is running lean at high speeds, test the VOV as described in this section.

### Inspection/Replacement (All Models)

Refer to **Figures 112-116** (for your model) for the components and the hose routing to the various parts. Before removing the hoses from any of the parts, mark the hose and the fitting with a piece of masking tape and identify where the hose goes.

1. Check all emission control lines or hoses to make sure they are correctly routed and properly connected.

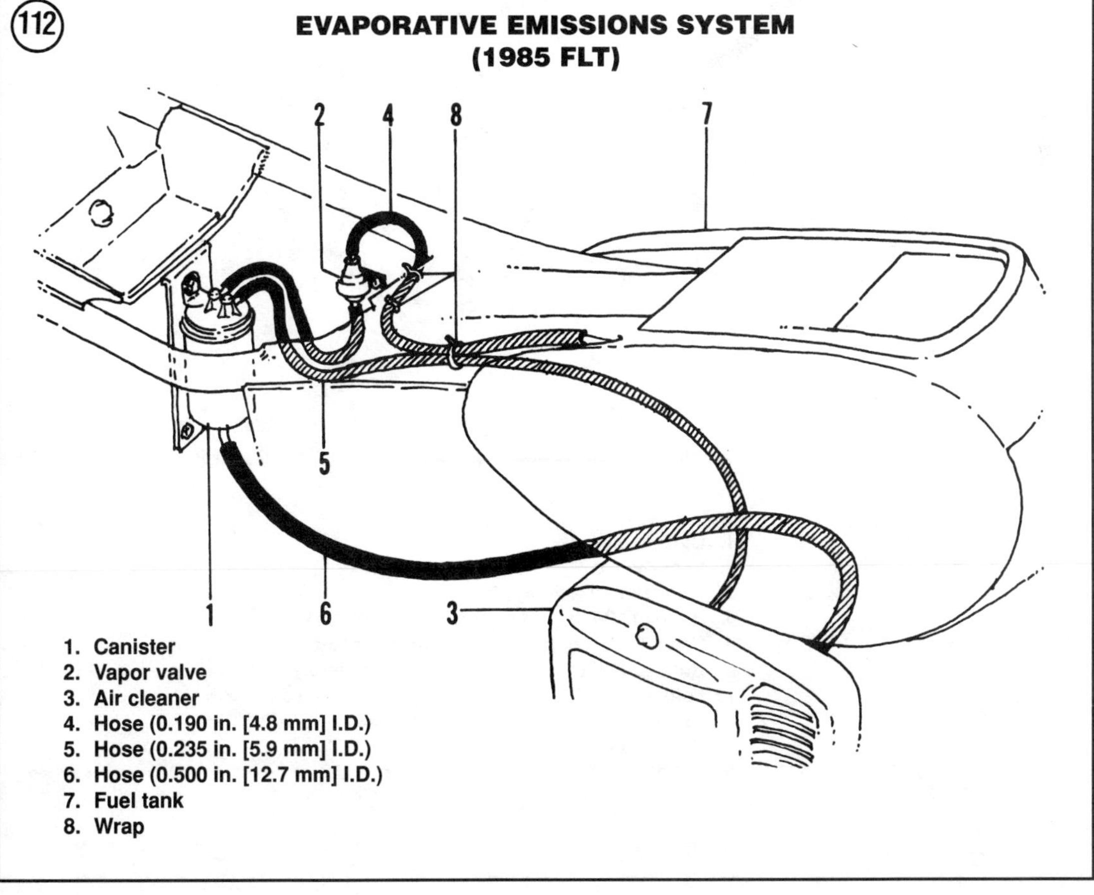

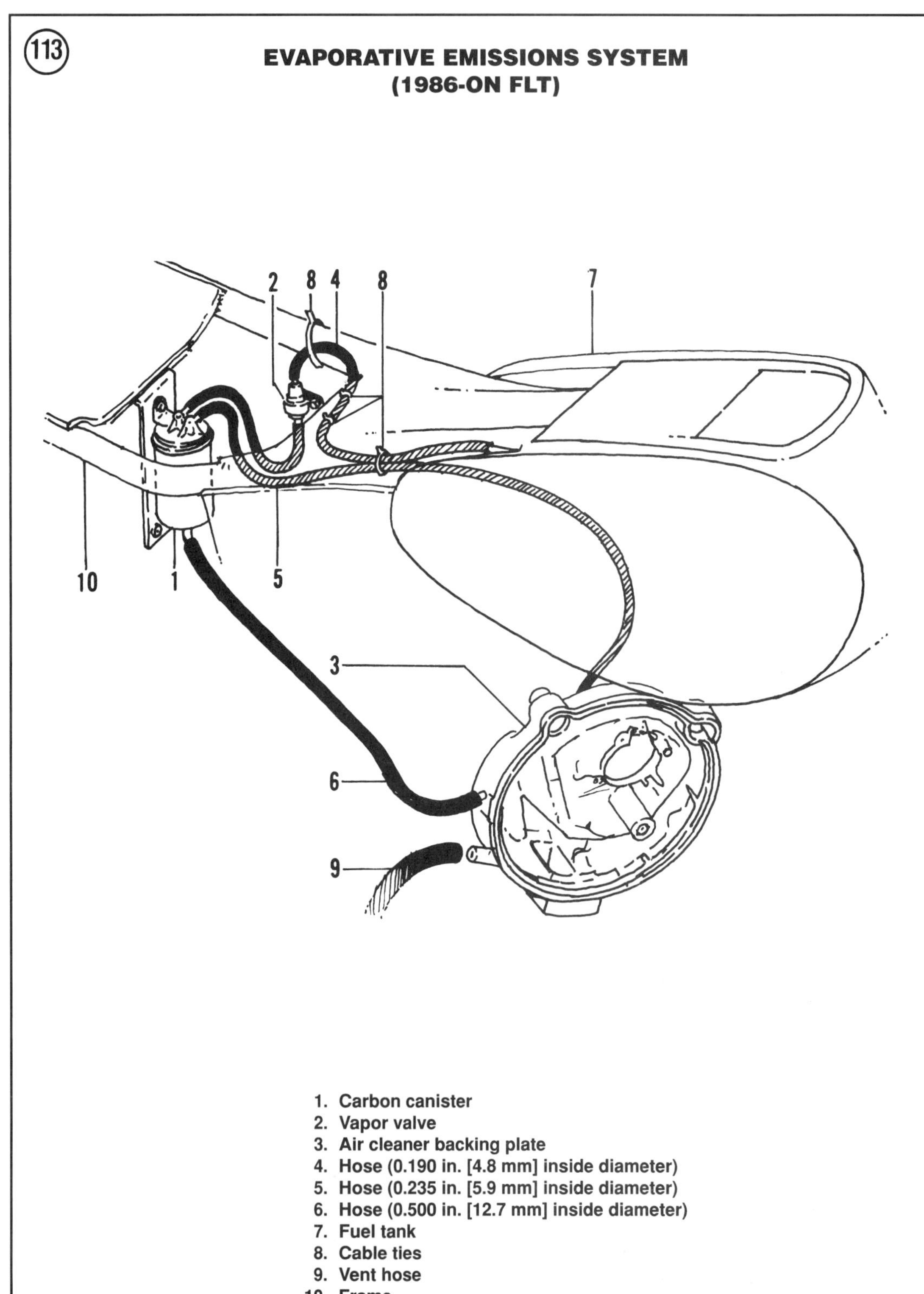


**EVAPORATIVE EMISSIONS SYSTEM (1986-ON FLT)**

1. Carbon canister
2. Vapor valve
3. Air cleaner backing plate
4. Hose (0.190 in. [4.8 mm] inside diameter)
5. Hose (0.235 in. [5.9 mm] inside diameter)
6. Hose (0.500 in. [12.7 mm] inside diameter)
7. Fuel tank
8. Cable ties
9. Vent hose
10. Frame

2. Make sure that there are no kinks in the lines or hoses and that there are no signs of excessive wear or burning on lines that are routed near engine hot spots.

3. Check the physical condition of all lines and hoses in the system for cuts, tears or loose connections. These lines and hoses are subjected to various temperature and operating conditions and eventually become brittle and crack. Damaged lines or hoses should be replaced.

4. Check all components in the emission control system for visible signs of damage, such as broken fittings or broken nipples on the component.

5. When replacing one or more lines or hoses, refer to the diagram for your model. Disconnect one end of the line from the component, then connect one end of the new line to the component fitting. Disconnect the other end of the line and connect the other end of the new line. In this way, you will not make any mistakes and will be able to follow the routing of the old line, correcting any improper placement that carries the line near components where it might rub and wear or be burned by hot components.

*NOTE*

*Emission control hoses with different inside diameters, come in bulk lengths and are cut to order by Harley-Davidson dealers and automotive parts stores. To assure that you get the right sizes, you should take a sample of each line with a different inside diameter, along with an estimate of the amount of each size that you will need.*

### Vapor Valve Replacement

Refer to **Figure 112-116** for your model when performing the following.

1. Label the hoses at the vapor valve and then disconnect them.

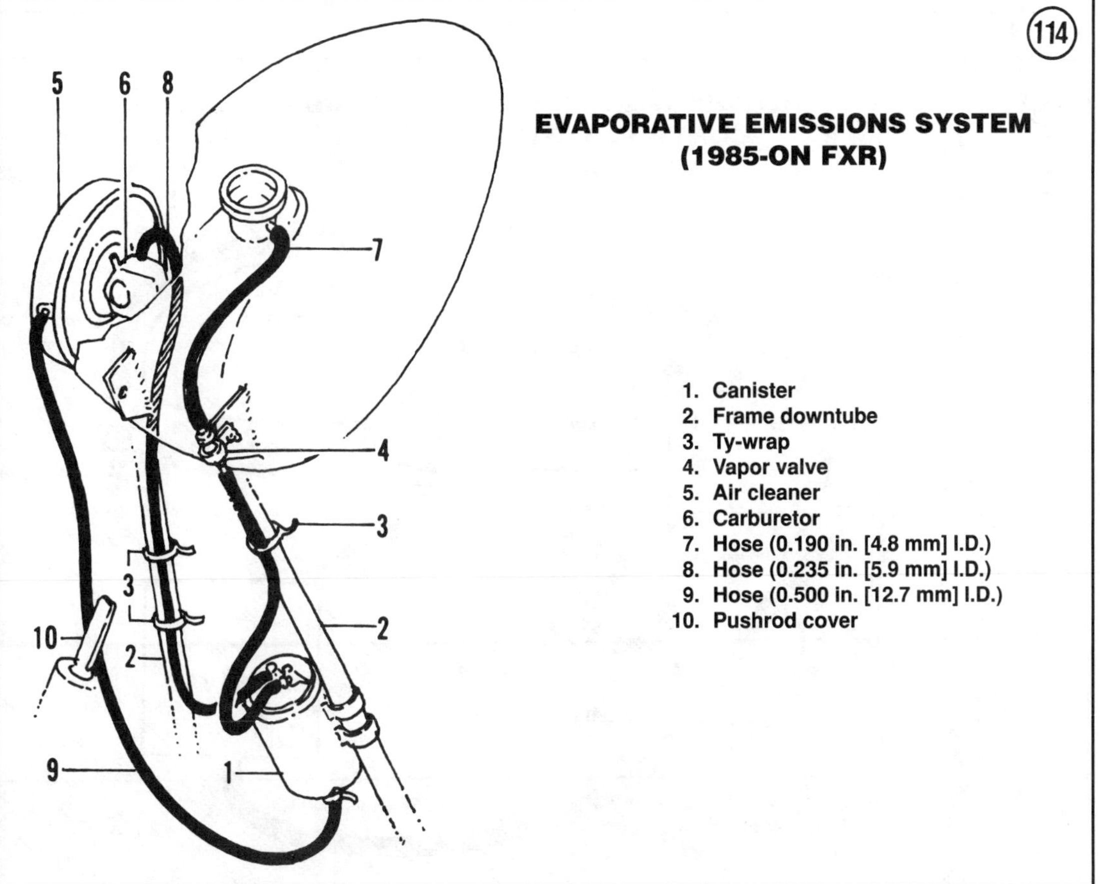

**115**

## EVAPORATIVE EMISSIONS SYSTEM (1985-1986 FX)

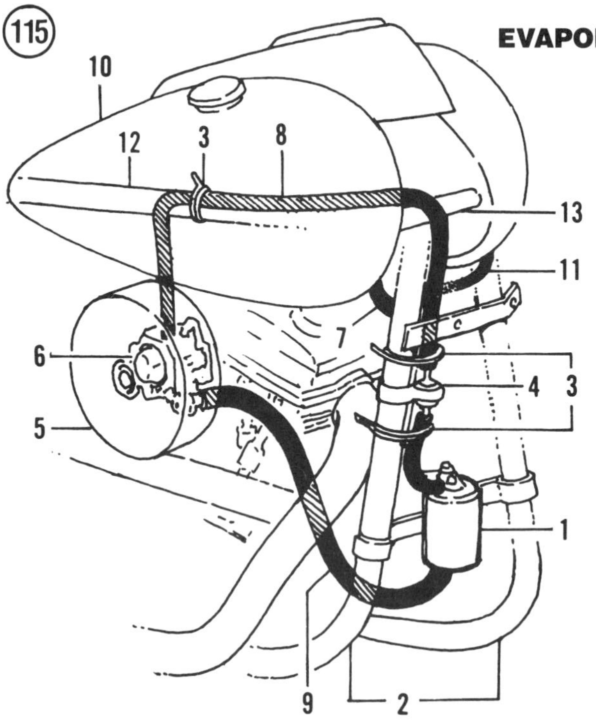

1. Canister
2. Frame
3. Wrap
4. Vapor cleaner
5. Air cleaner
6. Carburetor
7. Hose (0.190 in. [4.8 mm] I.D.)
8. Hose (0.235 in. [5.9 mm] I.D.)
9. Hose (0.500 in. [12.7 mm] I.D.)
10. Fuel tank
11. Crossover hose
12. Frame
13. Bracket

**116**

## CALIFORNIA EVAPORATIVE EMISSIONS CONTROL SYSTEM (1988-ON)

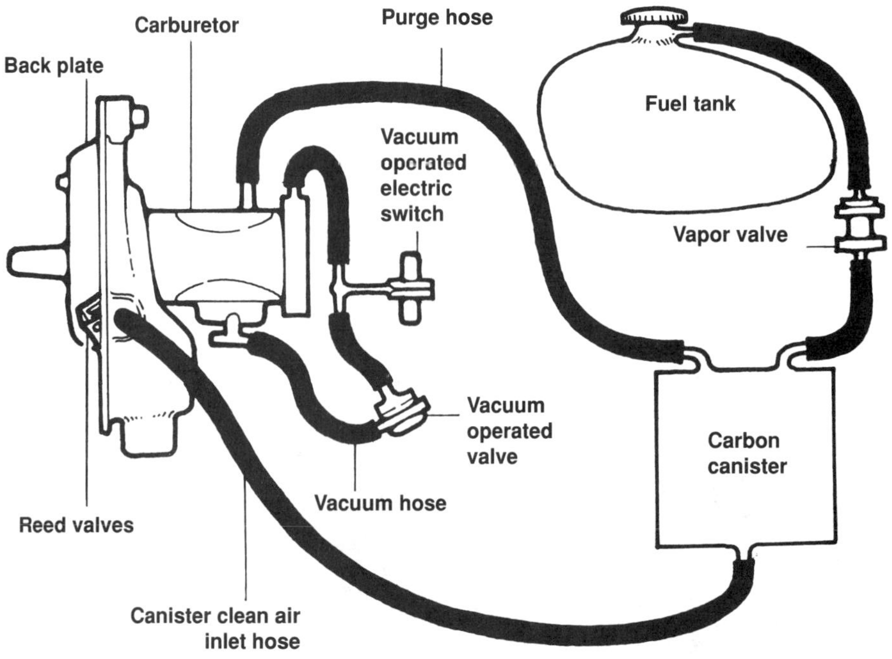

2. Note that one end of the vapor valve is longer than the other end. The longer end must face *up*. Remove and replace the vapor valve.

*CAUTION*
*The vapor valve must be installed in a vertical position with the **longer end** facing upward or excessive pressure will build in the fuel tank.*

### Carbon Canister Replacement

Refer to **Figure 112-116** for your model when performing the following.

1. Label and then disconnect the hoses at the canister.
2. Remove the canister mounting brackets, clamps, etc., and remove the canister.
3. Install by reversing these steps.

*CAUTION*
*Do not alter the carbon canister position. The canister must be mounted **below** the carburetor to work correctly.*

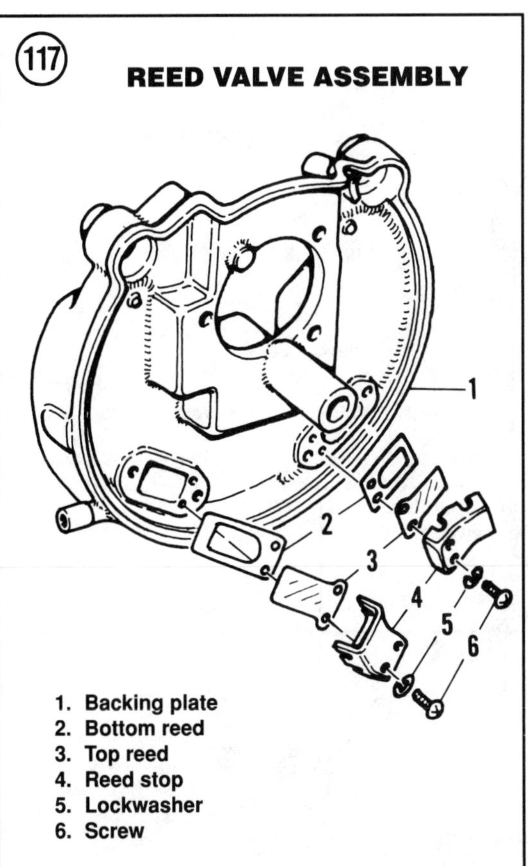


### Reed Valves (1988-on)

Whenever the air filter assembly is removed from the bike, check the reed valve assembly for broken reed valves. To replace damaged reed valves, perform the following.

1. Remove the air filter (Chapter Three).
2. Remove the screw and lockwasher securing the reed stop to the backplate. Remove the top and bottom reeds (**Figure 117**).
3. Install the reeds in the order shown in **Figure 117**. Install the screws and lockwashers and tighten securely.

### Vacuum Operated Valve (1988-on)

During engine operation, the vacuum operated valve (VOV) vents fuel vapors from the carburetor float bowl to the atmosphere. When the engine is turned off, the VOV closes off the carburetor vent tube, preventing vapors from escaping into the atmosphere. If the diaphragm in the VOV should become damaged and leak, a vacuum leak would occur and cause the engine to run lean at high speeds. The vapor operated valves can be tested with a hand vacuum pump (Harley-Davidson part No. HD-23738 or equivalent).

1. Disconnect the VOV from the emission control system.
2. Attach a vacuum pump to port A in **Figure 118**.

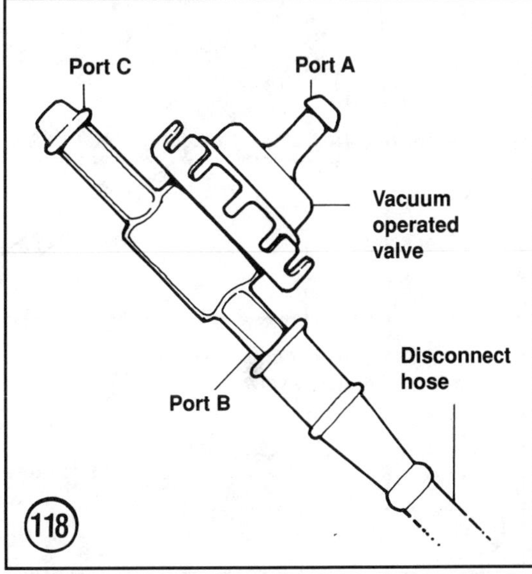


8

3. Apply 1-2 in. HG vacuum to the valve while watching the pump gauge. The vacuum should remain steady. If the vacuum reading decreases rapidly, the diaphragm is damaged.
4. If vacuum remains constant (Step 3), blow into port C; air should pass through the VOV. If air cannot pass through, the VOV is damaged.
5. Remove the vacuum pump and blow into port B; air should not pass through the VOV. If air can pass through, the VOV is damaged.
6. If the VOV failed to react as described in Steps 3-5, replace it with a new one.

## EVAPORATIVE EMISSION CONTROL SYSTEM (1992-ON CALIFORNIA MODELS)

All of the California models covered by this manual are equipped with an evaporative emission control system (**Figure 119**). This system is used to prevent gasoline vapors from escaping into the atmosphere. When the engine is not running, fuel vapor from the fuel tank is routed through the vapor valve and stored in a carbon canister. When the engine is running, these vapors are drawn through a purge hose and into the carburetor where they are to be burned in the combustion chambers. The vapor valve also prevents gasoline vapors from escaping from the carbon canister if the bike should fall onto its side.

### Solenoid-Operated Butterfly Valve Troubleshooting (1992-on)

On 1992-on California models, a solenoid-operated butterfly valve (**Figure 120**) is installed in the

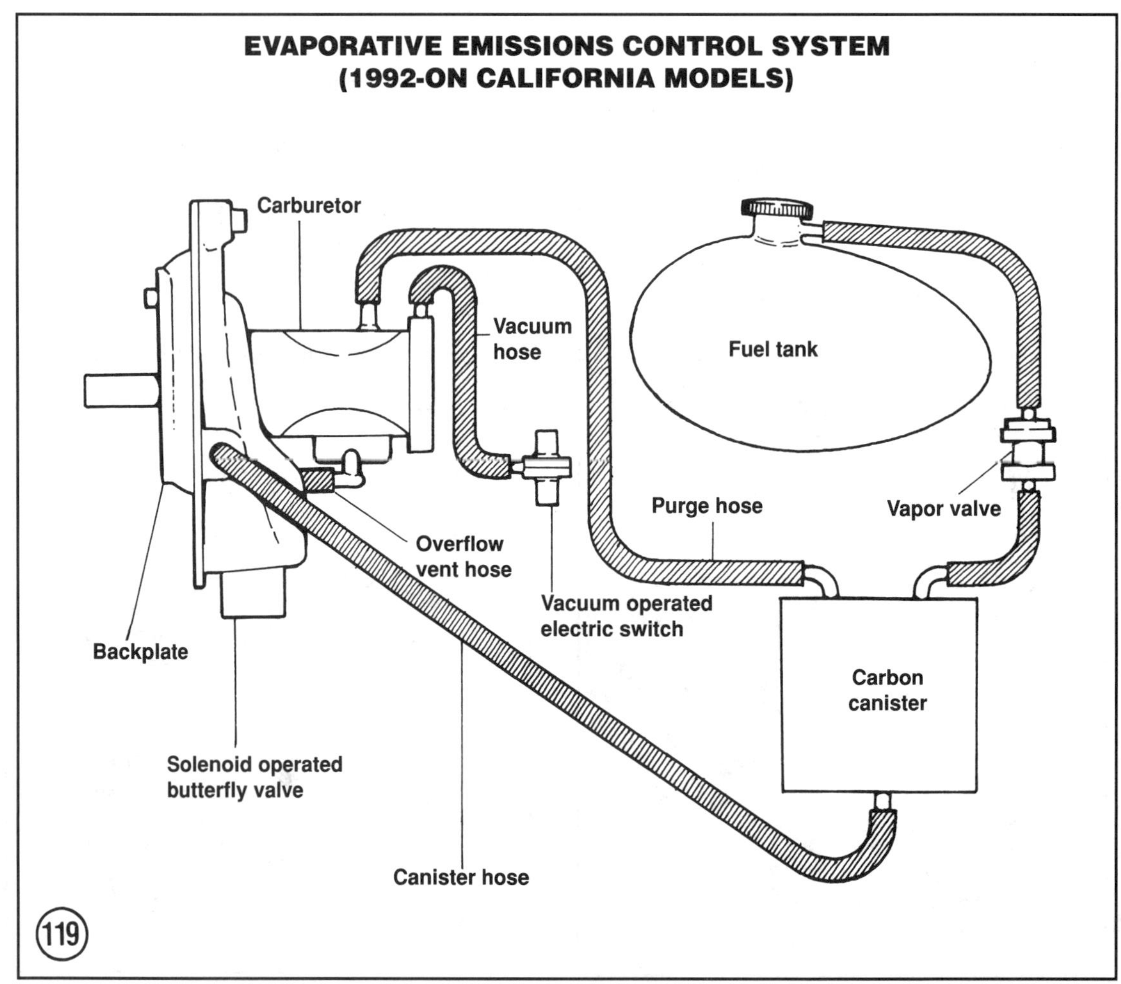

**SOLENOID-OPERATED BUTTERFLY VALVE (1992-ON CALIFORNIA)**

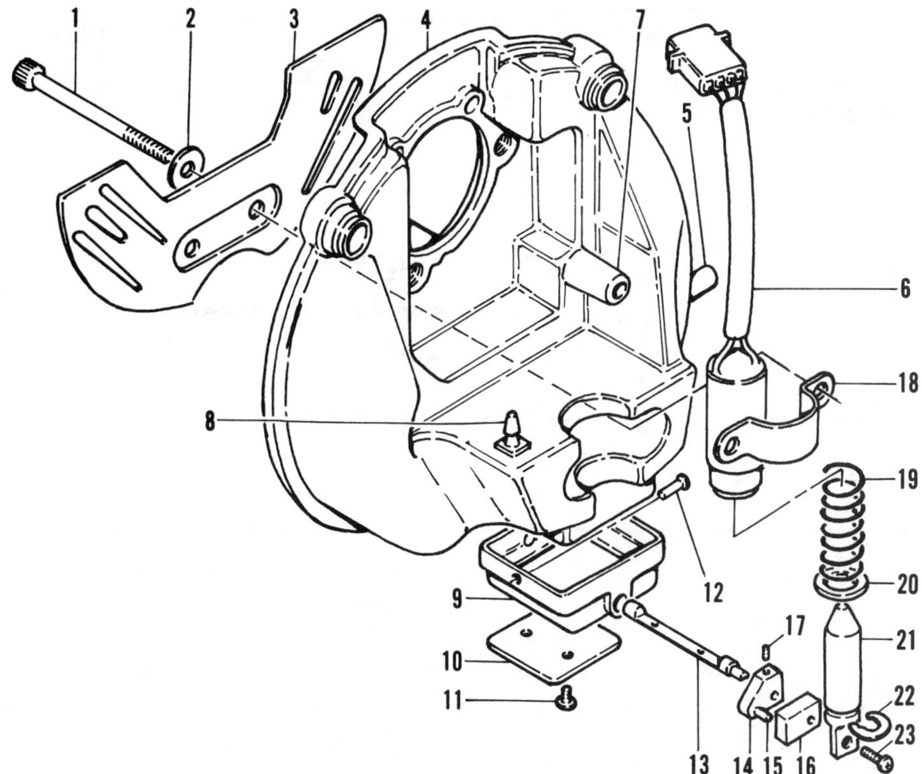


1. Solenoid mounting screws
2. Washer
3. Baffle
4. Backplate
5. Crankcase breather hose nozzle
6. Solenoid
7. Canister inlet hose nozzle
8. Fitting
9. Housing
10. Butterfly valve
11. Screw
12. Rivet
13. Butterfly valve shaft
14. Lever arm
15. Pin
16. Plastic link
17. Set screw
18. Solenoid clamp
19. Spring
20. Plastic washer
21. Plunger
22. E-clip
23. Screw

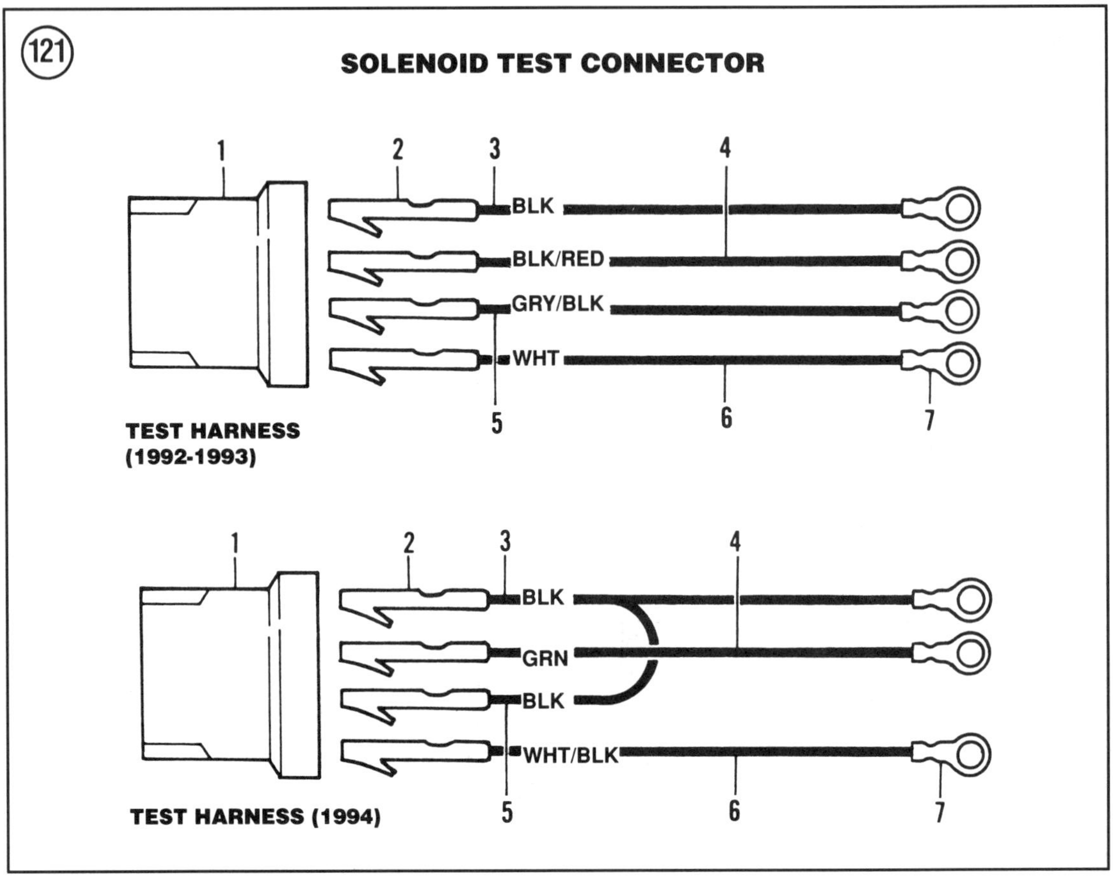

121
SOLENOID TEST CONNECTOR
1
2
3
4
BLK
BLK/RED
GRY/BLK
WHT
5
6
7
TEST HARNESS
(1992-1993)
1
2
3
4
BLK
GRN
BLK
WHT/BLK
5
6
7
TEST HARNESS (1994)

122
RESISTANCE TEST
4 place socket connector
Solenoid
Solenoid
test
connector
BLK
BLK/RED
GRY/BLK
WHT
1992-1993
Solenoid
Solenoid
test
connector
BLK
GRN
BLK
WHT/BLK
1994
4
3
2
1
WHT/BLK
BLK
GRN
BLK
A
To cycle
harness

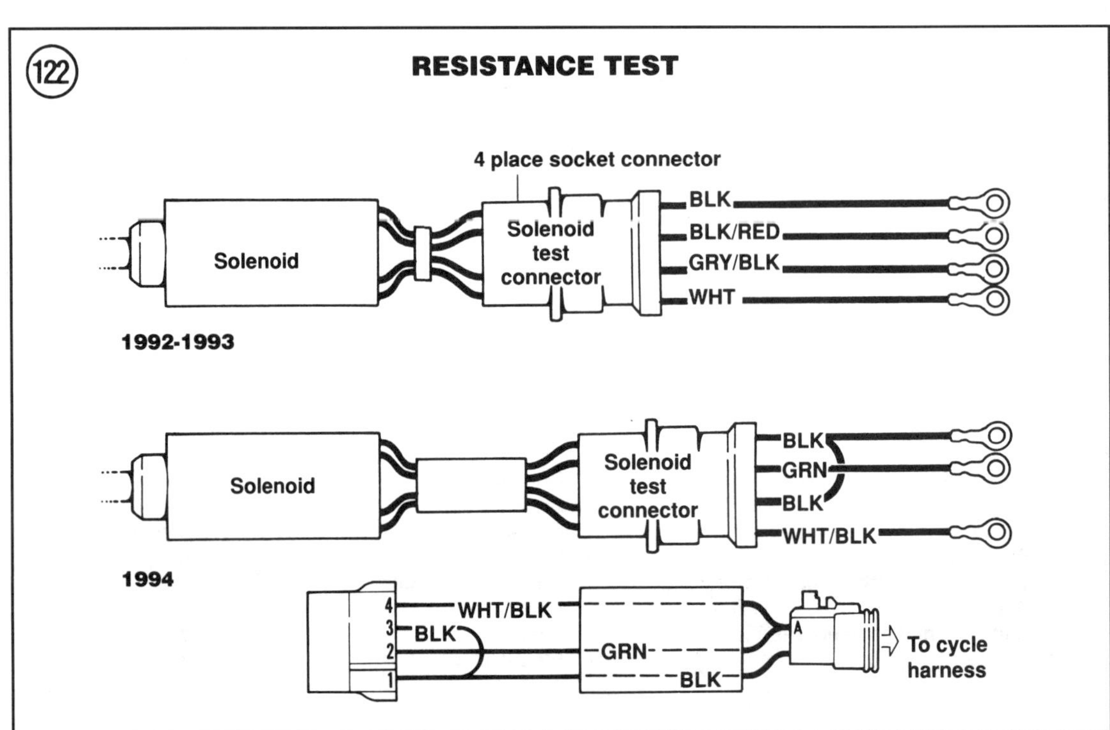

air filter backplate to seal off the backplate when the ignition switch is turned off to prevent fuel vapors from escaping into the atmosphere. Turning the ignition switch to the ON or IGNITION position energizes the solenoid hold-in windings. When the start switch is operated, the solenoid pull-in windings are energized. The hold-in windings will keep the butterfly valve open until the ignition switch is turned off.

Test the solenoid-operated butterfly valve if the engine suffers from sluggish acceleration and the engine's top speed tops out at 40 mph.

1. First check that all of the hoses are properly connected; see **Figure 119**. If the hoses are okay, proceed with Step 2.
2. Butterfly valve is not opening due to an electrical malfunction:
   a. Check that the solenoid valve electrical connector (**Figure 120**) is properly connected. If the connection is okay, disconnect the connector and check for dirty or loose-fitting terminals; clean and repair as required. If okay, continue with sub-step b.
   b. Test the solenoid as described under *Solenoid Testing* in this chapter.
3. Butterfly valve not opening and closing properly due to mechanical problem:
   a. Check the mechanical linkage assembly (**Figure 120**) for corroded, loose, broken or missing components. The butterfly valve linkage and plunger should be cleaned every 5,000 miles as described in this chapter.
   b. Check for a broken solenoid spring (**Figure 120**). If the spring is broken, replace the solenoid assembly. The spring cannot be replaced separately. Replace as described in this chapter.

### Solenoid Valve Electrical Testing (1992-on)

Prior to testing the solenoid valve, fabricate the test harness shown in **Figure 121**.

#### *Solenoid winding resistance test*

1. Remove the air filter and backplate as described under *Butterfly Valve Solenoid Removal/Installation/Adjustment (1992-on)* in this chapter.
2. Disconnect the solenoid valve 4 prong electrical connector (**Figure 120**).
3. Check for dirty or loose-fitting terminals and connectors.
4. Connect the solenoid test connector to the solenoid connector (**Figure 122**).
5. Refer to **Figure 123** for test connections and values and compare your meter readings to the stated values. If any of the meter readings differ from

**SOLENOID WINDING RESISTANCE**

| TEST | POSITIVE PROBE (+) | NEGATIVE PROBE (–) | RESISTANCE |
|---|---|---|---|
| | 1992-1993 | | |
| Pull-in | Back/Red | Gray/Black | 4-6 Ohms |
| Hold-in | White | Black | 21-27 Ohms |
| | 1994 | | |
| Pull-in | Green | Black | 4-6 Ohms |
| Hold-in | White/Black | Black | 21-27 Ohms |

the stated values, replace the solenoid as described in this chapter.

6. If the resistance readings are correct, proceed with the following dynamic tests.

### *Pull-in coil test*

A fully charged 12-volt battery is required for this test.

1. Remove the air filter and backplate as described under *Butterfly Valve Solenoid Removal/Installation/Adjustment (1992-on)* in this chapter.

2. Disconnect the solenoid valve 4 prong electrical connector (**Figure 120**).

3. Check for dirty or loose-fitting terminals and connectors.

4. Connect the solenoid test connector to the solenoid connector (**Figure 122**).

5. Connect a 12-volt battery to the 2 solenoid test connector wires shown in **Figure 124**. The butterfly valve should open when battery voltage is applied. Disconnect the battery connections and note the following:

   a. If the butterfly valve now opens but did not open when originally connected to the wiring harness, perform Step 6.

   b. If the butterfly valve did not open, check the linkage for corroded, missing or damaged parts. If the linkage assembly appears is okay, retest with a new solenoid.

6. Perform the following:

   a. Switch an ohmmeter to R × 1 and cross the test leads. Then check for ground at the grey/black (1992-1993) or black (1994) connector pin in the solenoid 4-prong connector. The ohmmeter should read 1 ohm or less.

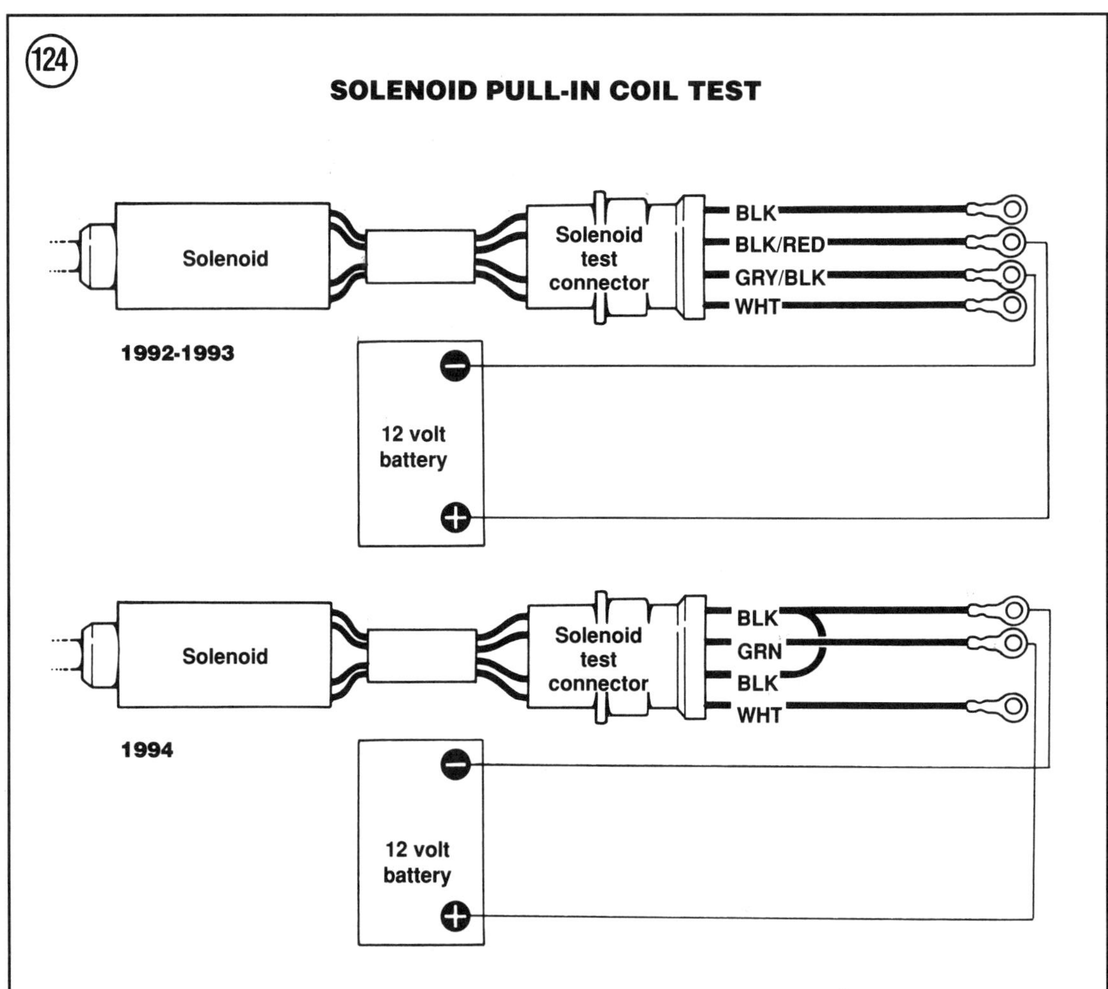

b. Reconnect the solenoid 4-prong connector.

c. Switch a voltmeter to the 12 VDC scale.

d. Connect the positive voltmeter lead to the black/red (1992-1993) or green (1994) lead in the 4-prong connector and the negative probe to a good engine ground. Press the start button while reading the voltage indicated on the voltmeter. It should be 12 volts.

7. If any of the meter readings differ from those specified in Step 6, there is a problem in the solenoid wiring harness. Use voltage and resistance checks to locate the damaged wire(s). After repairing the wire(s), repeat the above checks.

8. If the meter readings were correct as performed in Step 7, perform the following test.

### *Hold-in coil test*

A fully charged 12-volt battery is required for this test.

1. Remove the air filter and backplate as described under *Butterfly Valve Solenoid Removal/Installation/Adjustment (1992-on)* in this chapter.

2. Disconnect the solenoid valve 4 prong electrical connector (**Figure 125**).

3. Check for dirty or loose-fitting terminals and connectors.

4. Connect the solenoid test connector to the solenoid connector (**Figure 122**).

5. Connect a 12-volt battery to the 2 solenoid test connector wires shown in **Figure 126** and perform the following:

**125** **SOLENOID/BUTTERFLY VALVE ASSEMBLY (1992-ON CALIFORNIA MODELS)**

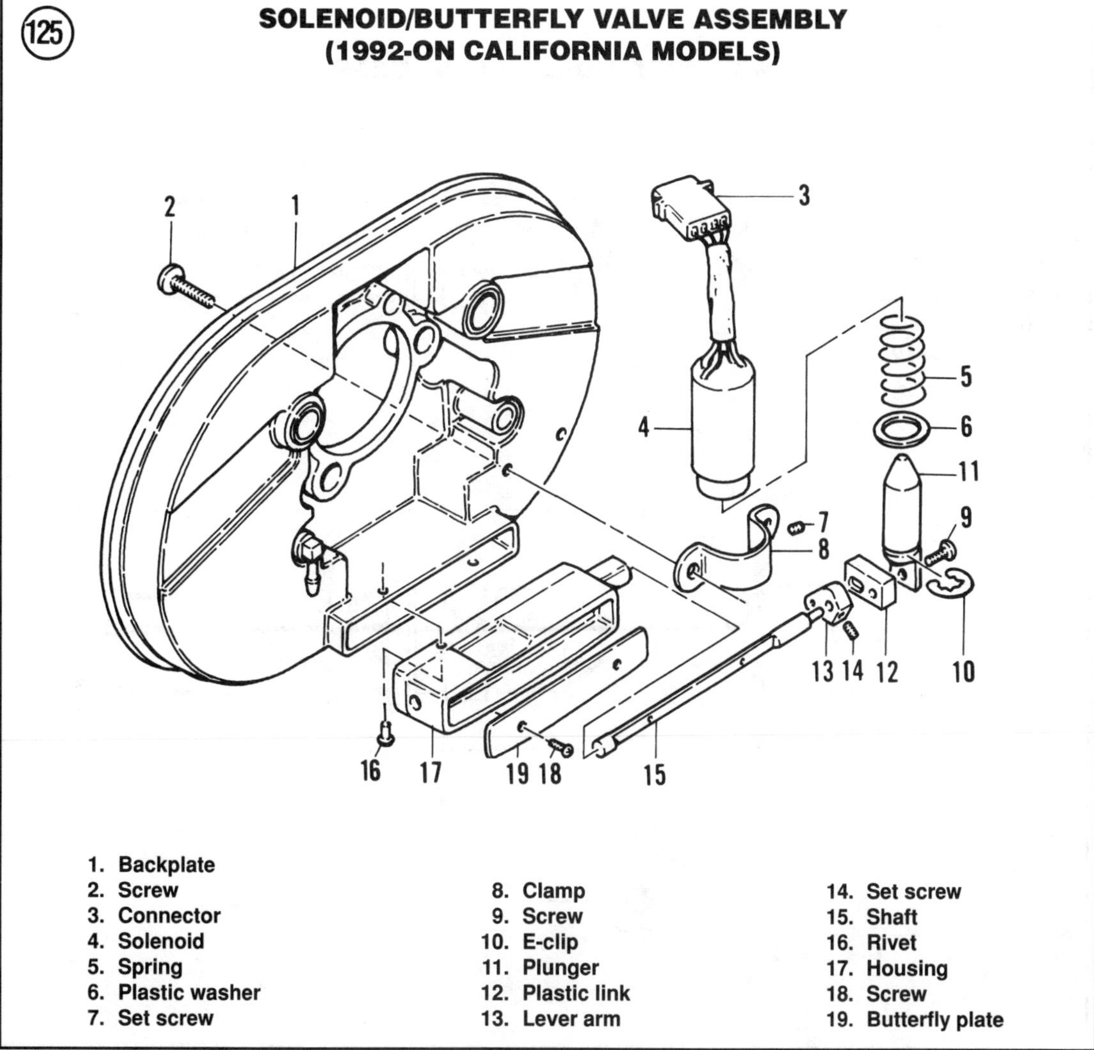


1. Backplate
2. Screw
3. Connector
4. Solenoid
5. Spring
6. Plastic washer
7. Set screw
8. Clamp
9. Screw
10. E-clip
11. Plunger
12. Plastic link
13. Lever arm
14. Set screw
15. Shaft
16. Rivet
17. Housing
18. Screw
19. Butterfly plate

a. Open the butterfly valve carefully with a screwdriver by pushing inward on the left-hand side of the butterfly valve.
b. Remove the screwdriver. The butterfly valve should remain open as long as the solenoid hold-in windings are energized.
c. Disconnect the negative battery cable from the solenoid test connector. The butterfly valve should close.
d. If the butterfly valve operated as described in sub-steps b and c, the solenoid hold-in windings are operating correctly.
e. If the butterfly valve failed to operate properly, perform Step 6.
f. Disconnect the positive battery cable from the solenoid test connector.

6. If the butterfly valve did not remain open in Step 5, sub-step b, perform the following:

a. Switch an ohmmeter to R x 1 and cross the test leads. Then check for ground at the black connector pin in the solenoid 4-prong connector. The ohmmeter should read 1 ohm or less.

*NOTE*

*On 1994 FLT models, make sure the 3-pin Deutsch connector is plugged together; refer to wiring diagram at end of book.*

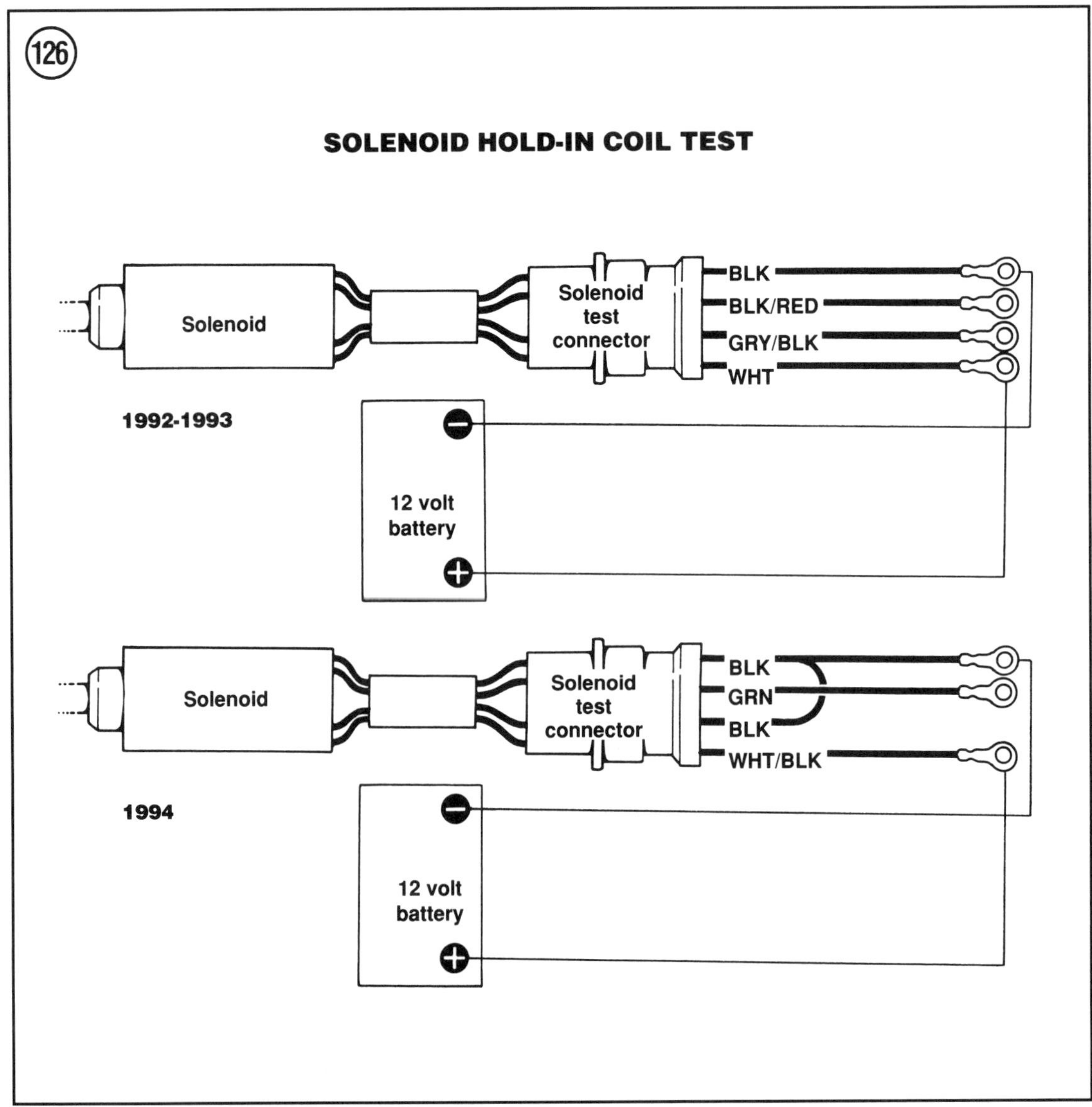

b. Reconnect the solenoid 4-prong connector.
c. Switch a voltmeter to the 12 VDC scale.
d. Connect the positive voltmeter lead to the white (1992-1993) or white/black (1994) lead in the 4-prong connector and the negative probe to a good engine ground. Turn the ignition switch to the ON or IGNITION position and read the voltage indicated on the voltmeter. It should be 12 volts.

7. If any of the meter readings differ from those specified in Step 6, there is a problem in the solenoid wiring harness. Use voltage and resistance checks to locate the damaged wire(s). After repairing the wire(s), repeat the above checks.
8. If the solenoid test readings were correct but the butterfly valve does not work properly, perform Step 3 under *Solenoid-Operated Butterfly Valve Troubleshooting (1992-on).*
9. Remove all test equipment and reconnect the solenoid 4-prong connector.

### Butterfly Valve and Solenoid Cleaning and Lubrication (1992-on)

Refer to **Figure 120**.

1. Remove the air filter and backplate as described under *Butterfly Valve Solenoid Removal/Installation/Adjustment (1992-on)* in this chapter.
2. At every 2,500 mile (4,022 km) interval, inspect the butterfly valve and solenoid for proper operation.
3. At every 5,000 mile (8,045 km) interval, spray the butterfly valve and plunger with carburetor cleaner. Then, after the carburetor cleaner evaporates, lubricate the linkage and plunger with a dry film spray lubricant.
4. Reinstall the air filter and backplate as described in Chapter Three.

### Butterfly Valve Solenoid Removal/Installation/Adjustment (1992-on)

Refer to **Figure 120**.

1. Remove the air filter as described in Chapter Three.
2. On FXR models, additional clearance must be made for backplate removal. Loosen the exhaust pipe crossover shield and pivot it downward or remove it from the exhaust pipe.
3. Disconnect the solenoid harness connector.
4. Disconnect the overflow hose from the backplate fitting.
5. Disconnect the canister inlet hose from the backplate fitting.
6. Remove the backplate mounting screws and backplate as follows (**Figure 120**):
   a. Remove the backplate mounting screws.
   b. Loosen the backplate-to-carburetor mounting screws in small amounts in a crisscross pattern. Continue until all of the screws are loosen, then remove the backplate and gasket.
7. To remove the solenoid:
   a. Remove the small screw securing the plunger to the plastic link.
   b. Remove the 2 long screws and washers securing the solenoid clamp to the backplate.
   c. Remove the solenoid assembly.
8. Clean the backplate and lubricate the butterfly valve linkage as described under *Butterfly Valve and Solenoid Cleaning and Lubrication (1992-on)* in this chapter.
9. Assemble the plastic link to the plunger screw as follows:
   a. Apply Loctite 222 (purple) to the plunger screw.
   b. Then secure the plastic link to the plunger's deep side with the plunger screw. When doing so, the link slot must face toward the pin on the lever arm.
   c. Tighten the plunger screw securely.
10. Install the solenoid into the backplate groove and install the lever arm pin into the plastic link.

*NOTE*
*Prior to installing the solenoid mounting screws, make sure the bottom of the baffle ( 3,* ***Figure 120****) is mounted behind the rib in the backplate. Otherwise, the solenoid plunger may bind when its mounting screws are tightened.*

11. Apply Loctite 222 (purple) to the solenoid mounting screws prior to installation. Install the screws, washers and clamp as shown in **Figure 120**. Do not tighten the screws at this time.
12. Adjust the solenoid plunger as follows:
   a. Push the solenoid plunger into the solenoid until it bottoms out. Hold it in this position.
   b. Check that the butterfly valve plate (10, **Figure 120**) is in its full-open position. Tighten

8

the solenoid mounting screws to 20-22 in.-lbs. (2.3-2.5 N•m).

*CAUTION*
*Do not overtighten the solenoid mounting screws; otherwise, the plunger may bind in the solenoid.*

c. Release the solenoid plunger and check the butterfly valve plate is closed.

13. Reverse Steps 1-6 to complete installation.

### Vapor Valve Replacement

1. Label the hoses at the vapor valve and then disconnect them.
2. Note that one end of the vapor valve is longer than the other end. The longer end must face *up*. Remove and replace the vapor valve.

*CAUTION*
*The vapor valve must be installed in a vertical position with the* ***longer end*** *facing upward or excessive pressure will build in the fuel tank.*

### Emission/Carburetor Hose Routing (All Models)

Refer to following figure for your model for emission hose routing:

a. **Figure 119**: Evaporative Emission Control System (1992-on California).

b. **Figure 127**: Hose routing at carburetor (1992-on FLT)

c. **Figure 128**: Emission hose and component location (1992-on FXR).

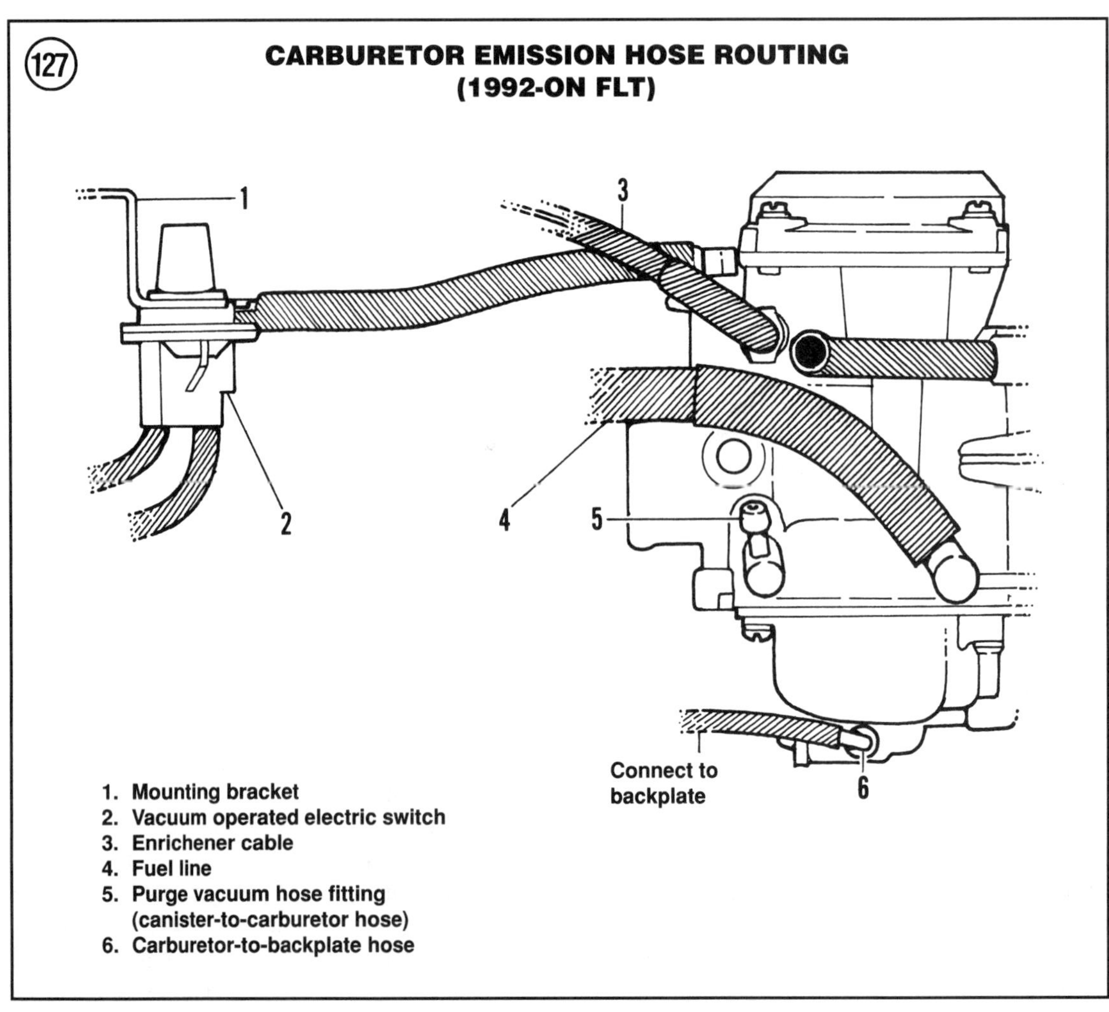

## EMISSION HOSE ROUTING AND COMPONENT LOCATION (1992-ON FXR)

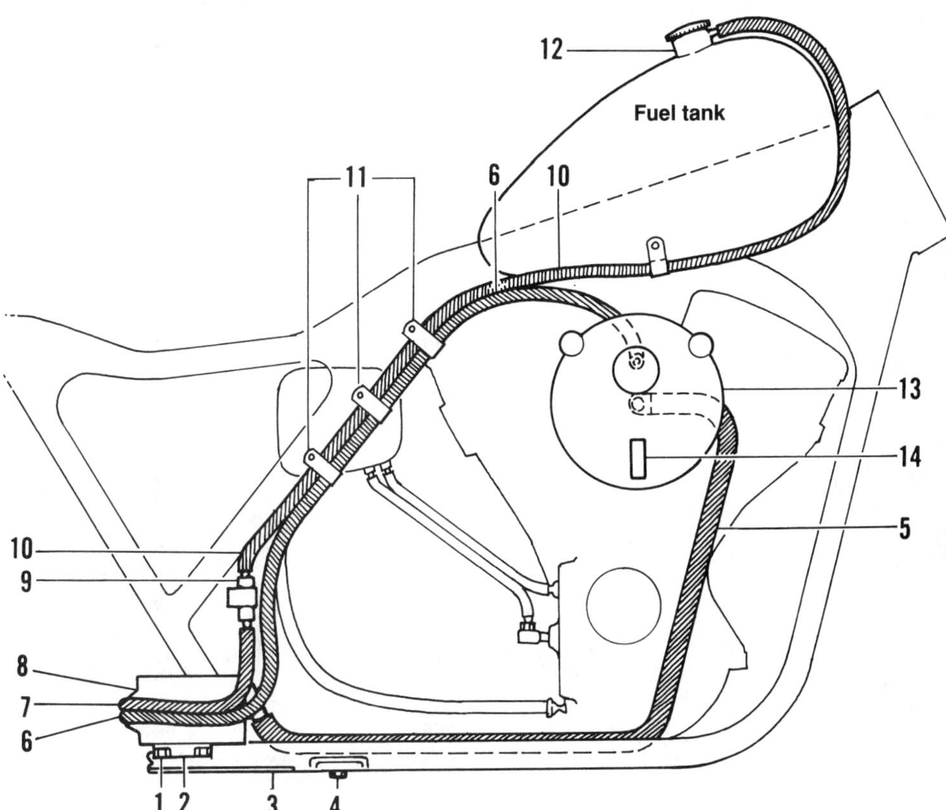


1. Screws
2. Canister mounting bracket
3. Canister bracket assembly
4. Screws
5. Canister-to-backplate hose
6. Canister-to-carburetor hose
7. Canister-to-vapor valve hose
8. Canister
9. Vapor valve
10. Vapor valve-to-fuel tank hose
11. Hose clips
12. Fuel tank filler neck
13. Air filter backplate
14. Solenoid

128

**Table 1 CARBURETOR SPECIFICATIONS**

| | Main jet | Pilot jet |
|---|---|---|
| FLT | | |
| Early 1984 | 165 | 50 |
| Late 1984-1986 | 175 | 50 |
| 1987 | 170 | 50 |
| 1988-1989 | | |
| 49-state | 165 | 52 |
| California | 140 | 42 |
| 1990-1991 | | |
| 49-state | 185 | 45 |
| California | 165 | 42 |
| 1992-1993 | | |
| 49-state | 175 | 40 |
| California | 160 | 40 |
| 1994 | | |
| 49-state | 175 | 42 |
| California | 165 | 42 |
| HDI* | 175 | 40 |
| FXR | | |
| 1984-1985 | 160 | 50 |
| 1986 | 170 | 50 |
| 1987 | 165 | 50 |
| 1988-1989 | | |
| 49-state | 165 | 52 |
| California | 140 | 42 |
| 1990-1991 | | |
| 49-state | 185 | 45 |
| California | 165 | 42 |
| 1992-1993 | | |
| 49-state | 165 | 40 |
| California | 160 | 40 |
| 1994 | | |
| 49-state | 165 | 42 |
| California | 165 | 42 |
| HDI* | 165 | 40 |
| FXWG | | |
| 1985 | 165 | 50 |
| 1986 | 170 | 50 |
| FXEF and FXSB | | |
| 1985 | 165 | 50 |

*HDI: International models.

## CHAPTER NINE

# ELECTRICAL SYSTEM

All models covered in this manual are equipped with a 12-volt, negative-ground electrical system. Many electrical problems can be traced to a simple cause such as a loose or corroded connection or frayed wire. While these are easily corrected problems, they can quickly lead to serious difficulty if allowed to go uncorrected.

This chapter provides service procedures for the battery, charging system, ignition system, starter, lights, switches and circuit breakers. Tune-up procedures involving the ignition system are described in Chapter Three.

**Tables 1-6** are found at the end of chapter.

## BATTERY

The battery is the single most important component in the motorcycle electrical system. Yet, most electrical system troubles can be traced to battery neglect. In addition to checking and correcting the battery electrolyte level on a weekly basis, the battery should be cleaned and inspected at periodic intervals. Battery capacity is listed in **Table 1**.

### Safety Precautions

When working with batteries, use extreme care to avoid spilling or splashing the electrolyte. This solution contains sulfuric acid, which can ruin clothing and cause serious chemical burns. If any electrolyte is spilled or splashed on clothing or skin, immediately neutralize with a solution of baking soda and water, then flush with an abundance of clean water.

*WARNING*

*Electrolyte splashed into the eyes is extremely harmful. Safety glasses should always be worn while working with batteries. If electrolyte is splashed into the eyes, call a physician immediately, force the eyes open and flood with cool, clean water for approximately 15 minutes.*

If electrolyte is spilled or splashed onto any surface, it should be immediately neutralized with baking soda and water solution and then rinsed with clean water.

While batteries are being charged, highly explosive hydrogen gas forms in each cell. Some of this gas escapes through filler cap openings and may form an explosive atmosphere in and around the battery. This condition can persist for several hours. Sparks, an open flame or a lighted cigarette can ignite the gas, causing an internal battery explosion and possible serious personal injury.

Take the following precautions to prevent an explosion:

1. Do not smoke or permit any open flame near any battery being charged or which has been recently charged.
2. Do not disconnect live circuits at battery terminals since a spark usually occurs when a live circuit is broken.
3. Take care when connecting or disconnecting any battery charger. Be sure its power switch is off before making or breaking connections. Poor connections are a common cause of electrical arcs which cause explosions.

4. Keep all children and pets away from charging equipment and batteries.

## Care and Inspection

For maximum battery life, it should be checked periodically for electrolyte level, state of charge and corrosion. During hot weather periods, frequent checks are recommended. If the electrolyte level is below the bottom of the vent well in one or more cells, add distilled water as required. To assure proper mixing of the water and acid, operate the engine immediately after adding water. *Never* add battery acid instead of water—this will shorten the battery's life.

On all models covered in this manual, the negative side is grounded. When removing the battery, disconnect the negative (–) ground cable first, then the positive (+) cable. This minimizes the chance of a tool shorting to ground when disconnecting the "hot" positive cable.

*WARNING*

*When performing the following procedures, protect your eyes, skin and clothing. If electrolyte gets into your eyes, flush your eyes thoroughly with clean water and get prompt medical attention.*

1. Access the battery as follows:
   a. *1984-1992 FLT:* The battery is located on the right-hand side of the vehicle, adjacent to the rear wheel. Remove the right-hand saddlebag and the right-hand side cover.
   b. *1993-on FLT:* The battery is located underneath the seat. Open Tour-Pak cover and remove screw securing seat to luggage rack. Remove seat.
   c. *FXR and 1985-1986 FX:* The battery is located underneath the seat.
2. Disconnect the negative battery cable from the battery. See **Figure 1**, typical.
3. Disconnect the positive battery cable from the battery.
4. Remove the battery hold-down strap and disconnect the battery vent tube at the battery.
5. Remove the battery from the motorcycle.

*CAUTION*

*Be careful not to spill battery electrolyte on painted or polished surfaces. The liquid is highly corrosive and will damage the finish. If it is spilled, wash it off immediately with soapy water and thoroughly rinse with clean water.*

6. Check the entire battery case for cracks or other damage.
7. Inspect the battery tray and cushion for contamination or damage. Clean with a solution of baking soda and water.
8. Check the battery hold-down strap for age deterioration, cracks or other signs of damage. Replace strap if required.
9. Check the battery terminal parts—bolts, spacers and nuts—for corrosion or damage. Clean parts thoroughly with a solution of baking soda and water. Replace severely corroded or damaged parts.
10. Cover the vent holes in each cap with small pieces of masking tape.

*NOTE*

*Keep cleaning solution out of the battery cells or the electrolyte level will be seriously weakened.*

11. Clean the top of the battery with a stiff bristle brush using the baking soda and water solution.

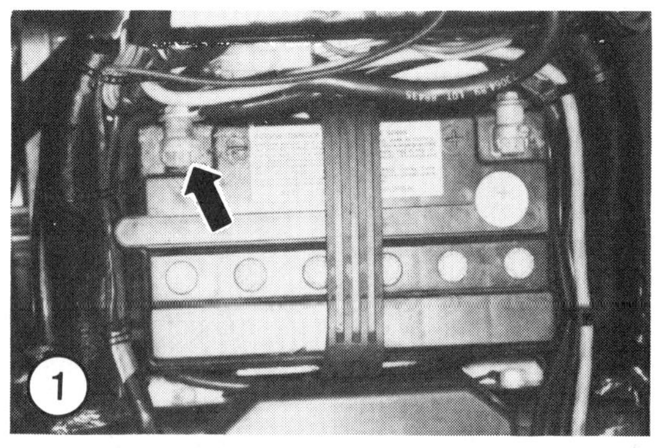
1

2

Rinse the battery case with clean water and wipe dry with a clean cloth or paper towel.

12. Check the battery cable clamps for corrosion and damage. If corrosion is minor, clean the battery cable clamps with a stiff wire brush. Replace severely worn or damaged cables.

*NOTE*
*Do not overfill the battery cells in Step 13. The electrolyte expands due to heat from charging and will overflow if the level is above the upper level line.*

13. On batteries with black housings, remove the caps (**Figure 2**) from the battery cells and check the electrolyte level. On batteries with clear housings, check electrolyte level through the side of the battery. Add distilled water, if necessary, to bring the level within the upper and lower level lines on the battery case (A, **Figure 3**).

14. Reposition the battery in the battery tray. Make sure the rubber cushion is installed in the bottom of the tray, if used, before installing the battery. Install the battery strap to secure the battery.

15. Reinstall the positive battery cable, then the negative battery cable. See **Figure 1**.

*CAUTION*
*Be sure the battery cables are connected to their proper terminals. Connecting the battery backwards will reverse the polarity and damage the rectifier.*

*WARNING*
*After installing the battery, make sure the vent tube (B, **Figure 3**) is not pinched. A pinched or kinked tube would allow high pressure to accumulate in the battery and cause the battery to explode. If the vent tube is damaged, replace it.*

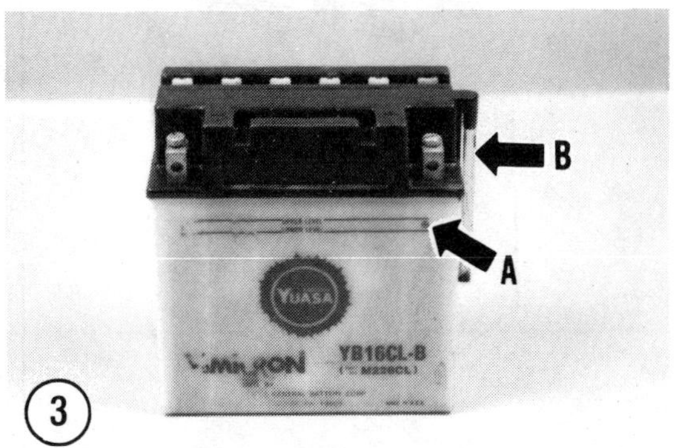

3

16. Coat the battery connections with a petroleum jelly such as Vaseline or a water resistant grease.

## Testing

Hydrometer testing is the best way to check battery condition. Use a hydrometer with numbered graduations from 1.100 to 1.300 rather than one with just color-coded bands. To use the hydrometer, squeeze the rubber ball, insert the tip into the cell and release the ball (**Figure 4**).

*NOTE*
*Do not attempt to test a battery with a hydrometer immediately after adding water to the cells. Charge the battery for 15-20 minutes at a rate high enough to cause vigorous gassing and allow the water and electrolyte to mix thoroughly.*

Draw enough electrolyte to float the weighted float inside the hydrometer. When using a temperature-compensated hydrometer, release the electrolyte and repeat this process several times to make sure the thermometer has adjusted to the electrolyte temperature before taking the reading.

Hold the hydrometer vertically and note the number in line with the surface of the electrolyte (**Figure 5**). This is the specific gravity for this cell. Return the electrolyte to the cell from which it came.

The specific gravity of the electrolyte in each battery cell is an excellent indication of that cell's condition (**Table 2**). A fully charged cell will read 1.260-1.280 while a cell in good condition reads from 1.230-1.250 and anything below 1.160 is discharged. Charging is also necessary if the specific gravity varies more than 0.050 from cell to cell.

*NOTE*
*If a temperature-compensated hydrometer is not used, add 0.004 to the specific gravity reading for every 10° above 80° F (25° C). For every 10° below 80° F (25° C), subtract 0.004.*

## Charging

A good state of charge should be maintained in batteries used for starting. When charging the battery, note the following:

a. During charging, the cells will show signs of gas bubbling. If one cell has no gas bubbles or if its specific gravity is low, the cell is probably shorted.

b. If a battery not in use loses its charge within a week after charging or if the specific gravity drops quickly, the battery is defective. A good battery should only self-discharge approximately 1% each day.

*CAUTION*
*Always remove the battery from the bike before connecting charging equipment.*

*WARNING*
*During charging, highly explosive hydrogen gas is released from the battery. The battery should be charged only in a well-ventilated area, and open flames and cigarettes should be kept away. Never check the charge of the battery by arcing across the terminals; the resulting spark can ignite the hydrogen gas.*

1. Remove the battery from the bike as described in this chapter.

2. Connect the positive (+) charger lead to the positive battery terminal and the negative (–) charger lead to the negative battery terminal.

3. Remove all vent caps (**Figure 2**) from the battery, set the charger at 12 volts, and switch it on. Normally, a battery should be charged at a slow charge rate of 1/10 its given capacity. See **Table 1** for battery capacity.

*CAUTION*
*The electrolyte level must be maintained at the upper level during the charging cycle; check and refill with distilled water as necessary.*

4. The charging time depends on the discharged condition of the battery. The chart in **Figure 6** can be used to determine approximate charging times at different specific gravity readings. For example, if the specific gravity of your battery is 1.180, the approximate charging time would be 6 hours.

5. After the battery has been charged for about 8 hours, turn the charger off, disconnect the leads and check the specific gravity. It should be within the limits specified in **Table 2**. If it is, and remains stable for one hour, the battery is charged.

### New Battery Installation

When replacing the old battery with a new one, be sure to charge it completely (specific gravity, 1.260-1.280) before installing it. Failure to do so, or using the battery with a low electrolyte level will permanently damage the battery.

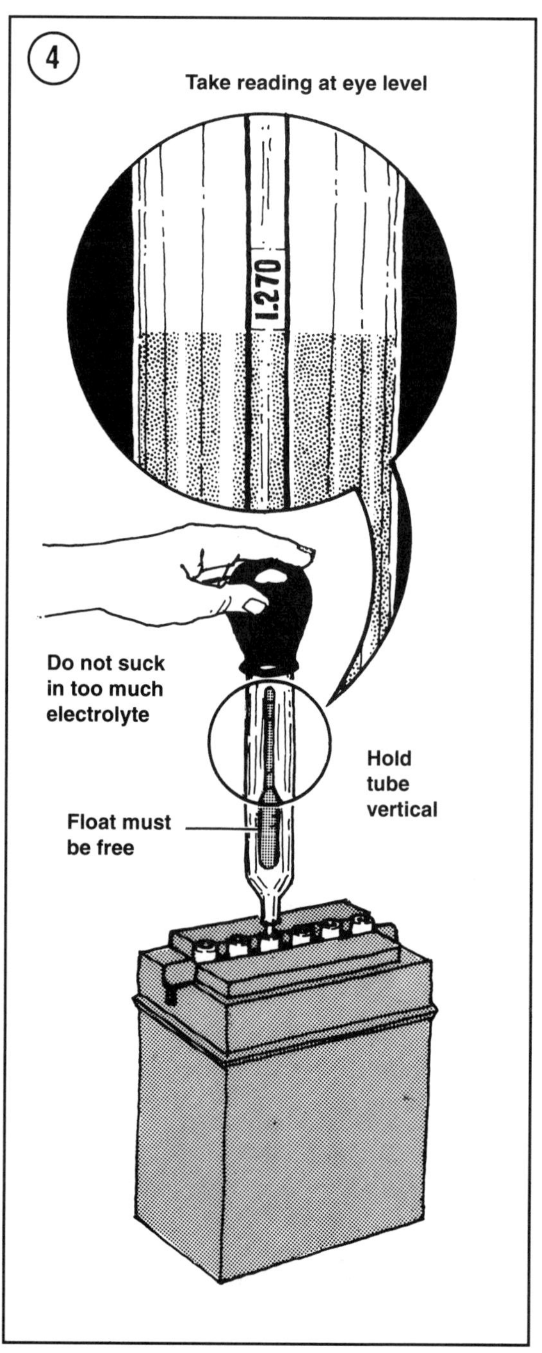

## Jump Starting

If the battery becomes severely discharged, it is possible to start and run an engine by jump starting it from another battery. If the proper procedure is not followed, however, jump starting can be dangerous. Check the electrolyte level before jump starting any battery. If it is not visible or if it appears to be frozen, do not attempt to jump start the battery, as the battery may explode or rupture.



The booster battery must be a fully charged 12 volt battery.

*WARNING*
*To avoid personal injury or damage to the electrical system, use extreme caution when connecting a booster battery to one that is discharged. Do not lean over the batteries when making the connections. Safety glasses should be worn when performing the following procedure.*

1. Position the 2 vehicles so that the jumper cables will reach between batteries. The vehicles must not touch.
2. Remove parts as needed to gain access to the dead battery. Remove parts as required to access the booster battery.
3. Make sure all electrical accessories are turned off.
4. Connect the jumper cables in the following order (**Figure 7**):
   a. Connect the positive (+) jumper cable between the 2 battery positive terminals.
   b. Connect one end of the negative (–) jumper cable to the booster battery negative terminal. Connect the opposite end to an unpainted engine case bolt on the bike with the dead battery. *Do not* connect the jumper cable to the negative battery terminal on the dead battery.

*WARNING*
*An electrical arc may occur when the final connection is made. This could*

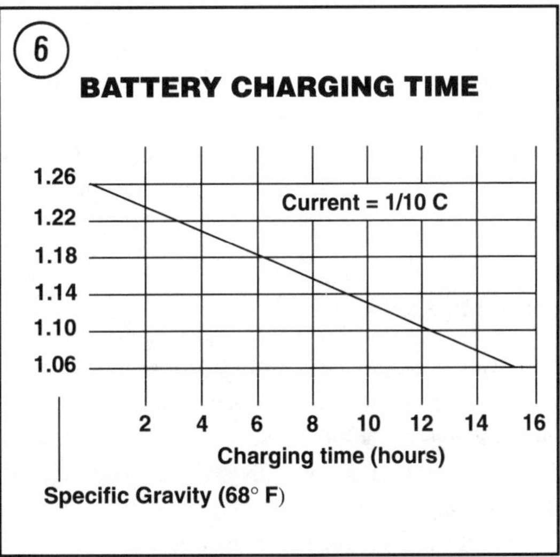

*cause an explosion if it occurs near the battery. For this reason, the final connection should be made to a good ground **away** from the battery and not to the battery itself. This includes keeping the connection away from the battery vent tube.*

*NOTE*
*Do not connect the negative jumper cable to a chrome or painted part as the connection may discolor it.*

5. Check that all jumper cables are out of the way.

*NOTE*
*When attempting to start the engine in Step 6, do not operate the starter longer than 6 seconds. Excessive starter operation will overheat the starter and cause damage. Allow 15 seconds between starting attempts.*

6. Start the engine. Once it starts, run it at a moderate speed.

*CAUTION*
*Racing the engine may damage the electrical system.*

7. Remove the jumper cables in the exact reverse order.

## CHARGING SYSTEM

The charging system consists of the battery, alternator, regulator, ignition switch, circuit breaker and connecting wiring.

The alternator generates an alternating current (AC) which the rectifier converts to direct current (DC). The regulator maintains the voltage to the battery and load (lights, ignition, etc.) at a constant voltage regardless of variations in engine speed and load.

### Service Precautions

Before servicing the charging system, observe the following precautions to prevent damage to any charging system component.

1. Never reverse battery connections. Instantaneous damage may occur.
2. Do not short across any connection.
3. Never attempt to polarize an alternator.
4. Never start the engine with the alternator disconnected from the voltage regulator/rectifier, unless instructed to do so in testing.
5. Never start or run the engine with the battery disconnected.
6. Never attempt to use a high-output battery charger to assist in engine starting.
7. Before charging battery, disconnect the negative battery lead.
8. Never disconnect the voltage regulator connector with the engine running.
9. Do not mount the voltage regulator/rectifier unit at another location.
10. Make sure the battery negative terminal is connected to both engine and frame.

### Testing

A malfunction in the charging system generally causes the battery to remain undercharged. Perform the following visual inspection to determine the cause of the problem. If the visual inspection proves satisfactory, test the charging system as described in Chapter Two.

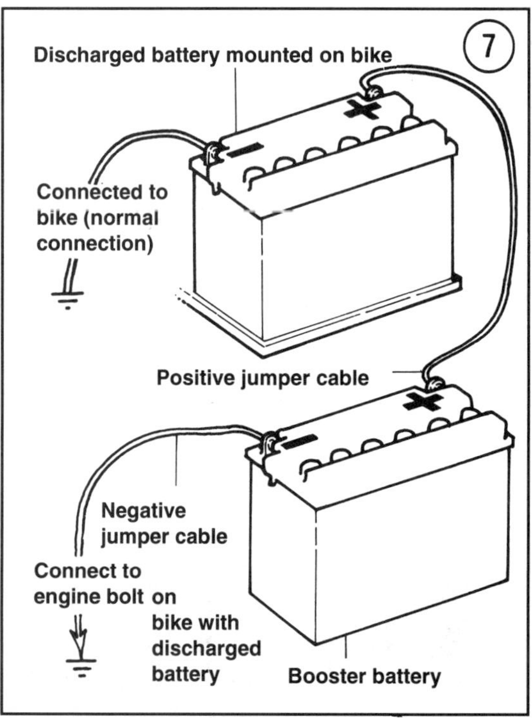

1. Make sure the battery cables are connected properly (**Figure 1**). The red cable must be connected to the positive battery terminal. If polarity is reversed, check for a damaged rectifier.

2. Inspect the terminals for loose or corroded connections. Tighten or clean as required.

3. Inspect the physical condition of the battery. Look for bulges or cracks in the case, leaking electrolyte or corrosion build-up.

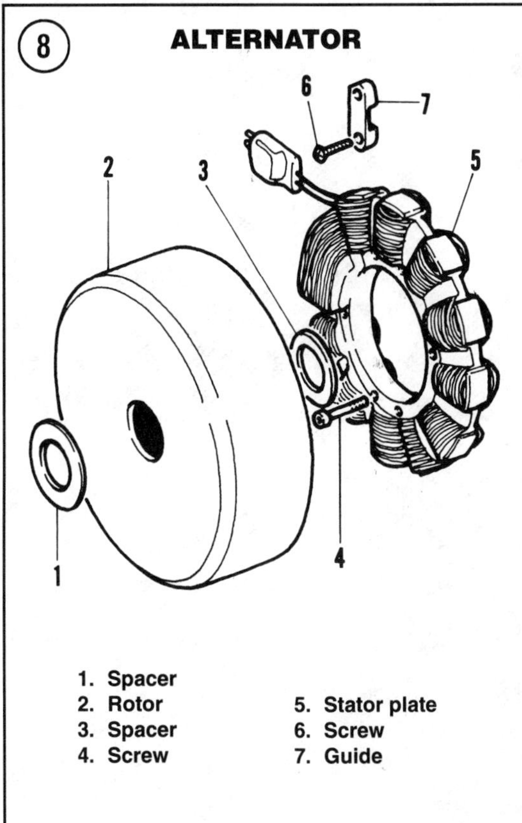


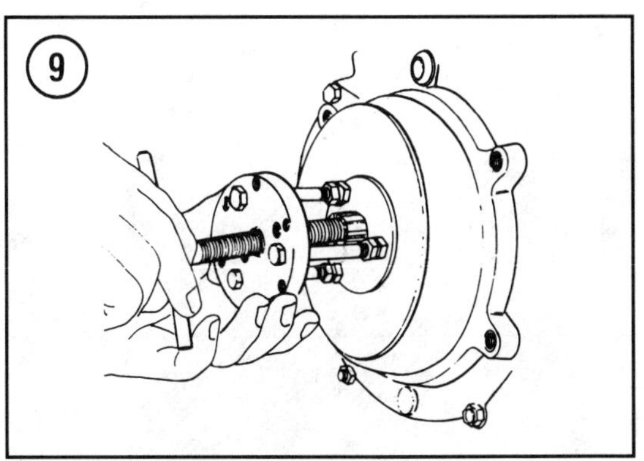


4. Carefully check all connections at the alternator to make sure they are clean and tight.
5. Check the circuit wiring for corroded or loose connections. Clean, tighten or connect as required.

## Rotor

### Removal/Installation

Refer to **Figure 8**, typical for this procedure.
1. Disconnect the negative battery cable at the battery.
2. Remove the primary cover, compensating sprocket, primary drive, clutch and primary case as described in Chapter Five.

*NOTE*
*Rotor removal will depend on the type of rotor used. Early model rotors have an internally splined boss. A rotor puller will be required to remove the rotor. Rotors on later models are a slip fit with large washers placed on both sides of the rotor.*

3A. *Rotors with internally splined boss*: Screw the rotor puller into the rotor as shown in **Figure 9**. Use the Harley-Davidson rotor puller (part No. HD-95-960-52B) or equivalent. Turn the rotor puller center bolt with a wrench until the rotor is free. Remove the rotor and puller.
3B. *Slip fit rotors*: The rotor installed on these models can either be slip fit or machined with splines. Spacers are installed on both sides of the rotor. These spacers are different, so ID each washer as you remove it. To remove the rotor, first remove the large O.D. spacer (**Figure 10**). Use 2 bolts as shown in **Figure 11** or slip 3 pieces of wire and hook it behind the rotor and remove the rotor from the end of the crankshaft. Remove the small O.D. spacer from behind the rotor (**Figure 12**).

### Inspection

1. Check the rotor (**Figure 13**) carefully for cracks or breaks.

*WARNING*
*A cracked or chipped rotor must be replaced. A damaged rotor may fly apart at high rpm, throwing metal fragments over a large area. Do not attempt to repair a damaged rotor.*

2. Check the rotor bore or taper for signs of scoring, cracks or other damage.

3. Replace damaged parts as required.

## Installation

*CAUTION*

*Carefully inspect the inside of the rotor (**Figure 13**) for small bolts, washers or other metal "debris" that may have been picked up by the magnets. These small metal bits can cause severe damage to the alternator stator assembly.*

1. Install the stator assembly, if previously removed, as described in this chapter.

2A. *Rotors without spacers*: Slide the rotor onto the crankshaft.

2B. *Rotors with spacers*: Install the rotor assembly as follows:

   a. Install the smaller O.D. spacer onto the crankshaft (**Figure 12**).
   b. Slide the rotor (**Figure 13**) onto the crankshaft.
   c. Install the larger O.D. spacer onto the crankshaft (**Figure 10**).

*NOTE*

*The small O.D. washer (A, **Figure 14**) shown next to the large O.D. rotor spacer (B, **Figure 14**) is used for primary chain alignment. This washer will be installed when you install the primary drive assembly in Chapter Five. Do not confuse it with the spacer used with the rotor assembly.*

10

11

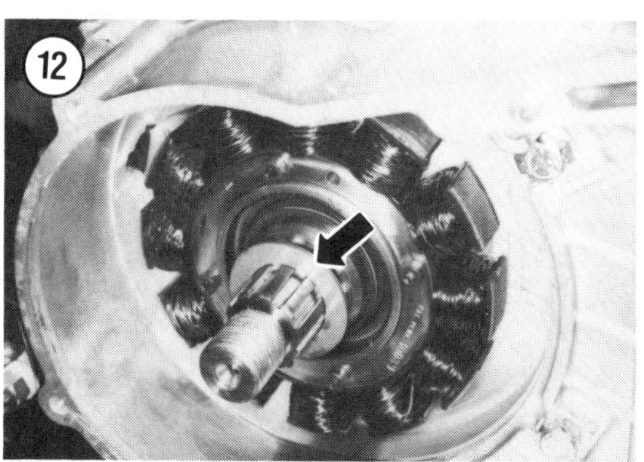
12

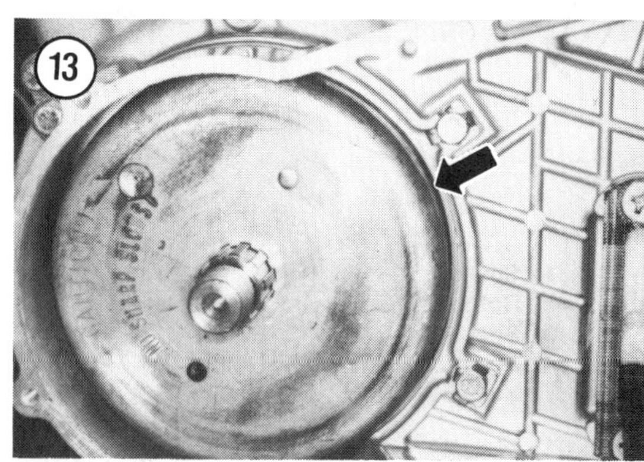
13

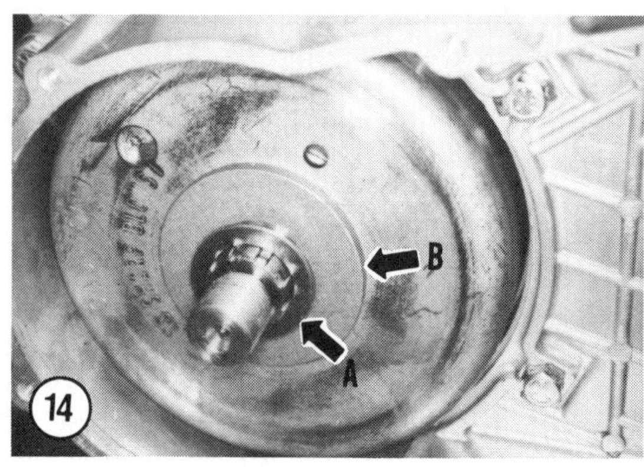

14

15

16

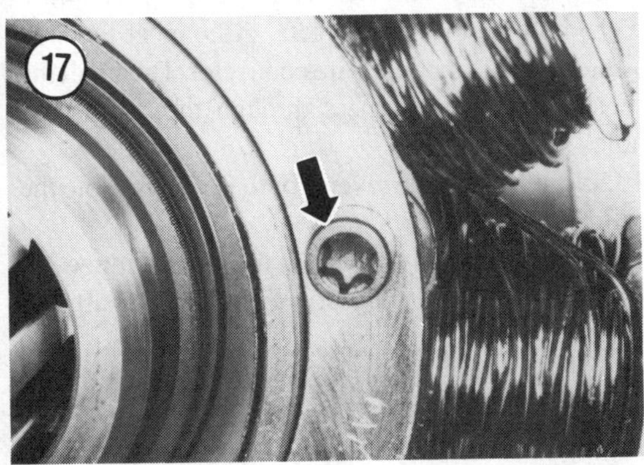
17

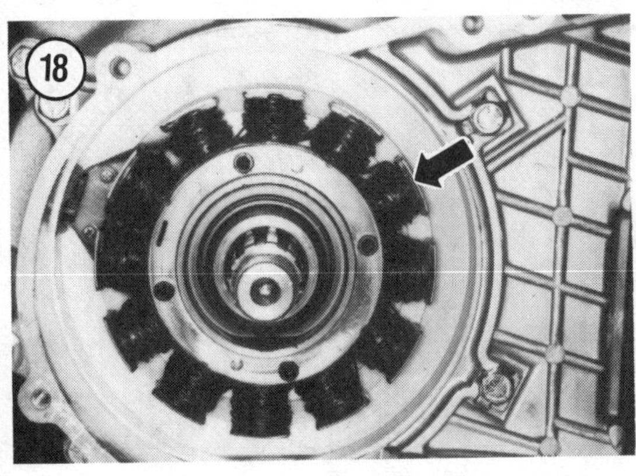
18

3. Install the primary drive components as described in Chapter Five. Make sure to torque the compensating sprocket nut as described in Chapter Five.

### Stator Removal/Installation

The stator (**Figure 8**) is mounted behind the rotor and bolted to the left-hand crankcase half. Early models used a lockplate and screw combination to secure the stator to the crankcase. Late models use Torx screws with a locking adhesive applied to the screw. Torx screws must be replaced after removal.

1. Remove the rotor as described in this chapter.

2. Disconnect the electrical connector at the stator (**Figure 15**).

3. Push the connector through the engine crankcase as shown in **Figure 16**.

4A. *Early models*: Bend the lockplates away from the stator screws. Then remove the screws and lockplates.

4B. *Late models*: Remove and discard the stator plate Torx screws (**Figure 17**).

5. Remove the stator assembly (**Figure 18**).

6. Inspect the stator wires (**Figure 19**) for fraying or damage. Check the stator connector pins for looseness or damage. Replace the stator if necessary.

7. Installation is the reverse of these steps. Note the following.

8. On early models, replace the lockplates if they cannot be reused. On late models, secure the stator plate with *new* Torx screws.

9. Install the rotor as described in this chapter.



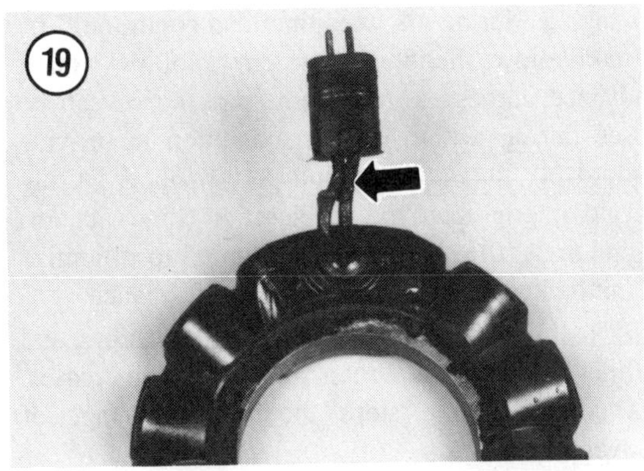
19

### Voltage Regulator Removal/Installation

The regulator cannot be rebuilt; if damaged it must be replaced.

*NOTE*
*Before disconnecting the voltage regulator electrical connectors in Step 1, diagram the wire routing and tag the electrical connectors so that you can correctly install the new voltage regulator.*

1. Disconnect the voltage regulator electrical connectors.
2. Remove the voltage regulator mounting fasteners and remove the voltage regulator. See **Figure 20**, typical.
3. Install by reversing these removal steps.

## IGNITION SYSTEM

The ignition system consists of a single ignition coil, 2 spark plugs, an inductive pickup unit, an ignition module and a vacuum operated electric switch (VOES). This system has a full electronic advance. The inductive pickup unit is driven by the engine and generates pulses which are routed to the solid-state ignition control module. This control module computes the ignition timing advance and ignition coil dwell time, eliminating the need for mechanical advance and routine ignition service.

The vacuum operated electric switch (VOES) senses intake manifold vacuum through a carburetor body opening. The switch is open when the engine is in low vacuum situations such as acceleration and high load. The switch is closed when engine vacuum is high as during a low engine load condition. The VOES allows the ignition system to follow 2 spark advance curves. A maximum spark curve can be used during a high-vacuum condition to provide improved fuel economy and performance. During heavy engine load and acceleration (low vacuum) conditions, the spark can be retarded to minimize ignition knock and still maintain performance.

The timing sensor is triggered by the leading and trailing edges of the 2 rotor slots. As rpm increases, the control module "steps" the timing in 3 stages of advance.

Refer to **Figure 21** (1984-1990), **Figure 22** (1991-1993 and 1994 FXR) or **Figure 23** (1994 FLT part 1 and part 2).

### Ignition Component Replacement

Refer to **Figure 24** for this procedure.

1. Disconnect the negative battery lead.
2. Drill out the outer cover rivets with a 3/8 in. (9.5 mm) drill bit (**Figure 25**).
3. Using a punch, tap the rivets through the outer cover and remove the outer cover. See **Figure 26.**
4. Using a punch, tap the rivets through the inner cover (**Figure 27**). Then remove the inner cover Phillips screws and remove the cover (**Figure 28**).
5. Remove the gasket (**Figure 29**).
6. Remove the screws (**Figure 30**) securing the sensor plate to the crankcase.
7. Disconnect the sensor wire connector at the crankcase. Then remove the connector from the wires. Withdraw the wires through the crankcase hole one wire at a time. Remove the sensor plate and wires. See **Figure 31**.
8. Remove the rotor screw and rotor (**Figure 32**).
9. To remove the sensor plate, disconnect the sensor-to-ignition module wire connector. Then pull the sensor plate wire harness through the chain case hole.
10. Installation is the reverse of these steps. Note the following.
11. Align the tab on the back of the rotor (**Figure 33**) with the notch in the end of the crankshaft (A, **Figure 34**).
12. Apply Loctite Lock 'N Seal to the rotor bolt and install it. Tighten the bolt to 75-80 in.-lb. (8.6-9.2 N•m).

20

13. Before riveting the cover in place, check the ignition timing as described in Chapter Three.

CAUTION

*Make sure to use the correct rivets in Step 14. These are special timing cover rivets which do not have ends that will fall into the timing compartment and damage the ignition components.*

14. Rivet the outer cover to the inner cover. Use only rivets (part number 8699) to secure the outer cover. See **Figure 35** and **Figure 36**.

### Ignition Module Removal/Installation (1984-1990)

1. Loosen and remove the ignition module ground wire.
2. Disconnect the ignition module wiring harness connector.
3. Remove the ignition module mounting bolts and remove the module assembly.
4. Install by reversing these removal steps. Clean ground wire connector at frame, if necessary.

### Ignition Module Removal/Installation (1991-on)

For 1991-1992 models, the ignition module location is as follows:

a. *FXR:* Under right-hand side cover.
b. *FLTC:* On left front fairing bracket.
c. *FLHTC and FLHS:* Left side of steering head.

For 1993-on models, the ignition module location is as follows:

a. *FXR:* Under right-hand side cover.
b. *1993 FLTCU:* On left front fairing bracket.
c. *1993 FLHTC/U and FLHS:* Left side of steering head.
d. *All 1994 FLT:* Under right-hand side cover.

1. On 1991-1993 and 1994 FXR, loosen and remove the ignition module ground wire.
2. Disconnect the ignition module wiring harness connector.

9

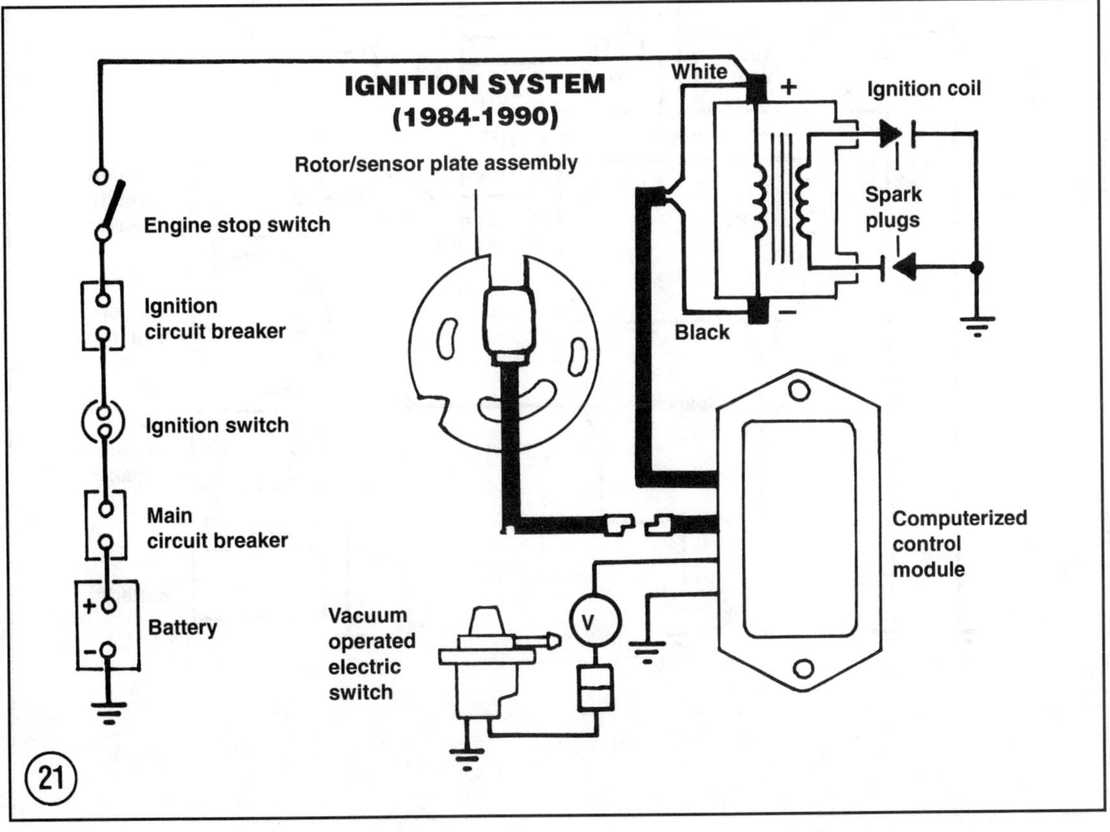

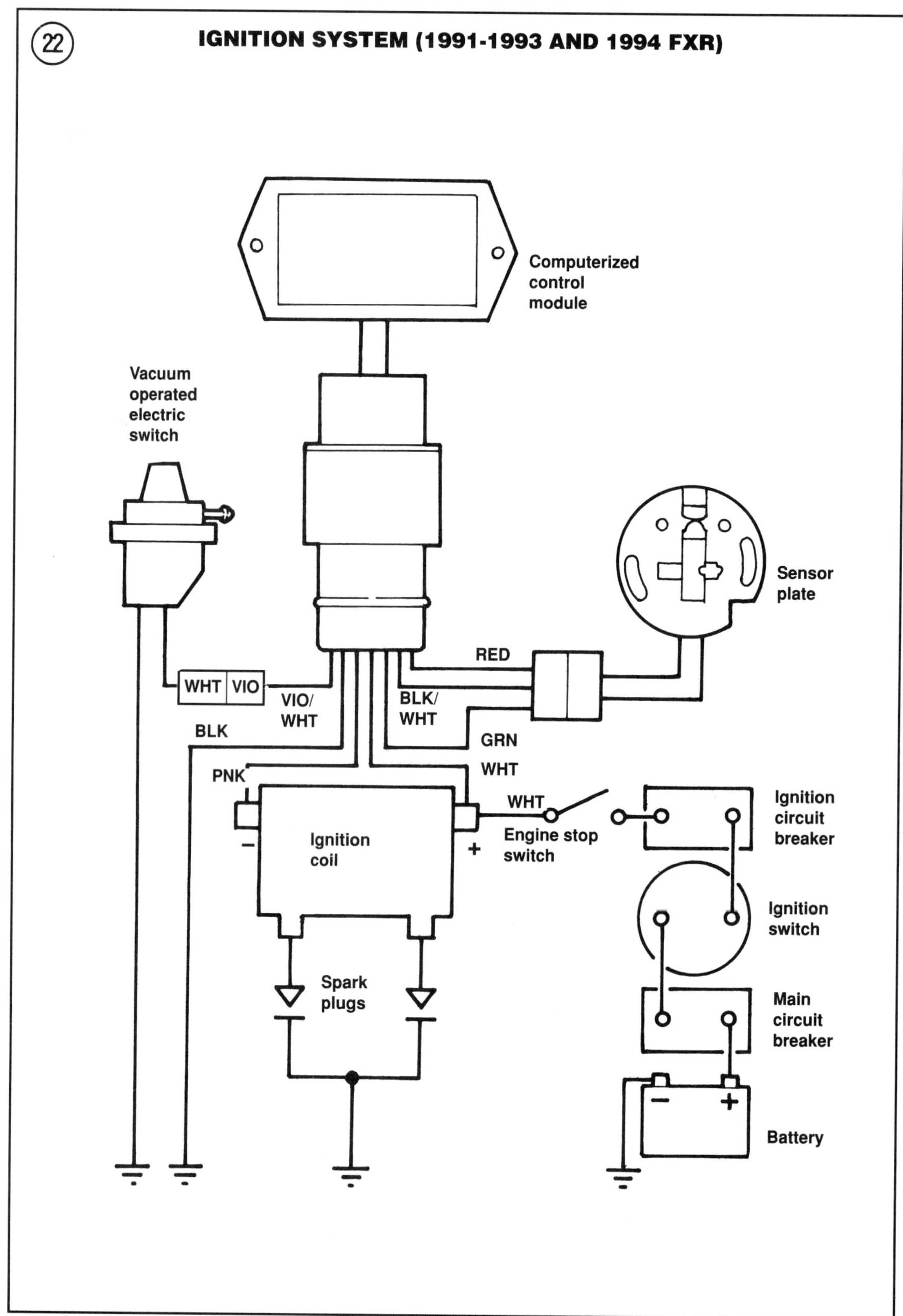
22
IGNITION SYSTEM (1991-1993 AND 1994 FXR)
Computerized control module
Vacuum operated electric switch
Sensor plate
RED
WHT
VIO
VIO/ WHT
BLK/ WHT
BLK
GRN
PNK
WHT
WHT
Ignition coil
Engine stop switch
Ignition circuit breaker
Ignition switch
Spark plugs
Main circuit breaker
Battery

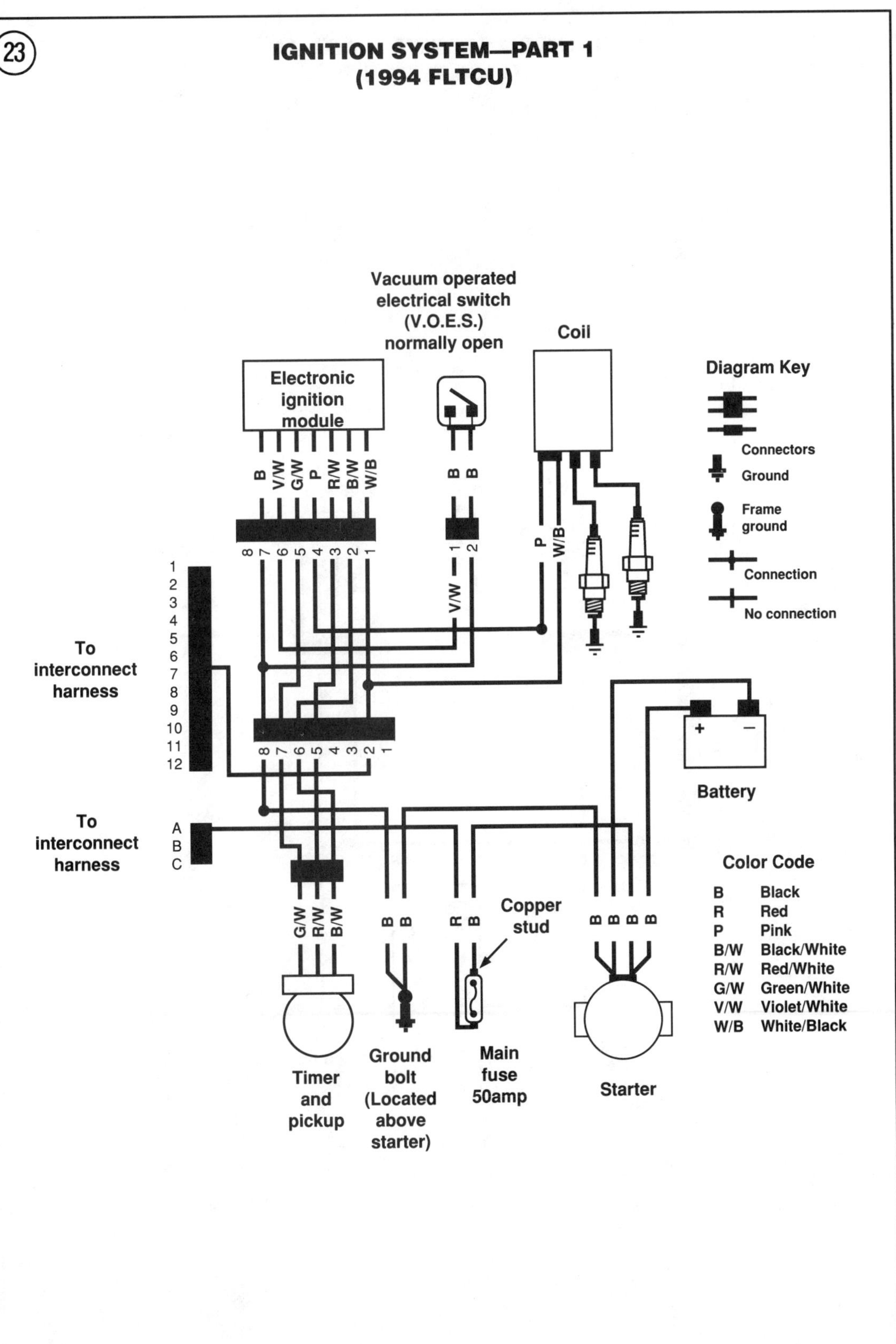
23
IGNITION SYSTEM—PART 1
(1994 FLTCU)
Vacuum operated
electrical switch
(V.O.E.S.)
normally open
Coil
Electronic
ignition
module
Diagram Key
Connectors
Ground
Frame
ground
Connection
No connection
B V/W G/W P R/W B/W W/B
B B
P W/B
V/W
To
interconnect
harness
1 2 3 4 5 6 7 8 9 10 11 12
+ −
Battery
To
interconnect
harness
A B C
Color Code
B Black
R Red
P Pink
B/W Black/White
R/W Red/White
G/W Green/White
V/W Violet/White
W/B White/Black
G/W R/W B/W
B B
R B
Copper
stud
B B B B
Timer
and
pickup
Ground
bolt
(Located
above
starter)
Main
fuse
50amp
Starter

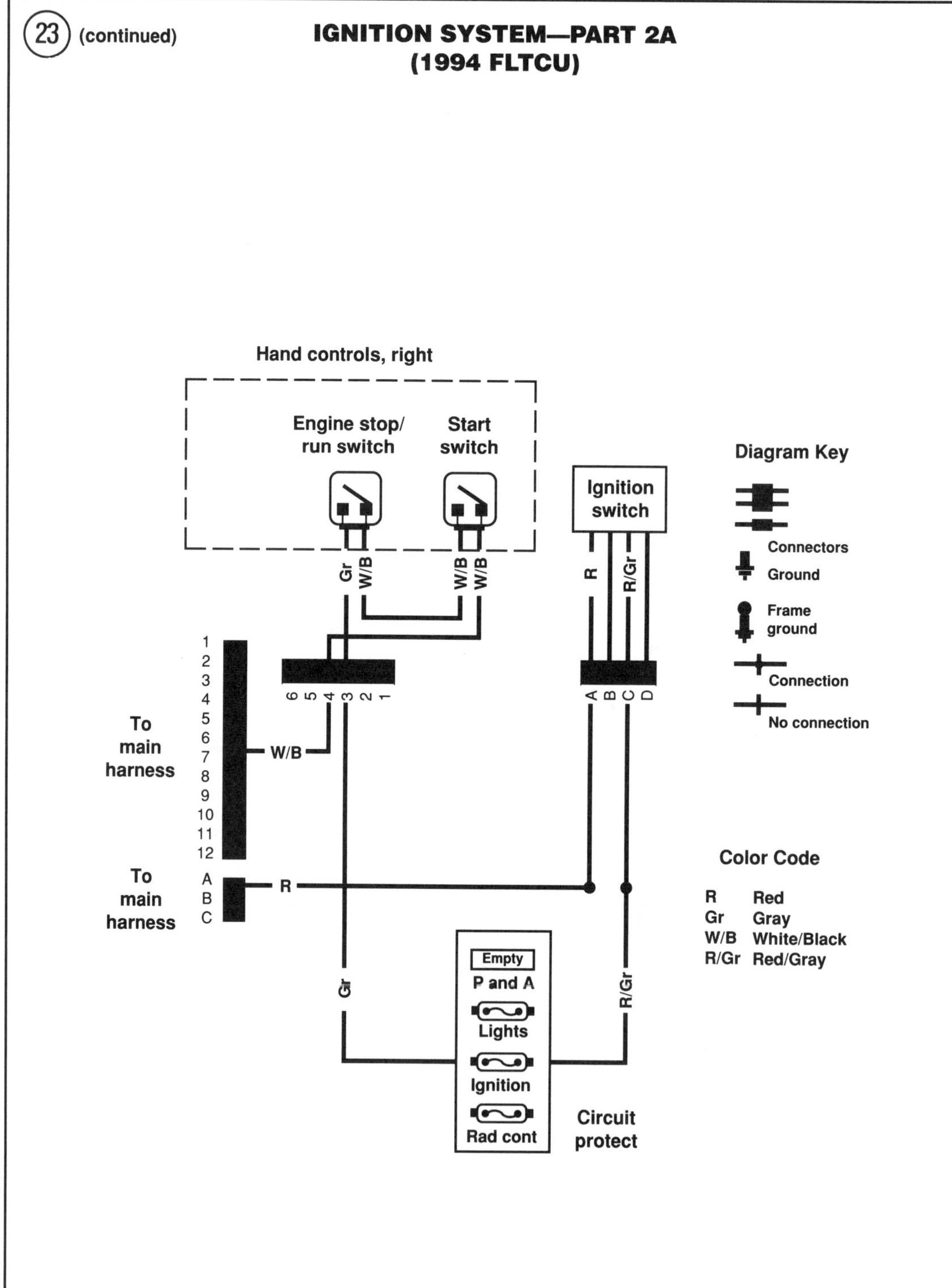

23 (continued)
IGNITION SYSTEM—PART 2A
(1994 FLTCU)
Hand controls, right
Engine stop/
run switch
Start
switch
Gr
W/B
W/B
W/B
Ignition
switch
R
R/Gr
1
2
3
4
5
6
7
8
9
10
11
12
To
main
harness
W/B
6 5 4 3 2 1
A B C D
To
main
harness
A
B
C
R
Gr
R/Gr
Empty
P and A
Lights
Ignition
Rad cont
Circuit
protect
Diagram Key
Connectors
Ground
Frame
ground
Connection
No connection
Color Code
R Red
Gr Gray
W/B White/Black
R/Gr Red/Gray

23 (continued)

## IGNITION SYSTEM—PART 2B (1994 FLHTC AND FLHTCU)

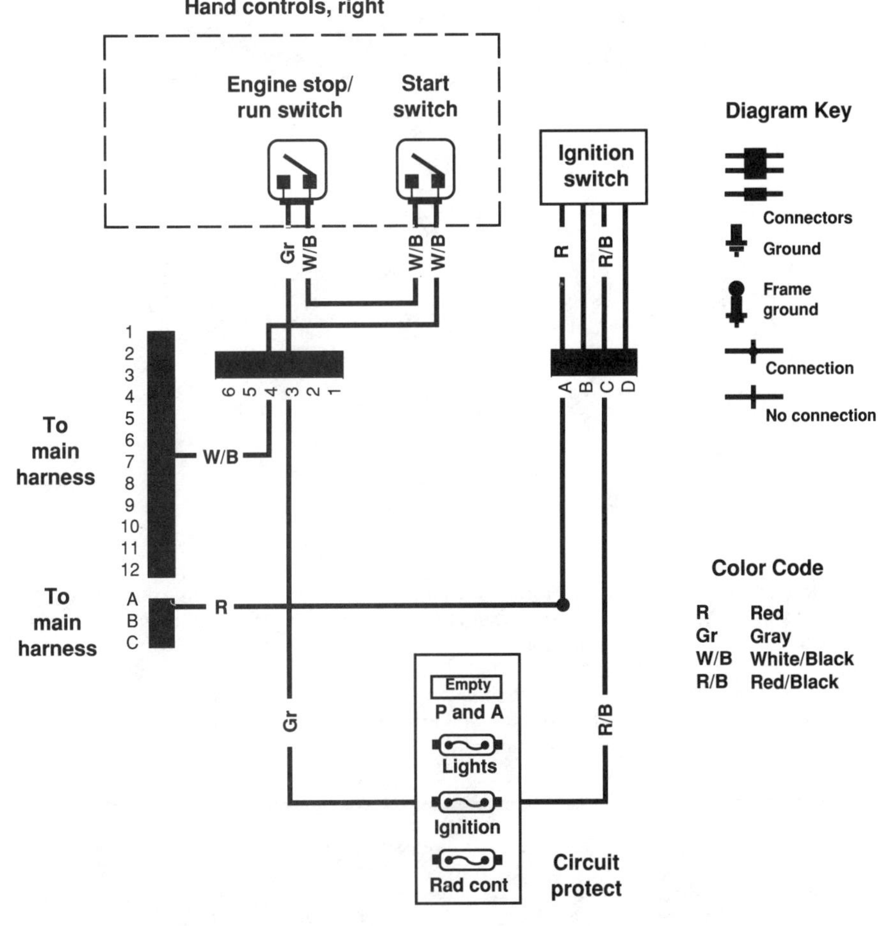

24

**IGNITION SYSTEM COMPONENTS**

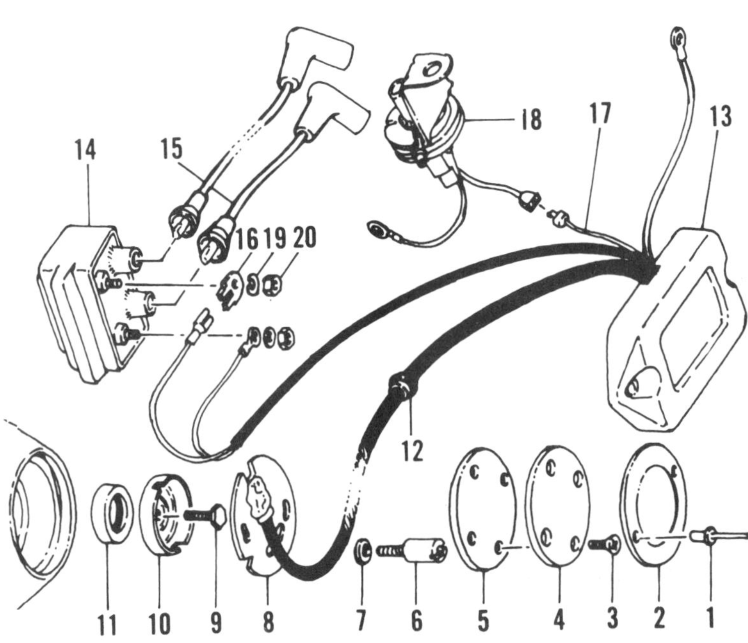


1. Outer cover rivet (2)
2. Outer cover
3. Inner cover screw (2)
4. Inner cover
5. Gasket
6. Sensor plate screw (2)
7. Washer (2)
8. Sensor plate
9. Rotor screw and star washer
10. Rotor
11. Camshaft oil seal
12. Connector
13. Ignition coil module
14. Ignition coil
15. Spark plug cable (2)
16. Ignition coil terminal
17. VOES wire
18. Vacuum operated electric switch
19. Washer
20. Nut

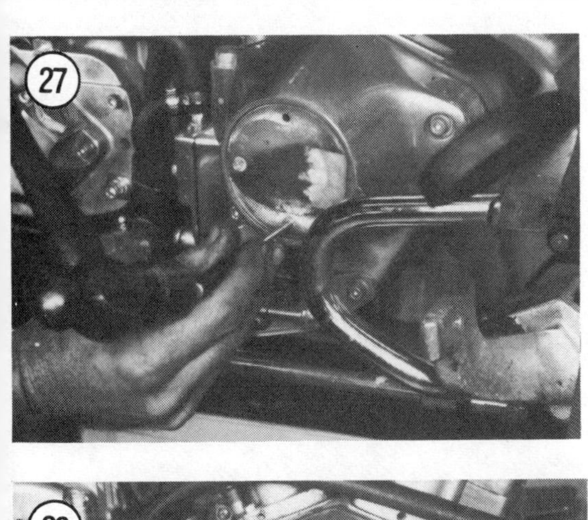
27

31

28

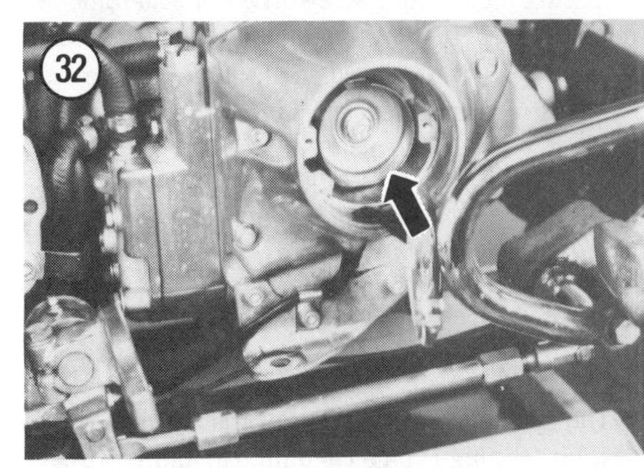
32

29
COPAC

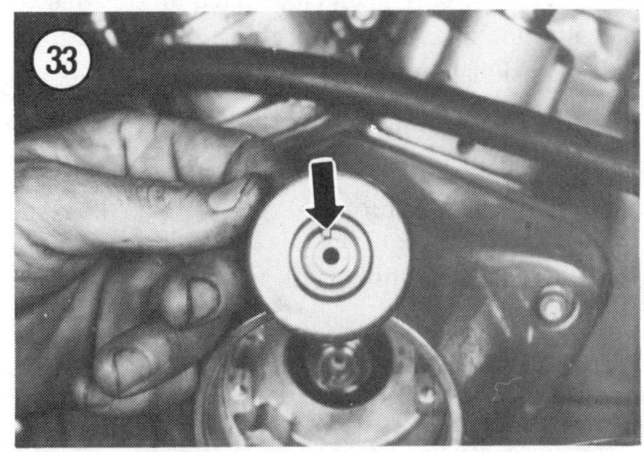
33

30

34
A
B

3. Remove the ignition module mounting bolts and remove the module assembly.
4. Install by reversing these removal steps. Clean ground wire connector at frame, if used.

### Inspection

1. If necessary, follow the procedures in Chapter Two to troubleshoot the ignition system.
2. Check the ignition compartment for oil leakage. If present, remove the crankcase seal (B, **Figure 34**) by prying it out with a screwdriver or seal remover. Install a new seal by tapping it in place with a suitable size socket placed on the outside of the seal. Drive the seal in until it seats in the crankcase.

*NOTE*
*If the crankcase seal is not installed all the way into the crankcase, it will leak.*

## IGNITION COIL

The ignition coil is a form of transformer which develops the high voltage required to jump the spark plug gap. The only maintenance required is that of keeping the electrical connections clean and tight and occasionally checking to see that the coils are mounted securely.

### Removal/Installation

1. Disconnect all ignition coil wiring.
2. Remove the coil cover, if so equipped.
3. Remove the coil mounting bolts and remove the coil.
4. Remove the coil cover (if so equipped).
5. Installation is the reverse of these steps.

*CAUTION*
*When replacing an ignition coil, make sure the coil is marked **ELECTRONIC ADVANCE**. Installing an older type ignition coil could damage electronic ignition components.*

## STARTER

The starting system consists of the starter motor, starter gears, solenoid and the starter button.

When the starter button is pressed, it engages the starter solenoid switch that completes the circuit allowing electricity to flow from the battery to the starter motor.

*CAUTION*
*Never attempt to operate the starter by pushing the starter button for more than 5 seconds at a time. If the engine fails to start, wait a minimum of 30 seconds to allow the starter to cool. Overheating the starter may damage it.*

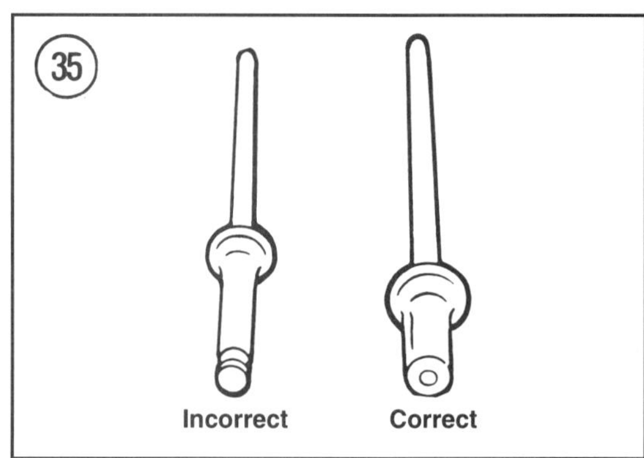

**Removal/Installation (1984-1988 FLT and FXR)**

1. Disconnect the negative battery cable.
2. Disconnect the solenoid cable at the starter (**Figure 37**)
3. Remove the bolts securing the starter to the transmission side door.
4. Remove the starter through-bolts.

*NOTE*

*Because the through-bolts are no longer holding the starter assembly together, hold on to the starter motor and both end covers to prevent the starter from falling apart when removing it in Step 5.*

5. Remove the starter housing and drive gear as an assembly (**Figure 38**).
6. Installation is the reverse of these steps, plus the following.
7. First install the drive gear onto the drive shaft and then install the starter motor onto the primary chaincase.

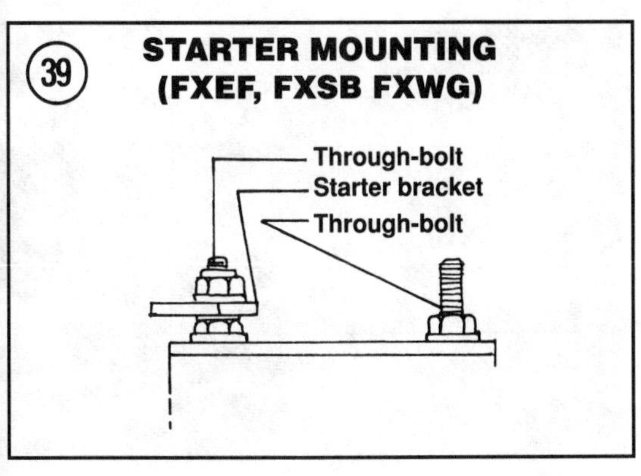


8. On FLT models, install the negative battery cable onto the left mounting stud. On FXR models, install the negative battery cable onto the right mounting stud.
9. Tighten starter bolts or nuts to 10-12 ft.-lbs. (13.8-16.5 N•m).
10. Tighten mounting bracket nuts to 20-25 in.-lbs. (2.3-2.8 N•m).
11. Tighten solenoid cable nut to 65-80 in.-lbs. (7.5-9.2 N•m).

**Removal/Installation (1985-1986 FXWG, FXEF and FXSB)**

Refer to **Figure 39** when performing this procedure.

1. Disconnect the negative battery cable.
2. Disconnect the solenoid cable at the starter.
3. Remove the fasteners securing the master cylinder reservoir bracket to the transmission housing.
4. Remove the starter bracket bolts at the rubber mount stud.
5. Remove the starter through-bolts.

*NOTE*

*Because the through-bolts are no longer holding the starter assembly together, hold on to the starter motor and both end covers to prevent the starter from falling apart when removing it in Step 6.*

6. Remove the starter motor.
7. Installation is the reverse of these steps. Tighten the following:
   a. Starter through-bolts: 20-25 in.-lbs. (2.3-2.8 N•m).
   b. Starter terminal nut: 65-80 in.-lbs. (7.5-9.2 N•m).
   c. Outer through-bolt nut (**Figure 39**): 20-25 in.-lbs. (2.3-2.8 N•m). Install a new nut during reassembly.
   d. Rubber mount stud: 6 ft.-lbs. (8.3 N•m).
   e. Master cylinder reservoir bracket: 13-16 ft.-lbs. (17.9-22.1 N•m).

### Removal (1989-on)

NOTE
*ID all electrical connectors at the solenoid so that you don't mix them up during reassembly*

1. Disconnect the negative battery cable.
2. Remove the primary chain case cover as described in Chapter Five.
3. Remove the rear exhaust pipe.
4. Pry the lockplate tab away from the jackshaft bolt. Then hold the pinion gear to keep it from turning and loosen the jackshaft bolt (**Figure 40**). Remove the jackshaft bolt and lockplate from the jackshaft.
5. Remove the fasteners securing the chrome cover to the end of the starter motor and remove the cover.
6. Remove the starter motor Allen bolts and washers and lift the starter out of the frame. Then disconnect the battery (**Figure 41**) and solenoid wires at the starter and remove the starter from the right-hand side.

NOTE
*On 1989-1993 models, the jackshaft-to-starter coupling may come off with the starter or it may stay attached to the jackshaft. If the coupling comes off with the starter, put it back onto the jackshaft. The coupling on 1989 is symmetrical; either coupling end can be installed over the jackshaft. The coupling on 1990-1993 models is asymmetrical; install the coupling so that the end with the counterbore faces the jackshaft. On 1994 models, the coupling will stay on the starter shaft.*

### Installation (1989-on)

NOTE
*Follow the ID marks made on the solenoid wiring connectors when connecting them in Step 1.*

1. Install the solenoid and battery cable over the solenoid stud and secure with the washer and nut.
2. Install the starter from the right-hand side, engaging the starter shaft with the jackshaft-to-starter coupling. If the coupling came off with the starter during removal and you didn't reinstall it, refer to the *NOTE* under *Starter Removal* when installing the coupling. On 1990 and later models, it is possible to install the coupling incorrectly.
3. Install the starter mounting bolts and washers and tighten to 13-20 ft.-lb. (17.9-27.6 N•m).

NOTE
*Install a new lockplate if the lock tab is cracked or broken.*

4. Slide the lockplate onto the jackshaft bolt and insert the bolt through the jackshaft assembly. Turn the lockplate so that the tab on the lockplate fits into the jackshaft keyway groove. Hold the pinion gear by hand and tighten the jackshaft bolt (**Figure 40**) to 7-9 ft.-lb. (9.6-12.4 N•m). Bend the lockplate tab over the bolt to lock it.
5. Install the primary chain case cover and fill the primary chain case as described in Chapter Five.
6. Install the chrome starter cover and secure it with its fasteners.
7. Install the rear exhaust pipe.
8. Reconnect the negative battery cable.

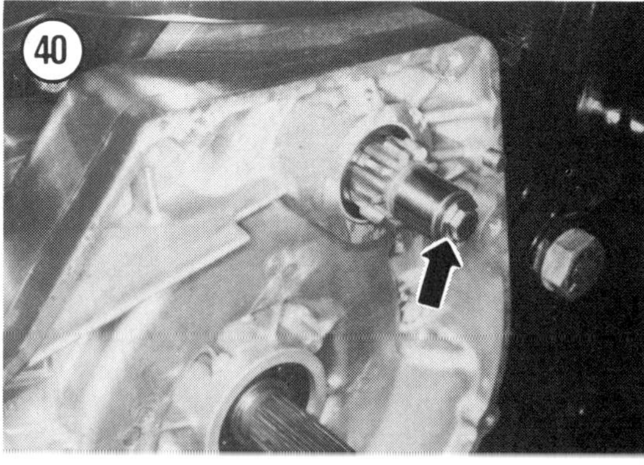
40

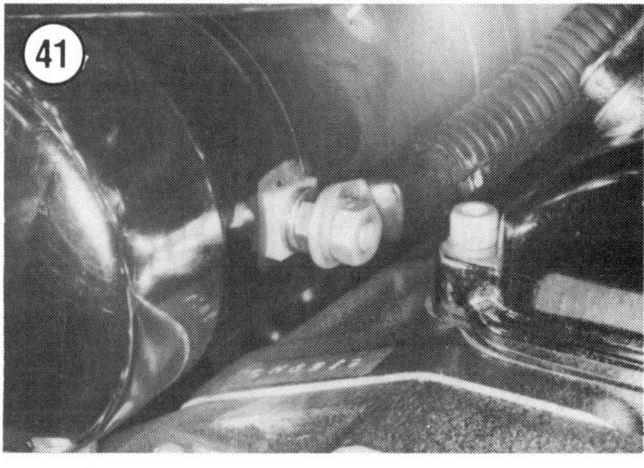
41

**Disassembly (1984-1988)**

Refer to **Figure 42** for this procedure.

1. Clean all grease, dirt and carbon from the case and end covers.

2. Remove the starter housing bolts (if they were reinstalled after removing the starter from the bike).

3. Remove the rear cover screws and remove the rear cover. The rear cover screws secure the brush holder to the rear cover.

4. Using a piece of wire, lift the brush springs and pull the brushes out of the holder.

*NOTE*

*Write down the number of thrust washers on the shaft next to the commutator. Be sure to install the same number when reassembling the starter.*

5. Remove the armature and field frame.

6. Inspect the starter assembly as described in this chapter.

**Reassembly (1984-1988)**

Refer to **Figure 42** for this procedure.

1. Prior to assembly, perform the *Inspection* procedure to make sure all worn or defective parts have been repaired or replaced. All parts should be thoroughly cleaned before assembly.

2. Install the armature into the frame so that the commutator side faces toward the brush holder side.

3. Install the front cover over the armature shaft and engage it with the frame.

4. Install the brush holder into the frame.

5. Install the 2 positive brushes as follows:

   a. The positive brushes are soldered to the field coil assembly.

   b. Pull a positive brush out of its brush holder. A piece of wire bent to form a small hook on one end can be used to access the brushes.

   c. Insert the positive brush into its brush holder.

   d. Release the spring so that tension is applied against the brush.

   e. Repeat for the other positive brush.

6. Install the 2 negative brushes as follows:

9

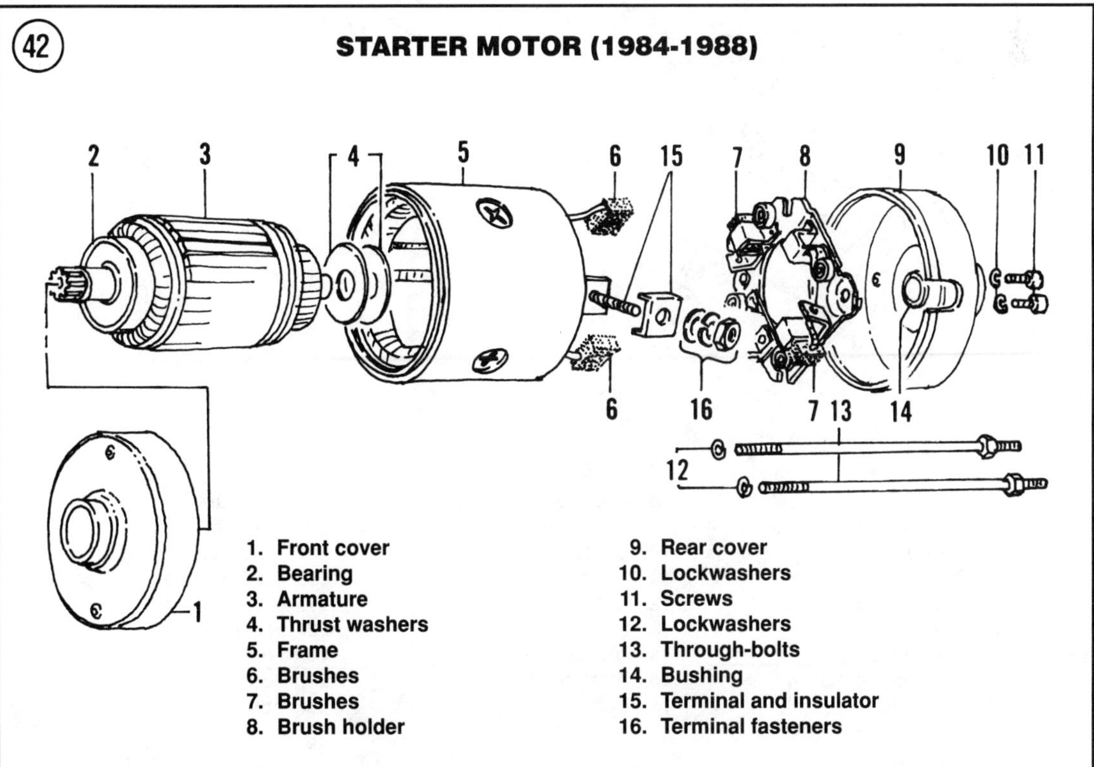

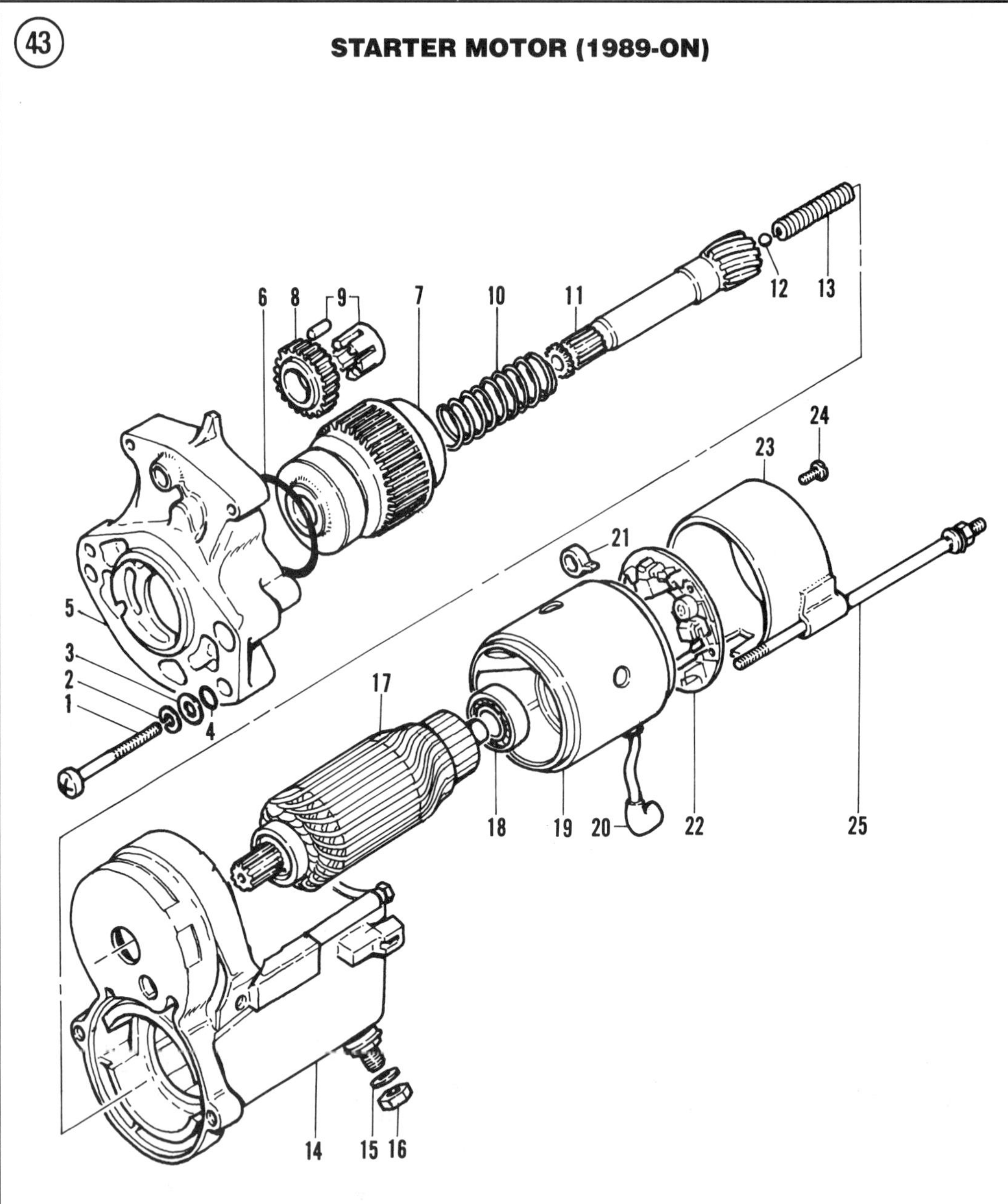


1. Bolt
2. Lockwasher
3. Washer
4. O-ring
5. Solenoid housing
6. O-ring
7. Drive assembly/ overrunning clutch
8. Idler gear
9. Idler gear bearing assembly
10. Spring
11. Shaft
12. Ball
13. Spring
14. Drive housing
15. Washer
16. Nut
17. Armature
18. Bearing
19. Field coil assembly
20. Starter cable
21. Brush spring
22. Brush plate
23. End cap
24. Screw
25. Bolt

a. The negative brushes are mounted onto the brush holder.
b. Pull a negative brush out of its brush holder. A piece of wire bent to form a small hook on one end can be used to access the brushes.
c. Insert the negative brush into its brush holder.
d. Release the spring so that tension is applied against the brush.
e. Repeat for the other negative brush.

7. Install the thrust washers onto the armature shaft.
8. Align the slot in the rear cover with the terminal in the frame and install the rear cover. Install the through-bolts through the starter assembly.
9. Secure the brush holder to the rear cover with the 2 screws and washers. Tighten the screws securely.

### Disassembly (1989-on)

Refer to **Figure 43** for this procedure.

1. Clean all grease, dirt and carbon from the case and end covers.
2. Disconnect the solenoid wire.
3. Loosen and remove the 2 starter housing through-bolts.
4. Remove the 2 screws securing the end cover to the brush holder. Remove the end cover.

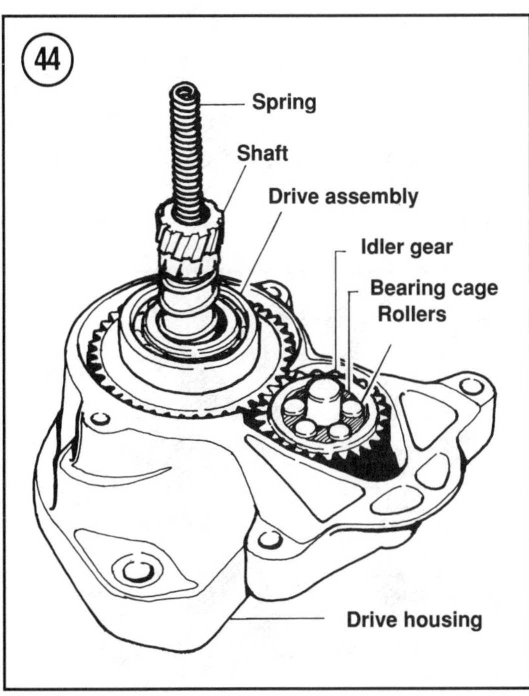


5. Lift the field coil brush springs out of their holders with a small hook and remove the brushes from their holders.
6. Slide the brush holder off of the commutator.
7. Remove the armature and field frame assembly. Slide the armature out of the field frame.
8. If necessary, remove and disassemble the drive housing (**Figure 44**) as follows:
   a. Remove the 2 screws and washers securing the drive housing to the solenoid housing. O-rings are installed on the screws used on 1989-1990 models.
   b. Remove the drive housing from the solenoid housing.
   c. Remove the ball and spring from the end of the shaft to prevent their loss.
   d. Remove the drive, idler gear and idler gear bearing assembly from the drive housing.
   e. Carefully pry the O-ring out of the groove in the bottom of the drive housing.
   f. Remove the spring and shaft from the drive assembly.
9. Inspect the starter assembly as described in this chapter.

9

### Assembly (1989-on)

Refer to **Figure 43** for this procedure.

1. Prior to assembly, perform the *Inspection* procedure to make sure all worn or defective parts have been repaired or replaced. All parts should be thoroughly cleaned before assembly.
2. Smear a thin film of Lubriplate 110 onto the drive housing O-ring and insert the O-ring into the groove in the bottom of the housing. Make sure that the O-ring seats squarely in the groove.
3. After the drive assembly components have been cleaned and dried, lubricate all components with Lubriplate 110.
4. Place the idler gear over the shaft in the drive housing. Then place the idler bearing cage in the gear so that the open cage end faces toward the solenoid. Install the bearing pins in the cage.
5. Insert the drive assembly into the drive housing, then slide the spring over the shaft and insert the shaft into the drive assembly (**Figure 44**).
6. Drop the ball into the shaft and slide the spring over the solenoid plunger shaft.

7. Align the drive housing with the solenoid housings and assemble both housings. On 1989-1990 models, secure the drive housing with the screws, lockwashers, flat washers and O-rings. On 1991 models, install the screws and lockwashers.
8. Pack the armature bearings with Lubriplate 110. Then insert the armature into the field frame housing and install the field frame housing onto the solenoid housing.
9. Install the brush plate into the end of the field frame and install the 4 brushes so that they ride over the commutator.
10. Install the 2 positive brushes as follows:
   a. The positive brushes are soldered to the field coil assembly.
   b. Pull a positive brush out of its brush holder. A piece of wire bent to form a small hook on one end can be used to access the brushes.
   c. Insert the positive brush into its brush holder.
   d. Release the spring so that tension is applied against the brush.
   e. Repeat for the other positive brush.
11. Install the 2 negative brushes as follows:
   a. The negative brushes are mounted onto the brush holder.
   b. Pull a negative brush out of its brush holder. A piece of wire bent to form a small hook on one end can be used to access the brushes.
   c. Insert the negative brush into its brush holder.
   d. Release the spring so that tension is applied against the brush.
   e. Repeat for the other negative brush.
12. Align the slot in the rear cover with the terminal in the frame and install the rear cover. Install the through-bolts through the starter assembly.
13. Secure the brush holder to the rear cover with the 2 screws and washers. Tighten the screws securely.
14. Reconnect the solenoid wire.

### Inspection (All Models)

1. The starter components should be cleaned thoroughly. Do not clean the field coils or armature in any cleaning solution that could damage the insulation. Wipe these parts off with a clean rag. Likewise, do not soak the overrunning clutch in any cleaning solution as the chemicals could dissolve the lubrication within the clutch and ruin it.
2. Measure the length of each brush with a vernier caliper (**Figure 45**). If the length is less than specified in **Table 3**, it must be replaced. Replace the brushes in sets of four, even though only one may be worn to this dimension.

*NOTE*
*The field coil brushes are soldered in position. To replace, first apply heat to the brushes' soldered joint to unsolder. Remove the old brushes. Solder the new brushes in place with rosin core solder—do not use acid core solder.*

3. Inspect the condition of the commutator. The mica in the commutator should be at least 0.008 in. (0.20 mm) undercut. If the mica undercut is less than this

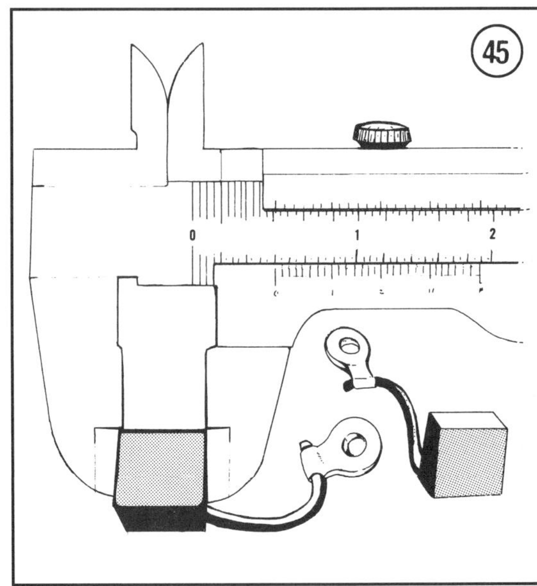


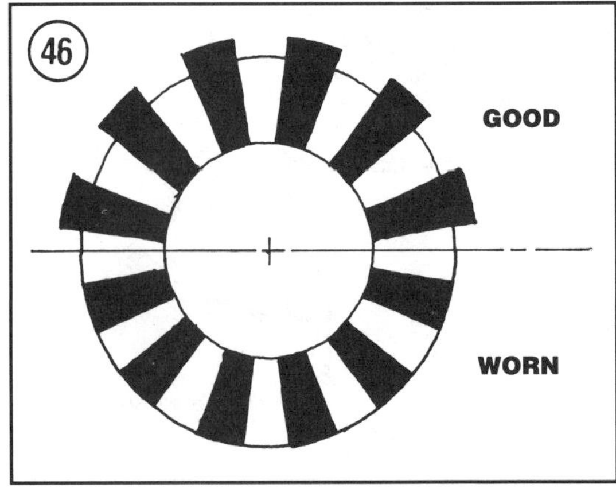

amount, undercut the mica with a piece of hacksaw blade to a depth of 1/32 in. (0.79 mm). This procedure can also be performed by a dealer or automotive specialist with a undercutting machine. When undercutting mica, each groove must form a right angle. Do not cut the mica so that a thin edge is left next to the commutator segment. **Figure 46** shows the proper angle. After undercutting the mica, remove burrs by sanding commutator lightly with crocus cloth.

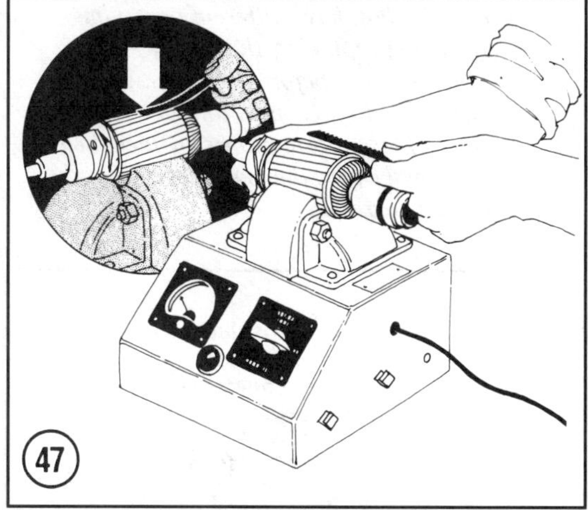

47

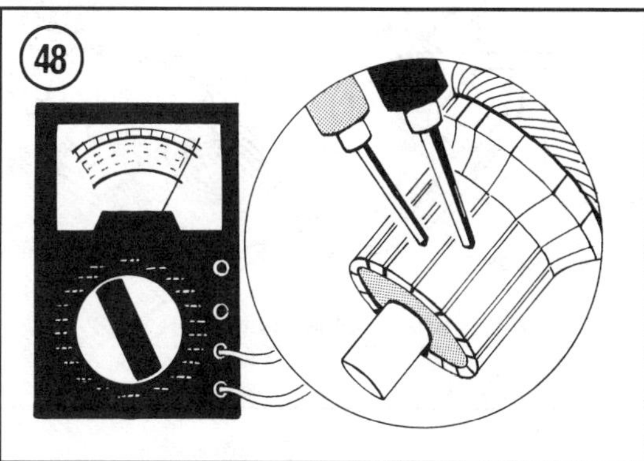

48

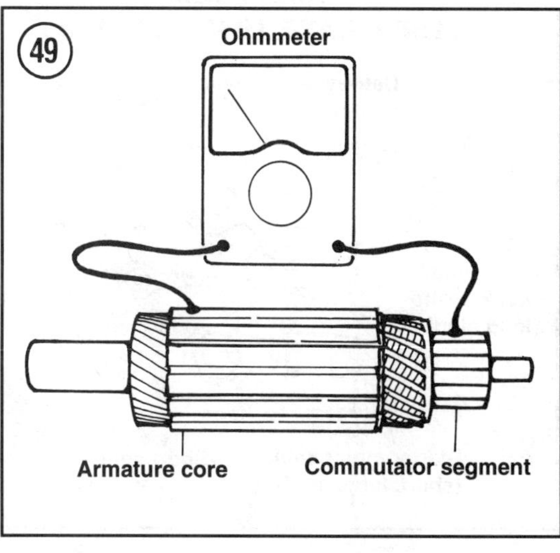


49

4. Inspect the commutator copper bars for discoloration. If a pair of bars are discolored, grounded armature coils are indicated.

5. The armature can be checked for winding shorts with a growler. To do this, the mechanic inserts the armature into a growler (**Figure 47**). The growler is then turned on while a hacksaw blade is held close to but not touching the armature. The armature is then rotated slowly by hand; if the blade vibrates and is attracted to the armature, an armature winding is shorted. If this is the case, the armature must be replaced. Refer this test to a Harley-Davidson dealer or automotive electrical specialist.

6. Place the armature in a lathe or between crankshaft centers and check commutator runout with a dial indicator. If runout exceeds 0.015 in. (0.38 mm), commutator should be trued on a lathe. When truing the commutator to eliminate the out-of-round condition, make the cuts as light as possible. Replace the armature if the commutator O.D. meets or exceeds the wear limit listed in **Table 3**.

7. Use an ohmmeter and check for continuity between the commutator bars (**Figure 48**); there should be continuity between pairs of bars. If there is no continuity between pairs of bars, the armature is open. Replace the armature.

8. Connect an ohmmeter between any commutator bar and the armature shaft (**Figure 49**); there should be no continuity. If there is continuity, the armature is grounded. Replace the armature.

9. Connect an ohmmeter between the starter cable terminal and each field frame brush (**Figure 50**); there should be continuity. If there is no continuity at either brush, the field windings are open. Replace the field frame assembly.

10. Connect an ohmmeter between the field frame housing and each field frame brush (**Figure 51**); there should be no continuity. If there is continuity at either brush, the field windings are grounded. Replace the field frame assembly.

11. Connect an ohmmeter between the brush holder plate and each brush holder (**Figure 52**); there should be no continuity. If there is continuity at either brush holder, the brush holder or plate is damaged. Replace the brush holder plate.

12A. *1984-1988*: Service the armature bearing and rear cover bushing as follows:

a. Check the bearing on the armature shaft. If worn or damaged, remove and install new bearing with a bearing splitter and a press.
b. Inspect the bushing installed in the rear cover. If the bushing is severely worn or damaged, replace the rear cover; replacement bushings are not sold separately.
c. Inspect the bushing surface on the armature shaft. If this surface is severely worn or damaged, replace the armature.
d. Check the bearing bore in the front cover. Replace the cover if this area is severely worn or damaged.

12B. *1989-on*: Service the armature bearings as follows:

a. Check the bearings on the armature shaft. If worn or damaged, remove and install new bearings with a bearing splitter and a press.

*NOTE*

*Note that the 2 bearings installed on the armature shaft have different part numbers. When replacing the bearings, ID the old bearings before their removal in relationship to their position on the armature. This information can then be used to make sure the new bearings are installed correctly.*

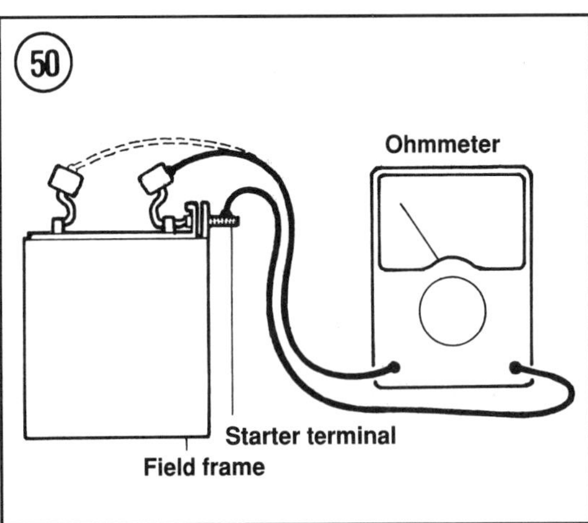


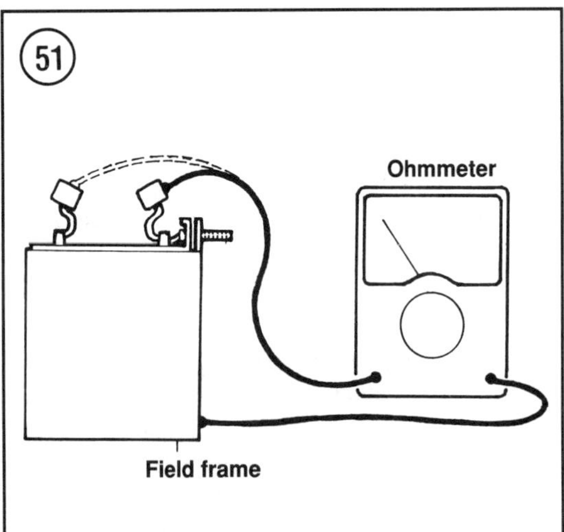


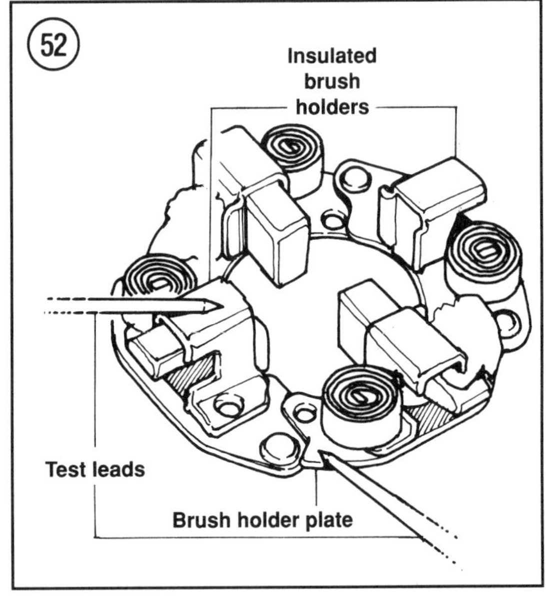


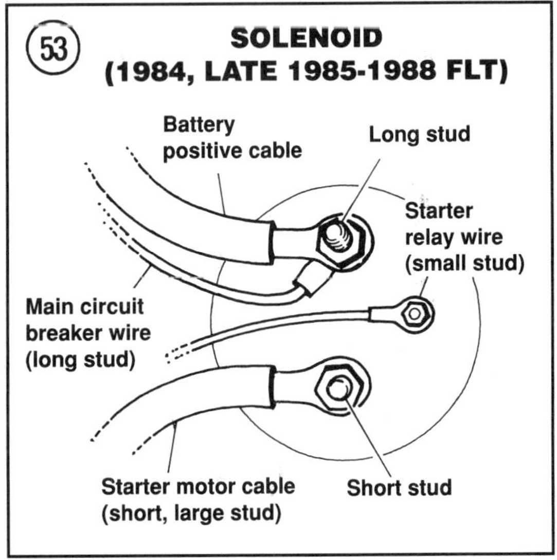

b. Check the bearing bores in the end cover and solenoid housing. Replace the cover or housing if this area is severely worn or cracked.

13. *1989-on*: The drive assembly is bolted onto the end of the solenoid housing. Inspect it as follows:

a. Check the teeth on the idler gear and drive assembly for wear or damage.

b. Check for chipped or worn bearing rollers. Damaged rollers would cause the pinion to turn roughly in the overrunning direction.

c. Replace worn or damaged parts as required.

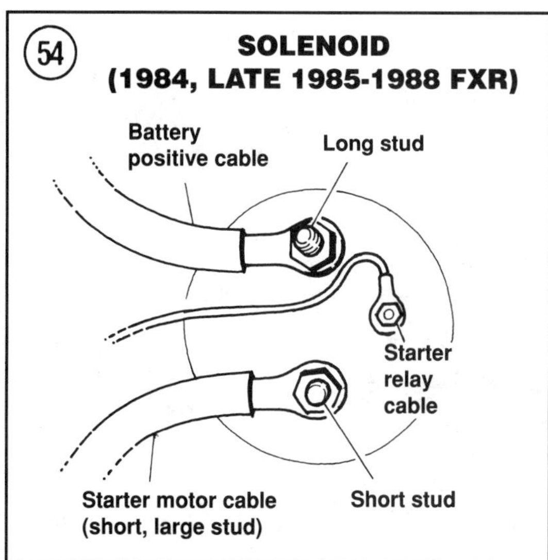


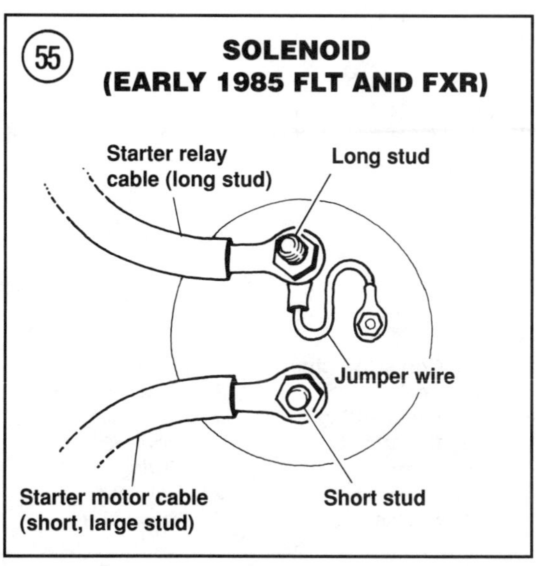


## STARTER SOLENOID (1984-1988)

The solenoid installed on 1984-1988 models is separate from the starter motor.

### Removal/Installation

1. Disconnect the negative battery cable.

NOTE

*Compare the wiring on your bike's solenoid with the wiring diagram in* ***Figures 53-57*** *for your model before disconnecting it.*

2. Label and disconnect the wiring cables at the solenoid. See **Figure 53** (1984, late 1985-1988 FLT), **Figure 54** (1984, late 1985-1988 FXR), **Figure 55** (early 1985 FLT and FXR), **Figure 56** (early 1985 FX) or **Figure 57** (late 1985-1986 FX).

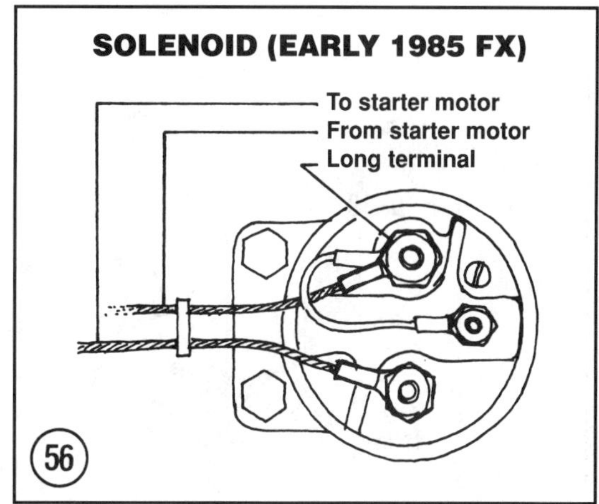


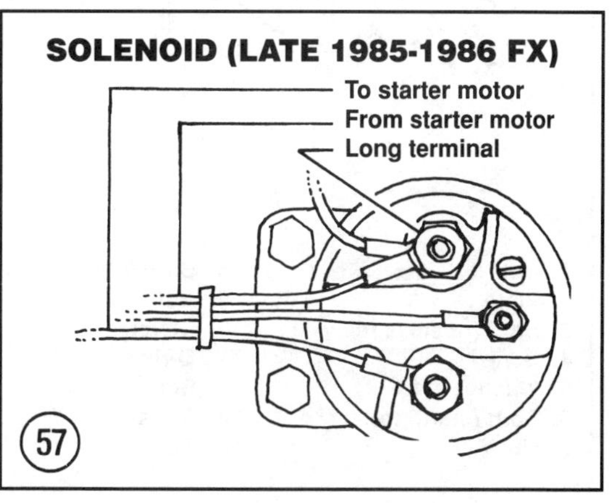


9

3. Remove the solenoid mounting bolts and remove the solenoid, spacer, spring and gasket.

4. Installation is the reverse of these steps. Tighten the mounting bolts securely.

### Disassembly/Reassembly

Refer to **Figure 58** for this procedure.

1. Clean the solenoid housing of all dirt and residue before disassembling it.

2. Remove the nut and lockwasher from the short large terminal.

3. Remove the nut and lockwasher from the small O.D. terminal.

4. Remove the 2 screws and washers securing the solenoid cover to the solenoid and remove the cover.

*NOTE*
*When disassembling the inner plunger assembly in Step 5, note the position and condition of the copper washer as it is*

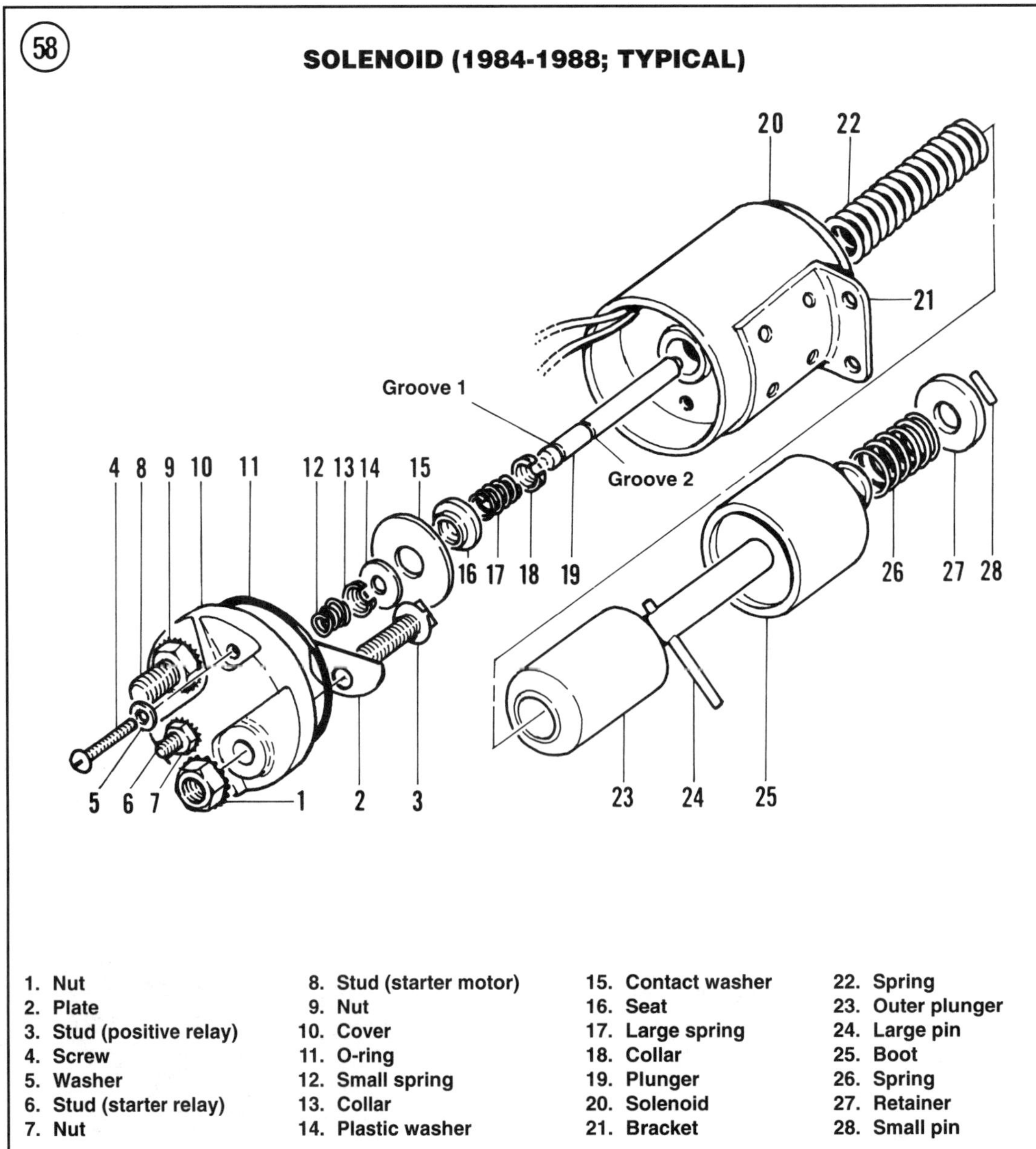


**SOLENOID (1984-1988; TYPICAL)**

1. Nut
2. Plate
3. Stud (positive relay)
4. Screw
5. Washer
6. Stud (starter relay)
7. Nut
8. Stud (starter motor)
9. Nut
10. Cover
11. O-ring
12. Small spring
13. Collar
14. Plastic washer
15. Contact washer
16. Seat
17. Large spring
18. Collar
19. Plunger
20. Solenoid
21. Bracket
22. Spring
23. Outer plunger
24. Large pin
25. Boot
26. Spring
27. Retainer
28. Small pin

*installed on the plunger between the plastic washer and seat. If one side of the copper washer is grooved or burnt, label the washer as to how it is positioned on the plunger, and then turn it around during reassembly so that the worn side is facing in the opposite direction. Because inner plunger assembly components are not available separately, this will extend the life of the copper washer.*

5. Referring to **Figure 58**, disassemble the solenoid assembly, keeping the outer and inner plunger parts separate.
6. Clean and inspect the solenoid components as described in this chapter.
7. Assembly is the reverse of these steps. Note the following.
8. Lightly wipe the plunger and the plunger bore with Lubriplate 110.
9. Assemble the inner plunger assembly as follows:
   a. Lay out the inner plunger components in the order shown in **Figure 58**. Note that the plunger has 2 grooves; these are identified as groove No. 1 and groove No. 2 in **Figure 55**. Note also that the 2 collars are identical.
   b. Install a collar into the No. 2 plunger groove so that the collar spring seat faces toward the No. 1 plunger groove.
   c. Slide the large spring over the plunger and seat it against the collar.
   d. Slide the seat over the plunger with the seat shoulder facing the No. 1 plunger groove.
   e. Slide the copper washer over the plunger and center it onto the seat shoulder installed in sub-step d.
   f. Slide the plastic washer over the plunger and seat it against the copper washer.
   g. Install the remaining collar into the No. 1 plunger groove so that the collar spring seat faces away from the assembled parts installed in sub-steps a-f.
10. Insert the plunger assembly into the plunger bore in the solenoid housing.
11. Stand the solenoid housing upright and slide the small spring over the plunger and seat it against the collar.
12. Install the gasket onto the solenoid housing.

*CAUTION*

*When installing the solenoid cover in Step 13, route the internal solenoid wires so that they cannot contact the copper washer as it travels with the plunger during solenoid operation. Contact of these parts will eventually wear away the wire insulation and cause the circuit to remain closed.*

13. Align the solenoid cover with the solenoid housing and place it into position, making sure the small plunger spring, plunger and terminal enter the cover bore properly.
14. Slide a washer onto each of the screws and install the screw through the cover and into the solenoid housing. Tighten the screws securely. Install the terminal nuts and washers previously removed.

### Cleaning and Inspection

1. Clean all parts thoroughly.
2. Visually check all parts for severe wear, cracks or other damage. The contact washer can be turned around during reassembly as described in the *NOTE* prior to Step 5 under *Disassembly/Reassembly*.
3. Replace all worn or damaged parts, if available, as required.

## STARTER SOLENOID (1989-1990)

Service procedures are not specified for these models.

## STARTER SOLENOID (1991-ON)

The starter solenoid, starter motor and drive assembly are assembled as one unit.

### Disassembly/Reassembly

Refer to **Figure 59** for this procedure.

1. Remove the starter motor as described in this chapter.
2. Three screws secure the cover to the solenoid housing. Mark the wire clip position on the cover, then remove the 3 screws, washers and clip.
3. Remove the cover and gasket.

9

4. Remove the solenoid plunger from the solenoid housing.
5. Inspect the parts for severe wear or damage. Replace parts as required.
6. Installation is the reverse of these steps. Note the following.

*CAUTION*
*Do not tighten the contact nut (8, **Figure 59**) until parts 2-7 have been removed or the contact will be damaged.*

7. Make sure the solenoid plunger shaft engages the spring in the drive assembly shaft.

## STARTER RELAY

### Removal/Installation

The starter relay is mounted at the following locations:

a. All FXR: Behind the right-hand side cover. See **Figure 60** (1984 and late 1985-on FXR) or **Figure 61** (early 1985 FXR).

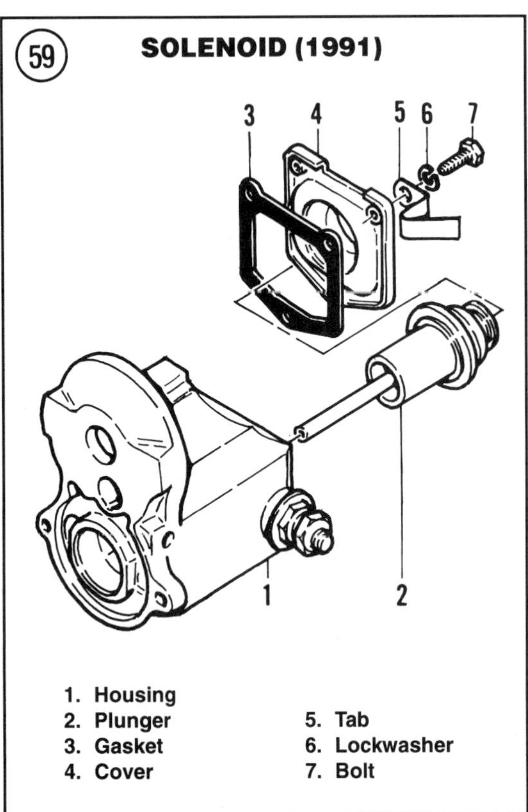


59 **SOLENOID (1991)**

1. Housing
2. Plunger
3. Gasket
4. Cover
5. Tab
6. Lockwasher
7. Bolt

b. 1984-early 1986 FLT: Underneath the seat. See **Figure 62** (1984, late 1985-early 1986 FLT) or **Figure 63** (early 1985 FLT).

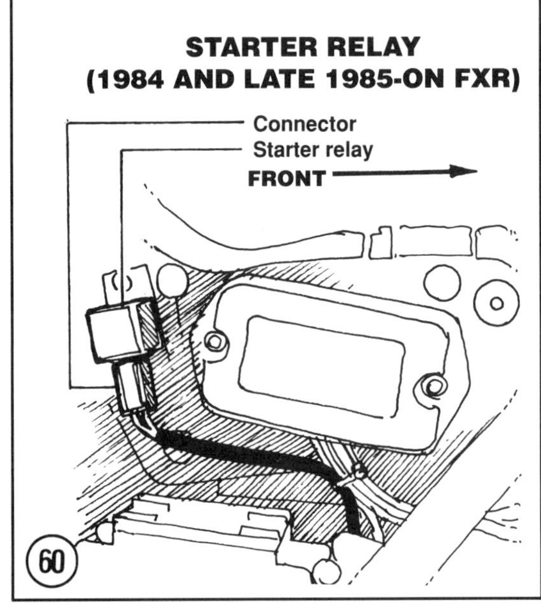


**STARTER RELAY (1984 AND LATE 1985-ON FXR)**

60

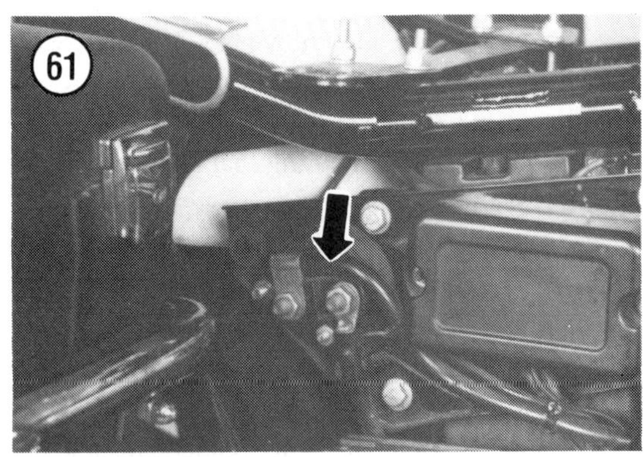

61

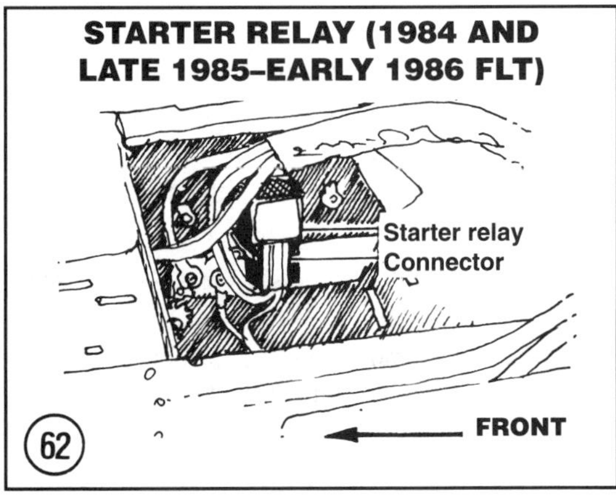


**STARTER RELAY (1984 AND LATE 1985–EARLY 1986 FLT)**

62

c. Late 1986 and later FLT: Behind the right-hand side cover. See **Figure 64**.

d. 1985-1986 FX: Behind the right-hand side cover.

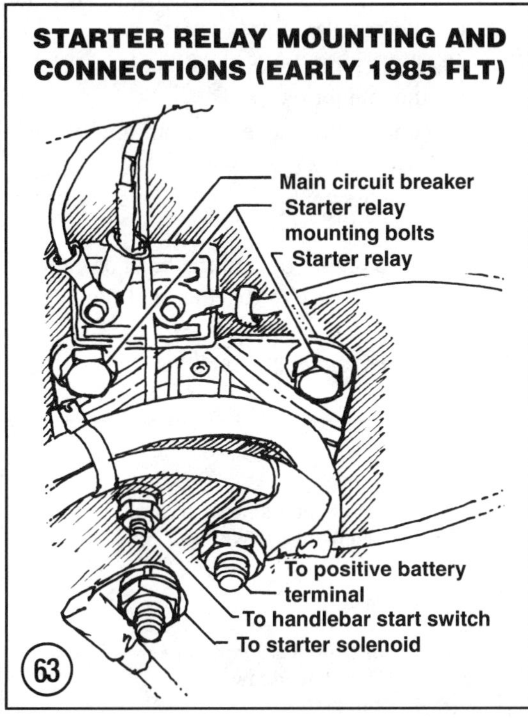


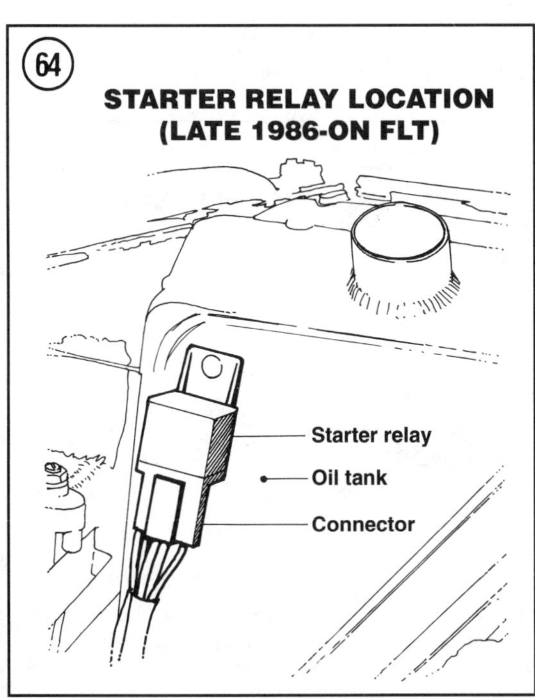


*NOTE*
*On early 1985 models, label the wiring at the starter relay before disconnecting it.*

1. Disconnect the wiring or the electrical connector at the starter relay.
2. Remove the starter relay.
3. Reverse these steps to install the new relay. Clean the wire or connector pins thoroughly with electrical contact cleaner before assembly.

## LIGHTING SYSTEM

The lighting system consists of a headlight, taillight/brake light combination, turn signals, indicator lights, speedometer illumination lights, running lights and fender tip lights.

Always use the correct wattage bulb. Harley-Davidson lists bulb sizes by part number. The use of a larger wattage bulb will give a dim light and a smaller wattage bulb will burn out prematurely. Replacement bulbs can be purchased through Harley-Davidson dealers by part number or by reading the number of the defective bulb and cross-referencing it with another supplier.

9

### Headlight Replacement

#### *FLT/C and FLTC ULTRA*

Refer to **Figure 65** for this procedure.

1. Remove the headlight cover plate screws and remove the cover plate. Do not lose the spacers at the upper corners.
2. Loosen the retaining ring screws. Then turn the retaining plate and remove it.
3. Pull the headlight partway out and disconnect the connector from the headlight and remove the headlight.
4. Install by reversing these removal steps.
5. Adjust the headlight as described in this chapter.

#### *FLHTC/U, FLHS, FXRT, FXRD and 1992-on FXLR*

Refer to **Figure 66** (FLHTC/U, FLHS and 1992-on FXLR) or **Figure 67** (FXRT and FXRD) for this procedure.

*CAUTION*
*These models are equipped with a quartz halogen bulb. Because of oil on your skin, do not touch the bulb glass with your fingers. Any traces of oil on the quartz halogen bulb will drastically reduce the life of the bulb. Clean any trace of oil from the bulb with a cloth moistened in alcohol or lacquer thinner.*

*WARNING*
*The quartz halogen bulbs contain halogen gas under pressure. During this procedure, wear eye protection to prevent injury.*

1A. *FLHTC/U:* Perform the following:

a. Remove the headlight door screw and remove the door.
b. Remove the retaining ring screws and remove the retaining ring.

1B. *FXRT and FXRD:* Disconnect the headlight connector at the rear of the fairing.

1C. *1992-on FXLR:* Perform the following:

a. Remove the outer headlight clamp screw and remove the clamp.
b. Carefully remove the headlight from the rubber mounting ring.
c. Disconnect the connector from the headlight and remove the headlight.

2. Pull the lens assembly out slightly and disconnect the connector.
3. Remove the rubber boot at the back of the lens. Then press the wire clip together and remove the bulb.
4. Install by reversing these removal steps.

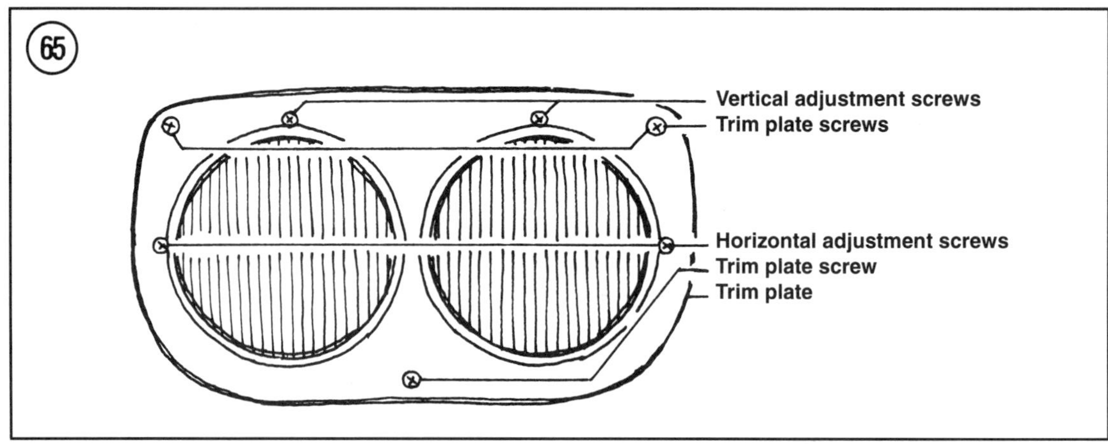


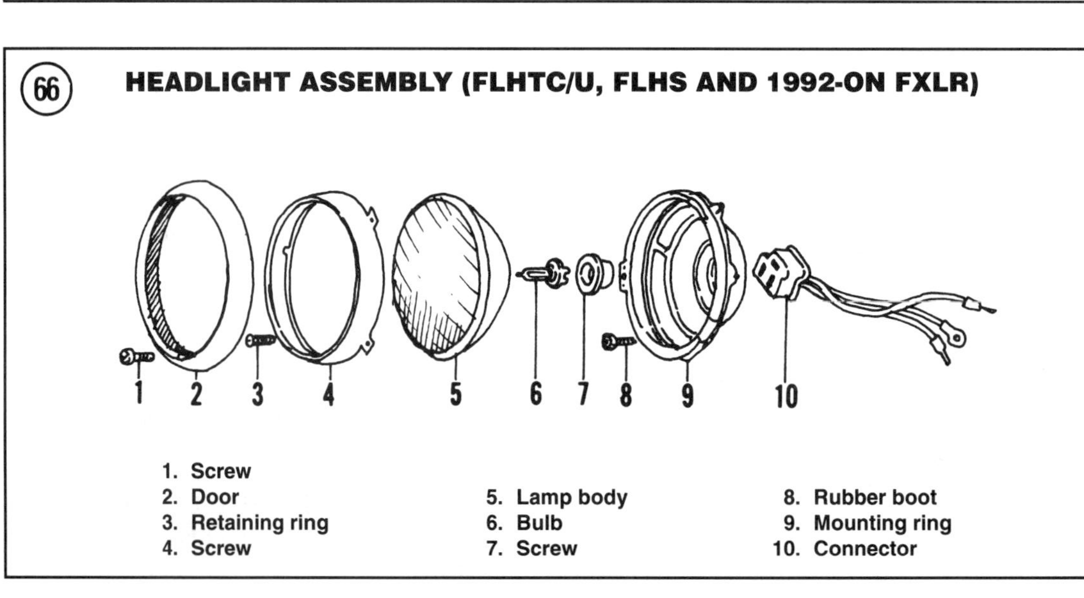

5. Install the rubber boot with the drain holes facing down.
6. Adjust the headlight as described in this chapter.

### *FXR, FXRS/SE/SP/CON and 1985-1986 FX*

Refer to **Figure 68** and **Figure 69**, typical for this procedure.
1. Remove the outer headlight clamp screw and remove the clamp.
2. Carefully remove the headlight from the rubber mounting ring.
3. Disconnect the connector from the headlight and remove the headlight.
4. Remove the retaining ring from the sealed beam unit and remove the sealed beam.
5. Install by reversing these removal steps while noting the following.
6. Clean the headlight electrical block with electrical contact cleaner.
7. Adjust the headlight as described in this chapter.

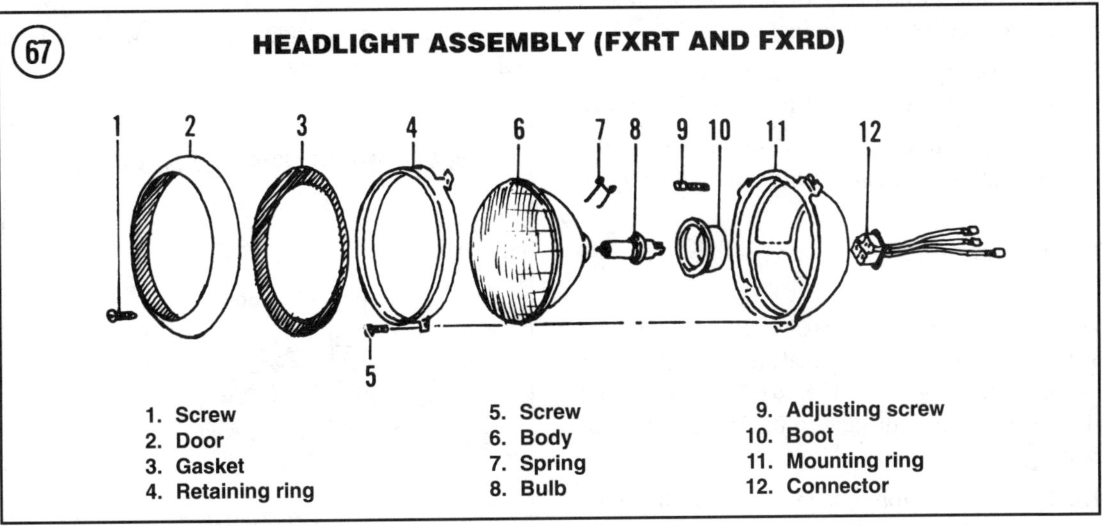


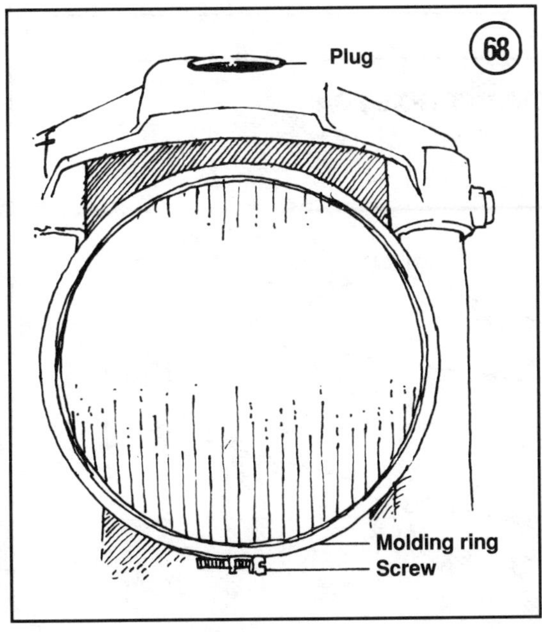


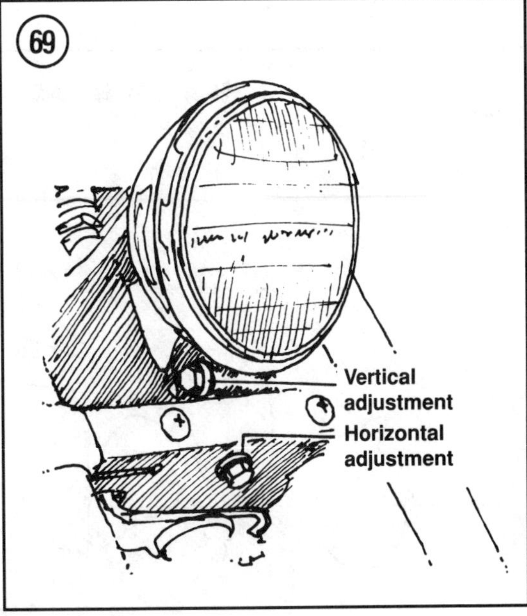

### Headlight Adjustment

Headlight adjustment will depend on the type of headlight assembly installed on your model. If your model's headlight lens has the NAL logo (North American Lighting) on the front of the lens (**Figure 70**), perform the steps under NAL headlight in the following procedures. If your headlight is not NAL marked, use procedures marked "all other."

1. Park the motorcycle on a level surface 25 feet (7.6 M) from a wall (test pattern). Have a rider (with same approximate weight as the vehicle's owner) sit on the seat and make sure the tires are inflated to the correct pressure when performing this adjustment. Make sure bike is facing straight ahead.

2A. *NAL headlight:* Draw a horizontal line on a wall which is 35 in. (0.89 M) above the floor (**Figure 71**).

2B. *All other:* Draw a horizontal line on the wall the same height as the center of the headlight (**Figure 72**).

3. Turn on the headlight. Switch headlight to high beam.

4A. *NAL headlight:* Main bean should be centered on the horizontal line with equal areas of light above and below line as shown in **Figure 71**. There should also be equal areas of light to the left and right of center.

4B. *All other:* The top of the main beam should be even with, but not higher, than the horizontal line drawn in Step 2B.

5. If the beam is incorrect, adjust as follows for your model.

#### *FLT/C and FLTC ULTRA*

Refer to **Figure 65** for this procedure.

1. Refer to *Headlight Adjustment* and then perform the following.

2. Turn the vertical adjustment screws so that the top of the main beam is even with the horizontal line.

3. Turn the horizontal adjustment screws so that the light beam shines straight ahead.

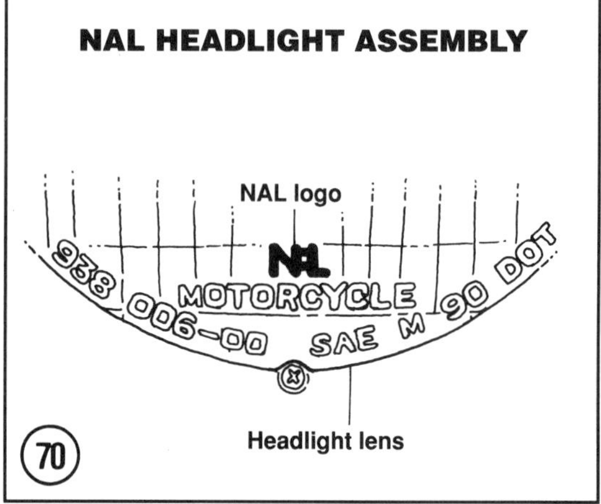


**NAL HEADLIGHT ASSEMBLY** (70)

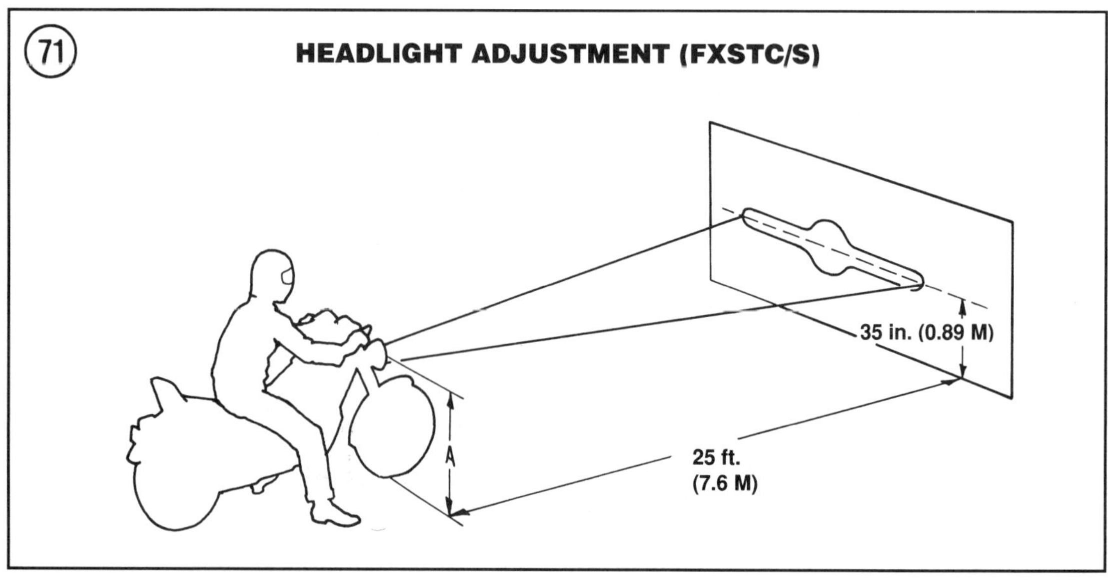


**HEADLIGHT ADJUSTMENT (FXSTC/S)** (71)

### *FLHTC/U and FLHS*

Refer to **Figure 66** for this procedure.

1. Refer to *Headlight Adjustment* and then perform the following.
2. Turn the top adjustment screw so that the top of the main beam is even with the horizontal line.
3. Turn the adjustment screw on the left side of the headlight housing so that the light beam shines straight ahead.

### *FXR, FXRS/SP/CON*

Refer to **Figure 68** for this procedure.

1. Refer to *Headlight Adjustment* and then perform the following.
2. Remove the snap plug on top of the headlight housing.
3. Loosen the clamp nut on the headlight bracket stud.
4. Tilt the headlight up and down and from side to side to adjust it.
5. Tighten the clamp nut to 10-20 ft.-lb. (14-27 N•m) and install the snap plug.

### *FXRT and FXRD*

Refer to **Figure 67** for this procedure.

1. Refer to *Headlight Adjustment* and then perform the following.
2. Remove the screws securing the headlight cover onto the fairing and remove the cover.
3. Turn the top adjustment screw so that the top of the main beam is even with the horizontal line.
4. Turn the adjustment screw on the left side of the headlight housing so that the light beam shines straight ahead.
5. Install the headlight cover.

### *FXLR and 1985-1986 FX*

Refer to **Figure 69** for this procedure.

1. Refer to *Headlight Adjustment* and then perform the following.
2. Loosen the bottom bolt to move the headlight beam from side to side.
3. Loosen the upper bolt to move the headlight beam up and down.
4. Tighten all bolts securely.

## Taillight/Brake Light Replacement

1. Remove the rear lens.
2. Push in on the bulb and remove it.
3. Replace the bulb and install the lens.

## Turn Signal Light Replacement

1. Remove the turn signal lens.
2. Push in on the bulb and remove it.
3. Replace the bulb and install the lens.



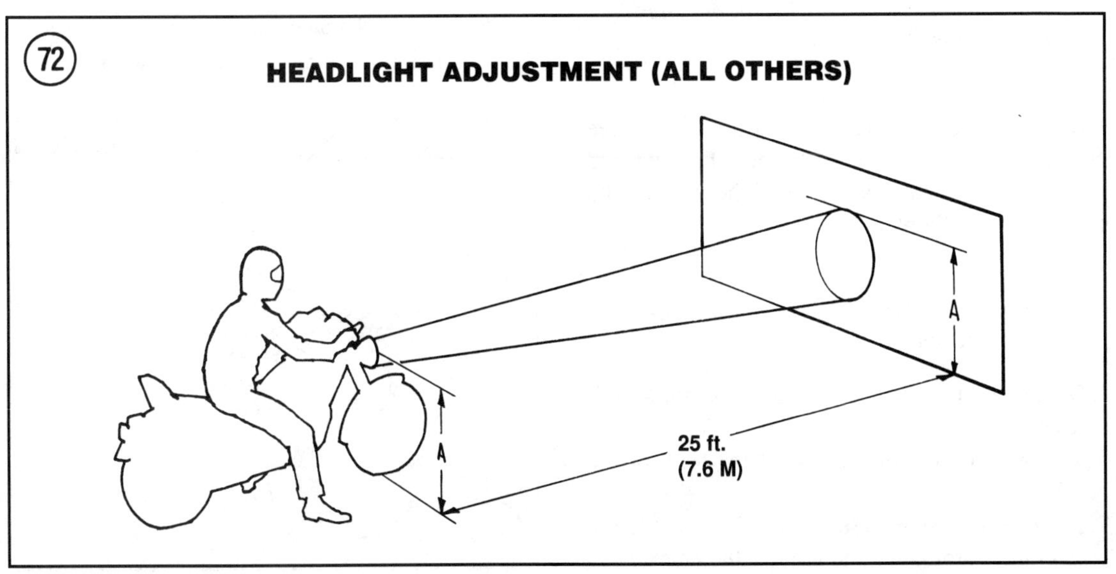

**Passing Light Replacement/Adjustment (FLHT/C and FLHS)**

Refer to **Figure 73** for this procedure.

1. Remove the sealed beam retaining ring screw and remove the retaining ring.
2. Pull the bulb partway out and disconnect the electrical connector.
3. Installation is the reverse of these steps.
4. Adjust the passing light as follows:
   a. Remove the 2 turn signal bracket screws and lift the turn signal off of the bracket.
   b. Loosen the nut on the inside of the turn signal bracket and turn the light so that it shines straight ahead and the top of the light is just below a line on a wall 25 feet (7.62 m) away.
   c. Hold the light in position and tighten the nut securely.
   d. Reinstall the turn signal assembly.

## INSTRUMENTS AND INDICATOR LIGHTS

**Removal/Installation (1984-on FLT/C and 1984-1985 FLHT/C)**

1. Remove the instrument panel screws.
2. Remove the screw securing the odometer trip knob and pull the knob out.

*CAUTION*
*Do not turn the instrument panel upside down when removing it in Step 3. Damping oil in the fuel gauge will leak out and damage the gauge plate.*

3. Carefully raise the instrument panel.
4. If a bulb is blown, you can replace it now. Remove the bulb holder from the instrument housing and replace the bulb. Reinstall the bulb holder into the gauge. Reverse Steps 1-3.

*NOTE*
*Proceed with Step 5 to replace a damaged instrument.*

5. Disconnect the speedometer cable from the speedometer.
6. Disconnect the wire harness at the back of the panel.
7. Remove the fasteners securing the bracket to the back of the instruments and remove the bracket.
8. Label the wires at the damaged instrument. Then remove the wires and the instrument.
9. Install by reversing these steps.

**Removal/Installation (1986-on FLHT/C and 1987-on FLHS)**

1. Remove the light bar and outer fairing as described in Chapter Fifteen.
2. If a bulb is blown, you can replace it now. Remove the bulb holder from the instrument and replace the bulb. Reinstall the bulb holder into the gauge. Reverse Step 1.

*NOTE*
*Proceed to Step 3 to replace a damaged instrument.*

3. Disconnect the electrical connectors at the back of the instrument panel and then disconnect the wire connectors.
4. Remove the screws securing the instrument panel to the fairing.
5. Remove the round nut securing the odometer trip knob to the fairing.
6. Disconnect the speedometer cable.
7. Remove the instrument panel from the bike.
8. Remove the fasteners securing the mounting bracket to the instrument panel and remove the bracket.
9. Label and then disconnect the wires from the damaged instrument.
10. Remove the damaged instrument.
11. Installation is the reverse of these steps.

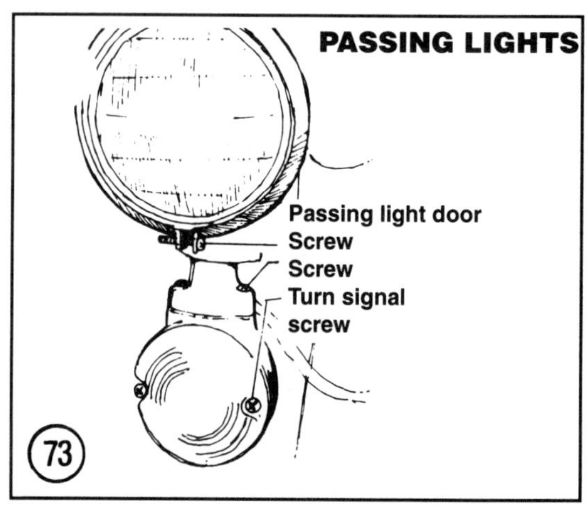

FUEL TANK INSTRUMENTS (FXR TYPICAL)

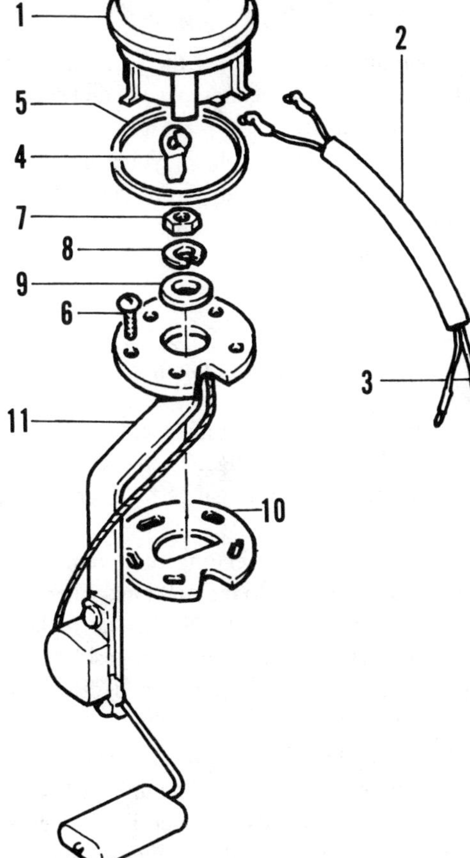


1. Fuel gauge indicator
2. Wire harness
3. Terminal ring
4. Bulb
5. Gasket
6. Screw
7. Nut
8. Lockwasher
9. Washer
10. Gasket
11. Fuel gauge

74

## Speedometer Removal/Installation (FXR)

1. Disconnect the negative battery cable.

2. Turn the odometer trip knob clockwise and unscrew it from the speedometer.

3. Remove the screws securing the instrument panel to the fuel tank and lift the panel off of the tank (**Figure 74**).

4. Disconnect the speedometer cable from the speedometer and remove the clamp nuts and clamp.

5. If the speedometer bulb is blown, you can replace it now. Remove the bulb holder from the speedometer and replace the bulb. Reinstall the bulb holder into the speedometer.

*NOTE*

*Proceed to Step 6 to replace the speedometer.*

6. Remove the speedometer, if necessary.

7. Installation is the reverse of these steps. Turn the odometer trip knob counterclockwise to install it into the speedometer.

9

## Removal/Installation (1984-1985 FXRS and FXRT)

1. Remove the fasteners at the rear of the instrument.

2. Remove the trip odometer knob screw and pull the knob out of the housing.

3. Remove the backing plate and the rubber bushings, then remove the instrument from its mounting bracket.

4. If a bulb is blown, you can replace it now. Remove the bulb holder from the instrument and replace the bulb. Reinstall the bulb holder into the gauge.

*NOTE*

*Proceed to Step 5 to replace a damaged instrument.*

5. Remove the speedometer cable from the speedometer.

6. Label and then disconnect all wires from the speedometer. Remove the speedometer.

7. Install by reversing these steps.

**Removal/Installation (1986-on FXRT and FXRD)**

1. Remove the screws securing the instrument panel to the fairing. Then pull the instrument panel outward and disconnect the speedometer cable.
2. Disconnect the electrical connectors at the back of the instrument panel and remove the panel from the bike.
3. Remove the nuts holding the clamps to the back of the instruments and remove the clamps.
4. If a bulb is blown, you can replace it now. Remove the bulb holder from the instrument and replace the bulb. Reinstall the bulb holder into the gauge.

*NOTE*
*Proceed to Step 5 to replace a damaged instrument.*

5. Label all of the wires at the back of the instrument, then disconnect them. Then remove the damaged instrument.
6. Install by reversing these steps.

**Removal/Installation (1988-on FXRS)**

1. Remove the screws securing the instrument console to the fuel tank.
2. Carefully lift the console away from the fuel tank to access the bulb sockets. Pull the bulb socket out of the instrument and replace the damaged bulb. Install by reversing these steps.

*NOTE*
*Continue with Step 3 to replace a damaged instrument.*

3. Disconnect the speedometer cable from the speedometer, if necessary. Remove the odometer trip knob by turning the knob clockwise.
4. Label all wires at the back of the instrument, then disconnect them. Remove the damaged instrument.
5. Install by reversing these steps.

**Fuel Gauge Removal/Installation (1989-on FLT and All FXR Except FXRS)**

1. Disconnect the negative battery cable.

*WARNING*
*Gasoline is extremely explosive and flammable. Work in a well-ventilated area at least 50 feet (15.2 m) from any sparks or flames, including gas appliance pilot lights. Do not smoke in the area. Keep a fire extinguisher handy.*

*NOTE*
*Work carefully around the fuel tank to avoid scratching it.*

2. Remove the screws holding the fuel tank center panel to the fuel tank. Then remove the fuel tank cap and center panel.
3. If the fuel gauge bulb is blown, you can replace it now. Remove the bulb holder from the fuel gauge and replace the bulb. Reinstall the bulb holder into the gauge. Reverse Steps 1-3.

*NOTE*
*Perform Steps 4 and 5 to remove the fuel gauge and the fuel sending unit.*

4. To replace the gauge, first make a diagram of the wires at the back of the gauge. Then disconnect the wires and remove the fuel gauge fasteners and remove the gauge.
5. To remove the fuel sending unit, remove the screws holding the unit to the fuel tank. Then carefully lift the sending unit out of the fuel tank, placing a rag underneath the unit to prevent gasoline from dripping onto the tank. Remove and discard the sending unit gasket.
6. Install the fuel sending unit as follows:
   a. Purchase a new fuel sending unit gasket from your Harley-Davidson dealer. The new gasket must be equipped with a grounding staple.
   b. Align the new gasket with the fuel tank, then guide the sending unit into the fuel tank and align it with the fuel tank and gasket mounting holes.

*NOTE*
*The fasteners used to secure the sending unit to the fuel tank must also prevent fuel from leaking past them. Early models used special sealing washers. Late models use screws that have a seal bonded underneath the screw head. Inspect these fasteners carefully and replace them if their seal appears worn or damaged.*

c. Secure the fuel sending unit to the fuel tank with its fasteners.

7. Repeat Steps 1-4 to install the fuel gauge. Check the fuel gauge for proper operation.

## Removal/Installation (1988-on FXRS)

1. Disconnect the negative battery cable.

*WARNING*
*Gasoline is extremely explosive and flammable. Work in a well-ventilated area at least 50 feet (15.2 m) from any sparks or flames, including gas appliance pilot lights. Do not smoke in the area. Keep a fire extinguisher handy.*

*NOTE*
*Work carefully around the fuel tank to avoid scratching it.*

2. Remove the fuel gauge by carefully pulling it up and out of the fuel tank. Do *not* twist the gauge when removing it.
3. If the fuel gauge bulb is blown, remove the bulb holder from the fuel gauge and replace the bulb. Reinstall the bulb holder into the gauge. Reverse Steps 1-3.

*NOTE*
*Perform Steps 4 and 5 to remove the fuel gauge and the fuel sending unit.*

4. To remove the fuel gauge, first make a diagram of the wires at the back of the gauge. Then disconnect the wires and remove the fuel gauge fasteners and remove the gauge.
5. To remove the fuel sending unit, remove the screws holding the unit to the fuel tank. Then carefully lift the sending unit out of the fuel tank, placing a rag underneath the unit to prevent gasoline from dripping onto the tank. Remove and discard the sending unit gasket.
6. Install the fuel sending unit as follows:
   a. Purchase a new fuel sending unit gasket from your Harley-Davidson dealer. The new gasket must be equipped with a grounding staple.
   b. Align the new gasket with the fuel tank, then guide the sending unit into the fuel tank and align it with the fuel tank and gasket mounting holes.

*NOTE*
*The screws used to secure the sending unit to the fuel tank have a seal bonded underneath their head. Inspect each screw for a missing, cracked or severely worn seal. Replace the screws as required.*

   c. Secure the fuel sending unit to the fuel tank with its screws.

7. Repeat Steps 1-4 to install the fuel gauge. Check the fuel gauge for proper operation.

## Removal/Installation (1985-1986 FX)

1A. *FXWG*: Perform the following:
   a. Remove the odometer screw and remove the odometer knob.
   b. Unscrew the choke knob and its locknut. Then remove the housing nut.
   c. Lift the panel up slightly.

1B. *FXSB and FXEF*: Remove the screws securing the instrument panel to the frame mounting tabs. Lift the panel up slightly.
2. If a bulb is blown, replace it now. Remove the bulb holder from the instrument and replace the bulb. Reinstall the bulb holder into the gauge. Reverse Step 1. 9

*NOTE*
*Proceed to Step 3 to replace a damaged instrument.*

3. Remove the speedometer cable from the speedometer.
4. Label and then disconnect all wires from the instrument being removed. Then remove the instrument mounting fasteners and remove the instrument.
5. Install by reversing these steps.

## SWITCHES

Switches can be tested for continuity with an ohmmeter (see Chapter One) at the switch connector plug by operating the switch in each of its operating positions and comparing results with the switch operation. When testing switches, consider the following:

   a. First check the circuit breaker.

b. Check the battery as described in this chapter and bring the battery to the correct state of charge, if required.

c. When separating 2 connectors, pull on the connector housings and not the wires.

d. After locating a defective circuit, check the connectors to make sure they are clean and properly connected. Check all wires going into a connector housing to make sure each wire is properly positioned and that the wire end is not loose.

e. To connect connectors properly, push them together until they click into place.

### Handlebar Switch Replacement (Non-Sound System Models)

Refer to **Figure 75** for this procedure.

1. Remove the screws securing the switch housing to the handlebar. Then carefully separate the switch housing to access the defective switch.

2. Remove the switch screw and pull the switch out of the housing. Cut the switch wires at the switch and discard the switch.

3. After purchasing the new switch, strip the new switch wire 3/4 in. (19.05 mm) from the switch. Make sure you don't cut into the wire strands themselves.

4. Install the switch into the housing and secure it with its mounting screw.

5. Cut a piece of shrink tubing to length and slide it over one of the wires.

NOTE

*Make sure the heat shrink is positioned away from the soldering gun when soldering the wires in Step 6.*

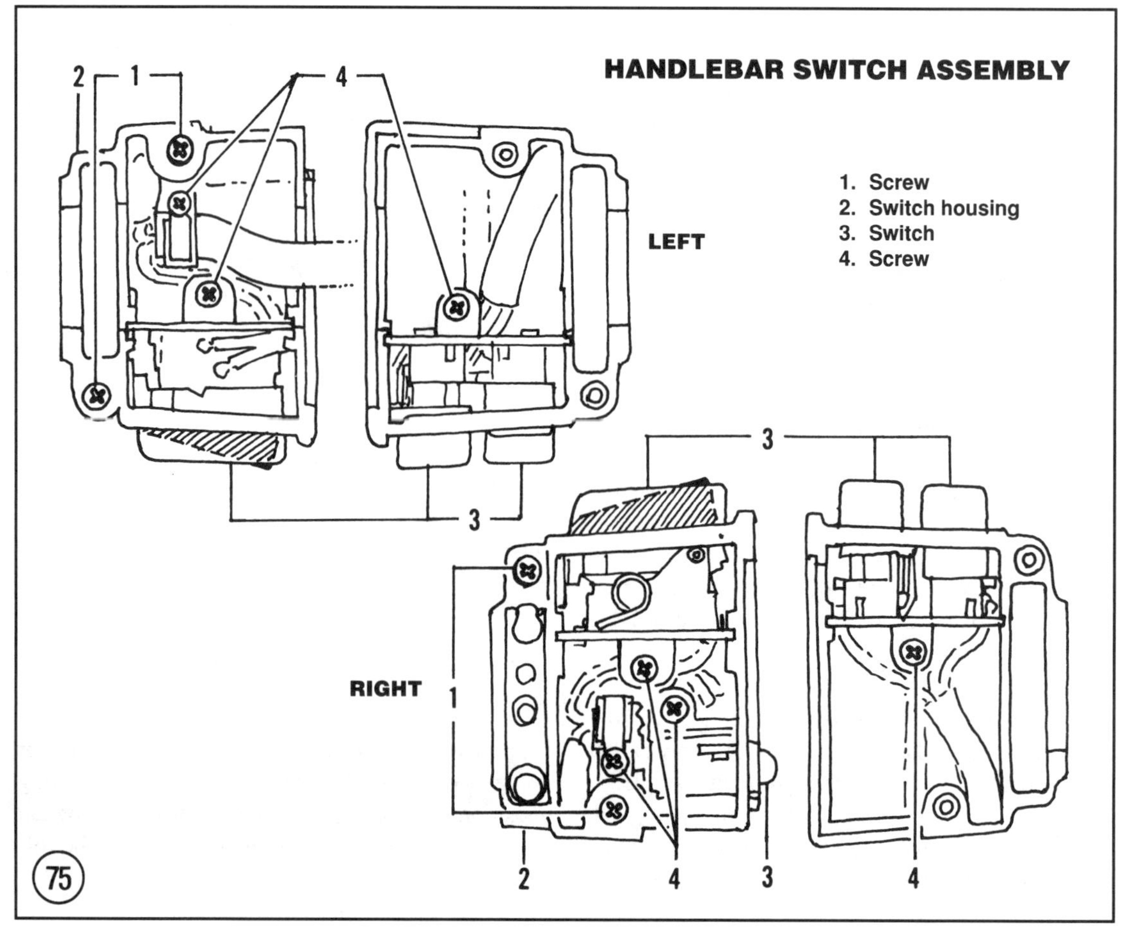

6. Join the 2 wire ends and solder them with rosin core solder—do not use acid core solder.

7. After the wires have cooled, slide the shrink tubing into position across the 2 wire ends. Then briefly apply heat to the shrink wrap. The wrap will shrink across the wire connection after the heat is applied. Check that the shrink wrap conforms tightly with the soldered joint and wire insulation.

8. Tuck the wire into the switch housing.

9. Install the switch housing and secure it with its mounting screws. Check wire routing to prevent them from damage.

10. Check throttle control and brake light operation.

## Left-hand Switch Replacement (Sound System Models)

Refer to **Figure 76** or **Figure 77** for this procedure.

1. Remove the switch screws and separate the switch halves.

2. If equipped with a volume control switch, first remove the set screw and knob from the switch.

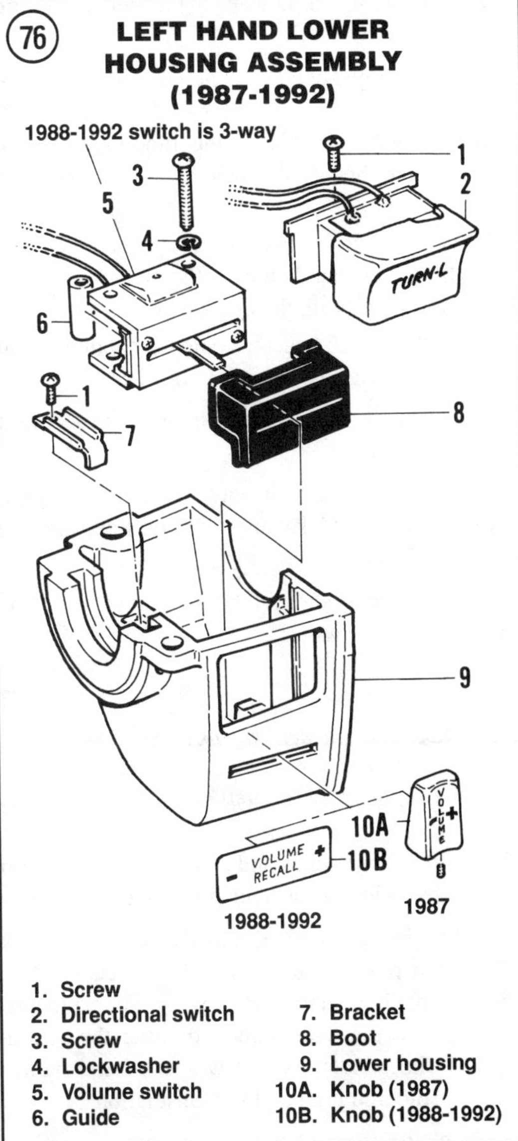


**LEFT HAND LOWER HOUSING ASSEMBLY (1987-1992)**

1. Screw
2. Directional switch
3. Screw
4. Lockwasher
5. Volume switch
6. Guide
7. Bracket
8. Boot
9. Lower housing
10A. Knob (1987)
10B. Knob (1988-1992)

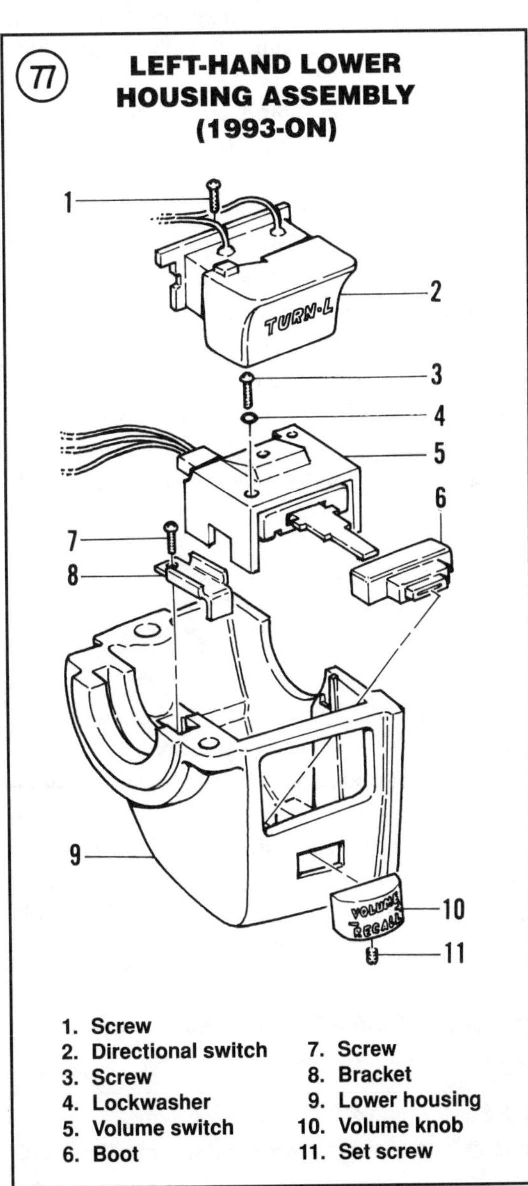


**LEFT-HAND LOWER HOUSING ASSEMBLY (1993-ON)**

1. Screw
2. Directional switch
3. Screw
4. Lockwasher
5. Volume switch
6. Boot
7. Screw
8. Bracket
9. Lower housing
10. Volume knob
11. Set screw

3. Remove the screws securing the left directional switch and the volume switch and remove the switches.
4. Cut the switch wire at the defective switch and discard the switch.
5. Take the volume control switch and install the guides between the switch surfaces so that the hole in the guides line up with the holes in the switch surfaces. Slide the rubber boot over the front switch arm and place the switch into the housing. Install the switch so that the boss on top of the switch faces up as shown in **Figure 76** or **Figure 77**. Secure the switch with its screws and washers.
6. Place the directional switch on top of the volume control switch and secure it with its attaching screws.
7. Route the volume control and directional switch wires together following the same routing path through the right-hand side of the switch housing. Secure the wires with the bracket and screw.
8. Install the switch housings onto the handlebar and secure with their mounting screws.
9. Install the volume knob onto the switch lever (if used) and secure it with its set screw.
10. Strip the new switch wire 3/4 in. (19.05 mm) from the switch. Make sure you don't cut into the wire strands themselves.
11. Cut a piece of shrink tubing to length and slide it over one of the wires.

*NOTE*
*Make sure the heat shrink is positioned away from the soldering gun when soldering the wires in Step 12.*

12. Join the 2 wire ends and solder them with rosin core solder—do not use acid core solder.
13. After the wires have cooled, slide the shrink tubing into position across the 2 wire ends. Then briefly apply heat to the shrink wrap. The wrap will shrink across the wire connection after the heat is applied. Check that the shrink wrap conforms tightly with the soldered joint and wire insulation.

### Right-hand Switch Replacement (Sound System Models)

Refer to **Figure 78** for this procedure.
1. Remove the switch screws and separate the switch halves.
2. If equipped with a radio control switch, first remove the set screw and knob from the switch.
3. Remove the screws securing the right directional switch, functional switch and brake light switch and remove the switches.
4. Cut the switch wire at the defective switch and discard the switch.
5. Slide the rubber boot over the functional switch and install the switch into the lower housing.
6. Install the brake light switch so that the mounting tab on the functional switch is placed on top of the brake light switch mounting tab. This alignment prevents the brake light switch from binding. Secure both switches to the housing with their mounting screws.
7. Place the right-hand directional switch into the housing and align the mounting tab on the switch with the threaded hole in the functional switch mounting tab. Secure the switch with its mounting screw.
8. Route the switch wires together so that they exit through the left-hand side of the switch housing. Secure the wires with the bracket and screw.
9. Install the switch housings onto the handlebar and secure with their mounting screws.
10. Install the functional switch knob and secure it with its set screw.
11. Strip the new switch wire 3/4 in. (19.05 mm) from the switch. Make sure you don't cut into the wire strands themselves.
12. Cut a piece of shrink tubing to length and slide it over one of the wires.

*NOTE*
*Make sure the heat shrink is positioned away from the soldering gun when soldering the wires in Step 13.*

13. Join the 2 wire ends and solder them with rosin core solder—do not use acid core solder.
14. After the wires have cooled, slide the shrink tubing into position across the 2 wire ends. Then briefly apply heat to the shrink wrap. The wrap will shrink across the wire connection after the heat is applied. Check that the shrink wrap conforms tightly with the soldered joint and wire insulation.
15. Check throttle control and brake light operation.

### Ignition/Lighting Switch Removal/Installation (FLT)

Refer replacement to a Harley-Davidson dealer.

### Ignition/Lighting Switch Removal/Installation (FXR and 1985-1986 FX)

The ignition/lighting switch on these models is not repairable. If switch is damaged, disconnect the wires from the switch. Then remove the switch mounting fasteners and remove the switch. Reverse to install.

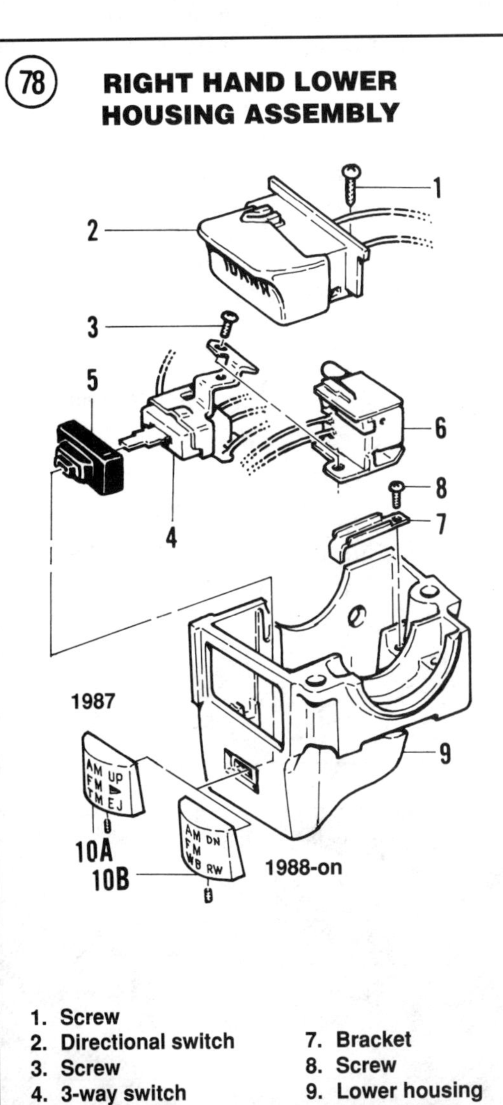


1. Screw
2. Directional switch
3. Screw
4. 3-way switch
5. Boot
6. Stoplight switch
7. Bracket
8. Screw
9. Lower housing
10A. Knob (1987)
10B. Knob (1988-on)

### Oil Pressure Switch Testing/Replacement

The oil pressure indicator light should come on when the ignition is turned on prior to starting the engine. When the engine is running, the oil pressure indicator light should go off when engine speed rises above idle. This procedure tests the electrical part of the oil pressure switch assembly. If the oil pressure switch, indicator bulb and related wiring are okay, inspect the lubrication system as described in Chapter Two.

The oil pressure switch is located on the right-hand crankcase next to the rear tappet guide (**Figure 79**). The electrical wire is connected to the switch with a lockwasher and nut.

1. Remove the rubber boot and disconnect the electrical connector at the switch.
2. Turn the ignition switch ON.
3. Ground the switch wire to the engine.
4. The oil pressure indicator light on the instrument panel should light.
5. If the signal indicator light does not light, check for a burned-out indicator light and inspect all wiring between the switch and the indicator light. If necessary, replace the light as described in this chapter.

6A. If the problem was solved in Steps 3-5, attach the electrical connector to the pressure switch. Make sure the connection is tight and free from oil. Slide the rubber boot back into position.

6B. If the problem was not solved in Steps 3-5 and the warning light remains ON when the engine is

9

running, shut the engine off. Check the engine lubrication system as described in Chapter Two.
7. To replace the switch, unscrew it from the engine and install a new one. Test the new switch as described in Steps 1-4.

## Neutral Indicator Switch Testing/Replacement

The neutral indicator switch is mounted on the shifter cover on 4-speed models (**Figure 80**) and on top of the transmission cover on 5-speed models (**Figure 81**). The neutral indicator light on the instrument panel should light when the ignition is turned ON and the transmission is in NEUTRAL.

1. Slide the rubber boot up the neutral switch wire and disconnect the electrical connector to the switch.
2. Turn the ignition switch ON.
3. Ground the switch wire to the transmission housing.
4. The neutral indicator light on the instrument panel should light.
5. If the signal indicator light does not light, check for a burned-out indicator light and inspect all wiring between the switch and the indicator light. If necessary, replace the light as described in this chapter.

6A. If the problem was solved in Steps 3-5, attach the electrical connector to the neutral switch. Make sure the connection is tight and free from oil. Slide the rubber boot back into position.

6B. If the problem was not solved in Steps 3-5, remove the neutral switch and its gasket and depress its plunger by hand. If the plunger does not return when depressed or if it moves roughly, replace the neutral switch.

7. When installing the neutral switch, check the neutral switch gasket for wear. Install the neutral switch gasket over the neutral switch threads and thread the switch into the cover and tighten securely. Reconnect the electrical connector, making sure the rubber boot on the end of the connector is positioned over the connector.

## Front Brake Light Switch Testing/Replacement

A mechanical, plunger-type switch is mounted in the front master cylinder. When the front brake lever is applied, the switch closes the brake light circuit and the rear brake light comes on. If the brake light does not come on when the front brake lever is applied and the ignition switch is turned ON, first check for a blown taillight bulb. If the bulb is okay, test the switch as follows.

1. Disconnect the electrical wires to the brake light switch.
2. Use an ohmmeter and check for continuity between the 2 terminals on the brake light switch connector. There should be no continuity (infinite resistance) with the brake lever released. With the brake lever applied there should be continuity (low resistance). If the switch fails either of these tests, the switch must be replaced.
3. Refer to *Front Master Cylinder Disassembly and Reassembly* in Chapter Thirteen to replace the switch.

*NOTE*
*On FLTC and FLHTC models, a stoplight relay is used. Refer to the wiring diagram at the end of this book for wire connections. The stoplight relay is mounted underneath the seat.*

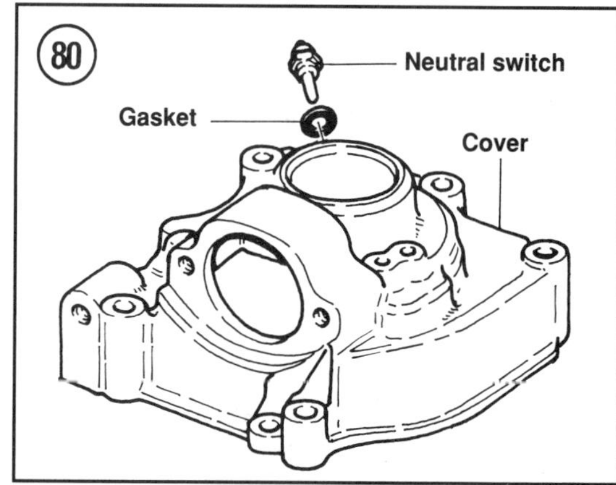

### Rear Brake Light Switch Testing/Replacement

On 1984-1991 FLT models, the rear brake light switch is mounted on the rear left side of the rear master cylinder. On 1992-on FLT, all FXR and 1985-1986 FX models, the rear brake light switch threads into a hole intersecting a brake fluid passageway in the rear brake line tee fitting; see **Figure 82**, typical. When the ignition switch is turned ON and the brake pedal is released, the brake switch contacts are open and the rear brake light is off. When the rear brake pedal is applied, hydraulic pressure closes the switch contacts, providing a ground path for the rear brake light to come on.

If the rear brake light does not come on when the ignition is turned ON and the rear brake pedal is applied (with sufficient hydraulic pressure to lock the brake), perform the following.

1. Turn the ignition switch OFF.

2. Use an ohmmeter and check for continuity between the 2 terminals on the brake light switch connector. There should be no continuity (infinite resistance) with the rear brake pedal released. With the rear brake pedal applied there should be continuity (low resistance). If the rear brake switch fails either of these tests, the switch must be replaced.

*NOTE*
*On FLTC and FLHTC models, a stoplight relay is used. Refer to the wiring diagram at the end of this book for wire connections. On 1993 and earlier models, the stoplight relay is mounted underneath the seat. On 1994 models, the stoplight relay is mounted inside the fairing (behind the headlight).*

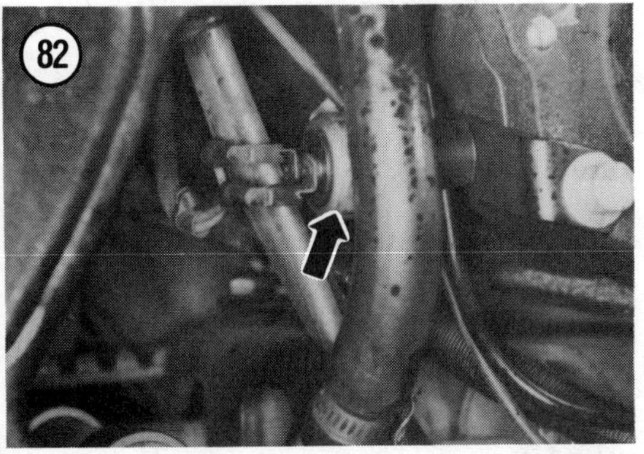


3. Purchase the new switch before removing the old switch.
4. Disconnect the wires at the switch.

*NOTE*
*There will be some brake fluid leakage after removing the old switch.*

5. Loosen and remove the old switch. Then cover the hole opening with your finger to prevent excessive brake fluid spillage.
6. Remove your finger from the hole opening and install the new switch. Tighten the switch securely.
7. Reconnect the switch wires.
8. Bleed the rear brake as described in Chapter Thirteen.

*WARNING*
*Do not ride the motorcycle until the rear brake is operating properly.*

## HORN

The horn is an important safety device and should be kept in working order. If the horn is damaged, it should be replaced immediately.



### Removal/Installation

1. If the horn fails to sound properly, check for broken or frayed horn wires. Also check the battery as described in this chapter.
2. Remove all components as necessary to gain access to the horn.
3. Disconnect the horn electrical connector.
4. Remove the horn mounting attachments and remove the horn.
5. Installation is the reverse of these steps.

## TURN SIGNAL MODULE

All 1989 and later FLT and all 1991-on FXR models are equipped with a turn signal module, an electronic microprocessor that controls the turn signals and the 4-way hazard flasher. The turn signal module receives its information from the speedometer and turn signal switches. The turn signal module is mounted onto the right-hand upper fork tube on FLT models and to the frame panel underneath the right-hand side cover on FXR models.

### Troubleshooting

The following basic troubleshooting procedures will help isolate some specific problems to the module.

***One or both turn signals do not flash. Light on front or rear side is lit, but does not flash***

1. Remove the lens and check for a damaged bulb. Replace bulb if necessary.
2. If the bulb is okay, check for one of the following problems:
   a. Check the bulb socket contacts for corrosion. Clean contacts and recheck. If you have a problem with corrosion building on the contacts, wipe the contacts with a dielectric grease before installing the bulb.
   b. Check for a broken bulb wire. Repair wire or connector.
   c. Check for a loose bulb socket where it is staked to the housing. If the bulb socket is loose, replace the light assembly.
   d. Check for a poor ground connection. If necessary, scrape the ground mounting area or replace damaged ground wire(s).

***Turn signals do not operate on one side***

1. Perform the checks listed under *One or both turn signals do not flash. Light on front or rear side is lit, but does not flash.* If these checks do not locate the problem, proceed to Step 2.
2. Inoperative handlebar directional switch. Perform the following:
   a. Turn the ignition switch ON.
   b. Disconnect the turn signal module electrical connector.
   c. Referring to **Figure 83**, locate pin 6 or 7 on 1994 FLT or pin 8 or 10 on all other models.
   d. With voltmeter set on DC scale, connect the negative lead to a good ground and the positive lead to pin 6 or 7 (1994 FLT) or pin 8 or 10 (all other models) and press the turn signal switch. The voltmeter should read 12 volts when the switch is pressed in.
   e. If the voltage is correct, proceed to Step 3.
   f. If the voltage reading is incorrect, proceed to Step 4.
3. Inoperative module. If 12 volts were recorded in Step 2, and the lights and connecting wires are in good condition, the module may be damaged. Replace the module and retest.
4. Damaged directional switch wire circuit. If no voltage was recorded in Step 2, check the handlebar switch and related wiring for damage. Tests can be made by performing continuity and voltage checks.
5. Reconnect the turn signal module electrical connector.

***Turn signals/hazard lights do not operate on both sides***

1. If none of the turn signals or hazard flashers operate, check the module for proper ground with an ohmmeter. Using the wiring diagram at the end of this book for your model, trace the ground connection from the module to the frame tab. If a ground is not present, remove the ground wire at the frame and scrape the frame and clean the connector. Check the ground wire for breaks. Repair as required. If a ground is present, perform Step 2.
2. Refer to the wiring diagram for your model and locate the accessory circuit breaker. Turn the ignition switch ON and check for voltage on the hot or load side of the circuit breaker with a voltmeter. If there is no voltage, check the following components:
   a. Accessory circuit breaker.
   b. Main circuit breaker.
   c. Starter relay.
   d. Ignition switch.
   e. Circuit wiring.
3. Check for an open ground wire connection at pin No. 1 (**Figure 83**). Repair broken wire, if required.

*NOTE*

*Operating the module without pin No. 1 grounded will permanently damage the module.*

***Turn signals do not cancel***

1. Support the bike so that the front wheel clears the ground.
2. Connect an ohmmeter to the speedometer switch white/green wire and ground. Spin the front wheel and watch the ohmmeter scale. The ohmmeter should alternate between 0 ohms and infinity.

83

## TURN SIGNAL MODULE

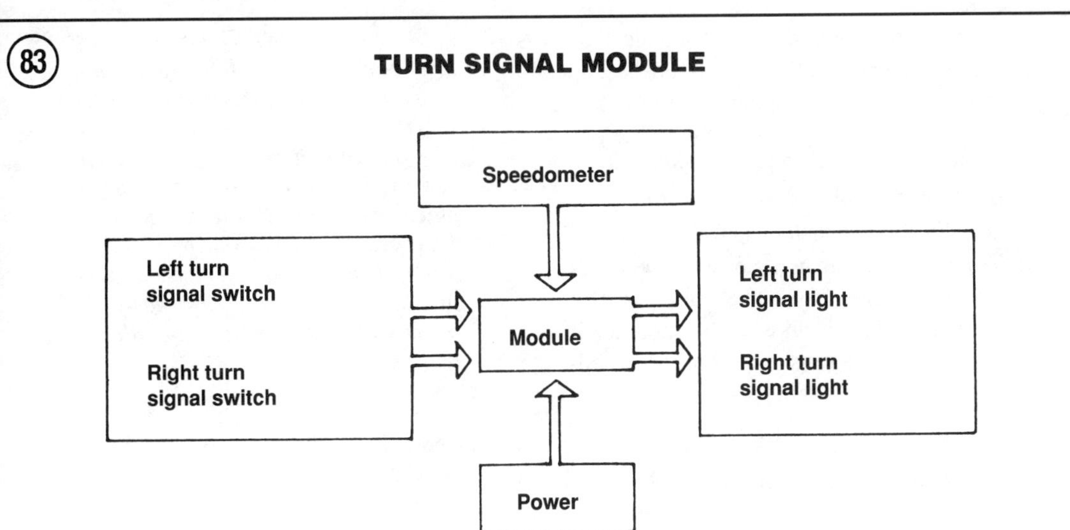


## 1989-1993 FLT AND 1991-ON FXR CONNECTOR BLOCK

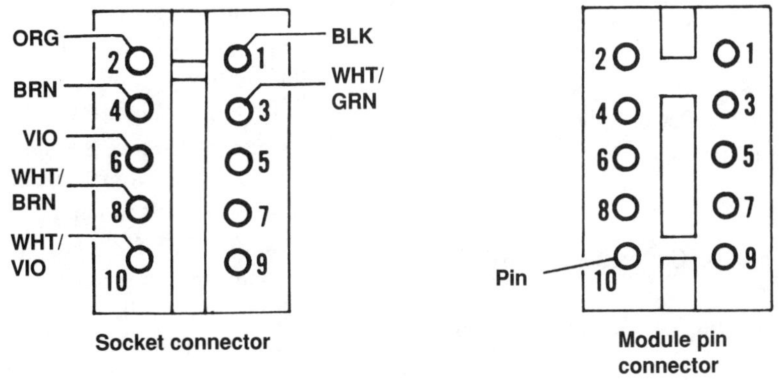


## 1994 FLT CONNECTOR 30A

| Pin No. | 1 | 2 | 3 | 4 | 5 | 6 | 7 | 8 |
|---|---|---|---|---|---|---|---|---|
| Color code | Blk | Org Wht | Wht Grn | Brn | Vio | Wht Brn | Wht Vio | Open |

a. If ohmmeter reading is correct, disconnect the module pin connector. With a voltmeter set on the DC scale, connect the negative lead to a good ground and the positive lead to the No. 3 pin socket connector. The voltmeter should read 12 volts. If ohm and volt readings are correct, the module is damaged.
b. If ohmmeter reading is incorrect, check for damaged wiring from the speedometer switch's white/green wire to the module. If wiring is okay, the reed switch in the speedometer may be damaged.

NOTE
*The reed switch signal also controls the sound system volume and the cruise control speed on 1990 and later Ultra models.*

### Removal/Installation

The turn signal module is mounted onto the right-hand upper fork tube on FLT models and to the frame panel underneath the right-hand side cover on FXR models.

1. Disconnect the harness plug from the module.

2A. *1994 FLHTC models:* Perform the following:
   a. Remove the headlight assembly.
   b. Cut straps securing module to fork tube and remove module.

2B. *All other FLT models:* Cut harness straps and remove module.

2C. *FXR:* Remove mounting bolt and remove module.

3. Install by reversing these steps.

## TURN SIGNAL AND 4-WAY FLASHERS (1984-1988 FLT AND 1984-1990 FXR)

FLT models are equipped with a turn signal flasher and a 4-way flasher. FXR models are only equipped with a single turn signal flasher.

NOTE
*If the turn signals do not work on 1986 models, check to see if both the left- and right-hand turn signal switches are turned on at the same time. This will overload the flasher and prevent it from operating properly.*

NOTE
*1984-early 1986 models are equipped with a rectangular shaped flasher. Late 1986 and later models are equipped with a round flasher with a blue stripe. See **Figure 84**. Do not use factory replacement round flashers that are not equipped with a blue stripe. These are 4-way flashers and will cause incorrect turn signal operation. 1984-early 1986 models can use the new style flashers with the blue stripe.*

### Replacement (1984-1988 FLT)

NOTE
*The turn signal and 4-way flashers must be installed in their original mounting positions. To prevent confusion when removing both flashers, record the position of the flashers before removing them.*

1A. *FLHT/C*: The turn signal and 4-way flashers are mounted on a bracket attached to the fork stem. Perform the following:
   a. Remove the headlight assembly.
   b. Working through the headlight opening, disconnect the wires from the flasher and remove the flasher from its mounting clip.

1B. *FLT/C and FLHS*: The turn signal and 4-way flashers are mounted on a bracket attached to the fork stem. Perform the following:
   a. Remove the instrument panel.

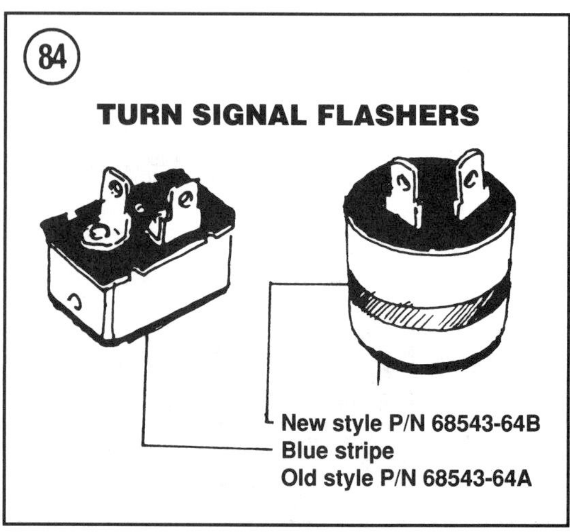

b. Working through the instrument panel opening, disconnect the wires from the flasher and remove the flasher from its mounting clip.

2. Install a new flasher in its original mounting position by reversing these steps. Check headlight adjustment on FLHT/C models as described in this chapter. Check flasher operation.

### Replacement (All FXR Except FXRT, FXRD and FXLR)

1. Remove the headlight sealed beam.

2. Remove the flasher and install a new one.

3. Reverse to install. Make sure the flasher is positioned in the headlight housing so that the electrical terminals on the flasher face toward the rear of the bike.

*CAUTION*

*If the flasher is installed with the electrical terminals facing forward, the terminals may become damaged from contact with the sealed beam unit.*

4. Check headlight adjustment as described in this chapter. Check flasher operation.

### Replacement (FXLR)

The flasher is mounted on the upper engine mount stabilizer bracket above the carburetor. Remove wires and replace flasher. Check flasher operation.

### Replacement (FXRT and FXRD)

The flasher is mounted inside the fairing above the headlight.

1. Remove the instrument panel.
2. Working through the instrument panel opening, disconnect the flasher and install a new one.
3. Install by reversing these steps.

## RADIO AND CB

Refer all service related to the radio and CB systems to your Harley-Davidson dealer.

## ELECTRICAL CIRCUIT PROTECTION

Electrical circuits are protected by circuit breakers and fuses (if so equipped).

Whenever a failure occurs in any part of the electrical system, always check the circuit breaker or fuse first. Usually, the trouble is a short circuit in the wiring. This may be caused by worn-through insulation or by a wire that has worked its way loose and shorted to ground.

A tripped circuit breaker or a blown fuse should be treated as more than a minor annoyance. It should serve as a warning that something is wrong in the electrical system.

*WARNING*

*Never replace a circuit breaker or fuse with one of higher amperage rating than that specified for use. Failure to follow this basic rule could result in heat or fire damage to major parts or loss of the entire vehicle.*

### Circuit Breakers

All models use circuit breakers (**Figure 85**, typical). Circuit breaker ratings for the different circuits are listed in **Table 4** and **Table 5**.

Whenever a failure occurs in any part of the electrical system, each circuit breaker is self-resetting and will automatically return power to the circuit when the electrical fault is found and corrected.

*CAUTION*

*If the electrical fault is not found and corrected, the breakers will cycle on and off continuously. This will cause the motorcycle to run erratically and eventually the battery will lose its charge.*

Replace a defective circuit breaker by disconnecting the wire(s) and pulling it out of its holder. Reverse to install.

### Fuses

The CB circuit on FLT models is protected by mini-fuses mounted in the fuse/filter board (**Figure 86**) on the left-hand side of the bike. The mini-fuse has 2 blades connected by a metal link encapsulated in plastic. When the fuse is installed, the end of each metal blade is exposed, allowing the fuse condition to be checked with test probes. To replace a mini-fuse, grasp the plastic covered top and pull the fuse from the fuse block. Insert a new one of the same amperage value in its place. **Figure 87** shows the difference between a good and a blown mini-fuse.

The radio memory and power circuits and the cruise control module on FLT Ultra models are protected by glass-capsule fuses. To replace a fuse, locate the in-line fuse holder and remove the blown fuse. Insert a new one of the same amperage value in its place and close the holder. See **Table 6**.

## DEUTSCH ELECTRICAL CONNECTORS (1994)

All 1994 FLT models use Deutsch DT Series Electrical Connectors. (Deutsch sealed connectors are also used on the 1993 Ultra CB transceiver-to-pod connectors). These connectors are designed to provide a superior seal, as compared to conventional connectors, to prevent dirt and moisture from entering the connector and shorting out the pin connections. The Deutsch connectors also provide better connector retention.

The following section describes service procedures that are required to remove, disassemble and reconnect the Deutsch electrical connectors.

### Disconnecting Deutsch Connectors

The pin housing on most connectors are secured with attachment clips. These clips are then fastened to T-studs on the frame that provide a more positive location when locating or routing the electrical connectors or wiring harness. This system improves serviceability and reduces electrical problems from chafing or other routing induced problems.

1. To remove a connector from its attachment clip, first push the connector toward the rear and lift the connector off the T-stud.

*NOTE*

*The Deutsch connectors have 1 or 2 locking tabs. When disconnecting the connectors in Step 2, both locking tabs (if so equipped) must be pressed in simultaneously.*

2. To separate the connector halves (pin and socket housings), depress the external latch on the socket housing with your fingers. Then, using a rocking motion, separate the socket halves.

### Connector Removal/Installation

To remove or replace many of the electrical accessories, the Deutsch electrical connector must be partially disassembled and then reassembled.

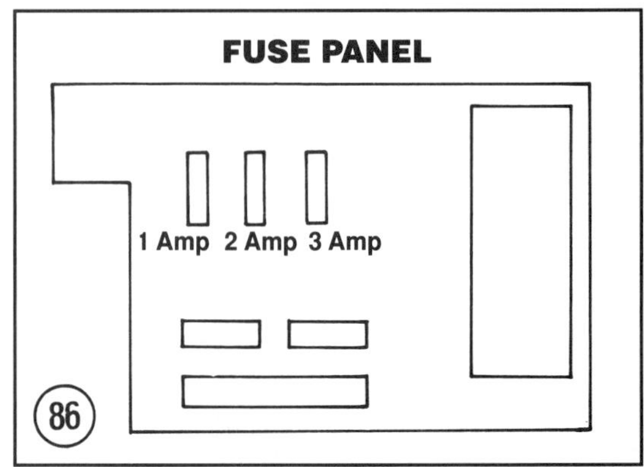


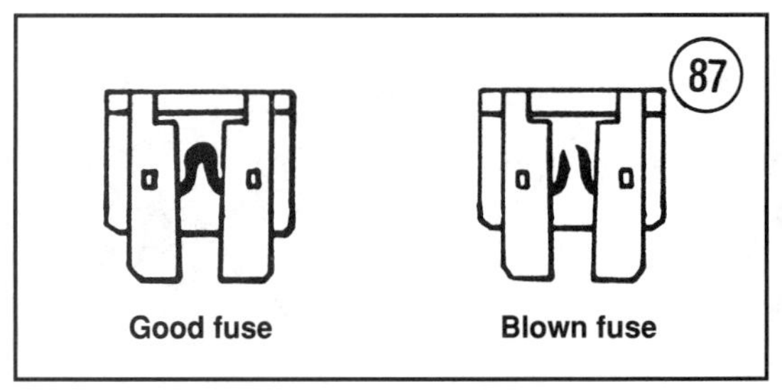

### *Socket terminal removal/installation*

This procedure describes how to remove and install the socket terminals from the socket housing connector half.

Refer to **Figure 88** or **Figure 89**.

*NOTE*
*This procedure is performed on a 12-pin Deutsch connector (**Figure 89**). Procedures can also be used for 2-, 3-, 4- and 6-pin connectors.*

1. Disconnect the connector housings.
2. Remove the secondary locking wedge (7, **Figure 89**) as follows:
   a. Locate the secondary locking wedge in **Figure 88** or **Figure 89**.
   b. Insert a wide-blade screwdriver between the socket housing and locking wedge and turn the screwdriver 90 degrees to force the wedge up (**Figure 90**).
   c. Remove the secondary locking wedge (7, **Figure 89**).

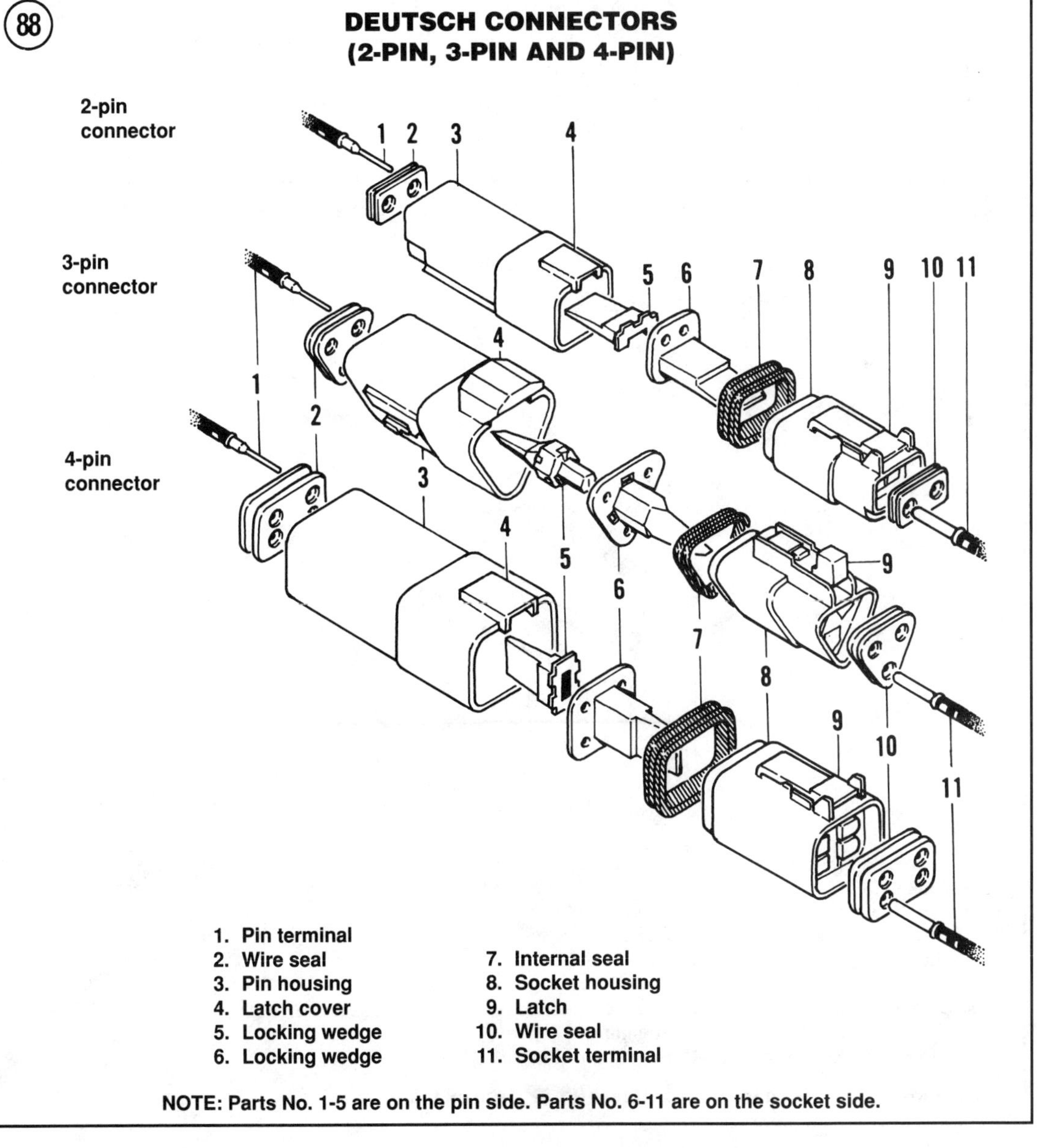

3. Lightly press the terminal latches inside the socket housing and remove the socket terminal (14, **Figure 89**) through the holes in the rear wire seal.

4. Repeat Step 3 for each socket terminal.

5. Remove the wire seal (12, **Figure 89**), if necessary.

*NOTE*
*Reassemble the socket housing, starting with Step 6.*

6. Install the wire seal (12, **Figure 89**) into the socket housing, if removed.

7. Hold the socket housing and insert the socket terminals (14, **Figure 89**) through the holes in the wire seal so that they enter their correct chamber hole. Continue until the socket terminal clicks in place. Then lightly tug on the wire to make sure that it is locked in place.

8. If removed, seat the internal seal (8, **Figure 89**) onto the socket housing as shown in **Figure 89**.

*NOTE*
*Except for the 3-pin Deutsch connector, all of the secondary locking wedges are symmetrical (both sides are the same). When assembling the 3-pin connector, the arrow on the secondary locking wedge must be installed so that it is pointing toward the external latch; see* ***Figure 91****.*

9. Install the secondary locking wedge into the socket housing as shown in **Figure 88** or **Figure 89**. Press the secondary locking wedge down until it snaps in place.

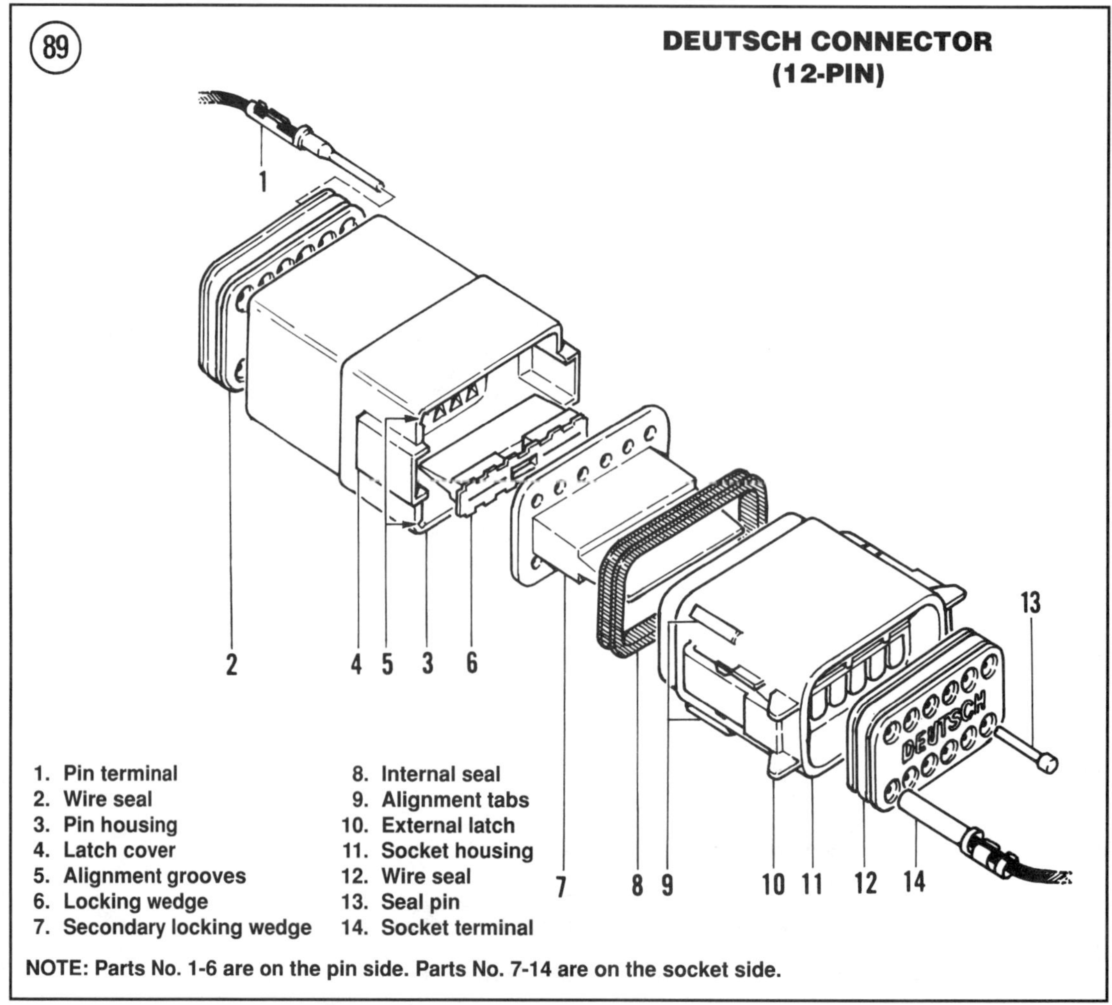


1. Pin terminal
2. Wire seal
3. Pin housing
4. Latch cover
5. Alignment grooves
6. Locking wedge
7. Secondary locking wedge
8. Internal seal
9. Alignment tabs
10. External latch
11. Socket housing
12. Wire seal
13. Seal pin
14. Socket terminal

NOTE: Parts No. 1-6 are on the pin side. Parts No. 7-14 are on the socket side.

*NOTE*
*If the secondary locking wedge does not slide into position easily, one or more of the socket terminals are improperly installed.*

***Pin terminal removal/installation***

This procedure describes how to remove and install the pin terminals from the pin housing (3, **Figure 89**) connector half.

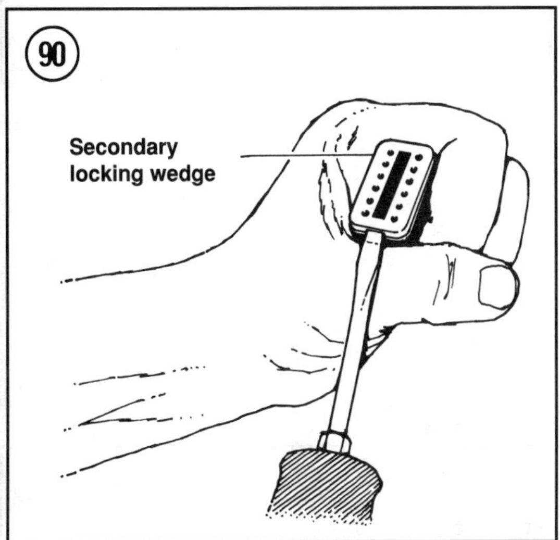


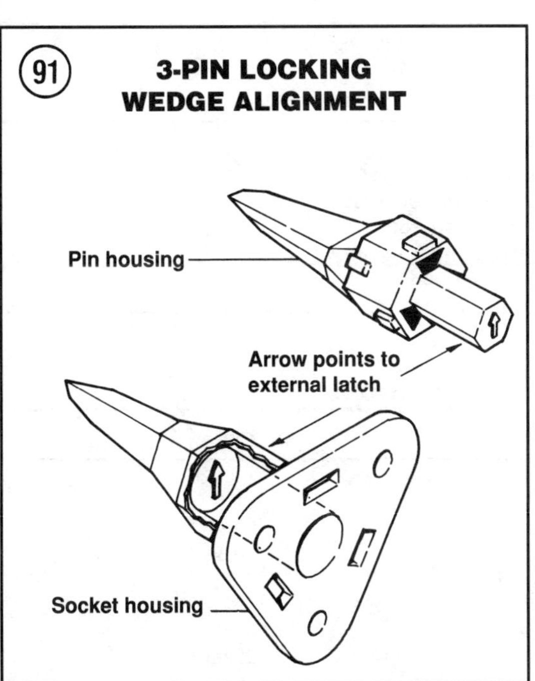


Refer to **Figure 88** or **Figure 89**.

*NOTE*
*This procedure is performed on a 12-pin Deutsch connector (**Figure 89**). Procedures can also be used for 2-, 3-, 4- and 6-pin connectors.*

1. Disconnect the connector halves.
2. Remove the secondary locking wedge (6, **Figure 89**) with needle nose pliers or a piece of bent safety wire.
3. Lightly press the terminal latches inside the pin housing and remove the pin terminals (1, **Figure 89**) through the holes in the wire seal (2, **Figure 89**).
4. Repeat Step 3 for each pin terminal.
5. Remove the wire seal (2, **Figure 89**), if necessary.

*NOTE*
*Reassemble the pin housing, starting with Step 6.*

6. Install the wire seal (2, **Figure 89**) into the socket housing, if removed.
7. Hold the pin housing and insert the pin terminals (1, **Figure 89**) through the holes in the wire seal so that they enter their correct numbered hole. Continue until the pin terminal clicks in place. Then lightly tug on the wire to make sure that it is locked in place.

*NOTE*
*Except for the 3-pin Deutsch connector, all of the secondary locking wedges are symmetrical (both sides are the same). When assembling the 3-pin connector, the arrow on the secondary locking wedge must be installed so that it is pointing toward the external latch; see **Figure 91**.*

8. Install the secondary locking wedge into the pin housing as shown in **Figure 88** or **Figure 89**. Press the secondary locking wedge down until it snaps in place. When properly installed, the wedge will fit into the pin housing center groove.

*NOTE*
*If the secondary locking wedge does not slide into position easily, one or more of the pin terminals are improperly installed.*

## Deutsch Pin and Socket Crimping Procedures

The Harley-Davidson electrical terminal crimp tool (part No. HD-39965) will be required to install new pin (1, **Figure 89**) and socket (14, **Figure 89**) terminals. Use the instructions included with the crimp tool.

When stripping the wire insulation prior to installing the socket or pin terminals strip away 5/32 in. (3.96 mm) of wire insulation. This ensures that the exposed wires will fill the terminal barrel.

After crimping the terminal and wire, tug lightly on the wire to make sure the crimp holds. **Figure 92** shows a properly crimped terminal and wire.

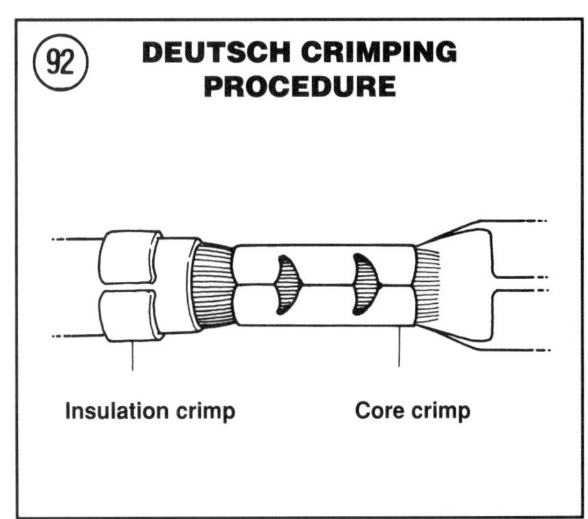


**Table 1 BATTERY CAPACITY**

| | |
|---|---|
| 1984-1990 | 12 volt, 19 amp hr. |
| 1991-on | |
| FLT | 12 volt, 20 amp hr. |
| FXR | 12 volt, 19 amp hr. |

**Table 2 BATTERY STATE OF CHARGE**

| | |
|---|---|
| 1.110-1.130 | Discharged |
| 1.140-1.160 | Almost discharged |
| 1.170-1.190 | One-quarter charged |
| 1.200-1.220 | One-half charged |
| 1.230-1.250 | Three-quarters charged |
| 1.260-1.280 | Fully charged |

**Table 3 STARTER SPECIFICATIONS**

| | in. | mm |
|---|---|---|
| Starter brush length | | |
| 1984-1988 | 0.438 | 11.1 |
| 1989-1990 | 0.354 | 8.9 |
| 1991-1992 | 0.413 | 10.5 |
| 1993-on | 0.354 | 8.9 |
| Commutator diameter wear limit (minimum OD) | | |
| 1984-1988 | — | — |
| 1989-on | 1.141 | 29.98 |

**Table 4 CIRCUIT BREAKER RATINGS**

| Circuit | Rating (amps) |
|---|---|
| Main (battery) | 30 |
| Ignition | 15 |
| Lights | 15 |
| Accessory | |
| FLHS | 10* |
| Accessory | 15 |
| Radio | 15* |
| Constant | 15* |
| Cruise | 15* |

* FLT and FXR models only.

**Table 5 CIRCUIT BREAKER RATINGS (1994 FLT)**

| Circuit | Rating (amps) | Color code | Terminal |
|---|---|---|---|
| Main | 50 | None | Threaded |
| Lights | 15 | Light blue | Blade type |
| Accessory | 15 | Light blue | Blade type |
| Ignition | 15 | Light blue | Blade type |
| Constant | 15 | Light blue | Blade type |

**Table 6 BLADE TYPE FUSES (1993-ON FLT)**

| Circuit | Rating (amps) | Color code |
|---|---|---|
| CB power | 3 | Violet |
| CB memory | 1 | Charcoal |
| Fender tip | | |
| 1994 FLHT/U | 1 | Charcoal |
| Pod power | 5 | Tan |
| Radio | | |
| 1994 Ultras | 10 | Red |
| Radio memory | | |
| 1994 | 1 | Charcoal |

# CHAPTER TEN

# WHEELS, HUBS AND TIRES

This chapter describes disassembly and repair of the front and rear wheels, hubs and tire service. For routine maintenance, see Chapter Three.

Models can be equipped with either wire spoke, cast or disc wheels. Make sure you use the procedure and illustrations applicable to your bike.

Tire service is a critical aspect to the overall operation and safety of your motorcycle. Tires should be properly mounted, balanced and maintained while in service.

**Tables 1-3** are found at the end of the chapter.

## FRONT WHEEL

Proper front wheel maintenance and inspection is critical to the safe operation of your Harley. The following section describes complete service to the front wheel. Service to the front hub and bearings is described later in this chapter.

### Removal

NOTE

*Due to the number of models and years covered in this manual, this procedure represents a typical front wheel removal and installation.*

1. Support the bike so that the front wheel clears the ground.

2. Remove the brake caliper mounting bolts (**Figure 1**) and lift the caliper away from the brake disc. Support the caliper with a cord so that the weight of the caliper is not supported by the brake line. Repeat for the opposite brake caliper, if so equipped.

NOTE

*Insert a piece of wood or vinyl in the calipers between the brake pads. That way, if the brake lever is inadvertently squeezed, the piston will not be forced out of the cylinder. If this does happen, the calipers might have to be disassembled to reseat the piston and the system will have to be bled.*

NOTE

*Prior to removing the front axle nut, record the side the front axle is installed*

*from. The axle must be reinstalled through the same side.*

3. Remove the axle nut (**Figure 2**), lockwasher and flat washer.
4. Loosen the fork slider cap nuts (**Figure 3**). It should not be necessary to remove the nuts and slider cap.
5. Tap the end of the axle with a soft-faced mallet and remove it from the wheel. If the axle is tight, tap the end of the axle with a brass or aluminum drift.

*NOTE*
*Record the position of any axle spacers that come off with the wheel. Generally, one spacer will be free while the opposite spacer will stay inside its oil seal; a shoulder on the inside of the spacer holds it in place.*

6. Pull the wheel away from the fork sliders slightly and remove the speedometer drive gear from the wheel. Remove the rubber washer-type seal installed between the speedometer drive and oil seal, if so equipped.

2

3

*CAUTION*
*Do not set the wheel down on the disc surface, as it may be scratched or warped. Either lean the wheel against a wall or place it on a couple of wood blocks.*

7. When servicing the wheel assembly, install the axle fasteners and the speedometer drive assembly on the axle to prevent their loss.
8. Inspect the front wheel assembly as described in this chapter.

### Installation

1. Clean the axle in solvent and dry thoroughly. Make sure the axle bearing surfaces on both fork sliders and the axle are free from burrs and nicks.
2. Apply an anti-seize lubricant to the axle shaft prior to installation.
3. If the front wheel oil seals or bearings were replaced, confirm front axle spacer alignment as described under *Front Hub* in this chapter.
4. Install the wheel as follows:
   a. Install the rubber washer-type seal between the speedometer drive and wheel, if so equipped.
   b. Align the speedometer drive dogs with the wheel gear case notches and install the speedometer drive into the wheel.
   c. Hold the speedometer drive in position and install the wheel between the fork tubes.
   d. Insert the axle through the front forks and wheel from the same side recorded prior to removal. When the axle is installed through the wheel, install the flat washer, lockwasher and axle nut finger-tight. Check that the left- and right-hand axle spacers are positioned correctly.
   e. Tighten the slider cap nuts securely to prevent the axle from turning and then tighten the axle nut to the torque specification listed in **Table 2**. Loosen the slider cap nuts and then retighten to the torque specification listed in **Table 2**. Make sure gap between the slider cap and fork slider is equal on both sides.
5. Perform the *Front Axle End Play Check* in this chapter.
6. Remove the vinyl tubing or pieces of wood from the brake caliper. Then *carefully* position the pads around the disc when installing the brake caliper. Be

careful not to damage the leading edge of the brake pads when installing the brake caliper. Tighten the brake caliper bolts to the specifications in **Table 2**. Install the second brake caliper, if so equipped.

7. After the wheel and brake are completely installed, rotate the wheel several times and apply the front brake a couple of times to make sure the wheel rotates freely and that the brake pads seat against the disc correctly.

### Inspection (All Models)

1. Remove any corrosion on the front axle with a piece of fine emery cloth.
2. Install the wheel in a wheel truing stand and spin the wheel. Visually check the wheel for excessive wobble or runout. If it appears that the wheel is not running true, remove the tire from the rim as described later in this chapter. Then remount the wheel into the truing stand and measure axial and lateral runout (**Figure 4**) with a pointer or dial indicator. Compare actual runout readings with service limit specifications listed in **Table 1**. Note the following:
   a. Cast or disc wheels: If the runout meets or exceeds the service limit (**Table 1**), check the wheel bearings as described under *Front Hub* in this chapter. If the wheel bearings are okay, cast and disc wheels will have to be replaced as they cannot be serviced. Inspect the wheel for signs of cracks, fractures, dents or bends. If it is damaged in any way, it must be replaced.

*WARNING*

*Do not try to repair any damage to cast or disc wheels as it will result in an unsafe riding condition.*

   b. Wire spoke wheels: If the wheel bearings, spokes, hub and rim assembly are not damaged, the runout can be removed by accurately truing the wheel. Refer to *Spoke Adjustment* in this chapter. If the rim is dented or damaged in any way, the rim should be replaced and the wheel respoked and trued by a Harley-Davidson dealer or a qualified mechanic familiar with Harley wheel service.
3. While the wheel is off, check the tightness of the brake disc bolts. Refer to the tightening torques listed at the end of Chapter Thirteen.

### Front Wheel Bearing End Play Check/Adjustment (1984-Early 1991 FXR and FX)

Proper wheel bearing end play is important to your Harley's steering and handling performance. Incorrect wheel bearing end play can cause poor handling or excessive bearing side loading and premature bearing wear.

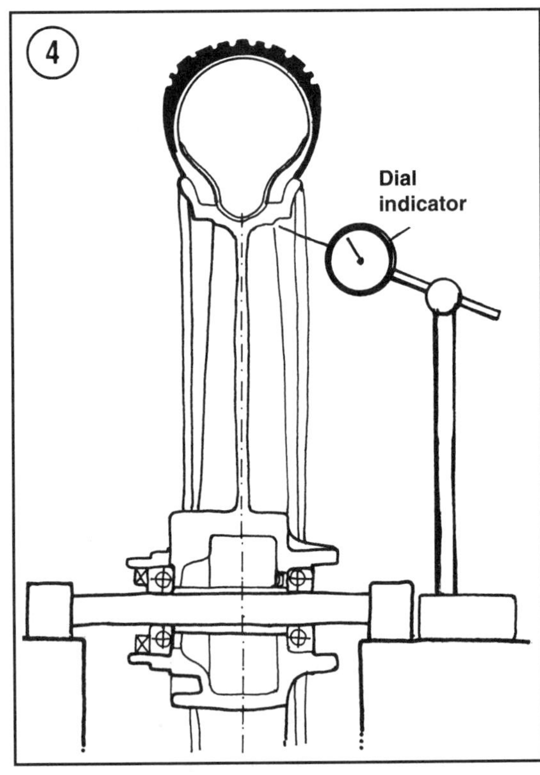


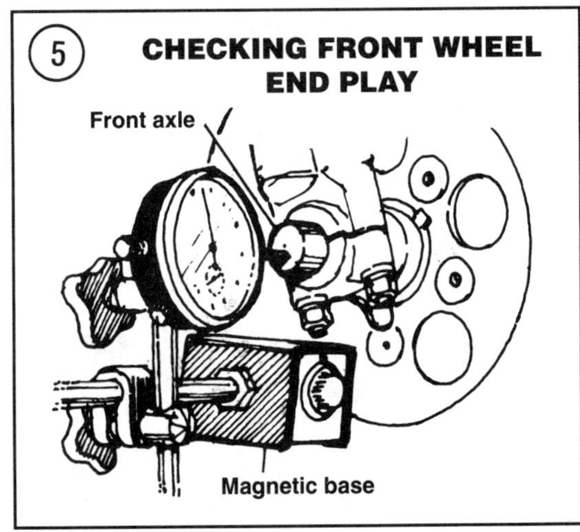

On these models, wheel bearing end play is controlled by the length of the center hub spacer; see **Figures 8-10** for your model. End play should be checked each time the front wheel is removed or whenever unstable handling is felt.

1. Support the bike so that the front wheel is off the ground.

2. Tighten the front axle nut to the torque specification in **Table 2**.

3. Tighten the slider cap nuts to the torque specification in **Table 2**.

4. Mount a dial indicator so that the plunger contacts the end of the axle (**Figure 5**). Grasp the wheel and move it back and forth by pushing and pulling it along the axle center line. Read axle end play by observing the dial indicator needle.

5. If the end play is incorrect, replace the center hub spacer; see **Figures 8-10** for your model. Install a longer spacer for less end play and a shorter spacer for more end play. Different length spacers can be purchased through Harley-Davidson dealers. To install a new spacer, remove the wheel and disassemble the front hub as described under *Front Hub* in this chapter. Reverse to install. Recheck end play after reinstalling the front wheel.

## Front Wheel Bearing End Play Check/Adjustment (FLT and Late 1991-on FXR)

Proper wheel bearing end play is important to your Harley's steering and handling performance. Incorrect wheel bearing end play can cause poor handling or excessive bearing side loading and premature bearing wear.

On these models, wheel bearing end play is controlled by the spacer installed between the spacer washer and the center hub spacer. End play should be checked each time the front wheel is removed or whenever unstable handling is felt.

1. Support the bike so that the front wheel is off the ground.

2. Tighten the front axle nut to the torque specification in **Table 2**.

3. Tighten the slider cap nuts to the torque specification in **Table 2**.

4. Mount a dial indicator so that the plunger contacts the end of the axle (**Figure 5**). Grasp the wheel and move it back and forth by pushing and pulling it along the axle center line. Read axle end play by observing the dial indicator needle.

5. If the end play is incorrect, replace the spacer; see **Figures 6-9** for your model. Install a thinner spacer

10

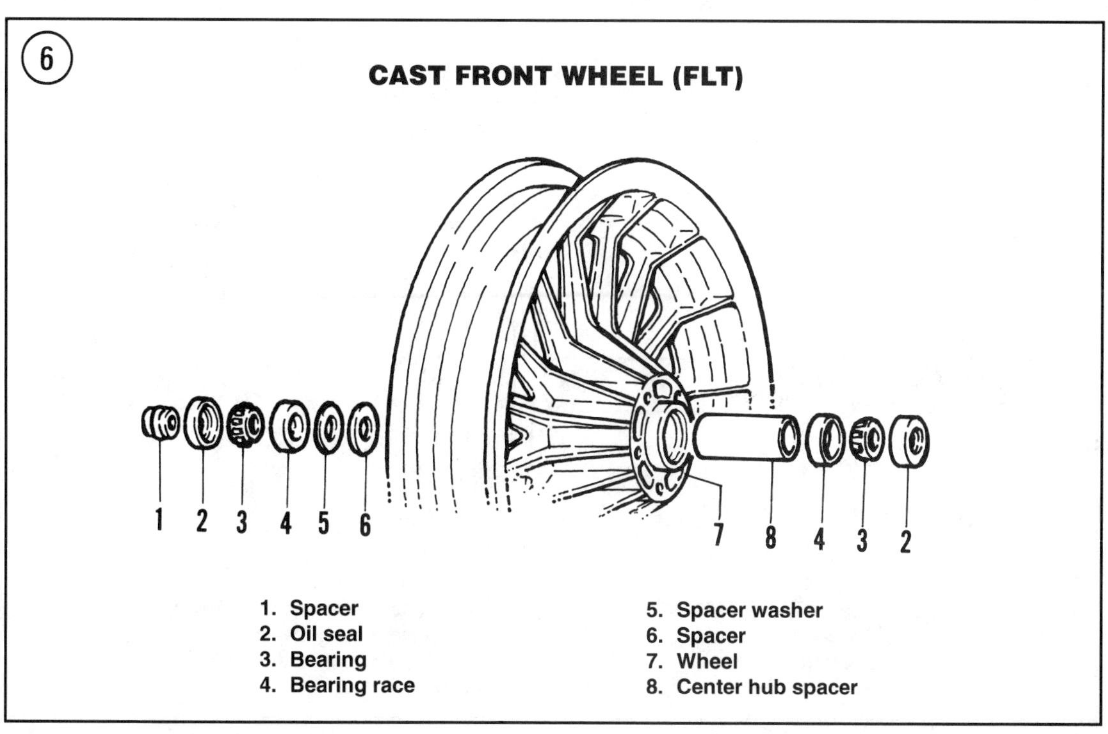

7

**LACED FRONT WHEEL (FLT)**

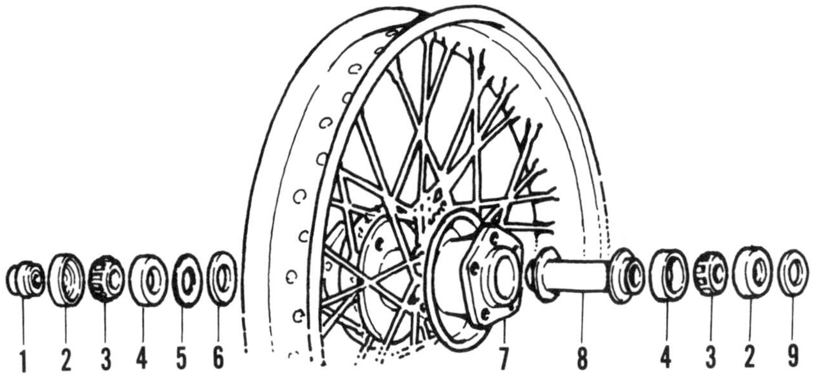


1. Spacer
2. Oil seal
3. Bearing
4. Bearing race
5. Spacer washer
6. Spacer
7. Wheel
8. Center hub spacer
9. Seal

8

**CAST FRONT WHEEL (FXR)**

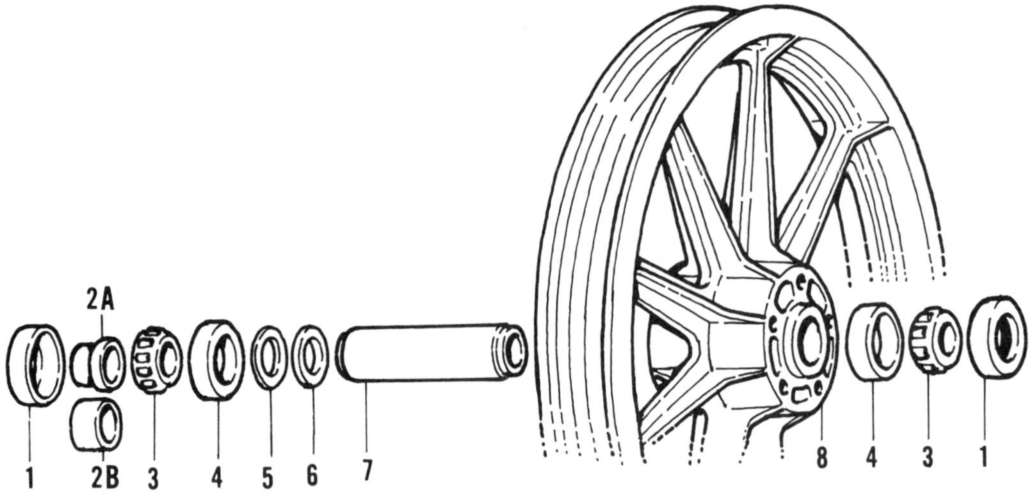


1. Oil seal
2A. Spacer (early models)
2B. Spacer (late models)
3. Bearing
4. Bearing race
4. Bearing race
5. Spacer washer (late 1991-on)
6. Spacer (late 1991-on)
7. Center hub spacer
8. Wheel

9

**LACED FRONT WHEEL (FXR)**

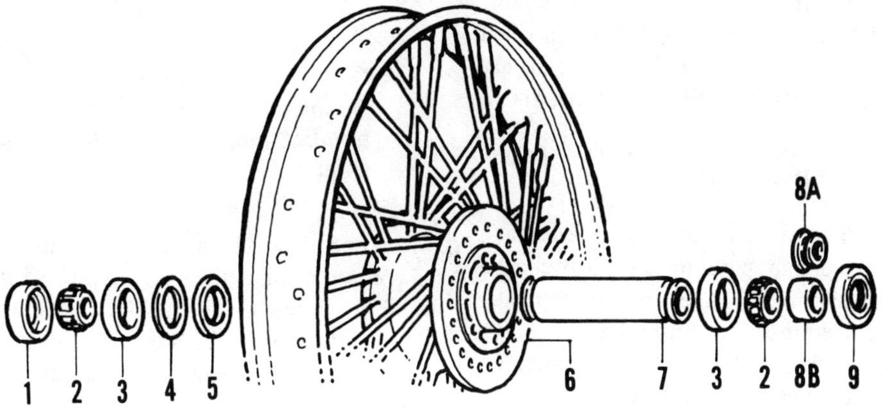

1. Oil seal
2. Bearing
3. Bearing race
4. Spacer washer (late 1991-on)
5. Spacer (late 1991-on)
6. Hub
7. Center hub spacer
8A. Spacer (early models)
8B. Spacer (late models)
9. Oil seal

10

**LACED FRONT WHEEL (FX)**

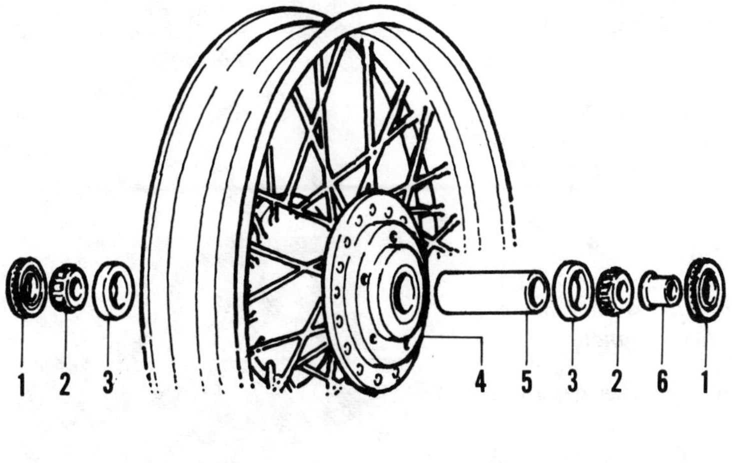

1. Oil seal
2. Bearing
3. Bearing race
4. Wheel
5. Center hub spacer
6. Spacer

for less end play and a thicker spacer for more end play. Do not replace the center hub spacer as this spacer is not used for end play adjustment. Different thickness spacers can be purchased through Harley-Davidson dealers. To install a new spacer, remove the wheel and disassemble the front hub as described under *Front Hub* in this chapter. Reverse to install. Recheck end play after reinstalling the front wheel.

## FRONT HUB

Tapered roller bearings are installed on each side of the hub. A center hub spacer installed between the bearings maintains front wheel bearing end play within a specified range; see *Front Wheel Bearing End Play* in this chapter. Oil seals are installed on the outside of each bearing to protect them from dirt and other contaminants. The bearings can be removed from the hub after removing the outer oil seals. The bearing races are pressed into the hub and should not be removed unless they require replacement.

### Disassembly/Inspection/Reassembly

Refer to the following for your model when performing this procedure:

a. FLT cast wheel (**Figure 6**).
b. FLT laced wheel (**Figure 7**).
c. FXR cast wheel (**Figure 8**).
d. FXR laced wheel (**Figure 9**).
e. 1985-1986 FX wheel (**Figure 10**).

*NOTE*
*If you are performing this procedure to replace or exchange the axle spacer, remove the bearing opposite the brake disc.*

*NOTE*
*The bearings and races are matched pairs. Label all parts so that they may be returned to their original position.*

1. Remove the front wheel as described in this chapter.
2. If necessary, remove the brake disc as described in Chapter Thirteen.

*NOTE*
*The outer axle spacers on some models may be different. ID each spacer when you remove it so you don't mix them up during reassembly.*

3. Remove the outer axle spacers from the oil seals in the hub.

*NOTE*
*On some models, a shouldered spacer is installed through one of the oil seals (**Figure 11**).*

4. Pry one of the oil seals out of the hub (**Figure 12**). If you are using a screwdriver, place a rag underneath the screwdriver to avoid damaging the hub. Remove the spacer from the oil seal, if necessary. Then identify and remove the bearing (**Figure 13**) from its race.

5A. *FLT and Late 1991-on FXR*: Remove the spacer washer, spacer and the center hub spacer from the hub. Note that the spacer washer has a shoulder. Wash these parts thoroughly in solvent.

5B. *All other models*: Remove the center hub spacer from the hub and wash it thoroughly in solvent.

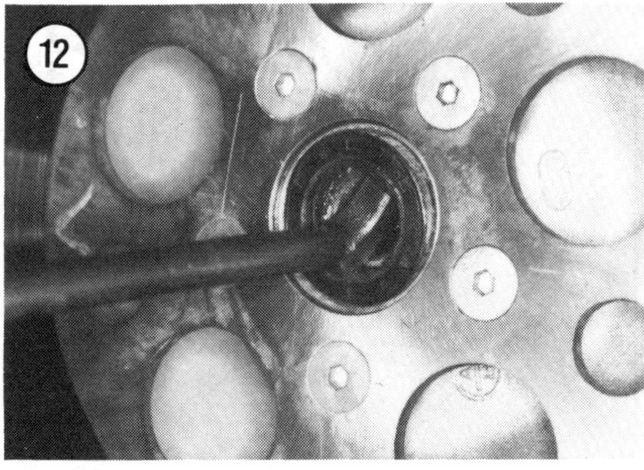

6. Repeat Step 4 to remove the opposite bearing. Remember, the bearings are matched to their races; label the bearings if they are going to be reused.

7. Wash the bearings thoroughly in clean solvent and dry with compressed air. Wipe the bearing races off with a clean rag dipped in solvent. Then check the roller bearings and races for wear, pitting or excessive heat (bluish tint). Replace the bearings and races as a complete set. Replace the bearing races as described in Step 8. If the bearing and its race don't require replacement, proceed to Step 9. If you are going to reinstall the original bearing(s), pack the bearing thoroughly with grease and wrap it in a clean, lint-free cloth or wax paper. Wipe a film of grease across the bearing race (**Figure 14**). If the bearings and races are not lubricated after cleaning them, they may rust.

8. Replace the bearing races (**Figure 14**) as follows:

a. A universal bearing remover should be used to remove the races from the hub. If this tool is unavailable, insert a drift punch through the hub and tap the opposite race out of the hub with a hammer. Move the punch around the race to make sure the race is driven squarely out of the hub. Do not allow the race to bind in the hub as this can damage the race bore in the hub. Severe damage to the race bore will require replacement of the hub.

b. Clean the inside and outside of the hub with solvent. Dry with compressed air.

c. Wipe the outside of the new race with oil and align it with the hub. Using a bearing driver or socket with an outside diameter slightly smaller than the bearing race, drive the race into the hub until it bottoms out on the hub shoulder. As you begin to drive the race into the hub, stop and check your work often to make sure the race is square with the hub bore. Do not allow the race to bind during installation.

*NOTE*

*If you do not have the proper size tool to drive the race into the hub, have a Harley-Davidson dealer or independent repair shop install the race. Do not attempt to install the race by driving it into the hub with a small diameter punch or rod.*

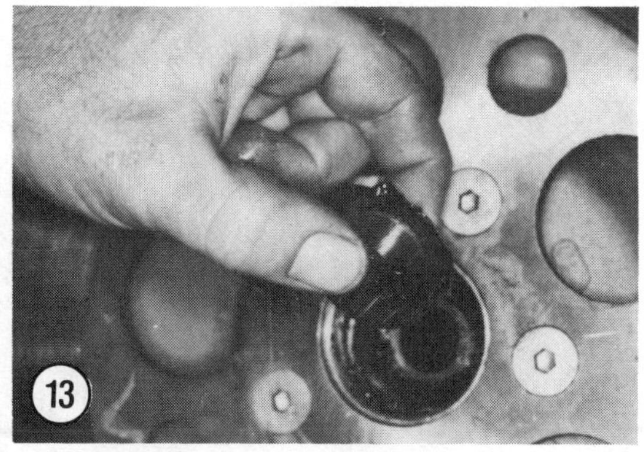

13

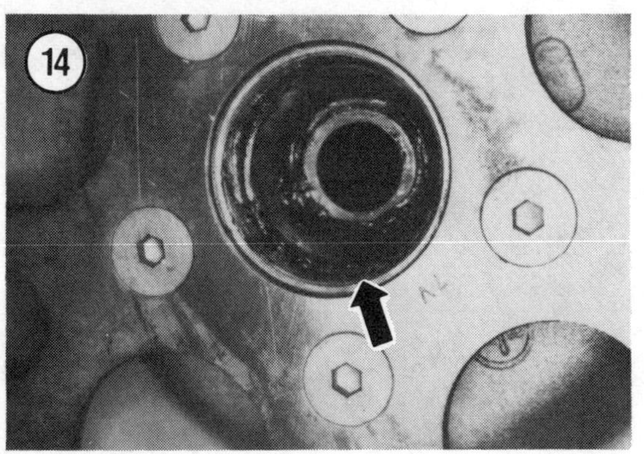

14

9. Blow any dirt or foreign matter out of the hub prior to installing the bearings.

10A. *FLT and late 1991-on FXR:* Wipe the ends of the center hub spacer with grease and install it into the hub. Then install the spacer and spacer washer as shown in **Figures 6-9** for your model. Install the spacer washer so that its shoulder faces away from the spacer and toward the bearing.

10B. *All other models*: Wipe the ends of the center hub spacer with grease and install it into the hub.

*NOTE*

*If you are performing this procedure to correct wheel bearing end play, make sure you install the correct length center hub spacer.*

11. Wipe each bearing race with grease.

12. Pack each bearing with grease. Then install each bearing in its respective bearing race. Pack the area between the bearing and oil seal (to be installed later) with grease; repeat for both sides.

13. Pack the seal lip cavity of each seal with grease.

14A. *1984-1990 FLT*: Install the oil seals and the 2 outer axle spacers as follows:

a. One of the outer axle spacers is longer than the other. Install the longer axle spacer into the valve stem side of the wheel. Install the shorter spacer into the opposite side.

b. Install the oil seals over the axle spacers and drive them into the hub, aligning the hole in the oil seal with the spacer shaft, until they are 13/64-7/32 in. (5.16-5.55 mm) below the outside edge of the hub.

14B. *1991-on FLT*: Install the oil seals and the 2 outer axle spacers as follows:

a. The 2 outer axle spacers are different. Install the outer axle spacer with the large chamfered end into the valve stem side of the wheel. Position the spacer so that the chamfered end faces toward the bearing. Install the other spacer into the opposite side.

b. Install the oil seals over the axle spacers and drive them into the hub, aligning the hole in the oil seal with the spacer shaft. On cast wheels, the oil seals should be driven into the hub so that the seal is flush or within 0.04 in. (1.0 mm) below the outside edge of the hub. On laced wheels, the oil seals must be installed so that they are flush or within 0.02 in. (0.51 mm). below the outside edge of the hub.

14C. *All other models*: Install the oil seals and the right-hand outer axle spacer as follows:

*NOTE*

*On 1984-1986 FXR and 1985-1986 FX models, the right-hand axle spacer has a shoulder. The axle spacer on 1987 and later FXR models does not. If the axle spacer on your model has a shoulder, install it so that the shoulder faces against the right-hand bearing.*

a. Install the right-hand axle spacer through a new oil seal and align the oil seal with the right-hand side of the hub. Install the other oil seal into the left-hand side (**Figure 15**).

b. Using a bearing driver or socket with an OD slightly smaller than the oil seal (**Figure 16**), carefully drive the oil seals into the hub until they are flush with the hub. On FX wheels, the oil seal may be installed so that its upper surface is flush or within 0.015 in. (0.38 mm) below the outside edge of the hub.

15. If the brake disc was removed, refer to Chapter Thirteen for correct procedures and tightening torques.

16. After the wheel is installed on the bike and the front axle tightened to the specified torque specification, the bearing end play should be checked as described in this chapter.

17. If the hub on wire spoke wheels is damaged, the hub can be replaced by removing the spokes and having a dealer assemble a new hub. If the hub on

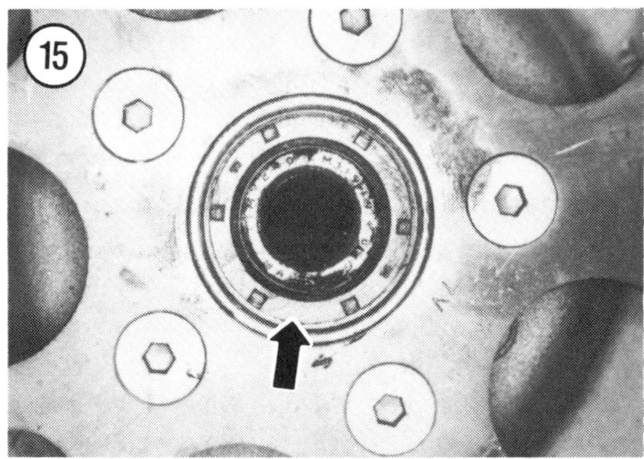


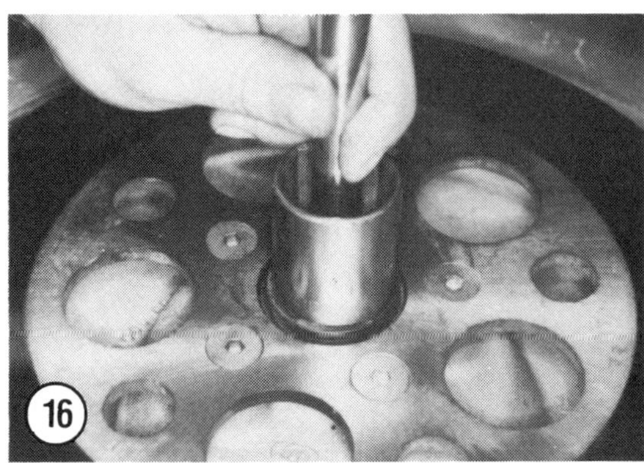

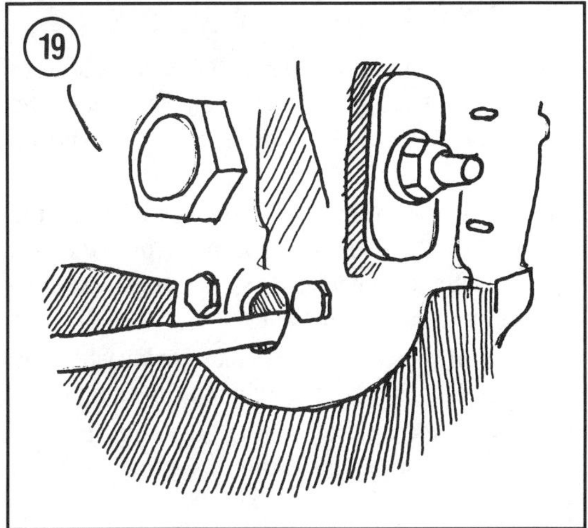

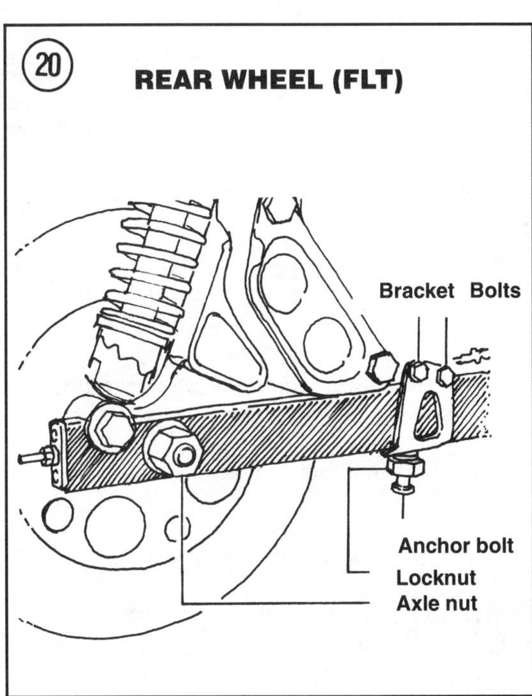


disc or cast wheels is damaged, the wheel assembly must be replaced; it cannot be repaired.

## REAR WHEEL

Proper rear wheel maintenance and inspection is critical to the safe operation of your Harley. The following section describes complete service to the rear wheel. Service to the rear hub and bearings is described later in this chapter.

### Removal/Installation (FLT/FXRT Models With Enclosed Sprocket)

You can remove the rear wheel in one of two ways. You can remove the rear wheel without removing the rear sprocket or you can remove the wheel and sprocket at the same time. Select the following procedure that is applicable to the required wheel or sprocket service.

#### *Service without disconnecting sprocket*

This procedure describes removal of the rear wheel without having to remove the rear sprocket.

1. Support the bike so that the rear wheel clears the ground by a minimum of 4 inches.
2. *FLT:* Remove the saddlebags (**Figure 17**). Remove the muffler bolts and remove the mufflers.
3. Remove the sprocket housing plug (**Figure 18**). Then remove the sprocket screws with a 3/8 in. Allen wrench. See **Figure 19**.

4A. *FLT:* Referring to **Figure 20**, perform the following:

a. Remove the lower shock bolts and lower the wheel to the ground.
b. Remove the brake anchor bracket bolts and anchor.
c. Remove the axle nut, lockwasher and washer.
d. Tap the axle out of the wheel far enough so that the axle clears the wheel but still supports the sprocket and drive chain housing.
e. Move the brake caliper up and away from the wheel.
f. Separate the rear wheel from the sprocket and chain housing. Remove the rear wheel.

4B. *FXRT:* Perform the following:

a. Remove the axle nut.

b. Tap the axle out of the wheel far enough so that the axle clears the wheel but still supports the sprocket and left chain adjuster.
c. Remove the spacer located between the brake caliper bracket and the swing arm.
d. Slide the caliper bracket to the right and lower the rear wheel to the ground.

*NOTE*
*Insert a piece of wood or vinyl tubing into the caliper between the brake pads in place of the disc. That way, if the brake pedal is inadvertently depressed, the piston will not be forced out of the cylinder. If this does happen, the caliper might have to be disassembled to reseat the piston and the system will have to be bled. By using the wood or vinyl tubing, bleeding the brake should not be necessary when installing the wheel.*

*CAUTION*
*Do not set the wheel down on the disc surface, as it may be scratched or warped. Either lean the wheel against a wall or place it on a couple of wood blocks.*

## Installation

1. Remove the vinyl tubing or pieces of wood from the brake caliper.
2. Apply a light coat of anti-seize or multipurpose grease to the rear axle prior to installation.
3A. *FLT*: Install the rear wheel as follows:
a. Make sure the right-hand axle spacer is installed through the oil seal.
b. Roll the rear wheel into position. The brake disc should be on the right-hand side.
c. Move the brake caliper into position between the wheel and swing arm.
d. Lift the wheel up and install the rear axle from the left-hand side. Push the axle in until it bottoms out. Make sure the axle centers the brake caliper.
e. Install the rear axle washer, lockwasher and axle nut. Tighten the axle nut finger-tight.
f. Install the brake anchor and its 2 bracket bolts onto the brake caliper (**Figure 20**). Then install the brake line and clip to the front anchor bracket bolt. Tighten the anchor bolt until it just starts to compress the rubber, then stop and tighten the locknut. Hold the anchor bolt when tightening the locknut.
g. Install the lower shock bolts and tighten securely.
3B. *FXRT*: Install the rear wheel as follows:
a. Roll the rear wheel into position. The brake disc should be on the right-hand side.

*CAUTION*
*When installing the rear wheel, carefully insert the brake disc into the caliper assembly. Do not damage the leading edges of the brake pads during installation.*

b. Lift the wheel up and install the rear axle from the left-hand side. Insert the axle through the wheel and stop it before it exits the opposite side.
c. Align the right-hand axle spacer with the brake caliper and swing arm and push the axle through the wheel, axle spacer and brake caliper until it bottoms out.
d. Install the rear axle washer, lockwasher and axle nut. Tighten the axle nut finger-tight.
4. Apply a light coat of engine oil to the sprocket screws and tighten to the torque specification listed in **Table 3**.
5. Perform the *Rear Axle End Play Check* in this chapter.
6. Adjust the drive chain as described in Chapter Three.
7. Tighten the axle nut to the torque specifications listed in **Table 3**.
8. Adjust the rear brake as described in Chapter Three.
9. Rotate the wheel several times to make sure it rotates freely and that the rear brake works properly.

*WARNING*
*Do not ride the motorcycle until the rear brake is working properly.*

10. Install the mufflers and saddlebags.

### *Wheel removal/installation with sprocket*

Refer to **Figure 21** for this procedure.
1. Support the bike so that the rear wheel clears the ground.

(21)

## ENCLOSED DRIVE CHAIN (FLT/FXRT)



1. Rubber boot
2. Rear wheel sprocket housing
3. Swing arm bracket
4. Bolt
4A. Washer
5. Bolt
6. Lockwasher
7. Nut
8. Bolt
9. Lockwasher
10. Nut
11. Bolt
12. Axle bracket
13. Screw
14. Drive chain
15. Spacer
16. Spacer
17. Bearing
18. Dust shield
19. Spacer washer
19A. Spacer
20. Bearing race
20A. Bearing shim
21. Bearing retainer
21A. Sleeve
22. Seal
23. Filler plug
24. Oil level plug
25. Sprocket screw plug
26. O-ring
27. Sprocket screw (5)
28. Screw

2. *FLT*: Remove the saddlebags (**Figure 17**). Remove the left-hand muffler bolts and remove the muffler.

3. Disconnect the upper and lower rear wheel housing rubber boots.

4. Position the boots so that you have access to the drive chain. Then rotate the rear wheel and locate the master link. Disconnect the rear drive chain master link. A chain breaker may be required to separate the chain.

5. Remove the bolts and washers securing the swing arm bracket to the sprocket housing and remove the bracket.

6. Loosen and remove the axle nut, lockwasher and flat washer.

7. Slide the axle out of the wheel and allow the wheel to drop to the ground. Locate and remove the right-hand axle spacer on FXRT models.

8. Remove the rear wheel and the rear wheel sprocket housing.

*NOTE*
*Insert a piece of wood or vinyl tubing in the caliper between the brake pads in place of the disc. That way, if the brake pedal is inadvertently depressed, the piston will not be forced out of the cylinder. If this does happen, the caliper might have to be disassembled to reseat the piston and the system will have to be bled. By using the wood or vinyl tubing, bleeding the brake should not be necessary when installing the wheel.*

*CAUTION*
*Do not set the wheel down on the disc surface, as it may be scratched or warped. Either lean the wheel against a wall or place it on a couple of wood blocks.*

9. If necessary, disassemble the sprocket housing assembly as described later in this chapter.

## Installation

Refer to **Figure 21** for this procedure.

1. Remove the vinyl tubing or pieces of wood from the brake caliper.

2. Apply a light coat of anti-seize or multipurpose grease to the rear axle prior to installation.

*CAUTION*
*When installing the rear wheel in Step 3, carefully insert the brake disc into the caliper assembly. Do not damage the leading edges of the brake pads during installation.*

3A. *FLT*: Install the rear wheel as follows:

a. Make sure the right-hand axle spacer is installed through the oil seal.
b. Roll the rear wheel into position, making sure the sprocket housing is facing forward. The brake disc should be on the right-hand side.
c. Lift the wheel up and install the rear axle from the left-hand side. Push the axle in until it bottoms out. Make sure the axle centers the brake caliper.
d. Install the rear axle washer, lockwasher and axle nut. Tighten the axle nut finger-tight.

3B. *FXRT*: Install the rear wheel as follows:

a. Roll the rear wheel into position, making sure the sprocket housing is facing forward. The brake disc should be on the right-hand side.
b. Lift the wheel up and install the rear axle from the left-hand side. Insert the axle through the wheel and stop it before it exits the opposite side.
c. Align the right-hand axle spacer with the brake caliper and swing arm and push the axle through the wheel, axle spacer and brake caliper until it bottoms out.
d. Install the rear axle washer, lockwasher and axle nut. Tighten the axle nut finger-tight.

4. Tighten the axle nut to the torque specification listed in **Table 3**.

5. Perform the *Rear Axle End Play Check* in this chapter.

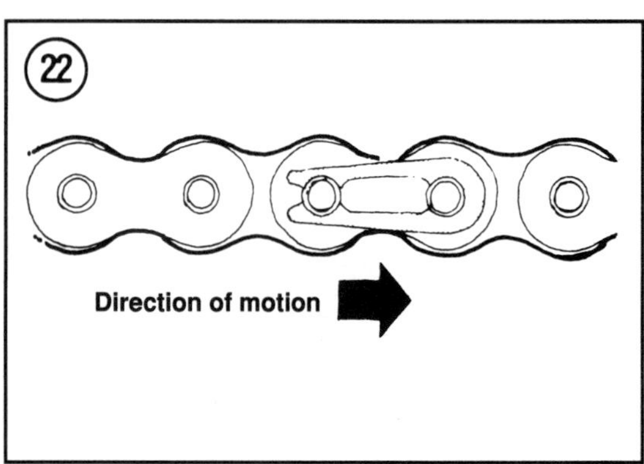

6. After performing Step 5, loosen the rear axle nut and reconnect the drive chain with a new master link. Attach the master link open clip so that the closed end faces in the direction of chain travel. See **Figure 22**.

7. Adjust the drive chain as described in Chapter Three.

8. Tighten the axle nut to the torque specification listed in **Table 3**.

9. Adjust the rear brake as described in Chapter Three.

10. Apply a coating of RTV silicone sealant to the rubber chain cover boots and to the chain housing mating surfaces. Secure the boots with its screws.

11. Secure the chain housing to the swing arm with the bracket and bolts. Tighten the bolts securely.

12. Rotate the wheel several times to make sure it rotates freely and that the rear brake works properly.

*WARNING*
*Do not ride the motorcycle until the rear brake is working properly.*

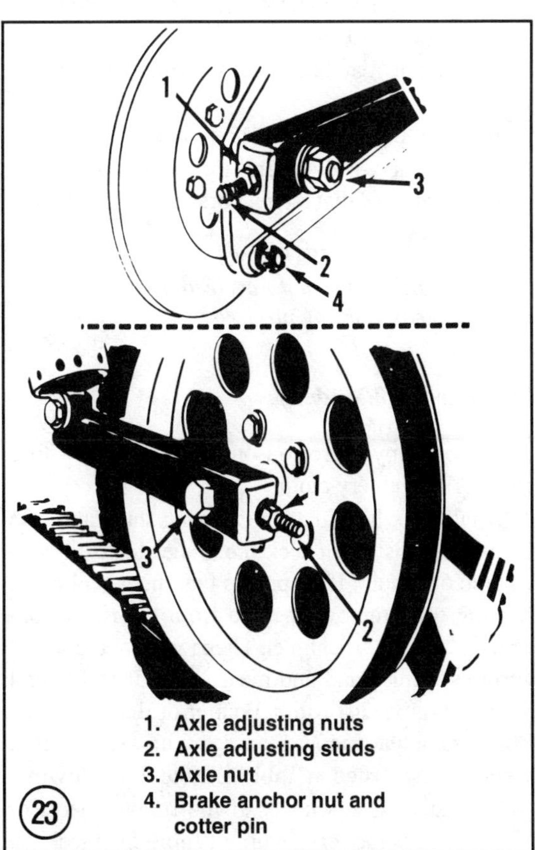


(23)
1. Axle adjusting nuts
2. Axle adjusting studs
3. Axle nut
4. Brake anchor nut and cotter pin

**Removal**
**(Open Drive Belt or Drive Chain Models)**

*NOTE*
*Due to the number of models and years covered in this manual, this procedure represents a typical rear wheel removal and installation.*

1. Support the bike so that the rear wheel clears the ground.
2. Remove the belt or chain guard.
3. Remove the saddlebags, if necessary.
4. Remove and discard the rear axle cotter pin, if so equipped.
5. Loosen the drive chain or belt adjusting locknuts and adjuster bolts. See **Figure 23**, typical.
6. Loosen and remove the axle nut and washers. See **Figure 23**, typical.
7. Slide the axle out of the wheel and allow the wheel to drop to the ground.
8. Remove the axle spacer.
9. Lift the drive chain or belt off of the sprocket and remove the rear wheel.

*NOTE*
*Insert a piece of wood or vinyl tubing in the caliper between the brake pads in place of the disc. That way, if the brake pedal is inadvertently depressed, the piston will not be forced out of the cylinder. If this does happen, the caliper might have to be disassembled to reseat the piston and the system will have to be bled. By using the wood or vinyl tubing, bleeding the brake should not be necessary when installing the wheel.*

*CAUTION*
*Do not set the wheel down on the disc surface. Either lean the wheel against a wall or place it on a couple of wood blocks.*

10. Inspect the rear wheel assembly as described in this chapter.

**Installation**

1. Clean the axle in solvent and dry thoroughly. Make sure the bearing surfaces on the axle are free from burrs and nicks.

10

2. Apply an anti-seize lubricant or wheel bearing grease to the axle shaft prior to installation.
3. Remove the vinyl tubing from the brake caliper.

*CAUTION*
*When installing the rear wheel in Step 4, carefully insert the brake disc into the caliper assembly. Do not damage the brake pad leading edges during installation.*

4A. *1984-1990 FLT and FXR belt drive*: Perform the following:
   a. Position the rear wheel into the swing arm, through the drive belt and install the axle spacer.
   b. Install the axle through the left-hand side.
   c. Install the washer and lockwasher (1984-1988) and the axle nut.

4B. *1984-1990 FLT and FXR chain drive*: Perform the following:
   a. Position the rear wheel into the swing arm and install the axle spacer.
   b. Install the axle through the left-hand side.
   c. Install the washer, lockwasher and axle nut.

4C. *1985-1986 FX*: Perform the following:
   a. Position the rear wheel into the swing arm, through the drive belt and install the axle spacer.
   b. Install the axle through the left-hand (wire spoke wheel) or right-hand (alloy wheel) side.
   c. Install the washer, lockwasher (if used) and the axle nut.

4D. *1991 FLT*: Perform the following:
   a. Position the rear wheel into the swing arm, through the drive belt and install the axle spacer.
   b. Install the axle through the left-hand side.
   c. Install the washer and the axle nut.

4E. *1991 FXR*: Perform the following:
   a. Position the rear wheel into the swing arm, through the drive belt and install the axle spacer.
   b. Install the axle through the right-hand side.
   c. Install the washer and the axle nut.

5. Tighten the axle nut to the torque specification listed in **Table 3**.
6. Perform the *Rear Axle End Play Check* in this chapter.

*NOTE*
*If it is necessary to tighten the axle nut a bit more to line up the axle nut slot with the cotter pin hole in the axle, make sure you do not exceed the maximum torque specification listed in* ***Table 3****.*

7A. *Drive chain models*: Perform the following:
   a. After performing Step 6, loosen the rear axle nut and reconnect the drive chain with a new master link. Attach the master link open clip so that the closed end faces in the direction of chain travel. See **Figure 22**.
   b. Adjust the drive chain as described in Chapter Three.
   c. Tighten the axle nut to the torque specification listed in **Table 3**.
   d. Install a new cotter pin (if used) and bend the ends over to lock it.

7B. *Belt drive models*: Perform the following:
   a. Adjust the drive belt as described in Chapter Three.
   b. Tighten the axle nut to the torque specification listed in **Table 3**.
   c. Install a new cotter pin (if used) and bend the ends over to lock it.

8. Adjust the rear brake as described in Chapter Three.
9. Install all parts previously removed.
10. Rotate the wheel several times to make sure it rotates freely and that the rear brake works properly.

*WARNING*
*Do not ride the motorcycle until the rear brake is working properly.*

### Inspection (All Models)

1. Remove any corrosion on the rear axle with a piece of fine emery cloth.
2. Install the wheel in a wheel truing stand and spin the wheel. Visually check the wheel for excessive wobble or runout. If it appears that the wheel is not running true, remove the tire from the rim as described later in this chapter. Then remount the wheel into the truing stand and measure axial and lateral runout (**Figure 24**) with a pointer or dial indicator. Compare actual runout readings with service limit specifications listed in **Table 1**. Note the following:
   a. Cast or disc wheels: If the runout meets or exceeds the service limit (**Table 1**), check the

wheel bearings as described under *Rear Hub* in this chapter. If the wheel bearings are okay, cast and disc wheels will have to be replaced. Inspect the wheel for signs of cracks, fractures, dents or bends. If a wheel is damaged, it must be replaced.

*WARNING*
*Do not try to repair any damage to cast or disc wheels as it will result in an unsafe riding condition.*

b. Wire spoke wheel: If the wheel bearings, spokes, hub and rim assembly are not damaged, the runout can be removed by accurately truing the wheel. Refer to *Spoke Adjustment* in this chapter. If the rim is dented or damaged in any way, the rim should be replaced and the wheel respoked and trued by a Harley-Davidson dealer or a qualified mechanic familiar with Harley wheel service.

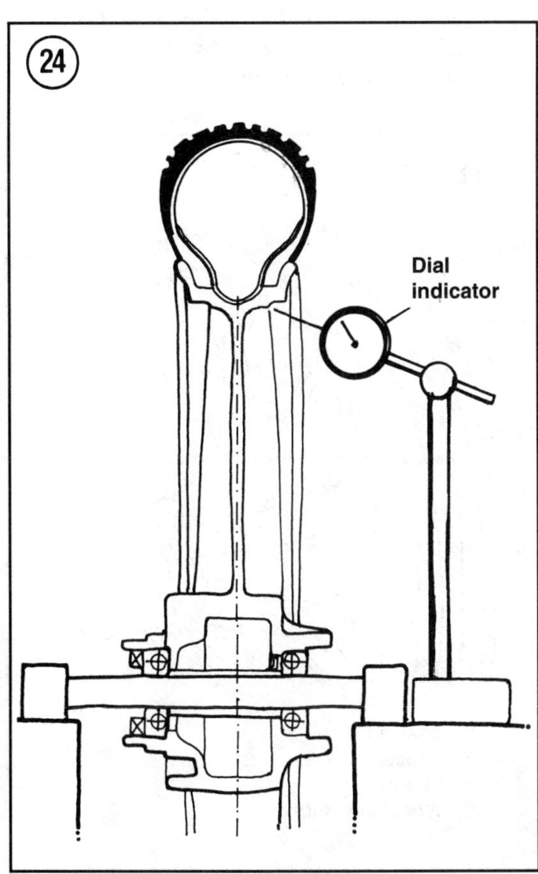


3. While the wheel is off, check the tightness of the brake disc bolts. Refer to the tightening torque listed at the end of Chapter Thirteen.

## Rear Wheel Bearing End Play Check/Adjustment (1984-Early 1991 FXR and FX)

Proper wheel bearing end play is important to your Harley's steering and handling performance. Incorrect wheel bearing end play can cause poor handling or excessive bearing side loading and premature bearing wear.

On these models, wheel bearing end play is controlled by the length of the center hub spacer; see **Figures 26, 28-30** for your model. End play should be checked each time the rear wheel is removed or whenever unstable handling is felt.

1. Support the bike so that the rear wheel is off the ground.
2. Tighten the rear axle nut to the torque specification in **Table 3**.
3. Mount a dial indicator so that the plunger contacts the end of the axle (**Figure 5**). Grasp the wheel and move it back and forth by pushing and pulling it along the axle center line. Read axle end play by observing the dial indicator needle and compare to specification in **Table 1**.
4. If the end play is incorrect, replace the center hub spacer; see **Figure 25, Figure 28, Figure 30A** or **Figure 30B** for your model. Install a longer spacer for less end play and a shorter spacer for more end play. Different length spacers can be purchased through Harley-Davidson dealers. To install a new spacer, remove the wheel and disassemble the rear hub as described under *Rear Hub* in this chapter. Reverse to install. Recheck end play after reinstalling rear wheel.



## Rear Wheel Bearing End Play Check/Adjustment (FLT and Late 1991-on FXR)

Proper wheel bearing end play is important to your Harley's steering and handling performance. Incorrect wheel bearing end play can cause poor handling or excessive bearing side loading and premature bearing wear.

On these models, wheel bearing end play is controlled by the spacer installed between the spacer washer and the center hub spacer. End play should be checked each time the rear wheel is removed or whenever unstable handling is felt.

1. Support the bike so that the rear wheel is off the ground.

2. Tighten the rear axle nut to the torque specification in **Table 3**.

3. Mount a dial indicator so that the plunger contacts the end of the axle (**Figure 5**). Grasp the wheel and move it back and forth by pushing and pulling it along the axle center line. Read axle end play by observing the dial indicator needle and compare to specification in **Table 1**.

4. If the end play is incorrect, replace the spacer; see **Figure 26, Figure 27** or **Figure 29** for your model. Install a thinner spacer for less end play and a thicker spacer for more end play. Do not replace the center hub spacer as this spacer is not used to adjust end play. Different thickness spacers can be purchased through Harley-Davidson dealers. To install a new spacer, remove the wheel and disassemble the rear hub as described under *Rear Hub* in this chapter. Reverse to install. Recheck end play after reinstalling the rear wheel.

## REAR HUB

Tapered roller bearings are installed on each side of the hub. A center hub spacer installed between the bearings maintains rear wheel bearing end play within a specified range; see *Rear Wheel Bearing End Play* in this chapter. Oil seals are installed on the outside of each bearing to protect them from dirt and other contaminants. The bearings can be removed from the hub after removing the outer oil seals. The bearing races are pressed into the hub and should not be removed unless they require replacement.

### Disassembly/Inspection/Reassembly (Enclosed Drive Chain)

Refer to **Figure 21** and **Figure 25** for this procedure.

*NOTE*
*The bearings and races are matched pairs. Label all parts so that they can be returned to their original position.*

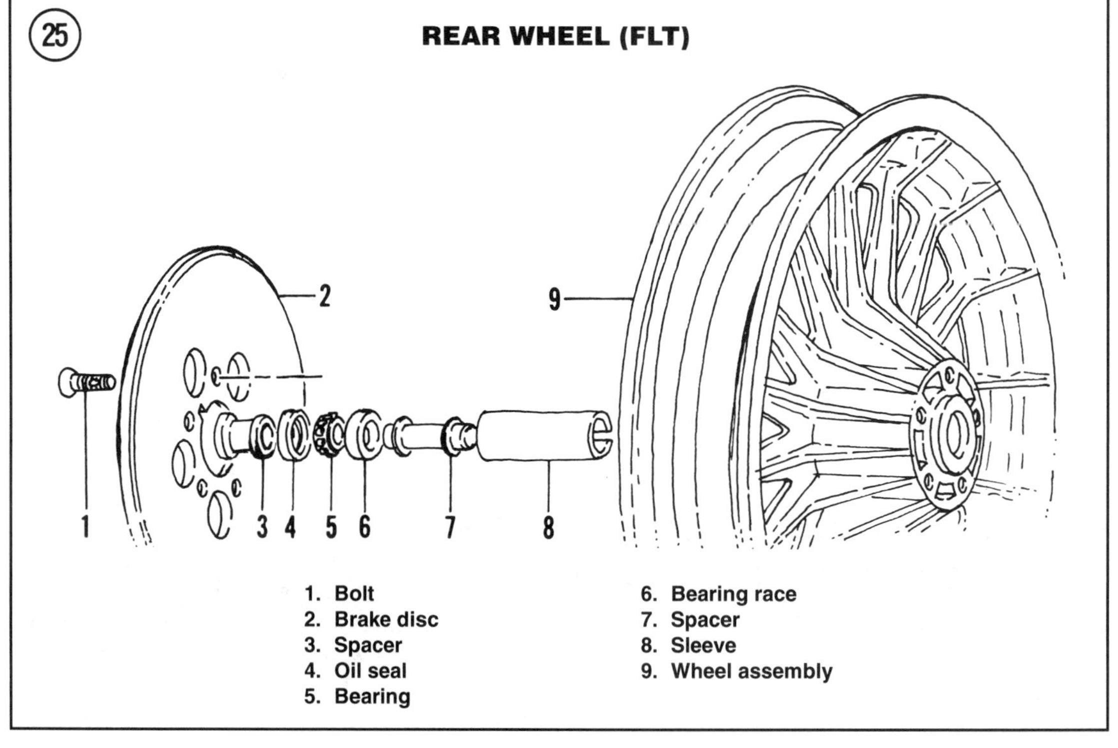

1. Remove the bearing assembly from the rear sprocket as follows:
   a. Remove the front and rear sprocket housing bolts. Then remove the bolts, lockwashers and nuts from the right-hand side of the housing.
   b. Remove the bolts, axle bracket and screws from the left-hand side of the housing and separate the housings.
   c. Remove the sprocket assembly and spacer from the wheel.
   d. Pry the left-hand oil seal out of the hub. Then remove the bearing, spacer washer and sleeve from the left-hand side.
   e. Pry the right-hand oil seal out of the hub.
2. Remove the bearing assembly from the rear wheel as follows:
   a. Remove the right-hand axle spacer. Then pry the oil seal out of the hub.
   b. Remove the bearing, hub spacer and sleeve from the hub.
3. Wash the bearings thoroughly in clean solvent and dry with compressed air. Wipe the bearing races off with a clean rag dipped in solvent. Then check the roller bearings and races for wear, pitting or excessive heat (bluish tint). Replace the bearings and races as a complete set. Replace the bearing races as described in Step 4. If the bearing and its race does not require replacement, proceed to Step 5. If you are going to reinstall the original bearing(s), pack the bearing thoroughly with grease and wrap it in a clean, lint-free cloth or wax paper. Wipe a film of grease across the bearing race. If the bearings and races are not lubricated after cleaning them, they may rust.

4A. *Sprocket bearing race replacement*: If the bearing race is worn, press the old race out of the sprocket. Reverse to install a new race.

4B. *Hub bearing race replacement*: Replace as follows:
   a. A universal bearing remover should be used to remove the race from the hub. If this tool is unavailable, insert a drift punch through the hub and tap the race out of the hub with a hammer. Move the punch around the race to make sure the race is driven squarely out of the hub. Do not allow the race to bind in the hub as this can damage the race bore in the hub. Severe damage to the race bore will require replacement of the hub.
   b. Clean the inside and outside of the hub with solvent. Dry with compressed air.
   c. Wipe the outside of the new race with oil and align it with the hub. Using a bearing driver or socket with an outside diameter slightly smaller than the bearing race, drive the race into the hub until it bottoms out on the hub shoulder. As you drive the race into the hub, stop and check your work to make sure the race is square with the hub bore. Do not allow the race to bind during installation.

*NOTE*

*If you do not have the proper size tool to drive the race into the hub, have a Harley-Davidson dealer or independent repair shop install the race. Do not attempt to install the race by driving it into the hub with a small diameter punch or rod.*

5A. *Sprocket assembly*: Perform the following:
   a. Pack the bearing with bearing grease.
   b. Wipe the bearing race with grease.
   c. Pack the seal lip cavity of each seal with grease.
   d. Assemble the bearing assembly in the order shown in **Figure 21**.

5B. *Hub assembly*: Perform the following:
   a. Blow any dirt or foreign matter out of the hub prior to installing the bearing.
   b. Wipe the ends of the bearing spacer with grease. Install the sleeve and spacer into the hub.

*NOTE*

*If you are performing this procedure to correct wheel bearing end play, make sure you install the correct length center hub spacer.*

   c. Wipe the bearing race with grease.
   d. Pack the bearing with grease and install it into the bearing race.
   e. Pack the seal lip cavity with grease.
   f. Install the oil seal so that it is flush with the hub bearing bore surface.
   g. Wipe the oil seal lip with oil and install the axle spacer into the seal.

6. If the brake disc was removed, refer to Chapter Thirteen for correct procedures and tightening torques.

7. If the driven sprocket was removed, install it as described in this chapter.

8. After the wheel is installed on the bike and the rear axle is tightened to the specified torque specification, the bearing end play should be checked as described in this chapter.

9. If the hub on wire spoke wheels is damaged, the hub can be replaced by removing the spokes and having a dealer assemble a new hub. If the hub on disc or cast wheels is damaged, the wheel assembly must be replaced; it cannot be repaired.

### Disassembly/Inspection/Reassembly (All Models Except Enclosed Drive Chain)

Refer to the following illustration for your model:

a. FLT models with open sprocket: **Figure 26**.
b. All 1991-on FLT models: **Figure 27**.
c. FXR models with open sprocket: **Figure 28**.
d. FX models with wire spoke wheels: **Figure 29**.
e. FX models with cast wheels: **Figure 30**.

*NOTE*
*If you are performing this procedure to replace or exchange the axle spacer, remove the bearing opposite the brake disc.*

*NOTE*
*The bearings and races are matched pairs. Label all parts so you don't mix them up during reassembly.*

1. Remove the rear wheel as described in this chapter.

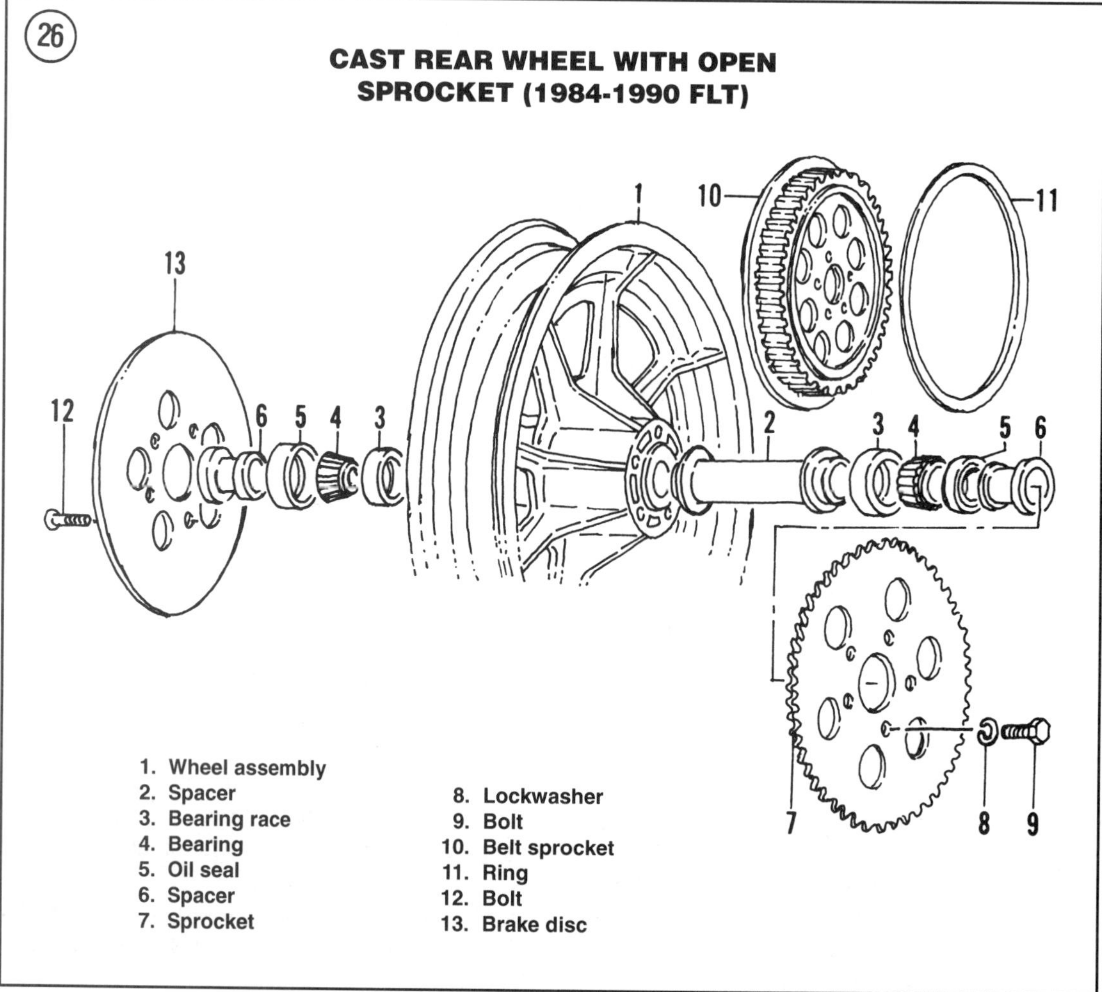

(27)

## REAR HUB (1991-ON FLT CAST AND LACED WHEELS)

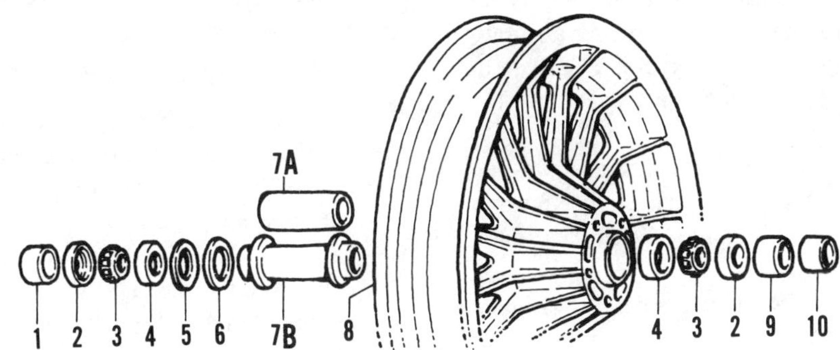


1. Spacer
2. Oil seal
3. Bearing
4. Bearing race
5. Spacer washer
6. Spacer

7A. Center hub spacer (cast wheel)
7B. Center hub spacer (laced wheel)
8. Wheel
9. Spacer
10. Outer spacer



## REAR HUB (1984-EARLY 1991 FXR EXCEPT ENCLOSED DRIVE CHAIN)

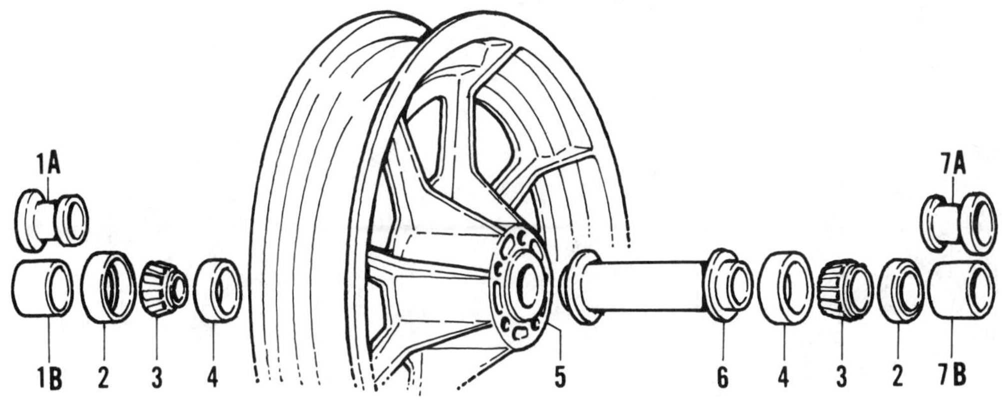


1A. Spacer (early model)
1B. Spacer (late model)
2. Oil seal
3. Bearing
4. Bearing race

5. Wheel
6. Center hub spacer
7A. Spacer (early model)
7B. Spacer (late model)

2. If necessary, remove the brake disc as described in Chapter Thirteen.
3. If necessary, remove the driven sprocket as described in this chapter.
4. Pry the right-hand oil seal (without the spacer) out of the hub (**Figure 31**). If you are using a screwdriver, place a rag underneath the screwdriver to prevent hub damage. Remove the spacer from the oil seal, if so equipped.
5A. *1991-on FLT*: Remove bearing, spacer washer, spacer and center hub spacer from the hub. Note that the spacer washer has a shoulder. Wash these parts thoroughly in solvent.
5B. *All other models*: Remove the bearing (**Figure 32**) from its race. Then remove the center hub spacer from the hub and wash it thoroughly in solvent.
6. Repeat to remove the opposite bearing. Remember, the bearings are matched to their races; label the bearings if they are going to be reused.
7. Wash the bearings thoroughly in clean solvent and dry with compressed air. Wipe the bearing races off with a clean rag dipped in solvent. Then check the roller bearings and races for wear, pitting or excessive heat (bluish tint). Replace the bearings and races as a complete set. Replace the bearing races as described in Step 8. If the bearing and its race does not require replacement, proceed to Step 9. If you are going to reinstall the original bearing(s), pack the bearing thoroughly with grease and wrap it in a clean, lint-free cloth or wax paper. Wipe a film of grease across the bearing race (**Figure 33**). If the bearings and races are not lubricated after cleaning them, they may rust.
8. Replace the bearing races (**Figure 33**) as follows:
   a. A universal bearing remover should be used to remove the races from the hub. If this tool is unavailable, insert a drift punch through the hub and tap the race out of the hub with a hammer. Move the punch around the race to make sure the race is driven squarely out of the hub. Do not allow the race to bind in the hub as this can damage the race bore in the hub. Severe damage to the race bore will require replacement of the hub.
   b. Clean the inside and outside of the hub with solvent. Dry with compressed air.
   c. Wipe the outside of the new race with oil and align it with the hub. Using a bearing driver or socket with an outside diameter slightly smaller than the bearing race, drive the race into the hub until it bottoms out on the hub shoulder. As you drive the race into the hub, stop and check your work to make sure the

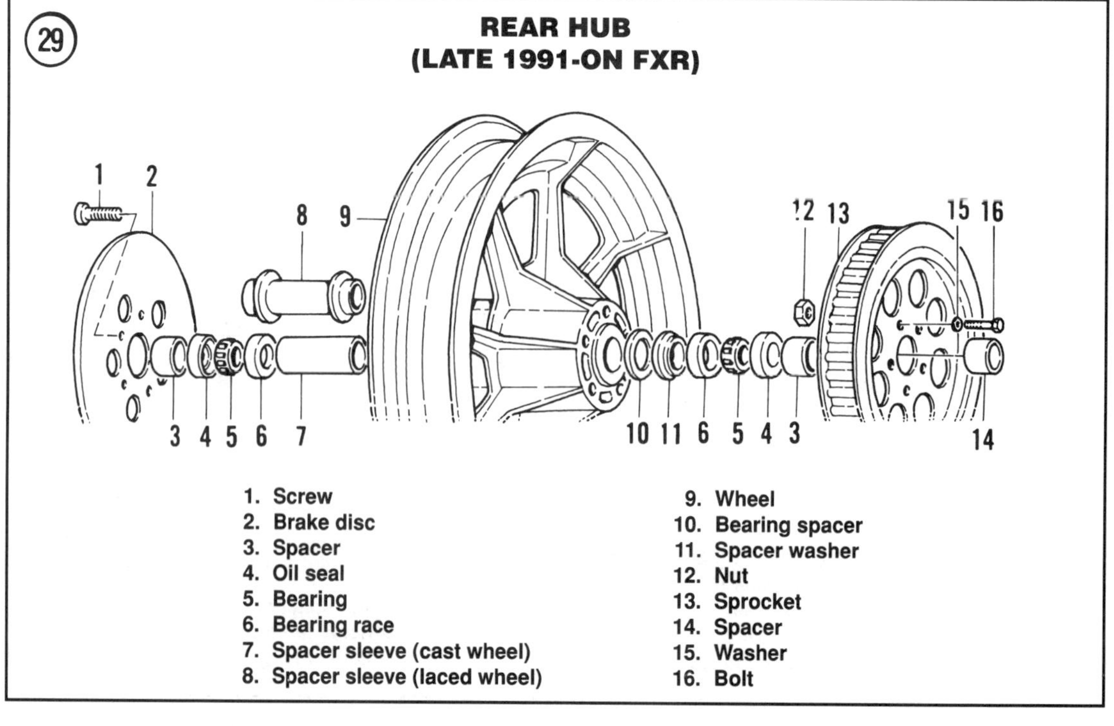

30 A

## LACED REAR WHEEL (FX)

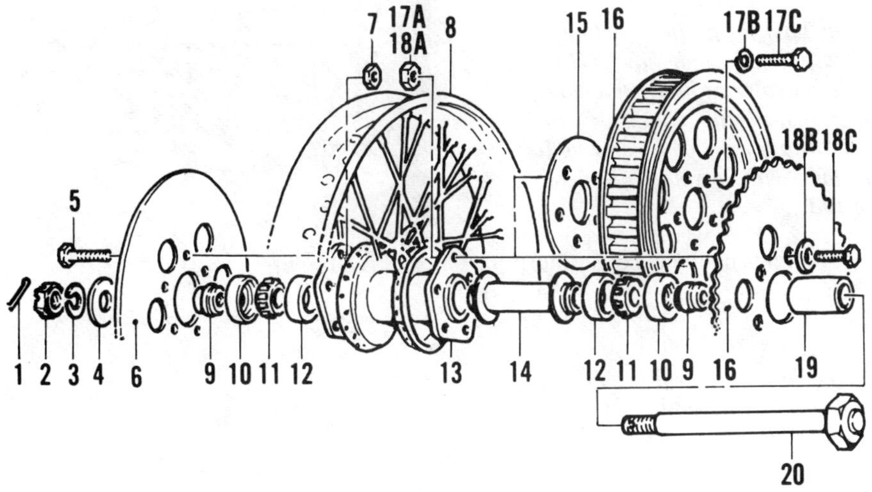

1. Cotter pin
2. Locknut
3. Lockwasher
4. Washer
5. Bolt
6. Brake disc
7. Nut
8. Rim
9. Spacer
10. Oil seal
11. Bearing
12. Bearing race
13. Rear hub
14. Spacer
15. Plate
16. Sprocket

17A. Nut
17B. Lockwasher
17C. Bolt
18A. Nut
18B. Washer
18C. Bolt
19. Spacer
20. Rear axle



30 B

## CAST REAR WHEEL (FX)

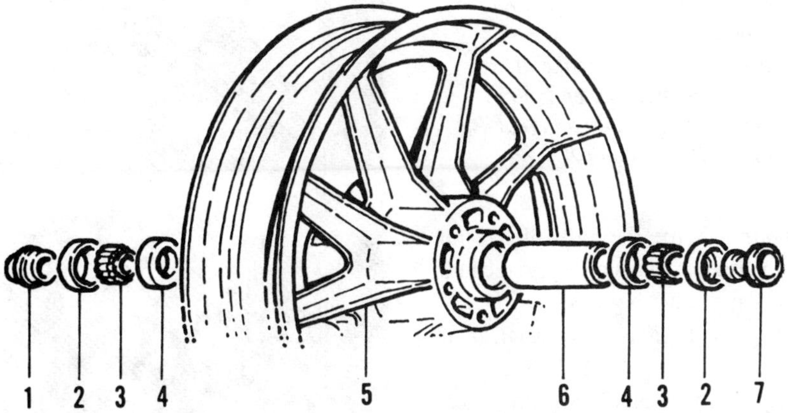

1. Spacer
2. Oil seal
3. Bearing
4. Bearing race
5. Wheel
6. Center hub spacer
7. Spacer

race is square with the hub bore. Do not allow the race to bind during installation.

*NOTE*
*If you do not have the proper size tool to drive the race into the hub, have a Harley-Davidson dealer or independent repair shop install the race. Do not attempt to install the race by driving it into the hub with a small diameter punch or rod.*

9. Blow any dirt or foreign matter out of the hub prior to installing the bearings.

*NOTE*
*If you are performing this procedure to correct wheel bearing end play, make sure you install the correct length spacer.*

10A. 1991-on FLT and late 1991-on FXR: Wipe the ends of the spacer with grease and install it into the hub. Install the spacer and spacer washer as shown in **Figure 27** or **Figure 29**. Install the spacer washer so that its shoulder faces toward bearing installed on same side.

*CAUTION*
*If the spacer washer is installed so that the large diameter faces the bearing, bearing damage may occur.*

*WARNING*
*On FXLR models with cast disc wheels, the spacer washer and spacer must be installed on the sprocket side of wheel. Installing these parts on the brake disc side will reduce wheel bearing end play. This may cause bearing seizure and rear wheel lock-up. Loss of control could cause personal injury.*

10B. *All other models*: Wipe the ends of the hub bearing spacer with grease and install it into the hub.
11. Wipe each bearing race with grease.
12. Pack the bearings with grease and install them in their bearing race.
13. Pack the seal lip cavity of each seal with grease.

*NOTE*
*When installing the oil seals in Step 14, use a bearing driver or socket with an OD slightly smaller than the oil seal (**Figure 34**) and carefully drive the oil*

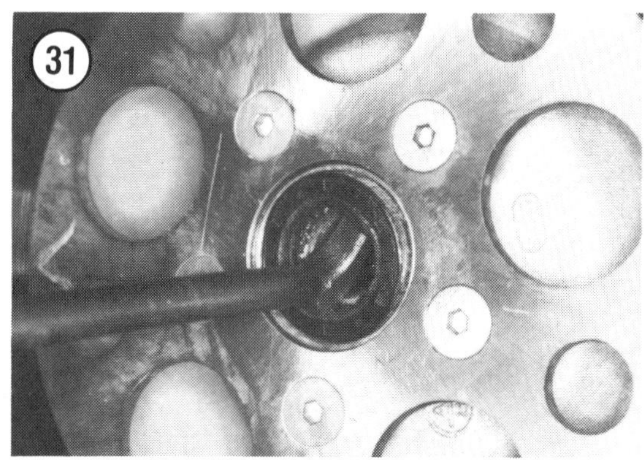
31

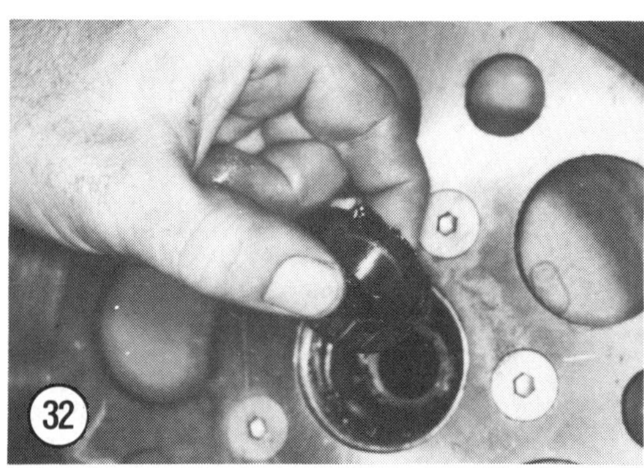
32

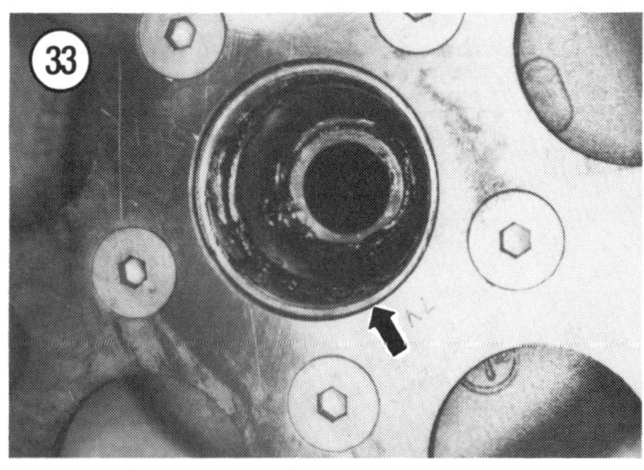
33

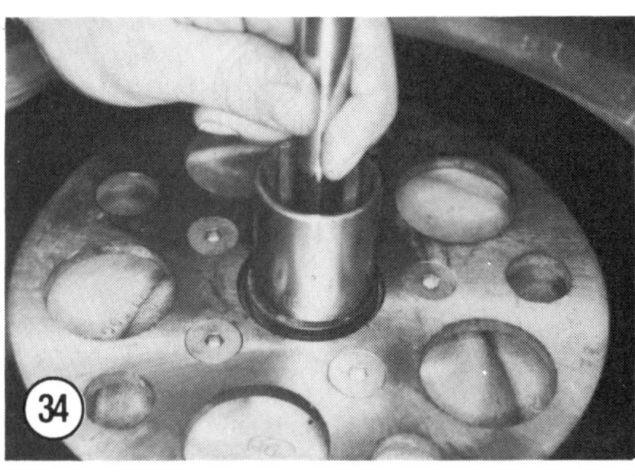
34

*seals into the hub. Install all oil seals so that their closed side faces out.*

14A. *1990 and earlier FLT*: Install both oil seals so that their outer surface is flush with the outer hub surface.

14B. *1991 FLT*: Install the oil seals as follows:

a. Cast wheels: Install the right-hand oil seal so that its outer surface is flush with the outer hub surface. Install the left-hand oil seal until its outer surface is 0.031 in. (0.79 mm) below the outer hub surface.

b. Wire spoke wheels: Install both oil seals so that their outer surface is flush with the outer hub surface.

14C. *1984-1990 FXR*: Install both oil seals so that their outer surface is 19/64-5/16 in. (7.54-7.94 mm) below the outer hub surface.

14D. *1991-on FXLR models with cast disc wheel:* Install the oil seals as follows:

a. Install the right-hand oil seal so that its outer surface is flush with the outer hub surface.

b. Install the left-hand oil seal until its outer surface is 0.31 in. (7.9 mm) below the outer hub surface.

14E. On all other 1991-on FXR models, install oil seals as follows:

a. *Cast wheels:* Install both oil seals so that their outer surface is 0.31 (7.9 mm) below the outer hub surface.

b. *Laced wheels:* Install both oil seals so that their outer surface is 0.26-0.28 in. (6.6-7.1 mm) below the outer hub surface.

14F. *FX*: Install the oil seals as follows:

a. Cast wheels: Install both oil seals so that their outer surface is 0.312 in. (7.9 mm) below the outer hub surface.

b. Wire spoke wheels: Install both oil seals so that their outer surface is 0.203-0.219 in. (5.16-5.56 mm) below the outer hub surface.

15. If the brake disc was removed, refer to Chapter Thirteen for correct procedures and tightening torques.

16. If the driven sprocket was removed, install it as described in this chapter.

17. After the wheel is installed on the bike and the rear axle tightened to the specified torque specification, the bearing end play should be checked as described in this chapter.

18. If the hub on wire spoke wheels is damaged, the hub can be replaced by removing the spokes and having a dealer assemble a new hub. If the hub on disc or cast wheels is damaged, the wheel assembly must be replaced; it cannot be repaired.

## DRIVEN SPROCKET ASSEMBLY

The driven sprocket is bolted to the rear wheel. On chain drive models, the sprocket is bolted to the hub using bolts, lockwashers and nuts. On belt drive models, the sprocket is bolted into the hub using threaded holes in the hub. A spacer is used between the sprocket and wheel hub on cast and disc wheel models.

### Removal/Installation

1A. *Models with closed drive chain*: Remove the rear wheel and sprocket as described in this chapter.

1B. *Models with open drive chain*: Perform the following:

a. Remove the rear wheel as described in this chapter.

b. Remove the bolts and nuts securing the sprocket to the hub and remove the sprocket. See **Figure 35**, typical.

c. Remove any sprocket spacer as required.

2. Installation is the reverse of these steps. Tighten the sprocket bolts to specifications in **Table 3**.

*NOTE*

*On some models, it will be necessary to check the bolt grade before tightening the bolts. Bolt grade can be determined by reading the bolt grade marks on the bolt heads. When replacing sprocket bolts, replace with the same grade bolt.*

### Inspection

Inspect the teeth on the sprocket. If the teeth are visibly worn, replace both sprockets and the drive chain or drive belt. **Figure 36** shows sprocket comparison for chain drive models. Never replace any one sprocket or chain as a separate item; worn parts will cause rapid wear of the new component.

## DRIVE CHAIN

### Removal/Installation

1. Loosen the rear axle nut, chain adjuster nuts and the anchor bolt (if so equipped).
2. Push the rear wheel as far forward in the swing arm as possible.
3. *Enclosed drive chain*: Remove the bolts holding the upper chain cover in place and slide the cover forward to expose as much of the upper chain run as possible. Use Bungee cords to hold the cover in place.
4. Turn the rear wheel and locate the drive chain master link on the rear sprocket.
5. Remove the master link spring clip and separate the chain. A chain breaker may be required to separate the chain.
6. If installing a new drive chain, connect the new chain to the old chain with the old master link. Pull the new chain through the front sprocket. If the original chain is to be reinstalled, connect it to an old chain or tie a piece of wire approximately 20 inches (50.8 cm) long to the drive chain. Pull the chain so that the old chain or wire is routed around the front sprocket. Disconnect the chain and remove it.
7. Install by reversing these removal steps while noting the following:
   a. Install a new drive chain master link spring clip with the closed end facing in the direction of chain travel (**Figure 37**).
   b. Adjust the drive chain as described in Chapter Three.
   c. Tighten the axle nut to the torque specification listed in **Table 3**.
   d. *Enclosed drive chain*: Apply a coating of RTV silicone sealant to the rubber chain cover and to the chain housing mating surfaces. Secure the boots with its screws.
   e. Rotate the wheel several times to make sure it rotates smoothly. Apply the brake several times to make sure it operates correctly.
   f. Adjust the rear brake as described in Chapter Three.

### Lubrication

For lubrication of the drive chain, refer to Chapter Three.

## DRIVE BELT

### Removal/Installation

1. Remove the rear wheel as described in this chapter.

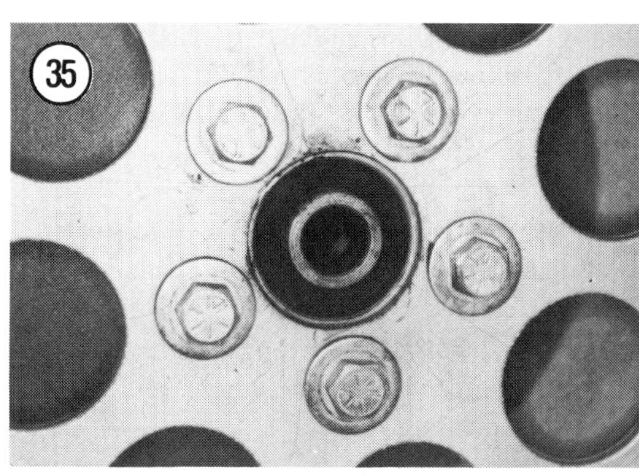


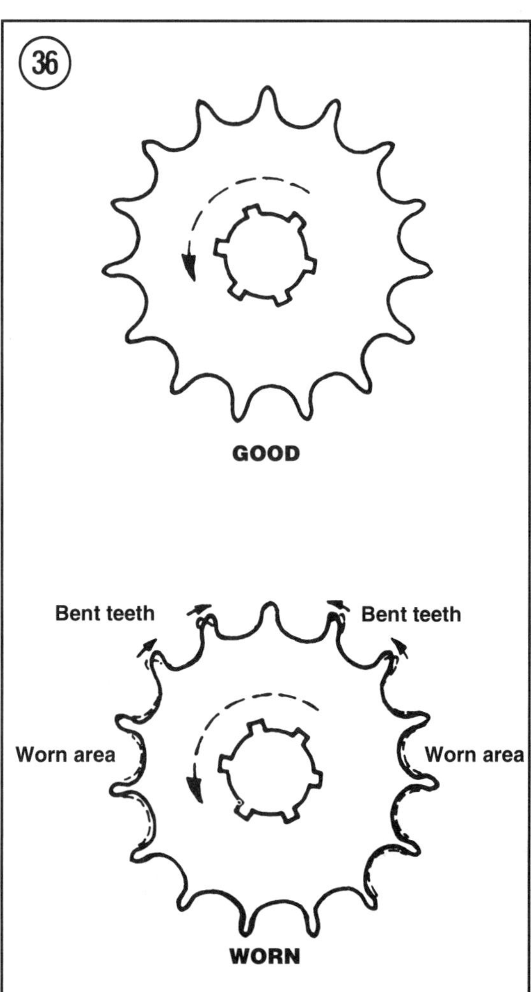

2. Remove the compensating sprocket and clutch as described in Chapter Five.
3. Remove the primary housing as described in Chapter Five.
4. Remove the swing arm as described in Chapter Twelve.
5. Remove the drive belt from the sprocket.
6. Installation is the reverse of these steps. Adjust the drive belt tension as described in Chapter Three.

### Inspection

The drive belt has a built-in polyethylene lubricant coating that burnishes off during break-in. Do not apply lubricants. Inspect the drive belt for wear or damage. Replace any belt that appears questionable. See **Figure 38**.

*CAUTION*
*When handling a drive belt, never bend the belt sharply as this will weaken the belt and cause premature failure.*

## WIRE SPOKE WHEELS

Wire spoke wheels consist of a rim, spokes and nipples and a hub (containing the bearings and the center hub spacer). The spokes are inserted through the hub and attached to the rim in a specific cross-over pattern. Spoke nipples secure the spokes to the rim. A rubber rim strip is inserted into the rim well.

Loose or improperly tightened spokes can cause hub damage and overall handling problems. Both wheels should be checked for looseness, missing or damaged spokes, rim damage, runout and balance at the maintenance intervals listed in Chapter Three. Wheel bearing service is described in this chapter.

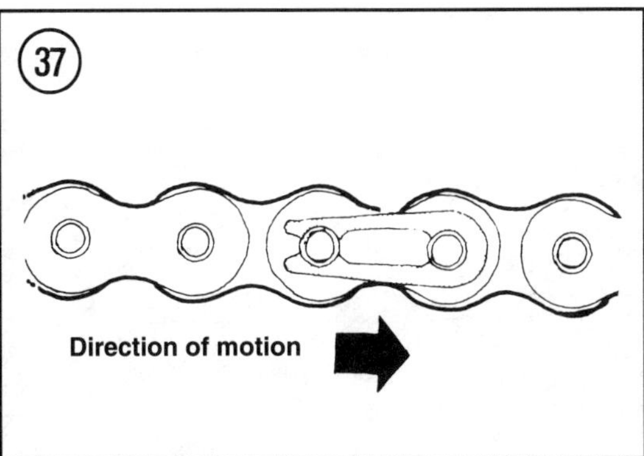


### Inspection and Replacement

1. To inspect the wheels, the wheel should be raised off of the ground so that it can spin freely. If you have access to a wheel truing stand, remove the wheel and mount it securely on the stand. If you do not have a stand, you can raise the front or rear off the ground and spin the wheel.

*NOTE*
*Wheel truing stands are expensive, but if you plan on servicing your Harley's wheels, you should either invest in a good truing stand or fabricate one. Another route you can take is to purchase a discarded swing arm from a motorcycle wrecking yard. The swing arm can be clamped securely in a vise and the wheel placed into position on the swing arm for servicing. When choosing a swing arm to be used as a truing stand, check the size of the swing arm to make sure that both of your Harley's wheels can fit into it with enough clearance for checking runout; measure the inside swing arm distance on your bike as a starting point. The rear wheel will be the wider of the two, though you may have to remove the tire from the front wheel for the wheel to fit into the swing arm.*

2. Check the rim for dents, cracks or other damage. Severe rim damaged is easily detected, though most small dents are discovered while the rim is spinning on a stand.
3. Check the hub for cracks or damage. Check closely where the spokes seat into the hub.
4. Check for bending, loose or broken spokes. Damaged spokes should be replaced as soon as they are detected, as they can destroy the hub. Replace a damaged spoke as follows:

*CAUTION*
*When replacing a broken spoke, do **not** bend the new spoke when installing it. If you cannot install a new spoke without bending it, you will have to loosen all of the spokes and then remove some of the spokes to provide clearance to install the new spoke. Because Harley wheels are laced to a specific offset dimension, wheel disassembly and retruing should be referred to a Harley-Davidson dealer or independent Harley repair shop.*

a. Remove the brake disc or rear sprocket as required.
b. Unscrew the nipple from the spoke and depress the nipple into the rim far enough to free the end of the spoke; take care not to push the nipple all the way in. Remove the damaged spoke from the hub and use it to match a new spoke of identical length.

*NOTE*
*Replacement spokes are generally sold through Harley-Davidson dealers in complete sets only, though you may find a dealer who stocks individual spokes, removed from damaged or discarded wheels, for sale in small quantities. If you purchase spokes in this manner, compare the replacement spoke with the corresponding spoke on the wheel. Spokes differ in length, size, head angle and length of spoke throat. Compare the spokes closely.*

c. If necessary, trim the new spoke to match the original and dress the end of the thread with a thread die. Install the new spoke in the hub and screw on the nipple; tighten it until the spoke's tone is similar to the tone of the other spokes in the wheel. After installing the spoke, seat its head into the hub as described in this chapter. Periodically check the new spoke; it will stretch and must be retightened several times before it takes a final set.

*NOTE*
*If a replacement spoke requires more than 2 turns to tighten it properly, the end of the spoke may protrude through the end of the nipple and puncture the tube. If necessary, remove the spoke and grind the end to a suitable length. To make sure that the spoke is not too long, remove the tube from the tire and check the end of the spoke.*

5. Spokes loosen with use and should be checked periodically. The "tuning fork" method for checking spoke tightness is simple and works well. Tap the center of each spoke with a spoke wrench or screwdriver (**Figure 39**) and listen for a tone. A tightened spoke will emit a clear, ringing tone and a loose spoke will sound flat or dull. All the spokes in a correctly tightened wheel will emit tones of similar

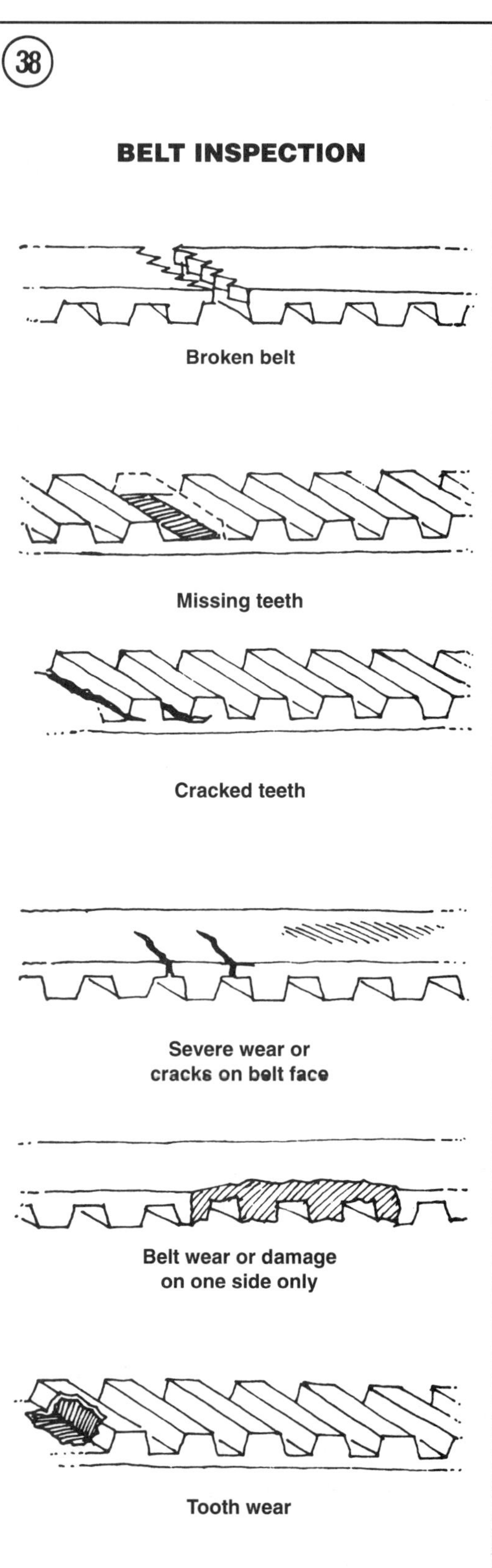

pitch but not necessarily the same precise tone. The tension of the spokes does not determine wheel balance.

## Spoke Adjustment

This section describes minor spoke adjustment. If a few spokes are loose, you can tighten the spokes with a spoke wrench. If there are many spokes loose, retruing will also be required. Wheels in which a large number of spokes were replaced or if the wheel is severely out of true should be serviced by a qualified Harley-Davidson mechanic as Harley wheels are laced to a specific offset dimension. This dimension must be adjusted, if required, when truing the wheel.

One way to check rim runout is to mount a dial indicator on the front fork or swing arm, so that it bears against the rim.

If you don't have a dial indicator, improvise one as shown in **Figure 40**. Adjust the position of the bolt until it just clears the rim. Rotate the rim and note whether the clearance increases or decreases. Mark the tire with chalk or light crayon at areas that produce significantly large or small clearances. Clearance must not change by more than 1/32 in. (0.8 mm).

To pull the rim out, tighten spokes which terminate on the same side of the hub and loosen spokes which terminate on the opposite side of the hub (**Figure 41**). In most cases, only a slight amount of adjustment should be necessary to true a rim. After adjustment, rotate the rim and make sure another area has not been pulled out of true. Continue adjustment and checking until runout is less than 1/32 in. (0.8 mm).

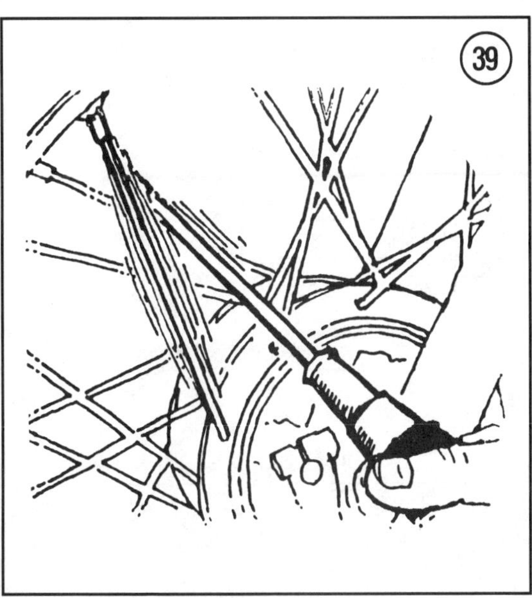


*CAUTION*
*Overtightening the spokes can cause spoke and nipple damage.*

## Spoke Seating

When spokes loosen or when installing new spokes, the head of the spoke should be checked for proper seating in the hub. If it is not seated correctly, it can loosen further and may cause severe hub damage.

If one or more spokes require reseating, hit the head of the spoke with a punch and hammer to seat it correctly in the hub.

True the wheel as described under *Spoke Adjustment* in this chapter.

## Rim Replacement

If the rim becomes bent or damaged, it should be replaced. A bent or distorted rim can cause serious handling problems.

If the spokes are not bent or damaged, they may be reused. Refer all service to a Harley-Davidson dealer or qualified Harley mechanic.



# CAST OR DISC WHEELS

The stock cast and disc wheels (**Figure 42**) consist of a single assembly equipped with bearings, oil seals and a hub spacer.

While these wheels are virtually maintenance free, they should be checked for damage at the maintenance intervals listed in Chapter Three. Wheel bearing service is in this chapter.

## Inspection and Replacement

1. Remove the wheel and mount it on a wheel truing stand.
2. Mount a dial indicator or pointer near the rim bead as shown in **Figure 40**. Spin the wheel and measure lateral and radial runout. The maximum lateral and

radial runout dimension is listed in **Table 1**. If the runout exceeds this dimension, check the wheel bearings as described in this chapter.

3. If the wheel's bearings are okay, the wheel will have to be replaced as the wheel cannot be serviced. Inspect the wheel for signs of cracks, fractures, dents or bends. If the wheel is damaged, it must be replaced.

*WARNING*
*Do not try to repair any damage to a cast or disc wheel as it will result in an unsafe riding condition.*

## WHEEL BALANCE

An unbalanced wheel is unsafe. Depending on the degree of unbalance and the speed of the motorcycle, the rider may experience anything from a mild vibration to a violent shimmy which may result in loss of control.

This procedure covers static balancing, which requires a wheel stand in which a wheel can be rotated. Dynamic balancing requires the use of a machine that spins the wheel. For dynamic wheel balancing, take the wheels to a motorcycle dealer.

On alloy wheels, weights are attached to the flat surface on the rim (**Figure 43**). On wire spoke wheels, the weights are attached to the spoke nipples (**Figure 44**).

Before you attempt to balance the wheel, check to be sure that the wheel bearings are in good condition and properly lubricated. The wheel must rotate freely.

1. Remove the wheel to be balanced.
2. Mount the wheel on a fixture such as the one in **Figure 45** so it can rotate freely.
3. Give the wheel a spin and let it coast to a stop. Mark the tire at the lowest point.
4. Spin the wheel several more times. If the wheel keeps coming to rest at the same point, it is out of balance.

5A. *Alloy wheels*: Tape a test weight to the upper (or light) side of the wheel (**Figure 43**).

5B. *Wire spoke wheels*: Attach a weight to the upper or light side of the wheel on the spoke (**Figure 44**).

6. Experiment with different weights until the wheel, when spun, comes to rest at a different position each time.
7. Remove the test weight and install the correct size weight.
8. When applying weights to alloy wheels, note the following:

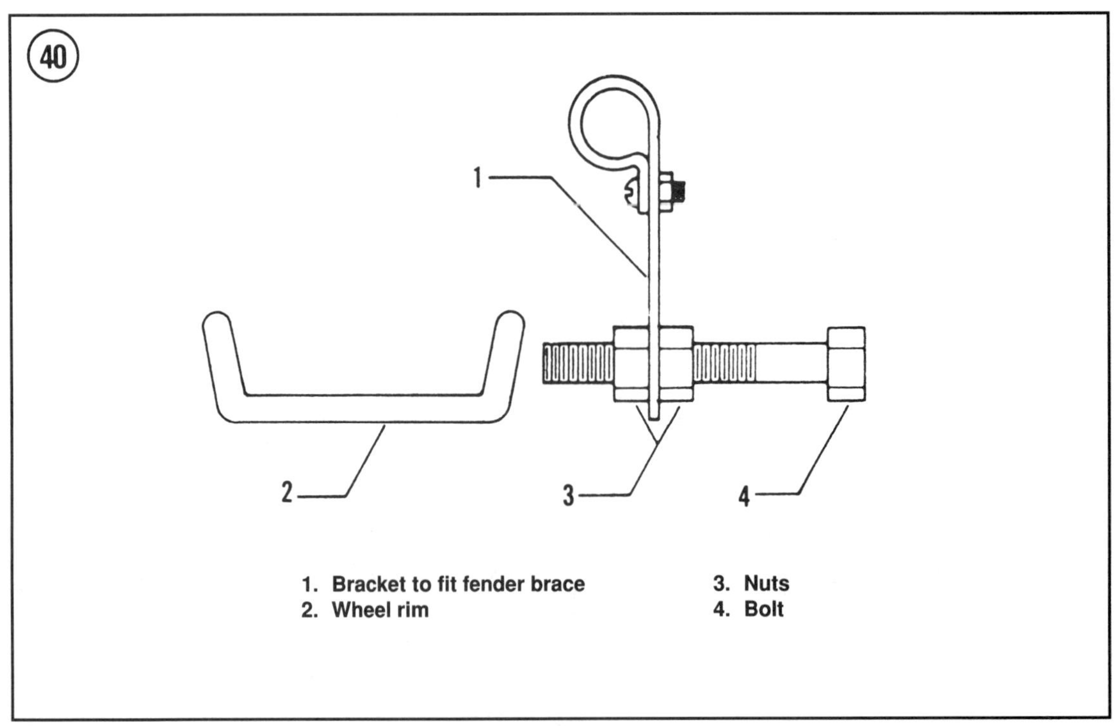


1. Bracket to fit fender brace
2. Wheel rim
3. Nuts
4. Bolt

a. Self-adhesive weights can be purchased through Harley-Davidson dealers in black, silver and gold colors.

b. Weights are attached to the flat surface on the rim (**Figure 43**). Clean the rim to remove all road residue before installing the weights; otherwise, the weights may fall off.

c. Weights should be added in 1/4 oz. (5 g) increments. If 1 oz. (10 g) or more must be added to one location on the wheel, apply half the amount to each side of the rim.

d. Harley-Davidson recommends that the wheel should not be used for 48 hours after installing weights to allow the weight adhesive to cure properly.

9. When fitting weights on wire spoke wheels for the final time, crimp the weights onto the spoke with slip-joint pliers.

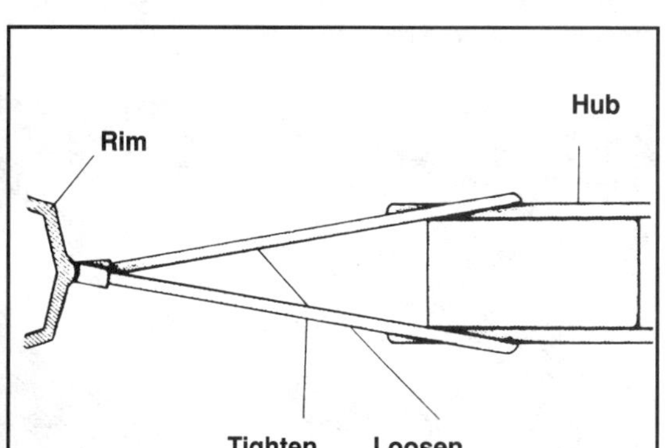

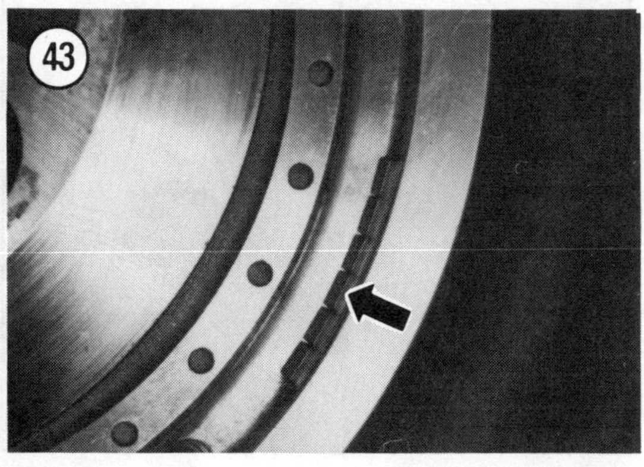


## TIRES

Proper tire service includes frequent inflation checks and adjustment as well as tire inspection, removal, repair and installation practices. By maintaining a routine tire maintenance schedule, tire damage or other abnormal conditions can be de-

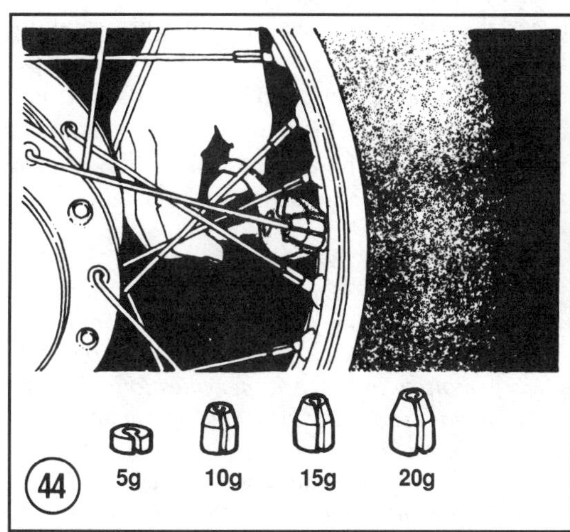


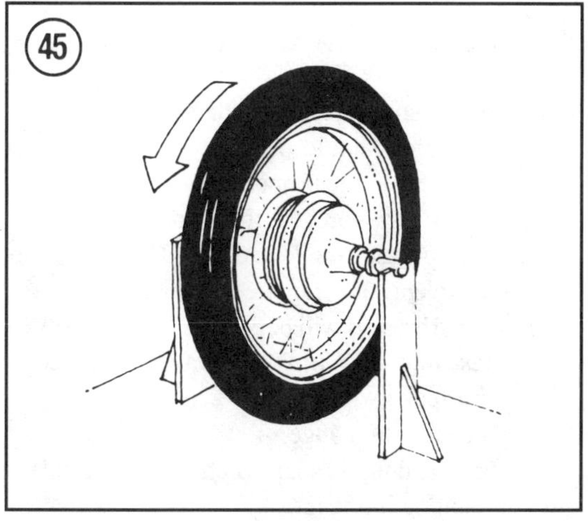


10

tected and repaired before they affect the operation and handling of your motorcycle. Refer to Chapter Three for general tire inspection and inflation procedures.

### Inspection

Visually inspect the tires for tread wear, cracks, cuts, aging and other damage. Check the tire for areas where the tread has broken or torn out. Stones imbedded between the tread rows can be carefully pried out with a key or screwdriver. Check the tread closely for secondary damage after removing the stone or other foreign objects. Uneven tread wear can be caused by improper inflation pressure, vehicle overloading or an unbalanced tire.

Run your hand along the sidewall and check for bulges or knots. If a bulge is noted, mark the area with chalk and then remove the tire from the rim; check the inside and outside of the tire carefully, looking for broken or separated plies. This type of damage can cause the tire to blow out. Likewise, if a tire is damaged on the outside, the tire should be removed from the rim and the inside checked carefully for broken or separated plies or other damage.

*WARNING*

*If you suspect tire damage, the tire should be removed from the rim and examined closely inside and out. Tires exhibiting bulges or other questionable damage should be inspected by a motorcycle technician before the tire is put back into use. A damaged or deformed tire can fail and cause you to lose control.*

### Service Notes

Before changing tires, note the following:

1. Tire changing should only be undertaken when you have access to the proper tools:
   a. At least 2 motorcycle tire irons.
   b. Rim protectors (part No. HD-01289 or equivalent) or scrap pieces of leather.
   c. A bead breaker will be required when breaking tires from alloy rims and may be required on wire spoke wheels.
   d. Accurate tire gauge.
   e. Water and liquid soap solution or a special tire mounting lubricant.
   f. Talcum powder for tube tires.
2. The alloy wheels can be easily damaged. Special care must be taken with tire irons when changing a tire to avoid scratches and gouges to the outer rim surface. Insert scraps of leather between the tire iron and the rim to protect the rim from damage.
3. When removing a tubeless tire, take care not to damage the tire beads, inner liner of the tire or the wheel rim flange. Use tire levers or flat handled tire irons with rounded ends—do not use screwdrivers or similar tools to remove tires.

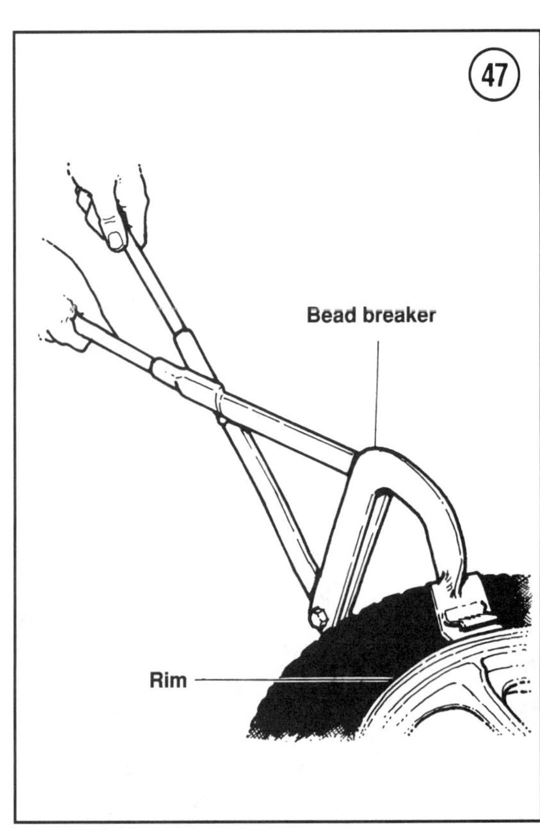

## Removal

*NOTE*
*If you do not have access to a motorcycle tire changer, you will probably be servicing the tire with the wheel placed on the ground. To avoid scratching or damaging the brake disc or wheel, place the wheel on a piece of plywood or other soft surface. If you do a lot of tire changing, you may want to construct a small wooden frame that, along with getting the wheel off the ground, will make it easier to work on the tire during changing.*

1. Remove the wheel from the motorcycle and place it on a suitable stand or surface.
2. Place a chalk mark on the tire aligning the tire with the valve stem (**Figure 46**). This helps to maintain tire and wheel balance during reassembly.
3. Remove the valve cap and unscrew the valve core to deflate the tire or tube. Block the valve core with your hand or the core removal tool to keep it from flying out. Remove the valve core and store it with the valve cap.
4. Press the entire bead on both sides of the tire into the center of the rim. If the bead is tight, a bead breaker (**Figure 47**) will be required.

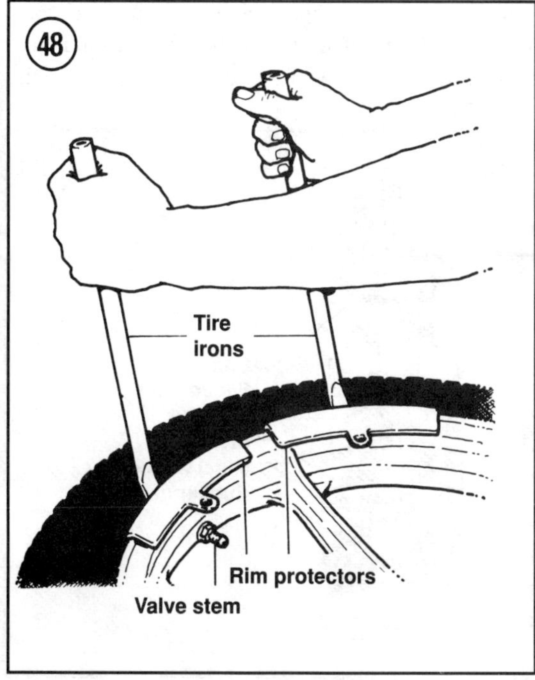


*CAUTION*
*Do **not** attempt to insert the tire irons between the tire bead and rim flange to break the bead. This can permanently damage both the tire and rim.*

5. Lubricate the beads with a tire lubricant or soapy water.
6. Place rim strips (**Figure 48**) along the rim near the valve stem and insert the tire iron under the bead next to the valve, making sure the tire iron contacts the rim strip and not the rim. Step on the side of the tire opposite the valve stem with your knee and pry the bead over the rim with the tire iron.

*CAUTION*
*Do not use excessive force when prying the tire over the rim or you may stretch or break the bead wires in the tire.*

7. Insert a second tire iron next to the first to hold the bead over the rim. Then work around the tire with the first tool prying the bead over the rim (**Figure 49**). On tube-type tires, be careful not to pinch the inner tube with the tools.
8. On tube-type tires, use your thumb and push the valve from its hole in the rim to the inside of the tire. Carefully pull the tube out of the tire and lay it aside.

10

*NOTE*
*Step 9 is required only if it is necessary to remove the tire from the rim completely, such as for tire replacement or tubeless tire repair.*

9A. *Tube-type tires*: Stand the wheel upright. Insert a tire tool between the second bead and the same side of the rim that the first bead was pried over. Force

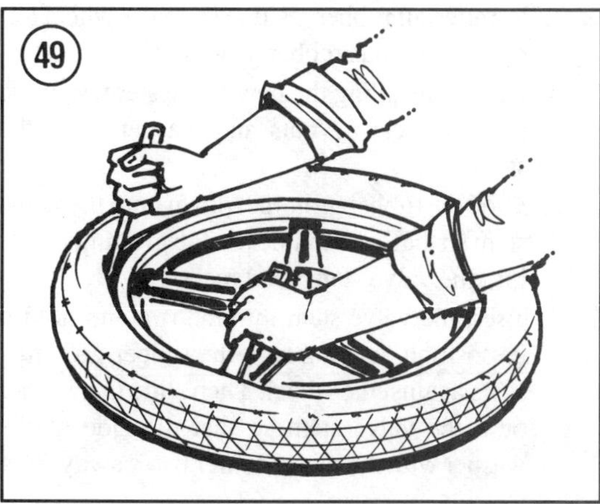

the bead on the opposite side from the tool into the center of the rim. Pry the second bead off the rim, working around the wheel with 2 tire irons as with the first. Remove the rim band.

9B. *Tubeless tires*: The second bead can generally be removed from the rim without having to use tire irons. Relubricate the second bead thoroughly and stand the wheel upright. Grasp the wheel at the top with one hand to steady it and then lift and pull the second bead over the top of the rim at the top of the wheel and remove the tire.

## Inspection

1. *Tubeless tires*: Alloy wheels use either a bolt-in type valve stem (**Figure 50**, typical) or an automotive snap-in valve stem (**Figure 51**). Inspect the rubber grommet or where the valve stem seats against the inner surface of the wheel. If it's starting to deteriorate or has lost its resiliency, replace the valve stem as this is a common location of air loss.

*NOTE*
*Because of weight and design configurations, valve stems should be replaced with O.E.M. Harley-Davidson valve stems. In addition, the bolt-in valve stems used on 16 in. (40.6 cm) and 19 in. (48.2 cm) wheels are different. Make sure to purchase the correct type of valve stem for your wheel. See your Harley-Davidson dealer.*

2A. *Bolt-in valve stems*: To replace the valve stem:

a. Loosen and remove the 2 valve stem nuts.
b. Remove the valve stem from the wheel, together with its washer and rubber grommet.
c. Remove all rubber residue from the wheel left by the previous rubber grommet.
d. Before installing the new valve stem, remove the valve cap, 2 nuts and washer from the stem.
e. Slide the rubber grommet down onto the valve stem so that the shoulder on the grommet seats into the valve stem head recess.
f. Insert the valve stem into the rim and hold it in position, making sure the rubber grommet seats against the wheel. Then slide the washer onto the valve stem so that the side of the washer with the raised center faces away from the rim.
g. Install the first valve stem nut and tighten to 20-25 in.-lb. (2.3-2.8 N•m).
h. Hold the first valve stem nut with a wrench, then install and tighten the second nut to 40-60 in.-lb. (4.6-6.9 N•m).

2B. *Automotive type valve stems*: To replace the valve stem:

a. Using a valve stem remover, pull the valve stem out of the rim.
b. Remove all rubber residue from the wheel left by the old valve stem.
c. Wet the new valve stem with water and insert it up through the rim. Thread a valve stem installation tool onto the end of the new valve stem and pull it through the rim until its indicator ring is visible all the way around the stem. See **Figure 51**.

3. Clean the rim thoroughly to remove all dust and dirt residue. Use steel wool, a stiff wire brush or sandpaper to remove rust from wire wheels.

*CAUTION*
*Work carefully when removing burrs or other rough spots from the rim flange on alloy wheels; otherwise, you may damage the air-sealing surfaces, requiring replacement of the wheel.*

4. Mount the wheel on a truing stand (if available) and check the rim-to-tire mating surface for dents, burrs or other rough spots. Emery cloth can be used to remove burrs on alloy wheels. A file or sandpaper can be used to remove burrs on wire spoke wheels.

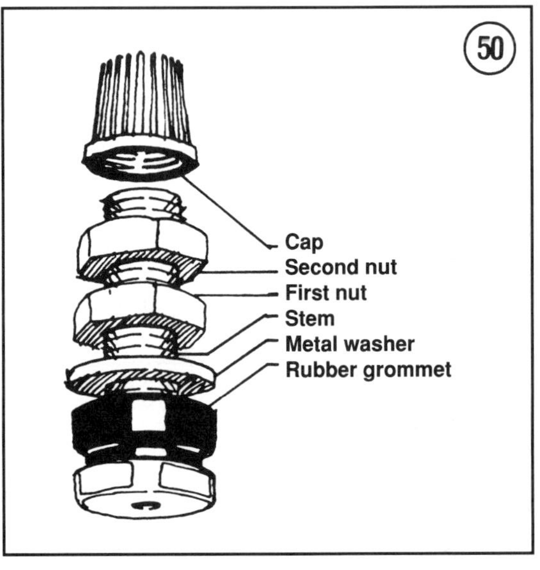

5. Check the wheel for dents or other damage. If the wheel has been dented by an accident or from running into a curb or other hard object, it should be replaced. On wire spoke wheels, the rim can be replaced by a qualified mechanic. On cast and disc wheels, the entire wheel assembly must be replaced.

*WARNING*
*Never operate your motorcycle with a bent wheel that has been straightened. The wheel may fail while under use and cause you to lose control.*

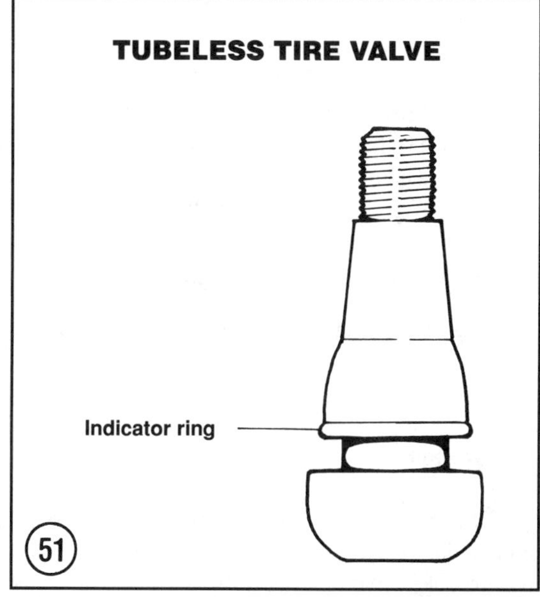

6. Check wheel runout as described in this chapter. Check for protruding spokes on wire wheels. File or grind the end of the spokes as required.
7. If you have access to compressed air, blow out the inside of the tire casing to remove all dust and dirt. Run your hand along the tire casing and check for small nails, cracks or other damage.
8. If a tire has been punctured, refer to *Tire Repairs* in this chapter.
9. *Tube-type tires*: Inspect the rim band for tearing or excessive wear. Replace the rim band if necessary. Install the valve core into the tube and then fill the tube with air. Check the tube for leaks. If the tube holds air, check the base of the valve stem for tearing or other signs of wear that may cause the tube to fail later. If the tube is damaged, replace it. Do not attempt to repair a tube unless you are in an emergency situation (i.e., you find yourself in the middle of Death Valley, a flat tire, no spare tube and vultures circling overhead). If you patch a tube, replace it with a new tube as soon as possible. Refer to *Tube Repairs* in this chapter.

## Installation

1. A new tire may have balancing rubbers inside. These are not patches and should not be disturbed. A colored spot near the bead indicates a lighter point on the tire. This spot should be placed next to the valve stem (**Figure 52**).
2. Install the rim band over the wheel (wire spoke wheels) and align the hole in the rim band with the hole in the rim. If you replaced the rim band, make sure it is the correct diameter and width for your wheel.
3. Align the tire with the rim so that the directional arrows molded in the tire's side wall face in the normal rotation position.

*NOTE*
*On some tires, the rotation arrow may have to be reversed, depending on whether the tire is mounted on the front or rear wheel. Follow the directions on the tire side wall or the tire manufacturer's instructions.*

4. Lubricate both beads of the tire with soapy water.
5. With the tire properly aligned with the wheel, press the first bead over the rim, working around the tire in both directions with your hands only (**Figure**

**53**). If necessary, use a tire iron (with rim protectors) for the last few inches of bead (**Figure 54**).

6. On tube-type tires, inflate the tube just enough to round it out. Too much air will make installation difficult. Wipe the outside of the tube with talcum powder to help reduce friction between the tire and tube during operation. Place the tube on top of the tire, aligning the valve stem with the matching hole in the rim. Then insert the tube into the tire. Lift the upper tire bead away from the rim with your hand and insert the tube's valve stem through the rim hole. Check the tube to make sure that the valve stem is straight up (90°), not cocked to one side. If necessary, reposition the tube in the tire. If the valve stem wants to slide out of the hole and back into the tire, install the valve stem nut at the top of the valve; do not tighten the nut yet.

7. Relubricate the upper bead with soapy water if necessary.

8. Starting 180° away from the valve stem, press the upper bead into the rim. Using tire tools and rim protectors, work around the rim to the valve. On tube-type tires, the last few inches will offer you the most difficulty and the greatest chance of pinching the tube. Work the tire tools carefully to prevent pinching the tube.

9. On tube-type tires, the valve stem should be straight up (90°). If the valve is cocked to one side, align the tube by sliding the tire along the rim one way or the other while holding the rim securely. When the valve stem is straight up, screw the valve nut onto the valve, but do not tighten it against the rim. After aligning the tube with the rim, check that the tube was not forced outward so that it rests between the tire bead and the rim. If so, push the tube back into the tire; otherwise, the rim will pinch the tube when the tube is filled with air.

10. Check the bead on both sides of the tire for an even fit around the rim.

11. Relubricate both tire beads.

*WARNING*

*When seating the tire beads in Step 12, never inflate the tire beyond the tire manufacturer's maximum pressure specification listed on the tire's side wall. Exceeding this pressure could cause the tire or rim to burst, causing severe personal injury. If the beads fail to seat properly, deflate the tire and relubricate the beads. Never stand directly over a tire while inflating it.*

12A. *Tube-type tires*: Inflate the tube to its maximum tire pressure to seat the beads in the rim. If the beads do not seat properly, release all air pressure from the tire and relubricate the tire beads. The tire is properly seated when the wheel rim and tire side wall lines are parallel (**Figure 55**). When the tire has seated properly on both sides, remove the valve core to deflate the tube; this allows the tube to straighten out, then reinstall the valve core and inflate the tire to the pressure reading listed in Chapter Three. Tighten the valve stem nuts and screw on the valve cap.

12B. *Tubeless tires*: Place an inflatable band around the circumference of the tire. Slowly inflate the band until the tire beads are pressed against the rim. Inflate the tire enough to seat it, deflate the band and remove it. The tire is properly seated when the wheel rim and tire side wall lines are parallel (**Figure 55**). Inflate the tire to the pressure reading listed in Chapter Three. Screw on the valve cap.

13. Check tire runout as described in this chapter.

14. Balance the wheel assembly as described in this chapter.

## Tire Runout

The tires should be checked for excessive lateral and radial runout after wheel mounting or if the motorcycle developed a wobble that cannot be traced to another component. The wheels should be

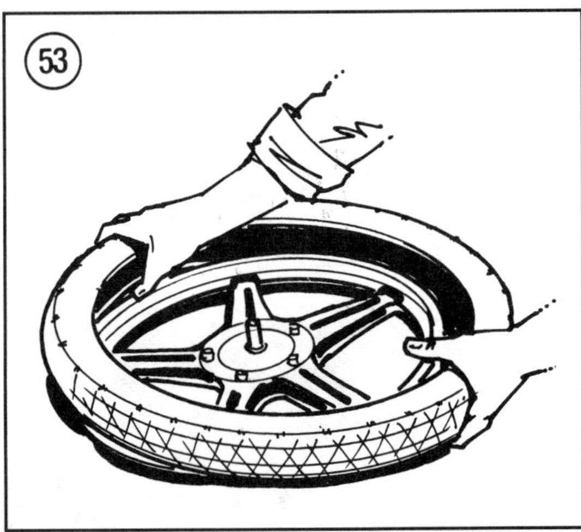

mounted on their axles when making the following checks.

1. *Lateral runout*: This procedure will check the tire for excessive side-to-side play. Perform the following:

   a. Position a fixed pointer next to the tire side wall as shown in **Figure 56**. The pointer tip should be located so that it is not directly in line with the molded tire logo or any other raised surface.
   b. Rotate the tire and measure the amount of lateral runout.
   c. The lateral runout should not exceed 0.080 in. (2 mm). If runout is excessive, remove the tire from the wheel and recheck the wheel's lateral runout as described in this chapter. If the runout is excessive, the wheel must be retrued (wire spoke wheels) or replaced (alloy wheels). If wheel runout is correct, the tire runout is excessive and the tire must be replaced.

54

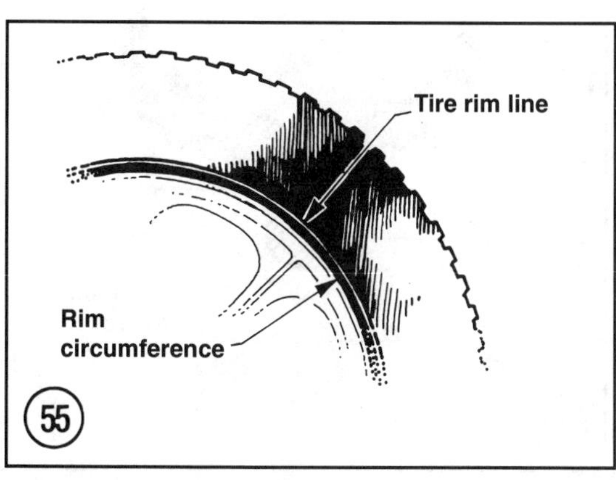


55

2. *Radial runout*: This procedure will check the tire for excessive up-and-down play. Perform the following:

   a. Position a fixed pointer at the center bottom of the tire tread as shown in **Figure 57**.
   b. Rotate the tire and measure the amount of radial runout.
   c. The radial runout should not exceed 0.090 in. (2.3mm). If runout is excessive, remove the tire from the wheel and recheck the wheels radial runout as described in this chapter. If the runout is excessive, the wheel must be retrued (laced wheels) or replaced (disc wheels). If wheel runout is correct, the tire runout is excessive and the tire must be replaced.

## TIRE REPAIRS (TUBE-TYPE TIRES)

Every rider will eventually experience trouble with a tire or tube. Repairs and replacement are fairly simple and every rider should know the techniques.

Patching a motorcycle tube is only a temporary fix. A motorcycle tire flexes too much and the patch could rub right off. However, a patched tube should get you far enough to buy a new tube.

### Tube Repair Kits

The repair kits can be purchased from motorcycle dealers and some auto supply stores. When buying, specify that the kit you want is for motorcycles.

There are 2 types of tube repair kits:

a. Hot patch.
b. Cold patch.

Hot patches are stronger because they actually vulcanize to the tube, becoming part of it. However, they are far too bulky to carry for roadside repairs and the strength is unnecessary for a temporary repair.

Cold patches are not vulcanized to the tube; they are simply glued to it. Though not as strong as hot patches, cold patches are still very durable. Cold patch kits are less bulky than hot and more easily applied under adverse conditions. A cold patch kit contains everything necessary and tucks easily in with your emergency tool kit.

### Tube Inspection

1. Remove the inner tube as described in this chapter.

2. Install the valve core into the valve stem and inflate the tube slightly. Do not overinflate.

3. Immerse the tube in water a section at a time. Look carefully for bubbles indicating a hole. Mark each hole and continue checking until you are certain that all holes are discovered and marked. Also make sure that the valve core is not leaking; tighten it if necessary.

*NOTE*
*If you do not have enough water to immerse sections of the tube, try running your hand over the tube slowly and very close to the surface. If your hand is damp, it works even better. If you suspect a hole anywhere, apply some water to the area to verify it.*

4. Apply a cold patch according to the manufacturer's instructions.

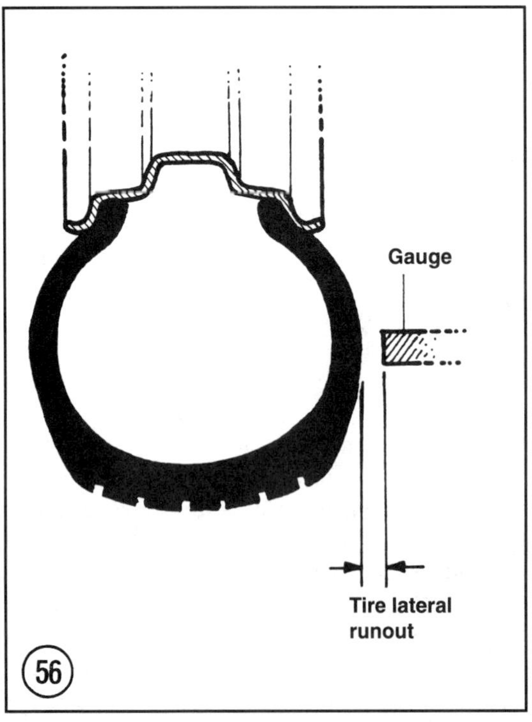


5. Dust the patch area with talcum powder to prevent it from sticking to the tire.

6. Carefully check the inside of the tire casing for small rocks or sand which may have damaged the tube. If the inside of the tire is split, apply a patch to the area to prevent it from pinching and damaging the tube again.

7. Check the inside of the rim.

8. Deflate the tube prior to installation in the tire.

## TIRE REPAIRS (TUBELESS TYPE)

Patching a tubeless tire on the road is very difficult. If both beads are still in place against the rim, a can of pressurized tire sealant may inflate the tire and seal the hole. The beads must be against the wheel for this method to work. Because an incorrectly patched tire might blow out and cause an accident, note the following:

a. Due to the variations of material supplied with different tubeless tire repair kits, follow the instructions and recommendations supplied with the repair kit.

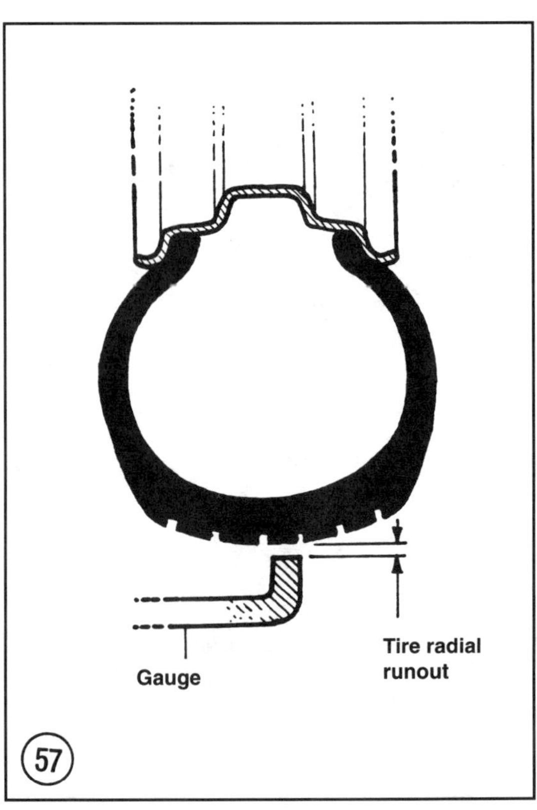

b. The tire industry recommends that tubeless tires be patched from the inside. Therefore, do not patch the tire with an external type plug. If you find an external patch on a tire, it is recommended that it be patch-reinforced from the inside or discarded.

c. Do not patch tires which have less than 1/16 in. (1.6 mm) of tread left.

d. Do not patch a tire in which the puncture hole is larger than 1/4 in. (6.35 mm).

e. Patches should only be applied to puncture holes in the tread area. Do not apply patches to holes in the tire's side wall.

f. When in doubt about whether or not to patch a tire, seek advice from your Harley-Davidson dealer or a qualified mechanic.



**Table 1 FRONT WHEEL SPECIFICATIONS**

| | |
|---|---|
| Alloy rim runout | |
| Lateral runout | |
| FLT and FXR | 0.047 in. (1.19 mm) |
| FXWG, FXEF and FXSB | 0.040 in. (1.02 mm) |
| Radial runout | |
| FLT and FXR | 0.031 in. 0.78 mm) |
| FXWG, FXEF and FXSB | 0.030 in. (0.76 mm) |
| Wire spoke rim runout | 0.031 in. (0.78 mm) |
| Wheel bearing end play | |
| FLT | |
| Front wheel | 0.002-0.006 in. (0.05-0.15 mm) |
| Rear wheel | |
| Enclosed drive chain models | 0.002-0.006 in. (0.05-0.15 mm) |
| All other models | |
| 1984-early 1991 | 0.004-0.018 in. (0.10-0.46 mm) |
| Late 1991-on | 0.002-0.006 in. (0.05-0.15 mm) |
| FXR | |
| 1984-early 1991 | |
| 1984 FXRT (rear wheel with enclosed drive chain) | |
| Front | 0.004-0.018 in. (0.10-0.46 mm) |
| Rear | 0.002-0.006 in. (0.05-0.15 mm) |
| All other models (front and rear wheels) | 0.004-0.018 in. (0.10-0.46 mm) |
| Late 1991-on | |
| Front and rear | 0.002-0.006 in. (0.05-0.15 mm) |
| FXWG, FXEF and FXSB | |
| Front and rear wheels | 0.004-0.018 in. (0.10-0.46 mm) |

**Table 2 FRONT WHEEL TIGHTENING TORQUES**

| | ft.-lb. | N•m |
|---|---|---|
| Front axle | | |
| FLT | 50-55 | 69-76 |
| FXR | | |
| 1984-1992 | 50 | 69 |
| 1993-on | 50-55 | 69-76 |
| FXWG, FXEF and FXSB | 50-55 | 69-76 |
| Front axle slider cap nuts | | |
| FLT | 9-13 | 12.4-17.9 |
| FXR | | |
| FXLR and 1987 FXRSE | 7-9 | 9.6-12.4 |
| All other models | 9-13 | 12.4-17.9 |
| FXWG, FXEF and FXSB | 9-13 | 12.4-17.9 |
| Front brake caliper | 25-30 | 34.5-41.4 |

**Table 3 REAR WHEEL TIGHTENING TORQUES**

| | ft.-lb. | N•m |
|---|---|---|
| Rear axle | 60-65 | 82.8-89.7 |
| Rear sprocket | | |
| FLT and FXR | | |
| 1984-1991 | | |
| Grade 5 bolts | 45-50 | 62.1-69 |
| Grade 8 bolts | 65-70 | 89.7-96.6 |
| 1992 | 45-55 | 55.2-75 |
| 1993-on | 55-65 | 75-88 |
| FXWG, FXEF and FXSB | | |
| Laced wheel | | |
| FXWG | 40-45 | 55.2-62.1 |
| FXEF and FXSB | 35 | 48.3 |
| Alloy wheel | | |
| Grade 5 bolts | 45-50 | 62.1-69 |
| Grade 8 bolts | 65-70 | 89.7-96.6 |

CHAPTER ELEVEN

# FRONT SUSPENSION AND STEERING

This chapter discusses service operations on the handlebar, suspension and steering components.

**Tables 1-3** are found at the end of the chapter.

## HANDLEBAR

The handlebars are clamped to the upper triple clamp with 2 caps and holders. Allen bolts are inserted through the caps and holders and secured with nuts to keep the assembly tight. Rubber bushings are mounted between the handlebar holders and the upper triple clamp to help reduce vibration. The handlebars are knurled where they fit between the clamps and holders; this machining process is used to provide additional holding power to help prevent the handlebars from slipping.

Handlebars are an important part in the overall comfort and safety of your motorcycle. The only maintenance required is to inspect the handlebar on regular intervals for signs of damage. The controls, master cylinder and turn signals, mounted on the handlebars, should be checked frequently for loose or missing fasteners.

The handlebars should be replaced when they become bent or damaged. Never try to heat, bend or weld bent handlebars. These efforts will seriously weaken the bars and may cause them to break.

When replacing a handlebar, you can order an exact replacement through Harley-Davidson dealers using their part numbers, or you can order bars through an accessory manufacturer. When ordering accessory bars, you will have to know the bars' outside diameter, width, bar height and sweep (**Figure 1**). When changing handlebars, make sure that the new bar has enough room to mount the controls, brake master cylinder, etc., without excessive crowding and that the controls feel comfortable when the front end is turned from side to side. In addition, if the new handlebars are higher, make sure the stock cables and switch wiring harnesses are long enough. If not, you will have to purchase longer cables and extend the wiring harnesses.

Incorrect mounting can put excessive stress on the handlebars. Always follow the installation and tightening procedures carefully as described in this chapter.

### Removal/Installation

NOTE

*Due to the number of models and years covered in this manual, this procedure represents a general guideline for removal and installation of the handlebar.*

1. Place the bike on the jiffy stand.
2. Unscrew and remove the mirrors.

NOTE

*Cover the fuel tank with a heavy cloth or plastic tarp to protect it from accidental spilling of brake fluid. Wash any spilled brake fluid off any painted or plated surface. Use soapy water and rinse thoroughly.*

NOTE

*Make a drawing of the clutch and throttle cable routing before removing them.*

3. Remove the bolts securing the master cylinder and support it with a Bungee cord. It is not necessary to disconnect the hydraulic brake line.

4. Separate the 2 halves of the start switch assembly. Disconnect the throttle cable from the twist grip.
5. Slacken the clutch cable and disconnect it at the hand lever.
6. Disconnect the clutch cable. Then separate the 2 halves of the directional signal switch assembly.
7. Remove the turn signals if mounted on the handlebar.
8. Remove the clamps securing the electrical cables to the handlebar.
9. Remove the handlebar cap bolts and nuts and remove the cap and handlebar.
10. Install by reversing these steps. Note the following.
11. Check the knurled rings on the handlebar for galling and bits of aluminum blocking up the rings. Clean this part of the handlebar with a wire brush.
12. Check the handlebar for cracks, bends or other damage. Replace the handlebar if necessary.
13. Clean the clamps and holders thoroughly of all residue before installing the handlebar.
14. After installing the handlebar, cap, bolts and nuts, reposition the handlebar while straddling the bike. Push it forward and backward to position it to best suit your riding style. Make sure, before tightening the cap bolts, that the knurled sections at the base of the handlebar are aligned with the cap and holder. Hold the Allen bolts with a wrench and tighten the nuts securely.

## STEERING HEAD AND STEM

The fork stem is mounted onto the lower triple clamp. A dust shield and a tapered bearing are installed onto the bottom of the fork stem. The fork stem is inserted through the steering head where another bearing is installed at the top of the steering head. Both bearings seat against races pressed into the steering head. Dust covers are used at both bearing areas to protect bearings from dust and other contaminants.

### Disassembly/Reassembly (FXR)

Refer to **Figure 2** or **Figure 3** for this procedure.

*NOTE*

*All 1992 FXR models have a grease fitting installed in the left-hand side of the steering head that allows periodic lubrication of the steering bearings without having to disassemble the steering assembly. See **Figure 5**. All 1993-on FXR models have a grease fitting hole installed in the right-hand side of the*

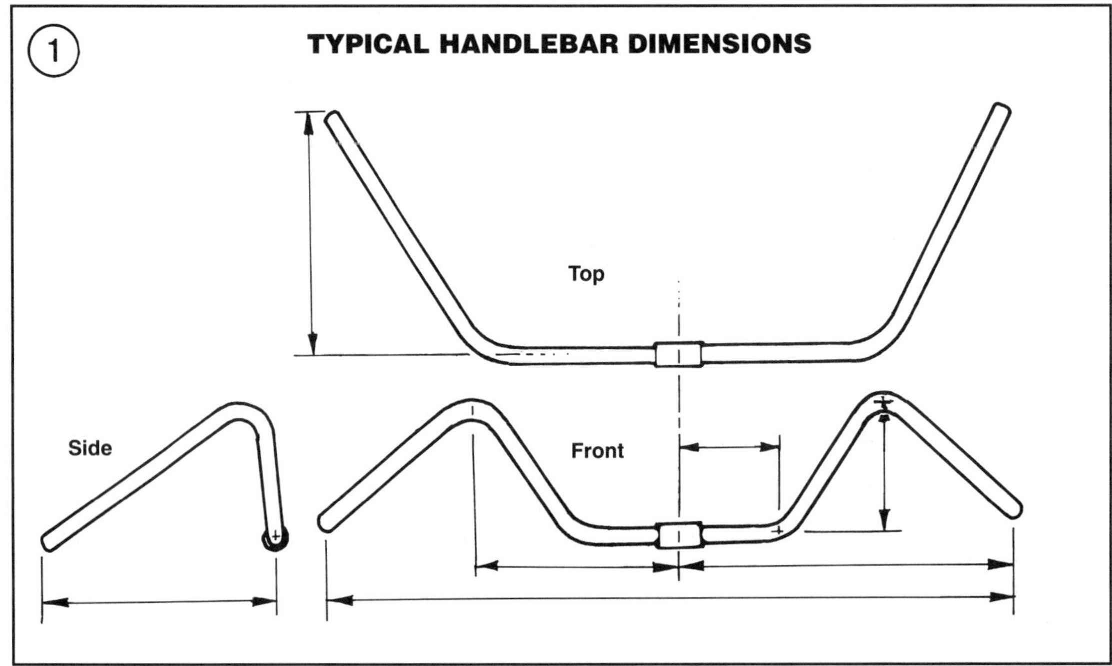

*steering head. The hole is tapped and sealed with a plug. To lubricate the steering bearings, remove the plug and install a grease fitting.*

1. Remove the front wheel as described in Chapter Ten.
2. Remove the fuel tank as described in Chapter Eight.
3. *Air control models*: Remove the air control system from the upper fork bracket as described in this chapter.
4. Loosen the fork stem nut (early models) or bolt (late models).
5. Remove the front forks as described in this chapter.

**2 FORK BRACKET (1984-1987 FXR AND FXRS)**

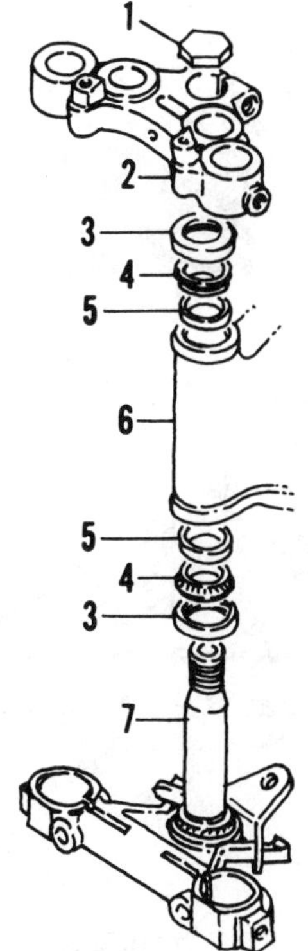


1. Fork stem nut
2. Upper bracket
3. Upper dust shield
4. Bearing
5. Upper bearing race
6. Frame
7. Fork stem and bracket

6. Remove the fork stem nut (early models) or the bolt and washer (late models) loosened in Step 4.

NOTE

*Hold onto the fork stem assembly when removing the upper fork bracket pinch bolt in Step 7. This will prevent the fork stem from falling out.*

7. Loosen the upper fork bracket pinch bolt and lift the bracket, together with the handlebars, off of the fork stem and set aside. Position handlebar so that the control cables are not kinked or damaged.
8. Remove the fork stem from the steering head.
9. Remove the upper dust shield.
10. Remove the bearing from the upper bearing race in the steering head.
11. Inspect the fork stem assembly as described later in this chapter.
12. After the fork stem assembly has been inspected and worn or damaged parts replaced, proceed to Step 13 to assemble the fork stem. If the bearing races were damaged, install them now as described under *Steering Head Bearing Race* in this chapter. Likewise, the lower bearing and dust shield must be installed onto the fork stem before installing the fork stem into the steering head. Refer to the same section to install these parts, if necessary.
13. Wipe the bearing races in the steering head with a clean lint-free cloth. Then wipe the face of each race with bearing grease.



NOTE

*Read the information listed under **Inspection** before packing bearings with grease.*

14. Pack the bearings thoroughly with bearing grease. The lower bearing and lower dust shield should be installed on the fork stem prior to installing the fork stem in the steering head. If necessary, install the lower bearing dust shield as described under *Steering Head Bearing Race* in this chapter. Place the upper bearing on a sheet of wax paper or other lint-free surface until it can be installed.
15. With the lower bearing and its dust shield properly installed on the fork stem, insert the fork stem up through the steering head until the bearing contacts the lower race and hold the assembly in position.

16. Install the upper bearing over the fork stem and seat it next to the upper race. Then install the upper dust shield.
17. Install the upper bracket together with the handlebar over the fork stem. Install the fork stem nut (early models) or the washer and bolt (late models) finger-tight.
18. Tighten the upper bracket-to-fork stem pinch bolt to the torque specification listed in **Table 1**.
19. Tighten the fork stem nut or bolt to remove all noticeable play in the fork stem.

*CAUTION*
*Do not overtighten the fork stem nut or bolt in Step 19 or you may damage the bearings and races. Final adjustment of the fork stem will take place after the front forks and front wheel have been installed on the bike.*

20. Reinstall the front forks as described in this chapter.
21. Install the front wheel as described in Chapter Ten.
22. Adjust the front steering as described in this chapter.
23. After the steering has been properly adjusted, install the air control assembly, if used, as described in this chapter.

**Disassembly/Reassembly (FLT)**

Refer to **Figure 5** for this procedure.

*NOTE*
*1991-on FLT models have a grease fitting installed in the steering head that allows periodic lubrication of the steering bearings without having to disassemble the steering assembly. See* ***Figure 4****. Refer to Chapter Three for lubrication procedures.*

1. Remove the front wheel as described in Chapter Ten.
2. *1986-on FLHT/C*: Remove the light bar and outer fairing (Chapter Fifteen).
3. *FLT/C*: Remove the instrument panel and handlebar.
4. Remove the front forks as described in this chapter.
5. Remove the air control unit as described in this chapter.

**3**

**FORK BRACKET (1987 FXLR, FXRS AND ALL 1988-ON FXR)**

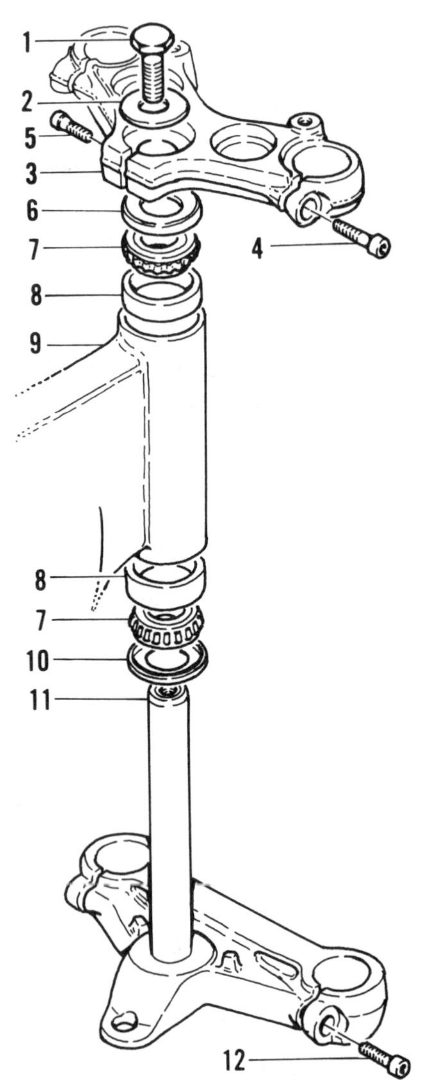


1. Bolt
2. Washer
3. Upper fork bracket
4. Bolt
5. Bolt
6. Dust cap
7. Bearing
8. Bearing race
9. Frame steering head
10. Dust shield
11. Steering stem and lower fork bracket
12. Bolt

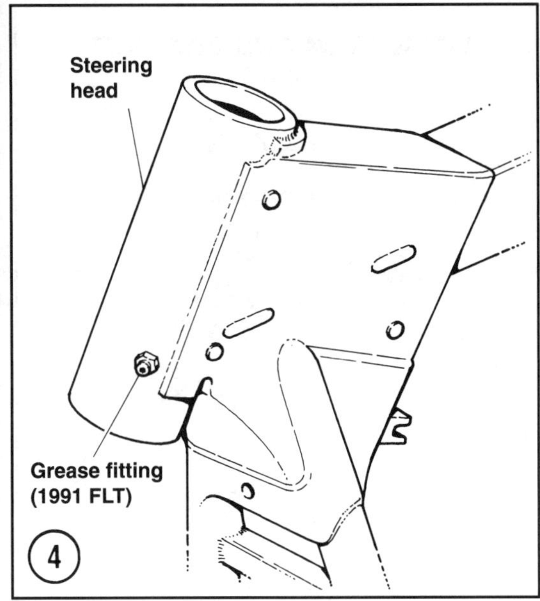


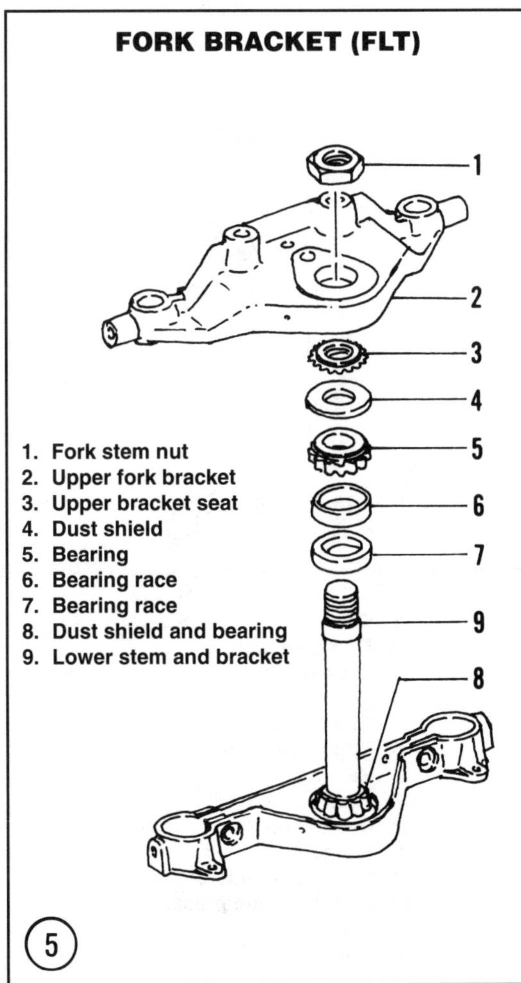


6. Remove the brake line bracket at the lower fork stem bracket.
7. Pry the lockwasher tab away from the fork stem nut, then loosen and remove the nut, lockwasher and circuit board.

*NOTE*

*If you are going to remove the circuit board, first disconnect its electrical connectors.*

8. Remove the upper fork bracket from the steering stem.

*NOTE*

*When the bearing adjust nut is removed in Step 9, there will be nothing holding the fork stem and bracket in position. Secure or hold the bracket to prevent it from falling out.*

9. Loosen and remove the bearing adjust nut, then slide the fork stem and bracket out of the frame tube.
10. Remove the upper dust shield.
11. Remove the bearing from the upper bearing race in the steering head cup.
12. Inspect the fork stem assembly as described later in this chapter.
13. After the fork stem assembly has been inspected and worn or damaged parts replaced, proceed to Step 14 to assemble the fork stem. If the bearing races were damaged, install them now as described under *Steering Head Bearing Race* in this chapter. Likewise, the lower bearing and dust shield must be installed onto the fork stem before installing the fork stem into the steering head. Refer to the same section to install these parts, if necessary.
14. Wipe the bearing races in the steering head with a clean lint-free cloth. Then wipe the face of each race with bearing grease.

*NOTE*

*Read the information listed under **Inspection** before packing bearings with grease.*

15. Pack the bearings thoroughly with bearing grease. The lower bearing and lower dust shield should be installed on the fork stem prior to installing the fork stem into the steering head. If necessary, install the lower bearing dust shield as described under *Steering Head Bearing Race* in this chapter. Place the upper bearing on a sheet of wax paper or other lint-free surface until it can be installed.

16. With the lower bearing and its dust shield properly installed on the fork stem, insert the fork stem up through the steering head until the bearing contacts the lower race and hold the assembly in position.

17. Install the upper bearing over the fork stem and seat it next to the upper race. Then install the upper dust shield and the bearing adjuster. Tighten the bearing adjuster to remove all bearing play.

*CAUTION*
*Overtightening the bearing adjuster can cause premature bearing wear or bearing damage. Step 17 is an initial adjustment only. Final adjustment of the fork stem will take place after the front forks and front wheel have been installed on the bike.*

18. Install the upper bracket over the fork stem, then install the circuit board, making sure to align the circuit board in its mounting bracket. Install the fork stem nut and tighten it to the torque specification listed in **Table 1**. Bend the lockwasher tab against one flat on the nut; tighten the nut, if required, to align it with the lockwasher.

19. On 1991-on FLT models, pack the frame tube with the same type of bearing grease originally used to pack the bearing during disassembly.

20. Install the fork tubes as described in this chapter.

21. Install the air control unit as described in this chapter.

22. Install the handlebar as described in this chapter.

23. Install the front wheel as described in Chapter Ten.

24. Bleed the front brake if the brake line or hose was opened.

25. Reverse Steps 1-6 to complete assembly.

26. Adjust steering play as described in this chapter.

## Disassembly/Reassembly (FXWG)

Refer to **Figure 6** for this procedure.

1. Remove the front wheel as described in Chapter Ten.

2. Remove the fuel tank as described in Chapter Eight.

3. Remove the front forks as described in this chapter.

4. Remove the headlight and headlight bracket.

**FORK STEM AND BRACKET (FXWG)**

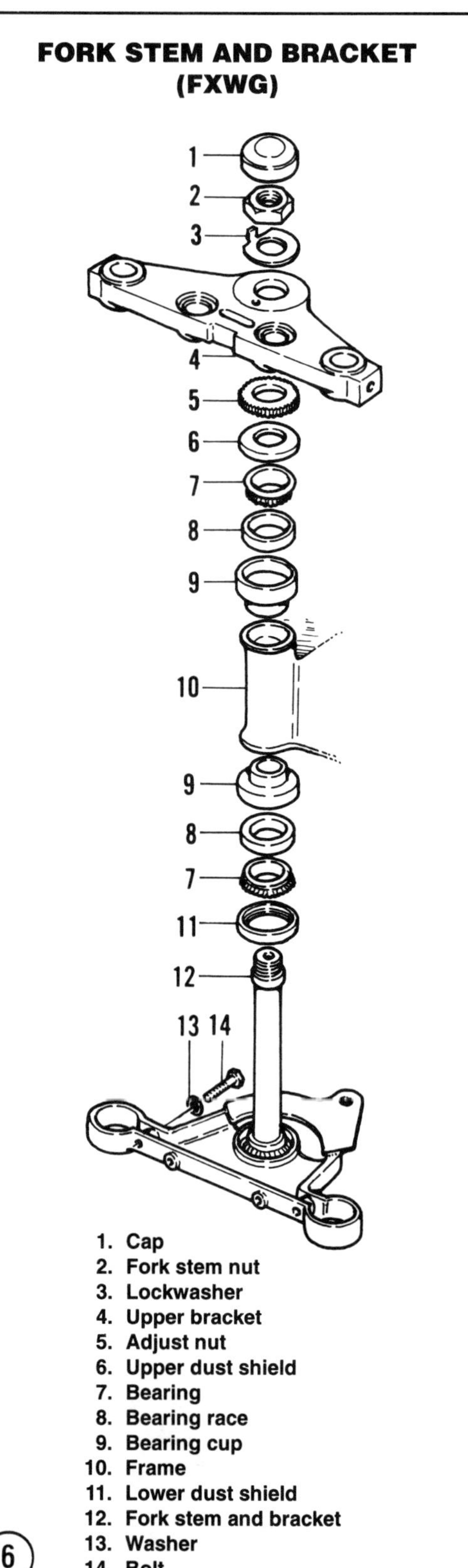


1. Cap
2. Fork stem nut
3. Lockwasher
4. Upper bracket
5. Adjust nut
6. Upper dust shield
7. Bearing
8. Bearing race
9. Bearing cup
10. Frame
11. Lower dust shield
12. Fork stem and bracket
13. Washer
14. Bolt

6

5. Remove the brake hose bracket at the bottom of the fork stem bracket. Do not disconnect the brake hose connection.
6. Disconnect the ground wire at the fork stem bracket.
7. Remove the fork stem cap from the fork stem nut.
8. The fork stem nut is secured with a tab lockwasher. The tab is bent up so that it seats against one flat on the nut. Bend the tab away from the nut.
9. Loosen and remove the fork stem nut and the tab lockwasher. Discard the tab lockwasher.
10. Remove the upper bracket together with the handlebar assembly from the fork stem. Position the handlebar so that the control cables are not kinked.
11. Remove the bearing seat and lower the fork stem out of the steering head.
12. Remove the upper dust shield.
13. Remove the bearing from the upper bearing race in the steering head cup.
14. Inspect the fork stem assembly as described later in this chapter.
15. After the fork stem assembly has been inspected and worn or damaged parts replaced, proceed to Step 16 to assemble the fork stem. If the bearing races were damaged, install them now as described under *Steering Head Bearing Race* in this chapter. Likewise, the lower bearing and dust shield must be installed onto the fork stem before installing the fork stem into the steering head. Refer to the same section to install these parts, if necessary.
16. Wipe the bearing races in the steering head with a clean lint-free cloth. Then wipe the face of each race with bearing grease.
17. Pack the bearings thoroughly with bearing grease. The lower bearing and lower dust shield should be installed on the fork stem prior to installing the fork stem in the steering head. If necessary, install the lower bearing as described under *Steering Head Bearing Race* in this chapter. Cover the upper bearing with a sheet of wax paper or other lint-free material until it can be installed.
18. With the lower bearing and its dust shield properly installed on the fork stem, insert the fork stem up through the steering head until the bearing contacts the lower race and hold the assembly in position.
19. Install the upper bearing over the fork stem and seat it next to the upper race. Then install the upper dust shield.
20. Thread the bearing seat onto the fork stem until the fork stem can pivot smoothly from side to side with no noticeable axial or lateral play.

*CAUTION*
*Do not overtighten the bearing seat in Step 20 or you may damage the bearings and races. Final adjustment of the fork stem will take place after the front forks and front wheel have been installed on the bike.*

21. Install the fork bracket over the fork stem. Install a *new* tab lockwasher over the fork stem. Insert the pin on the lockwasher into the hole in the fork bracket. Then install the fork stem nut until it is finger-tight. Check again that the pin on the lockwasher engages the hole in the fork bracket.

*NOTE*
*Final tightening of the fork stem nut will take place after the front wheel has been installed and you are adjusting front steering play.*

22. Install the brake hose bracket to the lower fork stem bracket and tighten to 11 ft.-lb. (15 N•m).
23. Install the headlight bracket and headlight. Adjust the headlight as described in Chapter Nine.
24. Reinstall the front forks as described in this chapter.
25. Install the front wheel as described in Chapter Ten.
26. Adjust the front steering as described in this chapter. After tightening the fork stem nut when adjusting the steering play, install the fork stem cap over the nut.

11

### Disassembly/Reassembly (FXEF and FXSB)

Refer to **Figure 7** for this procedure.
1. Remove the front wheel as described in Chapter Ten.
2. Remove the fuel tank as described in Chapter Eight.
3. Remove the front forks as described in this chapter.
4. Remove the brake hose bracket at the bottom of the fork stem bracket. Do not disconnect the brake hose connection.

*NOTE*
*Secure the fork stem before removing the fork stem nut in the following steps or it will fall to the ground.*

5. Loosen and remove the fork stem nut.
6. Loosen the upper bracket pinch bolt.
7. Remove the upper bracket together with the handlebar assembly from the fork stem. Position the handlebar so that the control cables are not kinked.
8. Lower the fork stem out of the steering head.
9. Remove the upper dust shield.
10. Remove the bearing from the upper bearing race in the steering head cup.
11. Inspect the fork stem assembly as described later in this chapter.
12. After the fork stem assembly has been inspected and worn or damaged parts replaced, proceed to Step 13 to assemble the fork stem. If the bearing races were damaged, install them now as described under *Steering Head Bearing Race* in this chapter. Likewise, the lower bearing and dust shield must be installed onto the fork stem before installing the fork stem into the steering head. Refer to the same section to install these parts, if necessary.
13. Wipe the bearing races in the steering head with a clean lint-free cloth. Then wipe the face of each race with bearing grease.
14. Pack the bearings thoroughly with bearing grease. The lower bearing and lower dust shield should be installed on the fork stem prior to installing the fork stem in the steering head. If necessary, install the lower bearing as described under *Steering Head Bearing Race* in this chapter. Cover the upper bearing with a sheet of wax paper or other lint-free material until it can be installed.
15. With the lower bearing and its dust shield properly installed on the fork stem, insert the fork stem up through the steering head until the bearing contacts the lower race and hold the assembly in position.
16. Install the upper bearing over the fork stem and seat it next to the upper race. Then install the upper dust shield.
17. Install the fork bracket over the fork stem and install the fork stem nut.
18. Install the fork tubes. Tighten the upper fork stem pinch bolts; do not tighten the lower fork stem pinch bolts until the steering assembly is adjusted as described later in this chapter.

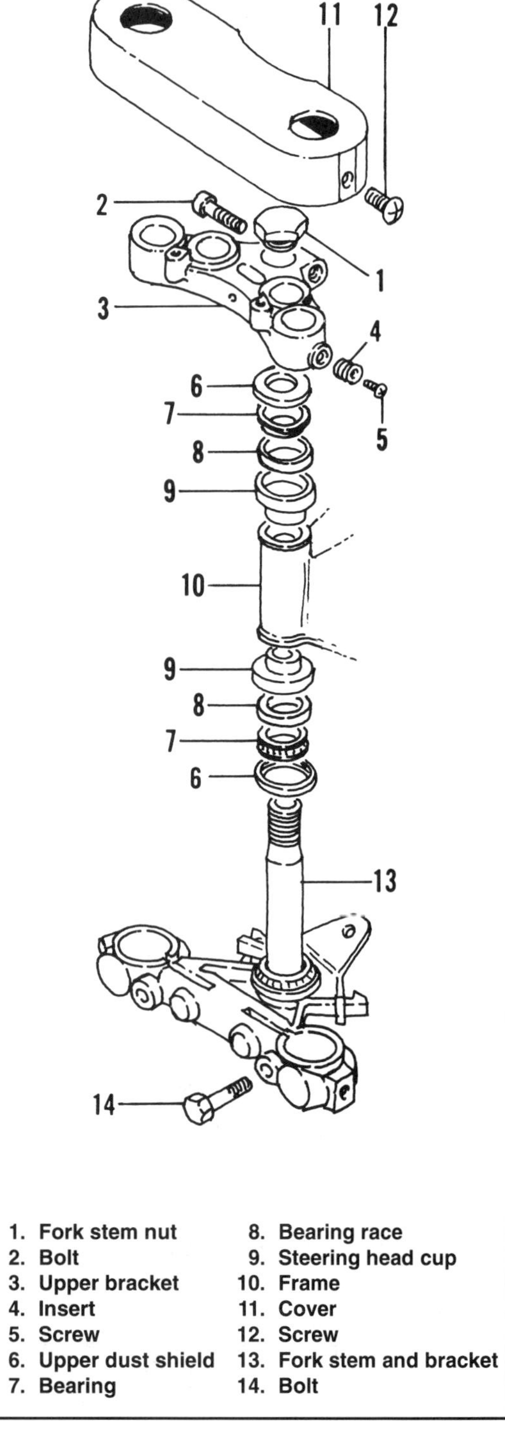


1. Fork stem nut
2. Bolt
3. Upper bracket
4. Insert
5. Screw
6. Upper dust shield
7. Bearing
8. Bearing race
9. Steering head cup
10. Frame
11. Cover
12. Screw
13. Fork stem and bracket
14. Bolt

19. Tighten the fork stem nut to remove all bearing play while at the same time the fork stem can turn freely from side to side.
20. Tighten the upper bracket-to-fork stem pinch bolt securely.

NOTE
*Final tightening of the fork stem nut will take place after the front wheel has been installed and you are adjusting front steering play.*

21. Install the brake hose bracket to the lower fork stem bracket and tighten to 11 ft.-lb. (15 N•m).
22. Install the front wheel as described in Chapter Ten.
23. Adjust the front steering as described in this chapter.
24. After adjusting the steering, tighten the upper fork stem to-fork tube pinch bolts securely.

## Inspection (All Models)

On FLT and FXR models, the bearing races are pressed into the frame's steering head. The bearing races should not be removed unless they are damaged and require replacement. On 1985-1986 FX models, the bearing races are pressed into a steering head cup that is pressed into the frame's steering head. The bearing races should not be removed unless they are damaged and require replacement.

A high quality wheel bearing grease should be used to pack bearings and races when performing the following steps.

NOTE
*The bearings were originally packed with Harley-Davidson Wheel Bearing Grease. Because different brands of grease are incompatible—mixing them may cause the grease combination to deteriorate, thus reducing bearing lubrication—all of the grease used in the steering head assembly should be cleaned out before packing the bearings, races and steering head with new grease.*

1. Wipe the bearing races with a solvent-soaked rag and then dry with compressed air or a lint-free cloth. Check the races in the steering head cups for pitting, scratches, galling or severe wear. If any of these conditions exist, replace the races as described in this chapter. If the races are okay, wipe the face of each race with grease.
2. Wipe the bearing with a lint free cloth to remove as much exposed grease on the bearing as possible. Then wash the bearing in solvent to remove all of the old grease. An aerosol type wheel bearing degreaser or carburetor cleaner can be used to blast residual grease from between the rollers that was not removed during the solvent bath. Blow the bearing dry with compressed air, making sure you do not allow the air jet to spin the bearing. Do not remove the lower bearing from the fork stem unless its replacement is required; clean the bearing together with the steering stem.
3. After the upper bearing has thoroughly dried, hold the inner race with one hand and turn the outer race with your other hand. Turn the bearing slowly, checking for any signs of roughness or resistance, indicating a worn, contaminated or damaged bearing. Visually check the bearing for pitting, scratches or visible damage. If the bearing is worn, check the dust shield for wear or damage or for improper bearing lubrication. Replace the bearing if necessary.
4. Repeat Step 3 to check the lower bearing while it is mounted on the steering stem, only turn the outer bearing race when checking it. If this bearing is worn or damaged, replace it as described later in this chapter.
5. If the bearings can be reused, pack them with grease as follows:
   a. Make sure the bearings are thoroughly dry. There should be no traces of solvent or cleaner anywhere on the bearing.

NOTE
*Because a trace of dirt can quickly damage a bearing, your hands should be clean when handling bearings, especially when packing them with grease.*

   b. Purchase a container of Harley-Davidson Wheel Bearing Grease (part No. 99855-89) or equivalent. Open the container and dip out a glob of grease onto one hand; install the cover to prevent contamination of the unused grease. Place the bearing in the grease and work the bearing and grease with your other hand to pack the bearing.

c. Rotate the bearing when packing it to make sure you pack grease throughout the entire bearing and that all bearing surfaces are covered.

d. After wiping your hands off, record the date, mileage and type of grease used, in the Maintenance Log at the back of this book. You shouldn't have to do this job for another 10,000 miles (16,000 km), at which time you won't have to guess at the type of grease used.

e. Wrap the bearing with wax paper or some other type of lint-free material until it can be reinstalled. Do not store the bearing for any length of time without lubricating it or it will rust.

6. Check the fork stem for cracks or damage. Check the threads at the top of the fork stem for strippage or damage. Check the mating fastener by installing it on the stem; make sure they screw together easily with no roughness. If necessary, clean the threads carefully with a brush and solvent or use a tap or die of the correct thread type and size.

7. Worn or damaged parts should be replaced. When discarding a bearing, both bearings and their races should be replaced. Replace bearing races as described in this chapter.

8. Check around the steering head for broken frame welds. If any are found, have them repaired by a competent frame shop or welding service familiar with motorcycle frame repair.

9. On 1991 FLT models, make sure the grease nipple installed on the frame tube is open.

## STEERING HEAD BEARING RACE

Whenever the steering stem and bearings are removed from the steering head, cover the steering head with a cloth to protect the bearing races from accidental damage. If a race is damaged, the bearing and race must be replaced as a set. Because the bearing races are pressed into place, do not remove them unless they are worn and require replacement.

### Fork Stem Bearing, Outer Bearing Race and Steering Head Cup Replacement

Each individual bearing assembly consists of a tapered roller bearing, bearing race, dust shield and steering head cup (FX models). When replacing a bearing, all of these parts must be replaced as a set. On FX models, the bearing races are first pressed into the steering head cups and then the cups are pressed in the frame steering head. On FLT and FXR models, the bearing races are pressed into the frame. The lower bearing is installed over the fork stem. The upper bearing is placed in the upper bearing race after the fork stem has been inserted through the frame steering head.

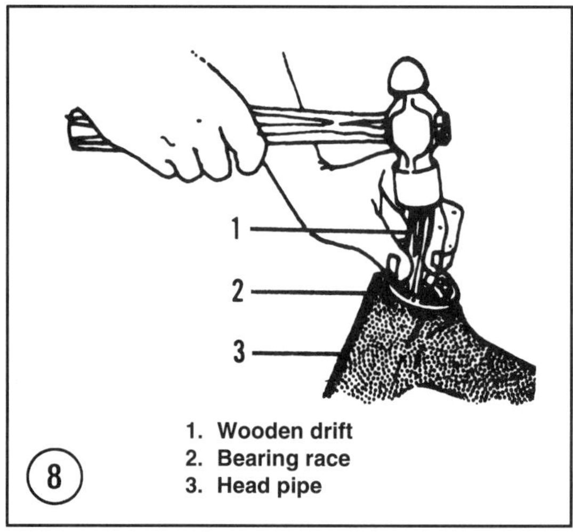


8

1. Wooden drift
2. Bearing race
3. Head pipe

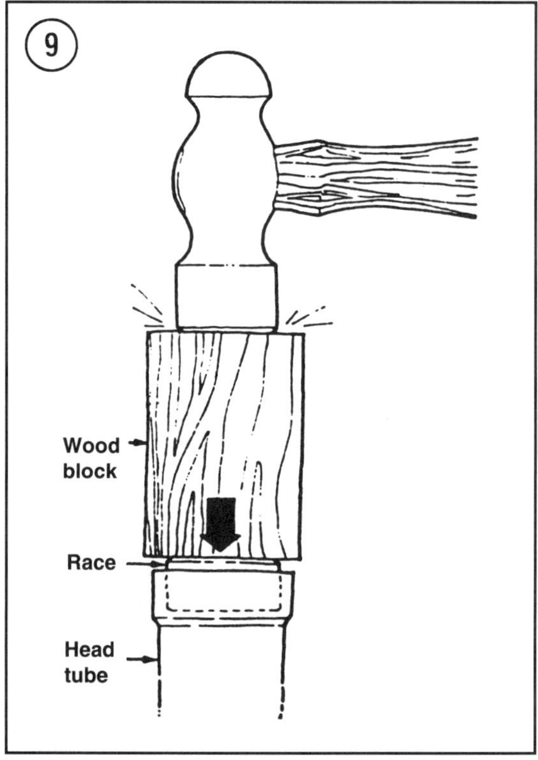


9

### *Outer bearing race and steering head cup*

1A. *Models with steering head cups*: To remove the steering head cup, insert a drift or similar tool into the frame steering head and carefully tap the cup out from the inside—tap around the cup every 90° to prevent it from binding in the tube bore. When the cup is removed, discard the cup and the race installed in the cup. Repeat to remove the other cup.

1B. *Models without steering head cups*: Insert a drift or similar tool into the frame steering head and carefully tap the race out from the inside—tap around the race every 90° so that it does not bind in the tube bore. See **Figure 8**. Repeat to remove the other race.

2. Clean the frame steering head with solvent to remove all old grease and dry thoroughly.

3A. *Models with steering head cups*: Assemble the steering head cups and races and install the cups as follows:

   a. After purchasing 2 new bearings and 2 new steering head cups, match a new bearing with one cup. Then align the new bearing race with the cup and tap it squarely into the cup until it bottoms out. Repeat to assemble the opposite cup and bearing race.
   b. Align the upper steering head cup with the frame steering head and tap the cup into the frame, using a wood block and hammer, until the cup bottoms out. Make sure to drive the cup squarely into the frame.
   c. Repeat to install the lower steering head cup.

3B. *Models without steering head cups*: Install the bearing races as follows:

   a. Clean the race thoroughly before installing it.
   b. Align the upper race with the frame steering head and tap it slowly into place with a block of wood, a suitable socket or piece of pipe, making sure you do *not* contact the bearing race surface; see **Figure 9**. If you saved an old race, grind its outer circumference so that it is a slip fit in the steering head, then use it to drive the new race into place. Drive the race into the steering head until it bottoms out on the bore shoulder.
   c. Repeat to install the lower race into the frame steering head.

4. Wipe the bearing races with bearing grease.

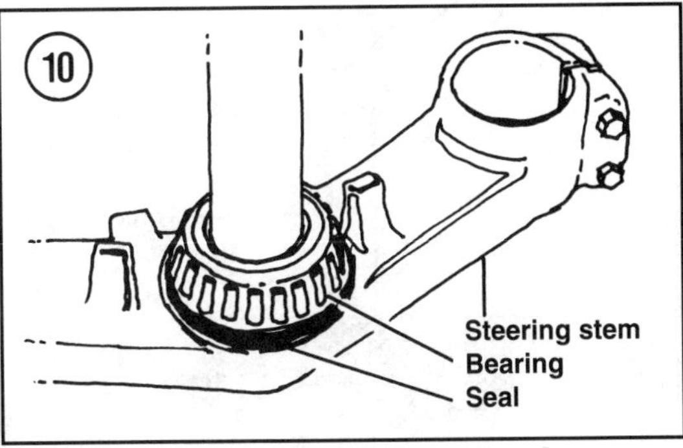


### *Fork stem lower bearing assembly*

*NOTE*

*Do **not** remove the bearing from the fork stem (**Figure 10**) unless it is going to be replaced with a new bearing. Do **not** reinstall a bearing that has been removed as it is no longer true to alignment.*

*WARNING*

*Safety glasses should be worn when using a chisel to break the bearing cage in Step 1. Likewise, insulated gloves should be worn when heating the fork stem.*

1. Using a chisel, break the bearing cage and rollers from the inner race. When the bearing cage and rollers are free, all you will be left with is the inner race on the fork stem. To remove the inner race, heat the race with a torch until it expands enough to slide off the fork stem. Remove and discard the old dust shield.

2. Clean the fork stem with solvent and dry thoroughly.

3. Pack the new bearing with grease before installing it as described in this chapter.

4. Slide a new dust shield over the fork stem until it bottoms out on the lower bracket.

5. Align the new bearing with the fork stem and press or drive it onto the fork stem until it bottoms out. When installing the bearing onto the fork stem, a bearing driver must be used against the inner bearing race (**Figure 11**). Do *not* install the bearing by driving against the outer bearing race.

## STEERING ADJUSTMENT

Steering adjustment must be performed at the specified intervals (Chapter Three, **Table 1**) or after reassembling the steering stem assembly.

### FXR and FX Models

1. Support the bike so that the front wheel clears the ground.
2. Remove the windshield (if used) and all other accessory weight from the handlebar and front forks that could affect this adjustment.

*NOTE*
*If any control cable affects handlebar movement, disconnect it.*

3. Apply a strip of masking tape across the end of the fender.
4. Swing the handlebar so that the front wheel faces straight ahead.
5. Place a pointer on a stand so that its tip points to the center of the fender when the wheel is facing straight ahead.
6. Lightly push the fender toward the right-hand side until the front end starts to turn by itself. Mark this point on the tape.
7. Repeat Step 6 for the left-hand side.
8. Measure the distance between the 2 marks on the tape. For proper bearing adjustment, the distance should be 1-2 in. (25.4-50.8 mm). If the distance is incorrect, adjust the steering bearings as follows.

*NOTE*
*Adjustment is made by loosening or tightening the fork stem nut or bolt or bearing seat on FXWG models.*

*NOTE*
*If the adjustment is less than 1 in. (25.4 mm), tighten the nut, bolt or bearing seat slightly. Loosen the nut, bolt or bearing seat if the adjustment is more than 2 in. (50.8 mm).*

9A. *1984-1987 FXR (except 1987 FXLR, FXRS Sport Edition, FXEF and FXSB)*: Loosen the upper fork bracket pinch bolt (**Figure 2**) and the lower bracket fork tube pinch bolts (**Figure 2**). Loosen or tighten the fork stem nut (**Figure 2**) until the fall-away distance is 1-2 in. (25.4-50.8 mm). Recheck adjustment then, when correct, tighten pinch bolts to torque specification listed in **Table 1**.

9B. *1987 FXLR, FXRS Sport Edition and all 1988-on FXR*: Loosen the upper fork bracket pinch bolt (**Figure 3**) and the lower bracket fork tube pinch bolts (**Figure 3**). Loosen or tighten the fork stem bolt (**Figure 3**) until the fall-away distance is 1-2 in. (25.4-50.8 mm). Recheck adjustment then, when correct, tighten pinch bolts to torque specification listed in **Table 1**.

9C. *FXWG*: Loosen the lower bracket fork tube pinch bolts (**Figure 6**). Turn the bearing seat located underneath the upper fork bracket (**Figure 6**) until the fall-away distance is 1-2 in. (25.4-50.8 mm). Recheck adjustment then, when correct, tighten pinch bolts to torque specification listed in **Table 1**.

10. Reinstall all parts previously removed.

### FLT Models

1. Support the bike so that the front wheel clears the ground.
2. Remove the windshield (if used) and all other accessory weight from the handlebar and front forks that could affect this adjustment.

*NOTE*
*If any control cable affects handlebar movement, disconnect it.*

3. Turn the wheel to the left as far as it will go and then let it go. If the steering adjustment is correct, the front wheel will swing from left to right 3 times and then stop near the center or straight-ahead position. If the adjustment is incorrect—the number of

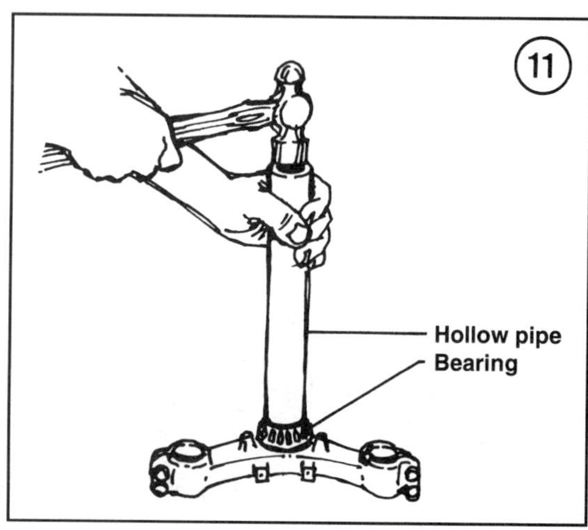

swings past center is less or more than 3 times—perform the following.

4. Loosen the lower bracket pinch bolts.
5. Slide both rubber fork stops a few inches up their respective fork tubes.
6. Pry the lockwasher tab away from the fork stem nut and loosen the nut.
7. Insert a drift punch into a notch in the bearing adjuster nut (**Figure 4**). Tighten the nut to decrease the number of swings or loosen the nut to increase the number of swings.
8. Tighten the lower bracket pinch bolts to the torque specification listed in **Table 1**.
9. Tighten the fork stem nut to the torque specification listed in **Table 1**. Bend the lockwasher tab against one flat on the nut; tighten the nut, if required, to align the nut flat and lockwasher tab.
10. Recheck the bearing adjustment.
11. When the adjustment is correct, reposition the rubber fork stops.
12. Reinstall all parts previously removed.

## FRONT FORK

The front suspension consists of a spring-controlled, hydraulically dampened telescopic fork tube assembly.

Before suspecting major trouble, drain the front fork oil and refill with the proper type and quantity; refer to Chapter Three. If you still have trouble, such as poor damping, a tendency to bottom or top out or leakage around the rubber seals, follow the service procedures in this section.

To simplify fork service and to prevent the mixing of parts, the legs should be removed, serviced and installed individually.

NOTE

*If you are going to disassemble the front fork assembly, check the condition of the fork tube bushings while the fork tubes are assembled and mounted on the bike. With the engine OFF, apply the front brake and then pull and push the handlebars forward and rearward and then up and down. If you note excessive play at the top of the slider, the fork tube bushings may be worn. Record any observations and check the bushings carefully after disassembling the fork tubes.*

### Removal (FLT)

1. Support the bike so that the front wheel clears the ground. Double check to make sure that the bike is stable before removing the front wheel and forks.
2. Remove the front wheel as described in Chapter Ten.
3. Remove the front fender as described in Chapter Fifteen.
4. Remove the instrument panel.
5. Remove the handlebar as described in this chapter.
6. Remove the front fork air control valve cap and bleed the air control system as described in this chapter. Then remove the banjo bolts attaching the air control system to the front fork tubes.
7. Remove the fork cap bolt and seal from each fork tube.
8. Loosen both fork tube pinch bolts.

NOTE

*The left- and right-hand fork sliders are different. ID the sliders before removal so you don't mix them up during reassembly.*

9. Remove the fork tube by twisting it back and forth as you slide it out of the fork stem and bracket assembly. Remove the rubber fork stop from the fork tube.
10. Repeat to remove the other fork tube.
11. If fork service is required, refer to *Disassembly* in this chapter.

11

### Installation (FLT)

1. Clean off any corrosion or dirt on the upper and lower fork bracket receptacles.
2. Make sure the fork cap screwed into the top of each fork tube is tight. Check also that the threads in the cap are not contaminated or damaged. Repair threads with the correct size tap before installing the fork tube.

NOTE

*The fork assemblies must be reinstalled on the correct side of the bike so the front axle can be installed from the right-hand side.*

3. Slide the fork tube up through the lower fork bracket and install the rubber fork stop, then continue to slide the fork tube upward until the fork cap bottoms out against the upper fork bracket; twisting the fork tube from side to side may ease installation.

4. Tighten the upper and lower pinch bolts to the torque specification listed in **Table 1**.

*NOTE*
*If the front fork oil was drained, refill the front fork now with the correct type and quantity fork oil specified in Chapter Three.*

5. Slide a seal on the fork cap bolt, wipe the cap bolt threads with fork oil, and thread the cap bolt into the fork cap threads. Tighten the fork cap securely.

6. Repeat to install the other fork tube.

7. Reverse Steps 1-6 to complete installation.

8. Apply the front brake and pump the front forks several times to seat the forks and front wheel.

### Removal (FXR)

1. Support the bike so that the front wheel clears the ground. Double check to make sure that the bike is stable before removing the front wheel and forks.

2. Remove the front wheel as described in Chapter Ten.

3. Remove the front fender as described in Chapter Fifteen.

4. Remove the headlight bracket and attach it to a cord to prevent the wires from pulling loose.

5. On models with air-assist front forks, remove the front fork air control valve cap and bleed the air control system as described in this chapter. Then remove the banjo bolts attaching the air control system to the front fork tubes.

6. *1984-1987 except 1987 FXLR and FXRSE*—Perform the following:
   a. Remove the lower bracket cover screws to uncover the lower bracket pinch bolts.
   b. Loosen the fork caps 2 turns, then tap the cap squarely with a plastic tipped hammer to loosen the fork tube-to-upper bracket taper fit.
   c. When the taper fit is broken, carefully remove the fork cap from the fork tube; the fork cap is under spring pressure, so remove it slowly.

*NOTE*
*On 1987 FXLR, FXRSE and all 1988 and later FXR models, removal of the fork cap is not required for fork removal.*

*NOTE*
*Label the left- and right-hand fork tubes so they can be reinstalled in their original position.*

7. Loosen the upper and lower fork bracket pinch bolts and slide the fork tube out of the fork brackets. It may be necessary to rotate the fork tube slightly while removing it.

8. Reinstall the fork caps on FXR models.

9. If fork service is required, refer to *Disassembly* in this chapter.

### Installation (FXR)

1. Clean off any corrosion or dirt on the upper and lower fork bracket receptacles.

*NOTE*
*The fork assemblies must be reinstalled on the correct side of the bike so the brake caliper and front fender can be installed. If the fork assemblies are installed on the wrong side, these components cannot be installed onto the fork sliders.*

2A. *1984-1987*—Slide the fork tube up through the lower and upper fork brackets until the fork tube bottoms against the upper bracket. Tighten the upper and lower bracket pinch bolts to the torque specification listed in **Table 1**. Refill the fork tube with the correct type and quantity fork oil; See Chapter Three for specifications. Install and tighten the fork cap.

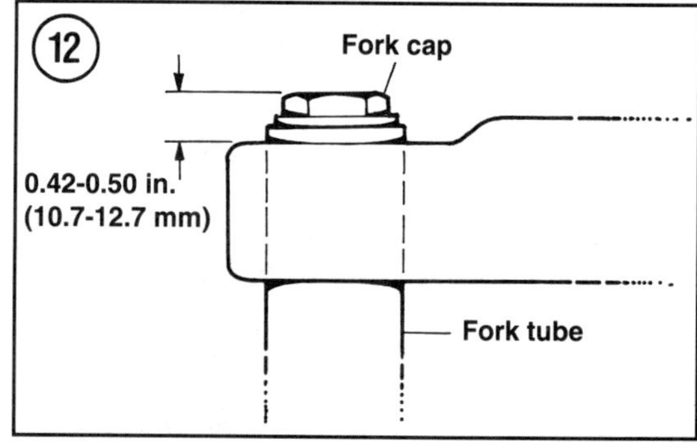

2B. *1987 FXLR, FXRSE and all 1988-on FXR*: Slide the fork tube up through the lower and upper fork brackets so that the fork tube extends 0.42-0.50 in. (10.7-12.7 mm). above the upper fork bracket as shown in **Figure 12**. Tighten the upper and lower bracket pinch bolts to the torque specification listed in **Table 1**. If the fork oil was previously drained, remove the fork cap and refill the fork tube with the correct type and quantity fork oil; see Chapter Three for specifications.
3. Reverse Steps 1-5 to complete installation.
4. Apply the front brake and pump the front forks several times to seat the forks and front wheel.

## Removal (FXWG)

1. Support the bike so that the front wheel clears the ground. Double check to make sure that the bike is stable before removing the front wheel and forks.
2. Remove the front wheel as described in Chapter Ten.
3. Remove the front fender as described in Chapter Fifteen.
4. Loosen the fork tube cap at the top of the upper fork bracket. Then remove the cap, washer and oil seal.

*NOTE*
*Label the left- and right-hand fork tubes so they can be reinstalled in their original position.*

5. Loosen the fork bracket pinch bolts and slide the fork tube out of the fork brackets. It may be necessary to rotate the fork tube slightly while removing it.
6. If fork service is required, refer to *Disassembly* in this chapter.

## Installation (FXWG)

1. Clean off any corrosion or dirt on the upper and lower fork bracket receptacles.
2. Make sure the fork tube plug screwed into the top of each fork tube is tight. Check also that the threads in the plug are not contaminated or damaged.

*NOTE*
*The fork assemblies must be reinstalled on the correct side of the bike so the brake caliper and front fender can be properly installed. If the fork assemblies are installed on the wrong side, the bolt holes on these components will not line up properly.*

3. Slide the fork tube up through the lower and upper fork brackets. Push the fork tube up until the fork tube plug bottoms out on the upper fork bracket. Then turn the fork tube so that one flat on the fork tube plug faces toward the inside of the fork tube.
4. Slide a flat washer and oil seal onto the fork stem cap threads, then thread the cap into the fork tube plug and tighten securely. After tightening the fork tube plug, check that one flat on the fork tube plug still faces toward the inside of the fork tube.
5. Tighten the fork bracket pinch bolt to the torque specification listed in **Table 1**.
6. Install the front fender as described in Chapter Fifteen.
7. Install the front wheel and front master cylinder as described in Chapter Ten.
8. Apply the front brake and pump the front forks several times to seat the forks and front wheel.

## Removal (FXEF and FXSB)

1. Support the bike so that the front wheel clears the ground. Double check to make sure that the bike is stable before removing the front wheel and forks.
2. Remove the front wheel as described in Chapter Ten.
3. Remove the front fender as described in Chapter Fifteen.
4. Remove the fork tube cover screws. Lift the cover to expose the lower bracket pinch bolts.

*NOTE*
*Label the left- and right-hand fork tubes so they can be reinstalled in their original position.*

5. Loosen the fork bracket pinch bolts and slide the fork tube out of the fork brackets. It may be necessary to rotate the fork tube slightly while removing it.
6. Loosen the fork tube cap at the top of the upper fork bracket 2 turns. Then tap the top of the fork tube cap with a plastic hammer to break the fork tube-to-

fork bracket taper loose. Remove the fork tube cap, washer and then remove the fork tube.

7. If fork service is required, refer to *Disassembly* in this chapter.

## Installation (FXEF and FXSB)

1. Clean off any corrosion or dirt on the upper and lower fork bracket receptacles.

*NOTE*
*The fork assemblies must be reinstalled on the correct side of the bike so the brake caliper and front fender can be properly installed. If the fork assemblies are installed on the wrong side, the bolt holes on these components will not line up properly.*

2. Slide the fork tube up through the lower and upper fork brackets. Install the washer and the fork tube cap. Tighten the fork tube cap to seat the fork tube taper against the upper fork bracket taper.
3. Tighten the lower bracket pinch bolts and the upper bracket pinch bolts to the torque specification listed in **Table 1**.
4. Install the cover and secure it to the lower fork bracket with its attaching screws.
5. Install the front fender as described in Chapter Fifteen.
6. Install the front wheel and front master cylinder as described in Chapter Ten.
7. Apply the front brake and pump the front forks several times to seat the forks and front wheel.

## Disassembly (FLT)

To simplify fork service and to prevent the mixing of parts, the legs should be disassembled and assembled individually.

Refer to **Figure 13** for this procedure.

1. Using the front axle boss at the bottom of the fork tube, clamp the slider in a vise with soft jaws. Do *not* clamp the slider at any point above the fork axle boss in a vise.

*NOTE*
*The Allen screw inserted through the bottom of the slider has been secured*

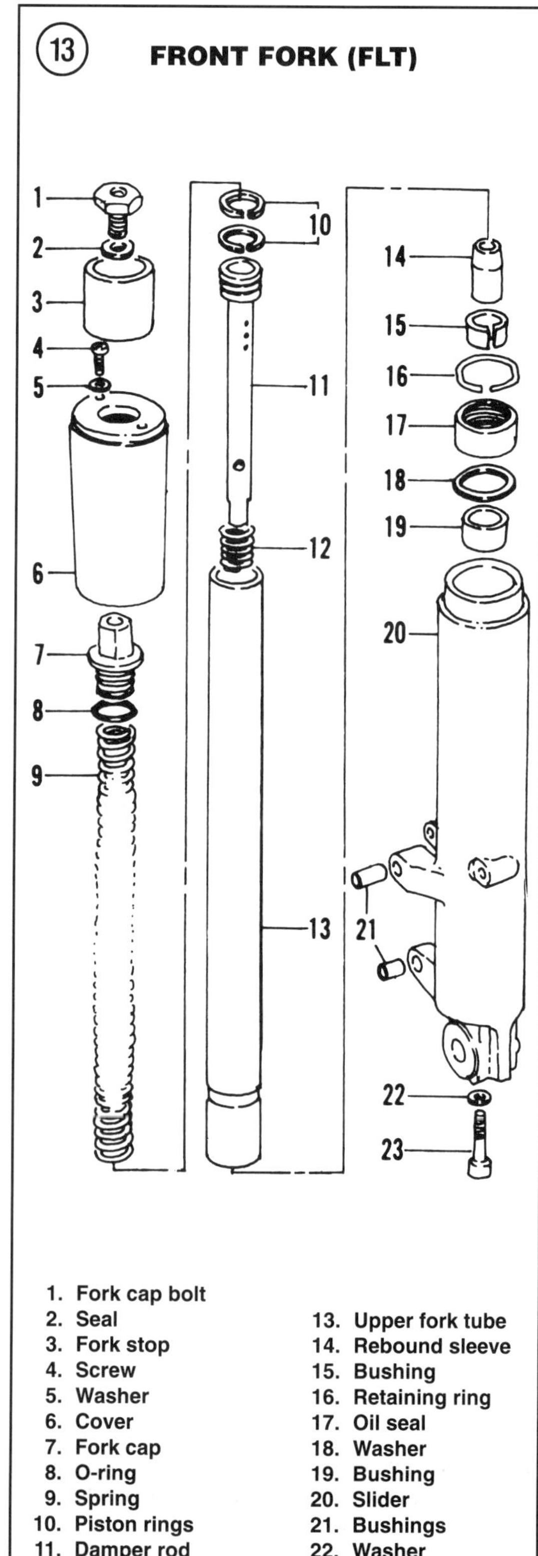

*with a locking compound and can be difficult to remove because the damper rod will turn inside the slider. If you have access to an air impact driver, you can remove the Allen screw after removing the fork spring in the following steps. If you do not have access to air tools, loosen the Allen bolt before removing the fork spring; the fork spring may offer enough resistance to allow removal of the screw. If you are unable to remove it, take the fork tubes to a dealer and have the screws removed.*

2. If you do not have access to air tools, loosen but do not remove the Allen screw at the bottom of the slider.

*WARNING*

*The fork cap is under spring pressure. When removing the cap, note that it may fly off. Keep your face away from the cap when removing it. In addition, make sure the fork tube is fully extended from the slider. If the forks are damaged and stuck in a compressed position, the fork should be disassembled by a dealer or qualified mechanic, as the cap and spring may fly out from the fork tube under considerable pressure when the cap is removed.*

3. Loosen and remove the fork cap at the top of the fork tube. Remove the fork cap and fork spring.
4. Remove the fork tube from the vise and pour the oil out of the fork into a clean container. Pump the fork several times by hand to expel most of the remaining oil. Check the oil for signs of aluminum debris, indicating worn or damaged parts. Discard the oil after examining it.

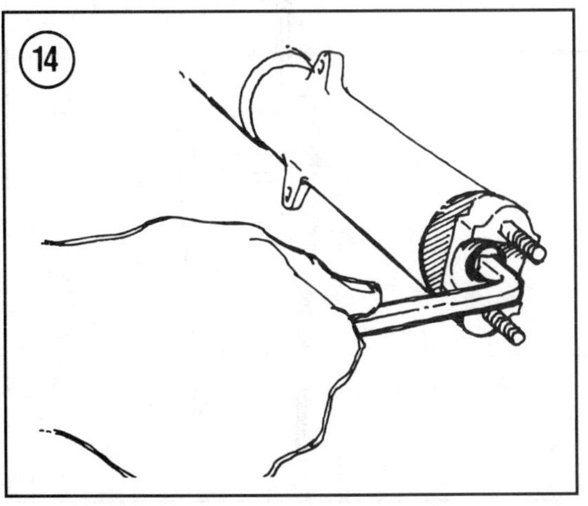


5. Remove the circlip securing the oil seal in the slider.
6. Remove the Allen bolt and washer (**Figure 14**) at the bottom of the slider.

*NOTE*

*The bushing installed in the slider is an interference fit. When separating the fork tube and slider, the bushing, washer and oil seal will be removed at the same time.*

7. While grasping the slider in one hand, work the fork tube up-and-down to knock the upper bushing, installed on the fork tube, against the lower bushing in the slider. As the lower bushing is knocked upward, it will push the oil seal and washer out of the slider.
8. Remove the rebound sleeve from the damper rod.
9. Insert a small rod into the end of the damper rod and push it out of the fork tube.
10. Inspect the fork assembly as described under *Inspection* in this chapter.

**Assembly (FLT)**

Refer to **Figure 13** for this procedure.

1. Prior to assembly, perform the *Inspection* procedure to make sure all worn or defective parts have been repaired or replaced. All parts should be thoroughly cleaned before assembly.
2. Coat all parts with Harley-Davidson Type E Fork Oil or equivalent before assembly.
3. If removed, install a new fork tube bushing as described under *Inspection* in this chapter.
4. If removed, install 2 new damper rod friction rings as described under *Inspection* in this chapter.
5. Slide the rebound spring onto the damper rod and insert this assembly into the fork tube.
6. Place the rebound sleeve onto the end of the damper rod.
7. Insert the fork spring into the fork tube so that the tapered side of the spring faces down (toward damper rod). Tension the spring to hold the damper rod in place and insert the fork tube into the slider. Make sure the rebound sleeve stays on the end of the damper rod.

8. Temporarily install the fork cap into the top of the fork tube. Tighten the fork cap.
9. Make sure the gasket is on the damper rod Allen screw.
10. Apply Loctite 271 (red) to the threads of the Allen screw prior to installing it. Install it through the slider and thread it into the end of the damper rod. Tighten the screw securely.
11. Remove the fork cap and the fork spring.

*NOTE*
*The bushing, seal spacer and oil seal are installed into the slider at the same time by knocking them into place with a driver. The Harley-Davidson fork seal driver (part No. HD-34634) can be used. A piece of pipe can be used to install the parts into the slider. If you are going to use pipe or a similar tool, care must be taken to prevent damaging the slider, oil seal and fork tube. If both ends of the pipe or tool are threaded, wrap one end with duct tape to prevent the threads from damaging the parts.*

12. Install the upper bushing, washer and oil seal at the same time. Perform the following:
   a. Coat the upper bushing with fork oil and slide the bushing down the fork tube and rest it short of the slider cavity.
   b. Install the washer over the fork tube. Rest the washer on the upper bushing.
   c. Slide a new oil seal over the fork tube (lettered side facing up). Rest the oil seal on the washer.
   d. Slide the fork seal driver down the fork tube (**Figure 15**).
   e. Drive the bushing, washer and oil seal into the slider until the groove in the slider can be seen above the top surface of the oil seal.
   f. Remove the installation tool.
13. Install the circlip into the slider groove. Make sure the circlip is completely seated in the groove.
14. Fill the fork tube with the correct quantity of Harley-Davidson Type E Fork Oil. Refer to Chapter Three for fork oil quantity.
15. Install the fork spring.
16. Install the O-ring onto the fork cap, if removed.
17. Align the fork cap with the spring and push down on the cap to compress the spring. Start the cap slowly, don't cross thread it.
18. Place the slider in a vise with soft jaws and tighten the fork cap securely.
19. Install the fork tube as described in this chapter.

## Disassembly (FXR)

To simplify fork service and to prevent the mixing of parts, the legs should be disassembled and assembled individually.

Refer to **Figure 16** (1984-1990) or **Figure 17** (1991) for this procedure.

1. Using the front axle boss at the bottom of the fork tube, clamp the slider in a vise with soft jaws. Do *not* clamp the slider at any point above the fork axle boss in a vise.

*NOTE*
*The Allen screw inserted through the bottom of the slider has been secured with a locking compound and can be difficult to remove because the damper rod will turn inside the slider. If you*

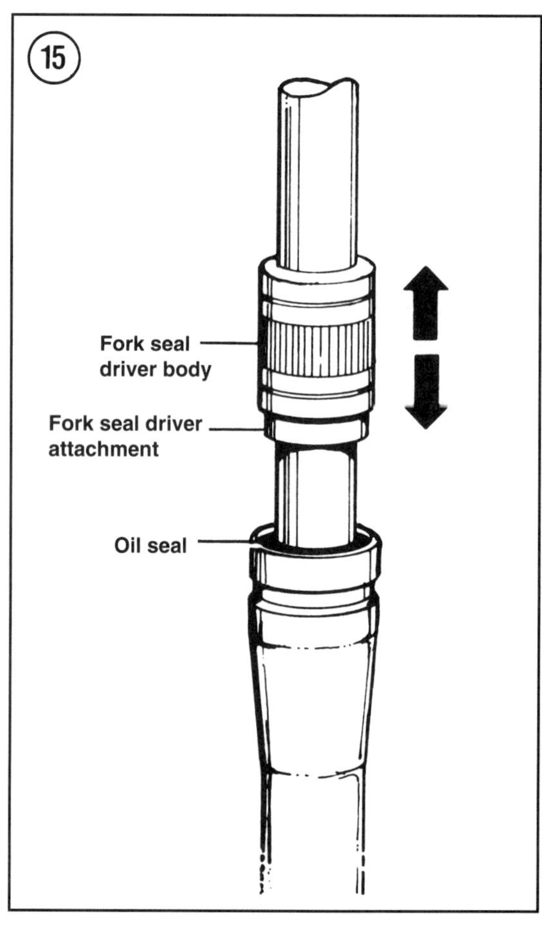

16

**FRONT FORK (1984-1990 FXR)**

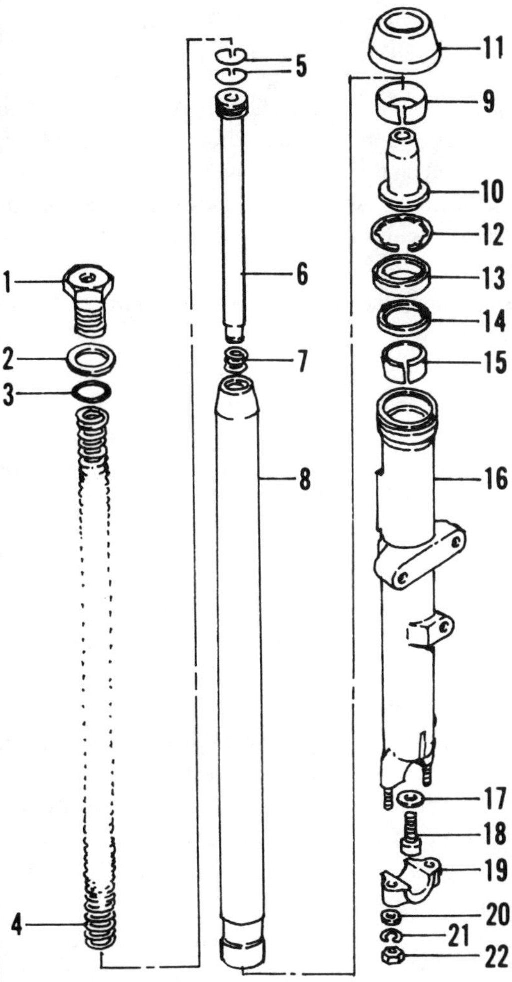

1. Cap
2. Washer*
3. O-ring
4. Spring
5. Piston rings
6. Damper rod
7. Spring
8. Upper fork tube
9. Bushing
10. Rebound sleeve
11. Boot
12. Retaining ring
13. Seal
14. Spacer
15. Bushing
16. Slider
17. Washer
18. Allen bolt
19. Cap
20. Washer
21. Lockwasher
22. Nut

*Not used on 1987 FXLR and FXRS and all 1988 FXR.

17

**FRONT FORK (1991 FXR)**

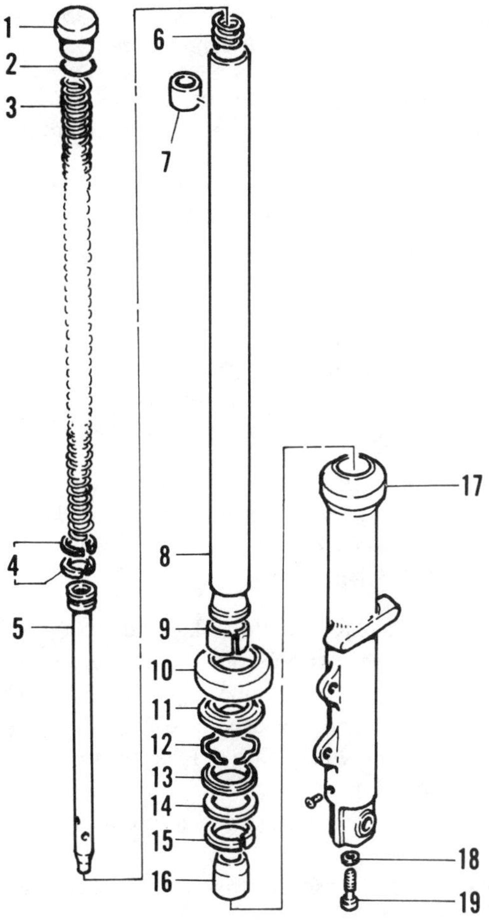

1. Cap
2. O-ring
3. Fork spring
4. Rings
5. Damper rod
6. Spring
7. Bushing
8. Fork tube
9. Bushing
10. Dust cap
11. Dust seal
12. Clip
13. Oil seal
14. Spacer
15. Bushing
16. Oil lock piece
17. Slider
18. Washer
19. Allen screw

*have access to an air impact driver, you can remove the Allen screw after removing the fork spring in the following steps. If you do not have access to air tools, loosen the Allen bolt before removing the fork spring; the fork spring may offer enough resistance to allow removal of the screw. If you are unable to remove it, take the fork tubes to a dealer and have the screws removed.*

2. If you do not have access to air tools, loosen but do not remove the Allen screw at the bottom of the slider.

*WARNING*

*The fork cap is under spring pressure. When removing the cap, note that it may fly off. Keep your face away from the cap when removing it. In addition, make sure the fork tube is fully extended from the slider. If the forks are damaged and stuck in a compressed position, the fork should be disassembled by a dealer or qualified mechanic, as the cap and spring may fly out from the fork tube under considerable pressure when the cap is removed.*

3. Loosen and remove the fork cap at the top of the fork tube. Remove the fork cap washer on 1984-1990 models. Remove the fork spring. Hold the bottom of the spring with a rag to avoid dripping oil on the floor as you remove it. Place the fork tube on clean shop rags or on newspapers spread over the workbench. This will help to absorb oil remaining on the spring.
4. Remove the fork tube from the vise and pour the oil out of the fork into a clean container. Pump the fork several times by hand to expel as much of the remaining oil as possible. Check the oil for signs of aluminum debris, indicating worn or damaged parts. Discard the oil after examining it.
5. Remove the Allen screw and washer at the bottom of the slider. If you loosened the screw prior to disassembly, you should be able to remove it now. If not, reinstall the fork spring and fork cap and loosen the screw.
6. Remove the cover (1991 models) and slide the fork boot off of the fork tube.
7. Secure the slider in a vise with soft jaws and remove the circlip from the groove in the top of the slider.

*NOTE*

*The bushing installed on the fork tube is larger than the bushing installed in the slider. When separating the fork tube and slider in Step 8, the slider bushing, washer and oil seal will be removed at the same time.*

8. While grasping the slider in one hand, work the fork tube up and down to knock the upper bushing, installed on the fork tube, against the lower bushing in the slider. As the lower bushing is knocked upward, it will push the oil seal and washer out of the slider.
9. Remove the rebound sleeve from the end of the damper rod.
10. Turn the fork tube over and slide the damper rod out. Remove the rebound sleeve from the damper rod.
11. Inspect the fork assembly as described under *Inspection* in this chapter.

## Assembly (FXR)

Refer to **Figure 16** (1984-1990) or **Figure 17** (1991) for this procedure.

1. Prior to assembly, perform the *Inspection* procedure to make sure all worn or defective parts have been repaired or replaced. All parts should be thoroughly cleaned before assembly.
2. Coat all parts with Harley-Davidson Type E Fork Oil or equivalent before assembly.
3. If the bushing was removed from the fork tube, install a new bushing as described under *Inspection* in this chapter.
4. If removed, install 2 new damper rod friction rings as described under *Inspection* in this chapter.
5. Slide the rebound spring onto the damper rod and insert this assembly into the fork tube.
6. Slide the rebound sleeve onto the end of the damper rod.
7. Insert the fork spring into the fork tube so that the tapered side of the spring faces down (toward damper rod). Tension the spring to hold the damper rod in place and insert the fork tube into the slider. Make sure the rebound sleeve stays on the end of the damper rod.
8. Temporarily install the fork cap into the top of the fork tube. Tighten the fork cap.

9. Make sure the gasket is on the damper rod Allen screw. Then install it through the slider and thread it into the end of the damper rod. Hold the slider in a vise with soft jaws and tighten the damper rod Allen screw securely.
10. Remove the fork cap and the fork spring.

*NOTE*

*The bushing, seal spacer and oil seal are installed into the slider at the same time by knocking them into place with a driver. The Harley-Davidson fork seal driver (part No. HD-34634) can be used. A piece of pipe can be used to install the parts into the slider. If you are going to use pipe or a similar tool, care must be taken to prevent damaging the slider, oil seal and fork tube. If both ends of the pipe or tool are threaded, wrap one end with duct tape to prevent the threads from damaging the parts.*

11. Install the upper bushing, washer and oil seal at the same time. Perform the following:
   a. Coat the upper bushing with fork oil and slide the bushing down the fork tube and rest it short of the slider cavity.
   b. Install the washer over the fork tube. Rest the washer on the upper bushing.
   c. Slide a new oil seal over the fork tube (lettered side facing up). Rest the oil seal on the washer.
   d. Slide the fork seal driver down the fork tube (**Figure 15**).
   e. Drive the bushing, washer and oil seal into the slider until the groove in the slider can be seen above the top surface of the oil seal.
   f. Remove the installation tool.
12. Install the circlip into the slider groove. Make sure the circlip is completely seated in the groove.
13. Install the dust seal and the cover (1991).
14. Fill the fork tube with the correct quantity of Harley-Davidson Type E Fork Oil. Refer to Chapter Three for fork oil quantity.
15. Install the fork spring.
16. Install the O-ring onto the fork cap, if removed.
17. Align the fork cap with the spring and push down on the cap to compress the spring. Start the cap slowly, don't cross thread it.
18. Place the slider in a vise with soft jaws and tighten the fork cap securely.
19. Install the fork tube as described in this chapter.

## Disassembly (FXWG)

To simplify fork service and to prevent the mixing of parts, the legs should be disassembled and assembled individually.

Refer to **Figure 18** for this procedure.

1. Using the front axle boss at the bottom of the fork tube, clamp the slider in a vise with soft jaws. Do *not* clamp the slider at any point above the fork axle boss in a vise.

*NOTE*

*The Allen screw inserted through the bottom of the slider has been secured with a locking compound and can be difficult to remove because the damper rod will turn inside the slider. If you have access to an air impact driver, you can remove the Allen screw after removing the fork spring in the following steps. If you do not have access to air tools, loosen the Allen bolt before removing the fork spring; the fork spring may offer enough resistance to allow removal of the screw. If you are unable to remove it, take the fork tubes to a dealer and have the screws removed.*

2. If you do not have access to air tools, loosen but do not remove the Allen screw at the bottom of the slider.

*WARNING*

*The fork tube plug is under spring pressure. When removing the plug, note that it may fly off. Keep your face away from the plug when removing it. In addition, make sure the fork tube is fully extended from the slider. If the forks are damaged and stuck in a compressed position, the fork should be disassembled by a dealer or qualified mechanic, as the plug and spring will fly out from the fork tube under considerable pressure when the plug is removed.*

3. Loosen and remove the fork cap at the top of the fork tube. Remove the fork cap and the fork spring.
4. Remove the fork tube from the vise and pour the oil out of the fork into a clean container. Pump the fork several times by hand to expel most of the remaining oil. Check the oil for contamination, in-

dicating worn or damaged parts. Discard the oil after examining it.

5. Slip the dust seal out of the lower fork tube and remove it.

6. Remove the circlip securing the oil seal in the slider.

7. Remove the Allen screw and washer at the bottom of the slider.

*NOTE*
*The bushing installed in the slider is an interference fit. When separating the fork tube and slider, the bushing, spacer seal and oil seal will be removed at the same time.*

8. While grasping the slider in one hand, work the fork tube up and down to knock the upper bushing,

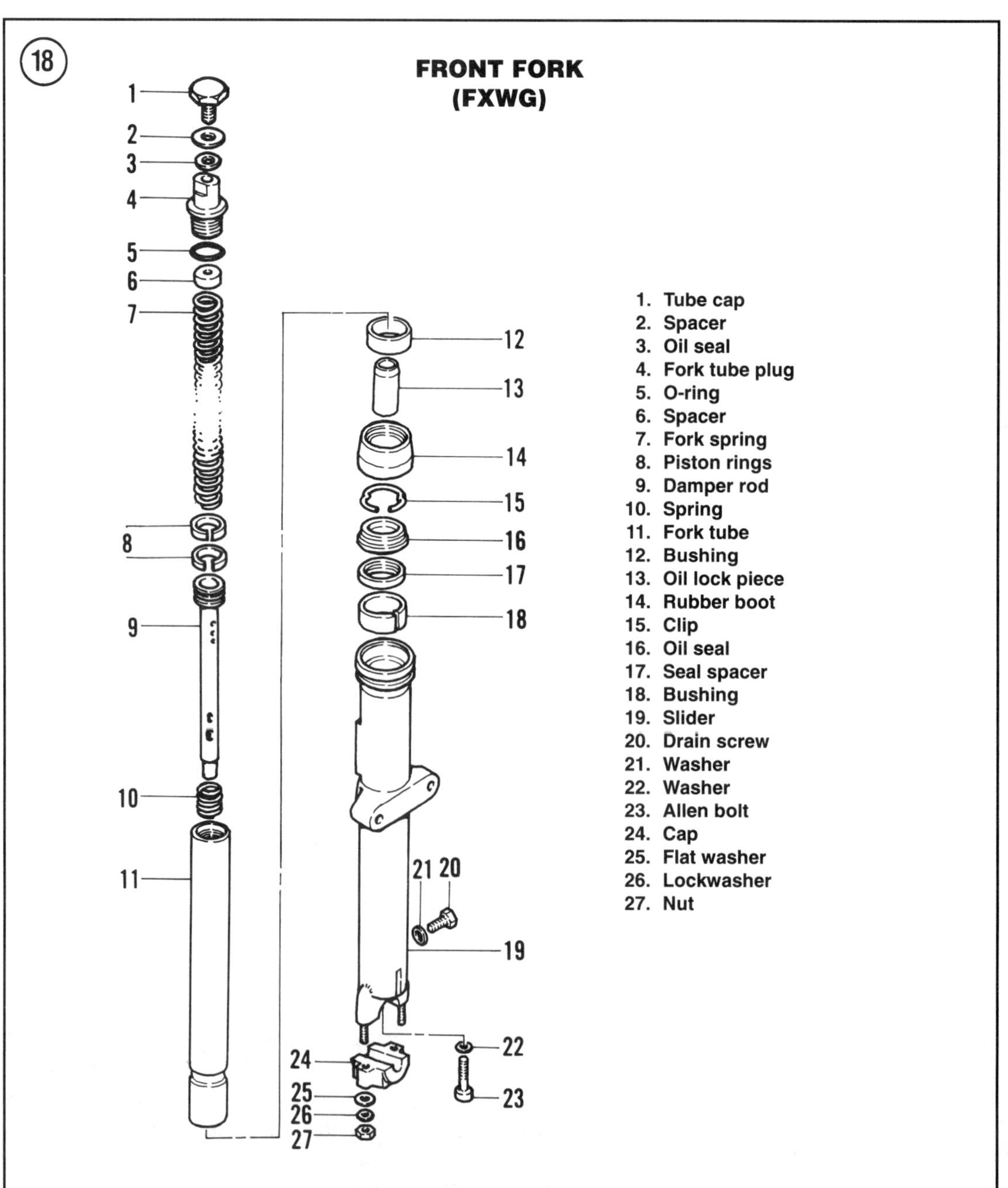

installed on the fork tube, against the lower bushing in the slider. As the lower bushing is knocked upward, it will push the oil seal and washer out of the slider.

9. Remove the rebound sleeve from the damper rod.
10. Insert a small rod into the end of the damper rod and push it out of the fork tube.

## Assembly (FXWG)

Refer to **Figure 18** for this procedure.

1. Prior to assembly, perform the *Inspection* procedure to make sure all worn or defective parts have been repaired or replaced. All parts should be thoroughly cleaned before assembly.
2. Coat all parts with Harley-Davidson Type E Fork Oil or equivalent before assembly.
3. If removed, install a new fork tube bushing as described under *Inspection*.
4. If removed, install 2 new damper rod friction rings as described under *Inspection*.
5. Slide the rebound spring onto the damper rod and insert this assembly into the fork tube.
6. Place the rebound sleeve onto the end of the damper rod.
7. Insert the fork spring into the fork tube so that the tapered side of the spring faces down (toward damper rod). Tension the spring to hold the damper rod in place and insert the fork tube into the slider. Make sure the rebound sleeve stays on the end of the damper rod.
8. Temporarily install the fork cap into the top of the fork tube. Tighten the fork cap.
9. Make sure the gasket is on the damper rod Allen screw.
10. Install the Allen screw through the slider and thread it into the end of the damper rod. Tighten the screw securely.
11. Remove the fork cap and the fork spring.

*NOTE*

*The bushing, seal spacer and oil seal are installed into the slider at the same time by knocking them into place with a driver. The Harley-Davidson fork seal driver (part No. HD-34634) can be used. A piece of pipe can be used to install the parts into the slider. If you are going to use pipe or a similar tool, care must be taken to avoid damaging the slider, oil seal and fork tube. If both ends of the pipe or tool are threaded, wrap one end with duct tape to prevent the threads from damaging the parts.*

12. Install the upper bushing, seal spacer and oil seal at the same time. Perform the following:
    a. Coat the upper bushing with fork oil and slide the bushing down the fork tube and rest it short of the slider cavity.
    b. Install the seal spacer over the fork tube (flange surface facing up). Rest the seal spacer on the upper bushing.
    c. Slide a new oil seal over the fork tube (lettered side facing up). Rest the oil seal on the seal spacer.
    d. Slide the fork seal driver down the fork tube (**Figure 15**).
    e. Drive the bushing, seal spacer and oil seal into the slider until the groove in the slider can be seen above the top surface of the oil seal.
    f. Remove the installation tool.
13. Install the circlip into the slider groove. Make sure the circlip is completely seated in the groove.
14. Slide the dust seal down the fork tube and seat it in the slider groove.
15. Fill the fork tube with the correct quantity of Harley-Davidson Type E Fork Oil. Refer to Chapter Three for fork oil quantity.
16. The fork spring is tapered at one end. Install the spring so that the tapered end faces toward the bottom of the fork.
17. Align the fork cap with the spring and push down on the cap to compress the spring. Start the cap slowly, don't cross thread it.
18. Place the slider in a vise with soft jaws and tighten the fork cap securely.
19. Install the fork tube as described in this chapter.

## Disassembly (FXEF and FXSB)

To simplify fork service and to prevent the mixing of parts, the legs should be disassembled and assembled individually.

Refer to **Figure 19** for this procedure.

1. Using the front axle boss at the bottom of the fork tube, clamp the slider in a vise with soft jaws. Do *not* clamp the slider at any point above the fork axle boss in a vise.

*NOTE*

*The Allen screw inserted through the bottom of the slider has been secured with a locking compound and can be difficult to remove because the damper rod will turn inside the slider. If you have access to an air impact driver, you can remove the Allen screw after removing the fork spring in the following steps. If you do not have access to air tools, loosen the Allen bolt before removing the fork spring; the fork spring may offer enough resistance to allow removal of the screw. If you are unable to remove it, take the fork tubes to a dealer and have the screws removed.*

2. If you do not have access to air tools, loosen but do not remove the Allen screw at the bottom of the slider.

*WARNING*

*The fork tube cap is under spring pressure. When removing the cap, note that it may fly off. Keep your face away from the cap when removing it. In addition, make sure the fork tube is fully extended from the slider. If the forks are damaged and stuck in a compressed position, the fork should be disassembled by a dealer or qualified mechanic, as the cap and spring will fly out from the fork tube*

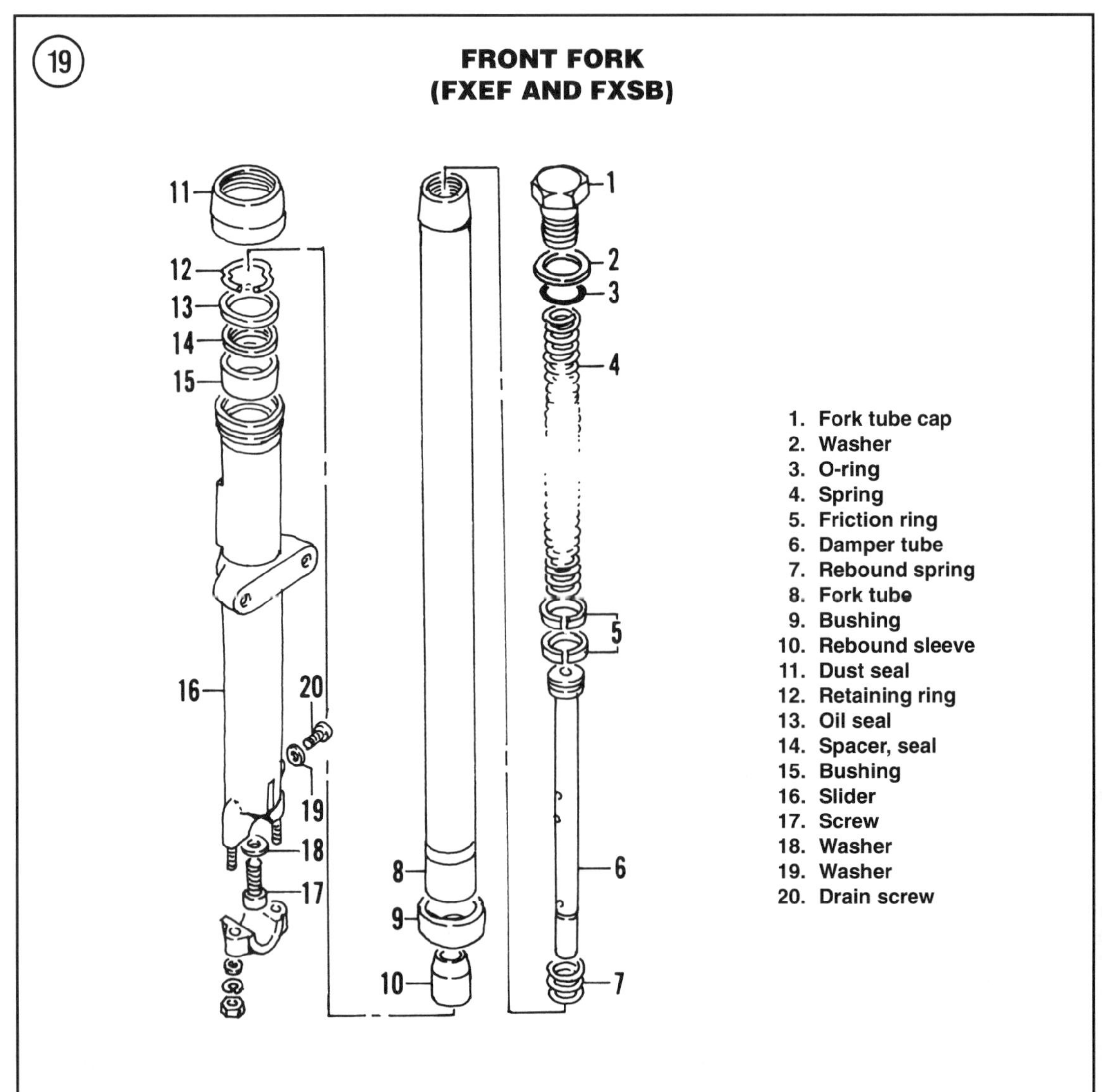

*under considerable pressure when the cap is removed.*

3. Loosen and remove the fork cap at the top of the fork tube. Remove the fork cap and the fork spring.
4. Remove the fork tube from the vise and pour the oil out of the fork into a clean container. Pump the fork several times by hand to expel most of the remaining oil. Check the oil for contamination, indicating worn or damaged parts. Discard the oil after examining it.
5. Slip the dust seal out of the lower fork tube and remove it.
6. Remove the circlip securing the oil seal in the slider.
7. Remove the Allen screw and washer at the bottom of the slider.

*NOTE*
*The bushing installed in the slider is an interference fit. When separating the fork tube and slider, the bushing, spacer seal and oil seal will be removed at the same time.*

8. While grasping the slider in one hand, work the fork tube up and down to knock the upper bushing, installed on the fork tube, against the lower bushing in the slider. As the lower bushing is knocked upward, it will push the oil seal and washer out of the slider.
9. Remove the rebound sleeve from the damper rod.
10. Insert a small rod into the end of the damper rod and push it out of the fork tube.

**Assembly (FXEF and FXSB)**

Refer to **Figure 19** for this procedure.

1. Prior to assembly, perform the *Inspection* procedure to make sure all worn or defective parts have been repaired or replaced. All parts should be thoroughly cleaned before assembly.
2. Coat all parts with Harley-Davidson Type E Fork Oil or equivalent before assembly.
3. If removed, install a new fork tube bushing as described under *Inspection*.
4. If removed, install 2 new damper rod friction rings as described under *Inspection*.
5. Slide the rebound spring onto the damper rod and insert this assembly into the fork tube.
6. Place the rebound sleeve onto the end of the damper rod.
7. Insert the fork spring into the fork tube so that the tapered side of the spring faces down (toward damper rod). Tension the spring to hold the damper rod in place and insert the fork tube into the slider. Make sure the rebound sleeve stays on the end of the damper rod.
8. Temporarily install the fork cap into the top of the fork tube. Tighten the fork cap.
9. Make sure the gasket is on the damper rod Allen screw.
10. Install the Allen screw through the slider and thread it into the end of the damper rod. Tighten the screw securely.
11. Remove the fork cap and the fork spring.

*NOTE*
*The bushing, seal spacer and oil seal are installed into the slider at the same time by knocking them into place with a driver. The Harley-Davidson fork seal driver (part No. HD-34634) can be used. A piece of pipe can be used to install the parts into the slider. If you are going to use pipe or a similar tool, care must be taken to avoid damaging the slider, oil seal and fork tube. If both ends of the pipe or tool are threaded, wrap one end with duct tape to prevent the threads from damaging the parts.*

12. Install the upper bushing, seal spacer and oil seal at the same time. Perform the following:
   a. Coat the upper bushing with fork oil and slide the bushing down the fork tube and rest it short of the slider cavity.
   b. Install the seal spacer over the fork tube (flange surface facing up). Rest the seal spacer on the upper bushing.
   c. Slide a new oil seal over the fork tube (lettered side facing up). Rest the oil seal on the seal spacer.
   d. Slide the fork seal driver down the fork tube (**Figure 15**).
   e. Drive the bushing, seal spacer and oil seal into the slider until the groove in the slider can be seen above the top surface of the oil seal.
   f. Remove the installation tool.
13. Install the circlip into the slider groove. Make sure the circlip is completely seated in the groove.

14. Slide the dust seal down the fork tube and seat it in the slider groove.

15. Fill the fork tube with the correct quantity of Harley-Davidson Type E Fork Oil. Refer to Chapter Three for fork oil quantity.

16. The fork spring is tapered at one end. Install the spring so that the tapered end faces toward the bottom of the fork.

17. Align the fork cap with the spring and push down on the cap to compress the spring. Start the cap slowly, don't cross thread it.

18. Place the slider in a vise with soft jaws and tighten the fork cap securely.

19. Install the fork tube as described in this chapter.

### Inspection (All Models)

*CAUTION*

*Before cleaning rubber components, make sure the cleaning solvent is compatible with rubber. Some solvents can cause permanent damage.*

1. Thoroughly clean all parts in solvent and dry them. Place cleaned parts on newspaper or lint-free towels until reassembly. Ordinary paper towels should not be used to dry parts because of the lint left on the parts.

2. Check upper fork tube exterior (**Figure 20**) for bending, scratches or other damage. The fork tubes can be checked for bending with a set of V-blocks and a dial indicator. If you do not have these tools, you can roll the fork tube on a large plate of glass to check runout. Harley-Davidson does not provide service limit specifications for runout. If a fork tube is slightly bent, it can be straightened with a press and special blocks; see your Harley-Davidson dealer. If a fork tube is bent so much that the metal has cracked or wrinkled, the fork tube should be replaced.

3. Check the slider for dents or exterior damage that may cause the fork tube to hang up when riding; extensive damage should be apparent. Check the circlip groove in the top of the fork tube for cracks, wear or corrosion. Clean out the groove if necessary so that the circlip can seat correctly during assembly. Replace the slider if the groove is cracked or damaged.

4. Check the axle bearing surfaces on the slider for wear or gouges. Check the cap for cracks or damage. Clean up the surfaces or replace the slider and/or cap if necessary.

5. Check the axle cap studs in the bottom of the slider(s) for thread damage or looseness. If necessary, replace the studs as described in Chapter One.

6. Replace worn or damaged washers as required.

7. Check the damper rod rebound sleeve and piston rings for wear or damage. Replace the piston rings by removing them from the damper rod and installing new ones.

8. Check the damper rod for straightness with a set of V-blocks and a dial indicator or by rolling it on a piece of plate glass. Harley-Davidson does not provide service limit specifications for runout. If the damper rod is bent, have it checked by your local Harley-Davidson dealer.

9. Make sure the oil passage holes in the damper rod and fork tube are clean. If clogged, clean out with solvent and dry with compressed air.

10. Check the threads in the damper rod for stripping, cross-threading or deposit buildup. The hole should be blown out with compressed air so that dirt

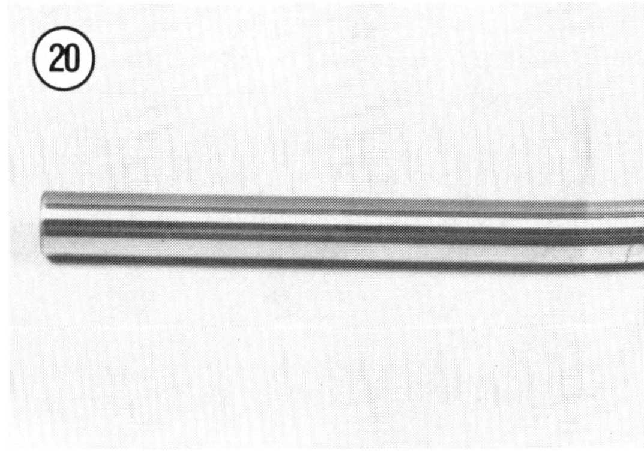
20

21

cannot prevent the Allen screw from being properly torqued. Use a tap to true up the threads and remove any deposits.

11. Check the damper rod rebound spring and the fork spring for wear or damage. Harley-Davidson does not provide service limit specifications for spring free length.

12. Check the upper bushing mounted in the slider and the lower bushing mounted on the fork tube for severe wear, cracks or damage. Worn bushings can cause the front forks to chatter or twitch during fork operation or when the front brake is applied. The upper bushing was removed together with the oil seal. The lower bushing installed on the fork tube should not be removed unless worn or damaged. To replace the bushing, perform the following:

a. Wedge a screwdriver into the bushing split to expand the bushing slightly and slide it off of the fork tube.
b. Install a new bushing by expanding the split as during removal. Expand the new split bushing only enough to fit it over the fork tube.
c. Seat the new bushing into the groove in the fork tube.

13. Inspect the outer dust seals for cracks, age deterioration or other damage.

14. The oil seals (**Figure 21**) should be replaced if removed. If you plan to install the original seals, inspect them closely for wear or deterioration. When in doubt, replace the seals as a set.

15. Any parts that are worn or damaged should be replaced. When replacing the fork springs (**Figure 22**), replace both springs as a set; do not replace only one spring. Simply cleaning and reinstalling unserviceable components will not improve performance of the front suspension.

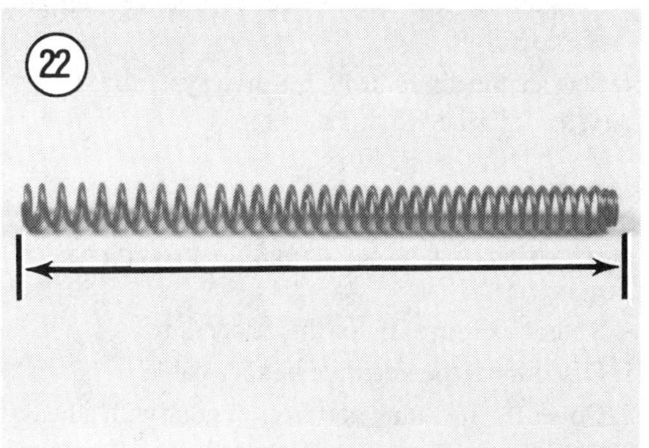


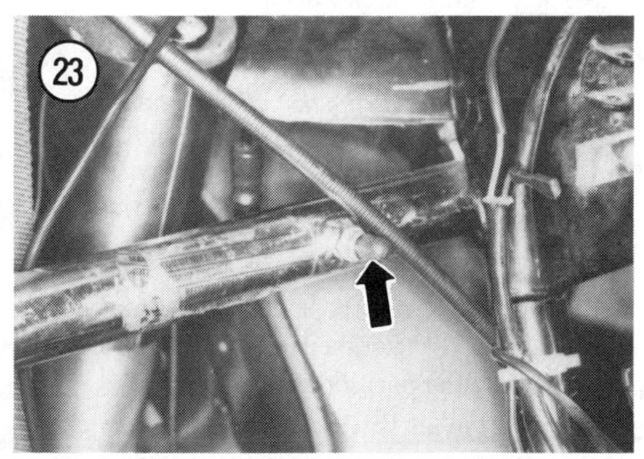


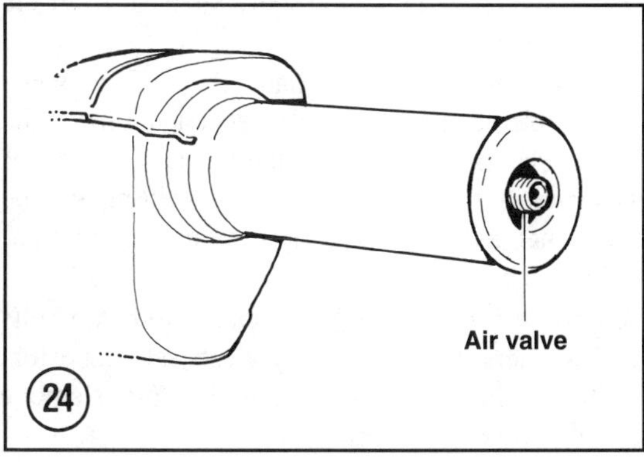


## FRONT FORK AIR CONTROL AND ANTI-DIVE SYSTEM

All FLT and some FXR models are equipped with a front fork air control/anti-dive system that uses air pressure to reduce fork compression during braking. The amount of anti-dive is dependent on the amount of air pressure used in the system.

### Air Pressure/Anti-Dive Adjustment

Anti-dive or fork compression can be controlled by regulating the amount of air pressure used in the front fork air control system. If you wish to obtain less fork compression (increasing the anti-dive), you should increase the system's air pressure. Reducing air pressure would result in more fork compression (less anti-dive).

To change air pressure, first remove the air valve cap from the air valve fitting. See **Figure 23** or **Figure 24**. To assure accurate readings, a no-loss air gauge should be used. Because high air pressure can fill the system quickly and damage it, add air with a hand or foot operated air pump. Do not fill the system with a hose connected to a large compressor. Harley-Davidson recommends a minimum and maximum air pressure setting for all models. Make sure that you maintain the air pressure in the system within these 2 limits. Insufficient or excessive air pressure readings can damage the system. Refer to **Table 2** or **Table 3** when adjusting the air pressure.

### Anti-Dive System Check

1. For the air control and anti-dive systems to work properly, the system must be closed—no leaks. If you are losing air pressure, there is a leak in the system. First check the tightness of the valve core in the air valve. If the valve core is tight, fill the system once again and put some saliva on the valve. If air bubbles appear across the face of the valve, the valve may be damaged. If air is not leaking from the valve core, tighten all of the air line fittings securely and recheck. Visually inspect the air lines for cracks or other signs of damage. If tightening the fittings does not stop the leak, you will have to remove the assembly and replace worn or damaged parts. Refer to **Figures 25-27** for your model.

*NOTE*

*If you have an FLT model, check the ground connector screwed onto the air manifold. If the screws holding the ground connector to the air manifold have backed out, air can leak out of the screw hole. If the screws are loose or suspect, remove them from the ground connector and apply Loctite Pipe Sealant With Teflon to the screw threads. Reinstall the screws and tighten securely. Check the system once again for leaks.*

*NOTE*

*When removing the air control system as described in this chapter, you should replace all of the O-rings and copper washers (if used) during reassembly.*

2. Anti-dive solenoid check: With the ignition switch turned ON, apply the front or rear brake while listening to the anti-dive solenoid. A faint click should be heard when the brake is applied. Because of the faint noise, touch the solenoid when applying the brake so that you can feel the solenoid vibrate (and click).

3. Check the anti-dive system as follows:
   a. Install a no-loss air gauge on the air control air valve fitting. The fitting location will vary depending on model. See **Figure 23** or **Figure 24**.
   b. With the ignition switch turned OFF, apply the front brake and bounce the front end while watching the air gauge. The air pressure should fluctuate as the front end is moved up and down.
   c. Now repeat sub-step b with the ignition switch turned ON. The air pressure should stay constant as the front wheel is bounced up and down.

4. Service the air control/anti-dive system, if necessary, as described in this chapter.

### Removal/Installation (All FLT Models Except 1986-on FLHT/C)

Refer to **Figure 25** for this procedure.

1. Disconnect the negative battery cable.
2. Cover the fuel tank and front fender with a heavy blanket to prevent damage from falling tools or parts when performing the following.

*CAUTION*

*When removing the instrument panel in Step 3, do not turn the panel upside down or damping oil in the fuel gauge will run onto the gauge face and stain it.*

3. Remove the instrument panel from the motorcycle and place it on a workbench so that it rests in its normal operating position.
4. Remove the air valve cap. Using a screwdriver, depress the air valve and bleed the system.

5A. *1984-1987*: Disconnect the air hose from the engine guard accumulator.

5B. *1988-on*: Remove the handlebar riser locknuts from underneath the fork bracket. Then remove the upper clamps and lift the handlebar up slightly. Disconnect the air hose from the fitting on the handlebar. Set the handlebar aside to prevent damaging the control cables.

6. Loosen and remove the air manifold banjo bolts and washers. Disconnect any electrical connectors at the manifold and remove the manifold. Remove and discard the O-rings.

(25) **FRONT FORK AIR CONTROL (FLT MODELS)**

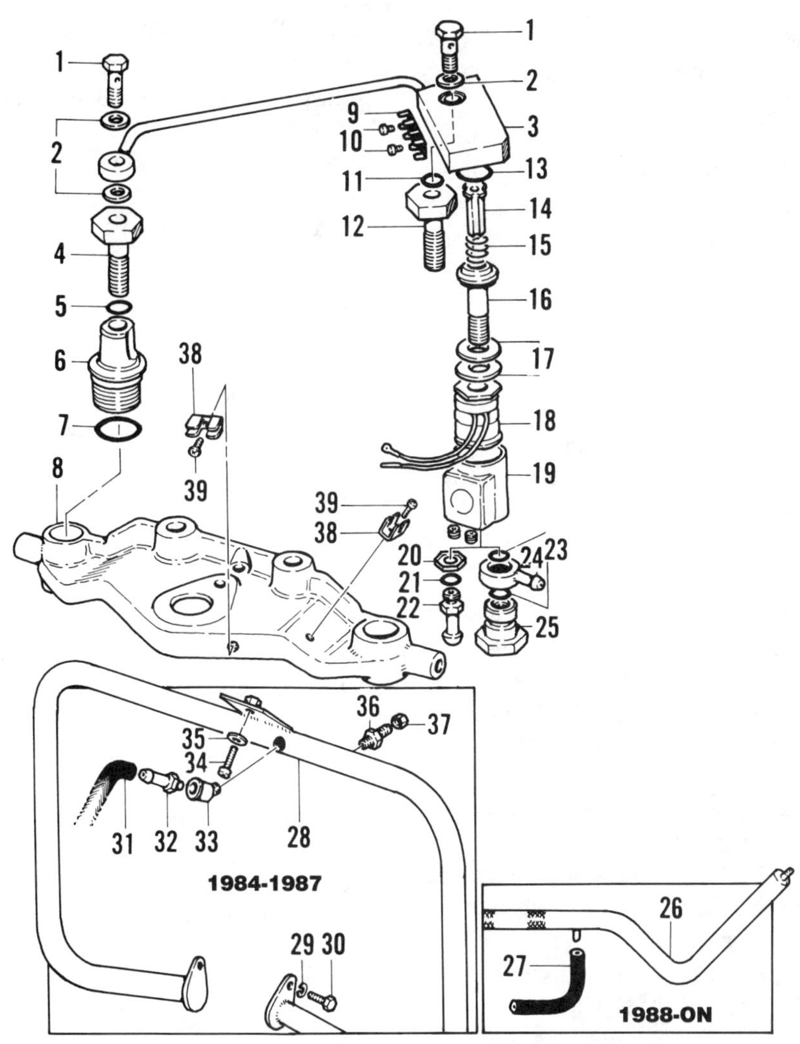


1. Banjo bolt
2. Washer
3. Air fork manifold
4. Fork tube cap
5. O-ring
6. Fork tube plug
7. O-ring
8. Upper fork bracket
9. Ground connector
10. Screws
11. O-ring
12. Fork tube cap
13. O-ring
14. Plunger
15. Spring
16. Plunger body
17. Spacer and rubber washer
18. Solenoid
19. Solenoid cover
20. Solenoid cover nut (1984)
21. O-ring (1984-1987)
22. Hose fitting (1984-1987)
23. O-rings (1988-on)
24. Hose fitting (1988-on)
25. Banjo bolt (1988-on)
26. Handlebar/air reservoir (1988-on)
27. Hose (1988-on)
28. Engine guard accumulator (1984-1987)
29. Lockwasher (1984-1987)
30. Bolt (1984-1987)
31. Hose (1984-1987)
32. Hose fitting
33. Engine guard plug (1984-1987)
34. Bolt (1984-1987)
35. Washer (1984-1987)
36. Valve stem (1984-1987)
37. Cap (1984-1987)
38. Ground terminal block (1993)
39. Screw (1993)

11

7. The anti-dive switch is now accessible. If necessary, remove it as described later in this chapter.
8. Installation is the reverse of these steps, plus the following.
9. Install a new O-ring in the bottom of the air manifold.
10. Position the anti-dive switch on the forks, if removed, and reconnect the switch electrical leads.
11. Install the upper banjo bolts using new washers. Tighten banjo bolts to 25-30 ft.-lb. (34.5-41.4 N•m).
12. Reconnect the air hoses after installing all air control components.
13. Pressurize the system and check for leaks.

### Removal/Installation (1986-on FLHT/C)

Refer to **Figure 25** for this procedure.
1. Disconnect the negative battery cable.
2. Cover the fuel tank and front fender with a heavy blanket to prevent damage from falling tools or parts when performing the following.
3. Remove the radio.
4. Remove the passing lamp bracket bolts and remove the bracket from the inner fairing; place the bracket onto the front fender. Reinstall the lower bracket bolts into the inner fairing to hold it in place.
5. Remove the outer fairing as described in Chapter Fifteen.
6. Remove the air valve cap. Using a screwdriver, depress the air valve and bleed the system.
7. The anti-dive valve is now accessible for removal. If necessary, remove the valve as described under *Inspection* in this chapter.
8. If you have a 1988 or later model, disconnect the air hose from the fitting on the handlebar.
9. Remove the handlebar riser nuts and move the handlebar back and lay it on the blanket covering the fuel tank.
10. Remove the ignition/fork lock assembly mounting bolts on the upper fork bracket.
11. Disconnect the electrical connectors from the anti-dive valve if the valve was not removed previously.
12. If you have a 1986-1987 model, disconnect the hose from the anti-dive valve.
13. Loosen and remove the 2 banjo bolts securing the air fork manifold to the fork tube bolts. Then lift the air fork manifold up and remove it. If the manifold contacts the inner fairing, gently push the fairing back by hand to make room for the manifold.
14. Installation is the reverse of these steps, plus the following.
15. Install a new O-ring in the bottom of the air manifold.
16. Position the anti-dive switch on the forks, if removed, and reconnect the switch electrical leads.
17. Install the upper banjo bolts using new washers. Tighten banjo bolts to 25-30 ft.-lb. (34.5-41.4 N•m).
18. Reconnect the air hoses after installing all air control components.
19. Pressurize the system and check for leaks.

### Removal/Installation (1984-1987 FXRD and FXRT)

Refer to **Figure 26** for this procedure.
1. Disconnect the negative battery terminal.
2. Remove the air valve cap. Using a screwdriver, depress the air valve and bleed the system.
3. Remove the instrument gauges from the handlebar.
4. Referring to **Figure 26**, note the banjo bolts and washers securing the air tubes to the fork cap. Remove both banjo bolts and their washers.
5. Remove the anti-dive valve solenoid housing bolts and washers.
6. Disconnect the anti-dive valve electrical connectors.
7. Remove the accumulator bracket bolts and washers.
8. Cut the plastic tie(s) securing the air hose to the fork tube. Remove the clamp securing the hose in position.
9. Check the air control assembly for any additional hose clamps or plastic ties and cut or disconnect them.
10. Remove the air control assembly from the front fork.
11. Installation is the reverse of these steps, plus the following.
12. If the air tubes were removed from the valve body, install them as described in this chapter.
13. Install the banjo bolts through the air tubes, making sure to place a washer on both sides of the air tube(s) as shown in **Figure 26**. Tighten the banjo bolts to 25-30 ft.-lb. (34.5-41.4 N•m).
14. When installing the accumulator mounting bracket and its bolts, place a flat washer so it is

(26)

## FRONT FORK AIR CONTROL UNIT (1984-1987 FXRD AND FXRT)

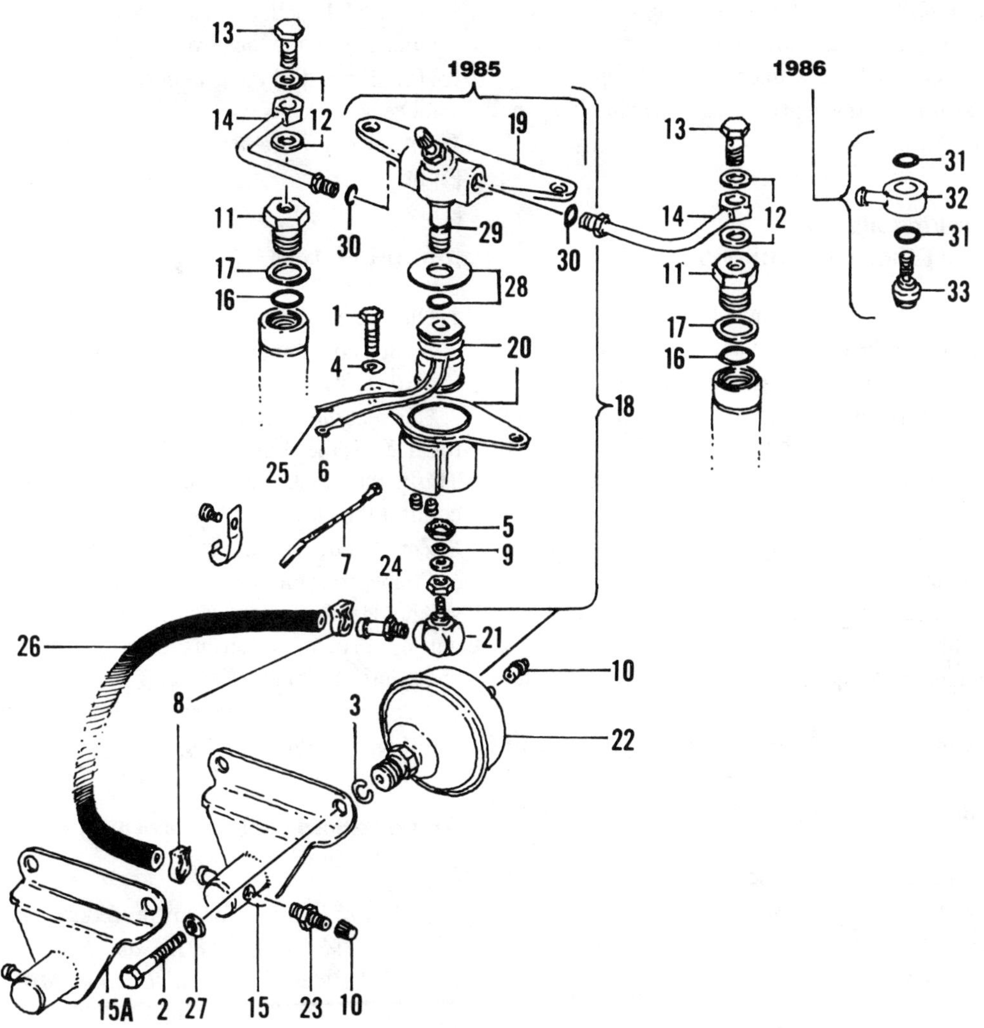


1. Bolt
2. Bolt
3. Lockwasher
4. Lockwasher
5. Nut (1985)
6. Wire terminal
7. Cable strap
8. Hose clamp
9. O-ring (1985)
10. Valve cap (1986)
11. Fork slider tube cap
12. Gasket
13. Banjo bolt
14. Tube
15. Bracket (1986)

15A. Bracket (1985)

16. Fork slider tube cap O-ring
17. Fork slider tube cap washer
18. Valve assembly
19. Valve body
20. Solenoid
21. Elbow (1985)
22. Accumulator
23. Valve stem (1986)
24. Fitting (1985)
25. Wire terminal, socket type
26. Hose
27. Flat washer
28. Spacer and washer
29. Plunger body
30. O-ring
31. O-ring (1986)
32. Banjo fitting (1986)
33. Banjo bolt (1986)

positioned between the bolt head and the bracket. Place a lockwasher so that it is positioned between the back of the bracket and the lower fork bracket. Tighten these bolts to 30-35 ft.-lb. (41.4-48.3 N•m).
15. Slide a lockwasher onto the anti-dive solenoid housing mounting bolts and tighten the bolts to 155-190 in.-lb. (17.8-21.8 N•m).
16. Reconnect the air hose, making sure to secure both ends of the hose with new hose clamps.
17. Pressurize the system as described in this chapter and check for leaks.

### Removal/Installation (1988-on FXRT and FXRS-SP)

Refer to **Figure 27** for this procedure.
1. Disconnect the negative battery terminal.
2. Remove the air valve cap from the air valve in the left-hand grip. Using a screwdriver, depress the air valve and bleed the system.
3. Remove the headlight from its mounting bracket and set it aside.
4. *FXRT*: Remove the upper cover screws. Then remove the cover and the 2 spacers.
5. *FXRS-SP*: Remove the headlight bracket and the manifold bolts.
6. Remove the banjo bolts and washers securing the air tubes to the fork caps.
7. Disconnect the air hose at the anti-dive valve connection.
8. Remove the air control assembly from the front fork.
9. Installation is the reverse of these steps, plus the following.
10. Position the air fork assembly into position on the fork tubes.

*NOTE*
*If the air tubes were removed, install them now.*

11. Install the air tubes onto the valve body as follows:
   a. Install a new O-ring into the valve body/air tube bore.
   b. Insert the flared end of the air tube into the valve body; align the end of the tube with the fork cap. Secure the end of the tube with the O-ring and valve body.
   c. Tighten the flare nut to 200 in.-lb. (23 N•m).

12. Install the banjo bolts through the air tubes, making sure to place a washer on both sides of the air tube(s) as shown in **Figure 27**. Tighten the banjo bolts to 25-30 ft.-lb. (34.5-41.4 N•m).
13. Reconnect the air hose, making sure to secure both ends of the hose with new hose clamps.
14. On FXRT models, make sure to install the spacers underneath the top cover.
15. Pressurize the system as described in this chapter and check for leaks.
16. Adjust the headlight as described in Chapter Eight.

### Anti-Dive Solenoid Testing

1. Disconnect the switch leads.
2. Switch an ohmmeter to R × 1 and touch the leads to zero the meter.
3. Connect the ohmmeter leads to both switch electrical leads; the ohmmeter should show 10-20 ohms. This is the resistance in the anti-dive solenoid. Disconnect the ohmmeter leads.
4. Zero the meter once again as described in Step 2.
5. Connect one ohmmeter lead to one of the anti-dive solenoid leads. Touch the other ohmmeter lead to the anti-dive solenoid housing. The ohmmeter should show infinity (high resistance).
6. Replace the anti-dive solenoid if it failed either test (Step 3 and/or Step 5).

### Anti-dive Solenoid Replacement (FLT Models)

Refer to **Figure 25** for this procedure.
1A. *FLT, 1984-1985 FLHT/C and FLHS*: Perform Steps 1-7 under *Removal (All FLT Models Except 1986-on FLHT/C)* in this chapter.
1B. *1986-on FLHT/C*: Perform Steps 1-7 under *Removal (1986-on FLHT/C)* in this chapter.
2A. *1984-1987*: Remove the hose fitting and O-ring from the bottom of the anti-dive solenoid.
2B. *1988-on*: Remove the banjo bolt, O-rings and hose fitting from the bottom of the anti-dive solenoid.
3. Remove the anti-dive valve cover nut, if used.
4. Remove the anti-dive valve case, anti-dive valve, spacer and rubber washer.
5. To remove the plunger body from the anti-dive valve:

(27)

**FRONT FORK AIR CONTROL (1988-ON FXRT, FXRS-SP)**

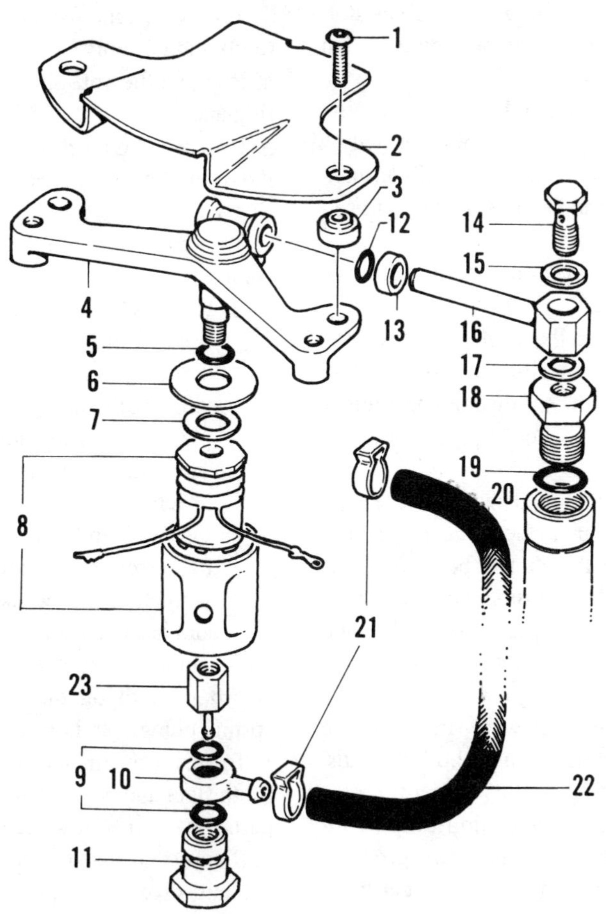


1. Screw
2. Cover (FXRT)
3. Spacer (FXRT)
4. Air manifold
5. O-ring
6. Washer
7. Rubber washer
8. Solenoid and case

15. Washer
9. O-ring
10. Banjo fitting
11. Banjo bolt
12. O-ring
13. Spacer sleeve
14. Banjo bolt
16. Tube

17. Washer
18. Fork tube cap
19. O-ring
20. Fork tubes
21. Hose clamp
22. Hose
23. Hose fitting (1992)

a. On 1984 models, a spanner wrench can be used to unscrew the plunger body from the anti-dive valve. If you do not have a spanner wrench, thread 2 jam nuts (thin nuts) onto the plunger body threads and lock them together. Then turn the inner nut with a wrench to unscrew and remove the plunger body.
b. On 1985 and later models, the plunger body has been redesigned with a screwdriver slot. Unscrew and remove the plunger body with a screwdriver.

6. After removing the plunger body, remove the spring, plunger and O-ring from the plunger body.
7. To ensure an air-tight system, replace all washers (both steel and copper) and O-rings. Installing used parts may cause the system to leak.
8. Remove all sealer residue from the plunger body and anti-dive valve threads.
9. Install a new O-ring into the air manifold recess.
10. One end of the plunger spring has a smaller OD than the other end. Install the spring onto the plunger so that the end with the smaller OD goes onto the plunger first.
11. Coat the plunger body threads with Loctite Pipe Sealant With Teflon and thread the plunger body into the air manifold. Tighten the plunger body using the same tool and method used for removal. See Step 5.
12. Install the spacer, washer, anti-dive valve and valve housing. Install the nut onto the end of the plunger body (early models only).
13A. *1984-1987*: Install a new O-ring into the groove machined above the plunger body threads. Then install the hose fitting on the plunger body.
13B. *1986-1987*: Assemble the banjo fitting by installing 2 new O-rings into the banjo fitting grooves. Then slide the banjo fitting over the plunger body and install the banjo bolt. Tighten the banjo bolt to 8-10 ft.-lb. (11-13.8 N•m).
14. The ground connector is secured to the air fork manifold with 2 screws. If it was necessary to remove or replace the ground connector, apply Loctite Pipe Sealant With Teflon to the screw threads before installing and tightening the screws. The sealant will help to prevent an air leak at the screw threads in the manifold housing. Tighten the screws securely.

### Anti-dive Solenoid Replacement (1984-1987 FXRT and FXRD)

Refer to **Figure 26** for this procedure.

1. Remove the front fork air control assembly as described in this chapter.
2A. *1984-1985*: Disconnect the hose from the hose fitting. Then unscrew and remove the hose fitting, nut, washer and O-ring.
2B. *1986-1987*: Disconnect the hose from the banjo fitting. Then unscrew and remove the banjo bolt, banjo fitting and O-rings.
3. Remove the nut from the end of the plunger body (early models only).
4. Remove the anti-dive valve and its housing, O-ring and spacer.
5. Unscrew the air hoses from the valve body. Remove the hoses and their O-rings. Discard the O-rings.
6. To remove the plunger body from the anti-dive valve:

a. On 1984 models, a spanner wrench can be used to unscrew the plunger body from the anti-dive valve. If you do not have a spanner wrench, thread 2 jam nuts (thin nuts) onto the plunger body threads and lock them together. Then turn the inner nut with a wrench to unscrew and remove the plunger body.
b. On 1985 and later models, the plunger body has been redesigned so that the spanner wrench cannot be used. Instead, a screwdriver slot has been added. Unscrew and remove the plunger body with a screwdriver.

7. After removing the plunger body, remove the spring, plunger and O-ring from the plunger body.
8. To ensure an air-tight system, replace all washers (both steel and copper) and O-rings. Installing used parts may allow the system to leak air.
9. Remove all sealer residue from the plunger body and anti-dive valve threads.
10. Install a new O-ring into the air manifold recess.
11. One end of the plunger spring has a smaller OD than the other end. Install the spring onto the plunger so that the end with the smaller OD goes onto the plunger first.
12. Coat the plunger body threads with Loctite Pipe Sealant With Teflon and thread the plunger body into the air manifold. Tighten the plunger body using the same tool and method used for removal. See Step 5.
13. Install the spacer, washer, anti-dive valve and valve housing. Install the nut onto the end of the plunger body (early models only).
14A. *1984-1985*: Install the nut, washer and O-ring onto the hose fitting. Then thread the hose fitting into

into the end of the plunger body. Tighten the nut, washer and O-ring securely.

14B. *1986-1987*: Assemble the banjo fitting by installing 2 new O-rings into the banjo fitting grooves. Then slide the banjo fitting over the plunger body and install the banjo bolt. Tighten the banjo bolt securely.

## Anti-dive Solenoid Replacement (1988-on FXRT, FXRS-SP and FXRS-CONV)

Refer to **Figure 27** for this procedure.

1. Remove the front fork air control assembly as described in this chapter.

2A. On 1988-1991 models, loosen and remove the banjo bolts, banjo fitting and 2 O-rings. Discard the O-rings.

2B. On 1992-on models, loosen and remove the fitting and O-ring.

3. Remove the anti-dive solenoid and its housing, rubber washer, washer and O-ring.

4. The plunger body threads into the bottom of the air manifold. To remove the plunger body, first thread 2 jam nuts (thin nuts) onto the plunger body threads and lock them together. Then turn the inner nut with a wrench and unscrew the plunger body.

5. After removing the plunger body, remove the spring, plunger and O-ring from the plunger body.

*NOTE*
*The 2 tubes installed at the top of the air manifold can be removed if necessary.*

*CAUTION*
*When removing the tube(s) in Step 6, do not remove the spacer sleeves.*

6. Carefully remove the air tube by pulling it out of the air manifold. Remove and discard the O-ring installed between the tube and air manifold seat. Repeat for the other air tube and O-ring.

7. To ensure an air-tight system, replace all of the O-rings used in the air control system. Installing used O-rings may allow the system to leak air.

8. Remove all sealer residue from the plunger body and anti-dive valve threads.

9. Install a new O-ring into the air manifold recess.

10. One end of the plunger spring has a smaller OD than the other end. Install the spring onto the plunger so that the end with the smaller OD goes onto the plunger first.

11. Coat the plunger body threads with Loctite Pipe Sealant With Teflon and thread the plunger body into the air manifold. Tighten the plunger body by reversing the removal steps.

12. Slide the washer, rubber washer, anti-dive solenoid onto the plunger body. Install the housing onto the anti-dive solenoid.

13. Install a new O-ring into the groove above the threads on the plunger body.

14A. On 1988-1991 models, perform the following:
   a. Install 2 new O-rings into the banjo fitting and slide the banjo fitting onto the plunger body. Thread the banjo bolt onto the plunger body until it is finger-tight.
   b. Turn the banjo fitting so that its hose nozzle faces in the direction shown in **Figure 27**. Tighten the banjo bolt to 8-10 ft.-lb. (11-13.8 N•m).

14B. On 1992-on models, install the fitting with a new O-ring.

15. If the air tube(s) were removed, install them as follows:
   a. Install a new O-ring into the air manifold.
   b. Carefully insert the air tube into the air manifold until the taper on the end of the tube touches the O-ring.
   c. Repeat for the other tube and O-ring.

**Tables 1-3 are on the following page.**

**Table 1 FRONT SUSPENSION TIGHTENING TORQUES**

| | ft.-lb. | N•m |
|---|---|---|
| Fork tube pinch bolts | | |
| FLT | | |
| 1984-1990 | 25 | 34.5 |
| 1991-on | 40 | 55.2 |
| FXR | | |
| 1984-1987 FXR, FXRS, FXRD, FXRT | | |
| Upper | 21-27 | 29-37.2 |
| Lower | 30-35 | 41.4-48.3 |
| 1987 FXLR, FXRSE and all 1988-1992 FXR | | |
| Upper and lower | 25-30 | 34.5-41.4 |
| 1993-on FXR | 30-35 | 41.1-48.3 |
| FXWG, FXEF and FXSB | 25-30 | 34.5-41.4 |
| Fork stem and bracket | | |
| FLT | | |
| Fork stem nut | 35-40 | 48.3-55.2 |
| FXR | | |
| Fork stem nut or bolt | See text | |
| Upper bracket-to-fork stem pinch bolt | | |
| 1984-1987 FXR, FXRS, FXRD, FXRT | 21-27 | 29-37.2 |
| 1987 FXLR, FXRSE and all 1988-1992 FXR | 25-30 | 34.5-41.4 |
| 1993-on FXR | 30-35 | 41-47 |
| FXWG | | |
| Fork stem nut | See text | |
| FXEF and FXSB | | |
| Fork stem nut | See text | |
| Upper bracket-to-fork stem pinch bolt | 20-25 | 27.6-34.5 |

**Table 2 FRONT FORK AIR CONTROL (FLT)**

| Ride | Amount of anti-dive | Recommended air pressure psi | $kg/cm^2$ |
|---|---|---|---|
| Firm | Stiff | 20 | 1.4 |
| Normal | Normal | 15 | 1.0 |
| Soft | Soft | 10 | 0.7 |

**Table 3 FRONT FORK AIR CONTROL (FXR)**

| | Recommended air pressure | | Accumulator 1984-1987 FXRD & FXRT | |
|---|---|---|---|---|
| Vehicle load | psi | $kg/cm^2$ | psi | $kg/cm^2$ |
| Rider weight not exceeding 150 lbs. | 4-8 | 0.3-0.6 | 25-30 | 1.7-2.1 |
| Each additional 25 lbs., add | 2 | 0.14 | | |
| Passenger weight for each 50 lbs., add | 1 | 0.07 | | |
| Maximum pressure | 20 | 1.4 | 30 | 2.1 |

## CHAPTER TWELVE

# REAR SUSPENSION

This chapter includes repair and replacement procedures for the rear suspension components.

**Tables 1-4** are found at the end of the chapter.

## REAR SHOCK ABSORBERS

Two shock absorbers connect the rear frame member to the swing arm.

When installing shorter shock absorbers or lowering kits, fender to tire clearance (with rider and passenger seated on bike) should be checked before riding bike.

### Spring Pre-load Adjustment (FXR Non-Air Shocks)

Hydraulically damped rear shocks are equipped with a cam at the base of each spring that allows spring adjustment to best suit different riding conditions and weight requirements. Cam positions range from off-cam position (solo rider with no luggage) to hard or maximum cam position (maximum loads).

Using a spanner wrench, engage the end of the wrench with one of the notches cut into the top of the cam and turn the cam to its desired position. A position is obtained when a cam ramp engages the tab fixed to the side of the shock body (**Figure 1**).

The cams on each shock absorber must be set to the same adjustment position. If you choose to set the cams into the off-cam position, rotate the cam from its hardest to its softest position. Do not turn the cam to the off-cam position directly from the hard or stiffest position as this could damage the cam and/or the positioning tab on the shock body.

*NOTE*
*A split rear shock absorber system is used on 1985 and later FXRT models. The shock absorber installed on the left-hand side is a non-adjustable hydraulically damped shock. The right-hand side is equipped with an air shock similar to the air shocks used on some FLT models.*

12

### Spring Pre-load Adjustment (FXWG, FXEF and FXSB)

The stock hydraulically damped rear shocks are equipped with a cam at the base of each spring that allows spring adjustment to best suit different riding conditions and weight requirements. Cam positions range from No. 1 (solo rider with no luggage) to No. 5 (maximum loads).

Using a spanner wrench, engage the end of the wrench with one of the notches cut into the top of the cam and turn the cam to its desired position. A position is obtained when a cam ramp engages the tab fixed to the side of the shock body (**Figure 1**).

The cams on each shock absorber must be set to the same adjustment position.

### Air Shock Adjustment (FXR and FLT)

A single air valve is used for air pressure adjustment on all air shock models. On 1985 and later FXRT models with one air shock, a single air line connects the air valve to the shock body. On all other models, separate air lines leading out from the air valve connects to the separate shock absorbers.

1. Locate and remove the air valve cap:
   a. 1984 FXRT: Air valve is located underneath the seat.
   b. 1985-on FLT: Air valve is located on the left-hand side cover.
   c. 1985-on FXRT and FXRD: Air valve is located underneath the right-hand saddlebag.

*CAUTION*

*Because the air lines and shock fill quickly, never fill the air shocks with a high pressure air supply; use a small manual or foot air pump. The maximum air pressure specification listed in* ***Tables 2-4*** *should not be exceeded or damage to the air shock or air lines may occur.*

2. Attach a small manual or foot air pump to the air valve fitting and inflate to the desired inflation pressure shown in **Tables 2-4**. To insure accurate readings, use a no-loss air pressure gauge when checking air pressure.
3. Reinstall the dust cap.

### Removal/Installation

Removal and installation of the rear shocks is easier if they are done separately. The remaining shock will support the rear of the bike and maintain the correct relationship between the top and bottom mounts. If both shock absorbers must be removed at the same time, first cut a piece of flat metal stock to length so that it is a bit longer than the shock absorber. Then drill two holes in the metal the same distance apart as the bolt holes in a shock absorber; select a drill bit that is slightly larger than the shock bolt OD The metal strap can be installed on the bike after the first shock absorber is removed. You can then move the bike around until the shock absorbers are reinstalled.

1. Place the bike on its jiffy stand. If both shocks are to be removed at the same time, support the bike so that the rear tire clears the ground. Slide a wood block between the rear tire and floor so that it just touches the tire.
2. Remove the saddlebags, if so equipped.
3. If necessary, loosen the muffler clamps and turn the muffler as needed to access the bottom shock mounting bolt. On some models, it may be necessary to remove the muffler from the bike.

*NOTE*

*A split rear shock absorber system is used on 1985 and later FXRT models. The shock absorber installed on the left-hand side is a non-adjustable hydraulically damped shock. The right-hand side is equipped with an air shock similar to the air shocks used on some FLT models.*

4. *Air shocks:* Bleed the air shock of all air pressure. Then disconnect the air line at the compression fitting.

*NOTE*

*Make a note of the washers used on each of the shock absorber bolts or studs so you can reinstall them in their original position.*

5. Remove the upper and lower bolts or nuts.
6. Pull the shock off of the frame and swing arm and remove it.

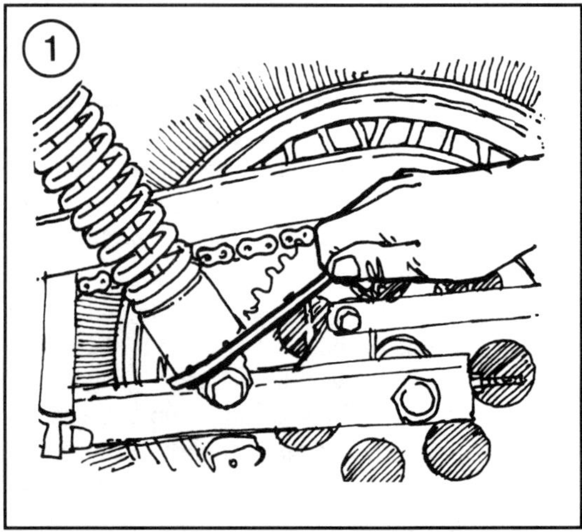

7. Inspect the shock absorbers and their mounting fasteners as described in this chapter.
8. Install by reversing these removal steps, plus the following.
9. If the spring was removed from a hydraulic shock, recheck the assembly to make sure the spring is properly installed.
10. Apply Loctite 242 (blue) onto the shock mounting bolt or stud threads.
11. Tighten the upper and lower shock fasteners to the torque specification listed in **Table 1**.

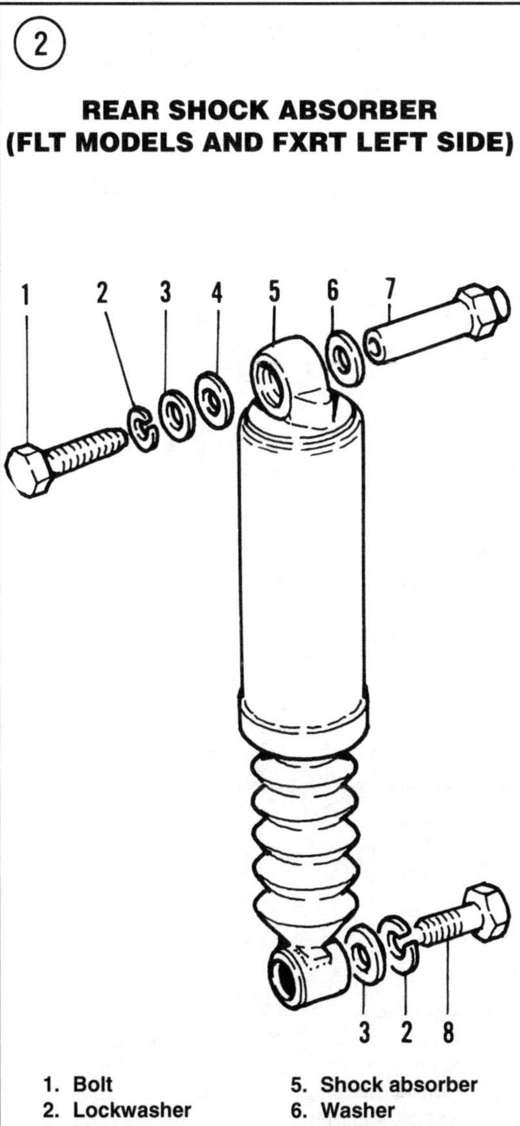


## Inspection (Air Shocks)

Other than replacing the shock bushings, the air shocks are not rebuildable. Refer to **Figure 2**.

1. Visually inspect the shock (**Figure 2**) for leakage or shaft damage. Check the rubber boot for deterioration, tears or other damage. If necessary, replace the shock absorber. See your Harley-Davidson dealer for the availability of replacement shock bushings.
2. Check the shock fastener threads for stripping, cross-threading or deposit buildup. If necessary, use a tap or die to true up the threads and to remove any deposits.
3. Check the washers for cupping, deformation, cracks or other damage. Replace the washers with the same size and thickness, if necessary.
4. If the air fittings on the shocks were removed or if they appear to be leaking, clean the fitting threads thoroughly to remove all sealant residue. Then reinstall the fitting(s) by first applying Loctite Pipe Sealant With Teflon to the fitting threads. Thread the fitting into the shock body and tighten securely.

## Disassembly/Inspection/Reassembly (Hydraulically Dampened Shocks)

The spring assembly on these models can be removed and worn or damaged parts replaced. The damper unit cannot be serviced.

Refer to the following illustration for your model when servicing the shock absorber.

a. 1984 FLT: **Figure 3**.
b. All 1984 FXR, all 1985-on FXR (except FXRT right-hand side): **Figure 4**.
c. FXWG, FXEF and FXSB: **Figure 5**.

1. Remove the shock absorber as described in this chapter.
2. Check the shock fastener threads for stripping, cross-threading or deposit buildup. If necessary, use a tap or die to true up the threads and to remove any deposits.
3. Check the washers for cupping, deformation, cracks or other damage. Replace the washers with the same size and thickness, if necessary.

*WARNING*
*Do not attempt to remove the shock springs without the proper spring compression tools.*

12

4. Mount the shock absorber in a spring compression tool so that the top of the shock absorber faces up. **Figure 6** shows the Harley-Davidson shock compressor (part No. 97010-52A). Variations of this tool can be purchased from motorcycle dealers and mail order houses; see **Figure 7**.

5. Compress the shock absorber spring enough to allow removal of the upper spring seat.

6. Release spring pressure, then remove the shock absorber assembly from the tool.

7. Disassemble the shock assembly as shown in **Figures 3-5** for your model. Do not attempt to disassemble the damper body.

8. Inspect the shock damper for leakage or shaft damage. The damper body is non-rebuildable and must be replaced if worn or damaged.

9. Hold the shock absorber on the workbench so that the top faces up. With your other hand, compress the shock pushrod and then pull it back up. The pushrod should compress slightly easier than when it extends. If you are unsure about its condition, compare its operation with a new one.

10. Harley-Davidson does not list spring free length specifications. Replace the spring if it is cracked or deformed. If you have access to a new spring, compare the spring lengths of the old and new spring.

11. Check the upper spring seat and the cam for cracks or other damage. Replace damaged parts as required.

12. Assembly is the reverse of these steps, plus the following.

13. To reduce spring tension when compressing the spring during reassembly, set the cam detent to its weakest position on the shock body. Then install the spring guide, spring and the upper cover over the

**(3) REAR SHOCK ABSORBER (FLT)**

1 2 3 4 5 6 7 8 10 9

1. Spring seat
2. Spring
3. Spring guide
4. Spring adjuster
5. Nut
6. Shock housing
7. Bushing
8. Washer
9. Bolt
10. Bolt

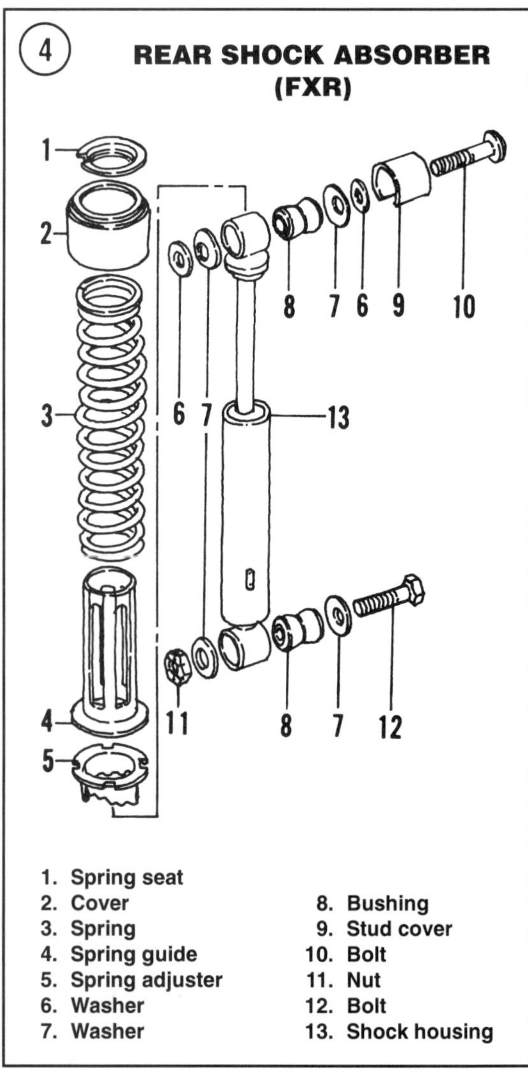


**(4) REAR SHOCK ABSORBER (FXR)**

1. Spring seat
2. Cover
3. Spring
4. Spring guide
5. Spring adjuster
6. Washer
7. Washer
8. Bushing
9. Stud cover
10. Bolt
11. Nut
12. Bolt
13. Shock housing

shock body. Compress the spring with the compression tool and install the spring seat. Make sure the spring seat engages the upper shock boss and the upper cover correctly, then release tension from the tool and allow the parts to seat together. Check the fit of the parts, especially at the top of the shock, before removing the tool.

### Shock Bushing Replacement

The shock bushings should be replaced as a set (all 4 at the same time) when they become worn or damaged.

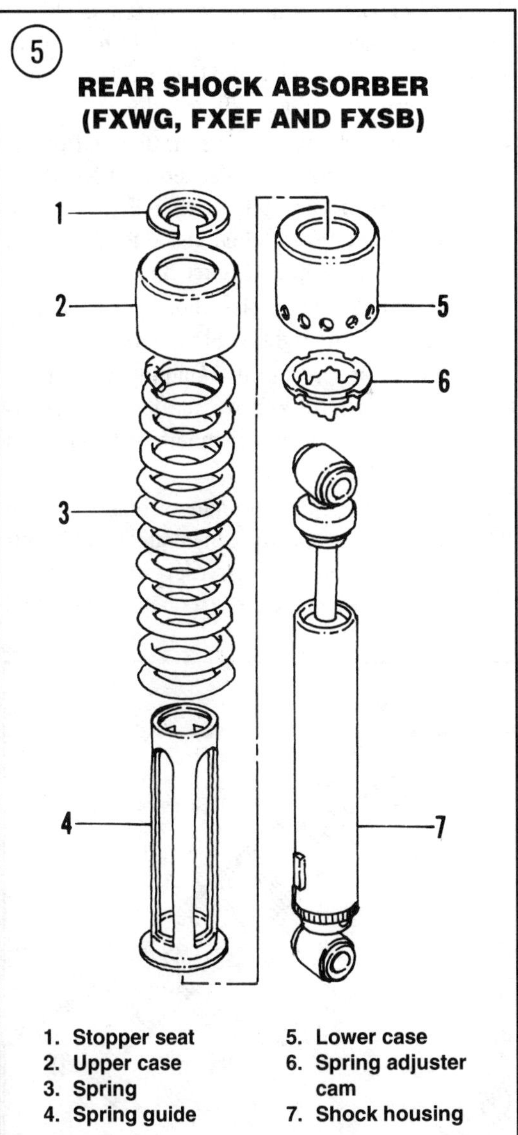


1. Before removing the bushings from the shock absorbers, purchase new bushings to have on hand.
2. Support the shock absorber in a press and press the bushing out of the eyelet.

CAUTION

*Failure to support the shock absorber correctly may damage it when pressure is applied to remove or install the bushing. Check the setup before and during bushing removal and installation. Work carefully so that you do not damage the shock shaft or deform the damper body.*

3. Clean the eyelet thoroughly before installing the new bushing.

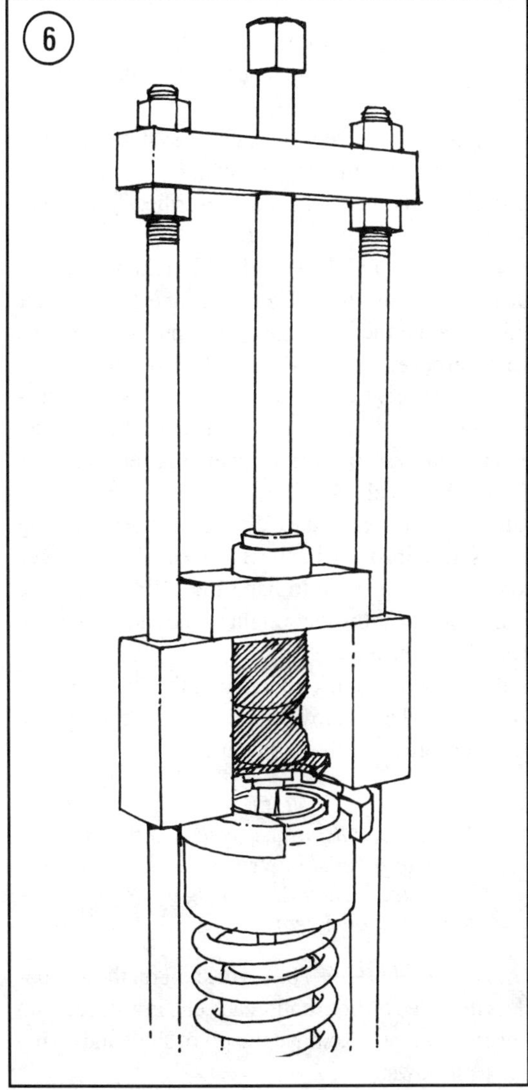


12

4. Press the new bushing into the shock eyelet.
5. Repeat for each bushing.

## SWING ARM (FLT AND FXR)

In time, the clevebloc bushings installed in the swing arm will wear and require replacement. Worn or damaged bushings can greatly affect handling performance and if worn parts are not replaced they can produce erratic and dangerous handling. Common symptoms are wheel hop, pulling to one side during acceleration and pulling to the other side during braking.

### Removal

Refer to **Figure 8** for this procedure.

1. Support the bike on a stand so that the rear tire clears the ground.
2. Remove the muffler or exhaust system if it will interfere with swing arm removal.
3. Remove the rear wheel as described in Chapter Ten.
4. *Drive chain models*: Turn the drive chain until you locate the master link. Then disconnect the master link, separate the drive chain and pull it off of the front sprocket. On models with drive boots that enclose the drive chain, it will be necessary to disconnect one of the rear chain boots from the sprocket cover to access the drive chain master link. See **Figure 9**, typical.
5. Remove the rear brake caliper from the rear swing arm as described in Chapter Thirteen. Use a Bungee cord or piece of wire to hang the caliper from the frame. Do not allow the weight of the caliper to hang from the brake hoses or lines.
6. Place a wood block underneath the swing arm to support it. Then remove the fasteners securing the shock absorbers to the swing arm.

*NOTE*

*Harley-Davidson has used 3 different types of pivot shafts since 1984. Refer to **Figure 8** and the following procedure for your model year.*

7A. *1984-early 1986*: The pivot shaft on these models is threaded on both ends; each end is secured with a washer and nut. Remove the pivot shaft and swing arm as follows:

a. Remove the cover plug from the end of the pivot shaft mounting brackets on FXR models.
b. Remove the right-hand pivot shaft nut and spacer.
c. Remove the pivot shaft mounting brackets on FXR models or remove the left- and right-hand passenger footpeg mounting brackets on FLT models.
d. Use an aluminum or brass rod and tap the pivot shaft out of the swing arm.
e. Remove the pivot shaft and swing arm. Note the position of the rubber and nylon washers as you remove the swing arm.

7B. *Late 1986-1988*: A dual pivot shaft assembly is used on these models. The left- and right-hand pivot shafts thread onto a center stud (**Figure 8**). Remove the swing arm and pivot shafts as follows:

a. Remove the cover plug from the end of the pivot shaft mounting brackets on FXR models. If you have a 1987 or 1988 FXR, remove the spring clips installed inside the mounting bracket access hole (**Figure 8**).
b. Hold the left-hand pivot bolt with a wrench and loosen the right-hand pivot bolt.
c. Remove the pivot shaft mounting brackets on FXR models or remove the left- and right-hand passenger footpeg mounting brackets on FLT models.
d. Select a piece of aluminum or brass rod with an OD larger than the center stud OD. Selecting the proper size rod to use will prevent you from damaging the threads on the center stud.

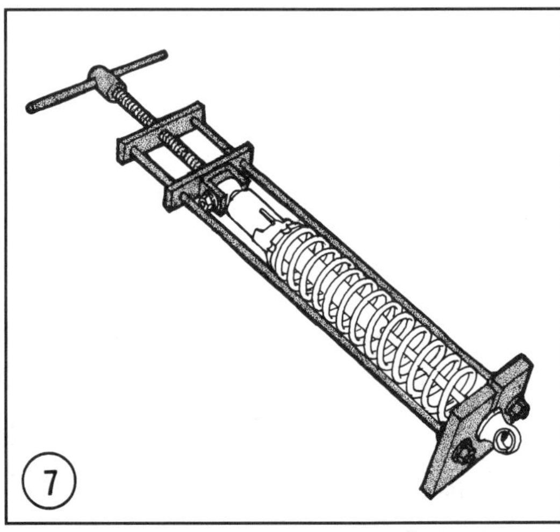
7

Insert the rod through the swing arm from the right-hand side, center it against the center stud and carefully tap the center stud and left-hand pivot shaft out of the swing arm.

e. Remove the swing arm assembly from the frame while noting the position of the rubber and nylon washers.

7C. *1989-on*: The swing arm pivots on a pivot shaft installed from the right-hand side (**Figure 8**). Remove the swing arm and pivot shaft as follows:

a. Remove the cover plug from the end of the pivot shaft mounting brackets on FXR models.

b. Hold the right-hand pivot shaft nut with a wrench and loosen the left-hand nut. Then remove the nut and the cup washer.

c. Remove the pivot shaft mounting brackets on FXR models or remove the left- and right-hand passenger footpeg mounting brackets on FLT models.

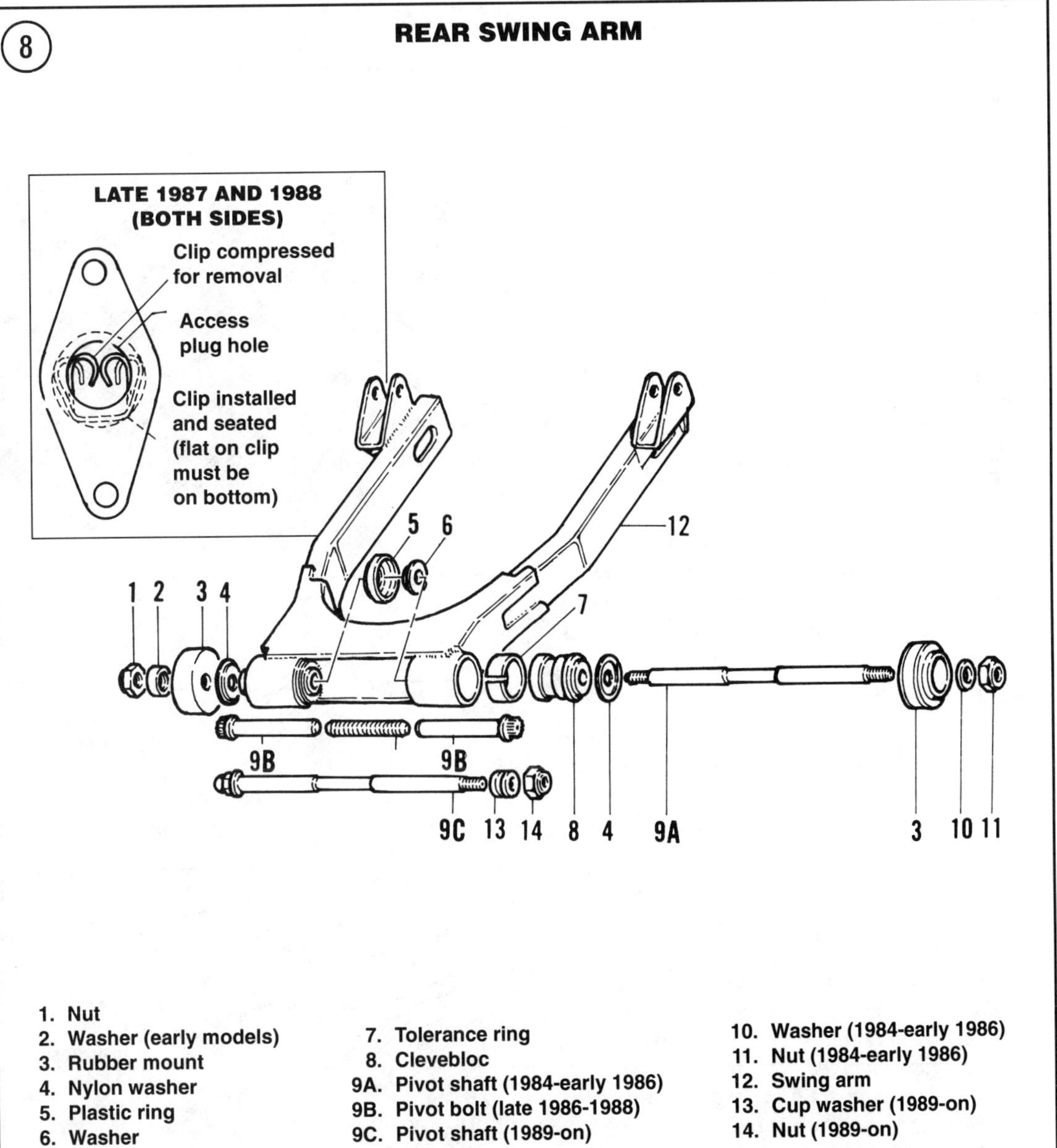


1. Nut
2. Washer (early models)
3. Rubber mount
4. Nylon washer
5. Plastic ring
6. Washer
7. Tolerance ring
8. Clevebloc
9A. Pivot shaft (1984-early 1986)
9B. Pivot bolt (late 1986-1988)
9C. Pivot shaft (1989-on)
10. Washer (1984-early 1986)
11. Nut (1984-early 1986)
12. Swing arm
13. Cup washer (1989-on)
14. Nut (1989-on)

d. Align the end of an aluminum or brass rod and tap the pivot shaft out of the swing arm.

e. Remove the pivot shaft and swing arm. Note the position of the rubber and nylon washers as you remove the swing arm.

8. Inspect the swing arm and pivot shaft assembly as described in this chapter.

## Inspection

1. Remove the rubber mounts from the outside of the swing arm, then remove the left- and right-hand nylon washers from the outboard side of each bushing.

2. Wash the swing arm in solvent and inspect it for cracks or other damage.

*NOTE*
*If paint was removed from the swing arm during cleaning, touch up areas as required before installing it onto the bike.*

3. Replace the rubber mounts if severely worn or damaged.

4. Inspect the pivot shaft(s) surface for cracks, deep scoring, excessive wear or heat discoloration.

5. Check the pivot shaft and center stud (late 1986-1988) threads for stripping, cross-threading or damage. Check the pivot bolts on late 1986-1988 models for deposit buildup in the end of the shafts. These areas should be blown out with compressed air. If necessary, use a tap or die to true up the threads and to remove any deposits.

6. The clevebloc bushings are filled with silicone. If a bushing is leaking or punctured, replace it as described in this chapter.

7. Replace worn or damaged pivot shaft(s).

*NOTE*
*Replacement parts used on the dual pivot bolt assembly installed on late 1986-1988 models are no longer available. If your Harley uses this pivot shaft assembly and one or both of the pivot shafts are damaged, you will have to install a late model pivot shaft assembly; see your Harley-Davidson dealer for further information.*

## Clevebloc Bushing Replacement

Bushing replacement will require the following tools:

a. Hydraulic or arbor press.

b. 1 1/4 in. socket.

c. Harley-Davidson Swing Arm Assembly (part No. HD-96200-80) or equivalent press adapters. These tools will be required to support the swing arm in the press when removing and installing the bushings.

d. Bench vise with soft jaws.

*NOTE*
*If you don't have access to a press, have the bushings replaced by a Harley-Davidson dealer.*

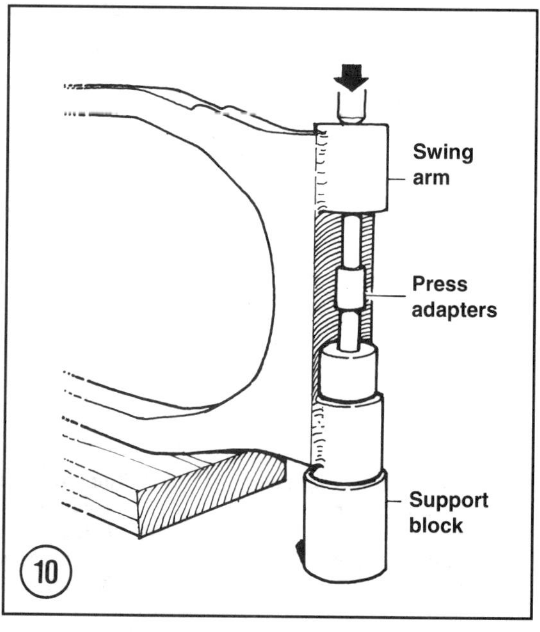

Refer to **Figure 8** when performing this step.

*NOTE*
*When it is necessary to support the swing arm in the following steps, a bench mounted vise works well. However, the vise should be equipped with removable soft jaws or wood blocks to avoid damaging the swing arm.*

1. Remove the rubber mounts from the outside of the swing arm, then remove the left- and right-hand nylon washers from the outboard side of each bushing.

2. Referring to **Figure 8**, note the washer and plastic ring installed in the inboard side of each bushing. Pry the washer and then the plastic ring from one bushing and remove them from the swing arm.

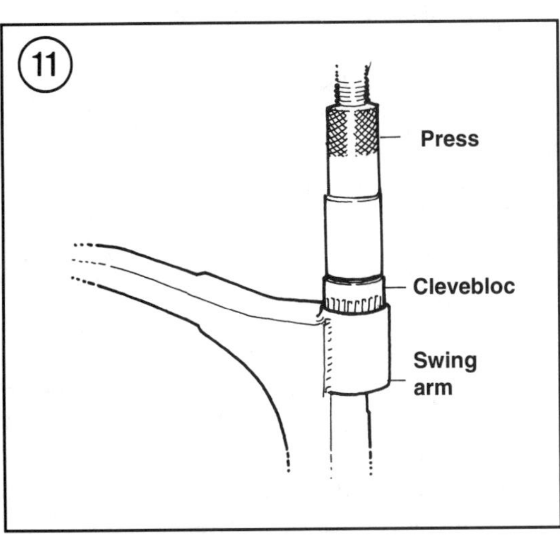


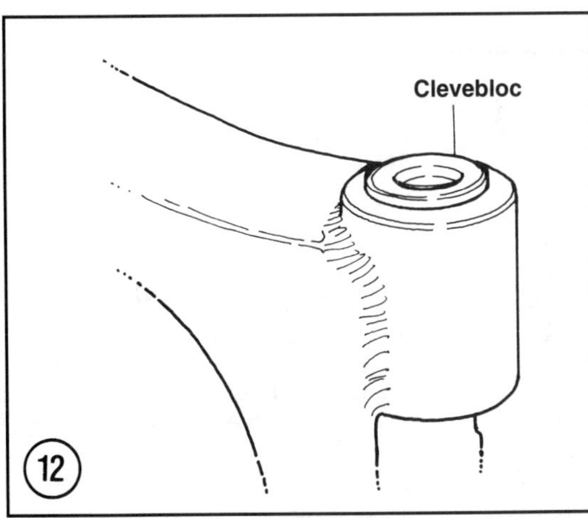


3. Support the swing arm in a press. If you have access to the Harley-Davidson Assembly Tool (part No. HD-96200-80), support the swing arm with the support block. If this tool is not available, support the swing arm with a suitable piece of pipe. See **Figure 10**.

*CAUTION*
*Do not apply pressure against the swing arm without supporting it as described in Step 3 or you could damage the swing arm assembly and reduce your bank account at the same time.*

4. Place a 1 1/4 in. socket against the outer clevebloc bushing outer sleeve, then place a long extension into the end of the socket and press the clevebloc bushing out of the swing arm from the outside in.

*CAUTION*
*The clevebloc bushing is filled with silicone. If the bushing is not leaking or damaged, it can be reused. If you press against the clevebloc instead of its outer sleeve as described in Step 4, you will damage the bushing.*

5. Remove the swing arm from the press and turn it over so that the opposite bushing is at the top. Repeat Steps 2-4 to remove the bushing from the swing arm.

6. Check the plastic rings and washers for cracks or damage. Replace damaged parts.

7. Remove and discard the tolerance ring from each bushing.

8. Install a *new* tolerance ring onto each bushing.

9. The clevebloc and its plastic ring and washer are installed at the same time. Assemble the plastic ring and washer onto the inboard side of the clevebloc shoulder.

10. Support the swing arm in the press as previously described and press one clevebloc bushing and its plastic ring and washer into the swing arm (**Figure 11**). Press the clevebloc bushing into the swing arm until the outer shoulder on the clevebloc is flush with the outer swing arm surface. See **Figure 12**.

11. Repeat to install the other clevebloc, plastic ring and washer.

### Installation

1. Prior to assembly, perform the *Inspection* procedures to make sure all worn or defective parts have been repaired or replaced.

*NOTE*
*Position the drive chain or drive belt over the sprocket before installing the swing arm. Leave the drive chain open; you can connect it later.*

2. Install the swing arm at the back of the transmission. If the swing arm will not fit into the transmission, it will be necessary to spread the clevebloc bushings apart. Perform the following:
   a. Place the swing arm on a workbench.
   b. Install the Clevebloc Spreading Tool (part No. HD-33805) between the cleveblocs as shown in **Figure 13**.

*NOTE*
*The clevebloc spreading tool is shown in **Figure 13**. If you don't have the Harley-Davidson tool, you can substitute with a piece of threaded rod, 2 large washers and 2 nuts.*

   c. Assemble the threaded rod, nuts and washers between the cleveblocs as shown in **Figure 13**, then turn the nuts with a wrench to spread the cleveblocs apart approximately 4 9/16 in. (115.9 mm).
   d. Remove the tool and check the swing arm fit at the back of the transmission. When the swing arm fits into the transmission correctly, proceed to Step 3.

3A. *1984-early 1986*: Install the pivot shaft assembly as follows:
   a. Lay the pivot shaft assembly out in the order shown in **Figure 8**. Reclean and dry parts as required before assembly.
   b. Identify the left side of the pivot shaft and slide the left-hand rubber mount (with shoulder facing outward) onto the pivot shaft. Then install the washer and nut onto the pivot shaft; tighten nut until it bottoms out on the shaft threads.
   c. Slide the nylon washer onto the pivot shaft and seat it against the rubber mount so that the smaller washer diameter faces inboard.
   d. Wipe the pivot shaft with Loctite Anti-Seize or equivalent.
   e. Install the pivot shaft through the swing arm from the left-hand side.
   f. Install the right-hand nylon washer (small washer diameter facing inward), rubber mount (shoulder facing outward), washer and nut. Tighten nut finger-tight at this time.

*NOTE*
*If you have a late 1986-1988 model and you replaced the swing arm pivot shaft assembly with a 1989 or later pivot shaft assembly, perform Step 3C.*

3B. *Late 1986-1988*: Install the pivot shaft assembly as follows:
   a. Lay the pivot shaft assembly out in the order shown in **Figure 8**. Reclean and dry parts as required before assembly.
   b. Install the left-hand pivot shaft onto the center stud.
   c. Coat the pivot shaft and center stud with Loctite Anti-Seize.
   d. Slide the left-hand rubber mount (with shoulder facing outward) onto the pivot shaft.
   e. Slide the nylon washer onto the pivot shaft and seat it against the rubber mount so that the small washer diameter faces inboard.
   f. Install the pivot shaft through the swing arm from the left-hand side.
   g. Coat the right-hand pivot shaft with Loctite Anti-Seize, then install the right-hand nylon washer (small washer diameter facing inboard) and the right-hand rubber mount (shoulder facing outward) onto the pivot shaft.

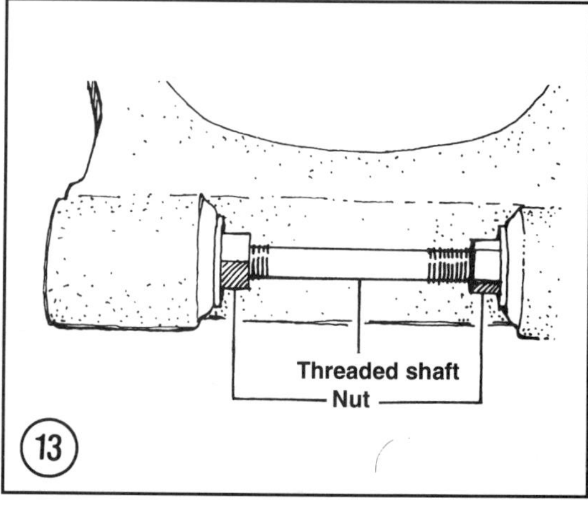

h. Insert the right-hand pivot shaft through the swing arm and thread it into the center stud finger-tight.

3C. *1989-on*: Install the pivot shaft assembly as follows:

a. Lay the pivot shaft assembly out in the order shown in **Figure 8**. Reclean and dry parts as required before assembly.
b. Wipe the pivot shaft with Loctite Anti-Seize.
c. Slide the right-hand rubber mount (with shoulder facing outward) onto the pivot shaft.
d. Slide the right-hand nylon washer (with small washer diameter facing inward) onto the pivot shaft.
e. Insert the pivot shaft through the swing arm from the right-hand side.
f. Install the left-hand nylon washer (small diameter facing inward), rubber mount (shoulder facing outward) and cup washer onto the pivot shaft. Then install the pivot shaft nut and tighten finger-tight.

4. Install passenger footpeg mounting bracket on FLT models. When installing mounting brackets, make sure roll pin in each bracket engages hole in rubber mount.
5. Install the pivot shaft mounting brackets on FXR models. When installing brackets, make sure roll pin in each bracket engages hole in rubber mount.
6. On 1984-early 1986 models, make sure the flat on the pivot shaft engages the flat on the right-hand rubber mount.
7. If passenger footpegs were removed, position footpegs so that they fold at a 45° angle, then tighten their mounting nuts to 20-25 ft.-lb. (27.6-34.5 N•m).

8A. *1984-early 1986*: Hold the left-hand pivot shaft nut with a wrench and tighten the right-hand nut to 45 ft.-lb. (62.1 N•m).

8B. *late 1986-1988*: Hold the left-hand pivot bolt with a wrench and tighten the right-hand pivot bolt to 85 ft.-lb. (117.3 N•m). After tightening pivot bolts, install the clip into each mounting bracket so that flat on clip faces toward the bottom of the bracket; see **Figure 8**.

*NOTE*

*If a 1989 or later pivot shaft assembly was installed on a late 1986-1988 model (to replace the 3-piece pivot shaft assembly), do not install the clips into the mounting brackets as described in Step 8B.*

8C. *1989-on*: Hold the right-hand pivot nut with a wrench and tighten the left-hand nut to 45 ft.-lb. (62.1 N•m).

9. After tightening the pivot shaft(s), move the swing arm up and down by hand. It should move smoothly with no sign of roughness or tightness.
10. Remount the rear brake caliper assembly onto the swing arm as described in Chapter Thirteen.
11. Install the drive boots, if used, making sure to route the drive chain through them. Coat the drive boot mating surfaces with RTV silicone sealant. Secure the drive boot to the cover with the mounting screws.

*NOTE*

*Install a new master link and reconnect the drive chain as described in Chapter Ten.*

12. Install the rear wheel and tighten the drive chain or drive belt as described in Chapter Three.
13. Install the muffler or exhaust system, if previously removed.

*NOTE*

*Check the pivot shaft torque every 5,000 miles (8,000 km).*

## SWING ARM (FXWG, FXEF AND FXSB)

### Removal

Refer to **Figure 14** for this procedure.

1. Support the bike on a stand so that the rear wheel clears the ground.
2. Remove the muffler or exhaust system if it will interfere with swing arm removal.
3. Remove the rear wheel as described in Chapter Ten.
4. Turn the drive chain until you locate the master link. Then disconnect the master link and separate drive chain with a chain breaker.
5. Remove the rear brake caliper from the rear swing arm as described in Chapter Thirteen. Use a Bungee cord or piece of wire to support the caliper. Do not allow the weight of the caliper to hang from the brake hoses.
6. Remove the rear shock absorber bolts at the swing arm.
7. Pry the pivot bolt lockwasher tab away from the bolt.

8. Loosen and remove the pivot bolt and swing arm.
9. Inspect the swing arm and pivot shaft assembly as described in this chapter.

## Inspection

NOTE
*ID each bearing as it is removed from the swing arm so you don't mix them up during reassembly.*

1. Tap a spacer and oil seal out of the swing arm with a long drift, then remove the bearing from its race. Repeat to remove the opposite spacer, oil seal and bearing.
2. Turn the bearing with your finger and check it for roughness or excessive play. If it appears that a bearing is damaged, replace both bearings and their races as described in this chapter.

NOTE
*If paint was removed from the swing arm during cleaning, touch up areas as required before installing it on the bike.*

3. Inspect the pivot shaft surface for cracks, deep scoring, excessive wear or heat discoloration.
4. Pack the bearings with grease.
5. Place one bearing in its race. Then install the oil seal and the spacer. Repeat for the opposite bearing.

## Bearing Race Replacement

Refer to **Figure 14** when performing this procedure.

1. Secure the swing arm in a vise with soft jaws.
2. Remove the bearing spacers and oil seals if they were not previously removed.
3. Drive a bearing race out of the swing arm from the opposite side with an aluminum or brass drift. See **Figure 15**.
4. Repeat Step 3 to remove the opposite bearing race.
5. Clean the swing arm with solvent and allow to dry thoroughly.
6. Press the new bearing races into the swing arm. Support the swing arm when installing the races.
7. Pack the new bearings thoroughly with grease before installing them.

## Installation

Refer to **Figure 14** when performing this procedure.

1. Clean the swing arm mounting holes in the frame thoroughly before installing the swing arm.

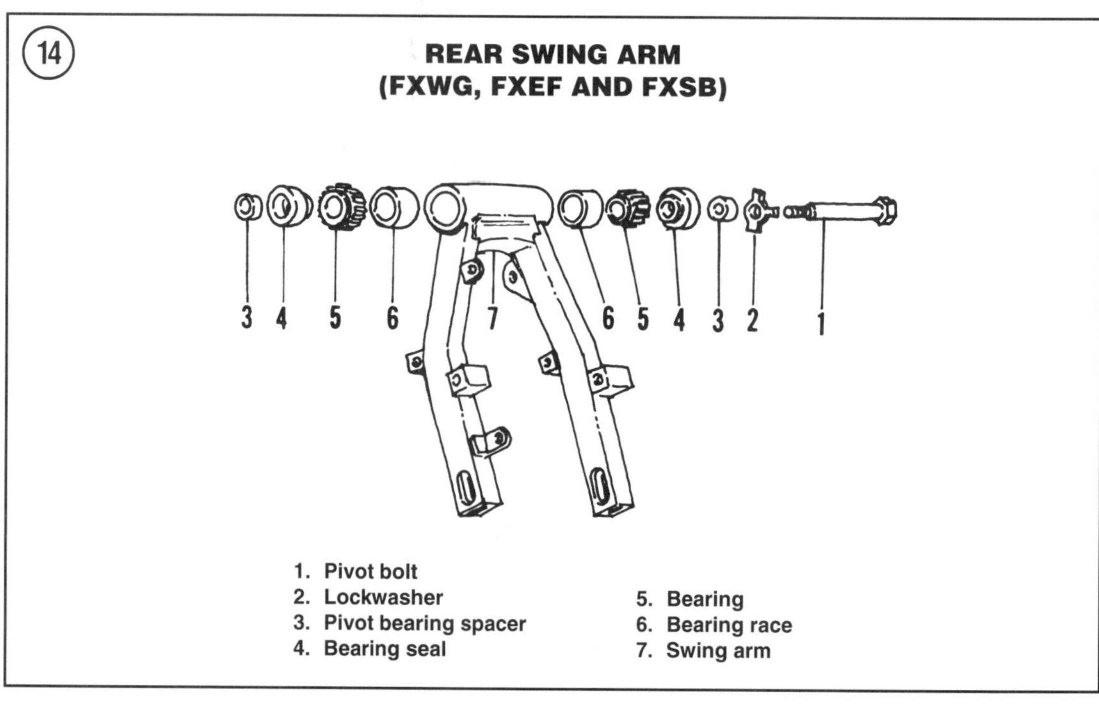

2. Slide a new lockwasher onto the pivot shaft. Then wipe the pivot shaft with grease.

3. Install the left- and right-hand spacers into the swing arm.

4. Position the swing arm into the frame and install the pivot shaft from the right-hand side. Thread the pivot shaft into the frame so that it supports the swing arm, but do not tighten the pivot shaft.

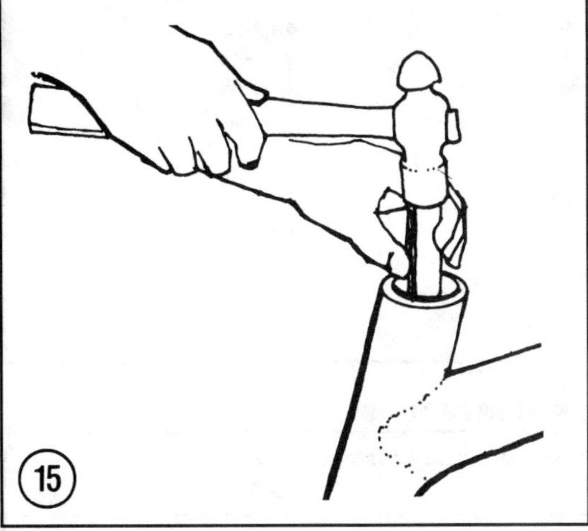


5. Preload the swing arm bearings as follows:
   a. Attach a spring scale to the rear of the swing arm.
   b. Lift the spring scale and note the reading on the scale as the swing arm is raised past horizontal.
   c. Tighten pivot shaft to pre-load bearings 1-2 lbs. (0.45-0.90 kg). For example, if scale reading is 5 lbs. (2.3 kg) when swing arm is raised in sub-step a, tighten pivot shaft until the spring scale reads 6-7 lbs. (2.7-3.1 kg) when the swing arm is raised past horizontal.
   d. When pre-load is set, bend the lockwasher tab against the pivot bolt head.

6. After pre-loading the bearings in Step 5, fill the area between the bearings with bearing grease. Apply grease with a grease gun at the swing arm grease nipple.

7. Install the shock absorbers and tighten their mounting bolts as described in this chapter.

8. Install the rear brake caliper as described in Chapter Thirteen.

9. Reinstall the rear wheel and reconnect the drive chain as described in Chapter Ten. Adjust the drive chain as described in Chapter Three.

**Tables 1-4 are on the following page.**

**Table 1 REAR SUSPENSION TIGHTENING TORQUES**

| | ft.-lb. | N•m |
|---|---|---|
| Swing arm pivot bolt | | |
| FLT and FXR | | |
| 1984-early 1986 pivot shaft nut | 45 | 62.1 |
| Late 1986-1988 (12-point head pivot bolt) | 85 | 117.3 |
| 1989-on pivot shaft nut | 45 | 62.1 |
| FXWG, FXEF and FXSB | See text | |
| Rear axle nut | 60-65 | 82.8-89.7 |
| Rear shock bolts | | |
| FLT | | |
| Upper | | |
| 1984-early 1988 | 35-40 | 48.3-55.2 |
| Late 1988-on | 33-35 | 45.5-48.3 |
| Lower | 35-40 | 48.3-55.2 |
| FXR | | |
| 1984 | * | |
| 1985 | | |
| Upper | 35-40 | 48.3-55.2 |
| Lower | 33-35 | 45.5-48.3 |
| FXWG, FXEF and FXSB | * | |

* Not available.

**Table 2 REAR SHOCK AIR CONTROL (FLT)**

| | Recommended air pressure | |
|---|---|---|
| Load | psi | $kg/cm^2$ |
| Solo rider | 0 | 0 |
| Rider and passenger | 5 | 0.35 |
| Rider, passenger and maximum luggage load | 10 | 0.70 |
| Maximum air pressure | | |
| 1992 and earlier models | 20 | 1.4 |
| 1993-on | 35 | 2.46 |

**Table 3 REAR SHOCK AIR CONTROL (1984 FXRT)**

| | Recommended air pressure | |
|---|---|---|
| Vehicle load | psi | $kg/cm^2$ |
| Rider weight not exceeding 150 lbs. (68 kg) | 4-8 | 0.28-0.56 |
| Each additional 25 lbs. (11.3 kg), add | 3 | 0.21 |
| Passenger weight for each 50 lbs. (22.6), add | 8 | 0.56 |
| For each additional 10 lbs. (4.5 kg) | | |
| luggage weight, add | 2 | 0.14 |
| Maximum pressure | 40 | 2.8 |

**Table 4 REAR SHOCK AIR CONTROL (1985-ON FXRT AND FXRD)**

| | Recommended air pressure | |
|---|---|---|
| Vehicle load | psi | $kg/cm^2$ |
| Rider weight not exceeding 150 lbs. (68 kg) | 0-5 | 0-0.35 |
| Each additional 25 lbs. (11.3 kg), add | 5 | 0.35 |
| Passenger weight for each 50 lbs. (22.6 kg), add | 10 | 0.70 |
| For each additional 10 lbs. (4.5 kg) | | |
| luggage weight, add | 3 | 0.21 |
| Maximum pressure | 60 | 4.2 |

# CHAPTER THIRTEEN

# BRAKES

The front wheel is equipped with a single disc or dual disc brakes. The rear is equipped with a single disc brake. This chapter describes repair and replacement procedure for all brake components.

The disc brakes are actuated by hydraulic fluid from the master cylinder. The master cylinder is controlled by the hand or foot lever. As the brake pads wear, the brake fluid level drops in the master cylinder reservoir and automatically adjusts for pad wear.

When working on hydraulic brake systems, the work area and all tools should be absolutely clean. Any tiny particles of foreign matter or grit on the caliper assembly or the master cylinder can damage the components. Also, sharp tools must not be used inside the caliper or on the caliper piston. If there is any doubt about your ability to correctly and safely carry out major service on the brake components, take the job to a Harley-Davidson dealer or qualified Harley repair shop.

**Table 1** and **Table 2** are at the end of the chapter.

### Disc Brake System Service Hints

Consider the following when servicing the front and rear disc brake systems.

1. Disc brake components rarely require disassembly, so do not disassemble them unless necessary.

2. Use only DOT 5 brake fluid from a sealed container.

3. Always keep the master cylinder's reservoir cover closed to prevent dust or moisture from entering.

4. Use only DOT 5 brake fluid to wash parts. Never clean any internal brake component with solvent. Solvents will cause the seals to swell and distort and require replacement.

5. Whenever *any* brake line has been removed from the brake system the system is considered "opened" and must be bled to remove the air bubbles. Also, if the brake feels "spongy," this usually means there is air in the system and it must be bled. For safe brake operation, refer to *Bleeding the System* in this chapter.

## FRONT BRAKE PADS

There is no recommended mileage interval for changing the friction pads in the front disc brake. Pad wear depends greatly on riding habits and conditions. The pads should be checked for wear initially at 500 miles (800 km), then every 2,500 miles (4,000 km) and replaced when the lining thickness reaches 1/16 in. (1.6 mm) from the brake pad backing plate. To maintain an even brake pressure on the disc, always replace both pads in the caliper at the same time. If your Harley is equipped with dual disc brakes, replace the brake pads in both calipers at the same time; always use brake pads from the same manufacturer in both calipers—never intermix different brands.

### Replacement

Refer to **Figure 1** for this procedure.

*NOTE*

*If your Harley has dual calipers, complete work on one caliper before beginning on the other.*

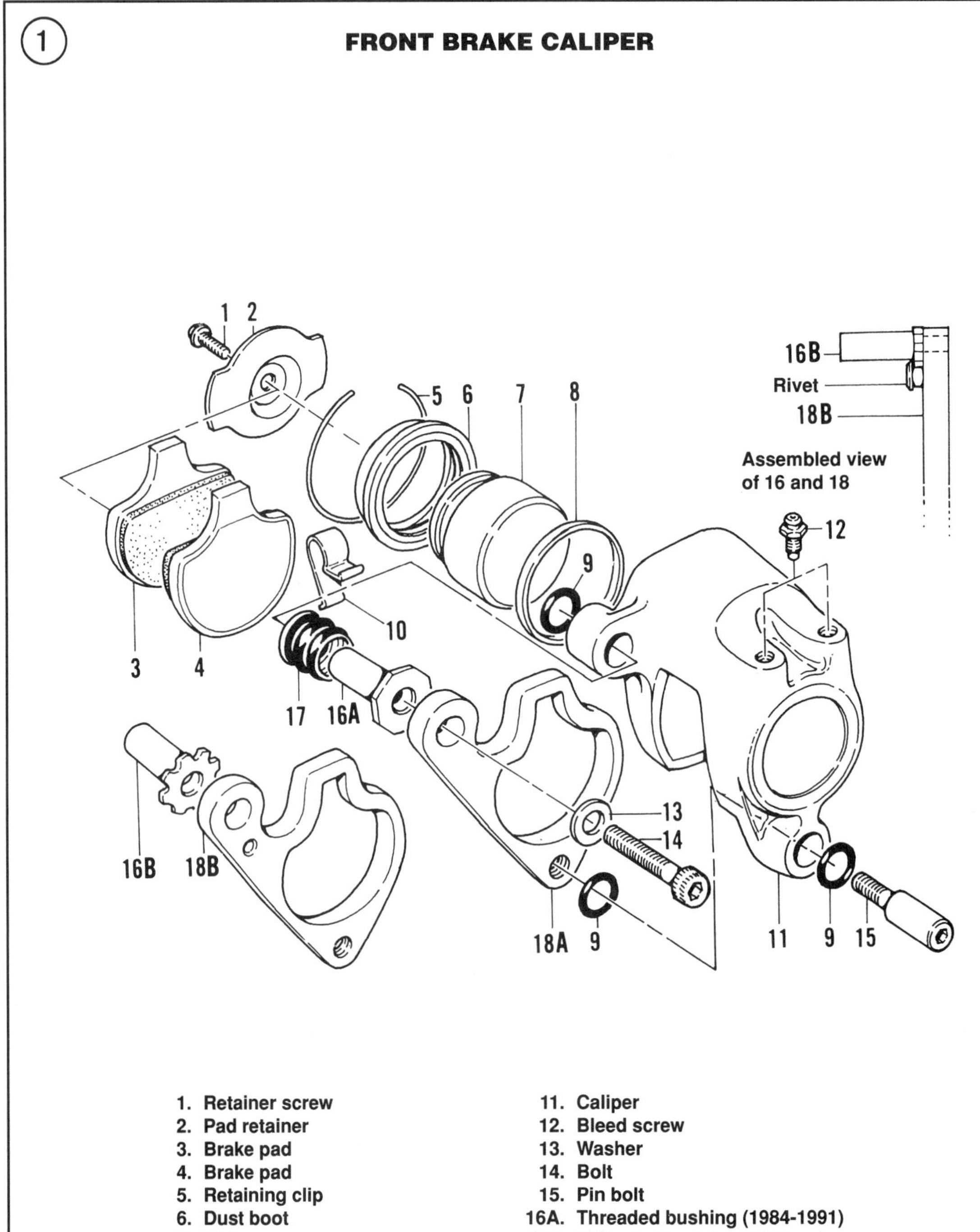


1. Retainer screw
2. Pad retainer
3. Brake pad
4. Brake pad
5. Retaining clip
6. Dust boot
7. Piston
8. Piston seal
9. O-rings
10. Spring clip
11. Caliper
12. Bleed screw
13. Washer
14. Bolt
15. Pin bolt
16A. Threaded bushing (1984-1991)
16B. Threaded bushing (1992-on)
17. Pin boot
18A. Pad holder (1984-1991)
18B. Pad holder (1992-on)

1. To prevent accidental application of the front brake lever, place a spacer between the front brake lever and the hand grip. Hold the spacer in place with a large rubber band or a tie wrap.

2. The front brake caliper is mounted on the front fork slider with 2 mounting bolts. Remove both bolts.

3. Lift the brake caliper off of the brake disc (**Figure 2**).

4. Remove the outer pad, pad holder and spring clip as an assembly (**Figure 3**).

5. Remove the screw (**Figure 4**) and remove the inner brake pad (**Figure 5**).

6. Push the outer pad free of the spring clip and remove it. See **Figure 6**.

7. Check the brake pads (**Figure 7**) for wear or damage. Replace the brake pads if they are worn to 1/16 in. (1.6 mm) or less (**Figure 8**). Replace both pads as a set.

8. Replace the caliper bolts (**Figure 9**) if necessary.

9. Check the pad retainer (**Figure 10**) for damage. Replace if necessary.

10. When new pads are installed in the caliper the master cylinder brake fluid level will rise as the caliper piston is repositioned. Clean the top of the master cylinder of all dirt and foreign matter. Remove the cap and diaphragm from the master cylinder and slowly push the caliper piston (**Figure 11**) into the caliper. Constantly check the reservoir to make sure brake fluid does not overflow. Remove fluid, if necessary, prior to it overflowing. The piston should move freely. If not, and there is evidence of it sticking in the cylinder, the caliper should be removed and serviced as described in this chapter.

11. Install the spring clip at the top of the pad holder as shown in **Figure 12**.

12. Place the brake pad with the insulator backing on top of the spring clip with the lower end of the pad slightly entering the pad holder opening. With the brake pad insulator backing facing toward the pad holder, push the brake pad down until it is held firmly in the pad holder by the spring clip.

13. Insert the outer brake pad/pad holder assembly into the caliper so that the brake pad insulator backing faces against the piston. See **Figure 3**.



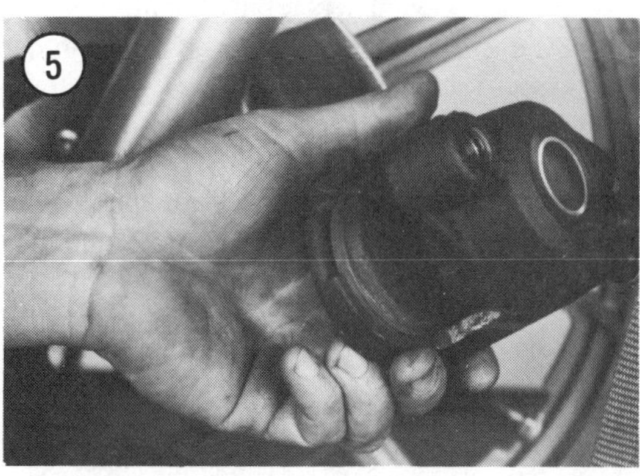

*WARNING*
*The spring clip loop and the brake pad friction material must face away from the piston. Brake failure will occur if the brakes are assembled incorrectly.*

14. Install the inner brake pad (without the insulator backing) in the caliper recessed seat (**Figure 5**).
15. Insert the pad retainer within the counterbore inside the caliper. Install the self-tapping screw through the pad retainer and thread into the brake pad (**Figure 4**). Tighten the screw securely.
16. Coat the lower mounting bolt with Dow Corning Moly 44 grease.
17. Install the brake caliper as follows:
   a. Install the caliper over the brake disc, making sure the friction surface on each pad faces against the disc.

*CAUTION*
*On 1992-on models, the splined head on the threaded bushing (16B, **Figure 1**) must be installed between the rivet head and the pad holder as shown in the assembled view drawing in **Figure 1**. In addition, one of the bushing head splined notches must engage the rivet head as shown in **Figure 1**. If the bushing is installed incorrectly, the rivet will be damaged when the caliper mounting bolts are tightened.*

   b. Align the 2 mounting holes in the caliper with the slider mounting lugs (**Figure 2**).
   c. Install a washer onto the upper mounting bolt (**Figure 1**) and insert the bolt through the slider lug and then thread into the caliper bushing. Install the bolt finger-tight.
   d. Insert the lower mounting bolt through the caliper and then thread into the slider lug. Tighten mounting bolt finger-tight.
   e. Tighten the lower mounting bolt to the torque specification listed in **Table 2**.
   f. Tighten the upper mounting bolt to the torque specification listed in **Table 2**.
18. Refill the master cylinder reservoir, if necessary, to maintain the correct fluid level. Install the diaphragm and top cap.

*WARNING*
*Use brake fluid clearly marked DOT 5 from a sealed container. Other types may vaporize and cause brake failure.*

6

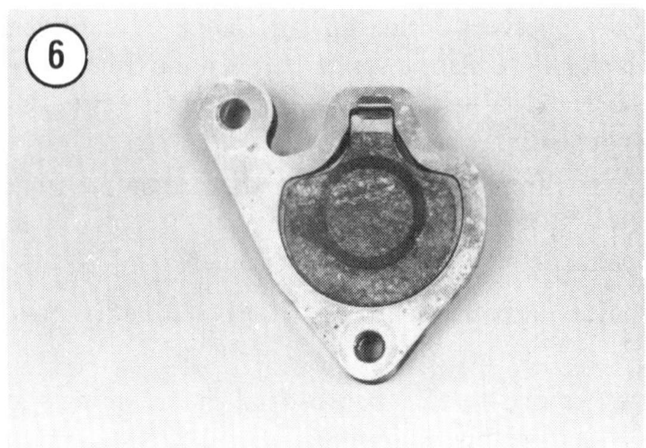

7

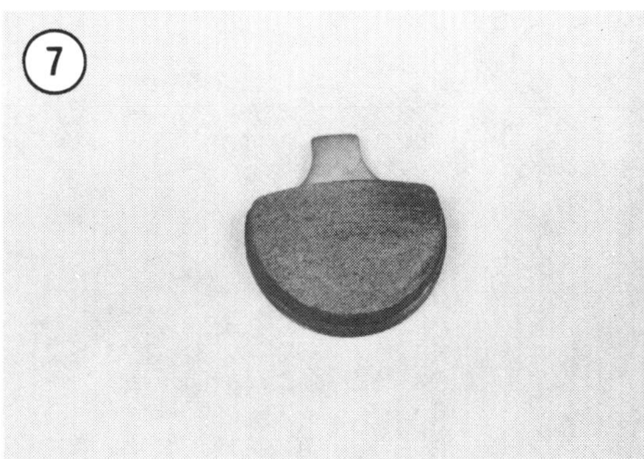

8

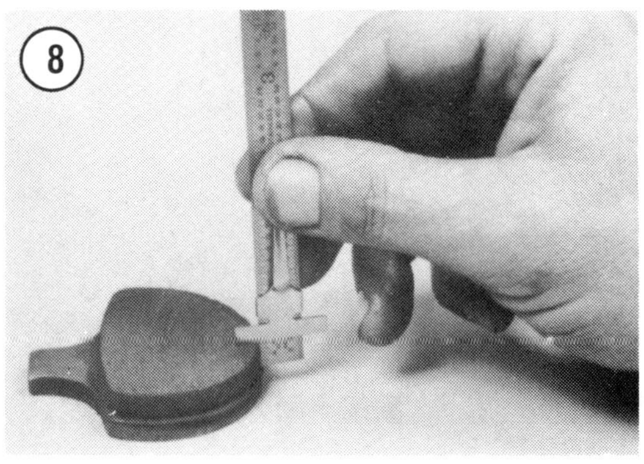

9

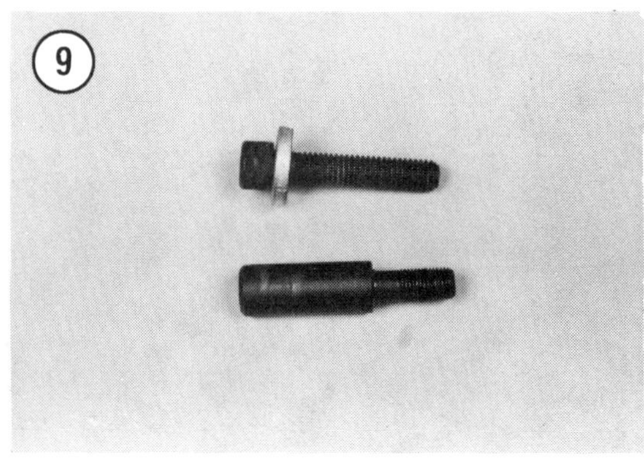

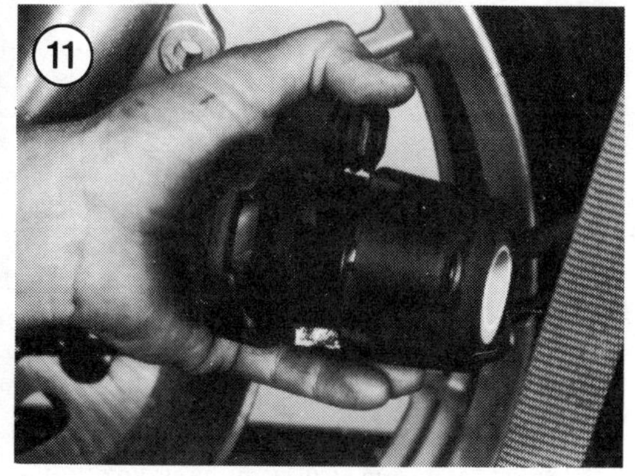


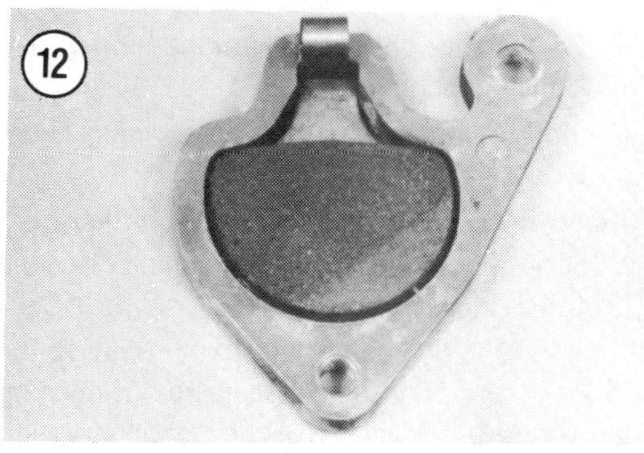

*Always use the same brand name; do not intermix, as many brands are not compatible.*

*WARNING*
*Do not ride the motorcycle until you are sure the brakes are operating correctly with full hydraulic advantage. If necessary, bleed the brake system as described in this chapter.*

## FRONT BRAKE CALIPER

This section describes overhaul of the front brake caliper. If you are removing the caliper to lubricate the caliper bolts, do not remove the banjo bolt from the caliper.

### Removal

1. Loosen and remove the banjo bolt holding the brake line to the caliper (A, **Figure 13**). Remove the bolt and the 2 washers. Place the end of the brake line in a plastic bag and secure the bag against the brake line with a plastic tie to prevent brake fluid from dripping onto the front wheel.
2. Remove the upper mounting bolt (and washer) and the lower mounting bolt and remove the brake caliper.
3. Remove the brake caliper from the disc.
4. Overhaul the brake caliper, if necessary, as described in this chapter.

### Installation

1. If removed, install the brake pads into the caliper as described in this chapter.
2. Coat the lower mounting bolt with Dow Corning Moly 44 grease.
3. Install the caliper over the brake disc, making sure the friction surface on each pad faces against the disc (**Figure 14**).
4. Align the 2 mounting holes in the caliper with the slider mounting lugs.
5. Install a washer onto the upper mounting bolt (**Figure 1**) and insert the bolt through the slider lug and then thread into the caliper bushing. Install the bolt finger-tight.
6. Insert the lower mounting bolt through the caliper and then thread into the slider lug. Tighten mounting bolt finger-tight.
7. Tighten the lower mounting bolt to the torque specification listed in **Table 2**.

8. Tighten the upper mounting bolt to the torque specification listed in **Table 2**.
9. Tighten the bleed screw (B, **Figure 13**) if it was previously loosened.

*WARNING*
*When installing replacement banjo bolts and washers used to connect the brake hose to the brake caliper, note that 2 different types of banjo bolt washers have been used. Washers used on early models were made of copper with a zinc coating (A, **Figure 15**). Late models use steel washers equipped with a rubber O-ring (B, **Figure 15**). Because the banjo bolts are designed to be used with a specific type of washer, make sure that replacement banjo washers or bolts match the original parts used. Using an incorrect washer or bolt may allow the brake hose to leak and result in loss of complete brake pressure. If necessary, ask your dealer's parts or service manager to identify the correct washers and banjo bolts used on your model.*

*NOTE*
*Install **new** banjo bolt washers when performing Step 10.*

10. Assemble the brake line onto the caliper by placing a washer on both sides of the brake line fitting, then secure the fitting to the caliper with the banjo bolt. Tighten the banjo bolt to the torque specification listed in **Table 2**.

*NOTE*
*The tightening torques for the copper and steel/rubber banjo bolts are different. Make sure to use the tightening torque for the type of washer installed on your bike (**Table 2**).*

11. Refill the system and bleed the brake as described in this chapter.

*WARNING*
*Do not ride the motorcycle until you are sure the brakes are operating properly.*

## Caliper Overhaul

Harley-Davidson does not provide any specifications or wear limits on any of the front caliper components (except brake pads). Replace any parts that appear to be worn or damaged.

Refer to **Figure 1** for this procedure.

1. Remove the caliper and brake pads as described in this chapter.
2. Carefully pry the retaining ring out of the caliper body with a small screwdriver inserted in the notched groove in the bottom of the piston bore. Do not pry elsewhere in the caliber bore or you may damage the caliper.
3. Remove the piston dust boot from the groove at the top of the piston.

*WARNING*
*When performing Step 4, the piston may shoot out like a bullet. Keep your fingers out of the way. Wear shop gloves and apply compressed air gradually.*

4. Place a rag or piece of wood in the path of the piston (**Figure 16**). Blow the piston out with compressed air directed through the hydraulic hole fitting. Use a service station air hose if you don't have a compressor.
5. Remove the piston seal from the groove in the caliper body.
6. Pull the threaded bushing out of the caliper, then remove the pin boot.
7. Carefully pry the piston seal out of the caliper bore groove.
8. Remove the 3 O-rings from the caliper body.
9. Inspect the caliper body for damage; replace the caliper body if necessary.
10. Inspect the hydraulic fluid passageway in the cylinder bore. Apply compressed air to the opening and make sure it is clear. Clean out, if necessary, with fresh brake fluid.

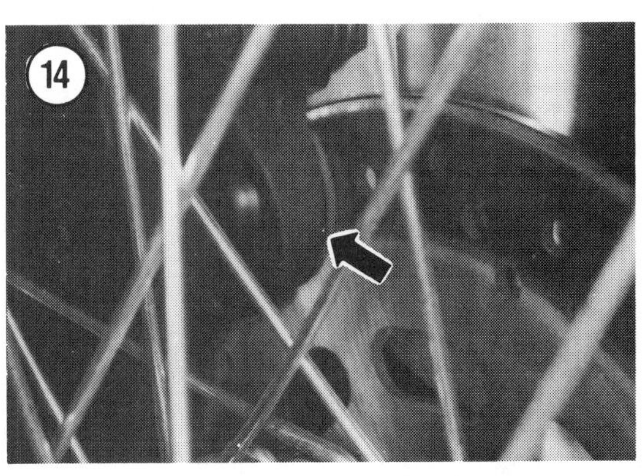

11. Inspect the cylinder wall and the piston for scratches, scoring or other damage. Replace worn, corroded or damaged parts.

12. Inspect the banjo bolt and bleed valve threads in the caliper body. If the threads in the caliper body are slightly damaged, clean them up with the proper size thread tap. If the threads are worn or damaged beyond repair, replace the caliper body.

13. Make sure the hole in the bleed valve screw is clean and open. Apply compressed air to the opening if necessary.

14. Check the mounting plate for cracks or damage. Check the threads in the plate for damage. If the threads are slightly damaged, clean them up with the proper size thread tap. If the threads are worn or damaged beyond repair, replace the mounting plate.

15. Check the threaded bushing, upper mounting bolt and the lower mounting pin for thread damage. Repair threads or replace damaged parts as required.

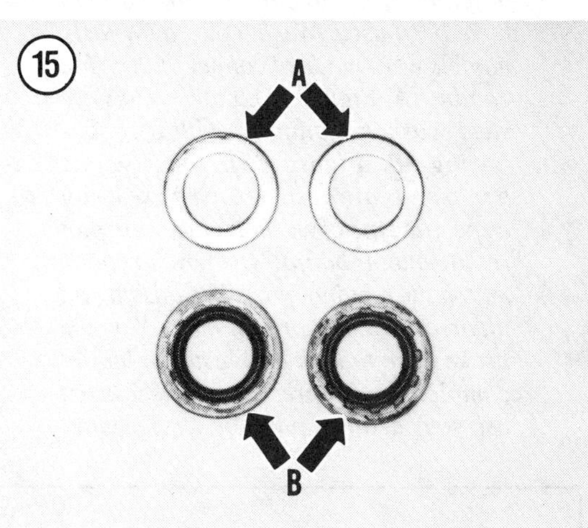


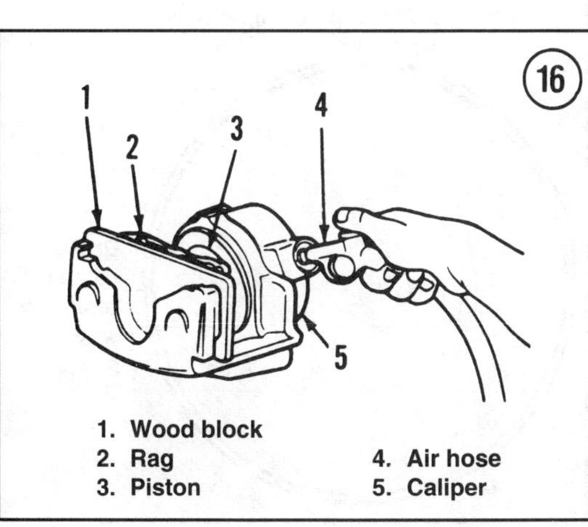


Check the mounting pin shoulder for deep scoring or excessive wear; replace if necessary.

16. Check the pad retainer for cracks or damage.

17. Check the brake pads (**Figure 7**) for wear or damage. Replace the brake pads if they are worn to 1/16 in. (1.6 mm) or less (**Figure 8**). Replace both pads as a set.

18. Check all of the rubber parts (dust boot, O-rings, piston seal, etc.) for cracks, wear or age deterioration. Because very minor damage or age deterioration can make these parts useless, questionable parts should be replaced. When reusing rubber parts, clean the parts in new brake fluid and place on a lint-free cloth until reassembly.

19. If serviceable, clean all metal parts with rubbing alcohol.

20. After replacing all worn or damaged parts, coat the following parts with new DOT 5 brake fluid. Place the parts on a clean lint-free cloth to prevent contamination before assembly.

a. Piston.
b. Piston dust boot.
c. Piston seal.
d. O-rings (3).

21. Make sure the retaining wire, piston and caliper bore are thoroughly clean. If necessary, reclean and allow to air dry before reassembly.

22. Install the piston seal into the caliper body groove.

23. Install the 3 O-rings into the caliper grooves.

24. Wipe the inside of the pin boot with Dow Corning Moly 44 grease. Then insert the boot into the bushing bore so that the flange end on the boot seats in the bushing bore internal groove.

25. The piston dust boot is installed on the piston *before* the piston is installed in the caliper bore. Perform the following:

a. Place the piston on your workbench so that the open side faces up.
b. Align the piston dust boot with the piston so that the shoulder on the dust boot faces up.
c. Slide the piston dust boot onto the piston until the inner lip on the dust boot seats in the piston groove.

26. Coat the piston and the caliper bore with DOT 5 brake fluid.

27. Align the piston with the caliper bore so that its open end faces out. Then push the piston in until it bottoms out.

*NOTE*
*If you are installing new brake pads, you will have to push the piston all the way into the bore. If necessary, use a C-clamp to push the piston into the bore.*

28. Locate the retaining wire groove in the end of the caliper bore. Then align the retaining wire so that the gap in the wire (**Figure 17**) is at the top of the caliper bore and install the wire into the wire groove. Make sure the retaining wire is seated completely in the groove and that it is pushing against the piston dust boot.
29. Wipe the caliper mounting lug bores with Dow Corning Moly 44 grease.
30. Insert the threaded bushing into the pin boot until the end of the pin boot seats in the groove adjacent to the threaded bushing hexagonal head.
31. Install the brake pads as described in this chapter.

## FRONT MASTER CYLINDER

The front master cylinder is mounted onto the right-hand handlebar.

### Removal/Installation

Refer to **Figure 18** for this procedure.

*CAUTION*
*Cover the fuel tank, instrument cluster and front fairing with a heavy cloth or plastic tarp to protect them from accidental brake fluid spills. Wash brake fluid off any painted or plated surfaces. Use soapy water and rinse completely.*

1. Flip the rubber cover off of the front caliper bleeder valve (B, **Figure 13**) and insert a hose onto the end of the valve. Insert the open end of the hose into a container. Open the front bleeder valve and drain the brake fluid from the front brake assembly by operating the hand lever. Remove the hose and close the bleeder valve after draining the assembly. Discard the brake fluid.
2. Place a couple of shop cloths under the banjo bolt and remove the banjo bolt and washers securing the brake hose to the master cylinder. See **Figure 19** or **Figure 20**.
3. Remove the screws securing the clamp to the master cylinder and remove the clamp and master cylinder housing.
4. Install by reversing these removal steps. Note the following.
5. Clean the handlebar of all brake fluid residue.
6. Clean the banjo bolt (**Figure 21**) fluid passage thoroughly. Use air to dry the bolt or allow it to air dry before installing it.
7. Check the clamp for cracks or damage. Replace if necessary.
8. Position the master cylinder onto the handlebar and install the clamp and its 2 screws. Tighten the screws to the torque specification listed in **Table 2**.

*WARNING*
*When installing replacement banjo bolts and washers used to connect the brake hose to the brake caliper, two different types of banjo bolt washers have been used. Washers used on early models were made of copper with a zinc coating (A, **Figure 15**). Late models use steel washers equipped with a rubber O-ring (B, **Figure 15**). Because the banjo bolts are designed to be used with a specific type of washer, make sure that replacement banjo washers or bolts match the original parts used. Using an incorrect washer or bolt may allow the brake hose to leak and result in loss of complete brake pressure. If necessary, ask your dealer's parts or service man-*

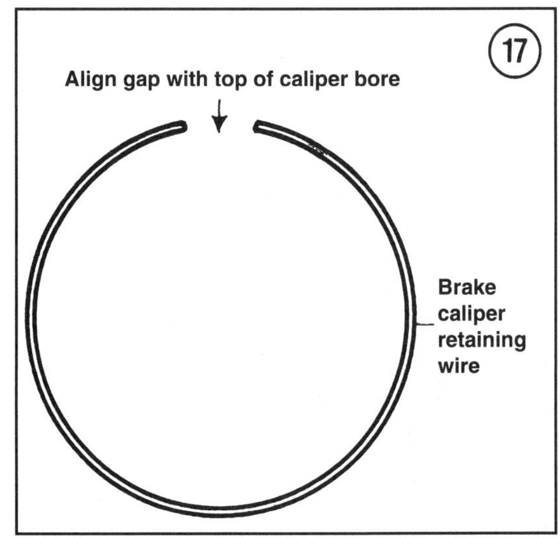

*ager to identify the correct washers and banjo bolts used on your model.*

*NOTE*
*Install **new** banjo bolt washers when performing Step 9.*

9. Install the brake hose onto the cylinder. Be sure to place a new washer on each side of the hose fitting when installing the banjo bolt; see **Figure 19** or **Figure 20**. Tighten the banjo bolt to the torque specification listed in **Table 2**.

*NOTE*
*The tightening torques for the copper and steel/rubber banjo bolts are different. Make sure to use the tightening torque for the type of washer installed on your bike (**Table 2**).*

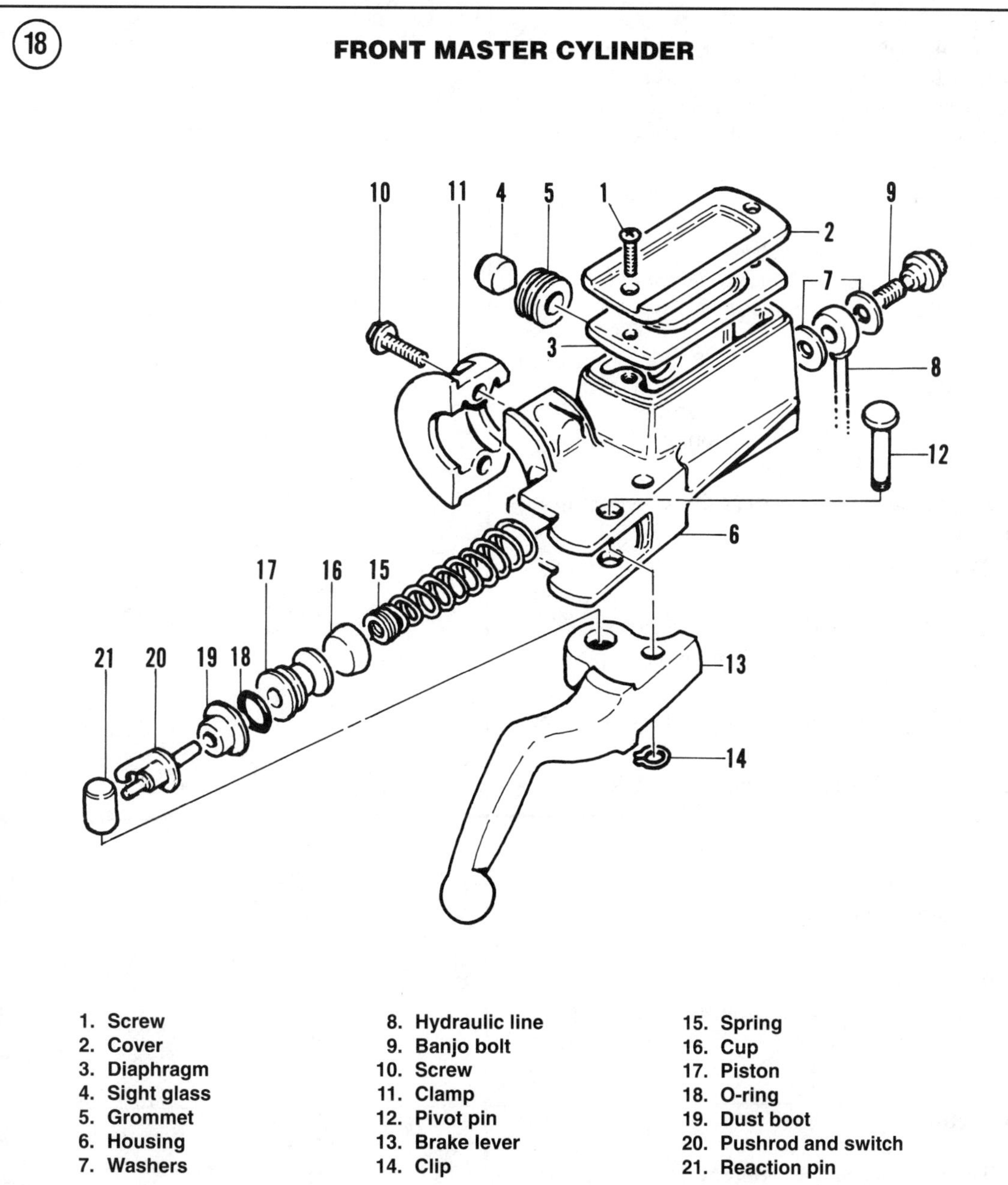

10. Fill the master cylinder with new DOT 5 brake fluid. Bleed the brake system as described in this chapter.

*NOTE*
*When actuating the brake lever in Step 10, a small spurt of fluid should break through the fluid surface in the master cylinder. This will indicate that all internal master cylinder components are working properly.*

11. Install the master cylinder gasket and cover after bleeding the brakes. Sit on the motorcycle and check that the brake lever position is suitable to your riding position. If necessary, loosen the clamp screws and reposition the master cylinder; retighten the clamp screws to the torque specification listed in **Table 2**.

*WARNING*
*Do not ride the motorcycle until the brake is working properly.*

### Disassembly

Refer to **Figure 18** when performing this procedure.

1. Drain and remove the master cylinder as described in this chapter.
2. Remove the screws securing the top cover and remove the cover and diaphragm.
3. The brake lever pivot pin is secured with a circlip. Remove the circlip and remove the pivot pin and brake lever (**Figure 22**).
4. Remove the reaction pin from the hand lever (**Figure 22**).
5. Referring to **Figure 18**, remove the following in order:
   a. Pushrod and brake switch actuator.
   b. Dust boot.
   c. Piston and O-ring.
   d. Cup.
   e. Spring.
6. If damaged, remove the grommet and sight glass from the rear side of the master cylinder housing.

### Inspection

Harley-Davidson does not provide specifications for wear limits on any of the master cylinder com-

**FRONT BRAKE HOSE ASSEMBLY**

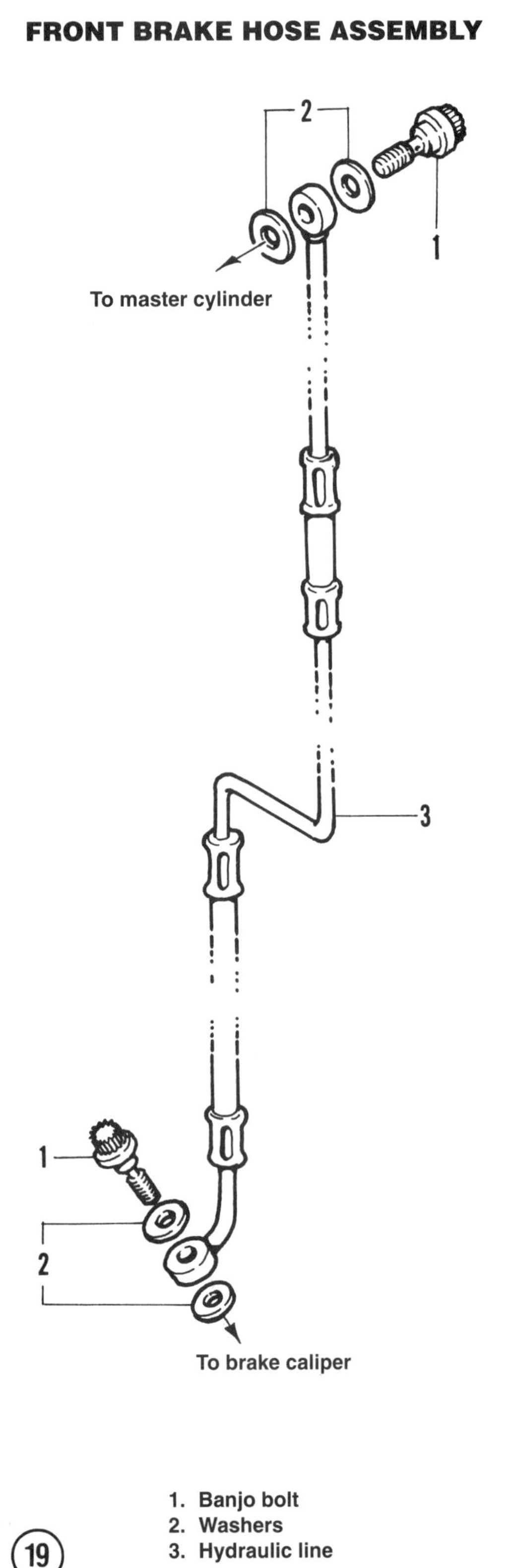


1. Banjo bolt
2. Washers
3. Hydraulic line

19

20

**FRONT BRAKE HOSE (DUAL CALIPER MODELS)**

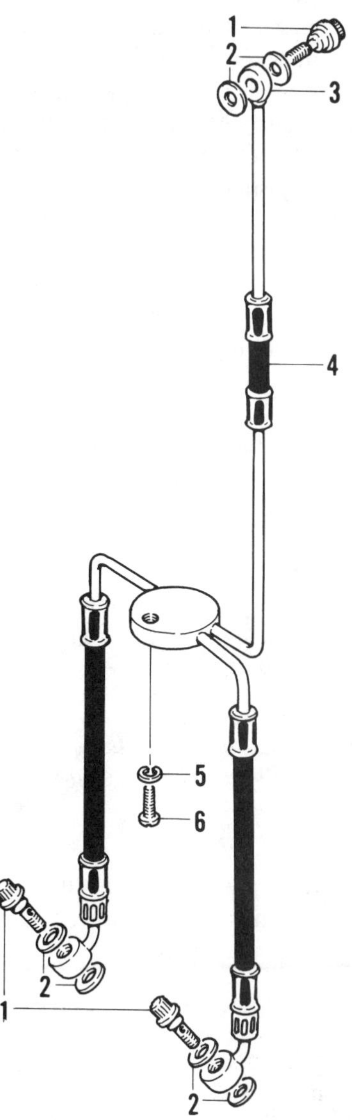


1. Banjo bolt
2. Washers
3. Hydraulic line
4. Hose
5. Lockwasher
6. Screw

21

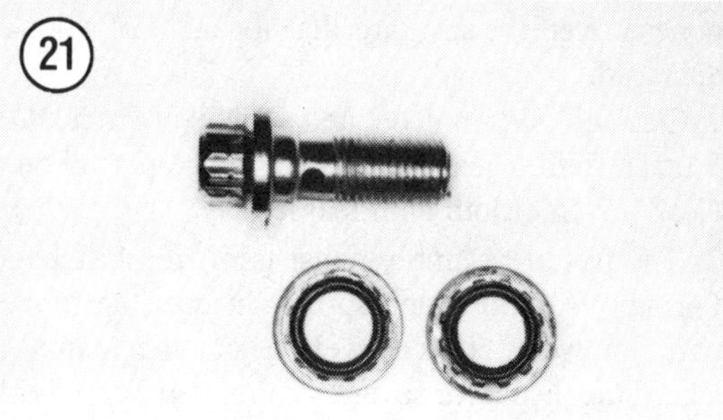

22

**FRONT BRAKE LEVER**

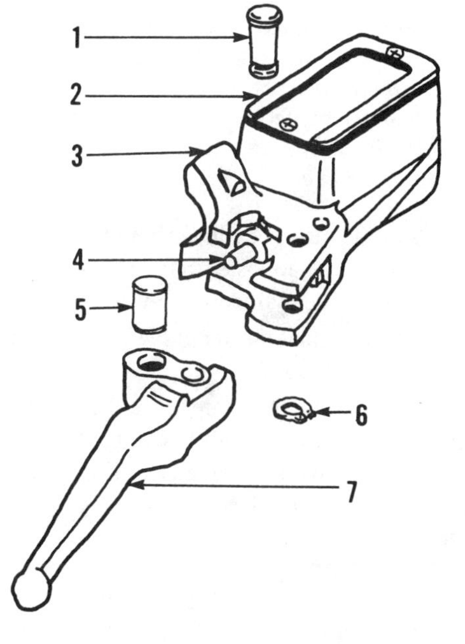


1. Pivot pin
2. Cover
3. Master cylinder assembly
4. Pushrod and switch
5. Reaction pin
6. Circlip
7. Brake lever

ponents. Replace any parts that appear to be worn or damaged.

1. Clean all parts in denatured alcohol or fresh DOT 5 brake fluid. Cleaned parts should be placed on a clean lint-free cloth until reassembly.

2. The piston assembly consists of the dust boot, O-ring, piston, cup and spring. Inspect the rubber parts for wear, cracks, swelling or other damage. Check the piston for severe wear or damage. Check the spring for fatigue or breakage. If any one part of the piston assembly is damaged, the entire piston assembly must be replaced; individual parts are not available from Harley-Davidson.

*NOTE*

*Do not remove the O-ring from the piston if you plan on reusing the piston and O-ring.*

*WARNING*

*When purchasing master cylinder rebuild kits, make sure to order the kit for your specific model. Because the master cylinder bore on FLT models is larger than the bore used on FXR and FX master cylinders, the parts are not interchangeable.*

3. Inspect the master cylinder bore for scratches or wear grooves. The master cylinder housing should be replaced if the cylinder bore walls are damaged.

4. Check to see that the vent hole in the cover is not plugged.

5. Check the banjo bolt threads in the master cylinder. If the threads are slightly damaged, clean them up with the proper size thread tap. If the threads are severely worn or damaged, replace the master cylinder body.

*NOTE*

*If you use a tap to clean the threads in the master cylinder, flush the master cylinder thoroughly and blow dry.*

6. Inspect the piston bore in the master cylinder for wear, corrosion or damage. Replace the master cylinder if necessary.

7. Make sure the fluid passage hole through the banjo bolt is clear. Flush bolt if necessary.

8. Check the reaction pin and pivot pin holes in the brake lever for cracks, spreading or other damage. Check the lever for cracks or damage.

9. Check the pivot and reaction pins for severe wear or damage. Check the fit of each pin in the brake lever. Replace worn or damaged parts as required.

### Assembly

1. Soak the piston O-ring and cup in fresh DOT 5 brake fluid for at least 15 minutes to make the cups pliable. Apply a thin coat of brake fluid to the cylinder bore before assembly.

2. Install the grommet and sight glass if removed.

3. Insert the cup onto the small end of the spring. The O-ring should be installed onto the piston before installing the piston.

4. Insert the spring and cup into the master cylinder as shown in **Figure 18**.

5. Install the O-ring onto the piston and insert the piston into the master cylinder.

6. Install the dust boot and reaction pin/switch.

7. Lightly coat the reaction pin with Loctite Anti-seize.

8. Referring to **Figure 18**, assemble the brake lever as follows:

   a. Install the reaction pin into the large hole in the brake lever.

   b. Position the brake lever into the master cylinder, making sure the end of the pushrod fits into the hole in the reaction pin.

   *NOTE*

   *Make sure the pushrod and switch are fully seated in the reaction pin hole. If the hand lever binds or pivots roughly, disassemble the parts and reassemble them correctly.*

   c. Insert the pivot pin through the master cylinder and engage the brake lever. Secure the pivot pin with the circlip.

## REAR DISC BRAKE

The rear disc brake is actuated by hydraulic fluid and is controlled by the right-hand foot-operated pedal that is linked to the master cylinder. As the brake pads wear, the brake fluid level drops in the reservoir and automatically adjusts for wear.

## REAR BRAKE PAD REPLACEMENT

There is no recommended mileage interval for changing the friction pads in the disc brake. Pad wear depends greatly on riding habits and conditions. The pads should be checked for wear initially at 500 miles (800 km), then every 2,500 miles (4,000 km) and replaced when the lining thickness reaches 1/16 in. (1.6 mm) from the brake pad backing plate. To maintain an even brake pressure on the disc, always replace both pads in the caliper at the same time.

### *1984-1985 FLT models*

Refer to **Figure 23** for this procedure.

1. Remove the 2 bolts and washers that mount the caliper to the bracket. Remove the pins into which the bolts thread and the spring washers and seals.

*CAUTION*

*To prevent brake hose damage, handle the brake caliper carefully while it is removed from the brake disc.*

2. Lift the caliper off of the brake disc.
3. Remove the plates, brake pads and springs.
4. Check the brake pads for wear or damage. Replace the brake pads if they are worn to 1/16 in. (1.6 mm) or less (**Figure 8**). Replace both pads as a set.
5. When new pads are installed in the caliper, the master cylinder brake fluid level will rise as the caliper pistons are repositioned. Clean the top of the master cylinder of all dirt and foreign matter. Remove the cap and diaphragm from the master cylinder and slowly push the caliper pistons into the caliper. Constantly check the reservoir to make sure brake fluid does not overflow. Remove fluid, if necessary, prior to it overflowing. The pistons should move freely. If the pistons are sticking in the cylinders, the caliper should be overhauled as described in this chapter.
6. Push the caliper pistons in all the way to allow room for the new pads.
7. Install the plates and brake pads in the order shown in **Figure 23**. Install the 2 springs. Line up the springs with the holes in the plates and pads.
8. Slide the caliper down over the brake disc, with the disc between the brake pads.
9. Coat the pins and the mounting bracket bores with Loctite Anti-Seize lubricant. Install a single spring washer on each pin.
10. Install the pins and bolts. Tighten the bolts to 12-15 ft.-lb. (16.5-20.7 N•m).
11. Refill the master cylinder reservoir, if necessary, to maintain the correct fluid level. Install the diaphragm and cover.

*WARNING*

*Use brake fluid clearly marked DOT 5 from a sealed container. Other types may vaporize and cause brake failure. Always use the same brand name; do not intermix as many brands are not compatible.*

*WARNING*

*Do not ride the motorcycle until the brake is working properly.*

### *1986-on FLT and Late 1987-on FXR*

Refer to **Figure 24** for this procedure.

*NOTE*

*There was a design change between early 1991 and late 1991-on brake pads and shims. When servicing the rear brakes on one of these models, refer to* ***Brake Pad/Pad Shim Identification*** *under* ***Rear Brake Caliper (1986-On FLT and Late 1987-On FXR)*** *in this chapter.*

1. To prevent accidental application of the rear brake lever, tie the pedal up to the frame so it cannot be depressed.
2. *FLT*: Perform the following:
   a. Remove the right-hand saddlebag; see Chapter Fifteen.
   b. Remove the right-hand side cover.
   c. Disconnect the negative and then the positive battery cable. Remove the battery and the battery carrier.
3. Remove the 2 caliper pin bolts and lift the caliper off of the mounting bracket. Do not disconnect the brake hose at the caliper.
4. Pull the retainer clip over the mounting bracket and remove it.
5. Slide the outer brake pad off the mounting bracket.
6. Slide the inner brake pad toward the wheel and off the mounting bracket.
7. Remove the 2 pad shims from the mounting bracket.
8. Check the brake pads (**Figure 25**) for wear or damage. Replace the brake pads if they are worn to 1/16 in. (1.6 mm) or less. Replace both pads as a set.
9. Clean the pad shims thoroughly and check for cracks or damage. Replace if necessary.

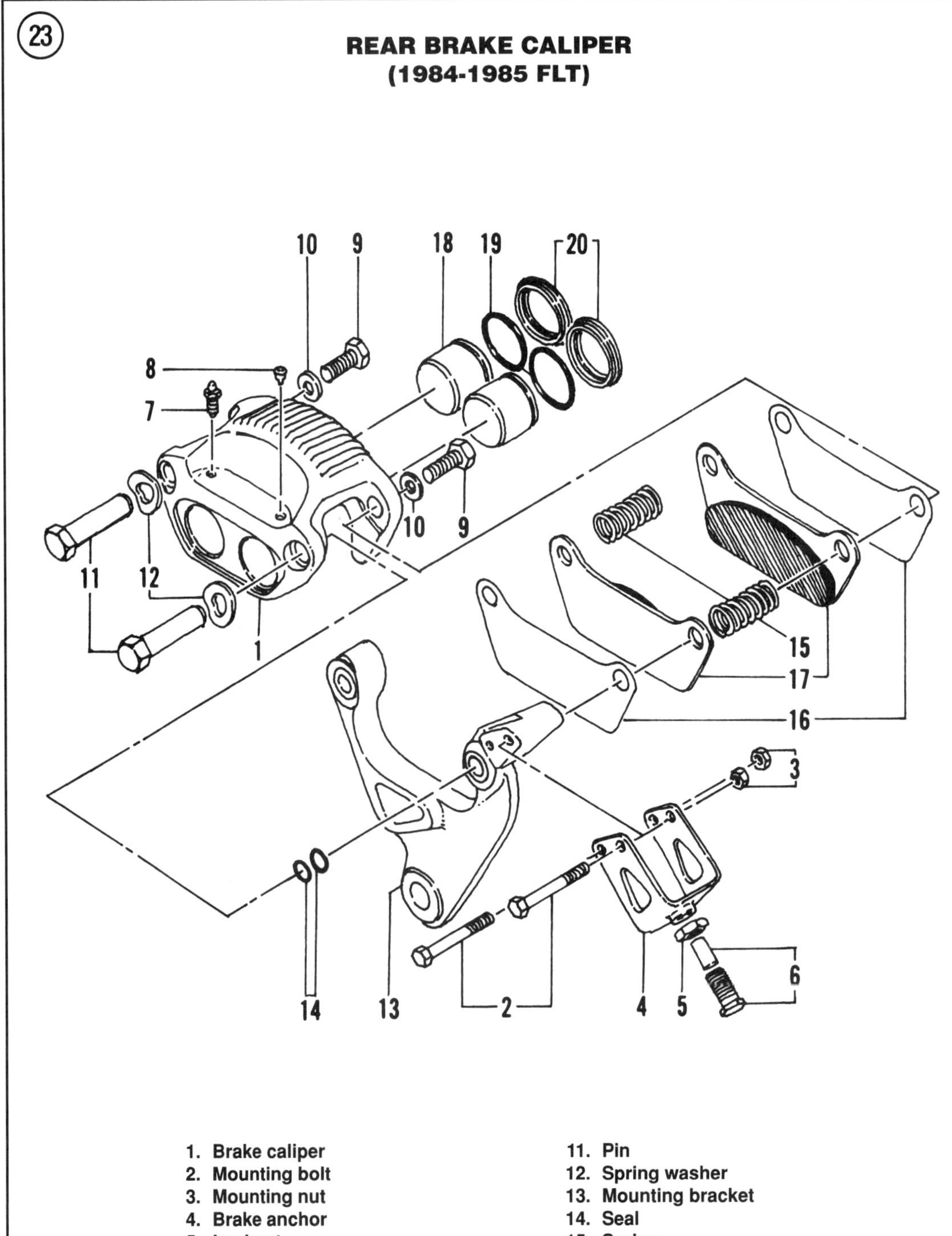


1. Brake caliper
2. Mounting bolt
3. Mounting nut
4. Brake anchor
5. Locknut
6. Bolt with spacer
7. Bleeder fitting
8. Brake hose seat
9. Pin bolts
10. Pin washer
11. Pin
12. Spring washer
13. Mounting bracket
14. Seal
15. Spring
16. Plate
17. Brake pad
18. Piston
19. Seal
20. Dust boot

10. Clean the shim mounting area on the mounting bracket thoroughly.

11. Check the pad clip for damage; replace if necessary.

12. When new pads are installed in the caliper the master cylinder brake fluid level will rise as the caliper piston is repositioned. Clean the top of the master cylinder of all dirt and foreign matter. Remove the cap and diaphragm from the master cylinder and slowly push the caliper piston into the caliper. Constantly check the reservoir to make sure brake fluid does not overflow. Remove fluid, if necessary, prior to it overflowing. The piston should move freely. If not, and there is evidence of it sticking in the cylinder, the caliper should be overhauled as described in this chapter.

13. Push the caliper piston in all the way to allow room for the new pads.

14. Install the pad shims onto the caliper mounting bracket rails as follows:

   a. On early 1991 and earlier models, insert the pad shim tabs (**Figure 26**) into the caliper bracket shim holes (3, **Figure 24**).

   b. On late 1991-on models, install the pad shims (**Figure 27**) so that their retaining loops face against the outer caliper mounting bracket rails as shown in B, **Figure 28** and **Figure 29**.

   c. On all models, hold the pad shims in place when installing the inner brake pad in Step 15.

15. Install the inner brake pad by sliding it over the pad shims so that it contacts the inside brake disc surface.

16. Install the outer brake pad by sliding it over the pad shims so that it contacts the outside brake disc surface.

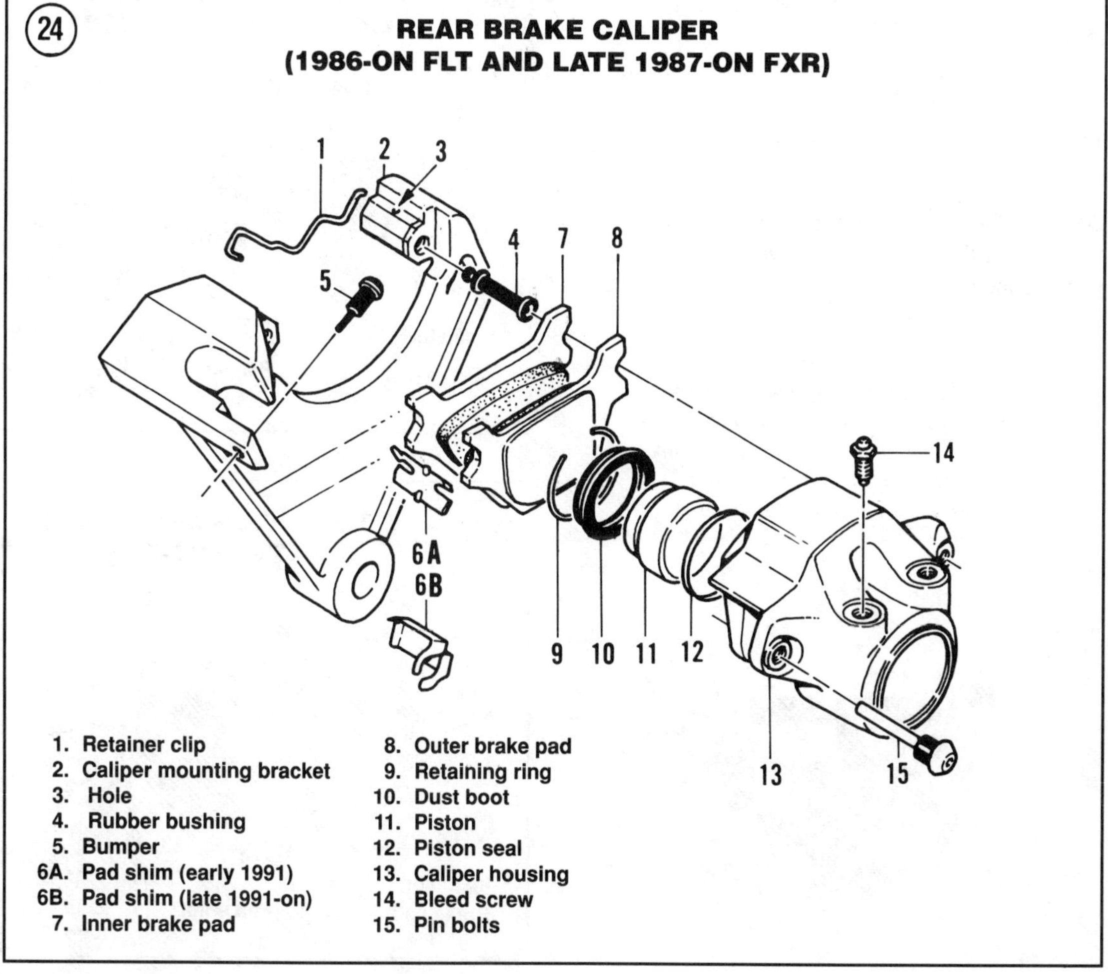


(24) **REAR BRAKE CALIPER (1986-ON FLT AND LATE 1987-ON FXR)**

1. Retainer clip
2. Caliper mounting bracket
3. Hole
4. Rubber bushing
5. Bumper
6A. Pad shim (early 1991)
6B. Pad shim (late 1991-on)
7. Inner brake pad
8. Outer brake pad
9. Retaining ring
10. Dust boot
11. Piston
12. Piston seal
13. Caliper housing
14. Bleed screw
15. Pin bolts

17. Working on the inside of the mounting bracket, insert the ends of the pad clip into the 2 holes in the mounting bracket. Then pivot the clip over the top of the brake pads until it seats against the outer brake pad as shown in **Figure 30**.

*WARNING*
*After installing the pad clip, check that the outer brake pad is still contacting the 2 pad shims. Failure of the outer pad to contact both pad shims can result in irregular pad wear, brake drag or mounting bracket damage.*

*NOTE*
*The caliper should be installed carefully over the brake pads so it does not knock against the brake pads and dislodge the pad shims.*

18. Align the caliper with the brake pads and install it over the pads. Align the holes in the caliper with the threaded holes in the mounting bracket and install the 2 pin bolts. Start the bolts by hand, then tighten with a torque wrench to the torque specification listed in **Table 2**.

19. If you tied the rear brake pedal to the frame, disconnect the wire.

20. Refill the master cylinder reservoir, if necessary, to maintain the correct fluid level. Install the diaphragm and cap.

*WARNING*
*Use brake fluid clearly marked DOT 5 from a sealed container. Other types may vaporize and cause brake failure. Always use the same brand name; do not intermix as many brands are not compatible.*

*WARNING*
*Do not ride the motorcycle until the brake is operating properly.*

### *1984-Early 1987 FXR and 1985-1986 FXWG, FXEF and FXSB*

Refer to **Figure 31** for this procedure.

1. To prevent accidental application of the rear brake lever, tie the pedal up to the frame so it cannot be depressed.

2. Remove the 2 brake caliper Allen bolts and lift the caliper off of the brake disc. Do not disconnect the brake hose at the caliper.

3. Remove the brake pads from the caliper body.

4. Remove the pad spring from inside the caliper.

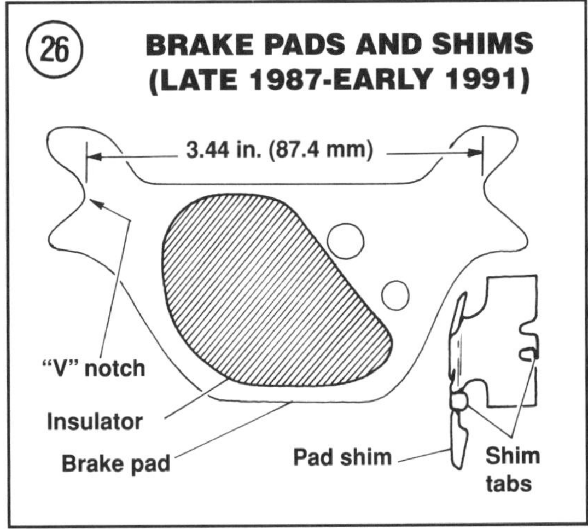


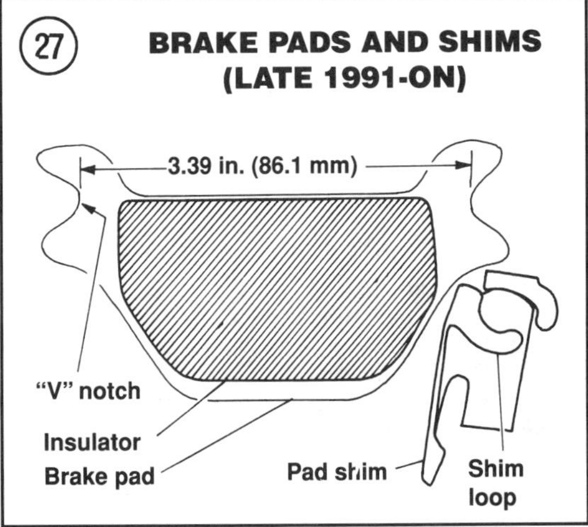

5. Check the abutment shim in the caliper frame (**Figure 32**). If it is worn or damaged, replace it as follows:

a. Pry the abutment shim away from the caliper.
b. Remove all adhesive from the caliper surface where the abutment shim is located.
c. Clean the abutment shim surface with denatured alcohol.
d. Apply silicone sealant to the abutment shim surface on the caliper and install the abutment shim. Hold the shim in position by installing the brake pads in the bracket.
e. Allow the silicone sealant to dry thoroughly before completing brake pad installation.
f. Check that the brake pads slide freely in the bracket.
g. Remove the brake pads after the silicone sealant has dried.

6. Check the brake pads for wear or damage. Replace the brake pads if they are worn to 1/16 in. (1.6 mm) or less. Replace both pads as a set.

7. When new pads are installed in the caliper the master cylinder brake fluid level will rise as the caliper piston is repositioned. Clean the top of the master cylinder of all dirt and foreign matter. Remove the cap and diaphragm from the master cylinder and slowly push the caliper piston into the caliper. Constantly check the reservoir to make sure brake fluid does not overflow. Remove fluid, if necessary, prior to it overflowing. The piston should move freely. If not, and there is evidence of it sticking in the cylinder, the caliper should be removed and serviced as described in this chapter.

8. Push the caliper piston in to allow room for the new pads.

9. Install the pad spring into the top of the caliper so that the spring's long tab extends above the piston. Hook the spring's short tab above the ridge on the caliper casting opposite the piston. See **Figure 33**.

*NOTE*
*Position the upper and lower pins so that the flat side on each pin is parallel with the bracket opening.*

10. Install the brake pads on the bracket. Then install the caliper body over the brake pads and onto the bracket. Make sure the upper and lower pins do not move when installing the caliper body.

11. Install the caliper screws and tighten to the torque specification listed in **Table 2**. Make sure the upper and lower pin flats are properly positioned. See *NOTE* prior to Step 10.

12. If you tied the rear brake pedal to the frame, disconnect it now.

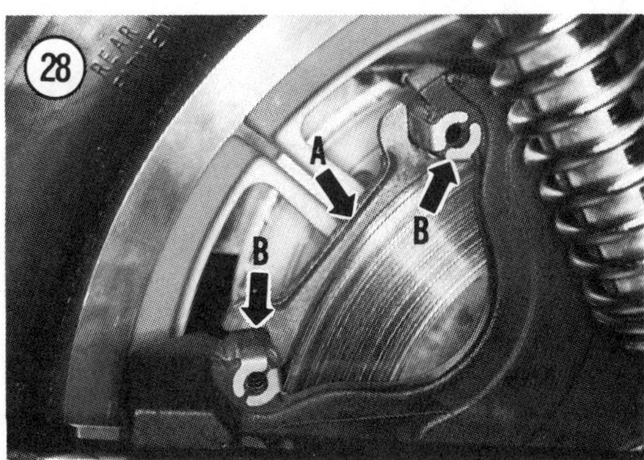


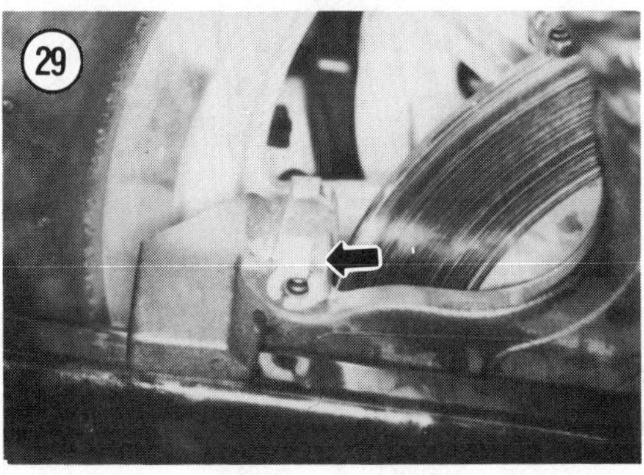


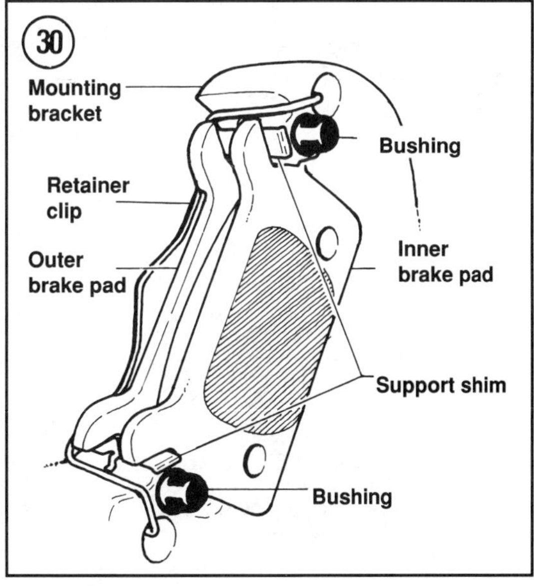


13

13. Refill the master cylinder reservoir, if necessary, to maintain the correct fluid level. Install the diaphragm and top cap.

*WARNING*
*Use brake fluid clearly marked DOT 5 from a sealed container. Other types may vaporize and cause brake failure. Always use the same brand name; do not intermix as many brands are not compatible.*

*WARNING*
*Do not ride the motorcycle until the brake is operating properly.*

## REAR BRAKE CALIPER (1984-1985 FLT)

### Removal

Refer to **Figure 23** when performing procedures in this section.

1. Remove the 2 bolts and washers that mount the caliper to the bracket. Remove the pins into which the bolts thread and the spring washers and seals.
2. Lift the caliper off of the brake disc.

*NOTE*
*If you are going to disassemble the brake caliper, remove the caliper pistons before disconnecting the brake hose at the caliper. Perform Steps 1 and 2 under **Caliper Overhaul** in this section.*

3. Disconnect the brake hose at the caliper.
4. Overhaul the brake caliper, if necessary, as described in this chapter.

### Installation

1. If removed, install the brake pads as described in this chapter.

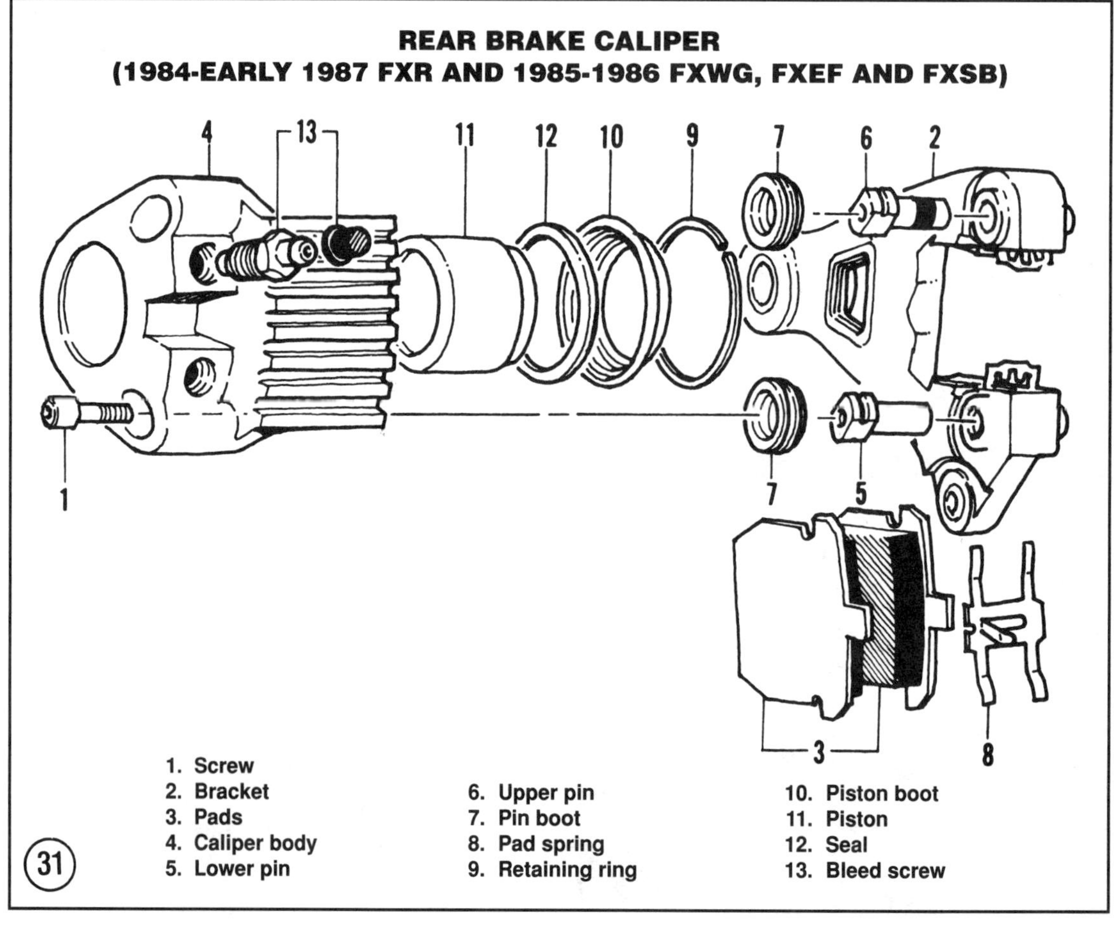

2. Slide the caliper down over the brake disc, with the disc between the brake pads.
3. Coat the pins and the mounting bracket bores with Loctite Anti-Seize lubricant. Install a single spring washer on each pin.
4. Install the pins and bolts. Tighten the bolts to the torque specification listed in **Table 2**.
5. Install the brake hose onto the brake caliper.
6. Bleed the brake system as described in this chapter.

### Caliper Overhaul

Harley-Davidson does not provide any specifications for wear limits on any of the rear caliper components (except brake pads). Replace any parts that appear to be worn or damaged.

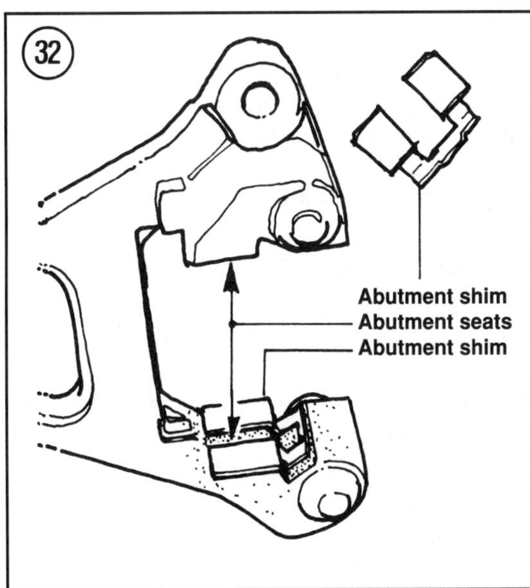


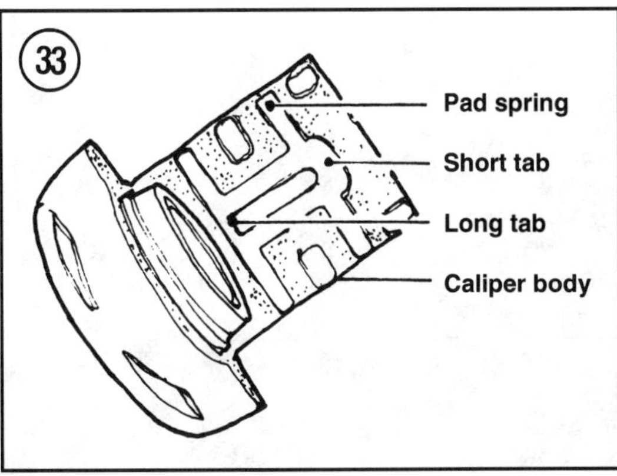


Refer to **Figure 23** for this procedure.
1. Remove the brake pads as described in this chapter.

*NOTE*
*Before removing the pistons in Step 2 or Step 3, ID the pistons by marking their inner bore with a black marker so you don't mix them up during reassembly. The pistons must be reinstalled in their original cylinders.*

2. With the brake hose still attached to the caliper, operate the brake lever until both pistons are forced out of the caliper as far as possible. Disconnect the brake hose from the caliper and take the caliper to your workbench for further disassembly. If the pistons did not come out, perform Step 3. If the pistons came out, perform Step 4.

*WARNING*
*When performing Step 3, the pistons may shoot out like a bullet. Keep your fingers out of the way. Wear shop gloves and apply compressed air gradually.*

3. If you were unable to remove the pistons as described in Step 2, perform the following:
   a. Disconnect the brake hose at the caliper.
   b. Place a rag or piece of wood in the path of the pistons (**Figure 34**) and place the caliper on the workbench so that the pistons face down.
   c. Blow the piston out with compressed air directed through the hydraulic hole fitting (**Figure 34**).
4. Remove the piston seals and dust boots.

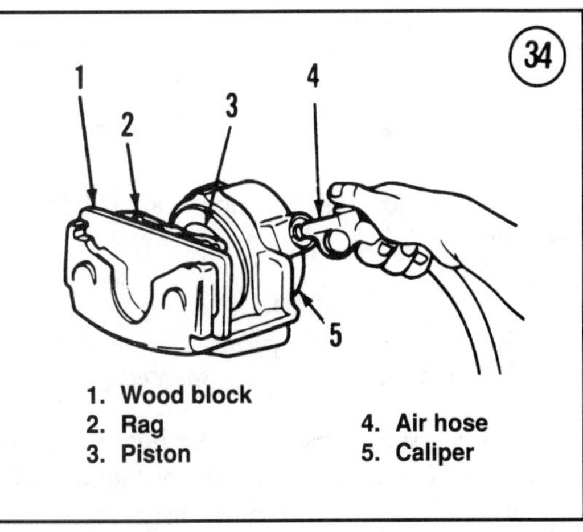

5. Inspect the caliper body for damage; replace the caliper body if necessary.
6. Inspect the hydraulic fluid passageways through the caliper body. They should be clean and open.
7. Inspect the caliper bore walls and the pistons for scratches, scoring or other damage. Replace worn, corroded or damaged parts. Do not bore or hone the caliper bore walls.
8. Make sure the hole in the bleed valve screw is clean and open. Use compressed air to clean it.
9. Check the mounting bracket for cracks or damage.
10. Check the pin bolt shoulders for deep scoring or excessive wear; replace if necessary.
11. Check the springs and wave washers for excessive wear or damage.
12. Check the brake pads for wear or damage. Replace the brake pads if they are worn to 1/16 in. (1.6 mm) or less. Replace both pads as a set.
13. Check all of the rubber parts for cracks, wear or age deterioration. Because very minor damage or age deterioration can make these parts useless, questionable parts should be replaced. When reusing rubber parts, clean the parts in new brake fluid and place on a lint-free cloth until reassembly.
14. If serviceable, clean all metal parts with denatured alcohol.
15. After replacing the piston seal and dust boot, as well as all worn or damaged parts, coat the following parts with new DOT 5 brake fluid. Place the parts on a clean lint-free cloth to prevent contamination before assembly.
  a. Pistons.
  b. Piston seals.
  c. Dust boots.
16. Make sure the caliper walls are thoroughly clean. If necessary, reclean in rubbing alcohol and allow to air dry before reassembly.
17. Install a new piston seal in each cylinder bore wall groove. Make sure the seals seat squarely in the grooves.
18. Coat the piston and the caliper bore with DOT 5 brake fluid.

*NOTE*
*When installing the pistons, follow the ID marks made prior to disassembly.*

19. Align a piston with the caliper bore so that its open end faces out. Then push the piston in until it bottoms out. Repeat for the other piston.
20. Install a piston dust boot onto the end of the piston. Repeat for the other piston.

*NOTE*
*If you are installing new brake pads, you will have to push the piston all the way into the bore. If necessary, use a C-clamp to push the piston into the bore.*

21. Install the brake pads as described in this chapter.

## REAR BRAKE CALIPER (1986-ON FLT AND LATE 1987-ON FXR)

Refer to **Figure 24** when performing procedures in this section.

### Brake Pad/Pad Shim Identification

There was a design change between early 1991 and late 1991-on models regarding the brake pads and pad shims (**Figure 24**). When purchasing replacement parts, note the following while referring to **Figure 26** (early 1991) or **Figure 27** (late 1991-on):

  a. Early 1991 pad shim thickness is 0.015 in. (0.38 mm).
  b. Late 1991-on pad shim thickness is 0.030 in. (0.76 mm).
  c. Early 1991 pad shims have a tab in the middle of each long side.
  d. Late 1991-on pad shims have an open loop at one end of the shim.
  e. Early 1991 brake pads measure approximately 3.44 in. (87.4 mm) between the "V" notches as shown in **Figure 26**. Late 1991-on

35

brake pads measure approximately 3.39 in. (86.1 mm) as shown in **Figure 27**.

f. Early 1991 outboard brake pads have an angle-cut, half-size insulator mounted on the back of the pad. The inboard brake pad has a full-size insulator.

g. Late 1991-on brake pads have full-size insulators mounted on the back of each pad.

*WARNING*

*When replacing brake pads, do not intermix early 1991 and late 1991-on brake pads and pad shims. Otherwise, improper rear brake operation will occur. This may cause brake failure and loss of control, resulting in personal injury. When purchasing new brake pads, take your frame's serial number to the dealer and have them verify your model as an early or late model.*

### Removal

1. Loosen and remove the banjo bolt holding the brake line to the caliper (**Figure 35**). Remove the bolt and the 2 washers. Place the end of the brake line in a plastic bag and secure the bag against the brake line with a plastic tie to prevent brake fluid from dripping onto the front wheel.
2. Remove the 2 brake caliper Allen bolts and lift the caliper off of the brake disc.
3. Overhaul the brake caliper, if necessary, as described in this chapter.

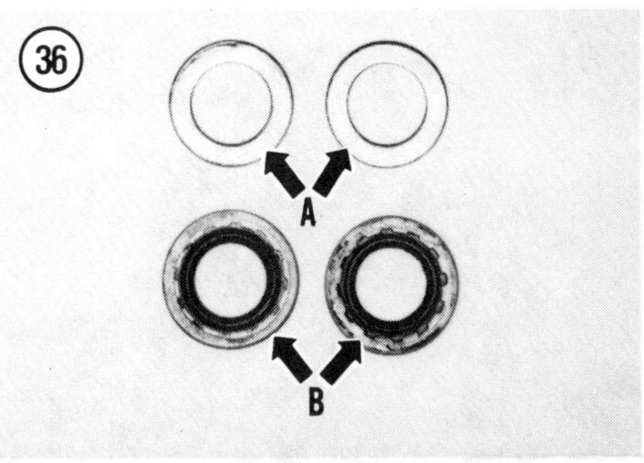

### Installation

1. If removed, install the brake pads as described in this chapter.
2. Install the caliper body over the brake pads and onto the bracket.
3. Install the caliper bolts and tighten to the torque specification listed in **Table 2**.

*WARNING*

*When installing replacement banjo bolts and washers used to connect the brake hose to the brake caliper, two types of banjo bolt washers have been used. Washers used on early models were made of copper with a zinc coating (A, **Figure 36**). Late models use steel washers equipped with a rubber O-ring (B, **Figure 36**). Because the banjo bolts are designed to be used with a specific type of washer, make sure that replacement banjo washers or bolts match the original parts used. Using an incorrect washer or bolt may allow the brake hose to leak and result in loss of complete brake pressure. If necessary, ask your dealer's parts or service manager to identify the correct washers and banjo bolts used on your model.*

*NOTE*

*Install **new** banjo bolt washers when performing Step 4.*

4. Install the brake hose onto the cylinder. Be sure to place a new washer on each side of the hose fitting (**Figure 37**) when installing the banjo bolt. Tighten the banjo bolt to the torque specification listed in **Table 2**.

*NOTE*

*The tightening torques for the copper and steel/rubber banjo bolts are different. Make sure to use the tightening*

13

*torque for the type of washer installed on your bike (**Table 2**).*

## Caliper Overhaul

Harley-Davidson does not provide any specifications for wear limits on any of the rear caliper components (except brake pads). Replace any parts that appear to be worn or damaged.

Refer to **Figure 24** for this procedure.

1. Remove the brake pads as described in this chapter.
2. Pry the retaining ring (**Figure 38**) out of the caliper body with a small screwdriver placed in the caliper notch. See **Figure 39**.
3. Remove the piston dust boot from the groove at the top of the piston (**Figure 40**).

*WARNING*
*When performing Step 4, the piston may shoot out like a bullet. Keep your fingers out of the way. Wear shop gloves and apply compressed air gradually.*

4. Place a rag or piece of wood in the path of the piston (**Figure 34**). Blow the piston out with compressed air directed through the hydraulic hole fitting. See **Figure 41**.
5. Remove the piston seal from the groove in the caliper body and discard it (**Figure 42**).
6. Replace the rubber bushings (**Figure 43**) in the mounting bracket if worn or damaged.
7. Inspect the caliper body for damage; replace the caliper body if necessary.
8. Inspect the hydraulic fluid passageways in the caliper body (**Figure 44**). Make sure they are clean and open.
9. Inspect the cylinder wall (**Figure 42**) and the piston (**Figure 45**) for scratches, scoring or other damage. Replace worn, corroded or damaged parts. Do not bore or hone the caliper cylinder.
10. Inspect the banjo bolt and bleed valve threads in the caliper body (**Figure 44**). If the threads are slightly damaged, clean them up with the proper size thread tap. If the threads are worn or damaged beyond repair, replace the caliper body.
11. Make sure the hole in the bleed valve screw (**Figure 46**) is clean and open.
12. Check the mounting bracket for cracks or damage. Check the threads in the plate for damage. If the threads are slightly damaged, clean them up with the proper size thread tap. If the threads are worn or damaged beyond repair, replace the mounting bracket.
13. Check the pin bolt shoulder for deep scoring or excessive wear; replace if necessary.
14. Check the pad retainer for cracks or damage.
15. Check the brake pads (**Figure 25**) for wear or damage. Replace the brake pads if they are worn to 1/16 in. (1.6 mm) or less. Replace both pads as a set.

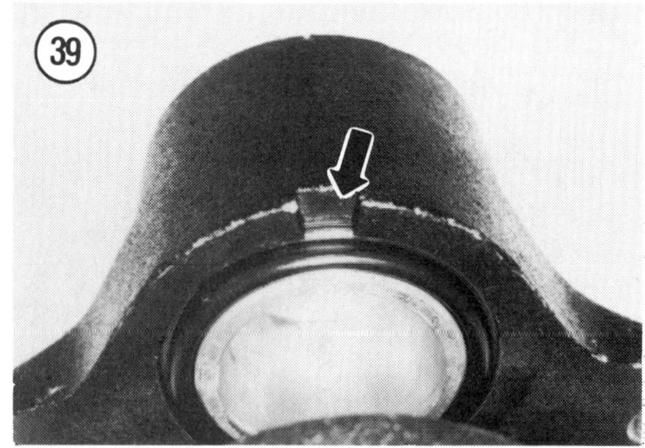

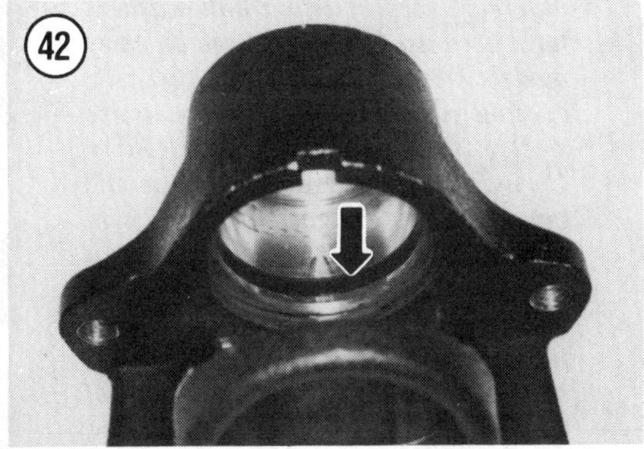


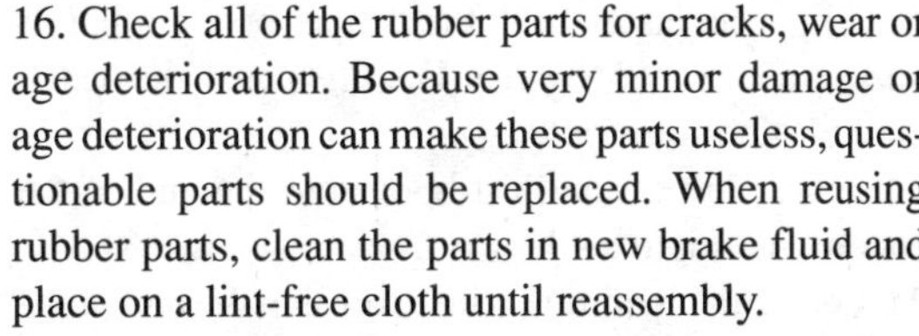

16. Check all of the rubber parts for cracks, wear or age deterioration. Because very minor damage or age deterioration can make these parts useless, questionable parts should be replaced. When reusing rubber parts, clean the parts in new brake fluid and place on a lint-free cloth until reassembly.

17. If serviceable, clean all metal parts with denatured alcohol.

18. After replacing the piston seal and dust boot, as well as all worn or damaged parts, coat the following parts with new DOT 5 brake fluid. Place the parts on a clean lint-free cloth to prevent contamination before assembly.

   a. Piston (**Figure 45**).
   b. Piston dust boot (A, **Figure 47**).
   c. Piston seal.

19. Make sure the retaining wire (B, **Figure 47**), piston and caliper bore are thoroughly clean. If necessary, reclean in rubbing alcohol and allow to air dry before reassembly.

20. Install the piston seal (**Figure 42**) into the caliper body groove.

21. Coat the piston and the caliper bore with DOT 5 brake fluid.

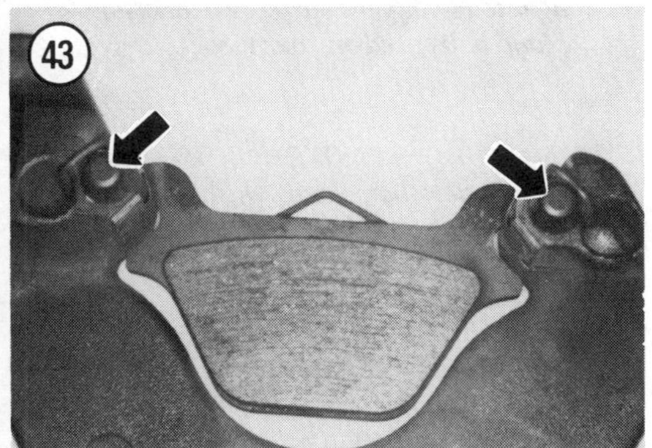


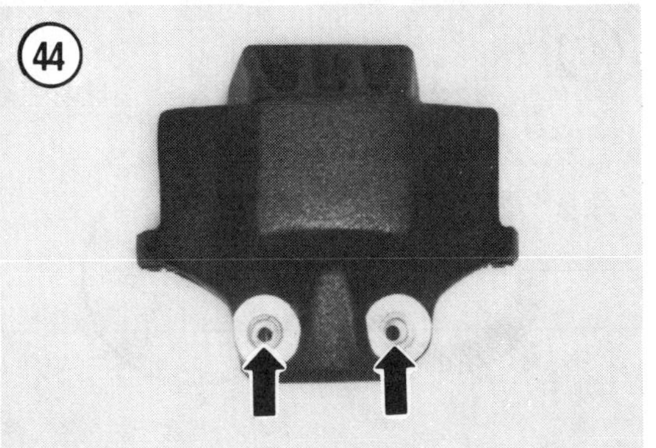


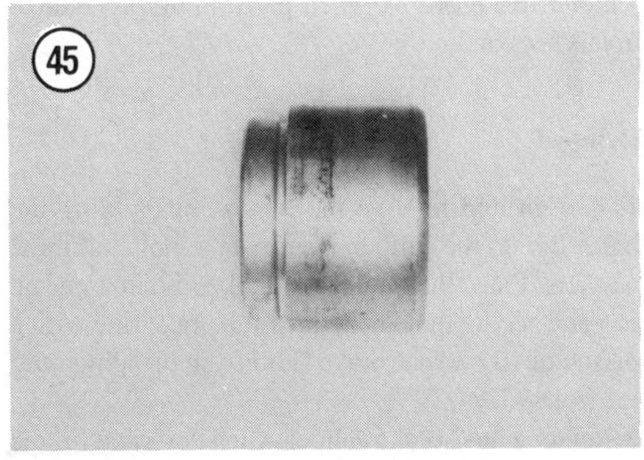


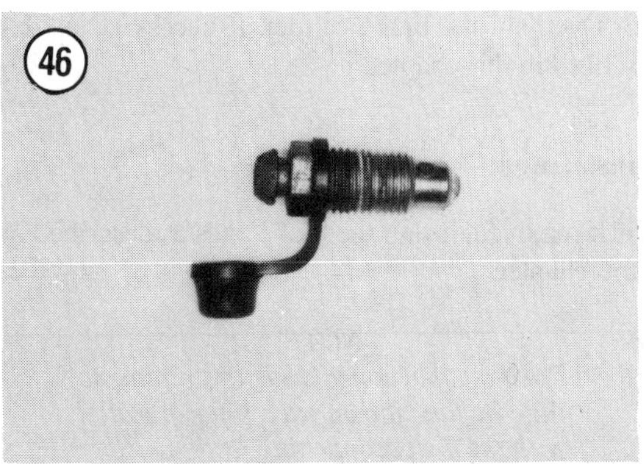

22. Align the piston with the caliper bore so that its open end faces out (**Figure 41**). Then push the piston in until it bottoms out.
23. Install the piston dust boot onto the end of the piston. See **Figure 40**.
24. Locate the retaining wire groove in the end of the caliper bore and install the wire into the wire groove (**Figure 38**). Make sure that the retaining wire is seated completely in the groove and that it is pushing against the piston dust boot.

*NOTE*
*If you are installing new brake pads, you will have to push the piston all the way into the bore. If necessary, use a C-clamp to push the piston into the bore.*

25. Install 2 new rubber bushings into the mounting bracket, if necessary.
26. Install the brake pads and pad shims as described in this chapter.

## REAR BRAKE CALIPER (1984-EARLY 1987 FXR AND 1985-1986 FXWG, FXEF AND FXSB)

Refer to **Figure 31** when performing procedures in this section.

### Removal

1. Loosen and remove the banjo bolt holding the brake line to the caliper. Remove the bolt and the 2 washers. Place the end of the brake line in a plastic bag and secure the bag against the brake line with a plastic tie to prevent brake fluid from dripping onto the front wheel.
2. Remove the 2 brake caliper Allen bolts and lift the caliper off of the brake disc.
3. Overhaul the brake caliper, if necessary, as described in this chapter.

### Installation

1. If removed, install the brake pads as described in this chapter.

*NOTE*
*Position the upper and lower pins so that the flat side on each pin is parallel with the bracket opening.*

2. Install the caliper body over the brake pads and onto the bracket. Make sure the upper and lower pins do not move when installing the caliper body.
3. Install the caliper screws and tighten to the torque specification listed in **Table 2**. Make sure the upper and lower pin flats are properly positioned. See *NOTE* prior to Step 2.

*WARNING*
*When installing replacement banjo bolts and washers used to connect the brake hose to the brake caliper, two different types of banjo bolt washers have been used. Washers used on early models were made of copper with a zinc coating (A, **Figure 36**). Late models use steel washers equipped with a rubber O-ring (B, **Figure 36**). Because the banjo bolts are designed to be used with a specific type of washer, make sure that replacement banjo washers or bolts match the original parts used. Using an incorrect washer or bolt may allow the brake hose to leak and result in loss of complete brake pressure. If necessary, ask your dealer's parts or service manager to identify the correct washers and banjo bolts used on your model.*

*NOTE*
*Install **new** banjo bolt washers when performing Step 4.*

4. Install the brake hose onto the cylinder. Be sure to place a new washer on each side of the hose fitting when installing the banjo bolt. Tighten the banjo bolt to the torque specification listed in **Table 2**.

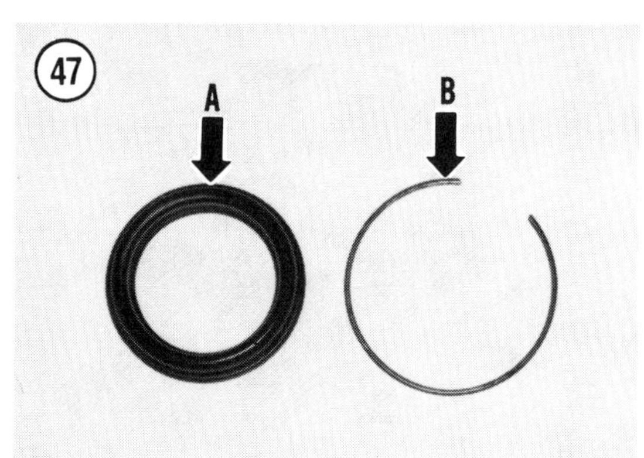

*NOTE*
*The tightening torques for the copper and steel/rubber banjo bolts are different. Make sure to use the tightening torque for the type of washer installed on your bike (**Table 2**).*

## Caliper Overhaul

Harley-Davidson does not provide any specifications for wear limits on any of the rear caliper components (except brake pads). Replace any parts that appear to be worn or damaged.

Refer to **Figure 31** for this procedure.

1. Remove the brake pads as described in this chapter.
2. Carefully pry the retaining ring out of the caliper body with a small screwdriver.
3. Remove the piston dust boot from the groove at the top of the piston.

*WARNING*
*When performing Step 4, the piston may shoot out like a bullet. Keep your fingers out of the way. Wear shop gloves and apply compressed air gradually.*

4. Place a rag or piece of wood in the path of the piston (**Figure 34**). Blow the piston out with compressed air directed through the hydraulic hole fitting. Use a service station air hose if you don't have a compressor.
5. Remove the piston seal from the groove in the caliper body.
6. Carefully pry the piston seal out of the caliper bore groove.
7. Remove the upper and lower pins and their rubber boots.
8. Inspect the caliper body for damage; replace the caliper body if necessary.
9. Inspect the hydraulic fluid passageway in the cylinder bore. Make sure it is clean and open.
10. Inspect the cylinder wall and the piston for scratches, scoring or other damage. Replace worn, corroded or damaged parts.
11. Inspect the banjo bolt and bleed valve threads in the caliper body. If the threads are slightly damaged, clean them up with the proper size thread tap. If the threads are worn or damaged beyond repair, replace the caliper body.
12. Make sure the hole in the bleed valve screw is clean and open.
13. Check the mounting bracket for cracks or damage. Check the threads in the plate for damage. If the threads are slightly damaged, clean them up with the proper size thread tap. If the threads are worn or damaged beyond repair, replace the mounting bracket.
14. Check the mounting pin shoulder for deep scoring or excessive wear; replace if necessary.
15. Check the pad retainer for cracks or damage.
16. Check the brake pads for wear or damage. Replace the brake pads if they are worn to 1/16 in. (1.6 mm) or less. Replace both pads as a set.
17. Check all of the rubber parts for cracks, wear or age deterioration. Because very minor damage or age deterioration can make these parts useless, questionable parts should be replaced. When reusing rubber parts, clean the parts in new brake fluid and place on a lint-free cloth until reassembly.
18. If serviceable, clean all metal parts with denatured alcohol.
19. After replacing all worn or damaged parts, coat the following parts with new DOT 5 brake fluid. Place the parts on a clean lint-free cloth to prevent contamination before assembly.
    a. Piston.
    b. Piston dust boot.
    c. Piston seal.
20. Make sure the retaining wire, piston and caliper bore are thoroughly clean. If necessary, reclean in rubbing alcohol and allow to air dry before reassembly.
21. Install the piston seal into the caliper body groove.
22. Coat the piston and the caliper bore with DOT 5 brake fluid.
23. Align the piston with the caliper bore so that its open end faces out. Then push the piston in until it bottoms out.
24. Install the piston dust boot onto the end of the piston.
25. Locate the retaining wire groove in the end of the caliper bore and install the wire into the wire groove. Make sure that the retaining wire is seated completely in the groove and that it is pushing against the piston dust boot.

*NOTE*
*If you are installing new brake pads, you will have to push the piston all the way*

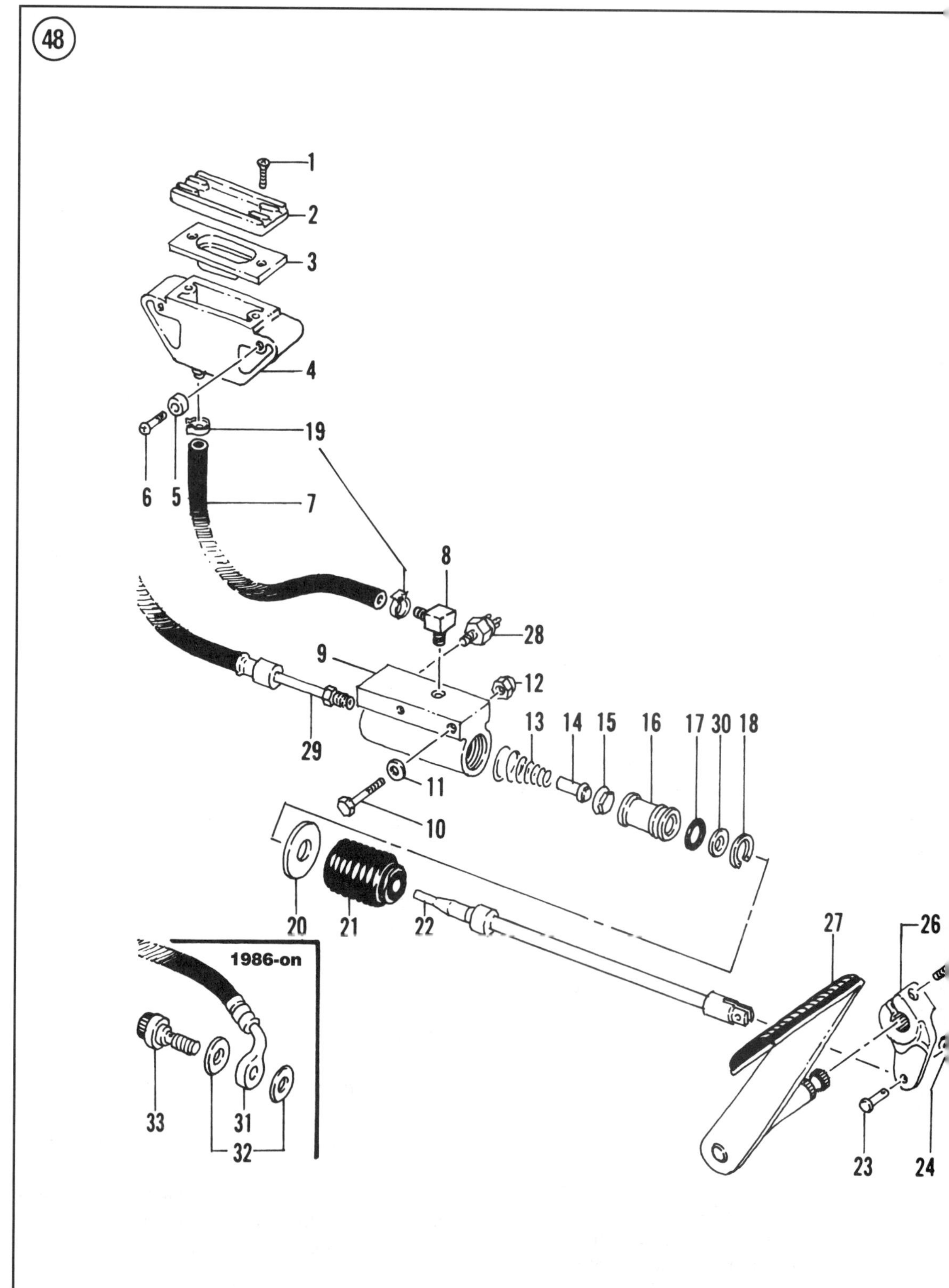
48
1
2
3
4
19
6
5
7
8
28
9
12
29
13
14
15
16
17
30
18
11
10
20
21
22
27
26
1986-on
33
31
32
23
24

**REAR BRAKE MASTER CYLINDER (1984-1991 FLT)**

1. Screw
2. Cover
3. Gasket
4. Reservoir
5. Spacer
6. Screw
7. Hose
8. Fitting
9. Master cylinder
10. Bolt
11. Washer
12. Locknut
13. Spring
14. Stop
15. Piston cup
16. Piston
17. O-ring
18. Circlip
19. Clamp
20. Nylon washer
21. Boot assembly
22. Pushrod
23. Pin
24. Washer
25. Cotter pin
26. Clevis and screw
27. Brake pedal
28. Stop light switch
29. Brake line
30. Washer (1986-on)
31. Banjo fitting (1986-on)
32. Washer (1986-on)
33. Banjo bolt (1986-on)

*into the bore. If necessary, use a C-clamp to push the piston into the bore.*

26. Install the boot onto the upper and lower pins. Then wipe the pin shafts and the pin bores in the mounting bracket with silicone grease. Insert the pins into the pin bores. Install the pin with the nylon sleeve into the top mounting bracket hole.

Each pin hole has a boss around the hole. Fit the boot shoulder on each boot onto their respective boss. Rotate the pins so that flat on both pins are parallel with the bracket opening.

27. Install the brake pads and abutment shims as described in this chapter.

## REAR MASTER CYLINDER AND RESERVOIR (1984-1991 FLT)

Refer to **Figure 48** when performing procedures in this section.

### Removal

1. To drain the hydraulic fluid from the rear brake system, perform the following:
   a. Attach a hose to the bleed valve on the caliper assembly.
   b. Place the loose end of the hose in a container to catch the brake fluid.
   c. Open the bleed valve and continue to apply the rear brake pedal until the brake fluid is pumped out of the system.
   d. Disconnect the hose and tighten the bleed valve.
   e. Dispose of this brake fluid—*never* reuse brake fluid. Contaminated brake fluid may cause brake failure.

*NOTE*

*If you only want to drain the master cylinder reservoir, disconnect the reservoir supply hose from the fitting on the master cylinder and drain the brake fluid into a container. Plug the hose opening.*

2. Cut the supply hose clamp at the master cylinder and disconnect the hose. Do not twist the hose back and forth sharply or you may damage the hose nipple on the master cylinder.

13

3A. *1984-1985*: Remove the brake hose at the master cylinder with a flare nut wrench. Pull the hose away from the master cylinder.

3B. *1986-on*: Remove the banjo bolt and washers securing the brake hose to the master cylinder.

*NOTE*

*Wrap the end of the brake hose with a plastic bag to prevent brake fluid from dripping onto the bike.*

4. Disconnect the electrical connector at the brake switch mounted on the master cylinder.

5. Remove the bolts, washers and locknuts securing the master cylinder to the frame or mounting bracket. Then pull the master cylinder back to disconnect it from the pushrod. Install the boot and nylon washer onto the pushrod if they came off when removing the master cylinder. See **Figure 45**.

6. Overhaul the master cylinder as described in this chapter.

### Installation

1. Install the boot and then the nylon washer onto the pushrod.

2. Insert the pushrod into the piston in the end of the master cylinder and position the master cylinder onto the frame. Install the bolts, washers and locknuts. Tighten bolts to the torque specification listed in **Table 2**.

3A. On 1984-1985 models, reconnect the brake hose to the master cylinder port. Tighten the fitting to 70-80 in.-lb. (8-9.2 N•m).

*WARNING*

*Two different types of washers have been used on oil hose banjo bolts on 1986 and later FLT models. Copper washers were used on 1986-1988 models (A, **Figure 49**). Steel washers with a rubber O-ring insert (B, **Figure 49**) are used on 1989 and later models. The banjo bolts are designed to be used with a specific type of washer. Make sure the replacement banjo washers and bolts match the original parts. Using the incorrect washer may cause fluid leakage and loss of brake pressure. If necessary, have your dealer's parts or service manager identify the correct washers and banjo bolts for your model.*

*NOTE*

*Tightening torques for copper and steel/rubber banjo bolts are different. Make sure to use the tightening torque for the type of washer installed on your bike (**Table 2**).*

3B. *1986-1988*: Reconnect the brake hose to the master cylinder with 2 new copper washers. Tighten banjo bolt to the torque specification listed in **Table 2**.

3C. *1989-1991*: Reconnect the brake hose to the master cylinder with 2 new steel/rubber washers. Tighten the banjo bolt to the torque specification listed in **Table 2**.

*NOTE*

*If the hose was removed or replaced, route the hose through the frame hose guide clip before reconnecting it onto the master cylinder in Step 4.*

4. Slide a new hose clamp onto the hose and fit the hose onto the hose reservoir nipple. Slide the clamp down so that it is against the hose where the hose fits onto the nipple. Close the hose clamp so that it is tight against the hose.

*NOTE*

***Figure 50** shows the type of pliers required to close stock hose clamps.*

5. Fill the reservoir with new DOT 5 hydraulic brake fluid. Bleed brake system as described under *Bleeding Hydraulic System* in this chapter.

6. Install the reservoir gasket and cover after bleeding the brakes.

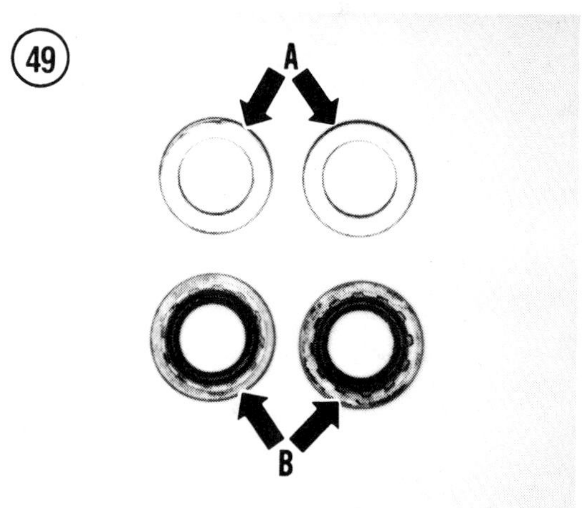

*WARNING*
*Do not ride the motorcycle until the brake is working properly.*

## Disassembly

1. Remove the master cylinder as described in this chapter.
2. Mount the master cylinder in a vise with soft jaws.
3. Insert a rod into the end of the piston and compress the piston to remove tension against the circlip. Remove the circlip and slowly remove tension from the piston. Remove the washer installed between the piston and circlip on 1986 and later models.
4. Remove the piston assembly, stop and spring from the master cylinder.

## Inspection

Harley-Davidson does not provide specifications for wear limits on any of the master cylinder components.

*NOTE*
*Harley-Davidson advises installing a new master cylinder repair kit whenever the master cylinder is disassembled.*

1. Clean all rubber parts in denatured alcohol or fresh DOT 5 brake fluid. Place cleaned parts on a clean lint-free cloth until reassembly.
2. Apply compressed air to all openings in the master cylinder body to dry it out thoroughly.
3. Inspect the cylinder bore and the piston contact surfaces for signs of wear and damage. If either part is less than perfect, replace it.

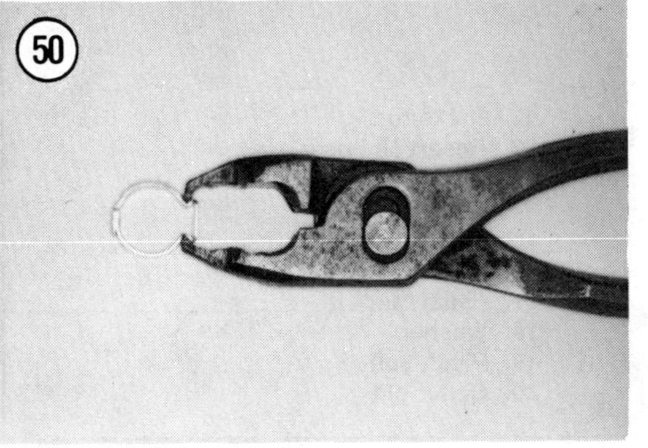


4. Replace the piston assembly if the cup and O-ring require replacement. The cup and O-ring can not be replaced separately.
5. Check the end of the piston assembly for wear caused by the pushrod. Replace if worn.
6. Inspect the rubber boot for deterioration, cracking and wear. Replace if necessary.
7. Inspect the dust boot nylon washer for wear or damage.
8. Remove the cover and gasket from the reservoir. Inspect the gasket for wear, deterioration or damage; replace if necessary.
9. Inspect the reservoir for cracks or damage.
10. Inspect the reservoir hose for deterioration or cracking. Replace if necessary and secure with new hose clamps.

## Assembly

1. Soak the piston assembly in fresh DOT 5 brake fluid for at least 15 minutes to make the primary cup pliable. Coat the inside of the cylinder with fresh brake fluid before assembly.
2. When installing a new piston assembly, coat the new O-ring with brake fluid and install it onto the piston.

*CAUTION*
*When installing the piston assembly, do not allow the primary cup to turn inside out. Cup damage will allow brake fluid leakage within the cylinder bore.*

3. Place the master cylinder in a vise with soft jaws. Do not overtighten the jaws or the master cylinder may be damaged.
4. Install the spring into the master cylinder so that the small spring end faces out.
5. Install the stop and piston cup into the cylinder.
6. Install the piston into the cylinder so that the end with the O-ring faces out.
7. *1986-on*: Install the washer onto the piston.
8. Compress the piston and washer (1986-on) into the cylinder and install the circlip into the cylinder groove. Release tension from the piston and check that the circlip seats in the groove completely.
9. Install the master cylinder as described in this chapter.

(51)

**REAR MASTER CYLINDER (1992-ON FLT)**

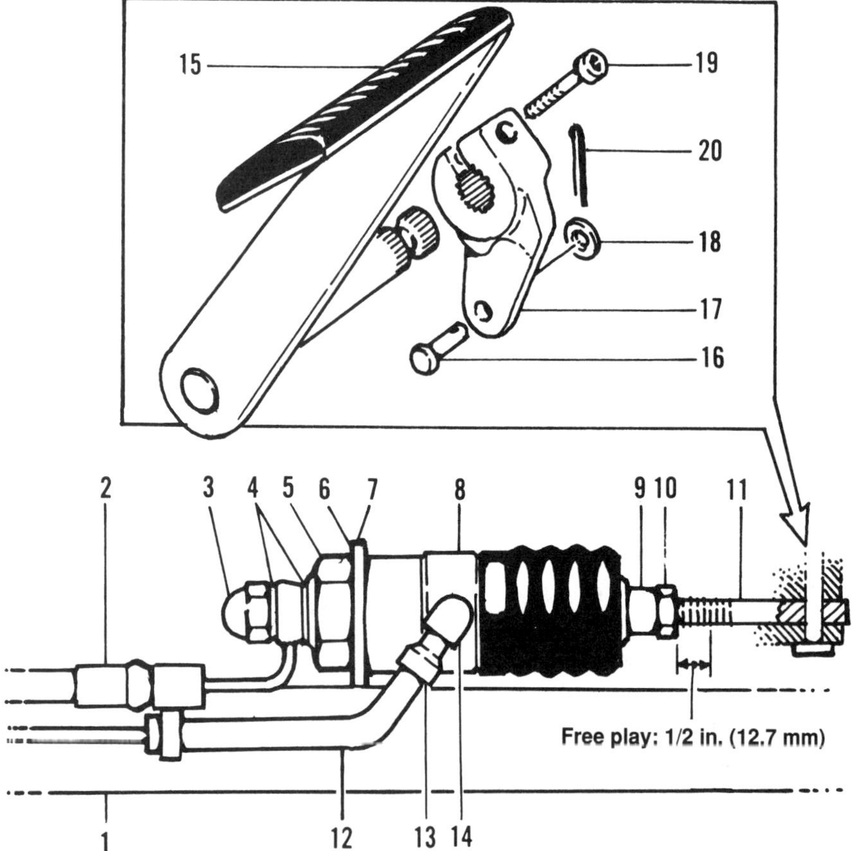


1. Frame tube
2. Brake line
3. Acorn nut
4. Washers
5. Nut
6. Lockplate
7. Frame bracket
8. Master cylinder assembly
9. Pushrod
10. Locknut
11. Brake rod
12. Reservoir hose
13. Clamp
14. Nipple
15. Brake pedal
16. Clevis pin
17. Pedal bracket
18. Washer
19. Pinch bolt
20. Cotter pin

## REAR MASTER CYLINDER AND RESERVOIR (1992-ON FLT)

Refer to **Figure 51** when performing procedures in this section.

*NOTE*
*Drain the brake fluid from the hose and discard it--never reuse brake fluid. Contaminated brake fluid may cause brake failure.*

1. To drain the hydraulic fluid from the rear brake system, perform the following:
   a. Attach a hose to the bleed valve on the caliper assembly.
   b. Place the loose end of the hose in a container to catch the brake fluid.
   c. Open the bleed valve and continue to apply the rear brake pedal until the brake fluid is pumped out of the system.
   d. Disconnect the hose and tighten the bleed valve.
   e. Dispose of this brake fluid—*never* reuse brake fluid. Contaminated brake fluid may cause brake failure.
2. Remove the brake line Acorn nut and washers at the master cylinder.
3. Remove the supply hose clamp at the master cylinder hose nipple and disconnect the hose. Do not twist the hose back and forth sharply or you may break the hose nipple on the master cylinder body.
4. Pry the lockplate tab away from the master cylinder nut. Then loosen and remove the master cylinder nut.
5. Remove the brake pedal clevis pinch bolt and remove the brake pedal from the clevis.
6. Loosen the pushrod locknut and turn the pushrod to disconnect it from the brake rod.
7. Pull the master cylinder out its mounting bracket and remove it.

### Installation

1. If the reservoir was removed, place it into position and secure it with its screws and washers. Install the hose onto the reservoir nipple and secure the hose with a new hose clamp.
2. Align the master cylinder square body with the square hole in the frame mounting bracket and install the master cylinder. The hose nipple should be facing as shown in **Figure 51**.
3. Thread the pushrod onto the brake rod. Do not tighten the locknut at this time.
4. Align the tab on the lockwasher with the notch in the master cylinder mounting bracket and install the lockwasher.
5. Install the master cylinder mounting nut and tighten to the torque specification in **Table 2**. Bend the lockwasher tab over flat on nut.
6. Install the brake line onto the master cylinder using the Acorn nut and 2 new washers. Tighten the Acorn nut to the torque specification in **Table 2**.
7. Slide the reservoir hose onto the master cylinder hose nipple and secure it with the hose clamp. Do not put excessive side force against the nipple or it may break.
8. Slide the clevis onto the brake pedal. Install the pinch bolt and tighten securely.
9. Adjust the brake pedal height as described under *Rear Brake Adjustment* in Chapter Three.
10. Fill the reservoir with new DOT 5 hydraulic brake fluid. Bleed brake system as described under *Bleeding Hydraulic System* in this chapter.
11. Install the reservoir gasket and cover after bleeding the brakes.

*WARNING*
*Do not ride the motorcycle until the brake is working properly.*

### Disassembly

Refer to **Figure 52** for this procedure.

*CAUTION*
*Keep all dirt and grease away from the cartridge body in the following steps. After cleaning the cartridge body in Step 2, all work on the cartridge body should be performed on a clean lint-free cloth.*

1. Remove the master cylinder as described in this chapter.
2. Clean the master cylinder cartridge body with denatured alcohol.
3. Screw the banjo bolt into the end of the cartridge body.

CAUTION

*The banjo bolt installed into the cartridge body in Step 3 will protect the end of the cartridge when removing it. Otherwise the cartridge may be damaged.*

4. Press down on the large washer and compress the spring. Put a wrench across the flat on the pushrod. Then use another wrench to loosen the pushrod locknut on the pedal rod and unscrew the rod from the end of the pushrod.

5. Set the cartridge body upright so that it rests on the banjo bolt. Then compress the large washer in the end of the cartridge body and remove the circlip from the groove in the pushrod. Release the washer and remove the washer, boot and spring.

6. Locate and remove the spring return retainer from inside the boot.

7. Remove the circlip from the cartridge body groove and remove the pushrod and its washer.

8. To replace the hose adaptor on the cartridge body:

   a. Stand the cartridge body upright so that it rests on the banjo bolt.

   b. Push down on the hose adaptor and slide it off of the cartridge body. Protect the cartridge body while it is exposed.

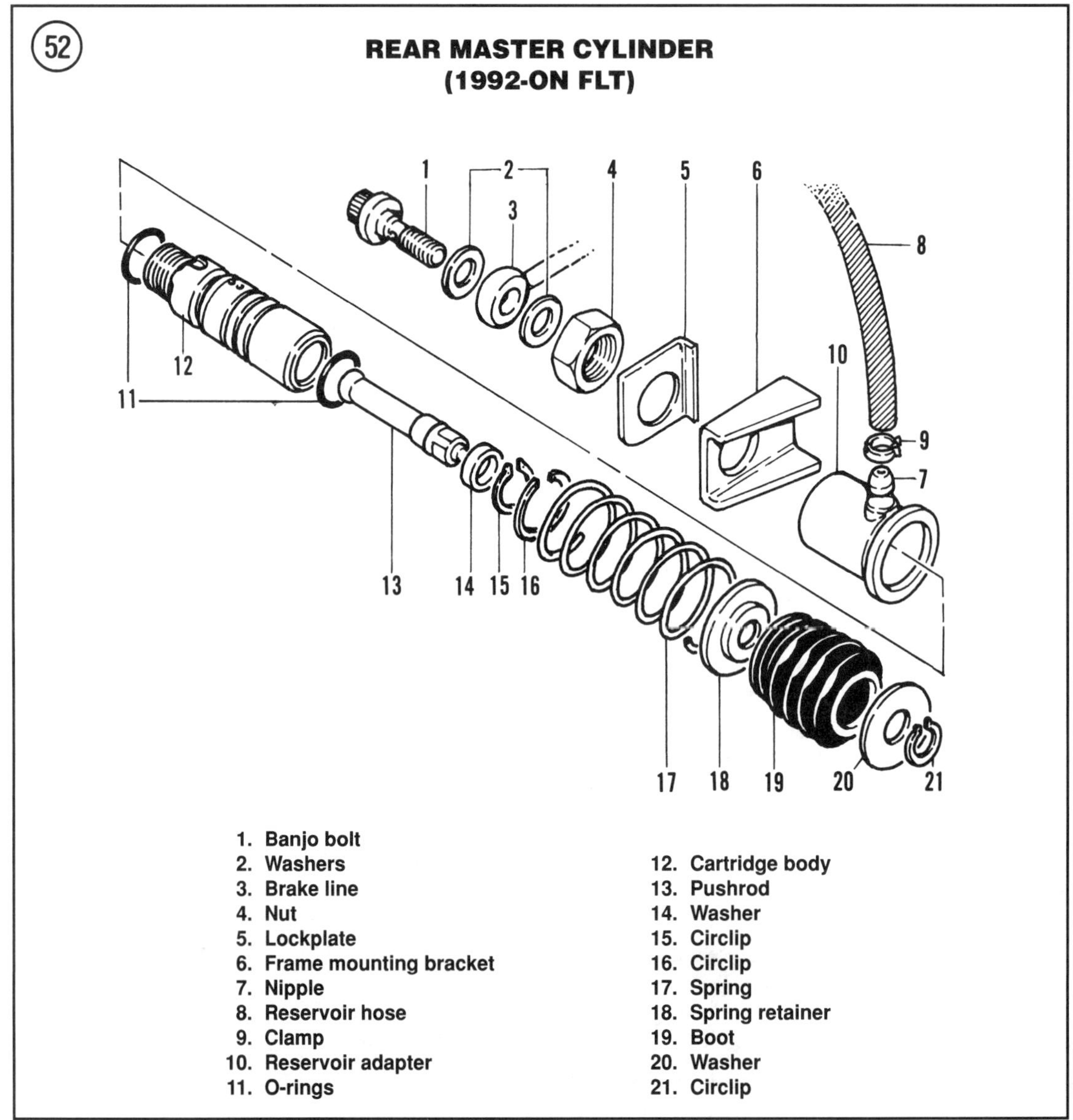

c. The O-rings should not be removed unless replacement is required.
d. Remove the outer cartridge body circlip.

*NOTE*
*Do not remove the piston assembly from the cartridge body. Replacement parts for the piston assembly are not available. If the piston and seals are damaged, the cartridge body assembly must be replaced.*

### Inspection

Harley-Davidson does not provide any specifications for wear limits on any of the master cylinder components.

1. Clean all parts in denatured alcohol or fresh DOT 5 brake fluid. Cleaned parts should be placed on a clean lint-free cloth until reassembly.
2. Inspect the cartridge body for cracks or damage.
3. Check the hose reservoir for damage.
4. Inspect the O-rings on the cartridge body for wear or damage. If the O-rings are worn, they must be replaced together with the hose reservoir.
5. Check the threads on the cartridge body, banjo bolt and pushrod. Replace damaged parts as required.
6. Check the dust boot for cracks, age deterioration or other damage. Replace if necessary.

### Assembly

1. Assemble the hose reservoir, if removed, as follows:
   a. Install the outer cartridge body circlip.
   b. When installing new cartridge body O-rings, soak the new O-rings in DOT 5 brake fluid. Then install the O-rings into the cartridge body grooves.
   c. The hose reservoir has a tab that must engage the notch in the cartridge body.
   d. Using hand pressure only, slide the hose reservoir over the cartridge body. Engage the tab in the hose reservoir with the notch in the cartridge body.

*CAUTION*
*Do not force the cartridge into the cartridge body. If the parts do not assemble easily, the cartridge and cartridge body are nor properly aligned. Forcing these parts together will damage them.*

2. Thread the banjo bolt into the end of the cartridge body and stand the assembly up so that it rests on the banjo bolt.
3. Install the washer onto the pushrod (opposite ball-end).
4. Insert the pushrod (ball-end first) into the cartridge until the pushrod washer is seated in the cartridge body bore. Then install the circlip into the cartridge body groove to secure the pushrod. Make sure the circlip seats in the groove completely. After installing the circlip, rotate the pushrod by hand; it should turn freely. If the pushrod is tight, disassemble the cartridge body to locate the damaged or improperly installed part.
5. Install the return spring and spring retainer onto the pushrod. Install the spring retainer so that the shoulder on the retainer faces away from the spring.
6. Install the dust boot over the pushrod and turn it so the drain hole in the boot faces down. Seat the lip on the dust boot into the groove in the hose reservoir.
7. Install the large washer over the end of the pushrod.
8. Push the washer down to compress the return spring and install the circlip onto the end of the pushrod. Make sure the circlip seats in the groove completely.
9. Thread the locknut onto the pedal rod and thread the rod into the pushrod. Do not tighten the locknut as it will be tightened after adjusting the rear brake pedal.

## REAR MASTER CYLINDER AND RESERVOIR (1984-EARLY 1987 FXR)



Refer to **Figure 53** when performing procedures in this section.

### Removal

1. To drain the hydraulic fluid from the rear brake system, perform the following:
   a. Attach a hose to the bleed valve on the caliper assembly.
   b. Place the loose end of the hose in a container to catch the brake fluid.

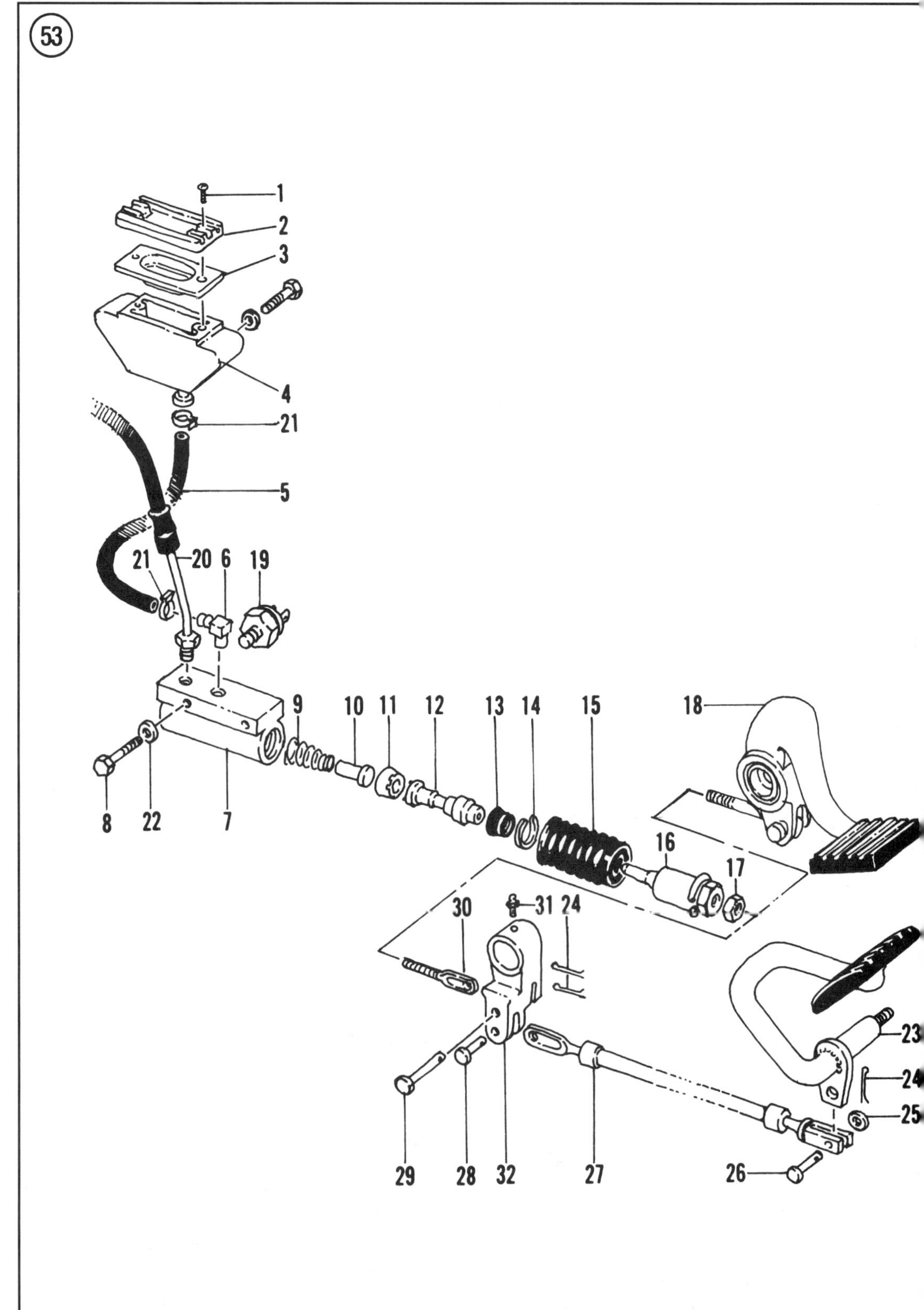
53
1
2
3
4
21
5
21
20
6
19
9
10
11
12
13
14
15
18
8
22
7
16
17
30
31
24
23
24
25
29
28
32
27
26

**REAR BRAKE MASTER CYLINDER (1984-EARLY 1987 FXR)**

1. Screw (2)
2. Cover
3. Gasket
4. Reservoir
5. Hose
6. Fitting
7. Master cylinder
8. Mounting bolt (2)
9. Spring
10. Stop
11. Piston cup
12. Piston
13. Seal
14. Retaining ring
15. Boot assembly
16. Pushrod and retaining ring
17. Locknut
18. Pedal assembly
19. Stop light switch
20. Brake line
21. Clamp
22. Washer (2)
23. Pedal (FXRD)
24. Cotter pin (FXRD)
25. Washer (FXRD)
26. Pin (FXRD)
27. Brake rod (FXRD)
28. Pin (FXRD)
29. Pin (FXRD)
30. Rod (FXRD)
31. Grease fitting (FXRD)
32. Pivot assembly (FXRD)

c. Open the bleed valve and continue to apply the rear brake pedal until the brake fluid is pumped out of the system.

d. Disconnect the hose and tighten the bleed valve.

e. Dispose of this brake fluid—*never* reuse brake fluid. Contaminated brake fluid may cause brake failure.

*NOTE*

*If you only want to drain the master cylinder reservoir, disconnect the reservoir supply hose from the fitting on the master cylinder and drain the brake fluid into a container. Plug the hose opening.*

2. Cut the supply hose clamp at the master cylinder and disconnect the hose. Do not twist the hose back and forth sharply or you may break the hose nipple on the master cylinder.

3. Remove the brake hose at the master cylinder with a flare nut wrench. Pull the hose away from the master cylinder.

*NOTE*

*Wrap the end of the brake hose with a plastic bag to prevent brake fluid from dripping onto the bike.*

4. Disconnect the electrical connector from the brake switch mounted on the master cylinder.

5. Remove the bolts and washers securing the master cylinder to the frame. Then pull the master cylinder back to disconnect it from the pushrod. Install the boot onto the pushrod if it came off when removing the master cylinder.

6. Overhaul the master cylinder as described in this chapter.



## Installation

1. Install the boot onto the pushrod.

2. Insert the pushrod into the piston in the end of the master cylinder and position the master cylinder onto the frame. Install the bolts and washers. Tighten bolts to the torque specification listed in **Table 2**.

3. Reconnect the brake hose to the master cylinder port. Tighten the fitting to 70-80 in.-lb. (8-9.2 N•m).

4. Slide a new hose clamp onto the hose and fit the hose onto the hose reservoir nipple. Slide the clamp down so that it is against the hose where the hose fits

onto the nipple. Close the hose clamp so that it is tight against the hose.

*NOTE*
***Figure 50** shows the type of pliers required to close the hose clamp.*

5. Fill the reservoir with new DOT 5 hydraulic brake fluid. Bleed brake system as described under *Bleeding Hydraulic System* in this chapter.
6. Install the reservoir gasket and cover after bleeding the brakes.

*WARNING*
*Do not ride the motorcycle until the brake is working properly.*

## Disassembly

1. Remove the master cylinder as described in this chapter.
2. Mount the master cylinder in a vise with soft jaws.
3. Insert a rod into the end of the piston and compress the piston to remove tension against the circlip. Remove the circlip and slowly remove tension from the piston.
4. Remove the piston assembly, stop and spring from the master cylinder.

## Inspection

Harley-Davidson does not provide specifications for wear limits on any of the master cylinder components.

*NOTE*
*Harley-Davidson advises installing a new master cylinder repair kit whenever the master cylinder is disassembled.*

1. Clean all rubber parts in denatured alcohol or fresh DOT 5 brake fluid. Place cleaned parts on a clean lint-free cloth until reassembly.
2. Apply compressed air to all openings in the master cylinder body to dry it out thoroughly.
3. Inspect the cylinder bore and the piston contact surfaces for signs of wear and damage. If either part is less than perfect, replace it.
4. Replace the piston assembly if the cup and seal are damaged. The cup and seal can not be replaced individually.
5. Check the end of the piston assembly for wear caused by the pushrod. Replace if worn.
6. Inspect the rubber boot for deterioration, cracking and wear. Replace if necessary.
7. Remove the cover and gasket from the reservoir. Inspect the gasket for wear, deterioration or damage; replace if necessary.
8. Inspect the reservoir for cracks or damage.
9. Inspect the reservoir hose for deterioration or cracking. Replace if necessary and secure with new hose clamps.

## Assembly

1. Soak the piston assembly in fresh DOT 5 brake fluid for at least 15 minutes to make the primary cup pliable. Coat the inside of the cylinder with fresh brake fluid before assembly.
2. If you are installing a new piston assembly, coat the new seal with brake fluid and install it onto the piston.

*CAUTION*
*When installing the piston assembly, do not allow the seal to turn inside out. A damaged seal will allow brake fluid to leak in the cylinder bore.*

3. Place the master cylinder in a vise with soft jaws. Do not overtighten the jaws or the master cylinder may be damaged.
4. Install the spring into the master cylinder with the small end facing out.
5. Install the stop and piston cup into the cylinder.
6. Install the piston into the cylinder with the seal end facing out.
7. Compress the piston into the cylinder and install the circlip into the cylinder groove. Release tension from the piston and check that the circlip seats in the groove completely.
8. Install the master cylinder as described in this chapter.

# REAR MASTER CYLINDER AND RESERVOIR (LATE 1987-ON FXR)

Refer to **Figure 54** when performing procedures in this section.

(54)

**REAR MASTER CYLINDER (LATE 1987-ON FXR)**

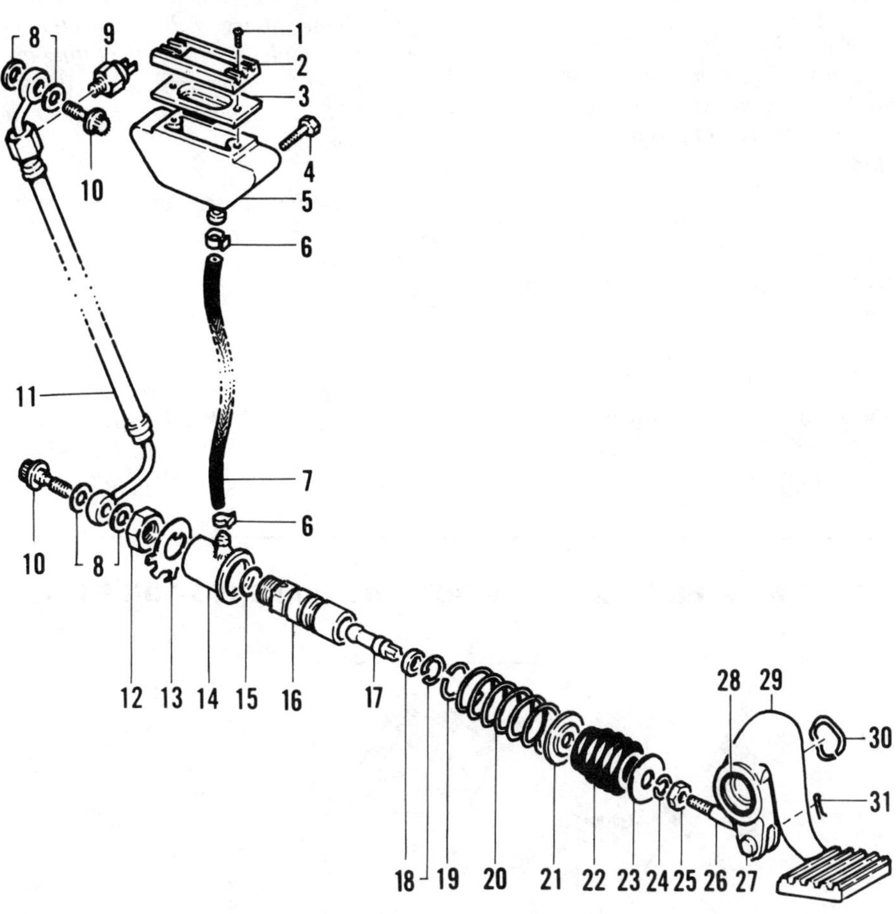


1. Screw
2. Cover
3. Diaphragm
4. Bolt
5. Reservoir
6. Hose clamp
7. Hose
8. Washers
9. Brake switch
10. Banjo bolt
11. Hose
12. Nut
13. Lockwasher
14. Adapter
15. O-ring
16. Cartridge body
17. Pushrod
18. Washer and Circlip
19. Circlip
20. Spring
21. Spring retainer
22. Boot
23. Washer
24. Circlip
25. Nut
26. Brake rod
27. Pin
28. Bushing
29. Brake pedal
30. Washer
31. Cotter pin

### Removal

Refer to **Figure 55** when performing these procedures.

1. Remove the exhaust system as described in Chapter Eight.
2. Remove the cotter pin and disconnect the brake pedal from the pedal rod. Discard the cotter pin.

*NOTE*
*Drain the brake fluid from the hose and discard it—never reuse brake fluid. Contaminated brake fluid may cause brake failure.*

3. To drain the hydraulic fluid from the rear brake system, perform the following:
   a. Attach a hose to the bleed valve on the caliper assembly.
   b. Place the loose end of the hose in a container to catch the brake fluid.
   c. Open the bleed valve and continue to apply the rear brake pedal until the brake fluid is pumped out of the system.
   d. Disconnect the hose and tighten the bleed valve.
   e. Dispose of this brake fluid—*never* reuse brake fluid. Contaminated brake fluid may cause brake failure.

*NOTE*
*If you only want to drain the master cylinder reservoir, disconnect the reservoir supply hose from the fitting on the master cylinder and drain the brake fluid into a container. Plug the hose opening.*

4. Cut the supply hose clamp at the cartridge body and disconnect the hose. Do not twist the hose back and forth sharply or you may break the hose nipple on the cartridge body.

*CAUTION*
*The banjo bolt (**Figure 56**) holding the metal brake line to the cartridge body is tightened to 30-40 ft.-lb. (41.4-55.2 N•m). Because of this high torque read-*

**REAR MASTER CYLINDER MOUNTING (LATE 1987-ON FXR)**

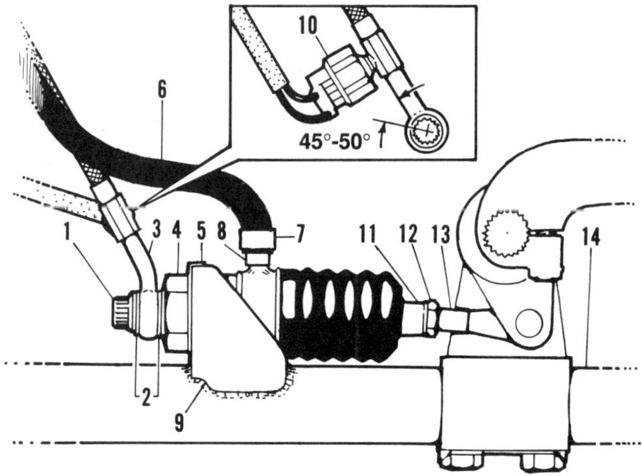


1. Banjo bolt
2. Washers
3. Brake hose
4. Nut
5. Lockwasher
6. Reservoir hose
7. Hose clamp
8. Adapter
9. Bracket
10. Brake light switch
11. Pushrod
12. Nut
13. Brake rod
14. Frame tube

*ing, the bolt will want to twist rather than turn when you loosen it. As the bolt twists, the metal brake line may turn with it; a condition that could damage or break the line. To prevent the bolt from twisting, shock it loose with a hand impact driver or hit the wrench with a hammer.*

5. Loosen the banjo bolt at the cartridge body and remove the bolt and the 2 sealing washers. Place the open end of the hose in a plastic bag to prevent brake fluid leakage.

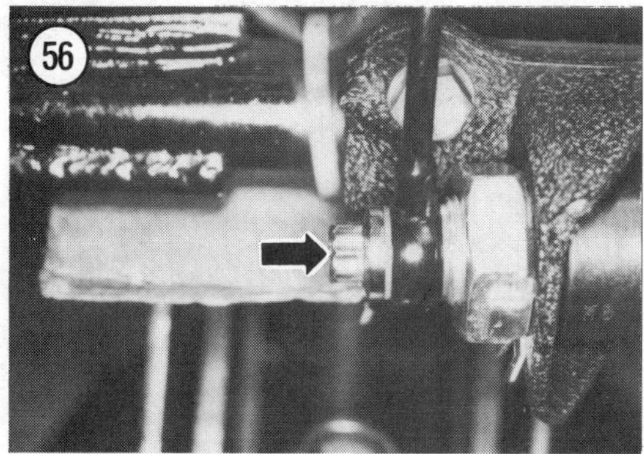
56

57

58

6. Bend the lockplate tab away from the cartridge body. Then remove the nut (**Figure 57**) and lockplate and remove the cartridge body.

## Installation

Refer to **Figure 55** when performing these procedures.

1. If the reservoir was removed, place it into position and secure it with its screws and washers. Install the hose onto the reservoir nipple and secure the hose with a new hose clamp.

*CAUTION*
*Handle the cartridge body carefully when installing it as the hose reservoir can be easily cracked or broken off.*

2. Align the tab on the lockwasher with the notch in the master cylinder mounting bracket and install the lockwasher (**Figure 58**).

3. Pivot the brake pedal as required to provide room when installing the cartridge body assembly into the frame mounting bracket. Then carefully insert the threaded end of the cartridge body through the frame mounting bracket, making sure the hose nipple is facing up. The square portion on the cartridge body must engage the square hole in the mounting bracket.

4. Screw the cartridge body nut (**Figure 59**) onto the cartridge body and tighten to the torque specification listed in **Table 2**. Bend the lockwasher arm over the nut to lock it.

*WARNING*
*Two different types of washers have been used to secure banjo bolts on 1986 and late 1987 and later FXR models. Early models used zinc coated copper washers (A, **Figure 49**). Steel washers with a rubber O-ring insert (B, **Figure 49**) are used on later models. Because the banjo bolts are designed to be used with a specific type of washer, the replacement banjo washers and bolts must match the original parts. Using an incorrect washer or bolt can allow the brake hose to leak and result in loss of complete brake pressure. If necessary, have your dealer's parts or service man-*

*ager identify the correct washers and banjo bolts used on your model.*

*NOTE*
*Install **new** banjo bolt washers when performing Step 5.*

5. Assemble the brake line onto the cartridge body by placing a washer on both sides of the brake line fitting (**Figure 60**), then secure the fitting to the cartridge body with the banjo bolt. Adjust the brake line so that it is at a 45-50° angle from horizontal (**Figure 55**). When the brake line is angled properly, tighten the banjo bolt to the torque specification listed in **Table 2**.

*NOTE*
*The tightening torques for the copper and steel/rubber banjo bolts are different. Make sure to use the tightening torque for the type of washer installed on your bike (**Table 2**).*

6. Slide a new hose clamp (B, **Figure 61**) onto the hose (A, **Figure 61**) and fit the hose onto the hose reservoir nipple. Slide the clamp down so that it is against the hose where the hose fits onto the nipple. Close the hose clamp so that it is tight against the hose (**Figure 62**).

*NOTE*
***Figure 50** shows the type of pliers required to close the hose clamp.*

7. Pivot the brake pedal into position and attach the pedal rod to the brake pedal (**Figure 55**) with the pin. Secure with a new cotter pin.
8. Adjust the brake pedal as described in Chapter Three.
9. Fill the reservoir with new DOT 5 hydraulic brake fluid. Bleed brake system as described under *Bleeding Hydraulic System* in this chapter.
10. Install the reservoir gasket and cover after bleeding the brakes.

*WARNING*
*Do not ride the motorcycle until the brake is working properly.*

### Disassembly

Refer to **Figure 54** for this procedure.

*CAUTION*
*Keep all dirt and grease away from the cartridge body in the following steps. After cleaning the cartridge body in Step 2, all work on the cartridge body should be performed on a clean lint-free cloth.*

1. Remove the master cylinder as described in this chapter.
2. Clean the master cylinder cartridge body with denatured alcohol.

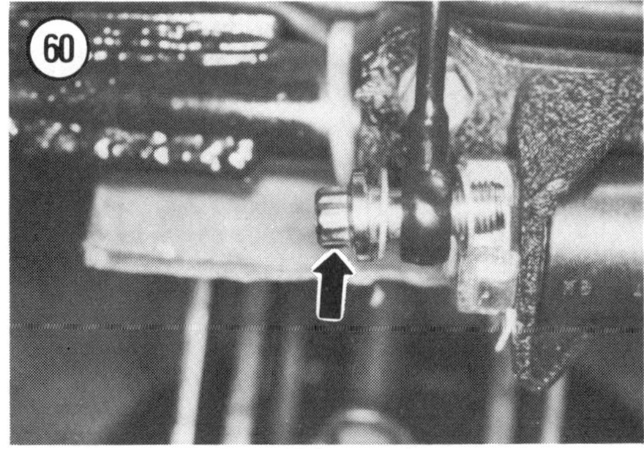


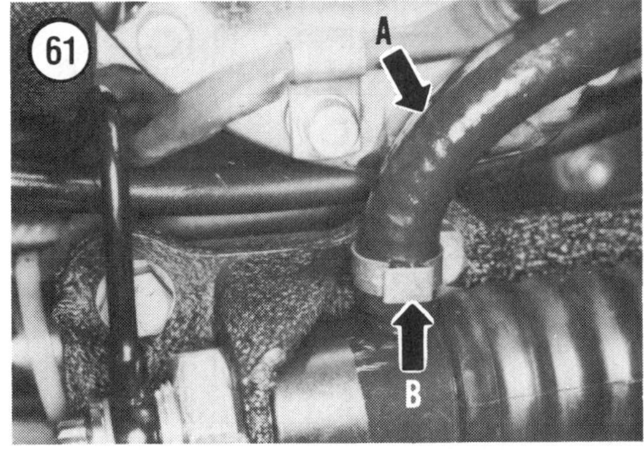

62

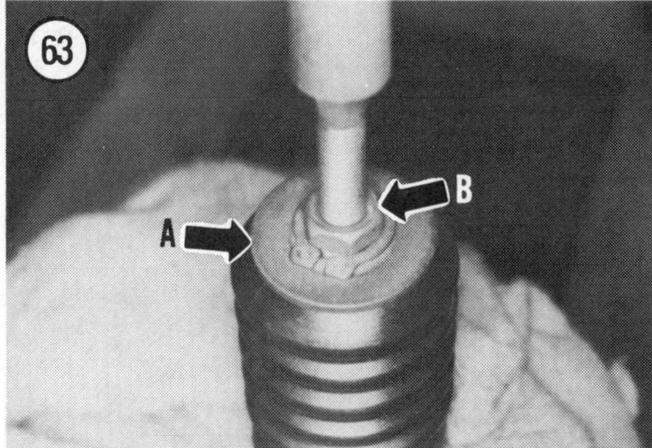

63

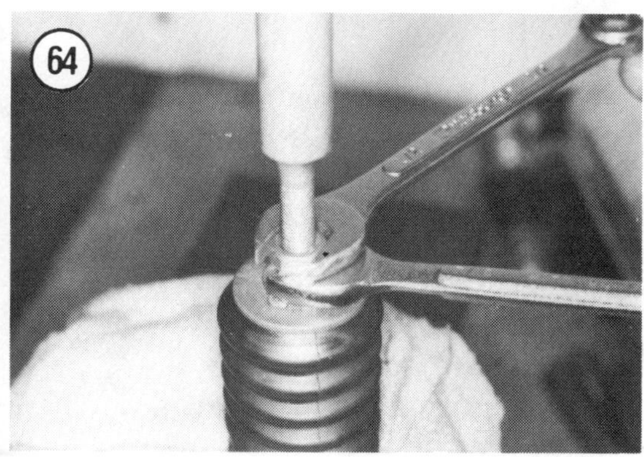
64

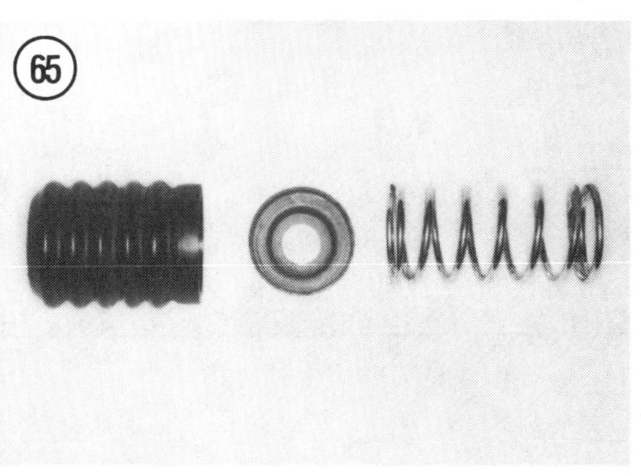
65

3. Screw the banjo bolt into the end of the cartridge body.

*CAUTION*
*The banjo bolt installed into the cartridge body in Step 3 will protect the end of the cartridge when removing it. Otherwise the cartridge may be damaged.*

4. Press down on the large washer (A, **Figure 63**) and compress the spring. Put a wrench across the flat on the pushrod. Then use another wrench to loosen the pushrod locknut (B, **Figure 63**) on the pedal rod and unscrew the rod from the end of the pushrod. See **Figure 64**.

5. Set the cartridge body upright so that it rests on the banjo bolt. Then compress the large washer (A, **Figure 63**) in the end of the cartridge body and remove the circlip from the groove in the pushrod. Release the washer and remove the washer, boot and spring.

6. Locate and remove the spring return retainer from inside the boot. See **Figure 65**.

7. Remove the circlip (**Figure 66**) from the cartridge body groove and remove the pushrod and its washer (**Figure 67**).

8. To replace the hose adaptor (**Figure 68**) on the cartridge body:

a. Stand the cartridge body upright so that it rests on the banjo bolt.

b. Push down on the hose adaptor and slide it off of the cartridge body. Protect the cartridge body while it is exposed.

c. The O-rings (**Figure 69**) should not be removed unless replacement is required.

d. Remove the outer cartridge body circlip.

*NOTE*
*Do not remove the piston assembly from the cartridge body (**Figure 70**). Replacement parts for the piston assembly are not available. If the piston and seals are damaged, the cartridge body assembly must be replaced.*

## Inspection

Harley-Davidson does not provide any specifications for wear limits on any of the master cylinder components.

1. Clean all parts in denatured alcohol or fresh DOT 5 brake fluid. Cleaned parts should be placed on a clean lint-free cloth until reassembly.
2. Inspect the cartridge body for cracks or damage.
3. Check the hose reservoir for damage (**Figure 71**).
4. Inspect the O-rings on the cartridge body (**Figure 69**) for wear or damage. If the O-rings are worn, they must be replaced together with the hose reservoir.
5. Check the threads on the cartridge body, banjo bolt and pushrod. Replace damaged parts as required.
6. Check the dust boot (**Figure 65**) for cracks, age deterioration or other damage. Replace if necessary.

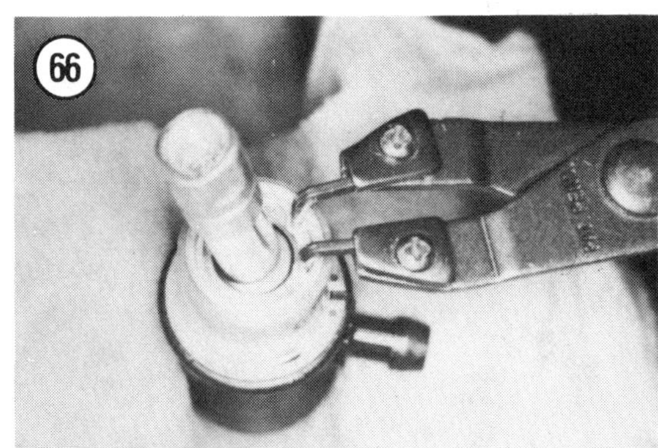


### Assembly

1. Assemble the hose reservoir, if removed, as follows:
   a. Install the outer cartridge body circlip.
   b. When installing new cartridge body O-rings, soak the new O-rings in DOT 5 brake fluid. Then install the O-rings into the cartridge body grooves (**Figure 69**).
   c. The hose reservoir has a tab (A, **Figure 72**) that must engage the notch in the cartridge body (B, **Figure 72**).
   d. Using hand pressure only, slide the hose reservoir over the cartridge body. Engage the tab in the hose reservoir with the notch in the cartridge body. See **Figure 73**.

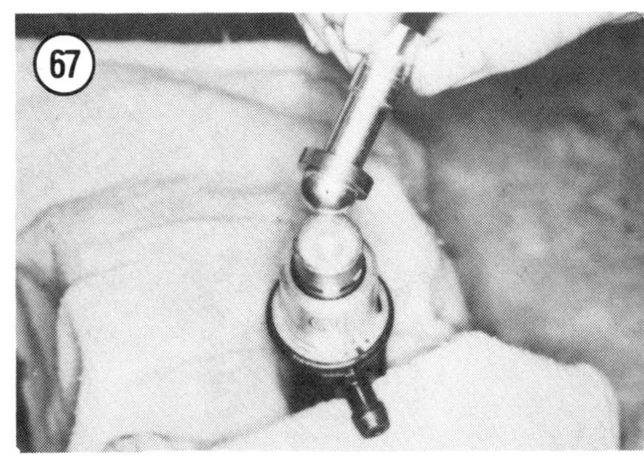


*CAUTION*
*Do not force the cartridge into the cartridge body. If the parts do not assemble easily, the cartridge and cartridge body are not properly aligned. Forcing these parts together will damage them.*

2. Thread the banjo bolt into the end of the cartridge body and stand the assembly up so that it rests on the banjo bolt.
3. Install the washer onto the pushrod (opposite ball-end). See **Figure 67**.
4. Insert the pushrod (ball-end first) into the cartridge until the pushrod washer is seated in the cartridge body bore. Then install the circlip into the cartridge body groove to secure the pushrod (**Figure 66**). Make sure the circlip seats in the groove completely. After installing the circlip, rotate the pushrod by hand; it should turn freely. If the pushrod is tight, disassemble the cartridge body to locate the damaged or improperly installed part.

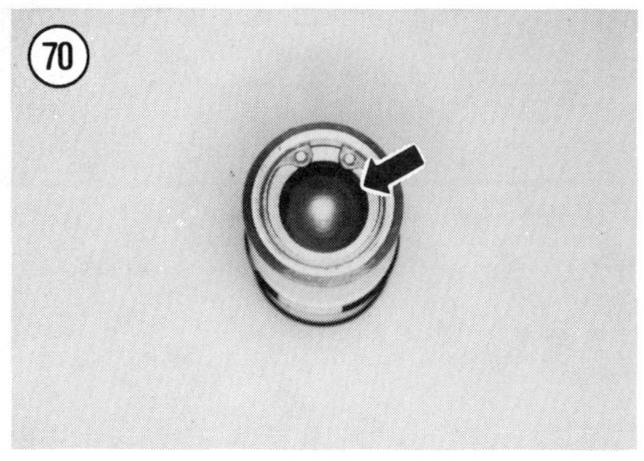

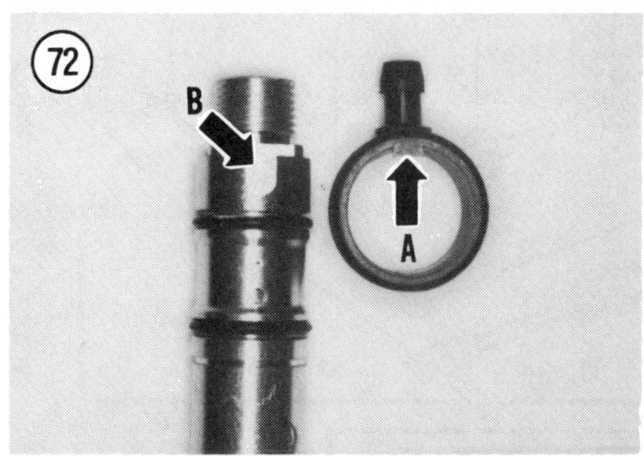


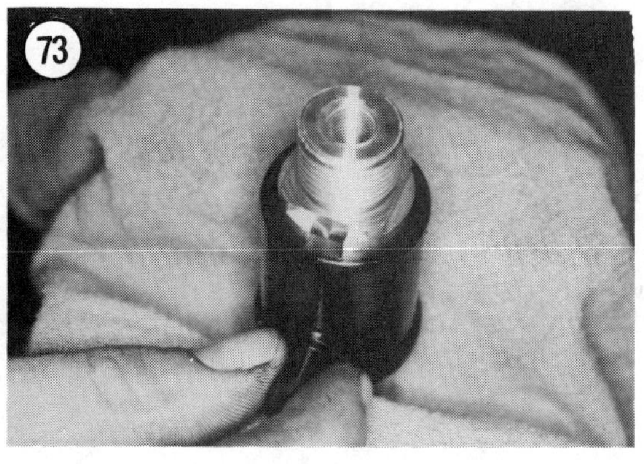


5. Install the return spring and spring retainer onto the pushrod. Install the spring retainer so that the shoulder on the retainer faces away from the spring.

6. Install the dust boot over the pushrod and turn it so the drain hole in the boot faces down. Seat the lip on the dust boot into the groove in the hose reservoir.

7. Install the large washer over the end of the pushrod.

8. Push the washer down to compress the return spring and install the circlip onto the end of the pushrod. Make sure the circlip seats in the groove completely. See **Figure 74**.

9. Thread the locknut onto the pedal rod and thread the rod into the pushrod. Do not tighten the locknut as it will be tightened after adjusting the rear brake pedal.

## REAR MASTER CYLINDER AND RESERVOIR (1985-1986 FXWG, FXEF AND FXSB)

Refer to **Figure 75** when performing procedures in this section.

### Removal

1. To drain the hydraulic fluid from the rear brake system, perform the following:
   a. Attach a hose to the bleed valve on the caliper assembly.
   b. Place the loose end of the hose in a container to catch the brake fluid.
   c. Open the bleed valve and continue to apply the rear brake pedal until the brake fluid is pumped out of the system.
   d. Disconnect the hose and tighten the bleed valve.



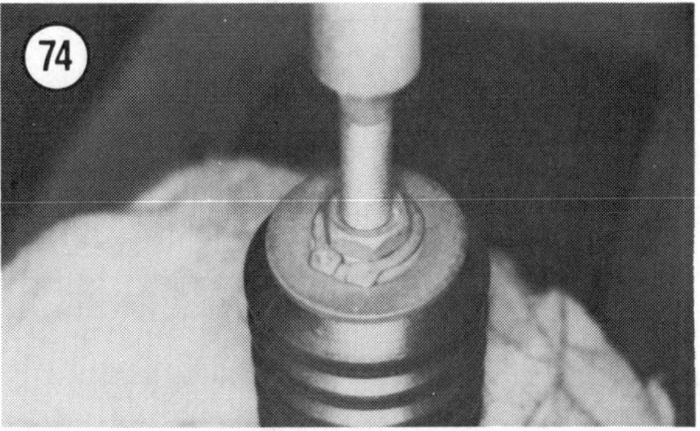

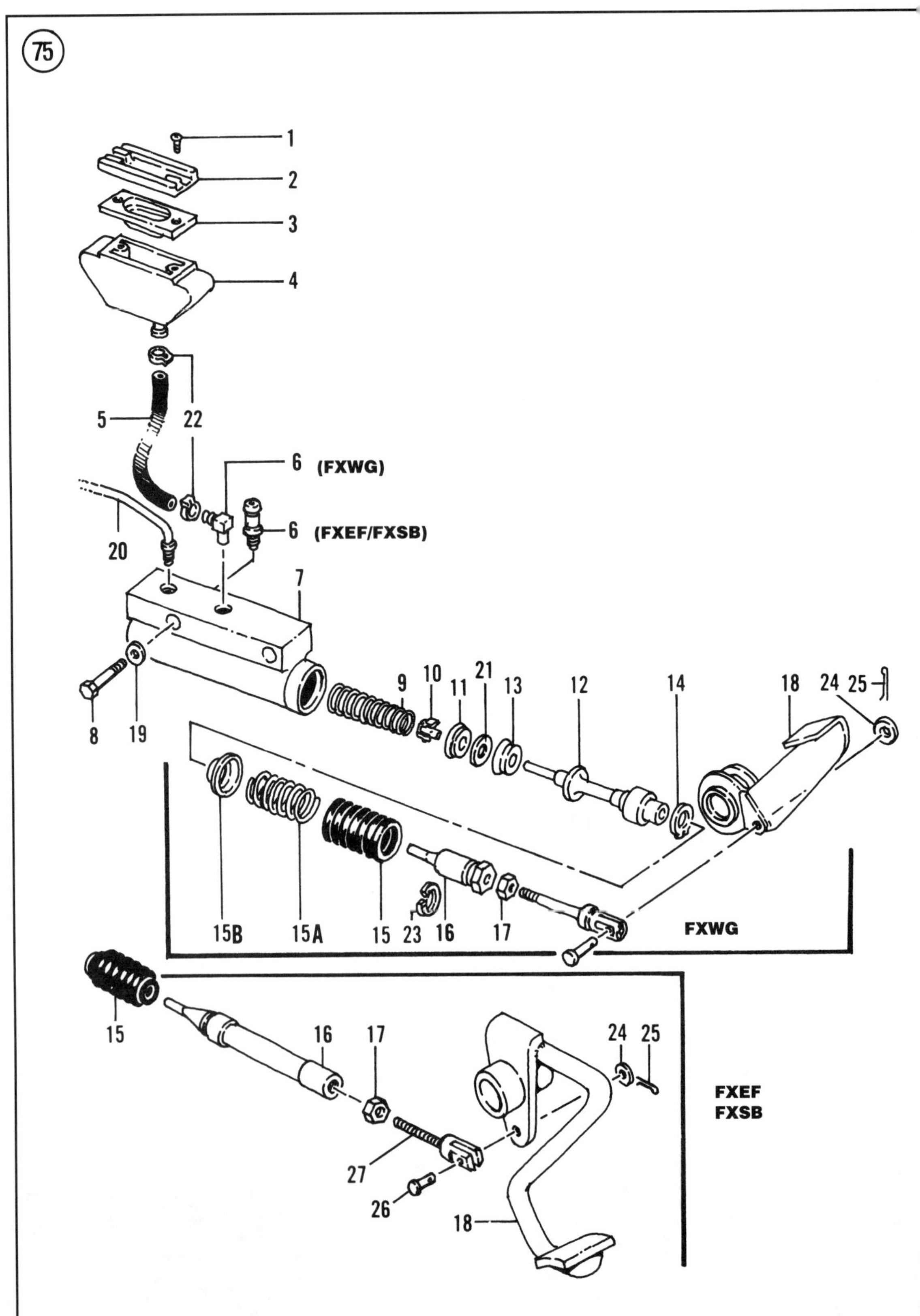
75
1
2
3
4
5
22
6 (FXWG)
6 (FXEF/FXSB)
20
7
8
19
9
10
11
21
13
12
14
18
24
25
15B
15A
15
23
16
17
FXWG
15
16
17
24
25
FXEF
FXSB
27
26
18

**REAR BRAKE MASTER CYLINDER 1985-1986 FXWG, FXEF AND FXSB)**

1. Screw
2. Cover
3. Gasket
4. Reservoir
5. Hose and clamp
6. Fitting
7. Master cylinder
8. Mounting bolt
9. Spring
10. Spring retainer
11. Piston cup
12. Piston
13. Seal
14. Circlip
15. Boot assembly
15A. Brake return spring
15B. Brake spring washer
16. Pushrod
17. Locknut
18. Pedal assembly
19. Washer (2)
20. Brake line
21. Piston cup washer
22. Clamp
23. Clamp
24. Washer
25. Cotter pin
26. Pin
27. Clevis

e. Dispose of this brake fluid—*never* reuse brake fluid. Contaminated brake fluid may cause brake failure.

*NOTE*
*If you only want to drain the master cylinder reservoir, disconnect the reservoir supply hose from the fitting on the master cylinder and drain the brake fluid into a container. Plug the hose opening.*

2. Cut the supply hose clamp at the master cylinder and disconnect the hose. Do not twist the hose back and forth sharply or you may break the hose nipple on the master cylinder.
3. Remove the brake hose at the master cylinder with a flare nut wrench. Pull the hose away from the master cylinder.

*NOTE*
*Wrap the end of the brake hose with a plastic bag to prevent brake fluid from dripping out and from dirt contaminating the open hose.*

4. Remove the bolts and washers securing the master cylinder to the frame. Then pull the master cylinder back to disconnect it from the pushrod.
5A. *FXWG*: Remove the boot, spring and spring washer.
5B. *FXEF and FXSB*: Remove the boot.
6. Overhaul the master cylinder as described in this chapter.

### Installation

1A. *FXWG*: Install the spring and spring washer over small end of pushrod. Then install boot over pushrod.
1B. *FXEF and FXSB*: Install the boot onto the pushrod.
2. Insert the pushrod into the piston in the end of the master cylinder and position the master cylinder onto the frame. Install the bolts and washers. Tighten bolts securely.
3. Reconnect the brake hose to the master cylinder port. Tighten the fitting to 70-80 in.-lb. (8-9.2 N•m).
4. Slide a new hose clamp onto the hose and fit the hose onto the hose reservoir nipple. Slide the clamp down so that it is against the hose where the hose fits

onto the nipple. Close the hose clamp so that it is tight against the hose.

*NOTE*
***Figure 50** shows the type of pliers required to close the hose clamp.*

5. Fill the reservoir with new DOT 5 hydraulic brake fluid. Bleed brake system as described under *Bleeding Hydraulic System* in this chapter.
6. Install the reservoir gasket and cover after bleeding the brakes.

*WARNING*
*Do not ride the motorcycle until the brake is working properly.*

### Disassembly

1. Remove the master cylinder as described in this chapter.
2. Mount the master cylinder in a vise with soft jaws.
3. Insert a rod into the end of the piston and compress the piston to remove tension against the circlip. Remove the circlip with circlip pliers and slowly release tension from the piston.
4. Remove the piston and seal, washer, piston cup, spring retainer and spring.
5. Remove seal from piston.

### Inspection

Harley-Davidson does not provide specifications for wear limits on any of the master cylinder components.

*NOTE*
*Harley-Davidson advises installing a new master cylinder repair kit whenever the master cylinder is disassembled.*

1. Clean all rubber parts in denatured alcohol or fresh DOT 5 brake fluid. Place cleaned parts on a clean lint-free cloth until reassembly.
2. Apply compressed air to all openings in the master cylinder body to dry it out thoroughly.
3. Inspect the cylinder bore and the piston contact surfaces for signs of wear and damage. If either part is less than perfect, replace it.
4. Replace the piston assembly if the cup and seal require replacement. The cup and seal can not be replaced individually.
5. Check the end of the piston assembly for wear caused by the pushrod. Replace if worn.
6. Inspect the rubber boot for deterioration, cracking and wear. Replace if necessary.
7. Remove the cover and gasket from the reservoir. Inspect the gasket for wear, deterioration or damage; replace if necessary.
8. Inspect the reservoir for cracks or damage.
9. Inspect the reservoir hose for deterioration or cracking. Replace if necessary and secure with new hose clamps.

### Assembly

1. Soak the piston assembly in fresh DOT 5 brake fluid for at least 15 minutes to make the primary cup pliable. Coat the inside of the cylinder with fresh brake fluid before assembly.

*CAUTION*
*When installing the piston assembly, do not allow the seal to turn inside out. A damaged seal will allow brake fluid to leak inside the cylinder bore.*

2. Place the master cylinder in a vise with soft jaws. Do not overtighten the jaws or the master cylinder may be damaged.
3. Install the seal, washer, piston cup, spring retainer and spring onto the piston.
4. Install the piston assembly into the master cylinder.
5. Compress the piston into the cylinder and install the circlip into the cylinder groove. Release tension from the piston and check that the circlip seats in the groove completely.
6. Install the master cylinder as described in this chapter.

## BRAKE HOSE AND LINE REPLACEMENT

A combination of steel and flexible brake lines are used to connect the master cylinder to its brake caliper. Where banjo bolts are used to connect a hose to a master cylinder or caliper, special sealing washers are used on both sides of the hose fitting. Where metal brake hoses are used, they screw directly into the brake caliper.

*WARNING*

*Two different types of washers have been used to seal banjo bolts on 1986 and later FLT models and late 1987 and later FXR models. Early models used zinc coated copper washers (A,* ***Figure 76****). Steel washers with a rubber O-ring insert (B,* ***Figure 76****) are used on later models. The banjo bolts are designed to be used with a specific type of washer. Replacement banjo washers and bolts must match the original parts. Using an incorrect washer or bolt can allow the brake hose to leak and result in loss of complete brake pressure. Ask your dealer to identify the correct washers and banjo bolts used on your model.*

There is no factory-recommended replacement interval, but it is a good idea to replace all flexible brake hoses every four years or when they show signs of swelling, cracking or damage.

Some brake hose assemblies consists of steel and flexible lines permanently attached together. This assembly should be replaced every 4 years as the flexible portion of the assembly will eventually swell, fatigue and crack.

All metal brake lines do not require routine replacement unless they are damaged or the end fittings are leaking. When replacing the flexible brake hoses, inspect the metal brake lines for damage. If they have been hit, the lines may be restricted, thus decreasing braking effectiveness.

*CAUTION*

*Cover the wheels, fenders, fuel tank and swing arm with a heavy cloth or plastic tarp to protect them from the accidental spilling of brake fluid. Wash any spilled brake fluid off of any painted or plated surface immediately. Use soapy water and rinse completely.*

## Front Hoses and Lines Removal/Installation

A combination steel/flexible brake hose is used to connect the front master cylinder to the front brake caliper. See **Figure 77** or **Figure 78**. When purchasing a new hose, compare it to the old hose to make sure that the length and angle of the steel hose portion is correct. New banjo bolt washers should be installed.

1. Drain the hydraulic brake fluid from the front brake system as follows:
   a. Flip the rubber cap off the caliper bleed valve and connect a hose over the bleed valve.
   b. Insert the loose end of the hose in a container to catch the brake fluid.
   c. Open the bleed valve on the caliper and apply the front brake lever to pump the fluid out of the master cylinder and brake line. Continue until all of the fluid has been removed.
   d. Close the bleed valve and disconnect the hose.
   e. Dispose of this brake fluid—*never* reuse brake fluid. Contaminated brake fluid may case brake failure.
2. Before removing the brake line, note how the brake line is routed from the master cylinder to the caliper. In addition, note the number and position of the metal hose clamps and plastic ties used to hold the brake line in place. The brake hose should be reinstalled following the same path and secured at the same position. The metal clamps can be reused. New plastic ties, however, will have to be installed.
3. Cut the plastic ties and discard them.
4. Remove the screw or nut holding the metal clamps around the brake line. Spread the clamp and remove it from the brake line.

*NOTE*

*After disconnecting the brake hose in Step 5 and Step 6, place the hose end in a plastic resealable bag and seal it around the hose.*

5. Remove the banjo bolt and washers securing the hose at the brake caliper.

13

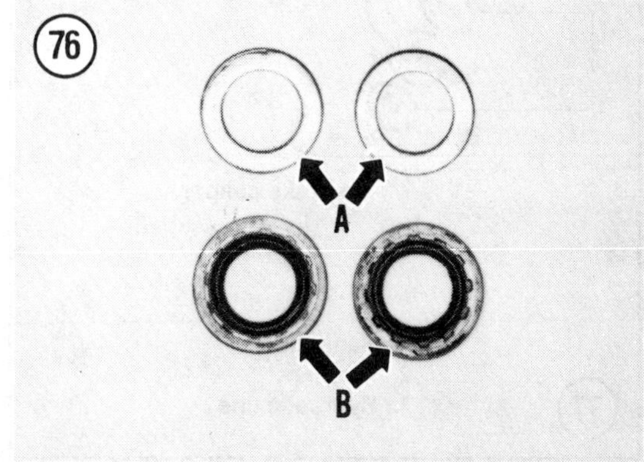

**FRONT BRAKE HOSE ASSEMBLY**

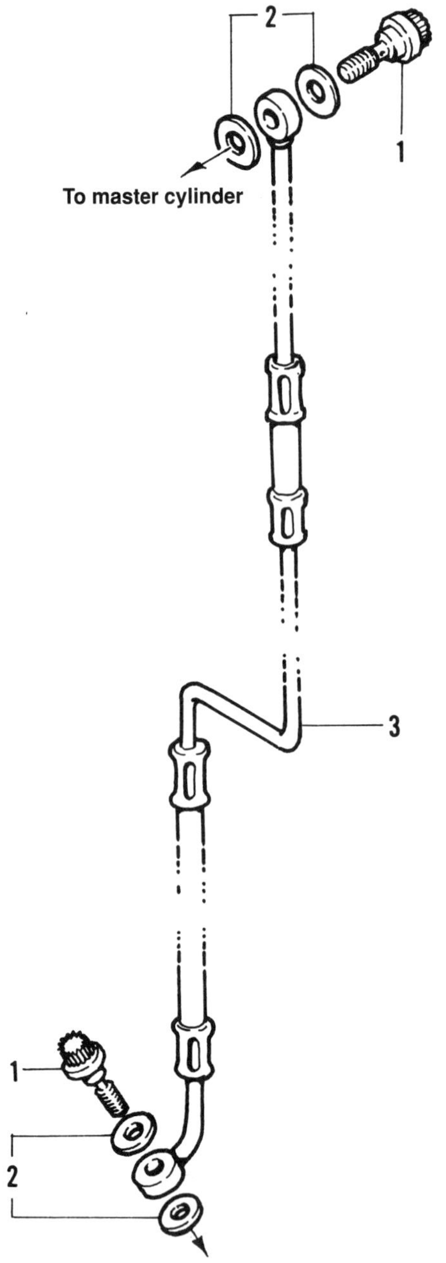

1. Banjo bolt
2. Washers
3. Hydraulic line

(77)

(78) **FRONT BRAKE HOSE (DUAL CALIPER MODELS)**

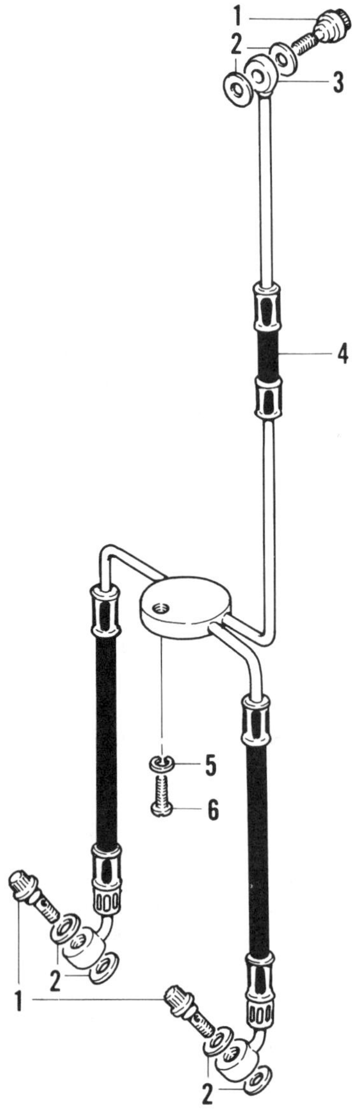

1. Banjo bolt
2. Washers
3. Hydraulic line
4. Hose
5. Lockwasher
6. Screw

6. Remove the banjo bolt and washers securing the hose at the master cylinder.

7. Remove the brake hose from the motorcycle.

8. If you plan on reusing the brake hose assembly, inspect it as follows:

a. Check the metal pipe portion for cracks or fractures. Check the junction where the metal pipe enters and exits the flexible hose. Check the crimped clamp for looseness or damage.

b. Check the flexible hose portion for swelling, cracks or other damage.

c. Replace the hose assembly, if necessary.

9. Install a new brake hose, sealing washers and banjo bolt in the reverse order of removal. Be sure to install new sealing washers on both sides of the hose fitting.

10. Tighten all banjo bolts to the torque specification listed in **Table 2**.

*NOTE*
*The tightening torques for the copper and steel/rubber banjo bolts are different. Make sure to use the tightening torque for the type of washer installed on your bike (**Table 2**).*

11. Refill the master cylinder with fresh brake fluid clearly marked DOT 5. Bleed the front brake system as described in this chapter.

*WARNING*
*Do not ride the motorcycle until the brakes are operating properly.*

**Rear Brake Hose Removal/Installation**

When purchasing a new hose, compare it to the old hose to make sure that the length and angle of the steel hose portion is correct. New banjo bolt washers should be installed where used.

1. Remove the saddlebags, if so equipped.

2. Drain the hydraulic brake fluid from the front brake system as follows:

a. Flip the rubber cap off the caliper bleed valve and connect a hose over the bleed valve.

b. Insert the loose end of the hose in a container to catch the brake fluid.

c. Open the bleed valve on the caliper and apply the front brake lever to pump the fluid out of the master cylinder and brake line. Continue until all of the fluid has been removed.

d. Close the bleed valve and disconnect the hose.

e. Dispose of this brake fluid—*never* reuse brake fluid. Contaminated brake fluid may case brake failure.

3. Before removing a brake line, note how the brake line is routed from the master cylinder to the caliper. In addition, note the number and position of the metal hose clamps and plastic ties used to hold the brake line in place. The brake hose should be reinstalled following the same path and secured at the same position. The metal clamps can be reused. New plastic ties, however, will have to be installed.

4. Cut the plastic ties and discard them.

5. Remove the screw or nut holding the metal clamps around the brake line. Spread the clamp and remove it from the brake line.

*NOTE*
*After disconnecting the brake hose in Step 5 and Step 6, place the hose end in a plastic resealable bag and seal it.*

13

6A. On early models, perform the following:

a. Loosen and then unscrew the metal brake line fitting at the master caliper and at the tee fitting. Remove the brake line. See **Figure 79**, typical.

b. Loosen and then unscrew the brake hose fitting at the tee fitting and at the brake caliper. Remove the brake line.

c. The tee fitting is mounted onto a bracket. If the brake fluid was contaminated, disconnect the brake light switch connector and remove the brake light switch at the tee fitting. Then unbolt the tee fitting and remove it from its mounting bracket. Clean the tee fitting with denatured alcohol and dry thoroughly with compressed air. Reinstall the tee fitting and the brake light switch.

6B. On late models, perform the following:
   a. Remove the banjo bolt and washers securing the hose at the brake caliper.
   b. Remove the banjo bolt and washers securing the hose at the master cylinder as described in this chapter.
   c. Remove the brake hose from the motorcycle.

7. If you plan on reusing the brake hose assembly, inspect it as follows:
   a. Check the metal pipe portion for cracks or fractures. Check the junction where the metal pipe enters and exits the flexible hose. Check the crimped clamp for looseness or damage.
   b. Check the flexible hose portion for swelling, cracks or other damage.
   c. Replace the hose assembly, if necessary.

8A. On early models, install new brake lines in the reverse order of removal. Tighten brake line fittings securely.

8B. On late models, install a new brake hose, sealing washers and banjo bolts in the reverse order of removal. Be sure to install new sealing washers on both sides of the hose fitting. See **Figure 80** and **Figure 81**.

*NOTE*

*The tightening torques for the copper and steel/rubber banjo bolts are different. Make sure to use the tightening torque for the type of washer installed on your bike (**Table 2**).*

9. Refill the master cylinder with fresh brake fluid clearly marked DOT 5. Bleed the front brake system as described in this chapter.

*WARNING*

*Do not ride the motorcycle until the brakes are operating properly.*

## BRAKE DISC (FRONT AND REAR)

Brake discs should be checked for runout and thickness. The minimum disc thickness is stamped on Harley-Davidson O.E.M. brake discs. **Table 1** lists disc brake specifications.

### Removal/Installation

1. Remove the front or rear wheel as described in Chapter Ten.

*NOTE*

*Place a piece of wood or vinyl tube in the caliper in place of the disc. This way, if the brake lever is inadvertently squeezed, or the brake pedal depressed, the piston will not be forced out of the cylinder. If this does happen, the caliper may have to be disassembled to reseat the piston and the system will have to be bled.*

*CAUTION*

*Do not set the wheel down on the disc surface, as it may get scratched or warped. Set the wheel on 2 blocks of wood.*

2. Remove the bolts (and nuts) securing the brake disc to the hub and remove the disc. See **Figure 82**, typical.

3. Install by reversing these removal steps while noting the following.

4. Check the brake disc bolts (and nuts) for thread damage. Replace worn or damaged fasteners.

5. Clean the disc and the disc mounting surface thoroughly with brake cleaner or contact cleaner. Allow surfaces to dry before installation.

6. Coat the disc mounting bolts with Loctite Stud 'N Bearing mount. Tighten the bolts to the torque specification listed in **Table 2**.

### Inspection

It is not necessary to remove the disc from the wheel to inspect it. Small marks on the disc are not important, but radial scratches deep enough to snag a fingernail reduce braking effectiveness and increase brake pad wear. If these grooves are found, the disc should be resurfaced or replaced.

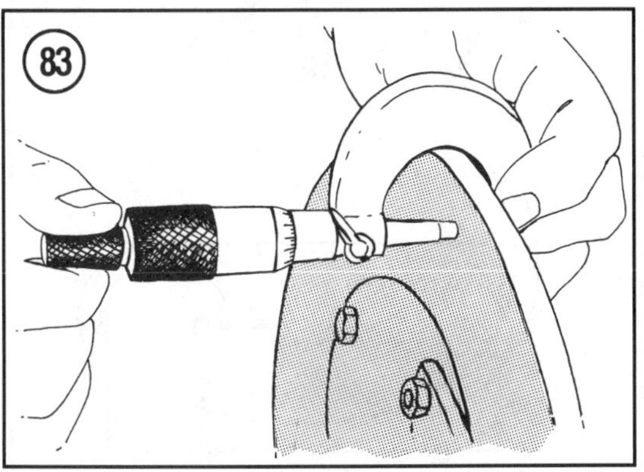


1. Measure the thickness around the disc at several locations with vernier calipers or a micrometer (**Figure 83**). The disc must be replaced if the thickness at any point is less than the minimum stamped on each disc.

*NOTE*
*Use the disc specifications listed in **Table 1** if the stamping on the disc is unclear.*

2. Clean the disc of any rust or corrosion and wipe clean with lacquer thinner. Never use an oil-based solvent that may leave an oil residue on the disc.

## BLEEDING THE SYSTEM

When air enters the brake system, the brake will feel soft or spongy, greatly reducing braking pressure. When this happens, the system must be bled to remove the air. Air can enter the system if there is a leak in the hydraulic system, a component has been replaced or the brake fluid has been replaced.

When bleeding the brakes, you can use one of two methods—manually or a brake bleeder. Both procedures are described separately.

### Bleeding the Brake with a Brake Bleeder

This procedure uses a commercial brake bleeder that is available from motorcycle or automotive supply stores.

*NOTE*
*Before bleeding the brake, check that all brake hoses and lines are tight.*

1. Remove the dust cap from the bleed valve on the caliper assembly.

2. Connect the brake bleeder to the bleed valve on the caliper assembly. See **Figure 84**, typical.

3. Clean the top of the master cylinder of all dirt and foreign matter.

4. Remove the screws securing the master cylinder top cover and remove the cover and rubber diaphragm.

5. Fill the reservoir almost to the top with DOT 5 brake fluid and reinstall the diaphragm and cover. Leave the cover in place during this procedure to prevent the entry of dirt.

*WARNING*
*Do not intermix brake fluid. DOT 5 brake fluid was originally installed at the time of manufacturer. Do not install DOT 3 or DOT 4 brake fluid as it can lead to brake system failure.*

6. Pump the pump handle 10-15 times to create a vacuum and then open the bleed valve until brake fluid begins to enter the jar. Allow approximately 1 inch of fluid to enter the jar and then close the bleed valve. As the fluid enters the system and exits into the jar, the level will drop in the reservoir. Maintain the level to just about the top of the reservoir to prevent air from being drawn into the system.

*NOTE*
*Do not allow the master cylinder reservoir to empty during the bleeding operation or more air will enter the system. If this occurs, the entire procedure must be repeated.*

*NOTE*
*If air is entering the brake bleeder hose from around the bleed valve, apply several layers of Teflon tape to the bleed valve. This should make a good seal between the bleed valve and the brake bleeder hose. Teflon tape can be purchased at hardware and plumbing supply stores.*

7. If the fluid emerging from the hose into the jar is completely free of bubbles, the system should be properly bled. If there are signs of bubbles being withdrawn with the brake fluid, air is still trapped in the line. Repeat Step 6, making sure to refill the master cylinder to prevent air from being drawn into the system.
8. When the brake fluid is free of bubbles, tighten the bleed valve and remove the brake bleeder assembly. Reinstall the bleed valve dust cap.

*WARNING*
*Do not reuse the brake fluid.*

9. If necessary, add fluid to correct the level in the master cylinder reservoir. When topping off the front master cylinder, turn the handlebar until the reservoir is level; add fluid until it is level with the reservoir gasket surface. The rear master cylinder should be filled until the level is 1/8 in. (3.2 mm) below the gasket surface.

10. Reinstall the reservoir diaphragm and cap. Secure the cap with its 2 screws.

11. Test the feel of the brake lever or pedal. It should be firm and should offer the same resistance each time it's operated. If it feels spongy, it is likely that there is still air in the system and it must be bled again. When all air has been bled from the system and the fluid level is correct in the reservoir, double-check for leaks and tighten all fittings and connections.

*WARNING*
*Before riding the bike, make certain that the brake is operating correctly by operating the lever or pedal several times.*

12. Test ride the bike slowly at first to make sure that the brakes are operating properly.

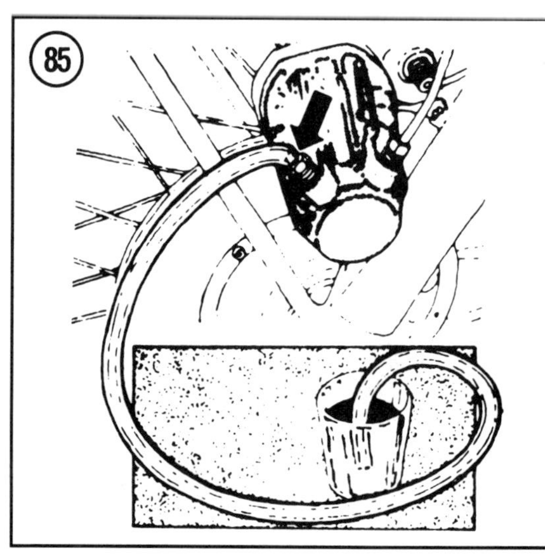

### Bleeding the Brake Manually

When bleeding the brake manually, a clean jar, a suitable length of clear hose and a wrench will be required.

*NOTE*
*Before bleeding the brake, check that all brake hoses and lines are tight.*

1. Flip off the dust cap from the brake bleeder valve.
2. Connect a length of clear tubing to the bleeder valve on the caliper. Place the other end of the tube into a clean container. Fill the container with enough fresh DOT 5 brake fluid to keep the end submerged. The tube should be long enough so that a loop can be made higher than the bleeder valve to prevent air from being drawn into the caliper during bleeding. See **Figure 85**, typical.
3. Clean the top of the master cylinder of all dirt and foreign matter.
4. Remove the screws securing the master cylinder top cover and remove the cover and rubber diaphragm.
5. Fill the reservoir almost to the top with DOT 5 brake fluid and reinstall the diaphragm and cover. Leave the cover in place during this procedure to prevent the entry of dirt.

*WARNING*
*Do not intermix brake fluid. DOT 5 brake fluid was originally installed at the time of manufacturer. Do not install DOT 3 or DOT 4 brake fluid as it can lead to brake system failure.*

*NOTE*
*During this procedure, it is important to check the fluid level in the master cylinder reservoir often. If the reservoir runs dry, you'll introduce more air into the system which will require starting over.*

6. Slowly apply the brake lever several times. Hold the lever in the applied position and open the bleeder valve about 1/2 turn. Allow the lever to travel to its limit. When this limit is reached, tighten the bleeder screw. As the brake fluid enters the system, the level will drop in the master cylinder reservoir. Maintain the level at about 3/8 in. (9.5 mm) from the top of the reservoir to prevent air from being drawn into the system.
7. Continue to pump the lever and fill the reservoir until the fluid emerging from the hose is completely free of air bubbles. If you are replacing the fluid, continue until the fluid emerging from the hose is clean.

*NOTE*
*If bleeding is difficult, it may be necessary to allow the fluid to stabilize for a few hours. Repeat the bleeding procedure when the tiny bubbles in the system settle out.*

8. Hold the lever in the applied position and tighten the bleeder valve. Remove the bleeder tube and install the bleeder valve dust cap.

*WARNING*
*Do not reuse the brake fluid.*

9. If necessary, add fluid to correct the level in the master cylinder reservoir. When topping off the front master cylinder, turn the handlebar until the reservoir is level; add fluid until it is level with the reservoir gasket surface. The rear master cylinder should be filled until the level is 1/8 in. (3.2 mm) below the gasket surface.
10. Install the cap and diaphragm and tighten the screws securely.
11. Test the feel of the brake lever or pedal. It should be firm and should offer the same resistance each time it's operated. If it feels spongy, it is likely that there is still air in the system and it must be bled again. When all air has been bled from the system and the fluid level is correct in the reservoir, double-check for leaks and tighten all fittings and connections.

*WARNING*
*Before riding the bike, make certain that the brake is operating correctly by operating the lever or pedal several times.*

12. Test ride the bike slowly at first to make sure the brakes are operating properly.

**Table 1 BRAKE SPECIFICATIONS**

| | in. | mm |
|---|---|---|
| Brake pad minimum thickness | | |
| Front and rear | 0.062 | 1.6 |
| Brake disc (front and rear) | | |
| FLT and FXR | See text | |
| FXWG, FXEF and FXSB | | |
| Minimum thickness | 0.205 | 5.21 |
| Outside diameter | 11.50 | 292.1 |

**Table 2 BRAKE TIGHTENING TORQUES**

| | ft.-lb. | in.-lb. | N•m |
|---|---|---|---|
| Brake disc screws | | | |
| FLT | | | |
| Front | | | |
| 1984-1990 | 16-18 | — | 22-25 |
| 1991-on | 16-24 | — | 22-33 |
| Rear | | | |
| 1984-1990 | 24-30 | — | 33-41 |
| 1991-on | 30-45 | — | 41-61 |
| FXR | | | |
| Front | | | |
| 1984-1990 | 16-18 | — | 22-25 |
| 1991-on | 16-24 | — | 22-33 |
| Rear | | | |
| 1984-1991 | 23-27 | — | 32-37 |
| 1992-on | 30-45 | — | 41-61 |
| FXWG, FXEF and FXSB | | | |
| Front | 16-18 | — | 22-25 |
| Rear | 23-27 | — | 32-37 |
| Brake line fitting @ rear caliper | | | |
| FLT | | | |
| 1984-1985 | — | 70-80 | — |
| FXR | | | |
| 1984-early 1987 | — | 70-80 | — |
| Banjo bolts* | | | |
| Copper washers | 35 | — | 48 |
| Steel/rubber washers | 17-22 | — | 23.5-30.3 |
| Brake bleeder nipple | — | 32-40 | — |
| Front brake caliper | 25-30 | — | 34-41 |
| Rear brake caliper | | | |
| FLT | | | |
| 1984-1985 | 12-15 | — | 16-21 |
| 1986-on | 15-20 | — | 21-27 |
| FXR | 15-20 | — | 21-27 |
| FXWG, FXEF and FXSB | 12-15 | — | 16-21 |
| Front master cylinder clamp screws | — | 70-80 | — |
| Rear master cylinder bolts | | | |
| FLT | — | 155-190 | — |
| FXR | | | |
| 1984-early 1987 | 13-16 | — | 17-22 |
| Late 1987-on | — | — | — |
| FXWG, FXEF, FXSB | — | — | — |
| Rear master cylinder mounting nut | 30-40 | — | 41-54 |

* See text for additional information.

# CHAPTER FOURTEEN

# CRUISE CONTROL

The cruise control system uses mechanical and electrical equipment to maintain a select speed set by the rider. This chapter covers service and troubleshooting procedures for the factory cruise control system installed on 1989 and later FLT Ultra models.

*WARNING*
*When testing and servicing the cruise control system, do not ride the motorcycle until the system is working correctly. When in doubt, park the bike and consult with a Harley-Davidson dealer.*

## SYSTEM COMPONENTS (1989-1992)

The Harley-Davidson cruise control system consists of a cruise module, servo motor, bellcrank system (1989), switches and related wiring. See **Figure 1** (1989) or **Figure 2** (1990-1992).

The cruise module receives command signals from the cruise ON/OFF switch. The cruise module receives information on operating conditions from the tachometer, servo motor, SET (1989) or RES/SET (1990-1992) switches, both brake light switches, throttle position and speedometer reed switch (1990-1992).

The cruise control will set and automatically maintain a speed starting at 40 mph (64 km/h). To set the cruise control, turn the cruise switch to ON; see **Figure 3** or **Figure 4**. Power is then supplied through the 2 amp fuse leading from connector 8A to the cruise module. After reaching your desired speed (minimum 40 mph [64 km/h]), momentarily press the SET switch on 1989 models or flip the RES/SET switch on 1990-1992 models down and release it. The cruise module will receive a signal input reading from the tachometer on 1989 models or from the reed switch on 1990-1992 models. The cruise module then sends a signal to actuate the servo motor.

During operation, the cruise module monitors engine rpm. On 1989 models, this is done through tachometer input. On 1990-1992 models, the tachometer and speedometer reed switch signals are used. Input received from the cruise module will signal the servo motor to vary the throttle position. Cruise disengagement will occur if engine rpm changes to a non-desired speed.

You can temporarily cancel the cruise control system by applying the front or rear brake, closing the throttle or disengaging the clutch. If you want to engage the cruise control again and your speed is above 40 mph (64 km/h), press the SET or RES switch. You can cancel the cruise control system by turning off the ignition switch or the cruise ON/OFF switch.

The cruise control system will not work if one or more of the following conditions occur:

a. Incorrect front brake light switch adjustment.
b. Brake light is on all of the time.
c. Blown brake light bulbs.
d. Incorrect throttle cable adjustment.
e. Vehicle speed is less than 40 mph (64 km/h).
f. A steep or extremely long uphill grade.

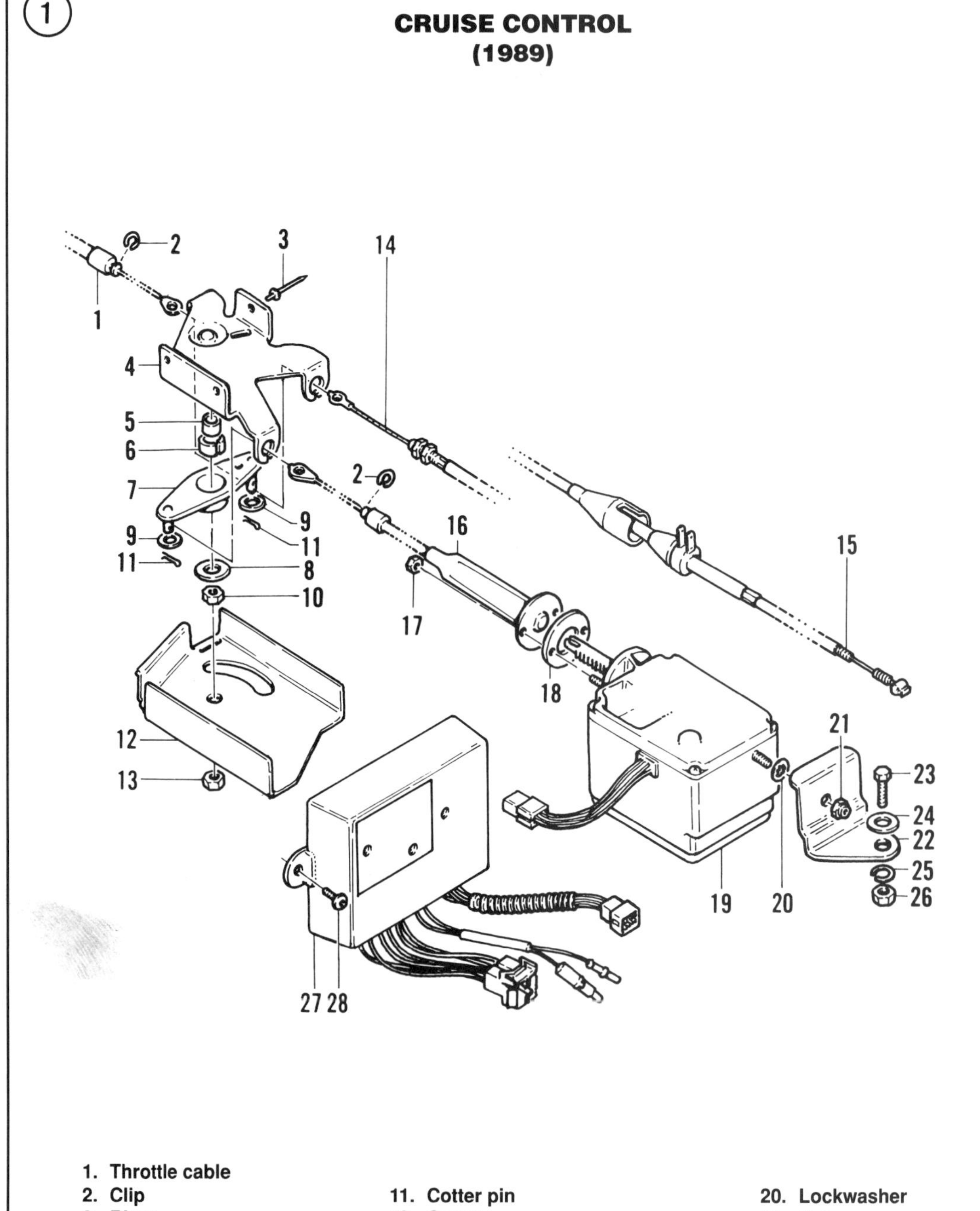


1. Throttle cable
2. Clip
3. Rivet
4. Bracket
5. Spacer
6. Bushing
7. Lever
8. Washer
9. Washer
10. Nut
11. Cotter pin
12. Cover
13. Nut
14. Throttle cable (short)
15. Idle cable
16. Servo cable
17. Nut
18. Gasket
19. Servo motor
20. Lockwasher
21. Nut
22. Mounting bracket
23. Bolt
24. Washer
25. Lockwasher
26. Nut
27. Cruise module
28. Screw

## SYSTEM COMPONENTS (1993-ON)

The Harley-Davidson cruise control system consists of a cruise control module (containing the stepper motor), switches and related wiring. See **Figure 5**.

The cruise module receives command signals from the cruise SET switch. The cruise module receives information on operating conditions by reading input from the speedometer reed switch.

The cruise control will set and automatically maintain a speed starting at 30 mph (48 km/h). To set the cruise control, turn the cruise switch to ON; see **Figure 4**. Power is then supplied through the 15 amp circuit breaker to the cruise control module.

After reaching your desired speed (minimum 30 mph [48 km/h]), momentarily press the RES/SET

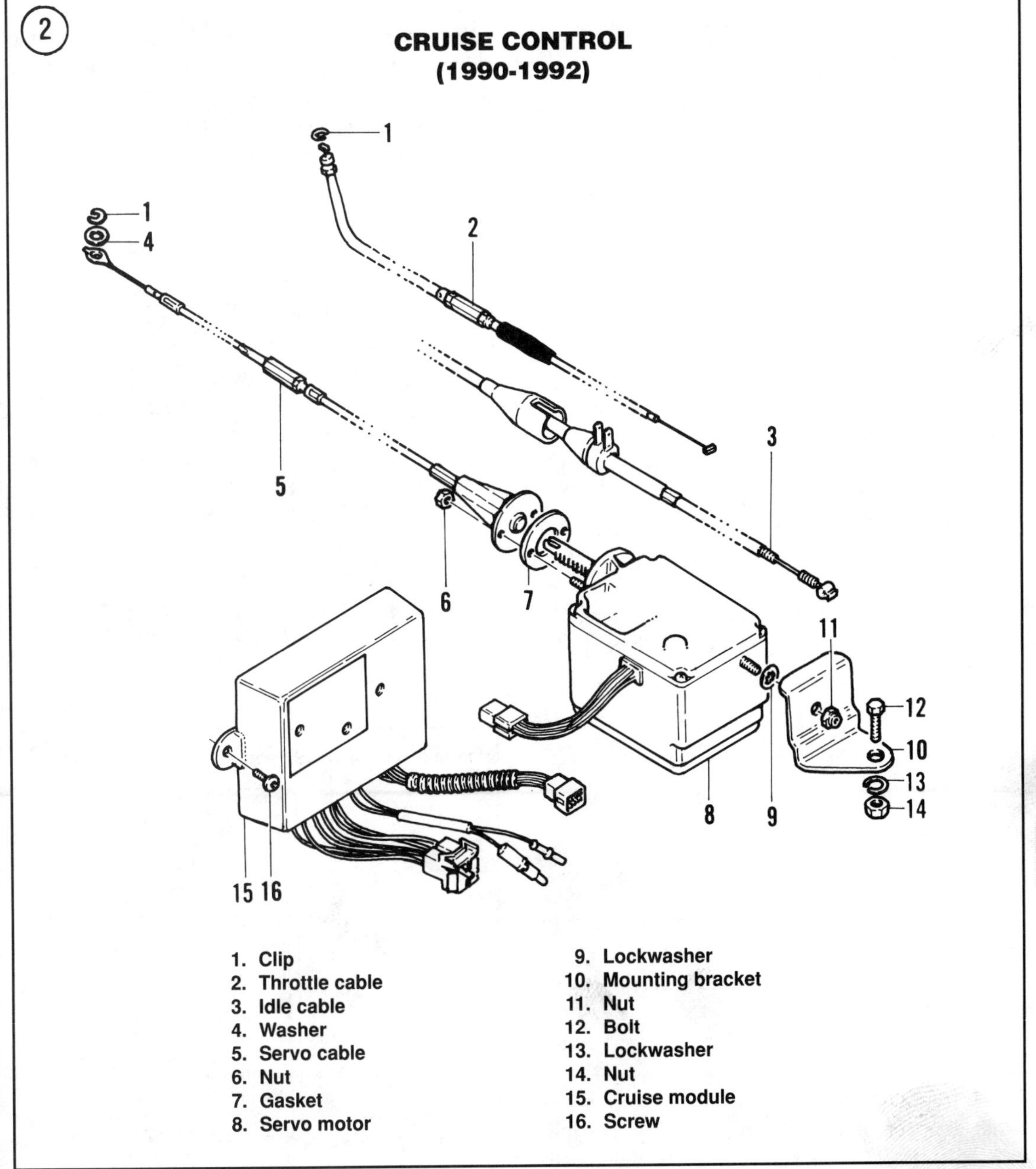


1. Clip
2. Throttle cable
3. Idle cable
4. Washer
5. Servo cable
6. Nut
7. Gasket
8. Servo motor
9. Lockwasher
10. Mounting bracket
11. Nut
12. Bolt
13. Lockwasher
14. Nut
15. Cruise module
16. Screw

switch. The cruise module will receive a signal input reading from the speedometer reed switch. The cruise module then sends a signal to the stepper motor. The stepper motor then drives the ribbon reel in the cruise cable housing to take up slack in the cruise cable.

During operation, the cruise module monitors engine rpm and the speedometer reed switch input signal. This information is used to signal the stepper motor to open or close the throttle, thereby keeping the speedometer reed switch input constant.

You can temporarily cancel the cruise control system by applying the front or rear brake, closing the throttle or disengaging the clutch. If you want to engage the cruise control again and your speed is above 30 mph (48 km/h), press the RES switch. You can cancel the cruise control system by turning off the ignition switch or the cruise ON/OFF switch.

The cruise control will disengage when the cruise control module receives any one of the following input signals:

a. Front or rear brake is applied.
b. Clutch disengaged.
c. Throttle is closed.
d. Cruise switch turned OFF.
e. Engine stop switch turned OFF.
f. RES/SET switch is pressed and held in this position for more than 6 seconds.
g. The RES/SET switch is pressed in SET position and held until vehicle speed drops below 30 mph (48 km/h). However, if switch is released with vehicle speed above 30 mph (48 km/h), system will re-engage cruise control.

## THROTTLE CABLES (1989)

To operate the cruise control on 1989 models, 4 cables are used:

a. Front throttle cable: Connects the throttle grip to the bellcrank.
b. Rear throttle cable: Connects the carburetor to the bellcrank.
c. Idle cable: Connects throttle grip to the carburetor.
d. Servo cable: Connects bellcrank to servo motor.

The front and rear throttle cables and the servo cable all attach to the bellcrank assembly. The idle cable does not. The bellcrank is mounted underneath the frame backbone. A cover protects the bellcrank during operation.

### Cable Adjustment

The idle cable must be loosened to full slack before adjusting the rear and front throttle cables. To adjust the cruise control cables properly, perform the following procedures in order. Failure to adjust the cables properly can cause cruise control malfunction.

Before adjusting the cables, check each of the cables for fraying, cracks, or severe bending. Check the cables for proper routing. Worn or damaged cables should be replaced before adjustment. Replace cable(s) as described in this chapter.

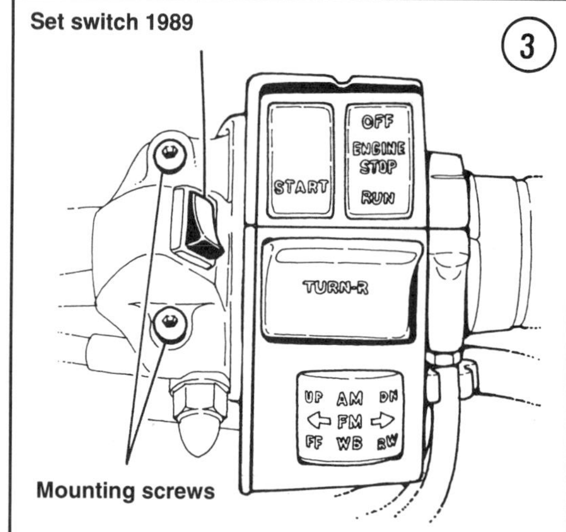


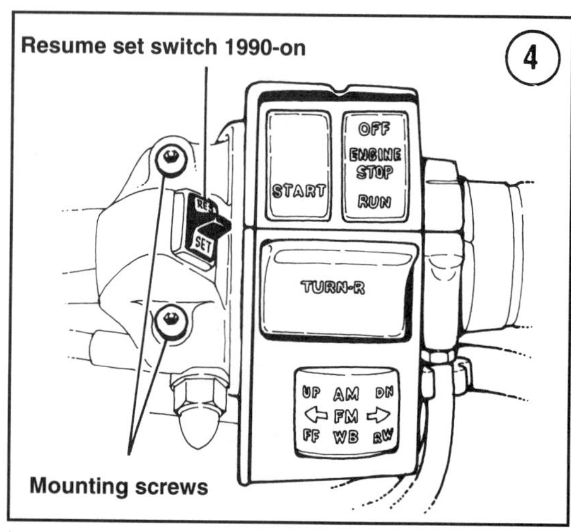

Access the bellcrank assembly by removing the seat and fuel tank.

### *Rear throttle cable*

Rear throttle cable adjustment is required if:

a. The rear throttle cable has been replaced.

b. The carburetor was removed from the bike.

Refer to the following *Front Throttle Cable* section for adjustment.

### *Front throttle cable*

The front and rear throttle cables are connected together at the bellcrank (**Figure 1**). The front throttle cable is attached to the bellcrank bracket with a C-ring. The rear throttle cable is inserted through the bellcrank bracket and held in position by 2 adjust nuts. These nuts are used to adjust the front and rear throttle cables.

1. Make sure all cables are properly installed.

*NOTE*

*Because the front and rear throttle cables are connected together, they will be referred to as the pull-open cable in the following steps.*

2. Loosen the idle cable adjuster locknuts and turn the adjuster to gain as much slack in the idle cable as possible.

3. Position the handlebar so that the front tire faces straight ahead.

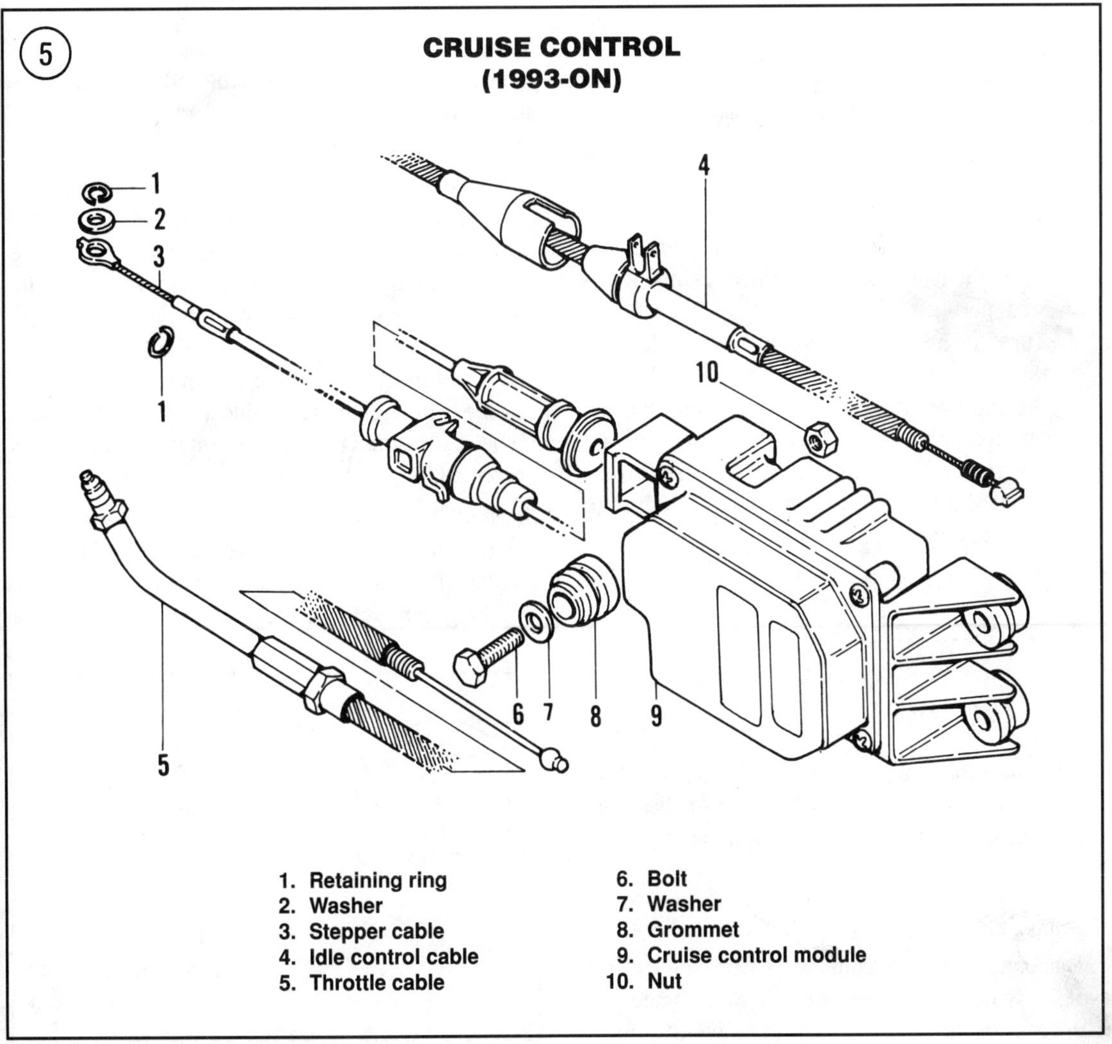


1. Retaining ring
2. Washer
3. Stepper cable
4. Idle control cable
5. Throttle cable
6. Bolt
7. Washer
8. Grommet
9. Cruise control module
10. Nut

14

4. Turn the throttle grip so that it is at wide open throttle.
5. The carburetor should be at wide open throttle. If not, adjust the pull-open cable until throttle opening at carburetor is completely open. Tighten the cable adjusters. Release the throttle and then open it again to wide open throttle and recheck the adjustment.
6. Twist the throttle grip by hand until the throttle is completely open and then close the throttle grip without releasing it (do not release it so that it snaps back). Check the idle stop screw; it should be touching its stop on the carburetor with the front wheel facing straight ahead. Then turn the handlebar from side to side (lock-to-lock). The idle stop screw should still be touching the carburetor. If the idle stop screw is not touching the carburetor, perform the following:
   a. First check that the cables are properly routed. If cables are properly routed, perform sub-step b.
   b. Loosen the pull-open cable adjuster just enough so that the idle stop screw touches the carburetor when the handlebars are turned from side-to-side. Tighten the cable adjuster locknuts and recheck the adjustment. When the idle stop screw touches the carburetor when the handlebars are turned from side-to-side, perform sub-step c.
   c. Turn the throttle grip so that it is at wide open throttle and hold it in this position. Measure the gap from the throttle cam stop to the carburetor stop boss. Harley-Davidson allows a maximum distance of 1/8 in. (3.2 mm) from the cam stop to the stop boss when the throttle grip is at wide open throttle.
7. Make sure pull open-cable adjuster locknuts are tight.
8. Perform the *Idle Cable Adjustment*.

### *Idle cable adjustment*

The idle cable and roll-off switch are manufactured as a closed assembly. If one part of the cable is damaged, the entire cable/switch assembly must be replaced.

An ohmmeter is required for this procedure. Refer to **Figure 6**.

1. Disconnect the wire connectors from the roll-off switch. Switch an ohmmeter to the R × 1 scale and then cross the test leads to zero the meter. Connect the 2 ohmmeter leads to the 2 switch contacts. There should be no continuity (infinite resistance). If ohmmeter shows continuity, the switch is damaged. Replace the idle cable/roll-off switch assembly as described in this chapter. If roll-off switch is operating correctly, proceed to Step 2.

*NOTE*
*Leave ohmmeter leads attached to the roll-off switch when performing the following. If necessary, connect the ohmmeter leads to the 2 black leads on the 8B 6-pin connector; see wiring diagram at end of book for 8B connector identification.*

2. Position the handlebar so that the front tire faces straight ahead.
3. Adjust the idle cable adjuster until there is approximately 0.06 in. (1.5 mm) of free play at the throttle grip. Tighten idle cable adjuster locknuts and recheck adjustment. When adjustment is correct, proceed to Step 4.
4. Rotate the throttle grip toward the closed throttle position and note ohmmeter reading; ohmmeter must show continuity (indicated resistance). If there is no continuity (infinite resistance), loosen the idle cable adjuster locknut and turn the adjuster to *decrease* cable free play; adjust until ohmmeter indicates continuity while there is some free play at the throttle grip. Tighten idle cable adjuster locknut and recheck adjustment. When continuity is indicated as described, proceed to Step 5.
5. Hold the throttle grip in its completely closed position (remove all free play) and then turn the handlebar from side to side (lock-to-lock) while watching ohmmeter scale; ohmmeter must indicate

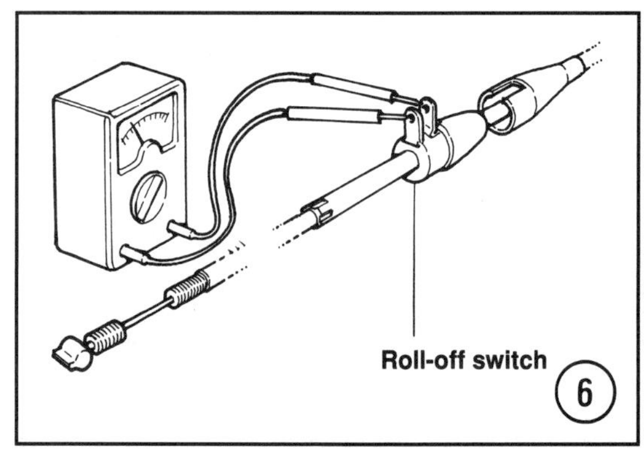

continuity while the handlebar is moved from side to side. If not, repeat Step 4.

6. Position the handlebar so that the front tire faces straight ahead. Rotate the throttle grip until it is at wide open throttle and release it. Throttle must return to idle position (idle stop screw touching carburetor). Repeat with the handlebar turned all the way to the left and then all the way to the right. Again, throttle must return to its idle position.

7. If the idle stop screw does not return properly when performing Step 6, repeat Steps 2-6.

#### *Servo cable adjustment*

There is no adjustment for the servo cable.

### Throttle Cable Replacement

Access the bellcrank assembly by removing the seat and fuel tank.

#### *Rear throttle cable replacement*

Refer to **Figure 1** when performing this procedure.

1. Remove the nut securing the bellcrank cover and remove the cover.
2. Loosen the locknuts securing the rear throttle cable to the bellcrank bracket.
3. Remove the cotter pin and washer securing the front throttle cable to the bellcrank. Then slip the front and rear throttle cables off of the bellcrank pin. Discard the cotter pin.
4. Cut the cable strap holding the rear throttle cable in position.
5. Disconnect the rear throttle cable at the carburetor and remove the cable.
6. Install a new cable by reversing these steps while noting the following:
   a. When installing the front and rear throttle cables onto the bellcrank pin, the rear cable end must be installed onto the pin first. Then install the front cable end onto the pin and install the washer and a *new* cotter pin. Bend the ends of the cotter pin over to lock it in place.
   b. Adjust the throttle cables as described in this chapter.
   c. When installing the bracket cover, make sure that the tab on the front of the brackets extends through the slot in the front of the cover.

#### *Front throttle cable replacement*

1. Remove the nut securing the bellcrank cover and remove the cover.
2. Remove the cotter pin and washer securing the front throttle cable to the bellcrank. Then slip the front throttle cable off of the bellcrank pin. Discard the cotter pin. Do not remove the rear throttle cable from the pin unless cable replacement is required.
3. Carefully pry the C-ring from the cable fitting at the rear of the bracket and free the cable from the bracket.
4. Remove the screws securing the throttle grip/switch housing assembly and separate them. Disconnect the front throttle cable from the throttle grip. Do not lose the ferrule from the end of the cable.

*NOTE*
*Note how the front throttle cable is routed so that you can install the new cable following the original cable path.*

5. Remove the front throttle cable.
6. Install a new cable by reversing these steps while noting the following:
   a. The front throttle cable should be installed onto the bellcrank pin so that it is positioned underneath the rear throttle cable (**Figure 1**). After both cables are installed on the bellcrank pin, install the washer and a *new* cotter pin. Bend the ends of the cotter pin over to lock it in place.
   b. Adjust the throttle cables as described in this chapter.
   c. When installing the bracket cover, make sure that the tab on the front of the brackets extends through the slot in the front of the cover.

#### *Idle cable replacement*

1. Remove the screws securing the throttle grip/switch housing assembly and separate them. Disconnect the idle cable from the throttle grip. Do not lose the ferrule from the end of the cable.

*NOTE*
*Note how the front throttle cable is routed so that you can install the new cable following the original cable path.*

2. Cut or remove all clamps holding the idle cable in position.
3. Disconnect the idle cable at the carburetor.
4. Installation is the reverse of these steps. Adjust the throttle cables as described in this chapter.

#### *Servo cable replacement*

The servo cable connects the bellcrank to the servo motor.

1. Disconnect the servo cable at the bellcrank pin by first removing the cotter pin and washer securing the cable to the pin. Then slide the cable off of the pin. Discard the cotter pin.
2. Pry the servo cable C-ring out of the cable conduit groove.
3. Remove the 2 nuts securing the servo cable to the servo motor. Then pull the servo cable forward to disconnect the cable from the servo motor rack and remove the cable and its gasket.
4. Installation is the reverse of these steps. Note the following:
   a. Replace the servo cable gasket if the old gasket is worn or damaged.
   b. Use a new C-ring to secure the servo cable to the bellcrank bracket. Make sure the C-ring seats in the cable conduit groove completely.
   c. After attaching the servo cable to the bellcrank pin, install the washer and a *new* cotter pin. Bend the ends of the cotter pin over to lock it in place.

## THROTTLE CABLES (1990-ON)

On these models, the bellcrank assembly is not used. Instead, the servo cable is connected directly to the carburetor. To operate the cruise control on 1990 and later models, 3 cables are used (**Figure 2**):

a. Throttle cable: Connects the throttle grip to the carburetor.
b. Idle cable: Connects throttle grip to the carburetor.
c. Servo cable (1990-1992): Connects servo motor to carburetor.
d. Cruise cable (1993-on): Connects stepper motor (cruise control module) to carburetor.

### Cable Adjustment

The idle cable must be loosened to full slack before adjusting the cruise control cables. To adjust these cables properly, follow the order listed below. Failure to adjust the cables properly can cause cruise control malfunction.

Before adjusting the cables, check each of the cables for fraying, cracks, or severe bending. Check the cables for proper routing. Worn or damaged cables should be replaced before adjustment. Replace cable(s) as described in this chapter.

#### *Throttle cable*

1. Loosen the idle cable adjuster locknuts and turn the adjuster to gain as much slack in the idle cable as possible.
2. Position the handlebar so that the front tire faces straight ahead.
3. Turn the throttle grip so that it is at wide open throttle.
4. The carburetor throttle valve should be at wide open throttle. If not, adjust the throttle cable adjuster until the carburetor throttle valve is completely open. Tighten the cable adjuster. Release the throttle and then open it again to wide open throttle and recheck the adjustment.
5. Twist the throttle grip by hand until the throttle is completely open and then close the throttle grip without releasing it (do not release it so that it snaps back). Check the idle stop screw; it should be touching its stop on the carburetor with the front wheel facing straight ahead. Then turn the handlebar from side to side (lock-to-lock). The idle stop screw should still be touching the carburetor. If the idle stop screw is not touching the carburetor, perform the following:
   a. First check that the cables are properly routed. If cables are properly routed, perform sub-step b.
   b. If the servo cable does not have enough slack, it will open the throttle cable. Loosen the servo cable adjuster locknut and loosen the cable, if necessary. Tighten cable adjuster locknut and recheck adjustment. If servo cable

is not causing the problem, perform sub-step c.

c. Loosen the throttle cable adjuster just enough so that the idle stop screw touches the carburetor when the handlebars are turned from side-to-side. Tighten the cable adjuster locknut and recheck the adjustment.

6. Perform the *Idle Cable Adjustment*.

### *Idle cable adjustment (1990-1992)*

The idle cable and roll-off switch are manufactured as a closed assembly; see 3, **Figure 2**. If one part of the cable is damaged, the entire cable/switch assembly must be replaced.

An ohmmeter is required for this procedure. Refer to **Figure 6**.

1. Disconnect the wire connectors from the roll-off switch. Switch an ohmmeter to the R × 1 scale and then cross the test leads to zero the meter. Connect the 2 ohmmeter leads to the 2 switch contacts. There should be no continuity (infinite resistance). If ohmmeter shows continuity, the switch is damaged. Replace the idle cable/roll-off switch assembly as described in this chapter. If the roll-off switch is operating correctly, proceed to Step 2.

NOTE

*Leave ohmmeter leads attached to the roll-off switch when performing the following. If necessary, you can connect the ohmmeter leads to the 2 black leads on the 8B 6-pin connector; see wiring diagram at end of book for 8B connector identification.*

2. Position the handlebar so that the front tire faces straight ahead.
3. Adjust the idle cable adjuster until there is approximately 0.06 in. (1.5 mm) of free play at the throttle grip. Tighten idle cable adjuster locknuts and recheck adjustment. When adjustment is correct, proceed to Step 4.
4. Rotate the throttle grip toward closed throttle position and note ohmmeter reading; ohmmeter must show continuity (indicated resistance). If there is no continuity (infinite resistance), loosen the idle cable adjuster locknut and turn the adjuster to *decrease* cable free play; adjust until ohmmeter indicates continuity while there is some free play at the throttle grip. Tighten idle cable adjuster locknut and recheck adjustment. When continuity is indicated as described, proceed to Step 5.
5. Hold the throttle grip in its completely closed position (remove all free play) and then move the handlebar from side to side (lock-to-lock) while watching ohmmeter; ohmmeter must indicate continuity while the handlebar is moved from side to side. If not, repeat Step 4.
6. Position the handlebar so that the front tire faces straight ahead. Rotate the throttle grip until it is at wide open throttle and release it. Throttle must return to idle position (idle stop screw touching carburetor). Repeat with the handlebar turned all the way to the left and then all the way to the right. Again, throttle must return to its idle position.
7. If the idle stop screw does not return properly when performing Step 6, repeat Steps 2-6.
8. Perform the *Servo Cable Adjustment*.

### *Idle cable adjustment (1993-on)*

An ohmmeter is required for this procedure.

1. Remove the left-hand side cover.

NOTE

*References to cruise harness connector 8A (1993) and connector 17A (1994) in Step 2 refer to the electrical connectors that plug into the electronic cruise control module (**Figure 7**). These connector references are labeled on the wiring diagram (end of book) and can be referred to when identifying wiring color codes.*

2. Disconnect cruise harness connector 8A (1993) or connector 17A (1994) at the cruise control module (**Figure 7**). Switch an ohmmeter to the R × 1 scale and then cross the test leads to zero the meter. Perform the following:

   a. On 1993 models, connect an ohmmeter to the black/red and black/orange leads on cruise harness connector 8A.

   b. On 1994 models, connect an ohmmeter to the violet/yellow and orange/violet leads on cruise harness connector 17A.

3. There should be no continuity (infinite resistance). If ohmmeter shows continuity, roll-off switch is damaged. If necessary, replace the idle cable assembly as described in this chapter.

*NOTE*
*Leave ohmmeter leads attached to connectors when performing the following.*

4. Position handlebar so front tire faces straight ahead.

5. Adjust idle cable adjuster (at handlebar) until there is approximately 0.06 in. (1.5 mm) of free play at the throttle grip. Tighten idle cable adjuster locknuts and recheck adjustment. When adjustment is correct, perform Step 6.

6. Rotate throttle grip toward closed throttle position and note ohmmeter reading; ohmmeter must show continuity (indicated resistance). If there is no continuity reading, loosen the idle cable adjuster locknut and turn the adjuster to *decrease* cable free play; adjust until ohmmeter indicates continuity while there is some free play at throttle grip. Tighten idle cable adjuster locknut and recheck adjustment. When continuity is indicated as described, perform Step 7.

7. Hold throttle grip in its completely closed position and them move handlebar from side to side (lock-to-lock) while watching ohmmeter; ohmmeter must indicate continuity while handlebar is moved from side to side.

8. Position handlebar so that front tire faces straight ahead. Rotate throttle grip until it is at wide open throttle and release it. Throttle must return to idle position. Repeat with handlebar turned all the way to the left and then all the way to the right. Again, throttle must return to its idle position.

9. If throttle does not return properly when performing Step 8, repeat Steps 4-8.

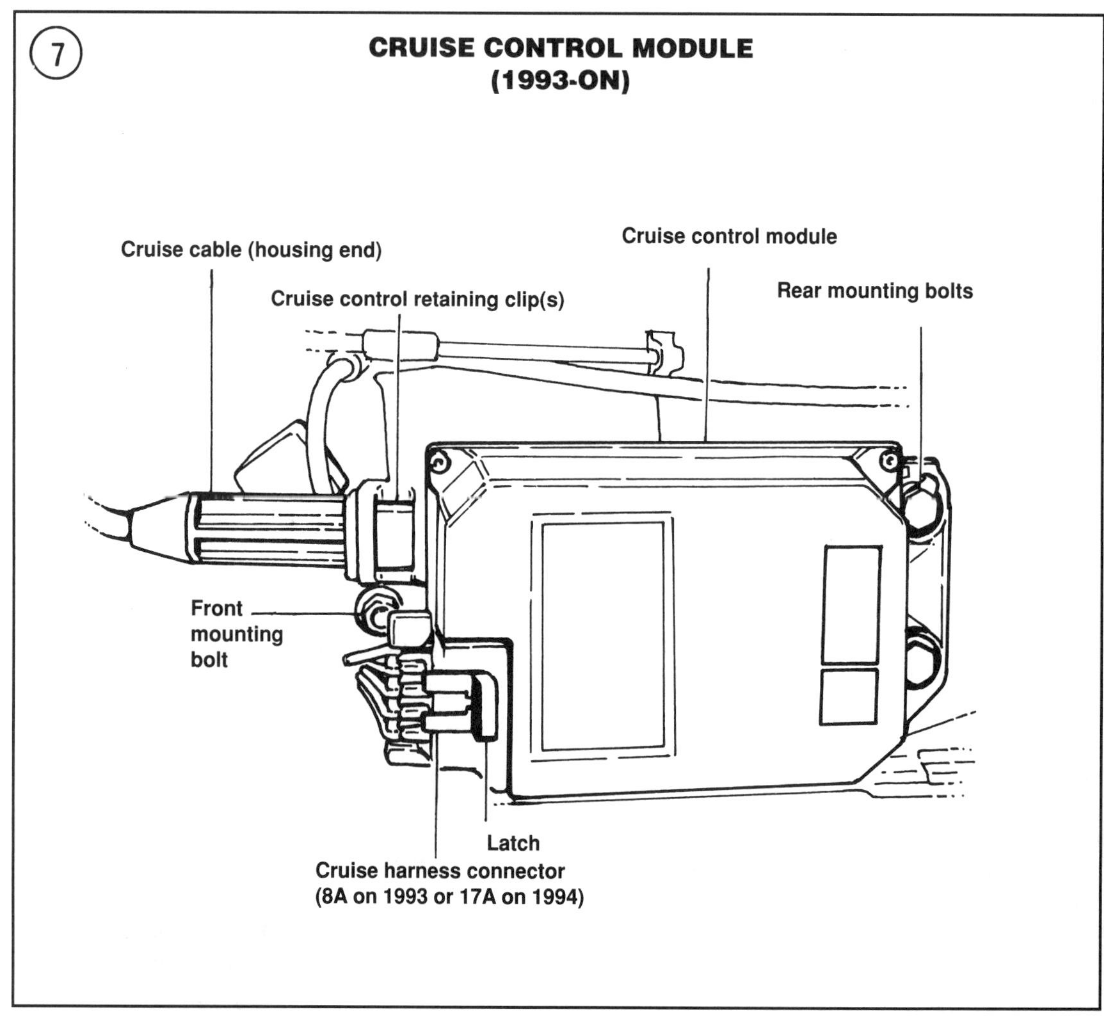

10. Perform *Cruise Cable Adjustment* as described in this chapter.

### *Servo cable adjustment (1990-1992)*

Refer to **Figure 2** when performing this procedure.

1. Adjust the throttle and idle cables as described in the previous procedures.
2. Disconnect the servo cable at the carburetor. This will require the removal of the 2 cable C-rings—one at the carburetor pin and one at the carburetor cable bracket.

*NOTE*

*The servo cable must be attached to the servo motor with the motor rack fully extended when performing the following procedures.*

3. Measure the servo cable with a vernier or dial caliper as follows:
   a. Insert the front caliper arm into the servo cable eyelet hole and the opposite caliper arm against the cable shoulder (**Figure 8**).
   b. The cable length should be 3.410 in. (86.6 mm).
   c. If the cable length is incorrect, loosen the servo cable adjuster locknut and turn the cable adjuster as required to obtain the correct length adjustment. Tighten the adjuster locknut and recheck the adjustment length.
4. If the servo cable was removed from its mounting position, insert the cable through its 2 mounting retainers. Then route the cable over the top of the engine stabilizer and drop it between the cylinder heads and toward the carburetor.
5. Insert the servo cable conduit into the cable bracket on the carburetor. Secure the cable by installing a new C-ring into the conduit cable groove. Make sure the C-ring seats in the groove completely.
6. Fit the servo cable eyelet over the carburetor pin (**Figure 9**), then visually check the cable fit on the pin. For the servo cable adjustment to be correct, the eyelet must fit against the pin so that the cable slack is at the back of the pin (i.e., a visible distance that is equal to 1/3 the eyelet hole diameter). See **Figure 10**. If necessary, loosen the servo cable adjuster and change the cable length until the specified clearance is obtained. Tighten the adjuster locknut and recheck adjustment.
7. Install the cable washer on the carburetor pin, then secure the cable onto the pin with a new C-ring. Make sure the C-ring seats in the pin groove completely.
8. Once the servo cable is installed and secured with the C-ring, snap the throttle grip a few times while turning the handlebars from side to side, then release the throttle grip and check that the idle adjusting screw touches the carburetor idle stop. If not, readjust the cable length starting at Step 6.

*NOTE*

*Proper servo cable adjustment is critical to cruise control and idle speed adjustment. If the servo cable adjustment is too loose, the servo motor will run nonstop when the cruise and ignition switches are turned ON as well as causing the overall speed of the motorcycle*

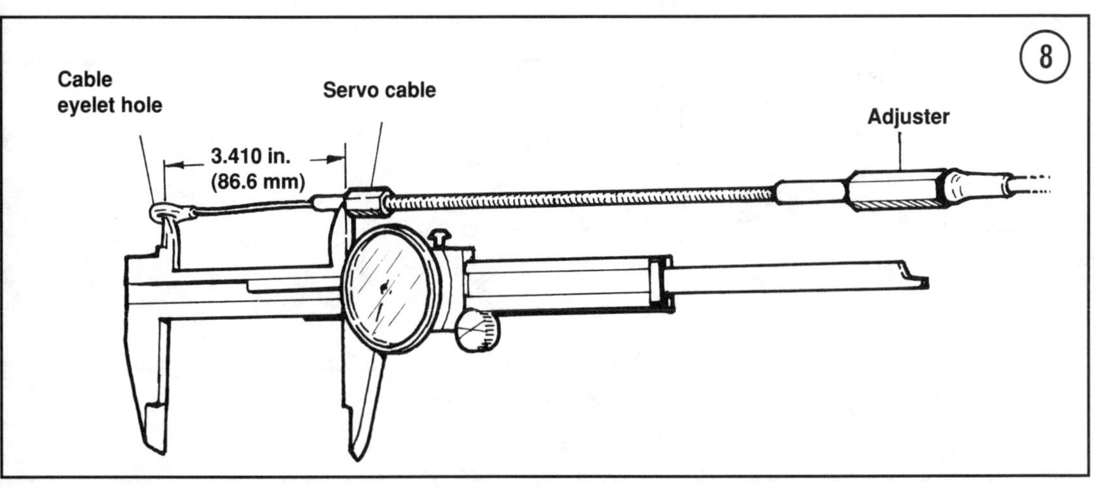

*to drop a few mph after the cruise control is set to run at a specified speed. If the servo cable adjustment is too tight, it will be difficult to adjust and maintain a correct idle speed. The bike will also gain an additional 1-2 mph (1.6-3.2 km) when the cruise control RES/SET switch is switched to SET speed.*

***Cruise cable adjustment***

Cruise cable adjustment is only required if cruise control module or cruise cable have been replaced.

1. Adjust the throttle and idle cables as previously described.

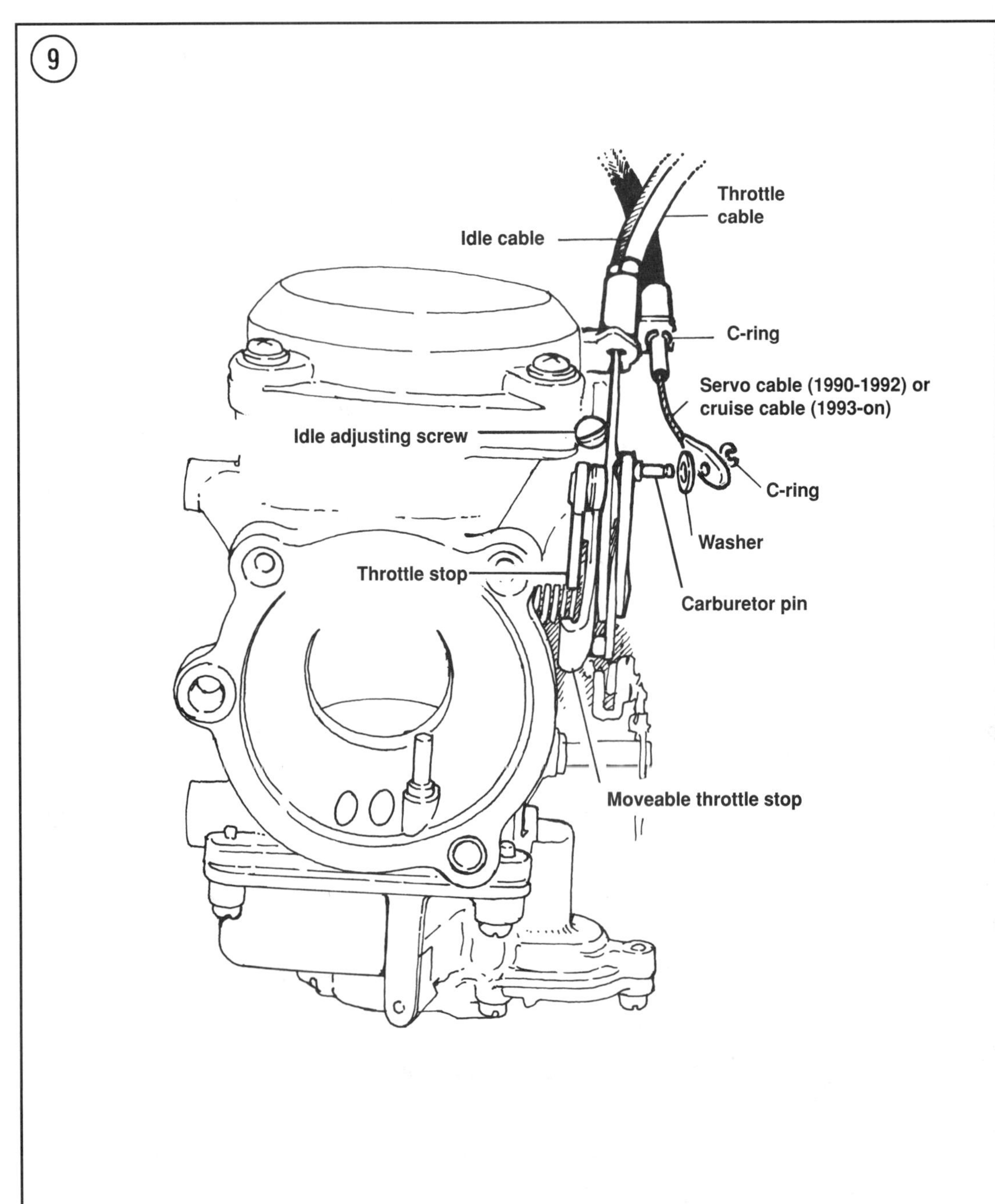

2. Disconnect the cruise cable at the carburetor (**Figure 9**). This will require the removal of the 2 cable C-rings—one at the carburetor pin and one at the carburetor cable bracket.

*NOTE*
*The cruse cable must be attached to the cruise control module (**Figure 7**) when performing the following; refer to **Cruise Cable Replacement** in this chapter.*

3. Set cruise cable length as follows:
   a. Push the square locking button on the cruise cable adjuster (**Figure 11**) and move the upper cruise cable housing in or out so that cable eyelet can be slipped on the carburetor pin as shown in **Figure 9**.

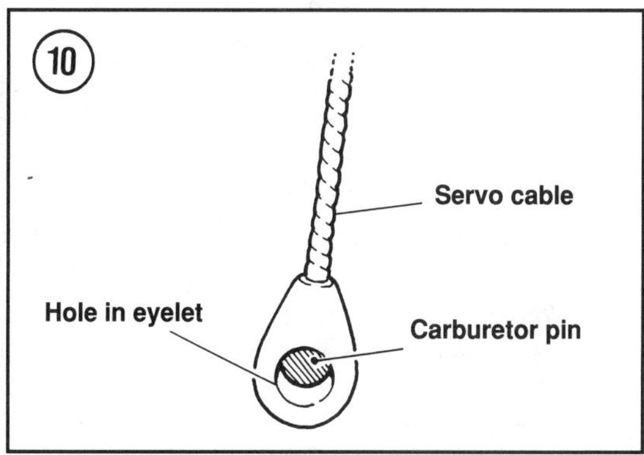


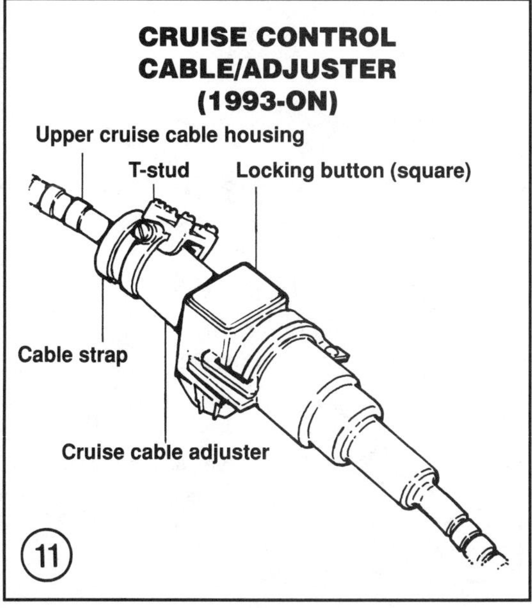


   b. For the cruise cable adjustment to be correct, the eyelet must fit against the pin so that the cable slack is at the back of the pin (i.e., a visible distance that is equal to 1/3 the eyelet hole diameter). See **Figure 10**.

4. Install the cable washer on the carburetor pin, then secure the cable onto the pin with a new C-ring. Make sure the C-ring seats in the pin groove completely.

5. Once the cruise cable is installed and secured with the C-ring, snap the throttle grip a few times while turning the handlebar from side to side, then release the throttle grip and check that the idle adjusting screw touches the carburetor idle stop (**Figure 9**). If not, readjust the cable length as described in Step 3.

*NOTE*
*Proper cruise cable adjustment is critical to cruise control and idle speed adjustment. If the cruise cable adjustment is too loose, the SET speed may be 1-2 mph (1.6-3.2 km/h) lower than the speed present when cruise was SET. If cruise cable adjustment is too tight, it will be difficult to adjust and maintain a correct idle speed. The bike will also gain an additional 1-2 mph when the cruise control RES/SET switch is switched to SET speed.*

### *Throttle and idle cable replacement*

Throttle and idle cable replacement is the same as for non-cruise control FLT models. Refer to Chapter Eight.

### *Servo cable replacement (1990-1992)*

Refer to **Figure 2** for this procedure.

1. Remove the C-ring securing the servo cable eyelet to the carburetor pin. Remove the washer and slide the eyelet off of the pin.
2. Remove the C-ring securing the servo cable to the carburetor cable bracket.
3. Discard both C-rings.
4. Remove the seat to access the servo motor.
5. Remove the 2 nuts securing the servo cable to the servo motor. Then pull the servo cable forward to disconnect the cable from the servo motor rack and remove the cable and its gasket.

6. Replace the servo cable gasket if the old gasket is worn or damaged.

7. Align the gasket with the servo cable and attach the cable to the servo motor rack. Secure the cable to the motor with the 2 mounting nuts.

8. Complete installation by performing the steps described under *Servo Cable Adjustment* for 1990-1992 models in this chapter. Install new C-rings.

#### *Cruise cable replacement (1993-on)*

1. Remove the air filter and backplate.

2. Remove the C-ring securing the cruise cable to the carburetor pin (**Figure 9**). Remove the washer and slide the cruise eyelet off of pin.

3. Remove C-ring securing cruise cable to the carburetor cable bracket.

4. Discard both C-rings.

5. Remove the 2 left-hand saddlebag mounting bolts and remove the saddlebag.

6. Remove the left-hand side cover mounting screw and remove the side cover.

7. Remove the T-stud mount strap securing the cruise cable to the frame (**Figure 11**). Then press the square button on the cruise cable and push the carburetor end of cable conduit into the cable adjuster to increase cable slack.

8. Lift the cruise harness connector latch at the cruise control module and disconnect the connector from the module (**Figure 7**).

9. Pull the cruise cable out and disconnect the cable end from the ribbon as shown in **Figure 12**.

10. Pull the ribbon out so that it is not twisted and connect the new cruise cable to it.

*CAUTION*
*Make sure the ribbon is not twisted when reconnecting the cable end.*

11. Push the cruise cable housing end (**Figure 7**) into the cruise control module. Make sure the latches lock the housing end securely.

12. Complete installation by performing the steps described under *Cruise Cable Adjustment* for 1993-on models in this chapter. Install new C-clips.

## SERVO MOTOR (1989-1992)

### Removal/Installation

Refer to **Figure 1** or **Figure 2** for this procedure.

1. Remove the seat.

2. Disconnect the servo motor 6-pin electrical connector.

3. Remove the 2 nuts securing the servo cable to the servo motor. Then pull the servo cable forward and disconnect the cable from the servo motor rack and remove the cable and its gasket.

4. Remove the locknut securing the servo motor to its bracket. Remove the servo motor and its external tooth lockwasher.

*NOTE*
*The lockwasher is installed between the servo motor and its mounting bracket.*

5. Installation is the reverse of these steps, plus the following.

6. Replace the servo cable gasket if damaged.

7. Replace the external tooth lockwasher if worn or damaged.

8. Make sure the external tooth lockwasher is installed between the servo motor and its mounting

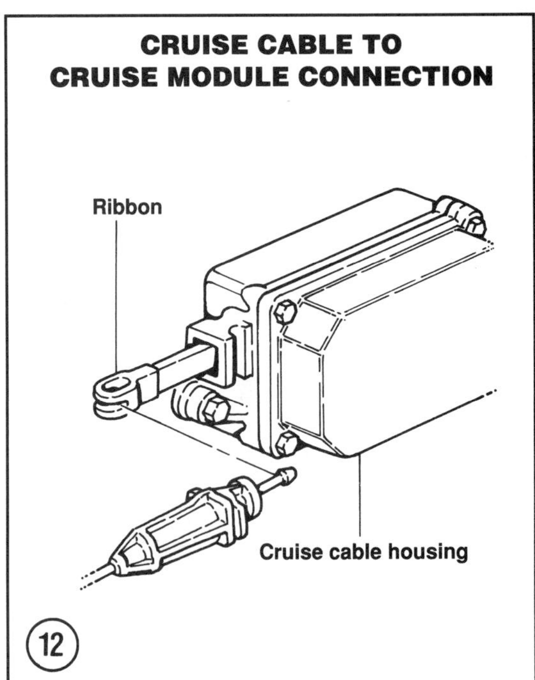

bracket when installing the motor into position. See 20, **Figure 1** or 9, **Figure 2**.

9. Clean the servo motor and servo module electrical connectors with electrical contact cleaner. After the cleaner evaporates, apply a dielectric electrical grease to the connector halves before connecting them.

10. On 1990 and later models, adjust the servo cable as described in this chapter. On 1989 models, servo cable adjustment is not required.

## SERVO MODULE (1989-1992)

### Removal/Installation

Refer to **Figure 1** or **Figure 2** when performing this procedure.

1. Remove the seat.
2. Disconnect all of the electrical connectors at the servo module.
3. Remove the 2 screws securing the module and remove the module.
4. Installation is the reverse of these steps, plus the following.
5. Clean the servo module electrical connectors with electrical contact cleaner. After the cleaner evaporates, apply a dielectric electrical grease to the connector halves before connecting them.
6. Make sure the servo module wire connector leads are properly connected.

## CRUISE CONTROL MODULE (1993-ON)

The cruise control module is mounted under the left-hand side cover; see **Figure 7**, typical. The cruise control cable adjuster is located just above the rear cylinder spark plug; see **Figure 11**.

### Removal/Installation

1. Remove the battery as described in Chapter Nine.
2. Remove the 2 left-hand saddlebag mounting bolts and remove the saddlebag.
3. Remove the left-hand side cover mounting screw and remove the side cover.
4. Remove the T-stud mount strap securing the cruise cable to the frame (**Figure 11**).
5. Disconnect the cruise control cable at the cruise control module as described under *Cruise Cable Replacement (1993-on)* in this chapter.
6. Lift the cruise harness connector latch at the cruise control module and disconnect the connector from the module.
7. Loosen, then remove the 2 rear cruise control module mounting bolts.
8. Loosen the front cruise control module mounting bolt until tension is released from the front module mount grommet.
9. Remove the cruise control module.
10. If you are replacing the cruise control module, transfer the grommets from the old module to the new one.
11. Install the module into position on the frame. Install the 2 rear mounting bolts. Tighten all mounting bolts to 9-11 ft.-lb. (12-15 N•m).
12. Reconnect the cruise harness connector.
13. Reconnect and adjust the cruise cable as described in this chapter.
14. Install the left-hand side cover and its mounting bolt.
15. Install the left-hand saddlebag and its mounting bolt.
16. Install the battery as described in Chapter Nine.

## CRUISE CONTROL SWITCHES

### ON/OFF Switch Replacement

On FLHTC Ultra models, the ON/OFF switch is mounted on the far right-hand side of the inner fairing. To remove the switch, carefully pry it out of the fairing, then disconnect the connector leads from the switch. Reverse to install a new switch.

On FLTC Ultra models, the ON/OFF switch is mounted on the right-hand front side of the instrument panel. Remove the instrument panel to access the switch. Remove the switch and disconnect the connector leads from the back of the switch. Reverse to install a new switch.

### Set Switch (1989)

The set switch is mounted onto the right-hand handlebar (**Figure 3**).

1. Remove the mounting screws securing the switch housing to the handlebar.

2. Disconnect the switch wires and remove the switch.

3. Install a new set switch by reversing these steps. Refer to **Figure 13** when connecting wires at the switch.

### Set/Resume Switch (1990-1992)

The set/resume switch is mounted onto the right-hand handlebar (**Figure 4**).

1. Remove the 2 mounting screws securing the switch to the handlebar.

2. Disconnect the switch wires and remove the switch.

3. Install a new set switch by reversing these steps. Refer to **Figure 14** when connecting wires at the switch.

### Set/Resume Switch (1993-on)

The set/resume switch is mounted on the right-hand handlebar (**Figure 4**).

1A. On FLTCU models, remove the instrument housing.

1B. On FLHTCU models, remove the headlight assembly.

2. On 1994 models, remove the 3-pin set/resume connector from its T-stud mount.

3. Disconnect the 3-pin connectors, then remove terminals from connector housing.

4. Remove the screws securing the set/resume switch to the handlebar and remove the switch.

5. Install the new switch onto the handlebar. Check and adjust front brake lever position prior to tightening set/resume switch screws. Then tighten switch screws securely.

6. Cut the new switch wires to length. Route wires from harness through the handlebar grommet. Crimp new connectors onto wires and reconnect.

7. Reverse Steps 1 and 2. Check switch operation.

## TROUBLESHOOTING (1989-1992)

This section describes troubleshooting of the cruise control system.

### Wiring Diagrams

Refer to **Figure 15** (1989) or **Figure 16** (1990-1992) when performing the following troubleshooting steps.

### System Inspection

A malfunction in the cruise control system will cause the system to be inoperative. Perform the following visual inspection to determine the cause of the problem. If the visual inspection fails to locate the problem, identify the complaint under *Troubleshooting* and perform the steps in order to locate the problem.

1. Make sure the battery cables are connected properly. The red cable must be connected to the positive battery terminal.

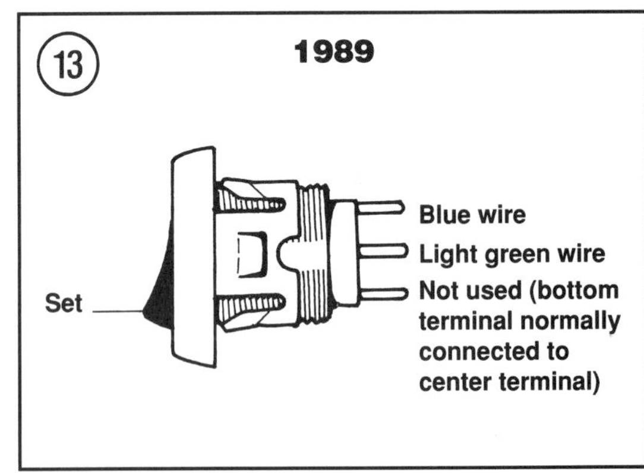


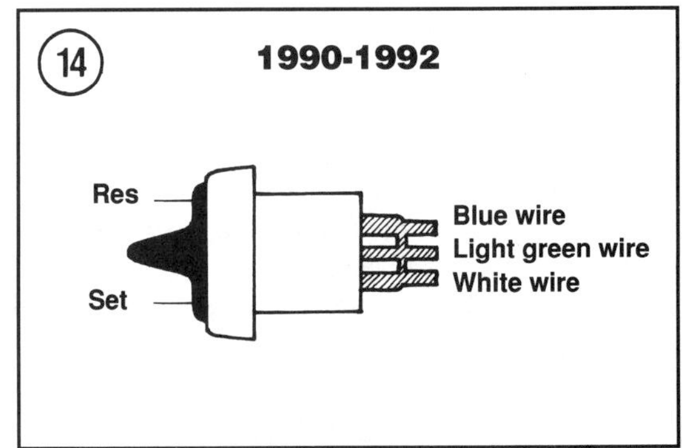

2. Inspect the battery terminals for loose or corroded terminals. Tighten or clean as required.

3. Carefully check the wiring leading to and within the cruise control system. Check the wiring for corroded, loose or disconnected connections. Clean, tighten or connect as required.

## Test Procedures

The following test procedures apply to the Harley-Davidson cruise control system. To find the test procedure you need, read through the following test list. Then locate the test procedure and read through the test before starting.

Proper testing and repair to the cruise control system is important to the safe and reliable operation of the system. If you cannot locate the problem or safely repair it, refer service to a Harley-Davidson dealer.

*WARNING*

*When testing or servicing the cruise control system, do not ride the motorcycle until the system is working correctly. When in doubt, park the bike and consult with a Harley-Davidson dealer.*

a. Test 1: Indicator Light Does Not Come On.

b. Test 2: Cruise Control Will Not Stay in SET Position.

c. Test 3: Cruise Control Will Not Stay in RES Position (1990-1992).

d. Test 4: Cruise Control Will Not Stay in SET or RES Position.

e. Test 5: Engine Speed Changes After Being SET. Vehicle Surges Constantly.

f. Test 6: Fast Engine Idle and/or Engine Speed Increases When Cruise Control SET (1990-1992).

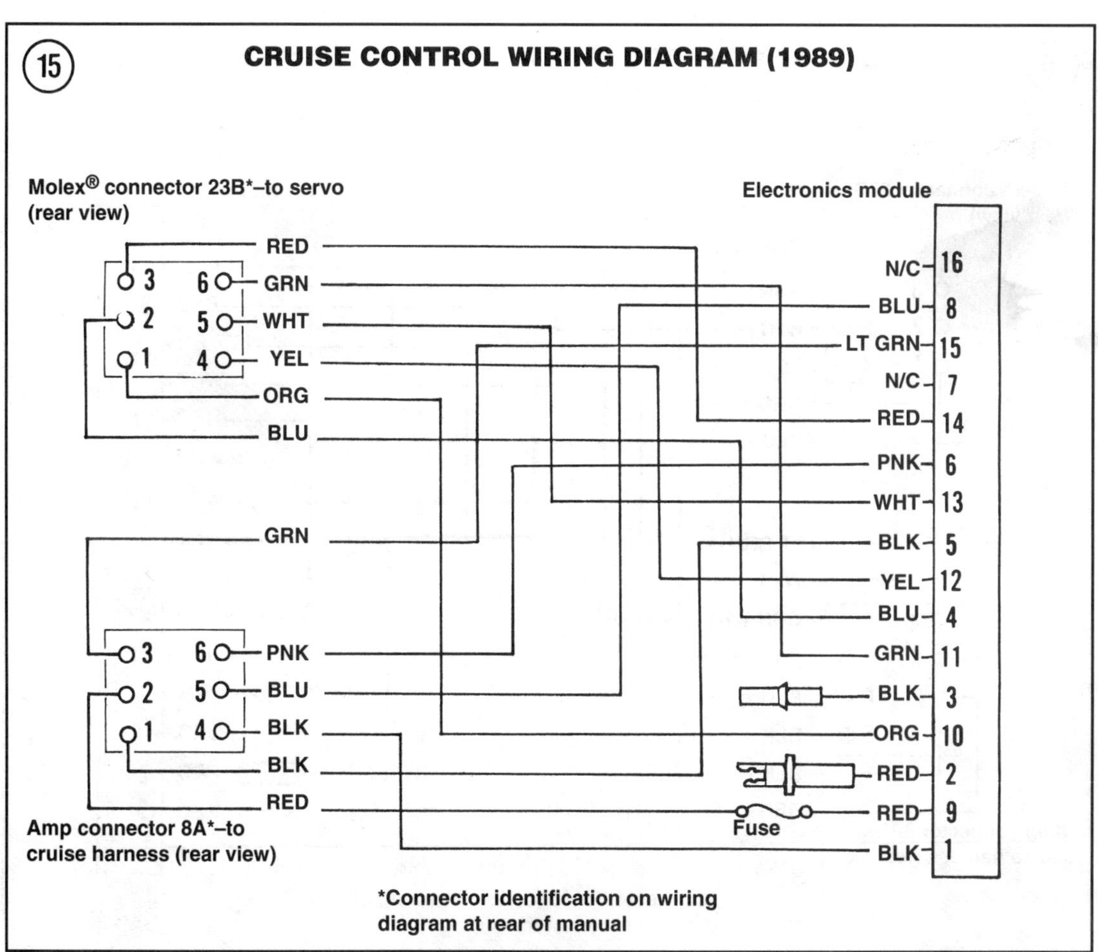

g. Test 7: Servo Motor Runs Continuously with Ignition and Cruise Switch ON and Engine at Idle (1990-1992).

### Test 1: Indicator Light Does Not Come On

1. If the cruise ON/OFF indicator light does not come on but the cruise control system works:

a. Check for a burned out indicator light filament. On FLHTC Ultra models, replace the rocker switch. On FLTC Ultra models, replace the indicator assembly.

b. If the indicator light filament is okay, check the indicator bulb circuit with a test light or ohmmeter. If the test lamp does not light or if the ohmmeter shows infinite resistance, there is an open in the indicator light wiring circuit.

2. If the cruise ON/OFF indicator light does not come on and the cruise control system does not work:

a. Remove the seat.

b. Connect a black voltmeter lead to a good ground and the red lead to the amp connector (8A) 6-pin connector red wire. See **Figure 15** or **Figure 16**.

c. Turn both the ignition switch and the cruise ON/OFF switch ON. The voltmeter should read 9-12 volts. Turn the cruise ON/OFF switch OFF. The voltmeter should read 0 volts.

d. If the reading is incorrect, remove the cruise ON/OFF switch to access the wiring connectors at the switch. If the switch was recently replaced, confirm that the switch is wired properly; compare actual wiring with wiring diagram at end of book. If switch is wired properly, test switch with an ohmmeter or test

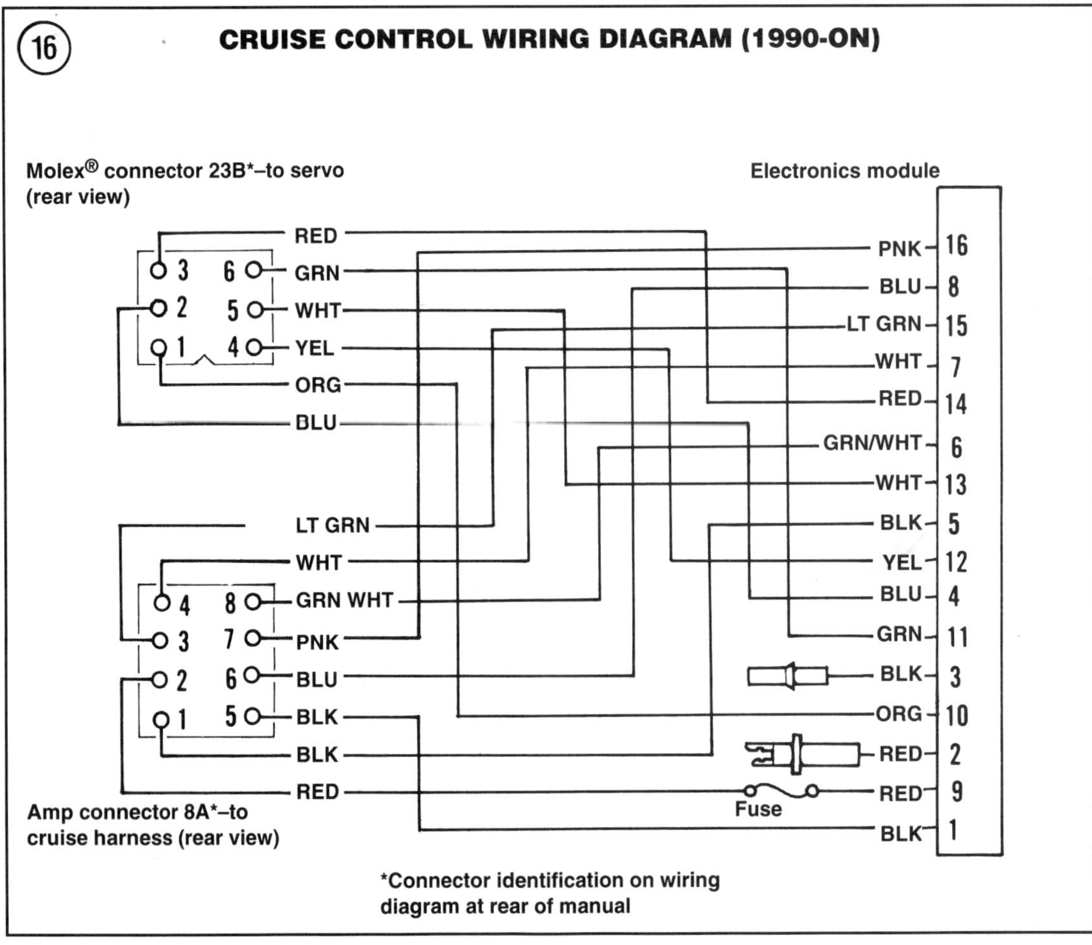

light. There should be continuity when the switch is in the ON position, and no continuity in the OFF position.

e. Replace switch if damaged.

f. If switch is okay, check switch wiring circuit.

### Test 2: Cruise Control Will Not Stay in SET Position

1. First check the electronic module 2 amp fuse. If the fuse is blown and a new one blows when installed, look for a short to ground in the wire circuit.

2. Turn on the lights and check for a blown taillight bulb. If this bulb is blown, also check the bulbs installed in the Tour-pack. If all three bulbs are blown, the cruise control system will be inoperative. Replace bulbs as required.

3. If the brake light stays on constantly, check for a shorted front or rear brake light switch; refer to Chapter Nine for switch testing. If both switches are okay, check the front brake light switch for binding in the brake lever. Refer to Chapter Thirteen under *Front Brake Caliper* for service procedures.

4. One way to deactivate the cruise control system under normal riding conditions is to roll-off the throttle (i.e., the throttle is closed). With this information, you can apply it to an incorrectly adjusted idle cable—if the idle cable does not have enough free play (adjusted too tightly), the roll-off switch (mounted in the idle cable) will close, simulating a closed throttle position. Check the idle throttle cable adjustment as described in this chapter.

5. Check the electronic module return ground as follows:

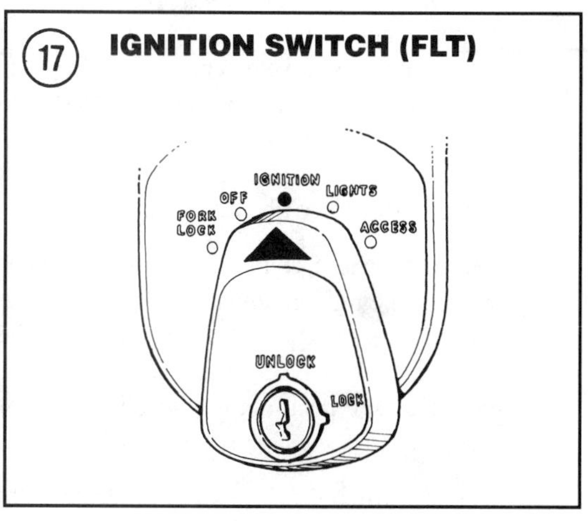


a. Connect the black ohmmeter lead to a good ground, then probe the electronic module No. 3 pin (black wire bullet connector) with the red test lead. The ohmmeter should show continuity (0.5 ohms or less).

b. If the ohmmeter reading is more than 0.5 ohms, check the electronic module ground wire for a loose or damaged connection.

6. Check the servo motor return ground as follows:

a. Connect the black ohmmeter lead to a good ground, then probe the electronic module No. 11 pin (green wire) with the red test lead. The ohmmeter should show continuity (0.5 ohms or less).

b. If the ohmmeter reading is more than 0.5 ohms, check the green wire from the electronic module, through the 23A and 23B connectors and to the servo motor. Check the wire for damage. Check the connectors for contamination or a damaged mating pin and socket.

7A. *1989*: Check the coil signal speed sense circuit as follows:

a. Turn the ignition switch ON but do not start the engine.

*NOTE*

*Ignition switch must be turned to IGNITION (ON) on the ignition switch. Do not perform following test with ignition switch turned to ACCESS. See* ***Figure 17*** *for switch contact identification.*

b. Connect the black voltmeter lead to a good ground, then probe the pink wire at the back of the 6-pin 8B connector with the red test lead. The ohmmeter should read 9-12 volts.

c. If the voltage reading is incorrect, the rotor may be perfectly aligned with the sensor. Turn the engine over with the starter button and recheck. If a reading of 9-12 volts is now obtained, proceed to Step 9.

d. If there was no recorded voltage in sub-step c, check for voltage at the pink wire connection on the ignition coil. If voltage is recorded, check the 8A and 8B connectors for contamination or a damaged pink socket and pin connection. If these are okay, check the pink 1-pin connector for a loose or damaged connection. If necessary, continue to check the pink wire from the 1-pin connector to the cruise module.

7B. *1990-1992*: Check the coil signal speed sense circuit as follows:

a. Turn the ignition switch to ON but do not start the engine.

*NOTE*
*Ignition switch must be turned to IGNITION (ON) on the ignition switch. Do not perform following test with ignition switch turned to ACCESS. See **Figure 17** for switch contact identification.*

b. Connect the black voltmeter lead to a good ground, then probe the pink wire at the back of the 8-pin 8B connector with the red test lead. The voltmeter should read 9-12 volts.
c. If the voltage reading is incorrect, the rotor may be perfectly aligned with the sensor. Turn the engine over with the starter button and recheck. If a reading of 9-12 volts is now obtained, proceed to Step 8.
d. If there was no recorded voltage in sub-step c, check for voltage at the pink wire connection on the ignition coil. If voltage is recorded, check the 8A and 8B connectors for contamination or a damaged pin socket and pin connection. If these are okay, check the pink 1-pin connector for a loose or damaged connection. If necessary, continue to check the pink wire from the 1-pin connector to the cruise module.

8. *1990-1992*: Check the reed switch signal as follows:

a. Support the bike so that the front wheel is off the ground.
b. Connect the ohmmeter lead to a good ground, then connect the red lead to the white/green wire at the 8A connector.
c. With the ohmmeter on the R × 1 scale, spin the front wheel to operate the speedometer. The ohmmeter needle should fluctuate between zero ohms and infinity.
d. If the ohmmeter needle does not fluctuate as described, check the white/green 20A and 20B connectors for a loose or damaged connection. If the wire connection is okay, the reed switch—mounted in the instrument panel—may be damaged. Refer further testing to a Harley-Davidson dealer.

9. Inspect the SET portion of the SET (1989) or the RES/SET (1990-1992) switch and its wiring as follows:

a. Connect an ohmmeter between the light/green and blue wire wires at the 8A connector. This should provide a reading of 0.5 ohms or less when the switch is pressed down on 1989 models (**Figure 3**) or set to the SET position on 1990-1992 models (**Figure 4**).
b. If the ohmmeter reading was higher than specified, check connector 17A and 17B for proper connection. Disconnect the 17A and 17B connectors and clean the connector plugs and sockets with electrical contact cleaner and retest. If the reading is still excessive, disconnect the connectors once again and check the switch operation with an ohmmeter.
c. To test the switch, connect the ohmmeter leads to the blue and light green wire switch terminals (1989) or between the blue and light/green switch terminals (1990-1992). There should be continuity when the switch is in the SET position, and no continuity in the OFF position. Replace the switch if necessary.

### Test 3: Cruise Control Will Not Stay in RES Position (1990-1992)

1. Inspect the RES portion of the SET/RES switch and its wiring as follows:

a. Connect an ohmmeter between the light green and white wires at the 8A connector. This should provide a reading of 0.5 ohms or less when the switch is set at the RES position.
b. If the ohmmeter reading was higher than specified, check connector 17A and 17B for proper connection. Disconnect the 17A and 17B connectors and clean the connector plugs and sockets with electrical contact cleaner and retest. If the reading is still excessive, disconnect the connectors once again and check switch operation with an ohmmeter.
c. To test the switch, connect the ohmmeter leads between the light green and white wire terminals. There should be continuity when the switch is in the RES position, and no continuity in the OFF position. Replace the switch if necessary.

2. Replace the switch if necessary and retest.

**Test 4: Cruise Control Will Not Stay in SET or RES Position**

1. On 1990-1992 models, consider the following when troubleshooting this complaint:
   a. The cruise control will not engage if vehicle speed is below 40 mph (64 km). Increase speed to above 40 mph (64 km) and reset control.
   b. If you increased or decreased the vehicle speed by more than 10 mph (16 km) since the last SET speed was set, the RES system will not activate. For system to activate, you must increase or decrease vehicle speed to within 10 mph (16 km) of the last SET speed.
   c. If the above situations do not account for system malfunction, proceed to Step 2.

2. Remove the seat and check that the servo 6-pin connector is not disconnected. If the connector halves are properly pushed together, disconnect them and clean both connectors with electrical contact cleaner. Check that all of the pins are straight and that the wires leading into both connector halves are tight. Assemble the connectors by pushing them together until they click into place.

3. If the brake light does not operate, remove the lens and check for a burned out bulb. If the bulb is okay, reinstall it and perform the following:
   a. Using the wiring diagram for your model (end of book), locate the red 1-pin connector leading from the rear brake light. Connect a black voltmeter lead to a good ground, then connect the red test lead to the red 1-pin connector. Voltmeter should read 9-12 volts with the ignition switch ON while applying either the front or rear brake.
   b. If there is no voltage reading, check the red brake wire for damage.

**CRUISE CONTROL SERVO TEST ADAPTER**

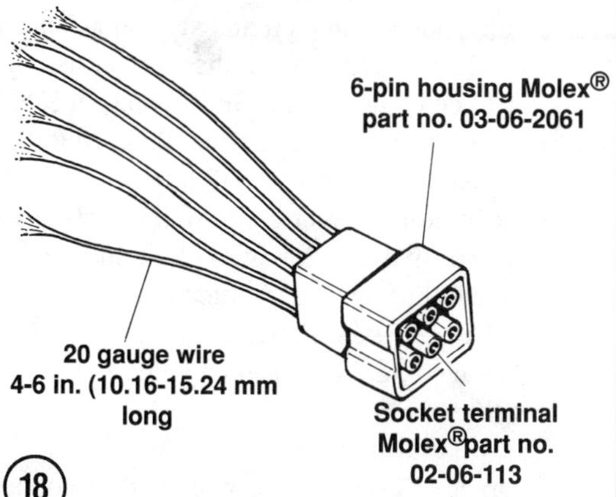

6-pin housing Molex® part no. 03-06-2061

20 gauge wire 4-6 in. (10.16-15.24 mm long

Socket terminal Molex® part no. 02-06-113

(18)

4. A malfunctioning servo motor can cause this complaint. Test the motor as follows:

*NOTE*

*Assemble a test adapter as shown in **Figure 18**. The 20 gauge wires installed in the test adapter should be the same color and placed in the same position as the cruise module-to-servo connector. See **Figure 15** (1989) or **Figure 16** (1990-1992) for servo motor connector wire colors.*

   a. Disconnect the cruise module-to-servo motor 6-pin connector.
   b. Connect the test adapter to the servo motor 6-pin connector.
   c. Connect an ohmmeter to the red and white test adapter wires; set the ohmmeter to its R × 1000 scale. With the throttle closed (servo motor cable rack extended), the ohmmeter should read 5-8 K ohms.
   d. Rotate the throttle grip until it is completely open and wire it so that it will stay in this position. Then remove the servo cable at the servo motor; see throttle cable information in this chapter. Using a stiff piece of wire, push the servo motor rack into the servo motor. With the rack all the way in and the throttle all the way open, the ohmmeter should read 1,500-2,500 ohms.

*CAUTION*

*Read the following test procedures through before testing. When battery voltage is applied, turn voltage OFF after servo motor rack travels approximately 1/2 in. (12.7 mm). If voltage input is continued, damage to the servo or throttle linkage may occur.*

*NOTE*

*It will be necessary to make 4 jumper cables with alligator clips when performing the following tests. A fully charged 12-volt battery is also required.*

e. With the cruise control adapter still connected to the cruise control 6-pin connector, connect the blue adapter wire to the positive battery terminal (+) and the green adapter wire to the negative battery terminal (–). Then connect the orange adapter wire to the positive battery terminal and the yellow adapter wire to the negative battery terminal. The servo rack should move in, simulating throttle opening. Disconnect the test leads.

f. Connect the orange adapter lead to the positive battery terminal and the yellow adapter lead to the negative battery terminal. The servo rack should extend, simulating the throttle returning to idle. Disconnect the test leads.

g. Replace the servo motor if it failed to operate as described in these tests. If the servo motor tested correctly, the cruise control module is damaged; replace it as described in this chapter.

### Test 5: Engine Speed Changes After Being SET. Vehicle Surges Constantly

1. First check for proper cruise control operation as follows:

a. *1989 models*: This condition can occur if the SET switch is pressed down and held too long.

b. *1990-1992*: This condition can occur if the RES/SET switch is held up (increased acceleration) or held down (decreased acceleration).

c. Refer to Owner's Manual for proper operation.

2. Incorrect throttle cable adjustment. Adjust cables as described in this chapter.

3. If condition continues after performing Steps 1 and 2, the cruise module may be damaged.

### Test 6: Fast Engine Idle and/or Engine Speed Increases When Cruise Control SET (1990-1992)

The servo cable adjustment is incorrect (adjustment too tight). Adjust throttle cables as described in this chapter.

### Test 7: Servo Motor Runs Continuously with Ignition and Cruise Switch ON and Engine at Idle (1990-1992)

The servo cable adjustment is incorrect (adjustment too loose). Adjust throttle cables as described in this chapter.

## TROUBLESHOOTING (1993-ON)

This section describes troubleshooting of the cruise control system.

### Wiring Diagrams

Refer to the cruise control wiring diagrams at the end of this book when troubleshooting a 1993 or later cruise control system.

**Table 1** lists cruise module connector numbers and wire color codes that should be referred to along with wiring diagrams (at end of book).

### Cruise Control System Check

The following steps should be followed in order when troubleshooting the cruise control system.

*NOTE*
*For the following system check to be accurate, the steps must be followed in order and with the engine turned off.*

1. Turn the ignition switch OFF.
2. Turn the cruise main switch ON.
3. Press the SET switch (**Figure 4**) down and turn the ignition switch to the ON position. The green cruise light should come on and stay on as long as the SET switch is held down. If the green cruise light stays on after releasing the SET switch, the SET switch and/or its wiring is shorted. Proceed to Step 4 if the light operates properly. If the cruise light did not come on after pressing the SET switch down, one or more of the following conditions may be causing the cruise light to malfunction:

a. SET/RES switch shorted.

b. Damaged SET/RES switch wires and/or connectors.

c. Blown cruise light.

d. Damaged cruise light wires and/or connectors.

e. Cruise harness connector (**Figure 7**) is disconnected or damaged.

f. Damaged cruise main switch.

g. Damaged cruise main switch wires and/or connectors.

h. Incorrect throttle cable adjustment.

i. Faulty module ground wire connection at Terminal E in 10-pin connector.

j. Brake light stays on constantly.

4. With the ignition switch in the ON position, press the RES switch (**Figure 4**) upward. The green cruise light should come on and stay on as long as the RES switch is pressed up. Proceed to Step 5 if the light operates properly. If the green cruise light did not come on after pressing the RES switch up, one or more of the following conditions may be causing the cruise light to malfunction:

a. RES switch wired incorrectly.

b. Loose or damaged wire to RES switch or cruise module.

5. To check the throttle grip switch, turn the throttle grip so that it is tightly closed. With the ignition switch turned ON, the green cruise light should light when the throttle switch is tightly closed and should turn off when the throttle grip returns to its free (relaxed-no hand pressure) position. Proceed to Step 6 if the light operates properly. If the green cruise light did not come on as described, one or more of the following conditions may be causing the cruise light to malfunction:

a. Throttle grip switch wires are damaged or switch is wired incorrectly.

b. Damaged throttle grip switch or cruise module wire or wire connector.

c. Faulty throttle grip switch.

6. Apply the front brake lever. With the ignition switch turned ON, the green cruise light should come on and remain on as long as the brake lever is applied. Proceed to Step 7 if the light operates properly. If the green cruise light did not come as described, one or more of the following conditions may be causing the cruise light to malfunction:

a. All brake light bulbs are disconnected (or burned out).

b. Faulty front brake light switch.

c. Faulty brake relay.

d. Damaged front brake light switch or cruise module wire or wire connector.

e. Front brake light switch or brake relay wires are damaged or component is wired incorrectly.

7. Press the rear brake pedal and hold it in this position for at least 5 seconds, then release it. The green cruise light should come on when the rear brake pedal is pressed and should turn off after 5 seconds. Then, when the brake pedal is released, the cruise module will momentarily pull the throttle open for approximately 20% of its travel. If the brake is applied with the throttle is being pulled open, the throttle should stop turning immediately. Proceed to Step 8 if the light and throttle grip operates as described. If not, one or more of the following conditions may be causing the malfunction:

*NOTE*

*If the green cruise light failed to operate properly, refer to sub-steps a, b and c. If the throttle did not operate properly, refer to sub-steps d and e.*

a. Faulty rear brake light switch.

b. Damage rear brake light switch or relay wires.

c. Rear brake light switch and/or relay incorrectly wired.

d. Incorrect throttle cable adjustment.

e. Faulty cruise control module.

8. While straddling the bike and with the transmission in NEUTRAL, roll the bike forward and then backward to activate the reed switch (mounted in speedometer). The green cruise light should come on. Proceed to Step 9 if the light operates as described. If not, note the following:

a. Speedometer cable/drive is damaged.

b. Reed switch wired incorrectly or wires damaged.

c. Faulty reed switch.

d. Disconnected reed switch ground wire.

9. Perform the following tests to simulate ignition sensor plate input:

a. Turn the main cruise switch OFF.

b. Disconnect the 3-pin ignition sensor-to-ignition module electrical connector.

c. Momentarily place a screwdriver across the ignition module black/white and green wire connectors (on ignition module side) while watching the green cruise light. Then repeat this step 10 times. The cruise light should flash on the 5th-10th attempts. If the cruise light fails to operate properly, refer further service to a Harley-Davidson dealer.

10. Terminate check procedure by turning the ignition switch OFF. If you have failed to locate the cruise control system malfunction, refer service to a Harley-Davidson dealer.

## Cruise Control Malfunctions

If the cruise control is not working properly, consider one of the following malfunctions that most closely resembles your vehicle's condition.

### *Vehicle gains speed*

Cruise cable is too tight. Readjust cable as described in this chapter.

### *Vehicle loses speed*

The cruise cable is too loose or the set switch was held on too long.

### *Speed surges*

a. Reed switch defective.
b. Cruise module defective.
c. Poor ground connection at reed switch or cruise control module (**Figure 7**).

*NOTE*
*If surging occurs when the cruise control is turned OFF, the air/fuel mixture may be too lean.*

### *Cruise disengages with RES switch in ON position*

The RES switch is being held ON for longer than 6 seconds.

**Table 1 MODULE CONNECTORS AND WIRE COLORS (1993-ON)**

| Terminal letter for connector 8A (1993) and connector 17A (1994)* | Wire color 1993 | Wire color 1994 |
|---|---|---|
| A | red/blue | red/green |
| B | blue | blue/black |
| C | white | white/blue |
| D | black/red | violet/yellow |
| E | black | black |
| F | black/orange | orange/violet |
| G | red/white | red/yellow |
| H | pink | pink |
| J | green | green/red |
| K | white/green | white/green |

*Terminal letters are printed on connectors, next to wires.

# CHAPTER FIFTEEN

# FRAME, BODY AND FRAME PAINTING

This chapter describes replacement procedures for frame and body components. Service information includes procedures for completely stripping and repainting the frame.

## FAIRING (FLTC)

### Removal

Refer to **Figure 1**, typical when performing this procedure.

1. Support bike on jiffy stand.
2. To remove the windshield, remove the screws and washers securing the windshield to the fairing. Then lift the windshield off of the fairing and remove it. Store the windshield in a safe place.
3A. On 1984-1985 models, disconnect the electrical connector at the back of the fairing.
3B. On 1986 and later models, disconnect the 2 electrical connectors at the back of the fairing.
4. Remove the screws holding the support bracket clamps to the engine guard (**Figure 2**). Remove the clamp from each support bracket.
5. Remove the headlight housing.
6. Working through the headlight housing opening in the fairing, remove the 2 fairing mounting bolts (**Figure 2**).

*NOTE*
*Check the fairing for any electrical connectors or fasteners that are still attached before removing the fairing in Step 7.*

7. Carefully lift the fairing off of the motorcycle.

### Installation

Refer to **Figure 1** when performing this procedure.

1. Clean all of the electrical connectors with electrical contact cleaner before installing the fairing.
2. Place the fairing into position on the motorcycle. Make sure it does not pinch or interfere with any wires or control cables.
3. Install the 2 fairing mounting bolts located behind the headlight housing (**Figure 2**).
4. Align the clamp with its support bracket and place it on the engine guard. Tighten the mounting screws finger-tight. Repeat for the other bracket and clamp. When both clamps are in position against the engine guard, tighten all of the bracket screws securely.
5. Reinstall the headlight housing. Check headlight adjustment as described in Chapter Nine.
6. Reconnect the electrical connectors.
7. Align the grooves in the bottom of the windshield with the fairing and place the windshield into position. Install the center screw first, then install the remaining screws by crisscrossing from left to right, working from the inside out. When all of the screws are installed, tighten the screws to a final torque of 4 in.-lb. (0.5 N•m). Overtightening the screws may crack the windshield.

8. Place a jack underneath the bike and raise the front wheel off the ground until the front forks are completely extended.

*NOTE*
*The fairing mounting bolts and the engine guard bracket screws must be tightened when making the clearance check in Step 9.*

9. Measure the clearance between the bottom of the fairing and the top of the fender as shown in **Figure 2**. The clearance should be 4 3/4-5 in. (120.6-127 mm).If the clearance is less than 4 3/4 in. (120.6 mm), perform the following:

a. Loosen the fairing bracket bolts identified in **Figure 2**.
b. Loosen the 4 engine guard bracket screws (**Figure 2**) approximately 1 turn.
c. Have an assistant lift the front of the fairing until the clearance between the bottom of the fairing to the top of the fender is 4 3/4-5 in. (120.6-127 mm). Hold the fairing in this position and tighten the bolts and screws loosened in sub-steps a and b.
d. Recheck the specified clearance.

*CAUTION*
*If the specified clearance is not maintained as described in Step 9, the fender will contact the fairing when the front forks bottom out. This may cause fender and fairing damage.*

10. Turn the front wheel all the way to the left and check throttle cable routing between the instrument housing and fairing. The cable must not be pinched or kinked in any way.

*WARNING*
*Do not ride the bike until you are sure that the throttle cable routing is correct.*

## Glove Boxes Removal/Installation (FLT Ultra)

Refer to **Figure 3** for this procedure.

1A. *Early 1989*: Remove the glove boxes as follows:

a. Remove the screw, lockwasher and clamp securing the clutch cable to the left-hand lower fairing.
b. Remove the screw, lockwasher and flat washer securing the left-hand glove box; remove the glove box.
c. Repeat sub-step b to remove the right-hand glove box.

1B. *Late 1989-on*: Remove the glove boxes as follows:

a. Remove the screws securing the lower cap onto the left-hand lower fairing. Remove the lower cap.
b. Remove the screw, lockwasher and clamp securing the clutch cable to the left-hand lower fairing.
c. Working through the front of the lower fairing, remove the screws securing the left-hand glove box to the lower fairing. Remove the glove box.
d. Repeat to remove the right-hand glove box.

2. Install by reversing these steps. Tighten the fairing bolt and the clutch cable nut to 12 ft.-lb. (16.5 N•m).

3. Check clutch cable routing before starting engine.

## Lower Fairings Removal/Installation (FLT Ultra)

Refer to **Figure 3** when performing this procedure.

1. Remove the glove boxes on early 1989 models as described in the previous section.

2. Remove screw, lockwasher and clamp securing the clutch cable to the left-hand lower fairing.

3. Remove the screw, lockwasher and flat washer from inside the lower fairing. This screw was previously removed on early 1989 models.

4. Remove the bolt and nut securing the clamp attaching the lower fairing to the engine guard.

5. Remove the lower fairing(s).

6. Installation is the reverse of these steps, plus the following:

a. The clamp on the engine guard must be positioned so that its flat tabs face to the rear of the motorcycle.
b. Tighten the fairing bolt and the clutch cable nut to 12 ft.-lb. (16.5 N•m).

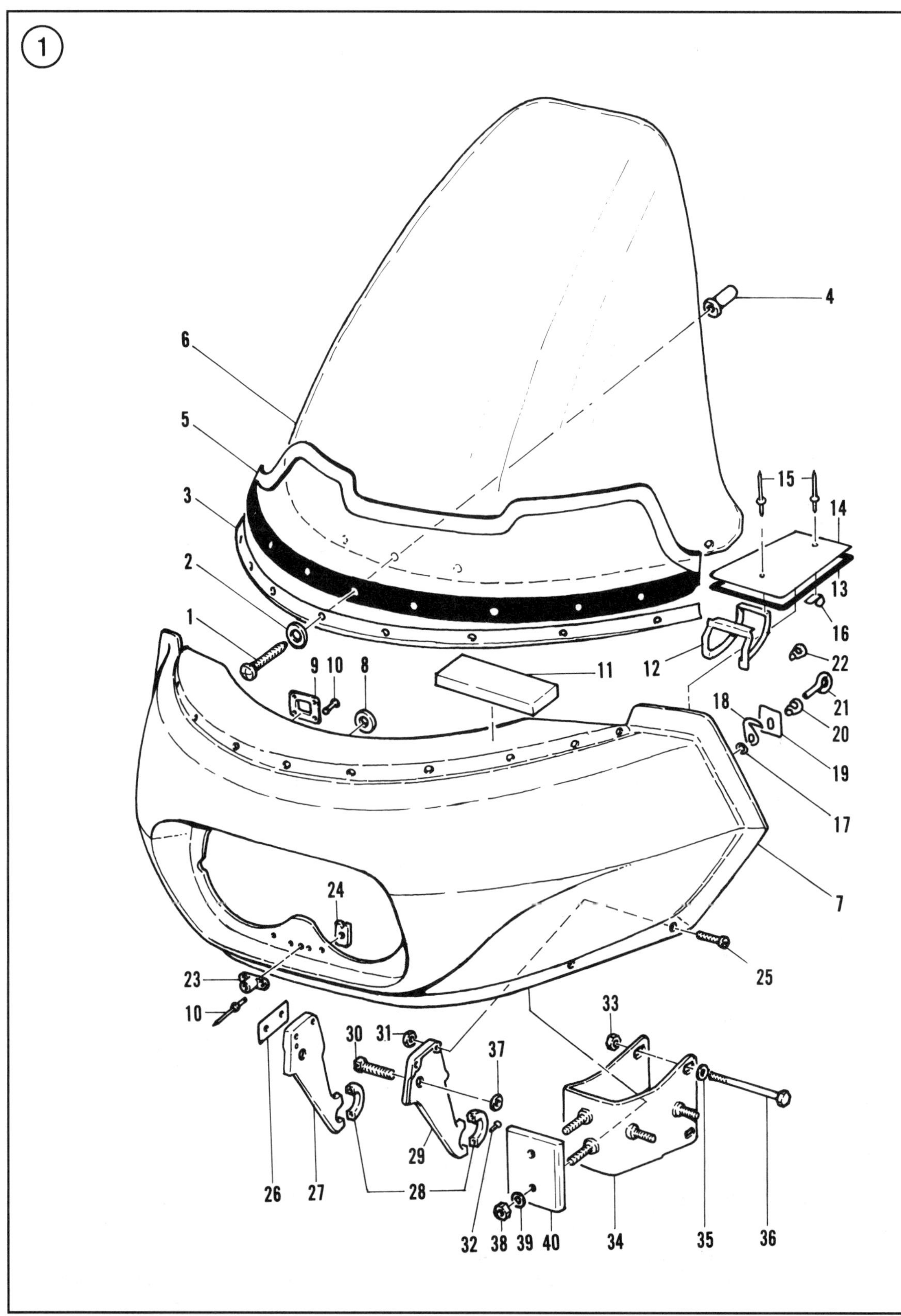
1
1
2
3
4
5
6
7
8
9
10
11
12
13
14
15
16
17
18
19
20
21
22
23
24
25
26
27
28
29
30
31
32
33
34
35
36
37
38
39
40

**WINDSHIELD AND FAIRING (FLTC)**

1. Screw
2. Washer
3. Foam tape
4. Well nut
5. Decal
6. Windshield
7. Fairing
8. Grommet
9. Mounting plate
10. Rivet
11. Pad
12. Cover hinge
13. Cover gasket
14. Cover
15. Rivets
16. Cover latch
17. Clip
18. Cam hook
19. Washer plate
20. Cam lock
21. Screw
22. Screw and washer
23. Mounting bracket
24. Clip nut
25. Screw
26. Gasket
27. Support bracket
28. Clamp
29. Support bracket
30. Bolt
31. Nut
32. Screw
33. Nut
34. Upper mounting bracket
35. Washer
36. Bolt
37. Washer
38. Locknut
39. Washer
40. Rubber pad

### Lower Fairings and Glove Boxes Removal/Installation (FLHTC-Ultra)

Refer to **Figure 3** for this procedure.

1. Remove the 2 screws securing the lower cap to the fairing. Remove the lower cap.
2. Remove the U-bolt nuts and retainer from inside the fairing. Then remove the U-bolt through the glove box opening. Remove the glove box.
3. Remove the bolt and nut securing the clamp that attaches the lower fairing to the engine. Remove the lower fairing.
4. Installation is the reverse of these steps, plus the following:
   a. The clamp on the engine guard must be positioned so that its flat tabs face to the rear of the motorcycle.
   b. Tighten the U-bolt nuts to 6 ft.-lb. (8.3 N•m).
   c. Tighten the engine guard clamp bolt and nut to 12 ft.-lb. (16.5 N•m).

## FAIRING AND WINDSHIELD (1986-1992 FLHT AND FLHTC)

### Outer Fairing Removal

Refer to **Figure 4** when performing this procedure.

1. Cover the front fender with a heavy blanket.
2. Disconnect the headlight electrical connector and remove the headlight.
3. Remove the bolts, nuts and washers attaching the outer fairing to the windshield and inner fairing.
4. Loosen the 4 bolts (2 bolts on each side) attaching the light bracket and outer fairing to the fork bracket. Remove the lower bracket bolt from each side, then lower the bracket and rest it on the front fender.
5. Remove the headlight trim ring mounting screw and remove the trim ring.
6. Remove the screws attaching the headlight assembly to the outer fairing. Remove the headlight assembly.
7. Working through the headlight opening in the fairing, loosen the locknuts securing the fairing studs to the fairing's mounting bracket. When the locknuts are loose, pull the fairing forward so that its mounting studs slide off of the mounting bracket slots, then remove the fairing.

## Windshield

### Removal

Refer to **Figure 4** for this procedure.

1. Remove the outer fairing as described in the previous procedure.
2. Remove the Acorn nuts, lockwashers, flat washers, nylon washers and screws securing the windshield to the inner fairing.
3. Lift the windshield off of the inner fairing.
4. Install by reversing these steps.

## Inner Fairing

### Removal

Refer to **Figure 5** when performing this procedure.

1. Disconnect the negative battery terminal.
2. Remove the outer fairing as described in this chapter.
3. Disconnect the speedometer cable at the instrument panel.
4. Disconnect the instrument, radio and gauge electrical connectors.

*NOTE*
*Record the routing path of the throttle and clutch cables so that you can route them the same way during installation.*

5. Disconnect the throttle and clutch cables. Then pull the cables back through their routing holes in the inner fairing. Do not bend or kink the cables when rerouting them.
6. Remove the screws securing the radio faceplate and cover to the fairing. Remove the faceplate and cover.
7. Remove the Allen screws securing the small fairing panel to the top of the handlebar.
8. Remove the radio.
9. Remove the handlebar clamp bolts and clamps and lift the handlebar away from the fairing.
10. At the ignition switch, pull the pin located underneath the switch bracket at the front of the inner fairing. Then remove the nut collar and lockwasher from the ignition switch.
11. Remove the ignition switch decal and then the screws securing the inner fairing to the ignition switch bracket.
12. Remove the screws securing the inner fairing to the upper fork bracket.
13. Check the inner fairing for any remaining wires, cables or fasteners. Then lift and remove the fairing from the motorcycle.

## Inner Fairing

### Installation

Refer to **Figure 5** when performing this procedure.

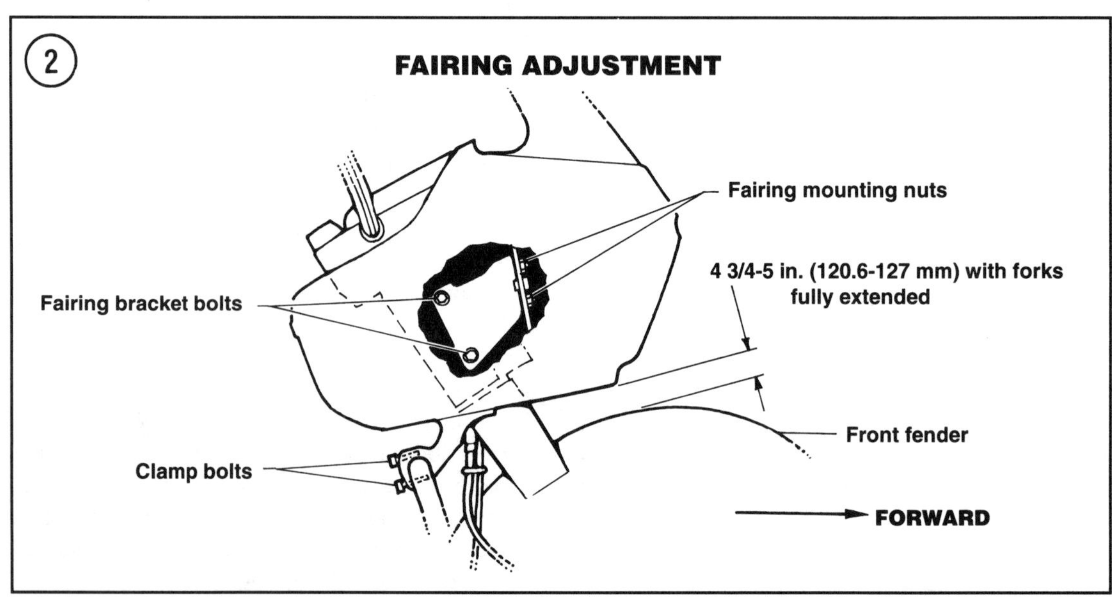

3

**GLOVE BOXES (FLT ULTRA AND FLHTC ULTRA)**

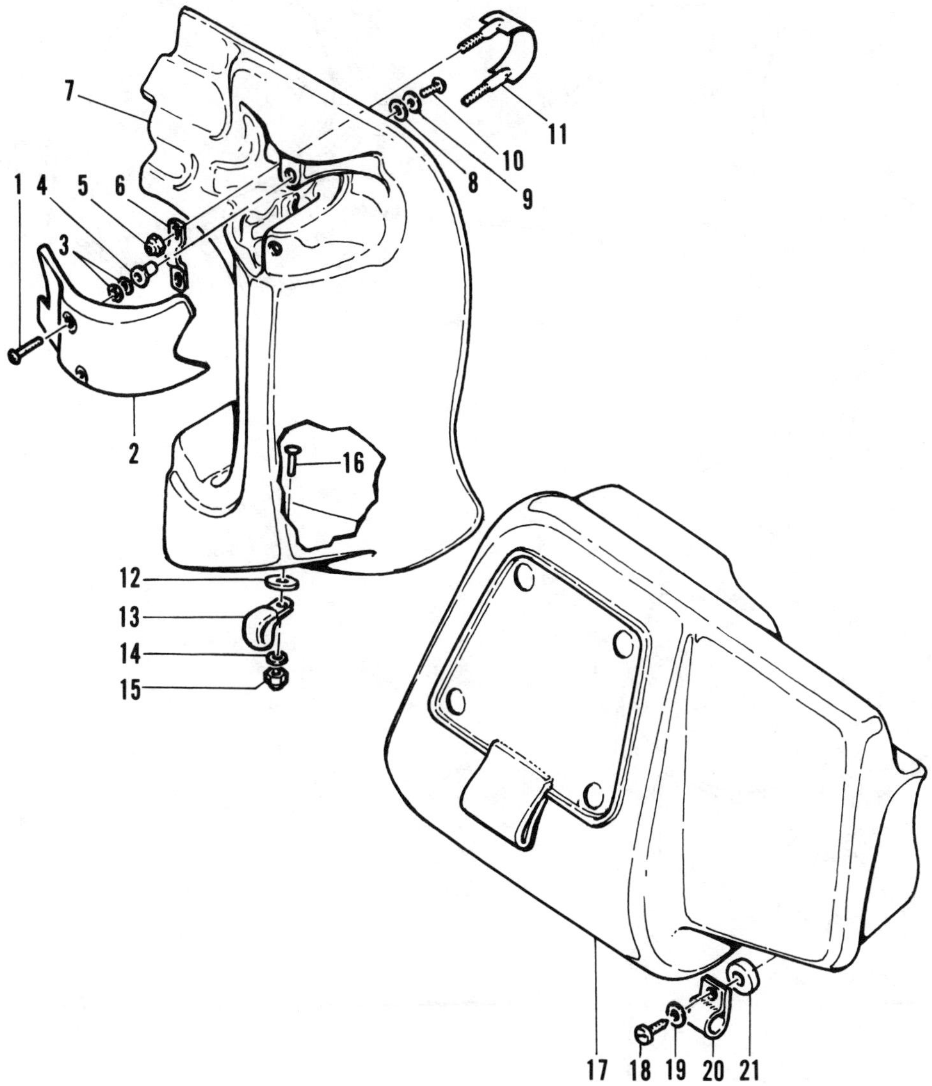

1. Screw
2. Cover
3. Washers
4. Bushing
5. Nut
6. Bracket
7. Box
8. Washer
9. Washer
10. Screw
11. Clamp
12. Washer
13. Clamp
14. Washer
15. Nut
16. Screw
17. Glove box
18. Screw
19. Washer
20. Clamp
21. Spacer

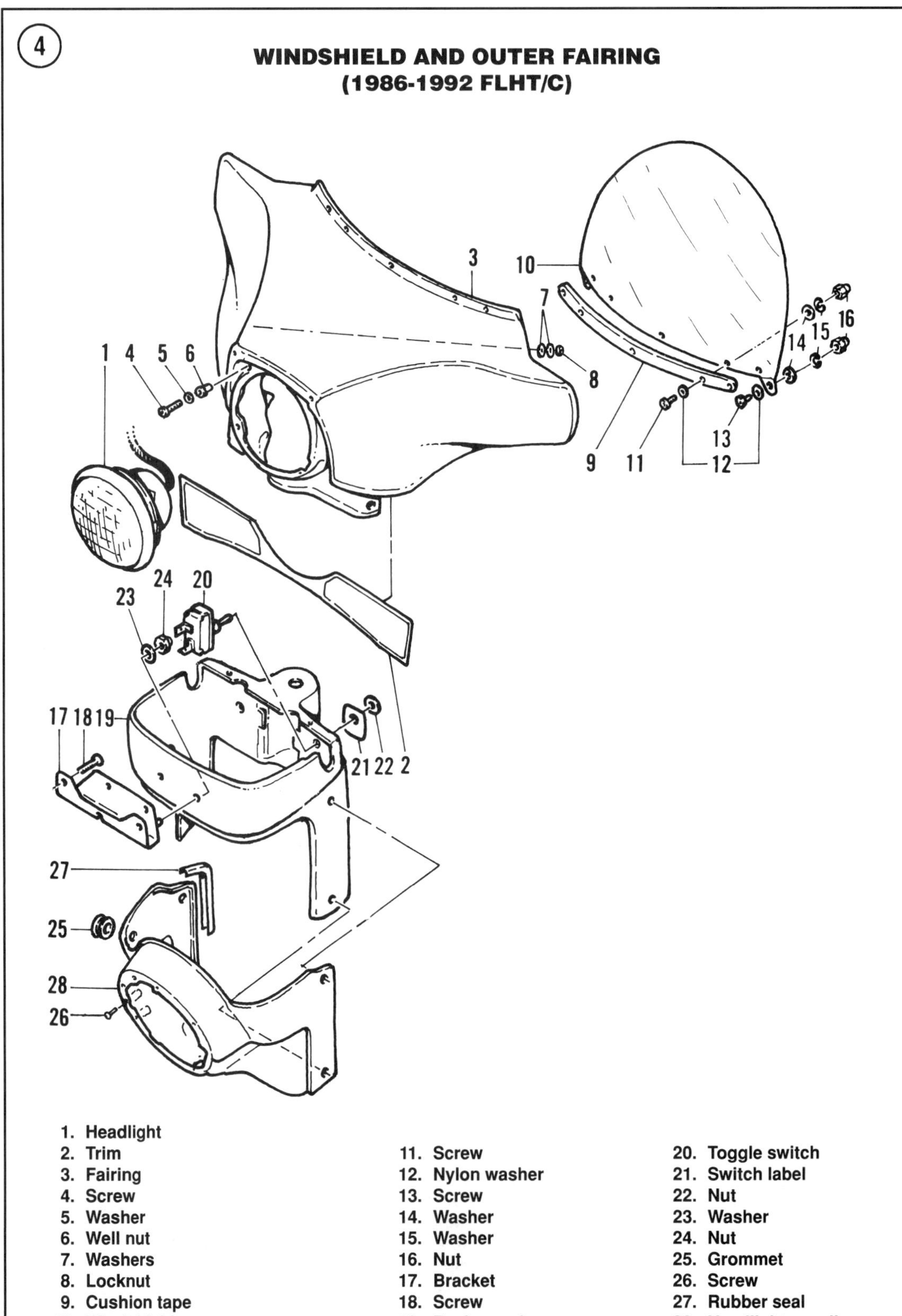


**WINDSHIELD AND OUTER FAIRING (1986-1992 FLHT/C)**

1. Headlight
2. Trim
3. Fairing
4. Screw
5. Washer
6. Well nut
7. Washers
8. Locknut
9. Cushion tape
10. Windshield
11. Screw
12. Nylon washer
13. Screw
14. Washer
15. Washer
16. Nut
17. Bracket
18. Screw
19. Dash panel
20. Toggle switch
21. Switch label
22. Nut
23. Washer
24. Nut
25. Grommet
26. Screw
27. Rubber seal
28. Headlight nacelle

1. Clean all of the electrical connectors with electrical contact cleaner.
2. Insert the throttle and clutch cables through the routing holes in the inner fairing.
3. Place the inner fairing so that it rests over the ignition switch. Snap the fairing support brackets into the bushings mounted on the lower fork bracket.
4. Install the screws securing the inner fairing to the ignition switch bracket. When the screws are tightened, their heads must be below the fairing surface. Then install a new ignition switch decal.
5. Install the lockwasher, collar and nut at the top threaded end on the ignition switch. Install the ignition switch knob.
6. Install the 2 inner fairing to upper fork bracket bolts finger-tight.
7. Place the handlebar into position along with its 2 clamps and screws. Position the handlebar and then tighten the clamp screws securely.
8. Install the radio.
9. Place the small fairing panel that mounts above the handlebar into position. Then install the radio faceplate and its cover and secure with its attaching screws.
10. Reconnect all of the electrical connectors previously disconnected.
11. Reconnect the speedometer cable.

### Outer Fairing/Windshield Installation

Refer to **Figure 4** when performing this procedure.
1. Install the inner fairing as described in the previous section.
2. Set the windshield into position next to the inner fairing, aligning the outer holes in the fairing with the corresponding holes in the fairing. Then slide a nylon washer onto the outer screw and insert the screw through the windshield and inner fairing. From the opposite side, slide a washer, lockwasher and Acorn nut onto the screw. Tighten the screw finger-tight and then install the opposite screw assembly. Tighten the Acorn nut finger-tight.
3. Place the outer fairing into position and install the remaining windshield fasteners; tighten fasteners finger-tight. Make sure to install the washers between the windshield and inner fairing as shown in **Figure 4**.
4. Install the locknuts onto the studs inside the headlight housing. Tighten the locknuts finger-tight, then check the inner and outer fairings where they meet. Reposition the outer fairing as required, then tighten the locknuts securely.
5. Position the light bracket in its mounting position by aligning the slots in the top of the bracket with the bolts installed in the lower fork bracket.
6. Install the lower fairing mounting bolts through the light bracket, outer fairing, inner fairing and into the lower fork bracket.
7. Before tightening the fairing mounting bolts, check the inner fairing rubber seal. The seal should seat evenly all the way around the inner fairing.
8. Tighten the fairing mounting bolts to 12-14 ft.-lbs. (16.5-19.3 N•m).
9. Tighten the windshield nuts and screws to 4 in.-lb. (0.5 N•m). Start with the inside fasteners and work toward the outside.

*CAUTION*
*Overtightening the windshield fasteners may cause the windshield to crack.*

10. Install the headlight assembly.
11. Reconnect the throttle and choke cables. Adjust both cables as described in Chapter Three. Check cable routing carefully before starting the engine. Then start the engine; do not shift the transmission out of NEUTRAL. Turn the handlebar from side to side without touching the throttle. If the idle speed rises at any time, the throttle cables are improperly routed. Reroute the cables as required.

*WARNING*
*Do not ride the motorcycle until the throttle and choke cables are routed correctly.*

### Lower Fairings and Glove Boxes Removal/Installation (FLHTC-Ultra)

Refer to **Figure 3** for this procedure.
1. Remove the 2 screws securing the lower cap to the fairing. Remove the lower cap.
2. Remove the U-bolt nuts and retainer from inside the fairing. Then remove the U-bolt through the glove box opening. Remove the glove box.
3. Remove the bolt and nut securing the clamp that attaches the lower fairing to the engine. Remove the lower fairing.

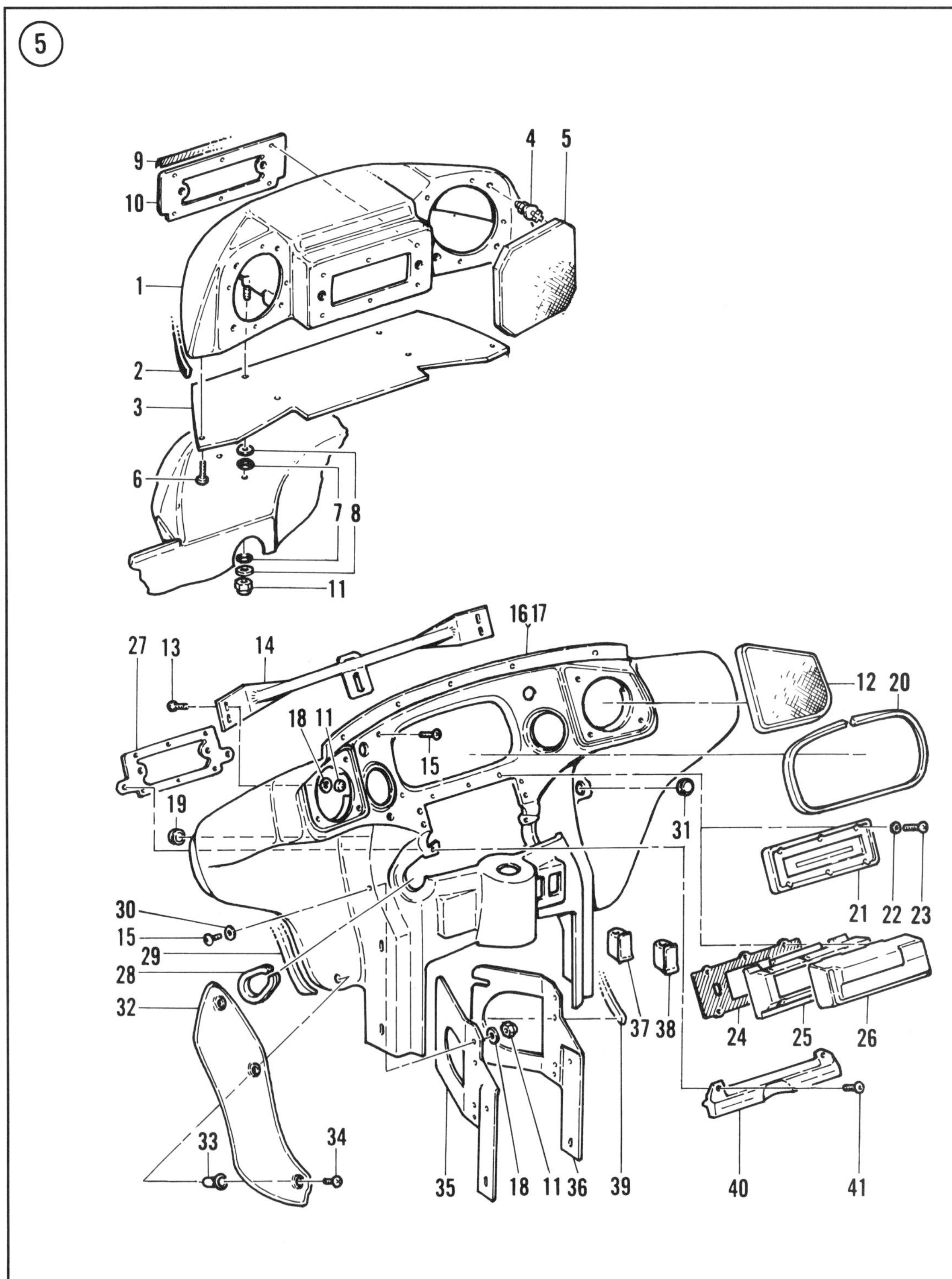
5
9
10
1
2
3
4
5
6
7
8
11
27
13
14
16
17
12
20
18
11
15
19
31
21
22
23
30
15
29
28
32
37
38
24
25
26
35
18
11
36
39
40
41
33
34

**INNER FAIRING (FLHT/C)**

1. Radio caddy
2. Trim
3. Bottom
4. Clip
5. Speaker grille
6. Screw
7. Rubber washer
8. Washer
9. Trim
10. Cover
11. Nut
12. Speaker grille
13. Screw
14. Bracket
15. Screw
16. Inner fairing
17. Trim
18. Washer
19. Grommet
20. Trim
21. Cover
22. Washer
23. Screw
24. Plate
25. Radio hood
26. Radio cover
27. Bracket
28. Grommet
29. Trim
30. Washer
31. Grommet
32. Air deflector
33. Well nut
34. Screw
35. Left bracket
36. Right bracket
37. Passing lamp switch
38. Hazard warning switch
39. Trim
40. Cover
41. Screw

4. Installation is the reverse of these steps, plus the following:
   a. The clamp on the engine guard must be positioned so that its flat tabs face to the rear of the motorcycle.
   b. Tighten the U-bolt nuts to 6 ft.-lb. (8.3 N•m).
   c. Tighten the engine guard clamp bolt and nut to 12 ft.-lb. (16.5 N•m).

## FAIRING AND WINDSHIELD (1993 FLHTC AND FLHTC ULTRA)

### Outer Fairing
### Removal

1. Cover the front fender with a heavy blanket.
2. Disconnect the headlight electrical connector and remove the headlight.
3. Remove the bolts, nuts and washers attaching the outer fairing to the windshield and inner fairing.
4. Loosen the 4 bolts (2 bolts on each side) attaching the light bracket and outer fairing to the fork bracket. Remove the lower bracket bolt from each side, then lower the bracket and rest it on the front fender.
5. Remove the headlight trim ring mounting screw and remove the trim ring.
6. Remove the screws attaching the headlight assembly to the outer fairing. Remove the headlight assembly.
7. Working through the headlight opening in the fairing, loosen the locknuts securing the fairing studs to its mounting bracket. When the locknuts are loose, pull the fairing forward so that its mounting studs slide off of the mounting bracket slots, then remove the fairing.

### Windshield
### Removal

Refer to **Figure 6**.

1. Remove the outer fairing as described in the previous section.
2. Remove the Acorn nuts, lockwashers, flat washers, nylon washers and screws securing the windshield to the inner fairing.
3. Lift the windshield off of the inner fairing.

### Inner Fairing Removal

1. Remove the seat.

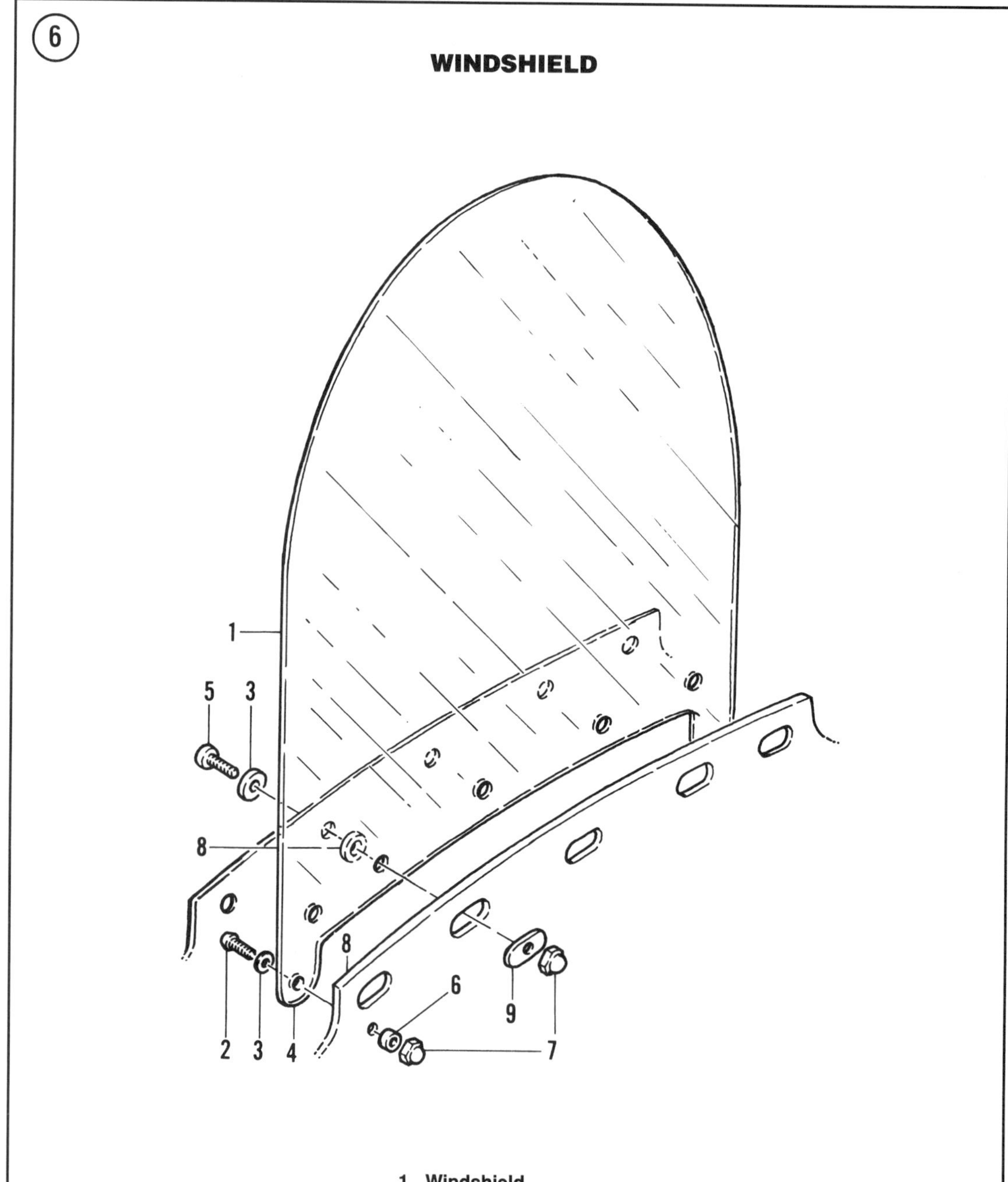


1. Windshield
2. Screw (12-24 × 11/16 in.)
3. Nylon washer
4. Mounting tab
5. Screw (12-24 × 7/8 in.)
6. Washer
7. Acorn nut
8. Inner fairing
9. Oblong washer

2. Disconnect the negative battery cable.
3. Remove the fuel tank as described in Chapter Eight.

NOTE

*While fuel tank removal is not required to remove the inner fairing, it will prevent accidental damage from occurring to the tank. If you leave the tank in place, cover it with a clean, thick towel or blanket.*

4. Remove the outer fairing as described in this chapter.
5. Disconnect the radio electrical connectors. Then remove the radio, mounting bracket and panel. Remove the mounting bracket and panel as an assembly.
6. Disconnect the throttle cables at the handlebar.
7. Disconnect and remove the front brake hose. Plug all hose openings to prevent contamination and brake fluid from dripping onto parts.
8. Disconnect the clutch cable at the handlebar.
9. Remove handlebar clamps.
10. Bleed pressure from anti-dive and remove anti-dive hose.
11. Disconnect the left- and right-hand handlebar switch electrical connectors. Set the handlebar assembly aside.
12. To remove the ignition switch knob:
    a. Insert the key in the ignition switch and turn the switch to the ACCESS position.
    b. Depress the small ignition switch button (on bottom side of switch) with a small screwdriver and then turn the key all the way counterclockwise. Then lift and remove the knob.
    c. Remove the ignition switch nut, collar, decal and screws (mounted underneath decal).
13. Remove the following components from the fairing assembly. To help with reassembly, label all of the wiring harnesses and their components as you remove and disconnect them. Use masking tape and a permanent type marking pen. Store fasteners in plastic bags, marked for reassembly.
    a. Wind deflectors and well nuts.
    b. Windshield.
    c. Speedometer cable.
    d. Left- and right hand radio speakers.
    e. Inner fairing cross bracket.
    f. Trip odometer.
    g. Lighter.
    h. Instrument panel, gauge and speaker wiring harnesses.
    i. Oil pressure and voltmeter gauges.
    j. Left- and right-hand outer fairing seals.
    k. Speaker grills.
    l. Rocker switches.
    m. Throttle cable and grommets.
    n. Clutch cable and grommets.
14. Check that all of the wiring harnesses and other components that will interfere with fairing removal have been removed.

NOTE

*When removing the inner fairing in Step 15, route the front brake hose through the radio opening in the fairing.*

15. Remove the inner fairing to upper fork bracket mounting bolts and remove the inner fairing.
16. If necessary, remove the fairing mounting brackets.
17. If replacing the inner fairing, remove the radio mounting bracket tabs.

### Inner Fairing Installation

1. If installing a new inner fairing, install the radio mounting bracket tabs, using a suitable adhesive or double-sided tape.
2. If removed install the fairing mounting brackets onto the fairing.
3. Position the fairing onto the fork brackets. Then route the front brake hose through the radio hole opening in the fairing.
4. Install the 2 inner fairing to upper fork bracket mounting bolts and tighten finger-tight.
5. Install the inner fairing components and accessories in the following order:
    a. Clutch cable and grommets.
    b. Throttle cable and grommets.
    c. Rocker switches.
    d. Radio speaker grills.
    e. Left- and right-hand outer fairing seals.
    f. Oil pressure gauge.
    g. Voltmeter.

NOTE

*The tripset cable strap should be installed on right-hand side of bulb on mounting bracket.*

h. Instrument cluster, gauge and speaker wiring harnesses.
i. Lighter.
j. Trip odometer.
k. Inner fairing cross brace.

*NOTE*
*Do not tighten the inner fairing cross brace mounting bolts until after the radio is installed.*

l. Radio speakers.
m. Speedometer cable.
n. Windshield.
o. Wind deflectors and well nuts.

6. Install the 2 inner fairing to ignition switch mounting screws (**Figure 7**).
7. Install a new ignition switch decal, collar (tab facing down) and nut. Tighten nut securely and install knob.
8. Place the handlebar onto the steering stem and reconnect the anti-dive hose.
9. Reconnect the handlebar switch connectors as follows:
   a. Insert the orange wire pin terminal into the violet 12-pin handlebar connector.
   b. Install a new 2-pin terminal bridge between the orange and yellow connector pins.
   c. On the left-hand side, connect the violet handlebar wiring connector and the 2-pin PTT switch wiring connector with the single-pin connector on the blue/yellow wire.
   d. On the right-hand side, connect the brown 12-pin connector housing. Then connector the 3-pin cruise set switch connector.
10. Install the handlebar grommets, handlebar and handlebar clamps. Tighten clamp bolts to 12-15 ft.-lb. (16-20 N•m).
11. Reconnect the clutch and throttle cables and adjust cables as described in Chapter Three.

*NOTE*
*On the clutch cable, adjust for a 1/8-3/16 in. (3.18-4.76 mm) gap between the cable's ferrule and bracket.*

12. Reconnect the front brake hose, using new washers, and tighten banjo bolt to 17-22 ft.-lb. (23-30 N•m).
13. To install radio:
   a. Install the radio mounting bracket and tighten mounting bolts to 4-6 ft.-lb. (5-8 N•m).
   b. Install the radio and reconnect the radio electrical connectors. Then tighten the fairing crossbrace.
   c. On Ultra models, tape the DIN connector with black PVC electrical tape.
14. Bleed the front brake as described in Chapter Thirteen.
15. Inflate the front suspension as described in Chapter Three.
16. Install fuel tank, if removed.
17. Reconnect the negative battery cable.
18. Turn on the ignition switch and check that all switches and lights operate correctly.
19. Install outer fairing and headlight. Check headlight operation.
20. Install seat.

## Outer Fairing/Windshield Installation

1. Install the inner fairing as described in the previous section.

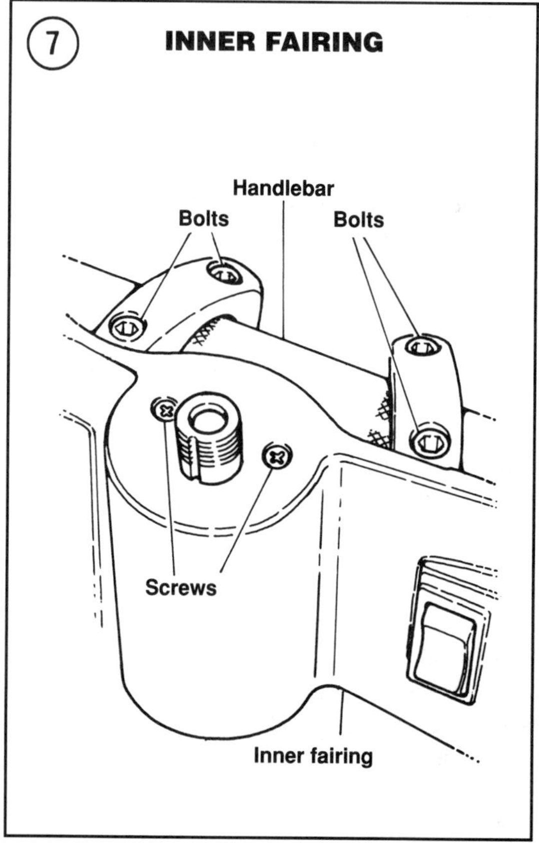

2. Set the windshield into position next to the inner fairing, aligning the outer holes in the fairing with the corresponding holes in the fairing. Then slide a nylon washer onto the outer screw and insert the screw through the windshield and inner fairing. From the opposite side, slide a washer, lockwasher and Acorn nut onto the screw. Tighten the screw finger-tight and then install the opposite screw assembly. Tighten the Acorn nut finger tight.

3. Place the outer fairing into position and install the remaining windshield fasteners; tighten fasteners finger-tight. Make sure to install the washers between the windshield and inner fairing as shown in Figure 6.

4. Install the locknuts onto the studs inside the headlight housing. Tighten the locknuts finger-tight, then check the inner and outer fairings where they meet. Reposition the outer fairing as required, then tighten the locknuts securely.

5. Position the light bracket in its mounting position by aligning the slots in the top of the bracket with the bolts installed in the lower fork bracket.

6. Install the lower fairing mounting bolts through the light bracket, outer fairing, inner fairing and into the lower fork bracket.

7. Before tightening the fairing mounting bolts, check the inner fairing rubber seal. The seal should seat evenly all the way around the inner fairing.

8. Tighten the fairing mounting bolts to 12-14 ft.-lbs. (16.5-19.3 N•m).

9. Tighten the windshield nuts and screws to 4 in.-lb. (0.5 N•m). Start with the inside fasteners and work outward.

*CAUTION*
*Overtightening the windshield fasteners may cause the windshield to crack.*

10. Install the headlight assembly.

11. Reconnect the throttle and choke cables. Adjust both cables as described in Chapter Three. Check cable routing carefully before starting the engine. Then start the engine; do not shift the transmission out of NEUTRAL. Turn the handlebar from side to side without touching the throttle. If the idle speed rises at any time, the throttle cables are improperly routed. Reroute the cables as required.

*WARNING*
*Do not ride the motorcycle until the throttle and choke cables are routed correctly.*

## FAIRING AND WINDSHIELD (1994 FLHTC AND FLHTC ULTRA)

### Outer Fairing Removal

1. Cover the front fender with a heavy blanket.
2. Disconnect the headlight electrical connector and remove the headlight.
3. Remove the bolts, nuts and washers attaching the outer fairing to the windshield and inner fairing.
4. Loosen the 4 bolts (2 bolts on each side) attaching the light bracket and outer fairing to the fork bracket. Remove the lower bracket bolt from each side, then lower the bracket and rest it on the front fender.
5. Remove the headlight trim ring mounting screw and remove the trim ring.
6. Remove the screws attaching the headlight assembly to the outer fairing. Remove the headlight assembly.
7. Working through the headlight opening in the fairing, loosen the locknuts securing the fairing studs to its mounting bracket. When the locknuts are loose, pull the fairing forward so that its mounting studs slide off of the mounting bracket slots, then remove the fairing.

### Windshield Removal

Refer to **Figure 6**.
1. Remove the outer fairing as described in the previous section.
2. Remove the Acorn nuts, lockwashers, flat washers, nylon washers and screws securing the windshield to the inner fairing.
3. Lift the windshield off of the inner fairing.



### Inner Fairing Removal

1. Remove the seat.
2. Disconnect the negative battery cable.
3. Remove the fuel tank as described in Chapter Eight.

*NOTE*
*While fuel tank removal is not required to remove the inner fairing, it will prevent accidental damage from occurring to the tank. If you leave the tank in place, cover it with a clean, thick towel or blanket.*

4. Remove the outer fairing as described in this chapter.
5. Remove passing lamp assembly.
6. Disconnect the radio electrical connectors. Then remove the radio, mounting bracket and panel. Remove the mounting bracket and panel as an assembly.
7. Remove the following electrical connectors from their T-stud mounts and then disconnect:
   a. 8-pin gray turn signal module connector.
   b. 3-pin front fender connector.
   c. 3-pin black main power connector.
   d. 12-pin gray main-to-interconnect harness connector.
   e. 12-pin black main-to-interconnect harness connector.
8. Remove the fairing crossbrace mounting fasteners and remove the fairing crossbrace.
9. On all models, remove the 6-pin gray handlebar switch connector from its T-stud and then disconnect.
10A. On Non-Ultra models, remove the 6-pin black radio control-to-interconnect harness connector from its T-stud and then disconnect.
10B. On Ultra models, remove the following electrical connectors from their T-stud mounts and then disconnect:
   a. 3-pin gray set/resume switch connector.
   b. 6-pin black radio overlay-to-radio control wiring harness.
   c. 6-pin black interconnect-to-radio overlay wiring harness.
11. On Ultra models, disconnect the red/green cruise switch terminal wire from the front interconnect harness.
12. Disconnect the 4-pin black ignition switch connector. On Ultra models, disconnect the 2-pin gray PTT switch connector. Remove the connector from its T-stud mount.
13. Remove the cable straps securing the interconnect harness to the anti-dive crossover tube.
14. Remove the 2-pin black anti-dive connector and the 12-pin gray handlebar switch connector from their T-studs and then disconnect.
15. Disconnect the blue/yellow and yellow/violet wires from the speaker switch.
16. Release pressure from the anti-dive assembly. Then remove the anti-dive hose.
17. Disconnect the throttle cables and clutch cable at the handlebar.
18. Remove the front brake hose at the handlebar.
19. Remove the handlebar holder mounting bolts and remove the handlebar.
20. To remove the ignition switch knob:
   a. Insert the key in the ignition switch and turn the switch to the ACCESS position.
   b. Depress the small ignition switch button (on bottom side of switch) with a small screwdriver and then turn the key all the way counterclockwise. Then lift and remove the knob.
   c. Remove the ignition switch nut, collar, decal and screws (mounted underneath decal).
21. If you are replacing the inner fairing assembly, remove the following components from the fairing assembly. To help with reassembly, label all of the wiring harnesses and their components as you remove and disconnect them. Use masking tape and a permanent type marking pen. Store fasteners in plastic bags, marked for reassembly.
   a. Wind deflectors and well nuts.
   b. Windshield.
   c. Speedometer cable.
   d. Left- and right hand radio speakers.
   e. 6-pin and 8-pin amp connectors.
   f. Trip odometer.
   g. Lighter.
   h. Instrument panel, gauge and other wiring harnesses.
   i. Oil pressure and voltmeter gauges.
   j. Left- and right-hand outer fairing seals.
   k. Speaker grills.
   l. Throttle cable and grommets.
   m. Clutch cable and grommets.
22. Check that all of the wiring harnesses and other components that will interfere with fairing removal have been removed.

*NOTE*
*When removing the inner fairing in Step 23, route the front brake hose through the radio opening in the fairing.*

23. Remove the inner fairing mounting brackets and remove the inner fairing.
24. If necessary, remove the fairing mounting brackets.
25. If replacing the inner fairing, remove the radio mounting bracket tabs.

## Inner Fairing Installation

1. If installing a new inner fairing, install the radio mounting bracket tabs, using a suitable adhesive or double-sided tape.
2. If removed install the fairing mounting brackets onto the fairing.
3. Position the fairing onto the fork brackets. Then route the front brake hose through the radio hole opening in the fairing.
4. Install the 2 upper inner fairing-to-upper fork bracket mounting bolts. Tighten bolts finger-tight.
5. Install and tighten the inner fairing bracket bolts.
6. If removed or disassembled, install the inner fairing components and accessories in the following order:
   a. Clutch cable and grommets.
   b. Throttle cable and grommets.
   c. Radio speaker grills.
   d. Left- and right-hand outer fairing seals.
   e. Oil pressure gauge.
   f. Voltmeter.

> NOTE
> *The tripset cable strap should be installed on the right-hand side of bulb on mounting bracket.*

   g. Instrument cluster, rocker switches and interconnect harnesses.

> NOTE
> *The ACC, spotlamp switch snap in and the cruise and speaker switch should be left loose when installing switches in sub-step g.*

   h. Lighter.
   i. Trip odometer.
   j. Amp 6-pin and 8-pin connectors.
   k. Radio speakers.
   l. Speedometer cable.
   m. Windshield.
   n. Wind deflectors and well nuts.

7. Install the 2 inner fairing to ignition switch mounting screws (**Figure 7**).
8. Install a new ignition switch decal, collar (tab facing down) and nut. Tighten nut securely and install knob.
9. Place the handlebar onto the steering stem and reconnect the anti-dive hose.
10. Install the handlebar grommets and holders. Tighten handlebar fasteners to 12-15 ft.-lb. (16-20 N•m).
11. Reconnect the clutch and throttle cables and adjust cables as described in Chapter Three.

> NOTE
> *On the clutch cable, adjust for a 1/8-3/16 in. (3.18-4.76 mm) gap between the cable's ferrule and bracket.*

12. Reconnect the front brake hose, using new washers, and tighten banjo bolt to 17-22 ft.-lb. (23-30 N•m) (steel and rubber washers) or 35 ft.-lb. (48.3 N•m) (copper washers).
13. Install the circuit breaker block and relays.
14. Align the handlebar grommets.
15. Reconnect the following connectors and secure them to the T-stud mounts:
   a. 2-pin black anti-dive connector.
   b. 2-pin gray handlebar switch connector. Route these wires behind the clutch cable prior to reconnecting the connector blocks.
16. Connect the speaker switch wires (blue/yellow and yellow/violet).
17. Install the speaker switch into position.
18. Connect the 4-pin black switch connector. Then insert the wires between the handlebar risers.
19. On Ultra models, connect the 2-pin gray PTT switch connector and secure to its T-stud mount.
20. Secure the interconnect harness to the anti-dive crossover tube.
21. Install the radio mounting bracket and fasteners; tighten fasteners to 4-6 ft.-lb. (5-8 N•m).
22. On Ultra models, connect the red/green wire (leading from the front interconnect harness) to the cruise switch terminal. Install the cruise switch.
23. On Ultra models, reconnect the following connectors and then attach to their T-stud mounts:
   a. 3-pin gray set/resume switch connector.
   b. 6-pin black radio overlay to radio control harness connector.
   c. 6-pin black interconnect to radio overlay connector.

24. On Non-Ultra models, connect the 6-pin black radio control-to-interconnect harness connector.
25. Install the fairing crossbrace and tighten its mounting fasteners finger-tight.
26. Reconnect the following connectors and then attach to their T-stud mounts:
   a. 8-pin gray turn signal module connector.
   b. 3-pin front fender connector.
   c. 3-pin black main power connector.
   d. 12-pin gray main harness-to-interconnect harness connector.
   e. 12-pin black main harness-to-interconnect harness connector.
27. Install the radio, then connect the following radio connectors:
   a. 8-pin black.
   b. 12-pin black.
   c. DIN cable.
   d. Antenna cable.

Connect each of the connectors to their T-stud mounts.
28. Tighten the fairing crossbrace bolts securely.
29. Bleed the front brake as described in Chapter Thirteen.
30. Inflate the front suspension as described in Chapter Three.
31. Install fuel tank, if removed.
32. Reconnect the negative battery cable.
33. Connect the passing light 8-pin connector. Then attach passing light cable onto the lower fork bracket and secure with cable straps.
34. Install the outer fairing, passing light and headlight. Check and adjust headlight aim as described in Chapter Nine.
35. Turn on the ignition switch and check that all switches and lights operate correctly.
36. Install seat.

### Outer Fairing/Windshield Installation

Refer to **Figure 6** when performing this procedure.
1. Install the inner fairing as described in the previous section.
2. Set the windshield into position next to the inner fairing, aligning the outer holes in the fairing with the corresponding holes in the fairing. Then slide a nylon washer onto the outer screw and insert the screw through the windshield and inner fairing. From the opposite side, slide a washer, lockwasher and Acorn nut onto the screw. Tighten the screw finger-tight and then install the opposite screw assembly. Tighten the Acorn nut finger tight.
3. Place the outer fairing into position and install the remaining windshield fasteners; tighten fasteners finger-tight. Make sure to install the washers between the windshield and inner fairing as shown in **Figure 6**.
4. Install the locknuts onto the studs inside the headlight housing. Tighten the locknuts finger-tight, then check the inner and outer fairings where they meet. Reposition the outer fairing as required, then tighten the locknuts securely.
5. Position the light bracket in its mounting position by aligning the slots in the top of the bracket with the bolts installed in the lower fork bracket.
6. Install the lower fairing mounting bolts through the light bracket, outer fairing, inner fairing and into the lower fork bracket.
7. Before tightening the fairing mounting bolts, check the inner fairing rubber seal. The seal should seat evenly all the way around the inner fairing.
8. Tighten the fairing mounting bolts to 12-14 ft.-lbs. (16.5-19.3 N•m).
9. Tighten the windshield nuts and screws to 4 in.-lb. (0.5 N•m). Start with the inside fasteners and work towards the outside.

*CAUTION*
*Overtightening the windshield fasteners may cause the windshield to crack.*

10. Install the headlight assembly.
11. Reconnect the throttle and choke cables. Adjust both cables as described in Chapter Three. Check cable routing carefully before starting the engine. Then start the engine; do not shift the transmission out of NEUTRAL. Turn the handlebar from side to side without touching the throttle. If the idle speed rises at any time, the throttle cables are improperly routed. Reroute the cables as required.

*WARNING*
*Do not ride the motorcycle until the throttle and choke cables are routed correctly.*

## FAIRING AND WINDSHIELD (FXRT AND FXRD)

### Windshield Removal/Installation

Refer to **Figure 8** when performing this procedure.

1. Remove the screws and washers securing the windshield to the fairing. Then lift the windshield and remove it.
2. Install by reversing these steps, plus the following:
   a. Install a nylon washer on each screw and install all of the screws finger-tight.
   b. Starting at the center of the windshield and working outward, tighten each screw to 4 in.-lb. (0.5 N•m).

*CAUTION*
*Overtightening the windshield screws may cause the windshield to crack.*

### Fairing Removal (All Models)

Refer to **Figure 8** when performing this procedure.

1. Support the bike so that the front wheel clears the ground.
2. *1986-on*: Disconnect the speedometer cable at the front wheel.

*NOTE*
*ID each of the mounting bolts and its washers so you don't mix them up during installation.*

3. Remove the upper and lower fairing mounting bolts.
4. Remove the bolts securing the fairing bracket to the steering head.
5. Slide the fairing forward to access the 12-pin electrical connector, then disconnect the connector and remove the fairing from the motorcycle.

*CAUTION*
*Do not allow the fairing to rest on the speedometer cable or it may kink the cable and damage it.*

### Installation (1984-1985)

1. Clean the electrical connectors with electrical contact cleaner.
2. With an assistant holding the fairing next to the motorcycle, reconnect the 12-pin electrical connector, then set the fairing onto its lower mounting brackets and align the fairing bracket lugs with the steering head threaded bushings.
3. Slide a 5/16 in. lockwasher on each of the 5/16 × 5/8 in. hex head bolts and insert the bolts through the bracket holes in the frame. Tighten the bolts finger-tight only.
4. Install the lower mounting support bolts as follows:
   a. Slide a flat washer and then a nylon washer on two of the 1/4 × 1 in. bolts.
   b. Place one nylon washer between the bottom of the fairing and the top of the lower mounting support at each hole in the support.
   c. Insert the bolts through the top of the fairing and through the lower mounting support, making sure the bolt passes through the nylon washer installed in sub-step b.
   d. Install the locknut and tighten to 8 ft.-lb. (11 N•m) while holding the bolt head with a wrench. Repeat to tighten the other locknut and bolt.
5. Tighten the 5/16 in. bolts installed in Step 3 to 19 ft.-lb. (26.2 N•m).
6. Align the fairing brace with the corresponding holes in the fairing on one side. Then install two 1/4 × 3/4 in. screws through the fairing and into the corresponding fairing brace holes. Install a lockwasher and nut. Tighten each nut to 10 ft.-lb. (13.8 N•m). Repeat for the other side.

*WARNING*
*Do not ride the motorcycle until the throttle and choke cables are routed correctly.*

### Installation (1986-on)

Refer to **Figure 8** for this procedure.

1. Clean the electrical connectors with electrical contact cleaner.
2. With an assistant holding the fairing next to the motorcycle, reconnect all of the electrical connec-

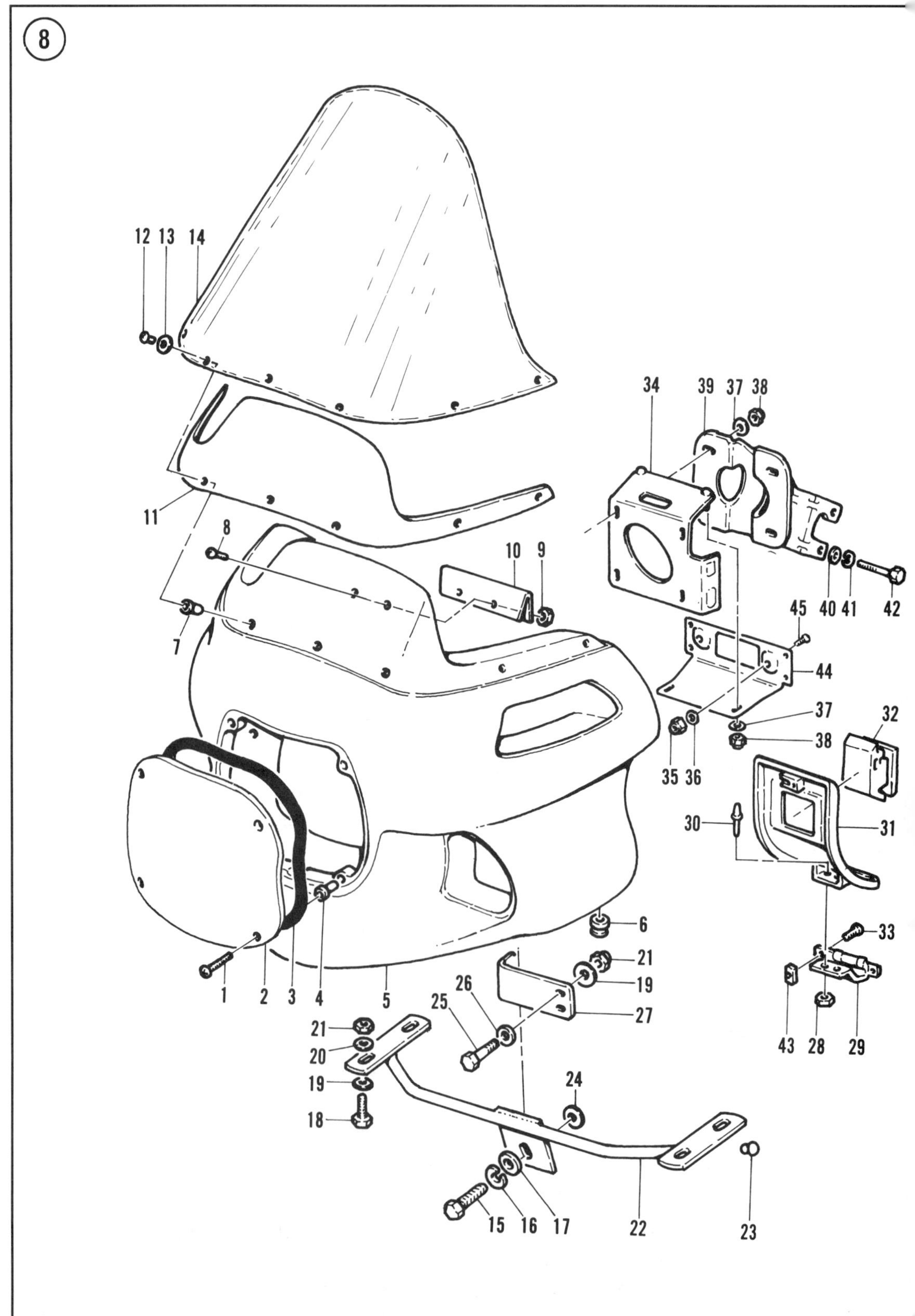
8
1
2
3
4
5
6
7
8
9
10
11
12
13
14
15
16
17
18
19
20
21
22
23
24
25
26
27
28
29
30
31
32
33
34
35
36
37
38
39
40
41
42
43
44
45

**WINDSHIELD AND FAIRING (FXRT AND FXRD)**

1. Screw
2. Cover
3. Seal
4. Screw
5. Fairing
6. Grommet
7. Well nut
8. Screw
9. Locknut
10. Bracket
11. Windshield seal
12. Screw
13. Washer
14. Windshield
15. Bolt
16. Lockwasher
17. Washer
18. Bolt
19. Washer
20. Washer
21. Nut
22. Mounting bracket
23. Plug
24. Washer
25. Bolt
26. Washer
27. Bracket support
28. Washer
29. Latch
30. Rivet
31. Fairing door
32. Door latch
33. Screw
34. Radio support bracket
35. Locknut
36. Washer
37. Washer
38. Nut
39. Bracket
40. Washer
41. Lockwasher
42. Bolt
43. Speed nut

tors, then set the fairing onto its lower mounting brackets and align the fairing bracket lugs with the steering head threaded bushings.

3. Slide a 5/16 in. lockwasher on each of the 5/16 × 5/8 in. hex head bolts and insert the bolts through the bracket holes in the frame. Tighten the bolts finger-tight.

4. Install the lower mounting support bolts as follows:

   a. The washers installed on the lower mounting support bolts have one plastic side and one metal side. Install the washers so that the metal side rests against the bolt head.
   b. The washers installed between the bottom of the fairing and the top of the lower mounting support are similar to those described in sub-step a. Install these washers so that the metal side rests against the lower mounting support.
   c. Insert the bolts through the lower support bracket and thread into the weld nuts inside the fairing, making sure each bolt passes through the washer installed in sub-step b.
   d. Tighten each bolt to 8 ft.-lb. (11 N•m).

5. Tighten the 5/16 in. bolts installed in Step 3 to 19 ft.-lb.

6. Align the fairing brace with the corresponding holes in the fairing on one side. Then install the bolts through the fairing and into the corresponding fairing brace holes. Then install a lockwasher and nut. Tighten each nut to 10 ft.-lb. (13.8 N•m). Repeat for the other side.

7. Reconnect the speedometer cable.

*WARNING*
*Do not ride the motorcycle until the throttle and choke cables are routed correctly.*

## WINDSHIELD (FXRS-CONV.)

### Removal/Installation

Refer to **Figure 9** when performing this procedure.

1. Support the bike on its jiffy stand.

2. Cover the headlight housing and the front turn signals with blankets before removing the windshield.

*NOTE*
*Use the key ring Allen wrench found in your tool kit to loosen and tighten the toggle bolt.*

3. Loosen the toggle bolt enough so that you can slip the toggle stop out of its notch in the toggle hinge. Repeat for the other side.

4. While supporting the windshield, disconnect the hinge from the fork tube; the toggle stop and bolt will remain with its toggle hinge. Repeat for the other side.

5. Lift the windshield off of the motorcycle.

*NOTE*
*When positioning the windshield onto the motorcycle in Step 6, make sure the lower portion of the windshield sits **behind** the front turn signals.*

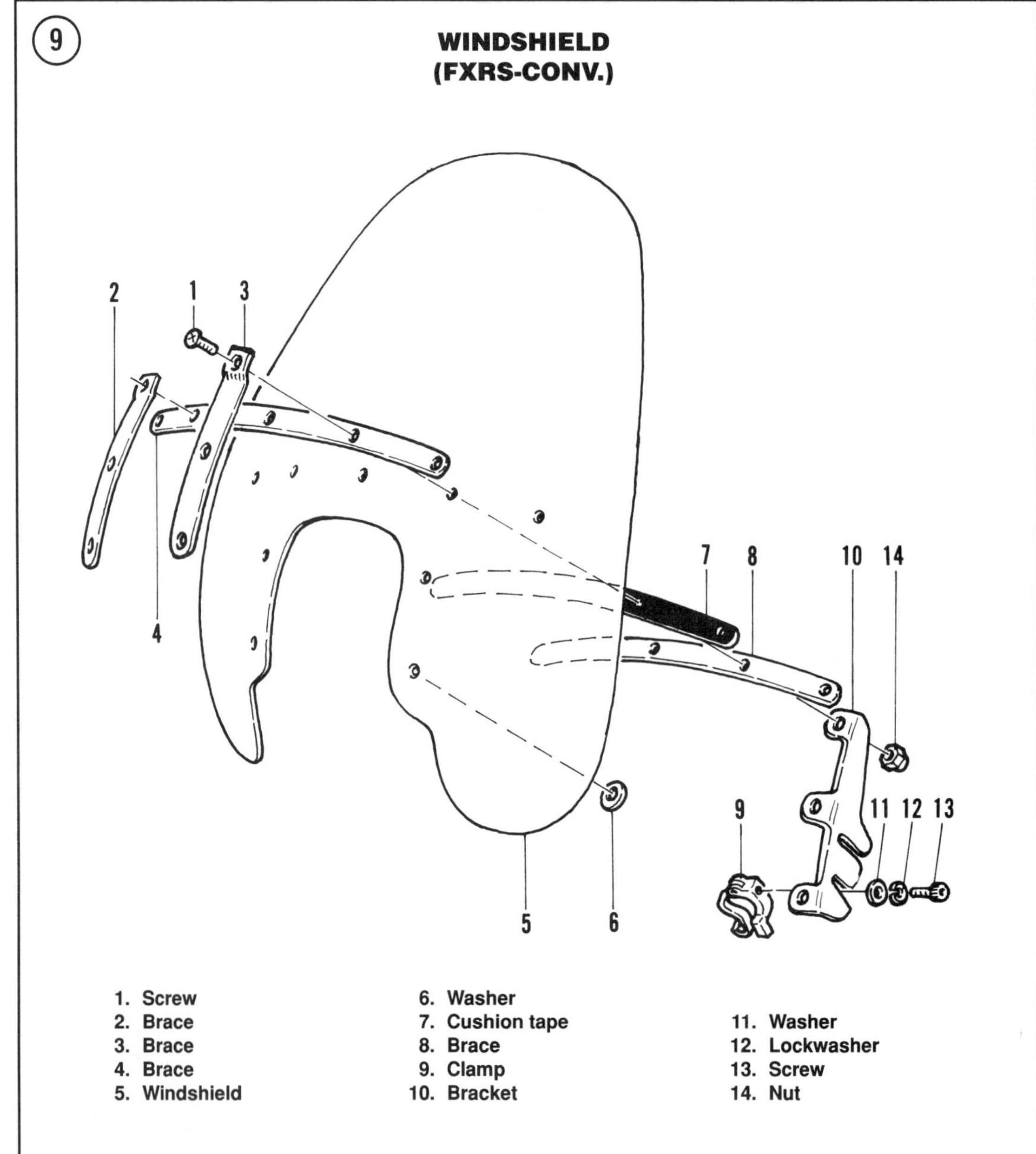

6. Set the windshield into position on the front fork, then wrap the hinges around the fork tubes and close them.

*CAUTION*
*The hinges must wrap around the fork tubes only. Do not allow them to close against a wiring harness or cable.*

7. Move the toggle stop on the toggle bolt into the notch in the hinge so that the lip on the stop faces out. Then tighten the toggle bolt finger-tight only. Repeat on the other side.
8. Check the position of the windshield, making sure no part of the windshield touches *any* part on the motorcycle. Reposition the windshield as required.

*CAUTION*
*The hinges holding the windshield to the fork tubes produce their maximum clamp load when the toggle bolts are tightened to a snug fit. To prevent overtightening the toggle bolts in Step 9, use the key ring Allen wrench supplied in your motorcycle's tool kit. Overtightening the toggle bolts will cause the hinge to loosen and the windshield to vibrate.*

9. Tighten the toggle bolts to a *snug* fit using the key ring Allen wrench (see previous *CAUTION*).

*NOTE*
*The Allen head bolts holding the hinge to the bracket can be used to make minor windshield adjustments. If necessary, loosen these bolts and adjust the windshield. Tighten the bolts after adjusting the windshield.*

10. Check that the hinge-to-bracket Allen head bolts are tight.

## WINDSHIELD (FLHS)

### Removal/Installation

Refer to **Figure 10** when performing this procedure.

1. Remove the bolts, flat washers, lockwashers and nuts holding the windshield to the outer bracket. Then remove the windshield.
2. Install the windshield by aligning the slots in the windshield mounting brackets with the holes in the outer mounting brackets. Install the bolts, flat washers, lockwashers and nuts. Tighten finger-tight only.
3. Adjust windshield as follows:
   a. Windshield is properly adjusted when rider, sitting on seat, can see over the top of windshield.
   b. Reposition the windshield at its adjusting brackets.
   c. Tighten nuts and bolts and recheck adjustment.

*CAUTION*
*The windshield must not touch the headlight housing. In addition, the lower edge on the lower window must align with the bottom of the instrument panel.*

*NOTE*
*If the outer spotlight brackets were removed, make sure to install the spacer between the outer bracket and light brackets during reassembly.*

## TOUR-PAK

The following procedures describe removal/installation of the factory Tour-Pak.

Because the passenger backrest is mounted onto the front of the Tour-Pak, check the Tour-Pak and backrest mounting bolts periodically for tightness. Missing fasteners should be replaced immediately.

*WARNING*
*Cargo packed into the Tour-Pak will change the handling of the motorcycle. Refer to your owner's manual on packing cargo and maximum allowable cargo weight.*

### Removal/Installation
### Ultra Models

Refer to **Figure 11** when performing this procedure.

1. Open the Tour-Pak and remove the liner to access the mounting bolts.
2. Disconnect the antenna cable and its ground lead from inside the Tour-Pak. Then remove the grommet and remove the cable by pulling it through the hole in the Tour-Pak.
3. Disconnect the 3-pin brake and taillight connector on the left-hand luggage rack.

4. To disconnect the speaker connectors:
   a. Remove the seat.
   b. Disconnect the left- and right-hand speaker wire connectors.
   c. Remove the cable straps, as required.

*NOTE*
*To remove the speakers from the Tour-Pak, remove the speaker bolts holding each speaker to the Tour-Pak. Then remove the speakers and secure them with wire or a Bungee cord. To remove the speakers from the motorcycle, remove the seat to access the speaker connectors (Step 4).*

*NOTE*
*The Tour-Pak can be moved forward or backward to adjust the passenger backrest position by approximately 1 1/4 in.*

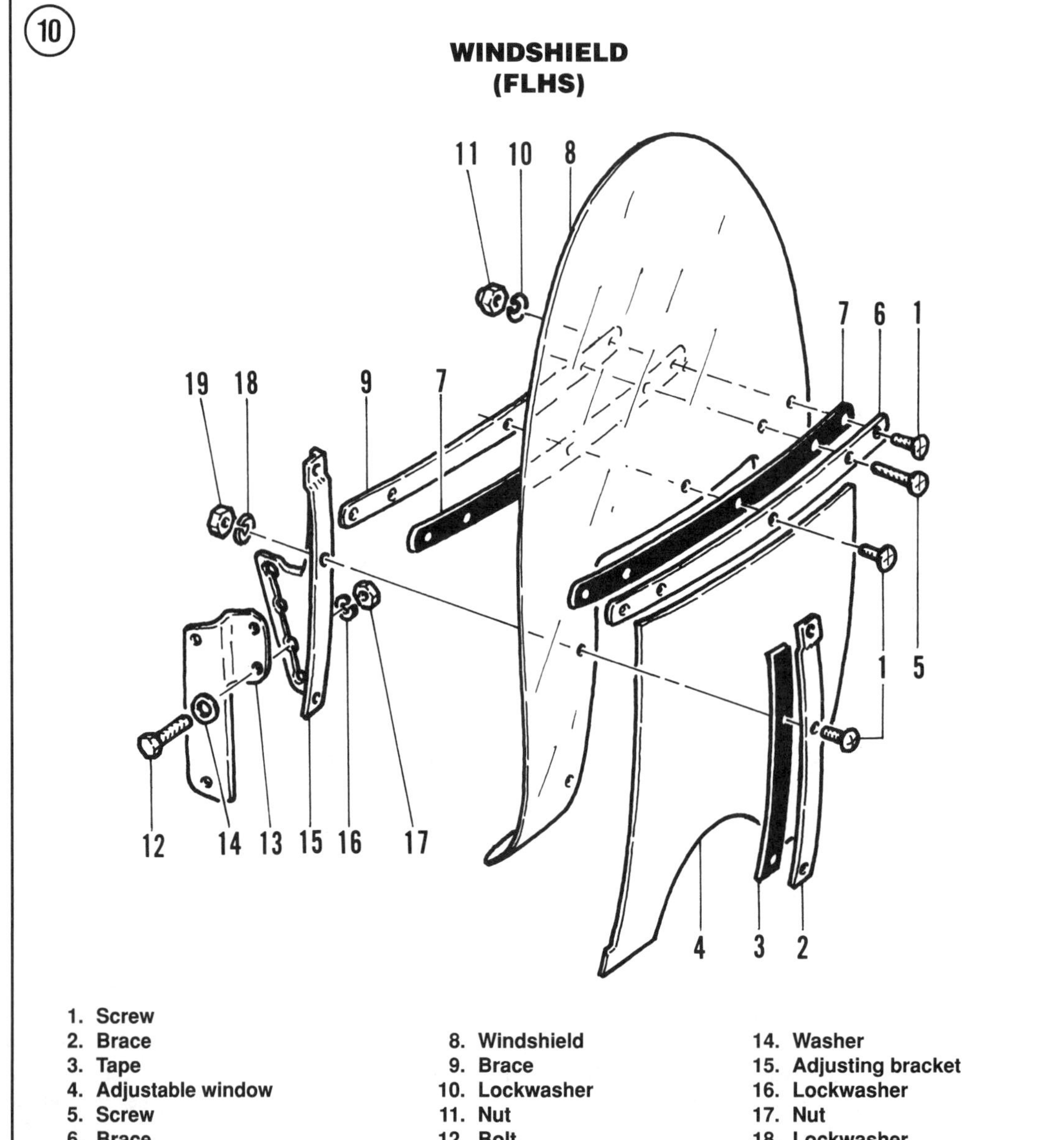


1. Screw
2. Brace
3. Tape
4. Adjustable window
5. Screw
6. Brace
7. Tape
8. Windshield
9. Brace
10. Lockwasher
11. Nut
12. Bolt
13. Bracket
14. Washer
15. Adjusting bracket
16. Lockwasher
17. Nut
18. Lockwasher
19. Nut

*(31.7 mm). Before removing the Tour-Pak mounting bolts, note the bolt holes used in the bottom of the Tour-Pak. You may want to reinstall the Tour-Pak into its original mounting position or change it. The Tour-Pak was originally installed in its forward mounting position.*

5. Remove the bolts retaining the Tour-Pak to the luggage rack and remove the Tour-Pak.

6. Installation is the reverse of these steps, plus the following:

   a. Clean all of the electrical connectors with electrical contact cleaner.

   b. Make sure the antenna and its ground lead are connected properly.

**Removal/Installation (All Models Except Ultra)**

Refer to **Figure 11** when performing this procedure.

1. Open the Tour-Pak and remove the liner to access the mounting bolts.

2. Disconnect the antenna cable and its ground lead and the light connectors.

*NOTE*
*The Tour-Pak can be moved forward or backward to adjust the passenger backrest position by approximately 1 1/4 in.*

*(31.7 mm). Before removing the Tour-Pak mounting bolts, note the bolt holes used in the bottom of the Tour-Pak. You may want to reinstall the Tour-Pak into its original mounting position or to change it. The Tour-Pak was originally installed in its forward mounting position.*

3. Remove the bolts holding the Tour-Pak to the luggage rack and remove the Tour-Pak.

4. Installation is the reverse of these steps, plus the following, if so equipped.

   a. Clean all of the electrical connectors with electrical contact cleaner.

   b. Make sure the antenna and its ground lead are connected properly.

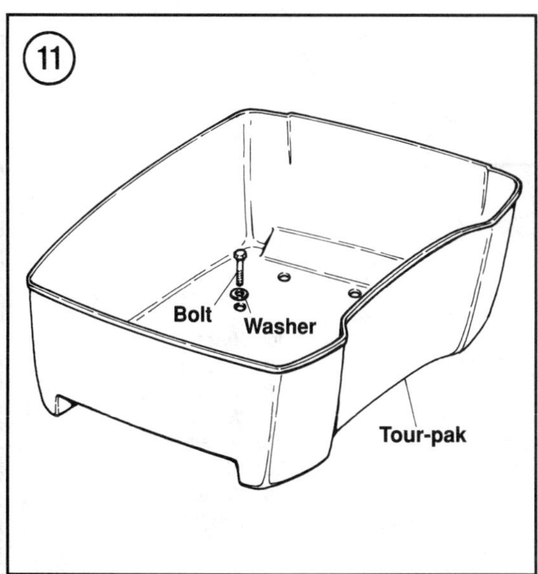


**Tour-Pak Passenger Backrest Removal/Installation**

1. Open the Tour-Pak and locate the fasteners securing the backrest to the Tour-Pak cover. Remove these fasteners and remove the backrest.

2. Install by reversing these steps.

## SADDLEBAGS

**Removal/Installation (FLT)**

Refer to **Figure 12**, typical when performing this procedure.

1. Remove the saddlebag cover.

2. Lift the wire loop on the 1/4 turn fastener and turn the fastener counterclockwise until they release from their retainer. Repeat for each 1/4 turn fastener, then lift and remove the saddlebag. Remove the rubber washers.

3. Installation is the reverse of these steps, plus the following:

   a. Reinstall the 1/4 turn fasteners along with their rubber washers. Make sure each of the 1/4 turn fasteners engage and lock with their retainer.

   b. Make sure the catches at the front of the saddlebag cover engage its latch properly. If not, the cover may come off.

15

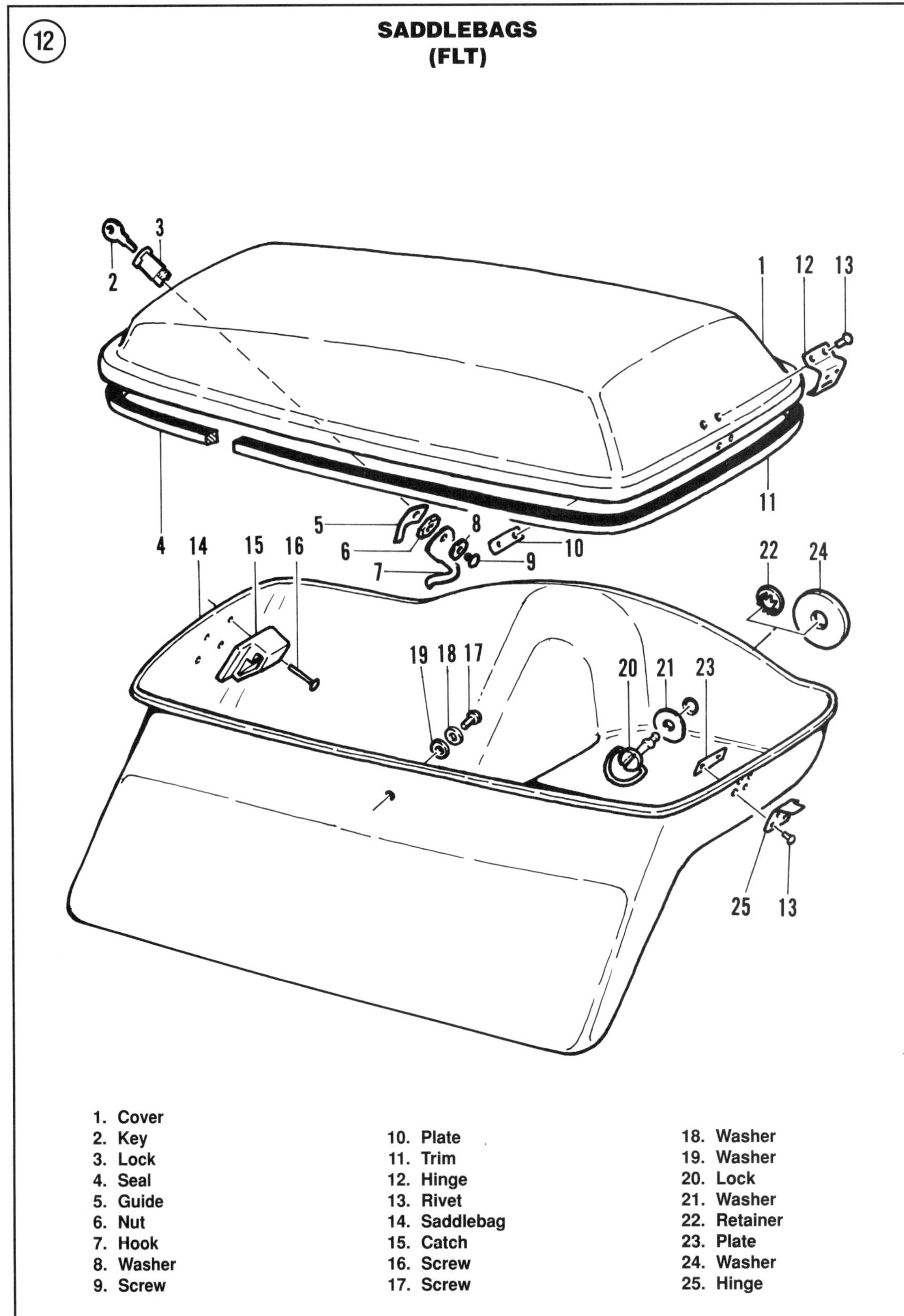


1. Cover
2. Key
3. Lock
4. Seal
5. Guide
6. Nut
7. Hook
8. Washer
9. Screw
10. Plate
11. Trim
12. Hinge
13. Rivet
14. Saddlebag
15. Catch
16. Screw
17. Screw
18. Washer
19. Washer
20. Lock
21. Washer
22. Retainer
23. Plate
24. Washer
25. Hinge

### Removal/Installation (FXRT and FXRP)

Refer to **Figure 13**, typical when performing this procedure.

1. Remove the saddlebag cover and the inner luggage bag.
2. Remove the bolts, washers and nuts holding the inner saddlebag cover to its support bracket and remove the saddlebag.
3. Install by reversing these steps, plus the following.
4. Each mounting bolt assembly used to secure the inner saddlebag to its support bracket consists of a bolt, 2 rubber washers, 2 steel washers, a lockwasher and nut. When installing the mounting bolt assembly, make sure to install the rubber washers so that they seat against the saddlebag. See **Figure 11**.
5. Tighten all of the mounting bolts finger-tight. Then tighten the bolts to 35 in.-lb. (4 N•m).

### Removal/Installation (FXRS-CONV.)

Refer to **Figure 14** when performing this procedure.

1. Pull the saddlebag handle out from underneath the fender brace.

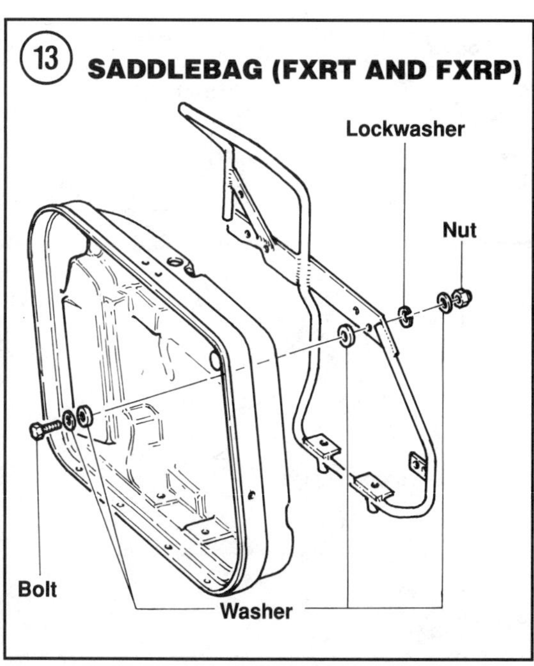


*NOTE*
*Use the saddlebag handle to support the saddlebag when removing the screws in Step 2.*

2. Unscrew and remove the saddlebag screws and remove the saddlebag.
3. Install the saddlebag screws into the fender brace sockets while the saddlebag is off the bike.
4. Install by reversing these steps. Make sure to tuck the saddlebag handles under the fender brackets.

*WARNING*
*The saddlebag handles are not designed to be used as passenger grab handles. Make sure to tuck the handles under the fender brackets. Do not allow passengers to grab the saddlebag handles.*

## SEAT

Seat removal is often required to access various components during service. Work carefully around the seat to prevent tearing it.

### Removal/Installation (FLT)

1A. On 1984-1990 models, remove the bolts and washers securing the seat to the handrail. Then pull the seat up and back and remove it.

1B. On 1991-on models, perform the following:

a. Open the Tour-Pak cover.
b. Remove the seat screw securing the seat to the luggage rack.

*NOTE*
*The rear seat screw is located in the middle of the seat between the rear of the seat and the Tour-Pak. To access the rear seat screw, the Tour-Pak must be positioned in its rear position.*

c. Remove the rear seat screw. Then pull the seat up and back and remove it.

2. Install by reversing these steps.

### Removal/Installation (FXR Fixed Seat)

1. Remove the rear fender pad screw, lockwasher and plastic washer.

2. Pull the seat back to clear its frame mounting bracket and remove the seat.

3. Install by reversing these steps. Install the plastic washer between the seat mounting bracket and fender.

### Removal/Installation (FXR Hinged Seat)

1. Raise the seat and remove the seat stop cord from the battery bracket bolt.

2. Remove the plastic sleeve from the seat pins, then slide the seat forward and remove it.

3. To remove the passenger seat, remove the rear bolt and slide the seat back and off of the fender. If your model is equipped with a factory installed sissy bar, remove the 2 front mounting bolts before removing the seat.

4. Install by reversing these steps.

### Removal/Installation (FXWG, FXEF and FXSB)

1. Remove the seat mounting bolt(s) and remove the seat.

2. Install by reversing these steps.

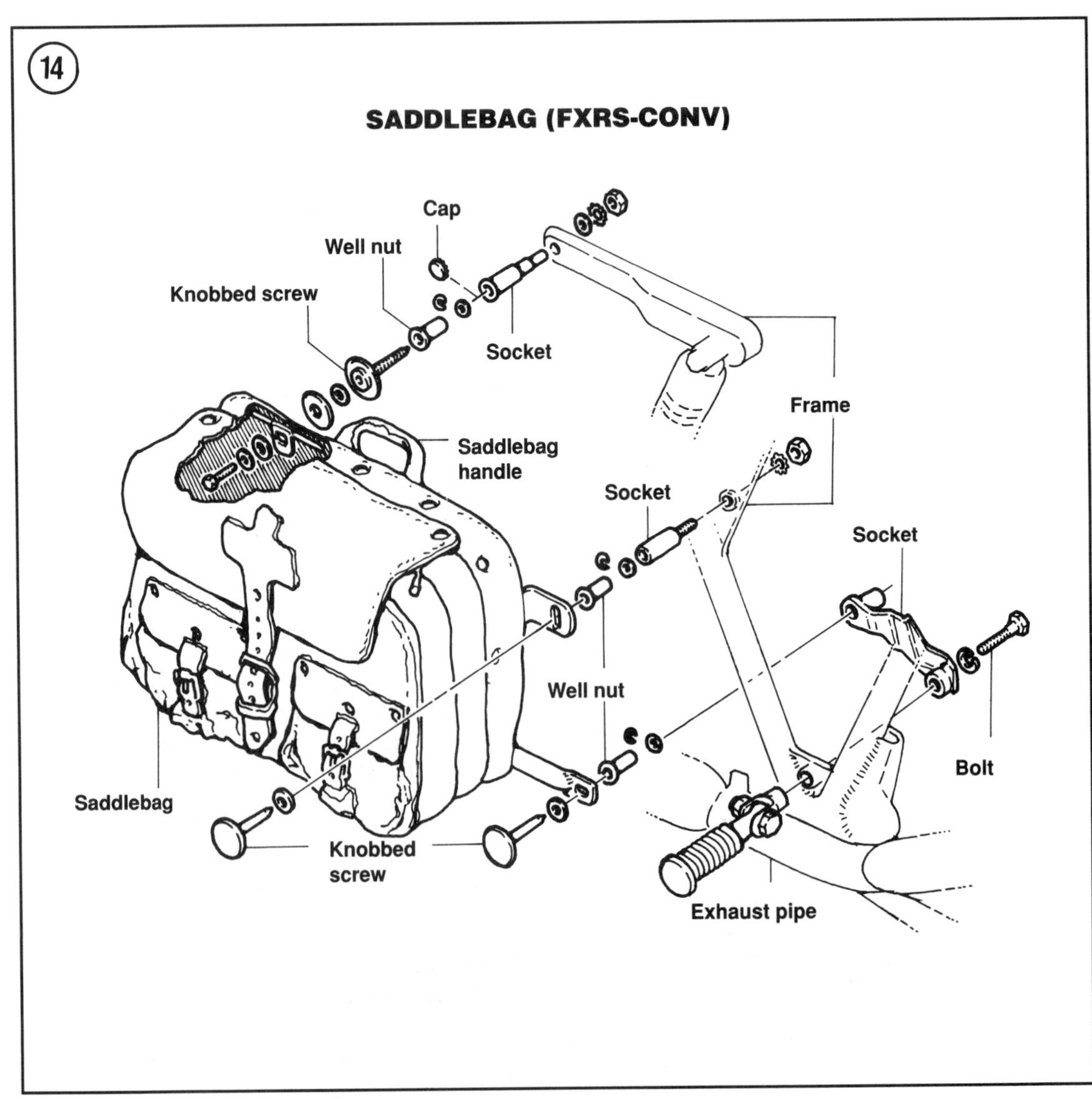

## FRONT FENDER

### Removal/Installation (FLT and FXR)

1. Place the bike on a stand so that the front wheel clears the ground.
2. Disconnect the speedometer cable and remove it away from the front fender.
3. Remove the front wheel as described in Chapter Ten.
4. *FLT*: Disconnect the fender tip light bulb connector.
5. If bolt tabs are used, bend the tabs away from the bolt heads.
6. Remove the fender mounting bolts and nuts and remove the front fender.
7. On FLT models, note the following:
   a. The bumper cushion mounted on the front of the fender can be replaced by removing the nut washer from inside the fender. The side reflectors installed on the bumper cushion can be replaced by removing the speed nut holding the reflector in place.
   b. The lamp assembly mounted on the top of the front fender can be removed by first removing the lens and gasket. Then remove the nut and lockwasher from inside the fender and lift the lamp off of the fender along with the mounting bolt and lockwasher.
   c. The fender skirt mounted on the rear of the fender is held in place with a number of screws, washers and nuts. Remove these to remove the fender skirt.
8. Installation is the reverse of these steps, plus the following:
   a. Tighten the fender mounting bolts to 16-20 ft.-lb. (22-27.6 N•m).
   b. If bolt tabs were used, bend the tabs flush against the bolt heads after tightening the bolts. Replace tabs that are weak or broken.

### Removal/Installation (FXWG, FXEF and FXSB)

1. Support the bike on its jiffy stand.
2. Remove the bolts, washers and/or nuts securing the front fender to the front sliders. Remove the front fender.
3. Installation is the reverse of these steps. Make sure the front fender lamp, if so equipped, works properly.

## REAR FENDER

### Removal/Installation (FLT)

*NOTE*

*ID all frame and fender fasteners as you remove them in the following steps so that you can reinstall them in their original position.*

1. Place the bike on a stand so that the rear wheel clears the ground.
2. Disconnect the negative battery cable.
3. Remove the Tour-Pak as described in this chapter.
4. Remove the saddlebags as described in this chapter.
5. Remove the seat as described in this chapter.
6. Remove the upper shock mounting bolts and washers.
7. Remove the bolt securing the fender to the frame cross member.
8. Remove the bolts, lockwashers and nuts securing the lower saddlebag guard to the fender bumper.
9. Remove the bolts and lockwashers securing the fender brace to the fender.
10. Remove the taillight and turn signal light wires from the terminal block. Slip the wires through the fender hole and remove them.
12. Carefully guide the rear fender out of its mounting position and remove it.
13. Installation is the reverse of these steps, plus the following.
14. Replace all worn or damaged fasteners as required.
15. After reconnecting the taillight and turn signal light wire electrical connectors, reconnect the negative battery cable and check the taillight and turn signals for proper operation.
16. Tighten the fender mounting bolts and nuts to 19 ft.-lb. (26.2 N•m).

### Removal/Installation (FXR)

*NOTE*
*ID all frame and fender fasteners as you remove them in the following steps so you can reinstall them in their original position.*

1. Place the bike on a stand so that the rear wheel clears the ground.
2. Disconnect the negative battery cable.
3. Remove the seat as described in this chapter.
4. Remove the left-hand side cover.

*NOTE*
*Label the taillight wires and their mounting position on the terminal block when removing them in Step 5.*

5. Disconnect the taillight terminal block and remove the terminal block from its mounting plate. Then disconnect the 2 gray wires from the terminal block using the Harley-Davidson Pin Terminal Tool (part No. HD-97363-71) or equivalent.
6. Place a block of wood underneath the rear wheel and remove the upper shock mounting bolts (both sides). Then remove the wood block and lower the rear wheel to the ground.
7. Remove the front fender to frame rail mounting bolt from underneath the fender.
8. Remove the side plate-to-rear fender mounting screws (both sides).
9. Remove the turn signal bracket bolts, then remove the bracket while pulling the signal wire through the hole in the fender.
10. Remove the remaining fender bolts (located underneath the fender) and remove the fender (and sissy bar side plates if so equipped).
11. Discard the 2 speed nuts securing the taillight to the fender.
12. Installation is the reverse of these steps, plus the following.
13. Install new taillight-to-fender speed nuts.
14. After reconnecting the taillight and turn signal light wire electrical connectors, reconnect the negative battery cable and check the taillight and turn signals for proper operation.

### Removal/Installation (FXWG)

*NOTE*
*ID all frame and fender fasteners as you remove them in the following steps so that you can reinstall them in their original positions.*

1. Disconnect the negative battery cable.
2. Remove the seat as described in this chapter.

*NOTE*
*ID all wires before disconnecting them in Step 3.*

3. Disconnect the wiring harness connector(s) interfering with rear fender removal.
4. Remove the screws securing the terminal block to the fender and set the terminal block aside.
5. Remove the taillight and license plate bracket from the rear fender.
6. Remove the rear fender mounting hardware and remove the rear fender. Pull the wiring harness connectors through the fender as required to remove the fender.
7. Installation is the reverse of these steps. Note the following.
8. After pulling the wiring harness through the fender, secure the wiring harness with the fender clips.
9. After connecting the negative battery cable, turn the ignition switch ON and check turn signal and taillight operation. Do not ride the motorcycle until these lights are operating properly.

### Removal/Installation (FXEF and FXSB)

*NOTE*
*ID all frame and fender fasteners and mounting brackets as you remove them in the following steps so you can reinstall them in their original positions.*

1. Disconnect the negative battery cable.
2. Remove the seat as described in this chapter.
3. Disconnect the taillight wiring harness connector.
4. Remove the circuit breakers from their mounting clips on the fender.

5. Remove the rear fender mounting fasteners and reposition the rear fender to access the taillight wires.

*NOTE*
*ID the wires and their mounting position before removing them in Step 6.*

6. Remove the taillight wire pins at the connector and pull the wiring harness through the fender. Remove the fender.
7. Installation is the reverse of these steps, plus the following.
8. If you are installing a new fender, drill out the pop rivets securing the circuit breaker clips to the fender with a 1/4 in. (6.35 mm) drill bit. Remove the clips and rivet them to the new fender.
9. If you are installing a new fender, install new speed nuts when transferring the parts to the new fender.
10. After connecting the negative battery cable, turn the ignition switch ON and check the turn signal and taillight operation. Do not ride the motorcycle until these lights are operating properly.

## FRAME

The frame is the "skeleton" of your motorcycle. It has been designed to support the engine, transmission and suspension systems and all other components in their proper relationship so that the motorcycle can operate as a unit. In addition, the frame is a determining factor in the overall styling of the motorcycle. Because of its importance in the overall operation of the motorcycle, proper frame care should include frequent cleaning and inspection. In addition, the frame should be inspected immediately after any accident or spill. If necessary, the frame should be mounted on a jig and checked for damage. Frame repair, which usually includes welding, should be performed by a dealer or frame specialist.

*CAUTION*
*Do not refer frame repair to an inexperienced repair shop or welder.*

### Frame Inspection

Certain areas on the frame are more susceptible to stress and wear damage. The following areas should be inspected on a yearly schedule or whenever the bike has been involved in an accident or spill.

1. Closely examine the paint on the frame. Flaking or chipping paint can be an early sign of frame bending or damage. Investigate these areas closely before repainting.

*NOTE*
*A bent frame tube can usually be straightened by heating and bending it back into shape. However, because this section may now be weaker than it was originally, the area may require additional repair in the form of tube sleeving, additional bracing or gusseting. Unless you are experienced in frame repair, do not attempt to straighten or weld a frame to repair it. Refer all frame repair to a frame specialist.*

2. All motorcycles vibrate to some degree. However, if you notice an increase in vibration, park the bike and go over it thoroughly. Abnormal vibration can be caused by loose or worn parts or from a broken or damaged frame member.
3. Loose or damaged engine mount bolts can cause frame breakage or engine mount damage. Check for loose or missing fasteners. Refer to the respective chapters for engine, transmission and primary drive bolt tightening torques. Replace worn or damaged engine mount fasteners.
4. The steering head is designed and constructed to withstand stress from braking and steering while supporting the weight of the front end. However, this area is very suspectible to damage from accidents. Inspect the steering head carefully for cracks, bending and other damage. The steering head bearings should be serviced as described in Chapter Eleven. Steering adjustment should be checked on a routine maintenance schedule and adjusted to remove all excessive bearing play. Worn bearings and races should be replaced as soon as they are detected.
5. The swing arm pivot area and the rear shock absorber mounting brackets are subjected to stress from acceleration, braking and turning. The swing arm and its bearings should be serviced as described in Chapter Twelve. Check the swing arm and the frame pivot area for cracks. Check and tighten the swing arm pivot bolts as described in Chapter Twelve.
6. Check all of the component mounting tabs for cracks, loose mounting fasteners or clamps and

other damage. Especially check the mounting brackets securing the footpegs, jiffy stand and rear brake master cylinder.

### Component Removal/Installation

If your bike has been involved in an accident, consult with the frame repair shop on how they want the frame delivered to their shop. The following lists steps required to strip the frame completely of all components. When stripping the motorcycle, note the following:

a. If you plan on removing all of the parts from the frame, you will be dealing with a large number of parts. Prepare your work area so that you have adequate storage space that can be left undisturbed for some time. It is important to store parts which can be damaged cosmetically (fuel tanks, seat, fenders, etc.), in a safe place.
b. Before removing the first bolt and to prevent frustration during assembly, get a number of boxes, plastic bags and containers and store the parts as they are removed. Also have on hand a roll of masking tape and a permanent, waterproof marking pen to tag and label each part or assembly as required. If your Harley was purchased secondhand and it appears that some of the wiring may have been changed or replaced, label each electrical connection before disconnecting it.
c. Note the condition of all threaded fasteners as they are removed from the bike. Replace worn or damaged fasteners with ones of the same size, type and torque requirements.
d. Make a list of worn, damaged or missing parts as you work on the bike so they can all be ordered at the same time. Then keep track of parts as they are ordered and note any missing or back ordered items. You don't want to find yourself in the middle of a procedure, only to find out that you have to stop because of an incorrect or missing part.

1. Support the bike in a manner such that both wheels clear the ground. Double check to make sure the bike cannot fall in either direction.
2. Remove the battery as described in Chapter Nine.
3. Remove the fuel tank, carburetor and exhaust system as described in Chapter Eight.
4. Remove the primary drive assembly as described in Chapter Five.
5. Remove the engine as described in Chapter Four.
6. Remove the transmission housing as described in Chapter Six or Chapter Seven.
7. Remove the headlight assembly as described in Chapter Nine.
8. Remove the front and rear brake caliper assemblies as described in Chapter Thirteen.
9. Remove the front and rear wheels as described in Chapter Ten.
10. Remove the handlebar, front forks and steering assembly as described in Chapter Eleven.
11. Remove the rear fender as described in this chapter.
12. Remove the rear shock absorbers and rear swing arm as described in Chapter Twelve.

*NOTE*

*Before removing the wiring harness in Step 13, photograph the harness as it is installed on the bike. The photographs can be used to good advantage during reassembly. Before photographing the wiring harness on the bike, place a piece of blue or grey cardboard behind the bike. The neutral background can help to unclutter the frame and wiring harness in your pictures.*

13. Remove all wire guides and other fasteners and remove the wiring harness from the bike. Do not pull on the wiring harness when removing it from a harness guide. If the bike was involved in a crash, check the harness for visible signs of damage. Check each wire for continuity with an ohmmeter.
14. Remove the jiffy stand and all other items left mounted or strapped to the frame.
15. Inspect the frame for bends, cracks or other damage, especially around welded joints and areas that are rusted. Check the frame swing arm pivot holes for elongation or other damage.
16. Check threaded holes in the frame for stripping, cross-threading or deposit buildup. Threaded holes should be blown out with compressed air as dirt buildup in the bottom of the hole may prevent the bolt from being torqued properly. If necessary, use a tap to true up the threads and to remove any deposits.
17. Clean all parts before reassembly.

*NOTE*
*If paint has been removed from parts during cleaning, touch up areas as required before assembly or installation.*

18. Make sure all worn or defective parts have been repaired or replaced.
19. Install by reversing these removal steps.

## Stripping and Painting

Remove all components from the frame. Thoroughly strip off all old paint. The best way is to have it beadblasted down to bare metal. If this is not possible, you can use a liquid paint remover and steel wool and a fine, hard wire brush.

*CAUTION*
*If you wish to change the color of molded plastic parts, consult an automotive paint supplier for the proper procedure. Do not use any liquid paint remover on these components as it will damage the surface. The color is an integral part of these components and cannot be removed.*

When the frame is down to bare metal, have it inspected for hairline and internal cracks. Magnaflux is the most common and complete process.

Make sure that the primer is compatible with the type of paint you are going to use for the finish color. Spray on one or two coats of primer as smoothly as possible. Let it dry thoroughly and use a fine grade of wet sandpaper (400-600 grit) to remove any flaws. Carefully wipe the surface clean and then spray a couple of coats of the final color. Use either lacquer or enamel base paint and follow the manufacturer's instructions.

A shop specializing in painting will probably do the best job. However, you can do a surprisingly good job with a good grade of spray paint. Spend a few extra dollars and get a good grade of paint as it will make a difference in how well it looks and how long it will stand up. It's a good idea to shake the can and make sure the ball inside the can is loose when you purchase the can of paint. Shake the can as long as is stated on the can. Then immerse the can upright in a pot or bucket of warm water (not hot-not over 120° F [49 ° C]).

*WARNING*
*Higher temperatures could cause the can to burst. Do* ***not*** *place the can in direct contact with any flame or heat source.*

Leave the can in the water for several minutes. When thoroughly warmed, shake the can again and spray the frame. Be sure to get into all the crevices where there may be rust problems. Several light mist coats are better than one heavy coat. Spray painting is best done in temperatures of 70-80° F (21-26° C); any temperature above or below this may give you problems.

After the final coat has dried completely, at least 48 hours, any overspray or orange peel may be removed with a light application of DuPont Rubbing Compound (red color) and finished with DuPont Polishing Compound (white color). Be careful not to rub too hard or you will go through the finish.

Finish off with a couple coats of good wax before reassembling all the components. It's a good idea to keep the frame touched up with fresh paint if any minor rust spots or scratches appear.

An alternative to painting is powder coating. The process involves spraying electrically charged particles of pigment and resin on the object to be coated, which is negatively charged. The charged powder particles adhere to the electrically grounded object until heated and fused into a smooth coating in a curing oven. Powder coated surfaces are more resistant to chipping, scratching, fading and wearing than other finishes. A variety of colors and textures are available. Powder coating also has advantages over paint as no environmentally hazardous solvents are used.

# INDEX

## F



## G



## H



## I

## K



## L



## M



## O



## P



## R



## S



## T

## V



## W

# EARLY 1984 FLHTC

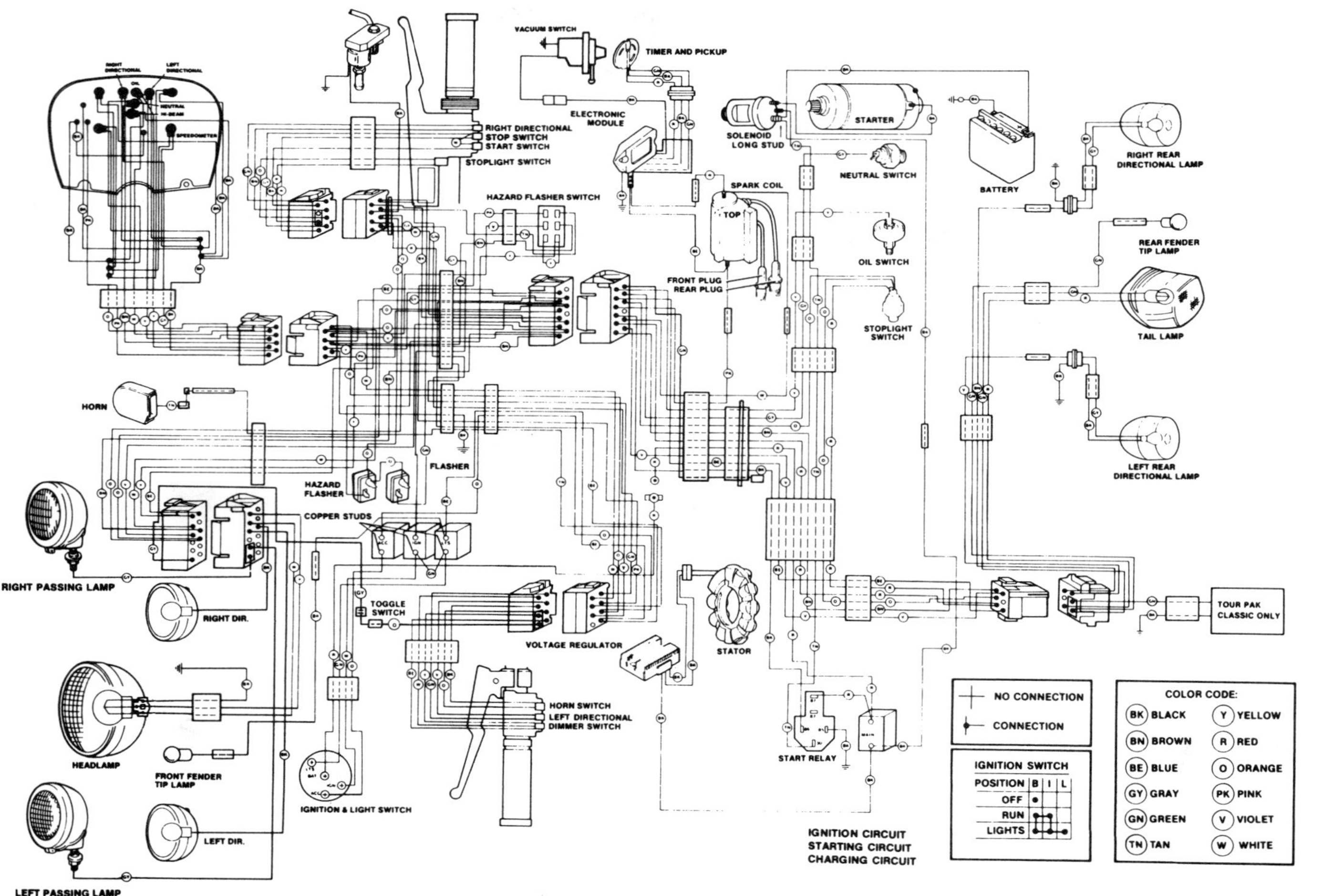

# EARLY 1984 FLTC

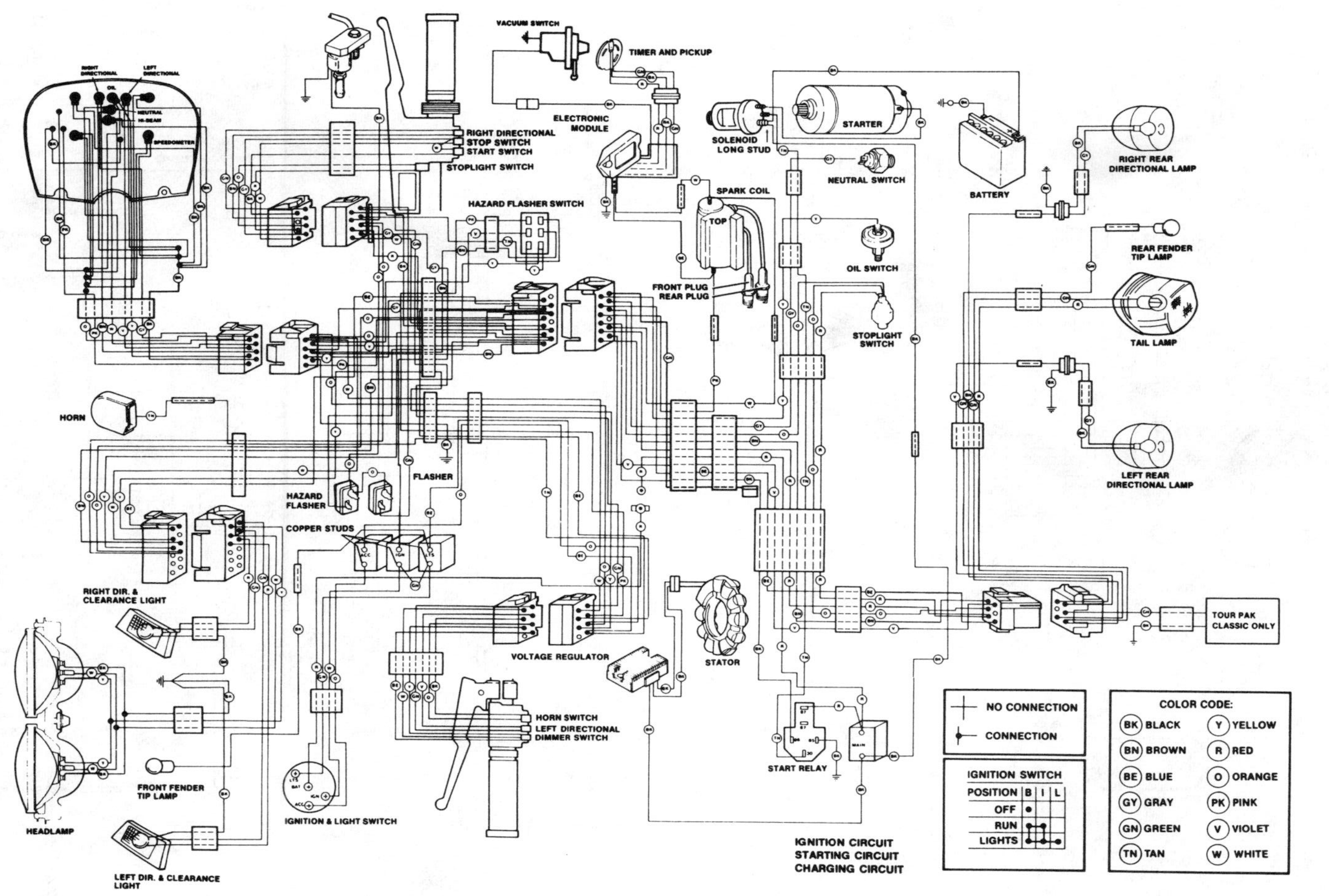

# EARLY 1984 FXRT

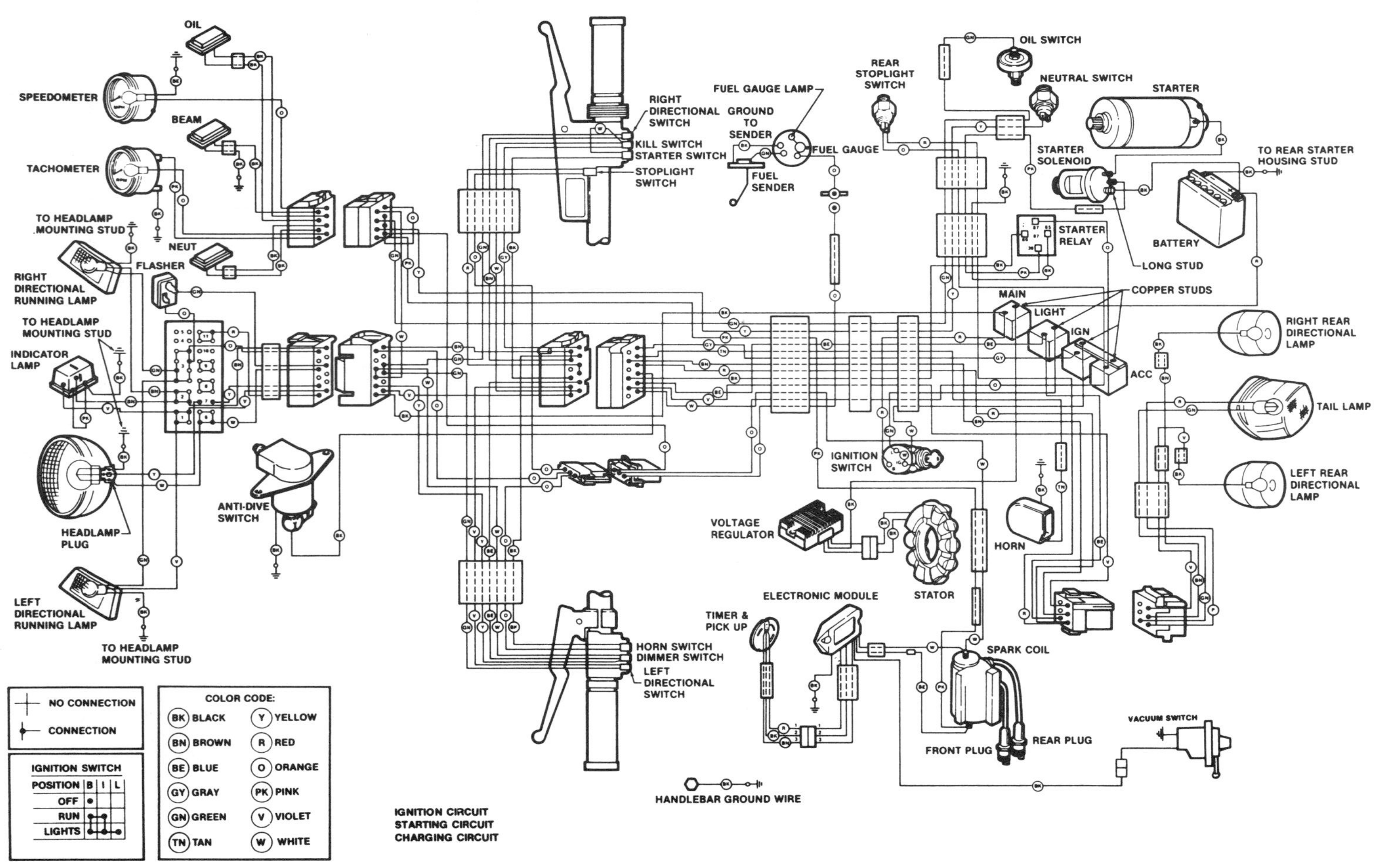

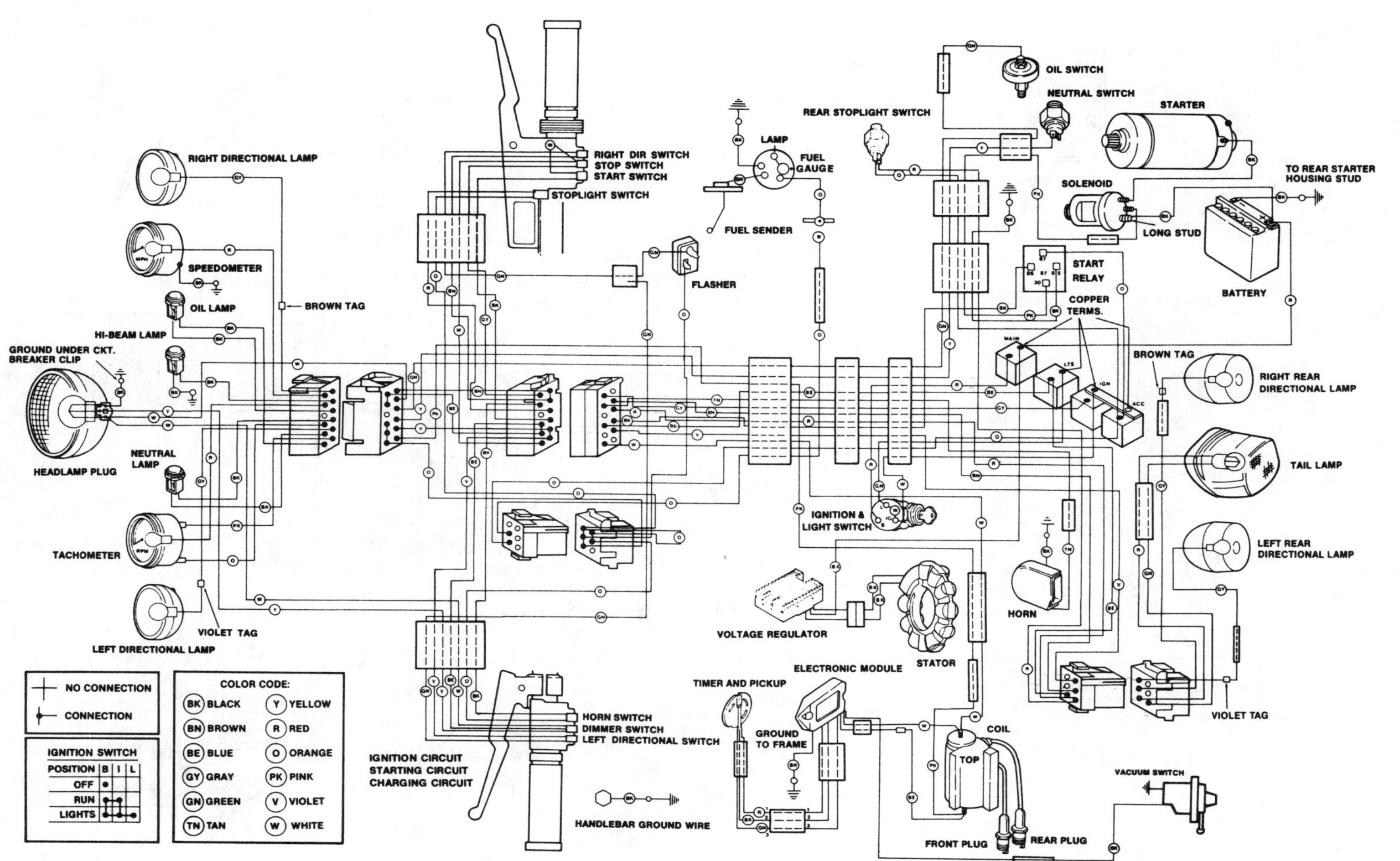
EARLY 1984 FXRS
RIGHT DIRECTIONAL LAMP
SPEEDOMETER
OIL LAMP
BROWN TAG
HI-BEAM LAMP
GROUND UNDER CKT. BREAKER CLIP
HEADLAMP PLUG
NEUTRAL LAMP
TACHOMETER
VIOLET TAG
LEFT DIRECTIONAL LAMP
RIGHT DIR SWITCH
STOP SWITCH
START SWITCH
STOPLIGHT SWITCH
LAMP
FUEL GAUGE
FUEL SENDER
FLASHER
REAR STOPLIGHT SWITCH
OIL SWITCH
NEUTRAL SWITCH
STARTER
TO REAR STARTER HOUSING STUD
SOLENOID
LONG STUD
BATTERY
START RELAY
COPPER TERMS.
BROWN TAG
RIGHT REAR DIRECTIONAL LAMP
TAIL LAMP
LEFT REAR DIRECTIONAL LAMP
IGNITION & LIGHT SWITCH
HORN
VOLTAGE REGULATOR
STATOR
ELECTRONIC MODULE
TIMER AND PICKUP
GROUND TO FRAME
COIL
TOP
FRONT PLUG
REAR PLUG
VACUUM SWITCH
VIOLET TAG
HORN SWITCH
DIMMER SWITCH
LEFT DIRECTIONAL SWITCH
IGNITION CIRCUIT
STARTING CIRCUIT
CHARGING CIRCUIT
HANDLEBAR GROUND WIRE
NO CONNECTION
CONNECTION
IGNITION SWITCH
POSITION B I L
OFF
RUN
LIGHTS
COLOR CODE:
BK BLACK
Y YELLOW
BN BROWN
R RED
BE BLUE
O ORANGE
GY GRAY
PK PINK
GN GREEN
V VIOLET
TN TAN
W WHITE

# LATE 1984 & 1985 FLHTC

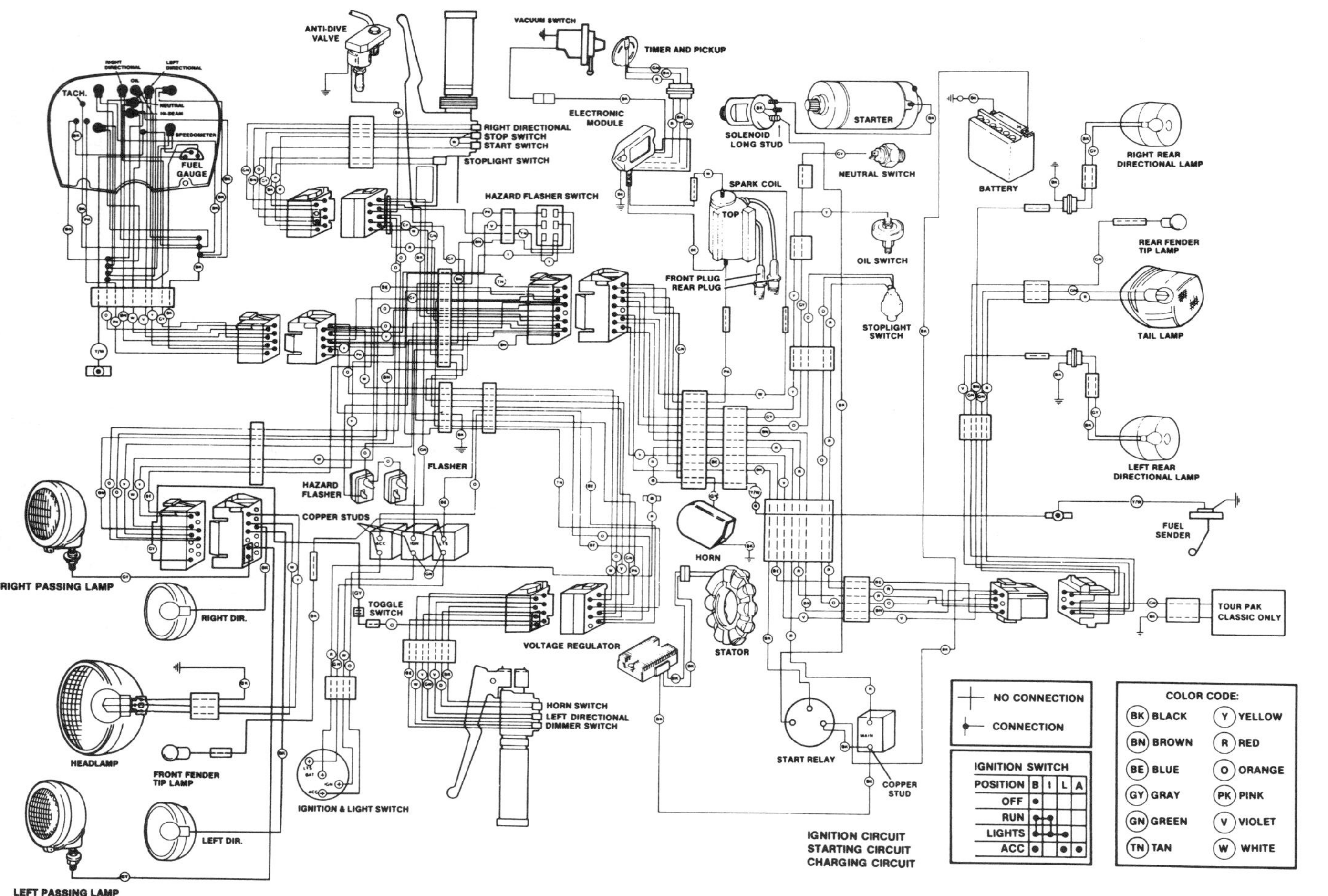

# LATE 1984 & 1985 FLTC

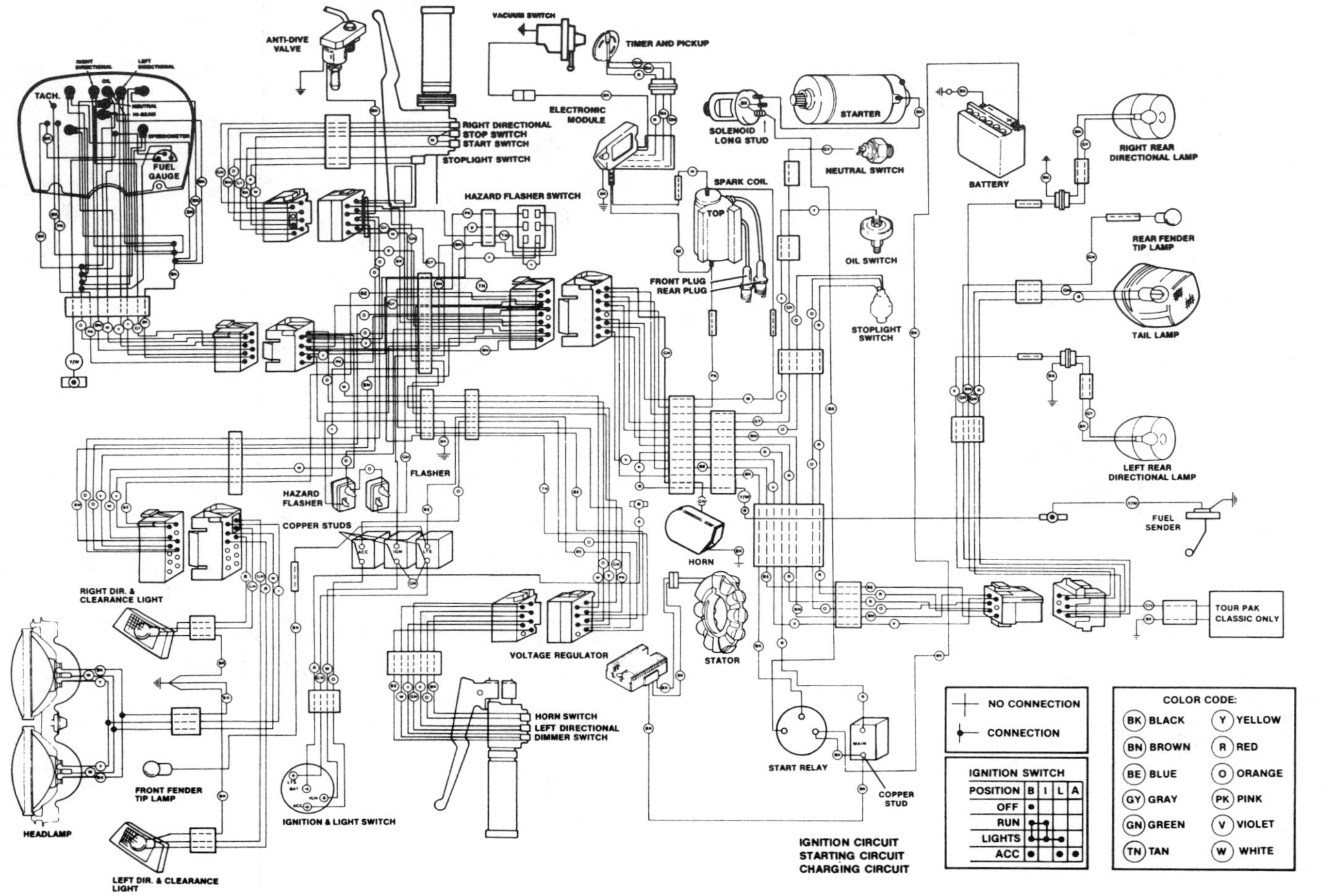

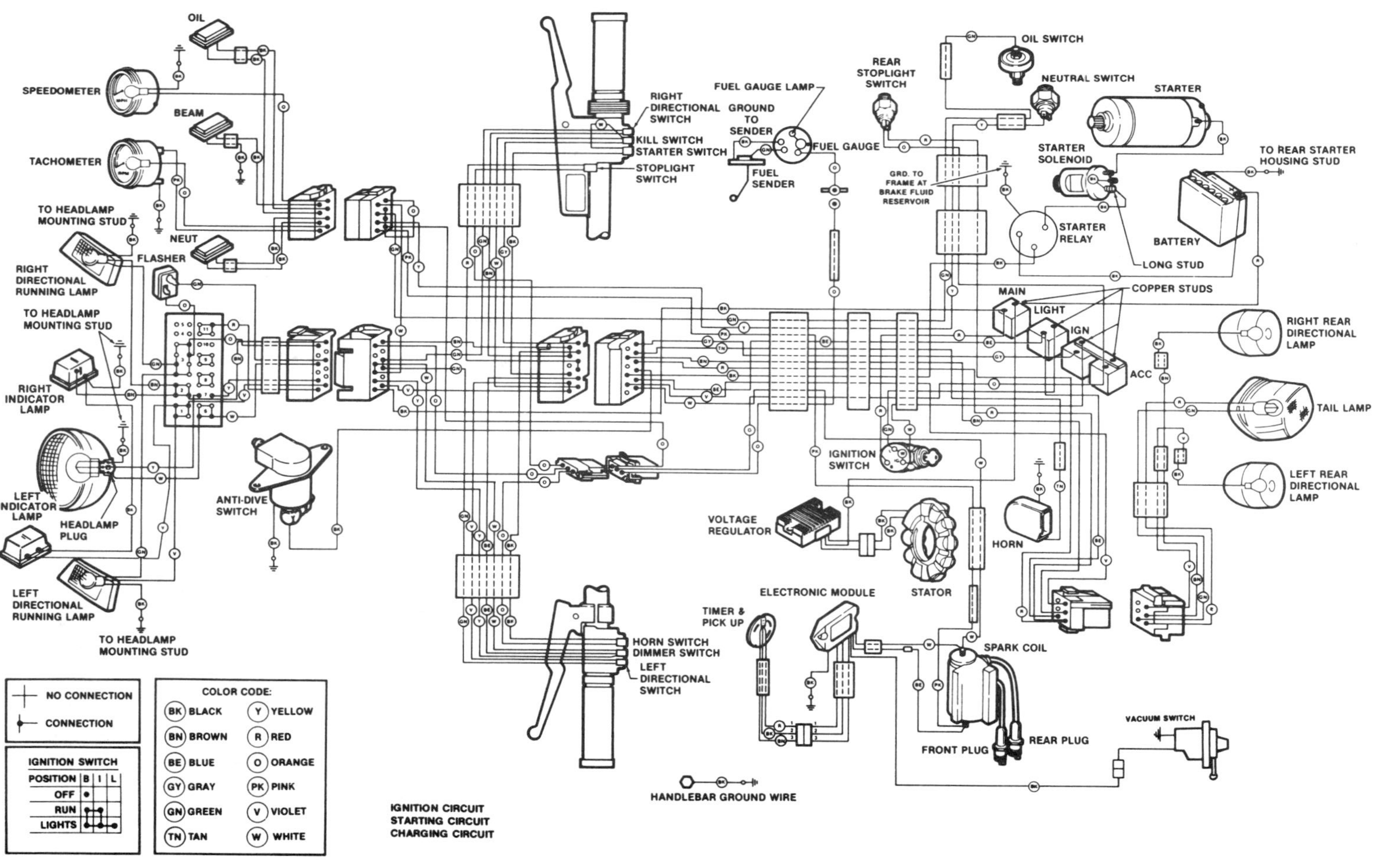
LATE 1984 & 1985 FXRT
OIL
SPEEDOMETER
BEAM
TACHOMETER
TO HEADLAMP MOUNTING STUD
NEUT
RIGHT DIRECTIONAL RUNNING LAMP
FLASHER
TO HEADLAMP MOUNTING STUD
RIGHT INDICATOR LAMP
LEFT INDICATOR LAMP
HEADLAMP PLUG
LEFT DIRECTIONAL RUNNING LAMP
TO HEADLAMP MOUNTING STUD
ANTI-DIVE SWITCH
RIGHT DIRECTIONAL SWITCH
KILL SWITCH
STARTER SWITCH
STOPLIGHT SWITCH
FUEL GAUGE LAMP
GROUND TO SENDER
FUEL GAUGE
FUEL SENDER
REAR STOPLIGHT SWITCH
GRD. TO FRAME AT BRAKE FLUID RESERVOIR
OIL SWITCH
NEUTRAL SWITCH
STARTER
STARTER SOLENOID
TO REAR STARTER HOUSING STUD
STARTER RELAY
BATTERY
LONG STUD
COPPER STUDS
MAIN
LIGHT
IGN
ACC
RIGHT REAR DIRECTIONAL LAMP
TAIL LAMP
LEFT REAR DIRECTIONAL LAMP
IGNITION SWITCH
VOLTAGE REGULATOR
HORN
STATOR
ELECTRONIC MODULE
TIMER & PICK UP
HORN SWITCH
DIMMER SWITCH
LEFT DIRECTIONAL SWITCH
SPARK COIL
VACUUM SWITCH
REAR PLUG
FRONT PLUG
HANDLEBAR GROUND WIRE
NO CONNECTION
CONNECTION
IGNITION SWITCH
POSITION B I L
OFF
RUN
LIGHTS
COLOR CODE:
BK BLACK
BN BROWN
BE BLUE
GY GRAY
GN GREEN
TN TAN
Y YELLOW
R RED
O ORANGE
PK PINK
V VIOLET
W WHITE
IGNITION CIRCUIT
STARTING CIRCUIT
CHARGING CIRCUIT

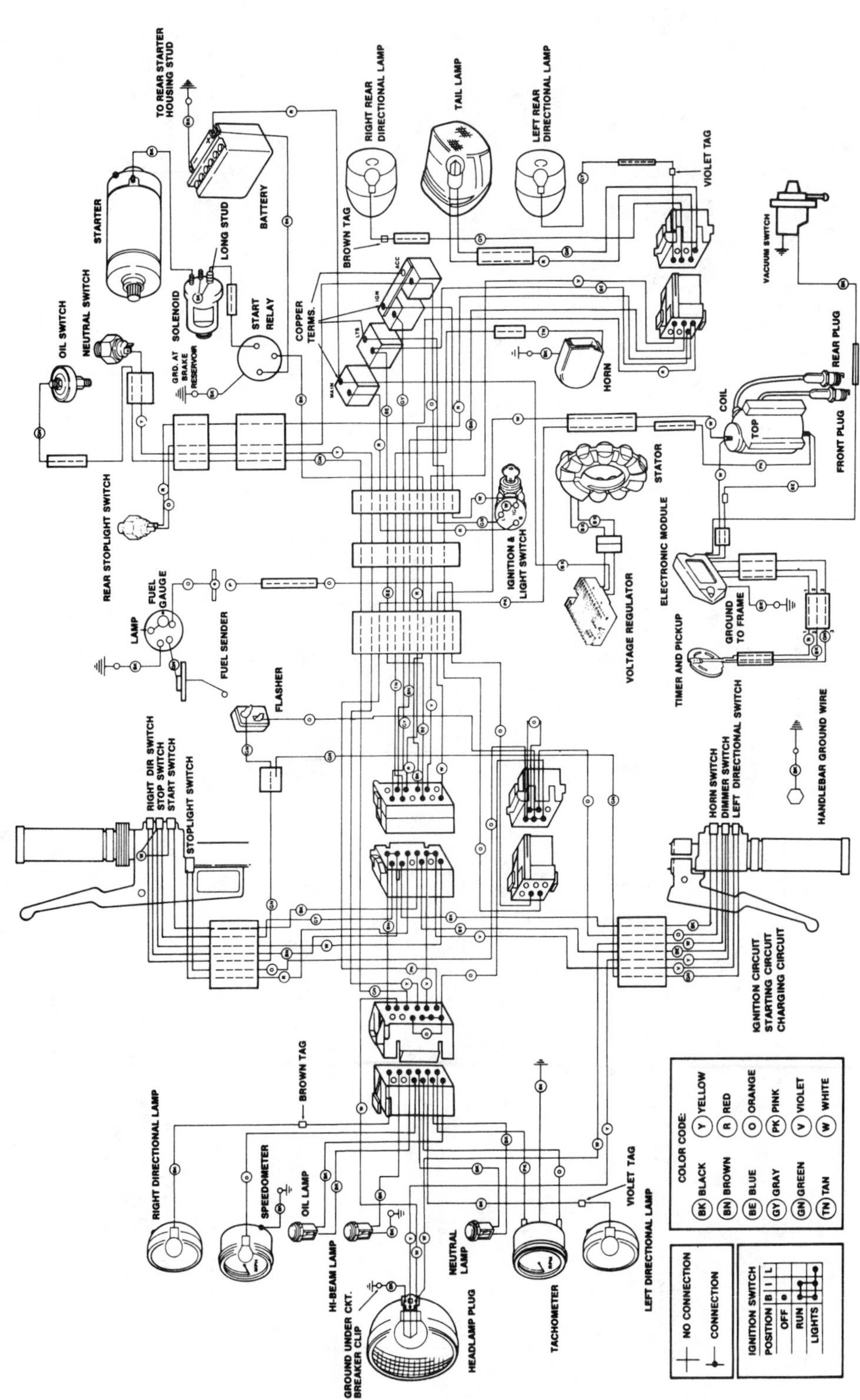
LATE 1984 & 1985 FXRS
TO REAR STARTER HOUSING STUD
RIGHT REAR DIRECTIONAL LAMP
TAIL LAMP
LEFT REAR DIRECTIONAL LAMP
VIOLET TAG
BROWN TAG
STARTER
LONG STUD
BATTERY
OIL SWITCH
NEUTRAL SWITCH
SOLENOID
START RELAY
GRD. AT BRAKE RESERVOIR
COPPER TERMS.
HORN
VACUUM SWITCH
REAR PLUG
COIL
TOP
FRONT PLUG
STATOR
ELECTRONIC MODULE
VOLTAGE REGULATOR
GROUND TO FRAME
TIMER AND PICKUP
IGNITION & LIGHT SWITCH
REAR STOPLIGHT SWITCH
LAMP
FUEL GAUGE
FUEL SENDER
FLASHER
RIGHT DIR SWITCH
STOP SWITCH
START SWITCH
STOPLIGHT SWITCH
HORN SWITCH
DIMMER SWITCH
LEFT DIRECTIONAL SWITCH
HANDLEBAR GROUND WIRE
IGNITION CIRCUIT
STARTING CIRCUIT
CHARGING CIRCUIT
RIGHT DIRECTIONAL LAMP
BROWN TAG
SPEEDOMETER
OIL LAMP
HI-BEAM LAMP
GROUND UNDER CKT. BREAKER CLIP
HEADLAMP PLUG
NEUTRAL LAMP
TACHOMETER
VIOLET TAG
LEFT DIRECTIONAL LAMP
COLOR CODE:
BK BLACK
BN BROWN
BE BLUE
GY GRAY
GN GREEN
TN TAN
Y YELLOW
R RED
O ORANGE
PK PINK
V VIOLET
W WHITE
NO CONNECTION
CONNECTION
IGNITION SWITCH
POSITION B I L
OFF
RUN
LIGHTS

# EARLY 1985 FXWG

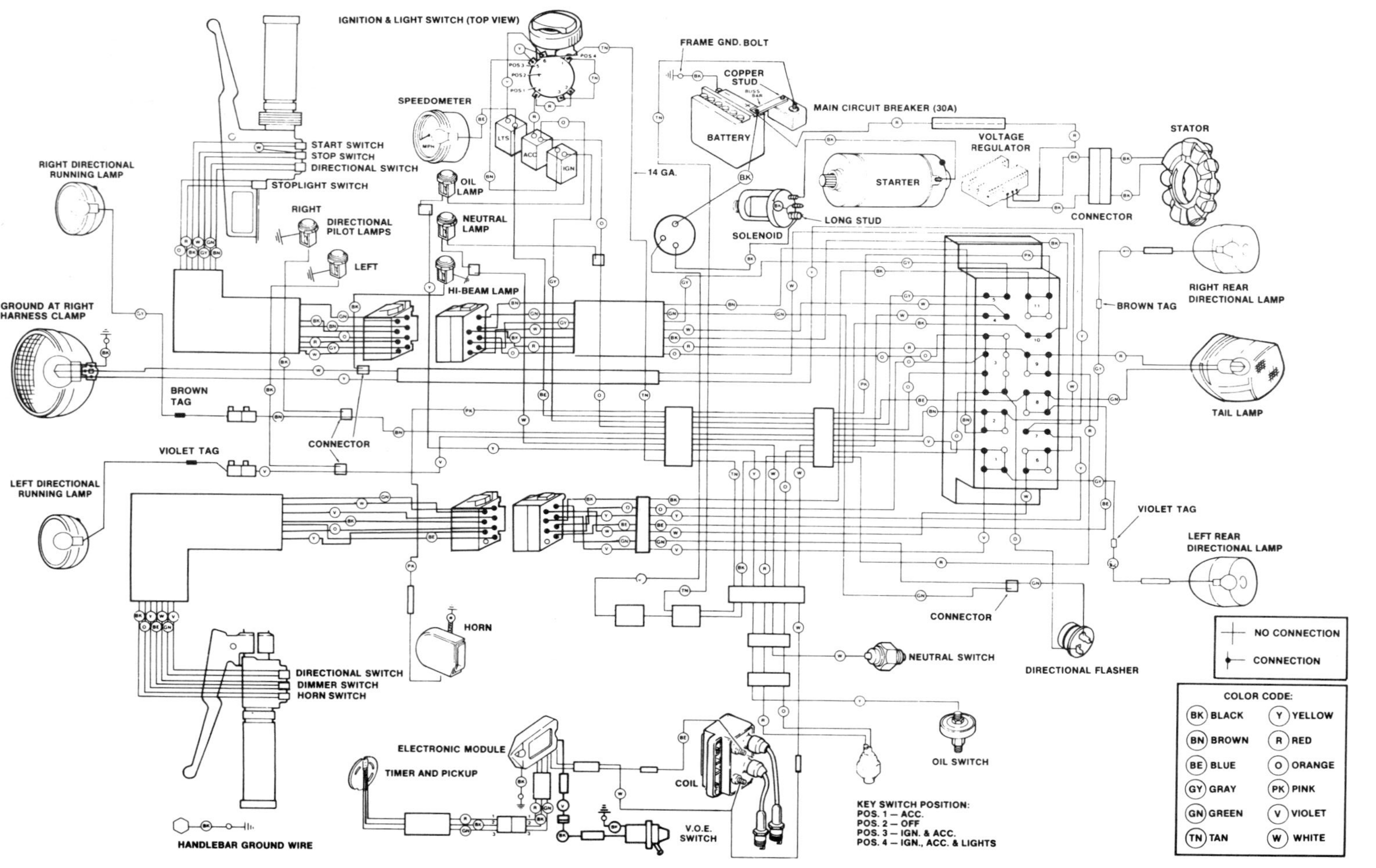

## EARLY 1985 FXSB, FXEF

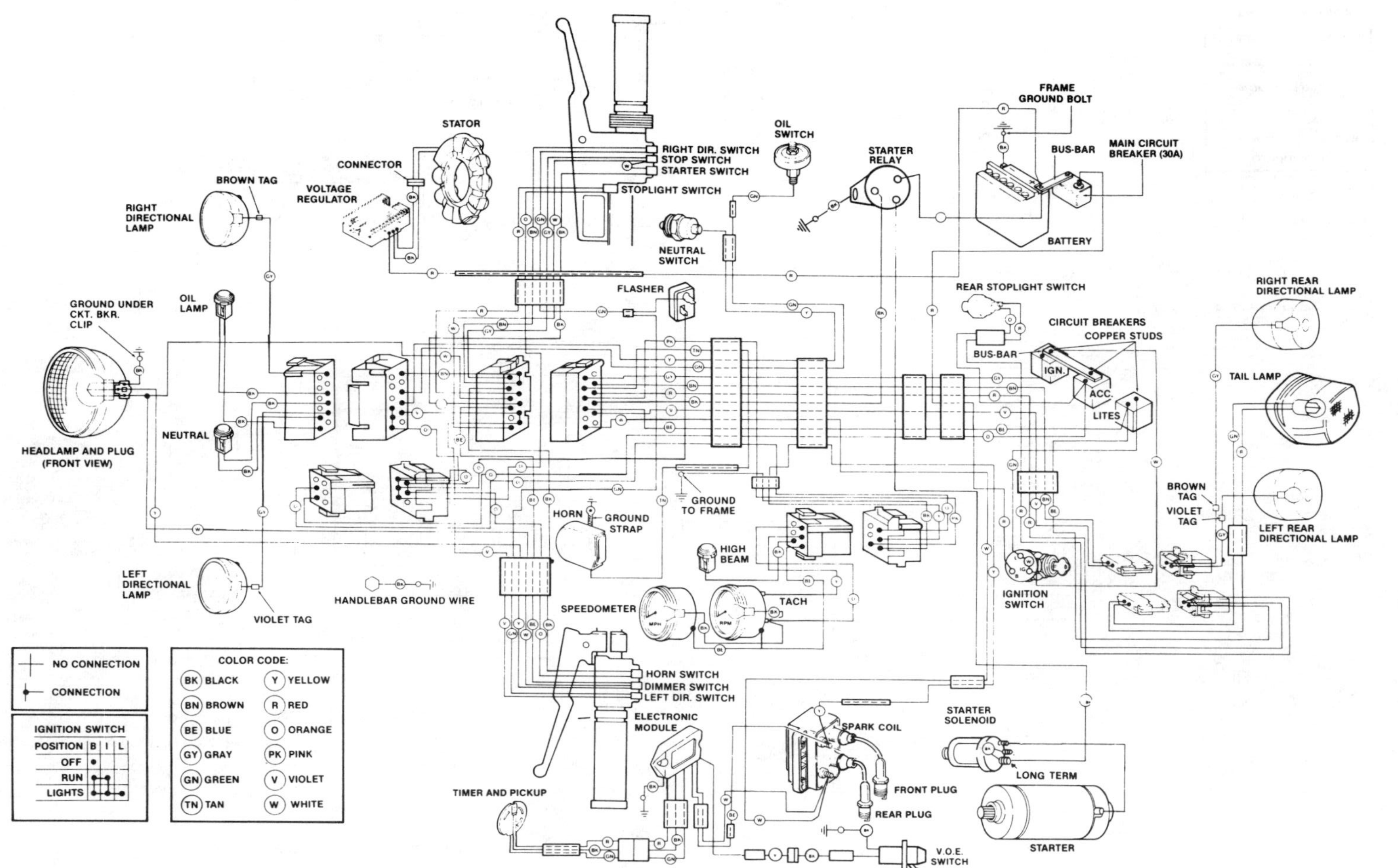

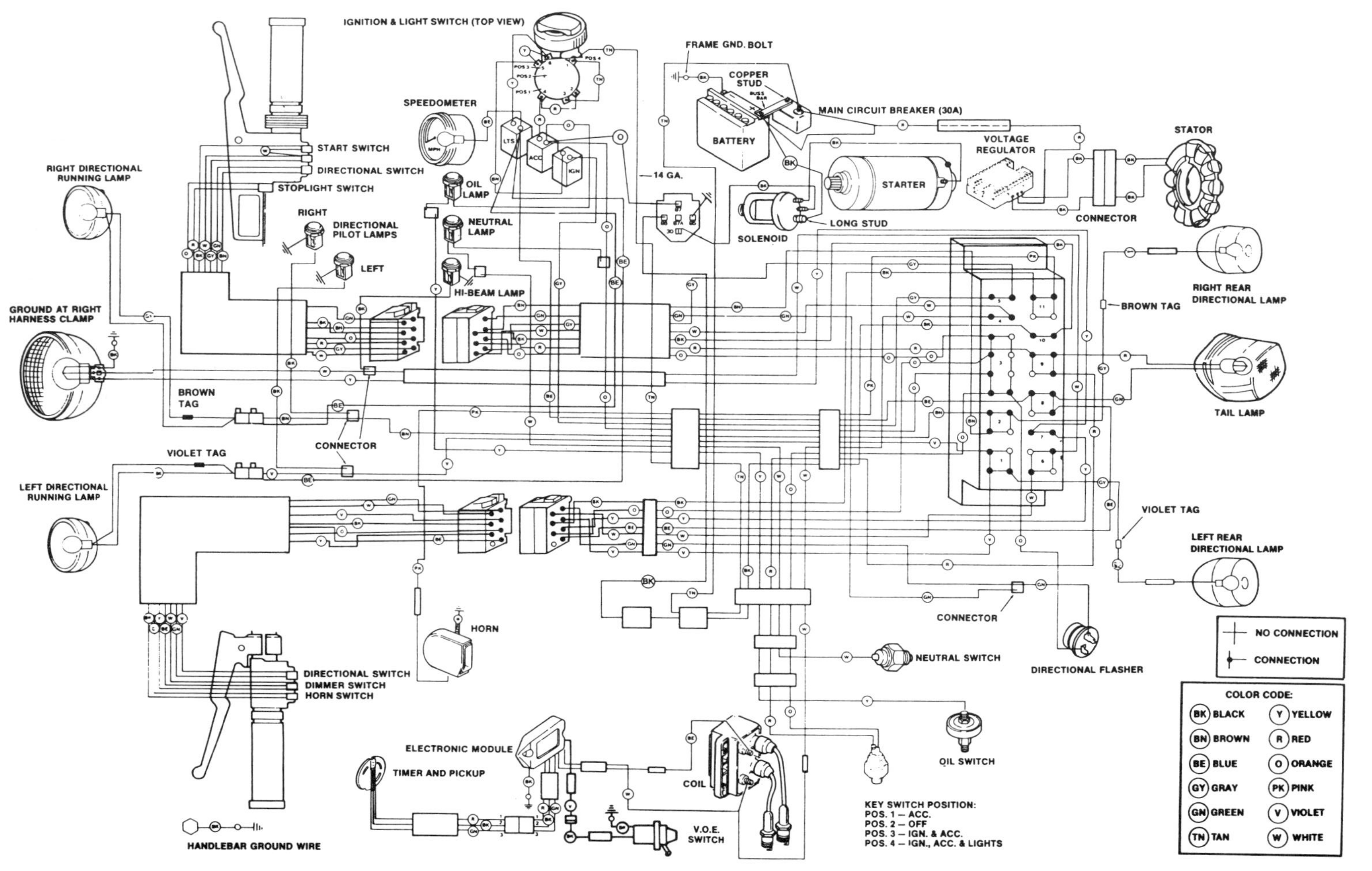
LATE 1985 TO 1986 FXWG
IGNITION & LIGHT SWITCH (TOP VIEW)
FRAME GND. BOLT
COPPER STUD
BATTERY
MAIN CIRCUIT BREAKER (30A)
VOLTAGE REGULATOR
STATOR
SPEEDOMETER
START SWITCH
DIRECTIONAL SWITCH
STOPLIGHT SWITCH
RIGHT DIRECTIONAL RUNNING LAMP
OIL LAMP
14 GA.
STARTER
LONG STUD
SOLENOID
CONNECTOR
RIGHT
DIRECTIONAL PILOT LAMPS
LEFT
NEUTRAL LAMP
HI-BEAM LAMP
RIGHT REAR DIRECTIONAL LAMP
BROWN TAG
GROUND AT RIGHT HARNESS CLAMP
TAIL LAMP
BROWN TAG
CONNECTOR
VIOLET TAG
LEFT DIRECTIONAL RUNNING LAMP
VIOLET TAG
LEFT REAR DIRECTIONAL LAMP
CONNECTOR
HORN
NEUTRAL SWITCH
DIRECTIONAL FLASHER
NO CONNECTION
CONNECTION
DIRECTIONAL SWITCH
DIMMER SWITCH
HORN SWITCH
COLOR CODE:
BK BLACK
Y YELLOW
BN BROWN
R RED
BE BLUE
O ORANGE
GY GRAY
PK PINK
GN GREEN
V VIOLET
TN TAN
W WHITE
ELECTRONIC MODULE
TIMER AND PICKUP
COIL
OIL SWITCH
V.O.E. SWITCH
KEY SWITCH POSITION:
POS. 1 — ACC.
POS. 2 — OFF
POS. 3 — IGN. & ACC.
POS. 4 — IGN., ACC. & LIGHTS
HANDLEBAR GROUND WIRE

# LATE 1985 FXSB, FXEF

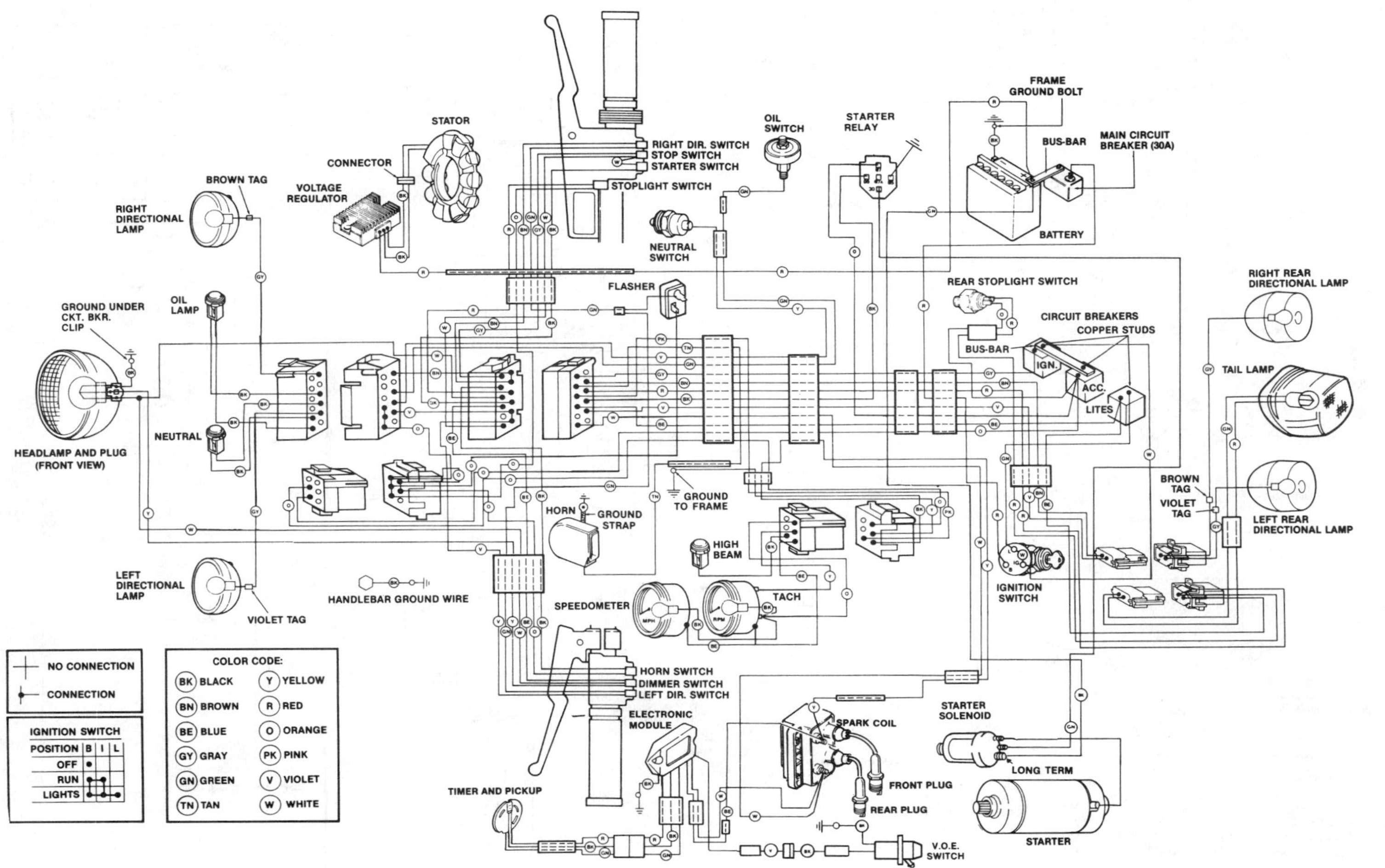

# 1986-1990 FXR

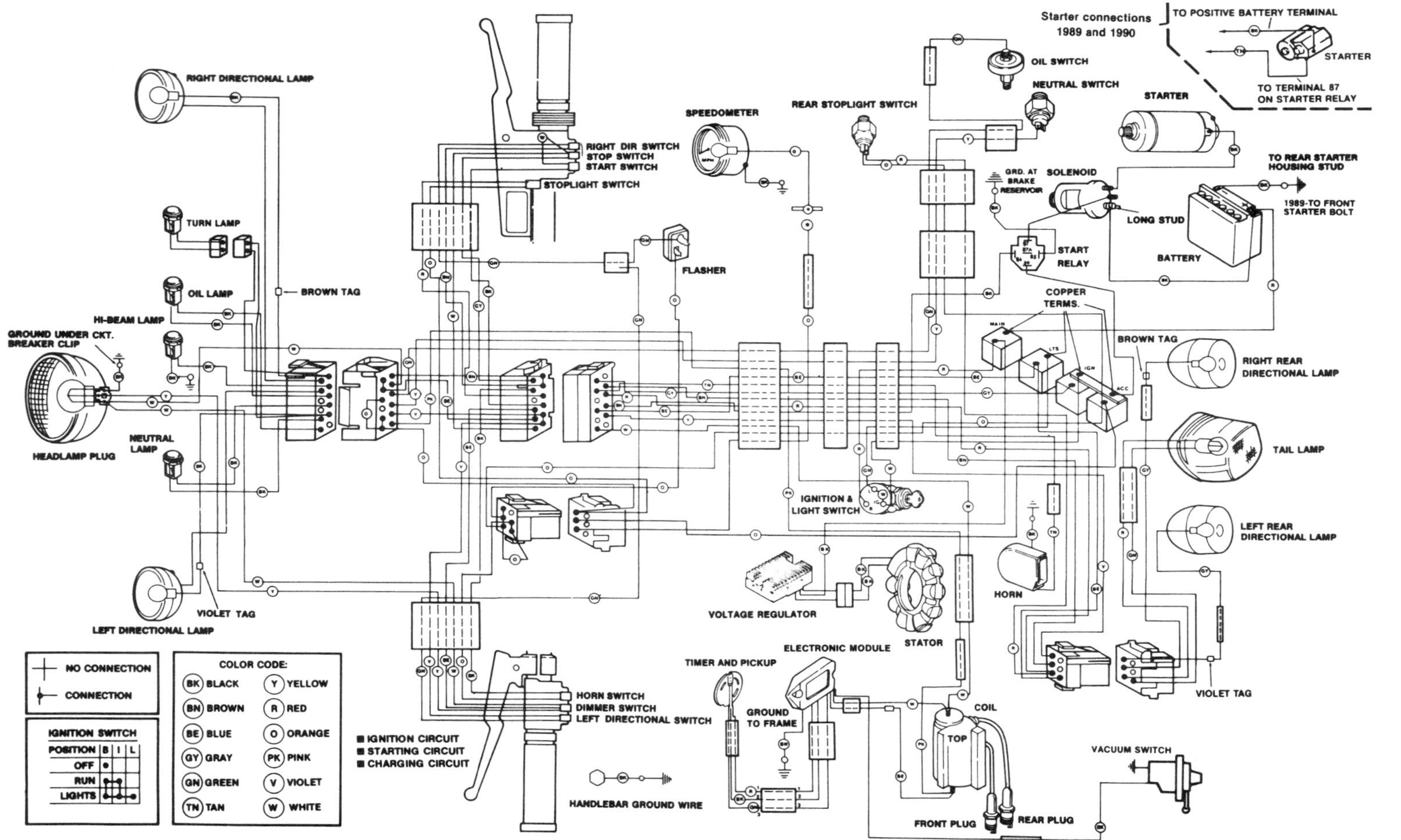

## 1986, 1987 FLHT/C FAIRING

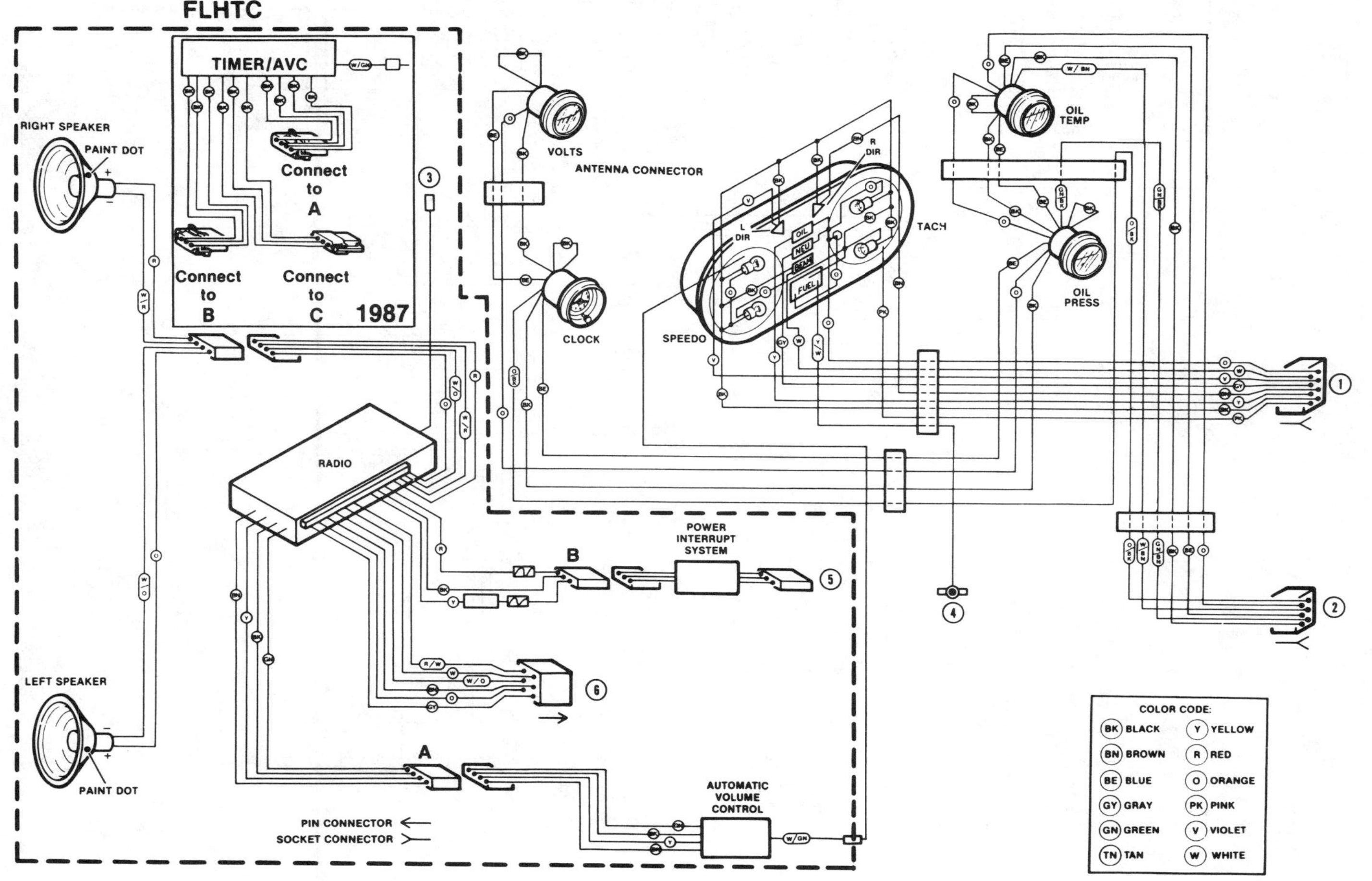

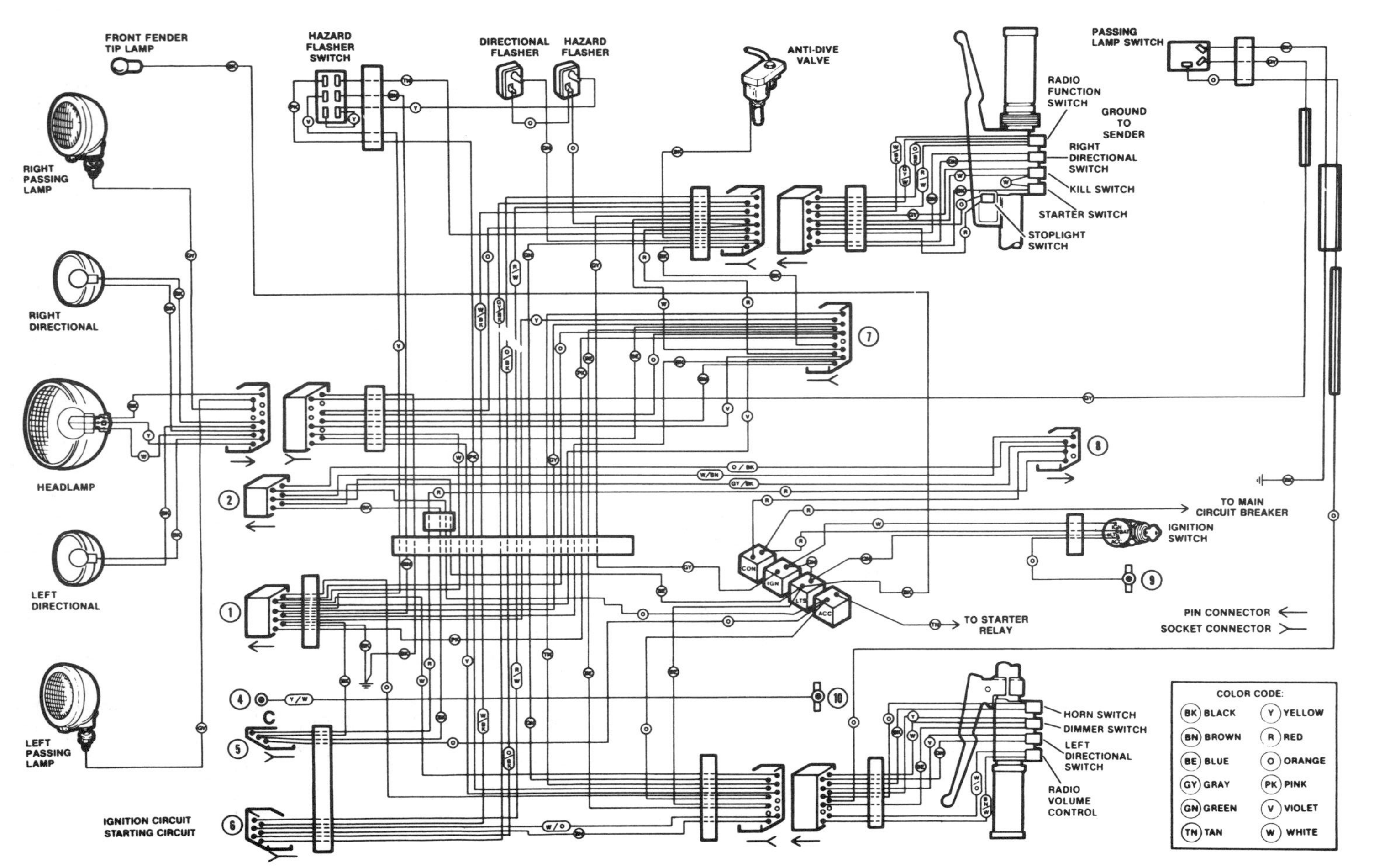
1986, 1987 FLHT/C CHASSIS (PART 1 OF 2)
FRONT FENDER TIP LAMP
HAZARD FLASHER SWITCH
DIRECTIONAL FLASHER
HAZARD FLASHER
ANTI-DIVE VALVE
PASSING LAMP SWITCH
RADIO FUNCTION SWITCH
GROUND TO SENDER
RIGHT DIRECTIONAL SWITCH
KILL SWITCH
STARTER SWITCH
STOPLIGHT SWITCH
RIGHT PASSING LAMP
RIGHT DIRECTIONAL
HEADLAMP
LEFT DIRECTIONAL
LEFT PASSING LAMP
IGNITION CIRCUIT
STARTING CIRCUIT
TO MAIN CIRCUIT BREAKER
IGNITION SWITCH
TO STARTER RELAY
PIN CONNECTOR
SOCKET CONNECTOR
HORN SWITCH
DIMMER SWITCH
LEFT DIRECTIONAL SWITCH
RADIO VOLUME CONTROL
COLOR CODE:
BK BLACK
Y YELLOW
BN BROWN
R RED
BE BLUE
O ORANGE
GY GRAY
PK PINK
GN GREEN
V VIOLET
TN TAN
W WHITE

# 1986, 1987 FLHT/C CHASSIS (PART 2 OF 2)

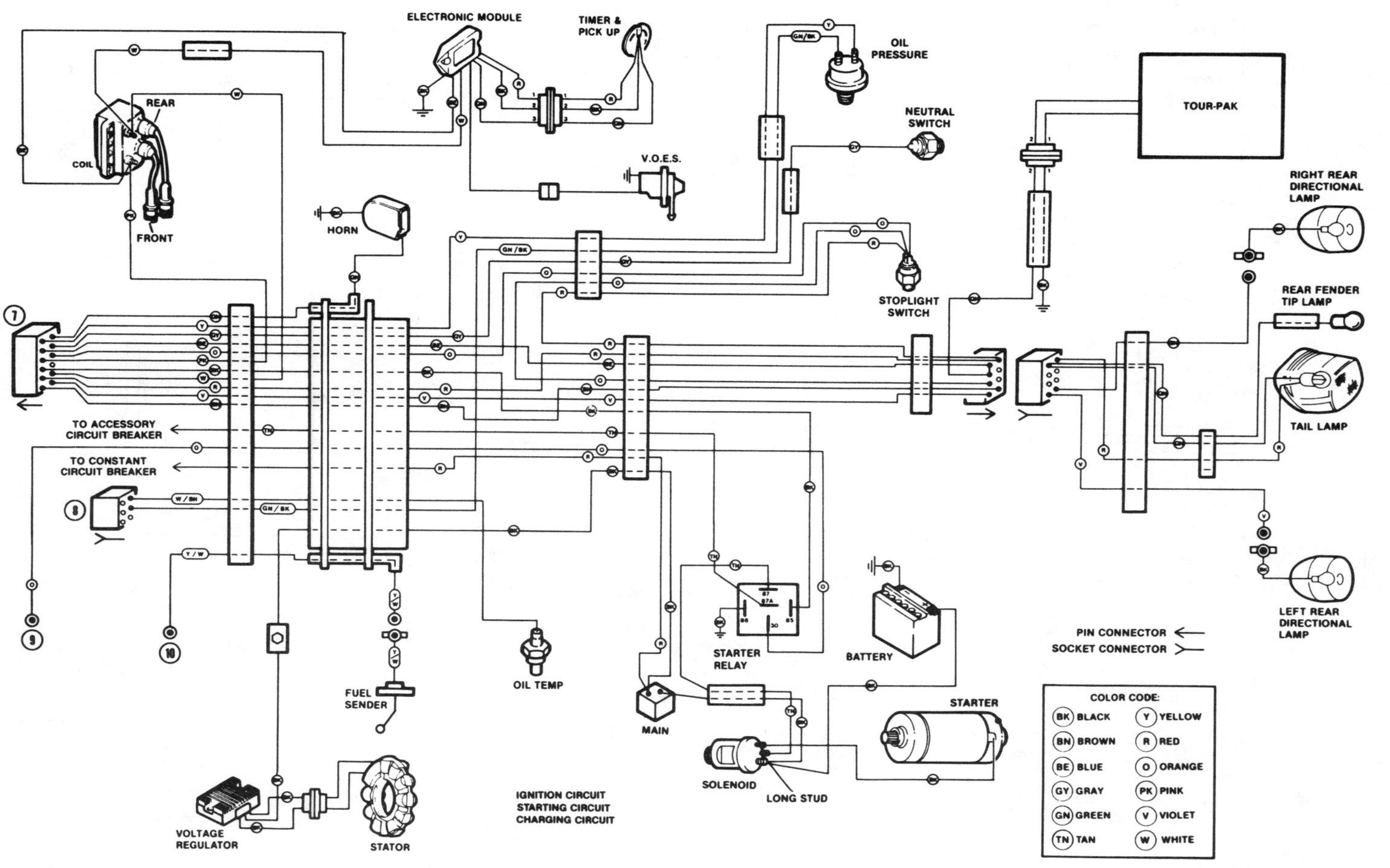


17

## 1986, 1987 FLTC FAIRING

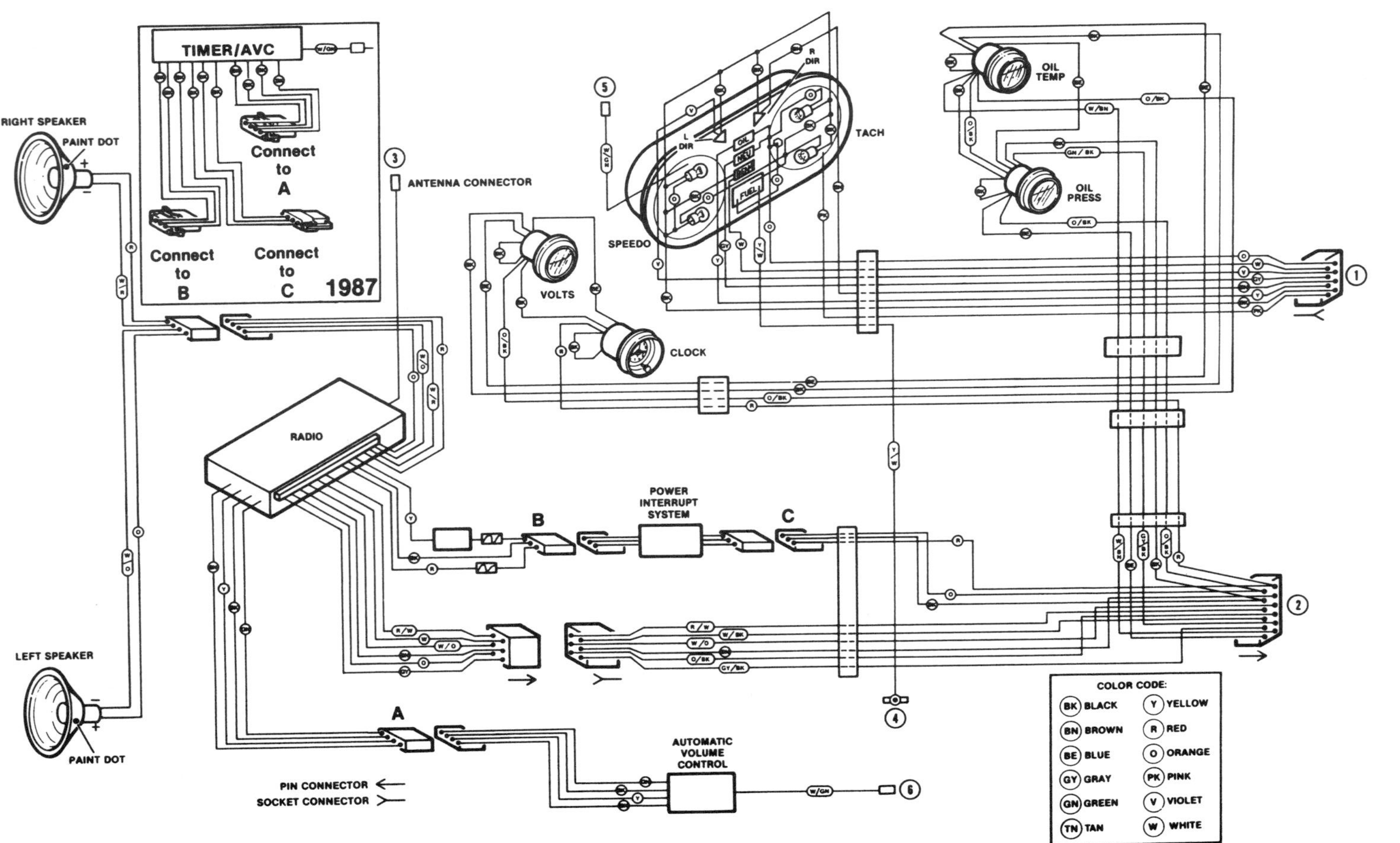

# 1986, 1987 FLTC CHASSIS

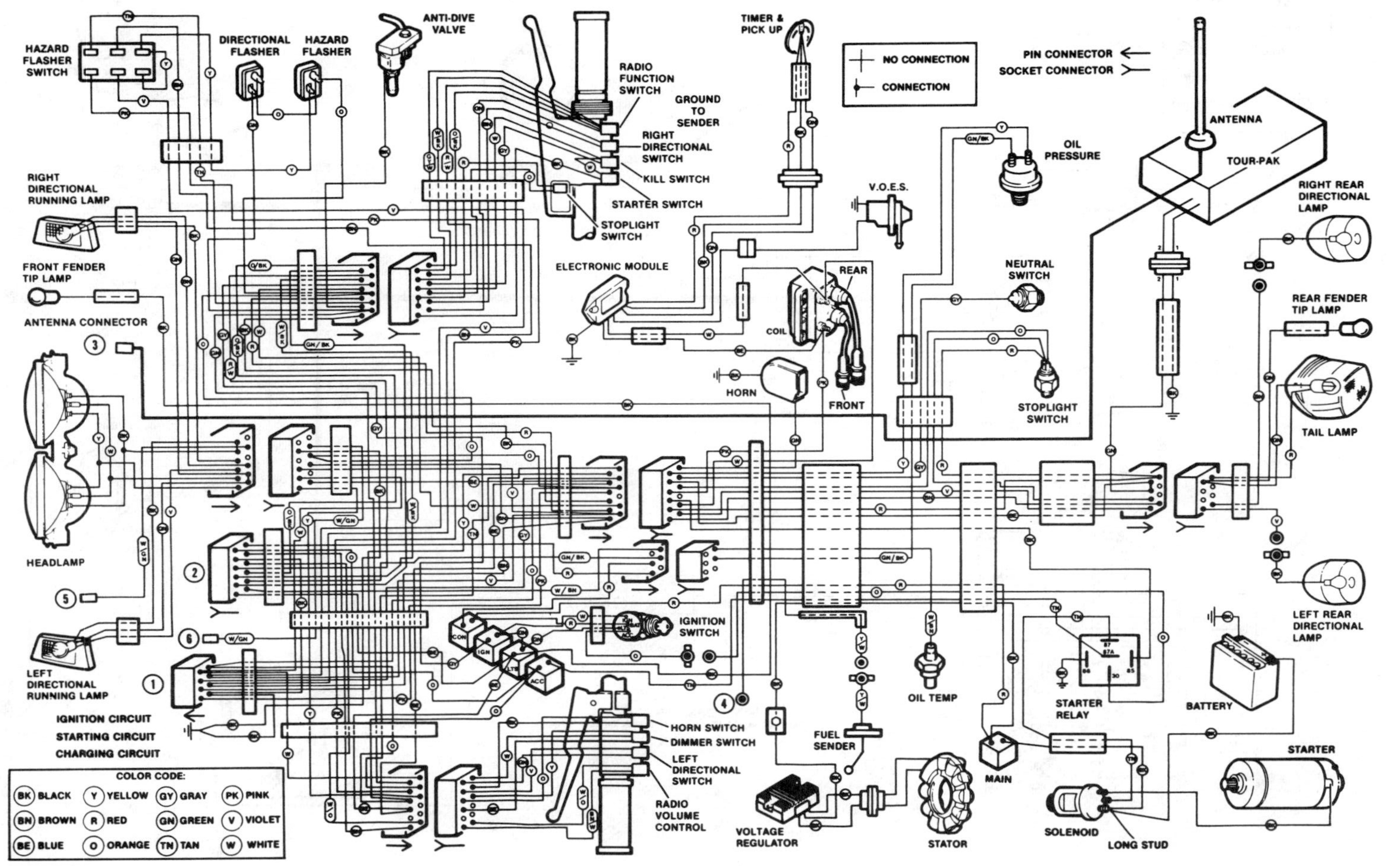

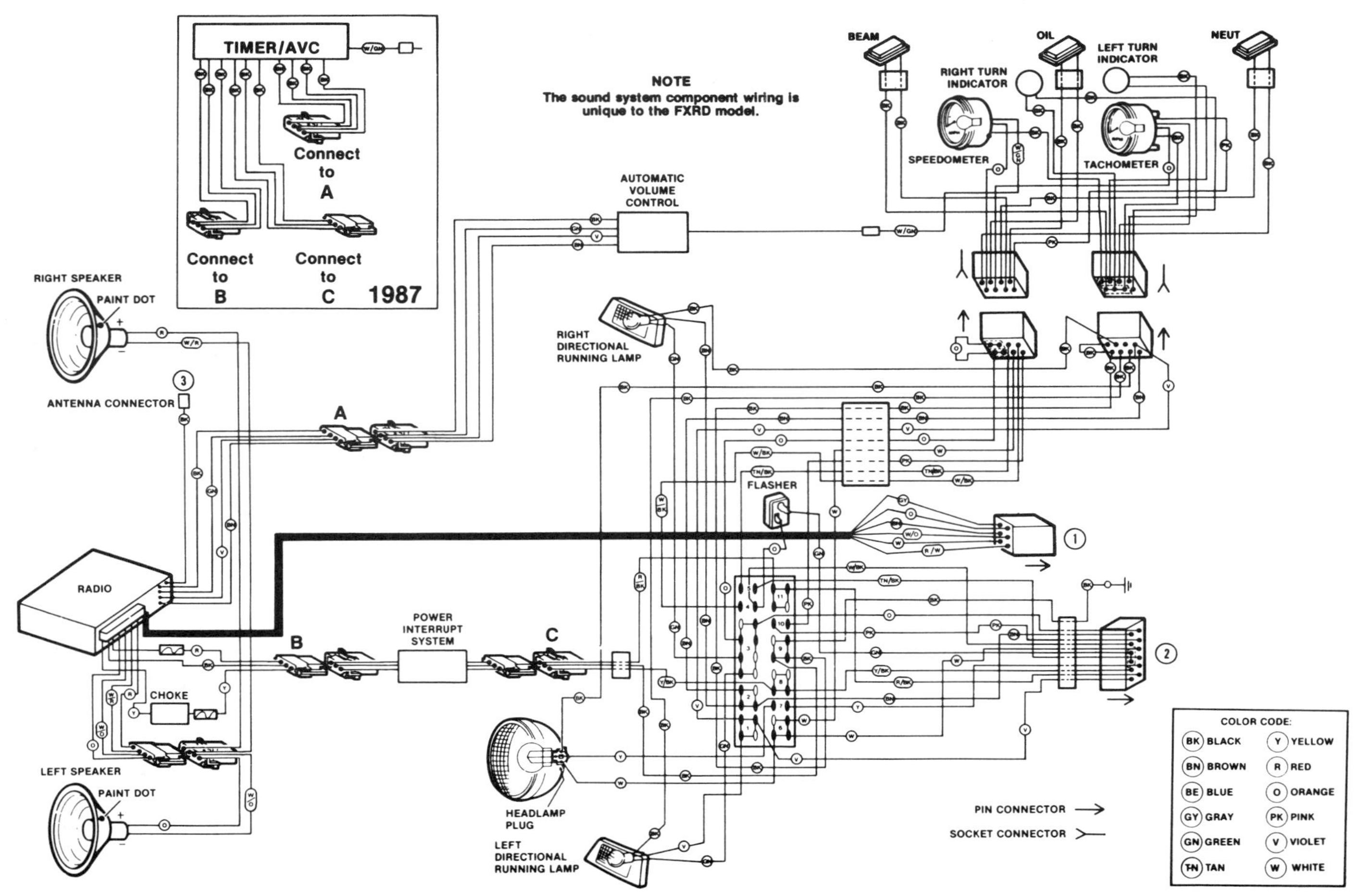
1986 FXRD/1986, 1987 FXRT FAIRING
NOTE
The sound system component wiring is unique to the FXRD model.
TIMER/AVC
Connect to A
Connect to B
Connect to C
1987
BEAM
OIL
NEUT
RIGHT TURN INDICATOR
LEFT TURN INDICATOR
SPEEDOMETER
TACHOMETER
AUTOMATIC VOLUME CONTROL
RIGHT SPEAKER
LEFT SPEAKER
PAINT DOT
ANTENNA CONNECTOR
RADIO
CHOKE
POWER INTERRUPT SYSTEM
A
B
C
FLASHER
RIGHT DIRECTIONAL RUNNING LAMP
LEFT DIRECTIONAL RUNNING LAMP
HEADLAMP PLUG
PIN CONNECTOR
SOCKET CONNECTOR
COLOR CODE:
BK BLACK
BN BROWN
BE BLUE
GY GRAY
GN GREEN
TN TAN
Y YELLOW
R RED
O ORANGE
PK PINK
V VIOLET
W WHITE

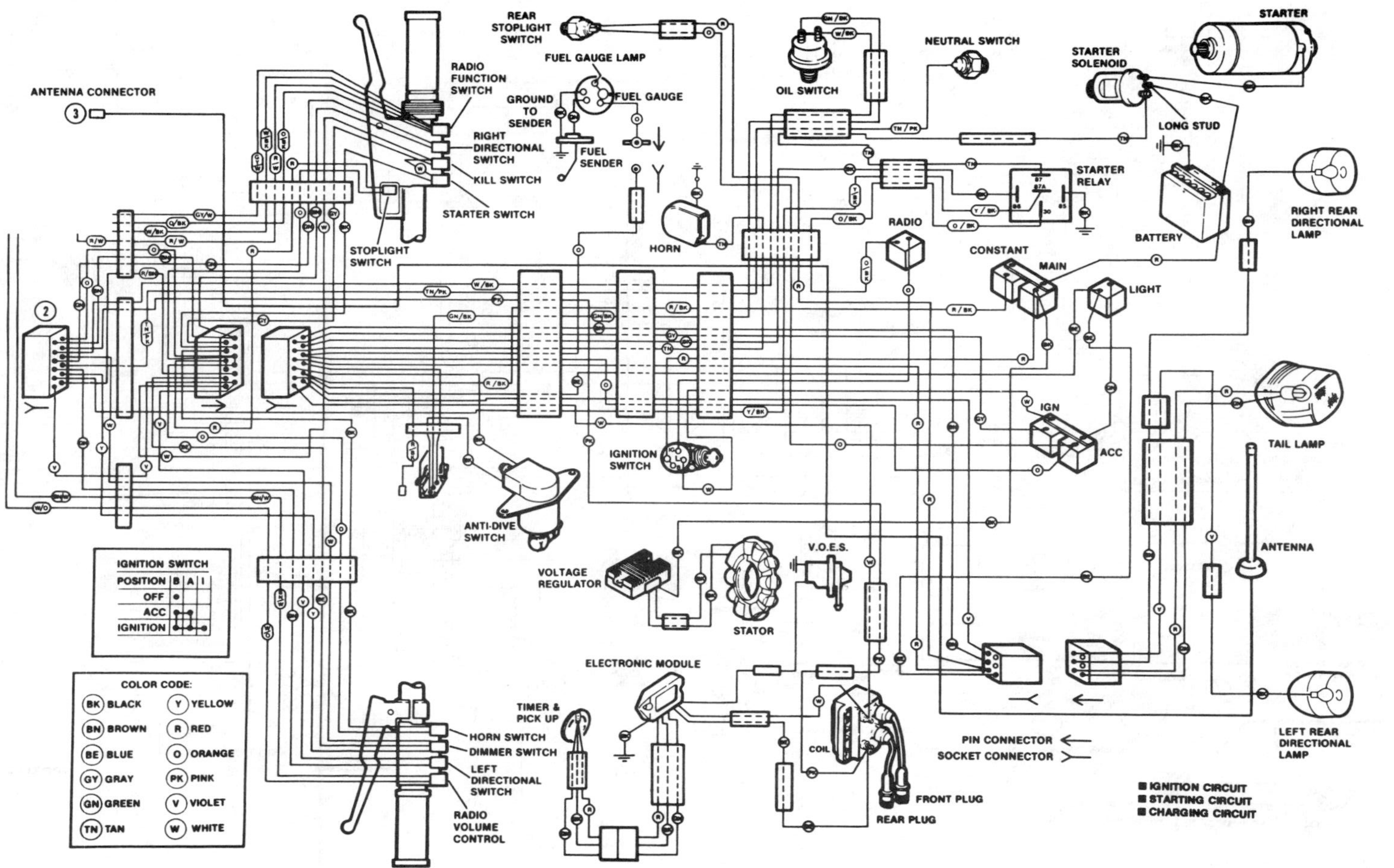
1986 FXRD/1986, 1987 FXRT CHASSIS
ANTENNA CONNECTOR
REAR STOPLIGHT SWITCH
FUEL GAUGE LAMP
RADIO FUNCTION SWITCH
GROUND TO SENDER
FUEL GAUGE
RIGHT DIRECTIONAL SWITCH
FUEL SENDER
KILL SWITCH
STARTER SWITCH
STOPLIGHT SWITCH
HORN
OIL SWITCH
NEUTRAL SWITCH
STARTER SOLENOID
STARTER
LONG STUD
STARTER RELAY
RADIO
BATTERY
RIGHT REAR DIRECTIONAL LAMP
CONSTANT
MAIN
LIGHT
IGN
ACC
TAIL LAMP
IGNITION SWITCH
ANTI-DIVE SWITCH
VOLTAGE REGULATOR
STATOR
V.O.E.S.
ANTENNA
ELECTRONIC MODULE
TIMER & PICK UP
COIL
FRONT PLUG
REAR PLUG
PIN CONNECTOR
SOCKET CONNECTOR
LEFT REAR DIRECTIONAL LAMP
IGNITION CIRCUIT
STARTING CIRCUIT
CHARGING CIRCUIT
HORN SWITCH
DIMMER SWITCH
LEFT DIRECTIONAL SWITCH
RADIO VOLUME CONTROL
IGNITION SWITCH
POSITION B A I
OFF
ACC
IGNITION
COLOR CODE:
BK BLACK
BN BROWN
BE BLUE
GY GRAY
GN GREEN
TN TAN
Y YELLOW
R RED
O ORANGE
PK PINK
V VIOLET
W WHITE

17

## 1986, 1987 FXRS & 1988-1990 FXRS-SP

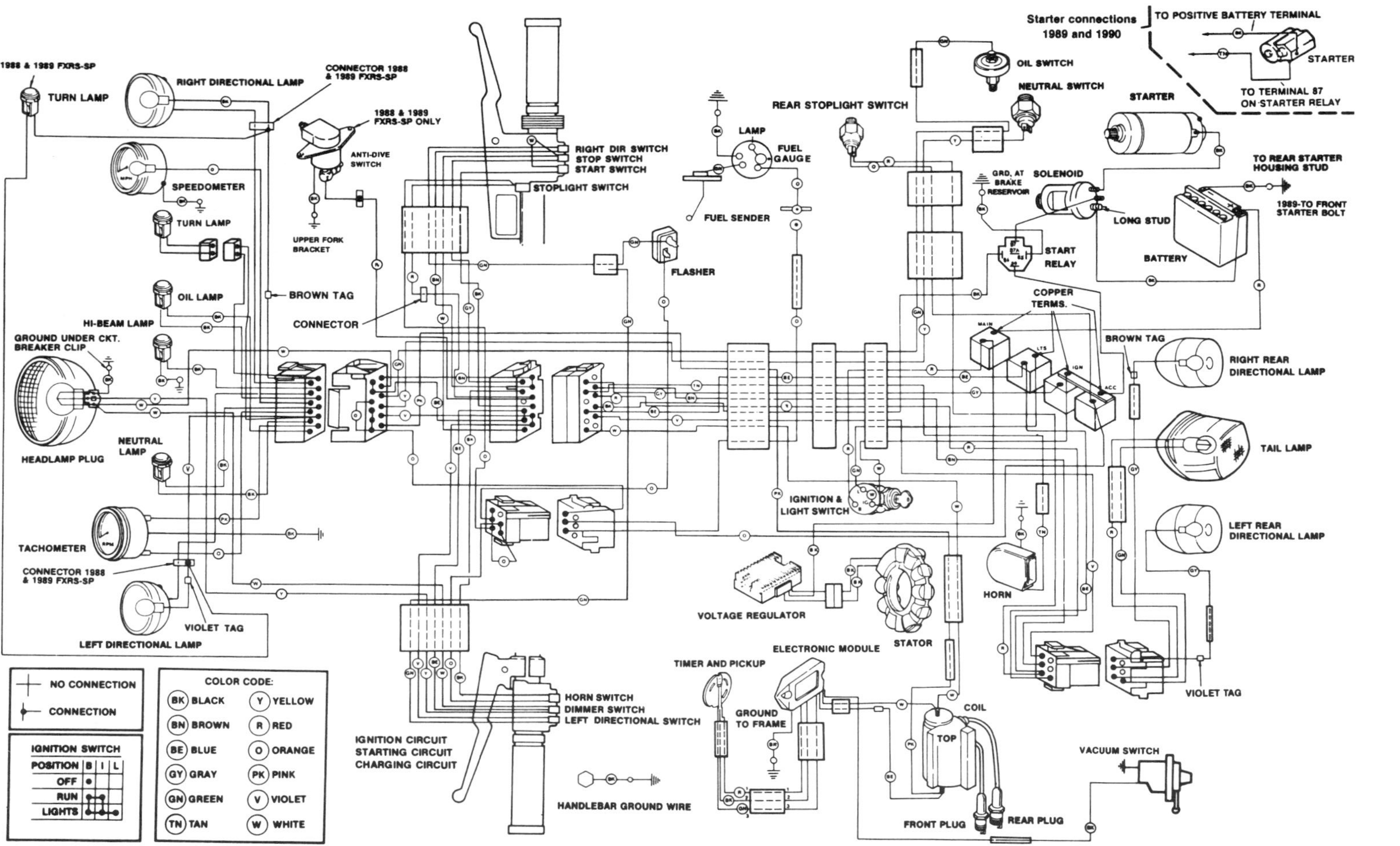

## 1987-1990 FXLR

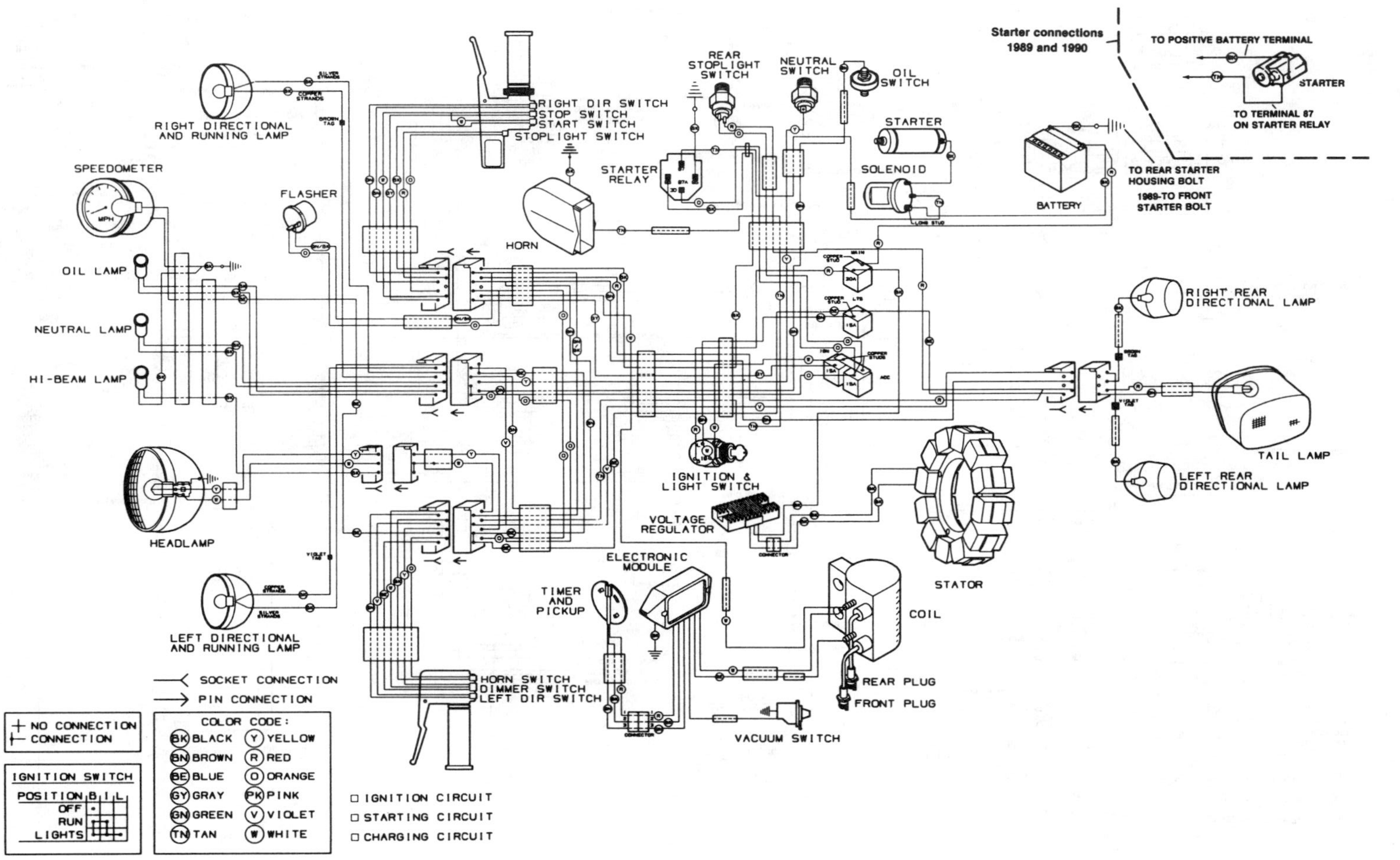

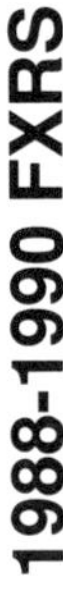

# 1988-1990 FXRS

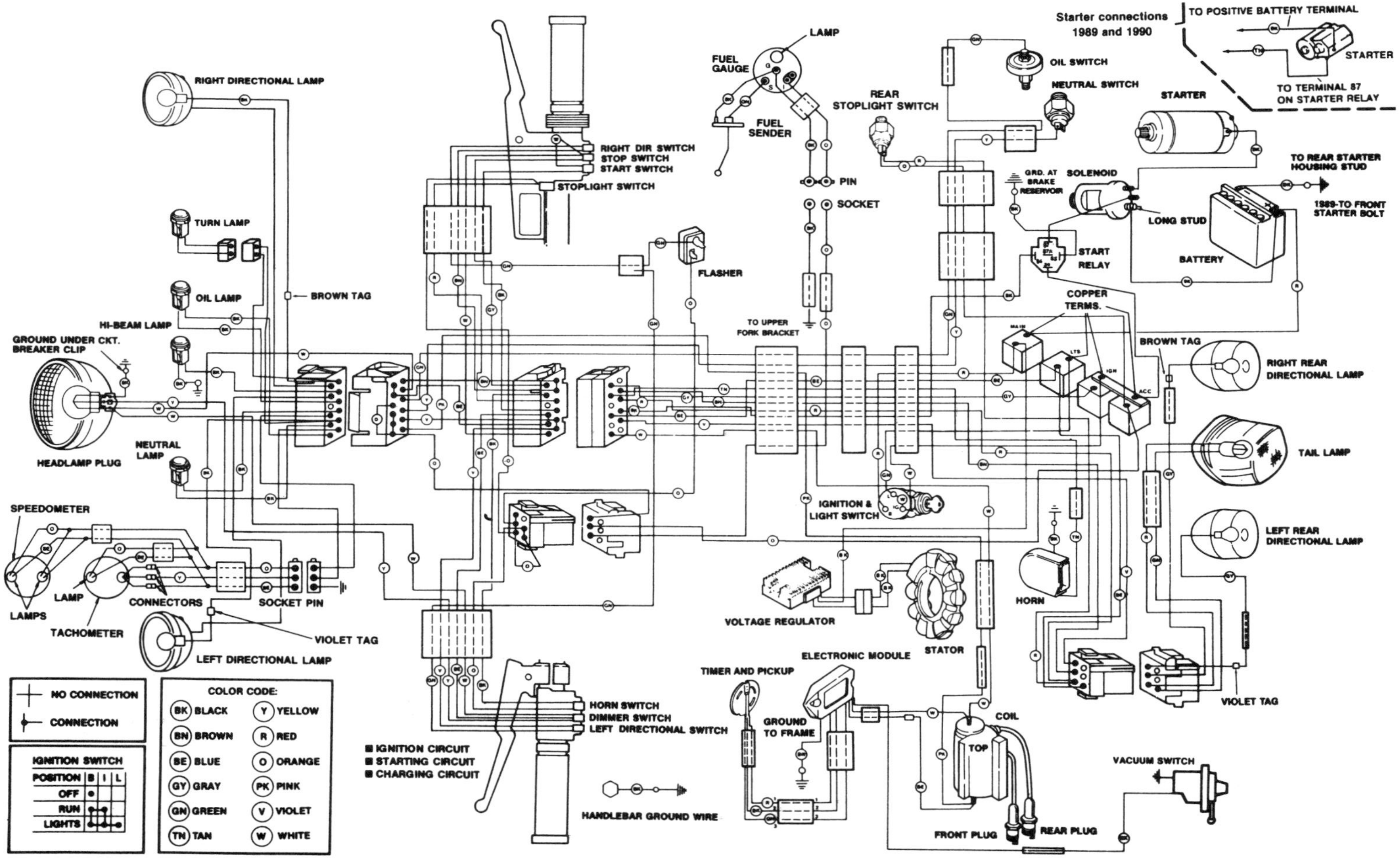

# 1988-1990 FXRT FAIRING

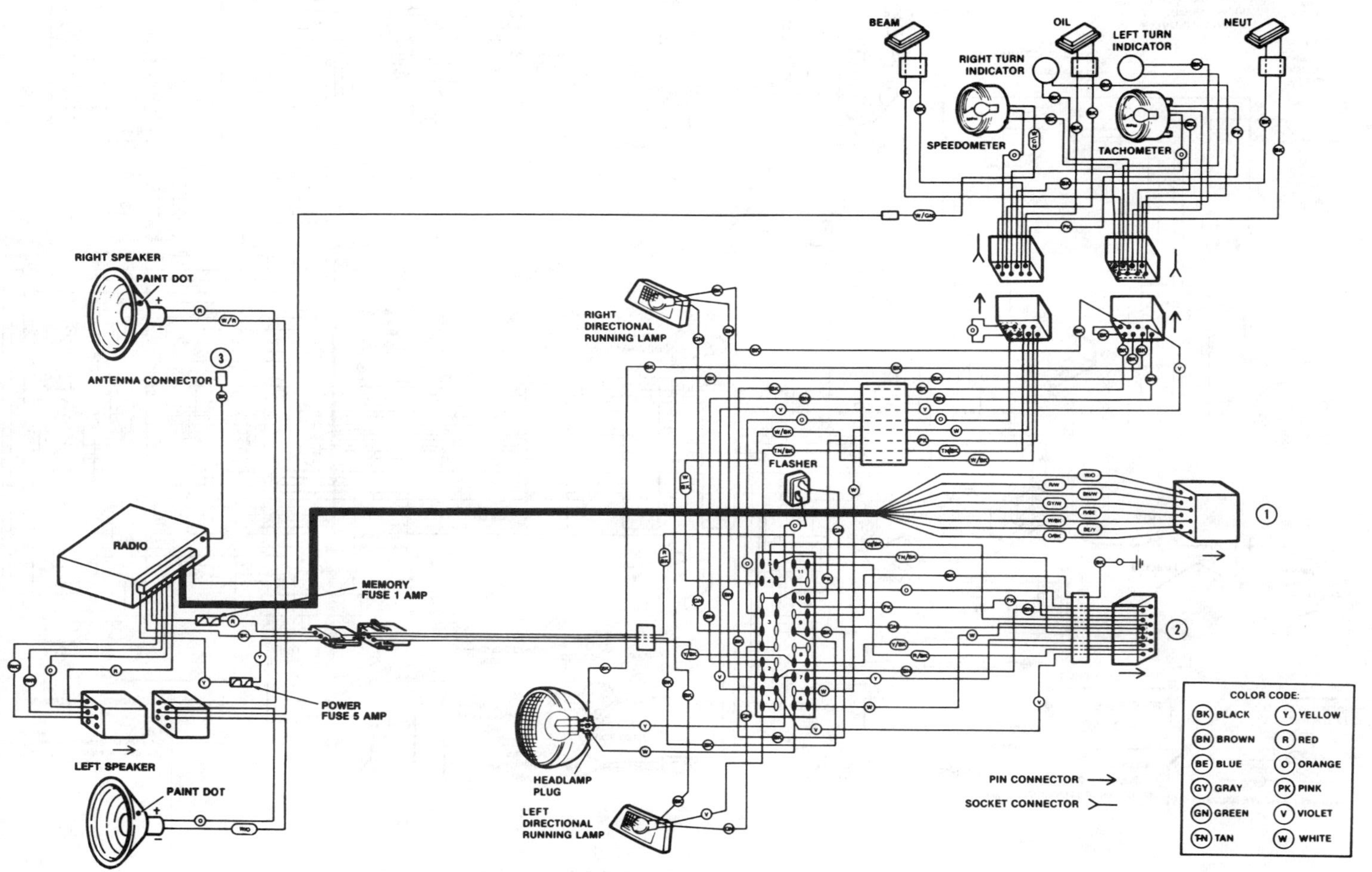

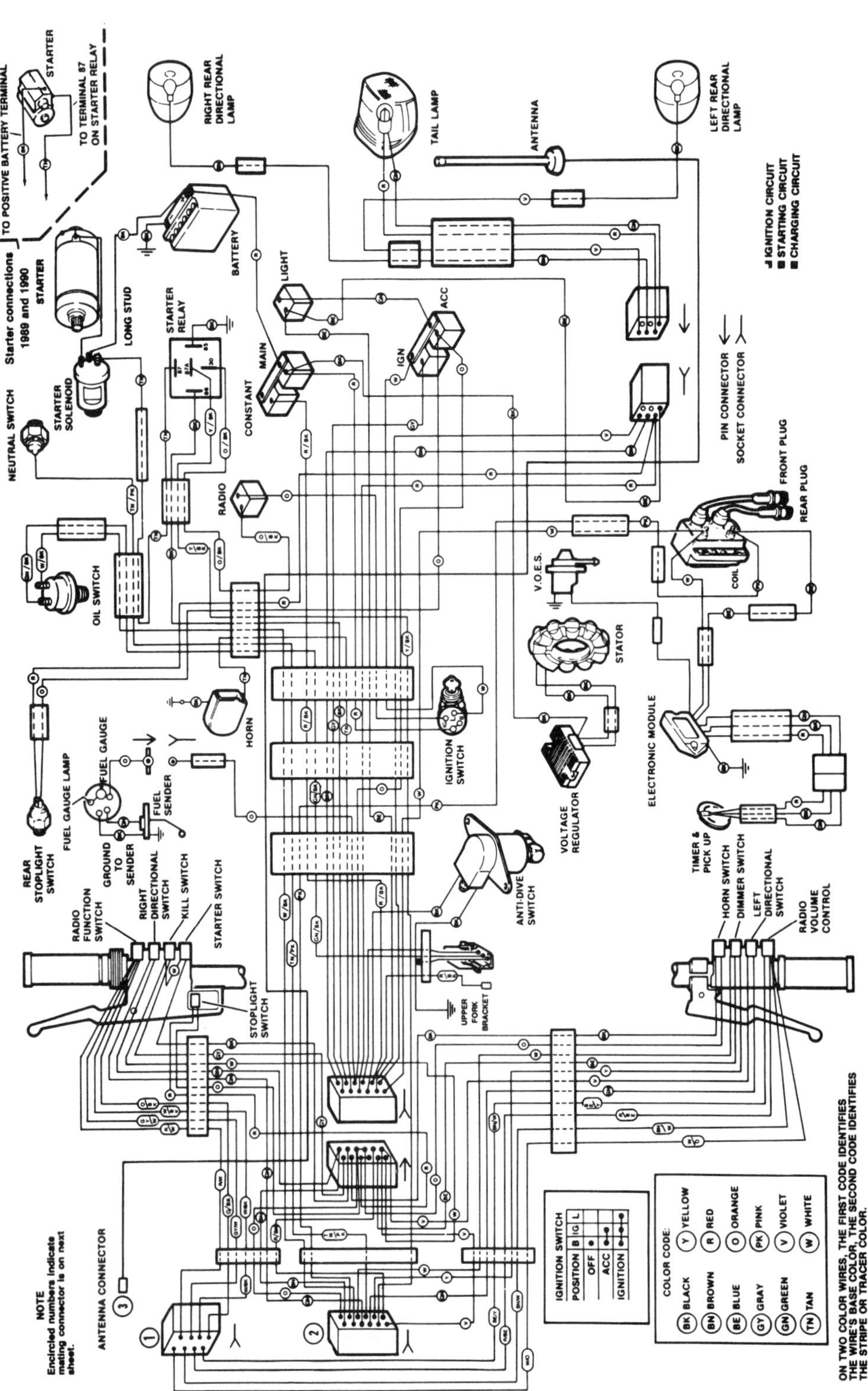

1988-1990 FXRT CHASSIS
Starter connections 1989 and 1990
TO POSITIVE BATTERY TERMINAL
TO TERMINAL 87 ON STARTER RELAY
STARTER
LONG STUD
STARTER SOLENOID
NEUTRAL SWITCH
OIL SWITCH
STARTER RELAY
BATTERY
RIGHT REAR DIRECTIONAL LAMP
TAIL LAMP
ANTENNA
LEFT REAR DIRECTIONAL LAMP
LIGHT
ACC
IGN
MAIN
CONSTANT
RADIO
PIN CONNECTOR
SOCKET CONNECTOR
IGNITION CIRCUIT
STARTING CIRCUIT
CHARGING CIRCUIT
FRONT PLUG
REAR PLUG
COIL
V.O.E.S.
STATOR
ELECTRONIC MODULE
VOLTAGE REGULATOR
TIMER & PICK UP
HORN
IGNITION SWITCH
ANTI-DIVE SWITCH
UPPER FORK BRACKET
FUEL GAUGE
FUEL GAUGE LAMP
FUEL SENDER
GROUND TO SENDER
REAR STOPLIGHT SWITCH
RADIO FUNCTION SWITCH
RIGHT DIRECTIONAL SWITCH
KILL SWITCH
STARTER SWITCH
STOPLIGHT SWITCH
HORN SWITCH
DIMMER SWITCH
LEFT DIRECTIONAL SWITCH
RADIO VOLUME CONTROL
NOTE Encircled numbers indicate mating connector is on next sheet.
ANTENNA CONNECTOR
IGNITION SWITCH
POSITION B IG L
OFF
ACC
IGNITION
COLOR CODE:
BK BLACK
BN BROWN
BE BLUE
GY GRAY
GN GREEN
TN TAN
Y YELLOW
R RED
O ORANGE
PK PINK
V VIOLET
W WHITE
ON TWO COLOR WIRES, THE FIRST CODE IDENTIFIES THE WIRE'S BASE COLOR, THE SECOND CODE IDENTIFIES THE STRIPE OR TRACER COLOR.

# 1988 FLTC FAIRING

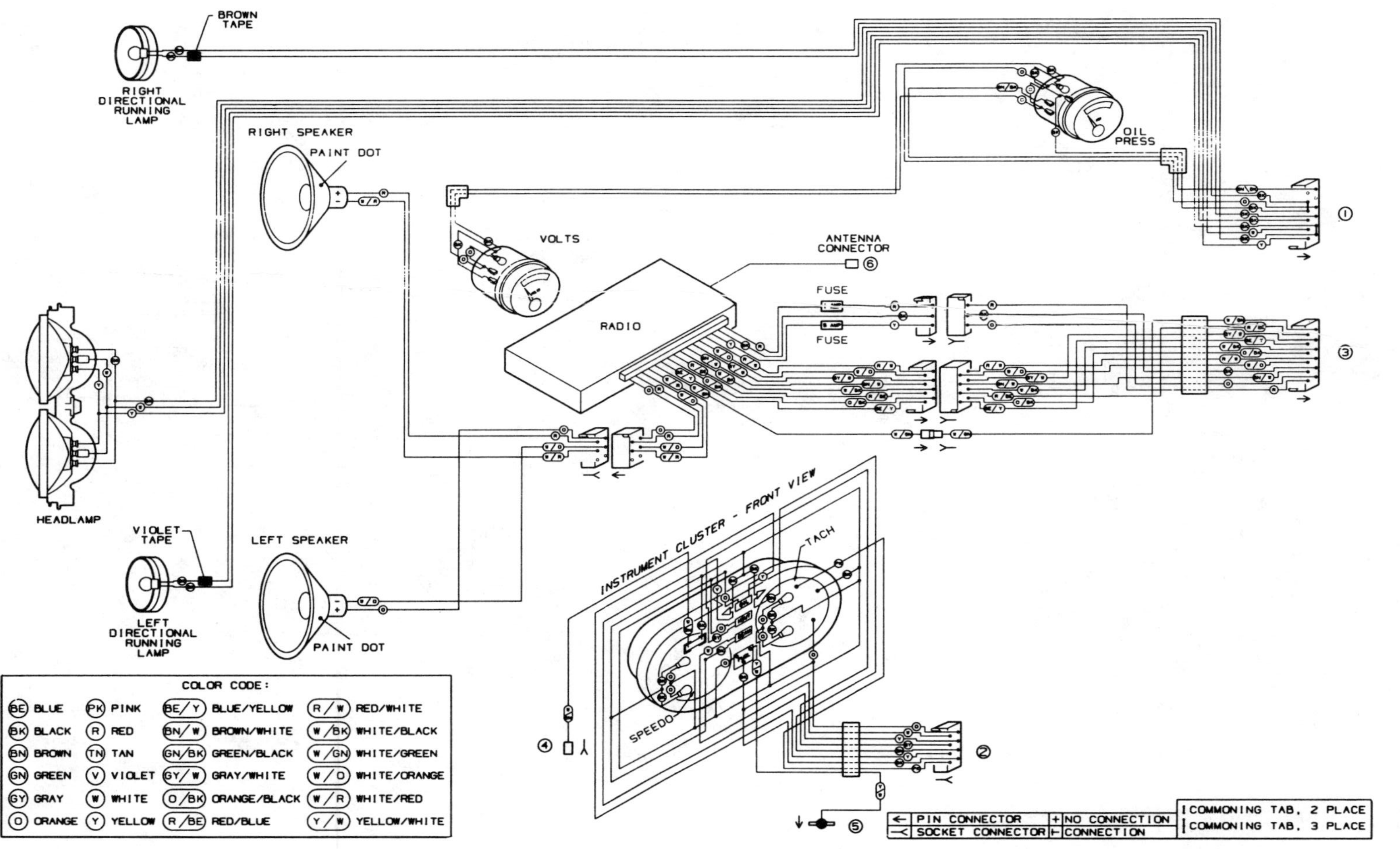


17

# 1988 FLTC CHASSIS

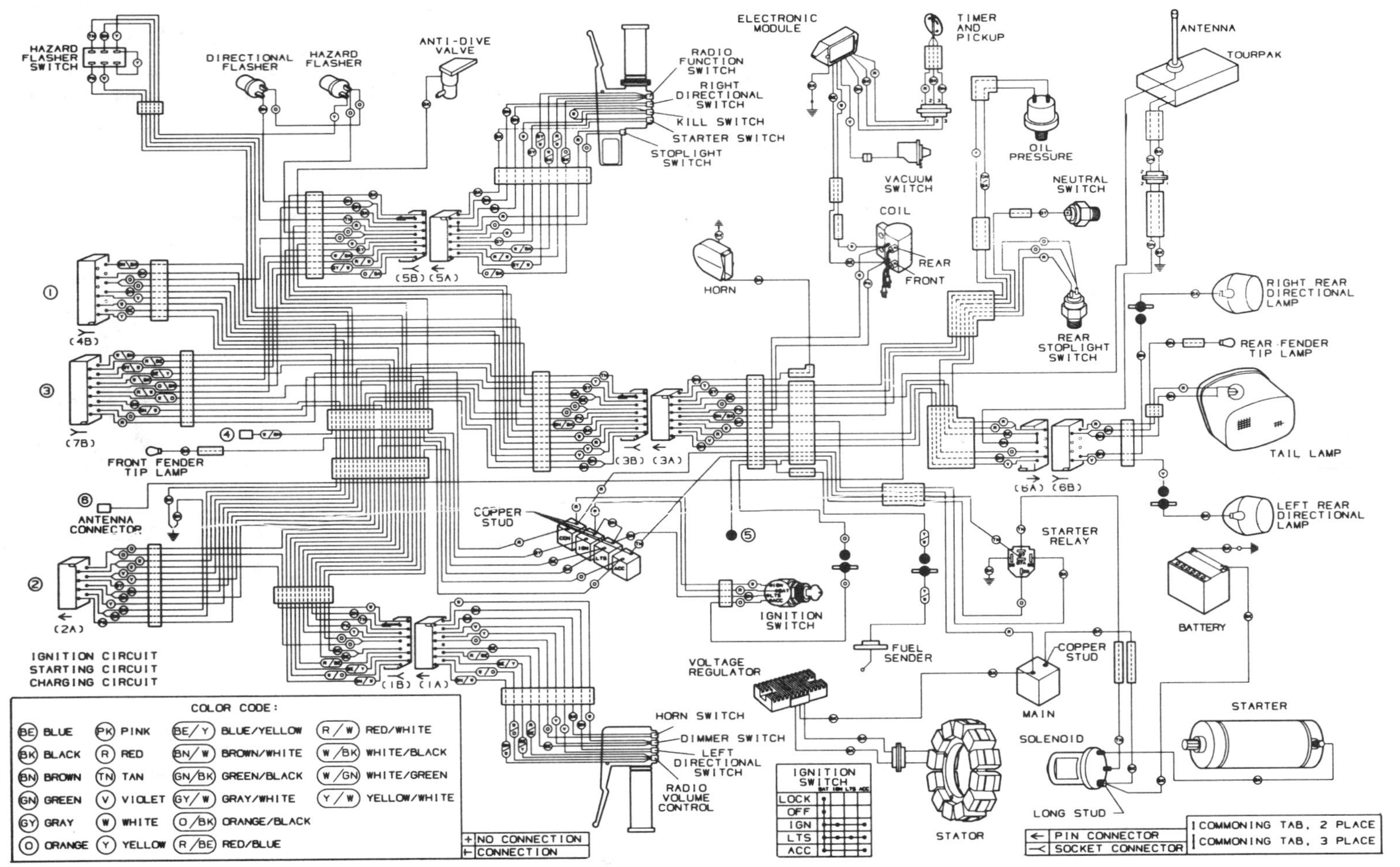

# 1988 FLHTC FAIRING

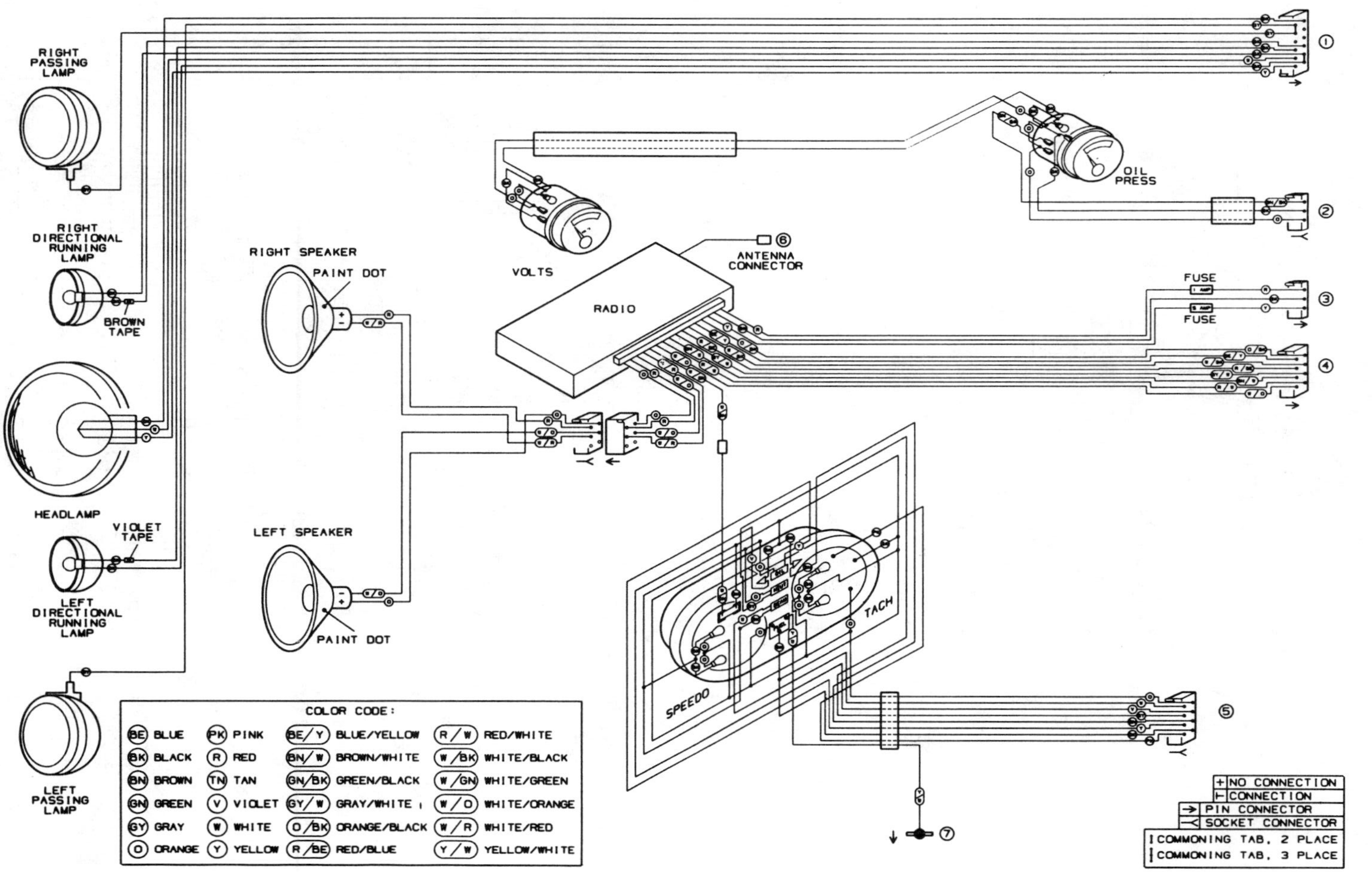

# 1988 FLHTC CHASSIS

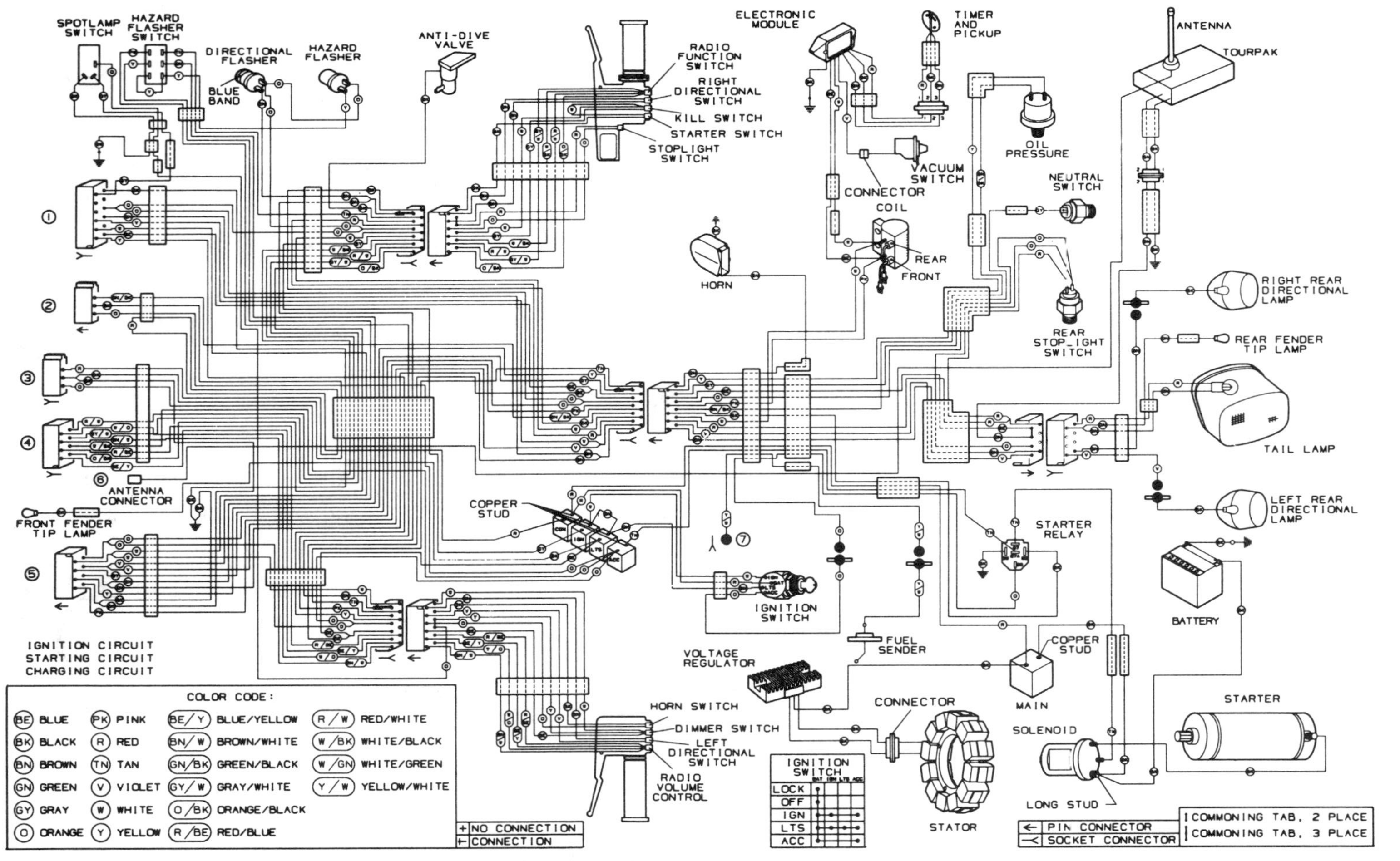

# 1988 FLHS CHASSIS (PART 1 OF 2)

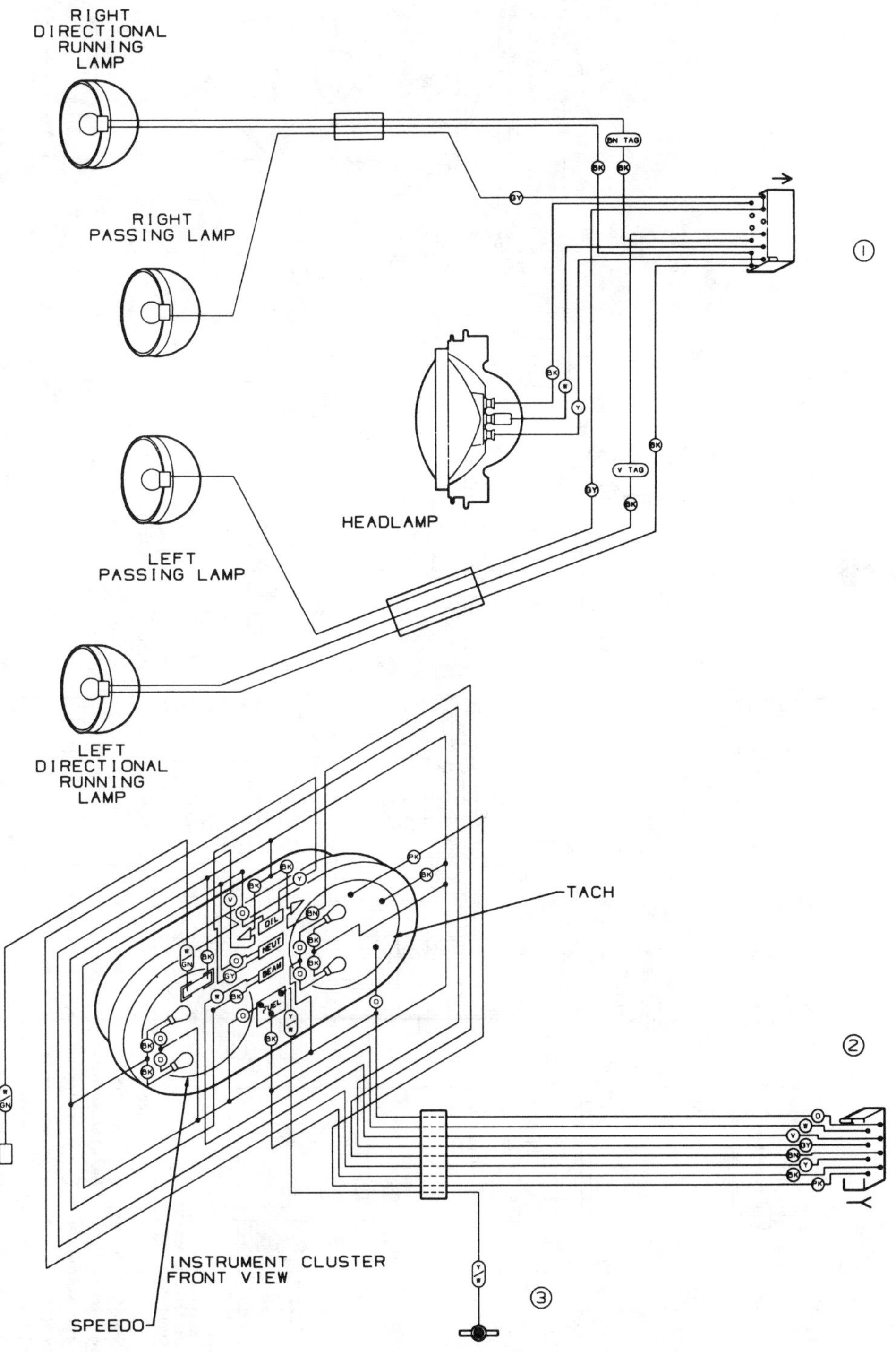

# 1988 FLHS CHASSIS (PART 2 OF 2)

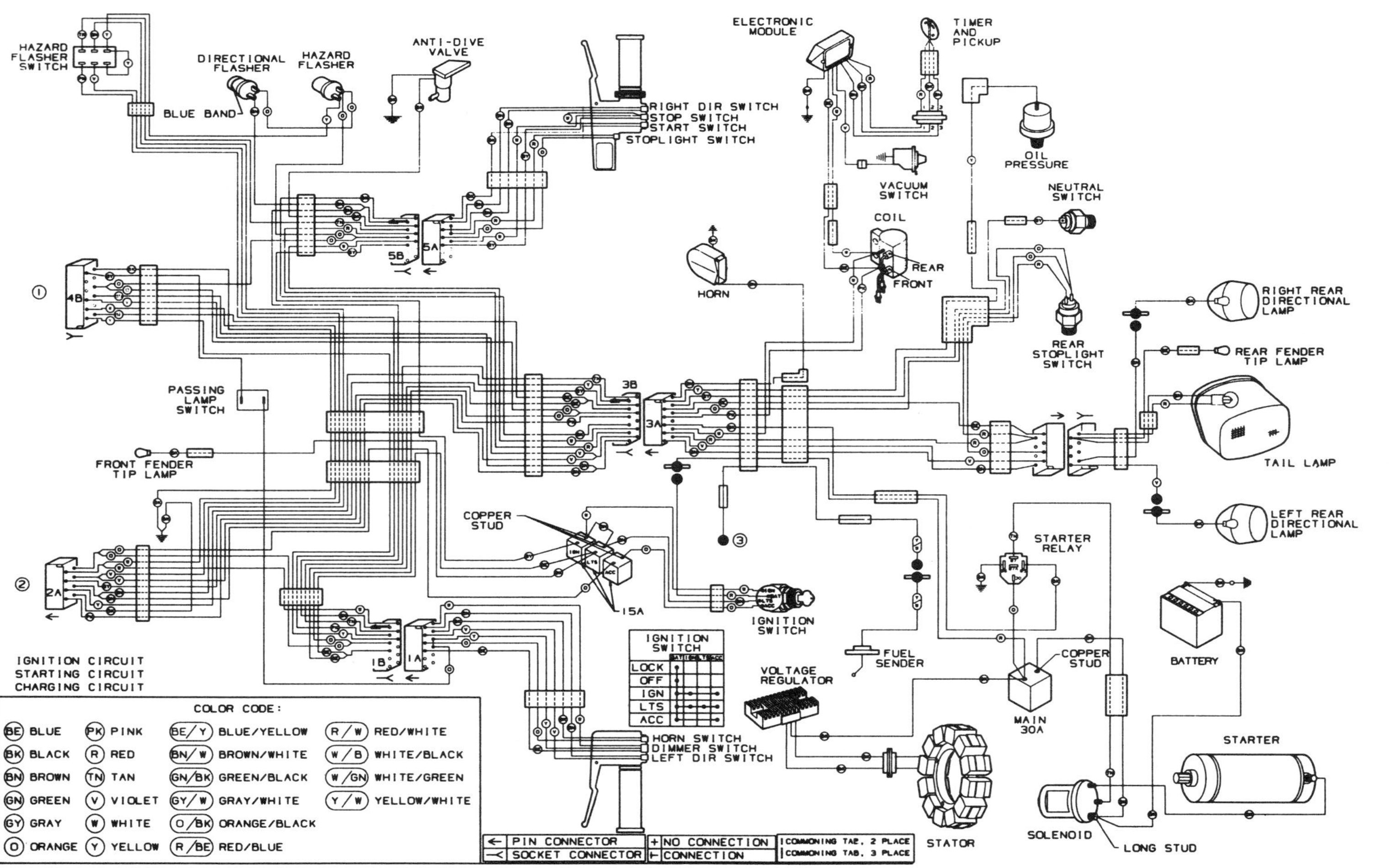

# 1989-1990 FLTC FAIRING

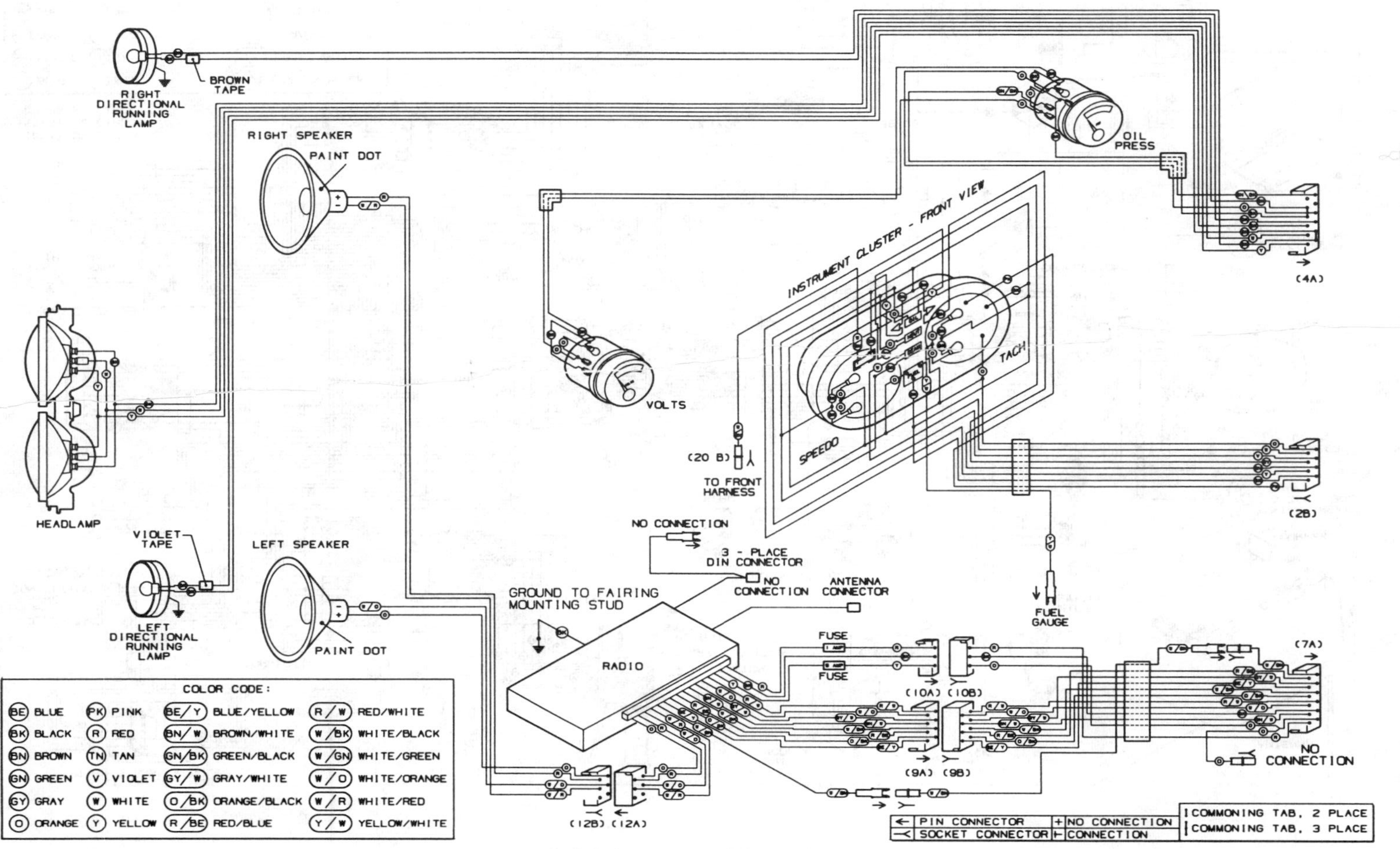


17

# 1989 FLTC, CHASSIS

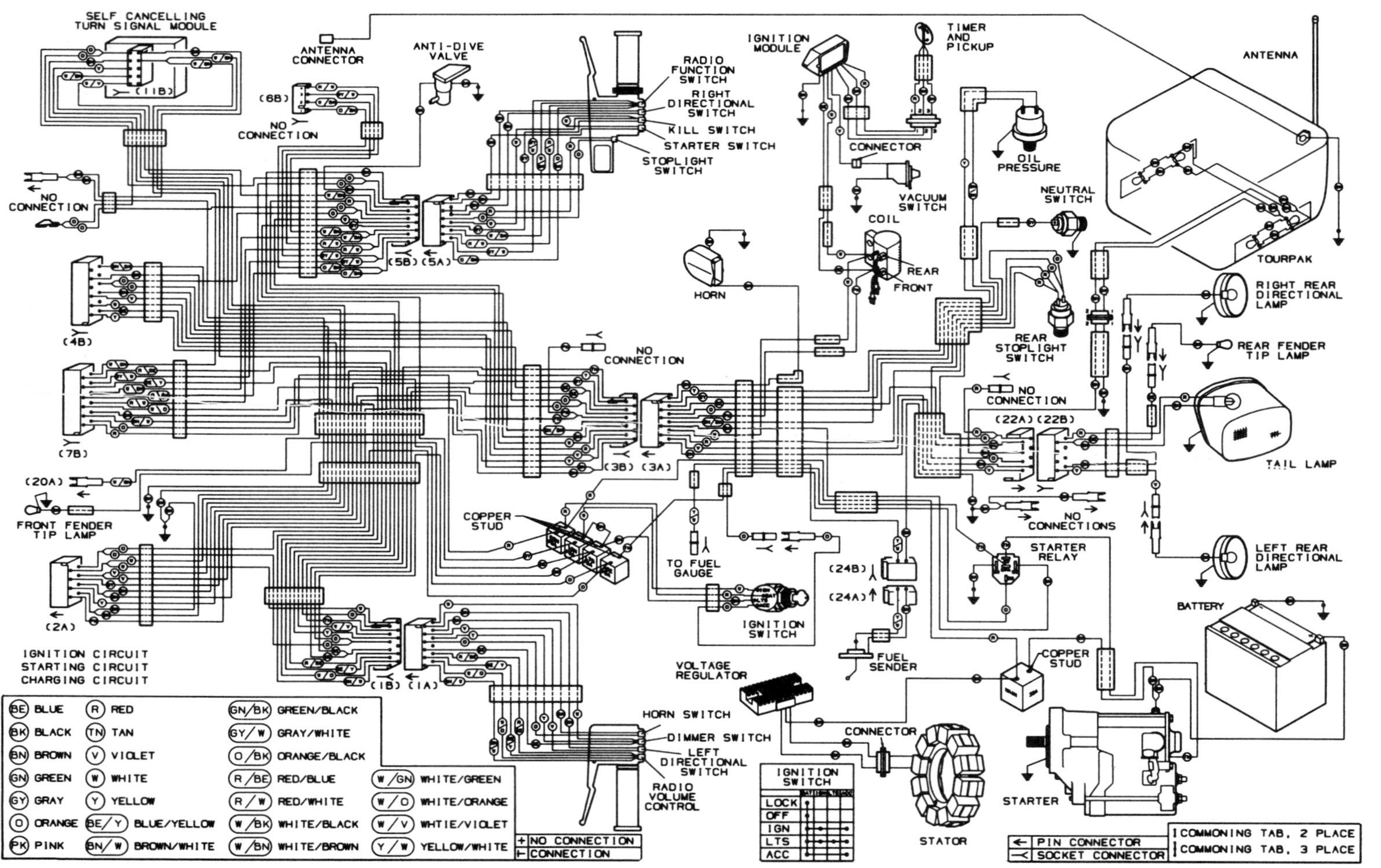

# 1989-1990 FLHTC FAIRING

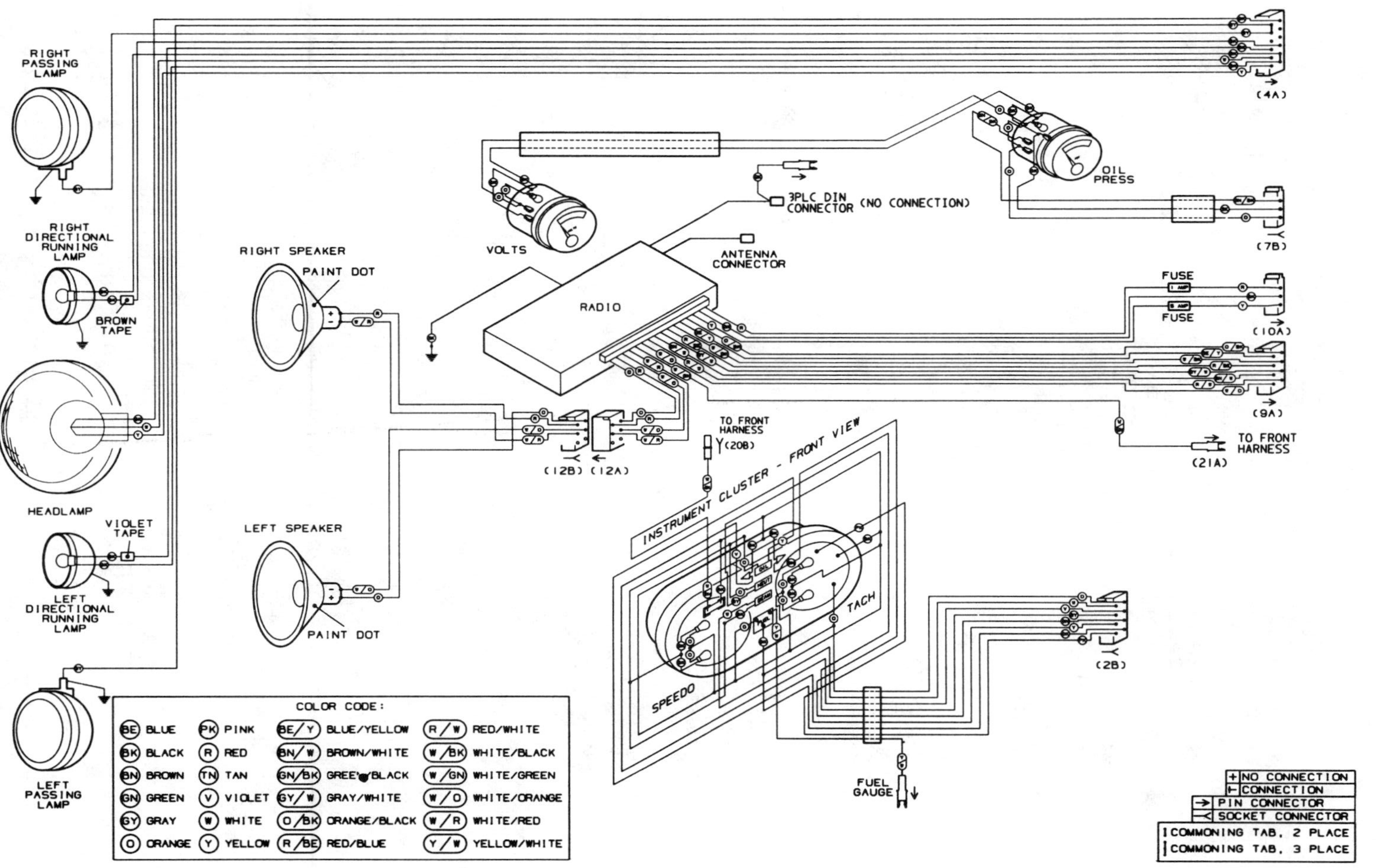


17

# 1989 FLHTC, CHASSIS

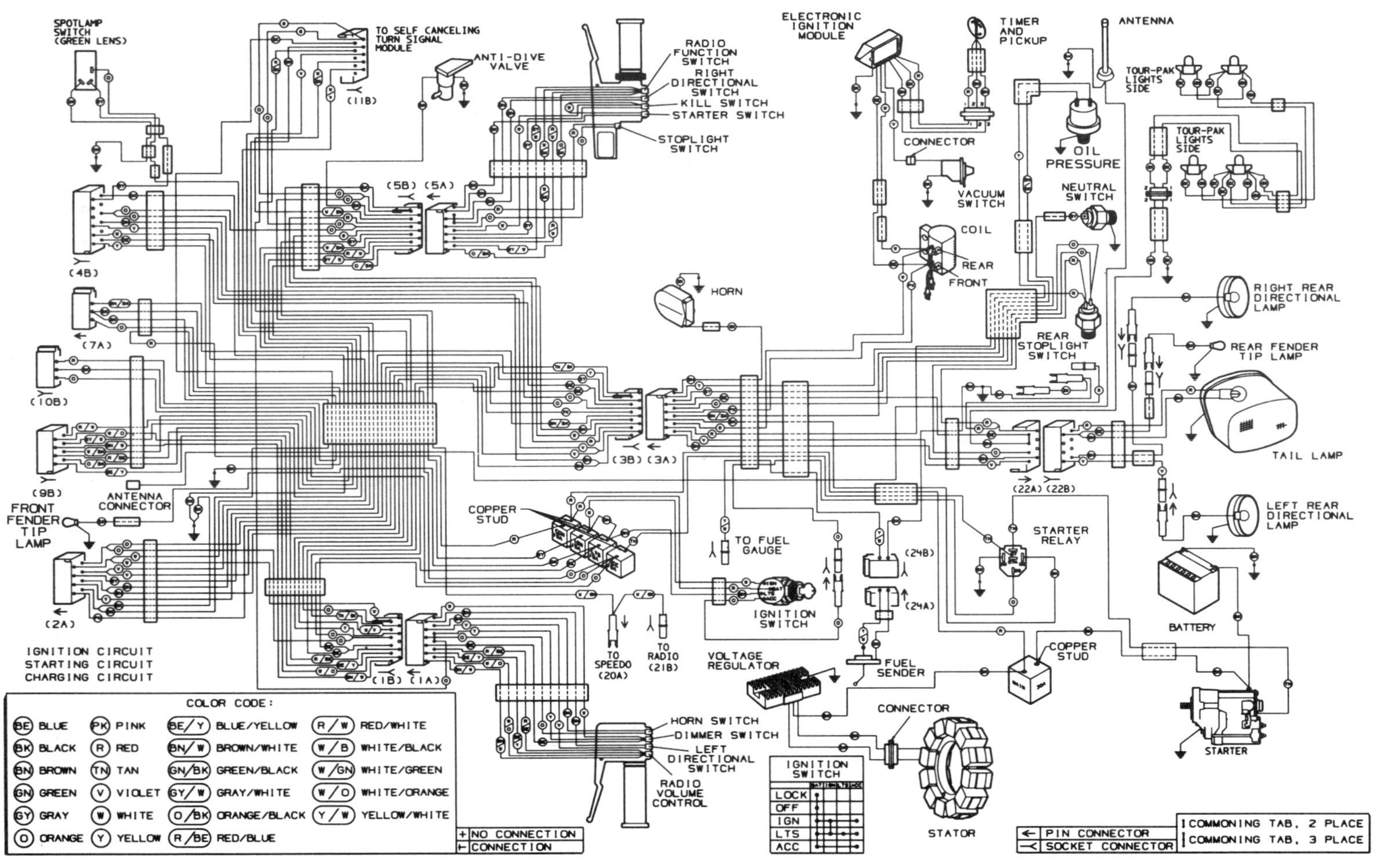

# 1989-1990 FLHS INSTRUMENTS

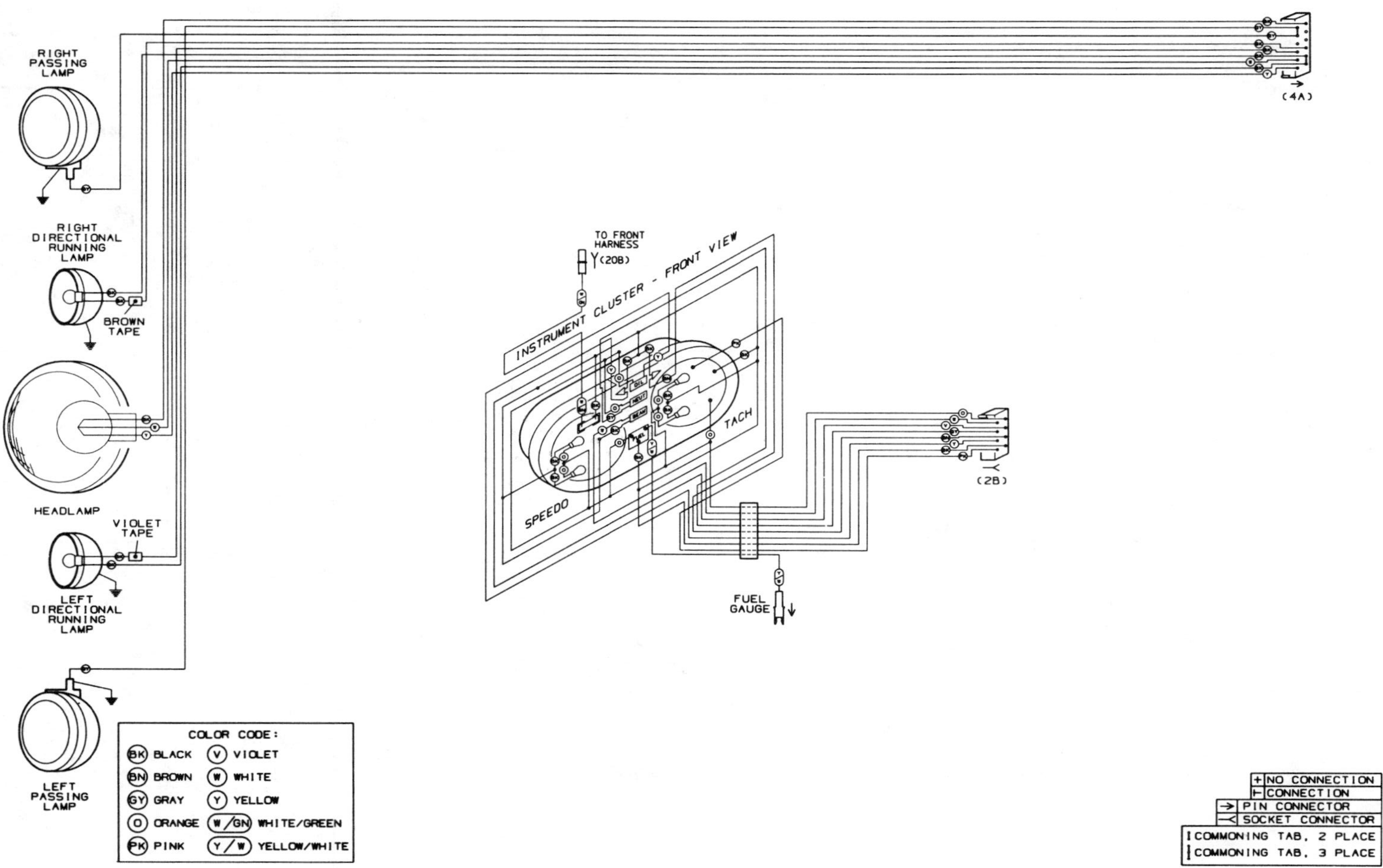

# 1989 FLHS CHASSIS

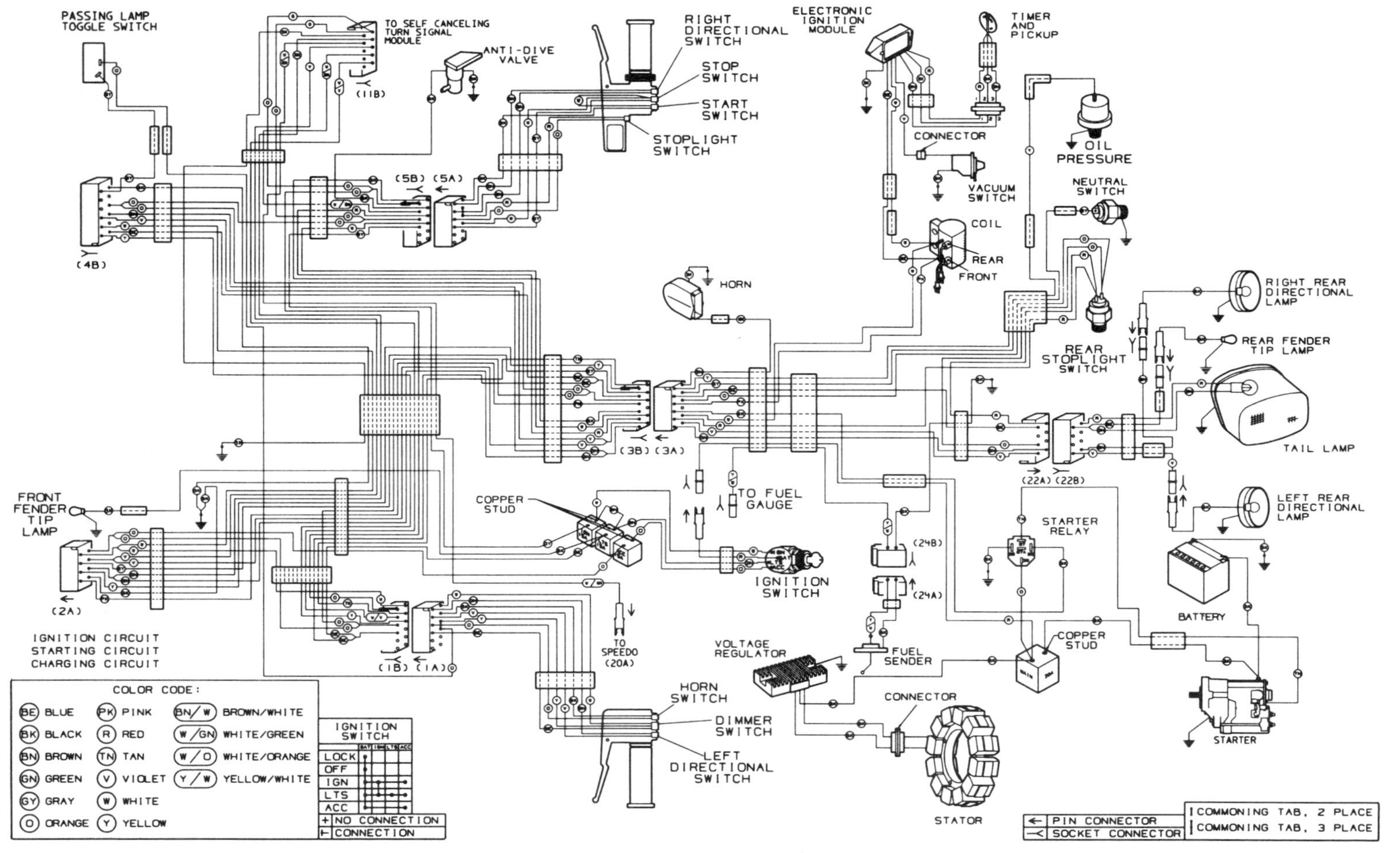

# 1989 FLTC ULTRA, CHASSIS (PART 1 OF 3)

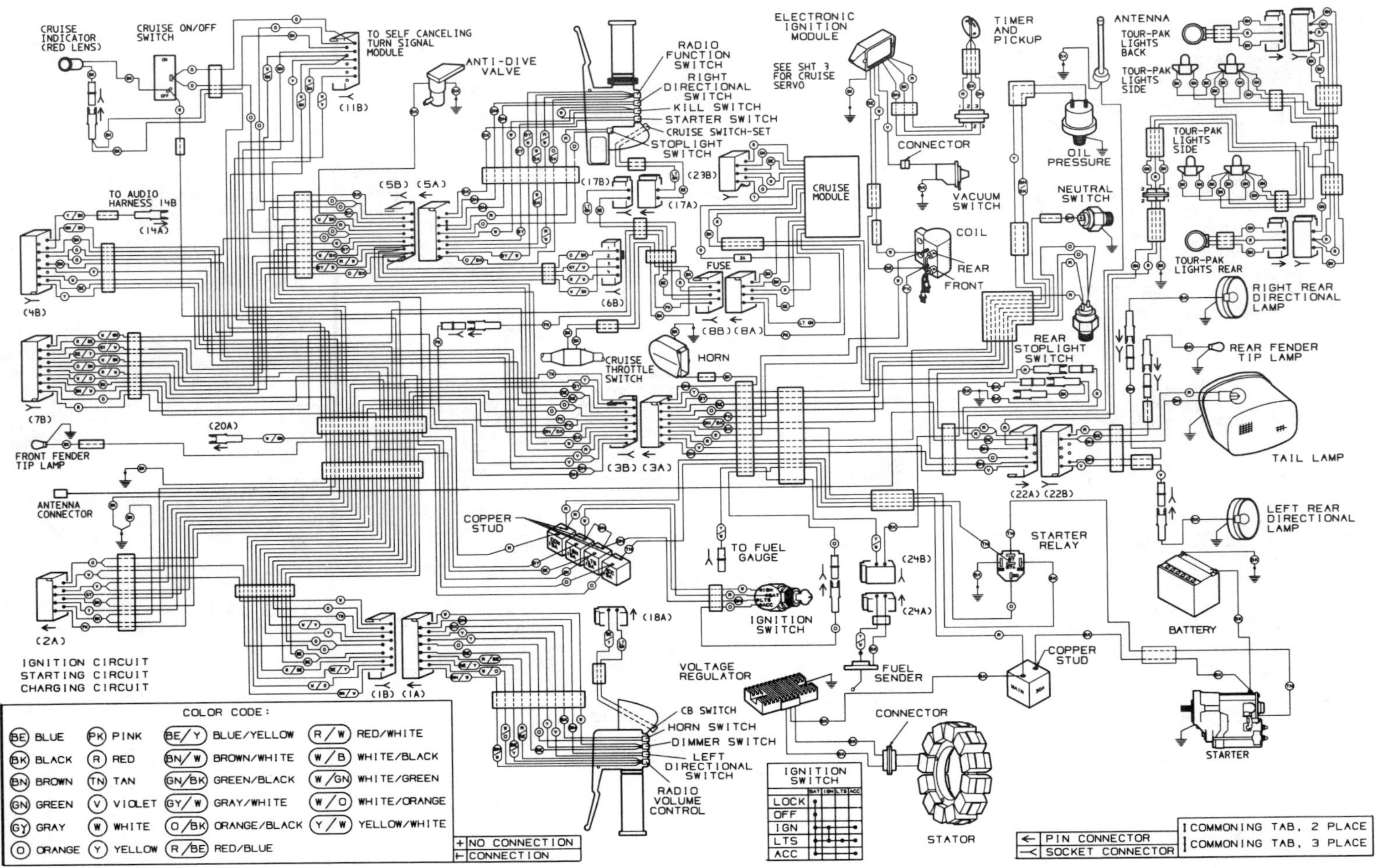

## 1989 FLTC ULTRA, FAIRING (PART 2 OF 3)

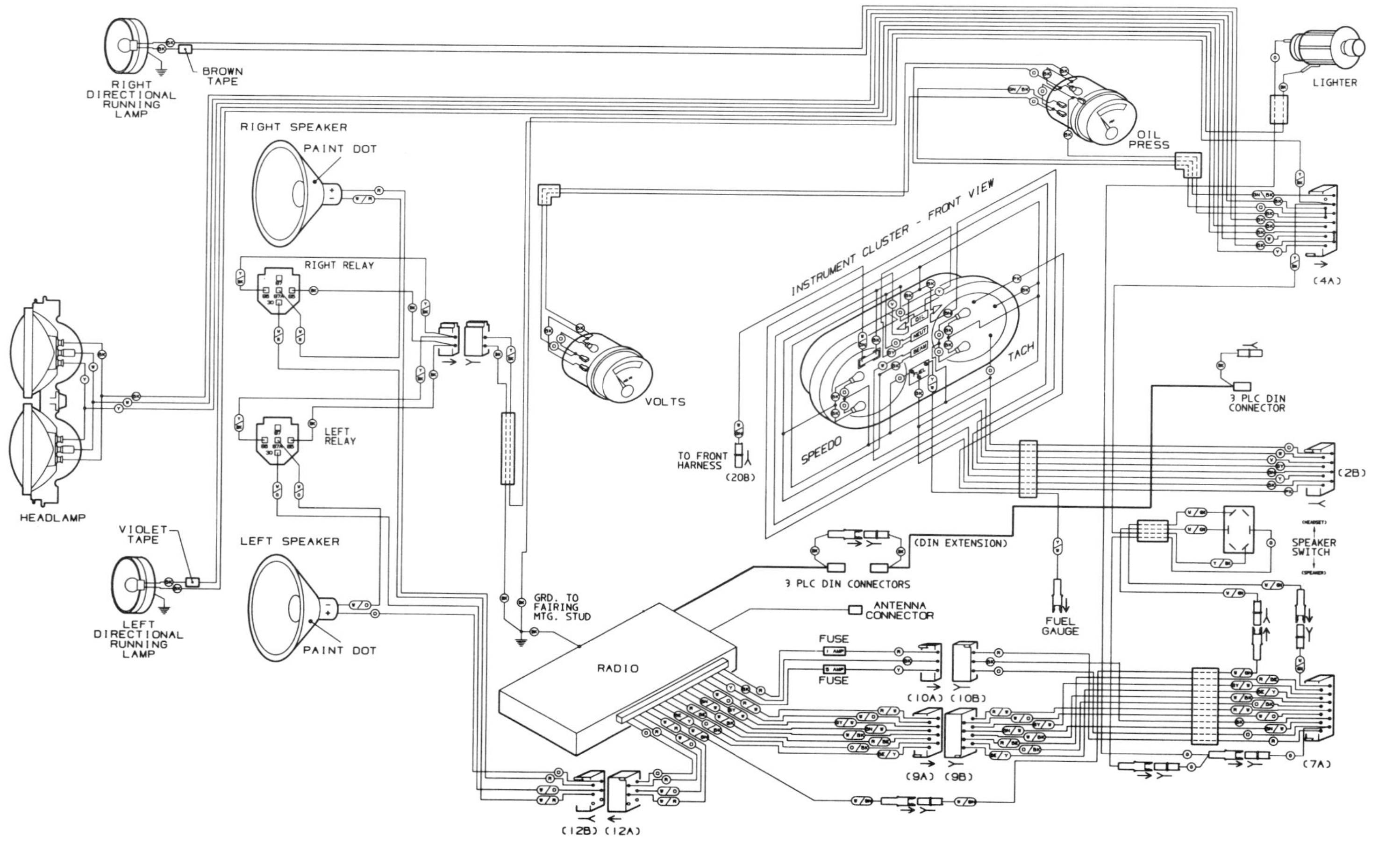

# 1989 FLTC ULTRA, CB/INTERCOM (PART 3 OF 3)

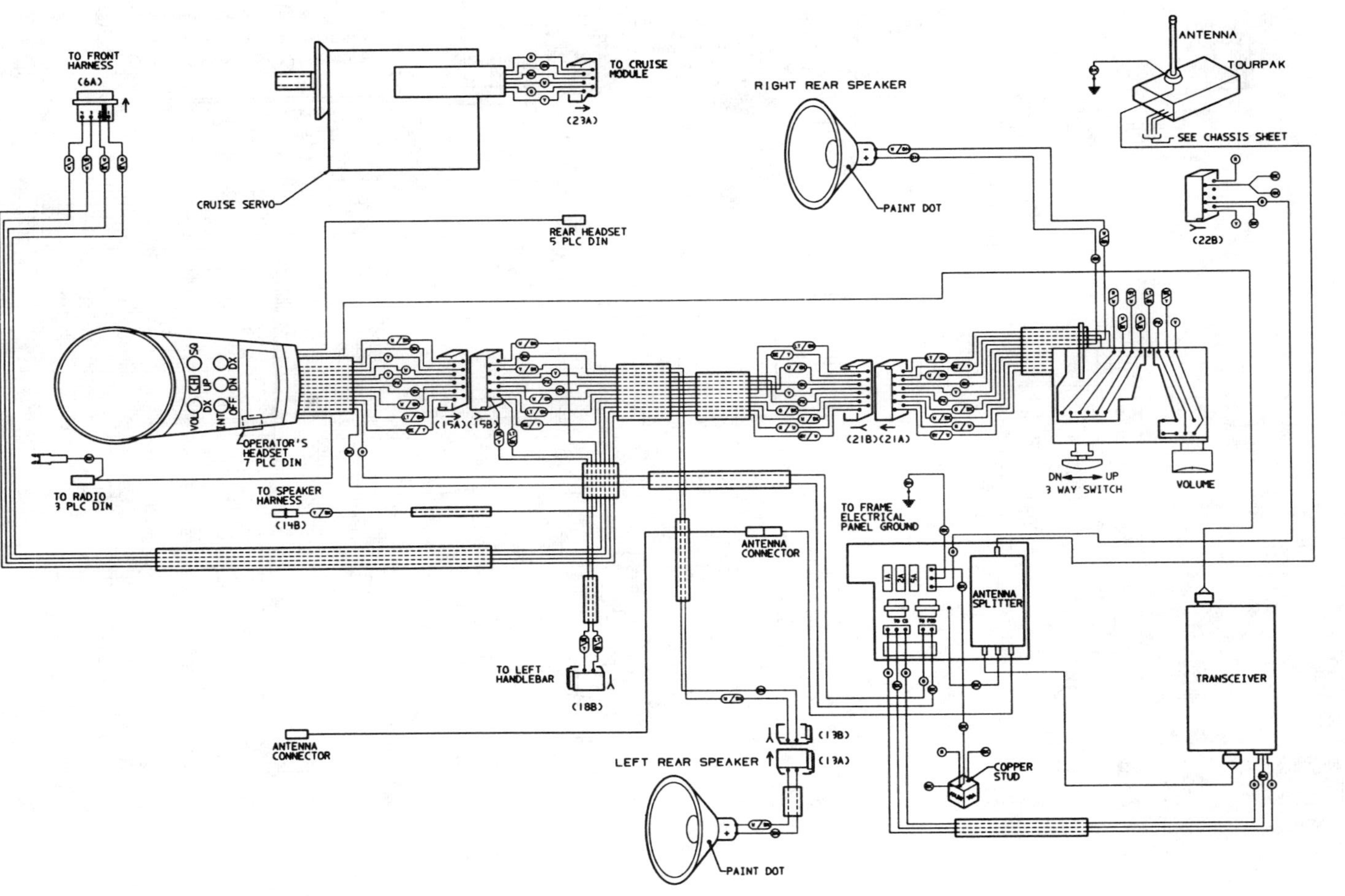

# 1989 FLHTC ULTRA, CHASSIS (PART 1 OF 3)

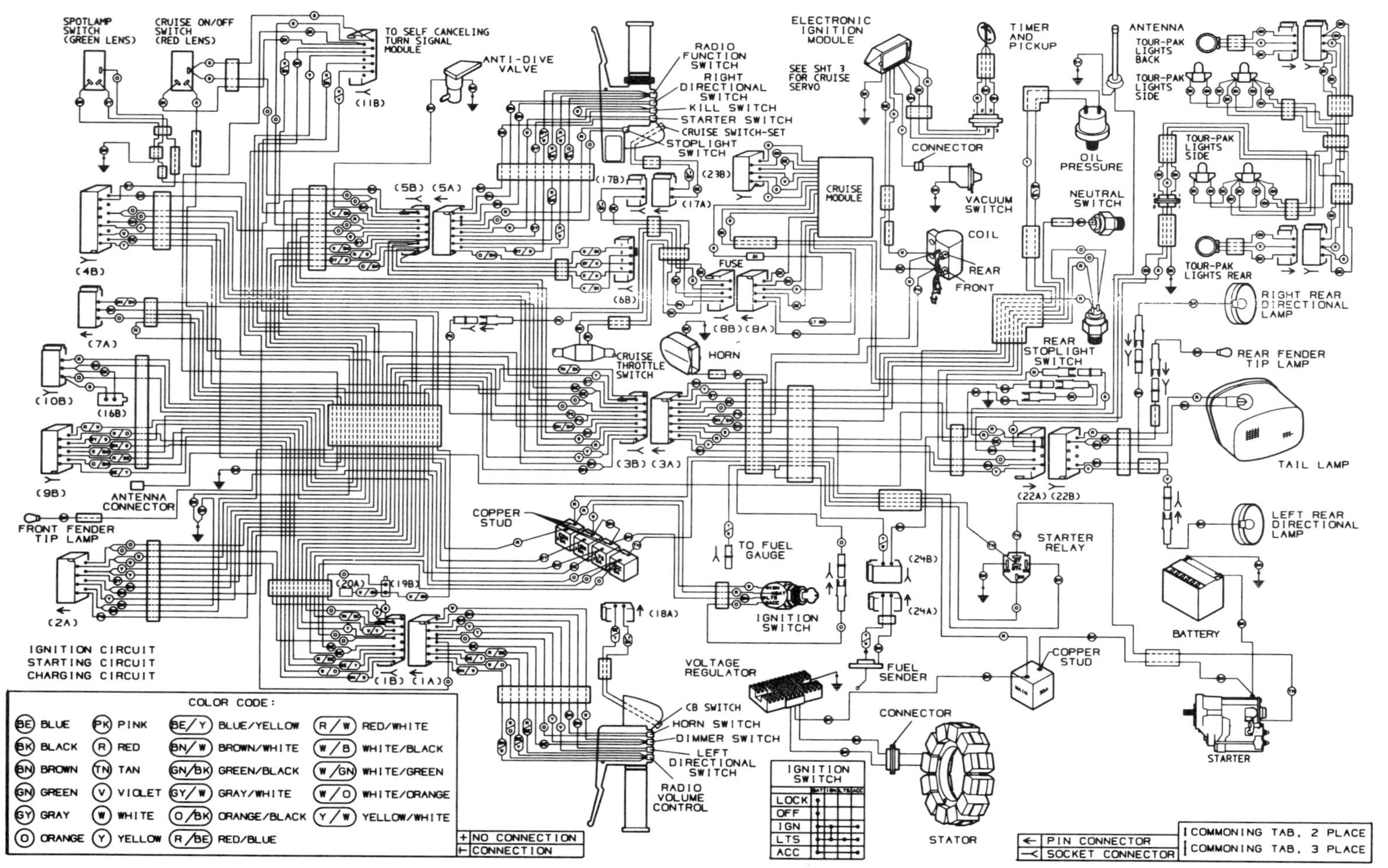

## 1989 FLHTC ULTRA, FAIRING (PART 2 OF 3)

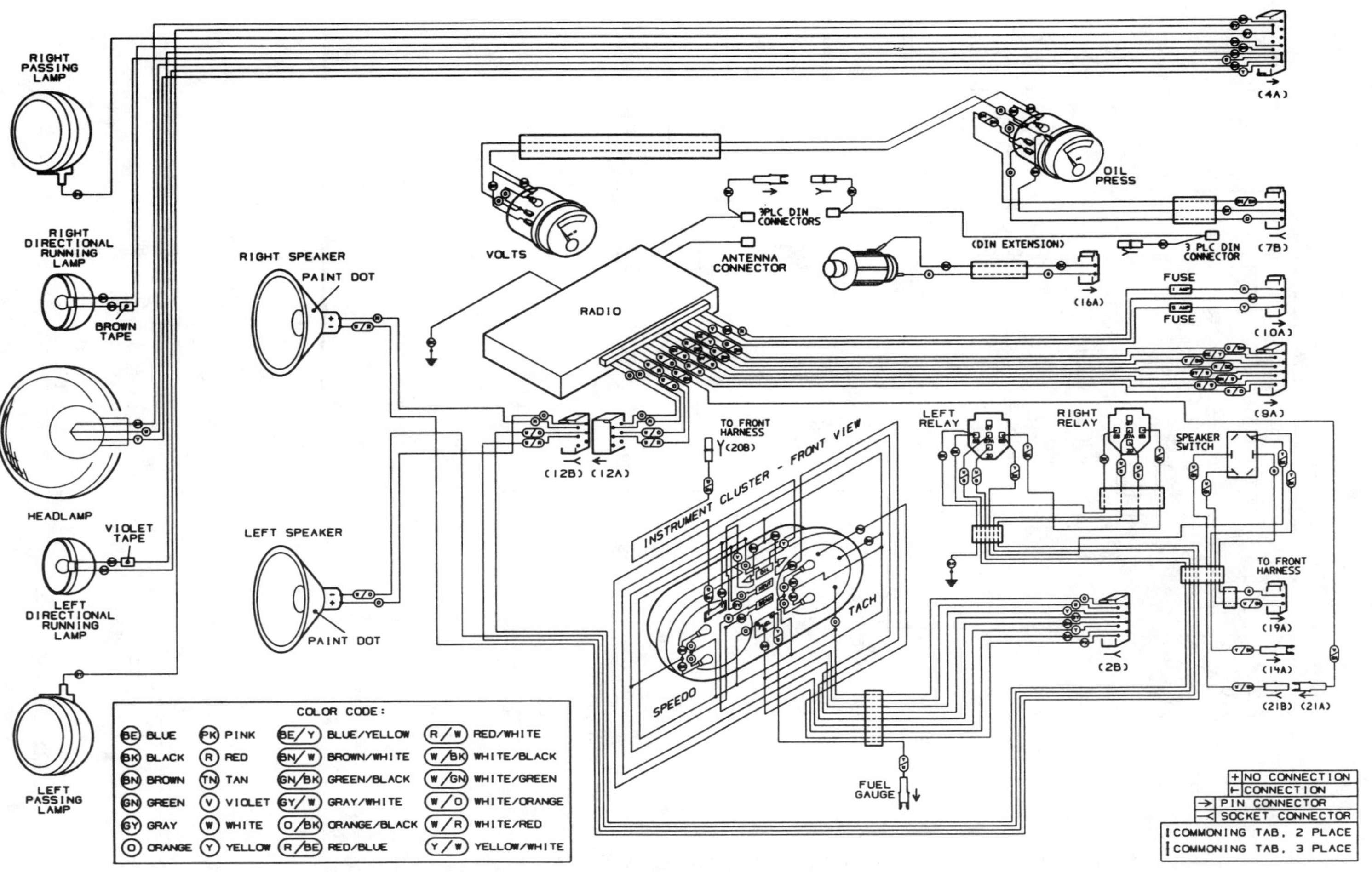

# 1989 FLHTC ULTRA, CB/INTERCOM (PART 3 OF 3)

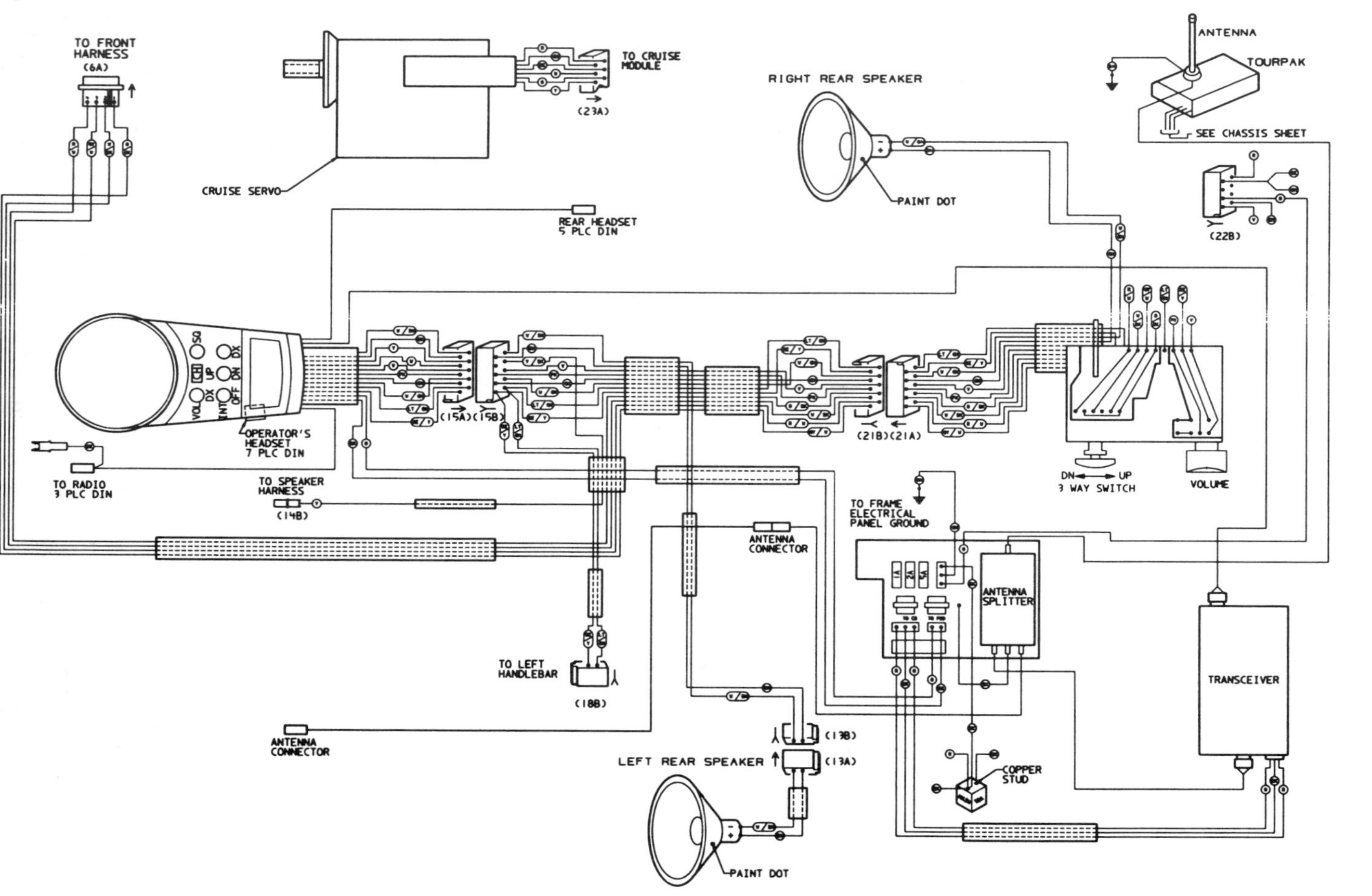

# 1990 FLTC CHASSIS (SEE 1989-1990 FAIRING)

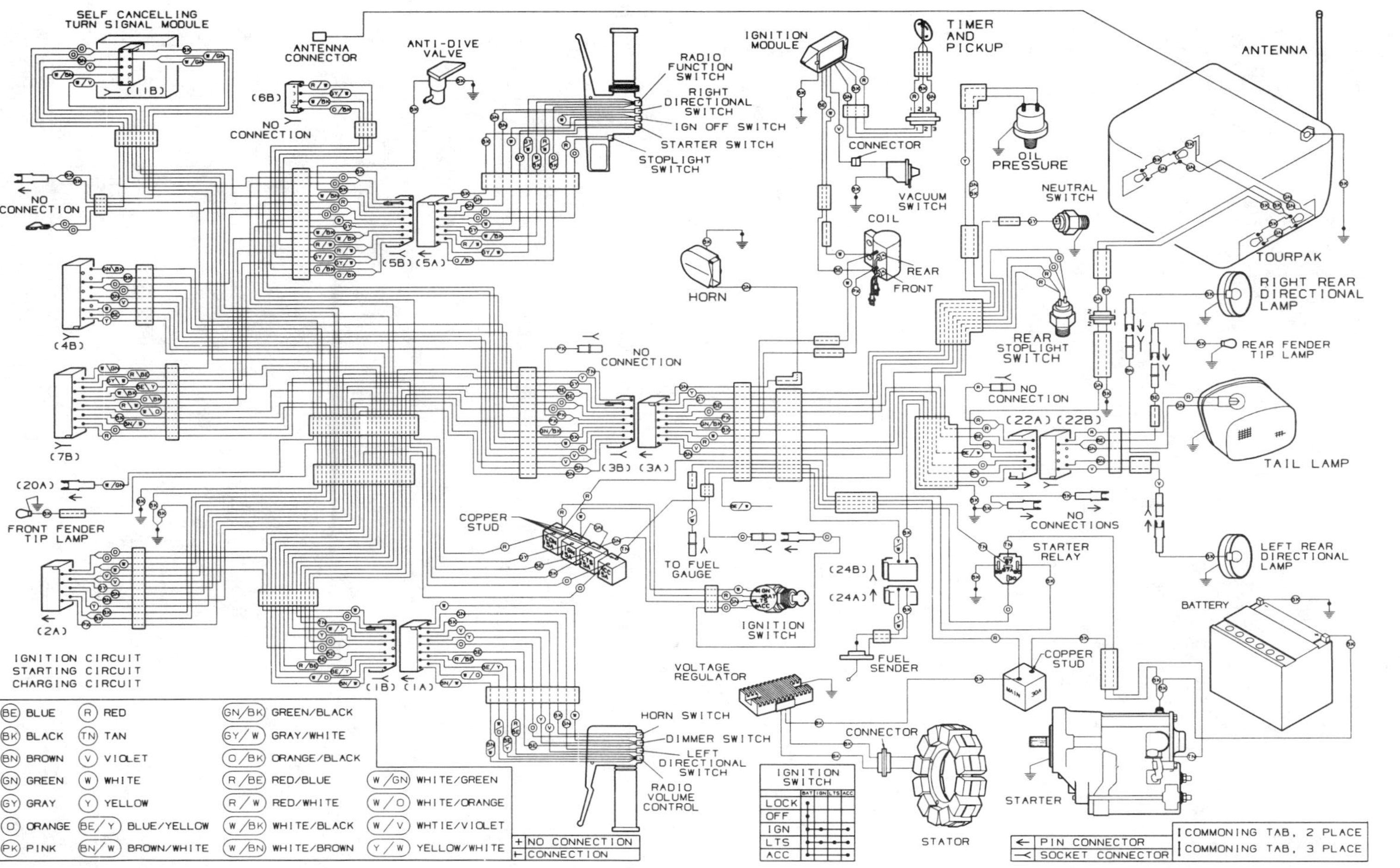

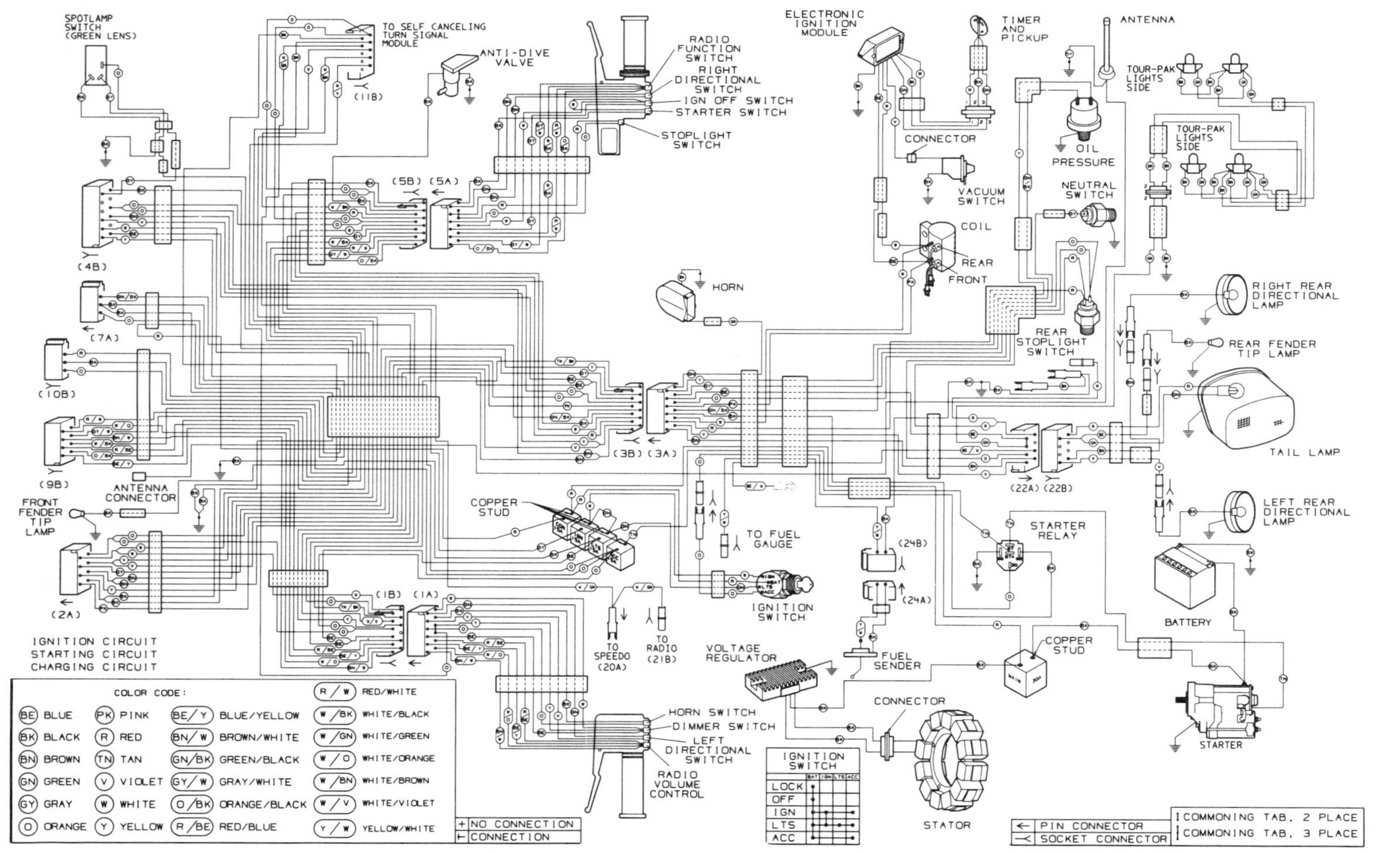
1990 FLHTC CHASSIS (SEE 1989-1990 FAIRING)
SPOTLAMP SWITCH (GREEN LENS)
TO SELF CANCELING TURN SIGNAL MODULE
(11B)
ANTI-DIVE VALVE
RADIO FUNCTION SWITCH
RIGHT DIRECTIONAL SWITCH
IGN OFF SWITCH
STARTER SWITCH
STOPLIGHT SWITCH
ELECTRONIC IGNITION MODULE
TIMER AND PICKUP
ANTENNA
TOUR-PAK LIGHTS SIDE
CONNECTOR
OIL PRESSURE
TOUR-PAK LIGHTS SIDE
VACUUM SWITCH
NEUTRAL SWITCH
(5B) (5A)
(4B)
COIL
REAR
FRONT
HORN
(7A)
RIGHT REAR DIRECTIONAL LAMP
REAR STOPLIGHT SWITCH
REAR FENDER TIP LAMP
(10B)
(3B) (3A)
TAIL LAMP
(9B)
ANTENNA CONNECTOR
(22A) (22B)
FRONT FENDER TIP LAMP
COPPER STUD
TO FUEL GAUGE
STARTER RELAY
LEFT REAR DIRECTIONAL LAMP
(24B)
(24A)
(2A)
(1B) (1A)
IGNITION SWITCH
BATTERY
TO SPEEDO (20A)
TO RADIO (21B)
VOLTAGE REGULATOR
FUEL SENDER
COPPER STUD
IGNITION CIRCUIT
STARTING CIRCUIT
CHARGING CIRCUIT
COLOR CODE:
BE BLUE
BK BLACK
BN BROWN
GN GREEN
GY GRAY
O ORANGE
PK PINK
R RED
TN TAN
V VIOLET
W WHITE
Y YELLOW
BE/Y BLUE/YELLOW
BN/W BROWN/WHITE
GN/BK GREEN/BLACK
GY/W GRAY/WHITE
O/BK ORANGE/BLACK
R/BE RED/BLUE
R/W RED/WHITE
W/BK WHITE/BLACK
W/GN WHITE/GREEN
W/O WHITE/ORANGE
W/BN WHITE/BROWN
W/V WHITE/VIOLET
Y/W YELLOW/WHITE
HORN SWITCH
DIMMER SWITCH
LEFT DIRECTIONAL SWITCH
RADIO VOLUME CONTROL
CONNECTOR
STARTER
IGNITION SWITCH
LOCK
OFF
IGN
LTS
ACC
STATOR
NO CONNECTION
CONNECTION
PIN CONNECTOR
SOCKET CONNECTOR
COMMONING TAB, 2 PLACE
COMMONING TAB, 3 PLACE

# 1990 FLHS CHASSIS (SEE 1989-1990 INSTRUMENTS)

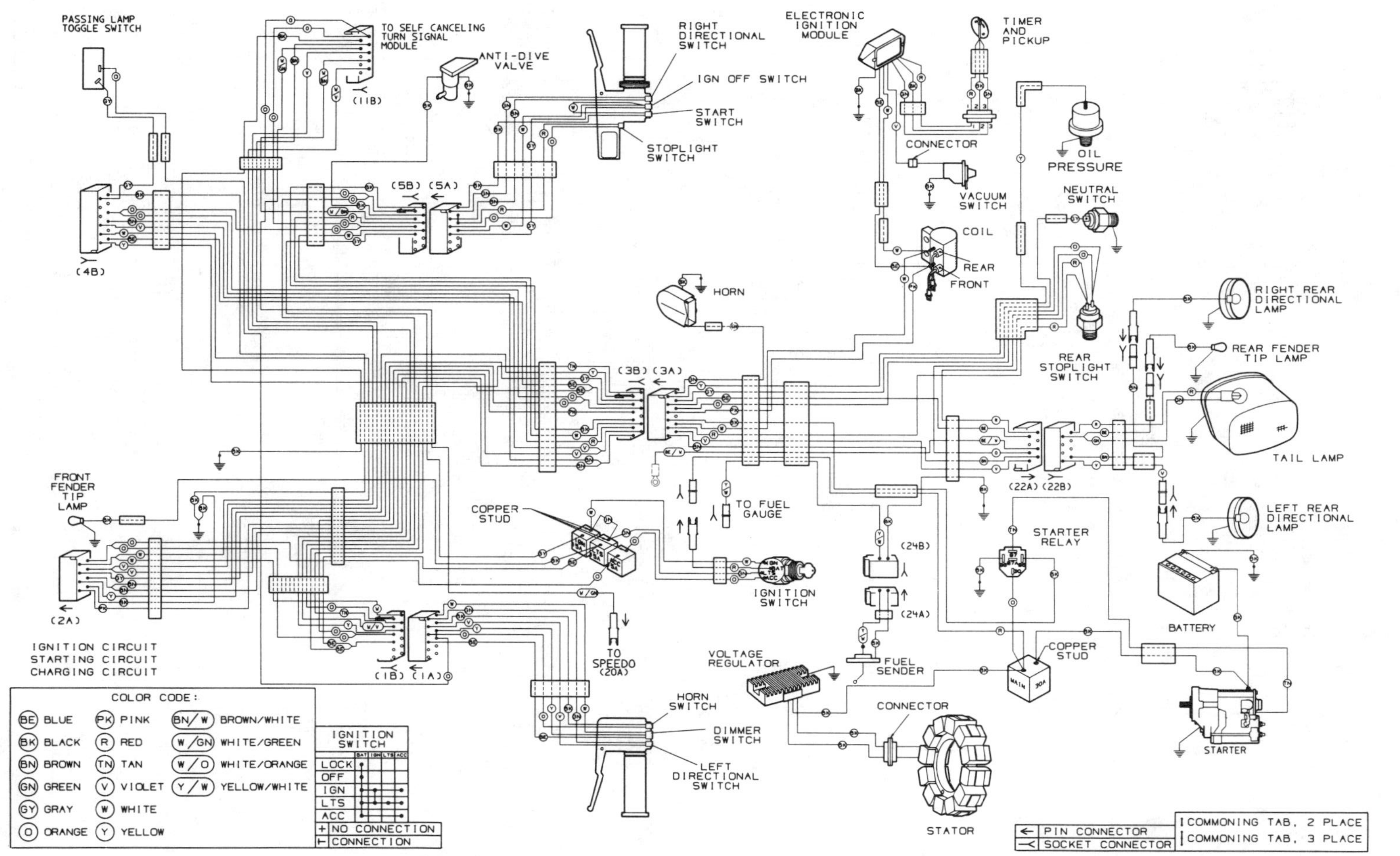


17

# 1990 FLTC ULTRA CHASSIS (PART 1 OF 3)

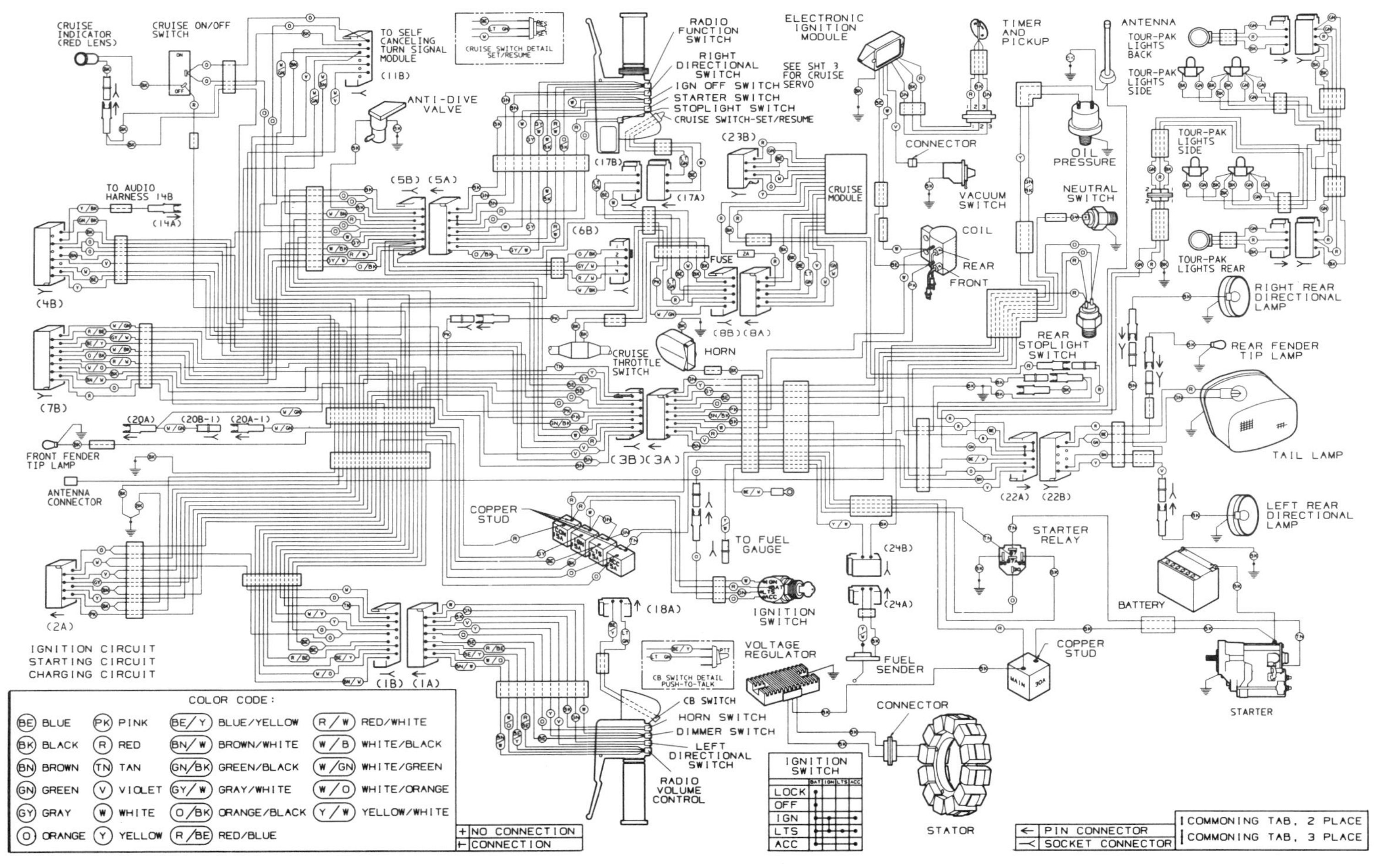

# 1990 FLTC ULTRA FAIRING (PART 2 OF 3)

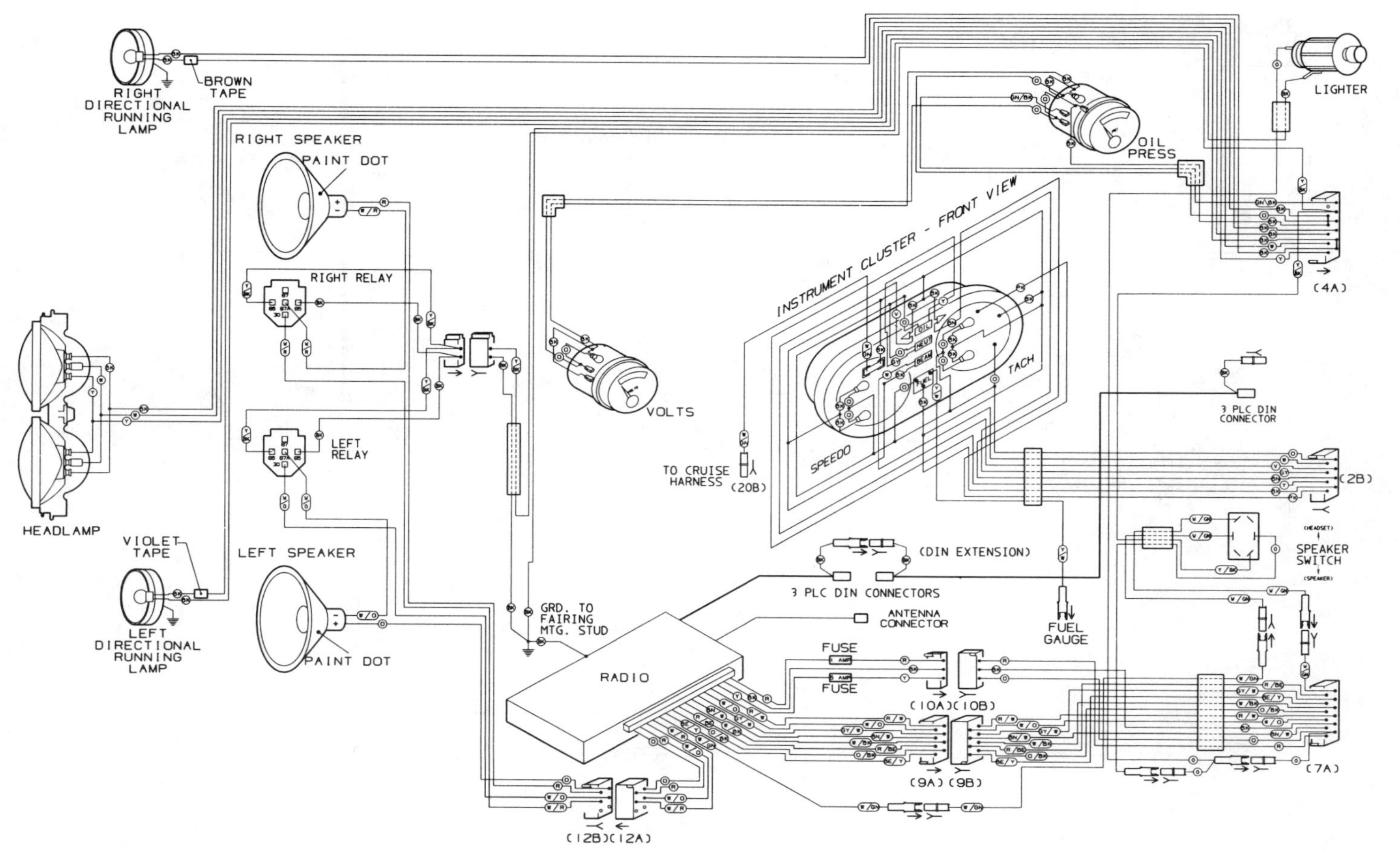

# 1990 FLTC ULTRA, CB/INTERCOM (PART 3 OF 3)

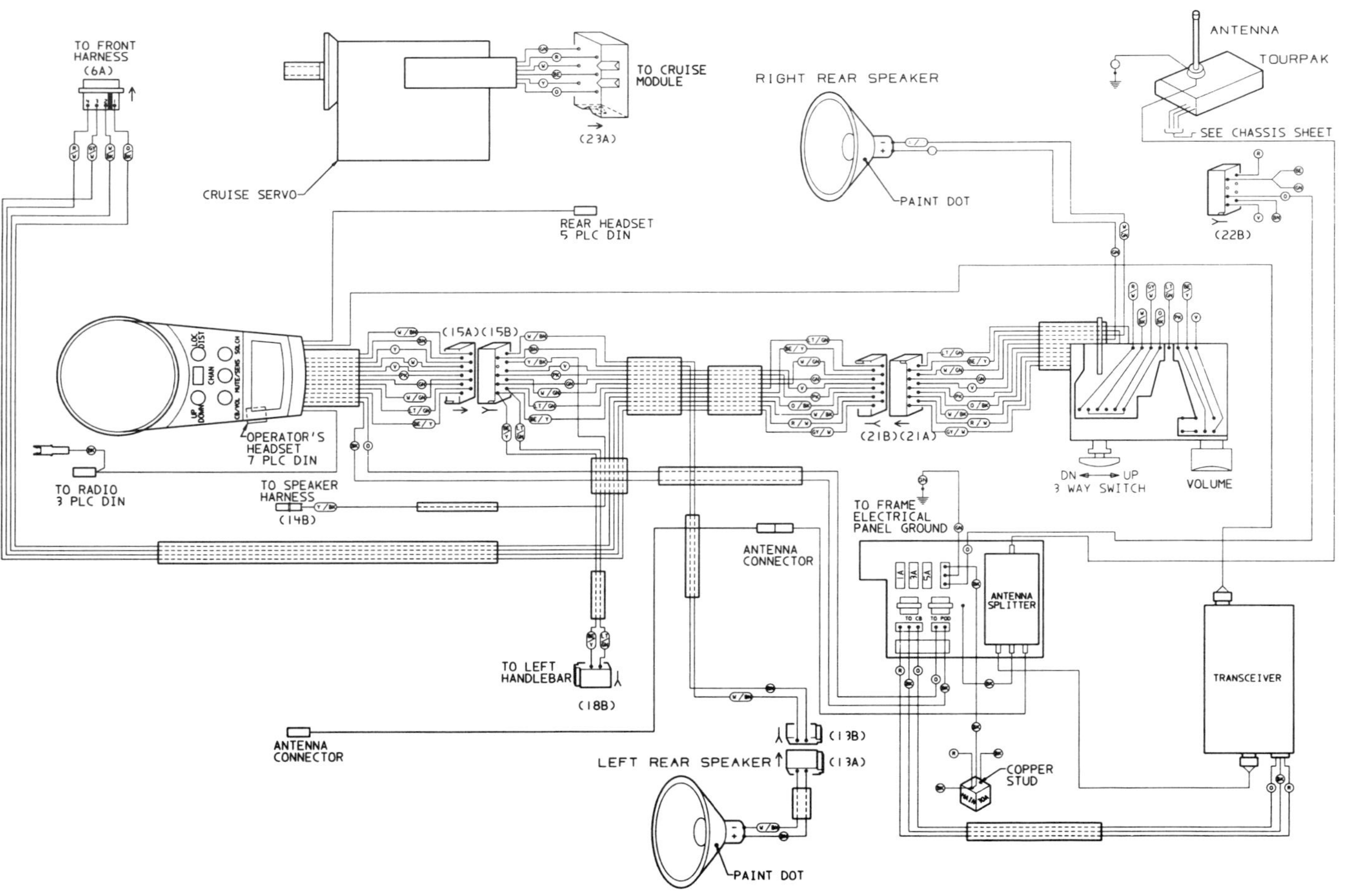

## 1990 FLHTC ULTRA CHASSIS (PART 1 OF 3)

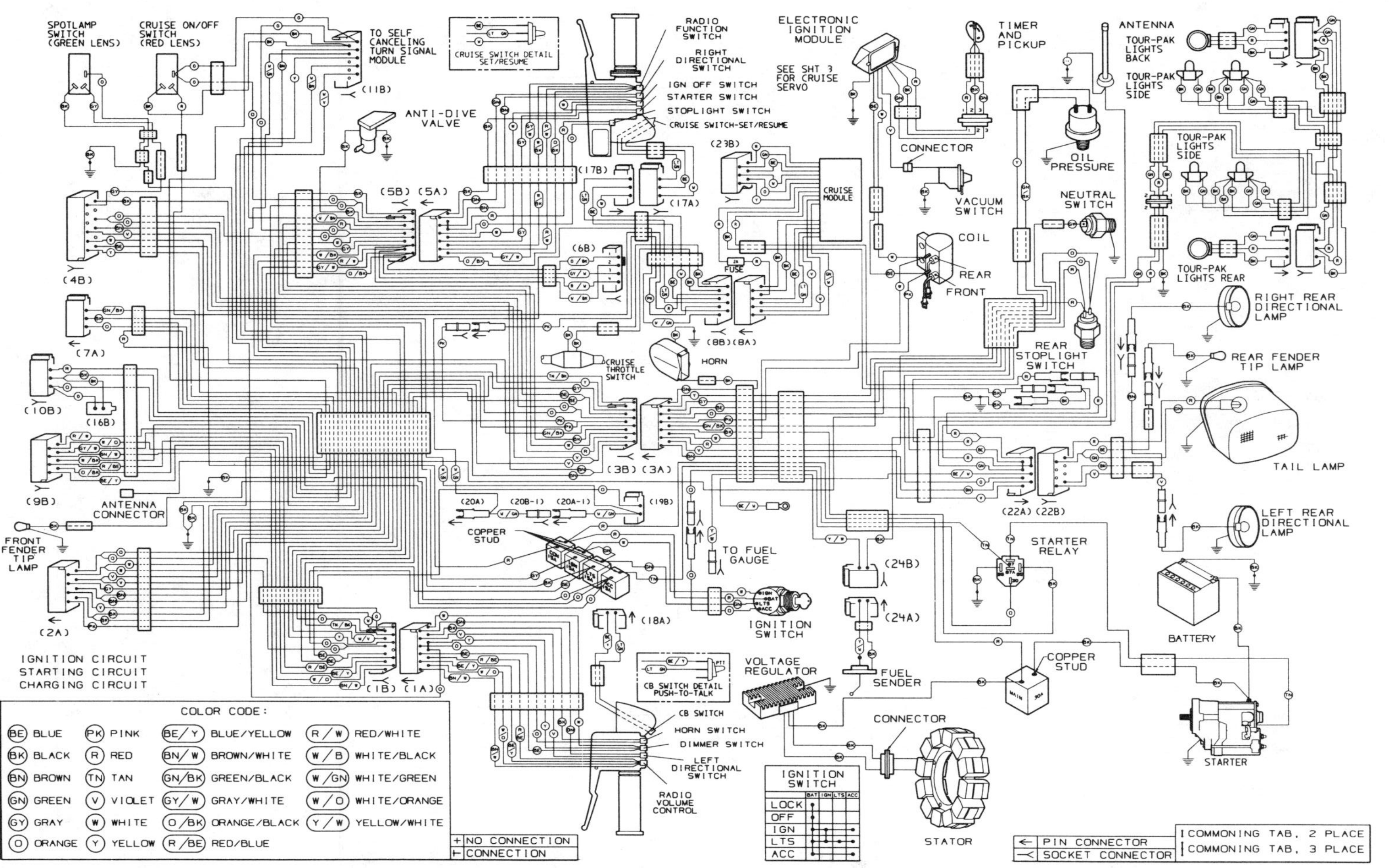

# 1990 FLHTC ULTRA FAIRING (PART 2 OF 3)

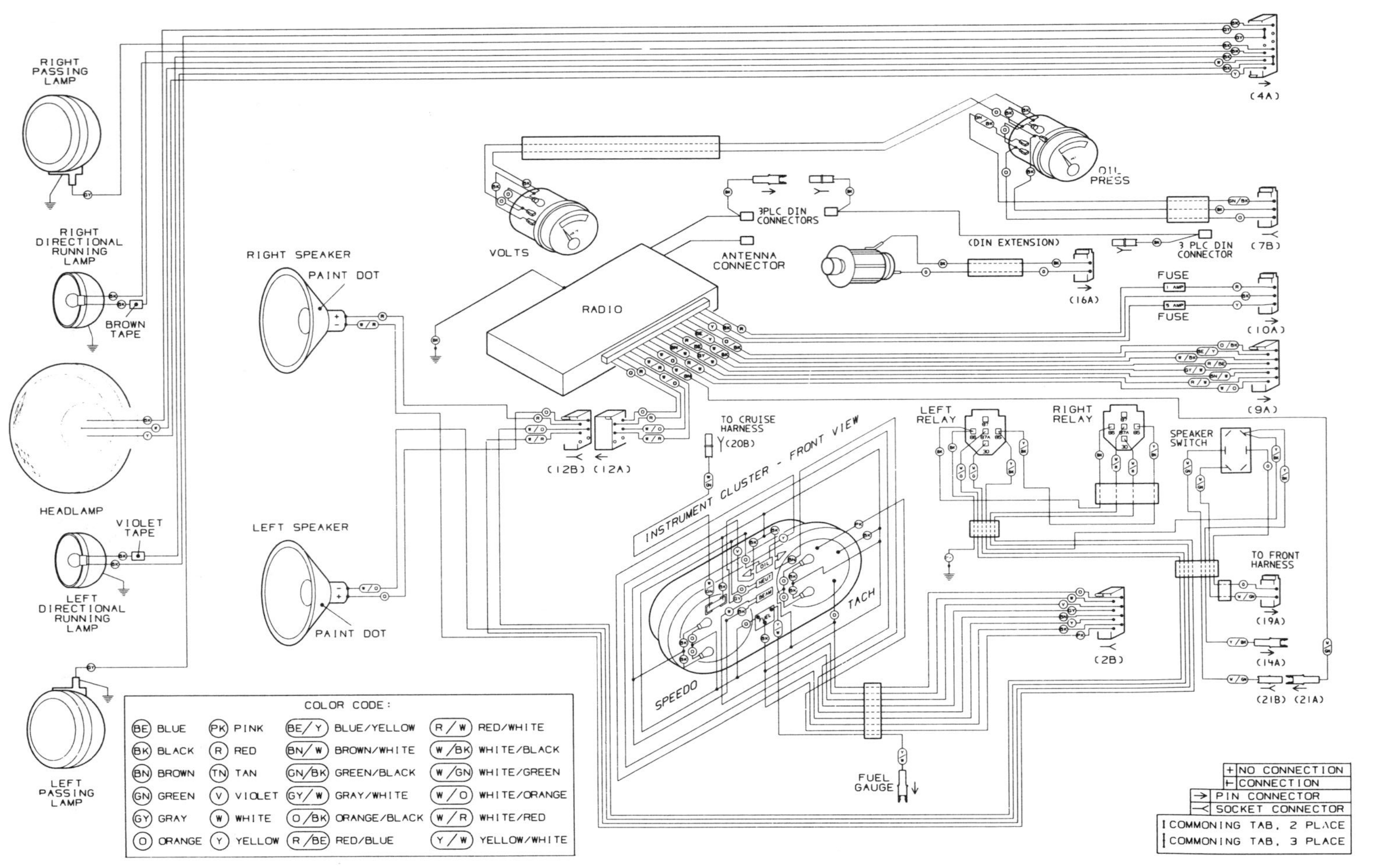

## 1990 FLHTC ULTRA, CB/INTERCOM (PART 3 OF 3)

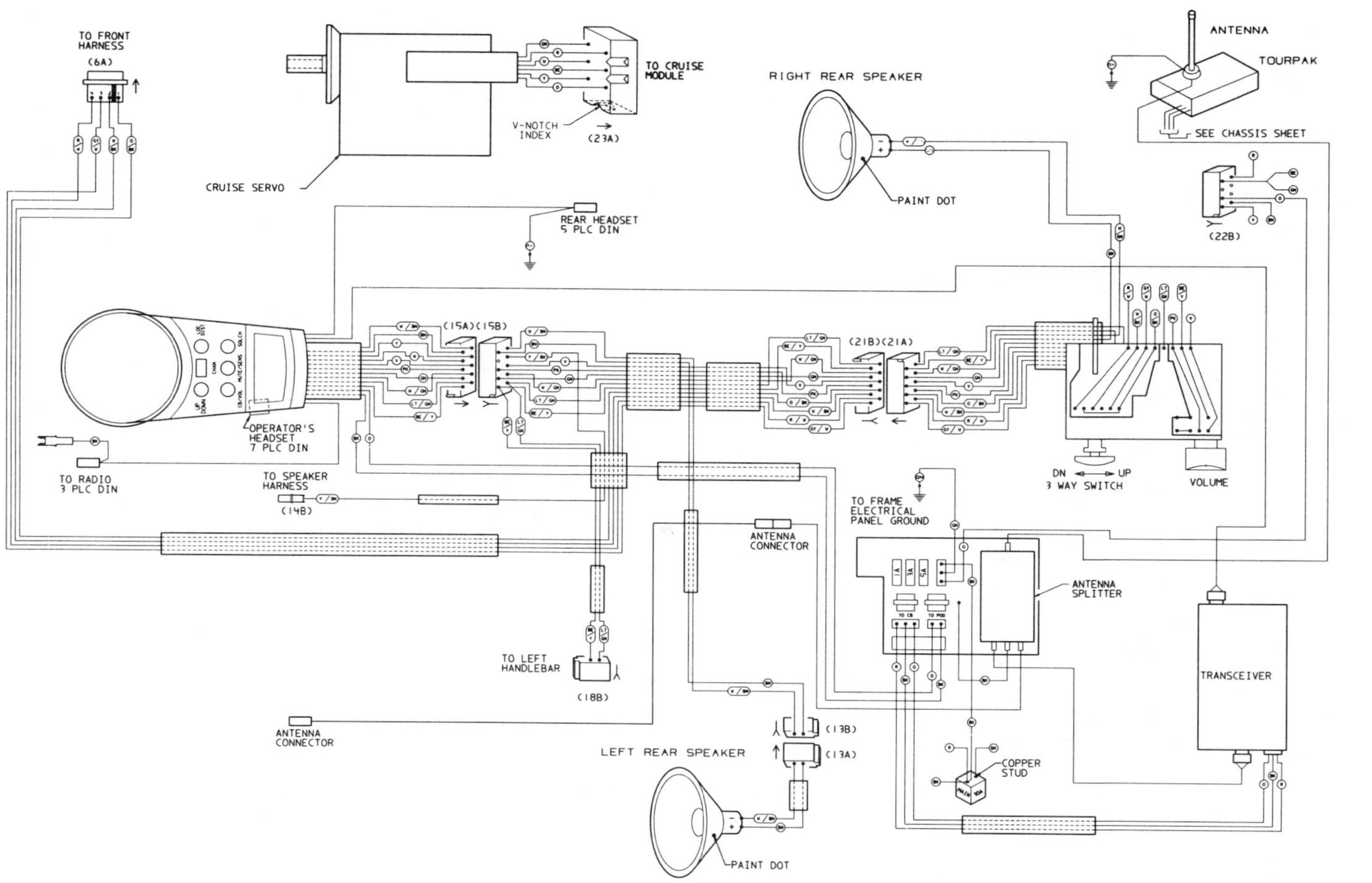

# 1991 FXR

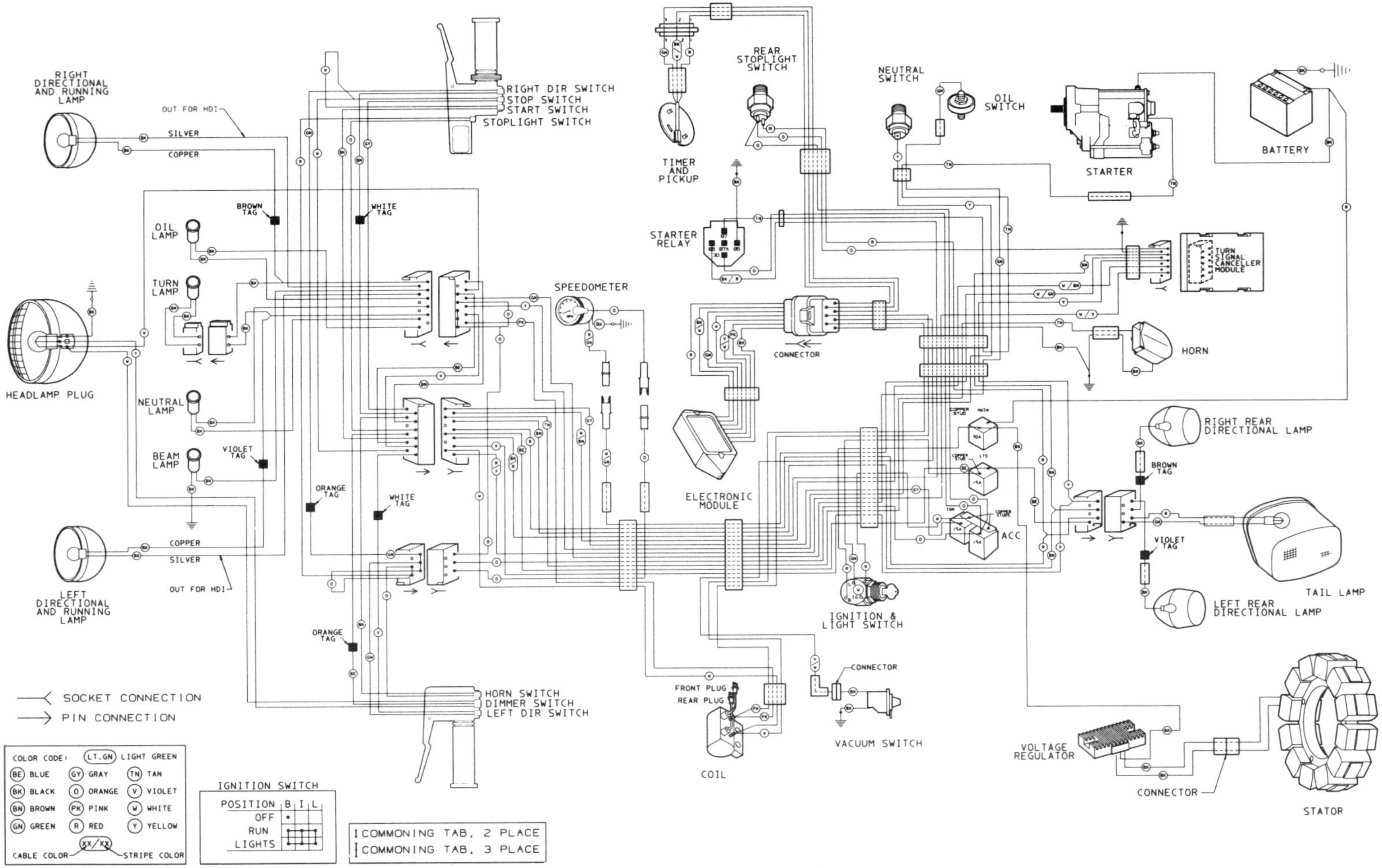
RIGHT DIRECTIONAL AND RUNNING LAMP
OUT FOR HDI
SILVER
COPPER
RIGHT DIR SWITCH
STOP SWITCH
START SWITCH
STOPLIGHT SWITCH
BROWN TAG
WHITE TAG
OIL LAMP
TURN LAMP
HEADLAMP PLUG
NEUTRAL LAMP
BEAM LAMP
VIOLET TAG
ORANGE TAG
LEFT DIRECTIONAL AND RUNNING LAMP
SPEEDOMETER
TIMER AND PICKUP
REAR STOPLIGHT SWITCH
STARTER RELAY
CONNECTOR
ELECTRONIC MODULE
NEUTRAL SWITCH
OIL SWITCH
STARTER
BATTERY
TURN SIGNAL CANCELLER MODULE
HORN
RIGHT REAR DIRECTIONAL LAMP
COPPER STUD
MAIN
LTS
ACC
IGNITION & LIGHT SWITCH
TAIL LAMP
LEFT REAR DIRECTIONAL LAMP
HORN SWITCH
DIMMER SWITCH
LEFT DIR SWITCH
FRONT PLUG
REAR PLUG
COIL
VACUUM SWITCH
VOLTAGE REGULATOR
STATOR
SOCKET CONNECTION
PIN CONNECTION
COLOR CODE:
BE BLUE
BK BLACK
BN BROWN
GN GREEN
LT.GN LIGHT GREEN
GY GRAY
O ORANGE
PK PINK
R RED
TN TAN
V VIOLET
W WHITE
Y YELLOW
XX/XX
CABLE COLOR
STRIPE COLOR
IGNITION SWITCH
POSITION B I L
OFF
RUN
LIGHTS
COMMONING TAB, 2 PLACE
COMMONING TAB, 3 PLACE

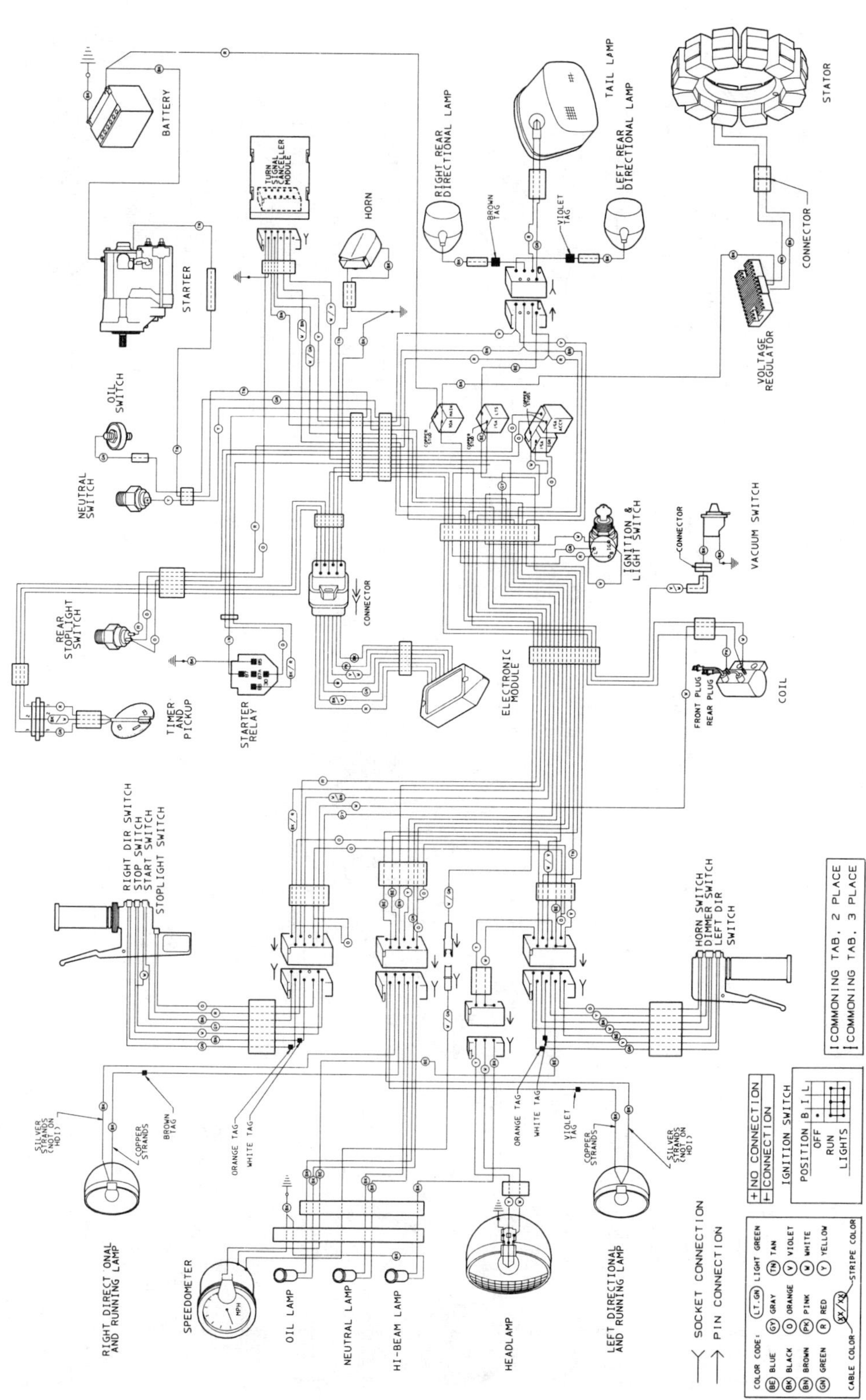
1991 FXLR
BATTERY
TURN SIGNAL CANCELLER MODULE
HORN
STARTER
OIL SWITCH
NEUTRAL SWITCH
REAR STOPLIGHT SWITCH
TIMER AND PICKUP
STARTER RELAY
CONNECTOR
ELECTRONIC MODULE
RIGHT REAR DIRECTIONAL LAMP
BROWN TAG
TAIL LAMP
VIOLET TAG
LEFT REAR DIRECTIONAL LAMP
STATOR
CONNECTOR
VOLTAGE REGULATOR
IGNITION & LIGHT SWITCH
VACUUM SWITCH
FRONT PLUG
REAR PLUG
COIL
RIGHT DIR SWITCH
STOP SWITCH
START SWITCH
STOPLIGHT SWITCH
HORN SWITCH
DIMMER SWITCH
LEFT DIR SWITCH
COMMONING TAB. 2 PLACE
COMMONING TAB. 3 PLACE
SILVER STRANDS (NOT ON HDI)
COPPER STRANDS
ORANGE TAG
WHITE TAG
RIGHT DIRECTIONAL AND RUNNING LAMP
SPEEDOMETER
OIL LAMP
NEUTRAL LAMP
HI-BEAM LAMP
HEADLAMP
LEFT DIRECTIONAL AND RUNNING LAMP
SOCKET CONNECTION
PIN CONNECTION
+ NO CONNECTION
⊥ CONNECTION
IGNITION SWITCH
POSITION B I L
OFF
RUN
LIGHTS
COLOR CODE:
BE BLUE
BK BLACK
BN BROWN
GN GREEN
LT.GN LIGHT GREEN
GY GRAY
O ORANGE
PK PINK
R RED
TN TAN
V VIOLET
W WHITE
Y YELLOW
CABLE COLOR
STRIPE COLOR

# 1991 FXRS

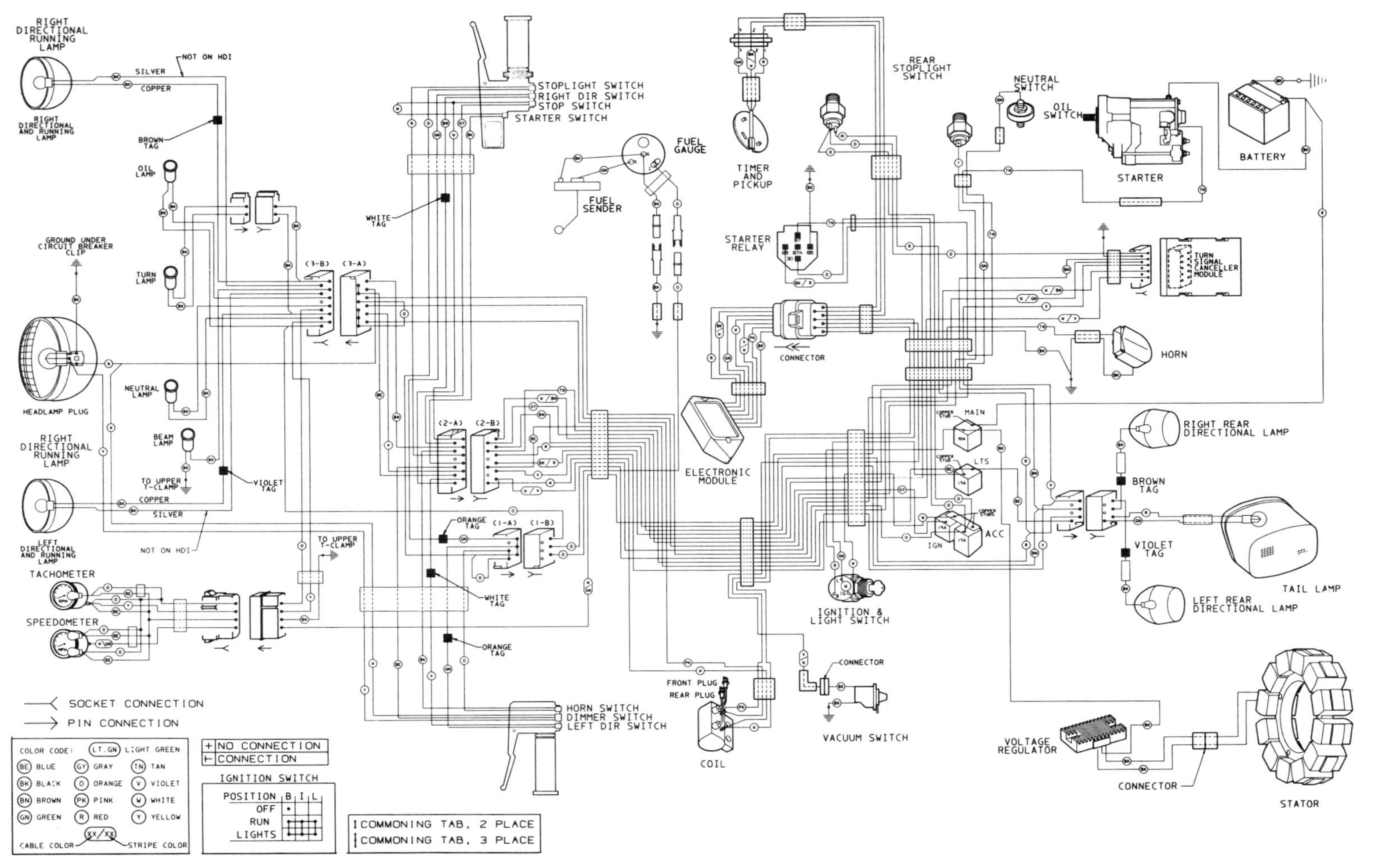
RIGHT DIRECTIONAL RUNNING LAMP
NOT ON HDI
SILVER
COPPER
RIGHT DIRECTIONAL AND RUNNING LAMP
BROWN TAG
OIL LAMP
TURN LAMP
GROUND UNDER CIRCUIT BREAKER CLIP
HEADLAMP PLUG
NEUTRAL LAMP
BEAM LAMP
TO UPPER T-CLAMP
VIOLET TAG
RIGHT DIRECTIONAL RUNNING LAMP
LEFT DIRECTIONAL AND RUNNING LAMP
TACHOMETER
SPEEDOMETER
STOPLIGHT SWITCH
RIGHT DIR SWITCH
STOP SWITCH
STARTER SWITCH
WHITE TAG
(3-B)
(3-A)
(2-A)
(2-B)
ORANGE TAG
(1-A)
(1-B)
TO UPPER T-CLAMP
WHITE TAG
ORANGE TAG
HORN SWITCH
DIMMER SWITCH
LEFT DIR SWITCH
FUEL GAUGE
FUEL SENDER
TIMER AND PICKUP
STARTER RELAY
CONNECTOR
ELECTRONIC MODULE
FRONT PLUG
REAR PLUG
COIL
REAR STOPLIGHT SWITCH
NEUTRAL SWITCH
OIL SWITCH
STARTER
BATTERY
TURN SIGNAL CANCELLER MODULE
HORN
MAIN
LTS
ACC
IGN
IGNITION & LIGHT SWITCH
CONNECTOR
VACUUM SWITCH
RIGHT REAR DIRECTIONAL LAMP
BROWN TAG
VIOLET TAG
TAIL LAMP
LEFT REAR DIRECTIONAL LAMP
VOLTAGE REGULATOR
CONNECTOR
STATOR
SOCKET CONNECTION
PIN CONNECTION
COLOR CODE:
BE BLUE
BK BLACK
BN BROWN
GN GREEN
GY GRAY
O ORANGE
PK PINK
R RED
LT.GN LIGHT GREEN
TN TAN
V VIOLET
W WHITE
Y YELLOW
CABLE COLOR
XX/XX
STRIPE COLOR
NO CONNECTION
CONNECTION
IGNITION SWITCH
POSITION B I L
OFF
RUN
LIGHTS
COMMONING TAB. 2 PLACE
COMMONING TAB. 3 PLACE

# 1991 FXRS-SP AND FXRS-CONVERTIBLE

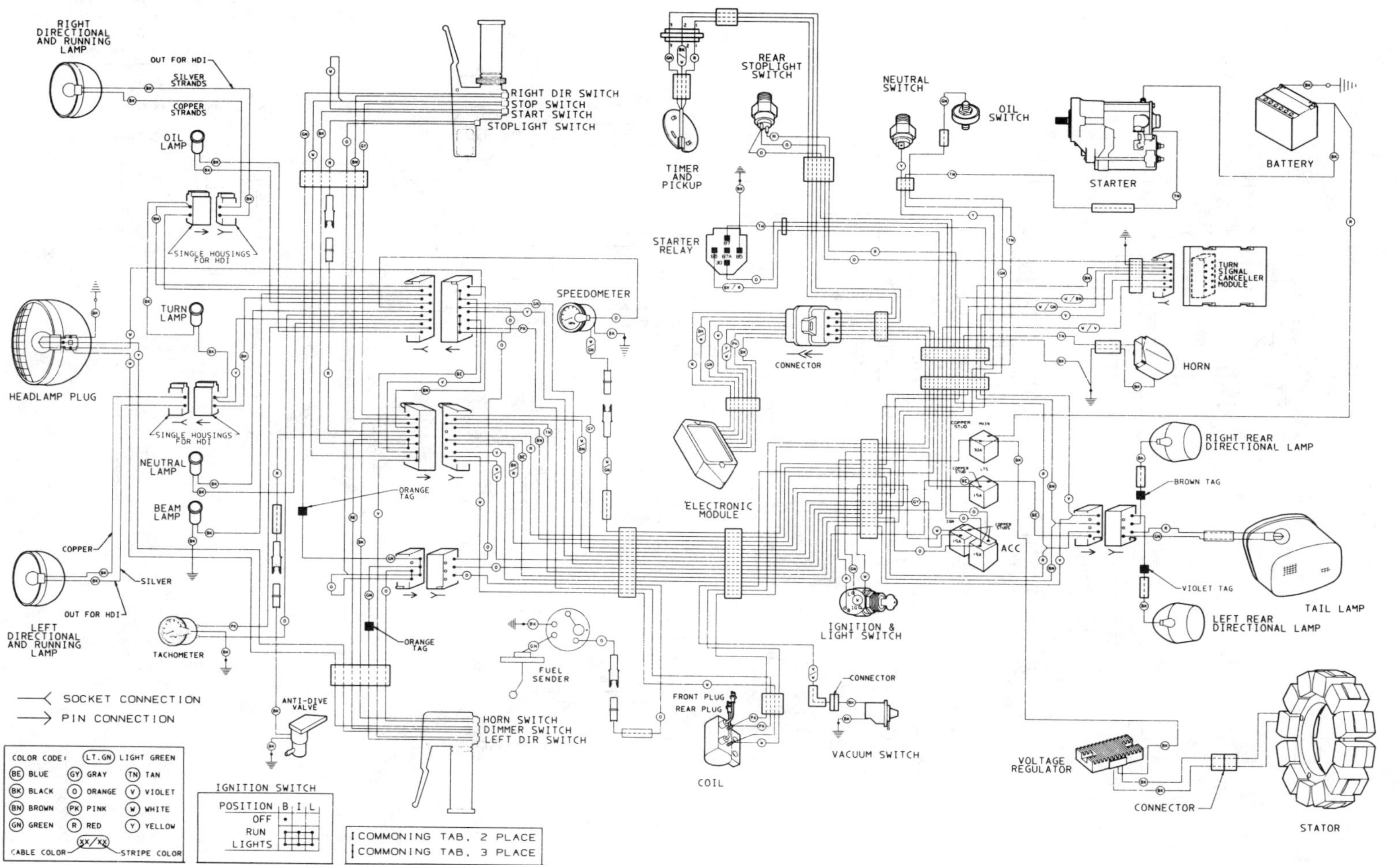

# 1991 FXRT FAIRING (PART 1 OF 2)

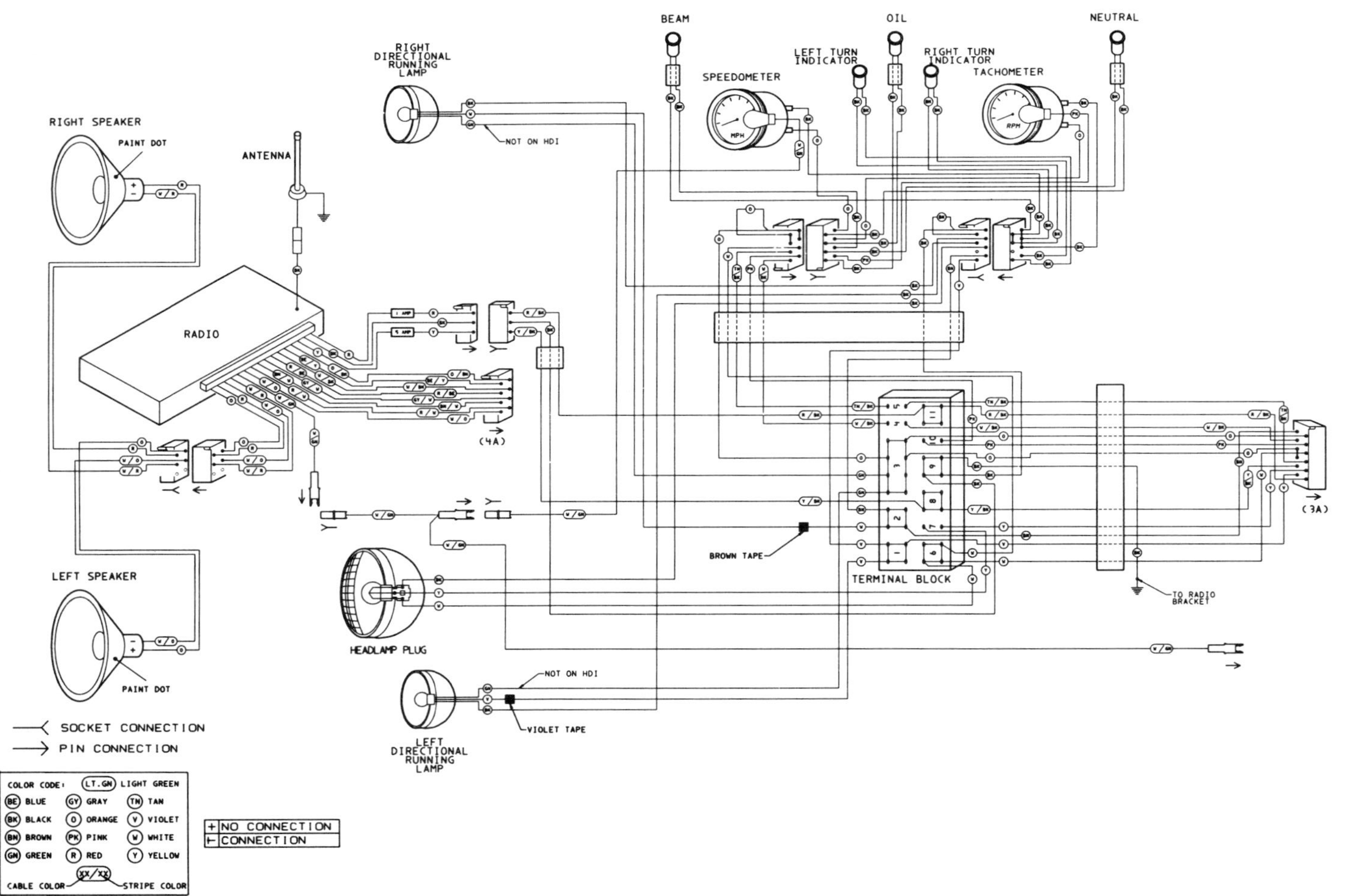

# 1991 FXRT CHASSIS (PART 2 OF 2)

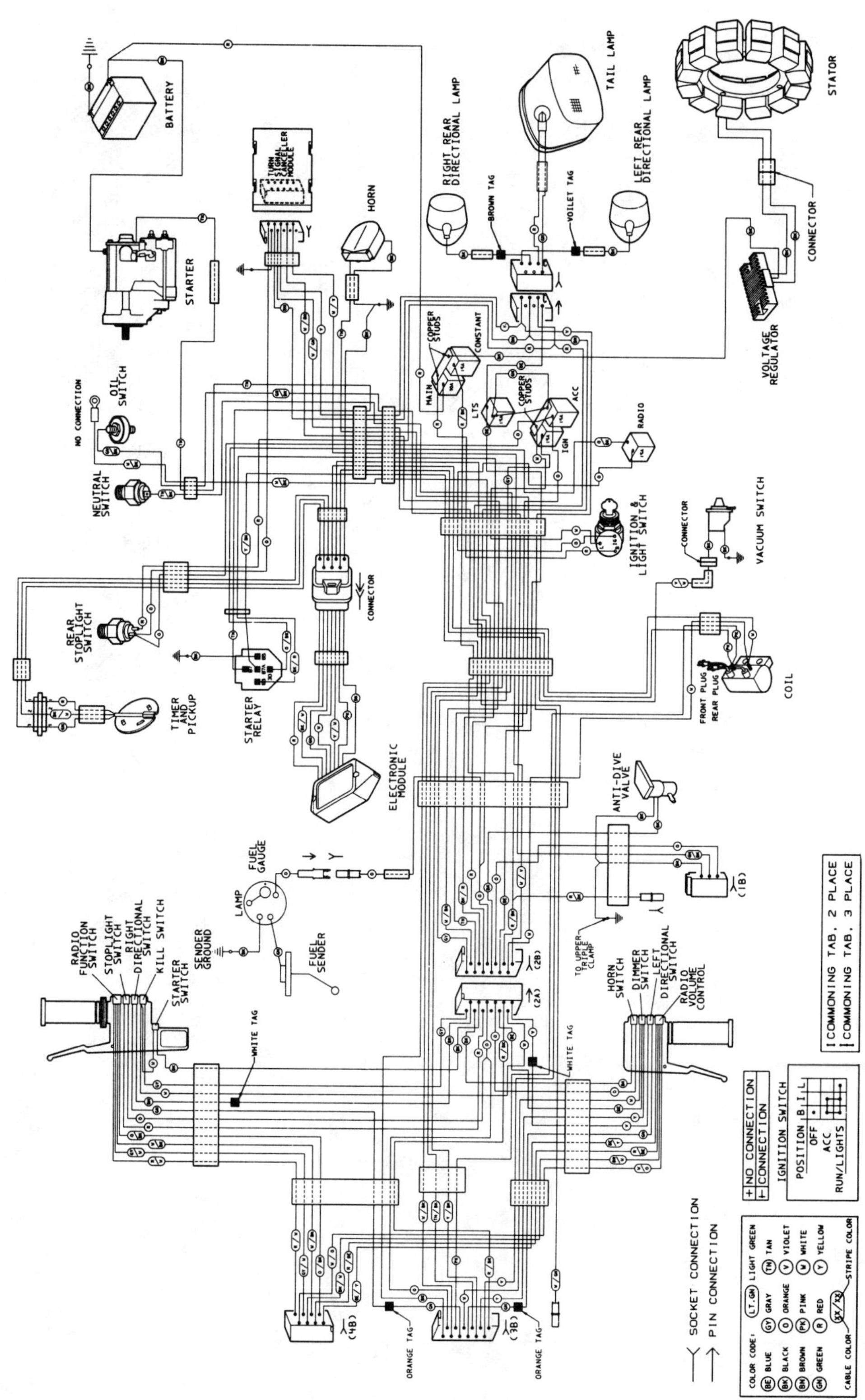

# 1991 FLTC FAIRING (PART 1 OF 2)

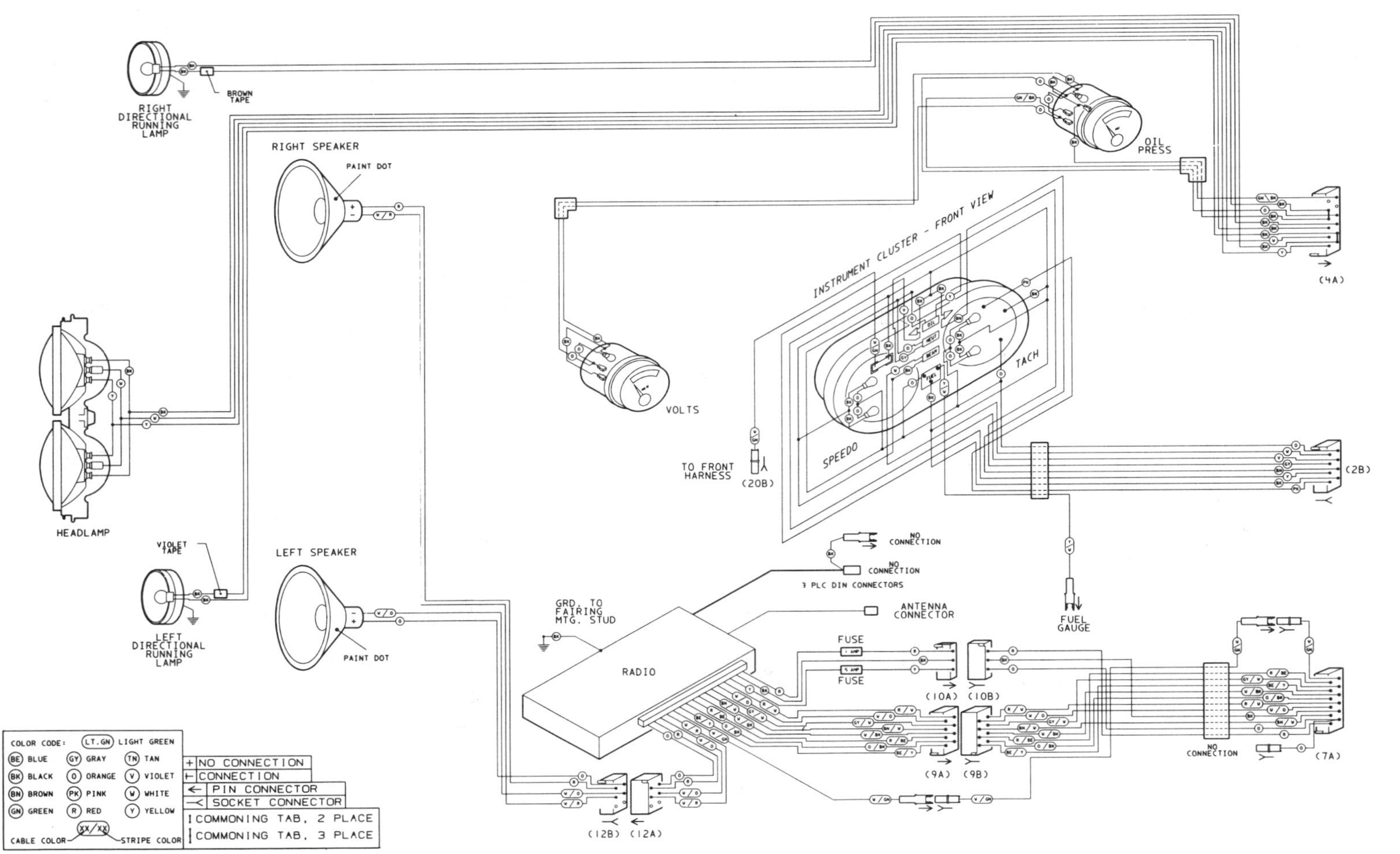

# 1991 FLTC CHASSIS (PART 2 OF 2)

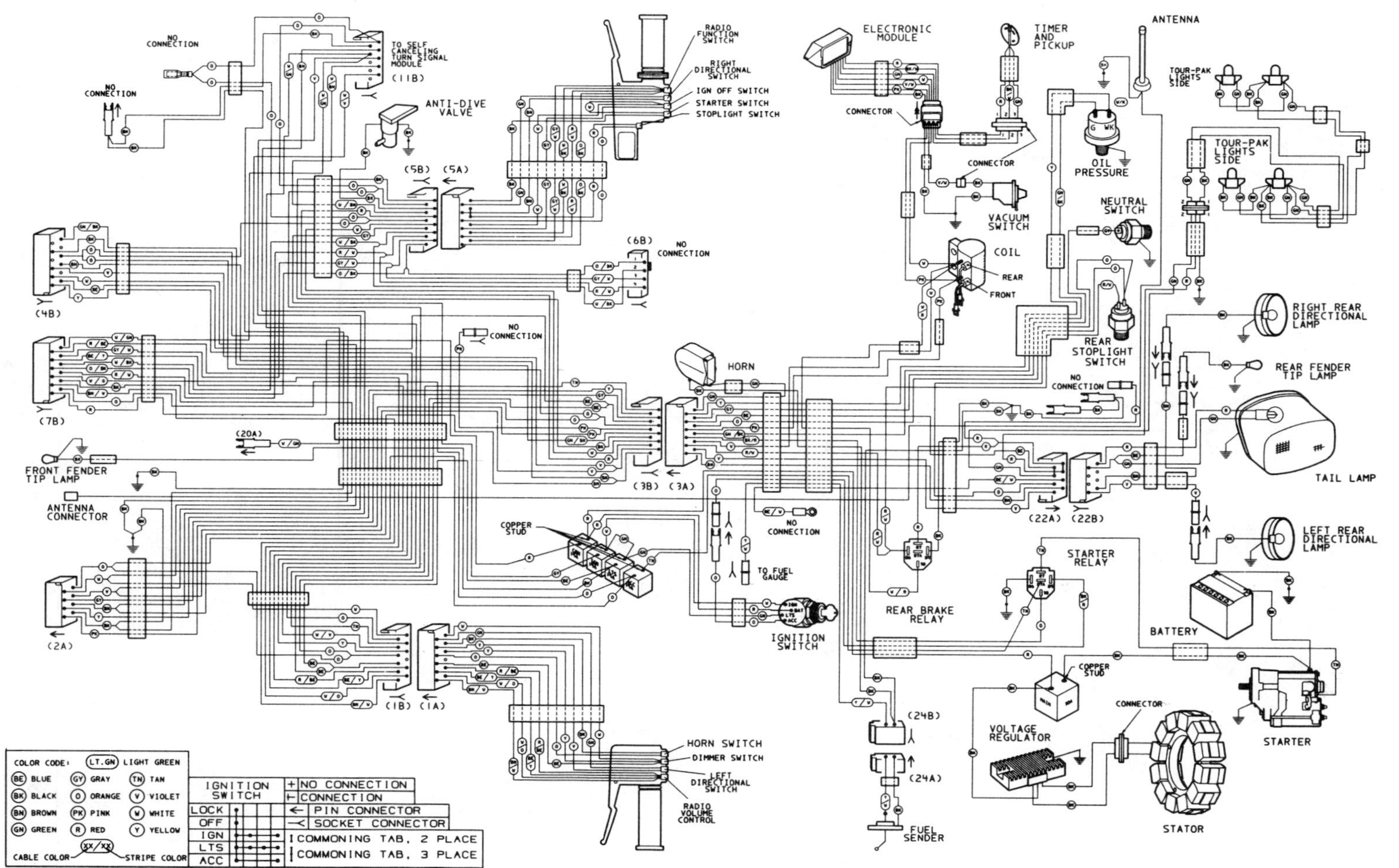

# 1991 FLHTC FAIRING (PART 1 OF 2)

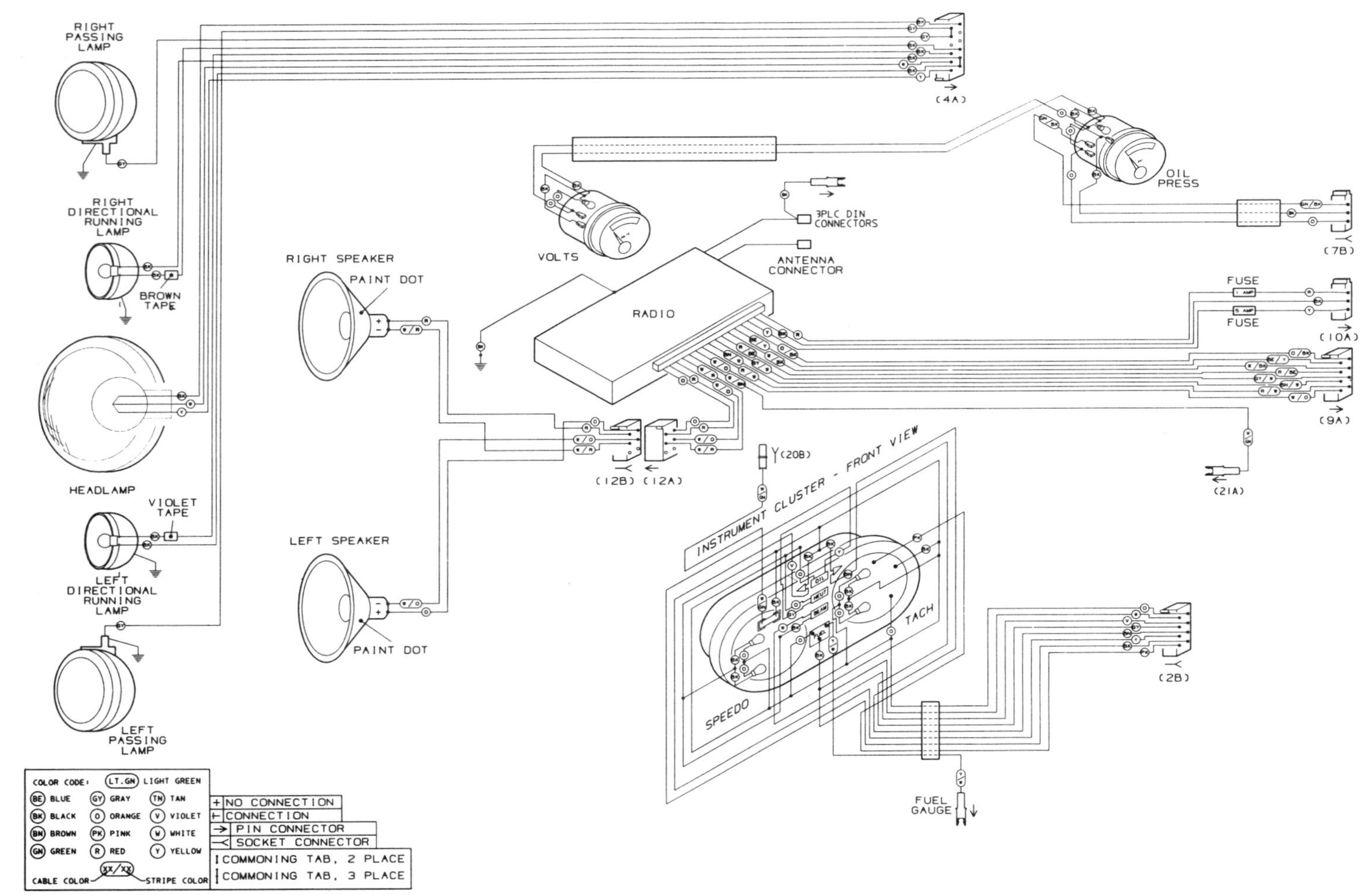

# 1991 FLHTC CHASSIS (PART 2 OF 2)

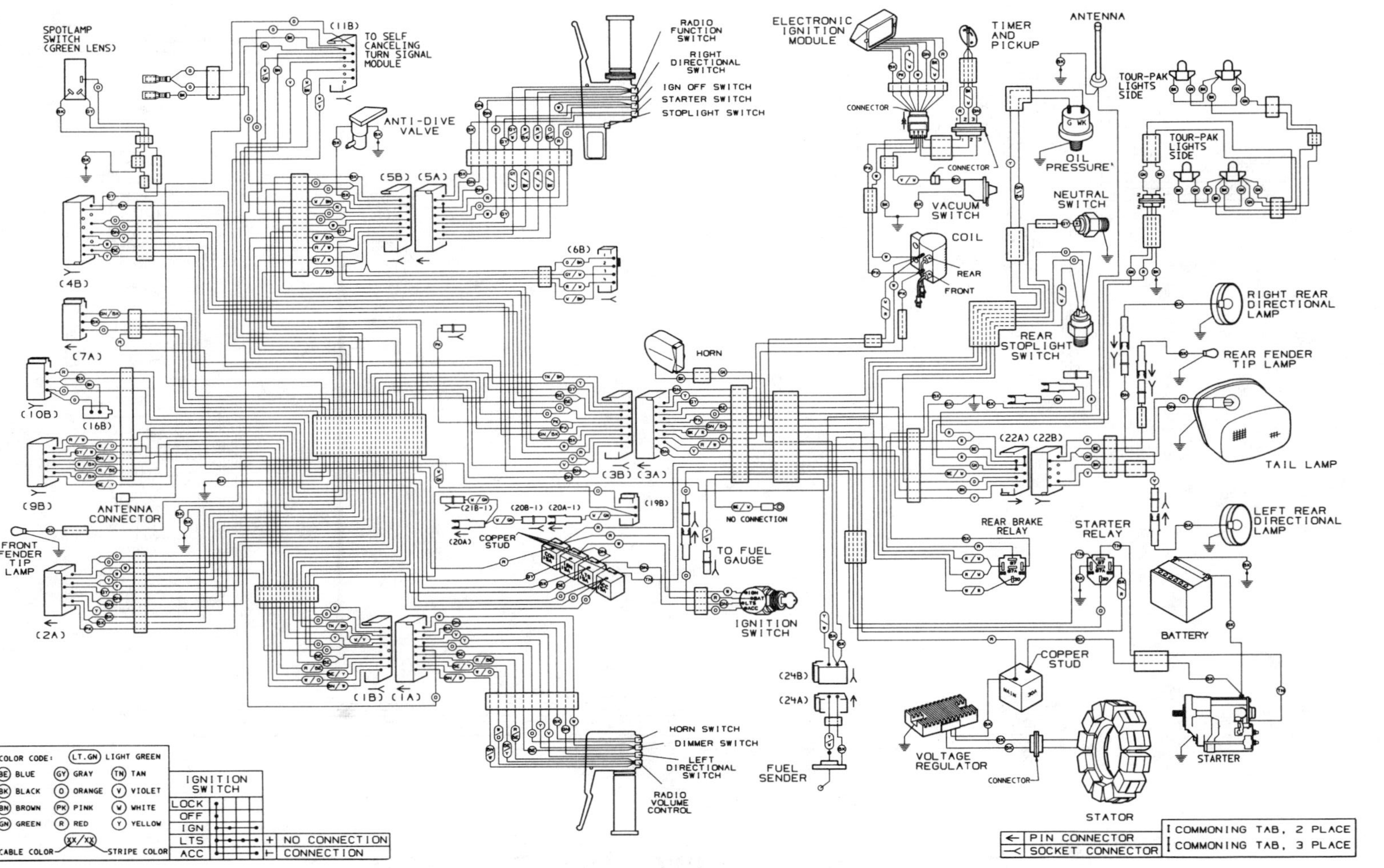

# 1991 FLHS INSTRUMENTS (PART 1 OF 2)

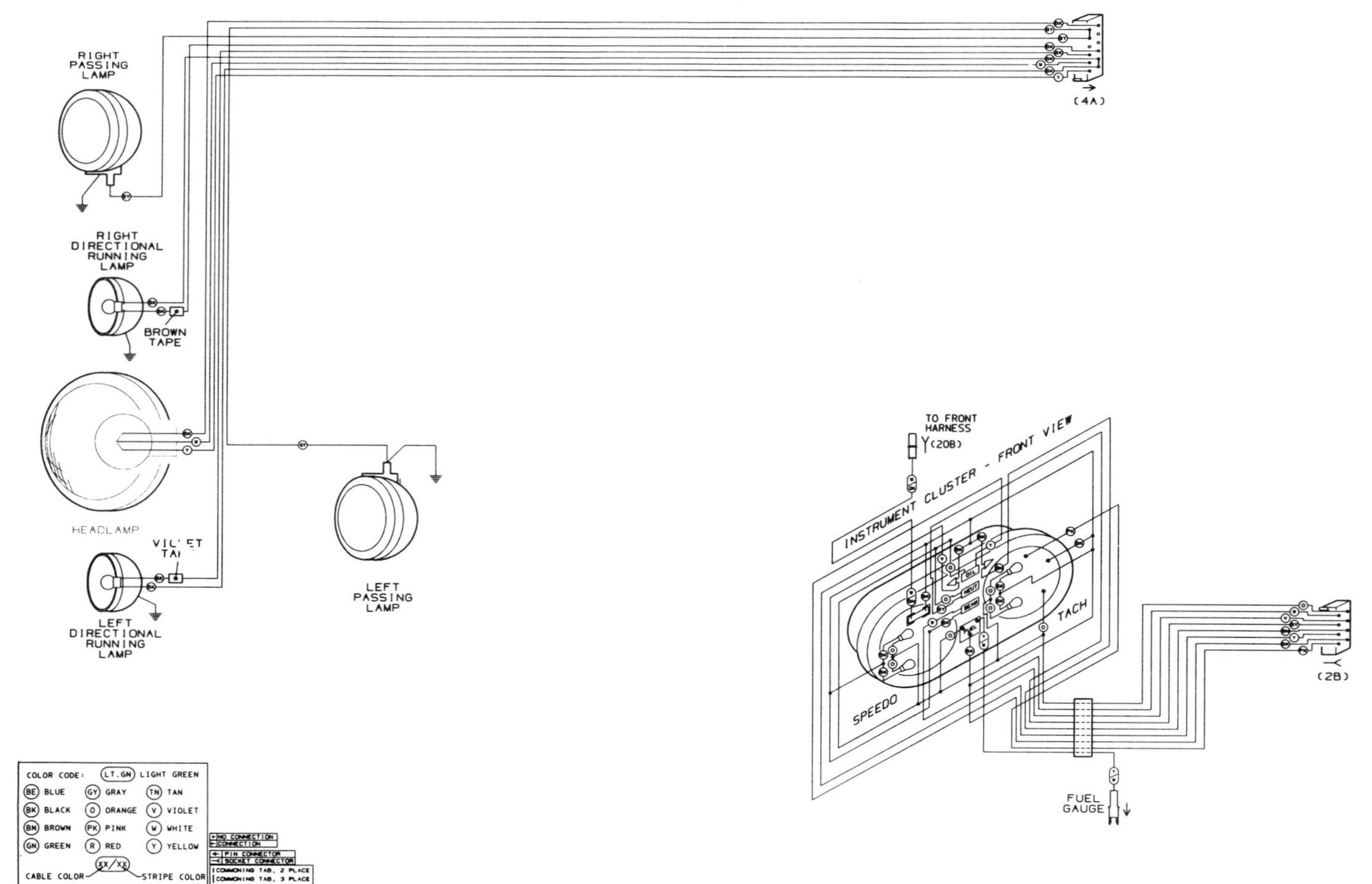

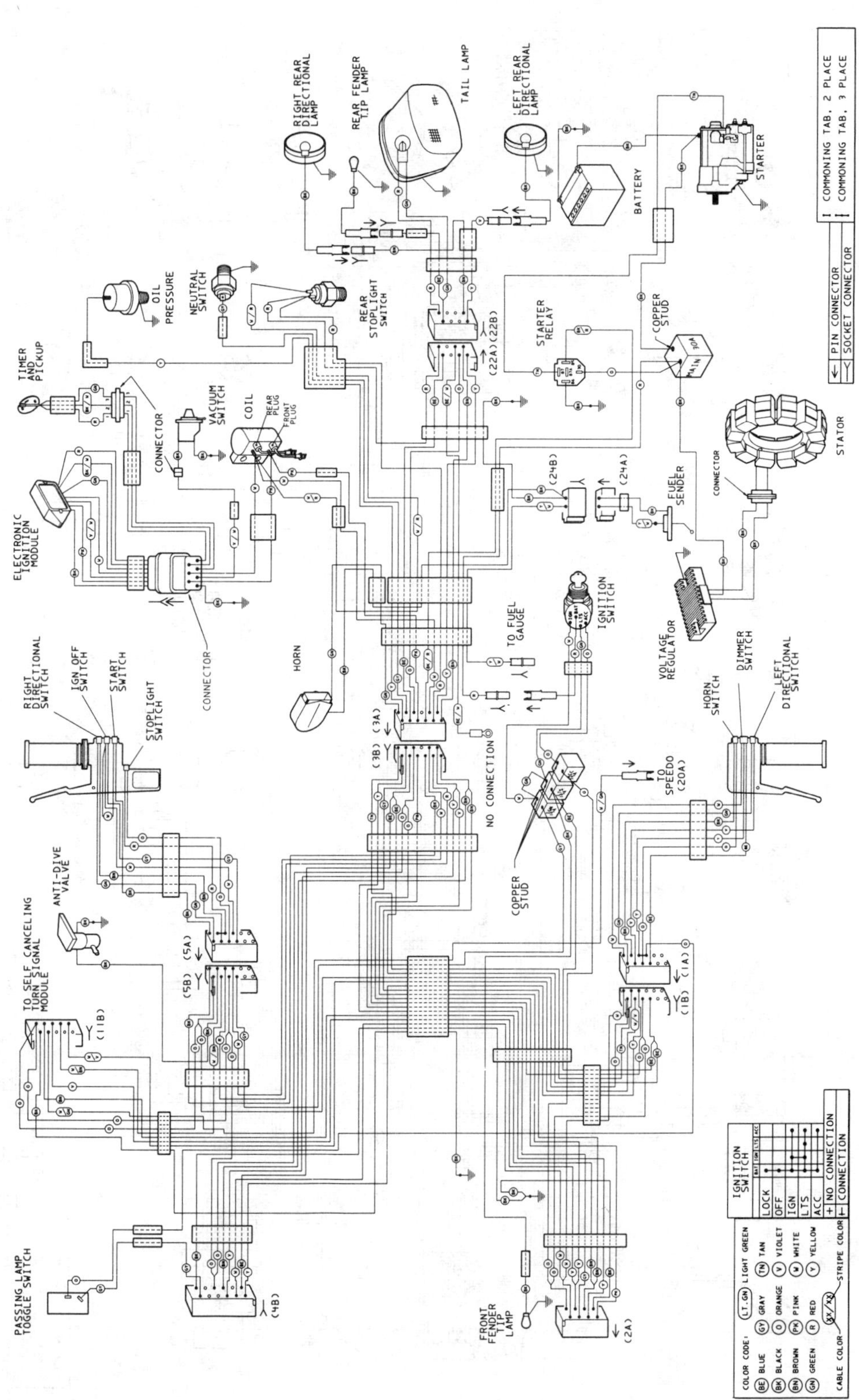
1991 FLHS CHASSIS (PART 2 OF 2)
RIGHT REAR DIRECTIONAL LAMP
REAR FENDER TIP LAMP
TAIL LAMP
LEFT REAR DIRECTIONAL LAMP
BATTERY
STARTER
OIL PRESSURE
NEUTRAL SWITCH
REAR STOPLIGHT SWITCH
TIMER AND PICKUP
STARTER RELAY
COPPER STUD
(22A)(22B)
VACUUM SWITCH
COIL
REAR PLUG
FRONT PLUG
CONNECTOR
ELECTRONIC IGNITION MODULE
STATOR
(24B)
(24A)
FUEL SENDER
TO FUEL GAUGE
IGNITION SWITCH
VOLTAGE REGULATOR
HORN
RIGHT DIRECTIONAL SWITCH
IGN OFF SWITCH
START SWITCH
STOPLIGHT SWITCH
(3B)
(3A)
NO CONNECTION
TO SPEEDO (20A)
COPPER STUD
HORN SWITCH
DIMMER SWITCH
LEFT DIRECTIONAL SWITCH
ANTI-DIVE VALVE
TO SELF CANCELING TURN SIGNAL MODULE
(11B)
(5B)
(5A)
(1A)
(1B)
PASSING LAMP TOGGLE SWITCH
(4B)
FRONT FENDER TIP LAMP
(2A)
PIN CONNECTOR
SOCKET CONNECTOR
COMMONING TAB, 2 PLACE
COMMONING TAB, 3 PLACE
IGNITION SWITCH
BAT IGN LTS ACC
LOCK
OFF
IGN
LTS
ACC
+ NO CONNECTION
— CONNECTION
COLOR CODE:
BE BLUE
BK BLACK
BN BROWN
GN GREEN
GY GRAY
O ORANGE
PK PINK
R RED
LT.GN LIGHT GREEN
TN TAN
V VIOLET
W WHITE
Y YELLOW
CABLE COLOR
STRIPE COLOR

# 1991 FLTC-ULTRA CHASSIS (PART 1 OF 3)

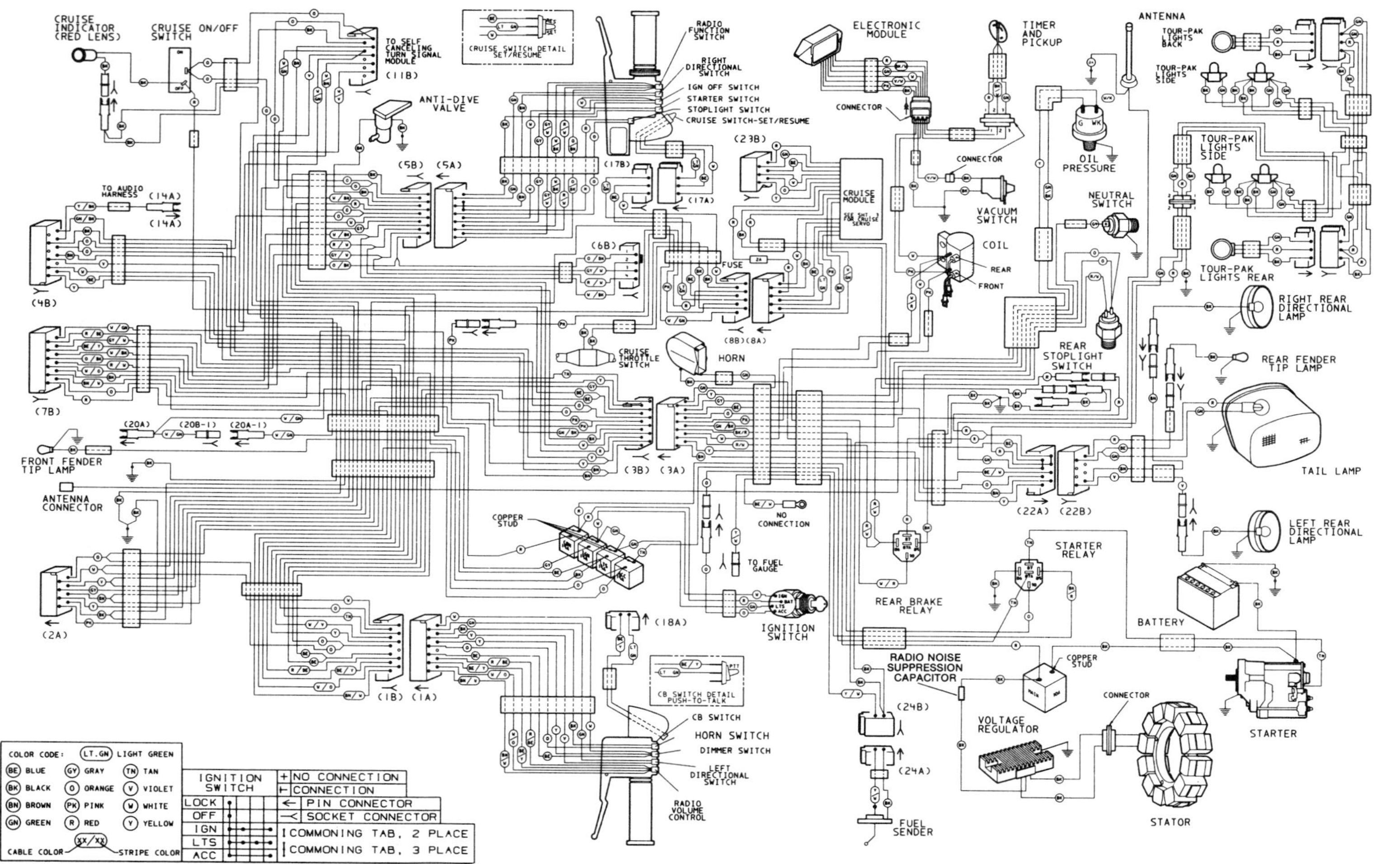

# 1991 FLTC-ULTRA FAIRING (PART 2 OF 3)

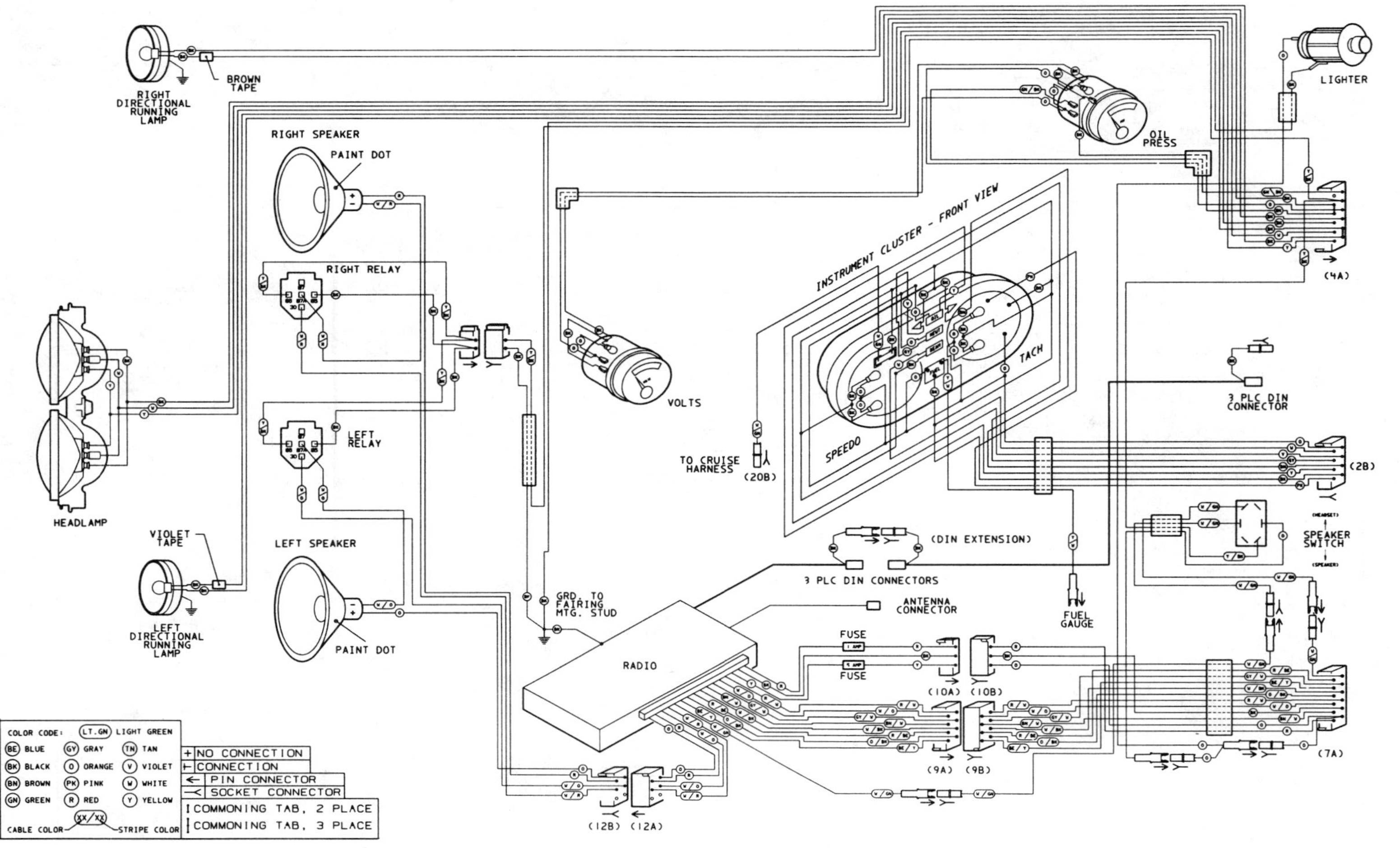


17

# 1991 FLTC-ULTRA, CB/INTERCOM (PART 3 OF 3)

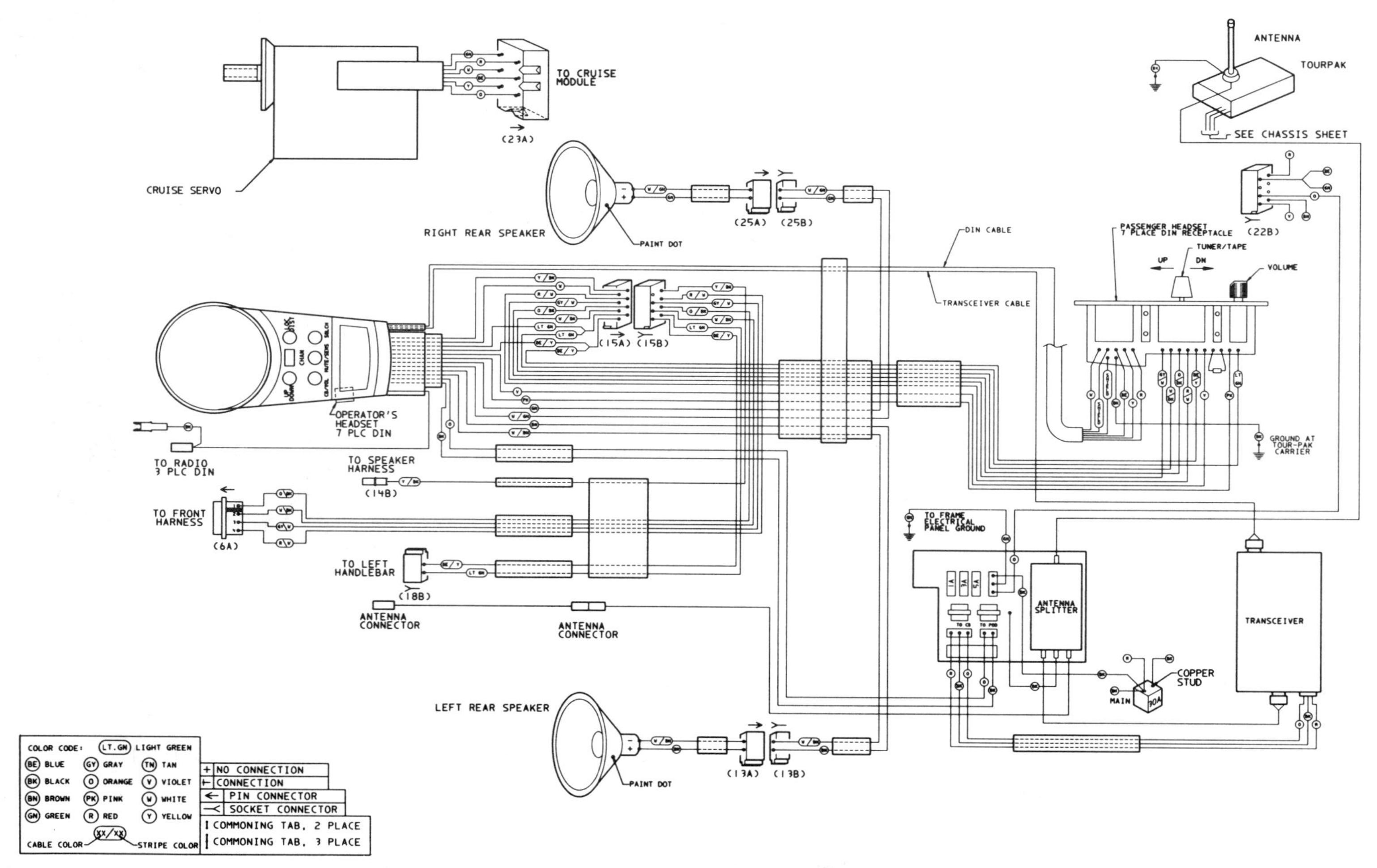

# 1991 FLHTC-ULTRA CHASSIS (PART 1 OF 3)

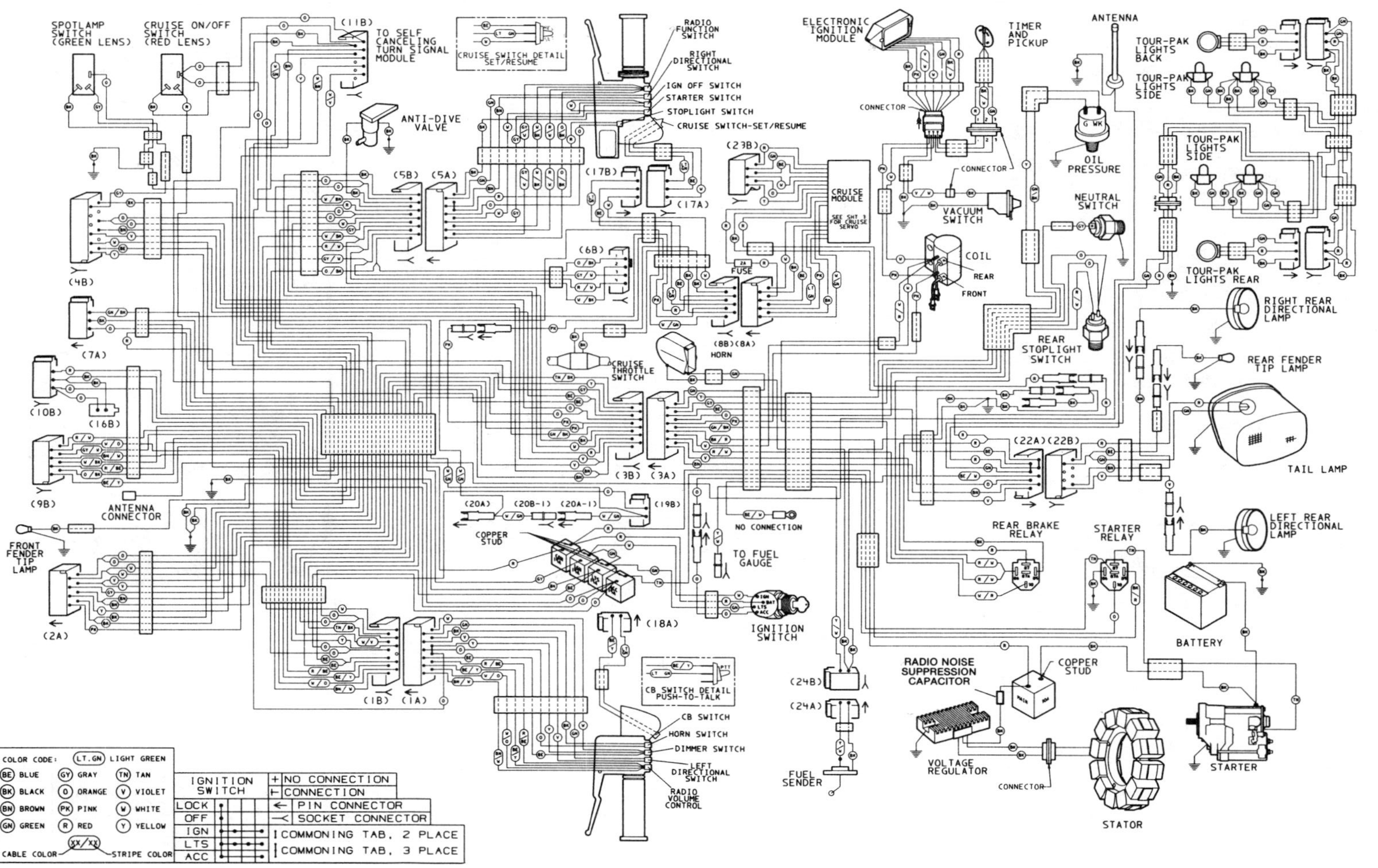

# 1991 FLHTC-ULTRA FAIRING (PART 2 OF 3)

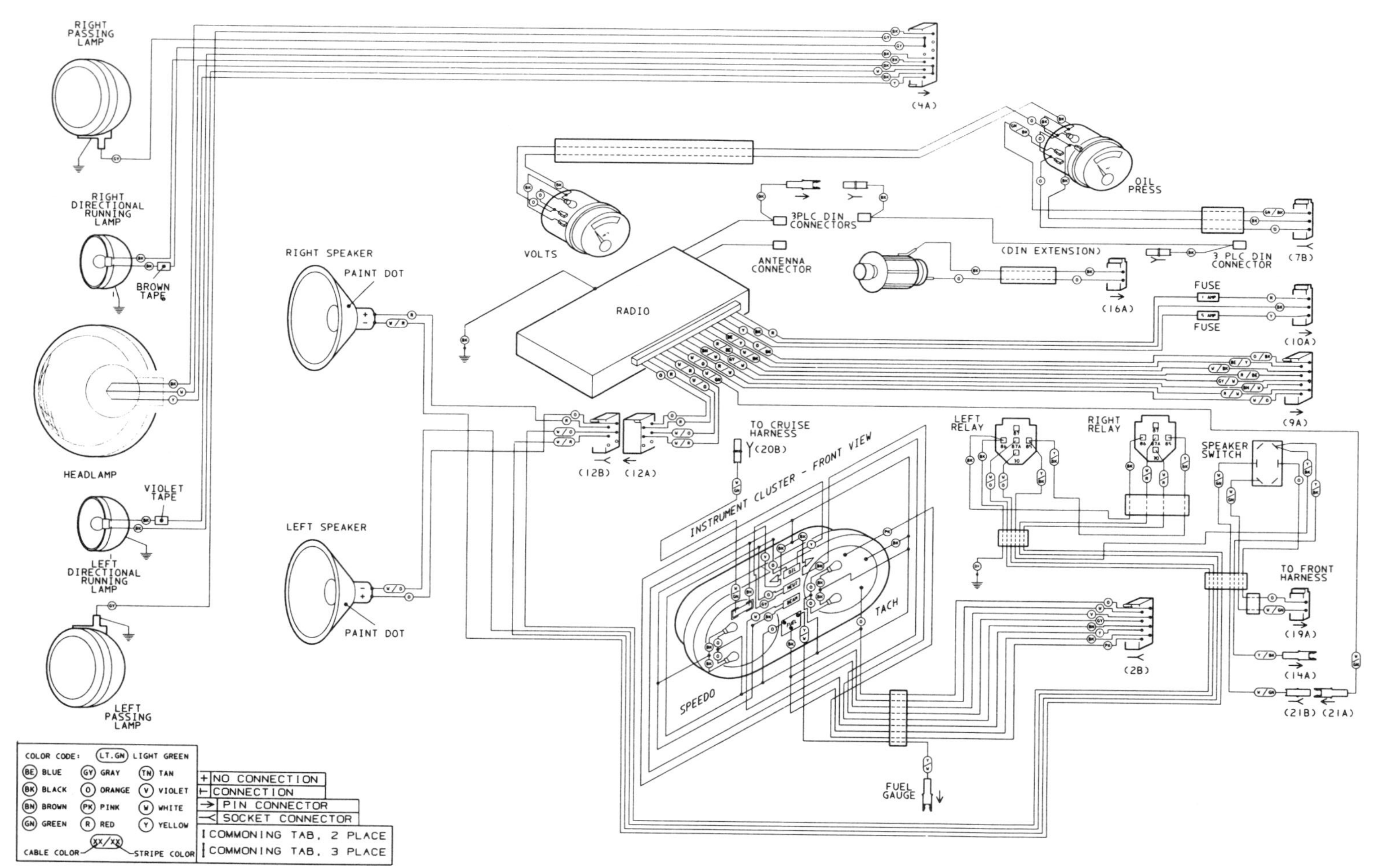

# 1991 FLHTC-ULTRA, CB/INTERCOM (PART 3 OF 3)

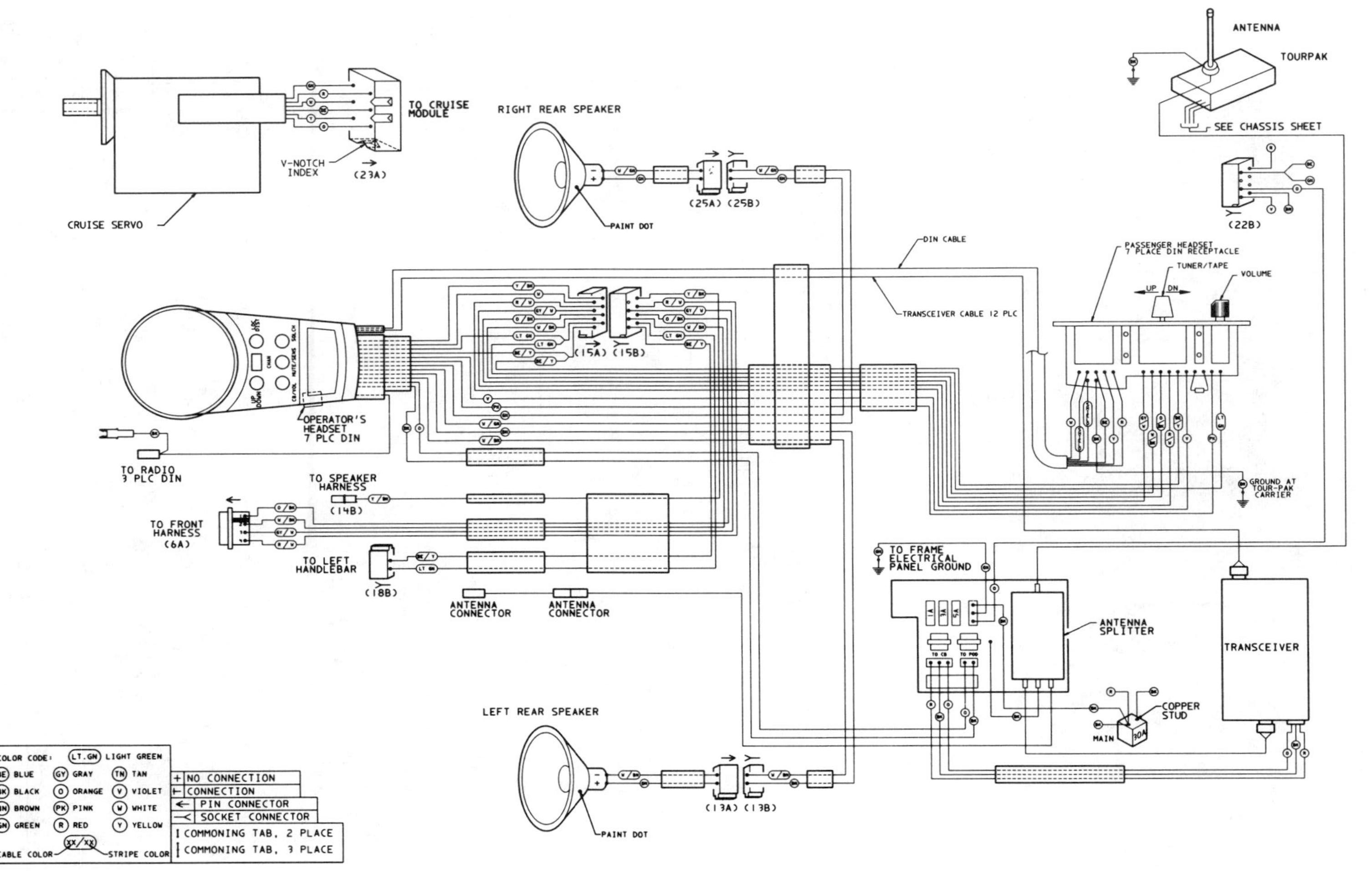


17

# 1992 FXR

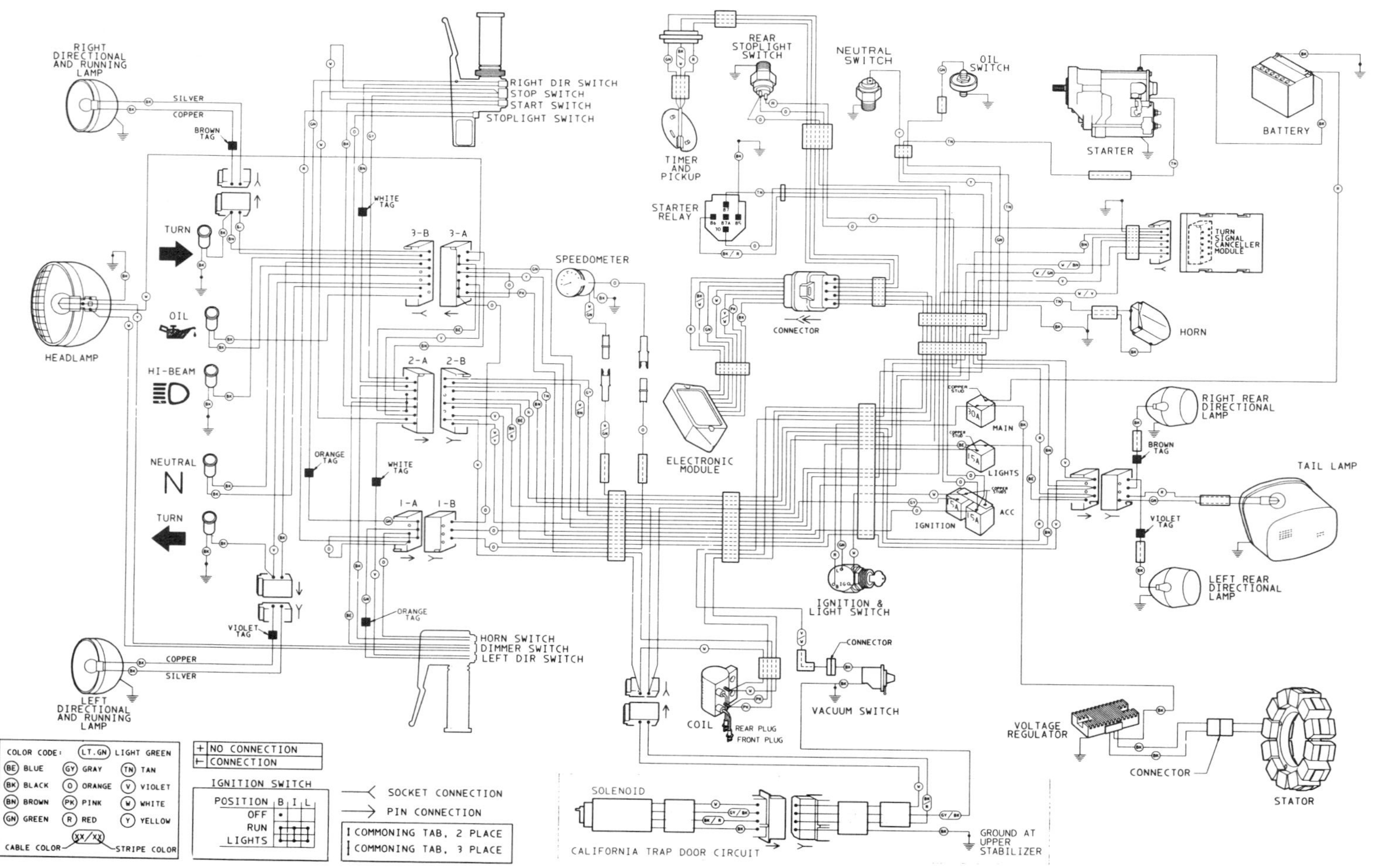
RIGHT DIRECTIONAL AND RUNNING LAMP
SILVER
COPPER
BROWN TAG
RIGHT DIR SWITCH
STOP SWITCH
START SWITCH
STOPLIGHT SWITCH
TIMER AND PICKUP
REAR STOPLIGHT SWITCH
NEUTRAL SWITCH
OIL SWITCH
STARTER
BATTERY
STARTER RELAY
TURN SIGNAL CANCELLER MODULE
WHITE TAG
TURN
3-B
3-A
SPEEDOMETER
HEADLAMP
OIL
CONNECTOR
HORN
HI-BEAM
2-A
2-B
ELECTRONIC MODULE
MAIN
LIGHTS
ACC
IGNITION
RIGHT REAR DIRECTIONAL LAMP
BROWN TAG
TAIL LAMP
ORANGE TAG
WHITE TAG
NEUTRAL
N
TURN
1-A
1-B
VIOLET TAG
LEFT REAR DIRECTIONAL LAMP
IGNITION & LIGHT SWITCH
VIOLET TAG
ORANGE TAG
HORN SWITCH
DIMMER SWITCH
LEFT DIR SWITCH
CONNECTOR
COPPER
SILVER
LEFT DIRECTIONAL AND RUNNING LAMP
COIL
REAR PLUG
FRONT PLUG
VACUUM SWITCH
VOLTAGE REGULATOR
CONNECTOR
STATOR
COLOR CODE:
BE BLUE
BK BLACK
BN BROWN
GN GREEN
LT.GN LIGHT GREEN
GY GRAY
O ORANGE
PK PINK
R RED
TN TAN
V VIOLET
W WHITE
Y YELLOW
CABLE COLOR
STRIPE COLOR
NO CONNECTION
CONNECTION
IGNITION SWITCH
POSITION B I L
OFF
RUN
LIGHTS
SOCKET CONNECTION
PIN CONNECTION
COMMONING TAB. 2 PLACE
COMMONING TAB. 3 PLACE
SOLENOID
CALIFORNIA TRAP DOOR CIRCUIT
GROUND AT UPPER STABILIZER

# 1992 FXLR

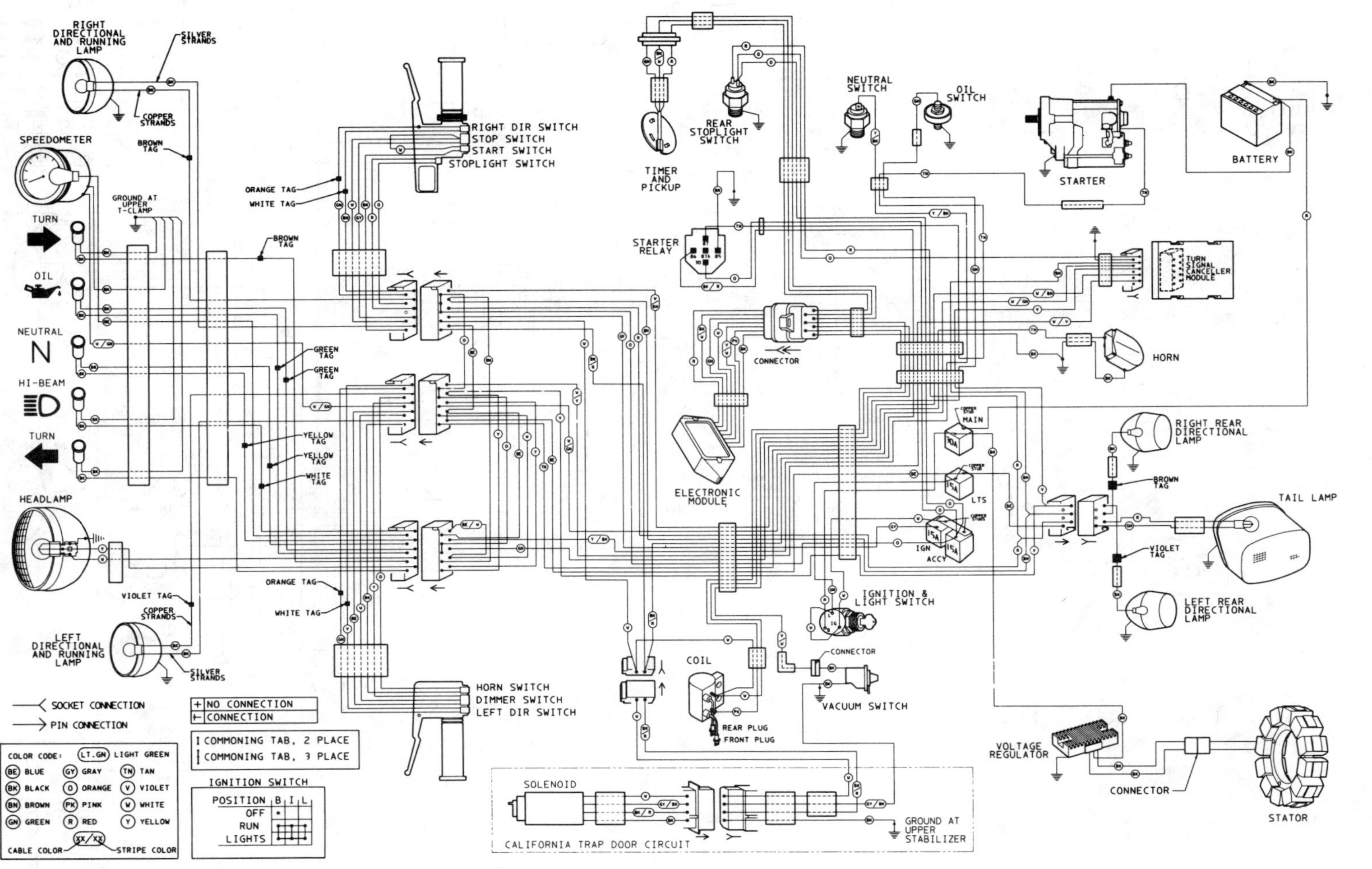
RIGHT DIRECTIONAL AND RUNNING LAMP
SILVER STRANDS
COPPER STRANDS
BROWN TAG
SPEEDOMETER
GROUND AT UPPER T-CLAMP
TURN
OIL
NEUTRAL
N
HI-BEAM
TURN
HEADLAMP
VIOLET TAG
COPPER STRANDS
LEFT DIRECTIONAL AND RUNNING LAMP
SILVER STRANDS
RIGHT DIR SWITCH
STOP SWITCH
START SWITCH
STOPLIGHT SWITCH
ORANGE TAG
WHITE TAG
BROWN TAG
GREEN TAG
GREEN TAG
YELLOW TAG
YELLOW TAG
WHITE TAG
ORANGE TAG
WHITE TAG
HORN SWITCH
DIMMER SWITCH
LEFT DIR SWITCH
TIMER AND PICKUP
REAR STOPLIGHT SWITCH
NEUTRAL SWITCH
OIL SWITCH
STARTER
BATTERY
STARTER RELAY
CONNECTOR
TURN SIGNAL CANCELLER MODULE
HORN
ELECTRONIC MODULE
MAIN
LTS
IGN
ACCY
RIGHT REAR DIRECTIONAL LAMP
BROWN TAG
TAIL LAMP
VIOLET TAG
LEFT REAR DIRECTIONAL LAMP
IGNITION & LIGHT SWITCH
COIL
REAR PLUG
FRONT PLUG
CONNECTOR
VACUUM SWITCH
VOLTAGE REGULATOR
CONNECTOR
STATOR
SOLENOID
CALIFORNIA TRAP DOOR CIRCUIT
GROUND AT UPPER STABILIZER
SOCKET CONNECTION
PIN CONNECTION
NO CONNECTION
CONNECTION
COMMONING TAB, 2 PLACE
COMMONING TAB, 3 PLACE
IGNITION SWITCH
POSITION B I L
OFF
RUN
LIGHTS
COLOR CODE:
BE BLUE
BK BLACK
BN BROWN
GN GREEN
GY GRAY
O ORANGE
PK PINK
R RED
LT.GN LIGHT GREEN
TN TAN
V VIOLET
W WHITE
Y YELLOW
CABLE COLOR
STRIPE COLOR

# 1992 FXRS-SP AND FXRS-CONV.

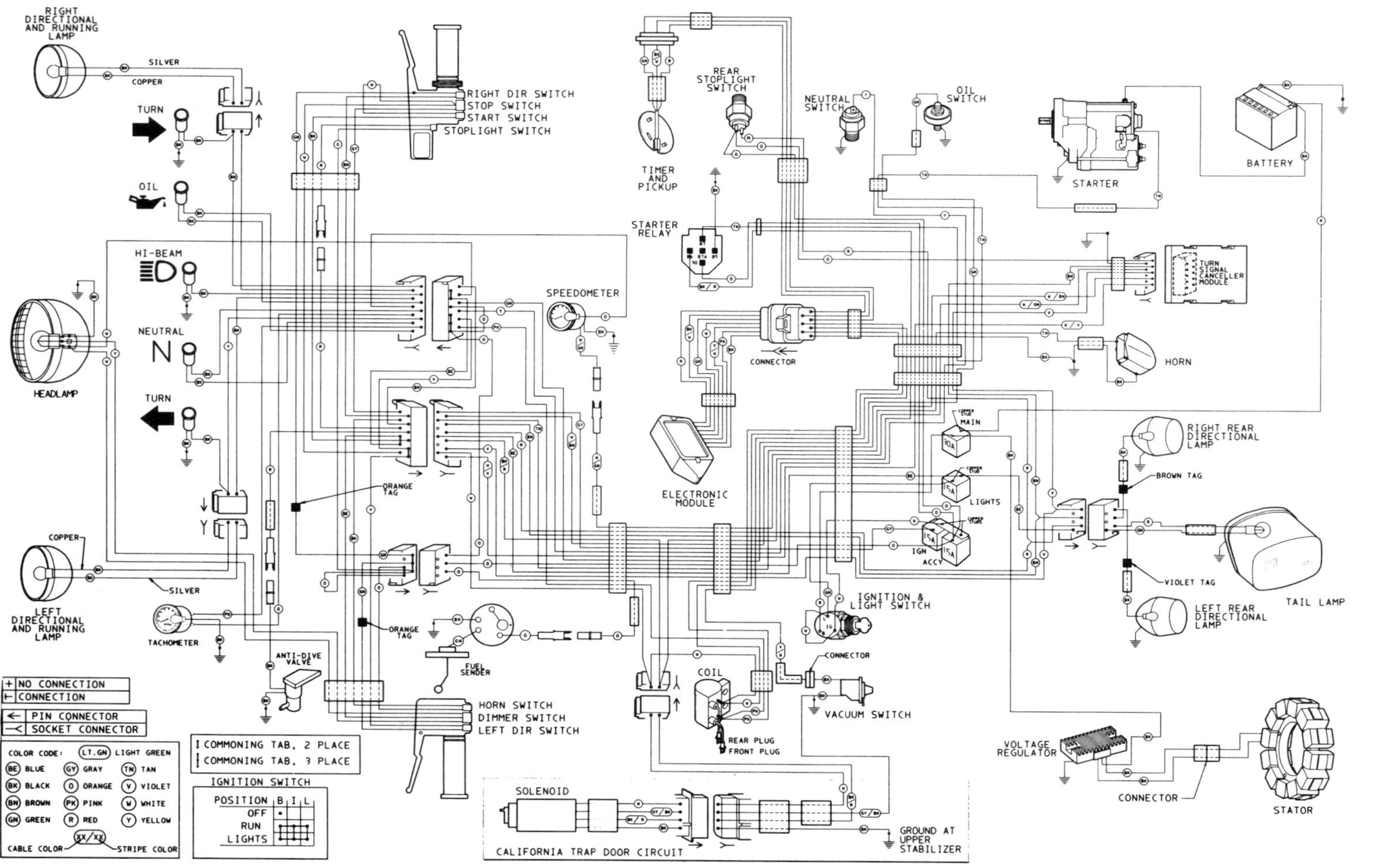

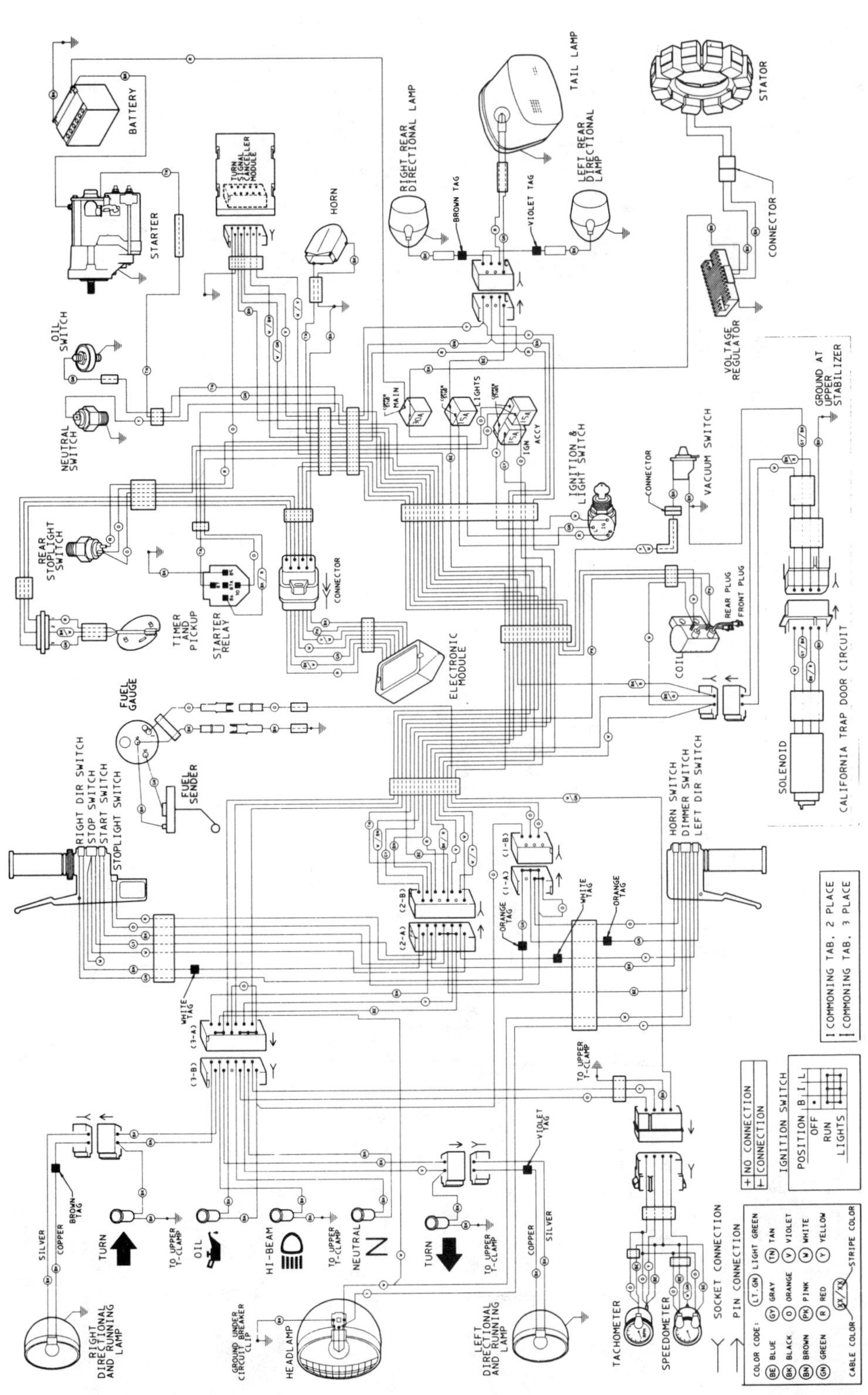
1992 FXRS
BATTERY
STARTER
TURN SIGNAL CANCELLER MODULE
HORN
RIGHT REAR DIRECTIONAL LAMP
BROWN TAG
TAIL LAMP
VIOLET TAG
LEFT REAR DIRECTIONAL LAMP
STATOR
CONNECTOR
VOLTAGE REGULATOR
OIL SWITCH
NEUTRAL SWITCH
MAIN
LIGHTS
IGN
ACCY
IGNITION & LIGHT SWITCH
CONNECTOR
VACUUM SWITCH
GROUND AT UPPER STABILIZER
REAR STOPLIGHT SWITCH
TIMER AND PICKUP
STARTER RELAY
CONNECTOR
ELECTRONIC MODULE
REAR PLUG
FRONT PLUG
COIL
FUEL GAUGE
FUEL SENDER
SOLENOID
CALIFORNIA TRAP DOOR CIRCUIT
RIGHT DIR SWITCH
STOP SWITCH
START SWITCH
STOPLIGHT SWITCH
HORN SWITCH
DIMMER SWITCH
LEFT DIR SWITCH
WHITE TAG
ORANGE TAG
COMMONING TAB. 2 PLACE
COMMONING TAB. 3 PLACE
TO UPPER T-CLAMP
IGNITION SWITCH
POSITION B I L
OFF
RUN
LIGHTS
NO CONNECTION
CONNECTION
SILVER
COPPER
BROWN TAG
TURN
OIL
HI-BEAM
NEUTRAL
VIOLET TAG
RIGHT DIRECTIONAL AND RUNNING LAMP
GROUND UNDER CIRCUIT BREAKER CLIP
HEADLAMP
LEFT DIRECTIONAL AND RUNNING LAMP
TACHOMETER
SPEEDOMETER
SOCKET CONNECTION
PIN CONNECTION
COLOR CODE: BE BLUE, BK BLACK, BN BROWN, GN GREEN, GY GRAY, O ORANGE, PK PINK, R RED, LT.GN LIGHT GREEN, TN TAN, V VIOLET, W WHITE, Y YELLOW
CABLE COLOR
STRIPE COLOR

# 1992 FXRT FAIRING (PART 1 OF 2)

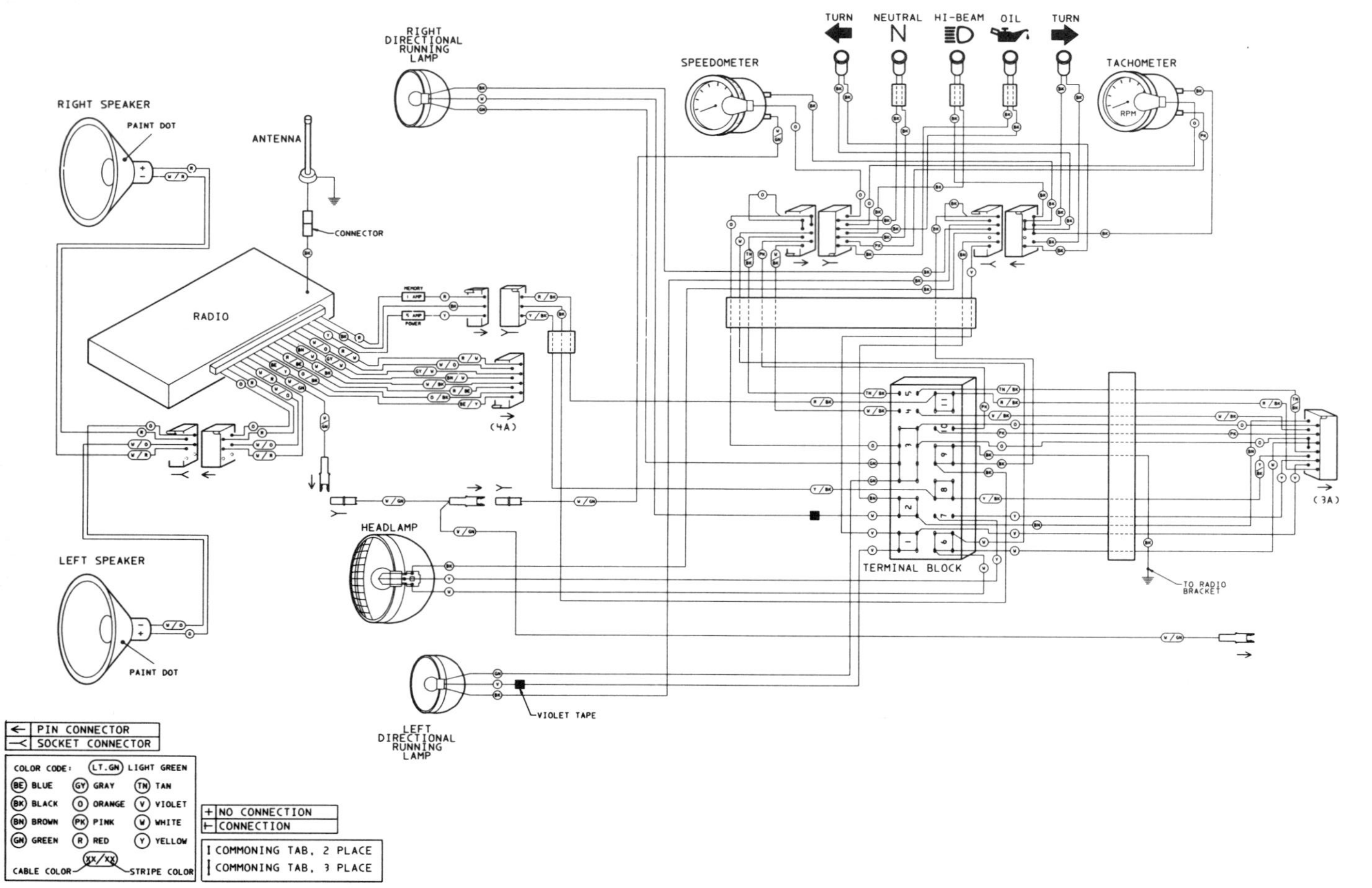

# 1992 FXRT CHASSIS (PART 2 OF 2)

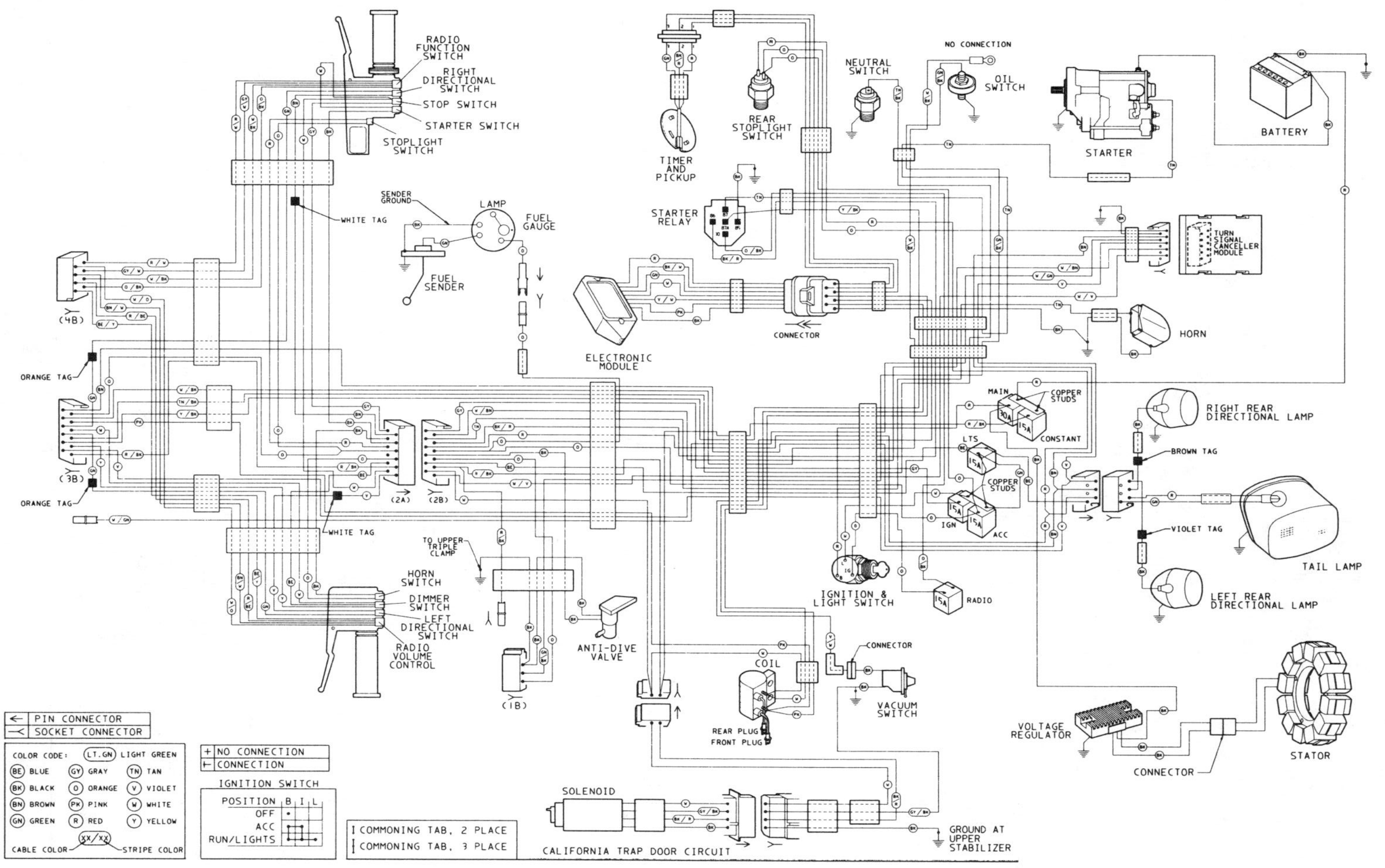

# 1992 FLHTC FAIRING (PART 1 OF 2)

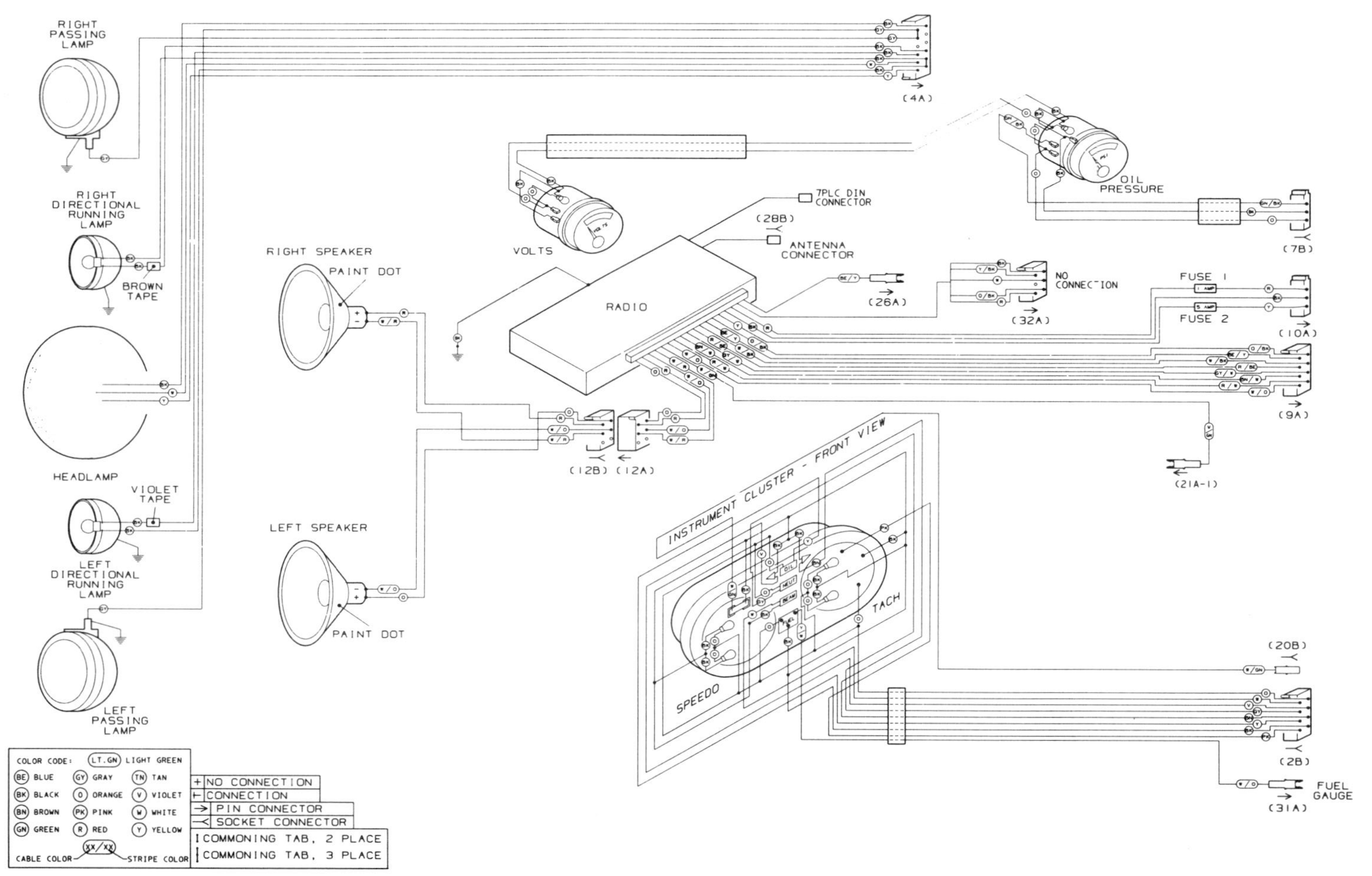

# 1992 FLHTC CHASSIS (PART 2 OF 2)

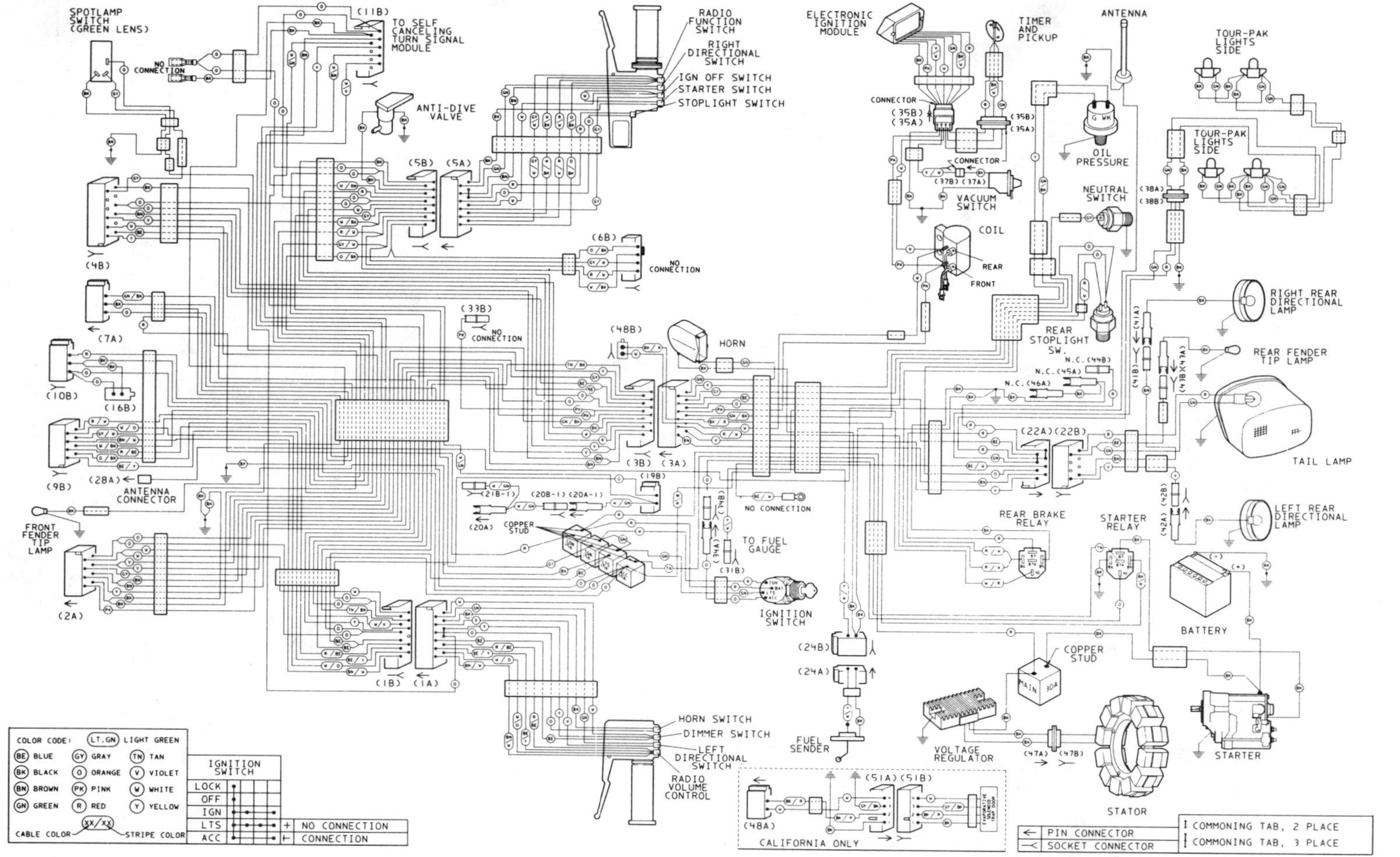

## 1992 FLHS INSTRUMENTS (PART 1 OF 2)

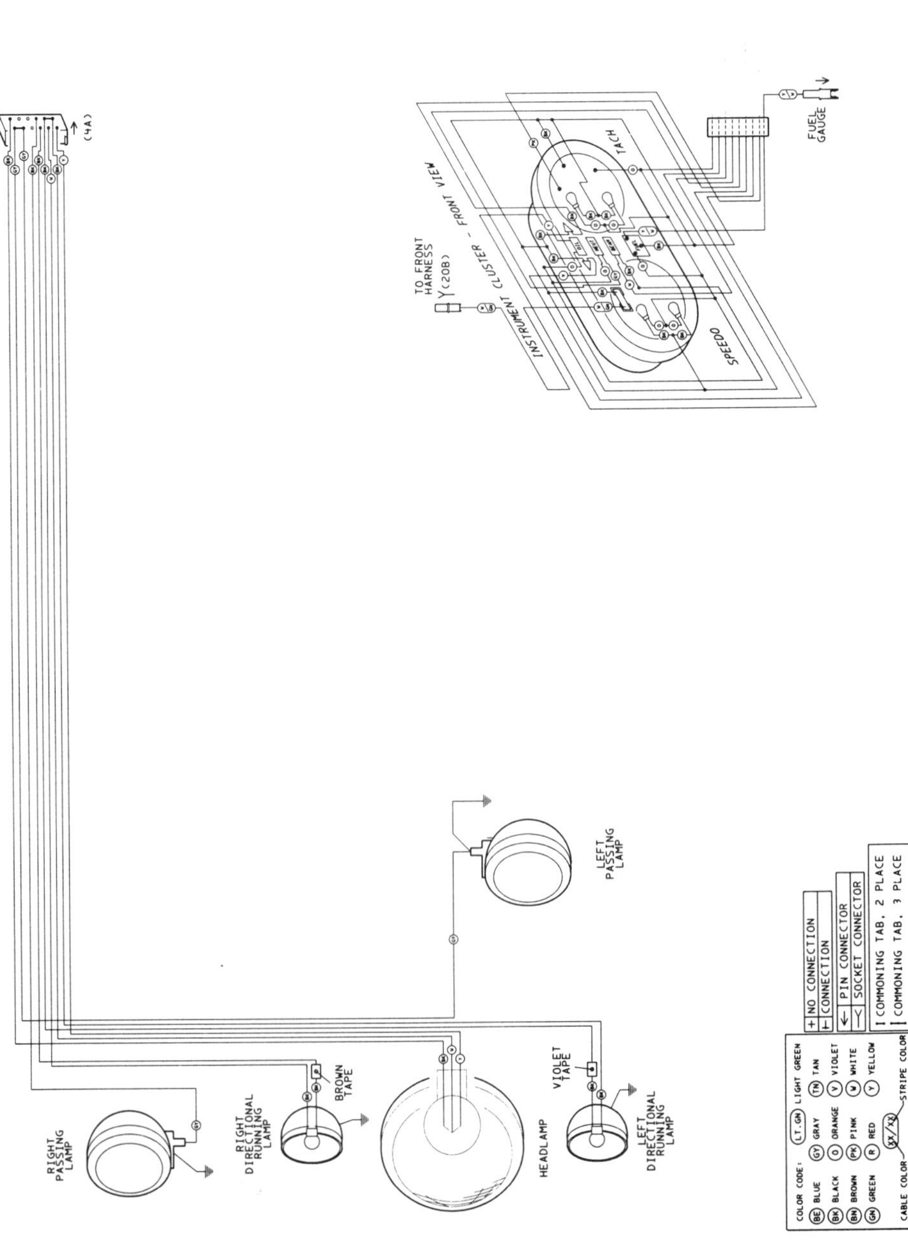

# 1992 FLHS CHASSIS (PART 2 OF 2)

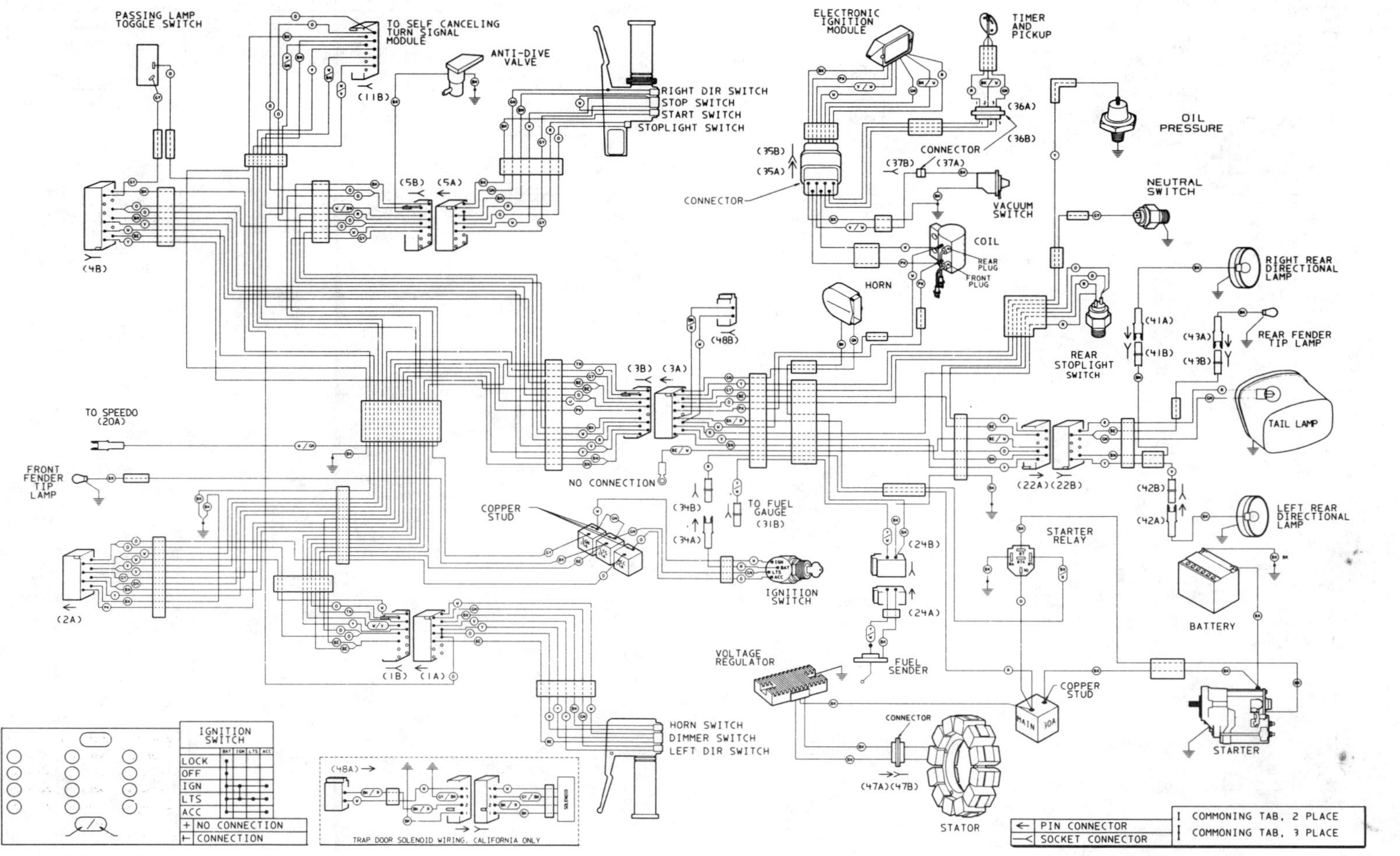

# 1992 FLTC-ULTRA CHASSIS (PART 1 OF 3)

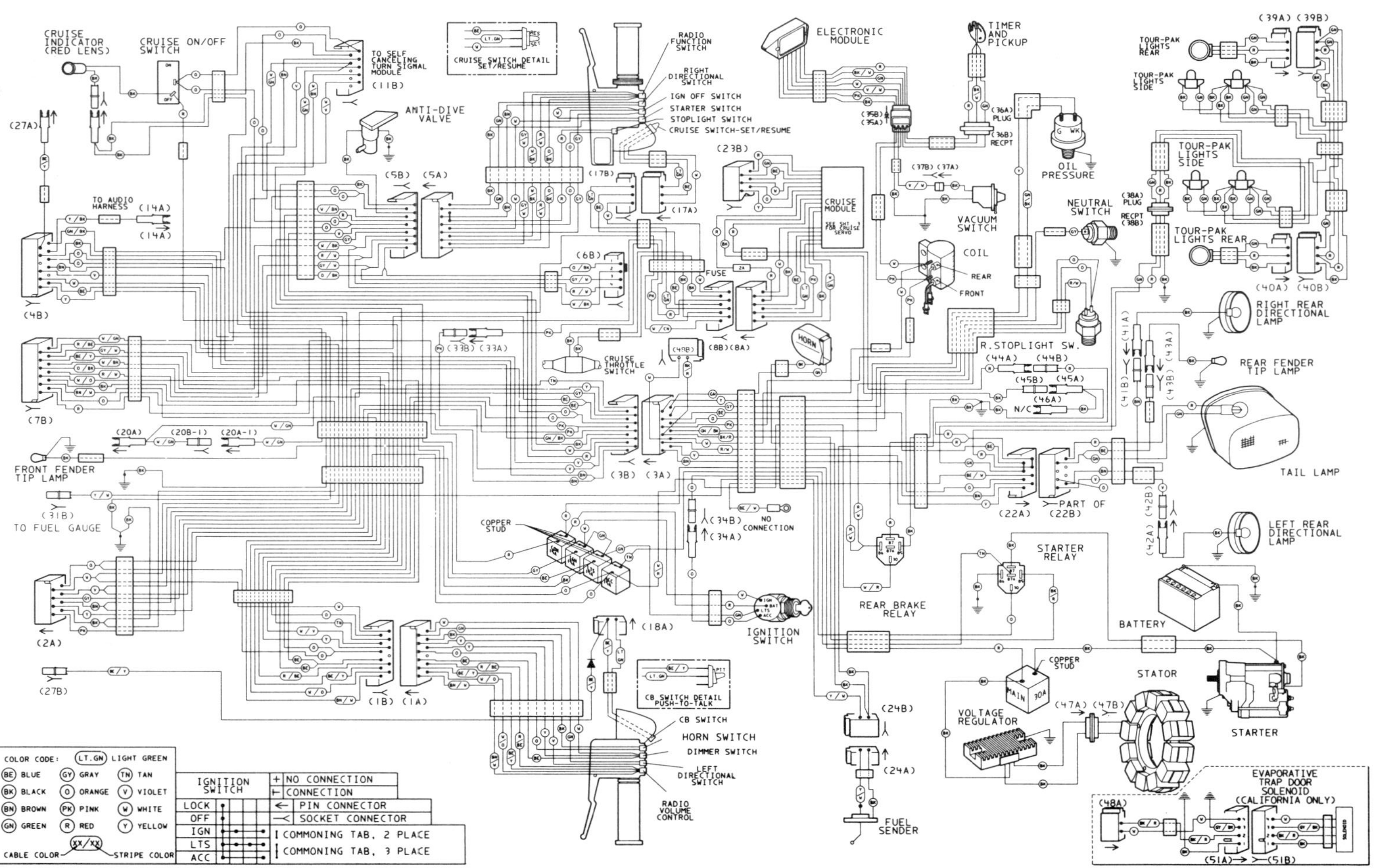

# 1992 FLTC-ULTRA FAIRING (PART 2 OF 3)

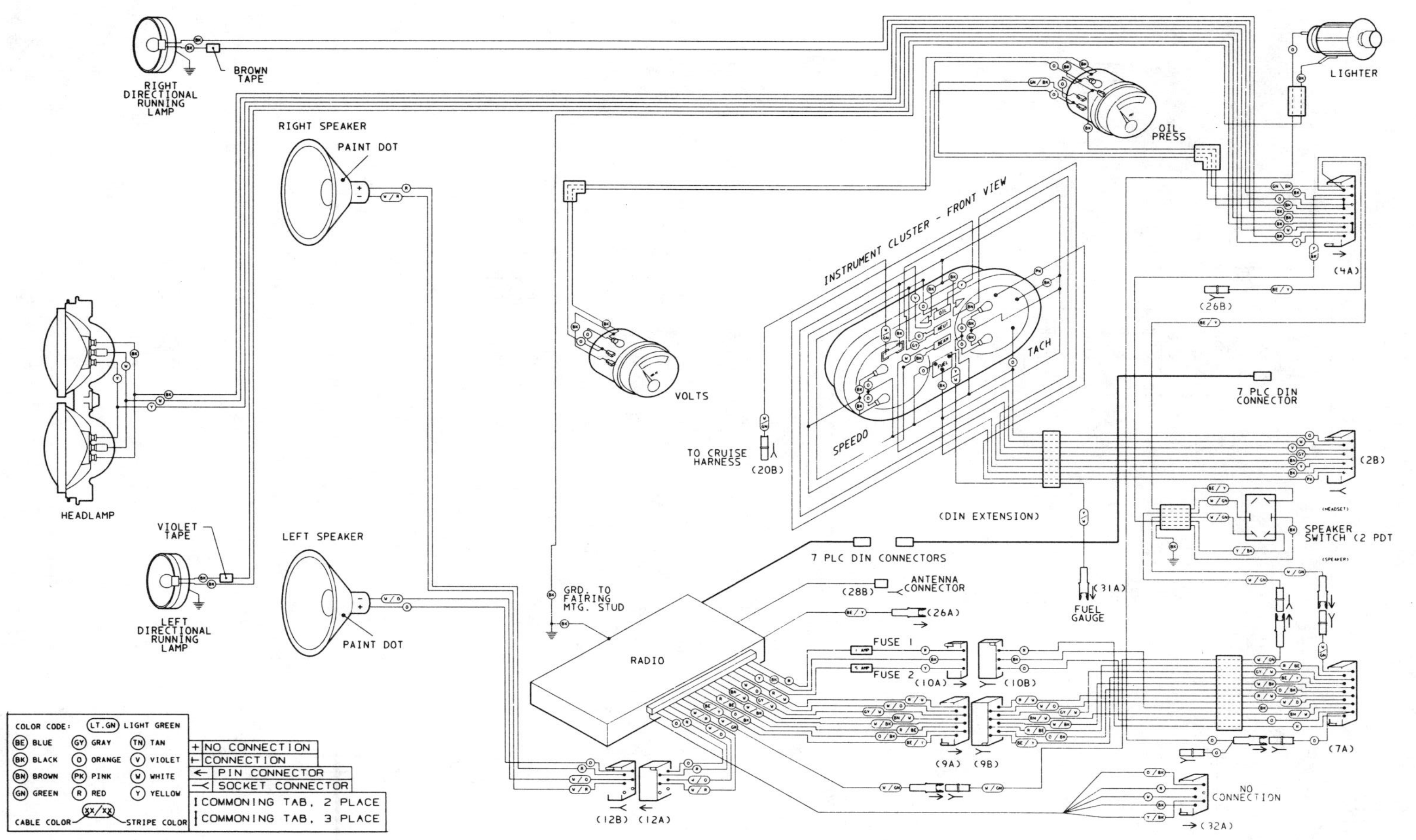

## 1992 FLTC-ULTRA CB/INTERCOM (PART 3 OF 3)

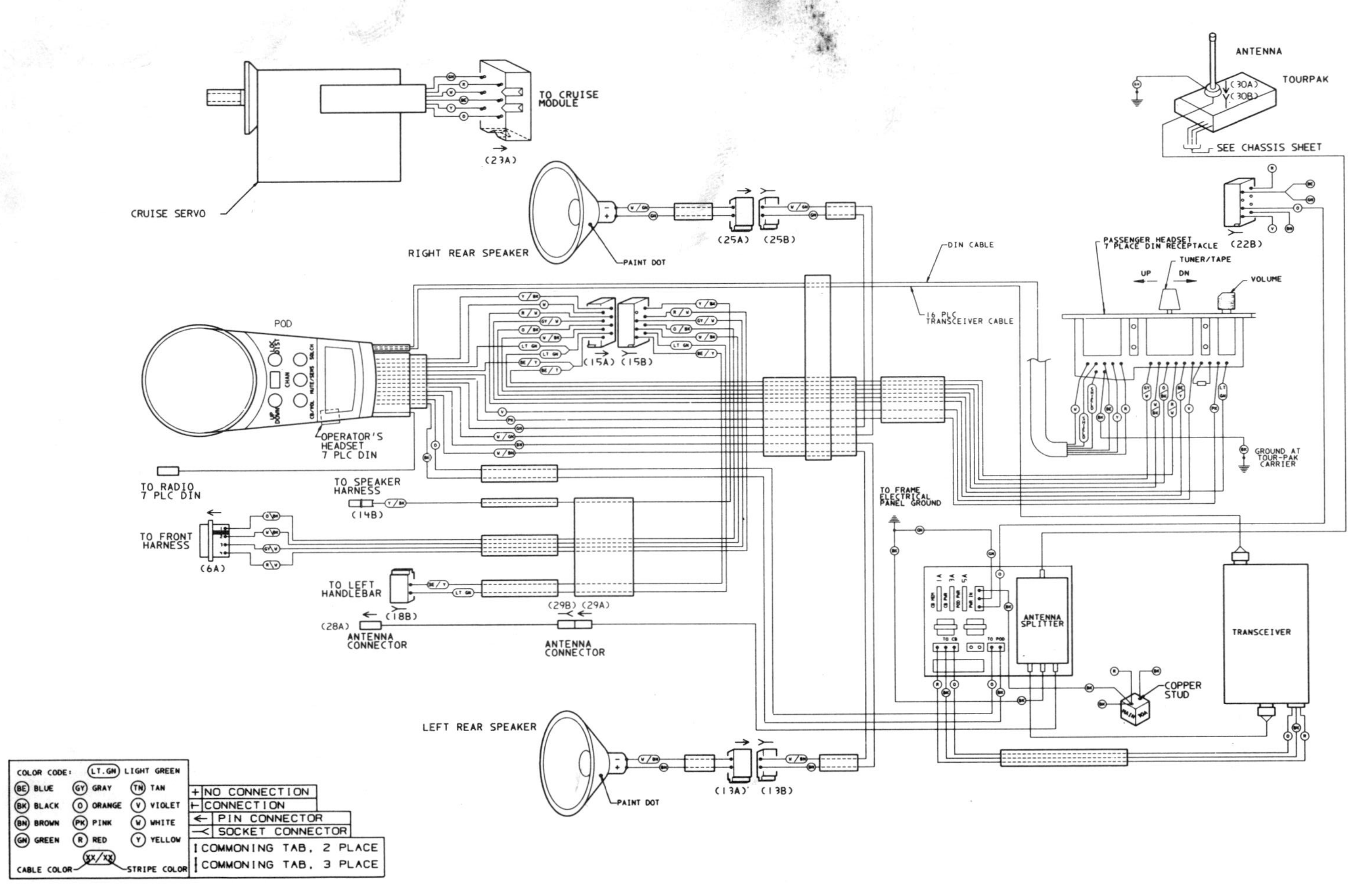

# 1992 FLHTC-ULTRA CHASSIS (PART 1 OF 3)

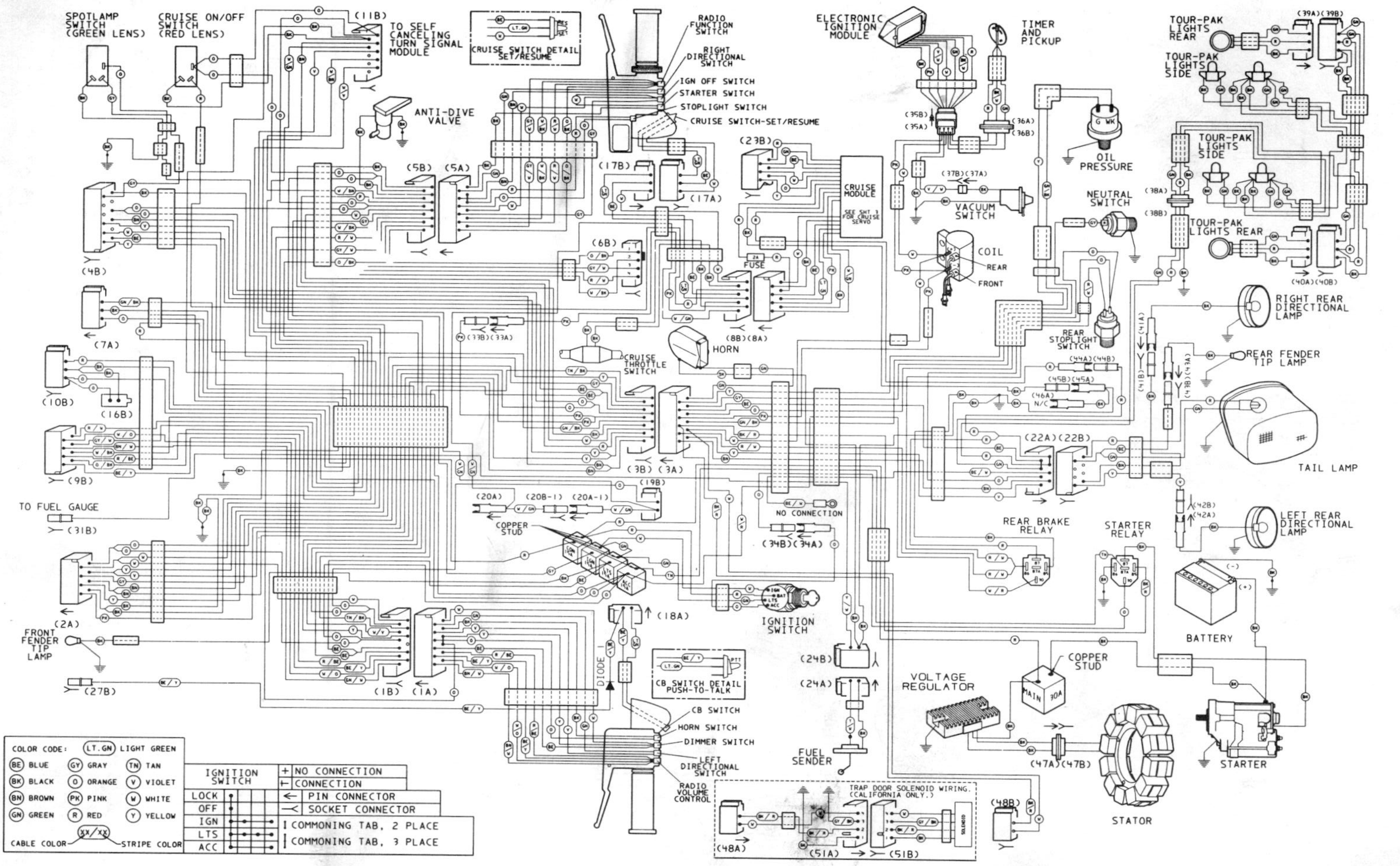

# 1992 FLHTC-ULTRA FAIRING (SHEET 2 OF 3)

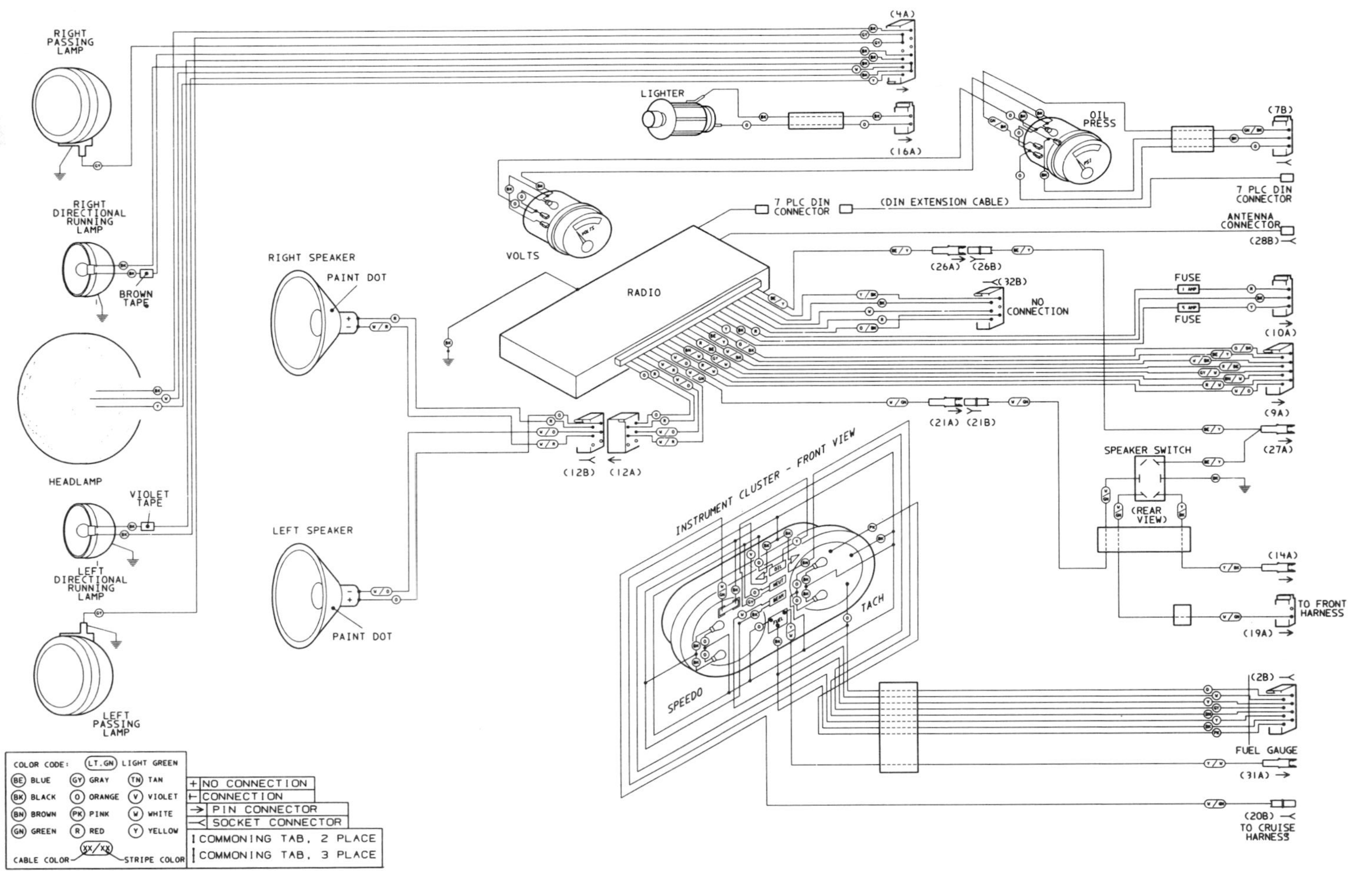

# 1992 FLHTC-ULTRA CB/INTERCOM (PART 3 OF 3)

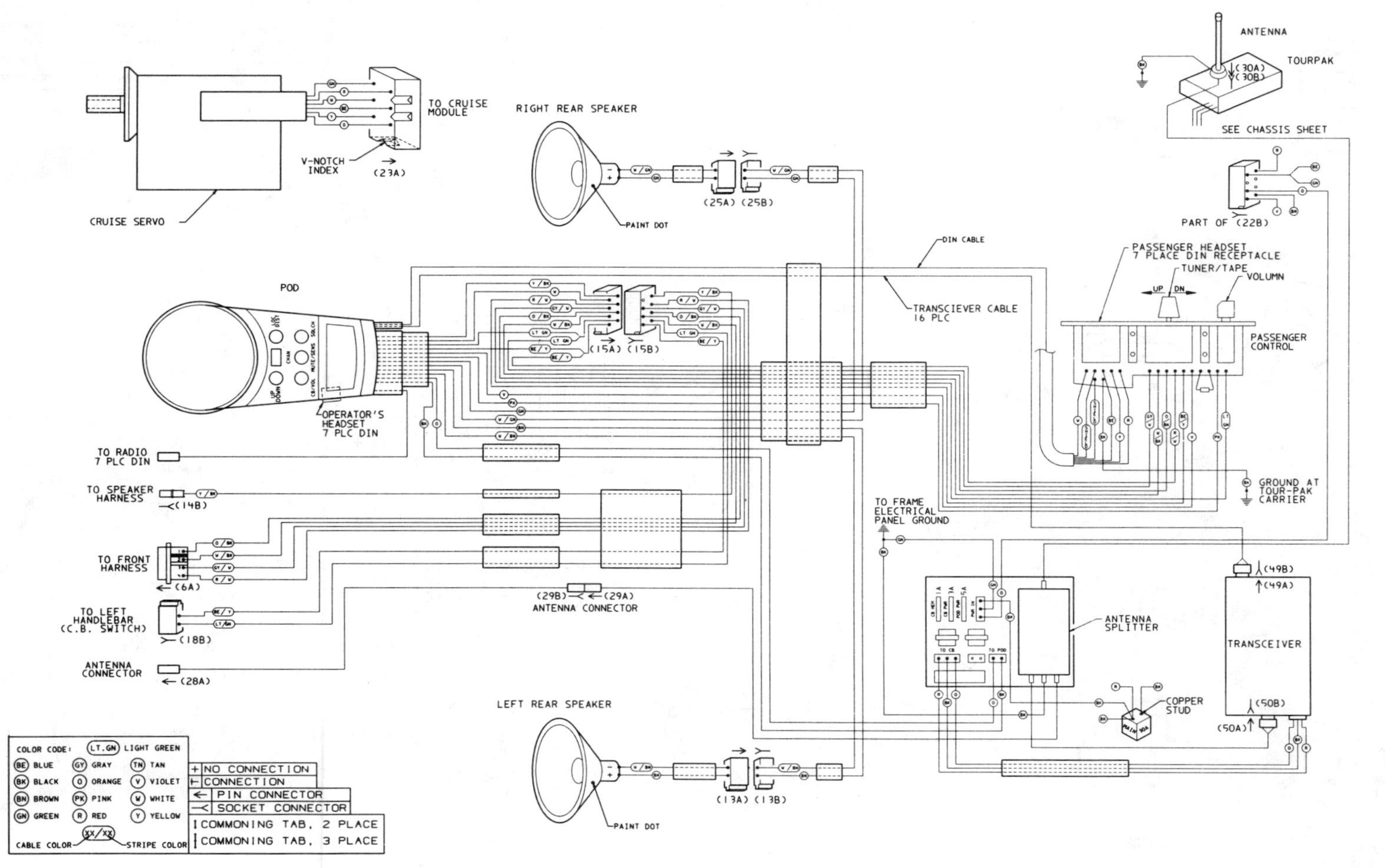


17

# 1993 FXR DOMESTIC AND INTERNATIONAL MODELS

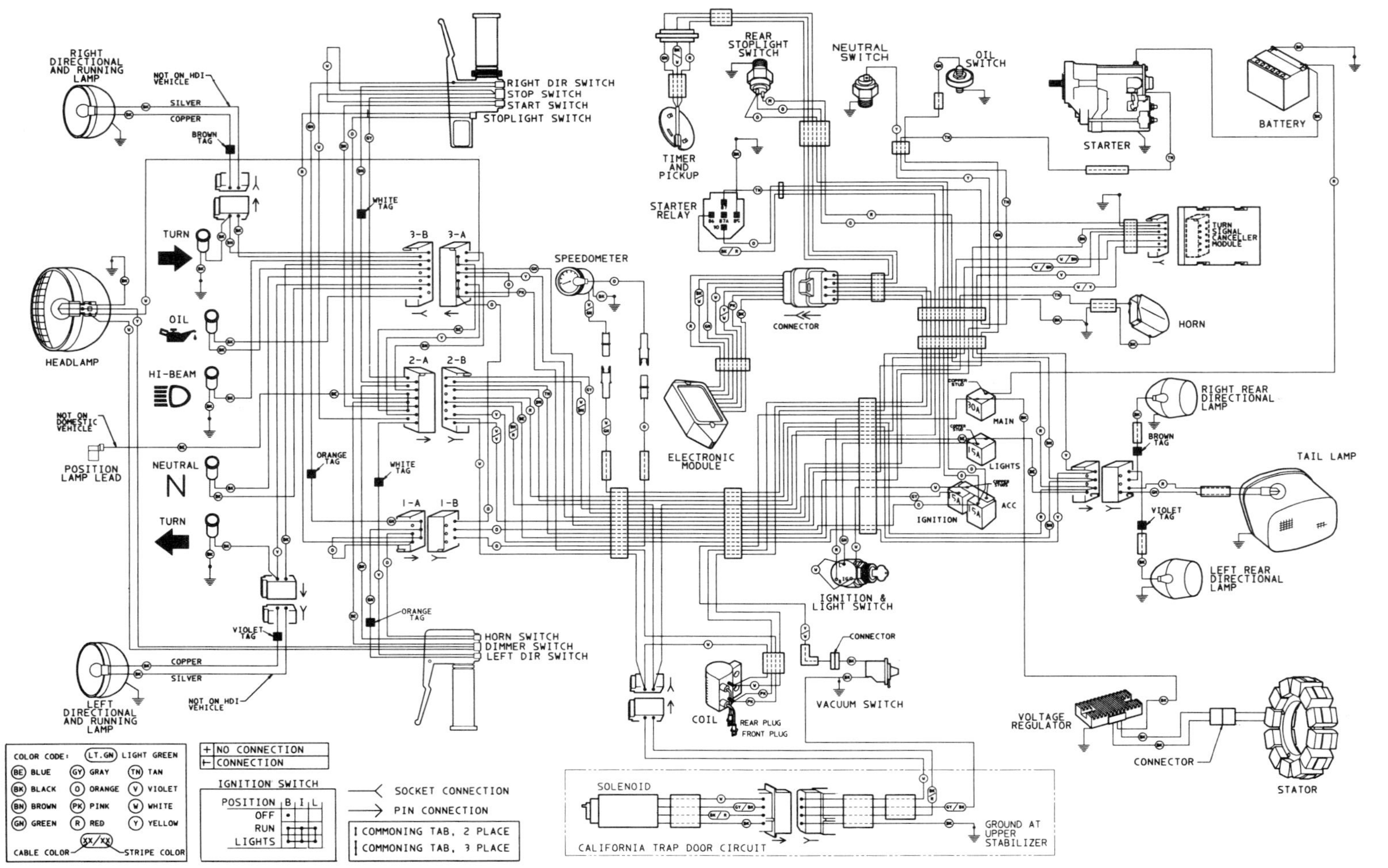

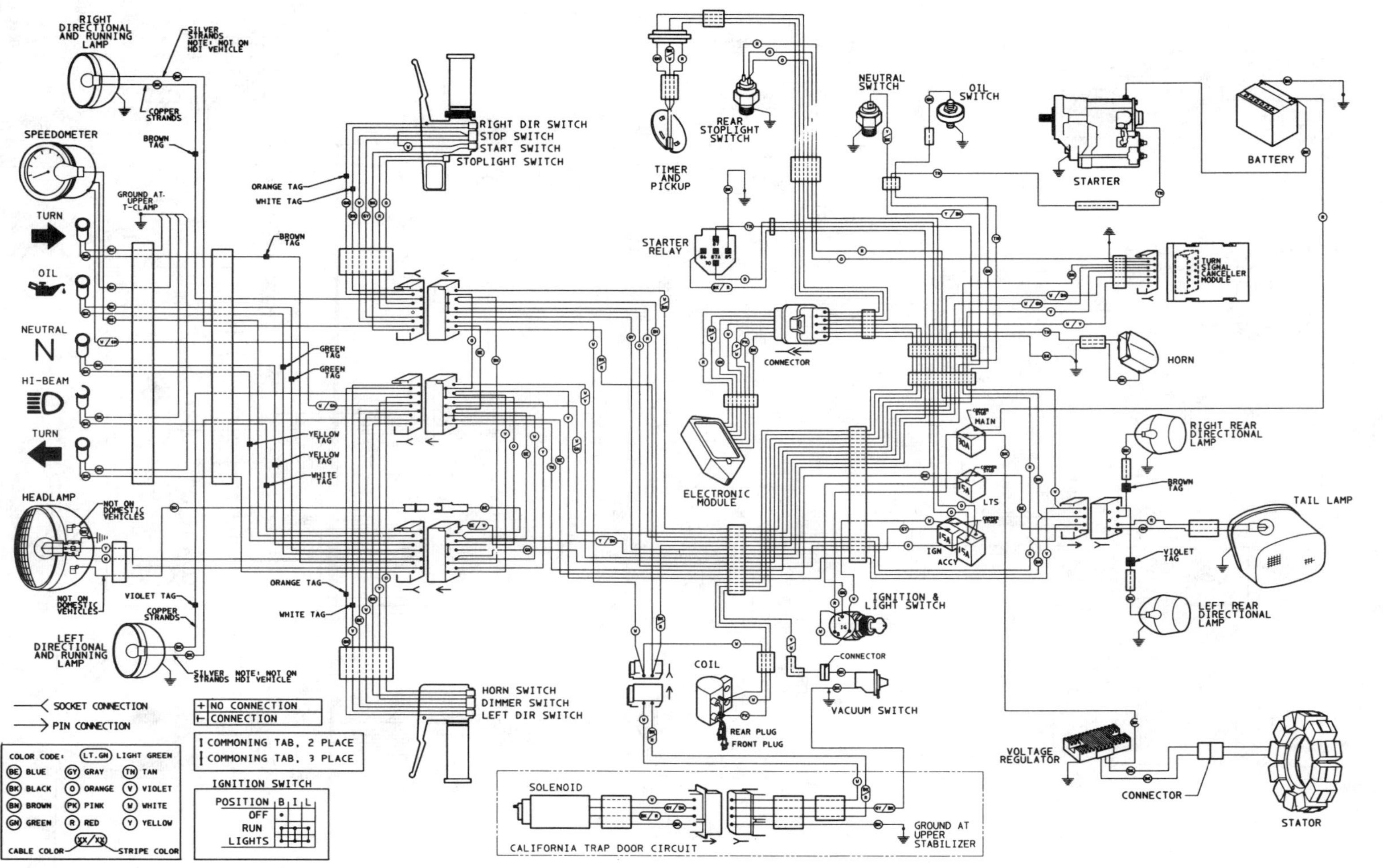
1993 FXLR DOMESTIC AND INTERNATIONAL MODELS
RIGHT DIRECTIONAL AND RUNNING LAMP
SILVER STRANDS NOTE: NOT ON HDI VEHICLE
COPPER STRANDS
BROWN TAG
SPEEDOMETER
GROUND AT UPPER T-CLAMP
TURN
OIL
NEUTRAL
N
HI-BEAM
TURN
HEADLAMP
NOT ON DOMESTIC VEHICLES
NOT ON DOMESTIC VEHICLES
VIOLET TAG
COPPER STRANDS
LEFT DIRECTIONAL AND RUNNING LAMP
SILVER STRANDS NOTE: NOT ON HDI VEHICLE
RIGHT DIR SWITCH
STOP SWITCH
START SWITCH
STOPLIGHT SWITCH
ORANGE TAG
WHITE TAG
BROWN TAG
GREEN TAG
GREEN TAG
YELLOW TAG
YELLOW TAG
WHITE TAG
ORANGE TAG
WHITE TAG
HORN SWITCH
DIMMER SWITCH
LEFT DIR SWITCH
TIMER AND PICKUP
REAR STOPLIGHT SWITCH
NEUTRAL SWITCH
OIL SWITCH
STARTER
BATTERY
STARTER RELAY
CONNECTOR
TURN SIGNAL CANCELLER MODULE
HORN
ELECTRONIC MODULE
MAIN
LTS
IGN
ACCY
RIGHT REAR DIRECTIONAL LAMP
BROWN TAG
TAIL LAMP
VIOLET TAG
LEFT REAR DIRECTIONAL LAMP
IGNITION & LIGHT SWITCH
COIL
REAR PLUG
FRONT PLUG
CONNECTOR
VACUUM SWITCH
VOLTAGE REGULATOR
CONNECTOR
STATOR
SOLENOID
CALIFORNIA TRAP DOOR CIRCUIT
GROUND AT UPPER STABILIZER
SOCKET CONNECTION
PIN CONNECTION
+ NO CONNECTION
CONNECTION
COMMONING TAB, 2 PLACE
COMMONING TAB, 3 PLACE
IGNITION SWITCH
POSITION B I L
OFF
RUN
LIGHTS
COLOR CODE:
BE BLUE
BK BLACK
BN BROWN
GN GREEN
GY GRAY
O ORANGE
PK PINK
R RED
LT.GN LIGHT GREEN
TN TAN
V VIOLET
W WHITE
Y YELLOW
XX/XX
CABLE COLOR
STRIPE COLOR

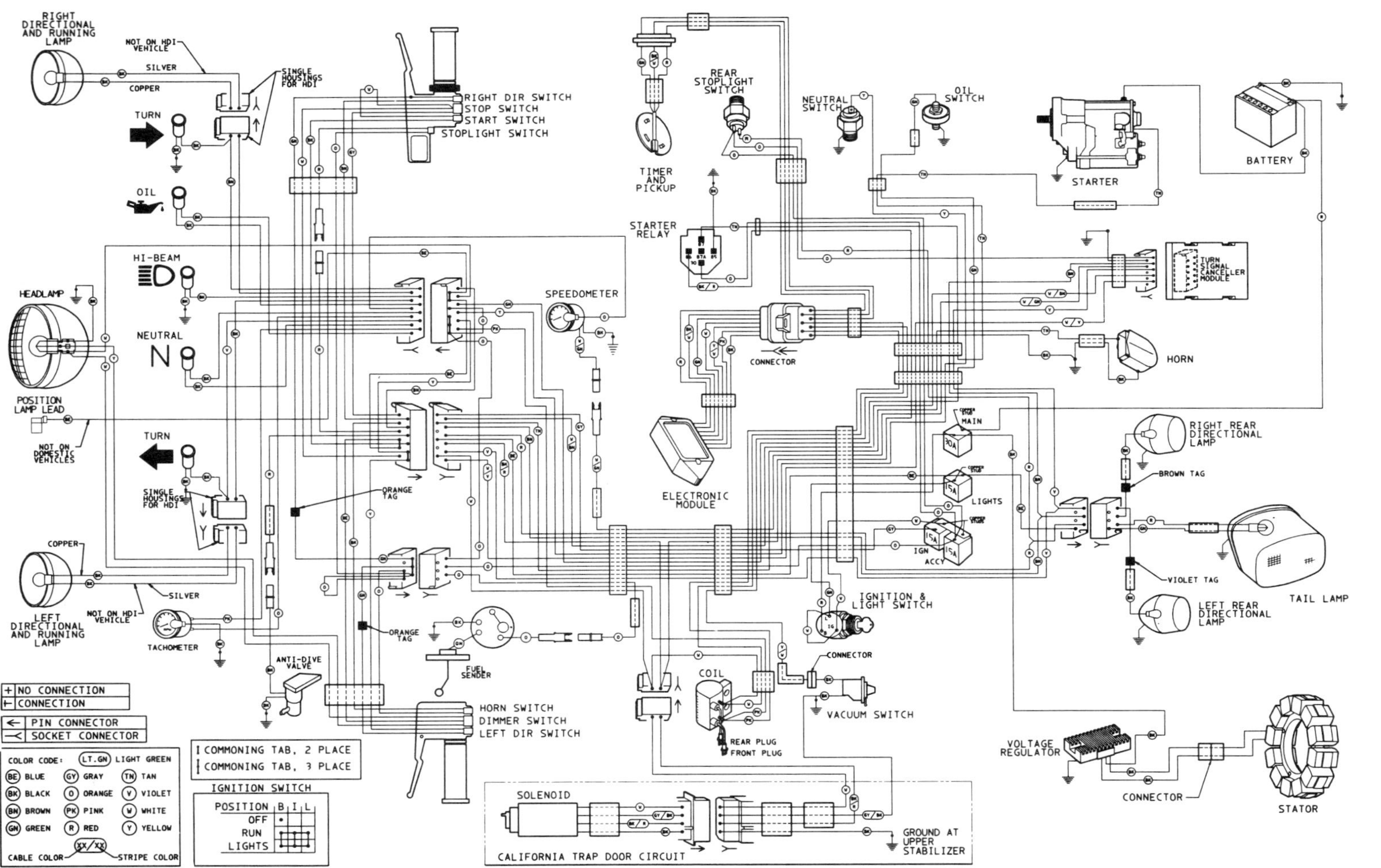
1993 FXRS-SP & FXRS-CONV. DOMESTIC AND INTERNATIONAL MODELS
RIGHT DIRECTIONAL AND RUNNING LAMP
NOT ON HDI VEHICLE
SILVER
COPPER
SINGLE HOUSINGS FOR HDI
TURN
OIL
HI-BEAM
HEADLAMP
NEUTRAL
POSITION LAMP LEAD
NOT ON DOMESTIC VEHICLES
LEFT DIRECTIONAL AND RUNNING LAMP
TACHOMETER
RIGHT DIR SWITCH
STOP SWITCH
START SWITCH
STOPLIGHT SWITCH
ORANGE TAG
ANTI-DIVE VALVE
FUEL SENDER
HORN SWITCH
DIMMER SWITCH
LEFT DIR SWITCH
SPEEDOMETER
TIMER AND PICKUP
REAR STOPLIGHT SWITCH
NEUTRAL SWITCH
OIL SWITCH
STARTER RELAY
STARTER
BATTERY
CONNECTOR
ELECTRONIC MODULE
TURN SIGNAL CANCELLER MODULE
HORN
MAIN
LIGHTS
IGN
ACCY
IGNITION & LIGHT SWITCH
COIL
REAR PLUG
FRONT PLUG
VACUUM SWITCH
RIGHT REAR DIRECTIONAL LAMP
BROWN TAG
VIOLET TAG
TAIL LAMP
LEFT REAR DIRECTIONAL LAMP
VOLTAGE REGULATOR
STATOR
SOLENOID
GROUND AT UPPER STABILIZER
CALIFORNIA TRAP DOOR CIRCUIT
+ NO CONNECTION
+ CONNECTION
← PIN CONNECTOR
≺ SOCKET CONNECTOR
COLOR CODE:
BE BLUE
BK BLACK
BN BROWN
GN GREEN
GY GRAY
O ORANGE
PK PINK
R RED
LT.GN LIGHT GREEN
TN TAN
V VIOLET
W WHITE
Y YELLOW
CABLE COLOR
XX/XX
STRIPE COLOR
COMMONING TAB, 2 PLACE
COMMONING TAB, 3 PLACE
IGNITION SWITCH
POSITION B I L
OFF
RUN
LIGHTS

# 1993 FLHTC DOMESTIC MODEL FAIRING (PART 1 OF 2)

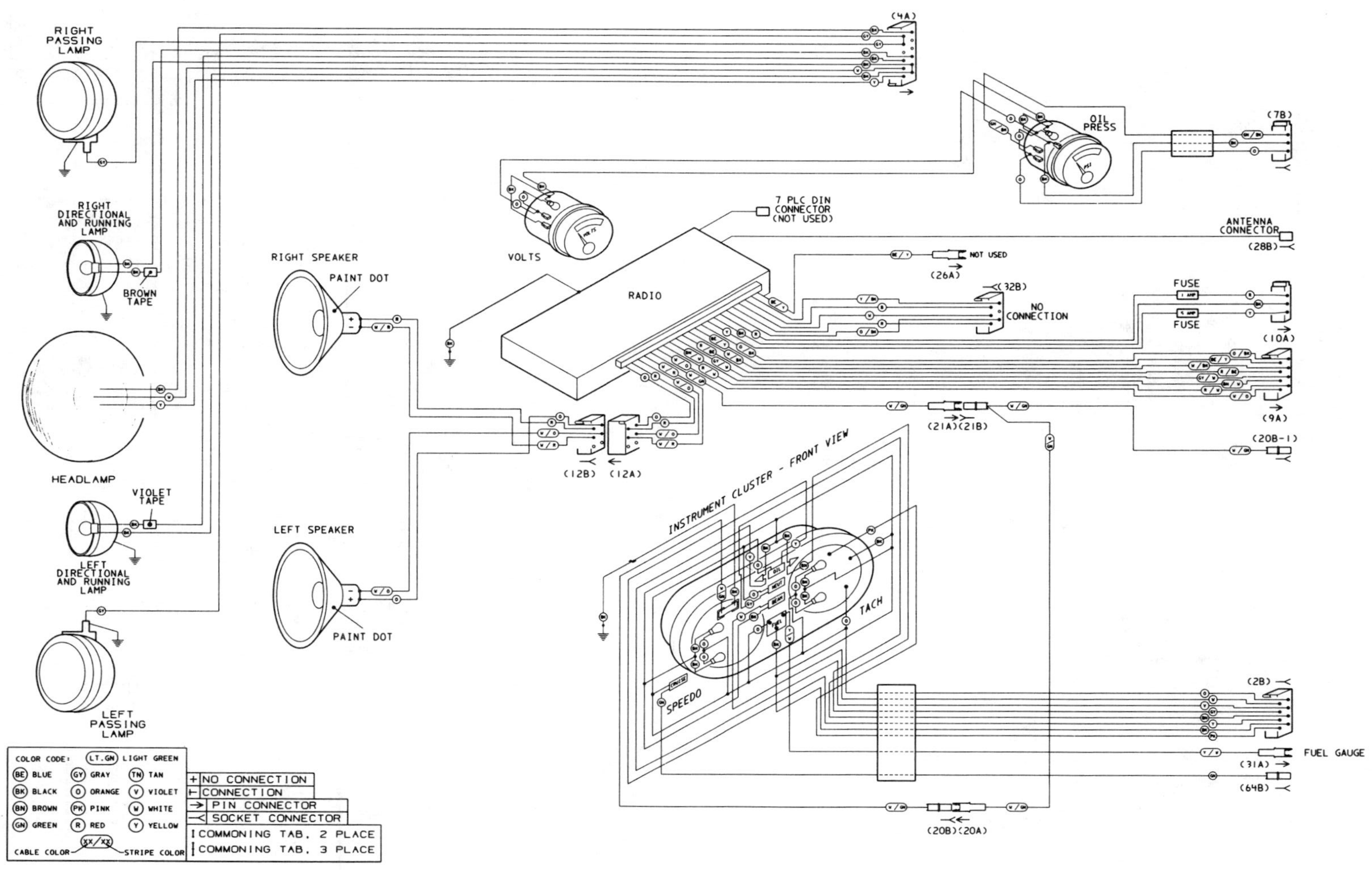

## 1993 FLHTC DOMESTIC MODEL CHASSIS (PART 2 OF 2)

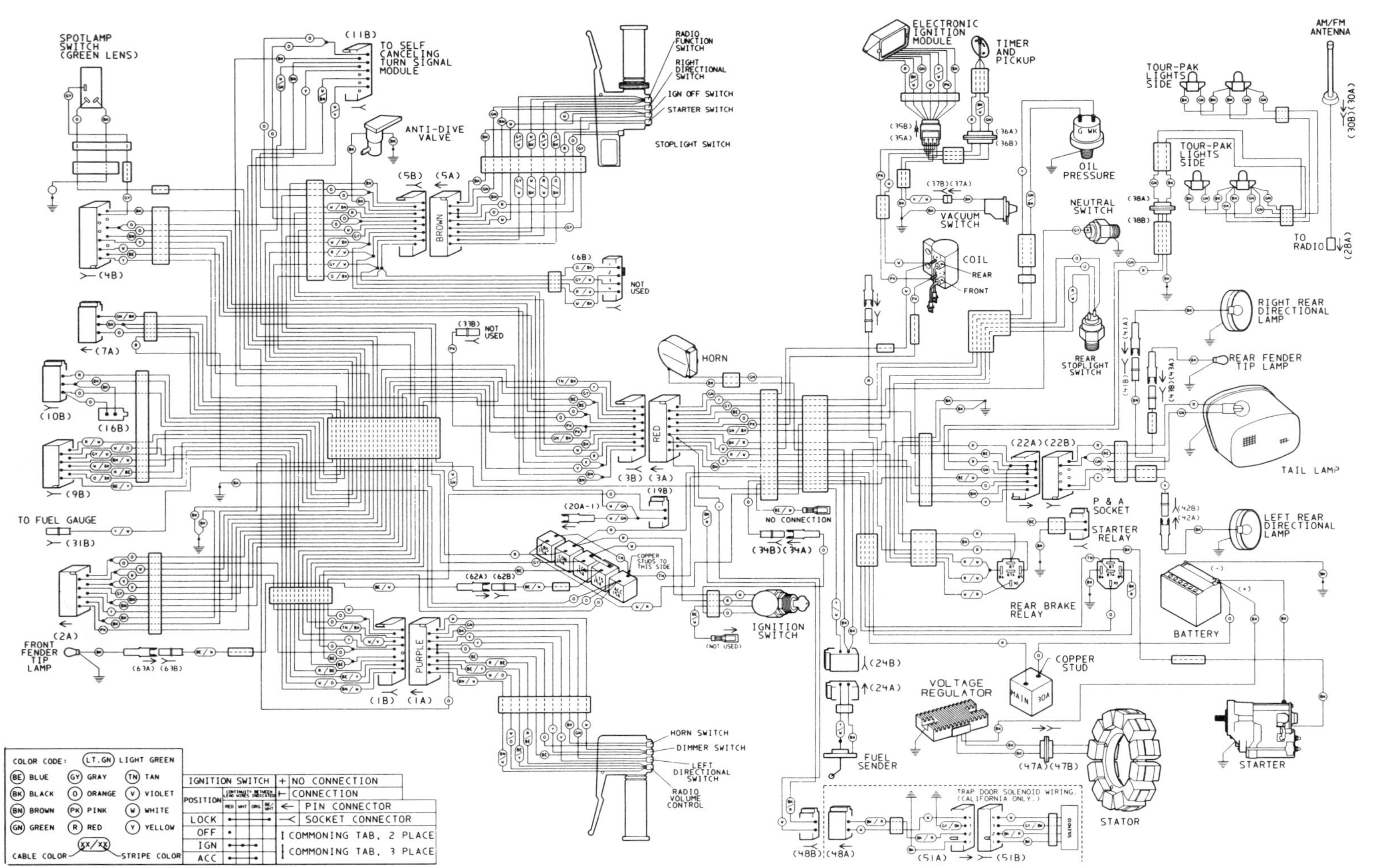

## 1993 FLHS DOMESTIC MODEL INSTRUMENTS (PART 1 OF 2)

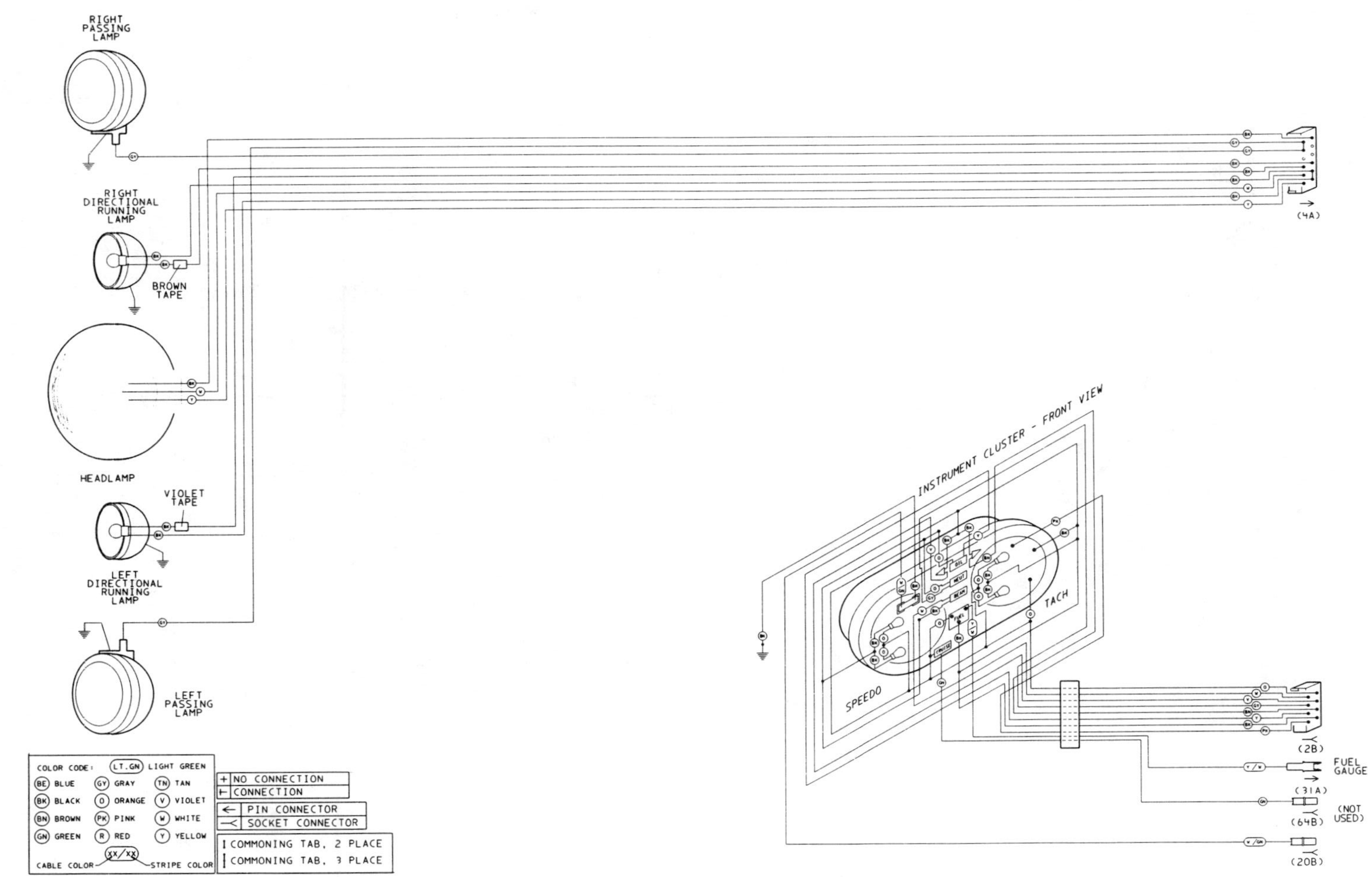

## 1993 FLHS DOMESTIC MODEL CHASSIS (PART 2 OF 2)

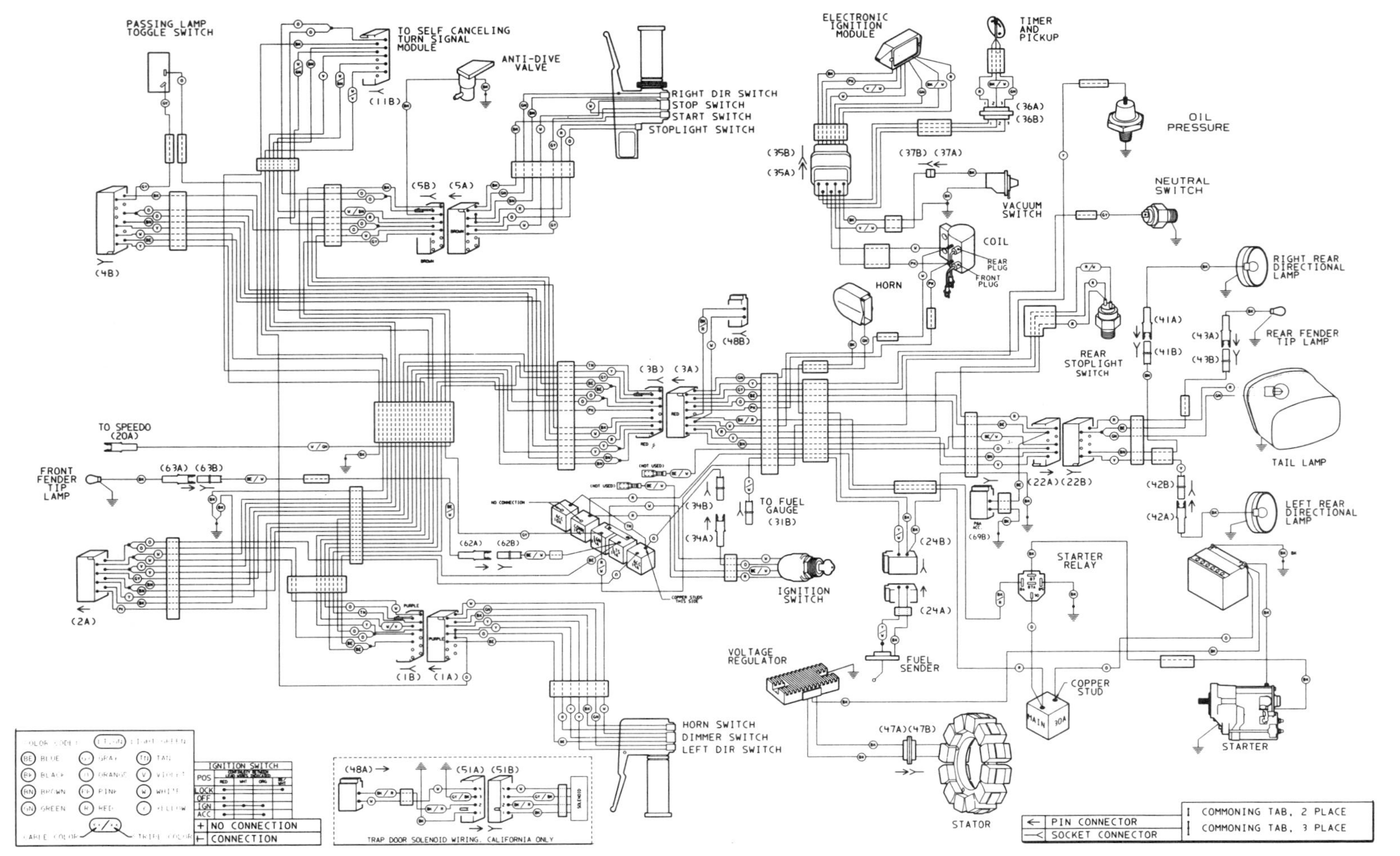

# 1993 FLTC-ULTRA DOMESTIC MODEL CHASSIS (PART 1 OF 3)

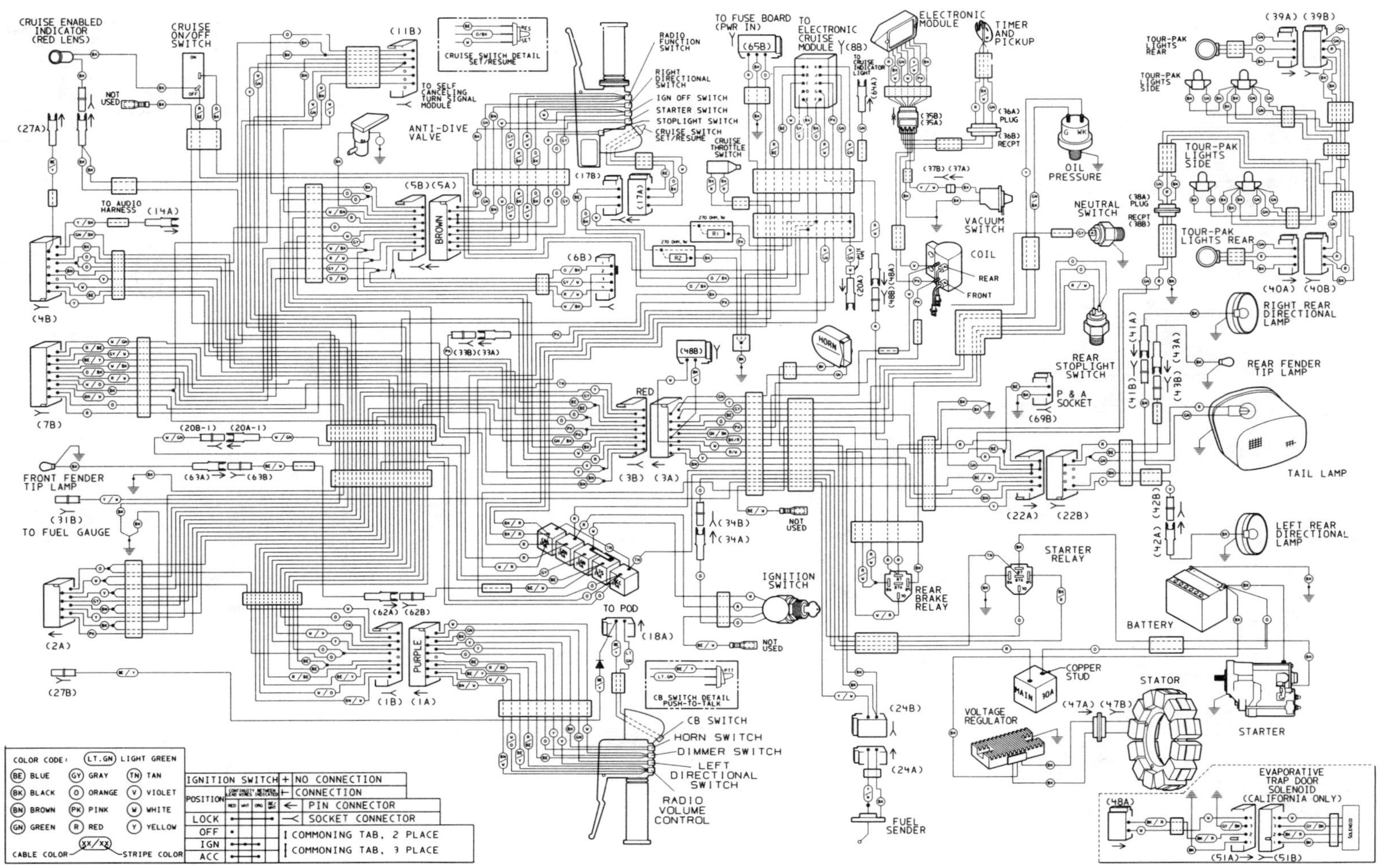


17

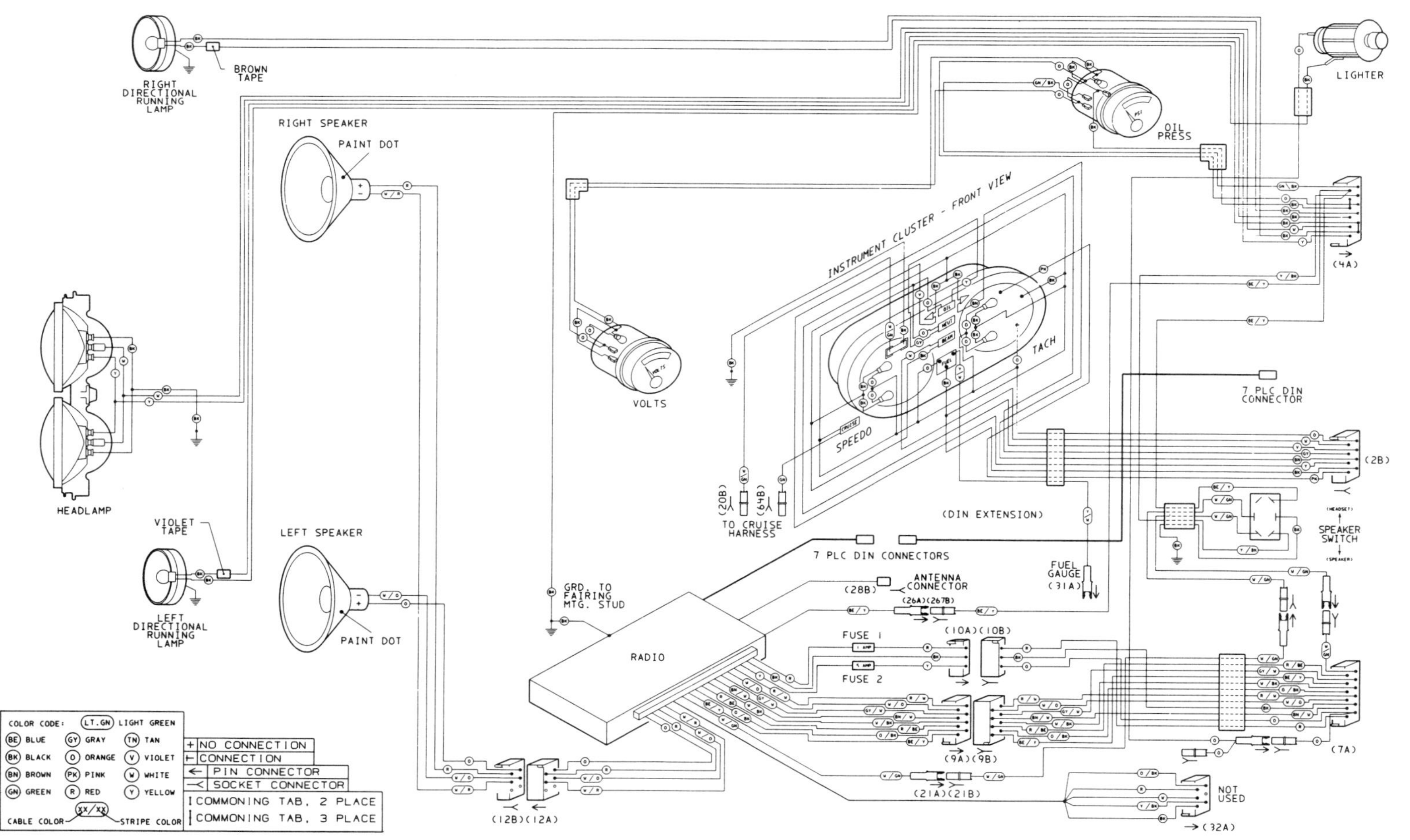
1993 FLTC-ULTRA DOMESTIC MODEL FAIRING (PART 2 OF 3)
RIGHT DIRECTIONAL RUNNING LAMP
BROWN TAPE
RIGHT SPEAKER
PAINT DOT
LIGHTER
OIL PRESS
INSTRUMENT CLUSTER - FRONT VIEW
TACH
SPEEDO
VOLTS
HEADLAMP
VIOLET TAPE
LEFT SPEAKER
LEFT DIRECTIONAL RUNNING LAMP
7 PLC DIN CONNECTOR
(2B)
(4A)
TO CRUISE HARNESS
(DIN EXTENSION)
SPEAKER SWITCH
7 PLC DIN CONNECTORS
FUEL GAUGE (31A)
ANTENNA CONNECTOR
GRD. TO FAIRING MTG. STUD
RADIO
FUSE 1
FUSE 2
(10A)(10B)
(9A)(9B)
(7A)
(21A)(21B)
NOT USED
(32A)
(12B)(12A)
COLOR CODE:
BE BLUE
BK BLACK
BN BROWN
GN GREEN
GY GRAY
O ORANGE
PK PINK
R RED
LT.GN LIGHT GREEN
TN TAN
V VIOLET
W WHITE
Y YELLOW
CABLE COLOR
STRIPE COLOR
NO CONNECTION
CONNECTION
PIN CONNECTOR
SOCKET CONNECTOR
COMMONING TAB, 2 PLACE
COMMONING TAB, 3 PLACE

## 1993 FLTC-ULTRA DOMESTIC MODEL CB/INTERCOM, CRUISE (PART 3 OF 3)

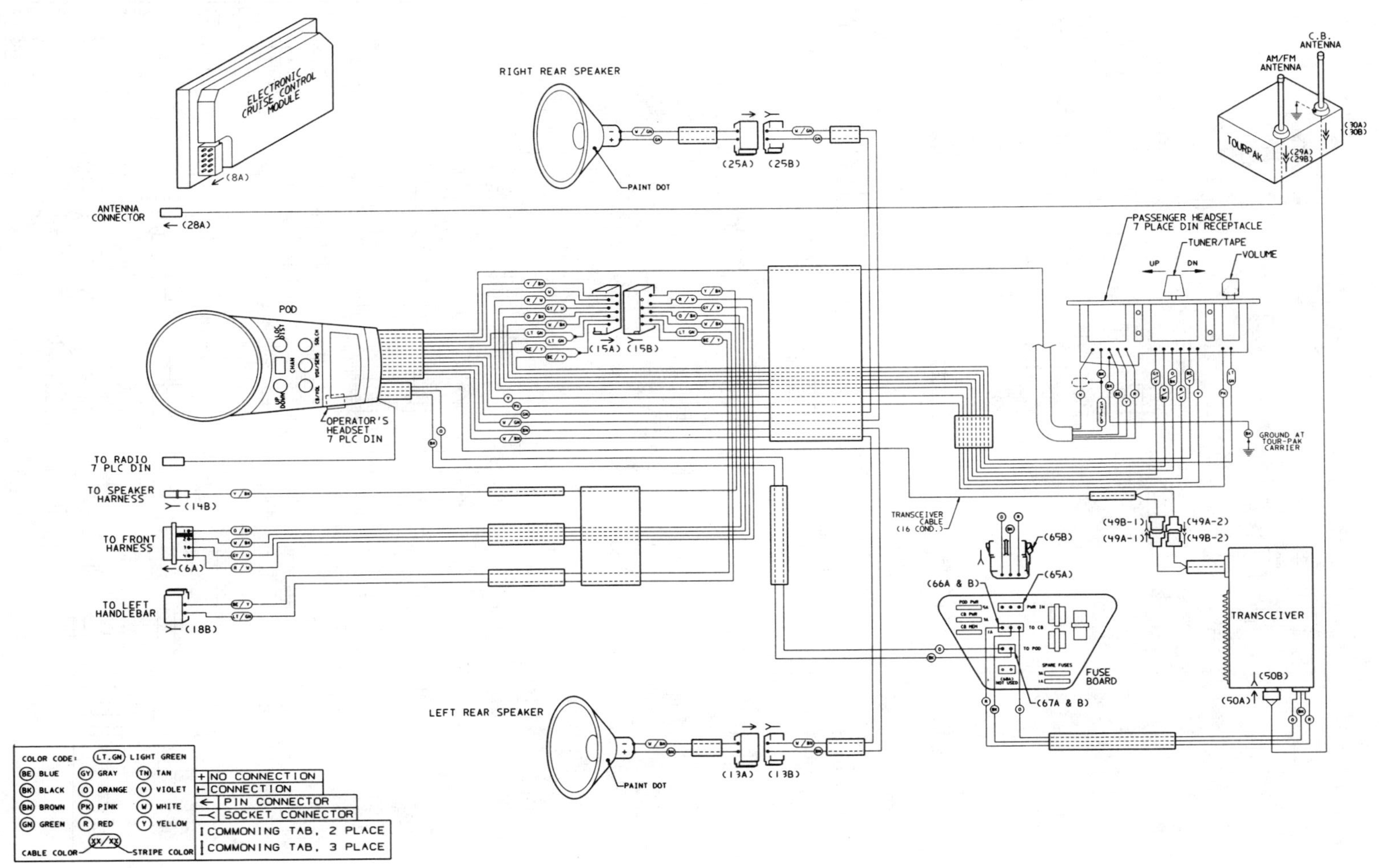

## 1993 FLHTC-ULTRA DOMESTIC MODEL CHASSIS (PART 1 OF 3)

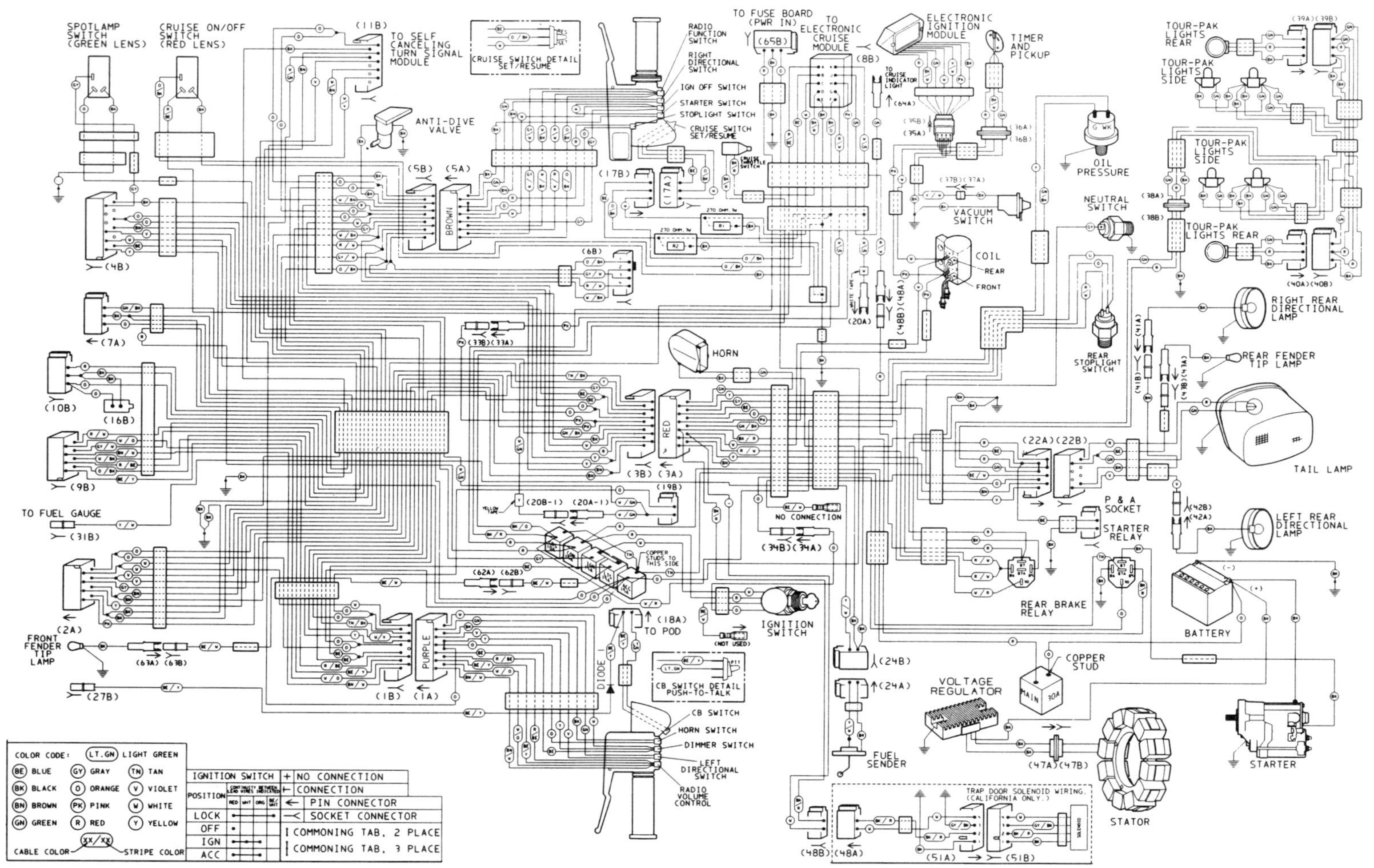

# 1993 FLHTC-ULTRA DOMESTIC MODEL FAIRING (PART 2 OF 3)

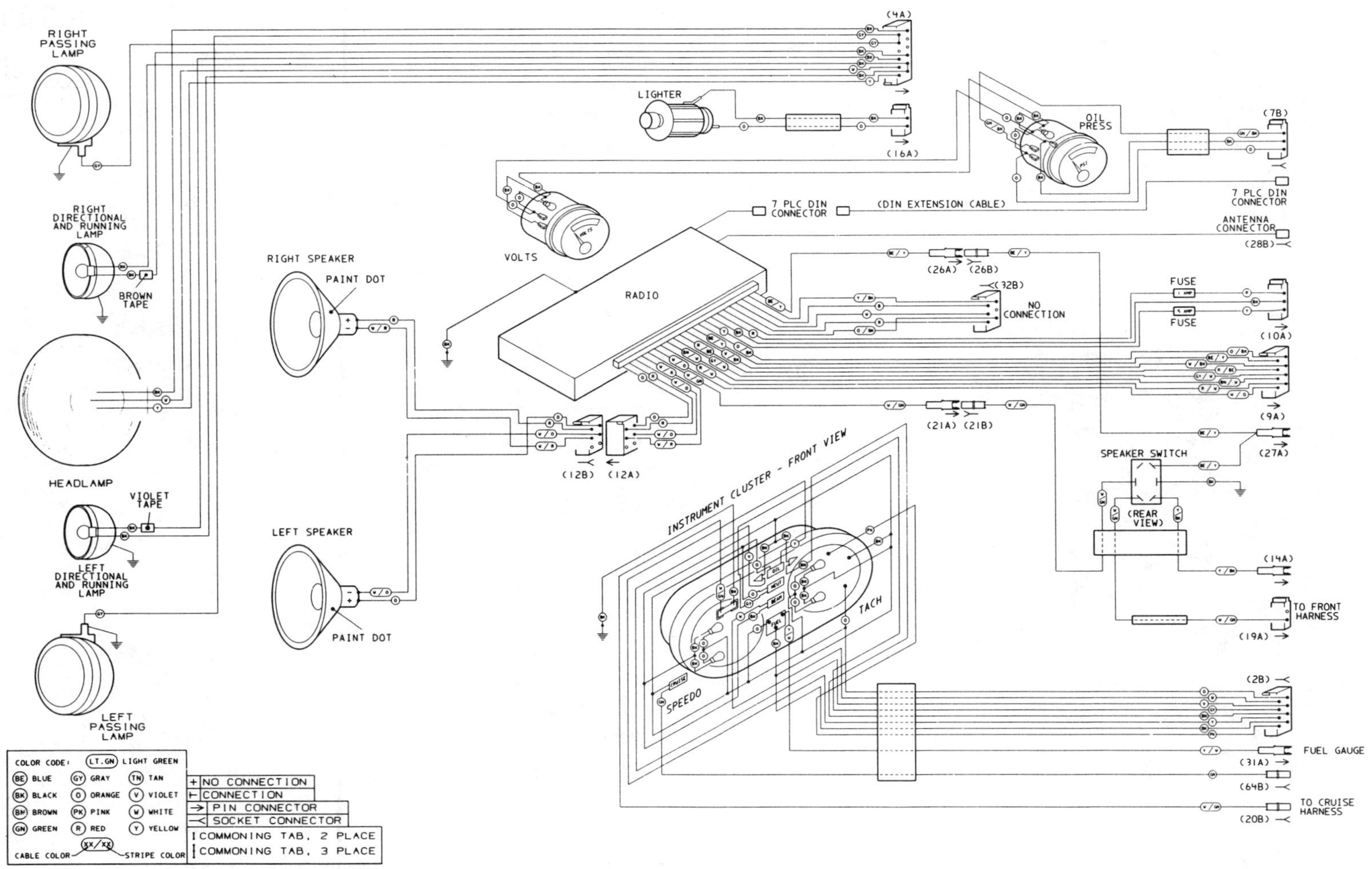


| COLOR CODE: | | LT.GN LIGHT GREEN |
|---|---|---|
| BE BLUE | GY GRAY | TN TAN |
| BK BLACK | O ORANGE | V VIOLET |
| BN BROWN | PK PINK | W WHITE |
| GN GREEN | R RED | Y YELLOW |
| CABLE COLOR | XX/XX | STRIPE COLOR |

|  |  |
|---|---|
| + | NO CONNECTION |
| ⊢ | CONNECTION |
| → | PIN CONNECTOR |
| ⤙ | SOCKET CONNECTOR |
| I | COMMONING TAB, 2 PLACE |
| ⁞ | COMMONING TAB, 3 PLACE |

# 1993 FLHTC-ULTRA DOMESTIC CB/INTERCOM, CRUISE (PART 3 OF 3)

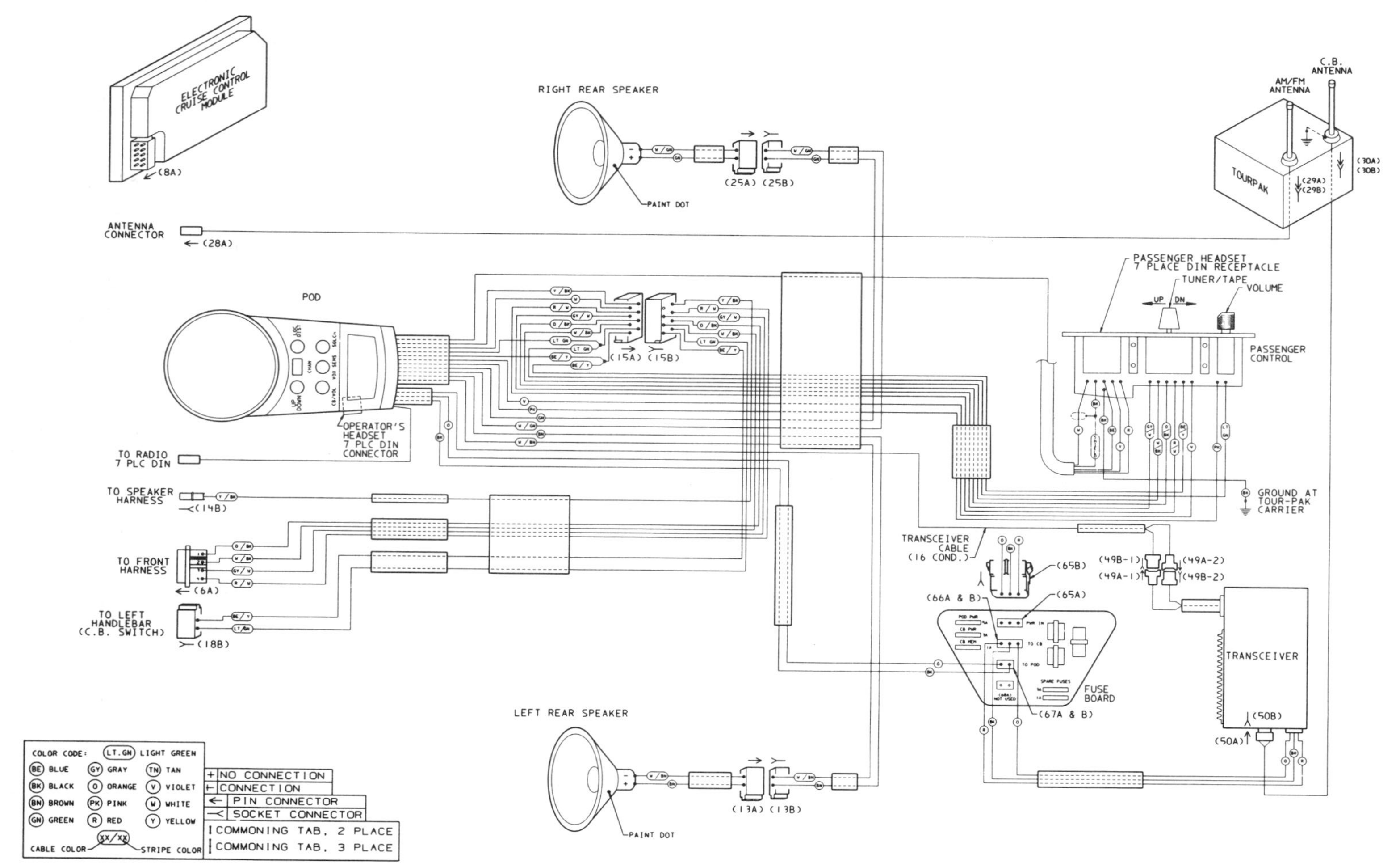

# 1993 FLHTC INTERNATIONAL MODEL FAIRING (PART 1 OF 2)

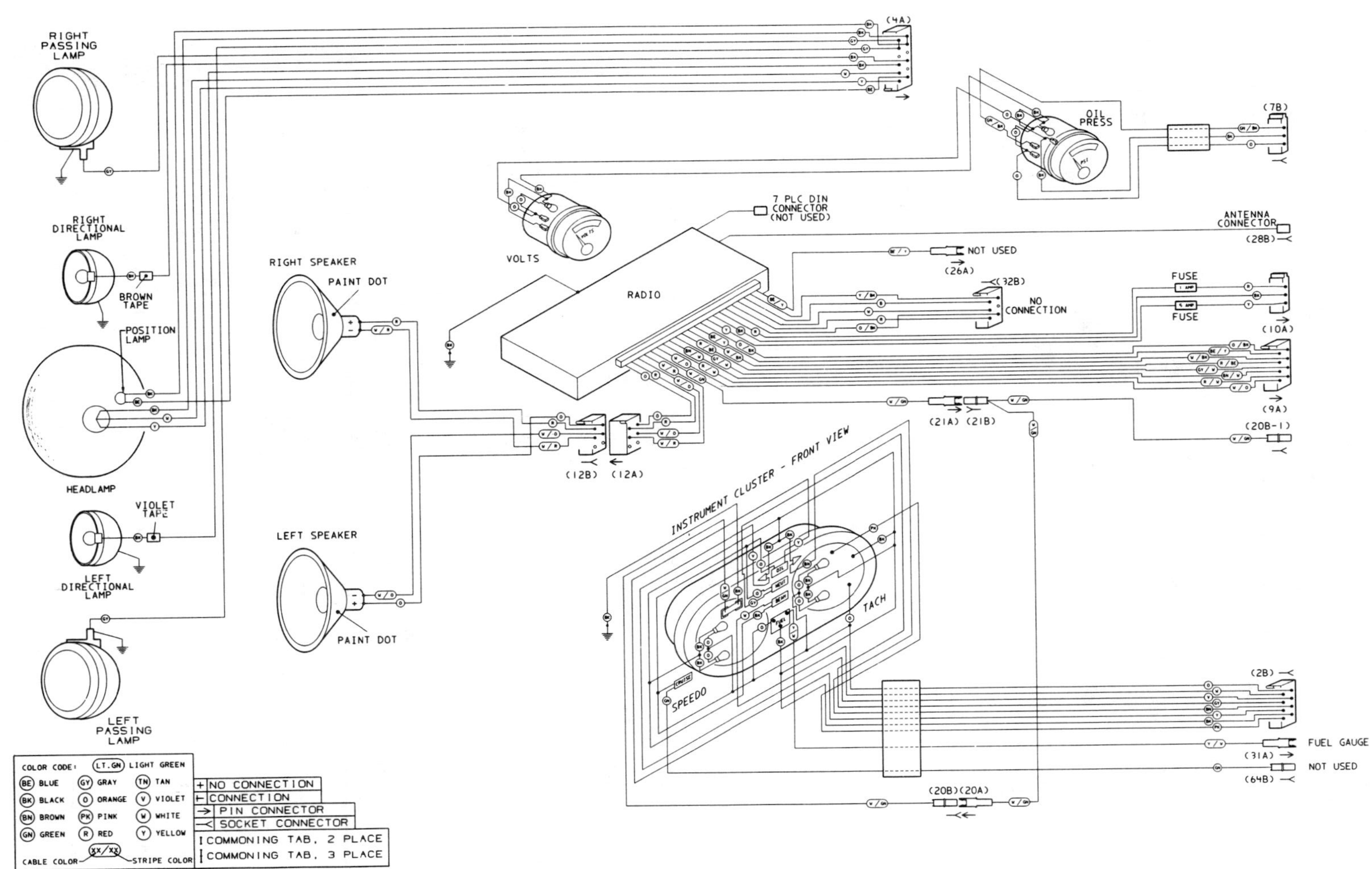

# 1993 FLHTC INTERNATIONAL MODEL CHASSIS (PART 2 OF 2)

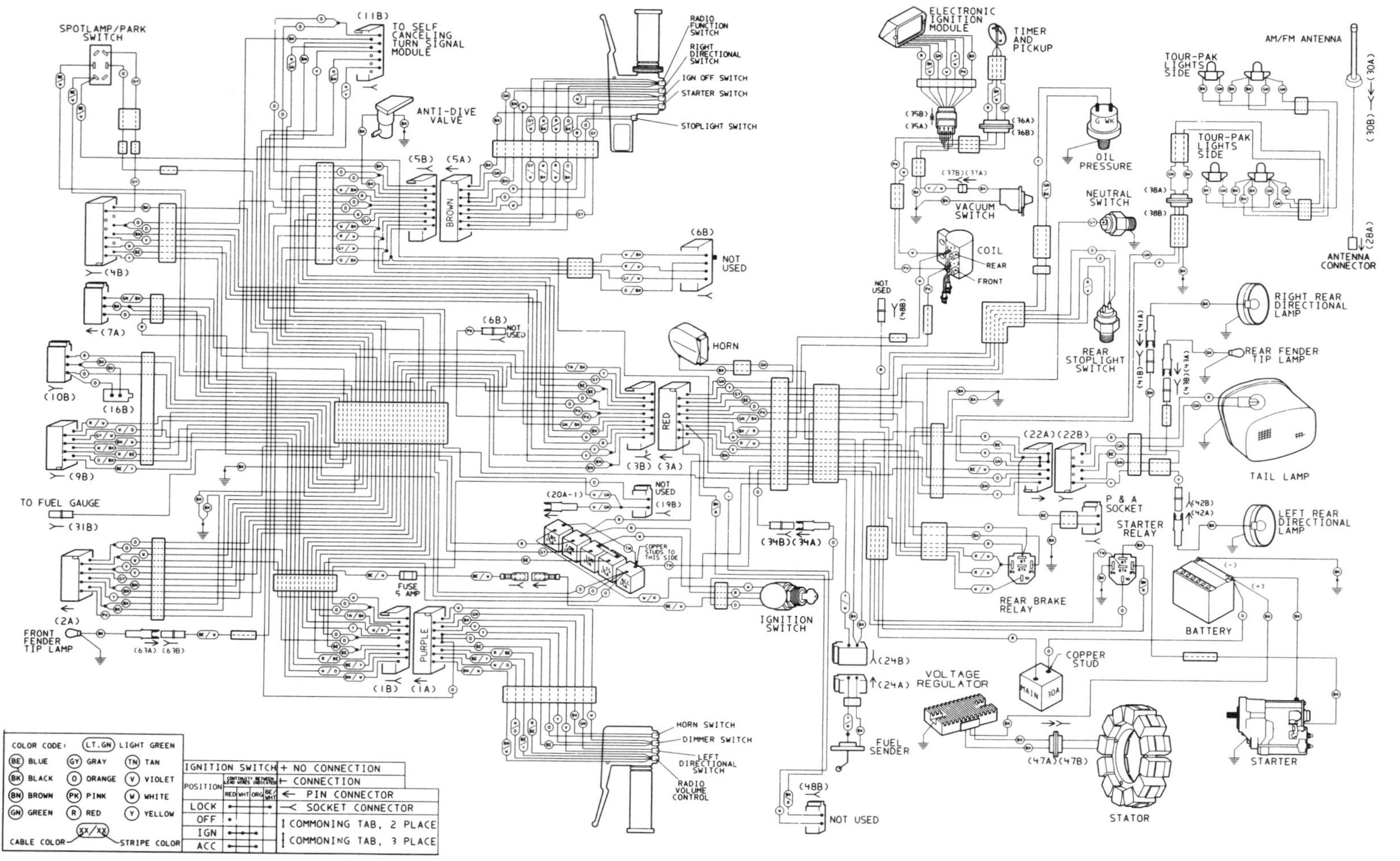

# 1993 FLHS INTERNATIONAL MODEL INSTRUMENTS (PART 1 OF 2)

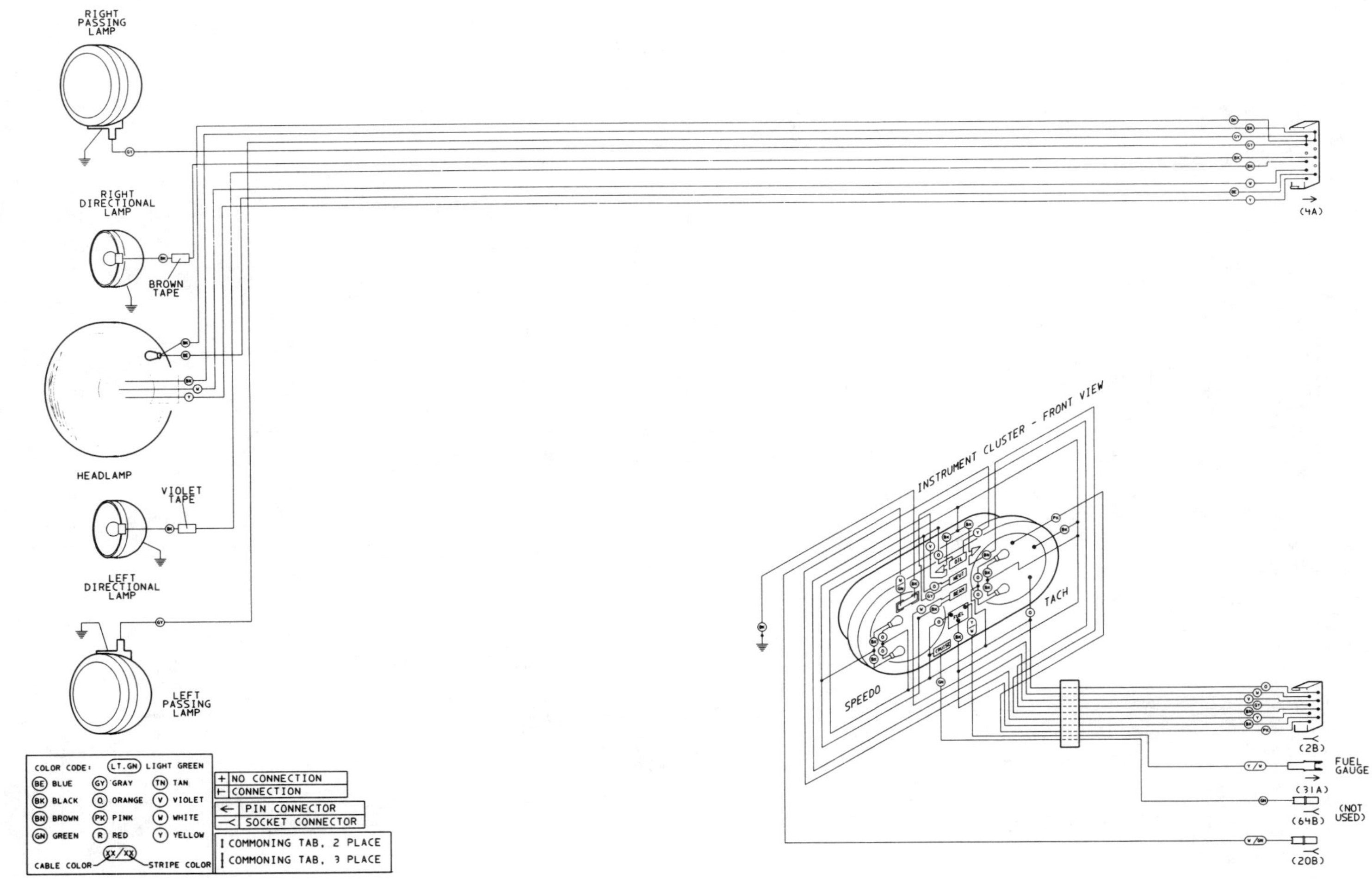

# 1993 FLHS INTERNATIONAL MODEL CHASSIS (PART 2 OF 2)

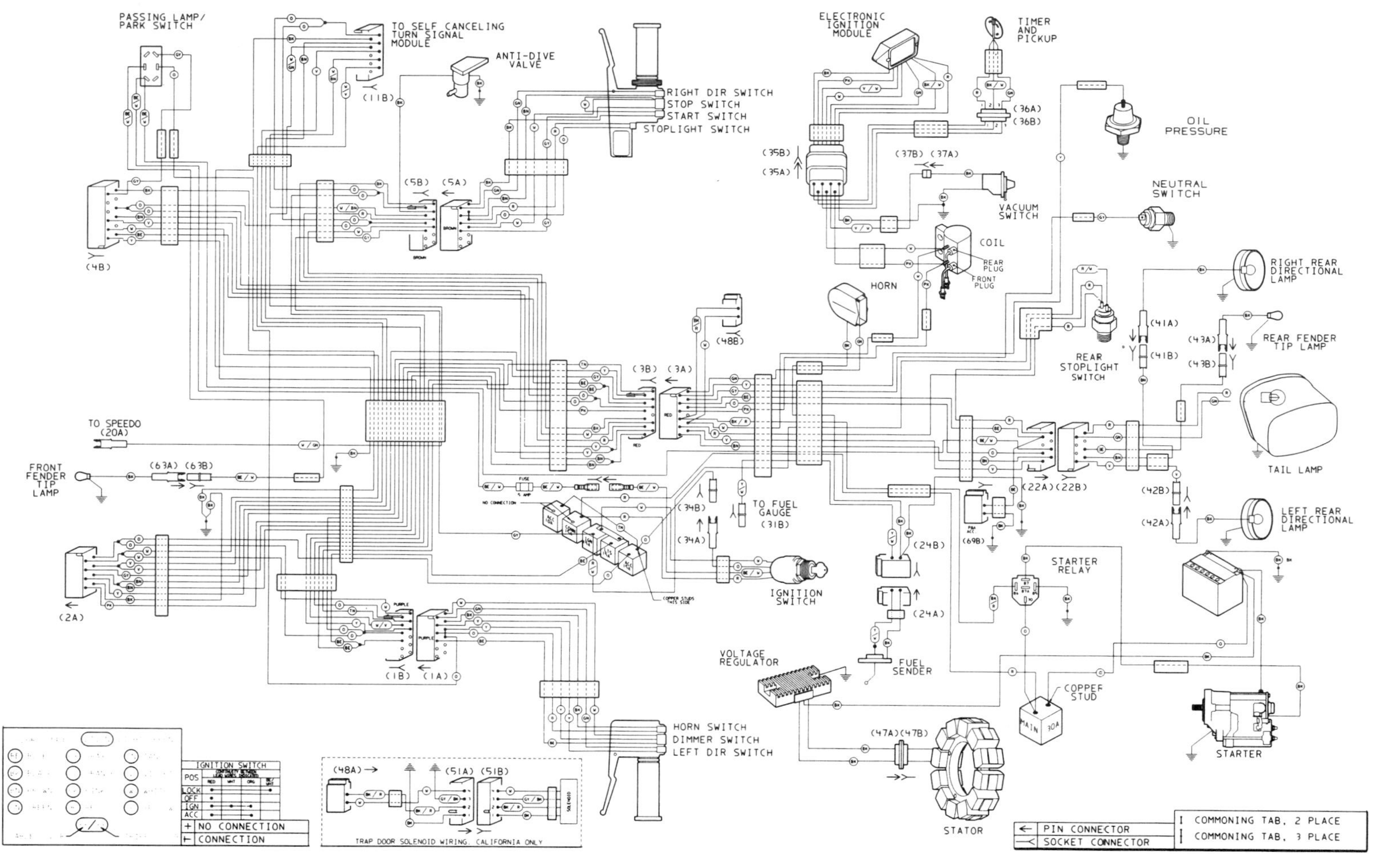

# 1993 FLTC-ULTRA INTERNATIONAL MODEL CHASSIS (PART 1 OF 3)

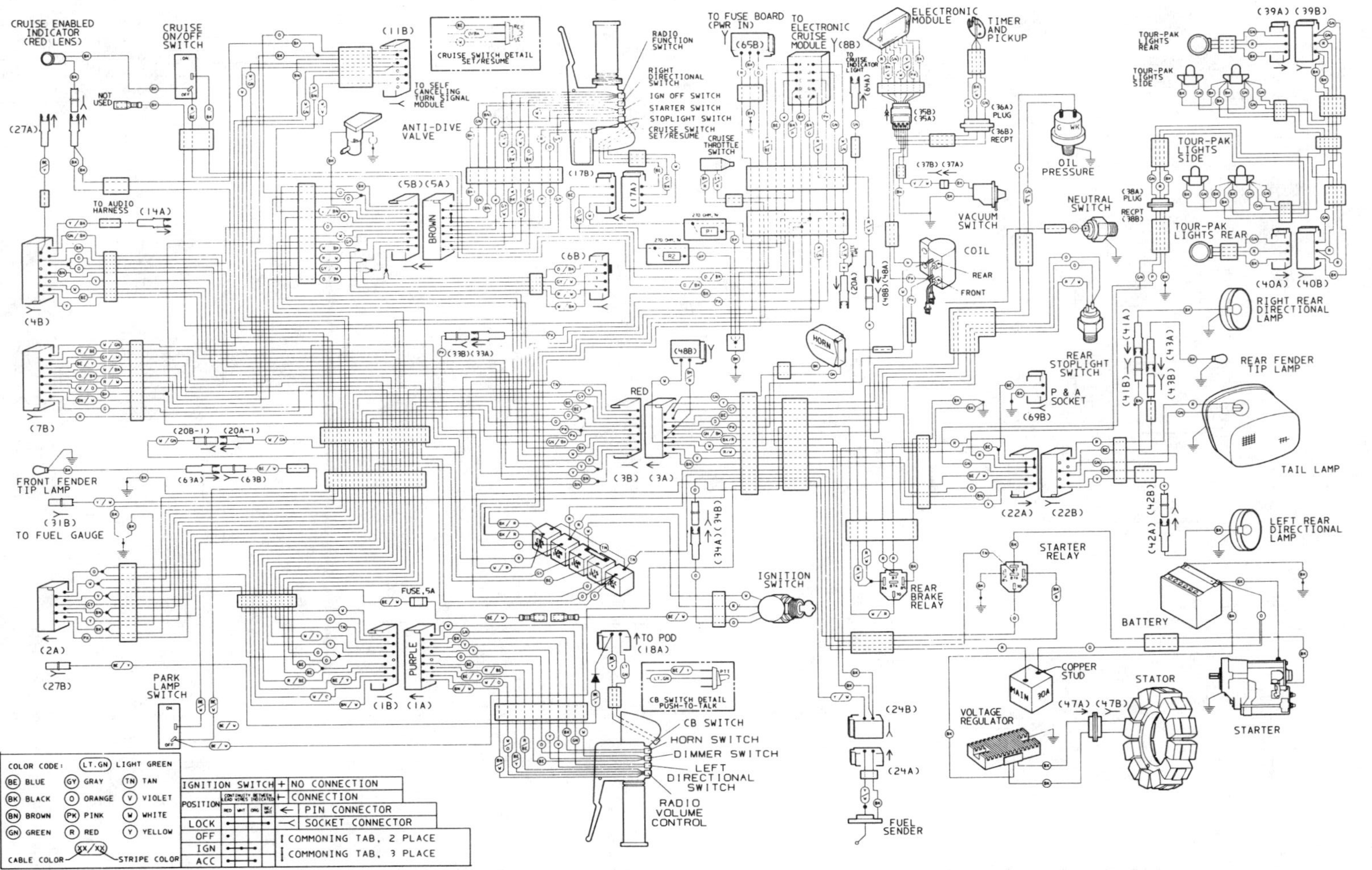

# 1993 FLTC-ULTRA INTERNATIONAL MODEL FAIRING (PART 2 OF 3)

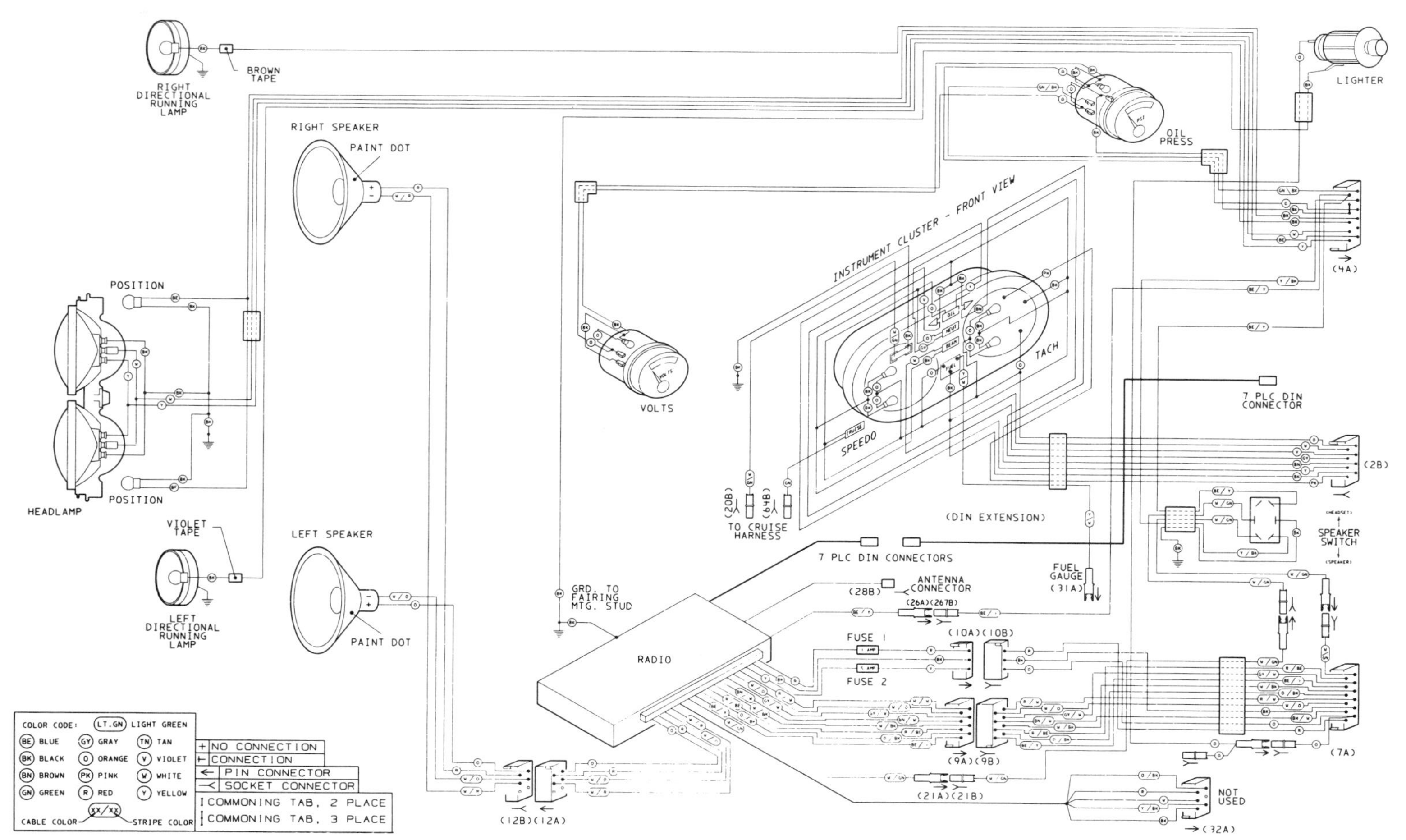

# 1993 FLTC-ULTRA INTERNATIONAL MODEL CB/INTERCOM, CRUISE (PART 3 OF 3)

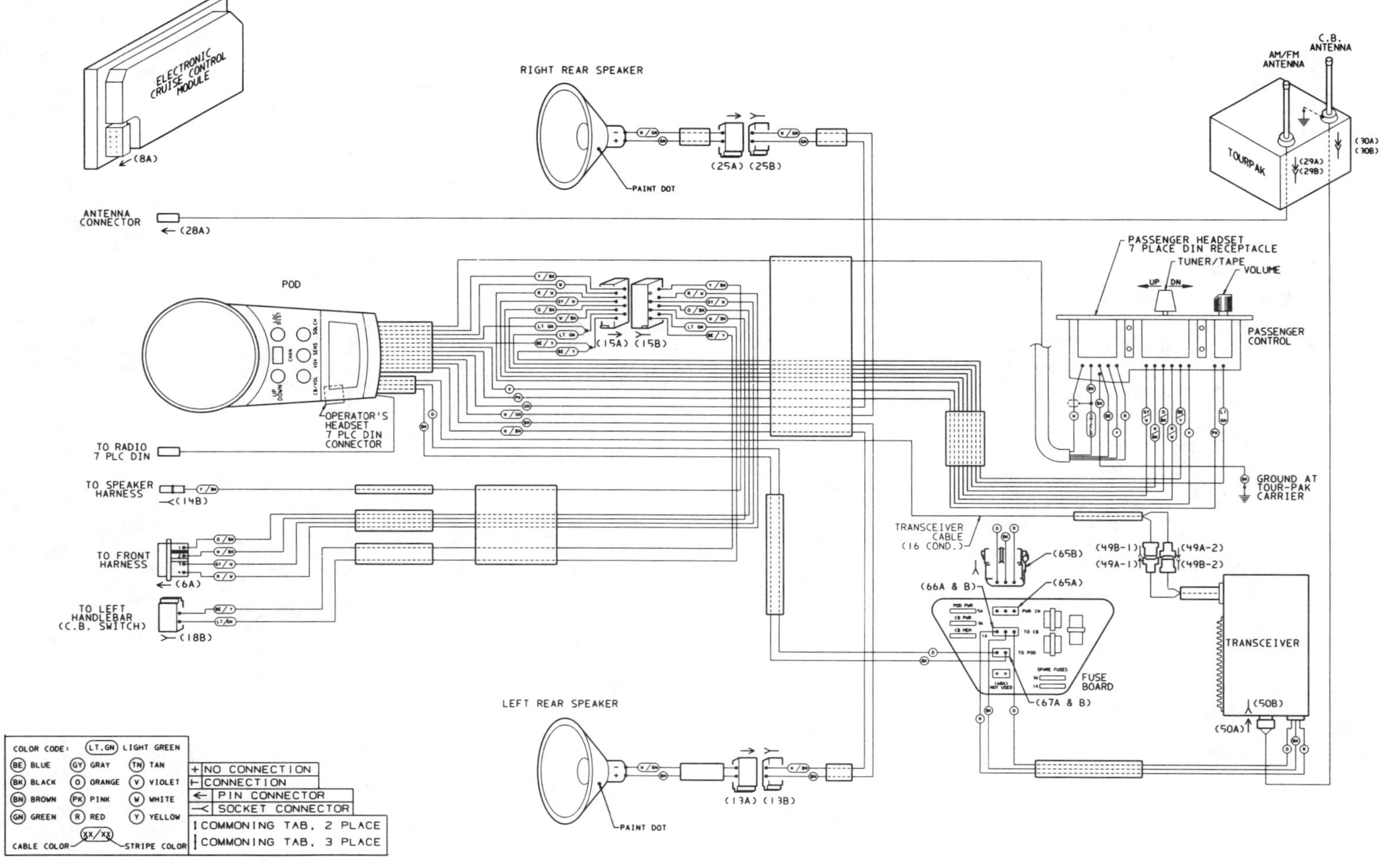

# 1993 FLHTC-ULTRA INTERNATIONAL MODEL CHASSIS (PART 1 OF 3)

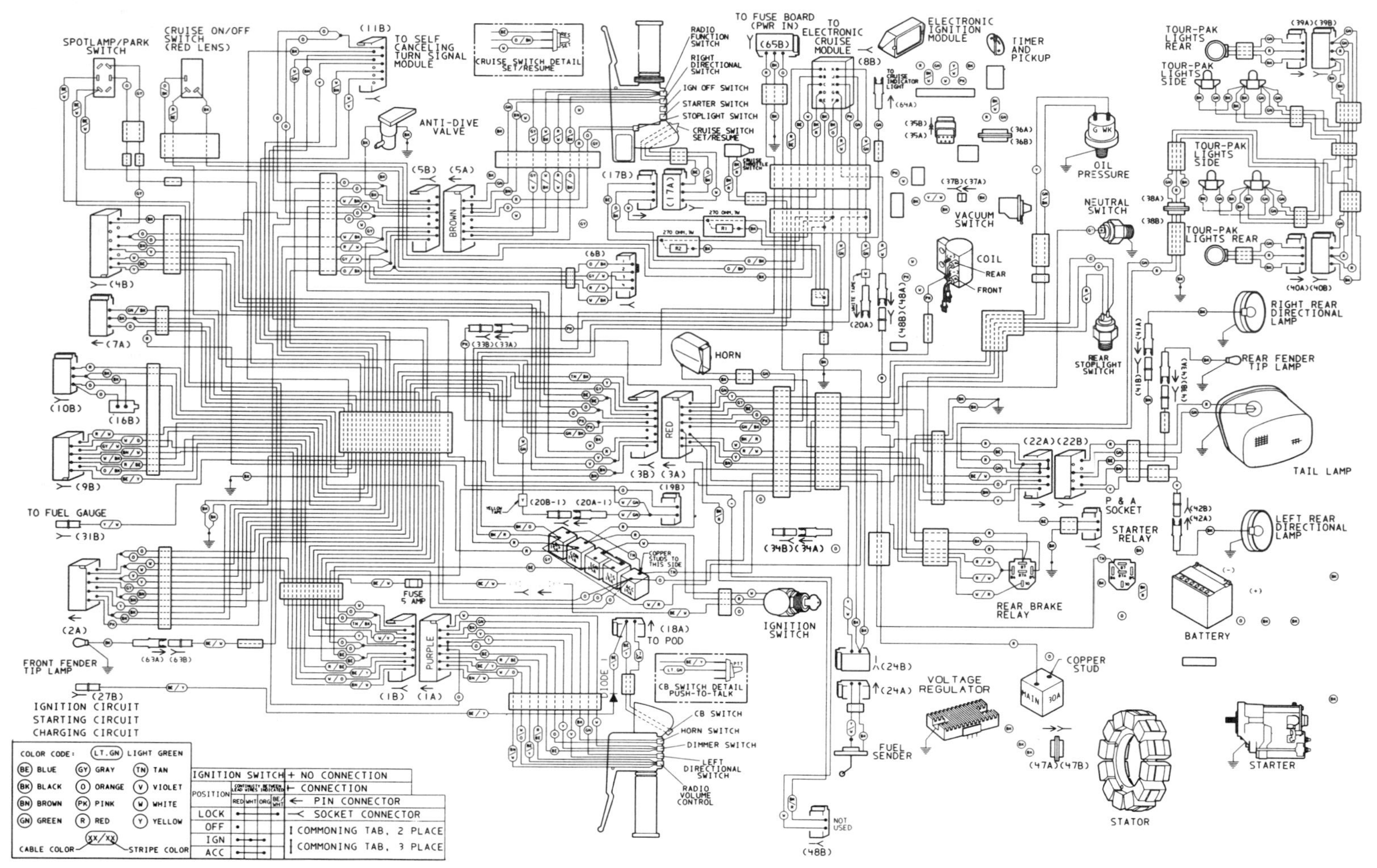

## 1993 FLHTC-ULTRA INTERNATIONAL MODEL FAIRING (PART 2 OF 3)

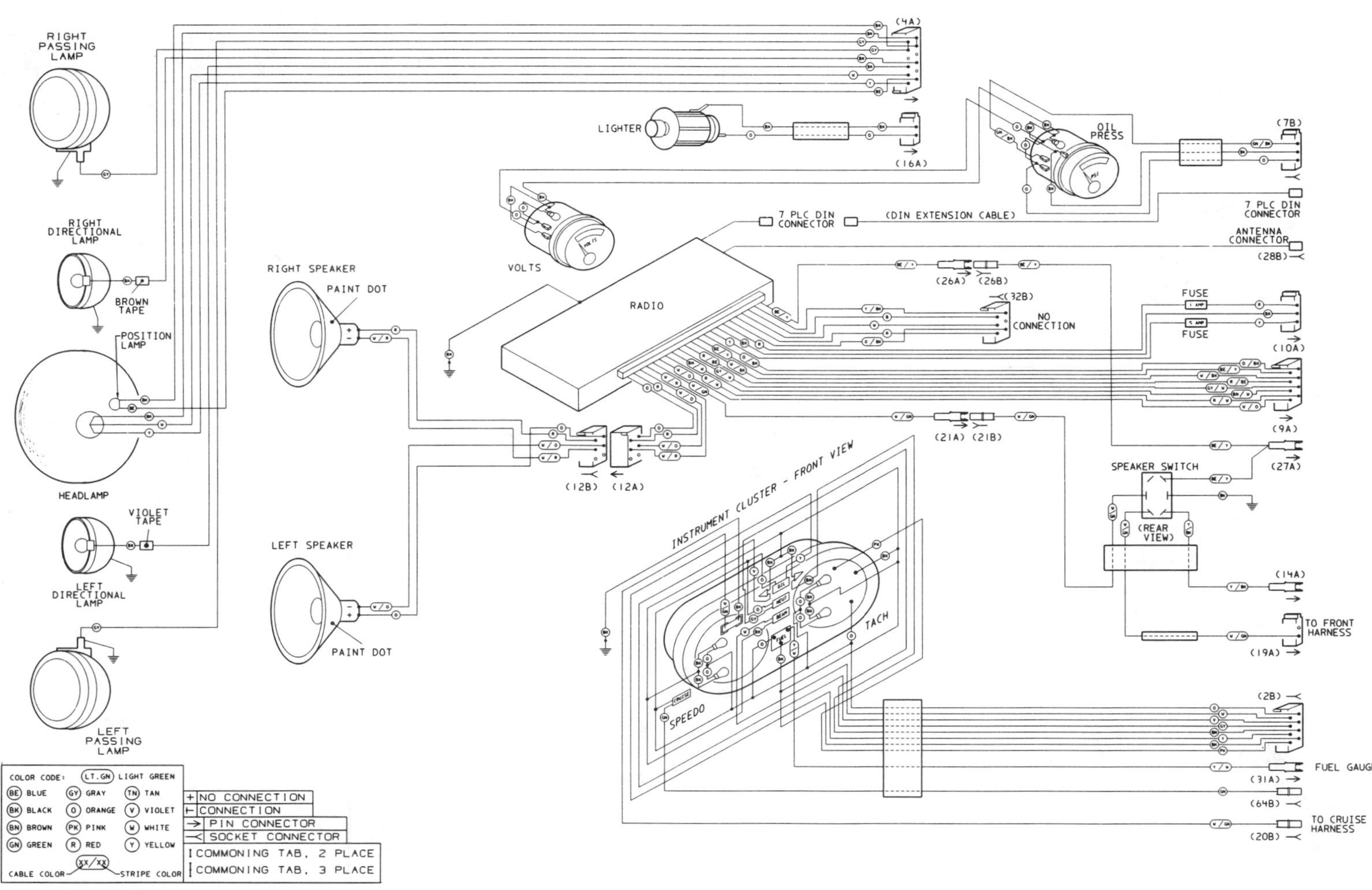


17

# 1993 FLHTC-ULTRA INTERNATIONAL MODEL CB/INTERCOM, CRUISE (PART 3 OF 3)

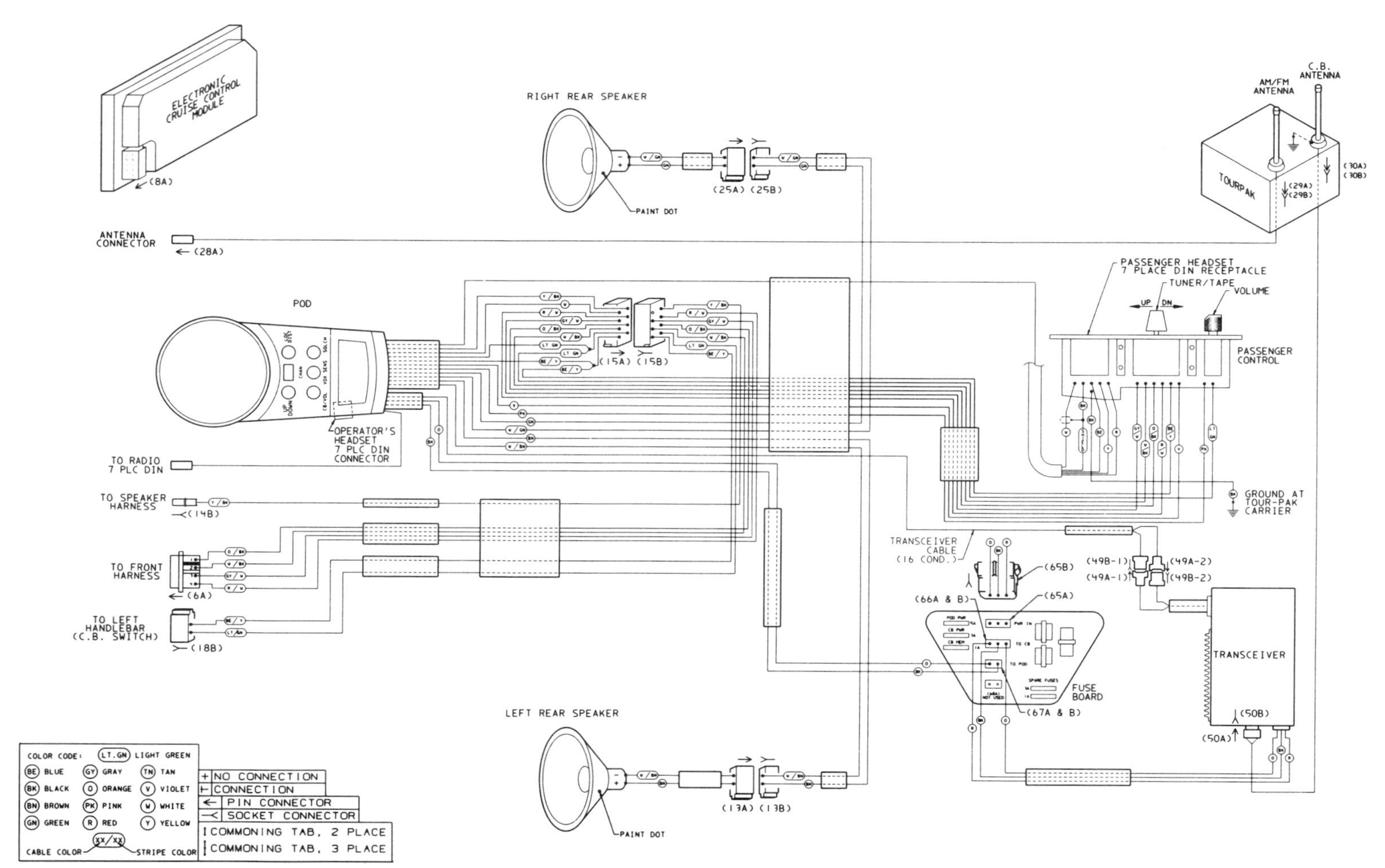

# 1994 FXR DOMESTIC AND INTERNATIONAL MODELS

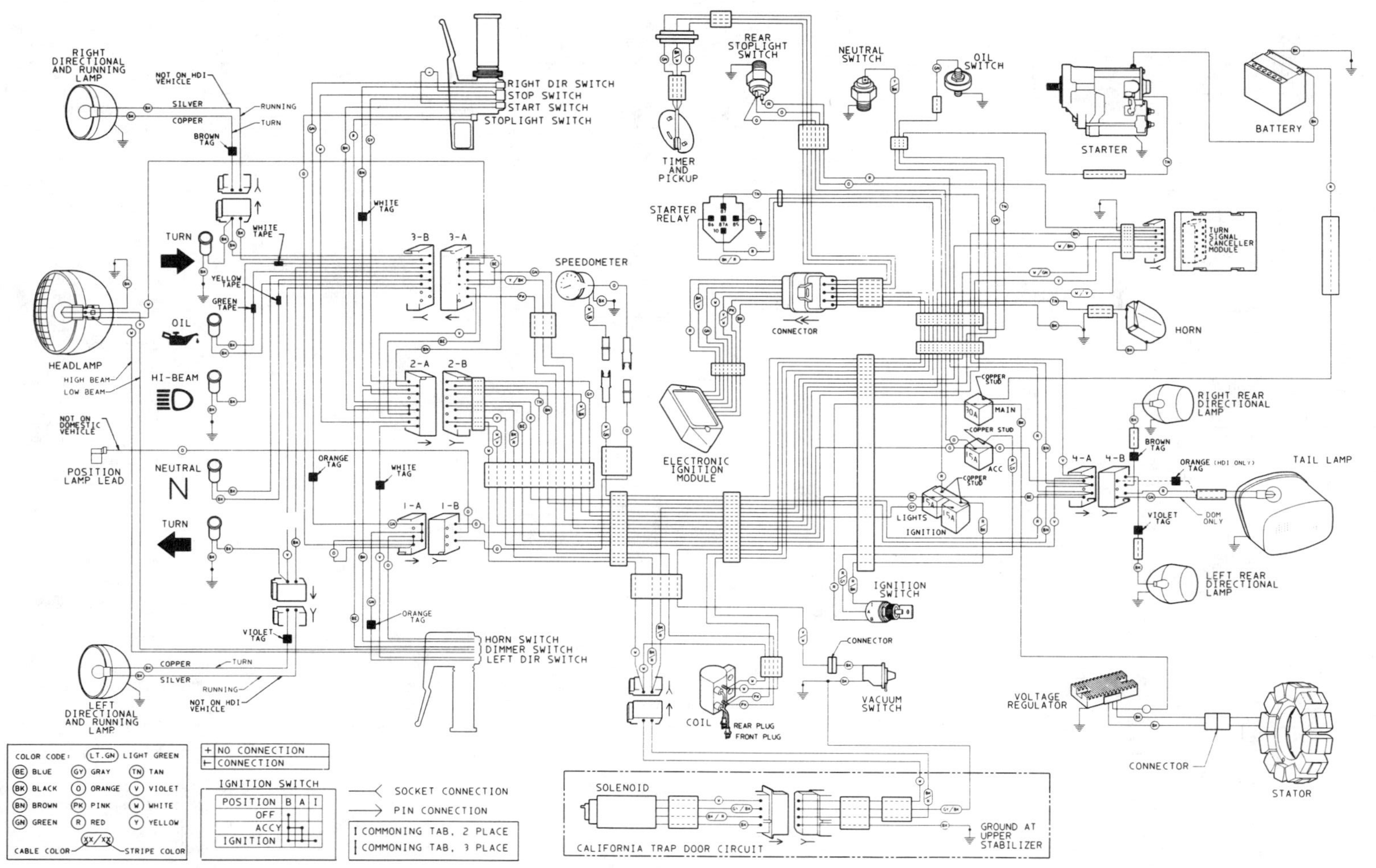

# 1994 FXLR DOMESTIC AND INTERNATIONAL MODELS

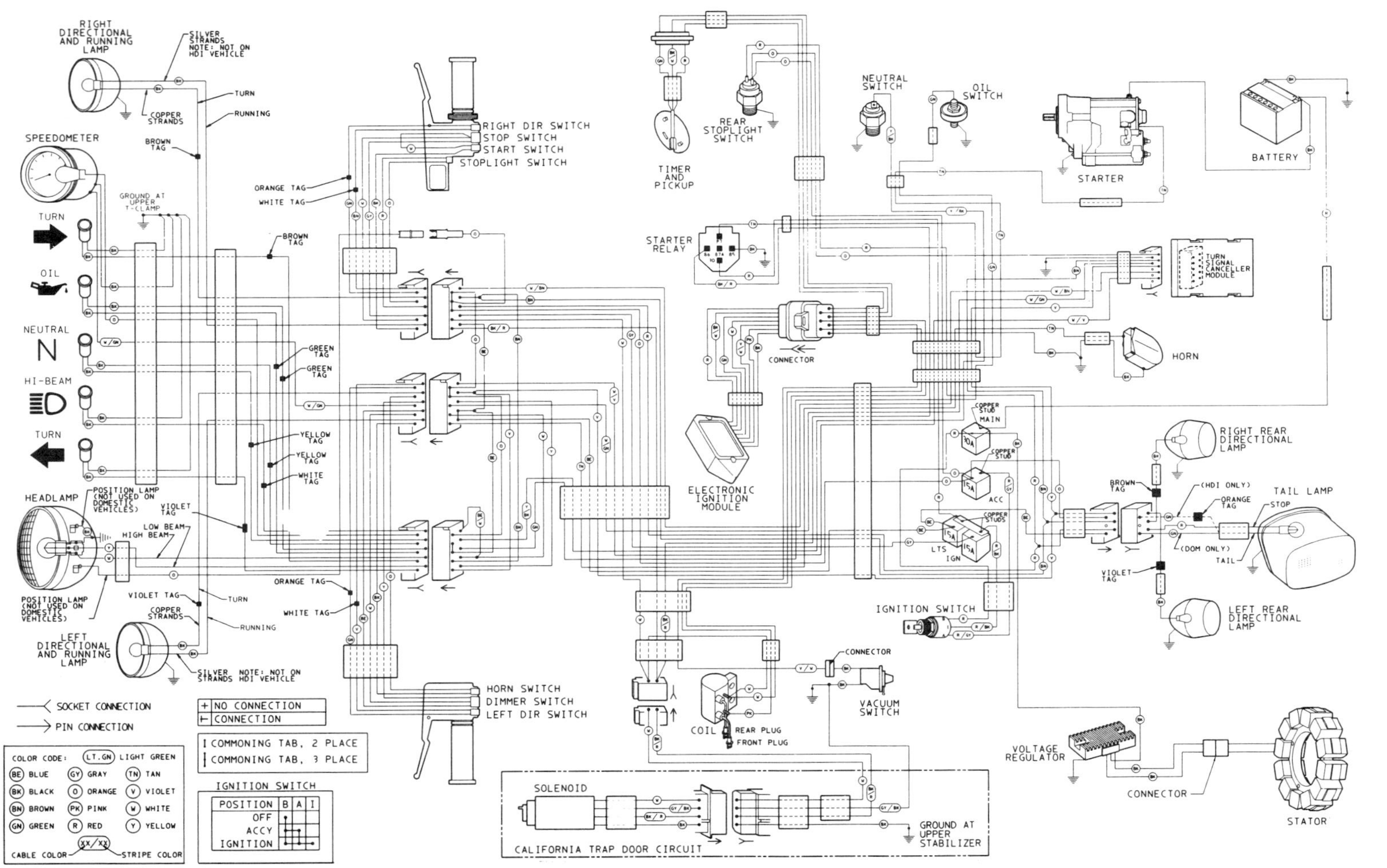

# 1994 FLHTC, FLHTC ULTRA & FLTC-ULTRA, DOMESTIC AND INTERNATIONAL MODELS, MAIN HARNESS

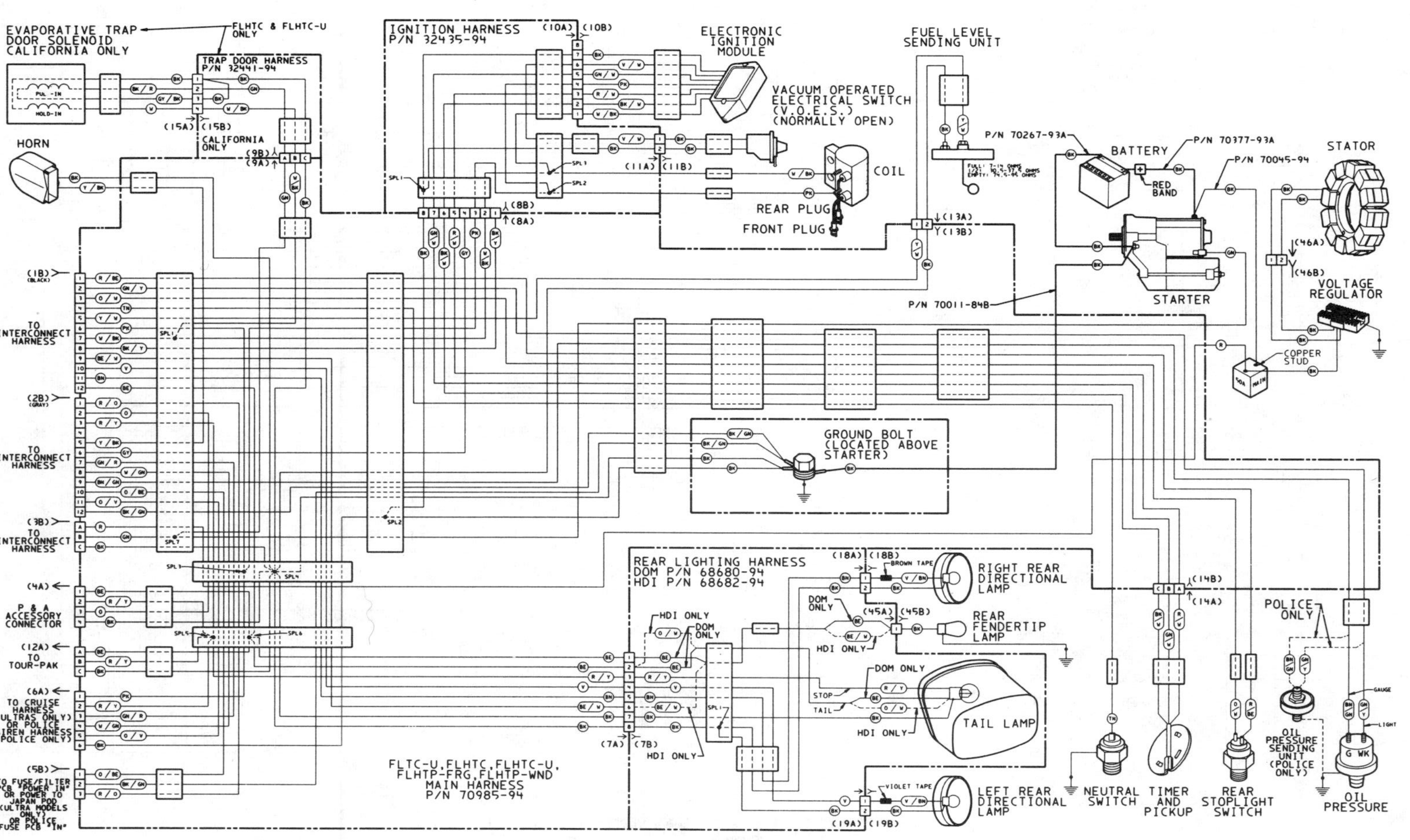

# 1994 FLHTC AND FLHTC ULTRA, DOMESTIC AND INTERNATIONAL MODELS, INTERCONNECT HARNESS

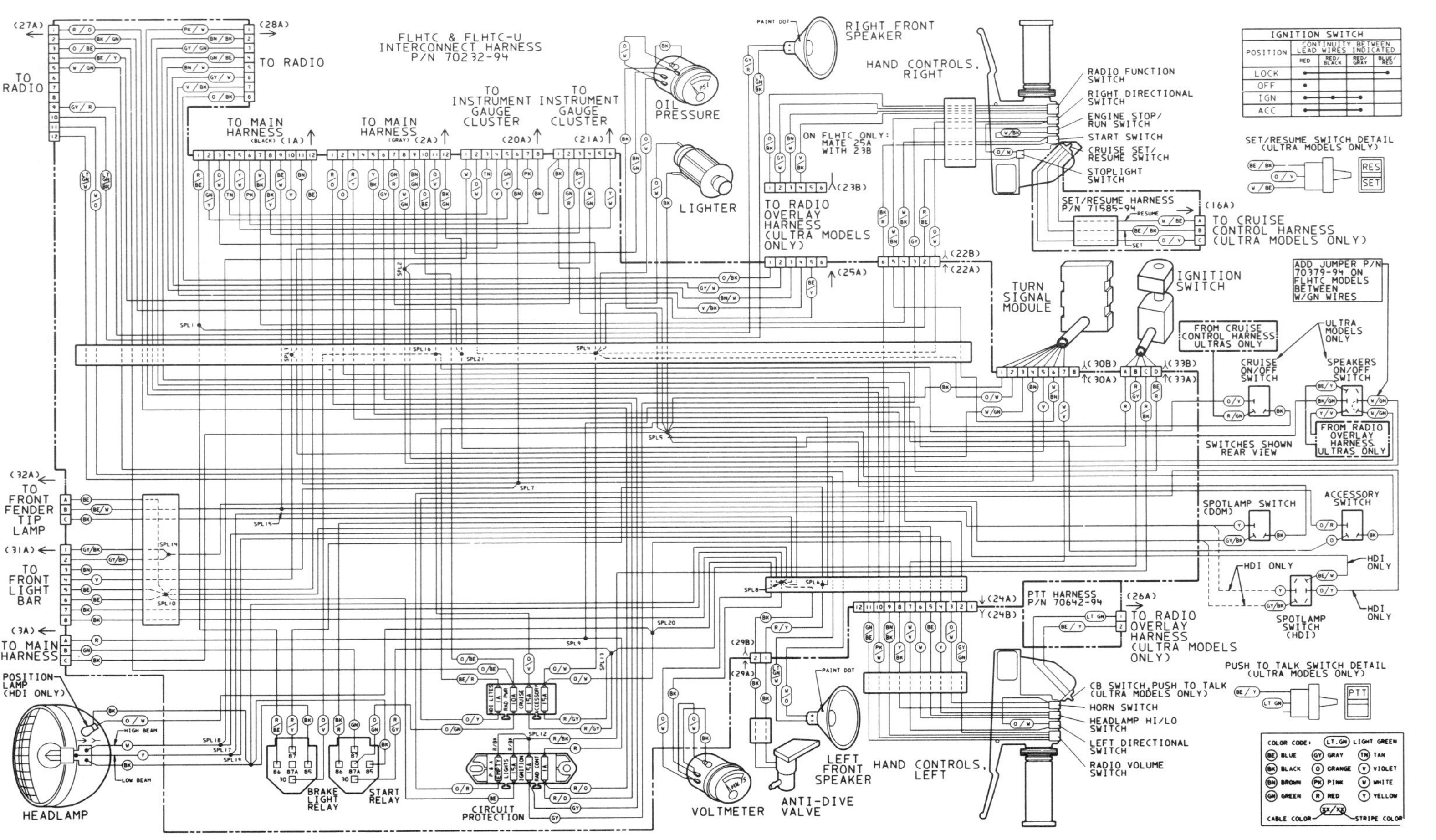

# 1994 FLHTC, FLHTC ULTRA & FLTC-ULTRA, DOMESTIC AND INTERNATIONAL MODELS, RADIO, FRONT LIGHTS, INSTRMENTS AND TOUR PAK

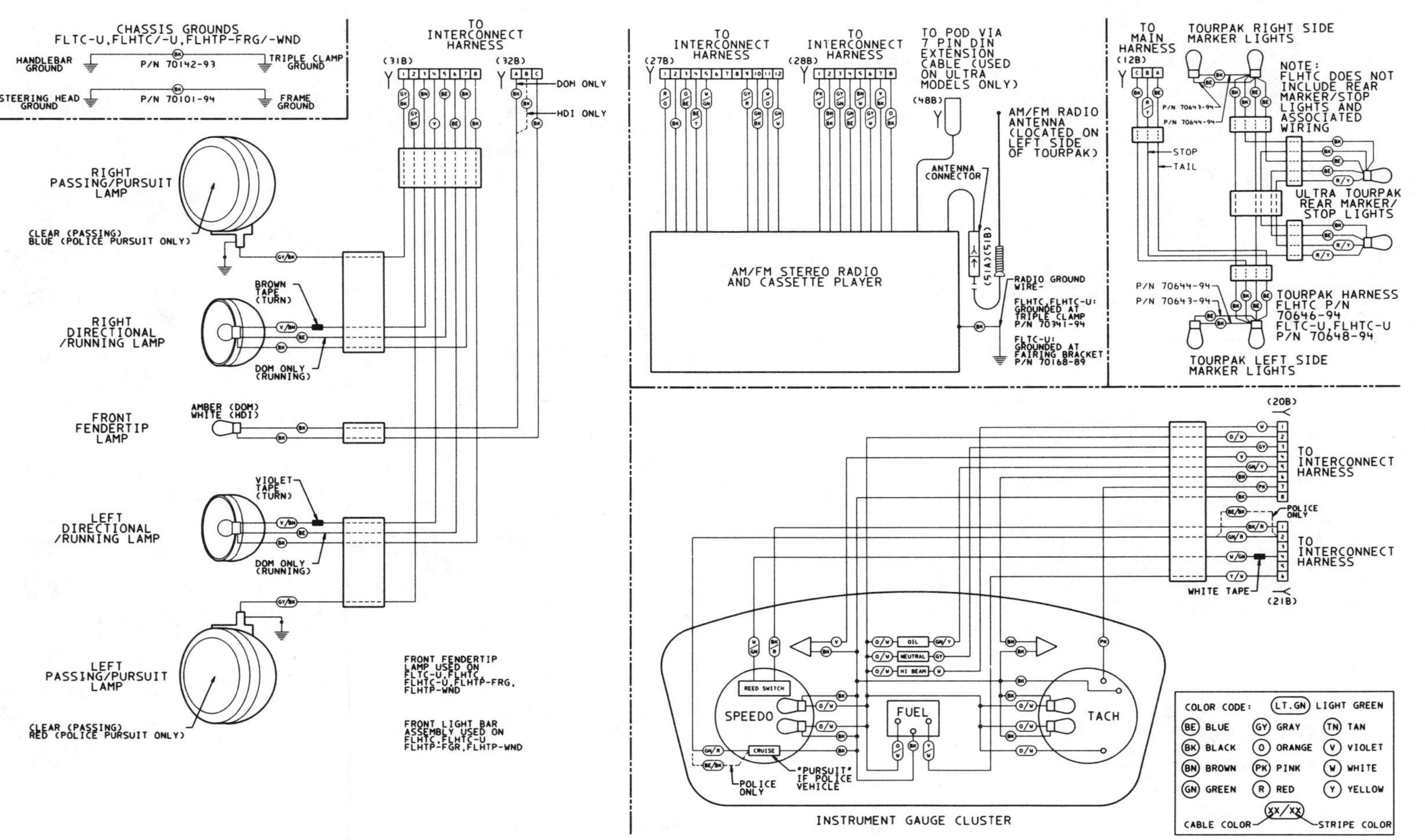

# 1994 FLHTC ULTRA AND FLTC ULTRA, DOMESTIC AND INTERNATIONAL MODELS, CB/INTERCOM, CRUISE

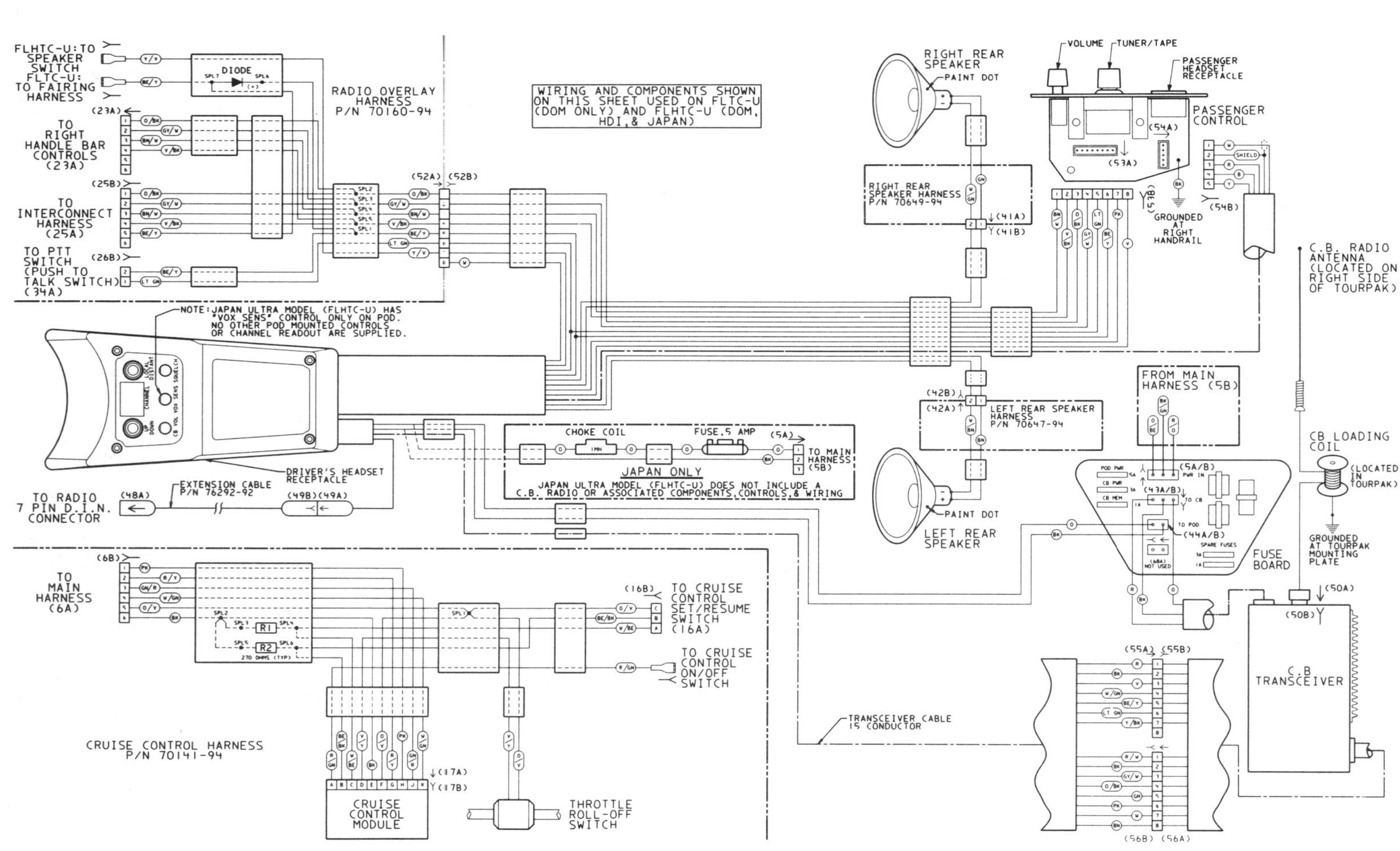

# 1994 FLTC ULTRA DOMESTIC MODELS, FAIRING HARNESS



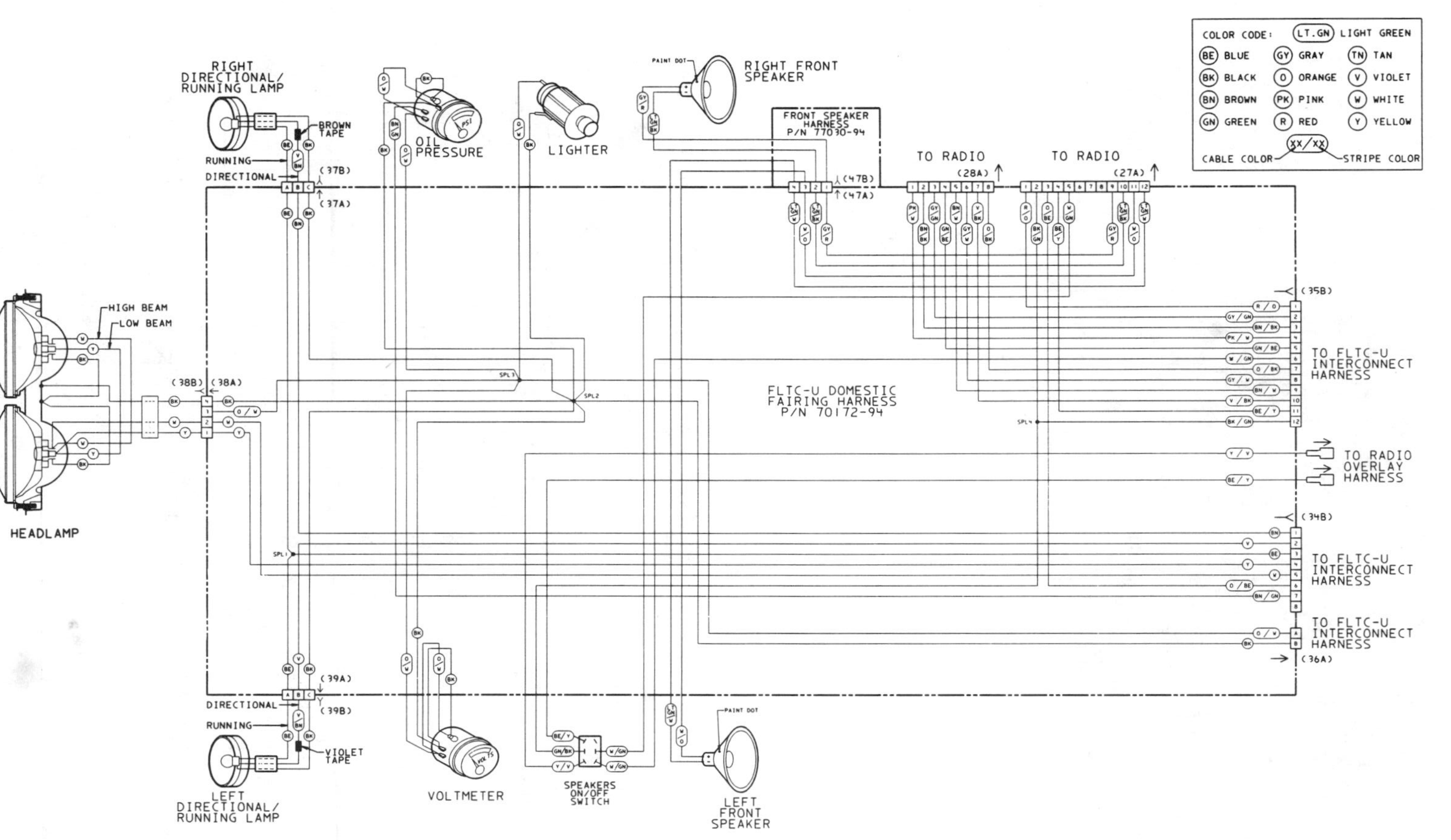

# 1994 FLTC ULTRA DOMESTIC MODELS, INTERCONNECT HARNESS

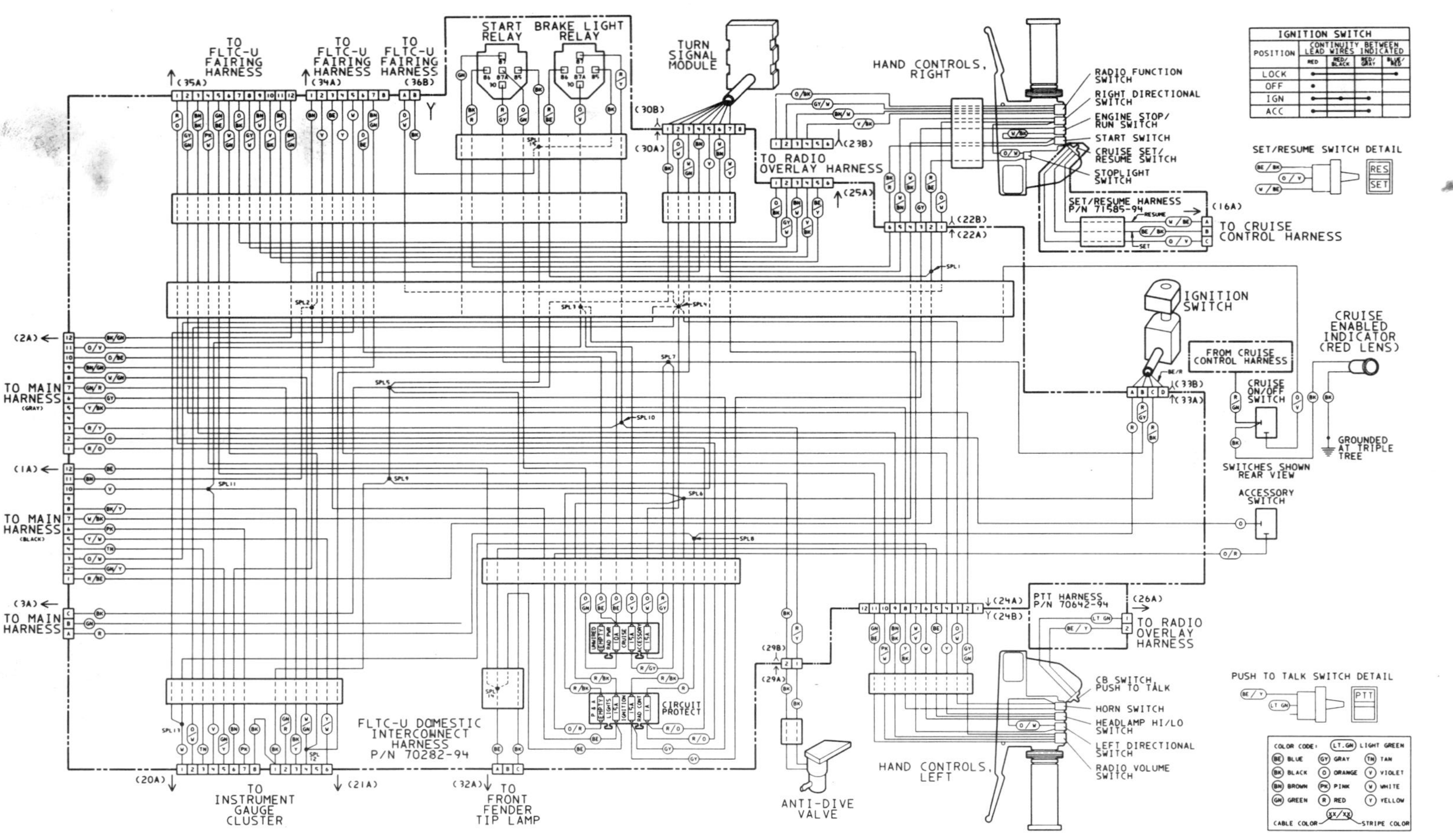